Here is the third volume in Gerald Bordman's acclaimed survey of American non-musical theatre. It deals with the seasons 1930-31 through 1968-69, a period which saw the number of yearly new plays decline at the same time as American drama fully entered the world stage and became a dominant presence.

With works like Eugene O' Neill's *Long Day's Journey Into Night*, Tennessee Williams's *A Streetcar Named Desire*, Arthur Miller's *Death of a Salesman*, and Edward Albee's *Who's Afraid of Virginia Woolf?*, American theatre finally reached adulthood both dramatically and psychologically. A number of distinguished theatrical careers reached their zenith during these years, including those of Alfred Lunt and Lynn Fontanne, Helen Hayes, Katharine Cornell, and Henry Fonda. And as many brilliant theatrical careers were launched, among them those of Julie Harris, Jessica Tandy, Hume Cronyn, Jason Robards, Uta Hagen, and Geraldine Page.

This volume chronicles every Broadway production as well as every major off-Broadway show as its coverage extends into the 50s and 60s. Noted theatrical historian Gerald Bordman moves from play to play and from season to season, offering plot summaries, production details, the names of directors, leading players and roles, as well as quotes from drama critics and any special or unusual aspects of individual shows.

Rich, comprehensive, and lively, this book will stand with the preceding two volumes of *American Theatre* as the premier survey of American drama.

AMERICAN THEATRE:
A Chronicle of Comedy and Drama, 1930–1969

AMERICAN THEATRE:

A Chronicle of Comedy and Drama, 1930–1969

GERALD BORDMAN

New York   Oxford
OXFORD UNIVERSITY PRESS
1996

Oxford University Press

Oxford   New York
Athens   Auckland   Bangkok   Bobotá   Bombay
Buenos Aires   Calcutta   Cape Town   Dar es Salaam
Delhi   Florence   Hong Kong   Istanbul   Karachi
Kuala Lumpur   Madras   Madrid   Melbourne
Mexico City   Nairobi   Paris   Singapore
Taipei   Tokyo   Toronto

and associated companies in
Berlin   Ibadan

Published by Oxford University Press, Inc.,
198 Madison Avenue, New York, New York 10016

Oxford is a registered trademark of Oxford University Press

Library of Congress Cataloging-in-Publication Data

Bordman, Gerald Martin.
American theatre : a chronicle of comedy and drama, 1930–1969
Gerald Bordman.
p.   cm.   Includes index.
ISBN 0-19-509079-9
1. Theater—United States—History—20th century.
2. American drama—20th century—Stories, plots, etc.
I. Title.
PN2266.B64   1996   792′.0973′0904—dc20   96-17572

1   3   5   7   9   8   6   4   2

Printed in the United States of America
on acid-free paper

PREFACE

This is the third volume in our series *American Theatre: A Chronicle of Comedy and Drama*. The first volume examined the seasons from 1869–70 through 1913–14, when, for the most part, the legitimate theatre remained the nation's primary entertainment milieu; the second, the halcyon theatrical years from 1914–15 through 1929–30. Since this volume deals with the seasons from 1930–31 through 1968–69, the three-work set covers what are assuredly the hundred most exciting years of American playwriting and playgoing.

In the early years surveyed here, "Broadway," that tiny, playhouse-packed enclave in mid-Manhattan, represented virtually all there was of real, enduring interest to theatre lovers. The shrinking road was confined almost wholly to tryouts and post-Broadway tours. But after World War II, what became known as "Off Broadway," which had bloomed tentatively in the 1920s, resurged and in a short while became a major factor. Considerations of space and time have precluded our examining it with the thoroughness with which we have looked at regular Broadway mountings, but we have tried to include many of the longer-run off-Broadway hits. Indeed, by the time we reach the end of this volume, much of the freshest, most interesting writing was coming from there.

It should be noted, too, that the same considerations of space and time have permitted us to look at only the main Federal Theatre offerings in Manhattan. Mountings by its Children's Theatre, its peripatetic Suitcase Unit, and some straightforward Harlem revivals have been ignored, as have a number of productions away from New York.

Once again, a few caveats. Programs were sometimes careless in spelling names, and, sometimes, people changed the spelling of their names. We have attempted to adopt a uniform spelling throughout, although a few instances may have slipped by us, and we have made a handful of exceptions. Some critics wondered aloud why Charlotte Armstrong shortened her name to the harsher Charl. We have kept her name as they were in the programs. So long as Bus-Fekete's works were presented in translation his name was spelled one way, but after he apparently began to write directly in English (was he a refugee?) an "h" was added. We have added it accordingly. When actors have dropped the "Jr." from their names, we have quietly dropped it, too. Other spellings, punctuation, and capitalization in quotations have been brought in line with accepted modern practice by our copy editor.

Special thanks must be extended to the excellent staff at the library of Millersville University, notably Ray Hacker, Leo Shelley, and Donald Tribit, as well as to John Schenke, who helped there with photocopying; to Geraldine Duclow and Elaine Ebo at the Theatre Collection of the Free Library of Philadelphia; to Robert Taylor at Lincoln Center's Library of the Performing Arts; to Ray Wemmlinger of the Hampden-Booth Library; to the distinguished theatrical historians Ian Bevan and Kurt Gänzl; to Jacques Kelly and to Richard Norton. Of course, my heartfelt thanks go to my friends and colleagues at Oxford University Press: India Cooper, Joellyn Ausanka, Leona Capeless, and to my incomparable, always understanding editor, Sheldon Meyer.

Kirk's Mills, Pa.
June 1996

Gerald Bordman

Act One, 1930–1944

The Waning of the Golden Age

Act Two, 1944–1959

A Silver Age?

Act Three, 1959–1969

Decline

ACT ONE
1930–1944

THE WANING OF THE
GOLDEN AGE

1930–1931

Without question the double whammy of talkies and the Depression took a sharp toll on Broadway in the new season. As usual, figures varied from one commentator to the next. *Variety* recorded 187 openings, of which 130 were new plays. The *Times* counted 197 and 124 respectively. Burns Mantle offered merely a total, without a breakdown. But he rationalized, "190 is enough." Whichever count was accepted, it represented a stunning drop of approximately 20 percent in one year. Yet bad times, ironically, did not discourage bad plays. In the 1920s many of these had been mounted to launder bootleg money, display some gangster's favorite, or assuage the ego of one of the more legitimately nouveau riche. While the illicit millions would soon disappear with the abolition of Prohibition, and many of the more honestly gained millions were already gone for good, by mid-season the need to keep houses lit prompted theatre owners to drastically slash rental terms. In the long run such cuts were unavailing, since no fewer than twenty of the season's new plays survived a week or less. Another twenty shuttered at the end of their second week; and twenty-four more could not run beyond their first month. Many of these were plays that theatre owners would have waved away contemptuously a season or two before. With some theatres remaining dark all season, it was not surprising that an increasing number of auditoriums soon were converting to films, becoming radio studios, and even giving way to parking lots.

One interesting phenomenon also seems to begin to emerge in the season. Critics on lesser papers long had given shows they did not like the shortest shrift. But now dismissive reviews of sometimes as little as one skimpy paragraph started to appear in tradesheets, which until now had felt obligated to offer extended professional analysis, and in the more prestigious dailies, such as the *Times*. Even the *Times*'s first-string critic, Brooks Atkinson, subscribed to the practice. Critics, moreover, appeared less tolerant of bad plays, even when they gave them lengthy notices. In later years, this was rationalized by suggesting critics of the period wished to prevent playgoers from squandering hard-to-come-by Depression dollars. Yet if that was their thinking, they were largely silent about it. At the same time, a growing number of reviewers became disenchanted with older plays. Faddists, extolling only the latest as good, were

nothing new, but over the next several years their chorus would grow louder, and behind much of the disparaging a political motive slowly became obvious—with more fervent left-wingers seeing it as their duty to whip any old play that dealt uncritically with princes and princesses, or carefree playboys and fun-loving debutantes, or simply the rich and happy.

For all the economic problems, the theatre retained more than a modicum of elegance. Playgoers, at least those in orchestra seats, continued to dress formally in the evenings, especially on weekends. On first nights tuxedoed men had to shoulder their way through "drifts of ermine, the tropical tangle of orchidaceous decorations, and the Guerlain mists." Careful dressing was in order even for later performances upstairs, although the soberly tailored, longer-skirted dresses women had begun to wear added a more somber note than heretofore.

A popular veteran, George M. Cohan, launched the new season with a revival of his comedy about a second-rate vaudevillian who nearly ruins what is left of his career by turning to crime to get money for a strapped friend, *The Song and Dance Man* (12-31-23), at the Fulton on June 16. However, his popularity could not pull in enough trade to prompt the show's remaining beyond its initially scheduled two weeks.

Four nights later the season's first short-lived disaster, Frank Martins's **Find the Fox** (6-20-30, Wallack's), began a three-performance run. Ostensibly a spoof of murder mysteries, it recounted how a group of actors, actually inmates at a home for the mentally ill, improvise a yarn in which they must determine who has committed three killings. The play was the last novelty to open at the house, which shortly afterwards became one of the first theatres on 42nd Street to turn to films.

More than a month passed before another play opened. Elmer Harris's rather coarse and obvious **Ladies All** (7-28-30, Morosco) was taken from Prince Antoine Bibesco's *Laquelle?* and featured one of New York's best operetta baritones, Walter Woolf. He was accorded little chance to sing as a notorious ladies' man trying to guess which of the women at a swank Westchester party—in a converted barn filled with the hostess's modernistic sculptures—came into his darkened bedroom last night and climbed into his bed. At one point or another each of the women claims it was she. Shortly before eleven o'clock he realizes the intruder was none other than his hostess (Violet Heming). A small cast and Woolf's celebrity helped the comedy run well into the fall.

David Belasco's first production of the season ran almost as long. He employed Frederic and Fanny Hatton to adapt an unidentified German play by Alexander Engel and Alfred Grunwald, and he called the result **Dancing Partner** (8-5-30, Belasco). Once again a comedy centered around a notorious ladies' man. Lord Robert Brummel (Lynne Overman) is pressed by his uncle, Lord George Hampton (Henry Stephenson), to abandon his rakehell life and marry a young lady named Roxy (Irene Purcell). Convinced marriage is an unnecessary hindrance, he agrees to wed only if he cannot seduce Roxy within a month. He poses as a M. Jolie and sets about his plan. One month later, having lost his wager, but having fallen in love with Roxy, he prepares to marry her. Belasco's mounting included magnificent reproductions of rooms in posh Paris and Biarritz hotels, and also one applauded scene near the end of the play set in an airplane. The plane swayed as it flew through the air, while audiences caught glimpses of passing clouds and stars outside its windows.

The next fortnight brought in two quick failures. Patrick MacGill's **Suspense** (8-12-30) was a British war drama blatantly patterned after *Journey's End* (which, coincidentally, had begun a return visit on the same night that *Dancing Partner* had premiered). Soldiers trapped in a dugout can hear German sappers laying mines ever closer to them, but when they make a run to apparent safety they are mowed down.

In Samuel Ruskin Golding and Paul Dickey's **Through the Night** (8-18-30, Masque) Inez Talbott (Helen MacKellar), unhappily wed to an unloving husband (George MacQuarrie) who serves as crime commissioner, thinks she has found a way to restore their marriage after she captures Tony Collister (Noel Tearle) attempting to burglarize the Talbott home. Instead she finds love, for Tony proves to be a detective, and he exposes Talbott as a mastermind who has been, in fact, commissioning crimes—a series of jewel thefts— in league with his mistress, a phony Spanish noblewoman (Francesca Destinn).

The Ninth Guest (8-25-30, Eltinge) was Owen Davis's theatricalization of Gwen Briston and Bruce Manning's novelette. All its action unfolded in a New Orleans penthouse, done up modernistically in black and silver, with geometric decorations and angular furniture. Eight well-known citizens discover they have accepted telegraphed invitations from an anonymous host to the same party. A butler turns on a radio, which announces they are listening to WITS and goes on, "This is the voice of one you know well. One who hates you bitterly and has planned a revenge on you because of deadly wrongs." The voice also tells them he has invited a ninth guest—Death. One by one the guests are tricked into confessing their wrongs and into killing themselves. The first guest (William Courtleigh) is killed when he cuts himself on a poisoned silver cork. Other deaths come about by drinking a poisoned cocktail, by touching an electrified doorknob, by jumping from the room, and by shootings. Two estranged lovers (Owen Davis, Jr., and Brenda Dahlen) are saved and reunited when they identify the killer as the remaining guest (Alan Dinehart), a demented, embittered engineer. The play, which ran nine weeks despite largely negative notices, was the last that Al Woods would present in the theatre he had built in more prosperous times.

Arthur Hopkins fared a mite better when his production of Kenyon Nicholson's **Torch Song** (8-27-30, Plymouth) lasted eleven weeks. At a cheap Cincinnati roadhouse whose cabaret is done up with fake latticework and equally fake, dusty roses, Howard Palmer (Reed Brown, Jr.) a traveling salesman, cannot muster enough nerve to tell a pretty, blonde singer, Ivy Stevens (Mayo Methot), that he is leaving her to marry his boss's daughter, so he writes a curt note and walks out. The news is certain to shock the girl, for, as the bartender says, the "palooka" has "got that kid on the merry-go-round for fair." Audiences never see her immediate reaction, but discover that a year later Ivy has joined the Salvation Army. She unexpectedly meets Palmer again at a small-town hotel, attempts to convert him to God, but instead spends the night with him. (The curtain fell briefly, and when it rose the freshly crumpled bed linens told all.) Distraught and convinced she is a hopeless sinner, Ivy prepares to go back to singing, until a fellow Army proselytizer (Russell Hicks), who has come to love her, convinces her that her lapse was momentary and that she can still be saved and save others. Even Howard, genuinely moved by the pathos of Ivy's singing of "Onward, Christian Soldiers," concurs.

More than one critic compared Marya Mannes's **Café** (8-28-30, Ritz) to Elmer Rice's *Street Scene*—at least in nature though certainly not in quality. For like that earlier drama, the whole of its story unfolded on a sidewalk, only this time the sidewalk was in Paris and the center of interest was not a brownstone tenement but the Café des Anges in the Latin Quarter. Throughout the evening all manner of Parisians and tourists stroll by as Maurice Larned (Rollo Peters), an American painter living in France, confronts a crisis in his relationship with his longtime mistress, Sally Burch (Georgia Caine). For one, a pretty and young new expatriate, Jane Geddes (Frances Fuller), also a painter, tempts him away. Then the wife (Marjorie Gateson) he deserted in America years before comes to stake her claim. Finally Maurice opts to remain with Sally.

On the first anniversary of their marriage, in Albert Hackett and Frances Goodrich's **Up Pops the Devil** (9-1-30, Masque), Steve and Anne Merrick (Roger Pryor and Sally Bates) realize that Steve's work keeps him from being the writer he longs to become. They agree to change places, with Anne turning breadwinner by dancing in the chorus at the Roxy and Steve staying home all day. But Steve soon comes to resent his position. Noting how men in other parts of the world and how many animals behave, he complains, "It won't be long now before men will get back to their rightful place in society—being purely ornamental." Furthermore, he grows suspicious of Anne's relationship with a publisher (John Martson), while she wonders about his relationship with an aggressive southern belle (Janet McLeay) who lives in the apartment upstairs. Steve's unhappiness and their mutual doubts nearly destroy the marriage, but their inherent love for each other and news that Anne is pregnant save the day. Much of the humor came not from the main plot, but from friends and neighbors popping in for endless partying. Thus one of the friends (Hackett), soured on southern belles who always talk of their plantations and mammies, remarks, "I'm living for the day when I meet some good old white trash." September's first hit, the play chalked up an eighteen-week stand and returned just over a year later in musicalized form as *Everybody's Welcome*.

Several duds came next. Bayard Veiller's **That's the Woman** (9-3-30, Fulton) could not override a critical split decision. Authorities are amazed that wealthy Richard Norris (Gavin Muir) will allow himself to be convicted of murder and sent to prison, since they are convinced that he is withholding the name of a person who could support his alibi that he was walking in Central Park at the time of the killing. Mercer Trask (A. E. Anson), a sly, adroit detective, is called out of retirement to find the truth. He eventually discovers that Norris was with his mistress, Margaret Erskine (Phoebe Foster), a married woman. But neither will own up. Then Trask has a prostitute claim she was with Norris, provoking Margaret to blurt out the truth. Who was killed and who the real killer was are never revealed.

Eva Kay Flint and Martha Madison failed to deliver another *Subway Express* in their latest offering, **The Up and Up** (9-8-30, Biltmore). Bee (Sylvia Field), a manicurist, loves Doggie (Donald MacDonald), although she knows he is a speakeasy manager and works closely with the underworld. She is also aware that he has a dying wife. For a time, she is almost lured away by Curley (Pat O'Brien), a decent, levelheaded bookie,

who gives Bee and Doggie an apartment he uses as a front for his betting game. In the play's most exciting scene, the apartment is raided. "In come the dicks, unmannerly brutes who sneer in the face of an honest bookmaker, yank phones from their boxes . . . , rip up cushions, knock over bookcases [and] pull down draperies." In the end Bee decides to remain faithful to Doggie. Most critics found O'Brien's quiet, honest-in-his-fashion bookie the evening's chief attraction.

Even the performances in Hugh Stange's **The Long Road** (9-9-30, Longacre) displeased many reviewers. Stange's hero, Tom Lovett (Otto Kruger), a doctor, no sooner goes off to serve in the war than his wife (Marion Wells) begins an affair with a musician (Howard Miller). But he, too, is called to the colors. When he is mortally wounded he is brought to Lovett's tent. Not recognizing Lovett, he dictates a letter to Lovett's wife, thereby alerting the doctor to the truth. But after the war, Lovett and his wife are reconciled.

Matters took an upturn with Frank Craven's **That's Gratitude** (9-11-30, John Golden). Robert Grant (Craven) is a small-time, backwater theatrical producer, the sort who calls a show *Rio Nita* so that playgoers will think he is offering them *Rio Rita*. But he can be thoughtful. When he hears his neighbor at an Iowa hotel groaning in pain, he comes to his rescue. The grateful man, Tom Maxwell (George W. Barbier), an ink manufacturer, invites him to visit his Kansas home. Grant does. In things small (like singing aloud while his host is on the phone) and large (like meddling in family affairs), he soon has his host climbing walls. Bill North (Ross Alexander) is engaged to the Maxwells' homely daughter (Myrtle Clark) but really prefers their pretty one (Thelma Marsh). For a mere $7000 in Depression money from the young man, Grant contrives to lure the unwanted girl into show business and actually makes her so attractive that she finds another romance. But somehow no one seems thankful to Grant. After all, as Maxwell says, "That's gratitude." The comedy, which *Variety* applauded for its "good detail and engaging humor," ran six months.

Three plays, all failures, opened the following Monday. The longest run—six weeks—went to Ruth Welty and Roy Hargrave's **With Privileges** (9-15-30, Vanderbilt). The play was set in the kitchen of a cheap New York rooming house and featured the usual mixture of tenants. Spotlighted were an idealistic young architect (Hargrave) from Ohio and a strange, depressed Jewish girl (Joan Madison). After he wins $5000 for one of his designs, the architect offers to take the girl for a fling in Atlantic City. She accepts, hoping that news of her affair will reach a man who has deserted her. Learning the man could not care less, she jumps off the rooming house's roof. The architect finds consolation with another roomer (June Justice), a girl who has silently admired him for some time. This time *Variety* found the play "strongly suggestive of vermin," influenced perhaps by the fact that the curtain falls as an exterminator is squirting poison around the roach-infested kitchen.

Louis K. Anspacher's **The Rhapsody** (9-15-30, Cort) studied a young composer, Lodar Baron (Louis Calhern), who has come to America after the war. He cannot dispel his deep, pathological hatred for a sadistic sergeant who had humiliated him and seduced the girl he loved, Delphine (Julia Hoyt). A psychologist (John R. Hamilton) arranges a meeting between the two men and hands Baron a gun. Baron fires at his former superior (Curtis Karpe) and is led to believe he has killed the man. Only later does the psychologist admit the gun contained blanks. Nonetheless, Baron's obsession seems cured. Delphine, who has followed Baron to America, recognizes that he now loves Majorie Kellam (Natalie Shafer), so she self-sacrificingly walks out of his life.

Insult (9-15-30, 49th St.) was J. E. Harold Terry and Harry Tighe's translation of Jan Fabricus's Dutch drama *Dolle Hans*. The action occurred in the Dutch East Indies and told a story somewhat similar to *The Rhapsody*'s. A half-caste officer (Leslie Perrins) in the Dutch Colonial Army is goaded by a sadistic superior (D. A. Clarke-Smith) into striking him and then is sentenced to death for insubordination. The superior has resented the half-caste's romance with his daughter-in-law (Lydia Sherwood). His actions cause his son (James Raglan) to accept a suicidal assignment. Although he comes to have doubts about his own behavior, the father does nothing to stop the half-caste's execution.

Another foreign play that failed to find acceptance was Ivor Novello's **Symphony in Two Flats** (9-16-30, Shubert). Two stories were recounted in alternating scenes. One concerned tenants of the Floor Above; the other, tenants on the Floor Below. In the first, a young wife (Benita Hume) and her lover (Ivan Samson) lie to her blind husband (Novello) that his symphony has gained a large award. He is subsequently disillusioned on hearing the truth, but manages to save his marriage. In the other apartment an impoverished widow (Lilian Braithwaite) deftly maneuvers to keep her daughter (Ann Trevor) from marrying until she herself lands a rich second husband (J. Lister Williams).

Dorothy Heyward and Dorothy DeJagers's **Cinderelative** (9-18-30, Comedy) rehashed a story that *The Rainbow* had told more to Broadway's liking two decades earlier. A young lady (Dorothy Chard) has been raised in Paris by her divorced mother (Marjorie De Voe) and not known her father (Edward Hogan). She runs off to New York to meet him, and the pair take to each other. Unlike the heroine of the earlier work, this youngster resorts to disguises, which lead to complications, and she is unable to reunite her parents. Moreover, unlike *The Rainbow*, the play was panned and was quickly withdrawn.

So was Laurence Stallings's dramatization of Ernest Hemingway's **A Farewell to Arms** (9-22-30, National). Curiously, the critics appeared to echo one another. Thus Atkinson in the *Times* noted, "Stallings has done as well by the novel as anyone could, yet what he has done is not very much," while Robert Littell wrote in the *World*, "Stallings has contrived ingeniously to pack as much of the book as possible into three acts. At times he has done it well, at others it seems to me he has got it quite wrong—but I doubt if it could have been done at all." The story of the doomed romance of an ambulance driver (Glenn Anders) and a nurse (Elissa Landi) in wartime Italy was removed after three weeks. It was produced by Al Woods.

Woods's former partner, Sam H. Harris, gave the season its first smash hit with his presentation of George S. Kaufman and Moss Hart's **Once in a Lifetime** (9-24-30, Music Box). Kaufman was a veteran from whom critics expected good things, but Hart was a virtually new name.

. . .

George S[imon] **Kaufman** (1889–1961) was born in Pittsburgh. He served as a journalist on newspapers in Washington, D.C., and New York City before collaborating with Marc Connelly on *Dulcy* (1921). Subsequent successes with Connelly or with other collaborators, but only once alone, included *To the Ladies, Merton of the Movies, Beggar on Horseback, Minick, The Butter and Egg Man, The Royal Family,* and *June Moon.* He also wrote librettos for the Marx Brothers' musicals. Besides being master of the barbed riposte, he was a skilled director and play doctor.

. . .

Moss Hart (1904–1961) was a native New Yorker, who received his earliest training as assistant to Augustus Pitou, famed for mounting plays catering to one-night stands. His first play failed to reach Broadway, but his collaboration with Dorothy Heyward on the musical *Jonica* (1930) did open in New York, only to shutter quickly.

. . .

Sam H[enry] **Harris** (1872–1941) was born on New York's Lower East Side and worked at a variety of jobs before becoming manager of Terry McGovern, a prizefighter. Between bouts McGovern had been appearing in a touring burlesque show, and when Harris purchased into the mounting he found himself in show business. Shortly afterwards he joined with Paddy Sullivan and Woods to send out touring melodramas, then formed a new partnership with George M. Cohan in 1904. Together they produced numerous hits. The partnership broke up in 1920, and, on his own, he produced many musicals and such straight play hits as *Six-Cylinder Love, Rain, Icebound, Cradle Snatchers,* and *Chicago.*

. . .

A small-time vaudeville team, Hyland, Daniels and Lewis (Grant Mills, Jean Dixon, and Hugh O'Connell) are so down and out that they are reduced to spending much of their time at the Automat. They would even sleep there "if they could get beds into them slots." In desperation, they abandon their act to try their luck in Hollywood. On the train heading west May Daniels bamboozles the famous, egomaniacal Hollywood gossip columnist Helen Hobart (Spring Byington) into wangling them a job at the Glogauer Studios coaching diction. The studios are a hectically busy, gaudily ultra-modernistic affair where nattily dressed page boys regularly appear carrying illuminated signs announcing the boss's whereabouts—such as "Mr. Glogauer is on Number Four." But since the Schlepkin Brothers brought out a sound film, Glogauer and all their other rivals are in trouble and in a quandary. Glogauer (Charles Halton) himself bemoans the loss of the good old days of silent films: "You couldn't stop making money—even if you turned out a *good* picture you made money." When their diction coaching fails, the old vaudevillians are fired, until George Lewis unthinkingly reminds Glogauer that he passed up the opportunity to have the first talking film. The stunned boss so admires George's candor that he makes him a director. Unfortunately, George's film seems headed for disaster, since George not only forgot to have the bright lights turned on while filming, but kept munching nuts during the takes, leaving a strange crackling sound throughout the picture. Worst of all, he filmed the wrong script. The trio are fired again. But to everyone's amazement the film receives rave notices, the critics comparing the incessant crunching to Eugene O'Neill's use of drums in *The Emperor Jones.* When news arrives that demolition crews are wrecking the studios, George announces he will build a bigger one.

In a notable departure, Kaufman took a role in the comedy. He played Lawrence Vail, a playwright brought out to the Coast with a wholesale lot of other New York writers, given a magnificent office, and then ignored. Frustrated at being unable to see Glogauer, he tells a page brandishing one of the illuminated signs signaling Glogauer's whereabouts, "I'm going to the

men's room and if anybody wants me I'll be in Number Three." The play had a huge cast of yes-men, glamor girls, Hollywood bit players, colorfully garbed extras, secretaries, pages, and even the twelve Schlepkin brothers (only one of whom had a single line).

Greeted by largely enthusiastic reviews—one notice calling it "the funniest, most searching play of the picture business"—the comedy ran a solid year.

Another big hit came in hot on its heels, although Zoë Akins's **The Greeks Had a Word for It** (9-25-30, Sam H. Harris) chalked up only a seven-month run. It achieved the run in the face of numerous nitpicking and unfavorable notices. In a sense, it looked at the lives, several years on, of characters like those in *The Gold Diggers.* Schatze (Dorothy Hall), Jean (Verree Teasdale), and Polaire (Muriel Kirkland) once had been *Follies* beauties. Today they still lead the good life thanks to rich men friends. For a time, Jean takes a fancy to Dey Emery (Don Beddoe), the weakling son of a wealthy banker, but Dey prefers Polaire. That could lead to unpleasantness until Jean lands a proposal of marriage from Dey's daddy (Frederic Worlock). Just before the wedding is to take place at a posh suite in the Ambassador Hotel, Jean confesses to the other girls that the elder Emery is "making me read Les Miserables through, and I get ten thousand dollars the day I can talk French to him fifteen minutes." Such forced learning does not sit well with her. So when Schatze and Polaire tell Jean they are joining some airline executives and heading for a carefree time in Paris, where the champagne "grows wild," Jean pulls off her lace veil and her wedding gown with the lemon blossoms on it, grabs her hat, her pocketbook, and a wrap-around cloak to hide her undies, and heads out with them.

John M. Kirkland's **Frankie and Johnnie** (9-25-30, Republic) was set in a splashily decorated waterfront dive in 1849 St. Louis. The pianist is trying to work out a tune, without much luck. Two of the bar's habitués are Frankie (Anne Forrest), a streetwalker, and Johnnie (Frank McGlynn, Jr.), a card sharp. Frankie and Johnnie are lovers. After Johnnie piles up $13,000 in winnings, Frankie suggests they head west and lead better lives. But Johnnie has been two-timing Frankie, having a free-spending affair with Nellie Bly (Roberta Beatty). So when Frankie learns that Johnnie has squandered his winnings on another girl, she shoots and kills him. The pianist uses the story to complete his song. During its tryout, the play had been raided by the police, who were offended by its story, its characters, and lines such as the one defending prostitution as "the only profession for which women are exclusively equipped." None of that bothered New Yorkers, who were indifferent to this "astonishing blending of desperate cynicism and boob sentimentality." Scuttlebutt gave out that Wells Root, F. S. Merlin, and Willard Keefe collaborated on the play. A few seasons down the road—a tobacco road, at that—Kirkland would have better luck with another drama about lowlifes.

Lynn Riggs, a young Midwest poet, would never have a major hit. But in the current season he found respected producers for two of his dramas. Arthur Hopkins's mounting of **Roadside** (9-26-30, Longacre) came first. Texas (Ralph Bellamy) is a wild, swaggering drifter, who saunters into Indian Territory, gets drunk, shoots up a courtroom, and then escapes from jail. He tells all this to Hannie (Ruthelma Stevens), a farm girl he meets and quickly falls in love with. Her taunting of him provokes him into surrendering, but his wild nature will not allow him to remain caged up. He once more shoots up the courtroom, then moves on to parts unknown with Hannie and her father (Frederick Burton).

There were no men in the cast of Philip and Aimee Stuart's English drama **Nine till Six** (9-27-30, Ritz). Set in a Regent Street dressmaking shop, what little story it had told of class differences among the employees and the search for someone who has been stealing dresses. When the culprit is found, her pathetic story causes her to be forgiven.

One, Two, Three (9-29-30, Henry Miller) was a double bill of Ferenc Molnár plays, taking its name from the longer of the pair. In Sidney Howard's faithful translation Nordson (Arthur Byron), a titan among Central European businessmen, learns that Lydia (Audray Dale), an American girl whose parents have entrusted her to his care, has secretly married a socialistic taxi driver and is pregnant. Since her parents are coming to pick her up, Nordson must turn the cabman (John Williams) into a rich nobleman. By some hook and more crook, he does. In Arthur Richman's translation of **The Violet** a producer (A. P. Kaye) is discouraged by the fact that every would-be chorus girl is willing to sleep with him to obtain work. So he is overjoyed to find a young lady (Ruth Gordon) who is attracted to him for himself and does not want to work in his show. Both titles were literal translations from the Hungarian, but neither piece found many enthusiastic supporters. On the other hand, Byron and Gordon were singled out for their superb performances.

September's last hit was yet another importation, Benn W. Levy's **Mrs. Moonlight** (9-29-30, Charles Hopkins). Reviewers discerned a touch of James M. Barrie in this saga of a young lady (Edith Barrett) who cannot grow old since she has wished for eternal youth on a magic necklace. She runs away from her marriage, returns years later to prevent her daughter (Katherine Standing) from making an unhappy one, then dies at seventy alongside her husband (Guy Standing), a doddering old man, although she is still young and beautiful.

Jed Harris found no good fortune in **Mr. Gilhooley** (9-30-30, Broadhurst), Frank B. Elser's dramatization of Liam O'Flaherty's novel. Since its co-star was Helen Hayes, the bitterness over Harris's suing her when she became pregnant during the tour of *Coquette* had obviously been set aside. Gilhooley (Arthur Sinclair) takes in a waif (Hayes) who is willing to be kept in grand style, even though she admits she loves another, younger man. Later, discovering the girl has been seeing her young man, he strangles her and shoots himself. While the play was dismissed, the leads were praised. Sinclair, a veteran of the Abbey, was lauded for his rich, mellifluous voice and range of characterization. The *Journal*'s John Anderson wrote of Hayes, "Her performance of the street girl is schemed out with such intuition and stated with such clarity that it becomes a major portrait."

Apart from one noteworthy revival, October came close to being a washout artistically. Commercially, its first novelty was a near miss. Although the heroine of Brian Marlow and Viña Delmar's provocatively titled **Bad Girl** (10-2-30, Hudson), a stage version of Delmar's novel, was not very naughty even by 1930s standards, the play itself raised some hackles. Like *Frankie and Johnnie*, the show had been raided by the police during its tryout in the Bronx. (The headlines helped the play gross a whopping $12,000 per week in both its Bronx and Brooklyn pre-Broadway stands.) Dot (Sylvia Sidney) and Eddie (Paul Kelly), a $40-a-week radio store clerk, agree to marry after Dot learns that she is pregnant. Each believes the other does not want the child, and neither, therefore, is willing to confess to his or her own interest. One friend (Sacha Beaumont) urges her not to have the child, but another (Charlotte Wynters) convinces her that she will come to want it. After giving birth, Dot admits she cares. In a taxi on the way home from the hospital, the driver takes a bump too speedily, provoking Eddie to scold angrily, "You ain't driving no hook-and-ladder!" So the pair realize they both love the baby. What shocked many playgoers and critics was a second-act childbirth scene, done in silhouette. Lit in such a manner that their outlines were sometimes grotesquely enlarged, nurses scurried about and a doctor attempted to reassure the pain-wracked Dot. The play ran ten and a half weeks.

Three weeks sufficed for **Stepdaughters of War** (10-6-30, Empire), Kenyon Nicholson's theatricalization of Helen Zenna Smith's novel. A socially prominent woman (Katharine Alexander), serving as an ambulance driver in France during the war, falls in love with a handsome captain (Warren William), even though she is engaged to another man. When the captain suffers

8

emasculating wounds and complains that he is now only the ghost of a man, the woman, herself deathly exhausted, convinces him that they should marry. Superb staging offered "the flicker of flame in a barracks stove, the long pageant of sunset through a window, the tread of feet off-stage—even the sounds of motors and airplanes, which are often so spurious in the theatre."

L. Allen Harker and F. R. Pryor's **Marigold** (10-8-30, 49th St.) was another of the London hits imported during the season that was rejected by American playgoers. In it, a Scottish girl slated to marry a stuffy lord finds her own true love in a dashing dragoon. The play was set in Victorian times.

On the 10th, the Civic Repertory Theatre offered Arthur Schnitzler's *The Green Cockatoo* as a companion piece for its mounting of *The Lady from Alfaqueque*. Schnitzler's Pagliacci-like tale, set in the French Revolution, had first been seen in New York twenty years earlier.

A few critics enjoyed Lawton Campbell's broad spoof of Southern traditionalism, **Solid South** (10-14-30, Lyceum). More did not. But most hailed the performances, especially that of Richard Bennett, got up in a Vandyke and flowing mustache, as an unreconstructed Confederate. His Major Follonsby is determined to protect the honor of Southern womanhood, especially when it is endangered by the presence of Yankees, and even more so when those damn Yankees are Republicans. So he runs for his gun when Edward Garrison (Moffat Johnston) and Garrison's son, Rex (Owen Davis, Jr.), appear on the scene and start to court Follonsby's widowed daughter-in-law, the languishingly coquettish Leila Mae (Jessie Royce Landis), and his sparkish granddaughter, Bam (Bette Davis). All's made right with the world after Garrison buys the rundown, mortgaged-to-the-hilt plantation, paying a price that assures the major a comfortable retirement.

That same evening, down in Greenwich Village, the old Provincetown Playhouse was temporarily renamed the Washington Arch Playhouse, and a group of young professionals, unimaginatively calling themselves the Washington Arch Players, offered a revival of John Galsworthy's 1912 hit, *The Pigeon*, in which a naively charitable man attempts to find a home for some street people.

There was cheering and hat-hurling when the beautiful Jane Cowl bounced onstage in tights and a tasseled cap as *Twelfth Night*'s Viola. Following her premiere at Maxine Elliott's on the 15th, the aging Percy Hammond cooed in the *Herald Tribune*, "I have dim memories of former Violas—Miss Julia Marlowe, Miss Annie Russell, and Miss Viola Allen, all of whom were acclaimed in their day. . . . But my happiest 'Twelfth Night'

recollections are those of Miss Cowl and her company." That company presented Walter Kingsford's applauded Sir Toby Belch, Arthur Hohl's Sir Andrew Aguecheek, Jerry Bowman's Sebastian, and, best of all, Leon Quartermaine's "fatuously graceful and exquisitely entertaining" Malvolio. However, Raymond Sovey's brilliant settings all but stole the show. He turned the stage into a huge Victorian picture book and had a clown in motley turn its gigantic pages for each scene change. Hard times and a slightly out-of-the-way location hurt business, but the play still chalked up sixty-five performances, eventually in repertory with another production.

The one novelty to open that same evening, Vera Caspary and Winifred Lenihan's **Blind Mice** (10-15-30, Times Square), was hooted and hurriedly removed. It was the second play in three weeks' time to have an all-woman cast. Taking place in a residential hotel for young ladies, it divided its large cast into "Those Who Stay Home Saturday Night"—the homely and the wallflowers—and "Those Who Go Out Saturday Night"—the brash and the beautiful. One of the beauties is pregnant Mae Thorpe (Claiborne Foster), who learns that her lover, like the man in *Torch Song*, has deserted her to marry his boss's daughter. She decides to accept the proposal of a compassionate, middle-aged pharmacist.

Geoffrey Kerr's **London Calling** (10-18-30, Little) focused on two brothers, Willie and George Craft (Charles Lawrence and Kerr), whose American mother (Anne Sutherland) and British father long have been divorced. Willie has been raised in America by his mother, George by his father in London. When George pops in for a surprise visit, he and Willie are soon vamped by a designing woman, Anne Hunter (Helen Flint). Mother uses all her wiles to be rid of the pest, but in the process decides that perhaps she should be reconciled with the boys' father.

The next Monday brought in four new plays, only one of which scored a modest success. William Du Bois's **Pagan Lady** (10-20-30, 48th St.) was compared—unfavorably—with *Rain*. Lenore Ulric's popularity and sultry performance accounted primarily for its nineteen-week run. She was seen as Dot Hunter, a voluptuous creature who boards at a seedy hotel in a small tourist town on Florida's east coast. Her roughneck, bootlegging lover, Dingo Mike (Russell Hardie), having gone off on a trip, she sets her net for Ernest Todd (Franchot Tone), a virgin missionary who, with his uncle (Thomas Findlay), has come all the way from the Dakotas to purge Florida of sin. She lands him after swimming with him to a deserted offshore island, only to have him slink away in shame. No matter to Dot, for Dingo is coming back, and Ernest may be a more understanding man for the experience.

Martin Mooney and Thompson Burtis's **Sisters of the Chorus** (10-20-30, Ritz) was yet one more yarn about stage folk. Anne Page (Dorothea Chard) shows up at a small apartment shared by three chorus girls, including her no longer young sister, Blanche (Enid Markey), who now has trouble earning a spot even in the back row of the least fancy choruses. Anne finds herself not only mixed up with underworld figures but accused of killing one of them. After a murder and a suicide, Blanche straightens matters out and sends the girl back home. Some critics were amused that all this was listed as a comedy. But then there was Edna Hibbard, as a typical wisecracking chorine, and Jean Malin, at the time a celebrated speakeasy m.c., as "a pansy who 'never resists the police.' "

The evening's other two openings were foreign plays. Frederick Lonsdale's **Canaries Sometimes Sing** (10-20-30, Fulton) told of two unsatisfactorily wed couples. When one (Mary Merrall) of the women finally agrees to a divorce, her husband (Robert Loraine) decides to live with the other couple (Athole Stewart and Yvonne Arnaud).

Jean Giraudoux's **Siegfried** (10-20-30, Civic Repertory) was offered in a translation by Philip Carr. The play looked at a wounded soldier (Jacob Ben-Ami) who rises to save Germany from its postwar hell and shame. He remembers nothing of his prewar past, until it is finally shown that he is actually a French writer who has been suffering from amnesia. He decides to return home, but hopes from there to help dissipate the hatred between the two nations.

The next evening brought in two more failures, but at least one of them contained a performance that thrilled the critics. Sidney R. Buchman's **This One Man** (10-21-30, Morosco) studied a pair of disparate brothers. Marvin Holland (Paul Guilfoyle) is a delicate, homely young man, filled with goodwill and thoughtfulness. His pampered brother, Saul (Paul Muni), is a virile, handsome criminal. After Saul escapes from jail and kills a man in a bank robbery, Marvin claims he himself is the guilty one. He is convicted and executed. Sitting alone in his cell, Saul learns of the execution and finally is overwhelmed with remorse and compassion. Once again Muni (who had abandoned the name he had been employing, Muni Wisenfreund) was showered with praise and hailed as an actor of surpassing promise— "overpowering and magnificent," "stunning and compelling," "remarkable."

The central figure in Frank Mitchell Dazey and Agnes Christine Johnston's **Sweet Stranger** (10-21-30, Cort) was Ann Norton (Linda Watkins), a slim blonde beauty so on her uppers that she decides to become a kept woman. She barges into the office of J. W. Marvin (Clyde Fillmore), the head of a giant utilities holding company and a notorious womanizer. Ann, who claims to be a judge's daughter, knows that Marvin's wife has long since left him and that he is having difficulties with his current "keptie," a girl named Pinkie Heath. Despite those problems, Marvin is about to sail for Europe with Pinkie, so he turns Ann over to his assistant, Albert Ruskin (Ralph Morgan), who is engaged to Marvin's daughter, until he returns. By the time he comes back, prepared to set up Ann as Pinkie's successor, Ann and Albert have fallen in love.

Another pair of flops premiered two nights later. Robert Wilder's three-performance fiasco, **Sweet Chariot** (10-23-30, Ambassador), was inspired by the notorious black self-promoter Marcus Garvey. Rechristened Marius Harvey, he was portrayed by Broadway's erstwhile Porgy, Frank Wilson. After fraudulently selling stock in a steamship company, he convinces his followers to sail with him to a promised land in Africa. There he is rejected by the authorities. Beaten and deserted by those who once had admired him, he is left to fend as best he can with a spiteful strumpet, Delia (Vivian Baber), and the still loyal, loving Lola (Fredi Washington).

Good performances by the willowy Miriam Hopkins and the adroit Anthony Kemble Cooper could not propel **His Majesty's Car** (10-23-30, Ethel Barrymore), which Fanny and Frederic Hatton adapted from an unspecified Hungarian play by Attila Von Orbok, beyond a week and a half. An attractive young lady is taken for a ride by an automobile salesman in the king's new car. Rumors fly that she is the king's new mistress. The king hears the rumors, comes to see just who the lady is, and is smitten.

On the 26th, Giuseppe Sterni's Teatro d' Arte began a seasons-long series of generally Sunday night performances at the Bijou (and later at other houses), offering Italian plays by Pirandello, Giuseppe Giacosa, Sem Beffi, and numerous additional Italian dramatists, as well as Italian translations of modern American and other European dramas.

Michael Grismaijer's **The Noble Experiment** (10-27-30, Waldorf) was a somewhat intemperate attack on Prohibition couched in melodramatic terms. Alexa Jovanovitch (Gordon Richard), an Austrian diplomat who studied at Oxford, sees a brighter future in running a speakeasy after his fiancée's bootlegger father is imprisoned. He tries to have the judge who convicted her father impeached, but before his plans come to fruition he is shot and killed by a disgruntled associate (Sidney Satvro) at the Club des Aristocrats he runs with the girl (Anne Lubow).

If it had nothing else, the Theatre Guild's mounting of S. Tretyakov's **Roar China** (10-27-30, Martin Beck)—in a translation by Ruth Langner—had some of the era's most memorable scenery. There was no curtain. Audiences entering the playhouse saw coolies slaving on a quay where the orchestra pit had been. Beyond them the Beck's stage had been converted into an ocean—with 1200 cubic feet of real water. Colorful, large-sailed sampans floated by. Only when they moved off did the audience see the gigantic, menacing battleship lurking in the background, its three huge guns pointed directly at playgoers. (In his *Part of a Lifetime,* Lee Simonson details the obstacles that had to be surmounted before everything worked as planned.) Tretyakov's blatantly anti-Western story told what followed after a brutal American exporter (William Gargan) falls or is pushed to his death from one of the boats. A British man-of-war is sent in to wreak vengeance. The captain (Edward Cooper), refusing to accept the local authorities' claims that the death was accidental, demands the killers must be put to death. Unable to find the real killers, if any, the authorities are forced to garrote two patently innocent boatmen, leading the other Chinese to rebel. The play ends with the battleship sailing slowly forward, the machine gun in its lookout blazing away. *Variety,* noting that the play's German production had been welcomed by Communists, remarked, "New York too has plenty of Reds. Just a question of whether they care much about the lowly workers of the far away China or will pay $3 if they have it loose." They didn't and they wouldn't, so the mounting was withdrawn after nine weeks. Although the play supposedly cost only $12,000, it lost $31,000. By season's end, with only one hit to its credit, the Guild was $180,000—in Depression values—in the red. Moreover, the arguments and losses associated with the show did the Guild irreparable damage. The rejection of Rouben Mamoulian as director sent him to Hollywood and temporarily ended his stage career. Right-wingers pointed to the play to suggest that the Guild was Communist dominated, while left-wingers, furious at the removal of some of the most offensive slanting in the original, denounced the Guild, and several joined the disaffected who were already planning a rival company. To help eradicate the loss, the Guild in future seasons embraced a more safely commercial policy, thereby alienating many who had hailed its artistic daring and integrity.

There were few takers for **Puppet Show** (10-28-30, Belmont), Samuel Ruskin Golding's venture into Pirandello-like drama. Sitting in his study and working on his new play, Anthony Davies (J. W. Austin) is assailed by the very characters he has created. They question the nuances and turns of plot in his latest work, in which an unhappy wife (Eunice Stoddard) is accused of killing her husband (Donald Blackwell) while attempting to kill her husband's mistress (Doris Un-

derwood). A trial elicits the fact that the mistress actually did the shooting. When the characters plead with the playwright "to strike one blow for truth in a world of eternal lies," he agrees to rework the play.

The month's biggest hit, Edgar Wallace's **On the Spot** (10-29-30, Forrest), ran only 167 performances and was one of only two October plays to step over the 100-performance mark. Wallace, a celebrated English mystery writer, claimed to have written the piece after a visit to America. Some critics saw it as a delicious send-up. Tony Perrelli (Crane Wilbur) is Chicago's most famous gangster. After he orders the killing of two thugs who belong to Mike Feeney's mob, which has been attempting to horn in on his territory, he hears from Feeney (Arthur R. Vinton). Feeney demands the killers be sent into his territory, so he can wipe them out. Since one of the men has been trying to steal Perrelli's girl, Minn Lee (Anna May Wong), and Perrelli himself has his eye on the other man's moll, he agrees. But after the murders, Minn Lee, who had come to love the dead man, stabs herself to death, arranging it so that Perrelli is convicted for her murder. Wallace spoofed the gangster's pretensions—his love of opera, his playing an organ he has had installed in his lavish apartment, his 200 silk shirts, his burying his men in silver caskets, and his sending flowers to the funerals not merely of his own men but even of those whom he has had killed. Indeed, he sends so many wreaths that one cohort tells him, "It would pay us to grow our own flowers." (Another reviewer heard the line in a slightly different way, quoting it as "It would be much cheaper if we raised our own flowers.")

The Last Enemy (10-30-30, Shubert), Frank Harvey's four-performance dud, was a weirdo. It begins with two explorers, Alexander McKenzie and James Churchill (George Merritt and Donald Eccles), freezing to death in the Antarctic. Climbing a ladder to the Pearly Gates, they are advised by a heavenly janitor (Cecil Ramage) that, although they are dead, they can still influence the living. The one sees to it that Cynthia Perry (Jessica Tandy) is reconciled with Jerry Warrender (Derrick de Marney), who had attempted to rape her while he was drunk. The other man consoles Harry Graham (Robert Douglas), whose love for Cynthia was never reciprocated and who now is dying in a shell-hole. He helps Harry to start up the ladder.

November compensated in some measure for October's drought. Its first show, H. M. Harwood's English comedy **The Man in Possession** (11-1-30, Booth), was a near miss. As such it was one of the few among the many shows the Shuberts imported during the season that was not a major money-loser for them. But they were chided for offering the short play, which had been part of a double bill in London, as a whole evening's entertainment. A scapegrace (Leslie Banks) is disowned by his snooty family after he serves time for selling an automobile he did not own. He takes employment as a bum bailiff, a man assigned to look after someone in financial trouble. That someone is a lovely lady (Isabel Jeans), so when she expects visitors he agrees to pretend to be a butler. The visitors turn out to be his brother, who is engaged to the lady, and his parents. His outraged family pay him to disappear. He does, taking with him the lady, who has fallen in love with him.

The Theatre Guild's only money-maker during the season was Maxwell Anderson's **Elizabeth the Queen** (11-3-30, Guild). Rival courtiers are jealous of the handsome, haughty, ambitious young Essex (Alfred Lunt), who has become the favorite of the aging queen (Lynn Fontanne). They cleverly lure him into taking his troops to Ireland, a futile campaign which Elizabeth has told him he must not participate in, then intercept letters between him and the sovereign to force a breach. Called before the queen, he appears with his men and, in effect, makes the queen his prisoner. He confesses that he does want power and thinks himself better fit to rule England—but only in conjunction with her. The defiant Elizabeth tells him, "I could have given freely—/ But not now. Not surrendering. Not to a victor." They nonetheless profess their love for one another until Elizabeth convinces Essex to send his men away. When he does, she orders him arrested and sent to the Tower. Shortly before he is to be executed, she calls him to her and gives him a chance to redeem himself, but he feels that for all their love, sooner or later she will discard and kill him. He jokes, "I have an appointment near-by with a headsman./ He comes sharp on the hour," She laments, "I could be young with you, but now I'm old./ I know how it will be without you. The sun/ Will be empty and circle an empty earth." After Essex leaves, the grief-stricken queen covers her ears so as not to hear the bells that chime the time of his execution. For her part, Fontanne hid her beauty by shaving her eyebrows, adding a putty nose and a layer of false skin to make her flesh seem to sag, and donning an ugly red wig. She won by far the evening's best notices, typified by the *Post*'s John Mason Brown's observing, "Her Elizabeth, with her amazing make-up, her booming chest tones, her imperiousness, her lusty oaths, her good nature and her pathetic craving for Essex, is a glorious, vigorous portrait." Lunt was also praised, but obviously took second place. The play divided the critics, many of whom questioned how genuinely poetic Anderson's blank verse was. Atkinson also complained that it was "no more dramatic than a tone-poem." Still, Burns Mantle called the drama "forthright and eloquent." Whatever its shortcomings,

the evening consolidated the fame of its playwright and his stars.

. . .

[James] **Maxwell Anderson** (1888–1959) was born in Atlantic, Pa., and educated at the University of North Dakota and at Stanford. He served as a teacher and journalist before his first play, *The White Desert,* was produced in 1923. He soon found success with *What Price Glory?* (1924), written in collaboration with Lawrence Stallings. His only other hit among his offerings that followed was *Saturday's Children* (1927).

. . .

Lynn Fontanne [née Lillie Louise Fontanne] (1887–1983) was born in England and studied there with Ellen Terry before making her debut in 1905 in *Cinderella.* She came to America briefly in 1910 to appear in *Mr. Preedy and the Countess,* then returned permanently in 1916. She met Lunt, her future husband, that year when they performed in Washington in *A Young Man's Fancy,* but did not make a major name for herself until *Dulcy* (1920). Beginning with *The Guardsman* (1924) she usually appeared opposite Lunt. However, he was not in the cast when she created the role of Nina in *Strange Interlude* (1928). Fontanne was a slender, dark-haired, and sharp-eyed actress with a throaty contralto voice and a regal bearing. One associate compared her to "a brilliant and beautiful tiger."

. . .

Alfred [David] **Lunt** (1892–1980) was born in Milwaukee and educated at Carroll College. Abandoning plans to become an architect, he made his theatrical debut in 1912 with the Castle Square Theatre stock company in Boston. He then toured with Lillie Langtry and Margaret Anglin before first appearing in New York in *Romance and Arabella* (1917). He scored a major success in *Clarence* (1919). Among later plays in which he did not appear with Fontanne after their 1924 triumph in *The Guardsman* were *Ned McCobb's Daughter* (1927) and *Marco Millions* (1928). A handsome man, he had a distingushed voice and "luminous brown eyes, with their always-startled expression."

. . .

While younger artists continued to make their mark, one older playwright, Thompson Buchanan, bid farewell to Broadway with **As Good as New** (11-3-30, Times Square). A happy tryst between Tom Banning (Otto Kruger) and Violet Hargrave (Vivienne Osborne) is interrupted when Banning's wife (Marjorie Gateson) and two detectives storm into Tom's supposedly secret apartment in Greenwich Village. The Bannings' children are appalled when their mother says she will sue for divorce. Mary (Dorothy Libaire) announces she will live in sin with her fiancé, while Tommy (Billy Quinn) plans to run away rather than live with a stepparent. The Bannings decide to forget and forgive. But all may not go well in the future, for as the curtain falls Tom is on the phone furtively arranging a new liaison. He gave up the struggle after seven weeks.

A much quicker failure was **Room of Dreams** (11-5-30, Empire), which Daniel Coxe, James Burrell, and Anne MacDonald took from an unidentified Viennese play by Ernest Raoul Weiss. A man attempts to lure away a friend's wife by redecorating his own apartment to resemble hers. The husband learns of the scheme and attempts to break it up, but, since he was drunk, the next day he is made to believe the whole contretemps occurred in his own flat. With the play's closing, the New York Theatre Assembly, which had been founded the previous season in hopes of competing with the Guild, also folded.

Mr. Samuel (11-10-30, Little), Winthrop Ames's adaptation of Edmond Fleg's *Le Marchand de Paris,* was withdrawn after just one week. Samuel Brisach, a wealthy New York businessman, has a heart attack after his family and his associates, who fear the man is overextending himself and are concerned with his costly, socialistic effort to provide all his employees with a guarantee against joblessness, attempt to oust him. From his sickbed, he buys back enough shares to reassume control, make a $750,000 profit, and save the company. The play was tedious, and even Edward G. Robinson's "whirlwind style of acting" could not truly enliven it. Shortly after the play closed, Robinson headed for Hollywood and was not seen in another play on Broadway for a quarter of a century.

That same night saw a revival at the Waldorf of Aaron Hoffman's 1923 comedy, *The Good Old Days.* This tale of two former buddies who take opposite stances on Prohibition was now called *Light Wines and Beer* and featured Sam Bernard II (actually the first Bernard's nephew) and Al Shean (of Gallagher and Shean fame) in the roles once played by Charles Winninger and Charles Bickel.

Five performances were all New York would allow Jack Larric's **Made in France** (11-11-30, Cort), with a plot very like that of *The High Cost of Loving* (8-25-14). For years a French girl (Lya de Putti) has been milking former doughboys by claiming that each had fathered her twins. When the men coincidentally appear at the same time to see their offspring, they find they were not totally taken advantage of, since the girl has been using their funds to support war orphans.

Rafael Sabatini's **The Tyrant** (11-12-30, Longacre) sent its colorful period costumes and settings to Cain's warehouse after a mere week and a half. In that time, Panthasilea Degli Speranzoni (Lily Cahill), the daughter of the Count of Solignola, whose territory is being menaced by Cesare Borgia (Louis Calhern), attempts to seduce Borgia and lure him to his death. Instead, she falls in love with him and drinks the poison planned for him.

One of the season's biggest hits—444 performances at a high $4.40 top—was **Grand Hotel** (11-13-30, National). Originally a German novel, *Menschen im Hotel,* by Vicki Baum, it had been theatricalized by its author and presented in Berlin under Max Reinhardt's auspices. W. A. Drake did the American translation. The action transpires over three days at a great Berlin hostelry. A lovelorn, timeworn ballerina (Eugenie Leontovich), a rich businessman (Siegfried Rumann), a thieving aristocrat (Henry Hull), and a dying bookkeeper (Sam Jaffe) out for a final fling are all staying there. The aristocrat uses the bookkeeper's room to enter into the ballerina's apartment in order to steal her jewels. He falls in love with her, so attempts instead to rob the businessman. He is caught and killed. The play, which was subsequently made into a popular film with Greta Garbo and John Barrymore, and which returned to Broadway in a musical version in 1989, helped boost the career of its young producer, Herman Shumlin.

. . .

Herman Shumlin (1898–1979) was born in Atwood, Colo. He worked at the *Clipper* and at *Billboard* before serving first with Schwab and Mandel, best known for their musicals, and afterwards with Jed Harris. He produced his first major hit, *The Last Mile,* the previous season.

. . .

Alfred H. White and P. William Tell's **Pressing Business** (11-17-30, Republic) might well have been called *Abie's Irish Ward,* not only because of its subject but because many of its players had appeared in one company or another of *Abie's Irish Rose.* Abie Goodman (White) and Izzy Small (Bernard Gorcey) have enough trouble moving from their small tailor's shop into the cloak and suit business without Abie's son, Ben (Alan Lowe), falling in love with Peggy O'Day (Nina Walker), a girl whom Abie had promised her long-absent father to look after. To worsen matters, Izzy's daughter (Mildred Elliott) has been making goo-goo eyes at a boy who is not Jewish. But old man O'Day (Andrew Mack) turns up in the last act after a sixteen-year absence to set things right. The play was the last to play the Republic before it was turned first into a Minsky burlesque house and then into a cinema. The comedy, and the other play that opened the same evening, both ran two weeks.

In **Marseilles** (11-17-30, Henry Miller), which Sidney Howard took from Marcel Pagnol's *Marius,* a

French girl (Frances Torchiana) gives herself to a boy (Alexander Kirkland) she loves even though she knows he will soon run off to his beloved sea. Although she is pregnant, she self-sacrificingly presses him to leave. The boy's father (Dudley Digges), who runs a seaside bar, persuades an old widower (Guy Kibbee) to wed the girl. Although New Yorkers rejected the play, they subsequently embraced a musical version (officially based on Pagnol's later film trilogy), *Fanny* (1954).

Two more foreign plays premiered the next evening. For their third effort of the season, the busy Hattons turned Lili Hatvany's *Ma este vaga soha* into **Tonight or Never** (11-18-30). The program listed the characters by such generic names as the Prima Donna, His Excellency, and the Unknown Gentleman, but they had names in the play. Nella Vargo (Helen Gahagan), angling for a contract with the Metropolitan, is warned that her singing is passionless and is urged to have a love affair. Obviously the elderly Count Albert (Warburton Gamble), who has helped her, has not been sufficient inspiration. But then she meets Fletcher (Melvyn Douglas), and one night with him provides the requisite ardor. Afterwards, he turns out to be an agent for the Met, but that does not hinder their marriage plans. Gahagan had trained for a time to be a singer, so was able to warble at least one aria onstage. The play's producer was David Belasco, and he filled the production with Belasco touches. A second-act hotel suite was replete with all the latest Continental hotel atmosphere and gadgetry. But Belasco had taken ill during the tryout and, for the first time in his career, was not well enough to attend one of his New York openings. Although he subsequently saw the finished mounting, he died in May, before the comedy completed its seven-month run.

Jane Cowl brought out Benn W. Levy's **Art and Mrs. Bottle** (11-18-30, Maxine Elliott's) to alternate in repertory with her Shakespearean comedy. Mrs. Bottle returns to her family twenty years after she ran off with an artist (Leon Quartermaine). In that time, she had remarried when the artist in turn deserted her. Now she finds her daughter (Katharine Hepburn) in love with the same artist, and her son (G. P. Huntley, Jr.) enamored of a shallow model (Joyce Carey). She rids her children of these undesirable relationships and even contemplates reunion with her mundane ex (Walter Kingsford).

Writing in the *World-Telegram*, Robert Garland hailed Paul Osborn's **The Vinegar Tree** (11-19-30, Playhouse) as "a sustained and sophisticated comedy, possessing the breath of bitterness and the touch of tragedy without which comedy is never quite complete." Nonetheless much of the credit for the play's season-long run had to be given to Mary Boland: "She times her lines perfectly; she calculates every gesture and

grimace to the exact point of intelligibility and she sweeps the audience furiously before her." Boland played Laura Merrick, a flighty, fortyish woman married to a cantankerous man (H. Reeves-Smith) in his sixties. When she is told how wonderfully peaceful her world is, she retorts ruefully that it is "the peace of the grave." At the same time that the Merricks' daughter, Leone (Helen Brooks), returns home from college lamenting that the boy she loves has rejected her for lacking experience, Laura's much-married, globetrotting sister, Winifred (Katherine Wilson), turns up for the first time in fifteen years. Laura is embarrassed that while she believes she recognizes Winifred's face, she cannot recall her name. But she soon happily embraces her dear Winky. Although Winifred's latest lover, Max Lawrence (Warren William), who years before had dated Laura, also comes, he comes separately for appearance's sake. Laura thinks he may have been the man she had a brief but passionate affair with before she was wed. After a while, Leone's beau, Geoffry Cole (Allen Vincent), also shows up, covered with soot, since for lack of money he hitched a ride on a train's coal car. Naturally Laura assumes he is talking about the Cole car, which must be a private railcar. Geoffry remains insistent that Leone gain more experience, prompting Leone to flirt with Max. A romance buds. Before long they agree to marry. Laura, who is unaware that Max has been Winky's lover and who has assumed that Max has come to woo her, is outraged: "Incest—that's what it is. Incest." But at three a.m. of a moonlight morning, out on the patio of the Merricks' brick, French-windowed mansion, everyone is paired off correctly, and even Laura and her husband admit that much of their old affection remains. Laura also realizes that her bygone lover was not Max Lawrence but Lawrence Mack, a pianist.

Some magnificently vaulted, gold-and-cream rooms at the summer palace of the Archduchy of B—— were the most attractive aspects of Robert L. Buckner's **An Affair of State** (11-19-30, Broadhurst). The citizens are up in arms since the archduke and archduchess (Wilfred Seagram and Florence Eldridge) have failed to produce an heir. Finally a dashing hussar (Edward Leiter), whom the archduchess prefers to a captain (Clifford McLaglen) initially selected, services the lady and all is well.

The next evening brought in another flop, A. W. Pezet and Carman Barnes's **Schoolgirl** (11-20-30, Ritz). The teenaged Barnes had been expelled from her own school after the novel on which the play was based had been published. The novel was said to have hinted at lesbian relationships at the school, but the play minimized these, touching on the issue gingerly only in the second act when one girl was said to have a "crush" on another. Sent to a strict private boarding school in order to put an end to her romance with Dave Montague (Michael Barr), Naomi Bradshaw (Joanna Roos) runs off from the school to spend a night with Dave and is caught. After she is returned home, she and Dave agree to wait until their schooling is finished before deciding if they will marry.

Howard Lindsay and Bertrand Robinson had fun with unethical lawyers and libidinous businessmen in **Oh, Promise Me** (11-24-30, Morosco), "a rowdy, hard-jawed, flaying farce." Aware of Jasper P. Ogden's habit of taking his pretty secretaries on trips, then firing them after he has had his pleasure with them, Mark Reed (Lee Tracy), an unscrupulous, headline-seeking attorney, foists his own fiancée, Connie Clark (Eleanore Bedford), on Ogden (Edward H. Robins), traps him in a compromising situation, and hauls him into court. Through clever publicity, the flippant Reed makes Connie a national heroine, who is inundated with floral tributes and telegrams. A flock of suborned witnesses happily perjure themselves, and Ogden is fined $250,000. Oldtimer Frazer Coulter as the judge "gave the trial scene a touch of authenticity that contrasted with the legal nonsense." Among the scene-stealers was Donald Meek as an out-of-work drummer in a jazz band, "a pathetic rascal with the worst of intentions and the strength of a jellyfish." The comedy, the month's last hit, ran sixteen weeks.

Scarlet Sister Mary (11-24-30, Ethel Barrymore) was dramatized by Daniel Reed from Julia Peterkin's Pulitzer Prize novel, and was one of the quirkiest flops in a long while. The play looked at life among the Gullah-speaking blacks on the southeastern coast. Shortly after giving birth to Unex—short for unexpected—Sister Mary is deserted by the boy's father, July. That does not stop her from having lots of other children by lots of other fathers. Twenty years later, Unex comes home to die. As he does, Sister Mary has a vision in which she is assured that she and Unex will have a welcome in Heaven. What made the evening so odd was that the players were all whites in blackface, and the star was Ethel Barrymore. Her support included Estelle Winwood (as a somewhat Piccadilly-accented husband-snatcher), William B. Mack (in his last Broadway role, as "an old darky who makes love charms"), Horace Braham (as a kind but deformed man), and Barrymore's daughter, Ethel Barrymore Colt (as Sister Mary's equally man-chasing child). The day when whites could routinely play blacks had gone, and critics were highly critical (many noting that the all-black *Green Pastures* was playing across the street). They probably would have been openly scathing had not the beloved, respected Barrymore been involved. The play had enjoyed a long, profitable tryout and, after just

three weeks in New York, went back on tour, hoping to cash in on the star's reputation.

• • •

Ethel Barrymore (1879–1959) was born in Philadelphia, the daughter of Maurice and Georgiana Drew Barrymore. She made her debut in 1894 playing opposite her famous grandmother, Mrs. Drew, in *The Rivals*. She spent time in London, performing with William Gillette and in Henry Irving's celebrated troupe. Back in America, her imperious beauty, fluttery eyes, and throaty voice singled her out for stardom, which Charles Frohman first accorded her in *Captain Jinks of the Horse Marines* (1901). Among her later vehicles were *Alice Sit-by-the-Fire, The Silver Box, Mid-Channel, The Twelve-Pound Look, Déclassée, The Constant Wife*, and *The Kingdom of God*.

• • •

Audiences entering the theatre to see Frederick Rath's **First Night** (11-26-30, Eltinge) were ushered to their seats by men in convict uniforms, for the play was purportedly being given to inmates and invited guests at Sing Sing. Joan Reid (Emily Graham) has written the play to recreate the killing for which her brother Stanley (Donald Blackwell) was convicted and to introduce evidence proving he is not guilty and should not die in the chair tomorrow night. The governor (John F. Morrisey) at first attempts to stop the play, but is induced not only to let it go on but to watch it, albeit grudgingly. The play points an accusing finger at one of the ushers, who is grabbed when he rushes onstage. After the play left, that stage never again heard the tread of actors' feet, for the Eltinge became the third house on 42nd Street to switch to films during the season.

Robert Sherwood's **This Is New York** (11-28-30, Plymouth) opens as South Dakota's Senator Harvey L. Kroll (Robert T. Haines) and his wife (Virginia Howell) are dining on steak and pie in his suite at New York's Hotel Roosevelt. He despises New York, telling a reporter (Sam Wren) who has come to interview him, "I'd consider the secession of New York to be an unmitigated blessing." He later expresses the hope that the city could be towed over to Europe, where he feels it belongs. His equally unsympathetic wife informs the newspaperman that she is "heartily ashamed" of New York. In part their noisy protestations are a cover-up, for they know that the reporter is really there to look into a rumor, made public by Walter Winchell, that their daughter, Emma (Lois Moran), at school nearby, is in love with a notorious playboy, Joe Gresham (Geoffrey Kerr). The sanctimonious Krolls couldn't care less that his wealthy family were upper-echelon Americans before the first Kroll set foot in the New World. Emma discovers that Joe has had a mistress, Phyllis Adrian

Act One: 1930–1944

(Audrey Dale), who is demanding $100,000 to keep quiet about her past relationship with him. She even goes to call on the woman at the lady's self-consciously modern apartment, which is soon invaded by Phyllis's louche neighbors escaping from a party upstairs in which a bootlegger's drug-addicted girl is creating mayhem. Before long the bootlegger (Robert Baratt) joins the group, only to be followed by the police, who announce that the girl has jumped or been pushed to her death from a window. Realizing the scandal that could embarrass her father if she is seen to be involved in such carryings-on, Emma calls the reporter whom her father had interviewed, and, when her father arrives, he convinces the senator to support his daughter. She cleverly points out that if she and Joe marry and buy a ranch in Dakota ("thereby relieving a lot of starving farmers that aren't too grateful to you, Pop, for what you haven't done for them"), and if Joe professes to be cured of all city vices (thus enlisting the religious and female votes), the senator will win reelection. Of course, the election over, she and Joe will head right back to New York. Even Phyllis, impressed by Emma and Joe's sincerity and resourcefulness, supports them. Although the play received a number of politely favorable reviews—"good entertainment in an unpretentious vein," "urbane, intelligently written"—it remained around for less than eight weeks.

Several of December's offerings were more welcomed by critics than by playgoers. To some small extent, that was the case with Susan Glaspell's **Alison's House** (12-1-30, Civic Repertory). The Alison of the play never appears and was recognized as a dramatic allusion to Emily Dickinson. Like her, Alison Stanhope was a lifelong spinster. She lived in her brother's house and wrote poetry which accorded her a posthumous fame. Now, on December 31, 1899, eighteen years after her death, her brother (Donald Cameron) is selling the home, so the family has gathered to claim keepsakes. They are shocked by the appearance of Stanhope's daughter, Elsa (Eva Le Gallienne), who has been ostracized by the family for running off with a married man. The excitement proves too much for another of Stanhope's spinster sisters, Agatha (Alma Kruger), who tries to burn down the house lest her sister's secret be discovered, but who dies from a heart attack. With the unearthing of Alison's lost poems that secret will now become public. Alison, like Elsa, loved a married man. Unlike her niece, she sublimated her yearnings by writing poetry about the romance. "It's here," Elsa proclaims. "She has written it, as it was never written before. The love that never died—loneliness that never died—anguish and beauty of her love." Although Atkinson's well-mannered rejection—"a disappointingly elusive play . . . it has not been sufficiently translated out

of ideas into theatre"—was typical of many notices, the play remained in the company's repertory until season's end. Then, to almost everyone's amazement, the play won the Pulitzer Prize. The Shuberts hurriedly moved it uptown, where two weeks utterly exhausted playgoers' interest.

Three weeks sufficed for **A Kiss of Importance** (12-1-30, Fulton), Arthur Hornblow, Jr.'s redaction of André Picard and H. M. Harwood's *Monsieur de St. Obin*. To win away the wife (Ann Andrews) of a political opponent (Frederick Kerr), a man (Montague Love) hires Christian St. Obin (Basil Rathbone) to act as corespondent. St. Obin performs his duties in so attractive a manner that the woman decides to stay with her husband and set St. Obin up as her lover.

A new group in Greenwich Village, the Dramawrights, brought out Ivan Sokoloff's **The Passion of Judas** (12-1-30, Cherry Lane). Whether Sokoloff was a Russian or an American was unclear, and so, to those who bothered to review it, was just what was achieved by having Judas moan and wail through thirteen scenes depicting biblical Jerusalem.

Maurice Moscovitch had gained initial recognition on the Yiddish stage and then had become successful in the West End, including an admired Shylock in *The Merchant of Venice*. On the 2nd he brought his interpretation to the Times Square. His was an essentially good-natured Jew, an approach which some reviewers felt vitiated the drama inherent in Shakespeare's comedy. His Portia, Selena Royle, was seen as lacking in poetry and too superficial. Another objection was to Moscovitch's sharp cutting and rearranging of the text, turning Shakespeare's five acts and twenty-three scenes into three acts and eleven scenes.

Probably no other play of the season divided critics as sharply as William Bolitho's **Overture** (12-5-30, Longacre). There seemed to be little middle ground. Robert Littell of the *World* spoke for its admirers when he called it a "stirring play on a good subject"; John Mason Brown stood for the naysayers when he branded it "an unsuccessful groping toward a new medium which was at all times nearer to the drier methods of a pamphlet . . . than it was to the warmer means of a dramatic statement." Bolitho was an Anglo-American journalist whose columns in the *World* had been exceedingly popular until his death in the summer of 1929. This was his only play. Shortly after World War I, revolutionaries seize the little German town of Herfeld after the town council demands workers accept longer hours and less pay. Among their leaders are Karl Ritter (Colin Clive), an idealistic army officer and a gentleman, Maxim (Pat O'Brien), a dedicated, brutal Communist, and Katie (Barbara Robbins), who had been Maxim's mistress but now loves Ritter. Although the three initially agree to offer themselves up when the army retakes the town, Maxim quietly disappears. At first Katie remains loyal to Ritter and to their agreement, and Ritter assures her that once they are dead they will have each other for "billions and billions of years, even after the sun gets cold again and the earth freezes. Even when our star itself flickers out from old age, we have only started our night together." Then Katie is made to witness a number of executions. The horror of them moves her to agree to reveal Maxim's probable hiding place. She is released. Now totally deserted, Ritter is led off to his own execution, remarking, "I shall not be sorry to be alone for the next million years." The public sided with the naysayers, so the play closed after five weeks.

Droll performances by Helen Hayes and her associates accounted in good measure for the twelve-week New York run of Neil Grant's London comedy **Petticoat Influence** (12-15-30, Empire). Hayes played the wife of a man (John Williams) expecting to be appointed a colonial governor. When he is passed over in favor of a patent incompetent (Eric Cowley), she does some snooping and brings to light an affair between the wife (Valerie Cowley) of a cabinet minister (Henry Stephenson) and the minister's secretary (Reginald Owen). The wife was the incompetent's niece. Hubby gets the appointment.

Jo Milward's **Life Is Like That** (12-22-30, Little) recounted the travails of Bill Courtney (Edward Pawley). Courtney is unhappily married to a basso-contralto harridan (Mary Morris). He keeps a mistress, Jane Barton (Peggy Shannon), and flirts with a showgirl, Delories (Helen Shipman). Mrs. Courtney appears and attempts to kill Bill, but kills his Chinese servant (Hanaki Yoshiwara) instead. Delories's wiles persuade a doctor (William H. Barwald) to claim the death was a suicide, leaving Jane to head for Russia with Courtney, who had once made a fortune there trading with the Communists and now hopes to make another. The play found few takers, although critics reported Shipman was encored when she belted out a vaudeville number in the second act.

But then Jed Harris came even more grievously a cropper with his revival of Nicolai Gogol's *The Inspector General,* as translated by John Anderson, at the Hudson on the 23rd. Romney Brent was the young traveler mistaken by frightened village authorities for the government inspector.

Christmas night brought in two more flops, one new and one old. **Purity** (12-25-30, Ritz) was Barre Dunbar and Ralph Roeder's translation of René Wachthausen's French original. A charwoman (Florence Reed) befriends a starving young man (Richard Bird), comes to love him, then attempts to throw herself in the Seine when she learns he has fallen for a younger woman. A

somewhat besotted Left Bank philosopher (Malcolm Williams) manages to talk her out of it.

Fritz Leiber brought back his Chicago Shakespearean mountings, which he had offered last season. He started at the Ambassador with *King Lear,* then followed with *Hamlet, The Merchant of Venice, Julius Caesar, Macbeth, As You Like It,* and *Richard III* but received such sour notices, when he received any notices at all, that he soon closed shop.

One rather offbeat entry was Sophocles' *Elektra,* which came in for a week's engagement at the New Yorker on the 26th. It was especially offbeat since it was performed in Greek by a cast with the then famous Marika Cotopouli in the lead and the up-and-coming Katina Paxinou and Alexis Minotis in support. But the Greek was not the original ancient Greek, for this was a modern translation of Hugo von Hofmannsthal's German version of the original. Several critics felt the acting was also modern, substituting violent emotionalism for the requisite grandeur.

Ivor Novello's second and more successful offering of the season, **The Truth Game** (12-27-30, Ethel Barrymore), was also set in Europe, but this time in Mayfair and other swank English locales. The widowed Rosine Browne (Phoebe Foster) loses her inheritance if she reweds. She nonetheless almost succumbs to the blandishments of Max Clement (Novello), her late husband's distant cousin, until she discovers he is the heir if she remarries. But when they realize they love each other, the pair also conclude it does not matter who has the money. For many, Billie Burke stole the show as a lady who lives by the commissions she receives leading "friends" to jewelry sellers and art merchants. When the fourteen-week stay ended, Burke headed west and returned to Broadway only briefly nearly a quarter of a century later.

Walter Damrosch, the conductor, was in the audience for the premiere of his daughter Gretchen's **The Life Line** (12-27-30, Vanderbilt). Interviewed afterwards, he professed to have enjoyed the play and hoped it would run. The critics felt differently, so the comedy lasted just two weeks. His minister (Shepperd Strudwick) returns a check for $5000 which Bronson Cutler (Carroll Ashburn) has given him and says Cutler should offer more personal charity to those in need. Mrs. Irving Ives (Rosalind Ivan) appears, laments that her husband (Herbert Delmore) is neglecting her for another woman, and is offered a refuge in the Cutler home. This brings problems when Mrs. Cutler (Helen Ambrose) takes umbrage and when Ives's new love proves to be Cutler's daughter (Eunice Stoddard). But all ends happily.

Shirley Warde and Vivian Crosby's **Queen at Home** (12-29-30, Times Square) also ran a mere two weeks. Although Jennifer Lee (Sylvia Field) is a stage star, her home life is beset by parasitic, live-in relations and by a vain, philandering husband (Franklyn Fox). Her buddy, Snip Haviland (Elizabeth Mears), arranges to frame the spouse and send him packing. Jennifer herself chases away the relations. Then she finds real love with Larry Scott (William Carey). Field was seen as an actress more suited to emotional roles than to comedy, but Jessie Crommette provided laughs as an acid-tongued grandmother.

The action of Claire and Paul Sifton's **Midnight** (12-29-30, Guild) took place in the modest living room of Edward Weldon (Frederick Perry), a florist who had been the foreman of the jury that convicted a woman of murdering her lover. Hours before her execution reporters swarm into the Weldon home, where Weldon insists justice has been done and the sentence must be carried out. Then his daughter, Stella (Linda Watkins), shows up with a smoking revolver and admits having killed her racketeer lover when he said he was leaving her. The heretofore sanctimonious Weldon acquiesces when a clever reporter (Glenn Anders) arranges a cover-up. The play ran only until the Theatre Guild's subscription list had been satisfied. Since the Siftons were journalists, many reviewers saw the play as an indictment of cynically manipulative newspapers. But the next night brought in a more searing indictment.

Louis Weitzenkorn had also been a journalist and had recently quit his post on the notorious *New York Graphic*. So many last-minute changes had been made in his **Five Star Final** (12-30-30, Cort) that players often tripped over their lines. (The published text differs from the opening night program in the order of scenes and also from some of the plot details mentioned by reviewers, suggesting that further alterations were made after the opening.) The sensation-mongering *Gazette* has fallen twenty thousand in circulation, and its owner, Hinchecliffe (Berton Churchill), demands something be done. The paper, it seems, "is getting too swell for the chewing gum trade." What is done is to resurrect the Nancy Vorhees scandal. She was a stenographer who killed her boss, "the Chocolate King," after he fathered her child and deserted her. The jury refused to convict. At first even the editor, Randall (Arthur Byron), agrees to go along, because there hasn't been a really good murder since the Snyder case. The paper unearths Nancy's whereabouts and learns that she (Merle Maddern) and her husband (Malcolm Duncan), a bank cashier named Townsend, have been living quietly on West 172nd Street, with Nancy's now grown daughter. The paper's hypocritical religious editor, the Rev. T. Vernon Isopod (Alexander Onslow), is sent to question them under false pretences. He learns that the daughter, Jenny (Frances Fuller), is about to marry Philip Weeks (King Calder), the son of upstart social climbers. The ghoulish headlines drive Nancy and her husband to poison themselves. This in turn provides more headlines. Reactions vary. An unhappy prostitute wishes she had the guts to kill herself. A hardworking Negress tells her shiftless husband, "You nevah heah of a man who killed hissel' from work." Randall, sickened by the turn of events, goes to a bar to get drunk. He repeatedly asks the bartender, "Did you ever kill a man?" But the most dramatic reaction comes when Jenny appears at the newspaper and brandishes a gun at Hinchecliffe and Randall. Philip wrests the gun from her but warns them that if they print another word of the story he himself will kill them. Angry at Randall's guilt about the matter, Hinchecliffe fires him. (Reviews suggest that on the first night, Jenny was left alone at the play's end since Philip's parents had talked him out of going through with the wedding.) A triple revolving stage was required to change the play's twenty-seven scenes. In what was a rare move at the time, lighting was hung from the front of the balcony and the boxes to illuminate the settings more imaginatively, and no footlights were employed. Although the increasingly dyspeptic Percy Hammond groaned that the show was "a morbid, depressing and often unskillful revelation of the so-called newspaper racket," Burns Mantle spoke for a majority when he wrote, "Because of its basic truth and the author's intense feeling for his play it overcame to a noticeable extent the handicap of being biased and extravagant." Al Woods's mounting ran twenty-two weeks.

At the New Yorker Marika Cotopouli and her troupe launched 1931 on January 6 with Euripides' *Iphigenia*. As before, the players performed in modern Greek since the offering was again a new translation of a German version—in this instance Goethe's—of the original.

The same evening saw a revival by the Civic Repertory Theatre of Jean Jacques Bernard's *Martine*, in a translation by Arnold Moss. Moss doubled in brass by playing Julian, the man who refuses to return the love of the title figure (Estelle Scheer).

The new year's first completely American novelty was Booth Tarkington's **Colonel Satan** (1-10-31, Fulton), which was subtitled "A Night in the Life of Aaron Burr." The story unfolded in Paris in 1811, while Burr (MacKay Morris) was living in a garret above a wineshop and hoping to obtain a passport that would allow him to return to America, whence he had fled after killing Alexander Hamilton. He stumbles on a band conspiring to topple Napoleon and restore a monarchy, courts the only lady (Jessie Royce Landis) in the group, and exposes her as an informer, but gets her to use her good offices to promote his passport. Reversing the tale of his duel with Hamilton, Burr fights a duel but is the one to shoot into the air. Luckily, his opponent's bullet barely grazes him. Landis, the only member of the cast to affect a French accent, was also the only one to receive generally good notices, while the play was perceived as filled "with flat fustian, with valentine emotions and mock-heroics."

Its ninety-seven performances meant that George Kelly's **Philip Goes Forth** (1-12-31, Biltmore) was almost a hit. Although she is puzzled that his college buddies had to show her nephew, Philip Eldridge (Harry Ellerbe), that he ought to be a playwright, Mrs. Randolph (Thais Lawton) supports him when he rejects the idea of going into his family's business and heads for New York to find fame as a dramatist. He takes a room at a cheap boardinghouse run by Mrs. Ferris (Marion Barney). Among the other boarders are a no longer young man who persists in seeing himself as a budding Beethoven, Haines (Harold Webster); a wan, clutter-prone girl, who dresses in shabby black crêpe de chine and announces, "I work in the poetic medium," Miss Krail (Dorothy Stickney); and an insincere, cliché-spouting, would-be critic, Shronk (Harry Gresham), who had been one of Philip's classmates and who professes to be awed by the "spiritual content" of Philip's writing. In her long-gone heyday, Mrs. Ferris had been the celebrated actress Estelle Mace. Her career was destroyed in good measure when she married a man who claimed to be a playwright but was only a noisy fraud. She takes one of Philip's plays to a friendly producer and learns what she has suspected—that Philip has no talent. "They said they were too busy an office to be interested in—practical jokes." Just as important, she tells Philip that he really doesn't want to write; rather he wants to have the glamorous reputation of being a famous playwright. "You're a business man, Philip,—gone wrong," she observes. Their conversation is interrupted by news that the unhappy Haines has killed himself. Since Philip has shown business acumen while supporting himself at the Ramona Novelty Company on Madison Avenue, she suggests he reconsider going into the family firm. He does. Quoting from the play, Atkinson dismissed it as "too much technique and not enough whimsey."

Having already listened to Greek and Italian, first-nighters could have heard some Bengali if they had attended the premiere of **Sita** (1-12-31, Vanderbilt), a dramatization of material from the Indian epic *The Ramayana*. "A Hindu in evening clothes steps in front of the curtain before each act, and, in unintelligible English, explains in a highly long-winded manner what is about to occur." What occurred was that a queen, newly released from captivity, is thought to have been

violated and so is considered impure and is exiled. When she is allowed back years later, the priests demand she take an oath attesting to her purity. She asks the gods to let the earth swallow her if she is untainted, and the gods grant her her wish.

Welcomed by Mantle as "sensitively and delicately wrought in both character and situation," Philip Barry's **Tomorrow and Tomorrow** (1-13-31, Henry Miller) embarked on a six-month run. Gail and Eve Redman (Harvey Stephens and Zita Johann) are childless after six years of marriage. They live in a college town founded by Gail's grandfather and are asked to put up Nicholas Hay (Herbert Marshall), a celebrated doctor coming to give a lecture series. During his stay, Nicholas and Eve fall in love. He describes her as "an artist without an art," and she thanks him for giving her, "for a little while, the illusion of being alive." After the doctor leaves, Eve realizes she is pregnant with his child. A few years later, the young boy (Drew Price) is taken ill, and doctors despair of his recovering. Eve calls in Nicholas, who comes and restores the boy to good health. He then asks Eve to leave Gail and live with him. But Eve comprehends that Gail, for all his faults, is a devoted husband and father. When Nicholas retorts that the truth is that he and Eve have loved each other and that the boy is theirs, Eve replies, "No—those are the facts . . . the truth is simply that I'm Gail's wife, and my place is here, because he needs me."

. . .

Philip [Jerome Quinn] **Barry** (1896–1949) was born in Rochester, N.Y., son of an immigrant Irish father who became a successful businessman and a mother of old Philadelphia Irish-Catholic stock. His father died when he was a year old. Although the frail youngster was plagued with myopia, he became an avid reader. He eventually entered Yale, but quit on America's entry into the war. Rejected by the armed forces, he took a post in the State Department's Communication Office in London. After returning to study with George Pierce Baker at Harvard, he launched his Broadway career. Among his early efforts were *You and I* (1923), *The Youngest* (1924), *Paris Bound* (1927), and *Holiday* (1928). He quickly established himself as a leading proponent of high comedy.

. . .

The play's producer was Gilbert Miller.

. . .

Gilbert [Heron] **Miller** (1884–1969) was the son of the famous actor and producer Henry Miller. He was born in New York and began his career as an actor. He first turned producer in London. Thereafter, with notable exceptions such as this comedy, he specialized in importing London plays to New York or New York plays to London, rarely producing the same work in both cities.

. . .

A revival at the Lyceum on the 16th of Schnitzler's *Anatol,* which John Barrymore had done nearly two decades earlier as *The Affairs of Anatol,* was on the receiving end of some harsh notices for both the play and its star, Joseph Schildkraut. Some claimed that New York's chauvinistic critics were getting revenge for his deserting live theatre, but the star himself, in his autobiography, said his poor performance stemmed from a bad cold on opening night.

In Lynn Riggs's **Green Grow the Lilacs** (1-26-31, Guild), Raymond Sovey's stylized settings again opened like cutouts in picture books to show interiors, all the while offering glimpses of the surrounding countryside. The time is 1900 and the place the Indian Territory that soon will be Oklahoma. At the Williams farm, where Aunt Eller (Helen Westley) looks after her orphaned niece, Laurey (June Walker), she is about to start churning butter when she hears the distant voice of Curly McLain (Franchot Tone) singing about "a-ridin' one morning for pleasure." He arrives and, though he pretends not to care, is really anxious to know if Laurey will accompany him to a play-party. When Laurey appears she, too, feigns indifference, even when Curly places one high-backed chair in front of another, covers them with one of Eller's aprons, and says that is the surrey he will take Laurey in. The real surrey, he adds, is a "yeller" rig, with fringe surrounding it, isinglass curtains, and two lamps "set on the dashboard, winkin' like a lightnin' bug." In a further show of independence Laurey says she will go with Jeeter Fry, their hired hand, who Curly knows is a "bullet-colored growly man." Curly goes to Jeeter's smokehouse and attempts to scare him off. Jeeter (Richard Hale) fires a wild shot at Curly. In turn Curly shoots out a tiny, far-off knothole to demonstrate his own skill. At the party Laurey becomes frightened by Jeeter. She and Curly run off to wed. The neighbors, learning of this, hoist the couple onto a haystack, but Jeeter attempts to set it on fire. In a fight with Curly, Jeeter falls on his own knife and is killed. Curly is arrested, escapes from jail, and returns to spend his wedding night with Laurey. When the deputy comes to rearrest Curly, Aunt Eller persuades him to wait until the morning, concluding, "Listen to that fool cowpuncher! His weddin' night—and there he is a-singin'." Besides the traditional western songs sung during various scenes, changes of scene were accomplished with a group singing in front of a high fence. Writing in the *New Yorker,* Robert Benchley, who shared his colleagues' reservations about the play's merits as melodrama, noted, "It is more in the nature

of a musical show, especially in the way the crowds dissolve instantaneously from swirling, shouting mobs of merrymakers into a suddenly silent offstage menace." Of course, the play was eventually reworked into the record-breaking musical *Oklahoma!* by Rodgers and Hammerstein, but this original Theatre Guild mounting ran only eight weeks.

By now many critics had taken to beginning any review of a Samuel Shipman play with suggestions that he take his pen and paper elsewhere. They most certainly felt that way about his one-week flop **She Means Business** (1-26-31, Ritz). Having helped her husband (Ernest Glendinning) build his ladies' bag business, Doris Roberts (Ann Davis) is outraged when he forces her to leave. After he runs off with his secretary, she is compelled to step in and save the company, which had been sinking following her departure. She makes it bigger and more profitable than ever, but refuses to take back Roberts when he returns hat in hand.

The Civic Repertory hit real paydirt with its revival of the younger Dumas's *Camille* on the same night, in Henriette Metcalf's translation, with Eva Le Gallienne as Marguerite, Morgan Farley as Armand, and Jacob Ben-Ami as his father. Despite some displeasure with certain miscastings, notably Farley, and some signs of creakiness they professed to discern, most critics felt this story of a courtesan who sacrifices her one chance for true love still could be genuinely touching.

One of the season's most memorable and often revived comedies was Noel Coward's **Private Lives** (1-27-31, Times Square). A divorced couple (Coward and Gertrude Lawrence), each with a new spouse (Jill Esmond and Laurence Olivier), meet on the terrace of a hotel in France. They decide they should never have separated, and run off to the woman's apartment in Paris. There they resume their quarreling, until the reappearance of the spouses they have jilted reconfirms their love for each other. The show offered a song that became one of Coward's standards, "Some Day I'll Find You." Performed with "consummate high style," the comedy ran for seven months, or until shortly after the original cast was replaced.

Luigi Pirandello's **As You Desire Me** (1-28-31, Maxine Elliott's), in a translation by Dmitri Ostrow, was also a hit—albeit a lesser one—despite the patent bafflement of many reviewers. Who is the real Lucia Pieri, who was raped by invading troops during the war and then disappeared? Is it the look-alike cabaret singer (Judith Anderson) found in a Berlin nightclub, who is willing to do anything to convince Bruno Pieri (Brandon Peters) that she is his long-lost wife? Or is it the madwoman (Amy Jonap) brought from a mental institution, who brandishes the hidden scars Lucia was known to have?

Apart from one importation, lifted to unforgettable heights by its star, February was, like October, a washout. Now and then throughout the month, one critic or another bewailed the state of the theatre, seemingly forgetful of the season's triumphs. Two of the month's entries managed runs of approximately four months apiece thanks to drastically cut prices and substantial concessions from theatre owners and players. One of these was Anita Hart and Maurice Braddell's **In the Best of Families** (2-2-31, Bijou), which some critics denounced as dirty while others saw it, at best, as "raw without actually naughty words." When an infant is deposited on the Hamilton doorstep with a note pinned to it saying the mother wanted the baby left with its father, Bronson Hamilton (Charles Richman) and his three grown sons all do some finger counting and allow that each of them might be guilty. They are not. The family's crusty old grandsire, Col. Hamilton (Henry Brooks), turns out to be the daddy.

Three fine players could do nothing for Kenneth Raisbeck's murky **Rock Me, Julie** (2-3-31, Royale). At a Satterlee family reunion, no one seems happy or truly successful. Some, like Charlotte (Helen Menken), have even lied over the years, sending letters back to Illinois boasting of New York's acclaim. But when she returns all Charlotte has to show for her time is her expectant motherhood. She attempts to get the family's adopted, malcontented son, Steven Moorhead (Paul Muni), to wed her. Since he himself is illegitimate, he is loath to repeat history. Mrs. Satterlee (Jean Adair) sends Charlotte off alone, with words of encouragement. Critics professed bafflement about what it all meant. The title was supposedly an old black song about the Mississippi.

Forcing allowed Howard Warren Comstock and Allen C. Miller's **Doctor X** (2-9-31, Hudson) to survive for ten weeks. A determined advertising campaign, which included large billboards and banners with the show's name hanging from buildings on Broadway, may have spurred some sales. The piece was a mystery packed with such traditional clichés as a knife-clutching hand emerging from sliding panels and a frightened, shrieking servant (the latter played by an actress famous for her frightened, shrieking servants, May Vokes). A maniacal, cannibalistic killer is at large. To aid the police, Doctor Xavier (Howard Lang) summons all the suspects to his Orange, New Jersey, laboratory, a room filled with the latest, pyrotechnical lie-detection equipment. There the scientist reenacts the crimes and watches for results. He is almost foiled, since a mad fellow scientist (Robert Lowing), the real killer, has cleverly talked an innocent newspaperman (Leslie Adams) into taking his place. Luckily, the newspaperman is cleared in time to propose to pretty Mavis (Eden Gray).

That same evening welcomed Rudolf Besier's London drama **The Barretts of Wimpole Street** (2-9-31, Empire). Harsh, puritanical Edward Moulton-Barrett (Charles Waldron) certainly verges on insanity, if he has not slipped over the line. There is nothing he will not do to keep his children unwed and with him. So it is not surprising that he attempts to prevent his eldest daughter, the invalid poet Elizabeth (Katharine Cornell), from meeting the famous young Robert Browning (Brian Aherne). To his consternation they not only meet but fall in love, and Browning persuades the adoring girl to run away with him from her father-imposed imprisonment. In a fury, Moulton-Barrett orders that Flush, Elizabeth's pet dog, be killed. But she has prudently taken the dog with her. Critical assessment of the play varied widely, but there was unanimity about Cornell. Admitting in the *New Yorker*, where she was substituting for Benchley, that she was "the little one in the corner who did not think *The Barretts of Wimpole Street* was a great play, or even a good play," Dorothy Parker nonetheless went on to coo, "Miss Katharine Cornell is a completely lovely Elizabeth Barrett—far lovelier than the original, I fear. It is little wonder that Miss Cornell is so worshipped; she has that thing we need, and we so seldom have, in our actresses; she has romance, or . . . glamour." Atkinson was more detailed and more specific: "By the crescendo of her playing, by the wild sensitivity that lurks behind her ardent gestures and her piercing stares across the footlights she charges the drama with a meaning beyond the facts it records. Her acting is quite as remarkable for the carefulness of its design as for the fire of its passion." The show, still doing excellent business, was removed after 370 performances so that Cornell could begin the first of several extended, famous tours she made with the play. She also appeared in two New York revivals in later years. The production marked her debut as an actress-manager, but perhaps more importantly assured her a niche as one of the first ladies (to many, *the* first lady) of the American stage.

. . .

Katharine Cornell (1893–1974) was the daughter of a onetime theatre manager and was born in Berlin, where her father had gone to study medicine. She made her debut with the Washington Square Players in 1916, afterwards continuing her apprenticeship in her hometown of Buffalo and in Detroit. Following a successful spell in London, she won attention on Broadway in *Nice People* in 1921. That same year she married the director Guthrie McClintic, with whom she worked closely for the rest of her career. Subsequently she appeared in *A Bill of Divorcement, Will Shakespeare, The Enchanted Cottage, The Green Hat, The Letter, The Age of Innocence,* and *Dishonored Lady.* She seemed tall and regal onstage but was actually not quite five feet, seven inches. Her dark complexion, dark hair, and broad features led some to suggest she seemed Oriental or negroid. In time she demonstrated the widest range of all the American stage's twentieth-century leading ladies.

. . .

Guthrie McClintic (1893–1961) was born in Seattle. He studied at the University of Washington and at the American Academy of Dramatic Arts before making his acting debut in 1913 and his New York debut a year later. Thereafter he spent time in Jessie Bonstelle's famous stock company and as assistant to Winthrop Ames. He embarked on his own career as producer and director in 1921 with *The Dover Road*. This was followed by such hits as *The Green Hat* (1925), in which he first directed his wife, Cornell, *The Shanghai Gesture* (1926), and *Saturday's Children* (1927). From the Besier play on, he directed all Cornell's plays as well as many others.

. . .

One fascinating setting and the clever revival of one bygone stage trick were all that William A. Grew and Harry Delf's **She Lived Next to the Firehouse** (2-10-31, Longacre) had going for it. Even the usually adroit Victor Moore came away empty-handed from this comedy set at the turn of the century. The boys in the firehouse, including the rotund, meek-mannered Captain O'Leary (Moore), know that Delilah Smith (Ara Gerald) is delighted to entertain them whenever her hardboiled, traveling salesman husband (William Frawley) is out of town—and he is leaving tonight on the 6:20. One by one the men come to Delilah's kitchen, all within minutes of one another. Delilah solves this problem by giving each a chore in a different part of the house as the next man knocks on the door. Thus one is put to beating rugs in the cellar, another is told to polish silver in the dining room, and the captain is set to knitting a sweater on the side porch. But all hell breaks loose when Mr. Smith returns unexpectedly, with the men's wives in tow. Luckily the fire alarm goes off, sending the firemen scurrying to their work. The first and third acts occurred in the firehouse, with a pair of real, white horses—one on each side of the room—flanking a seemingly genuine red fire engine. At the play's end, the men attached the horses to the engine and headed out, riding on a treadmill going from the front to the back of the stage, making it appear that the horses were heading directly for the audience as the firehouse setting receded into the background. But this old ploy, so clever and accepted in prefilm melodramas, created pacing problems when it was tagged on to the end of what was meant to be a slambang farce.

As was the case with *Rock Me, Julie,* critics panned Frank Merlin's **Hobo** (2-11-31) but sang praises for the cast, particularly Paul Kelly in the title role. The multiscened play depicted such settings as a railroad yard, the outside and inside of a boxcar, the exterior and interior of a jail, a courtroom, a tent during a religious revival, and a bordello. St. Louis Blackie (Kelly) is a tramp who hates all authorities, particularly the "bulls" (the police). To get them off his back after being nabbed for loitering, he tells them he lives with his sister, but the house he takes them to is a brothel, and the girl (Gwyn Statford) he says is his sibling is one of the employees. Fortunately, she goes along with the ruse. Later he is arrested for creating mayhem at a revival meeting and sentenced to road work. The girl helps him escape, and he hops a freight to who knows where.

The mounting of **Saturday Morning** (2-14-31, Waldorf) by "Rike Kass" exemplified the increasingly desperate situation on Broadway. The play was put on by a group of unemployed, largely untested actors, who leased the jinxed playhouse on exceptionally favorable terms. Although they announced a $2 top, most tickets were cut-rated to 50¢. The play dealt with the travails of a businessman destroyed by the 1929 Crash. Many critics did not review it, and it quickly departed. If the real name of "Rike Kass"—the quotation marks were in the program—was ever identified, the source is elusive.

An English offering was received almost as coolly. Roland Pertwee's **Heat Wave** (2-17-31, Fulton) was set in a British colony in the Orient. Hugh Dawltry (Basil Rathbone) has become a drunkard and scapegrace after Philippa (Selena Royle) rejected him in favor of George Marsh (Henry Daniell), who had lied to her about Hugh's past. Years later Philippa rushes to Hugh's bungalow to prevent her sister from having an affair with him. George finds her there, refuses to believe the truth, and shoots but does not kill Hugh. Philippa decides to leave George for Hugh.

Another group calling itself the Actors' Theatre (was this the third or fourth?) debuted at the Provincetown Playhouse on the 18th with a revival of Maxwell Anderson and Harold Hickerson's *Gods of the Lightning* (10-24-28), in which Wobblies are sentenced to death in a patently biased court. The few and meager notices the troupe received were favorable, but the group seems to have faded quietly into history.

Still one more of the season's short-lived bombs was Franklin L. Russell's **The Great Barrington** (2-19-31, Avon). The Barringtons are snooty bluebloods who hope to prevent their daughter from marrying a young engineer with no pedigree. Their plans are changed after the ghost of Prescott Barrington the First (Otto Kruger) appears in the old mansion the family has occupied for 300 years and shows them what an upstart and murderous scoundrel he was. Among his victims was an Indian servant named Ogu (George Probert), whose grunting, repeated professions of love for a white maiden—"Ogu want Phoebe," "Ogu love Phoebe"—brought embarrassing howls from the audience and a fatal stab in the back from Prescott. Although Kruger subsequently replaced Noel Coward in *Private Lives* and took over briefly in the following season from Paul Muni in another play, this was the last role he created before becoming a well-known character actor in films. He returned several times in the 1940s, but never again enjoyed the acclaim or occasional success he had been accorded when he was a rising star.

A revival at the Waldorf on the 20th of Patrick Kearney's dramatization of Theodore Dreiser's *An American Tragedy* (10-11-26), recounting the saga of a boy who kills his pregnant sweetheart so that he can make a richer marriage, surmounted innumerable dismissive notices and ran seventeen weeks, helped by deeply cut-rated tickets.

Mary Nash, approaching the end of her career as a beautiful leading lady, was starred in **A Woman Denied** (2-25-31, Ritz), taken by Jean Bart from Gennaro Mario Curci's unspecified Italian play. Nash was Barbara, an often besotted, unscrupulous Parisian model. But the statues she has inspired Paolo Vanni (McKay Morris) to create have brought him fame and fortune. So she attempts to seduce him into deserting his wife and children for her. She also becomes a forger. However, it is her attempt to bed every attractive man that crosses her path that leads one of them to strangle her.

A pleasant if not totally original idea was wasted in Claire Carvalho and Leighton Osmun's **Paging Danger** (2-26-31, Booth). Ronnie Van Horn, a booze-woozy playboy (Eric Dressler), having read a book on will power, decides he can make his parlormaid (Dolores De Monde) believe she is a Russian princess. So he lavishes money on jewels and a Rolls-Royce, only to discover that the girl and her family are exiled Russian nobles. Given some of the most scathing notices in a month filled with scathing notices, the comedy disappeared after four performances.

Mary Hay, heretofore better known as a diminutive entertainer in musical comedy, was co-author and leading lady of **Greater Love** (3-2-31, Liberty), a drama officially attributed to Bruce Spaulding (Hay) and Anthony Baird (Nella Steward). Hay played "Peter" Cornish, who stands by a brother (Douglas Gillmore) horribly disfigured in the war, after most of his family and his sweetheart (Brenda Dahlen) distance themselves from him. Only their ne'er-do-well father is also compassionate, but he commits suicide in the second act. It remains for Peter to help her brother become a successful novelist.

Edward J. Foran and Willard Keefe's **Privilege Car** (3-3-31, 48th St.) was set in a special car, reportedly becoming rare by 1931, that once had been part of all circus trains and served as a canteen and lounge for the employees. The Colton and Steel circus is filled with lowlife. The man who runs the concession in the car once killed another man. His son has just finished a sentence for forgery. The aerial artist had been a prostitute, and the cooch dancer's husband is a snow-bird (a drug addict). And somebody is divulging the troupe's plans to a rival circus. But the main plot concerns Cornets (Alan Bunce), a young man in the band, and Jean Steel (Ruth Easton), who has inherited half the show and has fallen in love with Cornets. The forger (Paul Guilfoyle) assaults a woman in one of the towns the circus visits, plants Cornets's cornet as evidence, and watches as the townsfolk attack the train and attempt to lynch Cornets. But after Cornets is cleared and the forger is fingered, the guilty man tries to flee only to be killed by a passing express. Cornets and Jean reveal they have been wed secretly. The aerial artist (Lee Patrick) is shown to be the squealer.

Many critics had kind words for A. A. Milne's **Give Me Yesterday** (3-4-31, Charles Hopkins), but it found only a limited public. However, it had been an even more abrupt failure when produced years before in London as *Success*. A cabinet member (Louis Calhern), who has been pushed to the top by his cold, ambitious wife (Gladys Hanson), encounters the great love (Sylvia Field) of his early, carefree years and almost runs away with her. But his wily secretary (Eric Blore) convinces him of his unhappy duty.

Along with *Tomorrow and Tomorrow*, Rachel Crothers's **As Husbands Go** (3-5-31, John Golden) was one of the season's two luminous high comedies. Like the earlier one, it took a wryly wistful look at a woman's aborted attempt to flout convention. Mantle hailed it a "light, pleasant, truthfully observed domestic comedy . . . an honest, amusingly human study of character." Emmie Sykes (Catharine Doucet), a forty-five-year-old widow, and Lucile Lingard (Lily Cahill), a beautiful, thirty-five-year-old married woman, have both found potential lovers while vacationing in Paris. Emmie's man is Hippie Lomi (Roman Bohnen), a sixtyish, suave, monocled hanger-on who tells the ladies that the most American thing about them is their guilt feeling over their newfound relationships. Lucile's man is Ronald Derbyshire (Geoffrey Wardwell), a twenty-five-year-old budding novelist. Lucile and Ronald have fallen so deeply in love that Ronald convinces her to ask her husband for a divorce. Back home, the unsuspecting, adoring Charles Lingard (Jay Fassett) tells his nephew that when he meets his aunt, "the flowers will be a little sweeter than you thought they were." Lucile returns home and, recognizing how good and loving her husband is, cannot bring herself to tell him about Ronald. Ronald appears, and he and Charles become good friends. Roland, too, understands Charles's virtues and, prompted by some hints the not altogether naive husband has dropped about his beloved wife's failings, quietly departs. He leaves a letter for Lucile, telling her, "I have seen the magnificent sympathy of a big man—the shining glory of a selfless love that has enveloped you and made you perfect in its own beauty." At least Emmie, having won over her initially hostile daughter (Marjorie Lytell), can latch on to Hippie. The comedy prospered until the hot weather came.

· · ·

Rachel Crothers (1878–1958) was born in Bloomington, Ill. She had dabbled in playwriting before enrolling in the State Normal School of Illinois, then studied acting at the Stanhope-Wheatcroft School. But she abandoned acting when she directed *Nora* (1903), her first play to be produced. Subsequently, she directed all her plays—which generally looked at life from their women's points of view and whose female characters were usually the most interesting. Among her better plays were *The Three of Us* (1906), *A Little Journey* (1918), *He and She* (1920), *Nice People* (1921), *Expressing Willie* (1924), and *Let Us Be Gay* (1929).

· · ·

A revival at the New Amsterdam on the 9th of James M. Barrie's *The Admirable Crichton* (11-17-03) received qualified notices, but did rather good business because of its star-packed cast. Walter Hampden played the butler who proved more skillful than his highborn employers when the group was shipwrecked. Fay Bainter was Lady Mary; Ernest Glendinning, the epigram-spouting Ernest; Effie Shannon, the sceptical countess; saucer-eyed Estelle Winwood, the vulgar kitchen wench.

The first and shorter-lived of the month's two English mysteries was Roger Wheeler's **Gray Shadow** (3-10-31, New Yorker), the latest opus to set critics to lamenting the dire state of the theatre. Edward Holden (William Townsend), alias the Gray Shadow, has an old crony, Dr. Peabody (Lewis Waller), write a phony death certificate for him and attempts to collect on a large insurance policy. A shrewd investigator (Richard Nicholls) clears the principal suspect, beautiful Diana Trent (Annabella Murray), then proposes to her. The doctor kills himself.

Down in Greenwich Village, Arthur Ebenhack's **School for Virtue** (3-10-31, Cherry Lane) cast its spotlight on Bud Heasley (Buford Armitage) and Clarinda Robbins (Evelyn Wade). She follows him all the way from Bucyrus, Ohio, where he once had saved her life, to the Village, where he has become a leader in the younger fast set. To keep her from abandoning the

straight and narrow, Bud renounces his own loose ways and decides to marry her. Although the play received less than enthusiastic notices, it was moved uptown in late April to the Longacre, but folded after a single week there.

Poor Ernest Truex! For all his charm and skills (which critics were ever pleased to enumerate), the tiny comedian could rarely find suitable vehicles. Certainly **Napi** (3-11-31, Longacre), which Brian Marlow took from Julius Berstl's German original, was not a good one. Truex was cast as Aristide Latouche, a lace-shop clerk, drafted by the blustering Marshal Duroc (Averell Harris) to double for Napoleon and, as the supposed Bonaparte, break off an impolitic liaison with La George (Peggy Shannon), an actress at the Comédie Française. News of the encounter is leaked to Napoleon's enemies, who, it is hoped, will attempt to kill him as he leaves and thus reveal themselves. La George sees through the deception and invites the man to stay the night. Josephine (Frieda Inescort) then helps him evade any further problems.

Still substituting for Benchley in the *New Yorker*, Dorothy Parker bequeathed theatre-lovers one of the most memorable of theatrical put-downs when she said of Channing Pollock's **The House Beautiful** (3-12-31, Apollo), "*The House Beautiful* is the play lousy." Of course, her reviews were becoming increasingly and all but unceasingly dyspeptic. Noting that the heroine of *A Woman Denied* had been strangled in the third act, she commented, "For me, the murder came too late." And reporting that Milne's cabinet member had been given yesterday, she added, "Me, I would have given him twenty years to life." She had taken to regularly ending her reviews, "Mr. Benchley, please come home. Nothing is forgiven," or "Mr. Benchley, please come home. A joke's a joke." Most other critics had something nice to say about the play. Arthur Ruhl of the *Herald Tribune* lauded its "nobility of sentiments," and the *American*'s Gilbert W. Gabriel called it "valiantly benevolent," but they and others felt its virtues did not quite add up to a fully effective play. As a result, the producer resorted to a ploy that had been used during earlier Pollock plays—quoting praises from famous figures, among them this time Nicholas Murray Butler, president of Columbia, and such celebrated clergymen as Harry Emerson Fosdick and Daniel A. Poling. They were not without effect. Of the month's entries, only *As Husbands Go* surpassed the drama's fifteen-week stand. The play's action moves from 1900 to 1930. Archie Davis (James Bell), a $40-a-week bond salesman, and his wife, Jen (Mary Phillips), buy a lot on a new development in West Hills, New Jersey, that until recently had been a farm. They agree to save to buy the neighboring lot, whose young pines should grow into a beautiful stand. Archie's co-worker, Guy (Roy Gordon), sneers at their dreams, seeing Archie as too unambitious and high-principled. Sure enough, Archie is passed over for promotion after he refuses to sell bonds he knows to be worthless. Guy sells them and is moved up. Time passes. When the Davises' son is ten years old, he is hurt in an automobile accident, and Archie must use the money he is saving for the pine lot to pay for the boy's medical expenses. Later Archie runs for mayor and wins narrowly. But Guy, who has risen to president of the company, fires him for refusing to sell out to a developer who would tear down the nice old houses and crowd the lots with cheap, tightly packed homes. Furthermore, Guy has bought the mortgage on Archie's home and orders him out. All this brings on a fatal heart attack. But, in a manner never explained, Archie's now grown son (Reed Brown, Jr.) buys out Guy. Nonetheless, sensing the inevitable he persuades Jen to move in with him and his wife. However, Archie's beckoning ghost appears to her. She admits, "Our work's done, Archie. I'm ready to go now and—I'm tired, too." Archie holds out his hand and bids her come with him. The action took place primarily in the Davis living room, but some scenes were performed on the forestage, and at times the paneling at the center of the living room moved away to allow for fantasies of Archie as a noble knight in medieval garments.

The Theatre Guild suffered a costly flop with **Miracle at Verdun** (3-16-31, Martin Beck), which Julian Leigh translated from the German of Hans Chlumberg. In 1934, on the twentieth anniversary of the outbreak of the World War, the dead German and French soldiers buried together at Verdun rise from their graves. But seeing what the world has become and understanding that they will no longer be welcome, they return to the cemetery.

The Dramawrights, the same group that had appeared earlier in the season at the Cherry Lane, briefly transferred its allegiance to another house where it offered Vladimir Mayakovski's **The Bed Bug** (3-19-31, Provincetown Playhouse), in which a bourgeois and a bed bug, frozen in ice from water used to fight a fire, are brought to life in a communist utopia to show how awful people once were. When the play soon folded, the Dramawrights also apparently packed their bags and sought other employment.

Jack De Leon and Jack Celestin's **The Silent Witness** (3-23-31, Morosco), heavily rewritten by Harry Wagstaff Gribble, was the month's second English mystery. It had enjoyed a six-month London run, a hugely profitable month-long Philadelphia tryout, and an enthusiastic first night, followed by numerous money notices. Yet, despite the lack of competition in its field, it survived only ten weeks on Broadway. *Variety* possibly touched

on the reason when it noted that while the thriller "may be the best of the English mystery dramas brought here in some time, it hardly rates with the best of the American kind, although the latter type of play has deteriorated in the last several seasons." Anthony Howard (Anthony Kemble Cooper) tells his parents he has strangled his faithless mistress. (A revolving stage allowed a flashback to show the strangling.) His father (Lionel Atwill) assumes the burden of guilt, and, in court, evidence suggests he may well be guilty. Then a man (Geoffrey Harwood), who had been sitting quietly in the courtroom, blurts out that he can prove the father's innocence. Escorted to Scotland Yard, he discloses that the supposedly murdered woman (Kay Strozzi) is still alive, and that she and her husband (Fortunio Bonanova) are wanted for various crimes. (In the London production the woman actually had been killed by a burglar.) For Atwill, who had clung to a somewhat precarious stardom over the years without winning widespread respect, the play represented his farewell to New York. His remaining career was as a Hollywood character actor.

For the second time in two weeks, the Theatre Guild found itself with a failure on its hands. This time it was George Bernard Shaw's tale of a young couple who talk themselves into a marriage they both hold reservations about. *Getting Married* (11-6-16) was restaged at the Guild on the 30th with a fine cast that included Peg Entwistle, Dorothy Gish, Helen Westley, Margaret Wycherly, Romney Brent, Reginald Mason, Hugh Sinclair, and Henry Travers. But playgoers were not lured in.

The month ended with yet another play that had critics wringing their hands and writing short, disparaging notices. In William Doyle's **Lady Beyond the Moon** (3-31-31, Bijou), a young lady (Ione Hutaine) who comes to Lake Como to surprise her fiancé (Donald McClelland) is led to think he has become engaged to another woman, so weds her host (John Goldsworthy). After a disastrous wedding night, she learns her lover is still true. She ditches her spouse and runs off with the happy fiancé.

April was certainly not the happiest of months, with only one of its numerous entries surpassing the 100-performance mark. Its string of failures was launched with Roy Davidson's **Right of Happiness** (4-2-31, Vanderbilt). Frustrated that Dr. Wardell (Herbert Rawlinson) cannot do anything for him, Nikolas (Robert DuRoy), a grotesquely crippled Russian youth, attempts to seduce the doctor's wife (Georgine Cleveland). He fails, so returns embittered to Russia, never learning that he is Wardell's son by an affair the doctor had there in his student days.

References to the disappearance of Judge Crater and

Mayor Jimmy Walker's travails suggested to some that John P. Leister's **The Rap** (4-6-31, Avon) held hidden topical meanings. The murder of a former district attorney brings both Inspector Garrison (Paul Harvey) and a reporter named Carter (Jack Marvin) to the scene. At first the dead man's secretary (Louise Flood) is suspected, but then Carter inadvertently tricks a professional hit man (Ernest Anderson) into admitting he killed the dead man on orders from government higher-ups. After the killer jumps out of the eleventh-story window, Carter would phone the facts in to his paper. So the inspector kills him to keep him quiet. The drama struggled along for eight weeks.

Osgood Perkins and Ruth Gordon did their often inspired best but failed to save Sheridan Gibney's **The Wiser They Are** (4-6-31, Plymouth). Bruce Ingram likes to play around, as does his ward Trixie. But that does not stop him from proposing marriage nor her from accepting the proposal. Still, both in his penthouse apartment after the proposal and in their honeymoon suite on the *Olympic,* many of their old flames pop up and are not asked to leave. The pair agree that they will never be able to fully trust one another. The play's failure—a five-week stay—was another black mark against Broadway's former "boy wonder," Jed Harris.

The shortest stay among the evening's openings—two weeks—went to **Joy of Living** (4-6-31, Masque), Americanized by Louise Carter from a German play by Rudolf Lothar and Hans Bachwitz. A rich upstart (Taylor Holmes) and an impoverished nobleman (Donald Brian), who serves as his valet, both fall in love with the same girl (Betty Hanna). The nobleman wins her after a good tip in the stock market makes him wealthy again.

Paul Hervey Fox's **The Great Man** (4-7-31, Ritz) had a still shorter life, opening on Tuesday and closing on Saturday. Walter Woolf, once more trying vainly to find a niche for himself outside the world of fast-fading operetta, exposed his hairy chest to play a notorious pirate, Captain O'Malley. (He nonetheless found a way for the pirate to sing one song.) Landing at a Central American port, he casts a lustful eye on the wife (Nedda Harrigan) of the governor, but the woman's niece, Lisa (Carla Hunter), determines to land the pirate for herself. She does—by hiding in a chest placed aboard O'Malley's ship just before he sails away.

The latest of the season's productions to receive sharply divided notices was the Shuberts' revival of John Raphael and Constance Collier's *Peter Ibbetson* (4-17-17) on the 8th at the Shubert, with Dennis King and Jessie Royce Landis as the lovers whose devotion transcends the man's imprisonment for murder. Perhaps surprisingly, some conservative stalwarts such as the *Herald Tribune*'s Percy Hammond joined those who

assailed the play as dated—a charge that would be leveled with increasing frequency on older plays. There was, however, general praise for Joseph Urban's romantic, spacious, and color-filled settings.

The 13th saw, but did not welcome, a revival of *Dracula* (10-5-27) at the Royale. The company was the sort that had been playing major touring stops (and generally doing good business) at sharply cut-rate prices. But New York wouldn't buy it.

The month's only offering to chalk up a respectable run was a sleeper—a surprise hit. Many critics and playgoers were growing weary of the amateurish, often shrilly propagandistic plays being mounted in the Village. The heyday of the Provincetown Playhouse was almost a decade in the past. Now suddenly the theatre sprang to life again with I. J. Golden's **Precedent** (4-14-31, Provincetown), which purported to show what really happened to Tom Mooney, a jailed California union rabble-rouser. The names were changed, not to protect the innocent, but to avoid libel suits. Mooney became Delaney (Royal Dana Tracey), who is trying to goad workers of the Queen City Railway Company into striking. He is a good man, who tells his work-weary wife (Ellen Hall) to take a vacation even if it means exhausting the couple's small savings and who contributes $15 of each $60 weekly income to help the strike fund. By contrast the president (Walter Green) of the rail company is a bad, bad man. He gratuitously snaps at his sweet, hardworking secretary (Lee Nugent), who is reading back his dictation, "Don't mumble. Read it distinctly," although the direction has said *"(Reading quite distinctly),"* and he not only bribes a senator but offers Delaney more than twice the $3000 a year he now earns as a unionist if he will work for the company. Naturally, Delaney, being a good man, stalks out. When a bomb is thrown at a parade, the president of the company and the local district attorney (William Bonelli) contrive to have Delaney framed for the crime. He is sentenced to death. A crusading editor (John Bennett) unearths the fact that Delaney was a mile from the scene and could not have been involved. Moreover, he shows the state's chief witness perjured himself. But the district attorney reneges on his promise to urge a pardon for the convicted man. Because of legal technicalities, the most the governor (Ben Roberts) will do is commute the sentence to life imprisonment. Fifteen years on, Mrs. Delaney and the editor, who have been visiting Delaney faithfully, can tell the prisoner no more than "We'll plan something new." When Mrs. Delaney responds ruefully, "Fifteen years we've been saying that," the editor can only lamely repeat himself. In the emerging liberal atmosphere of the time, the play was received favorably and soon was transferred uptown. Hopes were expressed that it might aid in obtaining a full pardon for Mooney. At one venue or another, the drama chalked up 186 performances.

The month's third revival, Pirandello's *Six Characters in Search of an Author* (10-30-22), which came into the Bijou on the 15th, was one more older play subjected to a whipping from Broadway's swelling coterie of faddists. But even those who could still enjoy the play deemed the new mounting undistinguished, so it was withdrawn after two weeks.

Edna Best, Basil Rathbone, and Earle Larimore brought some distinction to Arthur Pollock's translation of Henri Bernstein's **Melo** (4-16-31, Ethel Barrymore). Best played a wife who falls so in love with her husband's best friend (Rathbone) that she attempts to kill her husband. When she fails, she commits suicide in the Seine. The men remain close, with the husband unaware of what had happened between his friend and his wife.

Some nice ideas went down the drain in Alma Wilson's **Company's Coming** (4-20-31, Lyceum). The Janneys (Lynne Overman and Frieda Inescort) are planning to hold a posh bridge party in their apartment in a converted Philadelphia mansion, but Mr. Janney has not received his salary, and his wife has spent her cash on a wig and a pair of fancy pajamas. So they agree to hock the tennis cup Janney is to defend two days later. When they go to retrieve the cup, they realize the pawn ticket is in a tuxedo Mrs. Janney has lent to a neighbor (Sidney Riggs). Desperate, they decide to plan a robbery, only to have a real burglar interfere. The burglar, intrigued by the wig and gaudy pajamas, tries them on for size, then runs out when he hears people coming. The friend returns stewed and manages to give the Janneys the wrong pawn ticket—one for his own saxophone. The couple finally retrieves the cup, only to watch the weather turn rainy and to be advised the match has been delayed a week. The play had fun with the Janneys frantically trying to free a table stuck in a doorway while their guests were ringing the front-door bell, and cooking chops on a hot plate in a supposedly non-housekeeping apartment. *Variety* noted of one youngster in the cast, "Rosalind Russell as a girl from Atlanta used a broad Georgia cracker dialect that the first-nighters were doubtful about."

Last season's successful *Young Sinners* (11-28-29) was brought into the New Yorker on the same evening, not with a road company but, at a $1 top, with a troupe of lesser stock-company actors. The appeal of Elmer Harris's tale of young lovers defying convention and eloping had clearly been exhausted, forcing it to close after two weeks.

Two weeks was also all that **The Bellamy Trial** (4-22-31, 48th St.) could survive. But then this adaptation of Frances Noyes Hart's novel by Frank E. Carstarphen and Mrs. Hart had been released only shortly before as an early part-talking film. The State is trying Stephen Bellamy (Philip Tonge) and Susan Ives (Ellen Southbrook) for the murder of Mrs. Bellamy, who apparently was having an affair with Mr. Ives (Ben Hoagland). The defense is quick to show that virtually every prosecution witness had cause and opportunity to kill the dead woman. Its case is weakened somewhat when Ives demonstrates that seemingly incriminatory letters he wrote to her were actually written years before. The letters' references to dawn coming about four o'clock could not have been written after the more recent enactment of daylight-saving-time laws. Ives admits that well before his marriage he had loved Mrs. Bellamy, who now was in financial trouble and was attempting to sell him his old love notes. Just as the jury is about to announce its verdict, Ives's mother (Viola Roche) confesses to the killing, saying she, too, thought Ives was in love with Mrs. Bellamy and about to leave his family for the woman. Since her own husband had done just that to her, she did not want to see history repeated. The strain of the confession kills the old lady.

The action of DuBose Heyward's **Brass Ankle** (4-23-31, Masque) takes place in the Leamers' apartment, which sits over their general store in a small town in the Deep South. Larry Leamer (Ben Smith) has been a leader in shifting blacks into their own, isolated community and forcing whites with even a touch of black blood in them to remove their children from the white school. His wife, Ruth (Alice Brady), herself about to have her second baby, sympathizes with the victims of such segregation, who are referred to as brass ankles. Nor is Larry totally bigoted, recalling with some friendliness his late handyman, Davey. Davey is brought to mind because a dog is howling down below in the street. Larry asks a visiting minister, "You reckon there's anything to what all the niggers say that a dog can smell trouble?" Trouble comes fast enough when Ruth gives birth to a black baby. The understanding local doctor (Lester Lonergan) tells Larry that Ruth did not know she had any black blood. Larry is torn between his love for his wife and his refusal to accept a black child. Realizing that Larry could never move away and that she could never give up the baby, but that staying in their town would mean ostracism for her and Larry and their older child, she provokes Larry into killing her by claiming the baby was fathered by Davey. Many critics admired the play all the while qualifying their approval with various reservations, especially about the plausibility of its ending. Several who liked it suggested it would have had a better chance had it been brought in earlier in the season. As it was, it closed after five and a half weeks.

Not until mid-month did one of May's entries find an

audience, and even that play was not a huge success. Before its arrival, other newcomers fared poorly. **Devil in the Mind** (5-1-31, Fulton) was New York's first English-language production of Leonid Andreyev's Russian drama, which had been called *Thought* when the Moscow Art players offered it to Broadway years earlier. The translation was by William L. Laurence, with Leo Bulgakov producing, directing, and taking the leading part of a man who kills the husband of the woman he loves and hopes to claim he is insane to escape punishment. By play's end, his condemnation and rejection by everyone convinces him that he is mad indeed.

Despite the dollar sign in its title, Harold Sherman's **Her $upporting Cast** (5-4-31, Biltmore) could not lure in paying customers. Eleanor Curtis (Mildred McCoy) is a gold-digging, baby-talking ex-showgirl who has three men on her string: a young painter (Otto Hulett), an elderly stockbroker (Dodson Mitchell), and a likable pug (Jack Hartley). Convenient problems with an imaginary aunt from Boston allow her to break a date with one whenever she prefers to see another of the men. But in the end Eleanor proves good-hearted. She takes the money she has wheedled from the artist and the broker, along with $8000 she has won in a crap game with the prizefighter, makes some highly profitable investments, and splits the profits with the three startled men.

Willis Maxwell Goodhue, the author of **Betty, Be Careful** (5-4-31, Liberty), seems to have been less pleasantly startled. Just before opening night, he sent letters to all the major drama critics, claiming his play had been so distorted that he refused to take blame or credit. What first-nighters saw, whether his or not, was a comedy toying with the then voguish idea of eugenics. Betty West (Margaret Mullen), deemed a 98-percent-perfect specimen of American womanhood, sets her sights on Rollin North (Alan Goode), a close-to-ideal example of the American male. No matter to her that Rollin has been courting her sister, Judy (Mary Murray). But then Betty finds herself with Benito Calles (Frederic Tozere), an attractive but embarrassingly innocent Argentinian. After a few drinks, Benito dons boxing gloves and asserts his manhood, causing Betty to switch allegiances. Rollin and Judy are free to pursue their own romance.

Had they decided to pursue that romance by taking in a performance of Hutcheson Boyd's **Perfectly Scandalous** (5-13-31, Hudson), they would have had only five opportunities to do so. Oliver Drake (Grant Gordon) seems as preposterously naive as Benito Calles. He loves Fay (Jeanne Greene), the adopted daughter of his uncle, Sydney North (Henry W. Pemberton), but is unaware of what his feelings signify. So his uncle's new wife, Viva (Natalie Schafer), decides to take him

out for a night on the town and teach him what it is all about. This leads to suspicions that Oliver and Viva had been playing fast and loose before everything reaches a happy conclusion.

Only a performance by the Irish actor Arthur Sinclair was universally applauded in Patrick Kearney and Harry Wagstaff Gribble's **Old Man Murphy** (5-18-31, Royale). Sinclair was one of many fine players who regularly were embraced by the critics but who never achieved major stardom. In this instance, he played Patrick Murphy, a crusty old Irish pub-keeper who comes to America to help his son (Henry O'Neill) in the younger man's campaign for mayor of a midwestern city. He discovers that thanks to his snooty daughter-in-law (Gertrude Fowler), the family now calls itself Murfree and is putting on airs. He sets out to bring them back down to the sod. As might be expected, his behavior nearly does as much harm as good. But the son, with the help of a horde of working-class Irish whose support Patrick enlists, is victorious. Winning approval as the family's independent granddaughter was Peggy Conklin. Largely on the strength of Sinclair's notices, the comedy drew from New York's still sizable coterie of Irish playgoing loyalists to run until mid-July, close briefly, then run another six weeks in the fall. It was the only half-respectable showing among May's novelties.

A different ethnic group was the subject of the night's other opening. Mark Linder's **The Honor Code** (5-18-31, Vanderbilt) looked at life on the Lower East Side among first- and second-generation Italians, whose standards of conduct still reflected those of Sicily, where so many of them had come from. After Lillian Piccichanti (Betty Kashman) is raped by her uncle, Pietro (E. L. Fernandez), the family vows to be revenged. But that revenge comes about in a most unforeseen manner, for Lillian's aunt (Valerie Bergere), misunderstanding the situation, goes to kill Lillian and kills Pietro by error.

Elmer Harris, whose *Young Sinners* had confounded last season's naysayers and whose *Ladies All* did passably earlier in the now fading session, had no luck with **A Modern Virgin** (5-20-31, Booth). Although she is only seventeen, Teddy Simpson (Margaret Sullavan) has little time for old notions of propriety and lots of time for any man. Her spinster Aunty Weeks (Lola Raine) talks her into accepting a proposal of marriage from a wise, much older man, Rob Winslow (Herbert Rawlinson), but that does not stop Teddy from wanting to enjoy a fling with her husband-to-be's married friend, Hazard (Roger Pryor). This shocks Hazard. To teach her a lesson he pretends to go along but calls Rob so that Rob can find the pair in almost flagrante delicto at a camp in the woods. For all that, the marriage takes place, and Teddy finally realizes she will find contentment with Rob. Whatever critics thought of the play—and most thought little of it—many hailed the throaty-voiced and blonde Sullavan, with John Mason Brown proclaiming, "She has youth, beauty, charm, vivacity and intelligence" as well as "a bubbling sense of comedy" and "a veteran's poise." Still, it would be several seasons, and a stint in Hollywood, before she won more lasting recognition.

For their annual outing, the Players, one of the major clubs for theatrical people in New York, revived William Congreve's brilliant, cynical *The Way of the World* at the Guild on June 1. With many of its members apparently in Hollywood, the cast was not as star-studded as previous club mountings, albeit Walter Hampden was Mirabell and Fay Bainter, Millamant. Critics found the performance dissuadingly stolid.

The season's last longish run went to Barry Conners's **Unexpected Husband** (6-2-31, 48th St.). Waiting at a New Jersey roadhouse to tell her playboy lover (Robert Ober) that their affair is finished, a beautiful Texas runaway, Dorothy Atwater (Mary Howard), drinks a few cocktails, meets the personable Perry Morrison (Arthur Aylesworth), then drinks some more with him until they both pass out. Egbert Busty (Hugh Cameron), an alcoholic justice of the peace, and his tipsy wife (Josephine Hull) find the pair, assume they are married, so move them to a hotel and put them to bed. Dorothy's gun-totin' pa (Henry Pemberton) and a scribbler (Alan Bunce) for a notorious tabloid get wind of Dorothy's whereabouts and hurry to confront her and her new man. By that time Dorothy and Perry have fallen in love, so all ends happily, with Egbert performing the marriage service. All was not happy during the comedy's four-month stand. Most of the original players, balking at performing when paychecks were not forthcoming, soon quit. The play lingered thanks to cut-rate tickets and replacements willing to act for less or on trust.

A Regular Guy, which opened two nights later at the Hudson, proved to be a revival of Patrick Kearney's *A Man's Man* (10-13-25). Glenn Hunter and Charlotte Wynters now played the struggling young couple whose life is wrecked by a con artist (Edward Pawley). Brought in at cut-rate prices, the production found no audience and was withdrawn after thirteen performances.

But that was ten performances more than the short stay of Charles Conger Stewart's **Gasoline Gypsies** (6-6-31, Lyric), which collected some of the season's most damning notices. Even the shoddy scenery was assailed. Heading in her dilapidated flivver with her aunt and sister to Florida, where she hopes to go into business, Jean Warren (Gene Byron) finds her wealthy suitor, Wallace Frazer (Edmund Donald), has followed her in a snazzy new touring car. Jean and her companions

have camped out, without asking permission, on a New Jersey farm. The farmer (Roy Earles) tricks her into thinking there is oil under the farm. She buys the place. Though she soon realizes she has been hoodwinked, she is sure she and Wallace can make the farm pay.

The old battle between rich hill folk and poor valley folk—this time on an inlet of the Chesapeake—served as background for the season's final offering and final clinker, Harry Chapman Ford's **Ebb Tide** (6-8-31, New Yorker). Most of the action takes place in the shack of "Cove" Carrie Lee (Marjorie Main). Not all her children are legitimate, certainly not Ginnie (Adele Carpell), whose father was the rich Colonel Loughran. Now the colonel's black-sheep son, "Dandy" Dan (Samuel Flint), a dabbler in drugs smuggled in along the coast, casts an eye on Carrie's oldest daughter, Dossie (Eleanor Barrie). This infuriates Dossie's valley swain, Carl Blake (Sidney Eliot). He threatens violence. But Carrie sees that everything works out peacefully. Critics ridiculed not only the play but the players' bronze makeup and their strange, sometimes unintelligible dialects.

1931–1932

True, there was a slight increase in production in the current season. Along with a handful of revivals, *Variety* tallied 146 new plays; the *Times* and Burns Mantle, 134. But much of the other news was not good. With the shrinkage of the road, which often had allowed a show that failed in New York to recoup its costs on a post-Broadway tour, the percentage of out-and-out flops rose. Fewer than one in five productions closed in the black. *Theatre,* a popularly slanted magazine for playgoers since the beginning of the century, had shuttered in April 1931. Intermittent announcements that a new group had been formed to resurrect it finally were put to rest at the beginning of the new season. The more erudite *Theatre Arts* survived, suggesting that the theatre hereafter would be of interest to an increasingly elite audience. Survival was not in the cards for many of New York's playhouses, which continued to desert the legitimate fold to serve other purposes. So did numerous once reliable figures. In the case of some famous producers and theatre owners, bankruptcy also loomed ominously. A few, such as the gentlemanly, admired Winthrop Ames, confronted with a loss of their wealth, simply retired quietly. Some, like the brash, popular Al Woods, fought to build new fortunes. The Shuberts, who reneged on interest payments in June and admitted to insolvency in October, resorted to legal hanky-panky and, eventually, emerged proportionately stronger than they ever had been.

Artistically the season was not all that depressed. Any theatrical year that could bring forth *Mourning Becomes Electra, The Animal Kingdom,* or *Reunion in Vienna* was far from bankrupt. However, in a hint of a hardly suspected future, the Pulitzer Prize went to a musical for the first time—the Kaufman-Ryskind-Gershwin operetta *Of Thee I Sing.*

An amateur botch initiated the season. Anatole France's **Thais** (6-19-31, President), in an adaptation by Ellison Harvey, briefly rescued its small venue from films. Ostensibly presented by a new subscription-seeking group, the Drama Repertoire Players, it was actually produced and staged by the lady who also assumed the title role, one Dorothy Deer Horn. Her notices were so scathing—several critics refered to her merely as Deer Horn—that when the show closed after half a week, she attempted to poison herself.

Alexander Carr, Broadway's erstwhile Perlmutter, similarly attempted to wear more than one hat when he wrote and starred in **The Wooden Soldier** (6-22-31, Biltmore). He played David Kaufman, a war veteran who has never recovered from being gassed and who has been cheated out of his inheritance by his wicked brother, Moses (Robert Leonard). He has become a hobo. But his son, Arthur (Waldo E. Edwards), raised by Moses in ignorance of his true parentage, is grateful for David's assistance in his courtship of Sylvia (Billie Mae). Being a young lawyer, he forces Moses to restore David's moneys. Only Carr's small coterie of admirers kept the show going for a month.

No one attached to Bernard J. McOwen's **Paid Companions** (6-22-31, Masque) seemed to have any sort of loyal following, so the play lasted only a single week. During that time Lila Vaughn (Lee Smith), who had come to New York and let herself be kept in a swank penthouse by a rich man (Hal Clarendon), has a change of heart after her old Maine swain (Don Costello) comes to town and urges her to marry him. When her rich lover refuses to let her go, she kills him. The sympathetic police connive to call it a suicide. Oldtimer Cecil Spooner garnered the best notices as Lila's comic fellow gold digger.

All of June's openings had already closed before the new season began in earnest in August. By that time only seven non-musical holdovers were still playing on Broadway, and only three—*The Barretts of Wimpole Street, Grand Hotel,* and *The Green Pastures*—could report respectable grosses. Almost everything about Brock Pemberton's production of Valentine Davies's **Three Times the Hour** (8-25-31, Avon) was perceived as first-class, except the play itself. Each act took place on a different floor of Lawrence W. Blake's luxurious

Fifth Avenue mansion, starting on the ground floor and moving up. And all three acts covered the same period of time, so that each curtain fell to the sound of a gunshot. That shot does in Blake (Robert Strange), despite all his police protection after receiving a letter threatening to kill him if he does not save a failing bank instead of secretly buying up South American oil fields. It eventually is shown that Blake contrived the whole thing, but that the supposedly fake killing became real when the killer resented Blake's attentions to his mistress. As in *Paid Companions,* the police list the death as a suicide.

Producer John Golden shared credit with Hugh Stange for the authorship of **After Tomorrow** (8-26-31, Golden). In contrast to the posh settings in *Three Times the Hour,* the play unfolded in a shabby basement apartment in Washington Heights. Willie Taylor (Donald Meek) is a failed insurance salesman. His daughter, Sidney (Barbara Robbins), and her fiancé, Pete Piper (Ross Alexander), have scrimped and saved so that they can be married. Part of the reason Sidney is so eager to wed is that she cannot get along with her selfish, mean-mouthed mother (Marjorie Garrett). When she berates her mother for spending money on dresses for herself and forcing Willie to overwork himself, her mother retorts, "I suppose it's on account of me that he's a failure! Of course, it's got nothing to do with his being a jelly-fish, who lets people walk all over him!" Sidney suggests that her mother's actions nearly caused her father to have a stroke last year. But on the day before the wedding, Willie's wife runs off with their boarder (Joseph Sweeney), a man about to flee to Canada after stealing funds from the bank where he works. The shock of his wife's desertion brings on a real stroke. Partially paralyzed, Willie is looked after not only by Sidney and Pete, who have put off their wedding, but by Pete's absurdly grand, demanding mother (Josephine Hull). Willie realizes that he and Mrs. Piper are "stumbling blocks" to their children's happiness. He wheedles Mrs. Piper into wedding a widower, gives Sidney a $1000 bond that her guilt-ridden mother has sent, and quietly dies. Meek won applause not only for the "embarrassed giggles and worried optimism" that usually had characterized his playing, but in the last act for the "withered arm, the difficult articulation and the palsied mannerisms [that] were true to the point of painful realism." After the opening the ending was reportedly altered to allow Willie to live, but the published text retains the story as first-nighters saw it. Golden kept the play on the boards for ten weeks.

George M. Cohan had no such luck with his **Friendship** (8-31-31, Fulton), which closed at the end of its third week. When the curtain rose to disclose Cohan alone on the stage looking uncertainly up a staircase, playgoers might have guessed that this was not a typical Cohan vehicle. Besides eschewing a star's customarily delayed entrance, Cohan took the slightly unsavory role (for him) of a man who keeps a mistress, and he set aside his usual rapid-fire pacing. The widowed Joe Townsend's mistress is a beautiful nightclub hostess named Louise Dale (Lee Patrick), who is young enough to be his daughter. When she decides to turn to writing and becomes enamored of another writer, Cecil Steinert (Clifford Jones), who is young enough to be Joe's son, Joe launches his attack on the younger generation. His salvos send Cecil scurrying, and, after Joe allows that the older generation has its faults, too, Louise agrees to marry him.

The best notices of the season so far went to Floyd Dell and Thomas Mitchell's **Cloudy with Showers** (9-1-31, Morosco), but could not turn it into a hit. For the third time recently a playwright (or co-author, in this case) also took on the leading role. Mitchell played Professor Hammill of the all-girl Quiller College, who takes exception to one of his students writing about a modern girl's sex life. The student, "Cricket" Critchlow (Rachel Hartzell), bets her classmates she can get him to change his mind and bamboozles him into taking her for a ride in his Ford. After they go off the road in a downpour, they find themselves at a roadhouse "conducted by a wily Wop [Adrian Rosley] who had dug a ditch to force people to put up at his place." He serves them champagne and ignores the fact that Cricket has had to strip to her undies and wrap herself in a silken bed cover. Further complications arise after one gunman (Victor Killian) shoots another in the next room. But matters are resolved in time for Hammill to get to a function where he is to receive a prize for his own study of contemporary women's sex lives and to make a speech. Despite its encouraging reviews, the play left after nine weeks.

On the other hand, discouraging notices caused Owen Davis's **Just to Remind You** (9-7-31, Broadhurst) to be withdrawn after a fortnight. Jimmie Alden (Paul Kelly) has turned an old art gallery into a laundry and plans to marry Doris Sabin (Sylvia Field) once the business is on its feet. When Austin Jones (Harold Healy) threatens "to put a little laundry like this on the bum" if Jimmie fails to pay $100 a week protection, Jimmie orders him and his buddies to leave, telling them, "Don't trip on the 'welcome' mat as you're going out." Jimmie and Doris even refuse to heed the warnings of Eddie Mason (Owen Davis, Jr.), a young gangster who has loved Doris, that giving in is prudent. His fellow hoods mistake the meaning of Eddie's visit and kill him. They also bomb the window of the laundry, warn patrons not to use the shop, and pour acid into the machinery. Jimmie refuses to surrender and even

cooperates with the police in fingering some of the troublemakers. As a result, he is shot and killed on July 4th as a group of young schoolchildren outside sing about this "sweet land of liberty."

Another batch of unfavorable notices did not keep Gladys Unger's **Ladies of Creation** (9-8-31, Cort) from running just as long as the more favorably received *Cloudy with Showers*. Her story centered on a celebrated interior decorator, Sibyl Vanderlyn (Chrystal Herne), who long has used her feminine charms to promote her business. Unfortunately she has been something of a tease as far as her devoted assistant, Sam Hannigan (John B. Litel), is concerned. When they quarrel over this she fires him. Without him, the business starts to fall apart. At this point she succumbs to the blandishments of an old friend, Orme Willington (Charles Trowbridge), but just as they are about to run off the arrival of a lovely lady (Spring Byington) alerts her that Orme is a married man. Sybil has no choice but to call back Sam. Down the drain with the show went what several critics hailed as one of the best settings of the season, Sybil's ultra-modern offices.

Some reviewers expressed dismay that so distinguished a producer as Arthur Hopkins could sponsor so trite a comedy as Edwin and Albert Barker's **The Man on Stilts** (9-9-31, Plymouth). By the time Godfrey Block (Harry Ellerbe) arrives at his suite at New York's Belshazzar Hotel, the youngster is a national celebrity. Irked at not being paid for his work running a steam roller, he had filched the machine and headed east. His story was taken up by a beer-swilling reporter (Hobart Cavanaugh), and from city to city, politicians such as Senator Abner Tarbottom (Robert Cummings), mountebank press agents such as Joe Day (Raymond Bramley), and other opportunists have promoted the yarn for their own ends. Sick and tired, Godfrey goes on the air to blast the whole affair, only to find that the hero-seeking country thinks his honesty makes him even a greater hero. With a cast of nearly forty, Hopkins sensed the hopelessness of bucking bad reviews, so closed the play at the end of one week.

Slashing reviews indicated that Mae West had worn out her welcome when she arrived as star of **The Constant Sinner** (9-14-31, Royale), which she dramatized from her own novel. Babe Gordon has so exhausted Bearcat Delaney (Russell Hardie), her husband, who is also the middleweight champ, that she turns to Money Johnson (George Givot, a white playing in blackface), a Harlem policy king, until he goes to jail, then she snuggles up with Wayne Baldwin (Walter Petrie), the son of the owner of a department store where she works, sometimes illicitly selling drugs in cosmetic containers. After Money is released, Wayne discovers him in a clinch with Babe, so shoots and kills him. Bearcat is arrested for the murder, but a lawyer, paid for by Wayne, gets him off. Babe agrees to split her time between Bearcat and Wayne. Assuring them both of her loyalty, she attempts to recite a poem on the virtues of faith but, unable to get beyond the first line, exclaims, "Aw, I can't remember the God damn thing." Virtually all of the sixteen scenes, changed quickly on a revolving stage, occurred either in some bedroom or some speakeasy. *Variety,* summing up for the naysaying majority, suggested, "The only way to clean this one would be to eliminate all the objectionable lines. The remnants would make a good five-minute radio routine for Uncle Bob's Little Nephews, after the nephews grow up. This way the story is more bedside than bedtime, in fact it is under the sheets." The brash, buxom blonde's hardcore admirers sustained the show for eight weeks.

For several aisle-sitters, Jo Mielziner's superb settings walked away with the honors at **I Love an Actress** (9-17-31, Times Square), Chester Erskin's adaptation of László Fodor's Hungarian original. These began with his art-deco interior of a Budapest department store, complete with an elevator whose uniformed attendant calls out the items on sale on the floor, dapper clerks, and customers, and, after displaying rooms in an elegant home, concluded with a vast train terminal, crowded with scurrying porters and travelers. Hungary's richest man (Ernest Glendinning) desperately wants to marry the country's most glamorous actress (Muriel Kirkland), and she is not uninterested. But a lovesick young civil engineer (Walter Abel), who goes nightly to all her performances and even crashes her parties, wins her away just as she and her rich admirer are about to entrain to some romantic spot together.

As he had been with *I Love an Actress,* Chester Erskin was both adaptor and director of **He** (9-21-31, Guild), taken from Alfred Savoir's Paris hit. A man (Tom Powers) disrupts an Alpine convention of the International Society for Free Thought—a convention about to declare there is no God—declaring he is God. Strange occurrences make conventioners have second thoughts, until a doctor from a mental institution comes to take the intruder back. He jumps over the footlights and disappears. Claude Rains won laughs and fine notices as another madman, an elevator operator who dresses and behaves like Napoleon. The play lasted only until the end of the Theatre Guild's subscription list five weeks later.

A third successive importation fared no better, with critics bemoaning that Somerset Maugham's **The Breadwinner** (9-22-31, Booth) seemed like a dreary rehashing of ideas he had offered so compellingly in *The Moon and Sixpence.* Like his earlier hero, his unhappy businessman (A. E. Matthews), this time verg-

ing on bankruptcy, makes good on his threats to desert his self-involved family and goes off to another life somewhere far away.

Elizabeth Miele's **Did I Say No?** (9-22-31, 48th St.), an American play which opened the same evening, was an even shorter-lived flop. It featured Anna Appel, better known for her work in Yiddish theatre, as a widow who auctions secondhand furniture. After a painting she puts up proves to be a Rembrandt and brings $50,000, she must save her daughter (Miriam Stuart) from a young man who would have the girl steal the money and elope with him. As if that was not enough, a policeman (Gordon Hamilton) accidentally kills himself in her shop while examining a gun, and the police arrest her son (Herbert Rudley) for murder. Her warm, sensible plea, abetted by the eyewitness account of an Italian lady (June Mullin), convinces a jury that the boy is innocent, and so impresses her attorney (Maurice Freeman) that he proposes marriage. Her response: "Did I say no?" Minor characters represented a supposedly typical New York potpourri of Irish, German, and Italian neighbors.

Another story of Jewish life unfolded in Sholem Aleichem's **If I Were You** (9-23-31, Ambassador), as translated by Tamara Berkowitz. (The play's Yiddish title is generally translated more literally as *Hard to Be a Jew.*) The production was offered by the Shuberts and starred the great Yiddish actor Maurice Schwartz, who temporarily had closed his Yiddish Art Theatre to try a season on Broadway in English-language mountings. The story told of two Russian students, one Jewish (Harry Mervis) and one Christian (Edward Leiter), who agree to exchange places so the Christian can see what it is like to be Jewish in czarist Russia. As the supposed Jew, the Christian goes to live in the home of a modestly prosperous Jew (Schwartz) and falls in love with his daughter (Natalie Browning). Since the Jewish student also loves her, he must stop a marriage from taking place under the false assumption that the groom is a Jew. The ensuing brouhaha reveals that Jews and Gentiles are not perceived as equals. Sporting a beard for his fatherly role, Schwartz delighted audiences with his traditional bag of Yiddish stage tricks: "shrugs of the shoulder, gleams of mockery . . . and quizzical tones of voice." He kept playgoers coming for ten weeks.

Critics had begun to complain of how dull the season was, and Torvald Liljencrantz's **People on the Hill** (9-25-31, Comedy) provided nothing to mollify them. It centered on a pregnant, unmarried girl (Elaine Temple) whose lover (Alden Chase) drowns just before their marriage. Pressed by her sisters to marry an older man, she seemingly agrees, but as the wedding party gathers, news arrives that she has thrown herself into the sea.

Some relief from the artistic drought was provided

by Paul Green's **The House of Connelly** (9-28-31, Martin Beck). The Connellys had once been wealthy southern aristocrats, but now live in genteel shabbiness in their decaying mansion. No one takes the blustering, boozy, lecherous Uncle Bob (Morris Carnovsky) seriously. Nor is there much respect for young Will (Franchot Tone), heir apparent to the estate. As one loyal Negro servant (Rose McClendon) says, he cannot do anything but "let the world rot down." He, in turn, is well aware that "even the niggers laugh at me." However, Will meets and falls in love with Patsy Tate (Margaret Barker), the ambitious, farsighted daughter of a tenant farmer. His mother and sisters, who had hoped he would marry a Virginia heiress, attempt to poison his mind against her. They almost succeed, but the changes Patsy brings about and her well-reasoned arguments restore his will power. Shouting, "I've waked out of my sleep to see it all," Will tells his family the home truths they have avoided hearing. Uncle Bob shoots himself, the shock kills his mother, and his snooty sisters pack up and leave. Alone with his new bride, he assures her, "With you I'll go on—I'll go on." In the *Times*, Brooks Atkinson observed, "Without telling either an original or an exciting story, 'The House of Connelly' is wracked with passion," and he concluded that Green "has given us something exalting and beautiful with which to combat the cheap languor of Broadway." He also hailed "the best acting company in this town." That company consisted of members of the newly formed Group Theatre, which, while still officially "under the auspices of the Theatre Guild," would break away almost immediately to devote itself to plays with a more specific political agenda. Two more seasons would pass before the company hit full stride. Meanwhile, the new mounting, which had been directed jointly by Lee Strasberg and Cheryl Crawford—both of whom would move on to renown—chalked up ninety-one performances, the longest stand of the season to date and enough to allow the fledgling company to recoup its costs.

Less than one full week sufficed for Vincent Lawrence's savagely panned **Washington Heights** (9-29-31, Maxine Elliott's). For the second time in just over a month, a shabby Washington Heights apartment was the scene of the action. There, a lust-crazed railroad worker (William Harrigan) makes life difficult for his wife and neighbors, and ultimately drives a visiting niece (Jane Bramley) to kill herself by jumping from a fire escape.

Even a magnificent performance by Charles Laughton, making his American stage debut, could not turn Jeffrey Dell's theatricalization of C. S. Forester's **Payment Deferred** (9-30-31, Lyceum) into a hit. Laughton's William Marble, a bank clerk who has murdered his nephew, buried the body in his garden, and is living off the boy's wealth, is haunted by fear and constantly peering out at the hidden grave site. Yet he apparently has pulled off the perfect crime. Only after his wife (Cicely Oates) guesses what has happened and kills herself by drinking poison is Marble brought to justice—for supposedly murdering his wife.

A second London importation also failed. Critics felt Edward Knoblock and J. B. Priestley's dramatization of Priestley's best-selling novel **The Good Companions** (10-1-31, 44th St.) missed the warmth and spirit of the original. It followed an ultimately doomed enterprise of some amateur entertainers trying to eke out a living in English backwaters. Militating further against the show's success were one of the largest casts in a season of large casts and an elaborate mounting, which brought cars, trucks, and a brass band onstage and, in a throwback to bygone theatrical traditions, on occasion employed a panorama to help depict the players on their travels.

Don Mullally, still flailing for the brass ring, not only wrote but also produced and directed **The Camels Are Coming** (10-2-31, President). Terry Tracy (J. Anthony Hughes) is a cantankerous, gin-addicted playwright, whose drinking has all but ended his playwriting. His sweetheart (Shirley Booth) and agent (Earl Simmons) introduce him to a wealthy Jewish cloak-and-suiter, Milton Markowitz (Joseph Greenwald), who will pay him to create a play about religious interaction in the Middle East. Tracy accepts, but difficulties arise when Markowitz attempts to dictate much of the play, including a scene in which camels come onstage. By the final curtain, a compromise is reached. Not quite the straw that broke the author's back, the play's quick failure undoubtedly helped prompt Mullally to leave the theatre later in the season. He might well have looked for instruction to the author-producer-director of the next entry, which even featured a similar central figure.

One of the main characters in the season's first big hit, Elmer Rice's **The Left Bank** (10-5-31, Little), was another cantankerous writer. John Shelby (Horace Braham) and his wife, Claire (Katharine Alexander), have taken a room in a cheap Paris hotel so that John can write without distraction and in a congenial atmosphere, since, John claims, "no civilized man can live decently in America," which is "a spiritual vacuum, a cultural desert." Even Greenwich Village, with its kept women, Indiana poets, interior decorators, and advertising men, is out of the question. Claire longs not only for home but for her young son, whom John has insisted be placed in a Scottish school. So when their old friends, Waldo Lynde (Donald MacDonald), a home-loving, conservative young lawyer, and his wife, Susie (Millicent Green), a fun-loving, would-be sculptor, come to

Paris and take a room next to the Shelbys, it is not long before John and Susie head off for Vence, leaving Claire and Waldo to fend for themselves. That gives Claire and Waldo time to recognize they are affinities. Telling John that she is tired of exile and wants to live among her own people, Claire suggests a divorce. So does Susie. Claire and Waldo will head home, first stopping in Scotland to pick up Claire's boy. Critics, comparing the work to Rice's earlier hits, called it "his maturest play" and "a better play than *Street Scene*." The *Herald Tribune*'s Percy Hammond, despite reservations, was pleased that Rice "proves in a well-written, well-acted play, that the place for Americans is America." Enough Americans agreed to allow the comedy to run out the season, and, if any confirmation was needed, confirmed Rice's place among the leading dramatists of his time.

. . .

Elmer [Leopold] **Rice** [né Reizenstein] (1892–1967) was a New York native, who studied law and began practicing before switching to the theatre. His earliest work leaned heavily on his legal experiences, but also showed artistic daring. *On Trial* (1914), which made him famous and was credited with introducing the use of flashbacks to the stage, was followed by *For the Defense* (1919) and *It Is the Law* (1922), neither nearly as popular. His subsequent hits were the expressionistic *The Adding Machine* (1923) and his realistic *Street Scene* (1929).

. . .

Greeted by thumbs-down notices, Will Piper and Lois Howell's **Enemy Within** (10-5-31, Hudson) lasted a single week. Regan (George MacQuarrie) is a corrupt city boss with close ties to the underworld. One gangsterish associate, "Count" Muller (Herbert Ashton, Jr.), attempts to get a hold over Selma Wolfe (Anne Forrest), the woman he loves, by having her drive a car used in a murder. Selma, the honest daughter of a dishonest politician, loves an upright attorney, Don Candler (Walter N. Greaza), who rushes to defend her. In the courtroom, Muller attempts to shoot Candler, but kills Regan by accident.

While the Theatre Guild remained a major producer, its celebrated acting company had been jettisoned. One of the Guild's major figures, Lawrence Langner, attempted to rectify the problem by organizing the New York Repertory Company. After trying out at a summer theatre, the troupe brought New Yorkers its first offering, a revival of Dion Boucicault's 1857 look at how a scoundrel who has callously bankrupted a family gets his comeuppance, *The Streets of New York; or, Poverty Is No Crime*. Opening at the 48th Street Theatre on the 6th, its huge cast included Dorothy Gish, Fania Marinoff, Jessie Busley, Rollo Peters, and Moffat Johnston.

The old warhorse was played just tongue in cheek enough to delight critics and chalk up an eighty-seven-performance run in the face of the high costs of its cast and its elaborate, multi-scened mounting.

Although Arthur Wilmurt's **The Guest Room** (10-6-31, Biltmore) was listed as a comedy, more than one critic noted that Helen Lowell's performance, while expert and true to life, imparted a harsh, unfunny tone to the work. She played Charlotte Powers, a pestiferous spinster, who, as the play begins, has been asked to leave the home of her late sister, with whom she had lived and whom, it is implied, her nagging drove to an early death. She then invites herself, ostensibly for only a few days, to live with an old acquaintance (Beverly Sitgreaves). After a year, she is told she must leave. She next imposes herself on her niece (Joan Kenyon), driving the young girl's fiancé (Otto Hulett) to take work in South America. Rather than lose her sweetheart, the niece evicts Charlotte. The play ends with Charlotte's inviting herself to visit another old friend.

Katherine Roberts's **Divorce Me, Dear** (10-6-31, Avon) was one more of the season's numerous lone-week failures. When Veronica Vare (Violet Heming) insists she has found the young man (G. P. Huntley, Jr.) of her dreams, her husband (Reginald Mason) agrees not to stand in the way of a divorce. Her husband's casual acquiescence disturbs Veronica, and before long she is also disillusioned with her dreamboat. The divorce having gone through, Veronica has no choice but to start courting her ex again.

Robert Loraine headed an all-British company of players who were announced as launching a new repertory program at the 49th Street Theatre on the 8th. Their initial presentation, a double bill, consisted of *The Father*, Strindberg's study of a man driven to madness by his wife's refusal to tell him if he is truly the father of his child, and **Barbara's Wedding**, a James M. Barrie one-acter in which a doddering old veteran of the wars in India confuses fact and imagination, past and present, on the day of his granddaughter's marriage. Even at a low price of $2.50 top, the bill proved unattractive. No further productions were forthcoming.

"Of late," Robert Garland recorded in the *World-Telegram*, "each season has brought forth its shake-and-shudder drama dealing with some victim of the electric chair." As officials and newspapermen gather to watch the execution of John Allen (Edward Pawley) in Elliott Lester's **Two Seconds** (10-9-31, Ritz), a doctor (Leonard Jerome) tells them that an electrocuted man, like a drowning man, probably relives his life's highlights in the two seconds from the time the juice is turned on until he is dead. Allen, a riveter on high-rise construction, does just that. Angry at the fat blind date Bud

Clark (Preston Foster), his roommate and co-worker, has arranged for him, he runs off to a cheap dime-a-dance hall, meets pretty Shirley Day (Blythe Daly), and, believing her yarn that she is a struggling student trying to work her way through school and support her aged parents, falls in love with her. She gets him drunk and tricks him into marriage. Then she moves in and, of course, kicks Bud out. Bud has seen through Shirley and, one day as they are working high up on a new skyscraper, tries to warn John. John picks up a pincers and seems ready to throw it at Bud, who attempts to duck and falls to his death. Subsequently John catches Shirley in the embrace of the Italian (Harold Huber) who manages the dance hall where she worked. "You were born to lie to men an' trick 'em like you did to me—like you're doin' to him. It'll be the best thing for your soul an' mine if I stop it right now." He kills her. Detectives must climb the steel framework to nab him. Back at the prison, the doctor declares John is dead. Dismissive notices, coupled with the high costs of another large cast and another multiplicity of settings (changed on a revolve), doomed the play, which struggled along for fifty-nine performances. With its closing, Lester, the father of film director Richard Lester, said farewell to Broadway. Much of his later career was spent teaching at a Philadelphia high school for exceptional boys.

Curiously, although the reviews accorded **A Church Mouse** (10-12-31, Playhouse) were not much better, the play was only the season's second to score a respectable run—164 performances. Taken from László Fodor's Hungarian play by Fanny and Frederic Hatton and rewritten by producer William A. Brady, the comedy could be perceived as a version of Fodor's earlier *I Love an Actress,* with the sexes reversed. This time a homely, seemingly mouse-like young lady (Ruth Gordon) transforms herself into a beautiful, efficient secretary to win Hungary's greatest banker (Bert Lytell) away from a luscious rival (Louise Kirtland), the man's former secretary. No doubt a "swell performance" by Lytell, topped by an "absolutely captivating" performance by Gordon, aided in luring playgoers.

Ronald Jeans's **Lean Harvest** (10-13-31, Forrest) was an English drama with one highly lauded bit of staging. Nigel Trent (Leslie Banks) is too ambitious for his own good. So occupied with getting ahead, he neglects and loses the girl (Patricia Calvert) he loves, marries another woman (Vera Allen), who deserts him when she feels neglected in turn, and ignores his doctor's warnings. On an otherwise darkened stage, with only a spotlight from the flies on his face, he grimaces painfully as a cacophony of noises, voices, and bells symbolizes a fatal stroke. A final scene, which some deemed anticlimactic, showed the reading of Trent's

will, in which he left everything to his brother (Leonard Mudie), who had married Nigel's old sweetheart.

The New York Repertory Company's second offering was Ibsen's portrait of a supposedly model town official who was not as virtuous as he seemed, *The Pillars of Society.* Dismissive notices following its premiere at the 48th Street Theatre on the 14th may have actually prompted its immediate withdrawal, but in his autobiography Lawrence Langner blamed the abrupt closing on excessive demands by the stagehands' union, which insisted this one-set play employ as many grips as the multi-scened Boucicault drama. It would not be the only time that arrogant union demands ignored the plight of a depressed theatre and played havoc with hopes for repertory.

Somehow Edouard Bourdet's Paris hit *Le Sexe faible* arrived in New York in Jane Hinton's adaptation as the sound-alike, but not mean-alike, **The Sex Fable** (10-20-31, Henry Miller). Ostensibly it told a tale of a widowed mother's arranging soft-berthed marriages for her wastrel sons, while her daughter takes up with a gigolo no better than the brothers. However, in Paris Victor Boucher walked away with the evening as a panderishly obliging maître d'hotel. On Broadway attention centered on Mrs. Patrick Campbell, the once notorious English actress, who appeared in only one scene, playing an aging countess desperate for young lovers.

Talbot Jennings's **No More Frontier** (10-21-31, Provincetown) was billed as "an American chronicle" and followed four generations of a family as it moved from ever more crowded Indiana to the wilds of Idaho and onward, until the present generation, which hopes to be able to flee to another planet. Many critics found kind things to say about the play, but the consensus was that it remained insufficiently commercial for the big uptown stages it seemed to require, yet appeared constricted on its cramped Village stage.

The Unknown Warrior (10-29-28), which told of a soldier who must return to battle aware that the girl he loves does not love him anymore, failed when first produced. Its revival at the Morosco on the 22nd was announced as being only for four matinee performances, and, once notices appeared, everyone knew there would be no extension.

There may have been a hurtful irony in the failure of Edward Chodorov and Arthur Barton's **Wonder Boy** (10-23-31, Alvin), since its producer and director, Jed Harris, often had been called Broadway's wonder boy until his recent string of duds. Chodorov and Barton had, until lately, been publicists for Columbia Pictures, and their comedy seems to have been inspired by the abortive attempt of Harry Cohn, the studio's president, to make a major star of young Richard Cromwell. (*Variety*'s review itemized a number of telling, inside jokes.) In the show, the film company becomes Paragon Pictures, and its crass head is Phil Mashkin (Gregory Ratoff), the sort of man who barks over the phone to subordinates that when he wants something, then nothing is "in two words, im-possible." That is a statement his favorite yes-man, Schwartz (Sam Levene), would never dispute. It looks to Mashkin, and so to Schwartz, that a young man named Peter Hinkle (William Challee) has stolen Paragon's newest film, *Shadows,* from its star, Mabel Fenton (Hazel Dawn). Paying no attention to Hinkle's pleas that he is only trying to earn enough money to become a dentist, Mashkin and his cohorts order the film reshot to emphasize the youngster, now rechristened Buddy Windsor, rework all the publicity, and send Hinkle-Windsor on a big promotional tour. The boy is a complete flop, so the studio changes everything back to the original. Hinkle would be totally shoved aside, had not a thoughtful secretary (Jeanne Greene) talked the studio into offering him a cash settlement. Another huge cast (nearly forty) and another huge production (with numerous scene changes worked on a revolving stage and some scenes taking place on several levels at once) all but killed the comedy's chances to override mostly negative reviews.

The season's most awaited drama was Eugene O'Neill's **Mourning Becomes Electra** (10-26-31, Guild). A trilogy lasting over five hours (from 5:15 to 11:00), and with an intermission for dinner between the first and second plays, it reset the classic *Oresteia* in Civil War America. The first play was **Homecoming.** Christine Mannon (Alla Nazimova) has not been faithful to her husband, who is away fighting the war, but instead has been having an affair with his disowned cousin, Adam Brant (Thomas Chalmers), a sea captain. Lavinia (Alice Brady), Christine's daughter, hates her mother and suspects the truth, confirmation of which she finally wheedles from Adam. When Brigadier-General Ezra Mannon (Lee Baker) returns home he reveals his resentment of the attachment their son, Orin, has for his mother. His comments, coupled with her feelings for Adam, provoke Christine into poisoning her husband. Finding her father dead, Lavinia cries out, "Don't leave me alone! Come back to me! Tell me what to do!"

The Hunted has Orin (Earle Larimore) returning from the war. Lavinia recounts what had occurred and goads her brother into helping her be revenged. Interrupting a rendezvous between Christine and Adam, Orin kills his mother's lover. Christine commits suicide after she realizes that Adam is dead.

The Haunted takes place a year later, when Orin is hounded by guilt feelings. He comes to believe that his love for his mother was not entirely natural and that this love has been transferred to his sister. Unable to placate his furies, he kills himself. Once again Lavinia must don mourning. She orders the house shut, knowing she will live there alone for the rest of her life. A small figure in black standing between the high white pillars of the portico, she watches the sun go down and remarks, "It takes the Mannons to punish themselves for being born."

The production was greeted with virtually unanimous raves. John Mason Brown in the *Evening Post* hailed the play as "an achievement which restores the theatre to its high estate . . . an experiment in sheer, shuddering, straightforward story-telling which widens the theatre's limited horizons at the same time that it is exalting and horrifying its patrons." Most critics were delighted that so noble a tragedy had been presented, but the *New Yorker*'s Robert Benchley saw the ghost of O'Neill's father chuckling in the wings. Recognizing O'Neill's patrimony, the critic exclaimed that the new play was "a hundred times better than *Electra* because O'Neill has a God-given inheritance of melodramatic sense." The small, dark, often too sultry Nazimova and the frequently rambunctious Brady were both praised for reining in excesses that had marked some of their recent interpretations. Robert Edmond Jones's several interiors were commended, but his most memorable setting was the stark, white, columned portico on which much of the drama unfolded.

. . .

Robert Edmond Jones (1887–1954) was born in Milton, N.H., and educated at Harvard. He began designing sets in 1911 but did not call major attention to himself until his starkly modern, linear work for *The Man Who Married a Dumb Wife* (1915) was said to have "sounded the note that began the American revolution in stage scenery" by its rebellion against the heavy-handed realism fashionable at the time. Among his more memorable subsequent settings were those for *The Jest,* Barrymore's *Richard III* and *Hamlet, Desire Under the Elms,* and *The Green Pastures.*

. . .

So demanding a play, offered at a stiff $6 top, could not expect to repeat the success that *Strange Interlude* had enjoyed in a more prosperous, carefree time. Still, its run of 145 showings (with only six performances a week, since there was no room for matinees) was more than acceptable. A road company was subsequently sent out headed by Judith Anderson and Florence Reed. This troupe played two weeks at the Alvin in the spring.

Neither O'Neill nor his admirers could know that this would be the last dramatic triumph he would live to see. Only an atypical comedy would receive applause, while another long drama would garner a more divided press a decade and a half later. Still, there was no question of the writer's importance. Even though his reputation fell somewhat in his later years and for a time after his death, his high place in American drama would be confirmed by the premieres of several posthumously produced works.

. . .

Eugene [Gladstone] **O'Neill** (1888–1953) was the son of the celebrated actor James O'Neill, best known for his Monte Cristo. Born in New York, he spent much of his early years accompanying his drug-addicted mother and older brother as they followed his father on tour. He later spent a brief time at college, then went prospecting in Honduras, became assistant manager to a lesser touring company in the States, ran off to sea, and subsequently joined his father in vaudeville. While recuperating from tuberculosis he took to playwriting, then studied with the famous Professor George Pierce Baker at Harvard. He began to gain fame when his one-acters were produced in the teens in Greenwich Village. A production there of the experimental *The Emperor Jones,* with its incessantly throbbing drums, was moved uptown. *Beyond the Horizon* (1920) earned him his first Pulitzer Prize. Later significant plays included *Anna Christie* (1921), *The Hairy Ape* (1922), *Desire Under the Elms* (1924), *The Great God Brown* (1926), which remained his own favorite, and *Strange Interlude* (1928), which earned him another Pulitzer Prize. His plays emphasized the dark side of human nature and the seeming futility of seeking redemption.

. . .

Some commentators excoriated John Galsworthy's **The Roof** (10-30-31, Charles Hopkins) as a weak imitation of *Grand Hotel.* It recounted the reactions of a diverse group of English tourists after the small Paris hotel at which they are staying catches fire.

There was even less sympathy for Clifford Bax's **The Venetian** (10-31-31, Masque). When Bianca de Medici (Margaret Rawlins) learns that Cardinal Ferdinand de Medici (Alastair Sim) plans to kidnap her son she poisons the cleric's drink. Unaware of her actions, her husband (Wilfred Walter) drinks some of the wine to prove to the cardinal that it is safe. He dies, so Bianca also swallows the poison.

A third successive English importation, H. M. Harwood and R. F. Gore-Browne's dramatization of the latter's novel *An Imperfect Lover* as **Cynara** (11-2-31, Morosco), appealed to what one reviewer termed "the carriage trade," so ran a little more than six months. While his wife (Phoebe Foster) is away, a man (Philip Merivale) has a fling with a shopgirl (Adrianne Allen), who kills herself when he breaks off the affair. The wife listens understandingly to the husband's confession and forgives his straying. The play might have run even longer but for another extensive cast and multi-scened mounting.

Using a much smaller cast and a single setting, Rachel Crothers nonetheless came a cropper with her curious attempt to blend character study and mystery in **Caught Wet** (11-4-31, Golden). At a party thrown by stuffy young Clifford Vanderstyle (Michael Milan) and his shy sister, Julia (Dortha Duckworth), a waggish guest (Sylvia Field) suggests the group pretend to steal the Vanderstyle jewels. Another guest (Robert Lowes), a musician who is an amateur magician, removes them from the neck of Clifford's fiancée (Gertrude Michael) and hides them under some cushions. But when they go to retrieve the jewels, the guests cannot find them. A last-minute soul-unbaring by Julia, who has resented the lack of attention paid to her, clears up matters.

Sharply divided notices and a $5.50 top (the season's second highest for a non-musical) probably doomed the latest revival of *Hamlet,* at the Broadhurst starting on the 5th, to a three-week run. The production was the brainchild of designer Norman Bel Geddes, who doubled in brass by directing.

. . .

Norman Bel Geddes [né Norman Melancton Geddes] (1893–1958) was born in Adrian, Mich. After studying at art schools in Cleveland and Chicago, he saw his first settings mounted for a production of *Nju* in Los Angles in 1916. Otto Kahn brought him to New York to help create scenery for the Metropolitan Opera. Broadway soon admired his brilliant art-deco settings for many of the 1920s' best revues and musical comedies, as well as his conversion of the huge New Theatre into a seeming medieval cathedral for Max Reinhardt's *The Miracle* in 1924.

. . .

Bel Geddes's sparse settings were described variously as "an impressive series of platforms and cubes" or "a vaulted space with irregular column-like masses and other bulks with an entrance to the rear that is always left unexpressed and in shadows." Indeed, lighting (a good share of it from lamps on the front of the balcony, a practice still rare at the time) served to create much of the atmosphere and effect scene changes. Thus while one scene was played out on a part of the multi-leveled stage, actors could be discerned moving into place in the darkness on another part of the stage. So as to emphasize the thrust of the story, Bel Geddes cut the play severely, including several soliloquies. Raymond Massey, in his American debut, was seen as a sometimes grim-visaged, sometimes charmingly boyish but always energetic Hamlet. In one strange departure he was assigned the suddenly silent Ghost's lines, perhaps to make clearer that only Hamlet heard the words. Some of the best notices went to Celia Johnson, also in her American debut, for her sensitive Ophelia.

Act One: 1930–1944

Author-producer-director Elmer Rice had his second smash hit of the season with **Counsellor-at-Law** (11-6-31, Plymouth). George Simon (Paul Muni) has risen from the East Side tenements to become one of New York's most prominent lawyers. He is a charitable man, lending or even giving money to those in need, and gladly defending at no charge worthwhile clients who he knows cannot pay him. He is even willing to employ Charlie McFadden (J. Hammond Dailey), an ex-con, as his process server. Among his presumed rewards is his new wife, Cora (Louise Prussing), a lofty member of the Four Hundred. But things start to go awry for George, when he learns he is to be brought up for subornation of perjury and disbarred if convicted. Years ago to avoid a basically decent young man's having to go to prison for life, he had paid to have a witness give false evidence. As he tries to explain to his uncomprehending wife, "It was conniving at a lie, to prevent a conviction that nobody wanted, not the judge, nor the district attorney, nor the jury; but that the law made inevitable." Because the young man has lived a productive life since then, George feels his own long-ago lapse should be overlooked. But his hounder will not relent, so he puts Charlie on his opponent's trail and discovers that the man is leading a double life, with a second woman and child in Philadelphia. The charges are dropped. At the same time, however, Cora runs off to Europe with another man, leaving George to look with new interest on his devoted secretary (Anna Kostant). The play eschewed tryouts, and several commentators suggested after its opening that the nearly thirty-character drama still needed substantial cutting. (The published text, which seems more than a bit too long, leaves open the question of whether Rice responded to these critics.) Nonetheless, Robert Coleman, writing in the *Daily News,* spoke for a majority of his colleagues when he said the drama "has an inspired fire, a dramatic, compelling surge, a human realism and sufficient comedy relief." Muni, "less showily dramatic than usual," was hailed for his splendid performance. In slightly separated stands, and with Otto Kruger briefly spelling Muni, the show compiled 397 playings, the season's longest run.

Broadway showed no interest in Aben Kandel's **Hot Money** (11-7-31, George M. Cohan). Gar Evans (Leo Donnelly), a hot shot promoter, dashes from a speakeasy to a sobering Turkish bath upon being told by a Mr. Ginsburg (Robert C. Fischer) of a project to turn rubbish into rubber. From a lavishly furnished office, Gar launches a campaign to sell watered stock to gullible buyers and looks to make $100,000. The real rubber interests recognize him for a fraud but, even so, pay him a million dollars to be rid of the threat. He also promises his sweetie (Dorothy Vernon) and the au-thorities that he will never again indulge in pie-in-the-sky deals. Then he hears of a gold mine in Alaska.

After David Belasco's death, Katharine Cornell and her husband Guthrie McClintic, the director, took over his playhouse. Their first offering was S. N. Behrman's **Brief Moment** (11-9-31, Belasco). When the curtain rose the volley of applause that burst loose was not so much for Jo Mielziner's lovely setting of a penthouse sitting room as for the fat man comfortably ensconced on a sofa—the erstwhile critic Alexander Woollcott. He was cast as Harold Sigrift, a rather languorous sybarite, who is shocked to learn that his handsome, rich, socialite friend—and the owner of the penthouse—Roderick Dean (Robert Douglas) is about to marry a nightclub singer, Abbey Fane. He listens in growing dismay to Roderick's catalogue of Abbey's virtues, then, claiming he is "reluctant to blight this dewy romance," vainly attempts just that. Not even a visit from Manny Walsh (Paul Harvey), the fatherly gangster at whose club the strawberry-blonde beauty works, can dissuade Roderick. Even an admission by Abbey (Francine Larrimore), that while she is fond of Roderick, she does not love him, in no way proves discouraging. As Mrs. Deane, Abbey quickly displays "layers of adaptive coloring" and is soon a popular hostess. Unfortunately, she is something of a coquette, so cannot resist flirting with an old flame, Cass Worthing (Louis Calhern). Her behavior disturbs Roderick. They quarrel and split, with Abbey going to Cass's and Roderick threatening to give up his wealth and lead a spartan life. In the end they are reconciled. Abbey promises to goad him on to real success on his own, and he acknowledges that he can never "resist the eternal glamor of the illicit." Burns Mantle suggested that Behrman's "gift is for a pleasant wit and incisive characterization," and that his comedies were most admired "for the pungency of their comment on modern life rather than because of the emotional force of their situations." Capital acting added an earthiness to such a rarified atmosphere, allowing the play's 129 performances to go down in the record books as a modest hit for the author.

. . .

S[amuel] N[athaniel] **Behrman** (1893–1973) was born in Worcester, Mass. He studied first at Clark University before enrolling in Professor George Pierce Baker's 47 Workshop at Harvard. He next did graduate work at Columbia under Brander Matthews and St. John Ervine. Stints followed as a book reviewer, play reader, and press agent. Several early collaborations failed to reach Broadway. He scored a hit with his first solo effort, *The Second Man* (1927). *Serena Blandish* and *Meteor* (both in 1929) also had admirers.

. . .

38

That same night Anita Loos and John Emerson had a near miss (ninety-seven performances) with **The Social Register** (11-9-31, Fulton), which the pair took from Loos's sequel to *Gentlemen Prefer Blondes, But Gentlemen Marry Brunettes.* Tiny, dark Lenore Ulric, with her hoarse voice and often tempestuous mannerisms, helped their cause with a lively performance as Patsy Shaw. Patsy has risen from the carnivals to a place in the *Vanities,* and now looks to climb the social ladder by marrying Charlie Breene (Sidney Blackmer). Charlie's snooty family invites Patsy to dinner, hoping she will make a fool of herself. Instead, she wins over everyone but Mama Breene (Teresa Maxwell-Conover). Nevertheless, Patsy and Charlie quarrel, and, in a huff, Patsy runs off and marries a sleazy saxophonist (Alan Edwards). Charlie heads for foreign parts. But he returns, unhappy, about the same time Patsy decides to divorce her husband. Despite Mrs. Breene's attempt to sabotage the proceedings, Patsy wins the divorce and ties the knot with Charlie. Among the highlights of the evening was a dance Ulric did at the dinner party, stepping to the music of a black combo and displaying a bit of choreography fashioned for her by the then famous Billy Pierce.

Although Myron C. Fagan's comedy **Peter Flies High** (11-9-31, Gaiety) briefly rescued a fine house from films, critics could not muster any enthusiasm for it, so it went down as the evening's lone quick flop. By returning from Florida and claiming he saved several millionaire golfers from a mad dog, Peter Turner (John Hole) turns himself into a local hero, until his bubble is punctured. But one of the rich men, hearing of his story and feeling more pity than gratitude for the young man, helps him bring an airport to his New Jersey town, so all is not lost.

Ethel Barrymore's reputation recently had lost some of its old glitter, and, indeed, she would not have a single real triumph throughout the 1930s. But she recouped a small measure of her old acclaim when she appeared on the 10th at the theatre named for her as Lady Teazle in Richard Brinsley Sheridan's classic comedy *The School for Scandal.* She had been touring with it for some time and, on completing a three-week New York stand, returned with it to the road. She brought her poise and elegance as well as her gift for high comedy to her part, and several critics were delighted to proclaim the famous screen scene as the best version of it they had ever watched. (By this time most critics were apparently too young to have seen Ada Rehan in her heyday.) Moreover, Barrymore insisted that the text cling more closely to Sheridan's original than long had been the practice. Her supporting players delighted some critics and left others chagrined.

There was much more chagrin in evidence in the morning-after notices for Elmer Harris's **Marriage for Three** (11-11-31, Bijou). Many reviewers had become sated with what they perceived as his exploitive handling of sexual problems. The new play was no exception. It told bluntly of a woman (Jessie Royce Landis) who has lost her fertility, so is not disturbed when her husband (Terence Neil) has a child by a pretty young houseguest (Verree Teasdale). She is even willing to adopt the child and raise it as her own. At first the mother consents, then decides she will bring up the baby herself.

Two spoofs of the entertainment world came in the next evening. Both received a number of favorable notices and both ran sixty-eight performances, their runs undoubtedly shortened by the upkeep of large casts and, in one case, an elaborate, many-scened production. Norman Krasna, a former newsman and Hollywood publicist, made his playwriting debut with **Louder Please** (11-12-31, Masque). He was aided by the fast-paced direction of George Abbott and the exuberant histrionics of Lee Tracy, who had worked together so happily in *Broadway.* Robert Glecker, the snarling gangster of that melodrama, was now cast as a snarling, but decent and more than a little vain, detective. Herbert White, head of publicity at Criterion Pictures, hopes to rekindle interest in fading Polly Madison (Louise Brooks) by pretending she is lost at sea and launching a widespread search. Even the Coast Guard and the Navy are enlisted. The police are suspicious and do everything they can to expose the hoax. However, all ends peacefully after Detective Bailey is allowed to lead the phony rescue.

Murdock Pemberton (art critic for the *New Yorker* and brother of Brock Pemberton) and David Boehm were the authors of **Sing High, Sing Low** (11-12-31, Sam H. Harris), which took a comically jaundiced view of the opera world. Only in their version, the Metropolitan Opera became the Cosmopolitan, while glimpses of its famous director, Giulio Gatti-Casazza, and its well-known supporter, Otto Kahn, were discerned by some reviewers in the characters of Emilio Amalfi (Giuseppe Sterni) and Hugo Adams (Ralph Locke). Having won a hometown bathing beauty contest, a southern belle, Magnolia Jackson Wainwright (Barbara Willison), comes to New York convinced she deserves to be a great prima donna. Willie Northworth (Ben Lackland), an apprentice publicity agent for the company, talks Adams into talking Amalfi into giving Magnolia the lead in a new American opera. She is a disaster, losing her voice in the middle of the performance and having to mouth the role while another soprano sings it from the wings. Adams and Amalfi both still express some non-professional interest in the girl, but she runs off with Willie. William Lynn, as the opera's befuddled composer, ran off with the best notices. Besides a cast of twenty-six, an eight-member corps de ballet was on hand for a scene from the supposed opera. Sterni, along with appearing in the show, continued, as he had last season, to offer Sunday night performances of Italian classics and translations of non-Italian works into Italian—mostly at the Little Theatre.

Cutler Hatch's **If Love Were All** (11-13-31, Booth) departed quickly. When Janet Bryce (Margaret Sullavan) discovers her mother (Aline MacMahon) is having an affair with Frank Grayson (Hugh Buckler), she and Frank's son, Ronald (Donald Blackwell), connive to take their wronged parents (Mabel Moore and Walter Kingsford) away on vacation, in hopes the lovers will soon tire of each other. To their shock, the youngsters learn that the infidelities are an open secret.

The Theatre Guild's biggest money-maker of the season was Robert E. Sherwood's **Reunion in Vienna** (11-16-31, Martin Beck). Anton Krug (Minor Watson), a distinguished ''practitioner of Vienna's sole remaining industry,'' psychoanalysis, has advised a patient who cannot forget her first love to seek him and allow herself to be disillusioned. Knowing that his own wife, Elena (Lynn Fontanne), is similarly besotted by memories of her affair with the exiled Archduke Rudolf Maximilian von Hapsburg, he urges her to meet with him again after they learn that Rudolf has come quietly back into town to attend a reunion. She reluctantly agrees. The cigar-smoking Frau Lucher [read Sacher] (Helen Westley) greets the archduke (Alfred Lunt) effusively when he bursts in by way of the kitchen, disguised in Tyrolian touring clothes. He is anxious to see Elena again, and certain that, since ''I am constantly intoxicated with my own charm,'' Elena will still find him irresistible. But when Elena determinedly resists his advances and runs back home, he runs after her—first borrowing the cab fare from Frau Lucher. Realizing that Elena is not truly over her infatuation, Dr. Krug announces that he will have to spend the night at the police station arranging for Rudolf to be allowed to leave the country. When he returns the next morning, Rudolf is so happy and Elena so radiant that he wonders if he did the right thing. Several of the major morning papers had serious reservations about the play and, to a much lesser extent, about the Lunts. Other reviewers had no such doubts, with the *Sun*'s Richard Lockridge hailing the play as ''light and frisky'' and Garland praising it as ''adult in outlook, compassionate in its fun-poking, cumulative in the tale it has to tell.'' The *American*'s Gilbert Gabriel rejoiced that the Lunts ''play it to the hilt . . . swiftly, dashingly . . . and ornamentally.'' Aline Bernstein's fussily ornate hotel suite was sandwiched in between two acts featuring her up-to-date art-deco apartment. The comedy ran out the season

and helped reestablish Sherwood's renown following several disappointments.

· · ·

Robert E[mmet] **Sherwood** (1896–1955) was born in New Rochelle, N.Y., and studied at Harvard, including classes with Professor George Pierce Baker, although not his famous 47 Workshop. He spent World War I with the Canadian Black Watch, then served in a variety of positions with several major magazines. His first produced play was also his first success, *The Road to Rome* (1927).

· · ·

Ignoring the discouraging notices he had received in the last two seasons, Fritz Leiber brought his Chicago Civic Shakespeare back to Broadway, at the Royale on the 16th. Perhaps to fend off more criticism, he recruited such distinguished oldtimers as Tyrone Power, William Faversham, and Pedro de Cordoba, as well as the young, vibrant Helen Menken. Their repertory consisted of *The Merchant of Venice, Julius Caesar*, and *Hamlet*. Reviews were less damning than previously, but hardly money notices. When the troupe left after a single week, Broadway had seen the last of Leiber's Shakespearean mountings.

Elliott and J. C. Nugent were soundly chided for the rather off-color language they introduced into their **Fast Service** (11-17-31, Selwyn). Critics expected it of other playwrights but not of the gentlemanly father and son. Furious at the cavalier indifference of Bing Allen (Elliott), the tennis champion, Neila Anderson (Muriel Kirkland) marries the rich, much older John Blair (J. C.). Now it is Bing's turn to be upset. He buys the hotel in Baja California where the Blairs are honeymooning. Learning that their marriage has never been consummated, he persuades Nella to get an ʌnnulment and marry him.

Cries of ''sheer propaganda,'' ''overwrought [and] overwritten,'' and ''it screams with Marxian anger'' filled the notices of all but the furthest-left dailies following the opening of John Wexley's **Steel** (11-18-31, Times Square). Wexley's hero was Joe Raldny (Paul Guilfoyle), driven to become ''a union agitator'' following the death of his father (Egon Brecher), supposedly from overwork. At a union meeting, state troopers assault him and chase after him when he hurries home. His sister, Melania (Eleanor Phelps), shoots and kills one of the intruders, leading to her arrest along with her brother's. A shrill factory whistle, sounded indiscriminately throughout the evening, ended by eliciting hoots and laughter.

Some critics saw Carl Glick's **The Devil's Host** (11-19-31, Forrest) as a poorly minted reverse side of *He*'s coin. In this instance, a man (Gilbert Douglas), claiming to be the Devil, invites some prominent figures to a dinner, exposes their hypocrisies, and, whether as hush money or contrition, is given $100,000 by one of the guests. But is he truly the Devil or just a clever con man? Well, one of the guests pumps bullets into him—to no effect.

Another elaborate, large-cast drama from London, Reginald Berkeley's **The Lady with a Lamp** (11-19-31, Maxine Elliott's), found few takers. It retold the story of Florence Nightingale (Edith Evans) from her early years to her belated honoring as an old lady.

One curious venture was offered for a single matinee. Wilfred Walter, an English actor, was the author of **Happy and Glorious** (11-20-31, Bijou). It described how a young suffragette (Catherine Lacey) and young soldier (Walter) come to grips with life's stark realities. The two characters were the only figures in the play. Those few critics who deigned to review the piece seemed baffled. Their response was that two characters might make a dialogue but not a play. Of course, there had been a few similar pieces, such as *The First Fifty Years* (3-13-22) and *Jealousy* (10-22-28), but they had not met with much success. Time and a changing theatrical economy would force a later generation of critics to take a different view of two-player works.

When a memorial service for her husband, who has reportedly been lost in Africa, is interrupted by his (Ernest Glendinning) appearance and his denial of ever having married her, sweet, petite Sue (Claiborne Foster) is forced into a confession. Unfortunately, with so promising a start, Lea Freeman's **A Widow in Green** (11-20-31, Cort) thereafter fell apart. Flashbacks disclosed that though the couple had met briefly, the romance-seeking spinster had made up the story of their marriage and claimed his work kept him away. This time, he does propose. For Foster, whom many had long seen as one of Broadway's most promising actresses, the play marked her farewell.

A rehearsal is taking place on the stage of the Stuyvesant Theatre of a drama in which a theatre owner (Reginald Mason) is using his playhouse as a front for his drug dealings. He is abetted by his stage manager (Frank Shannon). A "dope-fiend" (Barry Macollum) is killed after the stage manager substitutes real bullets for blanks in a gun. In the end, the theatre owner reveals that he is really working with the police to trap the drug dealers. Critics were uncertain how much of Dodson Mitchell and Clyde North's **In Times Square** (11-23-31, Longacre) was meant to represent the play-within-the-play and how much was supposed to depict reality. Playgoers had only a week to decide for themselves.

Some "dainty and rapturous playing" by Helen Hayes kept Ferenc Molnár's **The Good Fairy** (11-24-31, Henry Miller), in a faithful translation by Jane Hinton, on the boards for nineteen weeks. Hayes played Lu, a "glow worm" or theatre usher (the nickname came from the small flashlights ushers used) who is impulsively given to good deeds. Rather than accept the offer of a rich man (Evelyn Roberts) to become his mistress, she claims she is married to a lawyer and picks an attorney's name from the telephone book. He (Walter Connolly) turns out to be a high-minded failure, so the rich man offers him a good-paying job in return for Lu's favors. Lu scotches the whole deal by spending the night with a headwaiter (Paul McGrath). An epilogue, ten years on, has Lu meeting all three men and introducing them to her husband, a young doctor (Douglas Wood). On opening night, the producer, Gilbert Miller, came before the curtain following the third act and claimed that he had persuaded Molnár to write the epilogue to tie together the loose ends. On subsequent evenings his stage manager made the same announcement. Critics and playgoers learned only later that the epilogue and the manager's comments were in the Hungarian original.

George Ford and Ethel Taylor's **Miss Gulliver's Travels** (11-25-31, Hudson) told of a group of second-rate English and American actors, calling themselves "Gulliver's Thespians," after their leader, Ned Gulliver (P. J. Kelly). They traipse from 1811 Albany to Washington in hopes of success. At best they get to perform *Romeo and Juliet* for President Madison, and their leading lady, Ned's daughter Julia (Taylor), finds true love. The play found even less success than the not dissimilar *Good Companions* earlier in the season.

Nor did H. A. Archibald and Don Mullally's **Coastwise** (11-30-31, Provincetown) find much luck, even though it was briefly hurried uptown, where it was rechristened *Coastwise Annie*. That second title at least spotlighted its central figure, a warm-hearted prostitute (Shirley Booth), who plies her trade out of Vancouver. She takes in and rehabilitates a derelict English gentleman (Richard Stevenson), and though he asks her to return to England with him, she recognizes that she will be out of place there, so resumes her old work. For Mullally, the drama's failure wrote "finis" to his playwriting career.

Two importations launched December; both flopped. England offered John van Druten's **After All** (12-3-31, Booth), in which a brother and sister are happy to leave their parents' home but, with time, come to appreciate how comfortable and reassuring it had been.

Maurice Schwartz continued his English-speaking season with **Bloody Laughter** (12-4-31, 49th St.), Forrest Wilson and William Schack's translation of Ernst Toller's *Hinkemann*. Egon Hinkemann returns from the war crippled and impotent. To support his faithless wife (Helen MacKellar), he takes work in a carnival as a freak who bites off the heads of live animals. His unhappy wife finally commits suicide, leading him to hang himself. Toller used his story to attack society's callous indifference to those it has maimed. Although Schwartz was praised, the play ran less than half as long as his earlier vehicle.

Life was not much better in America, if one took Gretchen Damrosch's **The Passing Present** (12-7-31, Ethel Barrymore) to heart. Page French (Hope Williams) is willing to borrow money to save her brother (Morgan Farley) from prison after he speculated with stocks he did not own and went bust. For the cash, she goes to her cousin's husband (Douglas Gilmore), whom she has secretly loved. Her father (Cyril Scott) gets wind of the problem and sells the family's home to pay off his son's debts. Then Page discovers that while her cousin's husband reciprocates her feelings, he is not willing to go through a messy divorce. She must pick up the pieces of her life on her own.

But if the public eschewed harsh histories of the modern world, it could also ignore sentimental views of bygone days. It did just that when William A. Brady revived Marian de Forest's 1912 adaptation of *Little Women* at his Playhouse on the same night. Even a cast including Lee Patrick (Meg), Jessie Royce Landis (Jo), Joanna Roos (Beth), and Peg Entwistle (Amy) was no attraction.

Just over a week after they had hustled down to Greenwich Village, critics had to return to the same playhouse to sit in judgment on George Bryant's **The Second Comin'** (12-8-31, Provincetown). Rev. Wilbur (Irving Hopkins), a white minister, has come to work among a group of lowly, "psalm-singing negroes." One black sceptic, Nicodemus (A. B. Comethiere), demands the minister prove his credentials by making a miracle come to pass, and he suggests that God send a black Jesus to save them. Wilbur spends time with Glory (Enid Raphael), Nicodemus's girl, and hypnotizes her into believing that she is to have a child by God. On Christmas day, the child is born. The hymn-singing is interrupted with the news and also with the information that Glory's child is a white baby. As the church bells peal angrily, Wilbur has a fatal heart attack. The new show left the playhouse after a single week but was not, unlike its predecessor, brought uptown.

The next evening saw the premiere of Benn W. Levy's London comedy, **Springtime for Henry** (12-9-31, Bijou). In an era of large casts and mammoth productions, it took only four actors and one simple setting to tell its tale. Henry Dewlip (Leslie Banks), an inveterate bachelor and playboy, who is having an affair with the wife (Frieda Inescort) of his best friend (Nigel Bruce), takes on a new secretary (Helen Chandler). Until now, Henry has been the sort of man who, after his late-morning breakfast and soda, can sit down and play the phonograph "rather well." He is proud of that. But his new secretary is a determined young lady, who gets him to abandon his decadent hours, his drinking, his gambling, and his philandering. Before long he is so enamored that he decides to propose marriage. Then he discovers that the girl has been married, and, when he asks what became of her husband, she blithely assures him that she had to shoot him. The girl is dismissed, and Henry resumes his old ways. The comedy ran for six months, but it had an especially long afterlife in frequent revivals on the road and in summer stock, more often than not with epicene Edward Everett Horton in the lead.

The course the Group Theatre would take became even clearer with its second presentation, Claire and Paul Sifton's **1931 –** (12-10-31, Mansfield). Adam (Franchot Tone), a trucker in a warehouse, is fired after a fistfight with his foreman. He is not too concerned since he is young, strong, and hardworking. But he finds there is no work. Too proud to stand in breadlines, he grows increasingly bitter. Cowardice overcomes him when he tries to rob a silk-hatted gentleman. His girl (Phoebe Brand) takes to the streets and contracts a social disease. They go to join a Communist meeting in Union Square, only to be greeted by machine-gun-wielding police. Throughout the play a line of dejected men kept reappearing during scene changes, standing before the large metal shutters of a warehouse, waiting for work. After only one or two would be chosen, the others would move slowly away. Soundly slated by most critics as a "bad play" filled with "bitter propaganda," it prompted *Variety* to comment, "Looks strictly for the balcony, if at all." Although Harold Clurman later claimed that curtain calls grew more enthusiastic with each performance, there were only twelve performances.

More traditional Broadway fare was rejected just as swiftly. In Doris Anderson and Joseph Jackson's **Cold in Sables** (12-23-31, Cort), John Hammond (Taylor Holmes) is so indiscreet about keeping his mistress, Lily La Mar (Dorothy MacKaye), that his wife, Victoria (Olive Reeves-Smith), takes up with a polo player (Brandon Peters) who lives in the apartment below theirs. When John buys both women sable coats, each claims the other's is better. The comic contretemps that follow are resolved after John decides to stick with his wife and Lily announces she is going to be married.

The Christmas season brought in a number of revivals, beginning on the 24th at the New Yorker with Aurania Rouverol's *It Never Rains* (11-19-29), in which a seemingly sour real estate deal nearly wrecks two couples' friendships and the romance of their children until the deal turns sweet.

Christmas night was busy, although hardly as busy

as Christmas-week evenings only a few seasons back. Three shows opened. The only true novelty among them was Lula Vollmer's **Sentinels** (12-25-31, Biltmore). Mallie (Laura Bowman) is a black maid who has served the Hathaways so long and so loyally that she considers their sons as much hers as her own son, Thunder (Wayland Rudd). So when young George Hathaway (Ben Smith), attempting to conceal a scandal relating to the girl (Elizabeth Love) his brother, Tom (Owen Davis, Jr.), is about to marry, kills a man, Mattie demands Thunder claim responsibility. George's confession prevents the black boy's being lynched. Disappointment that Vollmer could not recreate the excitement of her earliest successes doomed the play.

Ernö Vajda's saga of a young man's initiation into adult rites, *Fata Morgana* (3-3-23), came into the Royale with Douglass Montgomery as the boy and Ara Gerald as the cousin who loves and leaves him.

Throughout the season groups composed of child actors had sprouted up all over Manhattan. One such ensemble, the National Junior Theatre, braved Broadway for a week. Its first offering was Paul Kester's dramatization of **Tom Sawyer** (12-25-31, Alvin), which Kester had written some time earlier and which had toured the hinterlands without ever playing New York. However, New Yorkers had seen the group's second offering before, Jules Eckert Goodman's theatricalization of *Treasure Island* (12-1-15). Among the performers was a very young Ezra Stone.

The next evening witnessed the opening of the Kaufman-Ryskind-Gershwin spoof of American politics, *Of Thee I Sing,* which went on to become the first musical to win a Pulitzer Prize. As a result, second-stringers sat in judgment of the New York Repertory's final attempt to establish itself as an ongoing Broadway enterprise, Will Cotton's **The Bride the Sun Shines On** (12-26-31, Fulton). Their consensus was that while the comedy was "light and gay and frothy," it might have been better as a one-acter. Because of its notices, the comedy ran a good, but not good enough, nine weeks. All the action takes place in an elegantly paneled, flower-bedecked living room at the country home of the Marburys, just before, during, and after the wedding of their daughter, Psyche (Dorothy Gish). Psyche has had so many eligible suitors that Mrs. Marbury (Jessie Busley) isn't quite certain which one she is marrying. He turns out to be the handsome but curiously wimpy Alfred Satterlee (Sam Wren), who is distressed that guests might tie tin cans to the bridal limousine or otherwise embarrass him. One of the guests is Hubert Burnet (Henry Hull), who has come to play the organ at the ceremony. It becomes obvious during a tête-à-tête that Psyche and Hubert long have loved each other, even if the relationship is more love-hate

on the surface. He accuses her of having an evil mind; she accuses him of evil habits. Both are referring to his rumored affair with a married woman, Mrs. Lane (Fania Marinoff). Although Hubert admits he still worships Psyche, he announces that he will not play the organ for her. That job is assigned to an angry Mr. Lane (Nicholas Joy). As her father (Dudley Hawley) escorts her down the aisle, Psyche stops long enough to conk Hubert over the head with her bridal bouquet and bark, "You double-barreled fool!" (Critics agreed this second-act curtain earned the evening's biggest laugh.) Alfred's petulant behavior after the ceremony prompts Psyche to agree, as Hubert puts it, "to be of that great company the world adores, those lovers who dared." Psyche and Hubert elope.

There were more lovers who dared in Theodore St. John's **Adams' Wife** (12-28-31, Ritz). Peter Barrett (Eric Dressler), a New Yorker working as a farmhand to earn money for college, takes temporary employment on the Kansas ranch of Jim Adams (Victor Kilian). It is Ku Klux Klan territory. Yet even though a black boy (Alonzo Thayer) is lynched for kissing a white girl, that does not stop Peter from falling in love with Jim's wife, Jennie (Sylvia Field). The neighbors learn of this and organize another lynching party, but an understanding Jim holds them at bay until the lovers can escape. Despite a number of favorable reviews and almost universal praise for the acting, the play was taken off after a single week.

The history of Charles K. Gordon's **Papavert** (12-29-31, Vanderbilt) was not as simple. The play, which supposedly was loosely based on an unidentified German novel by George Froeschel, had been produced initially in a French translation in Paris by a celebrated Montmartre club owner, Joe Zelli. Zelli next brought the original version to New York, where it was hooted off the stage after two performances. Revised by H. S. Kraft, it reopened three weeks later as *Mr. Papavert* and closed in little more than a week. In one version or another it told of a simple workman (Edgar Stehli) who is released from prison after having wrongly had to serve time for a killing he did not commit. His daughter's lover (Edward Leiter), a determined Communist, tries to make capital of the situation. But Papavert is not interested. He would even prefer the peace and quiet of a nice prison to political agitation. His attempts to be rejailed fail, so he agrees to let himself be a symbol (and just possibly even head of the party), but he will use his newfound fame and power to argue for peaceful integrity and the virtues of quality workmanship.

By far the most successful of the end-of-year revivals was a return at the Avon on the same night of *Hay Fever* (10-05-25), Noel Coward's hilarious look at how guests are ignored by a self-involved actress and her equally self-involved family. With Constance Collier in the lead the comedy ran twelve weeks, although it was never to achieve the success in this country that it merited.

Valentine Williams's story "The Crouching Beast" was turned by Williams and Alice Crawford into **Berlin** (12-30-31, George M. Cohan), an American spy thriller about English agents in prewar Germany. But reviewers and the playgoing public perceived it as too little and too late. The man known as Abbott is really Nigel Druce (G. P. Huntley, Jr.), a top British operative assigned to retrieve documents the Royal Navy must have. He knows they are hidden in the gramophone of Floria von Pelligrini (Katherine Wilson), a prima donna who is also a German spy. But Druce obtains the papers and, together with a helpful and pretty English secretary (Helen Vinson), flees Germany, despite the machinations of the evil head (Sydney Greenstreet) of German security. Livingston Platt's quickly changed settings imparted an additional sinister element.

John Larkin, Jr.'s **Society Girl** (12-30-31, Booth) used only two settings, shuttling back and forth between Judy Gelett's art-deco penthouse and Johnny Malloy's less fancy training quarters. Judy (Claire Luce) is a spoiled, bored socialite, given to seducing then deserting any attractive male who catches her eye. Tired of the more or less effete men in her circle, she decides to pursue Johnny (Russell Hardie), a likable but no-nonsense prizefighter. His trainer (Brian Donlevy) attempts to talk him out of any fling. Judy has little trouble seducing Johnny, but when she attempts to walk away, he hands her a knockout punch, carries her to the training camp, and teaches her how to become the good girl his wife must be.

Walter Woolf, the popular operetta baritone, still seeking refuge in non-musicals since operettas were losing favor, tried, and almost succeeded, with **Experience Unnecessary** (12-30-31, Longacre), which Gladys Unger adapted from an unidentified German comedy by Wilhelm Sterck. Its story reversed the sexes of *Society Girl*. Woolf played a great automobile manufacturer who annually advertises for a lovely young lady to accompany him on an overseas trip. He loves them and leaves them, but, after all, he has paid them the $5000 he promised up front. A friend hints that he ought to choose his own secretary (Verree Teasdale), who for some time has had an unexpressed crush on him. The deal is agreed to, but in the bridal suite of the S.S. *Saturnalia*, the girl puts her foot down. She teaches her boss how to become the good man that her husband must be. At least she allows him one song—something about seeing the light in her eyes while they were waltzing—before putting him in his place.

The evening's fourth opening was a revival at the tiny President of Henry J. Byron's once popular English melodrama *The Lancashire Lass,* in which the machinations of a clever villain (Carl Benton Reid) nearly prevent the marriage of the heroine (Mercedes Desmore) to the hero (Herbert Ranson). The play had been a huge success following its opening on October 26, 1868, with Rose Eytinge and J. B. Polk as the lovers and Charles Fisher as their nemesis. But sixty-three years on, even at a low $1.50 top, it played to empty houses and was withdrawn after a less-than-three-week struggle.

New Year's Eve seemed an odd night to many critics to open Harry Hamilton and Norman Foster's **Savage Rhythm** (12-31-31, John Golden). Orchid (Vivian Baber), a black who has made a success in New York clubs and theatres, returns for a visit to her backwater village in the swamps of lower Mississippi, where her grandmother (Mamie Cartier) is a respected "conjur-woman." When Orchid's loose-moraled sister, Florabel (Venezuela Jones), flirts with a husky black man (Ernest R. Whitman) known as a "sweetback," the man's angry wife (Inez Clough) stabs her to death. The conjur-woman is called in to hold a trial. While tom-toms beat and frightened villagers sing fervently, she attempts to carry out the judgment but realizes her powers have deserted her. Suddenly Orchid falls screaming and writhing, and fingers the sweetback as the real cause of the tragedy. Hailed as the new conjur-woman, she agrees not to return to New York but to stay with her village. Poor staging and generally mediocre acting hurt what might have been an interesting entertainment.

The new year, 1932, got off to a pleasant enough start with Benn W. Levy's **The Devil Passes** (1-4-32, Selwyn). Unlike characters in several of the season's earlier plays, its central figure did not claim to be God or the Devil, but the story made clear he almost certainly was the latter. He is the Rev. Nicolas Lucy (Basil Rathbone), and at a dinner party he asks each guest what they most want in life. Then he tests them to see how far they will go to get their wish. The guests understand that they will not sacrifice their honor to achieve their dreams, so in a curious fashion the Devil has done God's work. Among the distinguished players were Arthur Byron, Ernest Cossart, Cecilia Loftus, Robert Loraine, Mary Nash, Ernest Thesiger, and Diana Wynyard. Good writing and superb playing kept the play going for twelve weeks, just under half the run enjoyed by Levy's lighter *Springtime for Henry*.

Broadway found T. C. Upham's **Lost Boy** (1-5-32, Mansfield) too unremittingly harrowing. Francis Demarco (Elisha Cook, Jr.), a lad in his early or mid-teens, is arrested for placing ties across some railroad tracks. Since he has a record of truancy, he is sent to a country Training School. A sympathetic psychiatrist

(Clyde Franklin), sensing the boy's artistic bent in his gift for woodworking, tries to set him on a constructive path and speed his release. But a sadistic superintendent (Joseph Eggenton) beats the boy for a minor infraction. Francis knocks out the man, steals his gun, and kills three guards in making his escape. When the police come to his home to arrest him, he shoots himself.

Maurice Schwartz brought his increasingly unprofitable season of plays in English to a close after his third offering, **Wolves** (1-6-32, 49th St.), chalked up the shortest run of all, twenty-nine performances. The play was taken by Barrett H. Clark from Romain Rolland's 1898 French original, which had been prompted by the Dreyfus Affair. Schwartz himself had offered a Yiddish version of the drama seven years before. He was seen as a scientist-turned-soldier who is sent to prison for attempting to prevent the guillotining of a general (Leslie Austin), who he realized was being unjustly railroaded by his jealous fellow officers. Several reviewers felt that Schwartz's Yiddish accent sounded singularly incongruous in a play about Frenchmen.

Neither the great black actress Rose McClendon nor one electrifying scene could draw playgoers to James Knox Millen's **Never No More** (1-7-32, Hudson). Mammy has raised six children, all but the youngest of whom have grown up decent and law-abiding. That youngest child, Solomon (Rudolph Toombs), is dangerously unruly. He has killed a white girl and is pursued by a lynch mob. They catch up with him just outside his mother's cabin, and she must watch and listen to his screams as the mob burns him to death. The flames from the pyre illuminate the cabin's window. But when the lynchers attempt to turn against Mammy and the rest of her brood, she brandishes dynamite sticks used to clear the woods. The mob flees.

While *The Devil Passes* was being performed in the evenings and at two weekly matinees at the Selwyn, the house devoted its free afternoons to a revival of Sophocles' *Electra,* in a translation by J. T. Sheppard, beginning on the 8th. The company had been touring college campuses with Blanche Yurka in the title part and with Alma Kruger leading the chorus. For Broadway, an added attraction was offered, with Mrs. Patrick Campbell cast as Clytemnestra. Critical comparisons with O'Neill's retelling of the tale, playing ten blocks north, suggested New York's aisle-sitters preferred O'Neill.

Billed as "a detective thriller," **Black Tower** (1-11-32, Sam H. Harris), Ralph Murphy and Lora Baxter's reworking of Crittenden Marriott's short story "The Wine of Anubis," employed all the requisite sliding panels, hidden passages, trap-door fireplaces, spectral lighting effects, and ingeniously contrived machinery a play about a mad scientist ought to have. Dr. Eugene

Ludlow (Walter Kingsford), a failed sculptor who is determined that critics will praise his figures, kidnaps people, brings them to his isolated mansion, and, with the help of his own diabolical invention, petrifies them. A detective (Raymond Bramley) on his trail is given proof positive by one of the madman's victims who has not yet become fully stone. But Ludlow is not brought to justice, since he is inadvertently trapped in his own machinery and starting to petrify as the play ends. The play ran nine weeks, but its co-author would have a chance to show another side of her talents the very next evening.

Frank Harvey's London drama **Three Men and a Woman** (1-11-32, Lyceum) told of the faithless wife (Franc Hale) of a New Zealand lighthouse keeper (William Desmond). She has an affair with his assistant (Walker Whiteside), then deserts him for a young man (Barrie O'Daniels) washed up on the beach. He turns out to be a wanted criminal who kills himself when the police arrive. The wife heads off with the policeman (Edward Carson), leaving her husband and his mate to fend for themselves. Some complaints were made about the persistent and ultimately annoying artificiality of offstage sounds of surf and storm. Whiteside had once been deemed among the most promising of young actors, but had frittered away his career starring in exotic hokum more acceptable to the road than to Broadway, where this play represented his swan song.

One of the season's brightest hits was Gilbert Miller and Leslie Howard's production of Philip Barry's **The Animal Kingdom** (1-12-32, Broadhurst). Tom Collier (Howard) has summoned his father (Frederick Forrester), his friend, Owen Arthur (G. Albert Smith), and Cecelia Henry (Lora Baxter) to his home. Mr. Collier surmises that Tom has some news about himself and the lady friend he has been seeing for many years. Embarrassed by this indiscretion, Cecelia confesses that Tom is to announce his intention of marrying her. Owen insists she and Tom have nothing in common. His father's slip forces Tom to tell Cecelia about Daisy Sage. Cecelia's reaction is chilly. Tom visits Daisy (Frances Fuller) to break the news, but, before he can, Daisy suggests that he and she marry. When she learns what is to happen she is understanding. However, seeing a picture of Cecelia, she warns, "Look out for that chin." Once married, Cecelia becomes possessive and intrusive. She forces Tom to fire his devoted houseman (William Gargan), whom she does not like, and interferes in Tom's publishing business. If she cannot have her way, she has convenient headaches and locks the door against her husband. Tom rehires the houseman and tells him he is leaving Cecelia. "I'm going back to my wife," he says, meaning Daisy. Welcoming it as "a sincere play, tender and amusing by turns," Atkinson concluded, "It brings great loveliness into the theatre." The comedy ran twenty-three weeks and further consolidated Howard's reputation both as a matinee idol and as a fine actor.

. . .

Leslie Howard [Stainer] (1893–1943) was born in England and made his American debut as the Prince of Wales's friend in *Just Suppose* (1924). His subsequent hits included *Outward Bound, The Green Hat, Her Cardboard Lover, Escape, Berkeley Square,* and *Candle Light.* A slender, handsome actor, he was known for the suavity, delicacy, and charm of his playing.

. . .

Another English actor and his American-born wife were less fortunate in their choice of a vehicle. **Jewel Robbery** (1-13-32, Booth) was the third play this season to be translated (in this case by Bertram Bloch) from one of Lászlo Fodor's Hungarian originals. Teri (Mary Ellis) happens to be in a swank jewelry store when it is robbed by a gentlemanly holdup man (Basil Sydney). She is dismayed when he demands that she hand over the ring she has just purchased. But she discovers it the next evening on her night table. Then the holdup man appears and takes her to his own place. Although she escapes, she first arranges to meet her new lover in Nice, far from the suspicious eyes of her fabulously rich husband (Clarence Derwent).

Many critics continued to hold out high hopes—hopes never realized—for Dan Totheroh. His latest work, **Distant Drums** (1-18-32, Belasco), had moments of great beauty but failed to add up to a completely satisfying drama. Having lost their way, a band of pioneers arrange their covered wagons in a circle (only half of which could be shown onstage) and ponder their future. Death has stalked the group, and the ceaseless pounding of not so far-off tom-toms suggests worse might be in store. Most of the band keep their distance from Eunice Wolfhill (Pauline Lord), the wife of their leader, since she is a strange woman, who claims she is descended from a witch and who is given to visions and dire prophecies. When Snake Indians appear, they offer to lead the band to safety in return for Eunice. The travelers agree and Eunice, seeing her worst prophecies fulfilled, accepts the sacrifice. Lord, with her tremulous gestures and her curiously jerky delivery, was perfectly cast, but could not impart her unique spell to the show.

By contrast, the comic talents of tiny Ernest Truex went a long way to turning Laurence Gross and Edward Childs Carpenter's **Whistling in the Dark** (1-19-32, Ethel Barrymore) into a hit. The critic for *Time,* the magazine, saw the evening's "wit and freshness" stemming from "a combination of facile playwrighting, skilled and humorous direction and notably high comedy

acting." Events unfold amidst the antique Victorian furnishings of an elegant mansion. The mansion is owned by Jacob Dillon (Edward Arnold), a mob boss, who has been trying unsuccessfully to sell it, and so has put it up for rent. But Dillon's chief preoccupation at the moment is how to bump off John B. McFarren, New York's incorruptible crime commissioner. In pop Wallace Porter (Truex) and his fiancée, Toby Van Buren (Claire Trevor), looking to rent the place. Porter is a best-selling detective-story writer. Not realizing whom he is talking to, he boasts that when it comes to crime, "I am probably the world's greatest living authority," adding, "The police seldom use their brains and the criminals, they haven't any." When he further boasts how easy it is to think up a perfect crime, Dillon and his fellow gangsters order Wally to work out a way to kill McFarren that will not throw suspicion on them. Wally and Toby understand they are prisoners. "From now on," he tells her, "I'm going to write nothing but bedtime stories." Wally's solution to Dillon's demand is to suggest they plant poison in McFarren's toothpaste—a poison that will kill quickly and leave no trace. When the men go to carry out the murder, Wally cleverly converts the mansion's radio into a two-way telephone and thereby gets the police to come to his and Toby's rescue. An operator tells Wally that McFarren would like to talk with him. All Wally can do is blurt out, "For God's sake, don't brush your teeth this morning!" The fluff delighted New York until June.

Killers were also featured in John McDermott's shortlived **Adam Had Two Sons** (1-20-32, Alvin). They were young brothers, Matt (Paul Kelly) and Kid (Raymond Hackett), who have escaped from prison and fled to Panama. There they both fall in love with the same Mexican beauty, Teresa (Raquel Torres), but get to fighting over her. Kid shoots Matt just as a pursuing detective (Preston Foster) appears. In front of witnesses, Matt tells the detective that he alone did the killing back in the States, and then, lest Kid then be arrested for his murder, shoots himself. Oddly enough, despite its unpleasant story, the play had such colorful settings, including a cheap, gaudy café and a ship passing through the locks, that several critics, possibly influenced by the fact that its two producers and their theatre were better known for musicals, suggested the drama might have been turned into a fun song-and-dance entertainment.

For the second time in recent seasons an enterprising producer attempted to bring the artistry of showboat players, out of work for the winter, to Broadway. Billy Bryant's troupe began a stay on the same night at the somewhat uptown John Golden. Although they announced the possibility of a large repertory, business warranted only two mountings before the band headed home. Those plays were William W. Pratt's 1858 temperance drama, *Ten Nights in a Barroom*—famous for its "Father, dear father, come home"—and Clifton W. Tayleure's 1863 tear-jerking saga of infidelity and mother love, *East Lynne.*

John Millington Synge's *The Well of the Saints,* which had not been made welcome in Greenwich Village nine years earlier, was waved away again when it was brought out on the 21st at the small but pleasant Barbizon Theatre (in the Barbizon Hotel). Augustin Duncan was seen as one of a pair of blind beggars who are restored to sight but ask to be made blind again after seeing the ugliness of the world.

Nor did New York have any time for the month's second mad scientist, the central figure in Charles K. Champlin's **The House of Doom** (1-25-32, Masque). Dr. Luther (Robert Brister) has invented a machine that can allow two people to exchange souls. He calls it a "Naturescope." As one critic described it: "Apparently manufactured out of fine kitchen aluminum ware and colored electric globes, it sputters and flickers rather noticeably when the current is turned on, and the patients bellow in sad tones from inside two inverted stewing pots." A second critic branded it more succinctly as "a cross between a gas range and an electric chair." The mad doctor attempts to forcibly switch the souls of Lionel Manning (Champlin) and a dithering lunatic. At that point Manning awakes to discover he was only having a nightmare.

The then young trio of "stage, screen, and radio" were combined in a sense in T. Reginald Arkell and Charles's Wagenheim's **East of Broadway** (1-26-32, Belmont). The title stood for the Lower East Side, where Herschel Solomon (James R. Waters), who peddles vegetables from a wagon, lives with his "zoftig wife" (Maude Elliott) and his children, Ida (Betty Worth) and Benny (Alfred Corn). Ida's flirtation with a bookie (Joseph Striker) is worrisome enough, but when Benny, who sells newspapers, innocently passes on a package of drugs, a crooked detective demands $250 to overlook matters. The Solomons' troubles end after a scout for Paramount Pictures selects Herschel as a perfect type for a minor role and pays him $750 to play it. The play's radio connection came from announcements in the program that Waters and Corn were appearing "by courtesy of Pepsodent and the National Broadcasting Company," since both were regulars on the NBC program *The Goldbergs.* Unfortunately, there were no Pepsodent smiles after reviews appeared, so the comedy lingered only five weeks.

A group calling itself the Afternoon Theatre announced a series of matinees at the Recital Theatre

(formerly Daly's 63rd St.) and launched its hoped-for series with Oscar Wilde's *Lady Windermere's Fan.* Notices were so dismissive that the troupe packed its bags and fled after four performances.

But four performances were twice the number played by Julian L. McDonald's **The Marriage of Cana** (2-2-32, Provincetown Playhouse). James Duncan High (Juano Hernandez), a barber who loves the sporting life, and Whyoming Hurtt (Wayland Rudd), a bricklayer who believes he is descended from the Queen of Sheba, both are courting Isabell White (Marjorie Lorraine) in their all-black community just south of Philadelphia. Whyoming's buddy, Willy (Hayes Pryor), convinces Whyoming that the only way to win Isabell is to tell her he has lots of money in the bank. The ploy works, but after the wedding the truth comes out. Although sparks fly (and at least one knife is drawn), Whyoming and Isabell are reconciled. Even more interesting than the notices the play received were the comments its playhouse evoked. *Variety* contended, "When the depresh hit show business it practically shut up those funny places they call theatres in the Village. Only now and then does one get dusted off by the arty people who do plays down there. The only thing that is missed through the dark downtown spots is that some of the terrible things offered on Broadway might have landed south of Eighth Street instead."

But back uptown (albeit at the bottom of the theatre district), a drama that received some of the season's highest praise—"an extraordinarily fine play," "a fascinating and unusual evening," "an interesting, provocative, moving play"—could not find an audience, either. No doubt the upkeep of its huge cast of more than thirty, plus twenty-five supers, and its many scenes, coupled with its less than ideal location, hurt Arthur Goodman's **If Booth Had Missed** (2-4-42, Maxine Elliott's). A group of important politicians, awaiting the president's arrival at Ford's Theatre, are discussing their plans to remove Lincoln from office. They are led by Thaddeus Stevens (John Nicholson), angry at the policy of leniency toward the South. Shortly after Lincoln (Daniel Poole) appears, an alert black porter, Sambo (Morris McKenney), prevents John Wilkes Booth (Fred Eric) from killing the president. Once Lincoln's party has left, Stevens returns to his obsession, remarking, "The South will be left undone. We will ruin them—and then let the niggers rule them." When Edwin M. Stanton (Royal Dana Tracey), the secretary of war, opposes Lincoln's policy at a White House cabinet session, Lincoln attempts to remove him, thus violating the Tenure-of-Office Act a hostile Congress has just passed. Lincoln is impeached. At his trial, with a gallery of cheering onlookers clearly on his side, Lincoln is acquitted by a single vote. But a notorious editor, Francis Hilton (John Burke), shoots and kills him. A wordless epilogue shows a statue of Lincoln silhouetted against an evening sky with a lighted city in the distance and a picket fence in the foreground. A choir is heard singing "America."

For the second time this season, a juicy performance by Charles Laughton failed to save a play he had performed successfully in London. **The Fatal Alibi** (2-9-32, Booth), called simply *Alibi* in the West End, was Michael Morton's dramatization of Agatha Christie's *The Murder of Roger Ackroyd*. Moving from a killer in his earlier part to the role of the famous sleuth Hercule Poirot, Laughton dressed in flamboyant clothes, used broad strokes, and spoke with "a mincing French dialect, adhered to as only a skilled actor does," to eliminate the many more obvious suspects in Ackroyd's stabbing and quietly point a finger at a largely unsuspected doctor (Moffat Johnston), whom he then talks into committing suicide.

Three more flops followed. Kenneth Webb's **Zombie** (2-10-32, Biltmore) was set in the mountains of Haiti, where ominous drums sound endlessly from afar. When Jack Clayton (Robert J. Stanley) insists on remaining for two more years to establish their fortune, his bored wife, Sylvia (Pauline Starke), considers running off with young Dr. Paul Thurlow (Hunter Gardner). Jack dies suddenly after downing a drink that may have been poisoned. Three nights later he returns as a zombie. Under the baleful influence of Clayton's overseer (George Regas), he not only terrorizes his wife but also filches their savings. Thanks to Paul's efforts, Jack is brought back from the living dead, and a professorial neighbor (Burr Caruth) is exposed as a villainous master of local voodoo rites. One creepy scene had a line of silent, stiff zombies surrounding the Clayton bungalow.

Nathaniel Davis's **Air-Minded** (2-10-32, Ritz) seemed even more inane to many critics. Having been jilted in New York, a young man (Stanley Ridges) flies to a resort in the Pennsylvania mountains, meets a girl (Charlotte Wynters), woos her, wins her, loses her after she discovers he is a rich playboy, and wins her back after (1) helping her brother and his friend make good on an invention, (2) flying out to get medicine for someone bitten by a rattlesnake, and (3) paying off the girl's mortgage.

Sam Janney's **Monkey** (2-11-32, Mansfield) was produced posthumously, so the author did not have to witness its quick closing. For the brief time it and *Zombie* survived, three mysteries were playing on West 47th Street. (The third was *Whistling in the Dark.*) Some critics thought this latest entry was designed as a spoof on mysteries; others suggested it only seemed so by accident. Murlein (Houston Richard), a house

detective, is certain that Joe Banning (Clifford L. Jones) killed Robert Kenmore (Wright Kramer). After all, Kenmore was doing everything in his power to stop Banning, a hoofer in the *Scandals,* from wedding his stepdaughter, Greta (Charlotte Denniston). Officer McSweeney (Edward McNamara) is not so sure. But then he has no respect for house detectives, who, he claims, spend most of their adult lives lurking on dark fire escapes. He calls in his superior, and, sure enough, Inspector "Monkey" Henderson (Richard Whorf), an oddball old man who notes, "Between the seventh commandment and the 18th amendment we're all having one hell of a time," thinks there is more to it. He proves that Banning was goaded by the lover (George Lessey) of Kenmore's mistress (Nedda Harrigan). Young Whorf, only twenty-five, won kudos for his garrulous, comically lip-smacking oldster.

Manuel Seff and Forrest Wilson's **Blessed Event** (2-12-32, Longacre) was the second play in as many seasons inspired by the famous columnist Walter Winchell, who was "out front with a massive bodyguard" on opening night. Alvin Roberts (Roger Pryor) is a brash young columnist famous for breaking the news about celebrities' pregnancies. (Winchell used to announce that the women were "infanticipating.") But he lands in trouble after he tells his readers that dancer Dorothy Lane (Isabell Jewell) is expecting, since her married lover is known to be a vicious gangster, Sam Gobel (Matt Briggs). A gunman whom Gobel orders to kill Roberts at a nightclub, shoots and misses, but Roberts's quick thinking saves Dorothy. Roberts also finds romance with Gladys Price (Lee Patrick). The play was filled with good lines and interesting minor figures. Roberts wires a rival columnist, "What do you know that I don't know," and receives a one-word answer—"Plenty." He asks his wiseacre secretary (Mildred Wall), "Do you know how many Jews there are in New York?" Her reply: "There must be dozens." Among subsidiary figures were Allen Jenkins as an amusingly dimwitted hood, and Charles D. Brown as a writer whose pet column in the *Daily Express* offers hints on how a reader's pet fleas can get rid of its dogs and who is grazed by the bullet meant for Roberts. Besides the third-act nightclub setting, the production offered a fine creation of a busy newspaper office in its first act, and Roberts's comfortable living room, with a radio blaring away a jingle for Shapiro's Shoes, in its second. A knowing combination of lighthearted humor (although in tryouts Roberts was killed) and tense melodrama, plus some special plugging from Winchell, kept the comedy on the boards into May.

John van Druten's London hit **There's Always Juliet** (2-15-32, Empire) ran almost as long, and might have run considerably longer had not a film studio paid producer Gilbert Miller to close the show so that Herbert Marshall could head for Hollywood. Unwisely, Miller elected to hold off putting in a replacement cast. By the time he brought the show back several months into the next season with Roger Pryor (currently of *Blessed Event*) and Violet Heming, Broadway had found new interests. In one respect Pryor may have been a more logical casting than the veddy British Marshall, since Marshall was playing an American architect, who finds romance in England. However, when he is called home, his new love (Edna Best) demurs at following him. Luckily, after she has had second thoughts, she discovers his sailing has been delayed, so they are able to depart for America together. There were only four characters in the play, the others being a minor suitor and a maid. Dame May Whitty played the servant.

Critics rejected both of the next evening's entries. The American work, Jerome Sackheim's **When the Bough Breaks** (2-16-32, 48th St.), served to rescue, albeit very briefly, Pauline Frederick from films. She played a possessive mother bitter that her son (William Post, Jr.) is closer to his father (Clyde Franklin) than to her. The father's death allows her to pounce. She wrecks her son's dreams of a business venture, and talks him into making a mistress out of the girl (Dorothy Libaire) he loves, rather than marry her. The girl commits suicide on learning that she is pregnant. After the mother attempts to destroy the relationship between her son and a longtime friend (Louis Jean Heydt) who hopes to become a business partner, it remains for the friend's telling off the mother to open the son's eyes.

Collision (2-16-32, Gaiety) was John Anderson's adaptation of an unidentified play by Rudolf Lothar and Erno Sebesi. A vividly imaginative young lady (June Walker) attempts to snare a timid young doctor (Geoffrey Kerr) by claiming she is being courted by a famous pianist. When the pianist is reported killed in a train wreck, the girl pretends to believe that the doctor is the pianist, and tricks him into wedding her. By the time the hoax is exposed, the pair are content to remain married. After the comedy closed, the Gaiety, which had been showing films on and off, went to films, and for a time burlesque, on a more permanent footing.

Many critics found Vivian Crosby, Shirley Warde, and Harry Wagstaff Gribble's **Trick for Trick** (2-18-32, Sam H. Harris) delicious hokum, but playgoers refused to support it. The tricks were those of two magicians, the younger of whom, Walter "Azrah" Lawrence (James Rennie), trained by the older, George La Tour (Henry O'Neill), is now accused of driving La Tour's pretty assistant to suicide. La Tour has come to resent Azrah's success. He invites him to a seance in which he promises to bring out the truth about the girl's death. Azrah is bound to a chair, then the lights go out.

When they come on again, it is La Tour who is bound to the chair, and he has been stabbed to death. His killer turns out to be the dead girl's father, a doctor who hid a knife in a stethoscope. Much of the entertainment was merely a succession of other tricks—levitations, objects changing shape or bursting into seemingly spontaneous flame, things caused to appear or disappear.

Out-of-town notices held great hopes for William Ford Manley's **Wild Waves** (2-19-32, Times Square), but Broadway felt the playwright, who was a successful writer for radio, could not make up his mind whether he wanted to bite the hand that fed him or merely tickle it. The golden voice of Roy Denny (Bruce MacFarlane) has won him admiring listeners from coast to coast. They don't know that Roy is a rat, currently being sued for desertion and child support. Nor do they know that Roy's singing voice isn't even his. It belongs to painfully shy John Duffy (John Beal), the young man who sounds the network chimes on the hour. Nancy Hodson (Betty Starbuck), an attractive programmer, and Mitch Gratwick (Osgood Perkins), WWVW's station manager, try to embolden John and get him to come out on his own. For their pains, Roy sees to it that the three are fired.

One of the season's shortest runs—three performances—was the lot of H. G. Buller's **New York to Cherbourg** (2-19-32, Forrest), in which a honeymoon couple (Taylor Holmes and Natalie Schafer) heading for Europe find they are pursued by two former flames (Eleanor Winslow Williams and Gerald Kent). At intermission the lobby buzzed with rumors that Buller was a pen name for Samuel Ruskin Golding, who in the late twenties had written a string of flops. Under the circumstances, the truth was immaterial.

Another of those arty ensembles that periodically brave Broadway—Living Theatre Productions—did not survive even three performances when it took over the troubled, out-of-the-way Recital Theatre and managed a single matinee performance (on the 22nd) of Nathaniel Irish's **Near to the Stars.** Set in a junkyard strewn with rusting automobiles, scrap metal, old tires, and ashcans, it told how the lives of the misfits who reside there were touched on by a visitor who had leprosy.

Al Woods long had been one of Broadway's most well-liked producers—a man who in warm weather often sat out in front of his Eltinge Theatre and addressed all comers as "sweetheart." So there was genuine sadness when Woods became among the first of a long line of celebrated producers driven by the Depression to declare bankruptcy (losing his playhouse in the process). As a result, *Variety* began its notice of George Bryant and Francis M. Verdi's **The Inside Story** (2-22-32, National) by reporting, "All Broadway seemed to be rooting for A. H. Woods' comeback production."

Unfortunately, critics could not join in the cheering, although they let the melodrama down easily. Louis Corotto (Louis Calhern) is the state's leading gangster, and he has all its politicians under his thumb. Angered at a rebuff by Mamie Gillette (Marguerite Churchill), one of his girlfriends, he decides to show her how mean he can be by sending her imprisoned lover, Gerald Stockton (Roy Roberts), to the electric chair. He arranges for the man to escape prison, then frames him for a murder. Despite holes in the evidence, judges and politicians are afraid to cross Corotto. The governor (William Courtenay) is sympathetic to the girl's plea until he is reminded of a receipt for $300,000 Corotto holds for his contribution to the governor's election. Mamie has no choice but to shoot and kill Corotto. Relieved officials agree there will be no charges against her or Gerald. Another huge cast (twenty) and another expensive multi-set production on another costly revolving stage militated against the drama's making a go of it.

Charles Hopkins had earlier found success with his importations of A. A. Milne's English plays, but saw his latest effort, **They Don't Mean Any Harm** (2-23-32, Charles Hopkins), hurry down the drain. Two young couples, all incorrigible do-gooders, destroy a family by trying to help it. The crippled mother dies in an operation the youngsters insist she must have, and the heartbroken daughter heads across the sea to Canada. The youngsters must look for someone else to help.

Apart from *Blessed Event*, the lone February entry to reach the supposedly charmed 100–performance mark was Daniel N. Rubin's **Riddle Me This** (2-25-32, John Golden). No small part of its success came from the playing of wide-eyed, exuberant Thomas Mitchell and the dry, homey, hands-in-pockets Frank Craven. A program note observed, "For the benefit of the latecomer, this is not a mystery play. In the opening scene we saw Dr. Tindal [Charles Richman] commit the murder [of his wife] and arrange the evidence to trap an innocent man." That man was Mrs. Tindal's lover, Frank Marsh (Robert Lowes). At first Detective Captain McKinley (Mitchell) sees no need to dispute the evidence. But a wily local newspaperman, Russell Kirk (Craven), slowly asks disturbing questions and begins to suggest doubts about the seemingly airtight case. For example, a piece of Marsh's watch chain was found in the dead woman's hand. Kirk insists a woman being strangled would attempt to break the stranglehold and not grasp at the chain. Typical of the play's humor was a scene in which Kirk and McKinley get into a crap game and enjoy some stiff drinks while they are throwing the dice. When the bull (a period epithet for a policeman) cautiously suggests the booze is obviously prewar (meaning pre-Prohibition), Kirk asks if he means

the Sino-Japanese affair (which had burst out into open warfare the previous September).

Even the Theatre Guild was not faring all that well in these hard times, so its production of Denis Johnston's Irish drama **The Moon in the Yellow River** (2-29-32, Guild) ran only until the Guild exhausted its five weeks of subscriptions. Johnston's play told of a German (Egon Brecher) forced to leave Ireland after the blowing up of a dam he had built and which had been opposed by rebels.

Although March was reasonably busy, it ushered in not a single success. The failure of his **Child of Manhattan** (3-1-32, Fulton) pushed Preston Sturges into abandoning theatre for films. Coming to check on the condition of the Loveland Dance Hall, which stands on land his aristocratic family owns, Otto Paul Vanderkill (Reginald Owen), a middle-aged widower, meets Madeleine McGonegal (Dorothy Hall), a dime-a-dance girl from "Greenpernt." Ignoring the differences in their speech and background, the pair take a liking to one another, especially after Otto slips $1000 into her stocking. He makes her his mistress until she becomes pregnant, then marries her. However, when the baby dies, she rushes off to Mexico to obtain a divorce. She asks for nothing from Otto. Panama Kelly (Douglass Dumbrille), a rambunctious Texas oil man, courts her, but she realizes that she still loves Otto, so agrees to become his mistress again.

If *Child of Manhattan* was a respectable failure, Deborah Beirne's **Park Avenue, Ltd.** (3-2-32, Provincetown Playhouse) was one of the worst among the season's many embarrassments. Unable to interest mainstream producers, Beirne, an elderly contributor of interviews to magazines, produced the play herself. A young Tenth Avenue promoter (Hugh Banks) ditches his Italian-American girlfriend (Dina Lanzi) when a Park Avenue debutante (Mildred Baker) shows interest in his idea of opening a fancy sanitarium. Marriage follows, and so do difficulties stemming from the couple's disparate backgrounds. For a time both think about rushing back to their old loves, but in the end decide to give the marriage a further try.

Thetta Quay Franks's **Money in the Air** (3-7-32, Ritz) was another vanity production, although the playwright did not produce it herself. According to lobby scuttlebutt, the producer was "an friend of long standing." Col. Jim Barton (Hugh Buckler) refuses to marry Penelope Worthington (Vera Allen) unless she renounces a fortune she is slated to inherit. Since she will lose the fortune if her long-lost nephew is found, she sets out to locate him. A villainous lawyer (Gordon Richards) tries to cut in on the deal and is murdered. Two comic detectives attempt a solution to the killing, and eventually reach one.

There were high hopes and crossed fingers when William A. Brady persuaded Laurette Taylor to return to the stage at the Playhouse on the same night in a James M. Barrie double bill of *Alice Sit-by-the-Fire,* in which a mother deftly deals with her daughter's belief that the woman has taken on a lover, and *The Old Lady Shows Her Medals,* in which a lonely charlady forges letters to herself from a soldier whose name she has picked from a list, and later finds satisfaction after the soldier adopts her as a surrogate mother. Taylor had not performed since the death of her playwright-husband, J. Hartley Manners, and her alcoholism was well known in the trade. Nonetheless, her notices were as ecstatic as always, with Gilbert Gabriel reporting in the *American,* "It was peculiarly thrilling to sense the immediate, almost pell-mell cordiality she established with the audience." Adjectives such as "glowing," "resplendent," and "magnificent" dotted other notices. But her drinking problems cropped up from the start, and, when she missed several performances, Brady was forced to close the production after one month.

Another revival also opened on the same night. Edmund Day's *The Round Up* (8-26-07) was brought into the large Majestic, telling of a woman (Gertrude Michael) who remains loyal to the man (Byron Shores) she has married even after she discovers he had tricked her into the wedding by falsely claiming her fiancé (Frank MacNeills) was dead. The show-stealing role of the sheriff, Slim Hoover, was taken by Herbert Corthell. Once again real horses trotted across some beautiful recreations of the Wild West, where Indians and soldiers still battled. A two-week engagement was announced, no doubt with every intention of extending the stay if trade warranted. Yet, in the face of sharply divided reviews, the play was withdrawn after a single week.

The Group Theatre's third mounting, Maxwell Anderson's **Night over Taos** (3-9-32, 48th St.), was its second quick failure. So long as Pablo Montoya is in charge, the gringos will not take Taos. They have overrun the rest of New Mexico and, angry that Montoya's men have killed the officer they sent to act as governor, are determined to complete the job. The Spanish community is horrified at the news that Pablo has probably been killed in an American ambush. Only a few people know that Pablo's son, Federico (Franchot Tone), told the Americans of his father's plans and has sold out in return for a guarantee of half of his father's old lands. He tells a priest (Morris Carnovsky) only that American rule is inevitable—"I wish I were as sure/ Of living through the next year, as I am of that"—and he is not receptive when the priest begs him to "take up the lance" of his fallen father. Of course, there are other more personal problems. Pablo, openly bigamous, was about to marry his fourth wife, a gringo who had been captured as a child and raised by the Spaniards. But the girl, Diana (Ruth Nelson), is really in love with Pablo's younger son, Felipe (Walter Coy), and is well aware that Federico, who has been having an affair with his father's third wife (Stella Adler), also lusts after her. The household is thrown into turmoil when Pablo (J. Edward Bromberg) appears and insists his wedding take place at once. He also ferrets out the truth about Federico and stabs him to death. But then he learns of Diana and Felipe's feelings. He orders them to drink some of the poison that Felipe and Federico's mother had prepared for him and which he had tricked her into drinking. But his condemnation of the young lovers turns everyone against him. "The news will spread/ That Pablo Montoya's raving in his house/ And murdering his sons," the priest warns. Sensing the hopelessness of the situation, he swallows the poison himself. Robert Edmond Jones's luminous setting of the Montoyas' adobe living room, gorgeous, colorful period costumes, and fine performances could not override Anderson's leaden, unpoetic blank verse, forcing the drama to close at the end of its second week.

Several years earlier Julian Thompson had won a prize for a one-acter. Now the play, with its original title retained, was expanded into a full evening. Although Robert Garland told his readers in the *World-Telegram* that "the evening turns out to be one of the most amusing in town," he and his colleagues agreed that **The Warrior Husband** (3-11-32, Morosco) was probably better when it was shorter. Theseus (Colin Keith-Johnston) and his companion, Homer (Don Beddoe), whom he introduces as "a war-correspondent and a writer of very snappy travel-books," are brought before Hippolyta (Irby Marshal), Queen of the Amazons. They present her with the gift of an urn, and, when she asks them what they would like in return, they cause consternation by requesting the girdle she is wearing. For the truth is that they are attempting to help Hercules (Al Ochs) complete his labors by winning the magic girdle that the goddess Diana once had presented to Hippolyta's foremothers. That's right, foremothers. The girdle has given women the ascendency, and everything in Pontus is therefore topsy-turvy. Why, the worst thing any soldier in the all-woman army can call another soldier is a "daughter of a dog!" Of course, Hippolyta refuses and orders the men expelled. War follows. Since her treasury is bankrupt, Hippolyta must agree to marry the coy, dainty Sapiens (Romney Brent), son of Hippolyta's rich, conniving prime minister (Jane Wheatley). During the war, Theseus manages to kidnap Hippolyta's sister, the feisty Princess Antiope (Katharine Hepburn), and, since she has exchanged girdles with her sister, he gets the sought-after garment, too. Antiope puts up quite a struggle, socking Ajax (Randolph Leymen) in the jaw and kicking Achilles (Alan Campbell)—in Achilles' heel. But she and Theseus are soon in love, and when peace is restored she agrees to remain with him. That may take her to foreign parts, since, as Theseus tells her, "a Trojan named Paris stole Helen, the wife of a friend of ours," and that means more war. Whatever reservations critics held about the comedy itself (and it reads delightfully today), they concurred with Garland, who continued his review, "It's been many a night since so glowing a performance has brightened the Broadway scene." He singled out Hepburn as "a young actress of alluring silhouette and tomboy manners." The play ran ten weeks, and some suggested it might have run longer and been a real hit had it not come in so near summer. A few years down the road it became the Rodgers and Hart musical *By Jupiter*.

Away from the mainstream, a semi-professional mounting gave New Yorkers their only chance to see Noel Coward's nine-year-old comedy **The Young Idea** (3-18-32, Heckscher). Its story was simple: two children lure their father from his second wife and reunite him with their mother. The comedy was presented for only three performances.

Arthur Hoerl's **A Few Wild Oats** (3-24-32, Forrest) were sown only four times. It, too, dealt with a child's reaction to a divorce. In this case, Rosemary Grayson (Mildred Van Dorn) responds to news of her parents' planned divorce by organizing an orgy. Luckily, a neighbor (Robert Allen), who is fond of her, sets matters aright and even proposes marriage to her.

John B. Hymer and William E. Barry's **Happy Landing** (3-26-32, 46th St.) was the latest in the season's exposés of inflated hero worship. It was also the latest of the season's many large-cast, multi-set productions, this time housed in a theatre normally reserved for grand-scaled musicals and which the resourceful Shuberts, who produced the play, had picked up for a song despite their own financial problems. Blin Gardner (Russell Hardie) of Old Orchard, Maine, using money lent to him by Phyllis Blair (Margaret Sullavan), a telephone operator who has sold her family farm to provide him with the cash, buys a plane and flies solo across the Pacific to Japan. He becomes a national celebrity and, in part through the machinations of a crass promoter, Russell Whiting (William David), soon forgets Phyllis. Of course, he finally comes to his senses and, after telling off Whiting and the inconsiderately demanding public during a nationally broadcast speech, flies back to Maine and to Phyllis. Harry Davenport, a generation ago a popular leading man, won laughs as a crusty hangar manager and repairman. What did not win laughs was the shoddy mounting. The Shuberts, like so many of their colleagues, had declared bank-

ruptcy, but, unlike Al Woods, apparently did not care if it showed. One reviewer noted, "Because of the receivership little money was spent to mount the show. Everything but the first scene [the hangar] seemed to come from the warehouse. Settings were never intended for a house with a proscenium opening the size of the 46th Street's, the result being that the scenes were masked in 10 to 12 feet on either side. What looked like an old sliding platform was employed for scene changes."

Although Mary Macdougal Axelson's **Life Begins** (3-28-32, Selwyn) ran only a single week, many critics considered it an honest, worthwhile endeavor, and Burns Mantle came close to including it as one of his ten *Best Plays*. All the action takes place in a maternity ward, filled with expectant and new mothers. These include a woman awaiting her sixth child, an unmarried nightclub singer told she will have twins, a woman worried that her baby will look like its father and not like her husband, an Italian who loses her baby, and another unwed mother, who jumps from the window after learning her lover has run off to South America. But the central figure was Mrs. Grace Sutton (Joanna Roos), who is brought by a policewoman to the hospital directly from the courtroom where she has been convicted of murder (the details of which are never made clear). The doctors tell her husband (Alan Bunce) that they can save only the baby or the mother, and he tells them to save the mother. But she demands the child be saved. The husband is given the news of his wife's death at the same time that he is shown the baby. Although Roos was lauded for her touching performance, some of the best notices went to Glenda Farrell as the caustic, secretly tippling nightclub performer. Some critics complained that none of the expectant mothers looked the least bit pregnant and wondered aloud why the women could not have employed pillows or some other stuffings.

Blanche Ring, so long a star in vaudeville and musical comedy, could not bring over her singular charm to a non-musical when she appeared in Earle Crooker's **Intimate Relations** (3-28-32, Ambassador). As the widowed Jane Marshall, she discovers that her late husband was a notorious philanderer. Over the protestations of her own nasty children she adopts his illegitimate son (Michael Barr) and finds the lad a suitable wife.

Crane Wilbur's **Border-Land** (3-29-32, Biltmore) was set in a hunting lodge owned by two brothers, Gene and Bert Cordovan (Robert Lowing and Alan Campbell). At a seance, Hugh Templeton (Lester Vail), a dabbler in spiritualism who is also Gene's rival for the hand of Maureen O'Dare (Lenita Lane), evokes the spirit of a man sent to the electric chair on Gene's testimony. Later Gene is found strangled with Hugh's tie. Hugh is convicted and sent to a mental institution, but a second seance reveals that Bert killed his brother in an effort to get his half of the family wealth.

Black-white relationships were dealt with in both dramas to open the next evening. Frederick Schlick's **Bloodstream** (3-30-32, Times Square) unfolded in a coal mine and a prison yard. Four black prisoners and one white, James Knox (Cecil Holm), are lorded over by a sadistic warden (Clyde Franklin). Among the blacks are a killer (Ernest R. Whitman) itching to kill again and the patently deranged Gypsy Kale (Frank Wilson), who believes he is God and who has hidden some dynamite in the mine for the time when he must destroy the world. The warden whips Knox to death for fatally shooting a guard in an attempt to escape. His killing provokes the blacks to mutiny. When Gypsy blows up the mine, the prisoners and the warden realize that they will all soon be suffocated. Jo Mielziner's mine setting heightened the feeling of impending doom, conveying "a sense of monstrous, shadowy terror and of ghoulish imprisonment that presses in from all sides."

By contrast, most of Annie Nathan Meyer's **Black Souls** (3-30-32, Provincetown Playhouse) took place in the comfortable office of Andrew Morgan (Morris McKenney), the founder and the principal of Magnolia College, a school for blacks. He is an advocate of improving the lot of his fellow blacks peacefully and gradually. His brother-in-law, David Lewis (Juano Hernandez), a poet and teacher of literature, believes only violence will improve their situation. Senator Verne (Alven Dexter) and his daughter, Luella (Guerita Donneley), both white, visit the campus. Verne has long had his eye on Mrs. Morgan (Rose McClendon), while, unbeknownst to her father, Luella had an affair with David when the two were in France. She induces David to take her to a cabin in the nearby woods, where they are spotted by some whites. David is lynched. Hiding his own miscegenetic inclinations, the senator disowns his daughter and walks away scot-free.

The husband-and-wife team of Englishman Geoffrey Kerr and American June Walker, having suffered a quick flop with *Collision,* suffered a second with **We Are No Longer Children** (3-31-32, Booth), which Ilka Chase and William B. Murray took from Léopold Marchand's French original. Former lovers, now unhappily married to new spouses, attempt to recapture their early ardor and find they cannot.

Aside from one surprise smash hit near month's end, April was even less rewarding than March. The procession of duds began with Harrison King's **The Decoy** (4-1-32, Royale), telling of a crusading newspaperman exposing his town's crooked political boss and courting the boss's daughter at one and the same time.

The evening also witnessed the arrival of the Guerrero-Mendoza Players of Madrid, who remained at the New Yorker for five weeks in a constantly changing program that mixed Spanish classics, more recent Iberian hits, and Spanish translations of foreign plays, such as *El Abanico de Lady Windermere.*

An entertainment billed as "a collection of stage sermons by a fellow of the Royal Society of Literature" would have had no chance at all on Broadway had not its producer been the Theatre Guild and the fellow been George Bernard Shaw. One of Shaw's most amorphous plays, **Too True to Be Good** (4-4-32, Guild) begins in a hospital room where a patient (Hope Williams) is beset by an outrageously unprofessional nurse (Beatrice Lillie), a minister-turned-burglar (Hugh Sinclair), and others. The group finally run off to continue their discussions at a beach just below some mountains. Several critics commented on the large number of playgoers who suddenly had to catch early trains, but the aisle-sitters' praise for the probably unshavian clowning of Lillie let the comedy run a little beyond the normal Guild subcription.

The other two entries for the same week both closed after their first Saturday night, although neither was satire. R. B. Lackey's **Angels Don't Kiss** (4-5-32, Belmont) employed a largely undistinguished cast to recount the tale of a wife who is repelled by her husband's sexual advances yet resents his seeking satisfaction with other women. She runs off to Paris, somehow hoping a chastened husband will pursue her there.

Gilbert Emery, a respected playwright and actor but one who had recently been devoting himself to the uncivilizing labors of Hollywood, fared no better with **Housewarming** (4-7-32, Charles Hopkins). Ignoring a history of family feuds, Mary Woollcott (Katherine Wilson) has wed Ned Sedgwick (Louis Jean Heydt). Years before, when a Sedgwick had painted their Connecticut town's new schoolhouse red, a Woollcott promptly had burned down the building. Now Ned's aunt (Molly Pearson), who had helped raise him and had paid for his education, presents the newlyweds with a fire-engine-red piano, covered with crimson plush. Mary's refusal to allow the thing to remain in the living room leads to a split, with Ned sleeping on his sailboat. To get rid of the piano, Mary burns down the house. In the end, Ned is forgiving, even if his aunt is not. The relentless drop in attendance at legitimate theatres appeared equally unforgiving, so after the play closed, the bandbox theatre became a film house.

An attempt to have fun with the stock market crash laid its own egg in Nat N. Dorfman's **Take My Tip** (4-11-32, 48th St.). Although she doesn't think much of him, cantankerous, eighty-year-old Mrs. Merrill (Helen Lowell) has allowed her somewhat rattlebrained son, Henry (Donald Meek), to run the family soap business.

On the side he has dabbled in the stock market and done so well with Triplex Oil that all his friends have bought the stock, too. Henry's $100,000 plunge has won him a position as thirty-second vice-president in the oil firm. But with the crash the stock plummets from 73 to 6. His angry, broke friends desert him, and mother takes over the running of the business. Fortunately, Henry has invented a process that will allow individual names to be imprinted cheaply on cakes of soap. He sells the patent at a tremendous figure, so he and mother are truly rich again. While some critics felt that Lowell's curmudgeon stole the show, most agreed that Meek gave another sterling performance in an unworthy play. For Broadway, it was the last unworthy play Meek would appear in. He left permanently for Hollywood.

Nor was there much more interest in a revival of A. A. Milne's story of a writer who finally admits he did not write his one highly admired book, *The Truth About Blayds* (3-14-22), which raised its curtain at the Belasco on the same evening. A superior cast included O. P. Heggie, Pauline Lord, Effie Shannon, Ernest Lawford, and Frederic Worlock.

Richard Maibaum's **The Tree** (4-12-32, Park Lane) was the latest in a spate of plays about lynchings, although unlike the others it was set "north of the Mason-Dixon Line." All the action unfolded around a gnarled, "gallows-like tree" standing alone in a bleak landscape. After a popular young girl named Ruth (Sylvia Lee) is found raped and strangled, suspicion falls on a black boy (Thomas Moseley) who was known to have mooned over her. He is lynched. Guilt feelings goad Matt (Barton MacLane) into confessing he is the actual killer, and he talks his friend Denny (Truman Quevli), who led the lynch mob, into hanging him from the tree. The Park Lane was the second new name given the old Daly's 63rd Street Theatre in recent months.

Some fine players were unable to turn Paul Hervey Fox and George Tilton's light comedy **Foreign Affairs** (4-13-32, Avon) into a hit. A countess (Dorothy Gish) and a diplomat (Henry Hull) check into a Tyrolian inn for a tryst only to learn that the countess's husband (Carl Benton Reid) has discovered the plan and is on his way to confront them. To divert suspicion, the countess pretends to flirt harmlessly with a rich businessman (Osgood Perkins) staying at the hostelry, and the diplomat befriends a kitchen maid (Jean Arthur). The husband is duly deceived, but the lovers are angry at the obvious interest each has displayed in the temporary pairings.

Critics and playgoers displayed no interest in Hale Francisco's **Angeline Moves In** (4-19-32, Forrest). Angeline (Suzanne Caubaye) is a tempestuous French-Canadian, with a dubious background. She comes to Burlington, Vermont, in search of an American boy she met and fell in love with back home. While seeking him she takes work at the home of the Weemses, whose daughter, Naida (Katherine Revner), is about to be married. The groom Naida's parents have selected for her is Jerry Dugan (Gerald Kent), the very man Angeline has come seeking, although she knew him by a different name. Jerry supposedly will lose his inheritance if he fails to marry Naida. Angeline overhears Naida tell Digby Struthers (Robert Brister), a bootlegger, that it is he she really loves and that she is marrying Jerry only for his money. By getting various people conveniently drunk and with the aid of a snooping but good-hearted neighbor (Mrs. Jacques Martin), Angeline sets matters aright and lands Jerry.

Given the encouraging reviews it received—"has an undeniable fascination," "stands out like a blaze," "an exciting political melodrama"—Albert Maltz and George Sklar's **Merry-Go-Round** (4-22-32, Provincetown Playhouse) might have been a hit had it opened earlier in the season or in more theatrically prosperous times. Critics were happy to make allowances for flaws in the writing by two young graduates of Professor George Pierce Baker's courses at Yale and for the cramping conditions required to put a thirty-odd-character, multi-scened (with revolving stage) play on the tiny Village stage. A young bellhop, Ed (Elisha Cook, Jr.), comes forward to say that he saw Jig Zelli (Harold Huber) kill a rival mobster. But the authorities find that Zelli has enough goods on top political figures to send them all to prison, so they elect to frame Ed for the killing. He is beaten, made to sign a phony confession, and hospitalized. When the true story is in danger of leaking out, the police and the district attorney's office have Ed killed and his death made to appear a suicide. Following the suggestion of several critics, plans were made to rush the drama uptown, and a second exciting political melodrama exploded. The play was initially to have been brought to the Cort, but rumored political pressure prompted the theatre to cancel the booking. The producers then booked the Avon, only to have authorities tell them and the theatre's owners that the playhouse's license would not be renewed. At this point the press intervened, and its articles forced the authorities to capitulate. They did so with ill grace, demanding, on a technicality, that the Avon remove fifty potentially profitable orchestra seats before it could receive the license. The drama lingered a little over a month at its new home.

The season's last major hit was Rose Franken's **Another Language** (4-25-32, Booth). The Hallams' dining room is a darkish affair, with heavy, ornately carved furniture. On Tuesday nights it is crowded, since, as the domineering Mrs. Hallam (Margaret Wycherly) assures listeners, "My sons never forget Tuesday nights." Neither do her daughters-in-law, except for Stella Hallam (Dorothy Stickney), who is married to the youngest son, Victor (Glenn Anders). So when Stella makes one of her rare appearances at the weekly affair, Mrs. Hallam is foolish enough to make snide remarks about Stella's interest in art school and other matters. Stella insists that every person knows what is best for himself or herself, provoking one (Margaret Hamilton) of her sisters-in-law to retort that her remark is "polite for 'mind your own business.' " But Stella finds a kindred soul in her nephew Jerry (John Beal), whom Mrs. Hallam and her obedient son (Herbert Duffy) have refused to allow to study architecture and have forced into the family business. After Stella presses the group to come to her house for a dinner, Mrs. Hallam reluctantly agrees to attend but has some sort of convenient seizure during the evening. Vickie rushes off to join his brothers at his mother's bedside, leaving Stella and Jerry to spend the night together. The next morning both have decided to do whatever they want, and, it seems, their remarks, coupled with the events of the evening and the following morning, may have opened Vickie's eyes, too. When Mrs. Hallam dramatically struggles down the stairs, wanting to know why Jerry hasn't come to her room, Vickie tells her, "Poor kid, he needs a break." Stella thanks her husband for trying to be helpful. Hailed by Atkinson as "a deep and illuminating play," it ran for more than ten months.

The late Edgar Wallace's London hit **The Man Who Changed His Name** (5-2-32, Broadhurst) headed a parade of flops that continued well into May. Selby Clive (Frank Conroy) smilingly denies reading anything suspicious into his wife's having had the room next to her onetime lover, Frank O'Ryan (Derek Fairman), at a hotel. The wife (Fay Bainter) and O'Ryan have learned that Clive had changed his name years ago and that his old name was identical to that of a man who had been acquitted of killing his wife and her lover, and who then had disappeared. Now a broken steering apparatus in O'Ryan's car and the collapse of a pergola where Mrs. Clive had been sitting moments before set them wondering. But after three acts of scares, Clive turns out to be a decent chap, who honestly had changed his name so as not to be confused with the suspected killer.

Some of the season's most brutal reviews were given to Wallace A. Manheimer and Isaac Paul's **Broadway Boy** (5-3-32, 48th St.). A young lawyer (Roy Roberts) decides to produce a play called *The Color Line*, a story about a "high yaller" in Harlem. To finance the mounting he steals $5000 in bonds from his uncle. His troubles have only begun. Extortionist unions demand extra wages for everything they can think of. His leading lady (Roberta Beatty) is so drunk on opening night that

the producer's secretary (Mildred Baker) is drafted into playing the lead at the last minute. And the producer is threatened with a lawsuit after he slugs a critic during intermission. But everything is forgiven after the press agent rushes in with rave reviews.

Another set of savage notices and the season's shortest run—two performances—was the lot of Milton Herbert Gropper's **Bulls, Bears and Asses** (5-6-32, Playhouse). His story looked at stock-mad Elsie Moore (Sally Bates), her more conservative but eventually amenable husband, Charlie (Hobart Cavanaugh), and their friends in the boom days of 1928, the bust of 1929, and in 1932, with Elsie and Charlie reunited after bitter recriminations had separated them following their losses in the crash. Elsie insists that if they start investing again, they will be rich when a new boom comes.

No writer came forth to accept blame for the next short-lived disaster, **The Lady Remembers** (5-10-32, Provincetown Playhouse). A barmaid turned baroness (Celia Haskell) threatens to publish her memoirs, which would reveal unpleasant things about Sir Jeremy Frayne (Gordon Fallows) and others. She not only wins over Sir Jeremy to allowing his nephew to marry a girl the uncle has opposed, she wins Sir Jeremy for herself.

For four performances playgoers wanting to see David Vardi's **Lenin's Dowry** (5-12-32, Chanin Auditorium) had to take an elevator to the fiftieth floor of the Chanin Building at Lexington Avenue and 42nd Street. The diminutive Russian expatriate was not only the author, he was the producer, director, and co-star (with his wife, Eva Yoalit) of this season's second two-character play. He was seen as an ex-soldier who leaves the Russian army to take up acting, tries out for the part of Napoleon in a play, and obtains not only it but his leading lady also.

A group from the Lambs, the famous theatrical club, banded together to produce and appear in a comedy by one of their fellow members, Roger Gray's **On the Make** (5-23-32, 48th St.). They reportedly cast their lady friends in the roles they themselves could not assume. While their fiancés are attempting an air flight endurance record, Christine Schroeder (Alice Cavanaugh) and her pals decide to have a fling. It turns sour when some crooked cops, out to win points for hauling in prostitutes, frame the girls. Christine takes the blame and is fined $500. She has some explaining to do when Bert Gibson (John A. Willarde) comes back to earth.

Jane Cowl paid no attention to the lateness of the season when she came in as star of Merrill Rogers's **A Thousand Summers** (5-24-32, Selwyn). The dark-haired, dark-eyed beauty took the role of Sheila Pennington, a thirty-six-year-old widow who has come to a small hostelry in the English Lake District to think over her fading affair with Laurence Hereford, a married man. She soon is courted by a young American art student, Neil Barton (Franchot Tone). Although she clearly is attracted to him, she tactfully rejects his advances, thereby pushing him into the arms of the local barmaid (Mary Newnham-Davis). Neil's fluttery, worry-hounded aunt (Josephine Hull) and restless uncle (Thomas Findlay) learn of the incident and rush off with him to Paris. After an unsatisfactory reunion with Laurence (Osgood Perkins), Sheila decides to kick over the traces and follow Neil. Neither Cowl's "loveliness and ardor" and "the romantic enchantment of her voice," nor her fine supporting cast, could sufficiently fire the play to turn it into a hit.

Apparently nothing redeemed Herbert Polesie and John McGowan's **Heigh-Ho, Everybody** (5-25-32, Fulton), the season's second send-up of radio and "boo-boo-boo-booing" crooners. It brought back for one final, extremely short-lived appearance before the footlights the former child star, musical comedy song-and-dance man, and sometime writer and producer Joseph Santley, who subsequently went on to a long career as a film director. Dave Frankel (Harry Rosenthal), a terse, cigar-chomping agent and frustrated composer, is convinced that the only reason for the sudden success of Buddy Baxter (Santley) as a radio crooner is that he had a terrible cold when he made his debut. So Dave keeps Buddy's feet wet and has him sit in drafts and in front of electric fans. Buddy has at least two other problems. He is kidnapped by the Mafia in hopes that an Italian crooner can take his place on *The Mellow Cigarette Hour,* and his wife, Pamela (Sue Conway), feels neglected. Buddy is rescued from the barn in the Berkshires where the mobsters have hidden him, and Pamela is signed to make commercials for a luxury soap. For many critics, Rosenthal, a former bandsman who had won laughs as the sarcastic Maxie in *June Moon,* stole the show with his hoarse barbs and his "supple tickling of the ivories."

The season's last successful novelty was Albert Hackett and Frances Goodrich's **Bridal Wise** (5-30-32, Cort). Ostensibly the show's stars were the popular comedienne Madge Kennedy and the suave, deep-voiced James Rennie, but a heretofore unknown youngster walked away with the comedy. Alan and Joyce Burroughs's marriage has hit the skids, especially after Alan has taken up with the horsey Babe Harrington (Blythe Daly), and Joyce, in revenge, finds solace with her sappy lawyer, Gidney Weems (Raymond Walburn). The couple divorce, marry their newfound loves, and are about to set out on their second honeymoons. Just then the Burroughses' obnoxious little son, Peter (Jackie Kelk), is sent home from his latest school. With the aid of his black buddy, Sam (Raymond Bishop), he unleashes all manner of hell—bells clanging, arrows flying

through a room. While Babe and Gidney demand the brat be sent away to another school, Alan and Joyce come to his defense and, in doing so, recognize that they belong together. Kelk never again found so rewarding a role on Broadway, but he did have a long career in radio. The comedy ran out the summer.

No future loomed for Hawthorne Hurst's **Christopher Comes Across** (5-31-32, Royale), in which the lazy, lascivious Christopher Columbus (Tullio Carminati) found a soft berth at the Spanish court until King Ferdinand (Walter Kingsford), concerned with the interested glances Isabella (Patricia Calvert) has cast at Columbus, provided the sailor with a fleet, in hopes he would plunge off the edge of the world.

Not a single June novelty garnered a cordial reception. Benson Inge's **Blue Monday** (6-2-32, Provincetown Playhouse) was set in a room at the Ideal Lamp-Shade Company. Having been despoiled by Frank (Frederic Tozere), a shade-design painter who had gotten her high on cheap wine, Lucy (Claire Carleton), a bookkeeper, agrees to marry him. But even before the wedding, Lucy realizes she prefers Paul (Theodore St. John), a more sensitive, articulate artist whose wife has left him because he has been such a poor provider. Frank, discovering what has occurred, kills both Lucy and Paul.

August L. Stern's **Hired Husband** (6-3-32, Bijou) was deemed another of the season's more embarrassing entries. Walter Brooks (Waldo Edwards) cannot marry before he is twenty-three without forfeiting his inheritance, but since he has gotten Nina Travis (Terry Carroll) pregnant, something must be done. The family lawyer (Paul Everton), convinces a handsome young drifter (Herbert Ashton, Jr.), whom he has picked up on a bench in front of his Gramercy Park apartment, to marry Nina long enough for her baby to be considered legitimate and Walter to come of age. Since the drifter is not only good-looking but a well-spoken graduate of the University of Montana, who took to the road after his ranch failed, he and Nina fall genuinely in love. But when the time comes to keep his bargain, he departs, recognizing that Walter is really the best man for Nina.

Gramercy Park was also called to mind when the Players, whose clubhouse is there, unveiled their annual offering at the Broadway on the 6th. For 1932 it was Shakespeare's **Troilus and Cressida,** supposedly in its first professional New York mounting. Neither Jerome Lawler nor Edith Barrett, who played the leads, were truly first-rate performers, but the cast had its share of notables, including Otis Skinner (Thersites), George Gaul (Patroclus), Charles Coburn (Ajax), Eliot Cabot (Agamemnon), Leo G. Carroll (Aeneas), Blanche Yurka (Helen), and Eileen Huban (Cassandra). Critics felt the performance of the heavily revised and cut tragedy was very uneven, and some complained of the actors' poor projection in the huge house. However, like all the Players' mountings, the staging was booked for only a single week, so reviews mattered little.

There were some colorful figures in John Montague's **The Boy Friend** (6-7-32, Morosco). Fat, aging Aunt Belle (Gertrude Maitland), who once had been in the chorus of *The Belle of New York,* now runs a boarding-house catering to a younger generation of chorus girls. Donnie (Miriam Stuart), one of the tenants, is pregnant by a slippery booking agent, Raincoat (Edward Leiter). As a result, Donnie's brother, a notorious gunman known as the Eel (Brian Donlevy), comes hunting for the guy. Raincoat flees up a fire escape, which, according to the Eel, is as close to heaven as he will ever get. Complicating matters, a sugar daddy (George Probert) drops dead in the room shared by Donnie and Daisy (Emily Graham), and the police come gunning for the gunman. Daisy's boyfriend, Roger (Walter Glass), a newspaper reporter, hurries to the scene in time to watch the Eel shoot Raincoat and the dead man come back to life to reveal both that he is a federal agent who was merely faking his death and that Raincoat was a dope peddler. Roger phones in the story, only to realize that in his excitement he has phoned it in to a rival paper.

The season's last new play was Jerrold Robert's **Back Fire** (6-13-32, Vanderbilt). It was an open secret that Jerrold Robert was a pen name for Robert Ober, who took the leading male role. In his story, George Davis breaks off his engagement to Sally Newton (Alice May Tuck) after he learns that the otherwise stainless girl had slept with his late brother, to whom she had been engaged before the man's death. On the rebound, he marries the much stained Doris Urquehart (Doris Packer). The marriage is a failure, and George recognizes that he truly loves Sally, but Doris is prepared to fight any divorce until the will of one of her old lovers is made public and discloses that the man left her $50 "for value received."

The month's longest run went to the season's final entry, a revival, initially slated for shorter road stands, of *That's Gratitude* (9-11-30) at the Waldorf on the 16th. With Taylor Holmes and J. C. Nugent in the roles once played by Frank Craven and George W. Barbier and aided by cut-rate tickets, the comedy outran its original stand by several performances.

1932–1933

It was not a good season. Broadway, like the rest of the nation, was mired deep in the Depression. The total number of productions plunged. Of new comedies and dramas, there were only somewhere between 109 and 124, depending on who counted what. And runs were shorter, too. Seventy-seven non-musicals ran a month or less, and of these, a whopping thirty-two lasted no more than one week. Prices also tumbled, with even hits having to shave figures. Burns Mantle rued, "The day of the $3, $4, $5 and $6 theatre is about over." Several playhouses, either determined to remain in the legitimate fold or poorly situated, stayed dark all season. And rather than help in such hard times, unions acted up, forcing a number of additional closings.

To gloss over the gloom, producers and writers leaned heavily toward comedy. A few more serious-minded playwrights hoped to profit from the ugly economic picture by propagandizing for left-wing causes (the far right had apparently abandoned the arts, preferring to sneer and growl rather than to contribute). A few producers, trusting that they were playing it relatively safe, fell back on revivals of recent hits.

Ignoring, as did virtually all critics, the season-long series of new plays mounted from June 18 onward downtown at the Cherry Lane Theatre, where most of the productions came and went in a week or two's time, the new theatrical year began inauspiciously with Frederick Herendeen's **The Web** (6-27-32, Morosco). Unlike a majority of contemporary plays, the new work was in only two acts. Set in the Florida Everglades, it spotlighted a pair of mad scientists who have bred a man-sized spider in hopes of using secretions from the animal to prevent birth defects in humans. One of the pair is a Japanese, and he further wants to find a method of making his fellow Japanese bigger, so that they can stand up to their Russian and Chinese adversaries. Two escaped criminals take refuge in the research facility and are strangled in the spider's web. A subplot recounted the romance of the American researcher's niece and a young neighbor who works on a snake farm.

Many of the critics did travel downtown for Leonard J. Tynan's **The Lingering Past** (6-29-32, Provincetown Playhouse). They did not like what they saw. Years ago Laura Pond, an adventuress, had deserted her husband and baby girl. Exhausted by her labors as a nightclub singer and a shill for gamblers, she takes a vacation at a summer resort, which, she discovers, is run by her ex and his second wife, who has raised Laura's child as her own. Laura attempts to win her former husband back, but her private life is exposed, and she leaves empty handed. Critics knocked not only the play but the acting and the staging. They reported the audience giggled at the "skipping entrances and exits" of the young daughter, and one reviewer was amused that the husband "always goes fishing with a rod minus hook and line." A character did get a laugh when, after lamenting all evening the fall in ATT stocks, she confessed she owned a single share.

Having trundled down to the Village, critics the next evening rode up toward the stars, for Bertha Wiernik's **Destruction** (6-30-32, Chanin Auditorium) was offered at a tiny venue high atop a modern skyscraper. After the critics came down to earth and wrote their notices, there was no second performance. What they saw was the preachy saga of a minister's son who is converted to a godless communism, until the father shows the son the light. The dertermined playwright reworked the drama and reopened it in late May as *Hate Planters,* with much the same results.

July's lone entry was **The Chameleon** (7-18-32, Masque), which Adam Gostony took from an unidentified Hungarian drama by Giza H. von Hessen. A beautiful screen star, smitten by a handsome but woman-hating doctor, pretends to be ill so that she can enter his sanatorium. She fails to ignite a spark until she feigns acute appendicitis. Somehow the operation makes the surgeon fall in love.

Confronted by harsh notices, Joseph Jay Ingerlid's **The Devil's Little Game** (8-1-32, Provincetown Playhouse) closed after a single week. During that time, a sleazy speakeasy in lower Manhattan played host to a motley crew of murderous gangsters, disillusioned intellectuals, a bank robber in hiding, loose ladies, and a rumpled, cashiered divinity student ("who should be made to comb his hair") torn between two of the painted women.

Matters weren't much improved in Carl Henkle's **Page Pygmalion** (8-3-32, Bijou). Tony Walton (Carleton Young), a wealthy young Oklahoman, who is engaged to one of Pittsburgh's rich Brownell girls, sets up as a sculptor in New York and falls in love with his model, Sally Gray (June Clayworth). Tony's cousin (Robert Emmett Keane) and an otherwise somewhat fatuous playwright (Percy Helton) goad Sally into pretending to be a statue come to life and speaking some home truths that cause Tony to send his fiancée (Doris Eaton) packing and propose to Sally.

Although Grace George adapted Marcel Achard's **Domino** (8-16-32, Playhouse), she did not appear in it. Had she, she would not have lost much time, since the comedy was gone after one week. Heller (Robert Loraine), discovering a letter signed François, realizes that François Cremone (Geoffrey Kerr) is the lover of his wife, Lorette (Jessie Royce Landis). To divert suspicion Lorette enlists Domino (Rod La Rocque) to pretend to be the François in question. Before long, she has fallen in love with Domino and prepares to desert both her husband and her former lover in his favor.

Given some of the delighted reviews George Oppenheimer's **Here Today** (9-6-32, Ethel Barrymore) received, it should have run far longer than the five weeks it actually played. Honing the skilled writing and sharp acting in Sam H. Harris's production was George S. Kaufman's brilliant direction (and, according to Broadway scuttlebutt, the pithy one-liners he added). One of these was a character's remark that he had been to Boston once, "but it was closed." Rumor also had it that the two principal characters were modeled after Dorothy Parker and Robert Benchley. Sweetly poisonous Mary Hilliard (Ruth Gordon), a divorcée who affects bohemian getups and sports a lorgnette "a foot away from the nose," and her playwright traveling companion, Stanley Dale (Charles D. Brown), come to Nassau, where they discover Mary's ex, the novelist Philip Graves (Donald Macdonald)—he's the one who found Boston shuttered—is courting a Boston socialite, Claire Windrew (Sally Bates). Claire's snooty, juggernaut mother (Charlotte Granville) is pressing her to marry the far more proper Spencer Grant (Paul McGrath). Mary and Stanley decide to aid Philip. Mary begins by attempting to take Mrs. Windrew down a notch or two. When the old gal admits that she likes lobsters but that lobsters don't like her, Mary responds, "Oh, you're modest." Mary and Stanley then move on to make it seem that there was more than meets the eye in Spencer's selling insurance to a notorious femme fatale. Mary even forges some sexy verses the lady and Spencer are supposed to have exchanged and, when these lines produce the requisite shock, deflates them by observing that the lines don't scan. However, Mary and Stanley do an about-face after Mary decides she wants Philip back. Even reviewers who held reservations about the play admired Gordon's "splendid acting, toying with the laugh lines enjoyably." Benchley, in his *New Yorker* review, took note of the rumor and observed, "I guess there must have been something in it, because if Stanley Dale wasn't meant to be Theodore Dreiser, then I must have been seeing things." Despite its immediate failure, the comedy became a decades-long favorite in summer stock and with little theatres.

Katharine Alexander's fine acting could not push Raymond Van Sickle's **Best Years** (9-7-32, Bijou) beyond its forty-fifth performance. Those best years were the ones Cora Davis has sacrificed to look after her demanding, hypochondriac mother (Jean Adair). Cora has spurned all her suitors but cannot discourage Fred Barton (Harvey Stephens). When her mother has a real stroke after an argument with her, it looks as if Cora will be doomed to many more years of spinsterhood. But then mother dies, leaving Cora free to wed Fred.

Another fine performance, this time by Claude Rains, could not help another weak drama, Jean Bart's **The Man Who Reclaimed His Head** (9-8-32, Broadhurst).

Several critics, influenced by Rains's masterful makeup, compared him to Lon Chaney. Paul Verin, a gruesomely ugly man with a twisted body (a raised shoulder, a shriveled arm) and a grotesque nose, appears with his young daughter (Evelyn Eaton) and a black bag at the office of a famous lawyer, and proceeds to tell his story. Back in 1911 he was a dedicated pacificist and socialist. Prodded by his ambitious peasant wife (Jean Arthur), he agrees to discard his principles and to help a rising young politician, Henri Berthaud (Stuart Casey). By persuading him to be the loudest among those crying for war, he engineers the man's rise to premier. As a captain in the war, Verin overhears his fellow officers joking about the premier's affair with Verin's wife. He abandons his post, rushes to the politician's apartment, and beheads the man with a bayonet. In the lawyer's office he goes to pull the head from the black bag. The lawyer deters him and prevents him from committing suicide by promising to win him an acquittal and reminding him that his daughter needs her father.

In more prosperous times Bella and Sam Spewack's **Clear All Wires** (9-14-32, Times Square) might have been a hit; as it was, its ninety-three performances made it a near miss. The action takes place in a once elegant Moscow hotel suite that has fallen into disrepair under the Soviets. A band of newsmen are chewing over the news that Buckley Joyce Thomas has lost his position as head of the Chicago *Press*'s foreign office because J.H., the paper's publisher, has learned that Thomas has been having an affair with Dolly Winslow, whom J.H. had sent to Europe for voice lessons. When one reporter, Kate Nelson (Dorothy Tree), comes to Thomas's defense, Pettingwaite (Charles Romano) of the *Times*, the renter of the suite, assures her, "You're a minority of one in the entire civilized world." Thomas (Thomas Mitchell) finally appears and, having pulled strings, takes over the suite—the only one with a working private bath—from the outraged Pettingwaite. Thomas is an impossible egoist and, it soon emerges, a total fraud. He writes articles about living with the Soviet army although he has done no such thing. And when, having demanded to be photographed with the Russian General Staff, he is advised they are in Manchuria, he insists the picture be faked with any officers available. Years earlier he had attempted to assassinate the Italian king for a news story, and now he proposes to kill a secretly returned Romanoff to make headlines. His plans go awry when the Russian foreign minister visits him and Thomas takes the bullet meant for the man. Thomas is declared a national hero. He receives mammoth bouquets from the Artificial Flowers Cooperative, is called on by a "delegation of morbidly grateful peasants," and learns that in accordance with the next Five-Year Plan, a new car barn will be named for him.

However, the affair is exposed and he is ordered to leave. At the same time, the comfort-seeking, demanding Dolly (Dorothy Mathews) deserts him. When he attempts to redeem himself with Kate and starts to talk of his "word of honor," Kate barks that she wouldn't touch his honor with a ten-foot pole. But she soon softens and proposes marriage. Thomas is happy to accept, doubly so because Hearst has just hired him to be his man in China, where Thomas appears ready to behave just as brashly and connivingly. A running gag throughout the comedy was the appearance of an English newspaperman (Philip Tonge) employing all manner of cajolery to use the suite's bath. In one unusual move, virtually all the Russian parts were cast with Russian emigrés for authenticity.

Philip Dunning and George Abbott failed to come anywhere near repeating the success they had enjoyed with *Broadway* six years earlier when they produced their latest collaboration, **Lilly Turner** (9-19-32, Morosco). Lil (Dorothy Hall) is the voluptuous queen of Dr. McGill's Health Exhibit, which tours tank towns, moving daily. Although she is married to Dave (James Bell), the troupe's barker and property man, she has an affair with the outfit's German strong man, Frederick (Robert Barrat), until he is committed to an insane asylum. Bob Cross (John Litel), a taxi driver who has delivered the physician (Joseph Creahan) needed to sign the papers for Frederick, is hired to replace him and in short order is also having an affair with Lil. Frederick escapes from the asylum, knocks out Bob, and throws Dave down a flight of stairs. For all that, Dave still loves Lil and attempts to persuade her to be true to him. Percy Kilbride walked away with some of the better notices for his bewildered, piping-voiced, backwater truck driver. The play lasted three weeks.

Two even shorter-lived flops followed quickly. In Robert Middlemass's **The Budget** (9-20-32, Hudson) Peter Harper (Lynne Overman) loses his job, then loses his $750 savings when his bank goes under. That does not stop his annoyingly well-bred sister-in-law (Olive Reeves-Smith) and her finicky husband (Raymond Walburn) from moving in with Peter and his wife (Mary Lawlor), or the Harpers' black cook, Calpurnia (Olive Burgoyne), and her mate, Theodore Roosevelt Smith (Paul C. Floyd), from also taking up residence. Matters are solved when Peter gets a new job, his brother-in-law makes him a gift of $800, and the cook leaves to have a baby.

Mark Linder's **Triplets** (9-21-32, Masque) received "the most severe panning in years." In Carbondale, Pennsylvania, three Irish triplets marry three Jewish triplets, and all their marital problems evaporate after each of the colleens presents her husband with triplets. *Variety* reported that on Friday night the author-producer split the week's receipts with the players, everyone getting a little over $3, but the stagehands' union refused to allow the play to continue until its members were paid in full. They were not, so the play closed after, appropriately, three performances.

Cecil Lewis's **Only the Young** (9-21-32, Sutton Show Shop) ran just one performance more in a bandbox auditorium inside an East 56th Street hotel. A twenty-one-year-old man discovers the thirtyish woman he adores is his father's mistress and then discovers that he is not really his father's son. That leaves him free to court a girl he thought was his sister. Grabbing attention in a cast that consisted largely of unknown mediocrities was Hilda Spong, decades ago a popular leading lady, as a garrulous grandmother called Squirrel.

Somewhat more adept players could do nothing with **The Stork Is Dead** (9-23-32, 48th St.), which Frederic and Fanny Hatton took from an unidentified Viennese play by Hans Kottow. Its producer was Al Woods, seeking renewed success with the sort of bedroom farce that had served him so well in the teens and the twenties. A count (Ross Alexander) promises his hectoring mistress (Ninon Bunyea) that he will not consummate his marriage to the naive young lady (Ethel Norris) whom he is marrying for her 10,000,000–franc dowry. He sleeps on a sofa in the newlyweds' sitting room until his mother-in-law (Nana Bryant) removes it. By the third act he has fallen in love with his bride, but when he goes to tell his mistress what has occurred, she surprises him by announcing she is going to marry his cousin.

Despite many fault-finding notices (particularly slamming the change of tone from stark realism to a certain mysticism in the last act and the infelicitous casting of secondary parts), the rising Group Theatre's production of John Howard Lawson's **Success Story** (9-26-32, Maxine Elliott's) pulled in attentive audiences for fifteen weeks, aided by a "pop price of $2.75" top. Actors accepting half salaries also prolonged the run. In booming 1928, Sarah Glassman (Stella Adler) is secretary to Raymond Merritt (Franchot Tone), the suave, socialite president of an advertising agency he founded and developed. She has persuaded Merritt to give a job to a neighbor she is fond of, Sol Ginsberg (Luther Adler), a coarse, blunt, ambitious young man. Merritt has just worked out an agreement with a shrewd but compassionate German-Jewish banker, Sonnenberg (Morris Carnovsky), who has cut short Merritt's smooth talk by stating, "I am a great admirer of glibness, but in close financial association I prefer candor." After briefly meeting Ginsberg, he has also warned Merritt that "the Russian Jews are the world's most gifted and most difficult people." Behind Merritt's back, Ginsberg sneers at his boss and vows, in the name of the revolu-

tion, to "bust up the whole place 'cause it smells of money." When Ginsberg makes his ideas public, Merritt fires him. Sarah talks Merritt into rehiring him. By the time the Depression hits, Ginsberg has shoved his way almost to the top of the firm. He discovers that Merritt has been using the firm's money to cover his personal losses in the stock exchange, so Ginsberg employs the knowledge nominally to make himself a partner but actually to force Merritt out, and he marries Merritt's pretty but money-grubbing mistress, Agnes (Dorothy Patten). His rise brings him no happiness, and he contemplates suicide. Sarah, still loyal and loving, attempts to stop him when he would make a pass at her. She grabs his revolver, and in the struggle it accidentally goes off, killing him. Merritt and Agnes rush in and, understanding the situation, call the police to tell them there has been a suicide.

The parade of out-and-out flops resumed with Lois Howell's **Bidding High** (9-28-32, Vanderbilt), which looked at another money-grubbing woman quick to change allegiances. Sylvia Chase (Shelah Trent) ditches her beau, Jimmy Stevens (King Calder), and marries Mark Ellis (Ivan Miller), the rich man her sister, Myra (Nedda Harrigan), had hoped to wed. But when the Depression hits, Mark goes broke, while Jimmy is now a wealthy bootlegger. So Sylvia deserts Mark and heads off with Jimmy, leaving Mark to make up as best he can with the waiting Myra.

Donald Heywood, a black composer whose work in Broadway musicals had always been panned, tried his hand at drama with **Ol' Man Satan** (10-3-32, Forrest). Critics saw his series of thirty-seven "jerky scenes" as a humorless, embarrassingly bad imitation of *The Green Pastures*. Mammy Jackson (Georgette Harvey), left alone in her log cabin with only one youngster after the rest of her children have gone off to camp, decides to tell the little boy the story of the Devil (A. B. Comatheire), how he caused all sorts of problems with biblical figures, and how he still motivates criminals. In the end, the Devil, having failed to win over mankind, sends hordes of myrmidons to earth to expound conflicting religious doctrines and thus confuse and thwart God's plans. Ironically, given their earlier responses to his works, some critics saved their kindest words for the music and choral material that Heywood either wrote or adapted.

Like Mary Lawlor, who also had made her name in musicals and tried straight theatre with *The Budget*, Helen Ford attempted to move from song-and-dance entertainments into drama. She, too, failed. In Henry Myers's "romantic ghost story" **The Other One** (10-3-32, Biltmore), she was seen as the sober-minded, evil Claire, who has murdered her gay, loving twin sister by switching the girl's medications. The dead girl's husband (George Baxter), unaware of Claire's treachery, marries her. When Claire demands they move because she fears their house is still haunted by her dead twin, he refuses. In an ending that confused critics, who offered varying interpretations, a figure—the sister's?—clad in a pink negligee was seen in the moonlight outside the window with arms extended in some possibly meaningful gesture.

Unwilling or unable to move away from the sort of sultry, sexy role that had rocketed her to fame, petite Lenore Ulric did nothing to boost her fading career when she essayed yet another such part in Gladys Unger's **Nona** (10-4-32, Avon). "Early in the first act she enters like a vexed tigress. From that heated moment onward she storms up and down the stage, shaking that busy mop of hair, tearing the air with passionate gestures, arranging the Ulrician torso in sinuous curves, smoldering with evil intentions and kissing like an acetylene torch." Backstage (audiences could see part of the performance supposedly taking place onstage) at Philadelphia's Symphony Hall the famed, hot-tempered Continental dancer Nona has just fired her accompanist and agrees to hire instead a slightly cynical, sophisticated local socialite, Henry Cade (Arthur Margetson), on the understanding that he will not make a pass at her. On tour, as her private Pullman is stalled in a snowstorm in Colorado, Cade teasingly violates the agreement. After all, he has seen a $50,000 check signed by his brother-in-law, whom he knew to be pursuing the dancer. He is kicked off the train, but at a small, rarely used station Nona comes after him and assures him that check was for a charity that supports musicians' orphans. Although he still feels she is a "promiscuous little push-over," they decide to wed.

To many the season's first real hit was Rachel Crothers's **When Ladies Meet** (10-6-32, Royale). Despite some implicit reservations, Brooks Atkinson welcomed this "endlessly refreshing" comedy in his *Times* review and saluted its best moments as "the high point of the season so far." For years Jimmie Lee (Walter Abel) has been asking Mary Howard (Frieda Inescort) to marry him, and she has refused. Mary is a writer whose latest book tells of a woman's falling in love with a married man and contriving to win him away from his wife. Jimmy cannot understand why Mary would write about such a creature: "If a woman pretends to be decent and isn't she's the worst kind." Mary's friend, Bridget Drake (Spring Byington), knows that Mary's story is essentially autobiographical. She is amused when Mary protests that her editor, Roger Woodruff, is a married man. "Of course he is. The good ones always *are*. Somebody has always beaten you to it." Nonetheless she consents to have both Mary and Roger to her weekend place. Jimmy, who has stumbled on the truth, contrives to have Woodruff called away and to bring Mrs. Woodruff (Selena Royle) to Bridget's converted barn. There the ladies meet. Mary realizes that Mrs. Woodruff is a warm, intelligent wife, and Mrs. Woodruff quickly recognizes that Mary is not a callous troublemaker. They both also realize how selfish Roger is and decide they can do very well without him. This leaves Mary a little pained, for she understands that she has destroyed another good woman's love and happiness. John Golden's production ran twenty-two weeks, went on a brief tour, and then returned for an engagement, still with its original cast, at a $1 top. Unfortunately this popular-priced return had to be curtailed when the stagehands' union again refused to make any concessions to the times.

A second hit came in several nights later. Edgar Wallace's London success *The Case of the Frightened Lady* was offered to New Yorkers as **Criminal at Large** (10-10-32, Belasco). As expected, the piece was filled with shots (though both killings are by strangulation), screams, ominous shadows, seemingly disembodied hands appearing through the drapery, and all the other requisite paraphernalia of the genre. An inspector (William Harrigan) from Scotland Yard and his humorous sidekick Sergeant Totty (Walter Kingsford) are assigned to investigate murderous doings at Mark's Priory, a secluded mansion. They meet the haughty Lady Lebanon (Alexandra Carlisle), her terrified, brooding son, Lord Lebanon (Emlyn Williams), her equally terrified niece, Isla (Katherine Wilson), and two glowering footmen who speak with American accents. It takes the inspector three acts to determine that the Lebanons are all a bit mad and that Lord Lebanon is a homicidal psychopath. The footmen are supposed to be his keepers. Superb performances and Guthrie McClintic's taut direction helped the thriller run for twenty weeks—almost as long as it had in the West End.

The closest thing to a success that the next night brought in was Molly Ricardel and William Du Bois's **I Loved You Wednesday** (10-11-32, Sam H. Harris). It told a story not unlike *When Ladies Meet*. Victoria (Frances Fuller) and Randall (Humphrey Bogart) had been lovers while they were students in Paris, until Victoria learned that Randall was married. Five years later Victoria has become a successful dancer, and Randall is doing well as an architect. When he comes across Victoria, Randall wants to resume their affair and promises to leave his wife. At the insistence of Victoria's barbed-tongued friend, Dr. Mary Hansen (Jane Seymour), Victoria and Cynthia (Rose Hobart), the wife, meet, after which Victoria sends Randall back to his spouse. Critics rejected Bogart and Fuller's lovemaking, one complaining "there isn't much fire" in it.

Two oldtimers, George Fawcett and his wife, Percy Haswell, made their final Broadway appearances in Leonard Ide's **Peacock** (10-11-32, 49th St). Fawcett also served as producer and director. He took the part of a dying, impoverished Parisian roué, whose grandniece, Suzanne (Virginia Curley), writes some of his former mistresses, reminding them of his generosity in his better years. The old gals (one of them played by Haswell) scrape up enough for him to be sent to the best hospital, but he takes the money and goes out for a fling on the town. This so restores his health that he is offered a diplomatic post in Syria.

The evening's third offering was a revival of Leo Ditrichstein and Frederic and Fanny Hatton's *The Great Lover* (11-10-15) at the Waldorf. Brought in by O. E. Wee and Jules J. Leventhal, producers who specialized in offering popular-priced revivals for the road, it starred Lou Tellegen as the aging opera singer who loses both his vocal powers and his hold on beautiful young women.

Barton MacLane, who went on to a long career playing tough guys in films and on television, was both the author and leading player of **Rendezvous** (10-12-32, Broadhurst). During the war, Private Oakley shoots a vicious officer who for no good reason has ordered a young soldier on a suicidal mission. "You asked for it, baby," he snarls over the dead officer's body. Back home he turns into a bootlegger, but a better-organized gang, supported by corrupt politicians, starts to decimate Oakley's associates. Oakley arranges to kidnap and kill some of the gang's principal backers, including a political boss, a venal judge, and the gangsters' attorney. Although the boss and the judge die, the former by his own hand, the other by a fright-induced heart attack, the rival gang stages a rescuing raid. To Oakley's surprise, one of his rivals' girls, Madge (Ruth Fallows), turns on her former pals and joins in shooting them. Oakley and Madge are arrested and sentenced to death. In the death house they promise each other they will rendezvous in the hereafter.

Elmer Rice suffered a humiliating setback when he produced one of his own early plays that other producers had rejected. **Black Sheep** (10-13-32, Morosco) tells of Buddy Porter (Donald Macdonald), a well-to-do young man who has spent several years vagabonding around the world. He startles and outrages his proper parents when he returns home with Kitty Lloyd (Mary Philips), another man's wife, in tow. The couple are ordered to leave until the family discovers that Buddy, under a pen name, has become a best-selling writer. In a complete turnabout, his family begins to coddle him. The coddling proves disastrous, with Buddy starting to play free and loose with the family's housemaid, with his brother's fiancée, and with every other skirt in sight.

To save him and let him return to his productive writing, Kitty drags him off to South America. Condemned as "thin entertainment, altogether lacking in the color that made 'The Left Bank,' " the play closed after four performances.

South America also figured in Reginald Lawrence and S. K. Lauren's **Men Must Fight** (10-14-32, Lyceum). But this was the South America of eight years on, in 1940, when, prodded by the Japanese, most of Latin America has united to fight Yankee exploitation. Edwin Seward (Gilbert Emery), the American secretary of state, and his wife, Laura (Janet Beecher), long have been ardent pacifists. So has their son, Robert (Douglass Montgomery). But after the war breaks out and the South Americans use poison gas, Edwin becomes a complete hawk. Robert is outraged and tells his father he will refuse to serve, thereby upholding the family's honorable tradition. That leaves Edwin no choice but to reveal that Robert is not his son, but the son of a British flier killed in the World War. An abashed Robert enlists and heads out to become a pilot. Several critics were put off by the change from a pro-pacifist slant to the more saber-rattling attitudes that followed the theatrically clichéd revelation. But if no sabers were actually rattled, some critics did applaud the authentic sounds of war planes and dirigibles flying above the Sewards' Fifth Avenue home.

Three nights later most first-string critics trudged uptown to evaluate **The Good Earth** (10-17-32, Guild), which Owen Davis and his son Donald theatricalized from Pearl Buck's award-winning novel. They rejected what they saw, suggesting the episodic stage version lacked the depth, the warmth, and the poetry of the original. Claude Rains, a last-minute replacement, played Wang Lung, the peasant farmer who marries a slave girl, O-Lan (Alla Nazimova), rises to riches, takes on a second wife (Gertrude Flynn), but only after O-Lan's death comes to understand that his simple fields and his first love were all that brought him genuine happiness. The performances were as troubling to critics as the adaptation. Rains was seen to be little more than adequate at best and certainly conveyed nothing Oriental, while Nazimova stirred a bit of controversy. One critic reported she "speaks her lines with flat bluntness and wears a countenance that is blankly expressive"; another lamented, "Her acting subsides into torturesome grimaces and her speaking becomes a series of primordial sounds." As with so many Theatre Guild failures, the play survived only until the Guild's subscription list was exhausted.

On that relatively busy night, the other American novelty, Francis De Witt's **Absent Father** (10-17-32, Vanderbilt), lured third-stringers. They, too, did not like what they saw, yet the new comedy somehow defied its dismissive notices and ran for eleven weeks. Set in a posh Park Avenue penthouse, the play recounts the plight of children of rich divorced folk. Ollie Townsend (Edward Crandall) loves his stepsister, Julie Boyden (Patricia Barclay), but after she rejects his proposal he gets drunk and marries a speakeasy cigarette girl, Janice Joy (Barbara Weeks), on the rebound. When the family threatens to disinherit Ollie, Janice retorts by threatening to blackmail the family. Julie's brother, Larry (Joseph Cotten), manages to trap Janice in a compromising situation, thus allowing Ollie to be rid of her.

Second-stringers and a few first-stringers attended the evening's third opening. Much of last season the Irish Players of the Abbey Theatre had toured the States; now they brought their repertory into the Martin Beck for a four-week stand and subsequent return. The program included revivals of *Autumn Fire, Birthright, Cathleen Ni Houlihan, Crabbed Youth and Age, Juno and the Paycock, The Playboy of the Western World, The Rising of the Moon, The Shadow of the Glen,* and *The White-Headed Boy.* Several new plays were also offered, beginning on opening night with Paul Vincent Carroll's **Things That Are Caesar's** (10-17-32), in which a dominating woman drives her husband into a fatal heart attack and forces her daughter into a loveless marriage. Lennox Robinson's **The Far-Off Hills** (10-18-32) tells of a girl who, frustrated that the man she loves and who professes to love her is married, longs to enter a convent. But when she has a chance to enter the convent she finds she is not interested, and when the man's wife dies he does not want a second marriage. George Shiels's **The New Gosoon** (10-21-32) tells how a young farm lad is taught responsibility after his father's death. In William Butler Yeats's **The Words upon the Window Pane** (10-28-32), a spiritualist recounts the history of Jonathan Swift's relations with Stella and Vanessa. Sean O'Casey's **The Shadow of a Gunman** (10-30-32) deals with a poet living in a Dublin tenement who is mistaken for a revolutionary and whose attempt to hide some bombs he discovers leads to an innocent girl's death. Robinson's **The Big House** (1-4-33) looks at an aristocratic family decimated by the Anglo-Irish war. **King Oedipus** (1-15-33) was Yeats's adaptation of the Greek tragedy. Among the players were Arthur Shields and Barry Fitzgerald.

William A. Brady and his clan had a squeak-by hit when he produced his wife's translation of Jacques Deval's **Mademoiselle** (10-18-32, Playhouse). Besides adapting the play, Grace George also assumed the title role. The Galvoisiers (A. E. Matthews and Alice Brady) are so involved in their social and professional worlds that they haven't much time for their children. They have no idea that their unwed daughter, Christine (Peggy Conklin), is pregnant. But the sour, spinsterish chaperon they have hired to look after the girl and whom they call Mademoiselle learns the truth. She takes Christine away to the country until the baby comes, and then, suddenly realizing how much she herself has always wanted to be a mother, quietly adopts the infant.

Seventy-three-year-old Margaret Crosby Munn reportedly spent fifteen or twenty years adapting her book *Will Shakespeare of Stratford and London* for the stage as **The Passionate Pilgrim** (10-19-32, 48th St.), only to watch it fold after a mere five performances. Shakespeare (Albert Van Dekker) leaves the nagging Anne Hathaway (Emily Ross) in Stratford and heads for London to write plays. At the home of the Earl of Southampton (George Macready) he falls in love with Elizabeth Vernon (Ara Gerald), who becomes the dark lady of his sonnets. But when she confesses it is Southampton whom she truly loves, he heads back to Stratford.

Montague Glass and Dan Jarrett's **Keeping Expenses Down** (10-20-32) lasted only seven performances longer, although it clearly tried to follow the advice of its title. Its small cast of unknowns meant that it had a weekly nut of a mere $3000, and the mounting had cost very little since its single setting of a modernistic office had been rented from William A. Brady, who had used it last season in *A Church Mouse.* Glass had wanted to write another Potash and Perlmutter farce but was stymied by the film studio that had purchased the rights to the series. So in the new play Abe Potash became Harris Fishbein (Louis Sorin), and Mawruss Perlmutter was rechristened (if that's an appropriate verb) Isaac Blintz (Solly Ward). The men are constantly feuding realtors who have been given $10,000 toward a property on the condition they return the money if title to the property is not clear. Since they have already spent $8000 of it to pay old debts, they stand to go to prison if the deal falls through. Placing an ad in the papers to seek any claimants, they are nearly hoodwinked by the crooked Thornbusch (Arthur Jarrett). But, being a typical comedy, all ends happily. One critic reported the line that got the biggest laugh was the remark "Payment in six months in 1932 is better than cash in 1929."

The season's first smash hit was Sam H. Harris's production of George S. Kaufman and Edna Ferber's **Dinner at Eight** (10-22-32, Music Box). Percy Hammond of the *Herald Tribune* hailed it as "one of the best of the shrewdly literate Broadway dramas," adding, "It is wise-cracking, philosophical, well told and intelligent." However, some critics were unhappy that there was so much drama or melodrama, and so little of Kaufman's expected wisecracks. Like *Grand Hotel,* to which a number of aisle-sitters compared it, the $50,000 production, with its eleven scenes requiring seven different settings, was played out on a revolving stage. Most reviewers felt the changes were made smoothly and swiftly, but *Variety,* noting that the curtain was lowered for each change, reported, "No special attempt for speed, nor did that seem necessary."

The guests invited to the dinner party of Millicent Jordan (Ann Andrews) all appear to have reached turning points in their lives. Larry Renault (Conway Tearle) is a broke, boozy, fading matinee idol, who has had a brief affair with Millicent's daughter Pearl (Marguerite Churchill). Millicent's husband, Oliver (Malcolm Duncan), is seriously ill, and his shaky shipping interests are in danger of being bought up by a ruthless upstart, Dan Packard (Paul Harvey). Packard's sluttish wife, Kitty (Judith Wood), a former hatcheck girl, finds her lover, Dr. Talbot (Austin Fairman), has tired of her and is going back to his wife, Lucy (Olive Wyndham). The long-retired star Carlotta Vance (Constance Collier), once Oliver's mistress, has sold her stock in his company, not fully aware of his precarious financial position. Even Millicent's servants come to blows. On the night of the dinner, the English lord and his wife who were to be the guests of honor abruptly beg off. The cook, upset by her fellow servants' fighting, announces that part of the dinner has been spoiled. Nevertheless, tired of waiting for Renault and unaware he has killed himself, the guests head for the dining room. Much of the melodrama was typified by a scene between Renault and his hapless agent, Max Kane (Sam Levene). The actor, frustrated by Max's inability to get him a starring part, calls him a "double dealing Kike." Max retorts with a bit of harsh truth, telling Renault that he never was an actor, but merely someone with looks. "Well, they're gone. And you don't have to take my word for it. Look in the mirror....Take a good look." Much of the humor was allotted to the imperious Carlotta, who is aware of the ravages of time and refuses to go back on the stage, stating, "I'll have my double chins in privacy." She also rues that unlike Langtry she never had a royal lover: "I picked the wrong period. Too young for Edward and too old for Wales. I fell right between princes." Kaufman and Ferber even gave the character an inside joke, having her mention that she saw Julia Cavendish last night. Regulars remembered that Julia Cavendish was the Ethel Barrymore–like character in the pair's *The Royal Family.*

The play's high upkeep prevented its spanning the summer, so it had to be content with a run of 232 performances. It was subsequently made into an all-star MGM film and given an all-star, albeit unsuccessful, revival on Broadway in 1966.

Two plays which opened the next Monday night both folded at the end of the week. The American novelty was John King Hodges and Samuel Merwin's **The Girl Outside** (10-24-32, Little). A young man (Horace Braham) who has become a painter and rented a basement studio in Greenwich Village over the opposition of his rich banker uncle (Charles Richman) takes in a girl (Lee Patrick) whom he has found faint and starving on the stoop outside. To avoid upsetting his mother (Helen Strickland), the youngsters pretend to be married. The two women eventually bring about a reconciliation with the uncle, thus restoring the young man's chance of becoming his uncle's heir.

From England came James Bridie's **The Anatomist** (10-24-32, Bijou), whose central figure was a famous anatomist (Frank Conroy) who is callously indifferent to the source of the bodies he works on. His assistant (Leslie Barrie), rebounding from a fight with a fiancée, dates a loose young girl, only to find he must dissect her corpse the next day. The murderers who regularly killed to provide the anatomist with bodies are brought to justice, but the anatomist remains not merely indifferent but defiant.

After a whole season's hiatus, the Civic Repertory Theatre relit its 14th Street playhouse on the 26th with an almost universally extolled revival of *Liliom* (4-20-21), a fantastic tragedy of a carnival barker and his doomed marriage. The original leads, Eva Le Gallienne and Joseph Schildkraut, returned to illuminate the star parts. The next night the same players appeared as Marguerite and Armand in the company's highly successful restoration of *Camille.*

Two novelties and one more revival competed for attention with Dumas's drama. The second revival was last season's *There's Always Juliet,* which elicited little interest at the Ethel Barrymore. The lone native effort was Anthony Young's **The Surgeon** (10-27-32, Belmont), produced and performed by a group which one critic devastatingly labeled "semi-amateurs." The play, "hobbled by some of the most pompous speeches of our time," centered on a plastic surgeon (Michael Randolf) who boasts he can make the ugliest person beautiful. He picks a homely vagrant (Helen Marley), turns her into a *Follies* beauty, and falls in love with her, only to find she is married to a crook. In the play's fourth act, the voice of the surgeon's conscience bellows at him from offstage until the doctor cries, "Enough! Enough!" He deserts the girl, making her so unhappy that she smears acid on her face to restore her ugliness.

There were sinister doings as well in J. B. Priestley's **Dangerous Corner** (10-27-32, Empire), but despite reviews which lamented that the play was filled with talk and was lacking in action, the London hit chalked up a six-month run. Like *Dinner at Eight,* the story revolved around a dinner party. This one is at the home of Robert and Freida Chatfield (Colin Keith-Johnston and Jean Dixon). Robert's brother, Martin, was said to have committed suicide after facing exposure for theft.

As the dinner guests talk, spurred on by a seemingly innocent remark about a cigarette box, it becomes clear that Robert's partner, Charles Stanton (Stanley Ridges), was the actual thief and that Martin was shot to death with his own gun by a secretary (Mary Servoss) defending herself against an attack from the drug-crazed young man. All the other guests also have dark secrets which come to light during the conversation.

Frank McGrath's **Carry Nation** (10-29-32, Biltmore) followed the crusading prohibitionist from her birth in 1846 to a demented mother and religiously fanatical father, through her unhappy marriages and hatchet-wielding escapades, to her final appearance at a lecture in 1910. Esther Dale, better known as a singer of art songs, won praise in the title role. The production had been mounted first in summer stock by a group of youngsters known as the University Players, several of whom took small parts in the Broadway mounting. These included Joshua Logan, Myron McCormick, Mildred Natwick, and James Stewart. But generally poor notices, coupled with the upkeep of a huge cast and a multi-scened story set on a revolve, forced the drama to call it quits after less than a month.

October's last entry proved one of the season's delights. Sidney Howard made a very free adaptation of René Fauchois's *Prenez garde à la peinture* and called it **The Late Christopher Bean** (10-31-32, Henry Miller). He moved the story from France to the dining room of the somewhat old-fashioned but comfortable home of Dr. Haggett (Walter Connolly), not far from Boston. The loyal maid of all works, Abby (Pauline Lord), "a Yankee villager, aged vaguely between youth and maturity," is sadly preparing to catch the five o'clock train from Boston and leave the Haggetts after fifteen years of faithful, if poorly paid, service to look after her newly widowed brother and his children. But the good doctor's interest is distracted by a telegram announcing that an admirer of the late Christopher Bean is coming to call. The telegram is signed Maxwell Davenport. The Haggetts had given shelter to Bean, a boozy, tubercular artist, who died ten years ago leaving behind only a batch of oils. One of these the doctor used to patch a leak in the chicken house; another to patch a leak in the roof. Most of the rest Mrs. Haggett (Beulah Bondi) threw on a bonfire. A young man (George Coulouris) arrives professing interest in Bean and, after the name Davenport is dropped, claims to be Davenport. He pays $50 for one of the surviving paintings and scampers off. He is hardly gone when an oily Jew named Rosen (Clarence Derwent) also arrives, interested in Bean's work. He is followed by the real Davenport (Ernest Lawford), who reveals that Bean has become the rage of New York, where one of his paintings can bring thousands of dollars. The first man is

exposed as a forger and Rosen as an unethical dealer. The doctor, who had been uninterested in money but suddenly has become uncontrollably greedy, hopes to trick Abby into leaving behind a portrait Bean had painted of her. Not telling her about what Bean's oil can bring, he looks at her as he starts the family's dinner prayer, "For what we are about to receive, O Lord, make us truly thankful." Abby not only refuses to part with the painting but reveals she rescued the seventeen paintings Mrs. Haggett had hurled on the flames. Sensing riches galore, Haggett insists that all the paintings really belong to him, since Abby was in his employ when they were painted and when she saved them. She ruefully reveals that she did so because Bean had been the only person ever to propose marriage to her. Of course, Dr. Haggett is certain she would never have accepted a proposal from such a pathetic figure, but she responds, "He was so sick, I couldn't refuse him nothing." As his widow, she is his indisputable heir. In the consternation that follows she takes the paintings and heads out. Some critics felt "Connolly's playing provoked most of the laughs," others that Lord's "buoyant and lighthearted and lovely" Abby stole the evening. The comedy played out the season.

By contrast, John Lyman and Roman Bohnen's **Incubator** (11-1-32, Avon) eked out just one week. Like last season's *Lost Boy* it looked at a juvenile delinquent who is sent to a reformatory. There Fred Martin (Charles Eaton) is persecuted by cruel administrators, falls in with a rough lot, is meanly punished after being forced to aid in a foiled escape plot, finally catches a guard and a matron in a compromising position which he uses to blackmail his way to freedom, and leaves a hardened criminal. Several critics were outraged by a scene which showed, in vivid terms for the time, an attempt by two other youngsters to have a homosexual relationship with Fred. It was berated as "a shocker" and "repulsive." Curiously, several critics had also expressed similar displeasure when one of the characters in *Dangerous Corner* was revealed, however discreetly, to be a homosexual.

In the middle and late nineteenth century it was not uncommon for New York to host several revivals of the same classic in a single season. By 1932 revivals of any classics had become exceedingly rare, and two of the same one all but unheard of. Yet the *Camille* which Robert Edmond Jones had designed for Lillian Gish at the Central City, Colorado, summer festival was brought in bravely at the Morosco on the same night to compete with the mounting downtown at the Civic Repertory. Jones created a consciously old-fashioned production, employing such long-superannuated devices as hooded footlights to suggest the play was being given as it might have been at the time of its first performances.

Act One: 1930–1944

Gish was deemed superior to the mechanical Le Gallienne. She was not quite as good as the haughty courtesan of the early scenes but bowled audiences over with her pathetic frailty and innocence in the later ones. Her supporting cast was not admired. Business did not warrant any extension of the original two-week booking.

A revival of *The Silent House* (2-7-28), in which a man can inherit a fortune only by spending time in a mysterious mansion that shelters some strangely ominous people, found no takers when it came into the Ambassador on the 8th. Playgoers picking up their newspapers the next morning to search for reviews undoubtedly took note of headlines announcing that Franklin Delano Roosevelt had been elected president.

Three plays opened the next Monday, and all of them flopped. The longest run—three weeks—went to Robert Keith's steamy melodrama **Singapore** (11-14-32, 48th St.). Suzanne Caubaye, who had won notoriety in 1926 as Nubi in *The Squall,* was cast in the not dissimilar role of Malaya, the adoring East Indian mistress of Eric Hope (Donald Woods), who shunts her aside when he marries Hilda Armstrong (Louise Prussing). But Hilda really loves the Sultan of Selernak (Brandon Peters) and plots to have some trained cobras kill Eric during an elegant dinner. Malaya learns of the plot and sees to it that the snakes kill Hilda instead. The "Dance of Death" at the dinner was choreographed by Ruth St. Denis and featured two girls reportedly naked from the waist up, if "slightly upstage and shaded by the dimmers." One critic bewailed that it looked like a production number at Minsky's.

Eleanor Holmes Hinkley's **Dear Jane** (11-14-32, Civic Repertory) was retained in the Civic's schedule for only eleven performances. In a loosely connected prologue, Samuel Johnson (Howard da Silva) tells David Garrick (Joseph Kramm) and his other buddies that "no woman is capable of creating an enduring work of art." Twenty-odd years on, Jane Austen (Josephine Hutchinson) is courted by three men: the Irish gallant Tom Lefroy (Robert F. Ross), the shy, devoted James Dickweed (Nelson Welsh), and the aristocratic Sir John Evelyn (Joseph Schildkraut). She almost accepts Sir John until he discloses his antipathy to her scribbling. Schildkraut was accused of posing rather than acting. Hutchinson garnered the best notices. Le Gallienne, who directed the play, also assumed the subsidiary role of Jane's sister.

The evening's shortest-lived opening was Don Marquis's passion play, **The Dark Hours** (11-14-32, New Amsterdam). Because of their admiration for the usually comic writer and because of the subject, critics let the offering down easily. Marquis required a cast of sixty-two to retell the story of Jesus from the time Caiaphas decides to demand his arrest until Golgotha.

An actor named Cliff Camp was glimpsed momentarily now and then as Jesus, but never spoke, while Jesus' words were sometimes heard from offstage pronounced by George Heller.

A cast replete with respected oldtimers, contemporary favorites, and future celebrities could not override the cool notices handed Rose Albert Porter's **Chrysalis** (11-15-32, Martin Beck). Many reviewers expressed incredulity at her story's intermingling of social ranks. Lyda Cose (Margaret Sullavan), a free-spirited rich girl who has returned home from college, where she was unhappy, is equally unhappy with her unresponsive beau, Don Ellis (Humphrey Bogart), who has been kicked out of Princeton. The pair go to a low-class speakeasy. There they meet Eva Haron (June Walker), a girl from the tenements, and Eva's paroled fiancé, Honey Rogers (Elisha Cook, Jr.). Honey's misbehavior lands him back in prison and causes Eva to be sent to a reformatory. To escape, Honey stabs a guard to death. Lyda then helps him rescue Eva from the reformatory. The three hole up in a dingy room in Hell's Kitchen. When the police appear, Honey and Eva commit suicide by jumping out the window, but Lyda's social position allows her to walk away from any trouble unscathed. Her uncle (Osgood Perkins) lectures her about going on with life as best as possible. Another revolve speeded changes for Cleon Throckmorton's realistic settings, albeit one critic thought the realism went too far with the presence of garbage cans in two scenes and with Honey stamping to death a cockroach with his shoe in the prison scene. Lily Cahill (as Lyda's rigid mother), Thurston Hall (as a judge), and a young player listed in the program as E. Kazan all had brief moments.

Arthur Goodrich found few admirers for his **The Perfect Marriage** (11-16-32, Bijou). To celebrate their fiftieth wedding anniversary, an old playwright (George Gaul) and his wife (Edith Barrett) invite the writer's onetime secretary (Fay Bainter) and his first star (George Baxter) to join them at lunch. The conversation brings out that forty-five years ago the secretary and the writer had enjoyed a fling, and so had the wife and the star. There are some heated words before everyone kisses and makes up. (The second of the three acts was a flashback, allowing all the players to doff their gray wigs and be young again.)

The same evening saw a revival at the Liberty of *Cradle Snatchers* (9-2-25), in which three dissatisfied matrons decide to have a good time with three college boys. A gem from the giddy Era of Wonderful Nonsense, it seemed out of place on a sober Depression night.

The large Jolson Theatre, just below Central Park, was renamed the Shakespeare Theatre and, beginning on November 17, housed a company of former Ben

Greet players and assorted American actors who announced their intention of offering a season of Shakespearean plays at a $1.10 top (the ten cents was tax). Balcony seats were a quarter (plus tax). Several arches served as the basic setting for all the plays, with drapes and bits of furniture altered to denote scene changes. The troupe opened with *A Midsummer Night's Dream,* then moved on to *As You Like It, The Comedy of Errors, Hamlet, Julius Caesar, King Lear, Macbeth, The Merchant of Venice, The Merry Wives of Windsor, Much Ado About Nothing, Othello, Romeo and Juliet, The Taming of the Shrew, The Tempest,* and *Twelfth Night.* Broadway's hardened critics could not become excited about the mountings, but they understood that many playgoers were hungry for these plays and that at so low a price no one could quibble, since the stagings were most definitely not incompetent. To the surprise of some more cynical Broadway pundits, the company played out the season, giving more than 200 performances.

The same night saw another revival appear at the Forrest. This was last season's *The Good Fairy,* with yet another former musical comedy favorite, Ada May, attempting to switch to non-musicals. Designed primarily for the road, it nonetheless stayed on in New York for two months.

The reviews accorded to Francis Lederer in his American debut seemed largely responsible for the six-month run enjoyed by C. L. Anthony's **Autumn Crocus** (11-19-32, Morosco). (It was an open secret that Anthony was a pen name for Dodie Smith.) In her story a spinster (Patricia Collinge) stops off at a Tyrolian inn during her vacation and falls in love with its young, handsome owner. He asks her to stay on, but after she discovers he is married, it is not hard for her Baedecker-lugging companion (Eda Heinemann) to convince her to continue her travels.

There was no matinee idol to beckon matrons to **Firebird** (11-21-32, Empire), taken by Jeffrey Dell from Lajos Zilahy's Hungarian original. Nor could some admired players gloss over the flaws of this mystery play that many felt cheated the public with its ending. Karola Lovasdy (Judith Anderson) attempts to have the famous actor Zoltan Balkanyi (Ian Keith) evicted from the apartment house her husband (Henry Stephenson) owns after Balkanyi makes unwanted advances to her. She fails, and when Balkanyi is found murdered she is the prime supsect. She confesses, and even her husband believes her. But to everyone's surprise (since not a hint has been dropped), an astute policeman (Reginald Mason) pins the killing on the Lovasdys' promiscuous daughter (Elizabeth Young). The play ran five weeks.

Two American plays that opened the same night had shorter stands—running four weeks and one week

respectively. G. N. Albyn's **Moral Fabric** (11-21-32, Provincetown Playhouse) told of a girl who is bribed by corrupt politicians to incriminate a reform candidate for mayor. Falling in love with the man, she instead uses the bribe money to embarrass the crooks and help the reformer win his election.

Sydney Stone wrote, produced, and directed **The Barrister** (11-21-32, Masque), which, as its title suggests, was set in England. When a rising young barrister throws over his fiancée, her gangster brother attempts to blackmail him. He kills the brother, gets away with murder, and decides to marry the sister after all.

Bessie Beatty and Jack Black, the latter a former convict, adapted Black's book *You Can't Win* and called it **Jamboree** (11-24-32, Vanderbilt). It spotlighted a white-haired madam, Mary Howard (Marie Kenney), who is more popularly known as Salt Chunk Mary. At her Board of Trade Hotel and Bar, in the Pocatello, Idaho, of the 1890s, she also acts as a fence for stolen goods and hides crooks needing shelter. Years earlier her vicious husband had helped frame her and send her to prison. While serving her time, she heard from him that their son had died. Now she sets about protecting a young streetwalker (Wanda Howard) and an attractive young hood, Jack (Carroll Ashburn). After discovering that Jack is her son, who actually had not died, she engineers the kids' escape, even taking a bullet meant for Jack. He will probably never know that his mother died in helping him. A raffish assortment of characters added color to the evening, but could not impart enough excitement to what more experienced hands might have turned into a ripsnorting oldtime melodrama.

A pair of quick failures launched December. The actor Romney Brent turned playwright with a comedy he clearly hoped would recapture the hilarious zaniness of Noel Coward's *Hay Fever,* **The Mad Hopes** (12-1-32, Broadhurst). Clytemnestra Hope (Violet Kemble Cooper), whose diplomat husband died of a heart attack brought on by her gaffes at an important state dinner, lives with her three children in a villa at Nice and struggles to maintain appearances in the face of a fast-dwindling bank account. Flighty Clytie puts on grand airs, such as communicating with her children by sending notes on picture postcards to be delivered to them by her maid. Her sons earn pin money working as extras on locally made films. Matters improve after one of the sons, Claude (Rex O'Malley), brings home a rich young New Yorker, Henry Frost (Harry Ellerbe), who falls in love with the Hope daughter, Geneva (Jane Wyatt), and after Clytie is won over by a wealthy Jew, Maurice Klein (Pierre Watkin).

Ben Hecht and Gene Fowler came a cropper with **The Great Magoo** (12-2-32, Selwyn). The title apparently was taken from a contemporary expression for a person someone loves. Nicky (Paul Kelly) is the "Caruso of spielers" for a cheap touring carnival and a young man who always has to have a woman with him. He is not above risking a tumble with Jackie (Dennie Moore), even though her husband (Victor Kilian) is a flagpole sitter who takes binoculars with him on his climb and insists that Jackie keep her shades up so that he can watch her. But Nicky's great magoo is the troupe's Salome dancer, Julie (Claire Carleton). After Julie leaves the show, first for a bandleader and afterwards to accept a big part in a new musical, Nicky quickly takes to drink. But then Julie flops in New York and herself hits the skids until a possibly reformed Nicky comes to her rescue. The episodic drama, clearly relishing its own sleaze, was not to the critics' liking. Writing in the *World-Telegram*, Robert Garland suggested the writers were behaving like "a pair of precocious boys showing off before company, plotting and planning just how far they will be allowed to go." All that remains popular from the show is a Harold Arlen and E. Y. Harburg song, known at the time as "If You Believed in Me" but subsequently retitled "It's Only a Paper Moon."

The two flops were followed by two of the season's brightest hits, which opened on the same night. Many theatregoers still regard S. N. Behrman's **Biography** (12-12-32, Guild) as his finest comedy. Marion Froude (Ina Claire), a portrait painter known as widely for her liaisons as for her paintings—the paintings often went hand in hand with the liaisons—has set herself up in an attractive, balconied New York studio. Two men are waiting to see her. One is Melchior Feydeck (Arnold Korff), an Austrian composer who has been signed by Hollywood in the mistaken belief that he is his more famous but long-dead brother. The other is a rude, impatient young man, Richard Kurt (Earle Larimore), a radical editor who is not appeased when Feydeck assures him that there is always someone waiting for Marion. A third visitor is Leander "Bunny" Nolan (Jay Fassett), once Marion's earliest love and now a candidate for senator from Tennessee. Although he is engaged to an influential publisher's daughter, he clearly is smitten again by Marion. And she still feels her own attraction to him. When the others have left, Richard talks Marion into writing her autobiography. Bunny learns of this several weeks later and comes storming back, demanding that Marion quash the story rather than imperil his chances. Richard is even more furious when he finds that Marion may agree. He is, as he tells her, determined "to laugh the powers that be out of existence in a great winnowing gale of laughter." Marion realizes that she has fallen in love with him, but that he is afraid to love her. With time, Bunny has come to resent the attitudes of his future bride and

father-in-law. He still loves Marion. This further angers Richard, leaving Marion to observe, "Studying you, I can see why so many movements against injustice become such absolute tyrannies." She burns her manuscript, politely sends both Bunny and Richard on their way, and orders her maid to pack. She will resume her wayfaring life alone.

The *Post's* John Mason Brown told his readers that Behrman had written "a play of witty tolerance, rippling over deeps and shallows and sparkling always." He added, "Miss Claire is the ablest comedienne our theatre knows. Her playing has about it the brilliance of a diamond." Numerous such notices helped the comedy run for eight months.

. . .

Ina Claire [Fagan] (1892–1985) was born in Washington, D.C., and made her debut in vaudeville as a singing mimic in 1905. Four years later she won New York's applause for her imitation of Harry Lauder. After more seasons in two-a-day she moved onto the musical comedy stage playing opposite Richard Carle in *Jumping Jupiter* (1911). During the next several years, in both New York and London, she played increasingly important assignments in musical comedies and revues, before accepting her first lead in a straight play—*Polly with a Past* (1917). Subsequent hits included *The Gold Diggers, The Awful Truth,* and *The Last of Mrs. Cheyney.* A svelte, blonde-haired, hazel-eyed beauty with a tipped-up nose and weak chin, she was generally considered the finest high comedienne of her generation.

. . .

Eva Le Gallienne and Florida Friebus's **Alice in Wonderland** (12-12-32, Civic Repertory)—which incorporated scenes from both the original story and *Through the Looking Glass*—might with time have chalked up as many performances as *Biography* had not the ugly intransigence of an arrogant union cut short its career. Most of the beloved scenes and characters were present. Some felt that the table and room growing as Alice seemingly shrank or the disembodied grin of the Cheshire Cat probably should have been left to the imagination, but with faithfully recreated Tenniel sketches, embellished with "story-book colors in limpid pastel shades," much of the tale came gorgeously to life. Sets on chariot-like platforms and drops kept the action moving apace. Josephine Hutchinson made a likable and not saccharine Alice—"just about a perfect Alice," one critic rejoiced. Joseph Schildkraut, in drag as the Queen of Hearts, stormed through a demented croquet game, shouting "Off with his head!" Tweedledum (Landon Herrick) and Tweedledee (Burgess Meredith) did everything in tandem, even to blinking their eyes simultaneously. Le Gallienne herself had fun with the far-seeing White Chess Queen. But for all its being hailed as "a money play," hard times and the theatre's out-of-the-way location hurt business. Monday nights and Wednesday matinees were as a rule discouragingly weak. So Le Gallienne, with the unanimous support of her company, asked the actors' union for permission to drop those performances and instead substitute a Sunday matinee and an early Sunday evening performance. The pleas were rejected out of hand. As a result, Le Gallienne moved the troupe to the New Amsterdam, where she had apparently been promised some subsidies. These were not forthcoming, so when the troupe ended its season it also ended its New York life. Le Gallienne toured with some of the players and the repertory during the next season, but it would be a decade and a half before she would be part of another, far less successful, attempt to establish true repertory in New York.

A third attraction came in the same night. A revival at the Hudson of George Kelly's *The Show-Off* (2-5-24) was produced by Wee and Leventhal, the same men who had brought in many of the recent revivals. This mounting was directed by and featured Raymond Walburn in the title role. Its 119 performances made it the longest-running of the season's revivals (as opposed to several longer-lasting return engagements which have been ignored).

For the lone week that it survived, John L. Balderston and J. E. Hoare's **The Red Planet** (12-17-32, Cort) told of an atheistic scientist (Bramwell Fletcher) and his deeply religious wife (Valerie Taylor) who believe they have made radio contact with Mars. To their amazement the Martian replies are filled with comments from the New Testament. But the replies are eventually shown to have been sent by a waggish, deformed old radio operator in the Alps. Disillusioned, the wife blows up the laboratory, killing herself, her husband, and the old man of the mountains.

Theatregoers read between the lines of the often laudatory notices handed to Katharine Cornell and her associates and concluded that they would not care for **Lucrece** (12-20-32, Belasco), which Thornton Wilder took from André Obey's *Le Viol de Lucrèce,* itself suggested by Shakespeare's poem. To everyone's surprise and delight, the officers who stage an unexpected visit to the home of the noble Collatine (Pedro de Cordoba), while he is away at the wars, find his lovely wife, Lucrece, dutifully and innocently weaving with her maids. When Brutus (Charles Waldron) reports this to Tarquin (Brian Aherne), the king's son, the prince burns with lust for the good woman. He enters her house by a ruse and during the night comes to Lucrece's bed, threatening to kill her and a young servant and then leave their naked bodies together if she does not submit to him. Lucrece summons her husband from

battle and, telling him what happened, commits suicide. Some of the action was in pantomime with the players employing imaginary props, and all of it was commented on by two figures who spent the evening on the sides of the stage. One (Blanche Yurka) was cowled in blackish gray and wore a silver mask; the second (Robert Loraine) had on similarly dark and drapy garments and hid his face with a mask of burnished gold. The other players were dressed in Robert Edmond Jones's sumptuous Renaissance costumes, while his simplified, formalized settings of Collatine's tent and various rooms in the officer's house were placed before a gray velvet curtain and flanked by fragmented colonnades. Guthrie McClintic and all his actors were praised, with the *Journal*'s John Anderson stating that the crucial moments between Cornell and Aherne were "played with such power and brilliance that the scene becomes fairly incandescent." Focusing on two of the star's later scenes—her contemplating suicide and her death when "she stabs herself gently but strongly"—he concluded, "Her performance reaches a mute eloquence that is incredibly sensitive and lovely." But the public's refusal to buy the static piece forced its removal after thirty-one playings.

A largely worthless comedy ran almost as long. The hero of Paul Barton's **Anybody's Game** (12-21-32, Bijou) was the dumb-as-they-come Jimmy Craig (Sam Wren). But after his old flame, Peggy Blake (Emily Lowry), wheedles him a job at the Delaney Advertising Agency, where she works as a telephone operator, every one of his stupid moves and suggestions is crowned with success. In his conceit, he drops her for a splashy typist and would-be hoofer (Edna Hibbard). But Peggy wins him back in the end.

Because it was set on the Left Bank, dealt with two unhappy couples, featured Katharine Alexander, who had appeared in Elmer Rice's earlier hit, and opened at the same playhouse, several critics compared Samuel Chotzinoff and George Backer's **Honeymoon** (12-23-32, Little) to *The Left Bank,* and compared it very unfavorably at that. Just as Leslie Taylor begins to play host in her Parisian flat to two squabbling honeymooners, the Chapmans (Ross Alexander and Rachel Hartell), Leslie's philandering ex, Bob (Thomas Mitchell), turns up, hoping to rekindle the old fire. But when Mrs. Chapman refuses to accompany her playwright husband back to watch a mounting of his latest highbrow opus, *Plethora,* a battle royal ensues. Leslie finds herself going out with the writer, and Bob takes Mrs. Chapman out for a spree. Of course, the newlyweds are soon reconciled, and so are the Taylors.

The night after Christmas brought in two offerings. Harold Sherman's **The Little Black Book** (12-26-32, Selwyn) was the first—and last—presentation by one of those ever hopeful groups that regularly popped up on Broadway. This one called itself the American Plays and Players. Their comedy was set in Washington. H. D. Porter (Jonathan Hole), a hick from the sticks, and his even more hickish wife Lulu May (Virginia Stevens), leave their Centerville home and take employment as civil servants. They are soon overrun by freeloaders. A local political boss and some local gangsters try to persuade the couple to help in bootlegging. By accident the visitors drop a little black book containing the names of and purchases made by important national figures. Porter is arrested, but after he hands over the black book to a worried senator (Dodson Mitchell), the senator not only swings his release but sees to it that Centerville gets the highway it long has wanted.

Like Le Gallienne, Walter Hampden had come to enjoy the dubious reputation of being more dedicated than inspiring. Still, his production of Rostand's *Cyrano de Bergerac* had won huge audiences and was still admired in many quarters. So when he brought it back the same evening at the New Amsterdam for a two-week stand, he himself received respectful reviews, although his supporting cast was not well liked. Moreover, the play was at an age when it was considered especially old hat, and several critics wondered about the value of reviving it.

The issue of *Variety* dated the next day—the 27th—presented a rather gloomy picture of the theatre world. Suggesting that the season had peaked and noting that only thirty-seven attractions were keeping playhouses lit, it decried "one of the dullest Christmases in many seasons." The tradesheet reported that *Dinner at Eight* was the only sellout, pulling in $23,000. *When Ladies Meet* trailed not far behind with $20,000. At the other end of the scale, *Absent Father,* in its eleventh week, had grossed a mere $2000. Among the newer arrivals it noted *Biography* had built to a rather strong $14,000. On the road, only thirty-odd playhouses were lit, and no fewer than five of those were presenting a film temporarily.

Two of the year's last three offerings brightened the picture a bit. Commentators had remarked that Walter Connolly and Osgood Perkins for some time had been the critics' favorite comedians, although both had gone through a string of disappointments. Now, with the jowly, avuncular Connolly delighting reviewers and audiences in *The Late Christopher Bean,* the slim, sophisticated Perkins also found a season-long success with Allan Scott and George Haight's **Goodbye Again** (12-28-32, Masque). The *American*'s Gilbert Gabriel spoke for many of his colleagues when he deemed the comedy "somewhat longish, somewhat fuddling, and mild, but . . . full of the patter of good little lines." Atkinson noted that Perkins had his best opportunity

since *The Front Page* to display his "whistling humors" and "to stride . . . violently across the stage, wheel suddenly and point a lean, accusing finger at somebody who really means something to him." He concluded, "In the final act, Mr. Perkins performs the almost impossible task—for a man—of playing all but a few minutes in bed. And that bed is in the Hotel Statler!" The Statler in Cleveland, he might have added, where Anne Rogers (Sally Bates), secretary to the best-selling author Kenneth Bixby, is busy signing his name to "autographed" copies of his latest. Bixby himself is a little vague about where they are, since Cleveland looks a lot like Pittsburgh—but then Pittsburgh looks like Cincinnati. They are interrupted by a Mrs. Harvey Wilson (Katherine Squire), who once had been Julie Clochessy, a college classmate of Bixby's, and had helped him lose his virginity beneath "the sequestered silence of the Horace P. Mortimer Memorial Arch." She hopes he will forgive her for running off and marrying, and also hopes that he will now have a fling with her. She and Bixby are hardly gone when her sister (Dortha Duckworth) and brother-in-law-to-be (Hugh Rennie) appear, hoping to avoid a scandal. Her husband (Leslie Adams) also turns up, clearly hoping to dump his wife on her old flame, and is happy to dance away the night with Anne waiting for the pair to return. The next morning Bixby manages to get rid of Julie and her ménage by claiming he is the father of a youngster (Jackie Kelk) who comes knocking at the door. In one scene, a young chauffeur barges in, demanding that Bixby immediately autograph Mrs. Bell-Irving's copy of Bixby's latest and that her name be spelled correctly. Kept waiting and then noticing the name is misspelled, he storms out barking, "Mrs. Bell-Irving is gonna be sore as hell." The chauffeur was played by young James Stewart. One of the few criticisms leveled against the no longer so young Perkins was that he was too old to be playing a man supposedly less than a decade out of college.

Several years earlier, Charles Bruce Millholland, Morris Gest's press agent, had written a play in which the central figure was a spoof of Gest. He turned it over to Jed Harris, who, in turn, handed it to Ben Hecht and Charles MacArthur for rewriting. They added a touch of Harris to the main character but left before completing the rewrite. Disgusted, Harris gave the property to Philip Dunning and George Abbott. By the time Dunning and Abbott produced **Twentieth Century** (12-29-32, Broadhurst), Hecht and MacArthur received the sole authors' credit, although it was generally known that Dunning had written the final version of the third act. But the result pleased Percy Hammond of the *Herald Tribune,* who told his readers, "Show business gets a cruel razzing from *20th Century,* a new prank . . . in which those impish bad boys of the Drama kick it urgently on its pants and inspire, thereby, much hilarity." He summed the entertainment up as "cold and glittering amusement." Having lost his last $75,000 on "a magnificent failure," the once great producer Oscar Jaffe (Moffat Johnston) stands on the brink of bankruptcy. His sole hope is to wangle his onetime star, the former Mildred Plotka and now the tempestuous, self-consciously glamorous Lily Garland (Eugenie Leontovich), into starring as the Magdalene in a mounting of the Passion Play. Of course, she is still furious after catching him making love to another woman. But he books a compartment next to hers on the Twentieth Century and goes to work. Complications and laughs come from Owen O'Malley (William Frawley), Jaffe's press agent; Oliver Webb (Matt Briggs), his general manager; two supposed fugitives from another Passion Play; and two supposed honeymooners, actually a businessman and his secretary. A $200,000 check from a religious fanatic (Etienne Girardot) seems to put Jaffe back on easy street, until the fanatic is shown to be a penniless nut. It takes Jaffe's faked death scene to get Lily to sign the contract. The settings carefully recreated the famous train and, for the final scene, the gate at Grand Central. George Abbott's brilliant direction signaled an important turn for him, his move from melodrama into farce.

. . .

George [Francis] **Abbott** (1887–1995) was born in Forestville, N.Y. At Harvard he studied under George Pierce Baker at the famous 47 Workshop and saw the Harvard Dramatic Club mount an early effort of his in 1913. That same year he made his acting debut in New York in *The Misleading Lady*. In 1918 his rewriting helped turn *Lightnin'* into a long-running hit. Another early hit collaboration was *The Fall Guy* (1925). He scored a huge success in 1926, when he co-authored and staged *Broadway*. In the next several seasons he staged and sometimes helped write more swift-moving melodramas, notably *Chicago* (1926) and *Coquette* (1927).

. . .

The play ran nineteen weeks, ran even longer in a 1950 revival starring Gloria Swanson and José Ferrer, and in 1978 became the musical *On the Twentieth Century*. It was also made into a popular film starring John Barrymore and Carole Lombard.

A contemporary German film, *Mädchen in Uniform*, based on Christa Winsloe's novel *Gestern and Heute*, had already won acclaim by the time Barbara Burnham's English-language stage version, **Girls in Uniform** (12-30-32, Booth), began its brief life in New York. A lovesick young girl (Florence Williams) in an austere Prussian school so describes her feelings for a kindly

teacher (Rose Hobart) that she is suspected of lesbian leanings and hounded into suicide by the rigid headmistress (Roberta Beatty). Two former stars, Ethel Jackson (America's first Merry Widow) and Charlotte Walker, had small parts as aristocratic ladies.

The new year began with another importation, since John Colton's **Saint Wench** (1-2-33, Lyceum) was reputedly based on a Croatian drama, Miliam Begovic's *Gat Incarnat*. A loose-moraled girl (Helen Menken) is married to a devout religious student (Russell Hardie), who spurns her after learning she has had an affair with a local brigand (Edward Leiter). The girl eventually finds religion and becomes saintly, while her husband loses the miraculous healing powers he possessed.

Down in the Village yet another aspiring group, the Provincetown Playhouse Guild, tested its wings and crashed with **Fantasia** (1-3-33, Provincetown Playhouse), John Eldon Fillmore's story of a would-be playwright reduced to begging in the subway and his girl who must take to the streets. Although there were two dozen players in the cast, three of them performed the fourteen most prominent parts.

Uptown, two entries fared no better. Audrey and Waveney Carten's English drama **Late One Evening** (1-9-33, Plymouth) told of a woman's marrying a drunken novelist (John Buckler) who, in his cups, had run her down with his automobile. Their life is filled with soap-operaish turns, such as losing their young son, until the woman (Ursula Jeans) is able to straighten out her husband's problems.

Dillard Long's **A Good Woman, Poor Thing** (1-9-33, Avon) also used some British-born players, albeit it was an American work. Claiming she needed the money, Lelia (Irene Purcell) had broken off with Bill (Arthur Margetson) and married a wealthy Englishman, John (John Williams). Now she tells Bill she has divorced John and wants to take up with him again, although she knows he has a mistress, Christine (Millicent Hanley). Bill gives Christine $20,000 as a supposedly parting gift, but soon is seeing her again. When John shows up, Lelia and he run off to Lake Placid. However, the couples are not happily paired, so after Bill meets up with Lelia and treats her rough, she agrees to remain with him.

That good woman, poor thing, was followed by **Two Strange Women** (1-10-33, Little), whose author, Edwin B. Self, suggested simple backwoods folk and city folk don't mix. The Martins (Jacqueline Logan and Houston Richards) and Robert Skinner (Douglas Gilmore) come to fish at the Jenkinses' Kentucky cabin, which sits high on the banks above the Dix River. The Jenkinses' twenty-year-old son, Mel (John Griggs), falls madly in love with Mrs. Martin, and when she mentions she wishes her husband were dead, he takes the man catfishing, throws him overboard, and pounds him with an oar until he sinks. On his return, Mel is horrified to discover that Mrs. Martin and Skinner are lovers. He turns himself in, but the liquor-loving Judge Whiffle (John Daly Murphy), who happened to witness the crime, promises to try to get the boy off. Meanwhile, the 100–year-old Greatgrandma Jenkins (Lida McMillan), who had raised Mel but had not spoken a word since the death of her daughter at Mel's birth, finds her voice and provokes Mrs. Martin into jumping out of the window to her death in the river below.

Many critics thought Gennaro Curci and Eduardo Ciannelli's **Foolscap** (1-11-33, Times Square) started off with a great idea. But the same critics concurred that the authors could not sustain it. George Bernard Shaw (Frederick Worlock) and Luigi Pirandello (Ciannelli) wake up in adjoining beds in a hospital. Seems they were distracted while driving by a figure that looked just like Shakespeare. Sure enough, it was Shakespeare (Geoffrey Kerr), but he is an inmate in the mental institution reserved for wealthy lunatics. Among the other patients are Eve, Cleopatra, Helen of Troy, and Marc Antony. The playwrights are persuaded to create a work for the inmates to stage, although Shaw is reluctant to reveal his idea for a plot until he can copyright it. He does admit, "I've written the same plot so many times, I'm tired of it." Pirandello proposes that they write a play without actors, while Shaw counters he would prefer to write one that did not require an audience. Shaw also comes up with a seventy-five-page preface to the play, putting the others to sleep as he reads it. In the end, when Shaw and Pirandello appear costumed as St. Peter and God, the chief physician assures his orderly that neither man is dangerous. Have we been dealing all this time with two more inmates? Pirandello remarks, "We are not as we are but only as we think we are."

But then who was Mr. Parker? There was no question that he was played by George M. Cohan, "the most beloved of the performers on Broadway and the most uncanny of theatrical prestidigitators." Still, he was seen in Cohan's **Pigeons and People** (1-16-33, Sam H. Harris) as an enigmatic figure. A young bachelor, Joseph Heath (Walter Gilbert), who for months has watched Parker feed and talk to the pigeons in the park, invites him home after listening to his story—"the most tragic story of a man's life I've ever heard," but one not without its comic side. Unfortunately, Parker, who insists that pigeons are "easier to understand than people," is a difficult guest, refusing all hospitality and asking his host how he can be certain that he—Parker—is not bamboozling him or is not a menacing criminal. He pulls the same routine on Heath's young lawyer buddy (Paul McGrath), the men's lady friends, Heath's

servants, a detective, and a doctor. His questions and comments often anger these folk, especially when he punctuates them by tapping his listeners on the shoulder with the hat he keeps folded in his hand. But he usually mollifies them with his assurance, "I'm straightaway." When he takes his leave, the detective (Edward Nannery) hurries after him, a short time later phoning Heath to say that he has discovered who Parker really is. But Heath promises not to tell anyone else—including the unmentioned audience. Nor is the audience ever told what Parker's story—referred to time and again—was about. Cohan played the role to the hilt: "He swings his knees as merrily as before; cocks his head knowingly from side to side; shoots piercing looks with his commanding eyes; cries 'Ha-ha-ha' triumphantly when he makes his points." Burns Mantle characterized the piece as "a lark, a stunt, an amusing mystery." It was unusual in other ways. The action was continuous and there were no intermissions, although the play was full-length (and not one of the down-sized ripoffs that so many later intermissionless plays became). Moreover, it was offered at a low $2.20 top when most hits were getting $3.30. Yet the low prices, the critical plaudits, and Cohan's much bruited popularity could not lure patrons. The play closed after seventy performances, and Cohan, as he so often did when frustrated, announced his retirement. Luckily, he changed his mind once again.

The still struggling Group Theatre had one of its worst fiascoes with Dawn Powell's **Big Night** (1-17-33, Maxine Elliott's). Powell was a then popular novelist whose works were soon forgotten, although an attempt was made to reintroduce them fifty years later. Her story, like that in the company's last offering, took a sour look at the advertising world. To assure his getting the Fortune Stores account, Ed Bonney (Lewis Leverett) demands his wife, Myra (Stella Adler), "be nice" to the chain's crass owner, Bert Schwartz (J. Edward Bromberg). Myra, who knew Bert years ago, had had to slap his face then and leave the café where their paths had crossed. At the Bonneys' noisy party, Bert again makes a pass and Myra attempts to repulse him until Ed demands she allow Bert to hug and kiss her. The next morning Bert awards Ed the account. He also snidely tells Ed he cannot recall what happened after the kiss. Myra, lying, claims she and Bert went much further, but that does not bother Ed since he has landed the account. His indifference to the lie she has just told so infuriates her that she packs her bags and leaves. The play's $2.20 top, like that of *Pigeon and People*'s, was no attraction.

Elmer Rice, still crankily insisting on being his own producer, had his second flop in short order with **We, the People** (1-21-33, Empire). The expensive mounting had a cast of sixty, including forty-four speaking parts, and a huge number of settings, all of which helped hurry it on its way after a majority of critics rejected it as a blatant "propaganda show." The play begins with Helen Davis (Eleanor Phelps), a young schoolmarm, berating an Italian immigrant (Egisto Visser) for blaming his failures on the capitalistic system and allowing his boy (Charles La Torre) to disparage the country publicly. Helen comes from a happy family. Her father (Ralph Theadore) works at the mills; her kid brother, Allen (Hubert Rudley), is about to go to college. But then Mr. Davis loses his job and, when the bank he has used collapses, his savings. Helen must put off any hopes of marrying Bert Collins (Blaine Corner) until he can save his family's farm. Then Allen is arrested for stealing coal to keep his family warm, becomes a militant radical, and, framed for killing a policeman, is sentenced to death. In a subplot a Jewish professor (David Leonard) is dismissed for expressing leftish sympathies while another professor (Maurice Wells), from old-line Wasp stock, is handed a verbal slap on the wrist for the same offense. Through all this, the rich Mr. Drew (Pierre Watkins), albeit shocked that any employee could ask for a raise in such hard times, is mainly preoccupied with his wife's purchase of a fine Titian, his daughter's wedding to an English aristocrat, and seeing that dividends are not cut. All the disaffected come together at a meeting where the young Wasp professor, who has joined their ranks, cries out, "America has forsaken justice for lynch-law, democracy for class-rule, and liberty for tyranny." Critics reported that the rich men's speeches were booed from the balcony and that the rabble-rousing speeches of the last scene were cheered from the same quarters but hissed from the orchestra.

Only the refusal of Noel Coward and the Lunts to play the comedy longer confined the run of Coward's **Design for Living** (1-24-33, Ethel Barrymore) to 135 performances. Gilda (Lynn Fontanne), an elegantly bohemian interior decorator, is courted and has been loved by both Leo (Coward), a playwright, and Otto (Lunt), a painter. The men's madcap antics and their rivalry over her finally provoke her into marrying a pompous art dealer, Ernest Friedman (Campbell Gullan). This does not prevent the other men from returning and cavorting with her as a threesome. Ernest is disgusted by such a "three-sided erotic hotch-potch," prompting Leo to point out that King Solomon was highly thought of although he had a hundred wives. Ernest exits, leaving the three to set up housekeeping together. The stars had a field day—"Miss Fontanne, with her slow, languorous deliberation; Mr. Lunt, with his boyish enthusiasm; Mr. Coward, with his nervous, biting charity." Subsequent biographies and autobiographies spoke of different figures, but *Variety* reported that the show

had cost $18,000 to mount and earned back all but $3000 of that during tryouts. A sellout opening night with a special $11.00 top ticket erased the remaining debt. The rest of the run was gravy, and since the play asked and got a $4.40 top at a time when other plays were cutting prices, the gravy was lush indeed.

One of the plays cutting prices was Isabel Dawn and Boyce de Gaw's **Marathon** (1-27-33, Mansfield), which harked back to bygone days by asking only a $1.65 top. The story was meant to spoof or expose the dance marathons sweeping the country. A single set depicted a large tent, with the dance floor in the center, the stands on one side, and the manager's canvased-off space on the other. Although a comic highlight told of a former five-and-ten salesgirl who becomes delirious under the strain, the main story focused on April Jones (Dawn). Having lost her job as a waitress, she enters the contest hoping to earn enough money to head west. The man she selects as a partner, Gilly Bray (Frank Rowan), turns out to be a racketeer. Both he and the dance promoter, "Too Soon" Decker (Robert Strange), proposition her. The men then get to fighting, and Decker kills Gilly. Dawn does not win, but she does sell her story to a newspaper for $500. Even at $1.65, playgoers were not interested, so *Marathon* folded after five performances.

Dana Burnet and William B. Jutte's **Bad Manners** (1-30-33, Playhouse) lasted three performances longer. One morning Craig Baldwin (Bert Lytell), a rising architect, tells Marion Lane (Leona Maricle) to take her kimono and go back to her own apartment. He is about to head out for the wedding of his best friend to Lois Aiken. Just then Lois (Margaret Sullavan) appears, saying she has decided not to marry Craig's friend. She and Craig agree that she will become Craig's secretary and they will live together—platonically. Anyone who could not fill in the rest of the plot had never been to the theatre before. Once again critics rued that the throaty-voiced, blonde and beautiful Sullavan had not found the sort of vehicle she deserved.

A play from England, Edward Knoblock and Beverly Nichols's **Evensong** (1-31-33, Selwyn), ran twice as long, and playgoers who missed it apparently missed some very fine acting. Its central figure is an aging prima donna, Irela (Edith Evans)—a totally vain and selfish woman who attempts to dominate and cruelly use everyone who crosses her path, including the niece (Jane Wyatt) who has come from Canada to be her secretary. Irela has trouble singing as beautifully and easily as once she could, so when her old lover, the Archduke Theodore, sends her a proposal of marriage she is tempted. But some truths from her brutally frank manager (Jacob Ben-Ami) convince her to reject the proposal and head out to offer concerts of the less demanding songs she is still able to sing. The curtain falls as she tearfully listens to a recording she made in her heyday.

At the Guild on February 5 a group calling itself the Stage Alliance began a handful of performances of Natalie Hays Hammond's modern adaptations of mostly French medieval miracle and morality plays.

Down in the Village, Percy Shaw and T. Wigney Percyval's **One Wife or Another** (2-6-33, Provincetown Playhouse) threw in the towel after three playings. Realizing her own marriage is in trouble, a woman suggests to several friends that they all change spouses. They give it a try, but wind up convinced their first choices were the best.

Another three-performance flop was **Low Bridge** (2-9-33, 57th St. Playhouse), which Frank B. Elser derived from Walter D. Edmonds's novel *Rome Haul*. The playwright was determined not to let the matter rest there. He sought out a more experienced dramatist, and their reworking, with a much better cast, would be one of the hits of the 1934–35 season as *The Farmer Takes a Wife*.

After a dismal parade of shows that ran no more than two weeks at best, Edna and Edward P. Riley's **Before Morning** (2-9-33, Ritz) managed to eke out a three-and-a-half-week run. Just before her marriage to a successful businessman, Elsie Manning (Jessie Royce Landis), an actress, is visited by her former lover, a married man. He drops dead in her apartment, so several of her friends, pretending to be helping a drunkard, take him to their car and deliver the body to a sanitarium. But the sanitarium's vicious doctor (McKay Morris) claims that the dead man was poisoned. The physician found a copy of the man's will in his pocket and demands as hush money half the $200,000 Manning is to inherit. Manning is off the hook when the dead man's wife (Louise Prussing) is shown to be the killer.

Wee and Leventhal next brought in a ten-year-old bit of hokum, *The Monster* (8-9-22), to the Waldorf on the 10th. The towering comedian De Wolf Hopper played the murderous, mad doctor who is finally brought to justice, a role originated by the late Wilton Lackaye.

Nan O'Reilly and Rupert Darrell's **Four O'Clock** (2-13-33, Biltmore) was based very loosely on the still unsolved murder a year earlier of a notorious blackmailer and dope peddler, Vivian Martin. A lovesick young man kills himself after he is caught stealing $25,000 from the bank where he works to give to Donna Mason (Ara Gerald), the woman with whom he is infatuated. As part of its news story, a tabloid prints a picture of Donna and her daughter. This drives the shamed daughter to commit suicide, too. Donna vows revenge on the tabloid's publisher. Along with an underworld connection, Edward Cannelli (Marc Loebell), she

sets out to trap and blackmail the man, but in a shootout is herself killed. Two weeks and the melodrama was gone.

Disdainful notices sealed the fate of Kenneth Phillips Britton's **The Sophisticrats** (2-13-33, Bijou) even more quickly. Nell Newsome (Helen Brooks), who lives in an arty community in Connecticut and publishes titillating poetry under titles such as *Bedroom Ballads,* has claimed to be romantically involved with a novelist named Lewis Beach, even though she is really a virgin. Beach's sudden arrival in her town exposes her hoax. But the man (Lewis Martin) is then himself exposed as not the real Beach. The son (Ben Lackland) of Nell's local publisher (Doan Borup) sets matters aright and proposes marriage to her.

The season's sleeper was James Hagan's **One Sunday Afternoon** (2-15-33, Little). Among those who admired the play, Richard Lockridge welcomed it in the *Evening Sun* by noting, "It is simple-hearted, and that disarms. Mr. Hagan has, by the sincerity and frequent delicacy of his writing, made the story real and affecting." Yet the comedy almost went down in the record books as a short-lived dud. Roosevelt's closing of the banks, coming on top of sharply divided notices and poor attendance, forced the show to close. Then the head of a large cut-rate ticket agency came to its rescue and reopened it at cut prices. Within a short time, it had caught on. Later it was rumored to have come within a single vote of capturing the Pulitzer Prize. Biff Grimes (Lloyd Nolan), a small-town dentist, and his drinking buddy, Snappy Downer (Percy Helton), are sitting one Sunday afternoon in Grimes's office, boozing and reminiscing. When Snappy remarks that Bill should have married Virginia Brush and not allowed Hugo Barnstead to steal her away, Grimes at first insists that he long has forgotten the affair. But after the manager of the local hotel phones to ask Grimes if he can take an emergency patient, a prominent out-of-town banker named Hugo Barnstead, Grimes agrees and gloats, "Hugo Barnstead—I've got you right where I want you." The scene flashes back many years earlier when Amy Lind (Francesca Bruning) and Virginia (Mary Holman) are waiting for their dates and Amy warns Virginia that Biff has a somewhat unsavory reputation; "I heard that he drinks and smokes." Biff is meant to be dating Amy, but he has eyes only for Virginia. On a later date with Virginia, Biff punches a boy who has made a smart-aleck remark about her, but she is upset at his public impetuosity and walks away. Afterwards a fight between Biff and Hugo over Biff's helping workers at the plant Hugo's uncle owns leads to Hugo's having Biff arrested. A short time later Biff learns that Hugo and Virginia are married. Back at Grimes's office an overpainted, crabby Virginia appears and complains of her husband, "God knows what I've suffered married to this death house buzzard." Biff realizes how lucky he had been to have married the right girl, Amy. According to some post-Broadway reviews, Grimes gets his revenge by extracting Barnstead's tooth without using gas, but the published text disagrees.

Arthur Hopkins, one of Broadway's most admired producers, had recently written an article for the magazine *Outlook* in which he gloomily predicted that the days of live theatre were numbered. Now, apparently unable to find a suitable play among those submitted to him, he produced one of his own, **Conquest** (2-18-33, Plymouth), which lasted little more than a week. It retold the Hamlet story in modern terms. Shortly after sending his son, Frederick "Fritz" Nolte, Jr. (Raymond Hackett) overseas to study engineering in Germany, the elder Nolte (Henry O'Neill), owner of a company manufacturing computing machines, drops dead of a heart attack on learning that his wife (Judith Anderson) has sold her controlling interest in the business to an industrial promoter, Cornelius Garvan (Hugh Buckley), whom she subsequently marries. The younger Fritz returns home and in the somberly lit family mansion hears the voice of his father's ghost demand vengeance. By raiding the stock market, Fritz regains control of the firm and forces Garvan to flee to Europe. Learning this, Fritz's mother seems to go mad. But at least Fritz is now free to marry his sweetheart (Jane Wyatt).

Having set aside their recent failure and needing an attraction for the theatre they had leased, Guthrie McClintic and Katharine Cornell turned to Sidney Howard's **Alien Corn** (2-20-33, Belasco). Elsa Brandt (Cornell) is a fine young pianist who has had to sacrifice her career and teach in a dreary, small-town midwestern school in order to support her crippled father (Siegfried Rumann). At the outbreak of the last war, her parents, a diva and a violinist, had been in America and had been interned as aliens. Her mother had succumbed in the flu epidemic, and her father had crippled his arm while attempting suicide. Elsa is courted by two men. One is the embittered, radical Julian Vardaman (Luther Adler), whom one colleague characterizes as "just another of the great army of academic refugees. They clutter up every college faculty because they're afraid to face real life." Her other suitor is a suave, rich married man, Harry Conway (James Rennie), who wants her as his mistress. An attempt to hold a joint concert with Mrs. Conway (Lily Cahill), who fancies herself a singer, leads to ugly complications. Elsa rejects both men, which provokes Julian into shooting himself. Aware of the scandal that could ensue, Elsa decides to leave the school. A policeman, investigating the suicide, asks Elsa if this is her home. She replies, "No. Vienna." Many critics thought the play, somewhat patently con-

trived with obvious foreshadowings and other such dramatic devices, was redeemed by its star. Mantle wrote in the *Daily News*, "Miss Cornell's Elsa is another of those luminous portraits of hers etched in ivory tints against a sort of dark velvet background. A saddened study and without much variety, but of deep feeling and convincing sincerity." Following a twelve-week stand the play toured briefly.

· · ·

Sidney [Coe] **Howard** (1891–1939) was born to pioneer stock in Oakland, Calif. He studied at the University of California and with Professor George Pierce Baker in his 47 Workshop at Harvard. For a time he supported himself writing for newspapers and magazines. His first play to reach Broadway, *Swords* (1921), was a failure. However, he scored a major hit with *They Knew What They Wanted* (1924). Later plays of interest included *Lucky Sam McCarver, Ned McCobb's Daughter,* and *The Silver Cord.*

· · ·

Virtually ignored by the critics was **Mighty Conlon** (2-20-33, Sutton), in which a politician must avenge his wife's being stolen from him yet not besmirch her reputation. In his study of the decade, Samuel L. Leiter lists the author as Oliver White.

George O'Neil's **American Dream** (2-21-33, Guild) was one of many Theatre Guild mountings able to remain before the footlights only as long as the Guild's subscription held out. It looked at three much separated generations of Daniel Pingrees. The first Daniel (Douglass Montgomery), in 1650, is ostracized for rebelling against his family's stern, Calvinist religious convictions. A later Daniel (Stanley Ridges), in 1849, heads West after becoming disgusted with the mills being built all over the area. In 1933, that Daniel's great-grandson, another Daniel (Montgomery), has, for all his wealth, become a Communist. He detests businessmen, asking, "Must not a business be operated by men who know what they want and how to get it? How, then, can we escape a dictatorship?" He has written a book on his beliefs which has become something of a best-seller for its kind, but, because he comes from old money, both it and he are rejected by the Communist Party whose acceptance he craves. His Communist friend, Jake Schwarz (Samuel Goldenberg), regretfully informs him that his upbringing leaves him "staring with a very correct look on your face at the big immaculate zero of life." The rejection and the discovery that his wife (Gale Sondergaard) not only loves Schwarz but has come to believe that Daniel is either impotent or a homosexual drive him to shoot himself. All this happens at a wedding anniversary party his wife has thrown and to which she has invited a motley assortment of bohemians and socialites. One of the guests, a notorious nymphomaniac

(Edith Van Cleve), looks at Daniel's body and exclaims, "I guess I know my Ibsen. People don't do such things." The action of all three acts took place in the main room of the Pingree home, modified only by the fashions and technology of each century.

More flops hurried in. The heroine of Stanley Kimmel's **Black Diamond** (2-23-33, Provincetown Playhouse) is a mine owner's wife who attempts to educate her lover. After her husband is killed during some labor troubles and her own brother is lynched for the killing, she and her lover run off.

Several critics thought that Livingston Platt's two views of the rotting hulk of an old ship, docked in an African river, were the best things about Norman Reilly Raine and Frank Butler's **Hangman's Whip** (2-24-33, St. James). The *Dei Gratia* had been in better condition thirty years before when Prin (Montague Love), a trader, had dropped anchor. Since that time he has brutalized the natives and his associates, and grown fat and slovenly. He seems to have finally met his match in young Ballister (Barton MacLane). But then the natives rise up. Ballister helps Prin's young wife (Helen Flint) and the man (Ian Keith) she really loves, a German fugitive, escape. The two men are left alone. A poisoned dart strikes and kills Ballister, so Prin prepares to die by himself in the natives' final onslaught.

J. Augustus Smith, a black, was the author of **Louisiana** (2-27-33, 48th St.), whose plot some reviewers thought followed last season's *Savage Rhythm* with suspicious closeness. Myrtle Simpson (Edna Barr) comes back from school in the North to her little black community in the swamps of Louisiana. Thomas Catt (Morris McKenney) is determined to have Myrtle work at his "juk," or free and easy cabaret, that he runs on the other side of the river. The Reverend Amos Berry (Smith), who once served on a chain gang with Catt and who is Myrtle's uncle, knows Catt is up to no good. Uncertain that his own prayers can deal with the situation, Berry approaches Aunt Hagar (Laura Bowman), the local voodoo priestess, and asks her to try her skills. She promises first to blind, then to kill, Catt. At a revival meeting, Catt attempts to take Myrtle, but he is struck sightless by a bolt of lightning. Rushing out, he becomes fatally mired in quicksand. Myrtle and her beau (Lionel Monagas), who is Hagar's nephew, promise Hagar to keep voodoo traditions alive. Just as white critics regularly spotlighted the "high stepping" and "risible dental displays" in black musicals, so they once again saved their highest praise for the moving singing in the revival scene and for the writhing voodoo ceremony.

Even Owen Davis could not put an end to the run of failures, although his **A Saturday Night** (2-28-33, Playhouse) brought the much liked Peggy Wood back to Broadway after several seasons in London. She and Hugh O'Connell played the middle-class, middle-aged James Langdons, who are about to go out for a rare evening on the town and enjoy the *Scandals*. But then Jim learns that his promotion will not go through, so dashes out for a few drinks. Their son, Ted (Richard Jack), is brought home with an injury sustained in a basketball game, and their daughter, Sally (Elizabeth Young), takes off with a seedy young man and soon comes back quite tipsy and disheveled. Dick Carrington (Arthur Margetson), a business associate of Jim's, picks that moment to tell Mrs. Langdon of his love for her and propose that they run off. Jim, in turn, picks that very instant to return and overhear Dick. An angry Jim tells his wife not to hesitate, since he also has had flings on the side. But in short order the couple is reconciled. In a telling comment on the times, *Variety* reported that this was William A. Brady's third offering of the season, and that no other old-line producer had as yet mounted three productions during the year.

Another youngish actress who had been spending time in London—the last eleven years, in fact—returned to Broadway the next evening. Tallulah Bankhead used her own money, though she allowed Arch Selwyn, an older producer, to take credit for mounting Edward Roberts and Frank Cavett's **Forsaking All Others** (3-1-33, Times Square). It takes the whole of the first act for Mary Clay to learn that her fiancé, Dillon Todd (Anderson Lawlor), has left her in the lurch at the altar and married someone else. When the minister (Robert Hudson) who was to perform the ceremony tries to comfort her, she whips back, "Thanks. I know. Jesus loves me." Mary, Jeff Tingle (Fred Keating), the man she had rejected in favor of Dillon, and Dillon and his new wife (Millicent Hanley) bump into each other at a speakeasy. The two women cross swords verbally, with Mary drawing all of the blood. Dillon has second thoughts about his marriage, agrees to a hurried Mexican divorce, and proposes to Mary again. She accepts, but come wedding-time she runs off with Jeff. Although Ilka Chase did some scene-stealing as a tipsy bridesmaid, the show was almost entirely Bankhead's. Gilbert Gabriel praised "her vitality, humor and her half gamin, half ladylike loveliness." Her popularity and notoriety kept the comedy alive for fourteen weeks. When the show closed, the Times Square became the latest house on 42nd Street to convert to films. While several major theatres on the street held out for a few more years, even then, as Bankhead noted in her autobiography, the once elegant street had begun to look "like the Bowery, cluttered up with flea circuses, grind picture theaters, orange drink stands and fake jewelry joints."

Another play opened the same night next door, Hall Johnson's **Run, Little Chillun** (3-1-33, Lyric). Johnson, who was much admired for his famous black choir, wrote not only the play but all the original music employed. In Hall's saga, Parson Jones (Harry Belden) of the Hope Baptist Church is upset when his son and anointed successor, Jim (Alston Burleigh), is lured to a revival meeting of the New Day Pilgrims by the infamous seductress Sulamai (Fredi Washington). Later, she claims she is pregnant with Jim's child. At a competitive revival led by the elder Jones, Jim is lured back into the fold, and Sulamai is killed by a bolt of lightning. Once again, critics insisted the fervor of the revival scenes was the best part of the show. *Variety* recorded that "dirge-like warbling of gibberish flows into choir singing, climaxing in a wild orgy of dancing. The picture is kaleidoscopic, a myriad of half-naked figures in frenzied action." The play outran Bankhead's by two weeks.

Critics liked Lyon Mearson and Lillian Day's **Our Wife** (3-2-33, Booth) no better than they had Bankhead's vehicle. But this time they found no dominating star to save the night, although several of them gave Humphrey Bogart some of the best notices he had yet received. Jerry Marvin (Bogart), a short-story writer, shares a Paris apartment and bed with Margot Drake (Rose Hobart), a newspaperwoman, even though Jerry is a married man, whose wife has remained in America. Jerry's "dizzy dame" wife, Barbara (June Walker), finally appears, prompting the lovers to run off to an island in the Bay of Naples. There Jerry is arrested after making fun of Mussolini, but, in a crap game with his guards, he wins his freedom, the soldiers' money, and one of their uniforms. Jerry then agrees to divorce Barbara and marry Margot.

Maxwell Anderson's **Both Your Houses** (3-6-33, Royale) took a theatrically jaundiced look at endemic corruption in Congress. After Alan McClean (Shepperd Strudwick) was fired for exposing the misappropriation of funds at the school where he taught, his muckraking publisher father used the story to help elect Alan to Congress. Aware of his history, members of the Appropriations Committee to which he has been assigned are alarmed. Their fears are quickly justified when Alan denounces the very contractors who had supported his election and argues against a dam in his own district. Solomon Fitzmaurice (Walter C. Kelly), a kind, understanding old congressman who had once been an idealist and nearly had been voted out of office because of it, tells Alan, "So I began to play ball, just to pacify the folk back home. And it worked. They've been reëlecting me ever since—reëlecting a fat crook because he gets what they want out of the Treasury." Alan is not swayed. After failing to defeat a carefully negotiated pork-barrel bill, he does an about-face and offers a bill which includes every congressman's request no matter

how absurd. To his disgust, the bill passes and he is hailed as a political genius. Praised by Atkinson as "the best of the latter-day propaganda plays and one of the best plays of the season," the drama barely ran past the Theatre Guild's subscription list and headed out for the road when it was awarded the Pulitzer Prize (the second year in a row a play about politics won the award). Hurried back in, it ran an additional four weeks for a total of 104 performances.

Elmer Harris's *Young Sinners,* a tale of a failed attempt to rehabilitate some flaming youth, was revived the same night at the Ambassador for the second time since its original production in November of 1929. This time it ran nine weeks.

A second revival that evening was the Civic Repertory's return of *The Cherry Orchard,* to be performed at the New Amsterdam when *Alice in Wonderland* was not on the boards.

Lou Tellegen, the matinee idol who had been Sarah Bernhardt's leading man in her last years, made a final and very short-lived Broadway appearance, before his sensational suicide, in Saxon Kling's **The Lady Refuses** (3-7-33, Bijou). His current leading lady was another favorite of bygone years, Cecil Spooner, also in her Broadway farewell. Nancy Whitehouse Parkes Rogers falls in love with Jacques Castel, who owns the apartment in Nice that she has rented, and not even the wooings of two of her former husbands can dissuade her from eventually marrying Jacques. The play received some of the season's most brutal notices.

Critics were just as harsh on Sophie Treadwell's **Lone Valley** (3-14-33, Plymouth). A former prostitute (Marguerite Borough) attempts to lead a quiet, respectable life on a ranch far from her old haunts. When her past is disclosed, she is forced to run off. A young farmhand (Alan Baxter), who had fallen in love with her and drew deep spiritual satisfaction from their friendship, decides to follow her.

The busy Wee and Leventhal brought in two more of their revivals on two succeeding nights. *Riddle Me This,* almost a return engagement since it initially had been one of the preceding season's novelties, came into the Hudson on the 14th. On the 15th at the Waldorf, David Gray and Avery Hopwood's *The Best People* (8-19-24), in which children of highfalutin parents rebel against their snooty ways, raised its curtain. Both plays ran for more than two months.

A lone novelty also appeared on the latter evening, and lasted a lone performance. Arthur Ebenhack's **Marilyn's Affairs** (3-15-33, Mansfield) had been done in late January at the tiny, out-of-the-way Sutton as *Cinderella's Brothers* and excoriated by those critics who bothered to review it. Why it was revamped is uncertain. The story told of a wealthy young lady determined to help and possibly to marry a lower-class young man. She singles out a cobbler, a cop, and a taxi driver. She aids the first two and, apparently, weds the hackie, who turns out to be the police commissioner's son.

Gertrude Tonkonogy's **Three-Cornered Moon** (3-16-33, Cort) collected the sort of "money reviews" that promised a long run, yet it survived less than eight full weeks. The widowed Mrs. Rimplegar (Cecilia Loftus), her sons—Ken (Ben Lackland), Douglas (John Eldredge), and Ed (Elisha Cook, Jr.)—and her daughter, Elizabeth (Ruth Gordon), are true oddballs. When Mrs. Rimplegar loses her $100,000 savings in the stock market, none of the youngsters is truly prepared to work, although they all try. Elizabeth's beau, Donald (Richard Whorf), a would-be novelist, becomes a non-paying boarder at the Brooklyn home after being dispossessed again. Actually he likes being dispossessed, since it brings out his "executive ability—running around and telling people to put my etchings down here and my book-cases there." A young family friend, Dr. Alan Stevens (Brian Donlevy), also comes to stay with the family—but as a paying boarder. He is quietly in love with Elizabeth. When family matters seem to go from bad to worse, Elizabeth sends the hopelessly unrealistic Donald packing, telling him, "Love is not a potato. You can't eat it." She proposes to Alan, who, after mastering his surprise, accepts. Gordon won the best notices, with Gabriel observing, "She has such an infinite art of turning her lines over and over with the lightest finger-flip, so that every glint of wit and wistfulness twirl and merge with spectroscopic ease." The production marked the debut of two producers, Richard Aldrich, who would eventually become known as Mr. Gertrude Lawrence, and Alfred de Liagre, Jr.

· · ·

Alfred de Liagre, Jr. (1904–19) was born in Passaic, N.J., and studied at Yale. He did not enter the professional theatre until 1930, when he took work at the Woodstock Playhouse, then served as a stage manager in New York.

· · ·

The season's second one-performance fiasco followed just three nights after its first. In A. J. Minor's **Masks and Faces** (3-18-33, Liberty), a woman believes she is really making love to another man whenever she sleeps with her husband. A lady psychiatrist tells the husband to leave the house for a while and let two men, one of whom must be the imagined lover, come to her. The dream man turns out to be the psychiatrist's own fiancé, but everyone is properly paired by eleven o'clock. When the play folded, the theatre joined the growing ranks of 42nd Street playhouses converting to films.

Only one play separated the next one-performance fiasco from *Masks and Faces,* and that play, Michael

Birmingham and Gilbert Emery's **Far-Away Horses** (3-21-33, Martin Beck), hurried away after four performances. Like *Three-Cornered Moon,* it told of a mother and her brood. But this time the action was set in Ireland, and there were six children and a besotted husband to boot. No sensible doctor joins the household, so by the play's end matters are just as hopeless as they were at the beginning, especially after one of the sons fritters away his mother's $400 savings and a daughter's savings are squandered on her pregnant sister and the sister's lazy spouse.

In Myla Jo Closser and Homer Little's **Raw Meat** (3-22-33, Provincetown Playhouse) the son of two famous animal hunters, disdained because he prefers photography to hunting, captures an escaped circus lion that his parents and the circus people have been trying vainly to retake.

Langdon Mitchell's *The New York Idea* (11-19-06) was revived at the Heckscher on the same night. There was no Mrs. Fiske to lend her singular authority to this mounting, which disappeared after three playings.

Robert Ober's **Ann Adams, Spinster** (3-25-33, Sutton) opened on one Saturday night and, apparently, closed the next Saturday. It told of a novelist (Ober) who runs off to India and lets his unwed mistress (Mabel Taliaferro) raise their child alone. He returns a quarter of a century later to somehow right the wrong.

By lasting six weeks, Daniel Kussell's **The Party's Over** (3-27-33, Vanderbilt) briefly broke the jinx of single-figure runs. Bruce Blakely (Harvey Stephens) has dutifully supported his shiftless father (George Graham), his snooty, DAR-obsessed mother (Effie Shannon), his Yaley brother (Geoffrey Bryant) who brings home a gum-chewing-waitress bride (Claire Trevor), his sister (Peggy Conklin), and her crooner spouse (Ross Alexander). But when his own business turns sour he tells them they are on their own and heads off with the divorcée (Katharine Alexander) he loves.

Shorter runs returned with Frederick Rath's **Her Tin Soldier** (4-6-33, Playhouse), which survived for a mere two performances. A dashingly handsome usher (Harry Ellerbe) is enlisted to serve as corespondent for the daughter (Emily Lowry) of a movie theatre magnate in her divorce. She wants to wed a West Point cadet. By evening's end, on daddy's sumptuous yacht, it is the usher whom the girl decides to marry.

At the Mecca Auditorium, which in afteryears became home to the City Center, the Reverend Joseph M. Congedo's passion play, **The Tragedy of the Ages,** was mounted starting on the 6th for a few showings, but caused no stir.

For Services Rendered (4-12-33, Booth) was one of Somerset Maugham's talkiest and least successful plays. It looked at an unhappy English family never able to recover from their experiences in the war. Among the cast were Jean Adair, Fay Bainter, Leo G. Carroll, Henry Daniell, Walter Kingsford, Percy Waram, and Jane Wyatt.

Jessica Ball's **Strange Gods** (4-15-33, Ritz) was the latest in the season's many single-digit flops. A young couple has come to the Florida wilds seeking a rare butterfly. The wife takes under her wing a young "cracker," and when he captures the butterfly, the frustrated, embittered husband shoots himself. Believing reports of the suicide will hurt the widow, the cracker claims he murdered the scientist. But the widow's college sweetheart, a still single lawyer, defends the cracker. Following the young man's acquittal, the lawyer proposes marriage to the widow and is accepted.

Susan Glaspell and Norman Matson's **The Comic Artist** (4-19-33, Morosco) managed to survive for two and a half weeks. Karl Rolf (Robert Allen) is a comic-strip artist who wonders aloud why his central figure must always get boffed in the last frame. He gets boffed himself when he and his wife (Lora Baxter) visit his brother (Richard Hale) and sister-in-law (Blanche Yurka) on Cape Cod, and his brother takes up with Karl's wife, whom he had known years before. But Karl's sister-in-law is a no-nonsense gal, so the couples are properly reunited.

A number of critics saw hints of the Montagues and the Capulets in J. N. Gilchrist's **Unto the Third** (4-20-33, Bijou). Lucien Case (Seth Arnold) is the vindictive, psalm-spouting patriarch of an old Massachusetts family. His wife and his son are weaklings, but his granddaughter, Muriel (Loretto Shea), has gumption. She defies him by announcing her engagement to George Talbot (Sam Wren), son of the Maine governor who is one of Case's bitterest political foes. Muriel's determination wins the day. But it couldn't win over any ticket buyers.

Playgoers also rejected the third reformatory drama to open in the last two seasons, Albert Bein's **Little Ol' Boy** (4-24-33, Playhouse). Cottage D at the Southwestern Reform School (located in the Midwest despite its name) houses a mixture of youngsters. Among the most hardened is Red Barry (Burgess Meredith). Robert Locket (Edwin Philips) is a relatively decent newcomer, committed for having tried to smuggle a gun to his imprisoned brother. He has caught the eye and aroused the mother instinct of Mrs. Sanger (Ara Gerald), the pathetically unhappy wife of the cottage master. She attempts to soften his position. When the authorities come across a letter of protest written to the governor, they blame Red. Robert steps forth to admit he wrote it. A fight with the guards ensues, and, after Robert knocks out one of the guards, he and Red attempt an escape. Robert is shot dead and Red recaptured. When

Mrs. Sanger asks Red if Robert had any last words for her, he barks, "He passed out a-hatin' everybody just like a man with any guts should." But when she responds, "If one ever quit this trainin' school without gall in his heart it'd be a wonder," Red is sufficiently moved to lie, "Well, he did have a word for yu, woman." Lionel Stander won applause as the reformatory's longest-resident inmate.

Don Lockbiler and Arthur Barton's **Man Bites Dog** (4-25-33, Lyceum) had some nifty ideas that neither the writers nor the director could capitalize on. Doc Sanger (Leo Donnelly) the managing editor of the *Daily Tab*, a newspaper awash in red ink, is told to shape it up or he will be shipped out. Luck comes his way in the person of pretty Renee Brennan (Dennie Moore), who hurries into the paper's bustling offices to warn her reporter-lover that her husband, Joe, the champ, who had entered the ring the previous night drunk and been knocked out, is on his way to show the reporter that he still has his stuff. Joe (Jack Stone) appears, drunk again, and kayos the man, but Renee pulls a gun and shoots him. Sanger and his staff hide the body in a closet, disguise Renee as an Indian squaw, and prepare to publish an exclusive telling of how an abusive Joe was killed in self-defense by Renee for the honor of her tribe. When Joe stumbles out of the closet, not quite as dead as everyone had imagined, Sanger has to stop the presses and faces ruin, until Renee picks up the gun again and this time shoots Joe for keeps. She needed only enough bullets for four performances.

Lillian Gish had to use her lethal weapons for nearly a month in John Colton and Carleton Miles's **Nine Pine Street** (4-27-33, Longacre), which was based on the Lizzie Borden story, with Lizzie rechristened Effie Holden. Effie blames a neighboring widow's breaking—accidentally on purpose, she claims—her mother's medicine bottle for her mother's death. On the day of her wedding to Warren Pitt (Raymond Hackett), the assistant pastor at her church, Effie learns that her banker-father (Robert Harrison) and the widow, Carrie (Roberta Beatty), have eloped. She puts off her own wedding. In short order Carrie has earned the disdain of all her neighbors. When Effie attempts to get an inheritance she is entitled to so that she can help Warren make good some church funds he used for other purposes, Carrie threatens to expose him. Effie follows her upstairs with a flatiron. She then tells her father not to expect dinner for "quite a while." After the bodies are found, Effie is put on trial, but, with the help of the church folk, she is acquitted. Many years later, a young reporter (Clinton Sundberg) comes to interview her. He tells her his editor "thinks the reason you never went away was some funny New England conscience idea of punishing yourself for something . . . as though you had put yourself in prison." But Effie stands by the story she told in court and continues to protest her innocence. "You will not soon forget," John Mason Brown predicted, "the moment when Miss Gish, shaking with hatred, follows her stepmother upstairs and kills her with the flatiron she has been using in the kitchen. Nor will you find it easy to banish from your memory Miss Gish's return down the stairs from the scene of the murder and the subsequent moment when she reaches for a heavy cane to brain her father as he sits on the sofa." (Although several other critics mentioned the cane, it is not in the directions in the Samuel French acting edition.)

Best Sellers (5-3-33, Morosco) was taken by Dorothy Cheston Bennett from Edouard Bourdet's *Vient de paraître*. A publisher (George Coulouris), furious that the author for whom he has pulled so many strings in order to win a major literary prize has signed with a rival house, convinces the judges to award the prize to a meek clerk's novel about a wife's early love affair. It turns out the clerk (Ernest Truex) has taken the material from the diary of his own wife (Peggy Wood). When he finds himself unable to write a sequel he suggests his wife have another affair. He then writes a book on his reactions—but so does his wife and so does her lover (Ian Keith). Truex, "always an expert in the whimsical pathos of a shrimp," won excellent notices, but Wood was perceived as wasted. Still, they helped the comedy survive for fifty-three performances.

The two plays that followed could not even chalk up such a modest run. Henry and Sylvia Lieferant's **Hilda Cassidy** (5-4-33, Martin Beck) told of an unusual triangle. Although Tom (Howard Phillips) marries Hilda (Stella Adler), he really loves Mamie (Sylvia Field). Not even a daughter by Hilda nor a prison sentence for bootlegging alters his affections. And when he attempts to prevent his daughter from marrying a racketeer, Hilda refuses to stand in the way of her daughter's happiness much as she has refused to put her foot down about Mamie.

Leo A. Levy and D. Frank Marcus set their **It Happened Tomorrow** (5-5-33, Ritz) in the distant future, when the United States has become the United Provinces of Mythica and is ruled by a Dictatrix (Helen Raymond), who, in hopes of preventing further wars, orders all male babies deported. Any woman having a male child will be considered a "babylegger." But Mythica's need for money eventually forces a return to the old, established ways.

The Theatre Guild ended its season with a revival of Luigi Charielli's *The Mask and the Face* (9-10-24), this time in a translation by Somerset Maugham. The story of a count who pretends to kill his wife because of her infidelity and, after spending time in jail for her sup-posed murder, later welcomes her back, had failed nine years before and failed once again.

Gladys Unger and Leyla Georgie's **$25 an Hour** (5-10-33, Masque) cast its limelight on Claude de Rozay (Georges Metaxa), whom stage fright had prevented from becoming an opera singer and who has settled for being a voice teacher in New York and something of a gigolo. When his mistress, Germaine (Olga Baclanova), a modiste, must spend some time in Paris, she asks quiet, shy Lucy (Jean Arthur) to look after him. By the time Germaine returns, a pretty, pert Lucy has won Claude away from her.

"There were mock cheers and hisses, there was ribald laughter in several wrong places" on the first night of John Washburne and Ruth Kennell's **They All Come to Moscow** (5-11-33, Lyceum). An American engineer (Jack Davis) working in Russia falls in love with Natalya Brikin (Tamara), a married woman. To the American's surprise and delight, Natalya's husband (Clifford Odets) has no objection to the affair. But a nefarious Russian (Boris Marshalov) scuttles it by raising all manner of difficulties.

June Moon (10-9-29), George S. Kaufman and Ring Lardner's send-up of the music business and middle-class strivings, was brought out again on the 15th at the Ambassador, with Harry Rosenthal, still in his original part of Maxie, the snide song arranger, given top billing. It ran until whammed by the heat at the end of June.

A second hit of the 1929–30 season, Laurence E. Johnson's *It's a Wise Child* (8-6-29), in which a young lady seeks to find a father to legitimatize a baby, was presented by the busy Wee and Leventhal at the Hudson on the next evening.

A third revival, this time Ibsen's *Ghosts,* was brought into the out-of-the-way Sutton on the 23rd with a cast of unknowns and quickly succumbed to thumbs-down notices.

The fourth revival in a row opened for an engagement of just one week, but highly welcoming reviews convinced its star-packed cast to keep it on the boards for three. *Uncle Tom's Cabin* (7-18-53) was the Players' annual outing and was presented at the Alvin on the 29th in a revised version by A. E. Thomas. Otis Skinner was Uncle Tom; Fay Bainter, Topsy; Elizabeth Risdon, Eliza; Thomas Chalmers, Simon Legree; and Pedro de Cordoba, George Harris. Other names in the cast included Malcolm Duncan, Sylvia Field, Ernest Glendinning, Minnie Dupree, and Gene Lockhart. Lois Shore was Eva. What delighted many reviewers was that the drama was played straight instead of being spoofed as some recent mountings had done. Although critics acknowledged the drama showed its age, they claimed the honest performances also showed how moving it still could be.

In Richard F. Flournoy's **Fly by Night** (6-2-33, Belmont) the young lady (Ruth Nugent) who runs the Ruth Clark Stock Company, a traveling tent show, has an abusive drunkard (Paul Guilfoyle) for a husband. His viciousness leads to a fight with a performer (Alan Bunce) in which the husband is killed when he falls and hits his head against a metal pole. His body is hidden away, but when it is discovered after a storm has knocked down the tent, the police assume the death was accidental.

Just before the premiere of Noel Pierce and Bernard C. Schoenfeld's **Shooting Star** (6-12-33, Selwyn), the principals involved all issued disclaimers, insisting the drama was not based on the life of the late Jeanne Eagels. Critics openly sneered. Stephen Rathbun of the *Sun* called the denial "foolish," while Mantle told his readers there was "no mistaking the intentions of either its authors or its star." That star was Francine Larrimore, who played the part of Julie Leander. Inspired by watching Duse, Julie abandons her husband and baby to become an actress. She moves from one manager to another on her ascent, even becoming one's mistress. Then she marries a handsome, socially prominent young lawyer (George Houston), who soon deserts her. His desertion drives her to drink and drugs. A sympathetic producer, Carl Hoffman [read Sam Harris] (Henry O'Neill), casts her as the man-baiting Carrie Smith in a South Seas drama, *Port of Call*. She makes a tremendous hit, but her addictions lead to her missing performances, and this in turn leads to Equity's censuring her. In a fit of depression she takes a fatal overdose. Larrimore, playing with "great force and effect," could not save the late-season entry.

The season ended the next evening when Edward J. Locke's *The Climax* (4-12-09), telling of a Svengali-like doctor who attempts to destroy a young singer's career, was revived at the Bijou. Unlike an earlier revival of the old hit, none of the original players recreated their parts. But Norma Terris, *Show Boat*'s first Magnolia, was cast as the singer.

1933–1934

Cautious optimism was the note of the hour. A singularly dreary summer prompted Broadway's incorrigible gaggle of keeners to wail that the theatre clearly was in its death throes. Then, in mid-September a spate of hits chased away the doom-criers. Business, too, began to look up—however hesitantly. Although the happy pace of late September and early October was not maintained, by season's end the record of new plays had not slipped further (*Variety*'s count was again 124), the proportion of flops had dropped slightly, and optimists sidled back into the driver's seat.

The dull summer began with Martin Mooney's **The Ghost Writer** (6-19-33, Masque). Bill Harkins (Hal Skelly), a failed author, desperate for cash, agrees to ghostwrite for a written-out creator of best-sellers. But then Bill is jailed for non-payment of alimony, the man for whom he has subbed dies, and Bill's girl, Peggy Winston (Peggy Conklin), is led to believe he is unfaithful. Fortunately, before she misconstrued the situation, Peggy had submitted one of Bill's stories to a magazine, and its publication leads to the expected happy ending. William Frawley received applause as Bill's ever resourceful buddy, while Ara Gerald was featured as a vamp.

June's only other entry was a revival of *A Church Mouse* at the Mansfield on the 26th, with Louise Groody becoming the latest musical comedy favorite to try her luck away from song-and-dance shows. The revival lasted one week.

July's only offerings were two more revivals (although one may have technically been a return engagement), both brought in by the busy team of Wee and Leventhal. On the 10th St. John Ervine's *John Ferguson* (5-13-19), telling of a kindly farmer who learns his weak son has killed the man who would foreclose on the farm's mortgage, came into the Belmont for seven weeks. Last season's *Dangerous Corner* began an eleven-week stay at the Waldorf on the 17th.

With settings that "looked to have come from the storehouse," the Shuberts brought out their first mounting of the season, William Miles and Donald Blackwell's **Going Gay** (8-3-33, Morosco). Since their son, George (George Walcott), has announced he will marry Ann Appleton (Diane Bourget), the very snooty T. Courtland-Smiths (Walter Kingsford and Thais Lawton) of Newport are resigned to entertaining her, her brash, vaudevillian mother, Daisy Appleton (Edith King), and Daisy's supposed secretary, Benny (Charles Halton), who is actually Daisy's husband. Daisy's presence is disruptive, and matters come to a head after Mr. Courtland-Smith attempts to sneak into her bed, only to find he has snuggled up with Benny. Ann and George's revelation that they have hurried off and been married reconciles the families. Reeling from poor notices, the play closed after three weeks.

Wee and Leventhal's third revival of the still young season was Howard Lindsay and Bertrand Robinson's *Tommy* (1-10-27), in which a wise uncle tricks a stubborn young lady into marrying the boy she is too proud to accept. The comedy began a three-week stand at the Forrest on August 7.

Act One: 1930–1944

More so than its inept writing, the tasteless jokes in Herbert P. McCormack's **Love and Babies** (8-22-33, Cort) offended many critics, who rued seeing such "expert players . . . hopelessly handicapped." Nona (Linda Watkins), frustrated at the refusal of her husband, Roddy (Ernest Truex), to have a child, invites a couple (Glenn Anders and Ruth Weston) to visit and to bring their baby. When that does not change Roddy's ideas, she threatens to find another man to father her child. Roddy then agrees to become a parent.

In London, Ivor Novello's **A Party** (8-23-33, Playhouse) was seen as a send-up of Tallulah Bankhead and Mrs. Patrick Campbell. So when William A. Brady decided to bring it to New York he attempted to enlist both ladies to, in effect, play themselves. Bankhead declined. At a party following the opening night of her latest West End play, Miranda Clayfoot (Lora Baxter), an actress who addresses everyone as "darling," attempts to vamp a former lover, now married, is nearly killed by his wife, turns her attention to a lord, then, after an aciduously worded but sensible lecture from the great old Mrs. MacDonald, decides to remain single and a star. Mrs. Campbell made her entrance in a long, elegant black gown, puffing on a huge cigar and cradling a white miniature Pekinese in her arm. She professed to want to play *King Lear,* so that she could get to wear a beard, and also recited some of Hecuba's lines from *The Trojan Women.* During the evening, entertainers (all playing themselves) at the party included Cissy Loftus in her famous imitations, and Gertrude Niesen and Leo Beers offering songs. The play was waved away as fourth-rate Noel Coward, but the *Evening Post*'s John Mason Brown did take time to observe that "Mrs, Patrick Campbell is one of those actresses who could bring majesty and subtlety to an Earl Carroll blackout." The five and a half weeks during which the play lingered were the oldtimer's last Broadway appearances.

Felicia Metcalfe's **Come Easy** (8-29-33, Belasco) was a largely unfunny comedy about a young Baltimore lady, Marcia Ward (Nancy Sheridan), who returns from attending a Philadelphia wedding with a handsome young count (Edward Raquello) in tow. Her newly impoverished, theatrically eccentric family is not pleased, and her boyfriend, Tobie (Bruce Evans), goes so far as to check out the count's credentials, only to learn there is no such man. But Tobie had misspelled the count's name. And the count proves he is a count just as the Wards once again regain their money. The play's humor ran to Mrs. Ward (Helen Lowell) telling a family member that she will make him a mustard plaster and his responding, "I don't think your mustard's so hot." Later, learning the count is just what he has

claimed he is, Mrs. Ward remarks, "He always did count with me."

Matters weren't any better at Marianne Brown Waters's **The Blue Widow** (8-30-33, Morosco), in which bantam Queenie Smith joined the parade of musical comedy stars showing off their skills in straight theatre. As Willie Hendricks, she made her entrance through some French doors at the Talbot home in Darien, Connecticut, and was soon being called "the poor little thing" after claiming to be the bereaved widow of a famous writer. But she is really a fraud and a man-hunter, who promptly sets about vamping Mr. Talbot (Albert Van Dekker). Exposed, she heads off with a millionaire (Ralph Locke) who was also a houseguest. In acknowledgment of her past celebrity, Smith was allowed to interpolate two songs into the evening.

All of the next three entries ran only a week or less. D. Hubert Connelly, a secretary to New York's police commissioner, based his play **Crucible** (9-4-33, Forrest) on a notorious breakout from the Tombs several years earlier. As luck would have it, a not dissimilar breakout took place two nights before the play opened, but notices condemning "some of the wordiest buncombe since 'Ten Nights in a Barroom' " erased whatever benefits the coincidence might have presented. Rejected by Rosemary (Genevieve Paul), Arlo Borsad (Edward Redding), a leading gangster, kidnaps the son of a Tombs guard and forces the guard (Don Costello) to smuggle guns to the inmates. After the bloody escape Arlo attempts to pin the blame on Rosemary's beau. The guard commits suicide, but Arlo is caught and held for trial.

Attempts to spoof radio, beer companies, advertising agencies, and gangsters in Albert G. Miller's **The Sellout** (9-6-33, Cort) got nowhere. The fanatically religious Mrs. Robbins (Minnie Dupree), who has inherited a failing advertising agency, is convinced by Emily Burke (Jane Seymour) that the only way to save the agency is to take on the Splitz beer account. The ploy is successful until snarling, gun-toting Big Mike Angelino (Robert H. Gordon), owner of a rival beer company, threatens mayhem if the account is not dropped. But the women manage to sell Angelino a 50 percent share in the agency, and the Splitz people the other 50 percent, thus making themselves rich and leaving the rivals as partners.

The Hatfields and the McCoys became the Holstons and McIntyres in Carty Ranck's **The Mountain** (9-11-33, Provincetown Playhouse). Zeke Holston (John Nicholson), a judge in Breathitt County, Kentucky, is patriarch of the Holston clan and long has participated in killing off the McIntyres. To his dismay, his college-educated son, Tom (William Lovejoy), has fallen in love with Molly McIntyre (Lois Jesson). Worse, the boy has been elected public prosecutor, and, in prosecuting the latest man to kill a McIntyre, he learns his father had ordered the killing. He decides he must bring his father to justice, but, before he can, the old man is shot dead by Molly's mother (Gertrude Fowler).

Leon Abrams and George Abbott's **Heat Lightning** (9-15-33, Booth) unfolded in an Arizona filling station lunchroom, probably not far from the petrified forest. Coming and going in the place are "hitchhikers, greasers [Mexicans], Reno divorcees," the last two ladies arguing over who will bed their handsome chauffeur. The place is run by two sisters, Olga (Jean Dixon) and Myra (Emily Lowry). Two gunmen, George (Robert Glecker) and the younger Jeff (Robert Sloane), appear, fleeing the police after killing someone in a Salt Lake City bank robbery. Years earlier George and Olga had been lovers, so George attempts to cozy up to her again. But when Olga realizes that he is merely trying to distract her in order that Jeff can burgle her safe, she shoots and kills George. Critics praised Glecker, especially his death scene in which he seemed flabbergasted that anyone would shoot him, but they found the usually comic Dixon sorrowfully miscast.

Virtually all the critics hailed Elizabeth McFadden's **Double Door** (9-21-33, Ritz) as the season's first nonmusical hit. (Earl Carroll's well-liked *Murder at the Vanities,* a revue with a murder mystery plot, had premiered two weeks earlier.) Richard Lockridge in the *Sun* proclaimed McFadden's thriller as "warranted to excoriate the nerves and send agreeable shivers up the spine." Since her father's death, cold, selfish Victoria Van Bret (Mary Morris) has lorded it over her sister, Caroline (Anne Revere), and her brother, Rip (Richard Kendrick), in the family's gloomily Victorian Fifth Avenue mansion. Appalled when Rip announced he would marry Anne Darrow (Aleta Freel), she subsequently refuses to attend the wedding even though it is held in the mansion, balks at handing over the pearls Rip's mother had left for whomever he wed, and then embarks on a plan of keeping Rip so busy he will have little time for his bride. She also hires a detective and tries to make it seem that Anne is having an affair with another man. Anne gives the charge the lie, and Rip berates his sister. In desperation, Victoria tricks Anne into entering a secret, soundproof room and locks her inside. She is rescued in the nick of time. Anne, Rip, and Caroline all leave the house for good. In her haste to depart, Anne forgets to take the pearls. Alone, Victoria sits gloating over them—"The pearls! . . . My pearls! . . . *Mine!*" The thriller ran eighteen weeks.

Sidney Kingsley's **Men in White** (9-26-33, Broadhurst) ran far longer, winning the Pulitzer Prize, playing into the following summer, and giving the Group Theatre its first smash hit. Because his father-in-law-to-be has agreed to become a trustee of St. George's Hospital, a young intern, Dr. Ferguson (Alexander Kirkland), is offered an associateship. His mentor, the distinguished Dr. Hochberg (J. Edward Bromberg), is dismayed, since he believes that the talented youngster should spend a year in Vienna and then further years of intensive study. Ferguson's fiancée, Laura (Margaret Barker), is all for his working less hard. When, for a second night in a row, he pleads work and backs out of a date, she is furious. Exhausted and unsettled by Laura's fury, the intern finds solace in the arms of an attractive nurse (Phoebe Brand). The girl becomes pregnant and dies following an abortion. Laura is not sympathetic, especially after Ferguson opts for the year in Vienna and additional study. He tells Laura, "It's not easy for any of us. But in the end our reward is something richer than simply living." When Laura can only say that maybe she'll be waiting on his return from Vienna, Ferguson bids her good-bye and turns to resume his work. Not all the reviewers were bowled over, though even the fault-finders saw the virtues of what the *American*'s Gilbert Gabriel called "an intensely phoney and intensely harrowing play" and the *Herald Tribune*'s Percy Hammond saw as "an honest, tricky and propaganda show that can be attended without a sacrifice of intelligence." Superb ensemble acting and the brilliant recreation of hospital life added to its public appeal. It also brightly launched Kingsley's career.

. . .

Sidney Kingsley [né Kirschner] (1906–95) was the Philadelphia-born son of a dentist. He began writing plays while studying at Cornell. After graduation he acted briefly before seeing this play reach Broadway.

. . .

For some time now both tradesheets and newspapers had been running stories about the plight of Jews in Nazi Germany, including the expulsion of the famed Max Reinhardt from his own theatre. In *Men in White* mention is made of Hochberg's having wanted Ferguson to study in Berlin, but that the doctor he was supposed to have worked under had been forced to flee. The same night that Kingsley's play premiered saw the opening of **Kultur** (9-26-33, Mansfield), which Adolf Philipp purportedly took from the German of Theodore Weachter. Broadway rumor said the two men were one and the same. It was, in any case, the first play to deal, however ineptly, with the situation in Germany, although no country was specified. Professor Koerner (Charles Coburn), a famous surgeon, is dismissed from his post after it is discovered his grandfather was named Kohn. But when the new chancellor is seriously injured in an automobile accident, Koerner is called in and saves his life. Some of the blood the patient was given was from a Jewish donor, and in the recovery room the chancellor is reported to be babbling about tolerance. His horrified associates offer to consider Koerner a full-blooded Aryan and restore his position if he will hush up the matter. Koerner prefers to leave and settle in Paris. Many critics felt the play was dull and, even worse, attempted to treat the whole matter as comedy, so much so that, as one paper reported, "the most ardent Nazi-baiters in a frankly partisan audience were hard put to keep properly inflamed." The piece was hurried away after little more than a week.

Clare Kummer, once so highly praised but recently long absent from Broadway, displeased New York with her latest work, **Amourette** (9-27-33, Henry Miller), expanded from her old vaudeville sketch "The Choir Singer." Scandal explodes in still puritanical 1840 Massachusetts after sweet little Amourette Tucker (Francesca Bruning) runs off in the same coach as the Rev. Hiram Hallowell (Byron McGrath), who was known to be one of her suitors. Her family demands the couple wed, but Amourette proves that nothing untoward occurred and announces she will marry the man of her choice, Parson Wylie (Charles Coleman).

The season's second smash hit was Kenyon Nicholson and Charles Robinson's **Sailor, Beware!** (9-28-33, Lyceum), which John Mason Brown applauded as "an uproariously funny and rowdy comedy" and which chalked up 500 performances. When Chester "Dynamite" Jones (Bruce MacFarlane) returns, after a leave, to the U.S.S. *Dakota*, docked in Panama, his sea bag contains forty-two letters, seven packages, and nine cards—each one from a different gal he has wooed. Such is his vaunted prowess that his fellow sailors quietly take bets on whether or not he can bed Billie "Stonewall" Jackson (Audrey Christie), the notoriously inaccessible hostess at the Idle Hour Café. His buddy, Barney (Edward Craven), has even bet his precious heirloom watch and leads the push to bring the pair together. The bets are made with the notorious gyrene Jake (Larry Fletcher). Dynamite has less than a week to work his wonders before the ship sails. The girls at the club also join in the betting, naturally taking Stonewall's side. When Dynamite, unaware of all the betting, meets Stonewall, he is immediately smitten and starts his pursuit, although she warns him that she long ago made up her mind that before any man can bed her he must wed her. Moreover, she notes, "I'd as leave marry a tom-cat as a sailor." Both are outraged to learn about the betting, and the whole thing seems off for good. But on the eve of the ship's departure, alone together in Stonewall's apartment, their reciprocal attractions prove too much. As they nestle on a sofa,

Stonewall turns out the lamp light. A few moments later there is an excited pounding on the door, and Barney's voice announces that he has got his watch back.

More huge hits followed in quick succession. One was the Irving Berlin–Moss Hart revue *As Thousands Cheer,* best remembered for "Easter Parade." The second was Eugene O'Neill's **Ah, Wilderness!** (10-2-33, Guild). Brooks Atkinson in the *Times* called it "one of his best works" and "a true and congenial comedy," then mused, "If Mr. O'Neill can write with as much clarity as this, it is hard to understand why he has held up the grim mask for so long." The Miller family lives in "a large small-town in Connecticut," where Nat Miller (George M. Cohan) publishes the town newspaper. Most of the family is preparing to celebrate July 4th, although their younger son, Richard (Elisha Cook, Jr.), calls the holiday "a stupid farce" and claims they are all slaves of the capitalistic system. Nat is amused by his son's youthful political ardor, but Mrs. Miller (Marjorie Marquis) is more upset by Richard's reading Shaw, Swinburne, and especially that awful Oscar Wilde. Richard's older brother, Arthur (William Post, Jr.), knows all about Wilde, who was arrested for "bigamy." Most upset of all is their neighbor Mr. McComber (Richard Sterling), who has come across some torrid poetry that Richard has sent to young Muriel McComber (Ruth Gilbert). He threatens to remove his advertising from Nat's paper unless the boy stops seeing the girl. In adolescent desperation Richard meets a "tart" at a local bar and gets hopelessly drunk. Nat and Richard's boozy Uncle Sid (Gene Lockhart), his mother's brother, who had been courting Nat's sister, Lily (Eda Heinemann), are understanding and forgiving, particularly after Richard wails, "It's lucky there aren't any of General Gabler's pistols around—or you'd see if I'd stand it much longer!" A letter from Muriel, saying she still loves him, calms him. And he promises to remain loyal to her when he leaves for Yale in the fall. Sitting together with his wife at the end of a wearying day, Nat quotes Omar Khayyam's lines about the brevity of spring, then concludes, "There's a lot to be said for autumn. That's got beauty, too. And winter—if you're together." Atkinson also praised Robert Edmond Jones's settings for recognizing "the humor in the stuffy refinement of 1906," while Burns Mantle, in the *Daily News,* noted that Cohan, often chided for the brashness of his playing, brought to his characterization "the utmost delicacy of technique, plus as true a feeling for sentiment as any American player possesses." The comedy ran out the season.

Before the next new hit came in, the Cherry Lane Theatre, which last season had offered a long list of novelties, reopened with a revival of *Strictly Dishonorable* (9-18-29) on the 3rd. Just as critics had ignored the new plays last year, they ignored the revival. But that didn't stop its running until mid-February.

A week later another season-long, successful novelty came in. Early playbills credited Alan Child and Isabelle Louden with the authorship of **The Pursuit of Happiness** (10-9-33, Avon), but it was an open secret that Child and Louden were actually Lawrence Langner and his wife, Armina Marshall. For the second time in recent weeks a comedy looked at puritanical New England, but in this instance it was set in Connecticut during the Revolution, in a small town still dominated by Calvinist doctrines. However strictly religious Comfort Kirkland (Eleanor Hicks) may be, her husband (Charles Waldron) is far more liberal and complains, "Church here is powerful set agin' folks enjoyin' themselves." But even Mrs. Kirkland cannot agree with rigid Reverend Banks (Seth Arnold), who opposes young lovers bundling—courting or "sparking" in a warm bed with the separating board to keep them chaste. Thaddeus Jennings (Raymond Walburn), the local sheriff and ardent head of the local militia, would not mind being able to spark and bundle with the Kirklands' pretty daughter, Prudence (Peggy Conklin). But his plans are frustrated by the arrival of a dashing young Hessian, Max Christmann (Tonio Selwart), who was forced into the British army by a Hessian grand duke and who longs to escape to a land which offers life, liberty, and "the running after happiness." Max and Prudence fall in love, but after she induces him to bundle, the snooping Banks and the furious Jennings demand Max be arrested. An officer (Hunter Gardner) from Virginia prevents the arrest by revealing he has gotten Max a position with the American army. Then Kirkland, by getting the lovers to pretend they will not marry, tricks the minister into "forcing" them to wed. The comedy was welcomed by Hammond as an "engaging bit of deviltry . . . a smart and bawdy satire."

Nancy Carroll, better known for her film roles, and playwright Leon Gordon, best known for *White Cargo* before also heading for the Hollywood hills, were handed thumbs-down notices when she starred in his **An Undesirable Lady** (10-9-33, National). Realizing that Sally Marsh is almost certain to be convicted for murder at her retrial, her lawyer, Charles Fennick (Lee Baker), persuades her to run off with him to his cabin in the Canadian wilds. There they are snowbound and Fennick loses his eyesight. An attractive trapper (Edward Leiter) comes to the cabin and has little trouble seducing Sally. Fennick regains his eyesight and exposes the trapper as a disguised Canadian Mountie. Sally commits suicide, while the men, having run out of food and beset by another storm, calmly await their own deaths together.

The fast-fading Lenore Ulric also came a cropper in **Her Man of Wax** (10-11-33, Shubert), which Julian Thompson translated from Walter Hasenclever's *Napoleon greift ein*. An actress cast as Josephine visits a wax museum where the figure of Napoleon (Lloyd Corrigan) comes to life and goes home with her. But he is so disgusted with the modern world that he soon hies back to his pedestal in the gallery.

The Theatre Guild followed *Ah, Wilderness!* with a second if much lesser hit, **The School for Husbands** (10-16-33, Empire), which Arthur Guiterman and Lawrence Langner took from Molière. The play was in rhymed verse and embellished with period songs, a ballet suggested by Molière's "Le Mariage forcé," created and danced by Doris Humphreys and Charles Weidman, and costumes and settings colorful enough for any musical. Once again the easygoing Ariste (Stuart Casey) wins the love of his ward (Joan Carr), while the suspicious, severe Sganarelle (Osgood Perkins) finds himself deceived by his ward (June Walker).

Anthony Armstrong's **Ten Minute Alibi** (10-17-33, Ethel Barrymore) had been a London hit, but had to be content with an eleven-week New York stay. To prevent the girl (Daphne Warren-Wilson) he loves from eloping with a man (Sebastion Braggiotti) he knows to be a scoundrel, Colin Derwent (Bramwell Fletcher) kills the rotter. By moving a clock back and forth, he gives himself a seemingly foolproof alibi. A team from Scotland Yard (Reynolds Denniston and John Williams) catch on to the trick but, misconstruing Derwent's remarks, exculpate him. At the end, he sits alone watching the clock tick on.

An even less satisfactory mystery was Valentine Davies's theatricalization of Earl Derr Biggers's **Keeper of the Keys** (10-18-33, Fulton). Its central figure was Charlie Chan, whose exploits Warner Oland had already brought to life on the screen. William Harrigan was the stage Chan, and was panned for his bland, unconvincing Oriental. Called to Nevada from Hawaii, Chan must solve the murders of a much married woman (Roberta Beatty) and one (Romaine Callender) of her husbands. Chan shows the killer to be another (Fleming Ward) of the husbands, the very man who called Chan in to investigate.

Blonde, throaty-voiced Jean Arthur received appreciative notices but could not turn B. M. Kaye's **The Curtain Rises** (10-19-33, Vanderbilt) into a hit. Elsa Karling is enamoured of the great actor Wilhelm Meissinger (Kenneth Harlan) and goes to him for acting lessons. Seeing nothing in her, he turns her over to his understudy, Franz Kermann (Donald Foster). She learns the part of Juliet and when Meissinger's leading lady becomes ill substitutes for her. Meissinger's kisses after her success leave her cold, but Kermann's make her wobbly, so she knows whom she really loves. Given the political situation in Europe, some commentators objected to an American comedy's being set in modern Germany, and to Kaye's employing a distinctly German pen name, Oskar Rempel, in the earlier programs.

The second all-English-born cast in four nights was lauded for its "excellent," "exceptional," "extraordinary" ensemble playing and helped make a success of Mordaunt Shairp's **The Green Bay Tree** (10-20-33, Cort). Jed Harris, recently so chided for his direction, won the highest praise for his deft staging. Young Julian Dulcimer (Laurence Olivier) has been kept in luxury by the elder Dulcimer (James Dale), a decadent who bought the boy from his real father, William Owen (O. P. Heggie). When Julian falls in love with Leonora (Jill Esmond), Dulcimer cuts him off. Owen, now a religious fanatic, murders Dulcimer to destroy all vestiges of degenerate influences. But with the huge inheritance Dulcimer has left him, Julian looks to become as unsavory in his own way as the elder man was in his. The play's fifth character, a butler, was played by Leo G. Carroll. Years earlier, *The Captive* (9-29-26) had been closed by the authorities for its hint of lesbianism, but in a changing climate there were apparently no strident calls to close the new play, and its discreet handling of homosexuality even may have lured in patrons. The play ran twenty-one weeks. Not quite the success that *The Captive* had been, but then times were not as prosperous as they were in 1926.

No suggestion of controversy embroiled the next play to arrive. Theatre folk were elated that Clare Kummer had found her old skills again. They could not know that **Her Master's Voice** (10-23-33, Plymouth) would be her last triumph. Gabriel purred, "Throughout the whole piece runs a really beautiful brand of humor, the stuff of grateful chuckles, of continuous pressure on the button that is midway between sympathy and absurdity. You not only gurgle at the people in this play, you love them dearly." Queena Farrar (Frances Fuller) sits at the piano of her modest New Jersey home accompanying herself in an aria from *La Boheme* and dreaming wistfully of what she might have been if she had not thrown up her singing lessons to marry. Her prim, flat-chested, dour mother, Mrs. Martin (Elizabeth Patterson), is happy to fuel the fire. Ned Farrar (Roland Young) returns home. He has asked for the raise his wife and mother-in-law have pressed him to demand and been fired for it: "I told Mr. Pearsall I thought I was worth more. He said he did too—and as he couldn't give it to me I'd better get it from someone else." But concerns about job hunting take second place, since their rich, busty Aunt Min (Laura Hope Crews) is expected. Min had helped pay for Queena's lessons and had cut her off when she married. She finds Ned cleaning house and mistakes him for a servant. She is anxious to break

up the marriage, so invites Queena to spend some time with her. Queena reluctantly agrees. At Min's estate, Queena is given a bed on the cold sunporch, an otherwise beautiful room overlooking the countryside. She is startled when Min's new houseman comes to fix a screen, since he is none other than Ned, whom Min knows only as George. That night Ned sneaks back onto the sunporch, unaware that Queena and Min have changed places. Min is thrilled that so excellent a young man would try to crawl into her bed. Meanwhile, Mr. Twilling (Frederick Perry), the Farrars' rich neighbor and a radio magnate, has proposed to Mrs. Martin. She has come to Aunt Min's undecided on whether to accept, but sporting the elegant new clothes he has bought her. She barges onto the sunporch, and Ned is forced to crouch and hide under a fur coat. When Twilling appears and Mrs. Martin accepts, he also has them listen on their radio to the new golden voice he has discovered— Sylvester Silverton. Sylvester turns out to be Ned by yet another name. So all ends merrily. The comedy ran seven months and added another fine credit to the list of its producer, Max Gordon.

• • •

Max Gordon [né Mechel Salpeter] (1892–1978) was born in New York and began his theatrical career as a press agent, then turned agent for vaudeville performers. For a time he worked withh Sam H. Harris. Most of his earliest hits had been musicals, but some months before he had scored with *Design for Living*. A tiny, professorial-looking man, he was known for his mercurial temperament, once threatening to jump from a window if money for a forthcoming production was not made available to him.

• • •

More Puccini was heard the next night in **Spring in Autumn** (10-24-33, Henry Miller), Blanche Yurka and Nene Belmonte's adaptation of Gregorio Martinez Sierra's Spanish play. Yurka played a fiery prima donna who is asked to reunite with her former husband (Richard Hale) for the sake of appearances at the wedding of their daughter (Helen Walpole). By evening's end singer and husband are permanently reunited even if the daughter has changed her mind about whom she will wed. The high point for many was a party in which Yurka sang a Puccini aria while standing on her head.

An American play that opened the same evening, Daniel N. Rubin's **Move On, Sister** (10-24-33, Playhouse), was a one-week failure. Eugene Greer (Ernest Glendinning) chases away the sycophants gathered around his deathbed and summons the only man he can trust, his old adversary, Paul Cromer (Moffat Johnston). He tells Cromer his history and dictates a will. It seems that long ago he had loved Alice Drave (Fay Bainter), but deserted her to make a self-serving marriage. Years afterwards, on business out of town, he had asked for a prostitute to be sent to his hotel room and Alice had come. He fled in dismay, but subsequently sent her $100. Now, still ashamed of himself, he would leave his fortune to her. In a scene some considered ghoulish, Alice appears at his viewing and places the $100 bill, which she had never spent, in the dead man's hand. But Cromer convinces her to accept the legacy and even goes to battle for her when the sycophants attempt to break the will.

Fifty years on, a play such as George F. Hummel's **The World Waits** (10-25-33, Little) would have elicited many snide comments, but in a more publicly decorous 1933 only a few papers, notably the *Times* and *Variety,* alluded to the comparisons of its story and Richard Evelyn Byrd's recent expedition. A group of scientists and explorers, led by the ineffectual if photogenic Hartley (Blaine Cordner), are stranded during their trip to Antarctica. Hartley's carelessness allows him to send a flyer (Donald Gallaher) on a fatal rescue mission and drives another associate (Philip Truex) to suicide. This prompts Brice (Reed Brown, Jr.) to take over the reins and keep the survivors alive until a rescue ship is able to break through the ice. At that point, he hands authority back to Hartley, remarking bitterly, "You're a national hero. You take the ticker tape." Critics found the play dull and tame but admired the "strange, wild atmosphere of an Antarctic encampment," including "the polar costumes, the coal stove, the bunks, the oil lamps, the sagging beams under the roof," and the howling winds.

Three and One (10-25-33, Longacre) was Lewis Galantiere and John Houseman's reworking of Denys Amiel's French original. A famous dancer (Ruth Shepley) has three sons, each by a different father. Arthur (Paul McGrath) resembles his banker-father; Paul (John Eldredge) is a musician much like his poet sire, and Charles (Brian Donlevy) is the virile image of his prizefighter-dad. When mother invites a beautiful girl (Lillian Bond) to visit, all three men court her. Charles would seem to be the victor, until mother takes all three boys away on a motor tour.

More than one critic felt that Mady Christians was the only reason for seeing **A Divine Drudge** (10-26-33, Royale), which Vicki Baum and John Golden dramatized from Baum's novel *And Life Goes On.* Christians was a celebrated German film and stage star who had left Germany in protest to the new regime there. In an obscure German town called Lohwinkel, Liza helps her husband (Walter Abel) work on a cure for a disease. One day Karl Kruppe (Minor Watson), a rich man, traveling with his glamorous movie-star mistress (Tamara Geva) and a prizefighter (Gerald Kent), is hurt in an automobile accident. He remains in the town to recuperate and with his cash enlivens the dull village. When he is about to leave, he asks Liza to come with him. She is ready to accept, but, learning that her husband's experiments have been in vain—that others have gotten the same results elsewhere—she elects to remain in Lohwinkel. Unlike *The Curtain Rises,* the new play touched on the situation in contemporary Germany, with the town's bigoted mayor (Roman Bohnen) refusing to invite the Jewish grocer (Ralf Belmont) to official festivities. Whatever virtues the play and the production had, they could not push it past twelve performances.

But that was twice as many playings as the next two entries combined, each of which lasted just three performances. Howard Koch's **Give Us This Day** (10-27-33, Booth) looked at a family waiting for its ailing, demanding matriarch to die. (She is never seen or heard, except when she pounds on her bedroom steampipe for attention.) In the years-long wait, one family member has committed suicide and another run off for an undesirable marriage. The heir apparent (Paul Guilfoyle), who has even sacrificed marrying for his grandmother's sake, finally fires a gun close to her head. The shock kills her. But he comes to feel so guilty that he gives the money to his relations and kills himself.

The other entry that evening was a revival of Harry Delf's *The Family Upstairs* (8-17-25) at the Biltmore. Once again Emma Heller (Helen Carew) nearly wrecks the chance of her daughter (Florence Ross) by dismissing the girl's suitors as unworthy of the family.

The long parade of failures continued with Percy G. Mandley's London success, **Eight Bells** (10-28-33, Hudson). In August of 1914 the camaraderie on the sailing ship *Combermere* is destroyed when Germany and England go to war. Six German sailors demand that they be put ashore in South America, but the unbending English captain (Colin Clive) refuses. In the mutiny that follows, the captain is killed. That allows the captain's wife (Rose Hobart), the lone woman aboard, to look with fresh interest at the kindly chief mate (John Buckler).

Eva Kay Flint and George Bradshaw's **Under Glass** (10-30-33, Ambassador) didn't even have a London imprimatur to aid it. Newlyweds Tony and Stephanie Pell (Ross Alexander and Ethel Barrymore Colt), who live with Stephanie's widowed father (Boyd Irwin), quarrel so much that they finally agree to a trial separation. When Tony immediately takes up with another woman, who happens to be his father-in-law's mistress (Leona Maricle), that proves too much. Stephanie packs for Reno, but then a reconciliation is arranged.

No other play in the long progression of failures received such good notices as Jean Ferguson Black's transcription of Christopher Morley's best-seller **Thun-**

der on the Left (10-31-33, Maxine Elliott's). Critics let it down easily, appreciating its high intentions and the difficulty of making fantasy come alive on the stage. At a party to celebrate the tenth birthday of Martin (Frank Thomas, Jr.) all the little guests—Joyce, who is Martin's favorite, Phyllis, Ruth, Ben, and Martin's sister, Bunny (Jeanne Dante)—exchange presents. In blowing out the candles on his cake, Martin wishes that he could see what they would all be like after they have grown up. When the lights come on again it is twenty years later. Phyllis (Katharine Warren) has married the grumpy, philandering George (Louis Jean Heydt) and has invited Ruth (Eleanor Audley) and Ben (Otto Hulett), whom Ruth has married, and Joyce (Hortense Alden) for a weekend. Martin (James Bell), now physically thirty but with a singularly child-like way of seeing things, also appears. To Phyllis, time is somehow out of joint, "As though yesterday never happened and tomorrow never will." Her conversations with Martin are odd, too. She tells him he does not have to finish his beans. He responds that he's glad he doesn't have to, prompting Phyllis to acknowledge that she also hates finishing things. "Specially carrots and beans," Martin adds. But Martin does not care for what he sees. The adults are vulgar or shallow or uncaring. Only Joyce seems to understand him, and only he and Joyce can see and hear Bunny, who, it turns out, drowned while still a child. Then Joyce points out that the obnoxious George is really what Martin could become. Back at the party, young Martin warns the others, "Don't grow up. Please. You won't like it. Really you won't."

The season's latest three-performance dud was **It Pays to Sin** (11-3-33, Morosco), taken by Louis Macloon and George Redman from Johan Vaszary's *Jó házbul való úrilány* (Young Girl of Good Family). In need of money, Greta (Jane Starr) responds to an advertisement by a doctor (Leon Waycoff) who is studying unwed but pregnant girls, even though she knows she is not pregnant. By the time the doctor discovers the fraud he has fallen in love with Greta.

A good cast, sparked by the flamboyant performance of Florence Reed, failed to save Doty Hobart's **Thoroughbred** (11-6-33, Vanderbilt). The widowed Petie Westervail, once rich but now having to watch her pennies, is determined to regain her fortune by having her horse, Lady Jane, win the Belmont Futurity. To do this she must keep secret the fact that Lady Jane's sire was a common workhorse, Tartar. Of course, fraud is nothing new to the old gal, since, finding her late husband impotent, she allowed the butler (Thurston Hall) to father her children, Rickey (Harry Ellerbe) and Mary (Claudia Morgan). Rickey is in love with a supposed *Follies* beauty, unaware she is a professional blackmailer. But Sylvia Van Horne (Lillian Emerson),

the sweet, pretty girl who loves Rickey, concerned that her flighty mother (Hilda Spong) has nearly spilled the beans about Lady Jane's pedigree, helps expose her rival and gets rid of Tartar. She wins Rickey, and, after Lady Jane wins the race, Petie wins the butler.

No one won with **Doctor Monica** (11-6-33, Playhouse), Laura Walker's adaptation of Marja M. Szczepkowska's three-character, anti-male Polish drama. Recuperating from surgery that will allow her to have children, Dr. Monica (Alla Nazimova) stays at the home of her friend Anna (Gale Sondergaard), a man-hating architect, and discovers that another friend (Beatrice de Neergaard) of Anna's is seeking an abortion since she is pregnant by Monica's husband. Monica attempts suicide, but Anna convinces her to make the best of a bad deal in a male-dominated world.

Lennox Robinson's Irish comedy **Is Life Worth Living?** reportedly had enjoyed some success at home and in the rest of Europe, but found no favor in New York. A seacoast hotel proprietor (Whitford Kane) hopes to elevate his small village by producing a season of highminded dramas—Chehkov, Strindberg, Ibsen, and the like. The guests and villagers are so depressed by the plays that the proprietor sends the actors on their way and brings in a circus.

In **I Was Waiting for You** (11-13-33, Booth), Melville Baker's translation of Jacques Natanson's Paris hit, the young mistress (Helen Brooks) of an older man (Glenn Anders) and the young lover (Bretaigne Windust) of an older woman (Vera Allen) fall in love and run off, leaving the oldsters, who themselves once had been lovers, to rekindle their former ardor. Critics divided on Anders's performance but pounced on his gray wig ("platinum dust," one sneered). Myron McCormick scored as "the rueful young man who lets the cat out of the bag." For most critics the best thing about the show was Jo Mielziner's beautiful settings—a bar, an elegant hotel room, and a Paris apartment—although no reviewer offered details.

The long sequence of flops was broken briefly with what *Variety* welcomed as "another real laugh show, fast, novel, modern," Howard Lindsay's theatricalization of Edward Hope's novel **She Loves Me Not** (11-20-33, 46th St.). The setting was so unique that virtually every critic mentioned it: "A double decked construction permits almost full width scenes on two levels. In addition the angled ends of the structure afford smaller scenes, upper and lower also." It is on one of those angled ends that Curley Flagg (Polly Walters), a dancer in a Philadelphia nightspot, watches Mugg Schnitzel (Harry Bellaver) mow down his rival. Not wanting to be held as a material witness, she throws a cloak over her skimpy costume and runs off. Having grabbed the first available bus, she soon finds herself in Princeton.

She seeks refuge in the room of a senior, Paul Lawton (John Beal), who, with Buzz Jones (Burgess Meredith), his buddy from the floor above, gives her boys' clothing, crops her hair, and introduces her as Buzz's cousin. Buzz even manages to get Curley a role in a film his uncle is making. Before long the film crew, Mugg and his cohorts, and the school authorites are involved in multi-leveled mayhem. At one point the boys even tie up Mugg and the dean (John T. Dwyer), and hide them in a closet. Finally, Curley lands a film contract, the boys are forgiven, and Paul finds romance with the dean's daughter (Florence Rice). The comedy ran eleven months.

If *Kultur* and *A Divine Drudge* had touched gingerly on Nazi Germany, Richard Maibaum's **Birthright** (11-21-33, 49th St.) pulled no punches. Unfortunately, the punches were not well aimed, theatrically. The Eisners are a well-to-do family of assimilated Jewish merchants in Berlin. But with Hitler's coming, the Christian fiancé (Harold Elliot) of their granddaughter (Sylvia Field) breaks off the engagement, and their grandson (Alan Bunce) is arrested and executed for killing an officer who would arrest him for a street protest. The survivors decide to wait out the madness.

Californian Aurania Rouverol once again looked at teenaged life in **Growing Pains** (11-23-33, Ambassador). Sixteen-year-old George (Junior Durkin) is willing to trade the gun he bought with the money he won for an essay on universal peace for a broken-down flivver, so he can impress the new local siren, Prudence (Joan Wheeler), especially since she seems taken by his buddy, Brian (Johnny Downs). George's tomboy sister, Terry (Jean Rouverol), is told that she is past "the mercurochrome age" and can no longer play baseball with the boys. So she dons high heels and goes after Brian herself. George, attempting to show Prudence how manly he is, gets in trouble speeding through a red light and sassing the cop who stops him. He is made to exchange the flivver back for the rifle. And since Prudence has been unimpressed, he looks with new interest on another girl.

Judith Anderson could do nothing for Howard Irving Young's **The Drums Begin** (11-24-33, Shubert). She played a bilingual French countess and movie star who has the lead in a film about the World War being shot, in part, in her château, with two casts, one for the German version and one for the French. An old officer realizes that she was a German spy in the war. This prompts the film's writer (Walter Abel) to walk out and exposes the latent enmities between the different nationals.

Although John Mason Brown branded it "hokum which revels agreeably in the special prerogatives of the species" and Mantle considered it "one of the happiest [murder mysteries] of recent seasons," enough critics qualified their reviews to doom Alexander Woollcott and George S. Kaufman's **The Dark Tower** (11-25-33, Morosco), particularly with so many hits vying for scarce Depression dollars. The Wellses, like Kaufman's Cavendishes, are a great acting family. But Jessica Wells (Margalo Gillmore) has been unable to act since coming under the baleful influence of her husband, Stanley Vance (Ernest Milton). Since he has now been reported dead, she decides to try a comeback, supporting her brother, Damon (Basil Sydney), in a play called *The Dark Tower*. Vance suddenly reappears and makes trouble. However, a famous foreign producer summons Vance to a suite at the Waldorf, and Vance is later found stabbed to death there, with the producer nowhere in sight. The police soon realize that the producer was merely Damon in disguise, but they take no action. One reason the play may have failed was that it was not filled with the wit playgoers expected of Woollcott and Kaufman. Only the early scenes abounded in the laughs playgoers probably sought. Thus Damon's aunt (Margaret Dale) replies to a remark that he is a great actor, "If you can call a man an actor who doesn't act. He's a great drinker." Later, Damon's ignored lady friend (Leona Maricle) complains he "forgets he's out with me half the time. Leaves me sticking in umbrella stands." Damon undoubtedly got a laugh when he greeted the family maid, "Well, if it isn't the Serpent of the Nile. Hattie, you grow more voluptuous every week." Hattie was played by dour, scrawny Margaret Hamilton.

November's second and last success was Maxwell Anderson's **Mary of Scotland** (11-27-33, Alvin). The Theatre Guild's third hit of the season, it ran into June. A delighted Brooks Atkinson informed his readers that the blank-verse tragedy "has restored the English language to its high estate as an instrument of lustrous beauty. It is an outspoken drama." When Catholic Mary Stuart (Helen Hayes) returns as Queen of Scotland, Protestant Queen Elizabeth (Helen Menken) rejects her courtiers' pleas to go to war and plans a more subtle downfall for her rival. She will spread rumors about Mary's chastity and trick her into marrying a worthless man. Mary refuses to heed the advice of her loyal Protestant lover, Bothwell (Philip Merivale), so Elizabeth's "crawling fog of whispers" soon takes effect. Mary exiles Bothwell and marries the irresponsible Darnley (Anthony Kemble Cooper). Before long Mary's courtiers are in revolt and she is captured. She and Elizabeth confront each other in Mary's prison cell, and Mary refuses to sign abdication papers. Even though Elizabeth will kill her, Mary gloats, "Still, *still* I win! I have been/ A woman, And I have loved as a woman loves,/ . . . I have borne a son,/ . . . A devil has no children." With Elizabeth gone, Mary stares out into the darkness. Brown praised the "eloquent and simple theatricality" of Robert Edmond Jones's settings, while Mantle particularly hailed his "sternest and wildest Caledonian coasts." Atkinson went into a bit more detail, writing of "scenes that vibrate with meaning and costumes that sharpen the alignment of forces. In the last act the simple black costume he has designed for Mary and the regal gold of Elizabeth's sweeping raiment visualize with great brilliance the opposition of will and the inequality of power that set the tone for the encounter." He also dwelt on Hayes's performance: "The girlish charm on her arrival in Scotland, the grimness with which she tries to control her destiny, the womanly horror in the murder scene, the bravery with which she defies the traitors and the rockbound resistance with which she meets Elizabeth summon emotions that none of her previous roles have required." For Hayes, more than any of those other roles, it confirmed her high rank.

. . .

Helen Hayes [Brown] (1900–93) was born in Washington, D.C. to a small-time actress and a traveling salesman. She made her debut there at the age of five in a local stock company before coming to the attention of Lew Fields, who cast her in a 1909 Broadway musical, *Old Dutch*. After several other Fields musicals she appeared as an ingenue in *Pollyanna* (1917), *Penrod* (1918), and *Dear Brutus* (1918), then moved on to somewhat more adult flappers in *Clarence* (1919), *To the Ladies* (1922), and *Dancing Mothers* (1924). More mature parts followed in *Caesar and Cleopatra* (1925), *What Every Woman Knows,* and *Coquette* (1927). Tiny of stature, she combined in her playing an almost cloying sweetness with a determined steeliness.

. . .

Bernard J. McOwen's creaky melodrama **The Scorpion** (11-27-33, Biltmore) was set in the Sudan. A plane crash deposits the sultry Illyana (Annette Margulies) in the midst of some British officers. One of them recognizes her as the wife who deserted him years ago. She flirts with another officer and with a local sheik, provoking the bloody ire of the sheik's paramour, who stabs the sheik and poisons the siren. Margulies had won fleeting fame as Tondelayo in *White Cargo,* but her new vehicle disappeared after a single week.

A single performance—the season's shortest stand—was the fate of a British drama, Rodney Ackland's **Strange Orchestra** (11-28-33, Playhouse), which told of the ordeal of a young girl (Edith Barrett), going blind and cruelly sponged on by a worthless cad (Ian Emery). Cecilia Loftus played the girl's Mae West–like mother, a boardinghouse keeper.

George Sklar and Albert Maltz's **Peace on Earth** (11-29-33, Civic Repertory) managed to run four months thanks to a $1.50 top ticket. A university professor (Robert Keith) supports longshoremen who refuse to load munitions. His best friend (Clyde Franklin) is shot by the police while they break up the strike. Later, the professor himself is arrested and sentenced to death for a murder he did not commit. He tells the judge, "You have no right to sentence me for murder because I haven't been found guilty of murder . . . if my crime was association with workers fighting against war, then I am guilty." Sitting in his cell he hears men outside shouting anti-war slogans. Black curtains and a few meager sets on platforms, lit by high-powered spots from the gallery, provided an appropriately austere background for the action.

"An ugly wallowing sort of drama," "a callow and unpleasant play," "ridiculously inept," "minor and squalid tragedy"—better assessments could not save better plays, but **Tobacco Road** (12-4-33, Masque) proved impervious to critical barbs and went on to run for eight years and to become the longest-running show in Broadway history to its day, accumulating 3182 performances. Just why it did is moot, although the play now reads more entertainingly than contemporary critics might have allowed, even if it does seem to be kidding what its original authors meant to be taken seriously. Those authors were Erskine Caldwell, who wrote the novel, and Jack Kirkland, who dramatized it. "Looks like about everything around here is wore out. Seems like the Lord just ain't with us no more at all." So wails Jeeter Lester (Henry Hull). But then Jeeter is a shiftless cuss, too lazy to even earn enough to buy turnips to feed his wife and the two of his seventeen children that still live in his shack. He has sold his oldest daughter, Pearl (Reneice Rehan), for $7 to Lov Bensey (Dean Jagger), who now complains she will neither sleep with him or even talk to him. Jeeter's blaspheming son, Dude (Sam Byrd), marries a prayer-spouting neighbor, Sister Bessie (Maude Odell), who has enough money to let him buy an old car. When Dude's mother, Ada (Margaret Wycherly) berates her son, he runs her over and kills her. In dying, she allows she will not be buried in the "stylish dress" she has longed for. Pearl runs off to the city, so Jeeter gives Lov his mute daughter, Ellie May (Ruth Hunter), by way of compensation. Then he goes back to lazing on his stoop and rubbing his hands in the dirt.

There were some very favorable notices for Laura and S. J. Perelman's **All Good Americans** (12-5-33, Henry Miller), which looked at the opposite end of the social scale from *Tobacco Road,* but the comedy failed after five weeks. The scene was Paris, including Jimmy's [read Harry's] Bar. There Pat Wells (Fred Keating) "hangs around all day," which June Gable (Hope Williams), who loves him, rationalizes is "better than doing nothing." But Pat seems too interested in the bottom of his martini glasses to care, and, besides, he seems to like a wealthy Southern belle, Mary-Louise Porter (Janet McLeay). When Mary-Louise is nabbed for smuggling and Pat suddenly sports a bankroll, June wonders if she misjudged Pat. She almost marries Rex Fleming (Coburn Goodwin), a wealthy New Rochelle snob, before Pat clears his name and lands her.

Tallulah Bankhead was to have starred in Owen Davis's **Jezebel** (12-19-33, Ethel Barrymore), but when she begged off because of illness, Miriam Hopkins was given the lead. The play was set in 1853 Louisiana, which allowed for beautiful scenery and costumes, even if the often reliable Davis could not muster the requisite tensions. Having loved but snubbed her cousin, Preston Kendrick (Reed Brown, Jr.), Julie Kendrick returns from Europe to find him married. She vows to make trouble, but when she provokes a duel between Preston and another man, Preston's brother, Ted (Owen Davis, Jr.), takes his place and kills his challenger, then drops the pistol in Julie's lap. She is snubbed by society, so when yellow fever breaks out Julie volunteers as a nurse, certain to die from the plague. Bette Davis scored in a later film version.

By the time that Robert Glecker made his final Broadway appearance in Herbert Ashton, Jr.'s **The Locked Room** (12-25-33, Ambassador), he was considered "the most flavorsome ruffian in the American theatre." In this case, however, he played the hero, a detective who must determine who shot, stabbed, and poisoned a man found dead in a room locked from the inside and with no windows. The man was nasty and rich, and several potential heirs are suspected, until the detective pins the killing on a seemingly helpful insurance agent who administered the crucial poison and other blows before the man entered the room.

One oddball attraction was a revival of Lillian Mortimer's oldtime melodrama *No Mother to Guide Her* (12-4-05), which told of the harrowing misadventures of a shopgirl after she is lured into marriage by a bank robber. It was odd not only as a selection but because midgets comprised the entire cast. It opened on Christmas night at the appropriately named Midget Theatre, but its subsequent history is vague.

Dorothy Massingham and Murray MacDonald's **The Lake** (12-26-33, Martin Beck) was an English play. Stella, rebelling against the domination of a selfish mother (Frances Starr), has fallen in love with a married man who refuses to divorce his wife. So her mother finally pushes her into marrying John Clayne (Colin Clive). By the time of the wedding Stella has begun to fall in love with him, and coaxes him into stealing away from the reception. The car careens into a lake, killing John and leaving Stella to contemplate suicide. *Variety*

noted, "There has been nothing in the recent annals of Broadway quite matching" the hubbub surrounding the premiere. This was not because of Jed Harris's inspired casting of two long-retired Belasco favorites, Starr and Blanche Bates (who played an aunt), but because the show's star, Katharine Hepburn, had become a major screen figure since her last Broadway appearance. Her welcome was hardly enthusiastic. Not everyone was as acid as Dorothy Parker, who observed that Hepburn ran "the gamut of emotions from A to B." The more gentlemanly Atkinson noted, "She has not yet developed the flexibility of first-rate acting and her voice is a rather strident instrument," while Parker's colleague and drinking buddy, Robert Benchley, said simply in the *New Yorker,* "She has a great deal to learn about acting." Harris withdrew the play after seven weeks.

Handsome but stiff Conrad Nagel also returned from Hollywood, in Lynn Starling's **The First Apple** (12-27-33, Booth), and ran just as long. After Gilbert Carey and Sylvia Carson (Irene Purcell) take shelter from the rain, he invites her back to his apartment and she accepts. Later, she feels guilty, decides to marry Calvin Barrow (Albert Van Dekker), but is brought to her senses and the altar by Gilbert.

A big hit in the Yiddish theatre failed when done in English on Broadway. **Yoshe Kalb** (12-28-33, National) was Fritz Blocki's translation of Maurice Schwartz's dramatization of I. J. Singer's story. Yoshe (Horace Braham) is forced to marry the daughter (Mildred Van Dorn) of Rabbi Melech (Fritz Leiber), has an affair with the rabbi's wife (Erin O'Brien Moore), becomes a wanderer, is brought before a rabbinical court, then continues his wanderings.

The first evening of the new year brought in 1934's first hit, Sophie Kerr and Anna Steese Richardson's **Big Hearted Herbert** (1-1-34, Biltmore). Herbert Kalness (J. C. Nugent) is something of a modern-day Scrooge, refusing to pay for his children's education and denying them all luxuries and even modest pleasures. So when Herbert invites an important client to dinner at his home, the family teaches him a lesson. With the kids doing the serving, Mrs. Kalness (Elisabeth Risdon) dishes up an embarrassingly spartan dinner. Herbert is properly humbled. The light comedy ran twenty weeks, despite numerous critical put-downs, such as Atkinson's dismissing it as "heavy-footed burlesque."

One waggish critic wondered aloud if the Captain Zebulon Brant who was the central figure in Crane Wilbur's **Halfway to Hell** (1-2-34, Fulton) was not a brother of Captain Adam Brant, whom Wilbur had played in *Mourning Becomes Electra*. This Brant (Carleton Macy) is a mean old codger, who, knowing he is dying, invites his possible heirs to visit him in the home he has made in an abandoned lighthouse. One by one the visitors are slaughtered, each in a different way, until Brant himself is exposed as the demented killer.

Samson Raphaelson's **The Wooden Slipper** (1-3-34, Ritz) spotlighted Julie Zigurny (Dorothy Hall), the ugly duckling of a beautiful acting family. When she is called in to substitute for an ailing Desdemona, her family consider her performance a disaster. But the kindly, loving Andre (Ross Alexander), a chef who is about to open a small restaurant, thinks otherwise, so Julie consents to marry him.

Cleon Throckmorton's colorful, modernistic penthouse may have been the only redeeming feature about G. H. McCall and S. Bouvet de Lozier's **The Gods We Make** (1-3-34, Mansfield). Because his wife has supposedly refused to divorce him, Dick Webster (Lloyd Hughes) insists he cannot marry his mistress, Merle Cavendish (Ara Gerald). When the Crash bankrupts him, the rich Merle continues to support him until she learns he has been divorced. But he explains that a man who lusts after Merle tricked him into pursuing another woman for a time. All is forgiven.

In Paul Osborn's **Oliver Oliver** (1-5-34, Playhouse) the free-spending but penny-short Constance Oakshot (Ann Andrews) is determined to marry off Oliver (Bretaigne Windust), her even more spendthrift idler of a son. So she has invited her friendly enemy, rich Judith Tiverton (Alexandra Carlisle), and Judith's quiet daughter, Phyllis (Helen Brooks), for a weekend. Oliver, in turn, invites Justin Stock (Thomas Chalmers), the wealthiest man in Ohio, to meet his widowed mother on the same weekend. Both plans succeed, despite the fact that both Constance and Oliver can only speak in barbs. Thus when another guest is abruptly shifted from a choice room to a lesser one and courteously responds that he is certain he will like the rooms at the far end of the house, Oliver assures him, "You *won't* when you see them." Several critics compared the play to Noel Coward's *Hay Fever,* but a collection of humorous remarks could not add up to a satisfying comedy.

In 1929 Robert Hare Powel's **A Divine Moment** (1-6-34, Vanderbilt), then called *Brief Candle,* won a prize in Professor George Pierce Baker's Yale class and subsequently received several mountings around the country. New York did not welcome its belated arrival. Its heroine, Cynthia Raeburn (producer Peggy Fears), is an unhappily married woman who has a brief fling with a likable young neighbor (Tom Douglas). Knowing she must break off matters, she says to him, "But remember this, *we've met!* And nothing as lovely as tonight could ever leave my heart. . . . So don't say goodbye!"

Having succeeded so handsomely with *Ah, Wilderness!*, Eugene O'Neill and the Theatre Guild suffered some rather sharp rejections with their second collabora-

tion of the season, **Days Without End** (1-8-34, Henry Miller). John Mason Brown characterized it as one of O'Neill's "feeblest" efforts, noting, "Almost everything that was simple, straight-forward and disarmingly poignant in the miracle plays of old becomes tedious . . . in this fakey preachment." John Loving is two men at once: John (Earle Larimore), the open, idealistic half, and Loving (Stanley Ridges), his baser side. Embittered by life, he has abandoned religion and made a god of love to the point of being unfaithful to his own wife (Selena Royle). Discovering this he becomes deathly ill. A mortified John prostrates himself before the cross and reembraces Catholicism. His reaffirmation kills Loving and saves his wife. He rejoices, "Life laughs with God's love again!" The damning reviews and growing health problems prompted O'Neill to withdraw for more than a decade from the commercial arena.

I. J. Golden's **Re-Echo** (1-10-34, Forrest) detailed the downfall of Richard Lord (Thurston Hall), one of the nation's leading bankers. His father had whipped his poetic yearnings out of him, and now he, for his part, would do the same thing to his son (George Walcott). His behavior loses him his son and his wife, and he is left alone with only his millions.

When a very young playwright in *The Dark Tower* points out that Noel Coward was only twenty-three when he wrote his first hit, the caustic actor spikes his ardor by retorting that Noel Coward was twenty-three for five consecutive seasons. Undaunted, the writer ripostes that Sheldon was only twenty-two when he wrote *Salvation Nell.* The actor comes back with the information that Chatterton was a mere eighteen when he hanged himself. According to Clemence Dane's **Come of Age** (1-12-34, Maxine Elliott's) Chatterton (Stephen Haggard) had second thoughts when he reached Hell, so bargained with the Devil to allow him to return to Earth for three more years. Since time had flown by, he returns to a modern world and falls into the clutches of so demanding a woman (Judith Anderson) that he is happy when the Devil comes to reclaim him. Contemporary party scenes were enlivened by some "vo-do-de-o" numbers done by young Muriel Rahn (years later the original Carmen Jones) "in a hybrid Florence Mills–Aida Ward manner." But even those scenes could not lure in playgoers.

The latest long procession of failures—one commentator called it mid-season perverseness—continued with Hugh Stange's large-cast (thirty-seven), many-scened (thirty-four) story of a *Titanic*-like disaster, **False Dreams, Farewell** (1-15-34, Little). Only in this case the ship was called the *Atlantia* and should never have tried to break speeds records on its maiden voyage since damage sustained in trial runs had not been properly fixed. As in *Grand Hotel,* the play looked briefly at many lives, some tenuously connected. Glenn Anders was the best-known player in the cast.

A number of reviewers, Mantle among them, were saddened by the poor response to Leopold Atlas's touching study of the effects of divorce on a young boy, **Wednesday's Child** (1-16-34, Longacre). He attributed it to "a divorce-conscious public that does not care to be reminded of its failures and a considerable public of playgoers that is frankly opposed to child actors, however talented." The central figure of Bobby Philips was assumed by Frank M. Thomas, Jr., who had also been seen as young Martin in *Thunder on the Left*. Bobby's mother (Katharine Warren) has grown tired of her marriage to a traveling salesman (Walter N. Greaza) and taken up with Howard Benton (Walter Gilbert). When her husband finds out, he strikes her, and she uses that as grounds for divorce. A judge awards her custody of Bobby during school months and his father custody in the summer. But both soon find it inconvenient to have the boy around, so he is shunted off to a military academy filled with other unwanted youngsters. When his fellow students confess to their dreams of someday having a place of their own, Bobby can only tell them, "Yeah.—Wait."

The titular **Mahogany Hall** (1-17-34, Bijou) of Charles Robinson's second play of the season was an exclusive Washington, D.C., brothel, run by the imperious Madame Paris (Olga Baclanova). She is not intimidated by corrupt police demanding protection money, since her little book of clients' names protects her. But she is distressed by the death of her hard-drinking lover, so turns for affection to her classy (no jazz) piano player (Eduardo Ciannelli). When he politely spurns her, she decides to sell her establishment and sail back to Europe.

Lewis Galantiere and John Houseman also had a second offering, **And Be My Love** (1-18-34, Ritz). It told of a man (Barry Jones) who preys on spinsters and widows, but when he falls in love with the niece (Renee Gadd) of one of his victims (Lily Cahill) is curtly rejected by her. She tells him she may allow her dog to visit him. The play had failed in London as *Women Kind* and managed only four performances in New York.

An English dramatist's English play on an American subject, Ronald Gow's **John Brown** (1-22-34, Ethel Barrymore), played in London as *The Gallows Glorious*, ran only half as long. George Abbott not only produced and directed it but took the title part. The story of Brown's returning from fighting in Kansas to set out for his raid on Harper's Ferry employed another huge cast and numerous settings—all to no avail.

January's lone hit was A. E. Thomas's **No More Ladies** (1-23-34, Booth). Although both Sheridan Warren (Melvyn Douglas) and Marcia Townsend (Ruth Weston) play free and loose, they decide to marry.

Marcia admits, "Getting married is as easy as bon jour. It's making it work, that's the catch." Sheridan agrees, "The rock-bound coast is strewn with wrecks." The following summer Marcia discovers that Sheridan is seeing a nightclub dancer (Marcella Swanson), so she holds a dinner party to which she invites the dancer, Sheridan's other girls, and their cuckolded mates, then at the end of the evening runs off for the night with the handsomest of the men. The next morning, after a heated argument, Marcia and Sheridan kiss and make up, but Sheridan still demands to know what happened that night. Marcia promises to tell him—as a Golden Anniversary present. The comedy played until the hot weather came.

The rest of the month was a wasteland. Carol Stone, Fred Stone's youngest daughter, braving New York's critics for the first time in John Haggart's **Mackerel Skies** (1-23-34, Playhouse), played a young woman who longs to be a singer, but whose mother (Violet Kemble Cooper) is opposed to her choice. The girl's father (Tom Powers) was not any of her mother's husbands, but an Austrian peasant who has since become a wealthy American, and he helps her to succeed.

Henry and Ellen Smith (Howard Lindsay and Dorothy Gish), the central figures in Gladys Hurlbut and Emma Wells's **By Your Leave** (1-24-34, Morosco), tell their flighty neighbor (Josephine Hull) that they have decided to go their separate ways for a week, with no questions asked afterwards. Henry's week of stag parties and an abortive attempt at paid love is a disaster, but Ellen has a satisfying fling with a Scottish explorer (Kenneth MacKenna). Lindsay, with his bone glasses and poker face, walked away with the best notices.

Hardwick Nevin's **Whatever Possessed Her** (1-25-34, Mansfield) attempted to spoof summer theatres. Millicent Bangs (Catherine Calhoun Doucet) converts her barn into a summer playhouse and hires a playwright (Richard Whorf) who has never written a play to be resident dramatist. On opening night the leading man accidentally gets drunk on spiked cider, the doors of the set refuse to work, the back of the set collapses, and the playwright attempts to commit suicide on the property's lake only to come dashing out bawling that the water is too cold. At the final curtain, Millicent is seen leading a cow back into the barn.

Like O'Neill three weeks earlier, Philip Barry turned to religion in his latest opus, **The Joyous Season** (1-29-34, Belasco), and quickly went down to defeat. John Anderson of the *Evening Journal*, almost echoing Brown on O'Neill, branded the drama "close to Mr. Barry's worst," observing that the writer "has taken leave of his good humor, his sense of proportion, and his peculiar felicities of technique." Barry had written the play in hopes of luring Maude Adams back to the stage but, when she balked, cast Lillian Gish in the leading role. Thus the Gish sisters were performing, albeit briefly, a few minutes' walk from one another. After a sixteen-year absence, Sister Christina, a nun, revisits her wealthy Irish family in Boston. She has come to choose between her late father's farm and his posh city home. But she finds her numerous siblings and in-laws in disarray and spiritually bankrupt. So she uses the Christmas season to rejuvenate the family as best she can.

Hotel Alimony (1-29-34, Royale) was taken by A. W. Pezet from a farce by Adolf Philipp and Max Simon. It related the problems encountered by a once flush songwriter (James Shelburne) after he is put in jail for non-payment of alimony. He finds anything can be bought in jail for a bit of cash and so arranges to have his collaborator jailed alongside him.

Florence Johns and Wilton Lackaye, Jr.'s send-up of the antiques trade, **American, Very Early** (1-30-34, Vanderbilt), met the same cold fate as last week's spoof of summer stock. Two idealistic, innocent gals (Johns and Lynn Beranger) attempt to enter the rural New England antique market and find themselves bamboozled by wily buyers and sellers. In no time at all they have caught on. Their once meticulous boutique is turned into a seeming junk shop, a truck parked outside suggests they are disposing of the business, and a phony dottering grandmother is seated on their front porch— all to lure in suckers.

An unidentified German drama by Wilhelm Speyer was the source of William A. Drake's **A Hat, a Coat, a Glove** (1-31-34, Selwyn). Jerry Hutchins (Lester Vail) brings a prostitute, Ann Brewster (Isabel Baring), to his apartment after stopping her attempt to drown herself in the river. He then seeks out his mistress, Felicia Mitchell (Nedda Harrigan), to help the girl. While he is away Felicia's husband (A. E. Matthews) appears, hunting Jerry. Ann grabs his gun and attempts to shoot herself, but when the man goes to stop her, the gun goes off and Ann is killed. Jerry is brought to trial, but Felicia's husband, who is an attorney and who has made her promise never to see Jerry again if he gets an acquittal, argues that the evidence fits himself as well as it might Jerry. Jerry is acquitted.

Programs were careful to point out that the "quean" in the title of Jo Milward and J. Kerby Hawkes's **Theodora, the Quean** (1-31-34, Forrest) meant a harlot. Theodora (Elena Miramova) is one of the most celebrated courtesans in old Byzantium until she meets Justinian (Minor Watson), then she falls truly in love. Not even the blandishments of the suave, persistent Prince Hypatius (Horace Braham) can make her disloyal.

February's first entry, Merton Hodge's **The Wind and the Rain** (2-1-34, Ritz), was an English success which found a modicum of favor in New York, running fifteen weeks. It focused on a young medical student (Frank Lawton), who leaves a sweetheart (June Blossom) in London when he goes to study in Edinburgh, finds a deeper love (Rose Hobart) there, and must return to London to break the news back home. Lawton received glowing notices but never lived up to his early promise.

Anne Morrison Chapin's **No Questions Asked** (2-5-34, Masque) begins on a Staten Island ferry, where a besotted Sonny Raeburn (Ross Alexander), who thinks he's on a liner for Europe, and a distraught, unwed mother-to-be, Noel Parker (Barbara Robbins), meet when he stops her from jumping overboard. He brings her home to his understanding mother (Spring Byington). Problems arise, especially after the mother and Noel quarrel and after Sonny realizes that Noel is expecting. Sonny inadvertently shoots himself in the arm, but finally accepts Noel although she is "eating for two."

Critics who had seen but had not reviewed **After Such Pleasures** (2-7-34, Bijou) when it had opened some weeks before at a small auditorium in the Barbizon-Plaza Hotel felt that the entertainment lost something in the larger, more demanding confines of even a tiny Broadway house. The series of seven vignettes was dramatized by Edward F. Gardner from Dorothy Parker's short stories. A snobbish white woman tells a friend of her interview with a black artist. A girl who hates dancing must waltz with an elephant-footed bore. On her honeymoon a bride starts to find fault with her husband and keeps on finding more and more fault. The best notices went to Enid Markey and Shirley Booth.

Amish country was the setting for Elmer Greensfelder's **Broomsticks, Amen!** (2-9-34, Little), which Lew Fields had performed in summer stock but had abandoned. As the seventh son of a Pennsylvania Dutch family, old Emil Hofnagel (William F. Schoeller) has served as a hex doctor. He refuses to accept money for his services and hates trained physicians. Naturally, he is angered when his daughter (Helen Huberth) marries a doctor (K. Elmo Lowe), so after the young couple's first baby becomes sick, he shoots his son-in-law and tends the baby himself. The baby dies. The wounded son-in-law decides to stay to rid the community of its old superstitions and practices. Humor often derived from Pennsylvania Dutch idioms. Thus, when the doorbell stops working, Hofnagel puts out a sign reading, "The bell don't make. Please bump!"

Although critics admired bantam Ernest Truex's comic skills, they regularly rued his infelicitous selection of vehicles. Milton Herbert Gropper's **Sing and**

Whistle (2-10-34, Fulton) was one more instance. Frank and Sylvia Jilson (Truex and Sylvia Field) are roused out of bed by the arrival of Hugo and Carol Dickens (Donald Macdonald and Dorothy Matthews). It appears that, ever since Hugo and Carol wed, Carol has not stopped talking about her old sweetie, Frank, and Hugo is determined to meet him. Since Frank has regularly annoyed Sylvia by dreamy references to Carol, she can sympathize with Hugo. She and Hugo decide to leave the old lovers on their own for an evening. A Murphy bed and large bottle of brandy, much of which gets poured over Frank, provide Carol and Frank with their entertainment. The next morning they are happy to return to their spouses.

Having been kept lit by a single revival for much of the season, on the 12th the Cherry Lane switched to an even older play, Clare Kummer's *A Successful Calamity* (2-15-17), in which a rich man pretends to be bankrupt to teach his money-mad family a lesson. It sufficed to keep the bandbox house lit until the hot weather.

Keith Winter's English drama **The Shining Hour** (2-13-34, Booth) was offered to Broadway before the West End saw it. It was a minor hit that also ran until the warm weather and might have run longer had it been brought in sooner. A new bride (Gladys Cooper) comes to live with the family of gentleman farmers into which she has married, falls in love with her brother-in-law (Raymond Massey), drives his wife (Adrianne Allen) to suicide, and runs off with him.

A second British play, this one already having run a year in London, was Gordon Daviot's **Richard of Bordeaux** (2-14-34, Empire). Daviot was a pen name for Agnes Mackintosh. The effete young King Richard II (Dennis King) surprises everyone with his political acumen and strength. But after his beloved wife (Margaret Vines) dies and his best friend (Francis Lister) is exiled, he falls to pieces, losing his once sound judgment and committing so many policy errors that he is overthrown. For all its beautiful and colorful mounting and despite its preopening publicity, the play failed to appeal to Americans.

Hal Skelly's second appearance of the season was in John Floyd's dramatization of Carroll and Garrett Graham's **Queer People** (2-15-34, National). As he did so often, Skelly played a hopeless boozer. Theodore Anthony "Whitey" White is a newspaperman who is willing to take the blame for a murder actually committed by a starlet who was repelling a director's advances. He does all sorts of other crazy things, too. But one hardnosed Jane (Gladys George) is always there to comfort him.

Two plays about the Scottsboro case premiered a week apart. The first was Dennis Donoghue's **Legal Murder** (2-15-34, President), which was slated by the critics and closed before the second play opened. That second play was the Theatre Guild's mounting of John Wexley's **They Shall Not Die** (2-21-34, Royale). Sitting in the Cookesville jailhouse, the redneck deputy sheriffs complain about how dull things are and talk bitterly about how arrogant "coons" are becoming—even attempting to use a white toilet. "Folks up No'th don't know how mean 'em niggers kin be," one asserts. Then all hell breaks loose after half a dozen white kid hoboes are thrown off a train by the blacks, who are left with two white girls. Although the original claim was that maybe a hundred blacks participated, only nine can be rounded up. A local doctor confirms that the girls recently had sex. The girls, Virginia and Lucy (Linda Watkins and Ruth Gordon), are bribed and cajoled into claiming the blacks raped them, while the boys are beaten into confessions. (A second act deals with the home life of Lucy, the weaker of the girls.) After the men are convicted, two Communist lawyers, a Jew (Louis John Latzer) and a black (Frank Wilson), approach the great New York defense attorney Nathan G. Rubin (Claude Rains), who agrees to take over the retrial if he is convinced the boys are innocent and if he feels they can win. When one of the white hoboes (Bob Ross) volunteers that he and another of the white boys had slept with the girls, Rubin feels his case is made. The state's jury commissioner (Ralph Sanford) insists there is no discrimination in the jury system, so Rubin retorts, "You say you have never in all your years as jury commissioner found one colored man qualified for jury service?" The commissioner agrees, and the judge (Thurston Hall) supports him. For all the white boy's evidence and Lucy's recantation, the entire court is clearly prejudiced. After a charge in which the judge insists with patent condescension, "We, the white race, must be just to our colored brethren," the jury goes off to vote. Raucous laughter is heard from the jury room, and when Rubin protests, the judge overrules him. Rubin cries out, "I'll make the fair name of this state stink to high heaven with its lynch justice . . . these boys, *they shall not die.*" (In reality, four were acquitted, four were given short sentences for minor offenses such as assaulting an officer, and the one sentenced to death was reprieved.) Atkinson hailed "one of the most stirring casts ever assembled" and continued, "None of the great causes of the last decade has received in the theatre such a calmly worded and overwhelmingly forceful defence as this." But others objected, with *Variety* warning that the brutality of the first act "comes close to the limit. Beatings administered the cringing colored boys roused the question among first-nighters whether such things constituted stage melodramatics." Playgoers agreed, and the drama found few takers beyond the Guild's subscribers.

Act One: 1930–1944

After several years in Hollywood, where he had attempted unsuccessfully to become a popular leading man (he later became an admired character actor), Walter Huston returned to Broadway in Sidney Howard's adaptation of Sinclair Lewis's **Dodsworth** (2-24-34, Shubert). Although Howard's work was deft and reasonably faithful, many critics felt Huston was the reason for its success: "The stoop of his head, the strength and modesty of his walk, the heartiness of his comradely greetings, the frankness of his eyes, the thoughtful hesitation in a scene that bewilders him, the easy spontaneity of his manner when he is among friends, the rudeness of his voice when he is aroused—all these aspects of his playing reveal Dodsworth completely." Sam Dodsworth is a retired businessman, who has embarked on a grand tour with his wife, Fran (Fay Bainter). But Fran seems more interested in indiscreet affairs with other men than in Europe's treasures. On the eastward sailing Sam had met Edith Cortright (Nan Sunderland), a woman Fran's age but more stable. When the time comes to sail back, Sam decides he cannot continue to live with Fran unless she "stops growing younger." He remains in Europe with Edith. Fran, alone on the ship, wails, "He's gone ashore. He's gone ashore." The play ran out the season and, after a break to allow Huston to honor other commitments, ran five more months next season.

Beulah Marie Dix, a name out of a fast-receding past, and Bertram Millhauser, a film writer, were the authors of a two-performance dud, **Ragged Army** (2-26-34, Selwyn). In the New England town of Dunbury, the leading citizens are preparing a pageant celebrating their ancestors' parts in a Revolutionary battle in the town. They have invited the descendant of the general who won the battle to participate, but when he (Lloyd Nolan) appears he brands them reactionaries and claims the "bohunks" who are striking at the town's mills are the true heirs to the Revolution. After the play closed, the Selwyn, which had already toyed with films and burlesque, went over to films on a more permanent basis.

The next two plays to arrive did better—each surviving a full week. Austin Major's **When in Rome** (2-27-34, 49th St.) recreated the Rome of Catiline in terms of New York's Tammany. A fusion reform group leads a rebellion.

There were reforms of a different stripe in Hiram Sherman's **Too Much Party** (3-5-34, Masque). With her husband away in Europe, Lettice Dean (Maude Richmond) falls under the sway of the mannish Edith (Claire Greenville), who persuades her to run for probation officer, even though both of Lettice's kids look like candidates for the officer's dossiers. Her daughter (Janet McLeay) is frighteningly loose-moraled, while her son

(Reed McClelland) has taken to gambling and forging. Mr. Dean (Pierre Watkin) returns, gets rid of Edith, and starts to straighten out his family.

Sidney Howard and Paul de Kruif had a near miss with their highly praised **Yellow Jack** (3-6-34, Martin Beck). In 1929, Dr. Stackpoole (Geoffrey Kerr) discovers that certain monkeys can contract yellow fever. The discovery prompts him to remind his colleagues what happened in Cuba three decades earlier. Back then Walter Reed (John Miltern) despairs of finding the microbe that causes the disease. Since only humans seem to suffer from it, the belief is that it is transmitted by person-to-person contact. But a much ridiculed Cuban doctor, Carlos Findlay (Whitford Kane), insists that mosquitoes are the culprits. Tragically, the only way to test the theory is on humans. Two doctors (Robert Keith and Barton MacLane) volunteer. At first, nothing happens, until the men realize the mosquitoes must first bite only newly infected sufferers. Both men come down with the disease, and one dies. But the test was not conducted under the "unimpeachable" conditions that Reed requires. To confirm the results for sceptics, four privates (James Stewart, Sam Levene, Myron McCormick, and Edward Acuff) are paid $300 apiece to act as guinea pigs. Two of the men are bitten by mosquitoes; two are confined with yellow fever victims. Only the two who have been bitten come down with the illness. The production was enhanced by Jo Mielziner's multi-leveled, skeletonized settings and poetic lighting (both shortly to become his trademarks), which permitted the action to move swiftly and sometimes to be seen at several places at once. Possibly only the lateness of the season, the somberness, if ultimate hopefulness, of the story, and the large, costly cast militated against a run of more than ten weeks.

At the American Music Hall, a revival of H. S. Smith's 1844 temperance drama, *The Drunkard*, was brought out on the 10th. It remained around for 100 performances. Coincidentally, a few months earlier another revival of the play, performed totally for laughs, was presented in Los Angeles, and by the time it closed had run for twenty years, establishing an American record unbroken until the New York run of *The Fantasticks* decades later.

Considering how many very short runs New York had seen and also taking into account the scathing notices handed Harry Wagstaff Gribble's **The Perfumed Lady** (3-12-34, Ambassador), it needed considerable forcing to keep this comedy on the boards for five full weeks. A young lady (Helen Brooks) barges in on her sweetheart (Brian Donlevy) while he is entertaining his secretary (Marjorie Peterson), who has nothing on but some lingerie. Matters are explained away two acts later.

Downtown runs were not so readily forced, so Eloise Keeler's **Wrong Number** (3-13-34, Provincetown Playhouse) lasted only a week and a half. It concerned a naive matron tricked by a flamboyant numerologist, King Karson, into handing over her fortune to him. Before he is caught and forced to return the money, he has disrupted the lives of her whole family.

Jacques Duval's *Etienne* was seen in New York in George Oppenheimer's translation as **Another Love** (3-19-34, Vanderbilt). Young Etienne (Alfred Corn), upset by the philandering of his pompous father (Raymond Walburn), wins his mother's admiration by stealing his old man's mistress (Suzanne Caubaye).

John Howard Lawson's **The Pure in Heart** (3-20-34, Longacre) looked at the downfall of a naively unprincipled girl (Dorothy Hall) from upstate who comes to New York City, lands a job in the chorus of a musical by sleeping with the director (Harold Vermilyea), becomes the mistress of the librettist (Tom Powers), loses her job because she has infuriated the star (Ara Gerald), takes up with the librettist's gunman brother (James Bell), and is killed with him in a police shootout.

The season's fourth anti-Nazi play, at a time when Hollywood still was ignoring the issue, was Leslie Reade's English drama called *Take Heed* in London but **The Shatter'd Lamp** (3-21-34, Maxine Elliott's) in New York. Apparently the British government shared Hollywood's timidity, since it forced the play to close in London for fear of offending the German government. Here, sympathetic but thumbs-down notices sent the drama packing after thirty-seven performances. The Opal family finds itself in trouble after it is disclosed that Frau Opal (Effie Shannon) is Jewish. The family's son (Owen Davis, Jr.) is deserted by his Aryan fiancée (Jane Bramley), Frau Opal commits suicide, and Herr Opal (Guy Bates Post), a professor, is shot by storm troopers.

For the second time in three nights a John Howard Lawson play opened on Broadway. But though **Gentlewoman** (3-22-34, Cort) was not as propagandistic as Lawson's other efforts, it received the sort of drubbing he was becoming accustomed to. Rudy Flannigan (Lloyd Nolan), the tenth child of an Illinois coal miner, has grown up to be an uncouth, soap-boxy writer, who hates all rich people. He meets wealthy Gwyn Ballatine (Stella Adler) just as she learns of her husband's suicide. Before long they are lovers. However, Gwyn's thoroughbred elegance in time rubs Rudy the wrong way. She comes home one day after learning she is pregnant to discover he plans to run off with another, less polished woman. In order not to make matters awkward for him, she does not tell him her news.

"Sure was a wet night, but the show was wetter," one critic wrote of Leo F. Reardon's **One More Honeymoon** (3-31-34, Little). His exterminating firm on the verge of bankruptcy, Richard Mason (Burford Hampden) weds a wealthy widow, Wanda Rutledge (Alice Fleming). They honeymoon in Iceland, where Richard meets Pookeelocodeecasomoko (Will H. Philbrick), an Icelandic Eskimo, if there is such a thing. The Eskimo's bug-killing fish oil saves Richard's company.

It took three writers—Nicholas Soussanin, William J. Perlman, and Marie Baumer—to author **House of Remsen** (4-2-34, Henry Miller). Arthur Remsen (James Kirkwood) has hated his son after discovering that the boy was fathered by his now dead wife's lover (Albert Van Dekker). Fortunately, Remsen also has a daughter he can dote on. Only when the children are grown and the boy is sent down from Harvard does he learn that the lover lied about the parentage. The son was Remsen's; the daughter, the lover's. Since the play spanned several decades, the younger children were played by different performers than those who played the offspring later in life.

Critics had become increasingly disillusioned about the promise Dan Totheroh had once shown. **Moor Born** (4-3-34, Playhouse) added to the disenchantment. The Brontë sisters live with their aged father (Thomas Findlay), their alcoholic, drug-addicted brother, Branwell (Glenn Anders), and their old servant, Tabby (Beverly Sitgreaves), in their Haworth parsonage. With the ailing Emily (Helen Gahagan) walking alone on the moors, superstitious Tabby warns the fairies will doom her—the milk she churns will be sour, and she will never get a husband. But Anne (Edith Barrett) is more concerned with Charlotte's return from a trip to Brussels, since she must alert Charlotte (Frances Starr) to Branwell's increasingly irresponsible behavior. When Charlotte returns and Branwell confronts his sisters, he tells them his poems and plays and novels will someday free them from their prison. But when he sneers at them, telling Anne she is only a woman, Charlotte snaps back, "Yes, the masculine mind! How superior it is, when it speaks through the fog of liquor and opium!" However, Branwell, then Emily soon die. Tabby was standing beside Emily when the young woman collapsed, and she cries, "She passed me . . . goin' out with the wind. . . . God rest her where she went." The surviving sisters refuse Emily's dying request to let her book be published in Branwell's name, and they resume their own lonely writing.

John Charles Brownell's **Brain Sweat** (4-4-34, Longacre) was something rare for the time, a domestic comedy about blacks. Henry Washington (Billy Higgins) has refused to work, insisting he needs to rest so that his brain can think up a "projeck" to make him rich. To support the family, his wife (Rose McClendon) takes in washing, and his son (Barrington Guy) becomes a delivery boy. When he hears his family wish him dead, he fakes a suicide, leaving only his battered hat by the stream bank. The mourners celebrate around the empty coffin, topped only by the hat, with a joyous wake (which allowed for the "familiar paraphernalia" of black shows, including a rousing sermon, a choir singing spirituals, and a jazz band). But matters are even more joyous when Henry returns. A voice had told him to go to Memphis, and there he had purchased the option on swampland that a steamboat company immediately paid him $10,000 for. Among his gifts to his family is a new car for his wife, with her initials painted boldly on the side. Critics acclaimed the show "nice, clean fun" and admitted it "had us all laughing," but white playgoers wouldn't accept it, so it folded after half a week.

That was also all Frederick Jackson's London comedy *School for Husbands* managed after opening in New York as **Wife Insurance** (4-12-34, Ethel Barrymore). When a philandering author (Harvey Stephens) contemplates eloping with the fiancée (Lillian Emerson) of a friend (Walter Abel), the wife (Ilka Chase) of another friend (Kenneth MacKenna) talks him out of it, but not before both male friends put the wrong construction on the matter.

A consciously mixed-race audience booed and cheered noisily on opening night of the left-wing Theatre Union's mounting of George Sklar and Paul Peters's **Stevedore** (4-18-34, Civic Repertory). To avoid revealing to her husband that she was beaten by her lover, a New Orleans woman claims "a nigger" attacked her. One of the blacks rounded up is Lonnie Thompson (Jack Carter), but he is released when the woman says she cannot identify him certainly. Lonnie is a troublemaker and a union advocate at the Organic Stevedore Company. Told he is stepping out of line, he growls, "Well, here one black man ain't satisfied being just a good nigger." Because of his insolence, the company conspires to frame him for the attack. When bands of whites attempt to seek him out, lynch him, and burn the Negro quarter, he helps set up and man the barricades. (This last setting was not unlike that in *Porgy and Bess,* with shabby houses on two sides of a courtyard and an arched gate in the back leading to the street.) The whites seem ready to carry out their plans until they are dispersed by Communist and union goons, but when the smoke clears Lonnie has been shot dead. The play ran thirteen weeks and returned in the following season for an additional two months.

Crane Wilbur's **Are You Decent?** (4-19-34, Ambassador) ran considerably longer—188 performances—albeit it garnered some of the season's most damning notices. When her granddaughter (Claudia Morgan) decides to have a baby out of wedlock but cannot choose between two potential fathers, grandmother (Zamah Cunningham) decides to "help." One boy (Eric Dressler) asks, "What can I lose?" But the other, a far more sentimental lad (Lester Vail) who dreams of someday having a honeymoon in Brittany, is persuaded by granny to become the father—after he makes the girl his wife. In the teens, settings on luxurious yachts were commonplace. The new comedy offered a variation, with all the action unfolding on a spiffy, wicker-furnished houseboat, with foghorns adding to the atmosphere.

Achmed Abdullah and William Almon Wolff met with disaster when they theatricalized Abdullah and Faith Baldwin's **Broadway Interlude** (4-19-34, Forrest). Broadway's rumor mill claimed that Abdullah, bitter after the late David Belasco had closed a play by Abdullah during tryout and never brought it to New York, meant the new piece as belated revenge. Belasco's former colleagues issued disclaimers, showing that Abdullah's central figure was very little like their old boss. Grant Thompson (Robert Emmett Keane) is a producer who rewrites other men's scripts, then demands the lion's share of royalties, and who prefers to star woman who sleep with him. He is also the sort who has his secretary keep a list of his bons mots for future use in his plays. Young Robert Foster (Arthur Pierson) is willing to lose out on the royalties, but when Thompson consents to star Foster's fiancée, Sally Cameron (Sally Starr), on his standard conditions, Foster balks. Thompson must find another play and make up with his former mistress (Suzanne Caubaye). Those few knowing playgoers who saw the production during its week-and-a-half run could read the Theatre Guild in references to the Playgoers Group and Al Woods in a remark about Al Stone.

The next of the season's two-performance duds was Nathan Sherman's **Late Wisdom** (4-23-34, Mansfield). A rubber magnate (Jay Fassett) and his secretary (Franc Hale) have an affair, which leaves the executive more open-minded but costs the girl her fiancé.

Luckless Ernest Truex found himself in good company, but in yet another bad play, in Dawn Powell's **Jigsaw** (4-30-34, Ethel Barrymore). Claire Burnell (Spring Byington) is a wealthy divorcée, always happy to spend time with her lover, Del Marsh (Truex), whenever he finds an excuse to leave his wife in Baltimore. But suddenly Claire falls in love with a man (Eliot Cabot) young enough to be her convent-trained daughter's husband. Who knows what might have happened had not the daughter (Gertrude Flynn) returned home and stolen the younger man away, leaving Claire to make it up with Del. Claire asks Del to tell her that he loves her, and he allows that he will tell it to her, "if you want to believe that stuff."

Claire's fate might have been that of Pearl Barton, the central figure in Ida Lublenski Ehrlich's **Love Kills** (5-1-34, Forrest). Pearl (Vivian Giesen) marries a rich man for his money, then jumps from lover to lover before jumping out of a window.

Another unhappy woman, almost seduced away from a comfortable home by a sailor she once loved, was the focus of Ibsen's *The Lady from the Sea,* which New York had first seen in November of 1911 and now was revived to unenthusiastic notices at the Little on the same night.

With the five-performance failure of her **Picnic** (5-2-34, National), Walter Damrosch's daughter Gretchen, now writing as Gretchen Damrosch Finletter, closed out her Broadway career. A soapbox revolutionist (Joanna Roos) is allowed to hide at the country home of a rich friend (Marvin Kline). The peace and gentility of the place, plus a kindly man named Robert (Percy Waram), lead her to question her own fire-breathing doctrines.

In Lionel Hale's short-lived **These Two** (5-7-34, Henry Miller) Simon (Bramwell Fletcher) agrees to marry Celia (Helen Chandler), who is pregnant by a faithless lover. But after the baby dies, Celia herself proves faithless to Simon. As a result, Simon takes up with Fay (Kay Strozzi). By the time Celia realizes that she truly loves Simon, it is too late. Their friend, Tom (A. E. Matthews), fails to reconcile the pair, so Simon walks out and Celia contemplates suicide.

One of the season's least explicable flops was Lynn Root and Harry Clork's **The Milky Way** (5-8-34, Cort). Allegedly based on the antics of a real middleweight champ, Mickey Walker, who was kayoed in a small fracas far from the ring, it received almost unanimous endorsements from the critics, with Robert Garland of the *World-Telegram* insisting, "If laugh piled on laugh, guffaw piled on guffaw, means anything, 'The Milky Way' is the spring's outstanding knockout. . . . Four stars would seem all too few for [its] laugh-provoking qualities." To this day, the play reads uproariously. Speed McFarland (Brian Donlevy), nursing a conspicuous shiner, is appalled to eye headlines proclaiming, "Speed McFarland, world's middleweight champion, knocked out by truck driver in street brawl." Actually the truck driver was a milquetoast milkman, Burleigh Sullivan (Hugh O'Connell), and he comes to Speed's rooms to apologize and explain. As a younger man he had been a professional ducker, ducking balls thrown at him at carnivals. On the night in question, when he tried to stop the fighter from dating his sister, Mae (Emily Lowry), Speed and Speed's trainer, Spider (William Foran), had both taken swings at him, Burleigh had ducked, and the two professionals had knocked each other out. Unfortunately for Speed and his corrupt, snarling manager, Gabby (Leo Donelly), the whole

affair is repeated just as newspapermen enter the room. The quick-thinking Gabby decides to have Burleigh turn professional, fix some fights to ensure he wins, then allow Speed to vindicate himself in an honest match with the milkman. He orders Spider to start training Burleigh. Spider groans that the best he could do is "make a dandy manicurist" out of him. Burleigh is finally talked into the plan—unaware, of course, that the fix will be in. He is so naive about boxing that when he enters the ring the first time, the fight is stopped until he can remove his bathrobe. The fixes all work, but at the bout between Speed and Burleigh, Burleigh ducks Speed's blows but in rising up inadvertently butts Speed, kayoing him. With his winnings as world champ Burleigh buys the dairy he worked for, while Mae and Speed become a pair. Much as the play was praised, O'Connell, with his irresistible innocence, his wide grin, and his hilariously halting gestures, was praised even more, Lockridge calling him the "foremost amiable idiot of our time and stage." Yet the play folded after just two months.

Adelyn Bushnell's **I, Myself** (5-9-34, Mansfield) was anything but light spring fare. A failed insurance salesman (Charles Trowbridge) arranges for a tramp (Harry M. Cooke) to kill him so that his family can benefit from his $50,000 policy. But when the wife (Regina Wallace) is held on suspicion of murdering her husband, the tramp comes forward to confess the truth.

Sweet, tiny, ungrammatical Sadie (Queenie Smith) comes once a week to clean for the Clarks in Doty Hobart's **Every Thursday** (5-10-34, Royale). So when she discovers that, while papa and mama are away, young Raymond Clark (Leon Janney) would take up with a streetwalker (Sheila Trent), she shoos off the girl and takes her place. Sadie loses her job but wins an understanding chauffeur (Jack Adams).

Richard Flournoy's **Come What May** (5-15-34, Plymouth) spanned more than three decades—which meant that characters played by children in early scenes were played by adults in later ones. In the late 1890s, Chet Harrison (Hal Skelly) marries Eve Hayward (Mary Philips), and their troubles begin. As a typesetter, Chet finds himself out of work when linotype machines come in. Their son is killed in the World War. But at least they now have $10,000 in the bank, and what more could go wrong in this year of grace, 1928? Skelly's appearance was his last before his untimely death at forty-three a month after the show opened.

Some good acting could not overcome some incredibly stilted dialogue and preposterous situations in Rufus King's **Invitation to a Murder** (5-17-34, Masque). In the great hall of the old Channing estate on the California coast, Lorinda Channing (Gale Sondergaard) can sit on her throne and by moving an armrest permit anyone in front of her to fall through a trapdoor down to certain death below. She is afraid her cousins, Walter and Horatio (William Valentine and Humphrey Bogart), are after her estate, so she persuades a young doctor (Walter Abel) to give her medication which will let her appear to be dead. While she supposedly is in her coffin, she sneaks out and kills Walter, then, discovering the doctor seeking her treasure, frames him for the killing. But her fingerprints on a cigarette case not introduced into the house until after she was supposedly dead convict her. Her loyal butler (James Shelburne) spares her capture by causing her to fall through the trapdoor.

Ragnhilde Bruland's **Furnished Rooms** (5-29-34, Ritz) told a "distressing story as drab as the lodging house in which it locales." Ann (Vicki Cummings) uses her last money to rent a room in a cheap guest house, whose landlord (John F. Morrissey) soon forcibly takes advantage of her. His son (Frank Reyman), falling in love with the girl, would be revenged on the man, but the landlord's discarded mistress (Violet Barney) does the job for him.

A London comedy, Anthony Kimmins's **While Parents Sleep** (6-4-34, Playhouse), ended the season on a down note. A snobbish elder brother (Alan Marshal) brings home a married noblewoman (Ilka Chase) to spend the night with him, while his playboy younger brother (Charles Romano) brings home a girl tellingly named Bubbles (Jane Bramley). The two life-styles clash at two in the morning, until an aroused old nanny (Jane Corcoran) orders the woman to pack.

1934–1935

The new season, described in one end-of-year survey as "neither good nor bad," saw the number of productions hold relatively steady for the third time in a row. Once again, depending on which survey was employed, somewhere between 101 and 110 new plays premiered. This led optimists to suggest that Broadway's decline had ceased. Alas, the optimists were wrong. In the very next season, the plunge would resume and continue headlong until, down the road, some seasons would introduce fewer than thirty non-musical productions. The doleful state of the road should have hinted at problems ahead. Week after week *Variety* reported touring houses converting to films or simply closing, and plays folding out of town for lack of trade. An inordinate number—at least for recent decades—of foreign plays could also have suggested a problem, in this case that native writers were more interested in trying their luck in Hollywood.

The lone, late June straggler, John Charles Brownell's **Her Majesty, the Widow** (6-18-34, Ritz), probably really belongs with the 1933–34 season, but since *Best Plays* and other records echoed theatrical contracts, which ran from one June 15th to the next, it is listed here. The play, with Hollywood favorite Pauline Frederick, had originated on the West Coast and been touring for more than a year. Frederick played a widowed mother who must prevent her son (Thomas Beck) from marrying a gold-digging floozie (Isobel Withers) and see him properly paired with a better girl (Laurette Bullivant). By inviting both girls to her home, she succeeds in opening her son's eyes. She also finds romance for herself. The comedy was brought in by Wee and Leventhal, who made a practice of touring oldies and occasional novelties at cheap prices. For the New York engagement, they flooded the city with "55¢ Oakleys" and refused to allow the box office to post prices so as not to embarrass or confuse ticket buyers. Neither the ploy nor the star availed much, so the play closed after one month.

The days of a rich summer theatrical harvest were gone. No other novelty appeared for more than two months. Then Harry Madden and Philip Dunning's **Kill That Story** (8-29-34, Booth) became the season's first modest success—chalking up 117 performances, thanks in part to George Abbott's taut direction. At a convention of newspaper folk and advertising executives, Duke Devlin (James Bell) learns that at the behest of some corrupt politicians, two unscrupulous promoters, Spike Taylor (Matt Briggs) and Paul Simpson (Royal Dana Tracy), are attempting to buy the crusading *Herald* in order to silence it. Years earlier Taylor had gotten a girl in trouble and pinned the responsibility on Devlin, causing him to lose his wife, Margaret McGuire (Emily Lowry), daughter of the paper's editor. With the help of the free-flowing liquor and playful young ladies who abound in such conventions, Devlin tricks Taylor into a confession. Threatening also to expose some of Taylor's illegal dealings, he gets the promoters to back away from the paper deal. And he wins back Margaret.

H. M. Harwood's **Lady Jane** (9-10-34, Plymouth), done first in England as *The Old Folks at Home*, told an almost similar tale to *Her Majesty, the Widow*. Only this time the mother (Frances Starr) must save her sex-starved daughter (Lila Lee) and her unhappy daughter-in-law (Frieda Inescort). To this end, she places the daughter's undesirable young man (Alan Marshal) and the daughter-in-law's lover (Paul McGrath) in rooms adjoining those of the women. She thus proves her notion that "an unsuccessful infidelity" is often the best tonic to keep a woman on the straight and narrow, and she confesses that she herself once took a lover. The play ran a week longer than the Frederick vehicle.

John Tainter Foote and Hubert Hayes's **Tight Britches** (9-11-34, Avon) had three strikes against it. First of all, it was not an especially good play. Second, it was so filled with regional idioms that a thirty-seven-word glossary was included in the program. Last, the Broadway actors picked to perform this tragedy of the North Carolina backwaters could not convey the requisite earthiness. The pious Ulys Palmer (Shepperd Strudwick) is about to preach his first sermon when it is revealed that he has had a child by a local trollop, Sallie Tabor (Joanna Roos). Since he believes he loves the girl and can change her ways, he agrees to marry her. But the baby dies, Ulys is shot by Sallie's indignant father (Arthur Hughes), who believes her honor has been soiled, and Sallie is driven out of town. Only Ethel Wilson, as a stern, sharp-tongued backwoods spinster, came away with praise.

The first of the season's nearly thirty one-week-or-less duds was **Too Many Boats** (9-11-34, Playhouse), which Owen Davis took from the novel by Charles L. Clifford. It was set in the Philippines during the World War at a camp reserved for enlisted men and officers whom the army feels unfit for combat. Most of the enlisted men are blacks; the officers, white. Yet the problem that arises is not a racial one, but rather personal enmity between the boozing Captain Coates (Earle Larimore) and the suspected Hun sympathizer Major Von Kurtz (Horace Braham), whose wife (Helen Flint) flirts openly with the captain. Von Kurtz attempts to provoke a riot among the blacks and blame Coates. The riot is quickly controlled and Von Kurtz subsequently shot dead. Suspicion falls on Coates, but there is no hard evidence. To be rid of him, he is sent to France. By chance Mrs. Von Kurtz, revealed as a former prostitute, is given passage on the same ship.

Elmer Rice, who had taken over the Belasco, returned to one of his favorite milieus, the courtroom, for his first offering there, **Judgment Day** (9-12-34, Belasco). However, this is not an American court where some innocent young lady is falsely accused; rather it is the kangaroo court in some unspecified Balkan country, where two citizens, Lydia Kuman (Josephine Victor) and George Khitov (Walter N. Greaza), and one drug-addicted foreigner (Eric Wollencott) are on trial for attempting to kill the country's dictator. The evidence is clearly trumped up and three of the court's five judges clearly in the leader's pocket. Lydia's brother (Vincent Sherman), who has returned from America where he now practices law, warns the court that ten thousand newspapers in a hundred countries are carrying extensive reports on the trial. Furious at the lack of speed and at calls for his appearance or abdication, Vesnic (House Jameson), the dictator himself, appears and warns, "If our courts do not know how to deal with their

country's enemies, the Government will be compelled to find more effective means of procuring justice." When a supposed priest is shown to be another alleged conspirator and Lydia's husband (Ryder Keane) in disguise, Vesnic demands he be killed then and there. Instead, one of the two unbiased judges (St. Clair Bayfield) grabs the gun a corrupt, obedient judge had pulled out, shoots Vesnic, then, shouting, "Down with tyranny! Long live the people!" kills himself. The fate of the accused is not shown. The play's fate was dismissive notices and a forced run of twelve weeks.

The Bride of Torozko (9-13-34, Henry Miller) was adapted by Ruth Langner from an unidentified play by Otto Indig, variously said to be of Hungarian, German, or Austrian provenance. Its heroine (Jean Arthur) finds her Catholic marriage is called off after it is discovered her parents were Jews. Under the tutelage of a local tavern-keeper (Sam Jaffe), she becomes a devout and totally idiomatic Jew, even to sneering at one former friend as a "goy." But when, on listening to the tavern-keeper's sad history of the Jews, she questions why Jews are called the chosen people, he replies: "Did I say what they were chosen for?" Matters take a final turn on the discovery that a clerk looked at the wrong records. The girl is not Jewish—she is a Protestant.

Since Charles Divine's **Strangers at Home** (9-14-34, Longacre) was billed as a comedy, critics decided it was meant to spoof those dear ladies who offer tourists a bed and a breakfast. They found it largely unfunny. In Kingston Mrs. Crosby (Eleanor Hicks) and her sister (Marie Bruce) decide to earn some additional moneys by catering to travelers. Before long, as a result of the constant comings and goings, the Crosby son (Philippe de Lacy) has run off to join the navy, a daughter (Joan Wheeler) has escaped to New York, and Mr. Crosby (Clyde Franklin) has had a nervous breakdown. At best, a second daughter (Katherine Emery) has found true romance with one (William Post, Jr.) of the guests.

The halcyon days of not long ago may have come to mind when critics and playgoers found themselves with three openings on the same Monday night. The shortest-lived was Alan Dinehart and Samuel Shipman's **Alley Cat** (9-17-34, 48th St.). A man (Dinehart) who has lost his fortune and whose wife has walked out on him is about to commit suicide when he is talked out of it by a young girl (Audrey Christie) who has smelled the gas. Later she confesses that she, too, was about to kill herself until she was diverted by her attempt to stop him. A romance blossoms before the man's ex (Kay Strozzi) hears that his fortune may be restored and so returns cradling a baby. But later, learning that the baby is not his, the man and his rescuer resume their affair. The affair lasted eight performances.

The other two entries fared a mite better, with both

lasting for five weeks. The American offering was Nat N. Dorfman's **Errant Lady** (9-17-34, Fulton). Clara Jessup (Leona Powers), a shrewish Westchester matron, is outraged on discovering not only that her daughter, Sylvia (Helen Walpole), wants to obtain a divorce in order to marry a dashing White Russian named Rachmananov (Donald Randolph) but that Mr. Jessup (Averell Harris) could not care less. So Clara attempts to chase away the Russian by vamping him herself, which gives the gleeful Mr. Jessup an opportunity to sue for a divorce from his harridan wife and spend the rest of his days duck hunting. That news brings Clara to her senses.

Immediately after its opening, Terence Rattigan and Philip Heimann's London comedy-drama **First Episode** (9-17-34, Ritz) changed its name to *College Sinners*. Neither title made the play attractive to Americans. A famous actress (Leona Maricle) falls in love with an Oxford student (John Halloran). When she believes his roommate (Patrick Waddington) is throwing obstacles in their path, she implies the roommate is homosexual. Then, discovering the boy illegally dating a girl off campus, she reports him and has him expelled. Her behavior loses her her lover's affection.

Joseph Anthony's **A Ship Comes In** (9-19-34, Morosco) begins in a Viennese coffee house and quickly moves onto the posh S.S. *Manhattan*. A rich American, H. Gordon Mortimer (Calvin Thomas), offers the famous Austrian psychologist Dr. Bard (Jacob Ben-Ami) a million dollars to establish a chain of clinics in the States. When Mortimer's love-starved niece (Virginia Stevens) makes advances toward Bard, the doctor slips an emetic in her whiskey. This outrages Mortimer until he discovers Bard has a serious psychological problem—he is terrified of being alone with women.

Eugene Charlier has no such problem, and that helps him pull off his scam in **The Red Cat** (9-19-34, Broadhurst), which Jessie Ernst took from an unspecified play by Rudolf Lothar and Hans Adler. Charlier (Francis Lister) is a nightclub imitator pressed into substituting for a famous banker (also Lister) who has run off rather than face bankruptcy. This even means spending a night with the banker's wife (Ruth Weston). When the banker returns after setting his affairs in order again, it seems as if he was never away.

Two hits followed in quick succession. The longer running of the pair—177 performances—was John van Druten's London comedy **The Distaff Side** (9-25-34, Booth), with beautiful, cello-voiced Sybil Thorndike's richly glowing performance immeasurably adding to its lure. She played a widowed matron who must deal with the numerous women in her life, including on the one hand her crotchety, cronish mother (Mildred Natwick) and her free-spirited sister (Estelle Winwood) and on

the other her troubled daughter (Viola Keats), caught between two lovers. She manages to work out most difficulties satisfactorily by the final curtain.

By coincidence the season's second play to carry George Abbott's directorial stamp ran exactly as long as the first—117 performances. **Small Miracle** (9-26-34, Golden) was a melodrama by Norman Krasna, who later would be better known for his comedies. One critic suggested it wanted to be "the 'Grand Hotel' of the theatre lobby." That lobby or, more accurately, downstairs lounge was in the 43rd Street Theatre. Among the playgoers is a faithless married woman (Ilka Chase) awaiting her lover. There is also a trampish usheress (Elspeth Eric) who is demanding $200 from the head usher and cloakroom attendant (Myron McCormick) to pacify her crooked mate (Owen Martin) when he discovers the usher has made his girl pregnant. And there is the usher's girl, who has sacrificed her virtue to find the $200 her fiancé needs. Somehow, a discreetly handcuffed Tony Mako (Joseph Spurin-Celleia) is present, too. He has escaped from a jail where he was being held for a killing in a gas station robbery. He manages to get free from his manacles and, when the man who squealed on him arrives, shoots him dead. He, in turn, is shot dead. It appears that the squealer was the usheress's mate. Now that he is dead she has no hold on the attendant. And his own girl realizes she made her sacrifice needlessly.

J. C. Nugent was author and star of **Dream Child** (9-27-34, Vanderbilt). He was seen as the dry-voiced, pudgy, balding "King Tut" Jones, who has lived a quietly ordered life in New Jersey, always ruing that he never eloped with the opera singer he once had a crush on. He is determined his son, Robert (Alan Bunce), shall not miss out on a good chance, so he takes him to New York City, where the boy meets a lovely artist (Ruth Nugent) and has a fling before the girl disappears. Years later Robert, now stolidly married much like his father had been, meets the girl again and wonders what might have happened had she not run off.

Those critics who liked George S. Kaufman and Moss Hart's **Merrily We Roll Along** (9-29-34, Music Box) liked it a lot. John Mason Brown of the *Evening Post* called it "superlatively good theatre," and Robert Garland of the *World-Telegram* acclaimed it as "brilliant." Other critics were a little less happy, with Burns Mantle in the *Daily News* finding it "not altogether satisfying" and the *Herald Tribune*'s old Percy Hammond, who wished the authors had written it from finish to start, confessing, "Something tells me that 'Merrily We Roll Along' may be a good show, even if I cannot rave about it with the fervor it no doubt deserves." Only the public seemed surprisingly cool, perhaps again because they expected a funnier play from Kaufman and Hart. It closed after less than twenty weeks. During that time it recounted, in reverse chronology, the life of a popular playwright, Richard Niles (Kenneth MacKenna), at forty at the peak of his career. But a party to celebrate his latest play ends in calamity when his latest wife, Althea (Jessie Royce Landis), throws iodine in the face of his latest star and mistress (Murial Williams). Seven years earlier, unhappy at a new portrait, he publicly punches his old buddy, the painter, Jonathan Crale (Walter Abel). A year before that he prepares to ditch the wife whom he married for love when he was a struggling writer and marry the glamorous Althea. Newly famous, he tells Crale he likes his new world and asks why he should set aside popular acceptance for art: "So that you and Julia [another old buddy] could tell me how great I was? I don't see myself writing plays for two people, and being miserable the rest of the time." And so a few years at a stretch Niles's life moves backward, with each backward move revealing him as more high-minded and more likable. So likable, in fact, that in 1916 he is chosen to speak for his graduating class, and he takes his theme from Shakespeare—"This above all; to thine own self be true." The character of the acid-tongued, besotted Julia (Mary Philips) was allegedly patterned after Dorothy Parker. Besides lauding the cast and Kaufman's direction, critics saluted the "nine highly illuminating scenes" created by Jo Mielziner (MacKenna's brother). These moved from a posh Long Island home, to a fashionable New York restaurant, to less and less luxurious surroundings, and finally to a corner of Madison Square Park at night with the surrounding skyscrapers lit and to a college chapel. Stephen Sondheim offered Broadway a musical version in 1981.

When the neighboring butcher (Joseph Greenwald) asks the widowed Mrs. Solomon (Helen Zelinskaya) to marry him in Bella and Sam Spewack's story of New York ghetto life, **Spring Song** (10-1-34, Morosco), she responds, "Soon the girls will be married, and then ask me again." Unfortunately, one of her girls, Florrie (Francine Larrimore), disgusted that her brash, traveling salesman beau (Sam Levene) is away so much, seduces Sid Kurtz (Norman Stuart), fiancé of her sister, Tillie (Frieda Altman). She becomes pregnant, attempts an abortion unsuccessfully, is forced by mama and the rabbi to marry Sid, but dies in childbirth. A heartbroken mama blames herself for the problem.

For the most part, second-string critics were sent to review the evening's other novelty, Emmet Lavery's **The First Legion** (10-1-34, 46th St.), called "a drama of the Society of Jesus." Impressed primarily by its honesty, the *Sun*'s Stephen Rathbun suggested that it

also "has a surprising amount of what is known as good theatre." In the *Daily News*, John Chapman hedged, "Not badly written and devoutly played." Aided by cut-rate tickets and some forcing, and by parishioners heeding the praises of their local priests, the play lingered, for its first month at the large musical comedy house, for fourteen weeks. Much of the action was set in the "towering, somber community room" at St. Gregory's Novitiate. Many of the older priests find themselves quietly or publicly questioning their own faith. Then one (Pedro de Cordoba) of the priests, who had become paralyzed, is able to walk again. The others begin to reaffirm their faith, until the novitiate's doctor (Harlan Tucker), who had proclaimed earlier that he had no faith to lose, confesses he tricked the father into walking again. The sick man's paralysis was psychosomatic. "All I had to do was let José think a miracle had touched him—and he was certain to walk." The vacillating priests find themselves disillusioned again. But then a youngster (Frankie Thomas) suffering from infantile paralysis comes, prays, and is cured. One (Bert Lytell) of the most doubting priests falls on his knees and, looking skyward, shouts, "Forgive me-Forgive me-how could I have doubted Thee?" Whitford Kane took the part of a non-Jesuit priest forever attempting sly digs at the order, while Charles Coburn was one of the more ardent clerics.

Margaret Leech (Mrs. Ralph Pulitzer) and Beatrice (Mrs. George S.) Kaufman collaborated on **Divided by Three** (10-2-34, Ethel Barrymore). Their story tells of a young man (James Stewart) who goes on a bender and almost goes to pieces on learning from his sweetheart (Hancey Castle) that his mother (Judith Anderson) has a lover (James Rennie). By the final curtain he recognizes that he must accept an imperfect world.

Paul Green's intermissionless "symphonic play of the Negro people" **Roll, Sweet Chariot** (10-2-34, Cort) was waved away politely by second-stringers sent to review it. The play had been floating around regional theatres for some years as *Potter's Field*. To incessant music and a choir singing from behind the back curtain, Green's story recounted the downfall of the black shantytown of Potter's Field and its leading citizen, John Henry (Warren Coleman), a former convict and self-proclaimed preacher whose misbehavior brings the wrath of his fellow blacks and neighboring whites down on himself and his community. In the end a chain gang is sent to dismantle the settlement.

The dominant figure in Owen Davis's **Spring Freshet** (10-4-34, Plymouth) was a family-proud New England grandmother, Isabel Levenseller (Esther Dale), willing to go to any lengths to keep the family name alive. To this end she forces her only grandson, Ned (Richard

Whorf), to marry a girl (Viola Frayne) he does not like. The unhappy marriage proves childless. So when she discovers that Ned has fathered an illegitimate son, she does not hesitate to adopt the child and make him her heir.

Some of the season's most damning reviews went to Henry Rosendahl's **Yesterday's Orchids** (10-5-34, Fulton), apparently written and produced to give his wife, Ann Whitney, a starring role. She played a girl who uses man after man before finding true love and mending her ways.

Kenneth Perkins's **Dance with Your Gods** (10-6-34, Mansfield) employed a racially mixed cast to suggest that whites could be affected by voodooism as much as blacks. To prove the point, Jacques Boyean (Ben Smith) asks Mother Bouche (Georgette Harvey), a woman the police are seeking after her followers have run amuck, to put a curse on Amos Juvenal, a name he believes he has picked at random. He then learns there is a gentleman (Charles Waldron) by that name who has just brought a daughter, Ninon (Pauline Moore), back from her convent school. Boyean goes to warn Juvenal of the curse, but instead locks the man up, kidnaps the daughter, and takes her to a voodoo ceremony in an old warehouse, where he hopes to rape her. Before he can, the police raid the place and take away Boyean, by now ravingly insane. The evening's only genuine excitement came from the voodoo celebration, with its "semi-barbaric, sensuous writhing of the colored players, beating of the native drums and the chaotic motion."

The Theatre Guild's first entry of the season, James Bridie's London drama **A Sleeping Clergyman** (10-8-34, Guild), received some quietly respectful notices but found no public beyond the Guild's subscribers. Bridie (otherwise Dr. O. H. Mavor) gave life to his contention that bad blood often contains the seeds of good blood by setting his drama in a gentlemen's club, where, while a clergyman sleeps in a nearby chair, another club member tells the history of the Camerons, whose earlier generations were troublesome but whose recent offspring have become productive and famous.

Variety complained that while hotel guests in **Order Please** (10-9-34, Playhouse), which Edward Childs Carpenter adapted from a play by Walter Hackett, were elegantly garbed, the cheap lobby setting made the hotel look little better than a fleabag. Nonetheless, Foxhall Ridgway (James Bell), a Wyoming rancher, books a suite at the Diplomat, hoping to find some excitement and a brunette to enliven his New York visit. The first thing he finds is a corpse in the adjoining room, but by the time the manager and the cops come the body has disappeared, only to be discovered later in Ridgway's trunk. A pricey necklace is found on the dead man's person, but it, too, does a disappearing act. The culprit

in both cases eventually turns out to be the murdered man's secretary. At least Ridgway does find romance with a beautiful girl (Vivienne Osborne), the hotel's telephone operator—even if she is a blonde.

The ghost of cruel Captain Morning hovers over Jay Doten's **Green Stick** (10-9-34, Provincetown Playhouse). His will decreed that any family member leaving his homestead before marriage would be disinherited. His Bible-spouting widow (May Gerald) keeps his dueling pistols on hand to enforce his wishes. Also kept at home are his son (Richard Boegner, the author's real name), a would-be poet crippled by a fall from a mast on his father's ship, and a meek, widowed daughter-in-law (Betty Worth). But a modern, cigarette-smoking, cocktail-drinking niece (Marguerite Walker) and her equally high-living beau (Thomas Anthony) defy the old woman. They are green sticks that bend but do not break.

Tom Powers again tried his skill at playwriting and came up empty-handed in **Bridal Quilt** (10-10-34, Biltmore), although several critics acknowledged that first-nighters had a good time. After Washburn Alexander (Blaine Cordner), a handsome hillbilly, rescues her when her car stalls in a fast-rising creek, Cathleen Hotchkiss Barton (Claudia Morgan) casually invites him to visit her if he ever comes to New York. Sure enough, he soon is knocking at her door just as she and her tuxedoed husband (Lester Vail) are awaiting dinner guests. It quickly becomes obvious that Washburn thought Cathleen was single. He hurriedly heads home. She follows to apologize and learns to her relief he has already fallen for his neighbor, Minnie Ella (Eleanor Lynn).

It took seventeen sets (and twenty scenes) on a revolving stage and two dozen actors (in forty roles) to help tell Harry Segall and John Hayden's **Lost Horizons** (10-15-34, St. James). An actress (Jane Wyatt), jilted by the ambitious young attorney (Arthur Pierson) she was about to marry, walks into her kitchenette and shoots herself. At the dignified Hall of Records, which "greatly resembles the reading room of a public library" and which may be in Heaven, Hell, or Limbo, a dapper, polite guide insists she must read the record of her life. When she asks if everyone must do this, he replies, "Only those, like yourself, who did not complete their earthly existence. Here they learn what the unfinished part of the story held in store for them." In her case, the story would have gone on to fame in the theatre, to a happy marriage with her director, Adam Thayer (Walter Gilbert), to bringing wealth and joy to many colleagues, and even indirectly to saving one girl (Betty Lancaster) from prostitution and another (Cynthia Rogers) from marrying a scoundrel (Gage Clarke). As she reads what might have been, the actress sees another apparent suicide enter and be handed his record of life—Thayer. The play gave rise to some of the sharpest critical disagreements of the season. Nor could the public seemingly decide. Two closing dates were announced, followed by spurts in attendance and extensions. But after seven uncertain weeks that play closed for good.

There was no uncertainty about the season's first if rather belated smash hit, Lawrence Riley's **Personal Appearance** (10-17-34, Henry Miller). The often nitpicking, snooty Hammond managed both to praise and to gently slap the comedy when he called it "the season's most crackling show, bright, impudent and not over the heads of the dullest drama lovers." John Mason Brown welcomed "the loud and sustained laughter that has not been heard in a New York playhouse since the merriest of last year's comedies." The curtain rose to show a darkened Scranton, Pennsylvania, film house and the end of a tearjerker called *Drifting Lady*. As soon as the film ends its star, the glamorous Carole Arden (Gladys George), comes onstage to say hello to the audience. Carole, it develops, is on a personal appearance tour, and her next stop is Wilkes-Barre. But her fancy Isotta-Franchini breaks down midway between the two burgs in front of a combination filling station and guest house. The guest house is run by Mrs. Struthers (Minna Philips), who, according to her sharp-tongued Aunt Kate (Eula Guy), is "always trying to be a duchess on nothing and a half a week." The filling station is managed by Bud Norton (Philip Ober), a handsome, hulking, inventive mechanic, who is engaged to Mrs. Struthers's daughter, Joyce (Merna Pace). Carole is furious when she learns that the Jiffy Service Garage cannot get to her car for several hours, but her attitude changes completely once she gets a look at Bud. This worries the observant Aunt Kate, who has read that Carole is susceptible to handsome men. But Carole's traveling factotum, Gene Tuttle (Otto Hulett), assures her, "The studio sends me along to see that she doesn't suscept too easily." Nevertheless, Carole, on learning that Bud has invented a gadget to make sound recording simpler, insists on heading for the barn—where his workroom is—with him alone. They return to announce he will accompany her back to Hollywood. The nose-in-the-air Mrs. Struthers will be delighted to have her daughter out of the embraces of a mere mechanic, but for everyone else there is consternation until Tuttle appeals to Carole's better nature and even lies that Joyce is expecting a child by Bud. The comedy, getting a special boost from the lack of much light-hearted competition, ran 501 performances. (The published version of the play was dedicated to its producer and director, Brock Pemberton and Antoinette Perry, with the remark, "I'd rather re-write than be President.")

There was no enthusiasm for John Crump's **Hipper's**

Holiday (10-18-34, Maxine Elliott's). Out of work and not very law-abiding, Jim Hipper (Burgess Meredith) persuades his buddy, Charlie Mason (Shelton Earp), who runs an orange-juice stand and whose girl is pregnant, to help him kidnap a well-dressed man and demand $1000 ransom. The man (John Boyd) they select turns out to be a cheat sought by the police and by those he scammed. The boys get their money not from their victim but from one (Carlos de Torre) of their victim's victims. It's small change compared to the $50,000 he forces the cheat to hand back.

Sean O'Casey's well-received **Within the Gates** (10-22-34, National) combined a large, mixed-bag *Grand Hotel*–style character list and the generic names (The Dreamer, The Young Whore, The Man in the Bowler Hat) of the no longer voguish expressionist drama with the sweeping poetic prose of so much Irish theatre to tell the story of a prostitute (Lillian Gish) who finds temporary satisfaction in the arms of a dreamy lover (Bramwell Fletcher) before finding death and redemption in the arms of her father (Moffat Johnston), the bishop. Gish received special praise for the diversity and poignancy of her performance. In two slightly separate engagements, the drama totted up 141 playings.

One of the season's shortest runs—two performances—was the lot of Edward Mendelssohn's **Good-Bye Please** (10-24-34, Ritz). Jack (Robert Keith), a young attorney, and Marian (Selena Royle), an interior decorator, live together for two years until Jack walks out. When he returns and asks Marian to take him back, she refuses, suggesting he head home to Mississippi and marry someone there. He does just that. Then Marian has a change of heart and appears on his doorstep. Critics felt the play's ending hinted at a possible reconciliation after Jack gets a divorce.

Elmer Rice's second offering of the season, **Between Two Worlds** (10-25-34, Belasco), was another in the *Grand Hotel* style, this one unfolding on an ocean liner heading for Europe. Aline Bernstein's admired setting showed a cross-section of a lounge and part of the sun deck. Despite the huge cast list two figures stood out. One was a blue-blooded American, Margaret Brown (Rachel Hartzell), whose friends include several exiled Russian aristocrats. The other was N. N. Kovolev (Joseph Schildkraut), a famous Russian film director returning home after an unsuccessful stint in Hollywood. The pair meet, and the Russian half cajoles and half taunts the American, who is engaged to be married, into a shipboard affair. Immediately afterwards he drops her, professing a prior allegiance to his country: "There are many women in the world, but for a Communist there is only one party." She is hurt, and he attempts dispassionately to explain his convictions. She finally forgives him, and when he says that if she visits Russia

Act One: 1930–1944

he will be her guide, she responds, "That alone would be worth the trip." Critics reserved the highest praise for Schildkraut's "class acting, his enunciation and faultless dialect." Although seen as better than *Judgment Day,* the drama itself was deemed essentially lifeless, so closed after four weeks.

Even shorter stands were in store for the two offerings that came in next. Samuel Ornitz and Vera Caspary's **Geraniums in My Window** (10-26-34, Longacre) featured the two players who had scored so heavily in *Sailor, Beware!*, Bruce MacFarlane and Audrey Christie. Toby Starr pretends to be a poor boy and, calling himself Slater Jones, applies for work at an employment agency. There he meets Nellie Quinn. After he fends off some mashers who were harassing her, she helps him get a job as a dishwasher. Love and marriage follow, until Nellie discovers the truth. Furious at being lied to, she walks out. Of course, there is an eleven-o'clock reconciliation.

Leigh Burton Wells's **Allure** (10-29-34, Empire) was even less attractive. As a child, Marion had crippled her baby sister by throwing her down the stairs. Now, as a grown woman (Edith Barrett), she marries a sculptor (Guido Nazdo), only to watch him fall in love with the sister (Florence Williams). She furiously smashes the statue he has made of the girl. This drives the girl to the brink of madness, but after the sister is cured by a famous Viennese psychiatrist (Robert T. Haines), the husband leaves Marion, who promptly shoots herself.

Nearly two years earlier Frank B. Elser had met with failure when he had dramatized Walter D. Edmonds's *Rome Haul* as *Low Bridge* (2-9-33). Now, in collaboration with Marc Connelly, he brought out a revised version, called it **The Farmer Takes a Wife** (10-30-34, 46th St.), and met with some success. The *Times*'s Brooks Atkinson embraced it as "a completely loveable play...out of the top of the cracker barrel." An old barrel stove sits smack in the middle of the lobby of Hennessy's Hotel, in 1853 a favorite watering hole for boatmen on the Erie Canal. It is opening day of a new season. Much of the crowd is watching Fortune Friendly (Herb Williams), a balding, bespectacled gambler and self-taught preacher, pull a young girl's tooth. Friendly won his dental equipment and an instruction manual in a card game. Unfortunately, in his anxiety to show his skill, he extracts the wrong tooth. But the real attention is soon centered on pretty Molly Larkins (June Walker), a lifelong "canawler" and the best cook on the waterway. Since her father's death, she has worked for Jotham Klore (Gibbs Penrose), a good-looking boatman who loves her but is also a braggart, a drunkard, and a bully. Molly meets Dan Harrow (Henry Fonda), a young man seeking work as a driver until he can save up enough to buy a farm. Molly takes an immediate interest

in the soft-spoken Dan, but assures him, "I couldn't stand a farm," adding it would be "too lonesome." Dan eventually becomes half owner of a boat, has Molly leave Jotham to work for him, and even proposes marriage. But Molly insists she will remain on the canal. Dan later leaves to buy a farm, handing over his boat to Molly. She is delighted with the boat but saddened that "he's gone away on a damned old railroad train!" Actually, the new railroads are quickly wrecking trade on the canal. When Dan, having established himself as a farmer, returns to ask Molly to marry him again, he must first fight Jotham for her. He throws his rival into the canal, then has Fortune Friendly wed him and Molly. Despite good notices, including praise for Fonda's "manly, modest performance in a style of captivating simplicity," the play rather quickly ran out of steam. One observer claimed the falling off after initially strong business reflected New Yorkers' ignorance of and indifference to the bygone cracker-barrel world. In any case, the play ran only thirteen weeks.

Even George Abbott met with rejection when he revised and staged Lawrence Hazard and Richard Flournoy's **Ladies' Money** (11-1-34, Ethel Barrymore). Boris Aronson's double-decked setting showed the dingy hallway and two rooms on each of two floors on a 46th Street brownstone converted into a boardinghouse. Two former vaudevillians (Hal K. Dawson and Eric Linden) and an out-of-work clerk (Robert R. Sloan) are supported by their wives. A little excitement enters their lives because one of the rooms is occupied by a crook (Jerome Cowan) who has gotten the landlady's daughter in trouble and is waiting to receive his share of the money from a kidnapping. While the police come looking for him, he is stabbed to death by the clerk, who mistakenly believes he was having an affair with his wife. A tipsy old biddy totters down the hall, gapes at the dying man, and says to him, "You can't take it, huh?" Still another plot concerned a gambler's attempt to raise money to treat his ailing wife.

With her former leading man receiving glowing notices for his work a block or two away, Eva Le Gallienne also won kudos for her revival of Edmond Rostand's *L'Aiglon* at the Broadhurst on the 3rd. Clemence Dane provided a fresh translation. No less than Ethel Barrymore assumed the subordinate role of Marie-Louise. In late 1900 Americans had been given the opportunity to see both Maude Adams and Sarah Bernhardt in the trouser role of Napoleon's ill-fated young son, and there were many still alive who could make comparisons. Granting that Bernhardt was in a class by herself, Adams was recalled as bringing more charm and tragic warmth to the part, while Le Gallienne's inherently taut masculinity made the doomed lad more genuinely believable. During her eight-week stand, Le Gallienne also resurrected *Hedda Gabler* and *Cradle Song* from her old Civic Repertory days.

Sinclair Lewis, the famed novelist, and Lloyd Lewis, who was no relation but was a well-known Chicago journalist, combined their efforts for **Jayhawker** (11-5-34), which allowed the beloved old musical comedy comedian Fred Stone to try his skills in the straight theatre. Ace Burdette, an opportunistic fire-eater, interrupts a religious service to confess his sins, take over the pulpit, and harangue his listeners with his hawkish, anti-slavery rhetoric. He soon is elected a senator from Kansas. When the Civil War breaks out he continues to be a hawk until the fraternal horrors of the war are brought home to him. Then he conspires with a former southern senator, Gen. Philemon Smallwood (Walter C. Kelly, a celebrated vaudevillian and brother and uncle of George and Grace), to unite the rebel and northern forces in order to fight the Mexicans. When his friends and constituents turn against him, he changes sides once again, returns to the civilwarpath, and proudly signs his letters "Jayhawker Burdette." "Jayhawker" was a term applied to the most violent of the anti-slavery Kansans. Thumbs-down notices removed the play after three weeks.

Irving Kaye Davis's **All Rights Reserved** (11-6-34, Ritz) managed to remain around for one more week. Philip Frampton (William Harrigan), a celebrated essayist but neglectful husband, discovers his wife (Violet Heming) is the author of a torrid novel. Peace is restored in the family after he is shown that the sizzling passages came not from her own experiences but were filched from other books.

Not even Tallulah Bankhead's "somber vivacity" and "intuitive stage intelligence" could keep George Brewer and Bertram Bloch's **Dark Victory** (11-7-34, Plymouth) before the footlights for two full months. She played Judith Traherne, whose only hope for life is a delicate operation. The operation would appear to be successful, and she marries the surgeon (Earle Larimore), only to learn that she still is doomed in the longer run. An attack of blindness will indicate the onset of the final hours. She has the attack just as he is about to head out on an emergency call, but she refuses to tell him about it. Alone, she sits by the fireplace to await the end. Bette Davis subsequently played in the film version, just as she had in *Jezebel,* which Bankhead had been slated to do in the theatre.

The Abbey Theatre Players began a five-week stand at the out-of-the-way Golden on the 12th. The company offered a repertory of fifteen more or less modern plays, some of which had never been seen before in New York, and most of which were given one to three performances. However, most of the time was devoted to three revivals: *The Plough and the Stars, Juno and the Paycock,* and *The Playboy of the Western World.* The troupe received good notices, but the obscurity of some of the plays, the theatre's location far north on 58th Street, and hard times combined to keep attendance disappointing.

The Gish sisters were once again performing a few minutes' walk from one another when Vincent York and Frederick Pohl dramatized Josephine Pollitt's biography of Emily Dickinson as **Brittle Heaven** (11-13-34, Vanderbilt). With Dorothy Gish as the poetess, the authors suggested a different lost love than the customary minister. This time it is Capt. Edward Bissell Hunt (Albert Van Dekker), a dashing officer who is also the husband of Emily's close friend, Helen (Edith Atwater). Helen gets wind of the attachment and sees to it she and her husband are transferred away. Though the captain is soon made a major, Emily senses something is awry. "Three days ago," she tells a friend, "I began hearing drums. Then a bugle sounding taps." She prepares to go in search of the officer, but moments later receives word that he has been killed while experimenting with a new torpedo.

The season's first smash hit drama was Lillian Hellman's **The Children's Hour** (11-20-34, Maxine Elliott's). Two young women, Karen Wright (Katherine Emery) and Martha Dobie (Anne Revere), have finally put their school for girls on a paying footing. A reading class there is interrupted by the late arrival of a troublesome pupil, Mary Tillford (Florence McGee), granddaughter of the influential Mrs. Tilford (Katherine Emmet). The girl's excuse is that she went picking wildflowers to present to the teacher. But Karen recognizes them as some thrown in the refuse that morning. The girl pretends to be ill, but Dr. Joe Cardin (Robert Keith), who is engaged to Karen, is called in and says nothing is really wrong. The vengeful Mary returns to her grandmother's home and whispers details about an "unnatural" relationship between Karen and Martha. At first disbelieving, Mrs. Tilford finally accepts the child's accusations and prevails on her friends to withdraw their children, thus destroying the school. Matters are made worse for the women when Mary forces a friend and fellow student (Barbara Beals) to corroborate her lies. Months later, in the empty school living room, Karen tells Joe that she wants to postpone the wedding, knowing in her heart that she will now never marry him and hurt his reputation. To make matters worse for her, Martha cries out distraughtly to her, "I have loved you the way they said," then shoots herself. Moments afterwards, a contrite Mrs. Tilford arrives to acknowledge that she was mistaken, but it is too late. Hammond assured his readers that that drama "will make your eyes start from their sockets as its agitating tale unfolds," but Mantle downplayed the lesbianism in the story, asserting, "The true theme is the curse of scandalmongering . . . the kind of vicious lying that may easily wreck the lives of innocent persons." The drama, based on a true incident in nineteenth-century Scotland, ran for 691 performances and immediately established its author's fame.

. . .

Lillian Hellman (1905–84) was born in New Orleans and studied at New York University, Columbia, and Tufts College before taking work as a press agent, a book reviewer, a film scenario reader, and a play reader for Herman Shumlin, who eventually brought this, her first produced play, to New York. One earlier collaboration—with Louis Kronenberger—was never mounted.

. . .

The heartbreaks of heterosexual affection were shown in Geraldine Emerson's **But Not for Love** (11-26-34, Empire), in which a woman (Hortense Alden) discovers her selfish, bank-clerk husband (Walter N. Greaza) has taken $50 of her own hard-earned cash to blow on booze and women at a convention. She would walk out on him, but the death of her sister-in-law in childbirth prompts her to remain in order to help raise the baby.

When three plays opened on the same Tuesday night, most first-string critics elected to attend Joseph Schrank and Philip Dunning's **Page Miss Glory** (11-27-34, Playhouse). A health salts company offers $2,500 for a photograph of America's most beautiful young lady, so two out-of-work wags (Charles D. Brown and James Stewart) take portions of pictures of famous beauties—Dietrich's legs, Shearer's smile—and combine them into one new picture. They submit it as a photo of Dawn Glory and win. Complications arise after they are asked to produce the girl and after others come with offers of more money—also if they can produce the girl. The sex-hungry girl (Dorothy Hall) they choose to personify the supposedly chaste Miss Glory only adds to their woes. The play ran eight weeks, far and away the longest run earned by any of the evening's premieres.

Part of Martha Madison's **The Night Remembers** (11-27-34, Mansfield) took place in a speakeasy (the use of the obsolescent term amused several reviewers). There Paul Ivins (Van Heflin) becomes so smitten by the mysterious Lola (Mary Holsman) that he runs out of the bar after her, even though she has overturned a chair to block his hasty exit. He follows her to the house of her even more mysterious father (Brandon Tynan), a patently mad sculptor. The house is replete with trapdoors, a body hidden under a bed, ghostly figures popping in and out of closets, and all other manner of hair-raising phenomena. He rushes off to the police, who can find no sign of the house or its people and who ship him off to a psychiatrist. What happened

next baffled even the critics: "the customary revelations just before the final curtain cleared up only a small portion of the eerie goings on"; "this spectator must confess that at the final curtain he didn't know just where he was."

The third-stringers were almost as baffled by the ending of Hatcher Hughes's **The Lord Blesses the Bishop** (11-27-34, Adelphi). An artist (Wilton Graff), married to the daughter (Claudia Morgan) of a bishop (Jack Soanes), is so infuriated by his wife's refusal to have a child that he comes to terms with a beautiful French lady (Ann Dunnigan) to have a baby with him. When the child is born, the chagrined wife offers the woman $20,000 for the tot, but the mother declines. "The play ends," one reviewer reported, "on a vague gag about how much fun it would be to have the Bishop pay for the illegitimate offspring."

Some critics, such as the *American*'s Gilbert Gabriel, were dazzled by the "vivid pageant" and the "zest for color and sheen and excitement" in the Group Theatre's mounting of Melvin Levy's **Gold Eagle Guy** (11-28-34, Morosco). Others, such as John Mason Brown, felt the glitter of the sets and costumes could not mask what was "no play at all" but at best a "feebly conceived" character study. Guy Button (J. Edward Bromberg) appears at the Mantic Barroom in 1862 San Francisco with little more than his vaulting ambition and a passion for gold eagle coins. He is soon heading higher by helping to import cheap Chinese laborers. On his rise, he ruthlessly steps one by one over his former colleagues. He has little time even for his wife (Margaret Barker) and weakling son (played by different actors in succeeding scenes). His one love, other than his money and gold eagles, would seem to be the actress Adah Menken (Stella Adler). By the late 1890s he is a wealthy man, though his fortune is threatened by hard times and Japanese competition. When an aging Menken turns up at his office, he forgets his hardness, confesses his love (all the while having no time to visit his dying wife), and gives her a handsome check. "I saw you, Adah Menken, the first day I come into this town. I reached out my hand to you and my bones ain't never lost that touch." Then, to save his fortune he arranges to steal money from one of his own ships and afterwards destroy any evidence of the theft by sinking the ship, regardless of the loss of life. Years later he thanks God for having helped him crush all his enemies, but just at that moment the 1906 earthquake strikes, crushing him. Whether critics liked them or not, Donald Oenslager's gaudy, intentionally overwrought settings of bygone San Francisco bars, homes, and offices caught the flavor of the time. The play, whose cast included Clifford Odets, Morris Carnovsky, and Luther Adler (as the celebrated Emperor Norton), managed to last for eight weeks.

Larry O'Connor's **A Roman Servant** (12-1-34, Longacre) survived for just over a single week. A doctor (Ernest Glendinning), who had convinced a rival (Leslie Denison) for his wife's attentions to disappear, encounters the man suffering from amnesia and knows that if he cures him the man will become a problem again. When he asks his wife (Helene Millard) to choose between them, she chooses the rival, so the doctor has his serving man (Charles H. Croker-King) prepare some poison and commits suicide.

"I'd like to know where I could get any excitement in this house," George Preble (Percy Kilbride) sighs early in Wilbur Daniel Steele and Norma Mitchell's **Post Road** (12-4-34, Masque). George, who lost his money in the Crash, and his wife, May (Mary Sargeant), have been taken in by May's sister, Emily Madison (Lucile Watson). Emily is a rather haughty lady reduced, like her counterpart in *Personal Appearance,* to turning her once lovely house into a tourist home. (Coincidentally, there is a filling station across the road, although it plays no part in the action.) Emily's problem at the moment is her laundress's retarded daughter (Ada May Reed), who has lost not only part of the laundry but the laundry list as well. Emily's only boarder has been a failed minister (Romaine Callender). But she soon has a houseful of guests: a slightly evasive doctor, his nurse, his chauffeur, and a young pregnant woman, who immediately gives birth. There is something odd about the group. Before long Emily realizes that the young woman did not give birth, that the baby was smuggled into the house when the others arrived, and that the baby is the one the police are seeking in a notorious kidnapping. By humoring and stalling the group, and seemingly clinging affectionately to the infant, she is able to sneak the infant out with the laundry and have it delivered to the police. The kidnappers realize her affections had been lavished on a doll. The comedy-thriller ran out the season.

A batch of failures and disappointments followed. Shortest-lived—four performances—was Hans Rastede's **Tommorow's Harvest** (12-5-34, 49th St.). Paula Goerlich (Kay Strozzi) has become a successful New York buyer after walking out of an unhappy marriage forced on her by her tyrannical father (Wm. F. Schoeller). When she returns home to Wetonka, Wisconsin, for a visit, she tries to help her siblings in their own struggles with the old man, but an argument with her father leads to his having a fatal heart attack. Her siblings, ungrateful for her help and jealous of her success, turn against her. She walks out again, this time with the prospects of marrying a Chicago doctor.

Norma Terris, *Show Boat*'s original Magnolia, tried her hand for a second time at non-musical theatre with Irving Kaye Davis's **So Many Paths** (12-6-34, Ritz)

and again failed. She played an ambitious singer who abandons the man who loves her (George Blackwood) and becomes the mistress of a rich man (Hermann Lieb) who pays for her training. But when she tries out for the Met, singing Mimi's first-act aria, she is rejected. She is also rejected by her former suitor when she attempts to return to him. The best she can do is look forward to a comfortable if loveless life with a rich man.

One of the season's major disappointments was Maxwell Anderson's blank-verse **Valley Forge** (12-10-34, Guild), which the playwright reputedly wrote after being challenged to create a blank-verse drama on an American rather than a European theme. Washington's starving, freezing soldiers live in rags and hovels in Valley Forge because the Continental Congress will not send him money or provisions. It is all Washington (Philip Merivale) can do to keep many a discouraged soldier from deserting. He finally decides to meet with General Howe (Reginald Mason) to discuss terms of surrender. But his most loyal troops rally to dissuade him, so he tells Howe and his colleagues, "Gentlemen, I am servant to these men in rags of homespun . . . This war, to your brief misfortune, is not mine to end, but theirs." With many critics characterizing the play in terms such as "a bore" or "dull," it lasted only until the Guild subscription list was exhausted.

At a $1.50 top, the left-wing Theatre Union was able to keep **Sailors of Cattaro** (12-10-34, Civic Repertory), Keene Wallis's translation of Friedrich Wolf's drama, on the boards for twelve weeks. The sailors on an Austrian battleship join with others in the harbor of Cattaro to mutiny against poor food and treatment. The rebellion is eventually put down and its leaders executed.

Smith and Dale, the popular Yiddish dialect vaudevillians, tried their luck with Pierce Johns and Hendrik Booraem's **The Sky's the Limit** (12-17-34, Fulton). They picked a sorry vehicle, another pale attempt to spoof radio and advertising. Lew Briskin (Smith), an out-of-work vaudeville booker, has taken over a small advertising agency and is attempting to land the Yeast Sweetie account. Yeast Sweetie is owned by his old pal, Abe Pinkel (Dale). Lew suggests a contest in which listeners to the firm's program will decide whether its crooner (John Kane) should marry his singing partner, pretty Peggy (Mary Mason), or the girl he has been dating, Olga (Ruth Altman). So, nu, vot can go wrong? Obviously, they will choose his yeastie sweetie, Olga. But, no, Peggy is vinning. Matters are made right only after the company and agency fudge the results.

Having toured for a season with *Romeo and Juliet,* Katharine Cornell brought her mounting into the Martin Beck on the 20th. Basil Rathbone was her Romeo, and Brian Aherne, Mercutio. Jo Mielziner designed the settings. More than one critic suggested that Aherne, whose Mercutio was like "forked lightning," would have made a better Romeo than the cold, correct Rathbone. There was no disagreement about Cornell. Typically, Richard Lockridge wrote in the *Sun,* "There can seldom have been a Juliet in whom the quality of youth was so pre-eminent. And it is chiefly because of that quality in Miss Cornell's playing, and the tenderness and pity it evokes, that Shakespeare is once again . . . lifted out of the library into our feelings." Mielziner was praised for "the rapturous blue-greens" of his garden, the gray and red tapestries of the Capulet mansion, and the "fearful blackness and ominous arches of the tomb scene." The play's ten-week-run was considered very good for Shakespeare and the times.

Ina Claire ran almost as long, but undoubtedly had hoped for an even longer stand, in **Ode to Liberty** (12-21-34, Lyceum), which Sidney Howard took from Michel Duran's *Liberté provisoire.* In Paris, Madeleine has left her stuffy husband and taken her own apartment, which is invaded one night by a Communist disguised as a policeman (Walter Slezak), who, among other things, is wanted for taking potshots at Hitler. She falls in love with him, gives him some polish, and even adopts some of his ideals.

There were echoes of *Gold Eagle Guy* in Dan Totheroh and George O'Neil's quick-closing **Mother Lode** (12-22-34, Cort). Hannah Hawkins (Helen Gahagan), ignoring the warnings of her shrewish mother (Beulah Bondi), stakes Carey Reid (Melvyn Douglas) to a share in a mine which proves to be the Comstock lode. He becomes rich, moves to San Francisco, and, like Guy Button, embarks on a torrid affair with an actress (Helen Freeman). He grows so wildly ambitious that when a panic strikes his friends desert him as a dangerous visionary. But Hannah and even her mother are there to keep on supporting him and to see him through his troubles.

S. N. Behrman's **Rain from Heaven** (12-24-34, Golden) missed the golden 100-performance mark by a single playing. As such it was still the longest run the Theatre Guild enjoyed in this unfortunate season. The problem was that for all Behrman's customary wit and literary brilliance, he waxed uncharacteristically preachy. The seemingly apolitical Rand Eldridge (Ben Smith), returned from a successful expedition to Antarctica which his rich, fascistic brother, Hobart (Thurston Hall), had underwritten, has come to England to propose marriage to Lady Violet (Jane Cowl). Of course, given Violet's penchant for liberal causes and her housing of refugees—all of whom Hobart instantly brands as Communists—Hobart is opposed to any such relationship. When Rand pops the question, Violet responds, "I have an awful foreboding that eventually I'll succumb

to you but I feel I owe it to my conscience to put up an *awful* fight." Actually her foreboding is groundless. One of the refugees is Hugo Willens (John Halliday)—kicked out of Germany because of his satiric writings and because his great-grandmother was Jewish. Hugo and Violet fall in love, and after Rand, mistakenly informed that Hugo and Violet long have been lovers, calls him a dirty Jew, the die is cast. Although Hugo says he must return to Germany to fight Nazism, Violet promises to be waiting for him when and if he still wants her.

Christmas night was busy and introduced one of the season's major delights, Samson Raphaelson's **Accent on Youth** (12-25-34, Plymouth). Mantle greeted it as "the happiest romance of the season." Steven Gaye (Nicholas Hannen) is a successful, fiftyish playwright who has written a play about a middle-aged man in love with a young girl. When actors hired to play in it openly express their disdain for the piece, Linda Brown (Constance Cummings), Steven's secretary, points out its virtues. Nonetheless, the playwright decides to abandon it and head for Europe. Linda changes his mind by agreeing to star in it herself. During the run, nudged by Steven's indifference, she falls in love with her leading man (Theodore Newton) and marries him. Alone now, Steven seems incapable of writing. Suddenly Linda appears, revealing she has left her handsome but vacuous young man. Steven and Linda recognize that, despite their differences in age, they were meant for one another. The thought awakens Steven's muse, so he begins to dictate a new play to Linda: "Act One . . . Scene One . . . A penthouse apartment in New York City—change that—The Bedroom of a Castle in Spain." The comedy ran well into the summer.

On the other hand, Sarah B. Smith and Viola Brothers's **Piper Paid** (12-25-34, Ritz) was the first in a string of very short-lived novelties. The play plunked Americans down in a fashionable European watering spa and in Paris. A popular, rather promiscuous dress designer (Edith Barrett) is engaged to one man (John Marston) and in love with another (Donald Douglas). Infuriated by a seeming snub from the latter, she rushes into a brief affair with his brother-in-law (Raymond Hackett), a newspaperman. When she breaks off the affair, the newspaperman attempts suicide, paralyzing himself. She agrees to help him on the road to recovery, but eventually marries the man she has loved all along.

Shakespeare competed with Shakespeare when Walter Hampden began a four-week stand at the 44th Street Theatre, also on Christmas night, offering *Hamlet, Macbeth,* and *Richard III,* as well as Bulwer-Lytton's *Richelieu.* By now Hampden's reputation as a sincere, thoughtful, but uninspired actor had been established, so business, while not bad, was not outstanding.

In London, Aimee and Philip Stuart's **Birthday** (12-26-34, 49th St.) had been known as *Sixteen*. It told of two teenaged girls (Antoinette Cellier and Jeanne Dante), enamored of their father's memory and reluctant to have their widowed mother rewed. She (Peggy Wood) is forced to show them he was not the saint they imagine him to have been.

Several reviewers wondered aloud if Benjamin Graham's **Baby Pompadour** (12-27-34, Vanderbilt) was a thinly veiled send-up of William Randolph Hurst. E. Silas Buchanan (Herbert Rawlison) is one of the nation's most influential editors and columnists. Those who count know that the best way to reach him is not directly or even through his wife (Nana Bryant), but through his voluptuous, blonde actress-mistress, Dorothy Hamilton (Gladys Shelley). At the moment he is calling for the marines to be sent to Nicaragua. At the same time, Dorothy is prepared to run off with Buchanan's secretary, only to change her mind and fall for a sailor. But Buchanan's stance is causing problems, so Mrs. Buchanan swallows her pride and sees to it that Dorothy and her husband are brought together again. Buchanan does a complete about-face on his Nicaraguan position. The evening's biggest laugh came when an assistant secretary of state calls on Dorothy to help change Buchanan's attitude. When she attempts to vamp him, he warns, "Diplomats are born, but not made."

The sensation caused by the kidnapping of the Lindbergh baby probably had inspired *Post Road*. Similarly, the upcoming trial of the accused kidnapper may have prompted Carleton Miles to write **Portrait of Gilbert** (12-28-34, Longacre). The husband of Anne Choate Whitman (Selena Royle) was dragged from the car in which they had been riding and subsequently murdered by his abductors, even though the ransom had been paid. The bodyguard (William Harrigan) she hires to watch out for her son begs her not to testify vindictively at the kidnapper's trial, saying more innocents will suffer. She does, anyway, then learns that after the man's conviction and sentencing his wife killed herself and their children.

Some of the season's shortest notices were handed to Bernard J. McOwen and Robert F. Adkins's **Slightly Delirious** (12-31-34, Little), in which a stodgy professor (Hall Shelton) comes home a victim of amnesia after spending time at a nudist colony. He has suddenly become a sexual athlete, to his wife's amazement and pleasure. When he finally confesses the amnesia was faked, his wife (Lee Patrick) claims she knew it all the time.

Two of the season's most memorable plays opened the first Monday of the new year. One was Robert Sherwood's **The Petrified Forest** (1-7-35, Broadhurst). Alan Squier (Leslie Howard), a world-weary idealist and wanderer, saunters into the isolated Mesa Bar-B-Q, a combination filling station and lunchroom near Arizona's petrified forest. To Squier, the landscape is a beautiful, welcome reminder of death. He is soon chatting with the owner's attractive daughter, Gabby Maple (Peggy Conklin), a girl filled with dreams of romance and hopes of studying art in Paris. When she reads some French poetry to Squier, he is not a little smitten. Their idyll is interrupted by the arrival of Duke Mantee (Humphrey Bogart) and his gang, who have decided to use the lunchroom as a hideout. Seeing some hope for Gabby's future and believing his own wanderings have reached the end of the road, Squier signs over his life insurance policy to the girl. Then, as the police close in and Duke is about to flee, he goads the startled Duke into shooting him. "O.K., pal," Duke says as he guns him down, "I'll be seeing you soon." Duke runs off, and the people at the lunchroom phone the police, telling them which way the gangsters went. The *Herald Tribune*'s Percy Hammond hailed the play as "a delightful improbability . . . made probable by Mr. Howard and his accomplices." Indeed, most reviews singled out Howard for the highest praise. Some totally ignored Bogart, while others bunched him in with their brief compliments for the entire cast. A few more observant, or prescient, reviewers had more to say. Thus Brown noted that Bogart, who "since 'Cradle Snatchers' has suffered a good deal from the drawbacks of typecasting, casts loose from the suave young worldlings he has played with varying success to act the killer in an excellent and quietly dominating 'tough guy' way," and Garland reported, "Bogart is Gangster Mantee to the tip of his sawed-off shotgun." The play ran out the season and was made into a popular film with both Howard and Bogart, who never again appeared on Broadway and never again was typecast as a suave young worldling.

Because of the opening night conflict, many critics accepted the producer's invitation to see Zoë Akins's adaptation of Edith Wharton's **The Old Maid** (1-7-35, Empire) at its final Baltimore matinee the previous Saturday. Most critics did not like what they saw. *Variety* summed up many of their sentiments when it called it "a bad play which should make money . . . a woman's play from every standpoint." So there was shock and dismay a few months later when the two-handkerchief tearjerker won the Pulitzer Prize and went on to a nine-month run. It is 1833. Not having heard for many months from her lover, Clem Spender, who is studying in Europe, Delia Lovell (Judith Anderson) marries another man, James Ralston (Frederick Voight). Her cousin, Charlotte (Helen Menken), runs a school for orphans and poor children. Ralston's brother, Joe (Robert Wallsten), is willing to marry her only if she abandons the school and the tots. But there is one child, Tina, that she refuses to abandon, so Joe withdraws his proposal. In time, Delia discovers that Tina (Margaret Anderson) is Charlotte's illegitimate daughter by Clem. Though she is appalled, after her husband's death she takes both Charlotte and Tina into her house, but refuses to allow Charlotte to reveal the truth to Tina. Tina thinks Delia is her mother and grows up to love her, not Charlotte. Charlotte knows that Tina considers her "a ridiculous, narrow-minded old maid." On the girl's wedding day, Charlotte decides to reveal the truth but finds she cannot. Understanding her pain, Delia quietly tells Tina to give her last kiss before parting to Charlotte. Whatever they thought of the play, the critics admired the stars. Mantle wrote of Menken, "Barring a familiar tendency to whiten and sadden her countenance beyond reason, [she] is splendidly expressive," and of Anderson, "Cramped in a role that gives little chance for that flaring emotionalism which she commands, [she] is as beautifully and still forcefully repressed as a fine actress can be."

In Samuel Shipman and John B. Hymer's **A Lady Detained** (1-9-35, Ambassador), toothy, slick-haired Oscar Shaw, the latest musical comedy favorite to try his hand at straight theatre, met with the same disappointment most transferring stars encountered. At his camp in the Adirondacks, Duke Bradford, a former bootlegger, foils the attempt of his old cronies to hold the millionaire aviatrix Joan Palmer (Claudia Morgan) for ransom after her plane crashes nearby. The men hoped to use the money they would obtain to buy and refurbish an old distillery. Duke's reward is Joan's hand.

There was no American market for Reginald Simpson and Frank Gregory's London drama **Living Dangerously** (1-12-35, Morosco). Two doctors split after one is shown to be crooked. The good one (Conway Tearle) sails to America with the other's wife (Phoebe Foster), whom he long has loved. When the crooked doctor (Percy Waram) follows, bent on mischief, his former partner shoots and kills him. The police refuse to press charges.

Conversely, enough New Yorkers and visitors enjoyed J. B. Priestley's **Laburnum Grove** (1-14-35, Booth) to keep it on the boards for sixteen weeks. When they come to him for loans, a respectable businessman (Edmund Gwenn) tells his brother-in-law (Melville Cooper) and prospective son-in-law (Lloyd Gough) that he will have no trouble providing the money, since he is really a counterfeiter. The appearance of a man from Scotland Yard (Reginald Denniston) seems to corroborate his story. But is it true?

Nan (Ann Mason), a busy Hollywood designer, writes to her precocious, free-spirited, teenaged children in Dorothy Bennett and Irving White's **Fly Away Home** (1-15-35, 48th St.), telling them to welcome James Masters (Thomas Mitchell), the father they have not seen since she separated from him twelve years earlier. He is coming to their New England home, where the kids live with a trusted maid, to help Nan get a divorce so that she can marry their summer neighbor, Professor Armand Sloan (Albert Van Dekker). The kids, to the extent that they think of their father at all, think of him as "half man and half captain of industry." He is a strict disciplinarian. By contrast, Armand boasts of his disdain for parental authority, love in marriage, and capitalism. At first the kids side totally with Armand. But after Nan's appearance and a series of mishaps which James deftly handles, they find themselves preferring his old-fashioned, comfortable ways. Armand, appalled at the cost and bother of a family, is sent packing. The "affable and diverting" comedy stayed around for five months.

Two failures opened the next evening. One was **Point Valaine** (1-16-35, Ethel Barrymore), a play Noel Coward had written for his friends the Lunts. For many years the gross, sensual Stefan has served as headwaiter at the tropical hotel run by the selfish, red-headed Linda Valaine. For many of those years he has also serviced her. But when he discovers her in an affair with a young English aviator (Louis Hayward) he spits in her face, slits his own wrists so that the blood will attract sharks, and jumps into the sea. Most critics had little liking for the play and even found themselves struggling to say something nice about the stars' skillful but inevitably unsympathetic performances. Garland wrote that Lunt was "sordid, self-conscious and intermittently superb," while Fontanne was "less spectacular, but courageously according to Coward." The play, which ran just seven weeks, was the worst fiasco the pair would have as a couple.

A vivid recreation of a mine disaster that reminded a few oldtimers of the sensation-scenes from bygone cheap touring melodramas was the lone highlight of Marie Baumer's **Creeping Fire** (1-16-35, Vanderbilt). When the explosion fatally injures John Connors (Maurice Wells), suspicion falls on Scotty (Eric Dressler), a rival for the affections of John's second wife (Marjorie Peterson), until John, on his deathbed, fingers his own son, Paul, who also lusted after his stepmother and wanted to be rid of Scotty. Scotty, not his father, was supposed to have been in the mine at the time of the explosion. The recreation of the rescue scene may have been inspired by the Floyd Collins incident, when publicity attending the rescue of a young boy from a well brought all manner of people to the site. In the play, a fortune teller and two hot dog stands are set up, and reporters start a big crap came, while rescue personnel rush back and forth.

A man arranging to be shot by gangsters so that his

suicide will seem like murder and who then has farcical difficulties calling off the killing was not a new idea (a more serious version had been a crucial theme in *The Petrified Forest* a few nights earlier), and it was clumsily told in Percival Wilde's **Little Shot** (1-17-35, Playhouse). This time around, Clyde Middleton (Donald Macdonald) sets up the killing with Big Shot Scarlatti (Robert Middlemass) so that Clyde's fiancée, Pat (Lillian Bond), can collect on his insurance. But then Clyde discovers he has inherited millions from his late uncle. Oddly, in the end he marries another girl, his secretary (Cynthia Rogers).

Frederick Hazlitt Brennan's **Battleship Gertie** (1-18-35, Lyceum) strutted her stuff for just two performances. Film-struck Gertie (Helen Lynd) steals a uniform from a sailor sleeping in her mother's Honolulu boardinghouse and sneaks aboard a Los Angeles–bound battleship. She is discovered in the quarters of Ensign Harris (Burgess Meredith). Her strange answers and some odd papers she has lead an officer to decide she is a Japanese spy. Before long war looms. (A screen flashed news bulletins from Washington, New York, Tokyo, and even interested European capitals.) But in the end the papers are shown to be "attabuoyant notes" sent by the likes of Mae West, Garbo, and Hepburn to encourage her screen ambitions. The warship returns to Hawaii, where she and the puzzled Harris are put ashore.

Tiny Elisabeth Bergner, once a reigning Berlin star and now a refugee, made her American debut in Margaret Kennedy's London success **Escape Me Never** (1-21-35, Shubert). She played Gemma Jones, a somewhat mysterious woman with an apparently illegitimate child. Gemma takes up first with one artistic brother (Hugh Sinclair), then with another (Griffith Jones), only to return to the first in the end. Bergner's singular charisma glossed over the flaws of the convoluted story and secured the piece a twelve-week run.

Dostoyevsky's **Crime and Punishment** (1-22-35, Biltmore), in Sonia Gordon Brown's translation of Victor Trivas and Georg Schdanoff's adaptation, was rejected by the critics and the public. Morgan Farley made an excessively emotional Raskolnikoff.

Some critics felt there was a good idea lost in Leo Birinski's **Nowhere Bound** (1-22-35, Imperial). The play was set in a Pullman car with landscape rushing realistically by. The train is packed with a theatrical variety of people—among them, a pathetic Jewish couple, a sweet Irish lass married to a nasty radical, a drug-addicted English actor, a leading Italian-American gangster. All they have in common is that the government is sending them east to be deported as undesirable aliens. Only the gangster (Edward Raquello) is anxious to leave, since he is now rich and will seem even richer

in Italy. But his fellow hoods don't want him to go, so they arrange for two "mutts" to board the train and kill someone, meaning the deportees will have to remain in the country as material witnesses. In the latter part of the play what appeared to be a *Grand Hotel*–style drama became farce after the killed man turns out not to have been killed.

The recent modest success of *The Green Bay Tree* prompted the production of an even older English drama on the same theme, J. R. Ackerly's **Prisoners of War** (1-28-35, Ritz). But this time there was only a quick failure. At a World War internment center in Switzerland, a not inelegant hotel, a captain (Barton Hepburn) finds himself falling in love with a second lieutenant (Ben Starkie). The reaction of the other prisoners is harsh, and by the play's end the isolated captain is increasingly demented, sitting alone and hugging a potted plant.

John Cecil Holm and George Abbott's **Three Men on a Horse** (1-30-35, Playhouse) consolidated Abbott's reputation as a master director of slambang farce as well as melodrama. Following a tiff with his wife (Joyce Arling) over her extravagant purchases of dresses, the meek-mannered greeting-card writer Erwin Trowbridge (William Lynn) seeks solace in a bar, where three down-and-out gamblers (Teddy Hart, Sam Levene, and Millard Mitchell) discover that, as long as he does not bet, he invariably picks the winners of the local horse races. They and one of the men's girls (Shirley Booth) sequester Erwin in a seedy hotel room, only to learn that he cannot make his picks unless he is riding a bus. They agree to let him take the ride. With his choices, they win big. But when they become mistrustful of him they force him to wager, thereby destroying his inspiration. Erwin returns to his frantic wife and boss (Frank Camp), who has been desperately awaiting Erwin's Mother's Day rhymes. The boss gives Erwin a handsome raise, and a grateful Erwin starts to work on his Father's Day jingles. To the *New Yorker's* Robert Benchley the farce was "distinctly low in tone, broad in method, and ostensibly mad in design, but there is an underlying comic truth running through it." The hit ran for two full years (835 performances) and served as the basis for a pair of musicals, *Banjo Eyes* (1941) and *Let It Ride!* (1961).

For the third time this season a private home catering to overnight travelers was the setting for a play, though, unlike the others, Courtenay Savage and Bertram Hobbs's **Loose Moments** (2-4-35, Vanderbilt) flopped. Ralph Merkes (Joseph Cotten), the local grocery delivery man, is wooed and adored by all the town's women except Mary Bartlett (Elizabeth Love), who is too busy running her tourist home. Naturally, Mary is the only one Ralph adores. Just as naturally, Mary wakes up to the situation and realizes she adores Ralph moments before the final curtain.

A second play to open the same evening, Lawrence Langner and Armina Marshall's **On to Fortune** (2-4-35, Fulton), had just as short a run—one week. It dealt with a less pleasant theme. An unbending, sanctimonious banker (Roy Atwell) is prepared to send a teller (Percy Helton) to jail for stealing $40,000, even though the man has already returned $15,000 and has promised to restore the rest. To teach his father a lesson in compassion, the banker's son (Myron McCormick) removes bonds from the bank and hides them in the family piano. With bank examiners coming, the banker is forced to take money from a niece's estate to cover the loss. The threat of exposure forces the banker to see the light.

Nor did George Bradshaw's Americanization of Maurice Bradell's London farce **It's You I Want** (2-5-35, Cort) meet with a cordial reception. Sherry Delaney (Earle Larimore), heading away for vacation, subleases his apartment to the husband (Taylor Holmes) of his mistress (Cora Witherspoon). The husband, in turn, gives it to his own mistress (Leona Maricle). Sherry returns unexpectedly just as a woman (Helen Chandler) who is pursuing him comes seeking him. Before long, and before a happy ending, the various characters are hiding in the apartment's bedrooms and even in the butler's quarters.

The latest string of failures continued with John Garrett Underhill's translation of Jacinto Benavente's **Field of Ermine** (2-8-35, Mansfield). A marchioness (Frances Starr) adopts a supposedly illegitimate nephew (Charles Bellin) and keeps him although he misbehaves for a time and is subsequently shown not to have been her late brother's child.

Eugenie Courtright's **The Eldest** (2-11-35, Ritz) spotlighted a woman (Lillian Foster) acquitted for murdering her husband. Despite the court's decision she is generally acknowledged to have poisoned her husband's soup so that she could marry her lover (James Spottswood). Her viciousness causes her mother (Minnie Dupree) to have a fatal stroke. Then she runs off with her lover, leaving her eldest daughter (Nancy Sheridan) to raise the family.

The second Spanish play of the month, this one done in the Village, was Federico García Lorca's **Bitter Oleander** (2-11-35, Neighborhood Playhouse), as translated by José A. Weissman. Its Spanish title is *Bodas de Sangre,* and today the play is usually offered more literally and dramatically as *Blood Wedding.* Shortly after their marriage, a bride (Eugenie Leontovich) runs off with her lover (William Lawson), thus provoking a duel fatal to both him and her husband (Edgar Barrier). Critics looked coolly on their first exposure to the great

contemporary Spanish dramatist and poet, but they gave high praise to the veteran Nance O'Neil's portrayal of the groom's anguished mother.

To Americans of a certain age Sadie Thompson meant the late Jeanne Eagels. Now Tallulah Bankhead, who had lost out on the part in London, allowed Sam H. Harris to revive *Rain* (11-7-22) for her. It was not a wise decision. Although Bankhead was a thoroughly skilled and often pyrotechnically stunning player, roseate memories of Eagels's performance, her golden beauty, and her moving fragility haunted and doomed the mounting, which opened on the 12th at the Music Box and survived for only six weeks.

A probably finer performance, that of Pierre Fresnay as the puzzled but obedient **Noah** (2-13-35, Longacre) in Arthur Wilmurt's translation of André Obey's biblical fantasy, could not help the much admired evening run any longer. The story told of the old man's dutifully constructing a rudderless ark, of his summoning the animals (played by costumed actors), of the nearly fatal mutiny of Ham (Harry Bellaver), and finally of Noah and his wife (Margaret Arrow) surveying the newly dried world from atop a mountain.

Under the aegis of Sol Hurok, a group of Russian emigrés who had been touring Europe under the hardly legitimate moniker of the Moscow Art Players opened a stand at the Majestic on the 16th with Nikolai Gogol's *Revisor* (*The Inspector General*). The company afterwards brought out a mixed bag of Russian classics, newer Russian plays, and one Swedish work (*The Deluge*). Scenery and costumes were often threadbare, but, despite their awareness of a certain illegitimacy on the group's part, critics generally lauded the performances.

Even the Theatre Guild and George Bernard Shaw felt the critics' winter blasts with **The Simpleton of the Unexpected Isles** (2-18-35, Guild), which dealt with the ultimately failed attempt of a priest (McKay Morris) and priestess (Alla Nazimova) to enlist a weak-brained English cleric (Romney Brent) in a plan to repopulate their tropical paradise with half-breeds.

A few weeks earlier as part of a mixed bill down at the Civic Repertory, some adventuresome playgoers had received their first taste of Clifford Odets. The play from that bill would be brought to Broadway in late March. Meanwhile, regular first-nighters had a chance to judge for themselves when another of his plays, **Awake and Sing!** (2-19-35, Belasco), was mounted by the Group Theatre. With their mother, Bessie (Stella Adler), a shrill, selfish shrew, and their father, Myron (Art Smith), a drudging failure, the Bergers of the Bronx are an unhappy, lower-middle-class family. Hennie (Phoebe Brand), an unmarried daughter, is pregnant with an unwanted child. The family's sole hope would seem to be its ambitious if embittered son, Ralph (Jules [later, John] Garfield). His grandfather, Jacob (Morris Carnovsky), who long ago found his consolation in philosophy, sees one way to help the young man. He makes him the beneficiary of his $3000 life insurance policy, then "accidentally" falls off the roof of their tenement. His death allows Hennie to run away with Moe Axelrod (Luther Adler), a crippled war veteran who offers her financial security. As Ralph sees it, "Did Jake die for us to fight for nickels? No! 'Awake and sing,' he said. . . . I saw he was dead and I was born!" He announces he will become a left-wing agitator. John Mason Brown saluted "a well-balanced, meticulously observed, always interesting and ultimately quite moving drama." Atkinson was a little less pleased, but nonetheless concluded, "The Group Theatre has found a genuine writer among its own members." Thanks to such praise the drama ran 184 performances and made Odets a name to be reckoned with.

· · ·

Clifford Odets (1906–63) was born in Philadelphia but raised in New York. His earliest theatre experiences were as an actor in stock, then playing for the Theatre Guild and eventually its breakaway Group Theatre. His first produced play, *Waiting for Lefty,* had created remarkable excitement when the Group mounted it in some special performances a few weeks earlier.

· · ·

The same evening brought in one short-lived failure, Noel Taylor's **Cross Ruff** (2-19-35, Masque). A middle-aged couple (Jay Fassett and Edith King) have been living happily for four years in their Manhattan duplex without benefit of clergy. When the woman's daughter (Helen Brooks) returns from Paris, and the man's son (Taylor), who has not seen his father for twelve years, arrives from London at the same time, the youngsters fall in love. Their elders are shocked to learn the children might want to live together but not marry. However, when the youngsters assure them they prefer the more conventional route, the older pair decide they will wed, too.

The next night brought another small hit, Frederick Jackson's **The Bishop Misbehaves** (2-20-35, Cort). It starred the popular, boxy Walter Connolly, who had recently won film celebrity playing another clerical detective. At an out-of-the-way pub, a suave socialite, Donald Meadows (Alan Marshal), and a bartender, Red (A. P. Kaye), plan a holdup. With the help of a chauffeur cohort they rob the Wallers (Reynolds Denniston and Phyllis Joyce), whose car has had a convenient flat right outside, of their jewels and papers, then lock the couple along with the supposedly innocent bartender in a room and leave. But first they hide the loot in a stein over the mantel. A fourth colleague will later appear and take the loot, but by that time they will

have alibis. A bishop and his sister, Lady Emily (Lucy Beaumont), enter the pub to make a phone call. He is an avid reader of mysteries and confesses, "I only regret that my duties to the church prevent my placing my gifts at the service of humanity. In fact, I sometimes feel that I might have done greater good if I had been a Scotland Yard man." The couple discover and release the trio, but the shrewd clergyman observes Red's glances at the stein. When no one else is looking, the bishop pockets the loot and replaces it with his calling card. Sure enough, a short while later the culprits are at the bishop's palace, demanding the swag. It does not take him long to discover that Meadows stole the jewels to be even with Mr. Waller for cheating Meadows's fiancée (Jane Wyatt) out of an inheritance. The bishop summons Waller and tricks him into a confession. He even demands a reward that the desperate Waller had promised earlier, and divvies that up among the others and his fund for the poor. That the comedy, despite its English setting, was designed for Americans could be heard in such gaffes as one character explaining that by Dartmouth he meant the prison and not the school. Whether Englishmen might have heard of Dartmouth College or not, they would know that the prison was at Dartmoor. Still, the comedy ran fifteen weeks.

Donald Blackwell and Theodore St. John's **The Distant Shore** (2-21-35, Morosco) found few buyers for its scarcely disguised retelling of the Dr. Crippen story. The authors called their man Dr. Bond (Roland Young). He murders his faithless, accusatory wife (Jeanne Casselle), buries her in his cellar, and flees overseas with his loving nurse (Sylvia Field), only to be apprehended by the first such use of a shore-to-ship radiogram.

There were not many more buyers for **Times Have Changed** (2-25-35, National), which Louis Bromfield redacted from Edouard Bourdet's *Les Temps difficiles.* Bromfield reset the scene in New England, where the once wealthy but now financially strapped Pentlands persuade the daughter (Elena Miranova) of the family black sheep (Moffat Johnston) to marry the weak-minded son (Eric Wollencott) of a millionaire. But soon after the wedding, the young man kills himself without having anything to bequeath to the girl.

Two revivals followed in short order. Katharine Cornell replaced her Shakespearean mounting with *The Barretts of Wimpole Street* at the Martin Beck for three weeks beginning on the 25th. The next night *Green Pastures* returned at the 44th Street with the incomparable Richard B. Harrison as De Lawd. But at the end of the first week tragedy struck. Harrison, who had played without missing a performance for five years, took ill and had to leave the cast. He died a few days later. An understudy finished the nine-week run.

March began with a modest success, Mark Reed's

Petticoat Fever (3-4-35, Ritz). Dascom Dinsmore (Dennis King), isolated at a Labrador wireless station for two years, is sex-starved. So when the priggish Sir James Fenton (Leo G. Carroll) and Sir James's fiancée, Ethel Campion (Doris Dalton), crash-land nearby, Dascom immediately sets out to steal Ethel. An attempt by the couple to flee is thwarted when Dinsmore has his Eskimo servant (Goo Chong) ride them about in a circle. Things should look up after the girl (Ona Munson) whom Dascom had been engaged to manages to break through the ice and come to the station after two years of silence. But Dascom realizes that she is now only after an inheritance he has just received. So he continues to woo and finally wins Ethel, leaving his ex to make eyes at the rich, pliable Sir James.

A cast that included Melvyn Douglas, Claudia Morgan, Violet Heming, Ann Andrews, Alan Bunce, and Blanche Ring was seemingly thrown for a loss by Louis Bromfield and John Gearon's **De Luxe** (3-5-35, Booth). It looked at the incessant interplay of lives of the determinedly expatriate Americans in Paris. Chief among these was Pat Dantry (Douglas), a dissipated young man who throws over the rich woman (Cora Witherspoon) who has kept him and finally settles for the hard-up Sabine Brandon (Heming), who until she falls for Pat has been rigorously seeking a rich husband. One interesting directorial trick has Pat start a phone call from his flat to Sabine, then the stage darkens and the conversation is heard from loudspeakers until the relit stage discloses Sabine's apartment and her concluding the conversation. The play was alleged to have been written in 1917 and optioned at the time by the Provincetown Playhouse but never produced there. Because of the relatively high-paid and large cast, the play needed to draw virtual capacity at the small Booth to just break even, and it could not do even that.

Archibald MacLeish's **Panic** (3-14-35, Imperial) was initially announced for only three special matinee performances. Two sufficed. McGafferty (Orson Welles) is a great banker who is certain he knows how to deal with the problems of the Depression. But his colleagues and the masses are too short-sighted and too greedy to listen. Realizing he is crushed, he cries out, "Christ! Must they knock us down with black-jacks—wring us with/ Midnight questions—twist our thumbs to make us/ Say we see them?"

The left-wing Theatre Union again relied on a $1.50 top ticket to lure loyalists to its productions. With Albert Maltz's **Black Pit** (3-20-35, Civic Repertory) they lured enough playgoers to keep the drama before the footlights for eleven weeks. A trouble-making miner, Joe Kovarsky (Alan Baxter), is fired and allowed to run out of cash to feed his family before a mine superintendent

(Clyde Franklin) persuades him to become a stool pigeon for the company. When Joe gets cold feet, the superintendent reveals that he made a recording of their meeting and will play it back to the miners. Somehow, word does seep through and he is ostracized. He decides to join his former buddies on the picket line, hoping they will eventually forgive him.

Only one play, John Charles Brownell's **A Woman of the Soil** (3-25-35, 49th St.), came between *Black Pit* and another play telling a similar story. In Brownell's work, a young, adopted woman (Ellen Brewster) feels she must marry her drug-addicted foster brother (Arthur Pierson), so her two suitors conspire to be rid of him. One of the suitors, the village parson (Maurice Wells), takes the man out in a boat and attempts to drown him, but is himself drowned. The foster brother, his body weakened from his drug usage, collapses and dies shortly after he is rescued. That leaves the second suitor, a farmer (Brandon Peters), free to pursue the girl.

Two more Odets plays came in the next evening to constitute both parts of a double bill. **Till the Day I Die** (3-26-35, Longacre) was set in Nazi Germany, where a dedicated Communist, Ernst Taussig (Alexander Kirkland), is arrested by storm troopers, who would beat him into betraying his colleagues. A sympathetic major (Roman Bohnen) warns him of the tortures that will follow and advises him, "Shoot yourself. There is peace and quiet in the grave." Moments later the major takes his own advice and kills himself when he is threatened with disclosure that he has Jewish blood. But, after his release, Ernst's former colleagues, even his own brother (Walter Coy), are now suspicious of him. Seeing no hope on either side, Ernst shoots himself. The evening's other play was the one that had created such a furor downtown, **Waiting for Lefty.** In her memoirs, Cheryl Crawford, one of the Group Theatre producers, recalled, "Never before or since have I heard such a tumultuous reaction from an audience. The response was wild, fantastic. It raised the roof." No doubt those left-leaning playgoers who had journeyed to 14th Street were easily provoked into such exuberance. Not all the critics were so overwhelmed, with *Theatre Arts* observing that the "writing is muddy, the thinking superficial and sentimental." Members of a taxi drivers' union await the return of their committeeman, Lefty Costello. Several calm heads address the gathering, pleading against a strike and its inevitable violence. But then the men are harangued by agitators, so when news arrives that Lefty has been killed, the men are readily goaded into joining a chorus yelling, "STRIKE, STRIKE, STRIKE!!!" The bill ran twenty-one weeks at a $1.65 top, with *Variety* noting, "Low admission scale indicates the type of patronage aimed at."

With her professorial husband (William Williams) about to have his first book published, Adelaide Willifer (Muriel Kirkland), the hopelessly scatterbrained heroine of Turner Bullock's **Lady of Letters** (3-28-35, Mansfield), decides she must have a book of her own, so she pays $500 for a manuscript that its writer (Shepperd Strudwick) warns her has received dozens of rejection slips. She gives the book a snazzier title and mails it to her husband's publisher, though that house has never published fiction. In need of cash, the publisher grabs the book, at the same time dropping all other projects, including Adelaide's husband's. The book is a wild success, which enrages Professor Willifer and puzzles Adelaide's mother (Anne Sutherland), who knows Adelaide "crosses her 'I's and dots her 'T's.' " Adelaide is even given a new honorary degree, Lady of Letters, before the hoax is exposed. Of course, Adelaide can see nothing wrong, since she paid for the manuscript. Dire consequences loom, but all ends happily.

Michael Egan's **The Dominant Sex** (4-1-35, Cort) failed to repeat its West End success on Broadway. A successful inventor (Bramwell Fletcher) wants to buy a farm and settle down quietly, but his wife (Helen Chandler) pushes him to make a fast quid by selling his invention to a huge corporation rather than trying to manufacture it himself. They compromise with his selling the rights, then buying the farm. In a subplot, an unfaithful wife (Ruth Weston) tells her husband (A. E. Matthews) to find a mistress. He not only does, he runs off with her (Rosalind Moore).

A revival at the Park on the 5th of *Potash and Perlmutter* (8-16-13) had to buck the same problem the revival of *Rain* had encountered, the memories of the original stars, in this instance Barney Bernard and Alexander Carr as the comically feuding Jewish business partners. Their successors had played the roles in London, but that was not good enough for Broadway's cloak-and-suit trade, even at a bargain $2.75 top.

Katharine Cornell ended her season on a down note with John van Druten's **Flowers of the Forest** (4-8-35, Martin Beck). Naomi is satisfactorily married to Lewis Jacklin (Moffat Johnston) but still lives in the past, cherishing her poet-sweetheart (Hugh Williams), killed in the 1914 war, and his child, which she bore and lost. It takes a dying young man (Burgess Meredith), himself a poet and blessed with second sight, to recall the dead lover's last words—the glory was in living—and give Naomi the wherewithal to enjoy life again. Cornell, having taken an uninteresting role, was on the receiving end of some polite dismissals. Hammond reported, "It is an unselfish role and Miss Cornell plays it unselfishly, permitting her collaborators to outshine her in many incidents of the drama."

There were no stars, but there was a "stunning" second-act close in **Ceiling Zero** (4-10-35, Music Box), written by the crippled flying ace Frank Wead. Talking about a frightened young pilot at Federal Air Lines who crashed his plane, some of the men worry that "crashes come in threes." That certainly does not worry Jake Lee (Osgood Perkins), the superintendent of Federal's eastern division, based at Newark's Hadley Field. He has summoned Dizzy Davis, "the best cockeyed pilot on this or any other line," to join him and their old war buddy, Texas Clark (G. Albert Smith). Never mind that others consider Dizzy "a flying fool," too preoccupied with chasing skirts and playing pranks in the air. No sooner does Dizzy (John Litel) arrive than he starts to proposition Tommy Thomas (Margaret Perry), even though he is told she is engaged to another pilot. To continue his pursuit of the girl, he allows Tex to take his place on a flight. With visibility nil and his radio malfunctioning, Tex is killed when he attempts to land his plane at the airport. (The others watching from the operations office and the crash effects outside the window provided the dramatic second-act curtain.) Abashed, Dizzy changes places with Tommy's fiancé (Allan Hale) and, against orders, takes off without a parachute into bad weather. The plane ices up and crashes.

A German play by Leo Perutz that had been making the rounds of producers' offices for several years, and even had been tried out a season or two earlier under a different name, was finally offered to New York in Arthur Goodrich's translation as **A Journey by Night** (4-16-35, Shubert). A young man (James Stewart) picks up a pretty woman (Greta Maren), steals money from a bank so he can elope with her, but afterwards learns she is the former wife of his much older brother (Albert Van Dekker), who kicked her out after finding her unfaithful. The younger brother drowns the girl in the river, then kills himself. When the play closed Stewart moved to Hollywood, not to return to Broadway for a dozen years.

David Arnold Balch's **Jackson White** (4-20-35, Provincetown Playhouse) was billed as "a folk play of elemental passion." Jackson White was not the name of a character, but the generic classification of the descendants of British soldiers and their camp followers who settled in the Ramapo Mountains after the Revolution. The Barks are inbred, mentally deficient examples. Ain't much Ma Bark (Marjorie Main) can do when Pa Bark (Frank McCormack) lusts after his daughter-in-law, Birdie (Ruth Conley). "You know what nature is, Birdie," he tells the girl, and she replies, "Yes, it's turrible." But the Bark son, Rance (John Galedon), nips trouble in the bud by shooting and killing his pa. At the same time, a social worker (Mary Talbot) and a snake-hunting biologist (Kirke Lucas) must protect the pregnant if unwed and mentally defective Ella Bark (Katherine Hirsch) from a lustful hex doctor (William Balfour).

Grace George returned to the stage after an extended illness and scored a memorable triumph in **Kind Lady** (4-23-35, Booth), which Edward Chodorov drew from a Hugh Walpole story. Because he did not beg for money but merely asked, "I wonder if I might have a cup of tea on Christmas Eve," old Mary Herries has invited Henry Abbott (Henry Daniell) into her house, where he shows himself to be an expert on fine art and where he steals a jade cigarette case on leaving. He soon returns the case, admitting shamefacedly that he stole it to provide food for his ailing wife and "nursing child." Mary invites all three to be her guests until the wife recovers. But before long, Abbott has chased away all of Mary's friends and servants, invited some of his own friends in, and made Mary a virtual prisoner. He gives out that she has gone away and sells off her art to support himself and his friends until Mary, left alone for once, finally manages to get word of her plight to a sympathetic visitor from her bank (Francis Compton). The unwanted guests can only look at each other in fear as a quietly victorious Mary goes to answer the persistent, firm knocking on her door. The play ran until George's recurring illness forced it to close during the summer. When it reopened in the fall its momentum had been lost, and it had to settle for 102 performances.

One of the season's shortest runs—three performances—was the lot of Charles March's **Symphony** (4-26-35, Cort). At the behest of a priest (Seth Arnold) who has listened to her confession at St. Patrick's, Prudence Chandler (Edith Barrett) marries for love rather than money. So when her husband (Herbert Warren) comes to consider himself a failure and kills himself, she can still gaze with contentment at their little baby and know she did the right thing. An intermittent, apparently canned, musical background drew snickers. It leaned heavily on Tschaikovsky but, at the end, in the scene with mother and child, resorted to "Ave Maria."

Even with Tallulah Bankhead as its star, Adelaide Heilbron's **Something Gay** (4-29-35, Morosco) wasn't. Its plot could have been seen as a variation on *The Dominant Sex*'s subplot. Learning that her husband, Herbert (Walter Pidgeon), is having an affair, Monica Grey seeks advice from an old flame, Jay Cochran (Hugh Sinclair). He suggests that since Herbert knows Jay is sailing for Europe the next day, he and Monica allow Herbert to overhear their planning to elope. Herbert duly overhears and smugly waves away the whole matter, unaware that what began as pretense on Monica and Jay's part has turned into the real thing. Only

Bankhead's allure—somewhat amazing considering she had yet to have a hit in America—kept the play going for seven weeks. Hammond described that allure: "She is ladylike, rowdy, wheedling, pathetic and comic, innocent and guilty, feeble and strong, which in the argot of dramatic criticism is running some gamut. She goddams and s.o.b.s., but always with a disarming Alabama delicacy."

Edward Knoblock and George Rosener's **If a Body** (4-30-35, Biltmore) was set in a remodeled brownstone in the Fifties. Since it was something of an old-fashioned mystery it was replete with shrieks, clutching hands, a body that kept disappearing then reappearing elsewhere, and eerie green lights. Its large, variegated cast of characters included a mincing ex-chorus boy, a religious maniac, a strange Chinese houseboy who plays doleful melodies on a clarinet, a stout lady with a Pekinese, and a bevy of crooks. It probably also had a plot, albeit not a single critic could fathom what it was. At best, the corpse (Hal Conklin) that is locked in chests, falls out of closets, or reappears under a bed turns out to be no corpse at all but a man who has been hypnotized while in pursuit of his unethical partner. What most critics did enjoy were Rollo Wayne's settings of the various rooms in the house. The settings opened and closed like pages in a book and were changed while the audience watched.

There was not even the compensation of unusual scenery in E. M. Delafield's London comedy **To See Ourselves** (4-30-35, Ethel Barrymore). A young, courting couple (Earle Larimore and Helen Trenholme) visit the girl's listless sister (Patricia Collinge) and stodgy brother-in-law (Reginald Mason) and ponder if they themselves will be any different after their marriage. But one torrid night between the younger man and his sister-in-law-to-be gives the older woman a new vitality, makes her husband take more interest in her, and alerts her sister to the need for understanding one's spouse.

W. D. Bristol's **Reprise** (5-1-35, Vanderbilt) earned the questionable distinction of the season's shortest stand—one performance. A man (Donald Randolph) finds himself falling in love with another young man (George Blackwood), whom he has dissuaded from committing suicide. The saved man shows little gratitude, not only wooing his rescuer's sister (Barbara O'Neil) but attempting to undermine his business. The rescuer's grandmother (Zamah Cunningham) talks the ingrate into jumping from the penthouse ledge after all.

Jack Lait and Stephen Gross were the authors of the latest attempt to spoof radio, **The Hook-Up** (5-7-35, Cort), which, like all its predecessors, failed. Like another similar spoof earlier in the season, *The Sky's the Limit*, it attempted to mix mockery and marriage. A. J. Lamb (Harold Moffat) is not convinced that he can expand the market for his Ponce de Leon pills, designed to rejuvenate amorous oldsters, if the Amalgamated Broadcasting Company's celebrated Down East country lawyer, Uncle Abe, will plug them. To nab the account, the man who plays Abe, Victor Vance (Ernest Truex), agrees to a romance with the program's Orphan Nell, baby-talking, bitchy, grasping Virginia Bryce (Helen Lynd). The romance is slated to end with Nell and Abe marrying on the final broadcast. But Victor soon realizes that Lamb believes the marriage should be in earnest. So at the final broadcast Vance arranges for everything to go wrong. The sound effects at the ceremony include the bride's galloping down the aisle, and these mishaps cause the bishop to drop his false teeth. When the smoke clears, Vance has actually wed his true love, Mary Bainbridge (Edith Taliaferro), and Virginia is overheard telling Lamb that his wife doesn't understand him. Arthur Tracy, the popular radio crooner, was cast as Bing Balboa and allowed to croon a few songs.

The central figure of Edward Sargent Brown's **Weather Permitting** (5-23-35, Masque) was a celebrity-struck young lady (Viola Frayne) who knocks on their doors, always on rainy days, hoping to let them seduce her. She fails with a polo player (Matthew Smith) and even with a fatherly racketeer (Len Doyle), so she heads off to the next figure in her scrapbook, a famous aviator.

For their annual outing the Players elected to revive George M. Cohan's *Seven Keys to Baldpate* (9-22-13), a comedy-mystery about a man who agrees to write a whodunit while confined alone in a snowbound resort. The mounting opened for the customary week at the National on the 27th. No less than Cohan himself took the leading role, supported by such fellow Players as Walter Hampden, Ernest Glendinning, James T. Powers, and such ladies as Josephine Hull and Zita Johann.

According to *Variety,* the Theatre of Action, which produced Peter Martin, George Scudder, and Charles Friedman's **The Young Go First** (5-28-35, Park), was an offshoot of the Communist-subsidized Workers Laboratory. Its offering told of unruly youngsters sent to a CCC camp to learn discipline. They remain so unruly that the camp officials decide to separate them, sending each to a different camp. But the youngsters promise each other that they will cause just as much trouble apart as together.

Allen Rivkin's **Knock on Wood** (5-28-35, Cort) was allegedly based on real Hollywood figures. Nick Hugo (James Rennie), a crass, corrupt agent, would force one client, Lurleen Marlowe (Sallie Phipps), to sleep with an important prospect (Nicholas Joy), until he discovers she is his brother's sweetheart. At that point his better nature wins out.

The season ended with a six-performance dud, Phil Kanter's **Them's the Reporters** (5-29-35, Ethel Barrymore). Like *The Front Page* (8-14-28), it took place in the newspapermen's room attached to a district police station and was filled with a motley crew of hardworking, hard-drinking, foul-mouthed reporters. In its principal story a cub reporter (Cledge Roberts), stunned that his buddies would publicize the fact that his girl (Helen Kingsley) was involved in a car crash with a notorious gangster, denounces them and resigns his post. But the show was stolen by young David Burns, as Cassady, a barely literate reporter who is usually drunk because his wife nags him and whose wife nags him because he is usually drunk.

1935–1936

After several seasons of holding more or less steady, the number of new plays plunged tellingly during the new theatrical year. The *Times,* which counted only unquestionably commercial Broadway productions, came up with the then startling figure of 89 (as opposed to 113 one season earlier). Mantle and *Variety,* casting wider nets, listed 102 and 108 respectively. However, never again after 1935–36 would any major accounting exceed 100 plays. Indeed, figures would continue to slip, and once the prosperous years of World War II were gone, the figures would never surpass 50.

By way of compensation, there was general agreement that the season was of high quality, with even the often pessimistic Mantle insisting that one could go far beyond the halcyon years of the twenties "without coming upon a record of plays more satisfying or more worthy of enthusiastic endorsement." The *Times,* looking at the other end of the list, was happy to observe far fewer instances "where shoestring operas usually roll up gloomy totals of seven performances or so." In short, there were proportionately more successes.

There were also two other interesting developments. Most important to contemporaries was the appearance of the subsidized Federal Theatre Project, which Congress had written into law earlier in 1935 and which began to relight darkened stages in mid-season. Second, New York drama critics, turning up their collective noses at many of the recent Pulitzer selections, decided to offer their own annual choice of best play. For several decades, until the nationally televised, if more commercially slanted, Tony Awards cast both in the shade, the competing prizes vied for hegemony over playgoers' tastes.

Only one novelty appeared in all of late June, July, and August, and that survived a mere week and a half. Far up in the little auditorium atop the Chanin Building, a triple bill of Grand Guignol–style one-acters was unveiled on July 11. The most harrowing of the trio was André de Lorde's **The Old Women,** in which three hags in a mental institution gouge out the eyes of a younger inmate who has been left alone in violation of a doctor's orders. The leader of the hags turns out to be a man in drag. The other plays dealt with the disposal of the body of a young boy who has died in a prostitute's bedroom and the manner in which some relations get around a dead man's will.

The season proper began with Nicholas Cosentino's **Moon over Mulberry Street** (9-4-35, Lyceum), which *Variety* characterized as "a once-over-light affair . . . okay until something else comes along." Fillipo Morello (Cornel Wilde), a janitor's son studying to become a lawyer, falls in love with a Park Avenue debutante, Helen Richards (Gladys Shelley), whose attorney father has been helping him. Helen, in turn, falls for Fillipo but finally concludes that their backgrounds are too disparate. Fillipo settles for an Italian girl (Olga Druce) from the apartment above his. Although other plays came along thick and fast, the comedy ran out the season.

Not so, Damon Runyon and Howard Lindsay's **A Slight Case of Murder** (9-11-35, 48th St.). It had to be content with a nine-week stay, since an assortment of raffish figures and some noisy mayhem too often were substituted for genuinely laugh-provoking comedy. Remy Marco (John Harrington), a former bootlegger turned legitimate brewer, takes a house at Saratoga for the season even though he is in debt to the banks and the banks are demanding payment. When he discovers the dead bodies of four armored-truck robbers in his new house, he orders his cronies to dump them on the porches of several neighbors who have snubbed him. But then he learns there is a $10,000 reward on each of the robbers' heads. So he regathers the bodies, plants them in a closet, and persuades his son-in-law-to-be (John Griggs), a state trooper, that the men are still alive and hiding there. They refuse to come out with their hands up, provoking the trooper to send a volley of machine-gun shots through the door. Marco collects the $40,000 reward.

There was double rejoicing after the opening of Ayn Rand's **Night of January 16th** (9-16-35, Ambassador), for not only had Broadway found a marvelous bit of theatrical hokum but the beloved Al Woods, so woefully beset since the Crash, had found himself a real money maker. The play was an unexceptional courtroom drama, but, in a novel, well-publicized departure, the jury was selected from members of the audience. (Since jurors were each offered a $3 service fee, they made a profit on an evening for which they had paid no more than $2.75. On opening night the jurors included Jack Dempsey.) Two endings—both extremely brief—had been prepared, one if the jury found the heroine guilty, another if they acquitted her. That heroine was Karen Andre (Doris Nolan), accused of murdering her millionaire employer and lover, Bjorn Faulkner, after hearing that he was bankrupt and about to marry another woman for the woman's money. Her trial seems to be going against Karen until the appearance of "Guts" Regan (Walter Pidgeon), who loves her and who testifies that the murdered man was not Faulkner and that Faulkner is probably hiding in South America. Karen admits she knew Faulkner was preparing to flee and that she intended to join him. What is the jury to believe? For many, the best performance in the play was the district attorney of the popular oldtimer Edmund Breese, "whose voice can scare the daylights out of a witness." Sadly, Breese died during the run. Others felt "it remained for Walter Pidgeon to walk off with the applause honors," though he left almost immediately for a role in another play. But these and other cast changes could not prevent the comedy-drama from chalking up a seven-month run.

Several flops followed. Nora Lawlor's **Few Are Chosen** (9-17-35, 58th St.) looked at the histories of seven novitiates in a convent. By play's end only two have concluded that their callings are true and that they can become nuns.

In John Whedon and Arthur Caplan's **Life's Too Short** (9-20-35, Broadhurst), Ed Fowler (John B. Litel) concludes that life is too short to worry about an unfaithful wife. He has lost his job and is down to his last cents when his wife (Doris Dalton) convinces his former superior (Leslie Adams), whose mistress she once had been, to give him another position. Fowler's reaction on learning the truth pushes his wife back into her old lover's arms, but Fowler can't decide whether to fight to get her back.

An unfaithful, egomaniacal husband was the central figure in Leonora Kaghan and Anita Philips's **A Touch of Brimstone** (9-22-35, Golden), but a number of critics suggested that Roland Young, so winning as a pathetically ineffectual character, was egregiously miscast in the leading role. He played a producer who drives his wife to leave him after he would bed an ingenue. In hopes of reclaiming his wife, he almost cancels a show he was to mount in London. But his belated efforts are probably in vain.

The Theatre Guild's first offering of the season, Dr. John Haynes Holmes—he was a celebrated minister—and Reginald Lawrence's **If This Be Treason** (9-23-35, Music Box), won critical praise for its integrity but little public support. After Japan, responding to apparently war-like gestures from the United States, invades the Philippines, President Gordon (McKay Morris), defying Congress and the press, travels to Japan to urge peace and mediation. At first the Japanese premier (Tom Powers) is unbending. But the people of both nations rise up to demand an end to war.

There was bloodshed on a more domestic level in James Warwick's **Blind Alley** (9-24-35, Booth), the first of three hits to open on two successive evenings. When the murderous Hal Stone (Roy Hargrave) and his fellow hoods seek forcible refuge in the home of Dr. Shelby (George Coulouris), a psychology professor, killing a young student (James Truex) in the process, the professor decides to bring Stone to heel by psychoanalyzing him. As Stone admits, "Before I know it, I finds myself in a spin—you know, it's that feelin' I gets. I tell yer, for a while I thought I was goin' screwy." Shelby gets Stone to see that his love-hate relationship with his sexually abusive mother shaped his criminal thinking, and he drives Stone to suicide. Several reviewers noted that by the play's close the audience had come to sympathize with Stone and to consider the coldly purposeful Shelby as the villain. The play ran fifteen weeks.

So did Philip Dunning and Philo Higley's **Remember the Day** (9-25-35, National), hailed by Robert Coleman in the *Daily Mirror* as "a tender and touching comedy . . . wholesomely and honestly sentimental, understanding and human." Fourteen-year-old Dewey Roberts (Frankie Thomas) falls in love with his seventh-grade teacher, Nora Trinell (Francesca Bruning), when he realizes that she shares his interest in old ships. But his idyll is shattered when he sees her kissing the school's athletic coach (Russell Hardie). His reaction is so strong that his parents decide to send him to another school. In saying good-bye, Nora tells him that while she does not care what he thinks about her now, she hopes that after he is old enough to understand he will remember her with kindness. When most critics reviewed the play at a special preview, the play's epilogue had a mature Dewey (Grant Mills) meet Nora years later, not remember her, and be indifferent when he is reminded who she is. There were so many complaints suggesting that the ending was false to the rest of the play that the epilogue was changed, with the grown Dewey, prompted by the younger Dewey, saying thoughtful things to her and buying her violets.

The reason for *Remember the Day*'s special preview was that its producers knew first-stringers would otherwise elect to attend the rival premiere, Guthrie McClintic's production of Maxwell Anderson's **Winterset** (9-25-35, Martin Beck). Anderson had co-authored a 1928 play, *Gods of the Lightning,* which dealt directly, if not

openly, with the Sacco-Vanzetti case. His new play touched on the matter more obliquely. Mio (Burgess Meredith), convinced his father was unjustly sentenced to death for the murder of a paymaster, attempts to appeal to the jurist (Richard Bennett) who sentenced his father, but recognizes that the judge has become hopelessly deranged. Mio decides that his best chance for bringing the truth to light is Miriamne (Margo), whose brother witnessed the crime. When the gangsters who were the actual killers hear of this, they kill Mio. Miriamne threatens to tell all and is killed, too. Esdras (Anatole Winogradoff), an old rabbi, begs the dead bodies to "forgive the ancient evil of the earth/ that brought you here." The *American*'s Gilbert Gabriel, speaking for an enthusiastic majority, observed, "It is, to date, Anderson's masterpiece. This, underneath all its full-flower eloquence, is melodrama, right, tight, trig melodrama, and immensely exciting melodrama, too." Reviewers also lauded the players and McClintic's staging, but reserved some of their loftiest praises for Jo Mielziner's two settings: a pipe-laden basement tenement and a riverbank directly under a huge bridge, with the span seemingly thrusting from the rear of stage right to lift out and disappear at left over the audience.

· · ·

Jo Mielziner (1901–76) was born in Paris but studied at the Pennsylvania Academy of Fine Arts and the National Academy of Design. His earliest professional jobs were as designer and actor with Jessie Bonstelle's stock company. He then served as an actor and stage manager for the Theatre Guild before designing sets for the Guild's mounting of *The Guardsman* (1924). At the beginning, many of his settings, such as those for *Strange Interlude* (1928) and *Street Scene* (1929), were starkly realistic. But by the mid-thirties he had begun to employ the poetic freedom that became his hallmark.

· · ·

The play was the first to receive the New York Drama Critics Circle Award and ran six months. It marked Richard Bennett's last Broadway appearances.

Arthur Hopkins found no takers for the season's second anti-war play, **Paths of Glory** (9-26-35, Plymouth), a Sidney Howard adaptation of a Humphrey Cobb novel. French officers order their troops on a suicidal mission and, when the sortie fails, arbitrarily execute three soldiers for supposed cowardice. The three doomed men were played by William Harrigan, Myron McCormick, and Jerome Cowan. Since the battles could not be properly shown onstage, critics felt the story was best left between the pages or else must await a more satisfactorily visual screen version.

Three respected performers came similarly a cropper when they presented a repertory of two Shakespearean plays at the Ethel Barrymore, bringing out *Othello* on the 27th and *Macbeth* on October 7. Philip Merivale assumed the title roles, Kenneth MacKenna was Iago and MacDuff, and Gladys Cooper essayed Desdemona and Lady Macbeth. Their interpretations were looked on by most critics as perfunctory or misguided.

By contrast, Shakespeare was to be hugely enjoyed starting on the 30th at the Guild, when Lunt and Fontanne raised the curtain on *The Taming of the Shrew* and kept New Yorkers delighted for sixteen weeks. Their interpretation made the comedy not just a battle of the sexes but at the same time a hilarious struggle of a group of strolling players to put on the work. Sly (Richard Whorf), ensconced in a box, mocked latecomers, and the actors stopped in their tracks to glare at the tardy arrivals. They also reacted to coughing from the audience. Since they were pretending to be not the best of players there were missed entrances onstage and actors going up on their lines, not to mention an assortment of dwarfs, acrobats, and trained animals brought on for additional color and laughs. Of course, the stars remained the center of attention. Fontanne, performing despite an injured knee, bellowed and stomped, a hellion as much as a shrew. John Mason Brown, writing in the *Post*, sang paeans to Lunt's "unfailing invention" and his "tremendous drive and variety."

John van Druten, soon to move permanently to America, set his **Most of the Game** (10-1-35, Cort) in New York, but that was no lure to local theatregoers. An English writer (Robert Douglas), who has been working in Hollywood, has fallen out of love with his aristocratic wife (Diana Campbell) and in love with a schoolteacher's daughter (Dorothy Hyson). In turn, his wife has fallen for a handsome film star (Robert Wallsten). All that would have been kept quietly under the covers had not the writer's secretary (James Bell), a former newspaperman, gone boozing and spilled the beans. So the couples are happily re-paired in the end.

Despite mostly thumbs-down notices, a much ballyhooed Soviet farce by Valentine Katayev, translated by Charles Malamuth and Eugene Lyons as **Squaring the Circle** (10-3-35, Lyceum), interested enough playgoers to survive for three months. Its plot was not dissimilar to Van Druten's. In it, two roommate bachelors (David Morris and Eric Dressler), without telling each other, marry. Four's a crowd, and the men soon realize they have married unwisely. A friendly poet (Albert Van Dekker), who knows the bureaucratic ropes, arranges for the men to switch brides, after which all is well.

Before the next straight play came in, *Porgy and Bess* opened. Although the Gershwins' folk-opera version of the Heywards' 1927 drama, *Porgy,* initially failed, it soon became recognized as one of the great landmarks of the American musical theatre.

Sweet Mystery of Life (10-11-35, Shubert) had no fewer than three authors, Richard Maibaum, Michael Wallach, and George Haight. So many cooks may well have helped spoil the froth. Aggravating matters was the fact that the authors called for no fewer than fifty changes of scene (nine different settings moved about on rollers). (The indifference to so many set changes may have come from the fact that the play was underwritten by a film company who planned to turn it into a movie.) After a hypochondriacal business executive (Gene Lockhart) is persuaded to make his company and associates the beneficiaries of his $5 million life insurance, those associates try everything they can think of to send the man to his reward. They even hire a voluptuous siren (Evelyn Allen) to vamp him to an early grave. Instead, she reinvigorates him.

Old traditions—such as white actors playing blacks in blackface—often die hard in the theatre. Just as Ethel Barrymore had attempted to play a black several seasons earlier, now Walter Hampden dared a like feat and met a like fate—rejection. John Anderson of the *Evening Journal* summed up the consensus when, after alluding to the actor's "smutty make-up," he continued, "I cannot, off-hand, think of any actor who looks less like a negro, except possibly Eddie Cantor, and Mr. Cantor is only joking." Hampden's vehicle was Martin Flavin's allegedly allegorical **Achilles Had a Heel** (10-13-35, 44th St.). Reviewers were at a loss to fathom the allegory, if indeed there was any. The play was set in a zoo. The Keeper of the Elephant is convinced there is no beast to touch his charge: "De lion, he jes' a great big cat. He hide hisse'f behind a bush and jump out on youah back. But *him!* He look you in de eye and teah you down—ef he git mad.—*He* king of all de beas'." Slats (John Wray), the white keeper of the monkeys, is jealous and tries everything to be rid of his rival. He finally gets a mulatto prostitute (Sylvia Field) to debauch him. Slats is made keeper of the elephant, but his mishandling goads the animal into killing him. The elephant would be put to death, but the Keeper calms him, wins his reprieve, and, apparently, also wins restoration to his old post. The play was the first of three successive openings to run a week or less.

In George Austin's **Triumph** (10-14-35, Fulton) two woman lawyers have a falling-out after one (Gladis Griswold) steals the other's fiancé (Douglas Gregory). The loser (Ruth Matteson) becomes a celebrated judge and wreaks a certain revenge when her ex-lover comes before her accused of serious peculations. She lets him sweat, but finally quashes the indictment. Austin was bruited to be a pen name for Elizabeth Miele, the show's producer and a sometime attorney.

Philip Barry, with his **Bright Star** (10-15-35, Empire), served Arthur Hopkins no better than Sidney Howard had. Quin Hanna (Lee Tracy) returns from newspaper work in New York to his New England hometown, hoping to help rejuvenate the area. The town's leading heiress (Julie Haydon) falls in love with him and, when he agrees to marry her, gives him the local newspaper as a wedding present. But his underlying ego destroys the marriage, and he decides to leave. His wife dies shortly after an unsuccessful childbirth. Most of the critics' encomiums were handed to Jean Dixon, as a wisecracking reporter, the sort of character Barry would later resurrect in a better play.

Variety ended its review of Henry Rosendahl's **Strip Girl** (10-19-35, Longacre) with what it termed a "fashion note": "Conspicuous in a front row seat at the premiere was Gypsy Rose Lee, a real-life taker-offer of top standing. In an ermine wrap and a flowing gown, she was the most dressed up woman in the house." There was no striptease in the play she sat through, although its heroine, Dixie Potter (Mayo Methot), was a stripper. Dixie lives in self-sacrificing squalor to earn enough to someday send her fourteen-year-old brother (Dick Wallace) to college. When he dies of cancer, she takes to drink. A fellow stripper (Doris Packer) convinces her that she will only get hold of herself again if she adopts a surrogate brother, so she decides to help an ex-paperhanger (Emmett Rogers), who is trying to become a decorator. This creates problems with Dixie's generous lover (Walter Gilbert), but all is resolved satisfactorily. Earlier in its review, the tradesheet had remarked on some of the play's difficulties: "Staging travels at a panicky pace through 23 scenes [done on a revolve] and with Miss Methot having practically that many changes of costume." The play survived four weeks.

That was one week more than Broadway would allow J. B. Priestley's **Eden End** (10-21-35, Masque). A woman (Estelle Winwood) who ran away from home a decade before to try her luck on the stage returns, hoping to become part of her English village once more. When she fails, largely because of the appearance of her hard-drinking actor-husband (Edgar Norfolk), she grudgingly agrees to go back to the footlights.

Homicide was only briefly contemplated in William Jourdan Rapp and Leonardo Bercovici's **Substitute for Murder** (10-22-35, Ethel Barrymore). When the widowed Audrey Hardy (Jessie Royce Landis) tells her children she intends to remarry, they rebel. Audrey's daughter, Cynthia (Tucker McGuire), idolizes her late father, and her son, Dick (Myron McCormick), has a sort of Oedipal feeling toward his mother. The children, after planning various ways to be rid of their prospective stepfather (Francis Lister), finally get him drunk and dump him in the back of a plane about to try to establish a non-stop-flying record. When the man, having forced the plane to land prematurely, returns, he puts

the kids in their place. Critics preferred the cast to the comedy.

Bertrand Robinson and Maxwell Hawkins's **Crime Marches On** (10-23-35, Morosco) was yet another failed attempt by live theatre to satirize radio. A Tennessee hillbilly, Russell Gibbons (Elisha Cook, Jr.), wins the Pulitzer Prize for poetry and is persuaded by a hustling agent (Charles D. Brown) to come to New York to read his poetry on *The White Swan Soap Hour*. He promises the youngster that his fan mail will be so voluminous that it will "pull Jim Farley out of the red." At the company's offices on the sixty-fifth floor of the Empire State Building, Russell's fear of heights causes him to pass out and dream of marrying the company's beautiful secretary, murdering his rival for her hand, the company president (by throwing him out the window), and hanging a radio announcer who could testify against him. He awakes from the nightmare to discover that the secretary (Mary Rogers) has, in fact, fallen for him. Mary Rogers was the daughter of the late Will Rogers.

The string of failures was snapped by an unlikely hit, Langston Hughes's **Mulatto** (10-24-35, Vanderbilt). By the time it closed it had tallied a remarkable 375 performances, the longest run up to its time for a black play. Yet Brooks Atkinson of the *Times* spoke for many of his colleagues when he noted, "Mr. Hughes has little of the dramatic strength of mind that makes it possible for a writer to tell a coherent, driving story in the theatre. . . . His play is pretty thoroughly defeated by the grim mechanics of the stage." In Hughes's story, Colonel Thomas Norwood (Stuart Beebe), a wealthy Georgia plantation owner, has fathered several children by his black housekeeper, Cora Lewis (Rose McClendon). Two of these mulattoes, Sally (Jeanne Greene) and Robert (Hurst Amyx), are so exceptional that they have been sent north to be educated. When Sally returns home, she is seduced by Norwood's vicious overseer (John Boyd). The colonel threatens to kill Robert after Robert demands to be treated like a white, so the son strangles him. The boy's suicide defeats a lynch mob. One point most critics were happy about was the performance of McClendon, "an artist with a sensitive personality and a bell-like voice" and generally acknowledged as the finest black player of her generation. Regrettably, this proved to be her last role before her early death.

Whether or not they recalled it, virtually no reviewers in their notices of Brian Marlow and Frank Merlin's **Good Men and True** (10-25-35, Biltmore) mentioned Mrs. Fiske's 1929 vehicle, *Ladies of the Jury,* in which she portrayed a lone holdout for acquittal who finally brought her fellow jurors around to her way of thinking. But the new play told the same story, ostensibly with a more serious purport. During prolonged deliberations, two jurors, Mary (Martha Sleeper) and John (Eliot Cabot), fall in love. But then Mary startles everyone by jumping out the window to her death. The other jurors, already furious at John for holding out alone for acquittal, blame him for the girl's suicide and threaten him. However, John gets them to agree that if he can show he was not responsible for Mary's death, they, in turn, will vote to free the defendant. He pulls out a letter Mary had written him, confessing she was a tramp and was pregnant by another man. John insists that in both cases circumstantial evidence was misleading. The play was the lone flop between two hits.

Few, if any, other settings of the period garnered as much attention or remain as memorable as Norman Bel Geddes's for his production of Sidney Kingsley's **Dead End** (10-28-35, Belasco). *Variety,* in its typical style, suggested, "Single setting showing the wharf end of a street in the Fifties as viewed from East River is as much the play as the script." A new luxury high-rise was seen on one side, with a uniformed doorman, while on the other was a dilapidating tenement. Construction equipment cluttered the area. The front of the stage was a pier, and the orchestra pit represented the river, into which characters occasionally jumped. (A number of commentators pointed out how appropriate it was for such scenery to be on display in the house that Belasco had built.) In this setting a crippled, failed young architect, Gimpty (Theodore Newton), sits sketching and studying street life. He watches, among others, Tommy (Billy Halop), who exercises a precarious hold on his gang of teenaged ruffians. Tommy's loving, well-meaning sister, Drina (Elspeth Eric), desperately tries to keep him on the straight and narrow, but Tommy and his hoodlums steal a rich boy's watch, and, when the boy's father attempts to recover the watch, Tommy stabs the man. At the same time, Babyface Martin (Joseph Downing), once a gang member on the same street and now a major racketeer and killer, returns on a secret visit to his mother. She (Marjorie Main) spurns him as a "no good tramp" and tells him, "Keep yer blood money." He is shot dead by the police, while Tommy, who looks to follow in Babyface's footsteps, is hauled off to jail. Gimpty, who as a youngster had admired Babyface but long since had rejected his ways, is left to comfort Drina and to continue his pointless sketching. Critics compared the play favorably to *Street Scene,* although several were dismayed at what, for the time, was its shocking language—so much of it coming from the mouths of youngsters. Nonetheless, the drama ran 687 performances, became a popular film with Humphrey Bogart, and gave passing celebrity to the Dead End Kids.

The procession of flops resumed when the inevitable comparisons between Benjamin M. Kaye's **On Stage** (10-29-35, Mansfield) and Pirandello's *Six Characters in Search of an Author* were less kind. Morgan Crawford (Osgood Perkins), a dramatist who has been told his characters do not ring true, falls asleep and dreams that he is living with the six figures from his play. To his annoyance, they refuse to behave the way he expects them to. (In performance, Morgan stepped from his dream to address the audience and explain why he made his characters do the things they were about to do—only to have them behave differently.) His lone compensation when he awakes is to find that the character he drew for his principal female role was based on a woman (Selena Royle) he had loved from afar and who, he now discovers, loves him.

A fictitious playwright gave way to a pair of fictitious musical geniuses. The plot of Joseph O. Kesselring's **There's Wisdom in Women** (10-30-35, Cort) was essentially simple. Margalo Nordoff (Ruth Weston) must decide whether to remain with her husband, Leon (Walter Pidgeon), a famous pianist and notorious philanderer, especially after he has an affair with Cecilia Wandover (Betty Lawford). Helped by the sensible advice of a family friend, Tony Cooke (Glenn Anders), she opts to stay. The play was Pidgeon's last for several decades, during which time he became a major Hollywood star. Kesselring would have a huge hit on Broadway a few seasons on, although who made it a hit would be in some dispute.

And a few seasons on another, superior drama would demonstrate that there were the makings of tragedy in a plot which Judith Kandel's **Play, Genius, Play!** (10-30-35, St. James) set up as comedy. Paul Carey's career as a child-prodigy violinist had been aggressively promoted by his selfish, greedy parents. Now twenty-three and bridling at the restraints imposed upon him by his enforced career, Paul (Hardie Albright) runs off for a night on the town with Diana Saunders (Judith Wood), a floozie in the ménage of his talentless, playboy brother (Sam Wren). A fight erupts at a nightclub during which Paul breaks his playing hand landing a sock on the jaw of a troublemaker. But when he returns home his parents assure him that everything will be all right. To one critic the comic lines sounded "like the captions under the cartoons in smart magazines."

The season's second musical genius was followed by the season's second stripper. She was Lulu Johnson (Polly Walters), heroine of Robert Rossen's **The Body Beautiful** (10-31-35, Plymouth). Her striptease is so classy that Boris Vassilevitch (Eugene Sigaloff), the burlesque-house orchestra leader, writes a concerto to underscore it, and before long Lulu is performing in Carnegie Hall. But she gives up her chance for ongoing fame to settle down with the stagehand (Oliver Barbour) she married. This time *Variety* failed to note if Gypsy

Rose Lee was in the opening-night audience, but it did report that "Garson Kanin, playing a Hebe candy butcher, with a pash for painting mustaches on posters, tops the cast in effectiveness." Like *Play, Genius, Play!,* the mounting lasted just half a week.

But a production most Broadway smart money had written off went on to pull in profits for six months. **Pride and Prejudice** (11-5-35, Music Box) was adapted brilliantly by Helen Jerome from Jane Austen's famous novel and presented by Max Gordon. A fine, largely British cast, headed by Adrianne Allen as Elizabeth Bennett and Colin Keith-Johnson as Mr. Darcy, played out the story amid gorgeous settings and costumes.

That same evening the historic old Fifth Avenue Theatre was rescued briefly (for just one week) from catering to less exalted tastes when it housed a revival of Charles Foster's sixty-four-year-old warhorse, *Bertha, the Sewing Machine Girl,* in a new adaptation by George Damroth. This noble and poetic drama of the plight of an innocent maiden in the evil big city was seen as too old hat and too poorly performed to elicit interest.

More modern melodrama was on view a few blocks uptown. Albert Bein had based his **Let Freedom Ring** (11-6-35, Broadhurst) on Grace Lumpkin's provocative novel *To Make My Bread,* which supposedly was based in turn on true incidents. Some critics questioned how objective the authors had been and lamented the extremely black-or-white characterizations, but most still agreed the new protest play made for strong theatre. When Carolina mill owners take advantage of hillbillies they have hired, the workers unionize and call a strike. The strike leads to bloodshed and the killing of the young organizer (Robert B. Williams). At the man's funeral, his younger brother (Shepperd Strudwick) stands before his simple pine coffin and vows to maintain the struggle. Tired businessmen who supported mainstream theatre had little time for such slanted stories, so after a month the radical Theatre Union took over the production and moved it to the much smaller Provincetown Playhouse in the Village, where the drama ran for two more months.

A second novel-turned-into-play was Rodney Ackland's **Night in the House** (11-7-35, Booth), which the dramatist took from Hugh Walpole's *The Old Ladies.* (London had seen it first, with Walpole's original title retained.) The three impoverished old gals live together in a ramshackle house. Agatha (Nance O'Neil), a ruthless, insane, and disheveled harpy, brazenly steals May's lone keepsake, an amber amulet, provoking the frail, jittery May (Mildred Natwick) into a fatal heart attack. Agatha would then turn her baleful attentions on sweet, harmless Lucy (Josephine Hull), but a pounding on the front door suggests Lucy's son may be coming to his mother's rescue. New Yorkers would not accept the play, thereby forfeiting their last chance to see Nance O'Neil.

England was also the setting for Elsie Schauffler's **Parnell** (11-11-35, Ethel Barrymore). The play received some macabre publicity when the playwright died just as rehearsals began, so she never read the generally embracing notices her drama earned. Parnell (George Curzon), a member of Parliament and a leader in the fight for home rule for Ireland, has had a passionate affair with Katie O'Shea (Margaret Rawlings), wife of a fellow M.P. (John Emery), who initially seemed to have no objection. But Gladstone, determined not to grant Ireland home rule, persuades Capt. O'Shea to start divorce proceedings. The move destroys Parnell politically and seemingly brings about his early death. Although many critics felt that Curzon, brought from England to play the lead, was a major disappointment, they had high praise for Guthrie McClintic's staging and for the acting of two of the ladies, Rawlings and oldtimer Effie Shannon, as Mrs. O'Shea's wise old aunt. The play missed the golden 100-performance mark by a single playing, but returned later in the season for another month with a somewhat different cast.

Two one-week failures came next. The first was Hugh Stange's **Mother Sings** (11-12-35, 58th St.). At the Westchester Court House, a lawyer, hoping to wangle an acquittal, tells of his client's tragic life. Dim-witted Ben Shermer (Wendell Phillips) grows up on the farm of his obsessively tight-fisted, possibly insane father (Ralph Theadore) and his patently demented mother (Mary Morris). After his father's death, his mother raises Ben in strict isolation and poisons his mind against other women. So when a dime-store salesgirl (Bernardine Hayes) rents a room on the farm for her summer vacation, Ben does not know how to behave and in short order kills her with his hatchet. The jury condemns him to death.

Better things were hoped for from Martha Hedman and Henry Arthur House's **For Valor** (11-18-35, Empire), especially with Frank Craven and June Walker in the leads. During the war, Wallace Brown had been captured by the Germans but managed to escape by stealing the clothes of an amorous fraulein. Now his wife has gotten wind of the story and, after coloring it more than a bit to exaggerate Wallace's heroism, starts a campaign to get him a medal. The noisy support he wins from the Rogue River Cirrhosis Club and other local boosters sends Wallace scurrying to a secret fishing hole until the bubble bursts and matters can return to normal.

The story of **Mother** (11-19-35, Civic Repertory) was not unlike that of *Let Freedom Ring,* only in this instance, instead of a brother, a mother (Helen Henry), initially opposed to the left-wing actions of her son, is prompted to take up his cause after he is shot dead by the police. The play, produced by the red-flag-waving Theatre Union, was Paul Peters's translation of a German drama based on a Gorky novel. The German dramatist was, according to Atkinson, "a playwright who signs himself plain Brecht," and several of Atkinson's colleagues could not get his first name correctly. Moreover, there was considerable bewilderment over what would eventually be recognized as a Brechtian style of staging. A large bare stage was lit by a battery of overhead lights in clear view. Multiple settings, placed on moving platforms, gave only skeletonized hints of what was represented. Brief films and titles were flashed on a screen at the rear of the stage, and the action was interrupted now and then by "revolutionary chants" accompanied by two pianos. Though it is doubtful that playgoers confused this work with *Mother Sings,* they were not receptive. The production was withdrawn after thirty-six performances.

Kerry Shaw and Joseph Mitchell's **Satellite** (11-20-35, Bijou) found that its first performance was its last—one of only two plays during the season to suffer such ignominy. A young college graduate (Stanley Smith) from Iowa comes to New York with $2000 to open a florist shop, but a gold-digging chorus girl (Noel Francis) soon bamboozles him out of the cash. Her two, more principled sisters help the lad recover the loot.

In a season rich in striking settings, a number of critics took time to laud P. Dodd Ackerman's "superb" library in **Abide with Me** (11-21-35, Ritz), though none deigned to describe it. They also had complimentary things to say about a small but first-rate cast that included Cecilia Loftus, Maria Ouspenskaya, James Rennie, Earle Larimore, Barbara Robbins, and Lee Patrick. However, they had little time for the play by a young lady who, as a tot, had acted under the name Joyce Fair and was now calling herself Clare Boothe Brokaw. While he plays the organ and sings hymns to please his uncritical mother (Loftus), Henry Marsden (Larimore) is actually a closet alcoholic and a twisted sadist, who loves to make life miserable for his devoted wife (Robbins). He even urges her to have a child by the doctor (Rennie) who saw him through a major illness and whom, he knows, his wife has taken on as a lover. When she does become pregnant and he refuses a divorce, he is shot—not by his wife but by the aggrieved old family servant (Ouspenskaya). The family agree to claim his death was a suicide.

Poor, star-crossed Ernest Truex met his usual fate—to be highly praised for his clowning in a play critics otherwise panned—when he arrived in Milton Lazarus's **Whatever Goes Up** (11-25-35, Biltmore). After Terrance J. Sweeney, a meek cigar-store clerk, wins $150,000 with a sweepstakes ticket given him in repay-

ment of a $2 loan, his ambitious wife (Leona Powers) moves him to the Waldorf. He is soon surrounded by money-grubbing hangers-on, most of all his wife's banker uncle (Edward H. Robins), a scam artist who bilks Terrance out of the cash by promising to invest it in what proves to be a nonexistent radio station. Luckily, the bellhop-beau (Fred Sherman) of Terrance's daughter (Peggy O'Donnell) gets half of it back for him. Nonetheless, by the time he has paid his taxes and hotel bills, Terrance has only $6000 with which to move back to Dyckman Street.

Another scam was featured in Mary Heathfield's **The Ragged Edge** (11-25-35, Fulton). To save his failing firm, Rodney Cole, Sr. (Robert Harrison), has appropriated the half million dollars due his son, Robert, Jr. (Glen Boles), on the boy's twenty-fifth birthday, a few weeks off. The youngster's sudden suicide presents problems, so the father decides to find a look-alike to impersonate the boy. He selects a young tramp (Boles) who has been living in a shantytown by the Hudson River. The impostor proves so attractive that he even wins over the dead boy's fiancée (Lillian Emerson). He is finally exposed, but, after the girl promises to wait, he heads for Australia to make his own way with the small sum the elder Cole has given him. He also agrees not to make waves for Cole. Most critics felt that Percy Kilbride, as a comic shantytown philosopher, stole the show.

The next two evenings brought in three hits. Katharine Dayton, a well-known Washington commentator, combined her efforts with those of the more experienced George S. Kaufman to delight sophisticated playgoers with **First Lady** (11-26-35, Music Box). The *World-Telegram*'s Robert Garland, bowled over by "some of the most brilliant topical dialogue ever spoken on an American stage," rejoiced, "This bright, this brittle, this frequently belligerent newcomer is a Juvenalian satire." Lucy Chase Wayne (Jane Cowl), the granddaughter of President Andrew Chase and the sharp-tongued doyenne of Washington society, dismisses an upstart rival, Irene Hibbard (Lily Cahill), as the "Ten Least-Dressed Women in Washington." Her niece, Emmy (Helen Brooks), is certain it does not matter, since people always laugh regardless of how terrible Aunt Lucy's remarks are. Lucy has had it in for Irene ever since Irene stole Lucy's celebrated chef. Now Lucy knows that Irene is preparing to walk out on her husband (Oswald Yorke), a Supreme Court justice, and marry young Senator Keane (Judson Laire), with whom she is having an affair and whom she is promoting as a candidate for president. Since Lucy hopes her own husband (Stanley Ridges) will be the candidate, she attempts to sidetrack Keane's campaign by promoting none other than the aged Justice Hibbard. Her attempt succeeds beyond expectations. Not only does Hibbard agree to become a candidate, but Irene ditches Keane to return to him. When Hibbard modestly tells Lucy that he hopes he can fill her grandfather's shoes, she assures him he can, but adds, "of course, it was the other end of grandfather that mattered." Fortunately, at the last moment Lucy discovers a legal fluke that means Irene has never been divorced from a prince she once married. Her marriage to Hibbard therefore has been bigamous. Hibbard is forced to withdraw from the race. But there is a stinger. Emmy returns home to announce her engagement to Keane, and Lucy says that maybe Emmy can someday be first lady. Emmy reveals that since Keane was born in Canada he can never be president. The comedy ran eight months.

Kaufman and his associates were at pains to deny that Lucy was patterned after Alice Roosevelt Longworth. They were not believed. Less credible still were the more strident disclaimers of Bella and Sam Spewack that the central figures in their **Boy Meets Girl** (11-27-35, Cort) were not caricatures of Ben Hecht and Charles MacArthur. Robert Law (Allyn Joslyn) and J. Carlyle Benson (Jerome Cowan) are two rambunctious, practical-joking screenwriters who cannot keep straight faces knowing they must create a script to save the fading cowboy star Larry Toms (Charles McClelland): "Even Wilkes-Barre doesn't want him, and they're still calling for Theda Bara." While Law is something of a would-be idealist, Benson is insistently pragmatic, convinced there is only one basic plot—boy meets girl, boy loses girl, boy gets girl. But it is a boy-meets-baby story they finally devise, since, learning that a studio waitress is about to become an unmarried mother, the pair obtain power of attorney then set out to make the baby, whom they christen Happy, Toms's co-star. The tot's popularity saves Toms's career. When the studio wrests away the men's power of attorney, the writers set out to destroy Happy's vogue by having a studio extra claim he is his father. The mother, Susie (Joyce Arling), had met the extra, Rodney (James MacColl), earlier and had fallen in love with him. But now she is furious, so she runs off with Toms, whose reaction is very uncharitable when he learns Happy has measles. Susie recognizes that she still loves Rodney. Only after she agrees to marry him does she learn he is a rich, titled Englishman. Law and Benson see a great story in that—boy meets girl, boy. . . . George Abbott's madcap direction filled the stage with all manner of moguls, yes-men, players, midgets, and blaring trumpeters. Appealing to a broader audience than the Kaufman-Dayton opus, the "extraordinarily hilarious" comedy compiled 669 performances.

If *First Lady* is one of Kaufman's least remembered gems, the third comedy hit is now totally forgotten.

Furthermore, Stephen Gross and Mrs. Lin S. Roots's **One Good Year** (11-27-35, Lyceum) had to override deprecatory notices by second-stringers before it could settle down for a season-long run. To earn $3000 so that she can pay off a loan on her home and go study music in Paris, Anne Haven (Gertrude Flynn) agrees to have another woman's baby with a eugenically selected father. Three candidates for fatherhood are offered, but Anne instead opts for an attractive piano tuner (Edward Woods) who comes to her house. By curtain time, the woman (Mary Sargent) who paid Anne learns that she herself is going to have a child, so Anne and her young man are able to marry and keep their own baby. Hilda Spong won laughs as an amiable lady doctor.

The brief flurry of successes was followed by a series of very short-lived failures. Wilbur Daniel Steele and Anthony Brown's folk drama **How Beautiful with Shoes** (11-28-35, Booth) was set, as were so many similar plays, in the Carolina hills. The wedding of Mare Doggett (Marie Brown) to Ruby Herter (Harry Bellaver) is interrupted by news of an escaped lunatic in the area. The groom and the neighbors all head off to hunt the madman. He himself (Myron McCormick)—a demented worshipper of beauty and poetry—finds Mare alone, about to take a bath, and awed by her loveliness recites his version of sensuous lines from the Song of Songs. He is arrested and later shot to death while trying to escape. But the experience has left Mare so inexplicably moved that she refuses to proceed with the wedding.

Few people wept over the quick demise of Nellise Child's **Weep for the Virgins** (11-30-35, 46th St.). Cecilia Jobes (Evelyn Varden), once a burlesque queen but long since married to a lowly worker in California's fish canneries, has clear and high ambitions for her three daughters. But one commits murder, a second becomes pregnant by a sailor who has quickly run off, and the third marries a morose old man who pays her father $200 for her. Ma Jobes is left to contemplate the hollowness of her dreams. The play was an embarrassing low mark in the history of its producer, the Group Theatre.

Impressed mostly by Thomas Mitchell's direction and performance, second-stringers let Frederick Hazlitt Brennan's **Stick-in-the-Mud** (11-30-35, 48th St.) down easily. There wasn't much of a plot. Thirty-one years ago the Mississippi steamboat *Dixie Belle* ran aground at Pike County Landing, Missouri, and has remained there ever since. Its captain, Dan Minor (Dudley Clements), has always blamed the wreck on false signals mischievously sent by workers on the Chicago, Burlington and Quincy Railroad. These many years the captain has lived in the wreck along with Buttinhead Adams (Rex Ingram), his Negro servant, Mrs. J. E. B.

Drumwright (Maida Reade), the tippling widow of the captain's late partner and a lady who never lets anyone forget she is related to Gen. "Jeb" Stuart, and Lucy (Sylvia Field), an orphan who has been raised on the ship and who has had a child by Adrian Reed (Bruce MacFarlane), a local boy who refuses to marry her until he can afford his own tugboat. One hanger-on is Paw Meriwether (Mitchell), a stubble-bearded, white haired loafer, who spends many of his waking hours fishing for catfish through a hole in the vessel's dining-room floor and the rest of his day telling stories. For example, he tells of the old fisherman livid at losing a huge king buffalo fish after a week-long struggle: "He quit fishin' for good, took to drink, and landed in Congress." It remains for Meriwether to win a lawsuit against the railroad after its pranksters set his old truck afire by hurling coals at it and to give away the money so that Adrian can buy his boat and make Lucy an honest woman. Virtually every major critic, extolling Mitchell, considered his character a Missouri version of *Tobacco Road*'s Jeeter Lester. But his playing and P. Dodd Ackerman's colorful setting of a derelict Victorian steamboat brought no line to the box office.

Without formally suggesting that she was attempting to establish another repertory company (indeed, one of her autobiographies implies she still felt she was continuing the old Civic Repertory), Eva Le Gallienne launched December with a series of revivals at the Shubert on the 2nd. She began with Ibsen's tale of a misguided idealist who brings about her own suicide and that of several acquaintances, *Rosmersholm.* She moved on, on the 4th, to Dumas fils's *Camille* and, on the 7th, to a double bill by Serafin and Joaquin Alvarez Quintero, *A Sunny Morning* and *The Women Have Their Way.* The last three plays had been in the repertory of Le Gallienne's earlier troupe. By now it was evident that the actress, for all her competence and dedication, lacked the alluring charisma and fire of great players such as Cornell, Hayes, or Fontanne. Nor were critics very happy with the rest of her company or her choice of plays, seeing the latter as old hat. As a result, Le Gallienne packed her bags after a disappointing fortnight. Shortly afterwards she disposed of her long-held settings and costumes and abandoned all surviving connections with her 14th Street heyday.

Hoping to recoup the losses of capital and prestige it had suffered with *Weep for the Virgins,* the Group Theatre brought out Clifford Odets's **Paradise Lost** (12-9-35, Longacre). While not such an immediate and dismal flop as the earlier drama, the new play was a clear disappointment. Leo Gordon (Morris Carnovsky), a handbag manufacturer, and his loving wife, Clara (Stella Adler), are middle-class New Yorkers (albeit the city is not specified in the text). Things go from bad to

worse for them. Among other matters, their daughter, Pearl (Joan Madison), a talented pianist, resigns herself to being a spinster. One son, Julie (Sanford Meisner), is dying of an incurable disease. Another boy, Ben (Walter Coy), hooks up with a small-time crook, Kewpie (Elia Kazan), and is gunned down by the police. Leo's business partner, the sexually impotent Marcus Katz (Luther Adler), is stealing large funds from the company. Yet Leo remains optimistic, telling his wife that better times lie ahead, and that "the world is in its morning . . . and no man fights alone." The drama's talkiness and diffuseness bothered critics. John Anderson observed in the *Evening Journal,* "Odets has said too much without saying quite enough. 'Paradise Lost' is three or four plays—and not completely one. It is a pity." As a result of such notices, the production had to be content with a nine-week run.

Joel W. Schenker and Allan Fleming's **This Our House** (12-11-35, 58th St.) was a two-performance dud. Beatrice Cenci (Edith Atwater) has her lover (Sherling Oliver) kill her incestuous father (Ian Maclaren). Rather than allow her innocent brother (Ben Starkie) to be tortured by the questioning authorities, she confesses to the crime and is executed. Her brother vows vengeance.

A revival of Ibsen's *Ghosts,* starring small, dark Alla Nazimova, opened on the 12th at the Empire as a three-week stopgap booking but was so ecstatically received that its engagement was extended, and, after heading out for a prebooked tour, it returned for a second stand later in the season. All told it played a remarkable ten weeks in Manhattan. Nazimova's Mrs. Alving was hailed as "great," "spellbinding," and "profoundly moving," while there was ample praise left over for her supporting cast, including the somewhat formal McKay Morris as Pastor Manders and the boyish Harry Ellerbe as Oswald.

Gilbert Miller, the late Henry Miller's son, had quickly earned a reputation for producing London plays on Broadway and New York plays in the West End. Now, one week apart, he brought in two British shows, both of which pleased New Yorkers. The lesser of the pair was Edward Wooll's **Libel** (12-20-35, Henry Miller's). A newspaper claims Sir Mark Loddon, M.P. (Colin Clive), is an impostor, having secretly taken the place of a captured British officer who died in a German prison camp during the war. Sir Mark sues, and, though the trial at first seems to go against him, he is vindicated. A refugee from postwar Germany, Otto Ludwig Preminger, made his American directorial debut with the drama, which ran twenty weeks.

Critics were baffled trying to find some meaning in Arthur Richman's **The Season Changes** (12-23-35, Booth). One reviewer quoted a line from the play to the effect "You make much of a trivial thing." While on summer vacation in New Hampshire, Alice Laming (Doris Dudley), apparently to upset her mother (Phyllis Joyce), becomes engaged to Jim Farringdon (Eliot Cabot), a lecturer almost old enough to be her father. Then she has second thoughts and breaks the engagement.

When, at the close of her cross-country tour, Katharine Cornell brought *Romeo and Juliet* back to New York for a two-week stand at the Martin Beck, beginning on the 23rd, several interesting replacements had been made. For one, Florence Reed was now the nurse. More interesting in the long run were three men who were making their Broadway debuts. The new Romeo was Maurice Evans; the new Mercutio, Ralph Richardson; and the new Tybalt, Tyrone Power. All three were favorably received (in fact, several critics felt they were better than Cornell's original choices), though no one could guess how illustrious their careers would be.

Another actor making his Broadway debut and subsequently moving on to stardom was Vincent Price. He had played the role of Prince Albert at a special performance (for copyright reasons) in London, but since the Lord Chamberlain would not permit a full West End staging of a play about a recent monarch, Americans in large numbers saw Laurence Housman's **Victoria Regina** (12-26-35, Broadhurst) long before most Englishmen did. In a sense, Gilbert Miller's production was a premiere. Of course, with this somewhat long and episodic look at Victoria from the time, as a young woman, she learns she has become queen into her old age, neither the play nor Price's debut has become the thing. What has counted in American theatrical history is Helen Hayes's now legendary monarch. Perhaps naturally, reviewers could not foresee history's judgment, so they gave far more attention to the play than to its star. And their praise for her might strike later readers as curiously perfunctory—albeit they all did praise her. True, Anderson reported that she displayed "a perfection of mood that yields warmth without familiarity, and suggests the unbending stiffness of the moral custodian of her time without making it seem either inhuman or impossible. . . . By the subtle cajolery of her own personality she illuminates Victoria." But most critics harped on her "triumph in makeup as the wizened widow of the last act," her "Make-up Triumph," and her "moment of sheer triumph" when she first appeared in her guise as an old woman and brought down the house. Indeed, Anderson complained that while her features aged remarkably, her voice aged not at all, and Brown wondered why she resorted to "the faintest suggestion of a German accent." Still, the playgoing public responded in droves, keeping the play on the boards for 517 performances.

One of the season's most highly applauded stage settings was that conceived by Marion Gering, a Meyerhold trainee, and executed by Donald Oenslager for Martin Flavin's second play of the season, **Tapestry in Gray** (12-27-35, Shubert). Done appropriately in various shades of gray and in an abstract, cubist style, it offered playing areas on several levels. A huge, curtained French window, the setting's only softening touch, was center stage. To its left a small, spiral staircase climbed from one level to another. Behind the slanting, angular walls of the various playing areas loomed a backdrop of stylized, windowless skyscrapers. During the war Eric (Melvyn Douglas) operates on his medical college buddy, Stephen (Minor Watson), to repair serious facial damage, but a nurse, hearing Stephen moan, loosens his bandages, thereby scarring him for life. Called a "half-baked débutante," she is fired. Some time later Eric marries Iris (Elissa Landi), unaware she is the nurse who ruined his surgery and scarred his friend. When Stephen reappears and Iris understands their relationships she attempts to turn the men against one another, but instead manages to drive Eric to suicide. She then attempts to destroy Stephen, only to repent when he says he loves her. She sends him on his way and cries, "Forgive me—Eric." The play's gray reception doomed it to a three-week run.

John Patrick's debut as a playwright, with **Hell Freezes Over** (12-28-35, Ritz), ran one performance more. Most members of a group set to explore Antarctica died when their dirigible crashed in the ice. Two by two the seven survivors also die. A drug-addicted doctor (Myron McCormick) kills himself after first giving poison to a young man (Richard Albert) with a gangrenous leg. Another pair (Frank Tweddell and George Tobias) go off to seek help and fail to return. Then one (John Litel) of the three survivors discovers another (Louis Calhern) has seduced his wife. The pair kill each other in a duel, leaving the last man (Lee Baker), who has broken down mentally and been handcuffed, to die of starvation.

Even George S. Kaufman's direction and playdoctoring could not save **Tomorrow's a Holiday** (12-30-35, Golden), which Romney Brent adapted from an unidentified Viennese play by Leo Perutz and Hans Adler. A man (Curt Bois) guilty of embezzling from his own bank seeks out a gambler friend (Joseph Schildkraut), who promises to win the money for him in a card game. The gambler wins it all, then loses it all, and finally wins everything back before the last curtain.

James Hagan's **Mid-West** (1-7-36, Booth), the new year's first entry, could be deemed a farm-belt *Paradise Lost*. The Zanhisers (Curtis Cooksey and Jean Adair) are farmers whose lives have been plagued by problems. Two sons were killed in the war. A son (Don Dillaway) married to a city girl (Bernardine Hayes) leaves the farm to please his wife. A fourth son (Van Heflin) is lynched by irate neighbors for his radical troublemaking. Drought has so aggravated the Zanhisers' losses that they may even lose their farm. But then the rains come, bringing at least a modicum of hope.

If rumor had several earlier plays based on real, living figures, Zoë Akins's **O Evening Star!** (1-8-36, Empire) was confessedly suggested by the life of the late Marie Dressler. In this instance, she was rechristened Amy Bellaire and played by a statuesque beauty of yesteryear, Jobyna Howland, in what marked her own Broadway swan song. The play begins in 1917 with Amy, once a musical comedy favorite but now a bankrupt, watching as her possessions are auctioned off. By 1931 she is living in poverty in Hollywood, taking work as an extra when she can get it. The young stars and directors have no memory of her and in their indifference are rude to her. But suddenly a producer (Frank Conroy) asks her to substitute for an actress who cannot take direction. Actually, Amy cannot either, but her casual clowning leaves everyone in stitches and she is made a star. However, with her new celebrity comes word that she is dying of cancer. Considered mawkishly sentimental, the play lasted only half a week.

The season's second and last single-performance fiasco was Irving Stone's **Truly Valiant** (1-9-36, 49th St.). Because Stone's book about Van Gogh had been a recent best-seller, critics were disappointed and, perhaps as a result, especially scathing. Berna Bowen (Margot Stevenson), working her way through college, accepts a position as maid in the home of Professor Cranby (Ian Maclaren). After some time, the professor's son (Alan Handley) falls in love with her and proposes marriage. She has to confess that she is pregnant by his father, who proposes to divorce his mother to marry Berna. But the son is not deterred, so he and Berna will wed, while the elder Cranbys kiss and make up.

When *Granite* raised its curtain at the Vanderbilt on the 13th, this revival of Clemence Dane's 1927 saga about a woman doomed to live on a lonely island with a man who has killed her first two husbands was rejected just as it had been the first time around. Mary Morris and Robert H. Gordon played the central figures.

Mystery writer Rufus King and comic writer Milton Lazarus unavailingly combined their talents for **I Want a Policeman** (1-14-36, Lyceum). Just as Eric Davidson (Dudley Hawley) accuses his young, second wife, Fern (Sylvia Field), of plotting to kill him, and when they come on again Eric has been shot dead. Later, a carefully flung knife kills his butler (Con MacSunday). The police naturally suspect Fern, but one of the detectives realizes that the handwriting on some threatening letters is the same as that on a bridge scorecard kept by Eric's son (Eric Wollencott), who is

bitter over his father's divorcing his mother. Estelle Winwood portrayed a comically haughty English aristocrat, visiting uncouth America.

Although Lynn Riggs's "modest, light, sensible and funny" comedy **Russet Mantle** (1-16-36, Masque) was hailed as "his fullest, maturest play" and "by all odds the best thing Mr. Riggs has done," it had to settle for a fifteen-week run in the face of so much excellent competition. Its story was straightforward and not new. Restless Kay Rowley (Martha Sleeper) and her mother (Margaret Douglas) are visiting her uncle and her aunt (Jay Fassett and Evelyn Varden) on their retirement ranch in New Mexico. When a rootless young poet, John Galt (John Beal), takes temporary work at the ranch, he shows Kay how shallow and unhappy the oldsters actually are, and he soon persuades her to run off with him.

Jo Mielziner's "brilliant setting . . . was pretty much all there was" to recommend Roy Hargrave's **A Room in Red and White** (1-18-36, 46th St.). As the play's title suggested, the modern room was done basically in white, with "searing scarlet draperies," a striking, steep staircase carpeted in "roaring red," and "ruddy gladioli" in the bay window. Aluminum furnishings and glass decorations accentuated the modernity. In that drawing room, Philip Crandall (Leslie Adams) so abuses his wife (Chrystal Herne) and son (Richard Kendrick) that they trick him into writing a suicide note, then poison his coffee. Only after he is dead do they discover he was dying of cancer.

Having recently delighted playgoers with his mounting of an adaptation of a classic English novel, Max Gordon earned their gratitude again with Owen and Donald Davis's theatricalization of an American masterpiece, Edith Wharton's **Ethan Frome** (1-21-36, National). Guthrie McClintic's direction and more fine Mielziner settings—this time capturing the wintry starkness of New England—gave further satisfaction. So did the illuminating performances of the play's three stars. When Mattie Silver (Ruth Gordon) comes to stay with her crabbed cousin, Zenobia Frome (Pauline Lord), and Zenobia's husband, Ethan (Raymond Massey), she and Ethan fall in love. Discovering this, Zenobia orders Mattie to leave. On the way to the station, Ethan and Mattie attempt suicide, but are instead crippled for life, leaving the now even more embittered Zenobia to care for them. The drama ran into May.

· · ·

Ruth Gordon [Jones] (1896–1985) was born in Wollaston, Mass. She studied at the American Academy of Dramatic Arts before making her debut opposite Maude Adams as Nibs in a 1915 revival of *Peter Pan*, then called attention to herself as Lola Pratt in *Seventeen* (1918). Among her subsequent major vehicles were

Saturday's Children (1927) and *Serena Blandish* (1929). She was a small woman with a gravelly voice and sometimes more than a hint of vulgarity in her acting.

. . .

Raymond [Hart] **Massey** (1896–1983) was born in Canada and made his professional debut in London in 1922. He met with disappointment when he made his first New York appearance in 1931, essaying nothing less than the role of Hamlet. Nor was his next appearance, in *The Shining Hour* (1934), very rewarding. But the tall, gaunt actor scored hugely in his latest outing.

. . .

A tiny theatre was rescued temporarily from films to house yet another dramatization of a novel, **The Puritan** (1-23-36, Belmont), which Chester Erskin derived from a Liam O'Flaherty work. A religious fanatic (Denis O'Dea), having killed a prostitute (Gertrude Flynn) in order to save her soul, concludes that he was goaded by his own lusts into the crime, so stabs himself to death. A large cast and multiple scene changes militated against any run at so small a house, even if reviews had been favorable.

Beautiful Oriental costumes and simple but equally lovely scenery helped S. I. Hsiung's redaction of an old Chinese theatre piece, **Lady Precious Stream** (1-27-36, Booth), overcome some clumsy acting by supporting players and some playgoers' antipathies to such Chinese theatrical conventions as imaginary or stylized props and inch beyond the 100-performance mark. An Honorable Reader (Mai-Mai Sze, the only Oriental in the cast) comes before the curtain in a gold-embroidered gown to elucidate the tale of the noble Lady Precious Stream (Helen Chandler), who rejects three suitors her father (Clarence Derwent) presents her and instead marries her gardener (Bramwell Fletcher). Her parents disown the couple, but the husband goes on to become a great general. He returns loyally to his wife after eighteen years in the field, and the two prepare to rule all China.

A slight English comedy ran almost twice as long. Dodie Smith's **Call It a Day** (1-28-36, Morosco) covered the mundane life of a middle-class British family over the course of a single day, from wake-up time to bedtime. Mother and father only briefly contemplate having flings, and the family's children are shown how to deal with their own love lives. Gladys Cooper and Philip Merivale, recovering from their unsuccessful Shakespearean mountings, headed the cast, supported by such fine players as Glenn Anders, Lawrence Grossmith, and Claudia Morgan.

Up in Harlem, the Lafayette Theatre, which had long brought all-black stage presentations to the area's black playgoers, played host on February 2 to New York's first Federal Theatre Project offering. Even before the initial production saw the footlights, controversy had exploded, with authorities applying sufficient pressure to have several projects dropped and Elmer Rice, who headed the New York office of the enterpise, resigning noisily in disgust. Nonetheless, something of a celebratory air was provided on opening night by red-capped, blue-gowned girls who served as ushers and a jazz band in the pit. The play, **Walk Together Chillun,** was by Broadway's original Porgy, Frank Wilson. A cast of approximately 100 was onstage to offer a drama whose top ticket price was 40¢. No commercial theatre could hope to compete. Wilson's story told of a small northern mill town which encourages Negroes from the South to emigrate from their homes in order to fill low-paying jobs. The town's whites make no distinctions between the newcomers and the town's old-line Negroes; they have contempt for all of them. Worse, the old-line Negroes look down on the late arrivals. A condescending Negro preacher (Oliver Foster) attempts to lecture the leader (Gus Smith) of the imported workers, only to be told, "Preachers ain't no better than anybody else. Jest got a job like me." Wilson pleaded for tolerance and understanding, but added, in any case, Negroes must never fall out among themselves. As with so many black shows, a church scene with blacks fervently singing spirituals and a wild dance hall scene provided special, if by now stereotypical, color. Those few critics who reviewed the production were more respectful than enthusiastic.

The hero of H. T. Porter and Alfred Henri White's **The Sap Runs High** (2-4-36, Bijou) is one of life's many nonentities, John J. Jennings (James Bell). For years now his wife, Maggie (Marie Nordstrom), has had to support their family by collecting and packaging local mud and selling it as Egyptian Beauty Clay. Having been tricked into buying some railroad stocks that soon became worthless, John grabs at the chance to sell them for $25,000 down when rumors say they will shortly be valuable again. But he squanders the money on a new car (which his son promptly wrecks) and on a swampland. After the stock collapses again, the buyer demands his money back. Maggie goads John into standing up for his rights, and, when the goverment purchases the swampland for a naval base, the Jenningses look to be on easy street for a while.

Margaret Anglin, reappearing after a prolonged absence, seems to have been responsible for Ivor Novello's **Fresh Fields** (2-10-36, Empire) eking out a ten-week stand, although the *Sun*'s Richard Lockridge felt her "measured stateliness" and timing were inimical to Novello's "elfin lines." On their uppers, two English ladies (Anglin and Mary Sargent), who are sisters, take in as boarders a giddy Australian widow (Elwyn Harvey), her daughter (Agnes Doyle), and her brother (Boyd Davis). In no time, the more commanding of the ladies has married off her son (Derek Fairman) to the Australian's daughter and her sister to the brother.

Comedian Ed Wynn also returned to the theatre, but as a producer rather than as a clown. The drama he presented suggested that if he could not play Hamlet, at least he could mount a serious piece. His public did not agree. **Alice Takat** (2-10-36, Golden) was José Ruben's free adaptation of Deszö Szomory's Hungarian original. After a young doctor (Mady Christians) practices mercy killing, her lover (Russell Hardie) accepts the blame and is sent to prison. On his release, he discovers the doctor is pregnant by another man. But he forgives her, even agreeing to accept the child as his own.

Although critics had lavished high praise on several of Jo Mielziner's earlier settings, when the designer co-produced Mildred Harris and Harold Goldman's **Co-respondent Unknown** (2-11-36, Ritz) most critics paid his latest work scant attention. But then most critics did not care for the comedy, either. Still, the play tickled the public's funny bone, so ran fifteen weeks. While his actress wife (Ilka Chase) is on tour, an author (James Rennie) of a best-selling book on modern economics has a fling with a pretty reviewer (Phyllis Povah) who praised his work. The actress demands a divorce, and her lawyer (Martin Wolfson) hires a sweet innocent (Peggy Conklin) to act as corespondent. Learning that the girl and the writer went beyond the call of duty, the reviewer storms out. Then the girl tells the actress all the loving things her husband said about his wife, so the divorce is called off.

Two one-week flops followed. Critics scoffed at the cliché-packed dialogue in Laura Walker's **Among Those Sailing** (2-11-36, Longacre). On board the *Aquitania* Calvert (Ted Trevor) and Sybil (Ruth Weston) light sparks, prompting Calvert to follow Sybil to the home of her sister, Marie (Selena Royle). Marie turns out to be Calvert's old flame. For a while it looks like Calvert and Marie might run off, but Marie finally decides to remain with her husband (William Harrigan), while Calvert and Sybil become a pair again.

A loathsome, headline-making Chicago murderer, Dr. Wynekoop, apparently inspired Samuel John Park's **Black Widow** (2-12-36, Mansfield). Only Park made his killer a woman. Because so many of her (Lucille LaVerne) patients have disappeared, police search Dr. Koloich's premises, including a furnace, for remains, but find nothing. Only after they discover an acid-filled vat beneath the furnace can they solve the crime. About to be arrested, the doctor stabs her accomplice and jumps into the vat. The writing was dismissed as amateurish and even the cast, including the often praised LaVerne, as no great shakes.

By contrast the season's most brilliant dialogue and some of its most scintillating performances were to be heard and seen in S. N. Behrman's **End of Summer** (2-17-36, Guild). Atkinson hailed the comedy as "one of those tolerant, witty, gently probing essays in modern thinking." Its leading lady, Ina Claire, he hymned as "all animation and crackle," adding, "and when there is need of it she is also politely moving." Leonie Frothingham is a rich woman of old stock, as her wise, world-weary mother (Mildred Natwick) is ready to point out. But she is a social butterfly, and her husband (Minor Watson), tired of living in *her house,* decides to divorce her. "Isn't is a pity," she laments, "I have no mind?" The fortune-hunting psychologist Dr. Kenneth Rice (Osgood Perkins) is ready to fill the gap. He is the sort of successful man who sneers, "It always satisfies the mediocrity to call the exceptional individual lucky." Meanwhile Leonie's daughter, Paula (Doris Dudley), proposes to and is accepted by a young radical, Will (Shepperd Strudwick), who promises merely revolution and a new social order. When Kenneth fears that Leonie will not marry him, he proposes to Paula. She in turn forces him to confess his duplicity to her mother. Leonie can only see all of this as the end of summer for her and her class. She agrees to underwrite a left-wing magazine for Will's even more radical buddy, Dennis (Van Heflin), who nonetheless assures her that when the revolution does come, she will have a friend in high office. Arriving late in the season, the comedy ran until the hot weather scared away playgoers.

In Dudley Nichols and Stuart Anthony's **Come Angel Band** (2-18-36, 46th St.) a psalm-spouting, hypocritical minster, Fate Shannon (Curtis Cooksey), who has buried four wives, buys fifteen-year-old Selah Hearn (Eleanor Lynn) for his fifth wife, paying her father (Robert Pitkin) a wagon, some mules, and some whiskey for the girl. Her lover, Bird (Elisha Cook, Jr.), kills the minister with a pitchfork, and the youngsters run off together. After they are caught, an understanding sheriff (Richard Taber) allows them to spend a night with each other before Bird is hanged. Two performances, and the drama was history.

The second Federal Theatre Project mounting to reach New York, and the first to use an old, established Broadway playhouse, was John McGee's **Jefferson Davis** (2-18-36, Biltmore), which was announced as embarking on an extended cross-country tour after a handful of New York performances. With a huge cast and multiple scenes, it was essentially a pageant recreating the salient moments in the life of the man (Guy Standing, Jr.) who presided over the Confederacy, with all its ugly backstage intrigues, and ending with an epilogue at his grave.

Like its two predecessors, Dan Totheroh's **Searching for the Sun** (2-19-36, 58th St.) ran less than a week.

Matt (Edwin Philips) and Dot (Olive Deering), two young hoboes, meet and fall in love. Dot hopes that the news that she is pregnant will keep Matt from following the criminal paths of his buddies, but the news merely terrifies him, and he flees. His conscience finally brings him back. They decide to seek out the unhappy Ohio family that Dot had run away from, but all they find is a deserted homestead. They resume their hobo ways.

Two plays that might well have opened on Halloween night opened concurrently the next evening—and both survived for less than two weeks. One, by Henry Myers, was called, appropriately, **Hallowe'en** (2-20-36, Vanderbilt). At a New England inn on Halloween, Joan (Mary Hone), who believes herself possessed of long-repressed powers, finds that the innkeeper (Ian Maclaren) is really the devil and that she is a reincarnated witch. Both a priest (Robert T. Haines) and a rabbi (Aristides de Leoni) attempt exorcisms, but only her fiancé (John Saeger), reciting the Lord's Prayer, succeeds. **The Devil of Pei-Ling** (2-20-36, Adelphi), Howard Chenery's adaptation of a Herbert Asbury novel, spotlighted an ancient Chinese bronze seemingly obedient to the malevolent will of a now dead murderer who once occupied the house to which it is brought. The killings are shown to have been done by the heroine (Nancy Crawford), stepdaughter of the hanged man and granddaughter of the new owner, who had been hypnotized by the murderer before his execution. Again, exorcism breaks the spell. O. E. Wee, the producer, apparently knew he was in trouble from the start. Although he announced a $2.20 top ticket, he also announced a "courtesy section" where all seats would be 40¢, and he flooded the city with these cheapies. To no avail.

A woman (Dorothy Gish), about to divorce her husband (Arthur Margetson) because he spends more time excavating mummies in Egypt than he spends with her, asks him to pretend for a few weeks that theirs is a happy marriage so that her sister (Rachel Hartzell) and the sister's fiancé (Leo G. Carroll) will have no qualms about wedding. The ploy fails when the fiancé joins the husband on his latest expedition. That was the plot of Philip Johnson's **Mainly for Lovers** (2-21-36, 48th St.), at least in London. In New York, the ending was altered to allow both couples a happy reconciliation. But even with the new curtain, New Yorkers would not buy the play. It ran only one week.

Far uptown, at what used to be Daly's Theatre on 63rd Street, a 55¢ top and a rechristened theatre could not nudge the latest Federal Theatre Project offering beyond two and half weeks. Remembering the recent Lindbergh trial in Flemington, New Jersey, and the not-long-gone Scopes trial in Dayton, Tennessee, Edwin L. and Albert Barker's **American Holiday** (2-21-36, Experimental) looked at how newsworthy American trials degenerate into circuses. The papers have been branding the trial of a young man who killed his sweetheart "the trial of the century." So the lobby of the Hollister House in Middletown is jammed not merely with the families of the central figures, their attorneys, and newsmen, but with popcorn peddlers and other cheap hucksters, with publicity seekers, and everyone else wanting to get in. The boy is acquitted and signs up with an evangelist for a promotional tour. While the play required only a single setting, it offered another of the huge casts that were fast becoming a signature of the Federal Theatre Project.

The beguiling charm and playing of a winsome young actress, Wendy Hiller, was largely responsible for Ronald Gow and Walter Greenwood's London success **Love on the Dole** (2-24-36, Shubert) enjoying a five-month New York visit. Hiller played a girl who is forced to become the mistress of a cynical gambler (Ross Chetwynd) after her fiancé (Brandon Peters) is killed during some labor strife. Both he and her family have been unemployed and on the dole.

The once popular silent-screen star Richard Barthelmess tried his luck on the stage and found his appeal was limited when he was cast in a mediocre play. His vehicle was **The Postman Always Rings Twice** (2-25-36, Lyceum), which James M. Cain theatricalized from his own best-seller. Critics felt that the play lacked the bite and thrust of the novel and that Barthelmess lacked the requisite toughness. He was seen as a drifter who falls in love with the wife (Mary Philips) of a roadstand operator (Joseph Greenwald). They conspire to murder the husband, and run off, scot-free. But when the woman is killed in a car accident while the drifter is driving, the police use her death to convict the man of homicide. Once again, Mielziner walked off with some of the best notices, this time for his "slatternly lunchroom, a wrecked car under the shoulder of an aloof mountain," and other settings.

A one-week revival of Austin Strong's old hit about a trio of aging bachelors who must raise an orphan girl, *Three Wise Fools* (10-31-18), at the Golden on March 1, might not have attracted much attention had not its star been eighty-year-old William Gillette, coming out of retirement for some special farewell appearances. James Kirkwood and Charles Coburn played his cohorts, while Elizabeth Love was the youngster. Among the oldtimers in the cast were such bygone favorites as Isabel Irving, John Blair, and Brandon Tynan. Critics insisted that Gillette's cool, crisp underplaying had lost none of its unique appeal. But for all the kudos, the star refused to extend the engagement.

Another "oldtimer"—he was a mere fifty-seven—probably hoped for a long run in his new vehicle, **Dear**

Old Darling (3-2-36, Alvin), but had to settle for a fortnight's stay. The story suggested melodrama. Wealthy, retired Calvin Miller has been hounded by a sweet girl (Marion Shockley) in her twenties, whom he met on shipboard and who has sent a photograph inscribed "To my dear old darling, with all the love of my heart and soul." Her mother (Theresa Maxwell Conover) appears soon enough, and the two gals prove to be blackmailers. This presents numerous problems for Miller, not the least that he has been courting the Widow Collins (Ruth Shepley). Matters are put in order only just before eleven o'clock. But the play was not melodrama. Indeed, it was billed as "A Comic Experience," and its author and star was George M. Cohan. While much of his public had faded away, Cohan had lost none of his popularity with critics, who let the play down gently and sang his praises as a performer. Thus Anderson dismissed the work as "a rattletrap piece of stage machinery," but detailed for his readers why Cohan made it "pretty fascinating," itemizing "that ridiculous skip, the bent-knee-action walk, the wink, the leer, the down-at-the-mouth voice, the face turning against the movement of the eyes, and all the assorted tricks that have endeared him to us."

That same evening saw another huge cast offer another production by the Federal Theatre Project, albeit in the Bronx. Samuel Jesse Warshawsky's **A Woman of Destiny** (3-2-36, Willis) was a variation of the earlier *If This Be Treason.* For political considerations, the Republicans nominate the pacifist Constance Goodwin (Alexandra Carlisle) to be vice-president on the ticket headed by a hawkish presidential candidate (Robert Harrison). After the election, the American ambassador to Japan is assassinated, and the president declares war on Japan, then drops dead of a heart attack. As president, Goodwin, goaded by her son (Robert Perry), who had been blinded in the last world war, bucks all the belligerent outcry and appeals to the emperor for reason and peace. Her appeal wins the day.

Jay Mallory's **Sweet Aloes** (3-4-36, Booth) was the third English play to arrive in two weeks' time. It told of a woman (Evelyn Laye) who had had a child out of wedlock by the son (John Emery) of an English lord (Charles Bryant), had been paid by the lord to move to America but leave the child behind to be raised as the family heir but, after suffering second thoughts years later, has been confirmed in her original decision by her abandoned son's family. Several critics were amused that Laye, who had been the American leading lady of *Bitter Sweet,* was starring in a play with so similar a title, but American playgoers were uninterested.

Harold A. Clarke and Maxwell Nurnberg's **Chalk Dust** (3-4-36, Experimental), the latest Federal Theatre Project mounting, recounted the problems of two radical schoolteachers (Katherine Standing and Mitchell Grayson) who fall in love but are hounded by a conservative school board and local gossips.

Another schoolteacher, this time a college professor (Reed Brown, Jr.), was the central figure of Francis Bosworth's **The Fields Beyond** (3-6-36, Mansfield). Professor Cameron comes to a midwestern school, where he marries the pliant daughter (Helen Claire) of the president (Herbert Duffy). But his demon mother-in-law (Merle Maddern), who has made life miserable for everyone on campus and has her daughter under her thumb, accuses him of harboring unnatural desires toward a young male student. Having enough of her, he tells her off and heads for a foreign school.

Katharine Cornell enjoyed one of her greatest triumphs when she and her husband, Guthrie McClintic, mounted a revival of Shaw's *Saint Joan* at the Martin Beck on the 9th. Cornell was no beauty and often had a curiously plodding gait, but captivated an audience within moments. Burns Mantle may have been alluding to this when he recorded in his review in the *Daily News,* "None of her scenes, it seems to me, was less than eloquent. Her entrance as the awkward but radiantly eager peasant was electric; her scene at court with the discovery of the Dauphin and her winning of the Archbishop were persuasively moving. . . . By the time she had reached the trial it seemed improbable that there was anything left in even her splendid equipment that could lift the episode above the others, but here the actress' sensitive command of a pathos that is heart reaching made of the trial a magnificently complete and forceful drama in itself." Her superb supporting cast included Charles Waldron as the Archbishop, Maurice Evans as the Dauphin, Brian Aherne as the Earl of Warwick, and Tyrone Power, Kent Smith, George Coulouris, Eduardo Ciannelli, and John Cromwell in lesser roles. The revival ran for eleven weeks.

Several critics thought that Robert Ardrey had a delicious idea and no knowledge of how to handle it in his **Star Spangled** (3-10-36, Golden). Greg Smith (George Tobias) has escaped from prison through a sewer. He is intent on killing the Polish-American political boss (Michael Visaroff) who helped send him up. His much married mother, Mrs. Dzieszienewski (Natasha Boleslasky), his brother, Stan (Millard Mitchell), a Texas Leaguer home after hurting his pitching arm throwing balls at a carnival at a girl who loses her clothing when hit, and another brother (Garson Kanin), a rising if unprincipled young politician, do everything they can to thwart him. They succeed, so Greg, who is president of the prison Killer's Club, sneaks back into prison in order to return the gun he borrowed from the club's vice-president. Whatever the play's failings, Tobias's performance as the likable, somewhat befuddled hood won loud applause.

The Federal Theatre Project's second mounting in Harlem was Rudolph Fisher's **Conjur Man Dies** (3-11-36, Lafayette). A scientist (Lionel Monagas), a detective (Dooley Wilson), and a bumbling amateur sleuth called Bubber (William Brown) combine forces to investigate the death of a popular voodoo conjur man, M'Gana Frimbo (Fritz Weller), who inconveniences everyone by turning up very much alive. It seems his assistant was killed. To unmask the killer, M'Gana decides to hold a seance in his gold-furnished, eerily lighted "Black Room." During the seance a shot rings out, and M'Gana drops down, really dead.

Just a little less than a decade earlier Broadway had accorded Patrick Kearney's dramatization of Theodore Dreiser's *An American Tragedy* a respectable run. Now the Group Theatre offered playgoers a more politically slanted and pretentiously staged version by Erwin Piscator and Lina Goldschmidt, retitled **Case of Clyde Griffiths** (3-13-36, Ethel Barrymore). With Morris Carnovsky serving as a modern-day chorus, the production professed to demonstrate how a callous, rich society drove Clyde (Alexander Kirkland) to murder his sweetheart (Phoebe Brand) so that he might marry a wealthier girl. Two and a half weeks exhausted Broadway's interest.

Playgoers did show more interest in another politically slanted production, but then they could afford to be lured into the auditorium by the Federal Theatre Project's low prices. The play was the first to be produced under a much ballyhooed cover-all title of **The Living Newspaper.** A previously announced mounting, *Ethiopia,* had made headlines when the State Department, worried about Mussolini's reaction, successfully pressured to have the production canceled. The new offering, **Triple-A Plowed Under** (3-14-36, Biltmore), was written by a slew of writers, featured another bloated cast, and was essentially a series of sketches denouncing the rich, big business, and big government for oppressing the farmer, the workingman, and the little consumer. The voice of a radio commentator connected the twenty-odd sketches. Farmers, for example, were shown to be encouraged in 1917 to expand production in order to satisfy war needs, then were left holding the bag. Farm strikes follow, bankrupt farms are forcibly auctioned off, and then, after the AAA begins subsidizing farmers, prices rise and hurt a woman trying to feed a family. Characters from Thomas Jefferson to the Communist leader Earl Browder, were depicted onstage. Lockridge wailed, "It is propaganda, as so many have asserted, it is propaganda in all directions. It is not a statement, but a chatter. . . . I regret to inform the 243 persons involved in this production of the 'living newspaper' that they will have to be more coherent than this."

Another Federal Theatre Project followed in short order, but this was not an American propaganda play. Rather it was a poetic English drama that London had hailed and that had been given its American premiere at Yale—T. S. Eliot's **Murder in the Cathedral** (3-20-36, Manhattan). The pseudo-Gothic architecture of the theatre (originally the Hammerstein) enhanced this recounting of the killing of Thomas à Becket (Harry Irvine) at the instigation of Henry II. After his death, his killers turn to the audience and, in startlingly modern terms, attempt to justify their action. Despite a mixed but generally good critical reception, playgoers showed little interest.

The anti-war sentiments that had been growing for some time found no more entertaining expression than Robert Sherwood's **Idiot's Delight** (3-24-36, Shubert). His comedy starred the Lunts, who had set aside their Shakespearean doings. The Hotel Monte Gabrielle, a former sanitorium, sits in Austrian territory ceded to Italy after the war. With another war looming, its handful of guests are stranded there by border closings. They are unsure when the war will begin and how sides will be chosen. As one Italian officer remarks, "The map of Europe supplies us with a wide choice of opponents. I suppose, in due time, our government will announce its selection—and we shall know just whom we are to shoot at." Into their midst come a mediocre American song-and-dance man, Harry Van (Lunt), and his six girls, following a failed Balkan tour. Among the other guests, Harry spots a supposed Russian countess, Irene [pronounced "Ear-ray-na"] (Fontanne), who is traveling with a rich munitions manufacturer, and recognizes her as a former trouper with whom he once had a brief fling in Omaha. As the war clouds darken they gingerly resume their old affair. The other guests leave, but Harry stays behind to convince Irene to flee with him and create a new mind-reading act. They share a bottle of champagne and sing "Onward, Christian Soldiers" as bombs begin to fall. *Variety* hailed the comedy as "Sherwood's best written and best acted play." The tradesheet also carried a slightly tongue-in-cheek nightclub review of "Harry Van and Les Blondes," commenting, "Van (Lunt) as a song and dance man is not so forte, per character, but okay per script. He looks and acts the part of a hoofer from the sticks." Fontanne, wearing a straight blonde wig and giving hints of cockney under her phony Russian accent, was applauded for an "uncanny" performance, "something to relish." To create an ominous air, Lee Simonson dwarfed the actors with an unusually high, expansive setting. The play had hardly opened when it was awarded the Pulitzer Prize. The notices and the award helped it to run 299 performances.

The next Federal Theatre Project offering, again in the Bronx, was Arthur Goodman and Washington Pezet's oddball **In Heaven and Earth** (3-26-36, Willis). To confirm his thesis of "returning personality," which suggests that people with personality disorders are often imbued with the spirit and mind of the dead, Dr. Littlefield (Allan Tower) hypnotizes an unconscious accident victim (Louise Kirtland) who reminds him of his late wife. For a time the woman believes she is the doctor's wife and behaves accordingly, even rejecting the pleas of her own fiancé (Mayon Pate). The doctor's son (Carl Emory) finally convinces his father to break the spell and allow matters to return to normal.

Of course, the Federal Theatre Project was not alone in offering theatregoers political tracts masquerading as plays. Even commercial producers did so, as witness *Idiot's Delight*. If that play had touched only tangentially on Mussolini, another was more direct. And on this occasion the State Department could bring no telling pressure to bear on the radical Theatre Union when it mounted Victor Wolfson's dramatization of Ignazio Silone's novel *Fontamara* as **Bitter Stream** (3-30-36, Civic Repertory). The seizure of much of their land and the imposition of higher taxes, all in the name of the "greatest good of the State," have riled Italian peasants. The final straw comes with a plan to divert a stream which supplies them with the little water they can depend on. Led by Berardo (Albert Van Dekker), the peasants rebel. Black-shirted troops put down the uprising and kill Berardo, but they cannot kill the peasants' dreams of justice.

All that Mark Linder and Dolph Singer's **Summer Wives** (4-13-36, Mansfield) had to offer was the popular vaudeville comedy team of Joe Smith and Charlie Dale, who, despite their Waspish stage names, performed with marked Yiddish accents. Even its title was no help, since it had nothing to do with the plot. Murray Lowen (Smith), operator of the Lowen-Green Country Club in the Catskills (at the time the famous Grossinger's called itself a country club), hires Mike Chisley (Dale), a broken-down vaudeville agent, to supply his resort with entertainment. All manner of contretemps ensue, especially when Mike learns Murray is nearly bankrupt and is threatened by a loan shark. The loan shark is arrested, and Mike and Murray grumpily go their separate ways. The evening included some bad singing and dancing at the resort's nightclub show, a burlesque golf lesson, and jokes on the order of "Don't make mountains out of moth balls."

A second attempt by the Federal Theatre Project to mount an English drama led to some highly disparaging

reviews and immediate artistic rather than political controversy, but nearly two-thirds of a century later remains one of the organization's best-remembered and most talked-about offerings. On the 14th, at Harlem's Lafayette Theatre, a twenty-one-year-old unknown named Orson Welles brought out *Macbeth* with an all black cast. This was no typical *Macbeth,* set in ancient Scotland. Instead it unfolded in torridly colored jungle settings, with women sometimes in scanty, bright tropical clothes and sometimes in equally gaudy Directoire gowns and the men often in uniforms lavishly gold-braided. There were voodoo rites, drums à la *The Emperor Jones,* a witch brandishing a huge bullwhip, and a Banquo (Canada Lee) who puffed away at a large cigar. Jack Carter was Macbeth and Edna Thomas his queen. Representative of the critical assessment was John Mason Brown's opinion that Welles's "version bastardizes the Bard but it does not establish him in the jungle. . . . The pity is that this 'Macbeth,' which should have been so interesting, wastes not only an exciting idea but murders an exciting play." Harlem, which Brown reported had been "dressed beyond the teeth" on opening night, rejected all the naysaying and packed the theatre for the rest of the season.

More traditional playgoers saw no reason to defy the critics who slated Hyman Adler and R. L. Hill's **Lady Luck** (4-15-36, Adelphi). They even paid no attention to a producer who offered them a chance to share in the play's profits if they bought a seat at the $2.20 top. As a result, there were no profits to share when the play closed after half a week. During those few performances it looked with some disdain on the Fraleys, a family of lazy California parasites. They depend on the income of their lone hard-working member, sister Alice (Viola Frayne). She abandons her stenographer's job, rejects an offer of marriage from a shady real estate promoter, "Whip" Lash (Jack Harwood), and takes a screenplay she has written to an agent, Robin Boyd (Hall Shelton). Alice and Robin fall in love. He later proves to be a disguised G-man, who arrests a racketeer (Hurst Amyx) courting Alice's sister (Eileen Myers).

The season had one more fine anti-war play up its sleeve. Irwin Shaw's **Bury the Dead** (4-18-36, Ethel Barrymore) was the major part of a double bill. Its first scene is a battlefield "Where Graves Are Being Dug for Soldiers Killed in an Advance During [the] Second Year of [a] War That Is to Begin Tomorrow." (Actually the graves were covered by army blankets.) The dead bodies are covered by army blankets. They are lowered into the pit, and a priest (Edwin **Cooper**) and a rabbi (Samson Gordon) say prayers. **Moans are** heard from the pit, and, one by one, the **dead arise** and beg the amazed survivors **not to bury them,** insisting they "want to hear the sound of men talking." The top brass are called in to assure them that wars can be fought and won only if the dead are buried and forgotten. The men's loved ones are brought over. Not all of them are gentle with the dead. One angry wife (Paula Bauersmith) berates her husband for never earning enough money while he was alive. Neither pleas nor machine-gunning has any effect. The living-dead head off to proselytize the world. Atkinson hailed the drama as "the most tormenting war play of the year." Its curtain-raising companion was J. Edward Shugrue and John O'Shaughnessy's **Prelude,** in which three soldiers crippled in a war reminisce about the horrors they encountered while from a radio come the rantings of statesmen proclaiming the glory of battle. The public did not want to be tormented, so the double bill's run of three months was somewhat forced.

On the 20th, the long-dark Comedy Theatre was relit briefly with a non-Equity company playing **Elizabeth Sleeps Out.** The play proved to be merely a retitled revival of Leslie Howard's 1927 failure, *Murray Hill,* in which a rich young man must resort to several impostures before landing the girl of his dreams. A low budget and some forcing allowed the revival to nearly double the original's short run.

Another show out of the past was Walter Hampden's revival of *Cyrano de Bergerac.* Hampden had first presented his mounting to great acclaim and success thirteen years earlier, and had brought it back several times since. This five-week stand, starting on the 27th at the New Amsterdam, was announced as the aging actor's farewell to the role. Once again he played to crowded houses.

The season's last hit, **Pre-Honeymoon** (4-30-36, Lyceum), was something of a surprise, with Anne Nichols, collaborating for this play with Alford Van Ronkel, again waving away a critical razzing. Since Senator Dexter (Clyde Fillmore) has not been able to stop his bride-to-be, Virginia Barnard (Jessie Royce Landis), from running off to Miami for a pre-honeymoon fling, he sees no reason why he should not have a similar fling with Millie Marlowe (Marjorie Peterson), a bubble dancer who is subletting Virginia's apartment with another girl. Never mind that the other girl (Sylvia Field) is the fiancée of Dexter's son (Louis Jean Heydt) or that Ken Arnold (Roy Roberts), Millie's betrothed, feels that he should have some say in the matter. Complications naturally arise before Virginia returns home and restores peace and order. Despite the critics' harrumphs, the comedy ran nine months.

The musical genre, the revue, was still flourishing in 1935–36, but few, if any, playgoers or critics recalled that it initially had been spelled "review" and had been, in fact, a review of the latest year. Omitting the songs, dances, and humor that had characterized the genre, the Federal Theatre Project attempted a more jaundiced,

tuneless look at the past year in **1935** (5-12-36, Biltmore), the newest edition of its *Living Newspaper.* Vignettes examined, among others, Huey Long; Bruno Hauptmann, the kidnapper; Dutch Schultz, the gangster; Barbara Hutton, the socialite; John L. Lewis; and Nazi Germany. They had little or nothing good to say about any of their subjects. The lone hopeful sign noted was Pan American's China Clipper initiating flights to Asia.

The Project had another offering ready the next evening, the 13th, at the Experimental Theatre. In fact, it was a triple bill of one-acters, starting with Alfred Saxe condensation's of Molière's *The Miser,* in which an obsessively greedy rich man receives his comeuppance. This was followed by Emjo Basshe's expressionistic, anti-war **Snickering Horses,** in which the head of the Fullerton Meat Packing Company encourages his employees to go off to battle but afterwards refuses to rehire one badly mutilated former employee. The evening concluded with Shaw's comic look at the old Russian court in *Great Catherine,* which a few New Yorkers may have seen twenty years before in some performances in the Village.

A single commercial offering intruded itself into the parade of federally subsidized presentations. The one-time musical comedy leading man Oscar Shaw continued his futile attempt to become a straight comedian in Gaston Valcourt's **A Private Affair** (5-14-36, Masque). A young fellow, looking to secure some papers his mother left behind when she rented her chalet to four American women, pretends to be a notorious burglar when he is discovered rifling drawers. Both complications and romance quickly blossom.

Two more mountings by the remarkably prolific Federal Theatre Project followed. Orrie Lashin and Milo Hastings's **Class of '29** (5-15-36, Manhattan) recounted the unhappy history of several men who graduated college just before the Crash. Ken (Jan Ulrich), an architect unable to find employment, is nonetheless resentful when his influential father (Harry Irvine) pulls strings to place him. Ted (Ben Starkie) is so humiliated at having to accept work as a uniformed elevator operator that he throws himself in front of a subway train. Martin (Robert Bruce), an illustrator, becomes a Communist. Only Tippy (Allen Nourse) seems unfazed, although the only work he can find is walking dogs for Park Avenue matrons.

Michael Blankfort and Michael Gold's **Battle Hymn** (5-22-36, Experimental), like the equally unsuccessful *John Brown* (1-22-34) before it, was a pageant detailing the long history leading up to the raid at Harper's Ferry.

Of course, the Federal Theatre Project was federal, active in large and small cities across the nation. Thus, at this time, on the West Coast, more than half the plays performing in Los Angeles were its mountings.

They included a musical revue, a revival of Hoyt's old *A Texas Steer,* and two original dramas. A pair of Chicago playhouses was given over almost exclusively to the Project. Even small theatre towns were affected. At this moment New Haven playgoers could attend the organization's stage version of *Wuthering Heights,* at an 83¢ top ticket.

With so many of the best performers now living in California, it was hard for the Players to enlist the sort of all-star cast the club once regularly had assembled for its annual outing. So although many critics enjoyed the revival at the National on the 25th of an amiable old piece of hokum, George Ade's 1903 hit, *The County Chairman,* reading between their lines clearly indicates some sense of comedown. For the one-week stand, the county chairman who opposes the campaign of shady Judge Rigby (Forrest Orr) for prosecuting attorney and wangles the election of his own young associate (Alexander Kirkland) instead was played by Charles Coburn. Since the club had no black members, it resorted to the old practice of a white in blackface for the role of the comic servant, Sassafras Livingstone. Ben Lackland acted the part. When attendance proved disappointing, the Players called a temporary halt to their annual productions.

As so often happened, the season ended on a down note. In William H. Fulham's **To My Husband** (6-1-36, Belmont) Sarah Vane has an interesting response to her husband's request for a divorce. She invites his inamorata, Iris (Madeline Clive), to dinner and offers to turn over to the woman not only her spouse (Donald McClelland), but her house and her kids. Surely, Iris won't mind that the kids all have whooping cough. It isn't long before Iris is out of the picture and hubby has gotten over his seven-year itch.

Despite a heat wave, business remained reasonably good at season's end. *Saint Joan* closed after establishing a box-office record in its final week of $24,000, the same figure *Idiot's Delight* was pulling in. *Victoria Regina* was doing almost as well, at $22,000. *Boy Meets Girl, End of Summer,* and *Dead End* reported grosses of $13,000, $12,000, and $10,500 respectively—which meant all were turning in good profits. Even *Tobacco Road,* in its 130th week, raked in a profitable $6500.

All in all, quite a season!

1936–1937

In the wake of so generally acclaimed a season as 1935–36, it could hardly be hoped that the new theatrical year would be as rewarding. It was not. Most sadly, there was a noticeable drop in quality. Moreover, the decrease in the number of new plays produced, which had begun with the coming of the Depression, had leveled off for a few seasons, then had resumed last year, continued. As usual, counts varied, with the *Times,* apparently excluding Federal Theatre Project offerings, tallying eighty-three and *Variety,* more inclusive, ninety-four. The reasons for both drops—numbers and quality—were laid by many pundits squarely at the feet of men three thousand miles away: Hollywood producers. In 1935–36 possibly half of Broadway's shows had been mounted with Hollywood money. But the Dramatists' Guild's new contract, which withdrew several major perks filmmakers had come to accept, so irked movie men that, with a handful of exceptions, they withheld backing. Conversely, by dangling attractive offers to players and to the same greedy playwrights who had supported their union's new contract, they lured away needed talent. Not only did Broadway producers bemoan the dearth of good new scripts, several plays announced for production were called off at the last moment because of "casting difficulties"—which may have meant the lack of a suitable performer or may have indicated a lack of cash.

Late June, July, and August each brought in one commercial novelty. All failed. Edwin Harvey Blum's **The Kick Back** (6-22-36, Ritz) initially had been done a few weeks earlier as a Federal Theatre Project mounting in Brooklyn and had been moved up by some untested commercial entrepreneurs. Sally Mason, a co-ed at Heath University, is found murdered in a nearby cabin. The police are stumped, so they call in the school's professor of criminology, Dr. Siska (Walet Scott Weeks). At first he suspects one of his colleagues, Mark Adams (Maurice Burke), but then comes across the written confession of another professor who had subsequently killed himself by driving his car over a cliff. The exonerated Adams finds romance with a student (Diane Tempest) whom he cures of a stammer.

The Federal Theatre Project also had several offerings ready for late June. A "third class beer parlor and dance hall" on West 52nd Street, called the Palm Garden, played host starting on the 23rd to a revival of George R. Sims's 1881 English melodrama, *The Lights o' London,* in which the hero finally triumphs over the dastardly machinations of his villainous cousin. Patrons were encouraged to hiss and boo and to pound their steins on their tables. But not enough came to make it worthwhile.

Up at Harlem the FTP unveiled J. A. Smith and Peter Morell's **Turpentine** (6-26-36, Lafayette), detailing how white bosses take advantage of black workers at a southern turpentine camp and abuse their women until the men unionize.

The FTP also brought in July's first offering, a light-hearted farce with, at best, a subtext that might have satisfied the group's more militant followers. **Help Yourself!** (7-14-36, Manhattan) was John J. Coman's adaptation of an unspecified Viennese play by Paul Vulpius. Out-of-work Christopher Stringer (Curt Bois), collecting payment as an extra after accidentally strolling onto a movie set, decides it is not hard to make one's own employment. He walks into a bank, sits himself at an empty desk, and begins behaving importantly. He is immediately accepted as a legitimate employee. In good time he becomes an officer in a big business and marries the daughter of the bank president.

There was no need for anyone to search for a subtext in **Injunction Granted!** (7-24-36, Biltmore), the season's first edition of the FTP's *Living Newspaper*. Sirens, loudly clanging bells, and screaming actors added to the shrill tone of an examination of labor strife from the days of seventeenth-century indentured workers to recent confrontations in the shipping, steel, and newspaper industries. Even the *Times*'s normally patient and tolerant Brooks Atkinson balked at such blatant, hysterical slanting, observing, "If it wants to give the Federal Theatre a bad name for political insurgence it has found the most effective method."

Dorian Gray (7-20-36, Comedy) was taken by Jeron Criswell from Oscar Wilde's *The Picture of Dorian Gray,* which told of a decadent man who sells his soul so that he can remain young and handsome while his portrait grows old and ugly. The adaptation was considered even more inept than one Broadway had rejected in 1928 and was atrociously acted. Closed after two weeks, it was rewritten and recast, then reopened in mid-August as *The Life and Loves of Dorian Gray,* but shuttered for good after a month of forcing.

A three-week run was all Philip Barry could point to when his revision of Eleanor Golden and Eloise Barragon's **Spring Dance** (8-25-36, Empire) reached Broadway. Alex Benson (Louise Platt) has invited Sam Thatcher (Richard Kendrick) to her big college dance, hoping he will finally propose. His radical buddy, The Lippincot (José Ferrer), has warned him that any such girls' school is "an absolute man-trap . . . teaching the young boas how to constrict." He gets Sam to agree to leave college and accompany him on a prolonged visit to Russia. But Alex's schoolmates unite to defeat The Lippincot and win Sam for Alex. After all, as Alex's closest friend, Kate (Ruth Matteson), points out, men are merely "the second-strongest sex." Sure enough, by wangling a good job for Sam and other ploys, the girls carry the day.

Edwin Gilbert's **The Golden Journey** (9-15-36, Booth) looked at three mediocre bohemians. Clayton Herrick (Alan Hewitt) gets his play produced only because his fiancée (Eleanor Lynn) puts up the money. It flops. Julian Verney (Alan Bunce) is branded a plagiarist after his novel is published, but discovers he has legally inherited the rights to the material. Ivan Black (Hugh Rennie), a poet, is left to have a fling with a publisher's wife (Leona Powers).

Marie Baumer and Martin Berkeley's **Seen But Not Heard** (9-17-36, Henry Miller's) cast its spotlight on the three Winthrop kids, fifteen-year-old Duke (Frankie Thomas), thirteen-year-old Elizabeth (Anne Baxter), and ten-year-old Tommy (Raymond Roe). They are convinced their beloved aunt was murdered by their wicked Uncle John (Paul McGrath), and they are right. But before they can uncover proof, their good Uncle Bob (Kent Smith) accidentally brings about John's death. That killing they would impute to a dour butler (John Winthrop). But when they learn the truth they connive to keep it from an inquiring sheriff (Ralph Theadore). Baxter's "cute kidlet" won many of the laurels.

The FTP had a competing entry the same night: **The Path of Flowers** (9-17-36, Daly's 63rd St.), which Irving DeW. Talmadge derived from the Russian of Valentin Katayev. A professor who considers himself a genius, and therefore above society's rules, sees no reason why he should be loyal to his wife or mistresses. Before long he finds himself alone and loveless.

Matters went further downhill with the next two commercial entries. First came Maxine Alton's **Arrest That Woman** (9-18-36, National). The assistant district attorney, Donald Drake (Hugh Marlowe), is the son of the judge (George Lessey) whom Marie Smith (Doris Nolan) is accused of murdering. Marie, the judge's illegitimate daughter and a former prostitute trying to aid her husband pay back money he had stolen to help his dying mother, had gone to the judge and threatened to kill herself there and thus smear his good name if he refused to assist. In the struggle that followed when the judge tried to grab her gun, the weapon fired and he was killed. Only by disclosing that she is his half-sister, can Marie get Drake to drop charges. Al Woods withdrew his production after a lone week.

A lone performance was all John Boruff's **Timber House** (9-19-36, Longacre) could manage. A dying, hate-filled man (Donald Cameron) decides to commit suicide but make it seem like his wife (Lenita Lane) and her lover (Robert Shayne) killed him. He plants the revolver from which he has shot a bullet into a sack of flour on the innocent man. A supposed hiker (Frieda Altman) comes to the Vermont summer cottage where the action takes place and exposes the hoax. The hiker proves to be a professional investigator for an insurance company.

The season's first hit, George Kelly's **Reflected Glory** (9-21-36, Morosco), was a modest one and its small success—127 performances—attributable wholly to its star, Tallulah Bankhead. "She is exciting and fascinating enough," John Mason Brown suggested in the *Evening Post*, "to make an otherwise uneventful evening worthwhile." He went on to add that she was "a kind of super-show in her own person . . . expert and glamorous and possessed of the kind of volcanic temperament which has ever been the mark of truly virtuoso players." There were a few dissenting voices, with the *World-Telegram*'s Douglas Gilbert ruing that "the subtle poignancy demanded here is beyond Miss Bankhead," but he noted, nonetheless, that she "proceeds, with forthright brass, to the curtain that for her will always be rising." Apparently it will always be rising, too, for Muriel Flood, although she is tired of learning new roles every season and traipsing from hotel to hotel and theatre to theatre. Her loyal maid, Hattie (Elizabeth Dunne), has assured her, "If I had *your* future on the stage, Miss Flood, I'd certainly leave marriage to the audience." She is courted by suave, handsome Leonard Wall (J. Herschel Mayall), but he turns out to be a married stage-door Johnny. The more likable Tom Howard (Alden Chase), despairing of her accepting his proposals, goes off and marries another woman. Left alone, Muriel can only beg her manager (Clay Clement) to show her where her onstage performance has been slipping.

A pair of dramas telling virtually identical stories opened five nights apart. In Joseph M. Viertel's **So Proudly We Hail** (9-22-36, 46th St.) Jim Thornton (Richard Cromwell), a sweet, relatively innocent, and artistically inclined young man, enters Stone Military Academy, where he is so brutalized that he ends up as a cold philistine but also an honor graduate. In Henry R. Misrock's **Bright Honor** (9-27-36, 48th St.), the youngster was called Thomas Briggs, Jr. (Charles Powers), and the school Newtown Military Academy, but his treatment there and its results were much the same. Critics found Misrock's play less vitriolic and less angry than Viertel's, with more comedy and humanity. Neither appealed to the public.

Some notion of just how many productions the Federal Theatre Project was mounting across the country was evident when its latest offering in New York was listed as "Project No. 891." Of course, not all projected productions made it to the footlights. Still, the figure is telling. This 891st project was **Horse Eats Hat** (9-26-36, Maxine Elliott's), Orson Welles and Edwin Denby's reworking of Eugène Labiche and Marc-Michel's *Un chapeau de paille d'Italie,* depicting the misadventures of a young man, on his way to his wedding, after his horse eats a girl's straw hat. Welles's sometimes frenetic staging was embellished by Nat Karson's colorful settings and costumes. (Karson had done last season's equally colorful *Macbeth* for Welles.) The cast, for a change among FTP offerings, enlisted a number of players who would go on to better things. Besides Welles himself, these included Joseph Cotten, Hiram Sherman, Paula Laurence, and Arlene Francis.

Just as two plays about life in military schools had followed in short order, now two very similar importations came in on successive nights. Both were from England; both dealt with psychopathic killers; both were written by relatively young men who assumed the leading roles; and both failed to find audiences in America. Emlyn Williams's **Night Must Fall** (9-28-36, Ethel Barrymore) centered on a charming but murderous bellhop, who kills not only guests at his hotel but also a dear old lady (May Whitty) who has given him employment. Her niece (Angela Baddeley) suspects the killer, but is so smitten by him that for a time she comes to his defense. In his own **Love from a Stranger** (9-29-36, Fulton) Frank Vosper played the part of an attractive, blond-haired man who attempts to murder the woman (Jessie Royce Landis) whose apartment he has leased and with whom he has fallen in love. She realizes he is a long-sought lady-killer, who has bleached his hair as a disguise. By tricking him into believing she has poisoned him, she provokes him into a fatal stroke. Williams's thriller ran two months; Vosper's, one.

Its setting of a prison death row caused a number of reviewers at Alfred L. Golden's **Mimie Scheller** (9-30-36, Ritz) to hark back to *The Last Mile*. But they all agreed the new play could not hold a candle to the 1930 hit. A notorious lady gangster, Mimie Scheller (Ara Gerald), who has eluded the police for years, is fingered by a stoolie (Edward Blaine) when she visits him in prison. She is arrested, sentenced to death, and placed in the death house. At first the redhead puts up a cocky, even tigerish facade, parading around with a hip-swinging strut and brazenly singing "The Last Round-Up." Experienced prison guards take bets on whether or not she will break. She finally does, but not without bringing down her curses on the whole world.

Another play to open the same night, Lynn Root and Frank Fenton's **Stork Mad** (9-30-36, Ambassador), ran only half a week. Its sole attraction was the deadpan comedy of Percy Kilbride in a principal role. The residents of the southern Ohio hill country are vying to see who can have the most children in ten years' time, the winner supposedly to collect a whopping $500,000. Leading contenders seem to be Matthew "Pa" Dever and Jed "Dad" Peters (Edward F. Nannary). At one point Jed contrives to have Matthew jailed on trumped-up charges in order to keep him out of Mrs. Dever's bed. At the decade's end both men claim ten offspring, but Dever's son (Root) steps in to pocket the winnings after his wife's last-minute delivery of quadruplets raises his own count to twelve.

George Kelly's brother, Walter C. Kelly, the famed "Virginia Judge" of bygone two-a-day, found no better luck in Philip Wood and Stewart Beach's **Lend Me Your Ears!** (10-5-36, Mansfield) than Kilbride had found in his vehicle. The stocky, moon-faced Kelly was cast as Jasper Beam, a small-town hardware-store owner with a penchant for speechmaking. A New York newspaper decides it can increase its circulation in his area by promoting him for a local office. His speeches soon put him in the national spotlight, especially when he invites a nudist convention to town. His wife, Willa (Jane Seymour), outraged at this and at his supposed fondness for the newspaper's female reporter (Mary Holsman), storms out, prompting him to go on the air with a tearful plea for her return. The broadcast wins him the election and brings on talk of his running for governor.

R. C. Sheriff and Jeanne de Casalis's **St. Helena** (10-6-36, Lyceum) was the latest London success to encounter far less favor in New York. Its story followed Napoleon's six-year exile, from his self-confident arrival on the isolated island, through his growing search for consolation in philosophy, to his lonely, embittered death. Max Gordon's fine production, with settings and costumes by Jo Mielziner, was universally lauded, but the highest praise was reserved for the play's Napoleon, Maurice Evans. On the second night, Gordon put Evans's name up in lights, launching Evans's decades-long career as a major Broadway player.

. . .

Maurice Evans (1901–89) was born in England and had established himself on the London stage, including a stint at the Old Vic, before coming to America to appear as Romeo opposite Katharine Cornell a year earlier. Small, with a slightly quizzical expression, he was hailed for the intelligence and clarity of his interpretations but also sometimes chastized for his singsong delivery.

. . .

Another young English actor, whose only other American appearance (in 1928) had gone largely unnoticed, scored an even greater triumph two nights later. The actor was haughty-miened, musical-voiced John Gielgud, who was bringing his highly touted *Hamlet* into the Empire on the 8th. Comparisons with John Barrymore were inevitable and rife. Barrymore was seen as far more forceful and direct; Gielgud, who played the prince as "an appealing young man, brimming over with grief," as more poetic and probing.

Certainly, Gielgud's supporting cast, especially as directed by Guthrie McClintic, far surpassed Barrymore's. Judith Anderson made a regal if painfully bewildered queen; Lillian Gish, a truly pathetic Ophelia. Highly admired oldtimers Arthur Byron and George Nash played Polonius and the First Grave-Digger; Morgan Farley was Osric; and John Cromwell, Rosencrantz. Perhaps suprisingly, some of the more negative notices were handed to Jo Mielziner, whose "dull, obvious" settings could not compare to Robert Edmond Jones's imaginative work of yesteryear. In a season that would bring a surprising amount of Shakespeare, including a rival *Hamlet,* this production chalked up a fine 132-performance run.

By contrast, the Theatre Guild, which had enjoyed a remarkable string of successes or at least critical triumphs last season, launched what proved to be a distressingly dismal new year with Julius J. and Philip Epstein's **And Stars Remain** (10-12-36, Guild). Cynthia Hope (Helen Gahagan), newly released from prison after serving time for a crime of which she was actually innocent, accessory to her husband's bank peculations, finds she is going to have trouble restarting her life. Her husband had committed suicide after his arrest, and now the family patriarch, Grandfather Trenchard (Charles Richman), is determined to revive the whole affair in hopes of vindicting his son. Appalled by the old man's increasingly reactionary pronouncements and his attempt to kill a relief program, Cynthia throws in her lot with Frederick Holden (Ben Smith), the radical-supporting prosecuting attorney who sent her to prison. When he tells her she is acting against all her instincts, she replies, "I'll get new instincts." For many critics and playgoers the star of the evening, in the role of an old family friend, was the epicene musical comedy dancer Clifton Webb, who, like Alexander Woollcott before him, spent much of the time lolling on a sofa, spouting witticisms. Thus, to a newspaperman telephoning to speak to Cynthia, he lies, "This isn't Mrs. Hope's apartment—This is a brothel—What?—No!—No special rates for newspapermen."

If importing a London hit was a risky business, importing a London flop had to be a form of commercial suicide. Nonetheless, producers who should have known better brought over Gordon Daviot's 1934 West End failure, **The Laughing Woman** (10-13-36, Golden). With a comparatively large cast and four scene changes hiking costs, it gave up the struggle after three weeks. Daviot was the pen name of Agnes Mackintosh, who had earlier written *Richard of Bordeaux*. In this play she turned to two modern bohemians, Henri Gaudier and Sophie Breska, who not long ago had scandalized London by flaunting their relationship. Rechristened René Latour (Tonio Selwart) and Ingrid Rydman (Helen

Menken), Rene goes to his death in the war, and Ingrid lives on in her tenement with only memories.

An even shorter-lived mounting was Robert Turney's **Daughters of Atreus** (10-14-36, 44th St.), although many critics applauded its "eloquent and poetic prose." The story begins as Klytaiminestra (Eleonora Mendelssohn) is preparing for the wedding of her daughter, Iphegeneia (Olive Deering), only to learn that Agamemnon (Gale Gordon) insists on sacrificing the girl so that the gods will grant good winds to carry his fleet to Troy. When he has gone, a vengeful Klytaiminestra takes Aegisthos (Hal Conklin) as a lover, and the two conspire to kill the king on his return. Another daughter, Elektra (Joanna Roos), goads her brother, Orestes (Eric Wollencott), into avenging their father's death. The deed done, Orestes is pursued by the furies: "They slip away before my sword and hide among the shadows there. I cannot kill them. I must hide." Some critics complained of a babel of accents including Mendelssohn's thick German one, Conklin's Irish brogue, the Russian of Maria Ouspenskaya, who played an old retainer, and the various British and American accents of the other performers. But there was praise for Mielziner's lofty sky-blue and gold settings of a courtyard, a palace, and a temple, all of which added to the then huge $50,000 it cost to bring in the drama.

The season's first, belated smash hit was **Tovarich** (10-15-36, Plymouth), Robert Sherwood's reworking of Jacques Deval's Paris success. Although Prince Mikail (John Halliday) has deposited millions of francs belonging to the czar in a bank, he refuses to touch the money, hoping to return it to the royal family after the Communists are overthrown. To keep themselves alive, he and the Grand Duchess Tatiana (Marta Abba) take employment as servants to a wealthy Parisian family. Eventually their true backgrounds are exposed and they are forced to hand over the bank account to the current Russian government. Their startled employers are reluctant to retain the pair, but they insist they are happy in their work and want to stay. Sherwood originally had translated the comedy as a vehicle for the Lunts, but they decided against it. When Cedric Hardwick and Eugenie Leontovich, who had played the roles in London, also proved unavailable, producer Gilbert Miller gave one principal part to the popular leading man Halliday and took a gamble on Abba, a famous Italian actress, for his leading lady. Both featured players led what *Variety* called "a corking performance," noting further, "They are a charming couple; in fact, charm is the play's chief lure." Part of that charm, the tradesheet insisted, came from White Russian mannerisms, such as friendly kisses on the forehead, touching the lips to the shoulder, and drinking vodka with arms intertwined. The comedy ran just short of eleven months.

Samson Raphaelson encountered no such good fortune with his **White Man** (10-17-36, National). Paul Grimm (producer Sam Byrd) had a white father and mulatto mother, but he is so light he passes for white. He proposes to Mary Nile (Louise Campbell) after learning to his relief that she does not want children. But when she becomes pregnant and refuses to have an abortion, he feels obligated to tell her the truth. Her father (Harold Gould) forces her to leave Paul and give up the baby to a black woman. Left alone, Paul heads for Harlem, but quickly learns the blacks do not want him, either. Except for a few extras in the Harlem scene, the entire cast was white, but Paul and the other blacks who passed for white supposedly showed their true color when, in one scene, they abruptly began "shouting and jumping around in what has come to be accepted as Harlem jungle rhythm."

Kenyon Nicholson and Charles Robinson hoped for another *Sailor, Beware!* with **Swing Your Lady** (10-18-36, Booth), but came up with only a squeak-by hit (105 performances). Critics allowed that some of the play was uproariously funny, but not enough of it. Bantam Joe Laurie, Jr., like Walter C. Kelly before him a refugee from defunct two-a-day, was cast as Ed Hatch, a small-time wrestling promoter, attempting to find work for his star attraction, Joe Skopapoulos (John Alexander), "the Greek Hercules." In desperation, he pits him against Sadie Horn (Hope Emerson), an Amazonian blacksmith looking for a father for her three children. She demands that Joe marry her if she wins the match. Joe, who has fallen in love at first sight, refuses to fight Sadie, lest he hurt her. So Hatch enlists Noah Wulliver (Al Ochs), who turns out to be the father of one of Sadie's kids, for the contest, with Sadie as the prize. Joe wins. One of the evening's biggest laughs came in the last scene, at the arena, when the referee (Jack Byrne), unsure how to call the falls, asks the wrestlers which of them is supposed to win that night.

Some superb Norman Bel Geddes settings could not save his production of Francis Gallagher's **Iron Men** (10-19-36, Longacre). Geddes not only presented remarkable recreations of a low-ceilinged, dingy workingman's bar and of steelwork for an unfinished skyscraper rising against a blue sky (with a crane hoisting new rust-colored beams into place on the sixty-fourth floor), but he went so far as to hire actual construction workers to play some of the principal roles. When the workgang boss, Andy (William Haade), learns that the wife (Kathleen Fitz) of Nils (Harold Moffet), one of his best men, has convinced her husband to quit his dangerous work, he arranges to make it seem that she is cheating on Nils. Nils kills her and then himself. Coming on top of another (Clark Twelvetrees) of his better young men accidentally falling to his death, the killings unhinge Andy. He goes to pieces atop the highest beam.

Not every critic was as harsh on George S. Kaufman and Edna Ferber's **Stage Door** (10-22-36, Music Box) as John Anderson of the *Journal,* who branded it "mechanical and stodgy stuff, lifeless in its efforts to be sharp and clever, and dreary in the soggy sentiment it sluices up." Even the majority of critics, who liked the comedy, lamented that it was a disappointment, not nearly as good as the pair's *The Royal Family.* To a man, however, they were delighted with its young leading lady, Margaret Sullavan, back before live audiences after a stint in Hollywood. She portrayed Terry Randall, an aspiring actress who boards with other youthful aspirants at the Footlights Club, where the girls are often packed three to a room. Her devotion to her art is sorely tested. For one, her fiancé is Keith Burgess (Richard Kendrick), a radical playwright who complains that he is fed up trying to live "on bread and cocoa for days at a time." He deserts both the stage and Terry to accept a big Hollywood offer. A sexy but untalented fellow resident is also grabbed by films, while another girl commits suicide after being dropped from a play. Support comes from David Kingsley (Onslow Stevens), who urges Terry to have the courage of her convictions. She follows his advice, thereby winning a juicy role and David. She tells the club's duenna (Leona Roberts) that she feels like Queen Victoria on learning she has ascended the throne and suggests that, like the young queen, she is entitled to a room of her own. Along with Sullavan, Lee Patrick won praise for her acid-tongued player. Despite all the critical reservations, the comedy enjoyed a profitable twenty-one-week run.

None of the five commercial plays that followed ran for more than two weeks. The first two offered highly praised scenery by Donald Oenslager. In Sidney Kingsley's **Ten Million Ghosts** (10-23-36, St. James) a young poet, André (Orson Welles), who loves Madeleine (Barbara O'Neil), scion of the munitions-manufacturing De Kruifs, enlists as a pilot in the war. Unable to comprehend why he has been ordered not to bomb certain war facilities and mines, he bombs them. He soon is killed, so Madeleine weds the great arms salesman Zacharey (George Coulouris). Playgoers found a special four-page insertion in their programs detailing the cynicism of the great arms manufacturers and merchants. Of course, the more knowledgeable playgoers had no trouble in matching character names in the play with such contemporary figures as Sir Basil Zaharoff, the Krupps, and the de Wendels. The play opened with Oenslager's "screaming, shrieking scene" in a cannon factory and moved on to realistic recreations of battle scenes. At one point, at the end of the second act, the moguls

gather in the de Kruifs' luxurious drawing room to watch motion pictures of the carnage they have helped spread. Baited by André and an acerbic newspaperman, they stand up to defend themselves and, silhouetted against the films, insist, "But this is our business!" During scene changes slides depicted cemetery crosses, close-ups of barbed wire, and telegrams urging that more armament be rushed to the front. But for all the fine scenery and playing, the *Herald Tribune*'s new man, Richard Watts, Jr., spoke for his colleagues when he complained, "Mr. Kingsley wastes great opportunities in his strangely colorless and elementary drama."

Between Oenslager's two efforts, the FTP brought out its latest offering. In a headline-grabbing departure it offered the production not just to Manhattan, but to twenty other communities across the country on the same night. These included Yonkers, Staten Island, and Newark, as well as Chicago, Boston, San Francisco, Los Angeles, Bridgeport, Birmingham, and Miami. There was even a Yiddish version at the Biltmore, and an Italian version was announced for a few weeks down the road. Hallie Flanagan, national director of the FTP, crowed that 1000 persons were employed in the companies, that productions cost only between a few hundred and two thousand dollars apiece, and that a record of more than 20,000 theatregoers attended the first night. **It Can't Happen Here** (10-27-36, Adelphi) was Sinclair Lewis and John C. Moffitt's dramatization of Lewis's novel. At a hilltop family picnic in Vermont, Doremus Jessup (Seth Arnold), the high-principled editor of a small-town paper, scoffs at the notion that Berzelius "Buzz" Windrip (Maurice Burke) can impose a fascist dictatorship on America. But immediately after his election, Windrip's uniformed thugs, the Corpos, begin making trouble. They bludgeon to death a local grocer who has refused to take down a sign for the opposition and shoot Jessup's son-in-law. Jessup is arrested, but escapes from the concentration camp and heads to Canada, where he starts up a resistance movement.

Oenslager had to switch his attention to the antebellum South for **Sweet River** (10-28-36, 51st St.). George Abbott's modern reworking of Harriet Beecher Stowe's *Uncle Tom's Cabin* was a curious affair, with no lawyer Marks and no dying Eva. A black chorus, directed by Juanita Hall, sang spirituals throughout the evening, and a large revolving stage turned the scenery. (The revolve was especially large since the stage belonged to a former film palace briefly turned over to legitimate theatre. Years later it would again become a playhouse and be called the Mark Hellinger.) Oenslager's sets included slave cabins surrounded by moss-hung oaks, sometimes with the sun shining in the background, and sometimes in a gentle moonlight. The St. Clare house had rich period furniture and drapes. At the end of Act

I a tavern setting turned to disclose an icy river (with what one critic said looked like "real river ice") over which Eliza (Margaret Mullen) fled her pursuers. Since Mullen was white and Juan Hernandez, who played Gabe, was not, they were not permitted to embrace at their farewell. Once again, a careful production could not override a critical feeling that the story's time had come and gone.

Gustav Blum, a producer who in the heyday of the twenties had kept shows going for months on end at the rooftop Bayes Theatre with the help of Leblang's cut-rate tickets, relit the long-dark auditorium and tried unavailingly to bring back the good old days. His vehicle, John Crump's **Don't Look Now** (11-2-36, Bayes), was no help, even though he brought the highly respected Yiddish comedian Joseph Buloff in to play the leading role of a film producer whom many saw as a spoof of Sam Goldwyn. Sam Stern becomes frantic after his great star, Nina Gay (Beverly Phalon), walks off a picture to follow her sweetie (Robert Shayne) to New York. "This picture is costing me two million dollars of the bank's money," he wails. But in New York Stern succeeds in separating the lover from a southern siren (Queenell Tucker) who has promised to back the man's new play, reunites him and Nina, and gets them to board a train heading west.

Max Catto's **Green Waters** (11-4-36, Masque) was an English drama set on the lonely Scottish coast. A young man (Denis O'Dea) loves his younger brother (Jackie Jordan), who, like him, is illegitimate, and hates his father (Reginald Bach), who has allowed them to be stigmatized. Shortly after the younger boy is accidentally shot and killed by a neighbor, the grieving older boy and the wife (Doris Dalton) of his legitimate half brother (Terence Neill) fall in love. At first the wife acquiesces in her husband's demand to break off the affair, but in the end she and the boy decide to continue the relationship.

Sophie Treadwell, still looking to repeat the acclaim accorded *Machinal,* tried and failed again with **Plumes in the Dust** (11-6-36, 46th St.). Her latest was a purple-prosed chronicle retelling the history of Edgar Allan Poe (Henry Hull) from his leaving his foster father's Richmond home in 1826 to his lonely death in 1849 in a Baltimore hospital, with a nurse (Juliet Fremont) reading biblical passages to him. Hull received the same sort of praise he had when he appeared as Jeeter Lester, but this time he could not bring about a run.

The latest English murder mystery, Gordon Sherry's **Black Limelight** (11-9-36, Mansfield), had been scheduled for simultaneous premieres in New York and London, but problems delayed the West End opening, allowing America to see the play first. America was not impressed, albeit Shaw's original American St. Joan, Winifred Lenihan, headed the cast. Naomi Charrington is certain her husband, Peter (Alexander Kirkland), did not commit the brutal murder of his mistress. Since evidence suggests the woman was killed in a dark room, Naomi finally pins the crime on the family lawyer (George Curzon), whose nyctalopia means he cannot see well in daylight but can see perfectly in the dark.

The next evening, the 10th, brought in the season's second *Hamlet,* this time at the Imperial and with Leslie Howard starred. Since Gielgud had been unknown to Americans before his return, while Howard long had been a major stage and screen star, Howard probably had an initial advantage. As his own producer, he undoubtedly hoped to profit by giving the tragedy a sumptuous mounting. Indeed, Stewart Chaney's sets and costumes represented a significant portion of the show's bruited $75,000 costs. But the sets were seen as heavy-handed and retarding the action, while Howard's supporting players, chosen largely from the ranks of the unknown, generally were considered no more than serviceable. (However, several critics thought Pamela Stanley's Ophelia better than Gish's.) But whatever advantage Howard had, he frittered it away with his own reading. His Hamlet displayed no thunderous passion nor any intense introspection. John Mason Brown reported, "He does not interpret Hamlet; he merely repeats the lines. He walks through Elsinor as if he were walking down Bond Street. . . . He plays Hamlet as if he were acting 'The Petrified Forest' in ancient dress." So chilly was his reception that Howard withdrew the production after five weeks. It marked his final Broadway appearance, since he was killed in the war a few years later.

Several more failures followed. In Doty Hobart and Tom McKnight's **Double Dummy** (11-11-36, Golden) Brains McGill (Charles D. Brown), a parolee who had been forced to learn bridge by a bridge-mad warden (Dudley Clements), arranges a highly publicized match between the warden and the warden's idol, the celebrated bridge expert Nullo Sykes (Hanley Stafford). Sykes hears that the warden may be a better player than he is, so he orders his two ex-con bodyguards to set on the man and send him to the hospital. Undaunted, McGill prompts Professor Gideon (John McGovern), a timid mathematical genius, to learn the game overnight and to trounce Sykes. The farce was played out on a double-decker set that allowed the action to unfold in several places at once.

Continuing her love of French boulevard entertainments, Grace George combined her efforts with James Forbes's to bring New Yorkers Louis Verneuil's *Le Mariage de maman* as **Matrimony Pfd.** (11-12-36, Playhouse). The actress, famous for her "fast-building, vivacious, chin up and tongue-sparkling" style, played a never-married lady who seems on the verge of matrimony until a vamp of a baroness (Rosemary Ames) attempts to lure away the man (A. E. Matthews). So the woman encourages her illegitimate son (Rex O'Malley) to seduce her rival. No matter that the boy is married to a jealous young woman (Sylvia Field). Naturally complications crop up, but the baroness is sent packing and all ends happily.

Some faddist critics were willing to dismiss *Hedda Gabler* as "a musty old play" or "a great pother about social trivialities," but even those who disdained the drama were impressed by tiny, dark Alla Nazimova's interpretation—"the most fascinating, the most plainly depraved, the most wantonly devilish" of all Heddas, according to John Anderson. Several in Nazimova's supporting cast had performed with her in last season's *Ghosts,* but critics seriously questioned Harry Ellerbe's boyish, superficial George Tesman and McKay Morris's sinister but speech-swallowing Brack. Since Edward Trevor was an eleventh-hour replacement as Eilert Lovborg, many reserved judgment. Opinion was divided on Stewart Chaney's dimly lit, somber green setting. The play did four weeks of slightly disappointing business at the Longacre, starting on the 16th.

Anti-war sentiments dominated Paul Green and Kurt Weill's **Johnny Johnson** (11-19-36, 44th St.), which straddled the fence between straight play and musical. It is treated as a musical in *American Musical Theatre: A Chronicle.*

The New Deal's disastrous attempt to resettle in Alaska some families on relief was depicted in Ellsworth Prouty Conkle's **200 Were Chosen** (11-20-36, 48th St.). When the families arrive they discover the promised housing has not been built and the army men in charge are bogged down in bureaucratic red tape. The families call a strike when the shacks they have built are ordered torn down and matters are made worse by a fever outbreak. In the end the colonists and the government agree to cooperate.

The month's second offering to be part musical theatre and part straight play, Noel Coward's **Tonight at 8:30** (11-24-36, National), was a series of nine one-acters, offered on three different bills of three plays each. Several were miniature musicals, but most were not. The plays varied in quality but were, for the most part, well received. With Coward and Gertrude Lawrence in the leads, the bills did good business for 118 performances, despite a $4.40 top, 33 percent higher than other non-musical shows were asking. *Hands Across the Sea* looked at a haughty lady who cannot or will not remember the names of people who were kind to her while she was traveling. In *The Astonished Heart* a fashionable psychiatrist cannot get over his passion for his mistress until she forces him to.

Fumed Oak watched as a milquetoast finally gets up the nerve to tell off and leave his impossible family. A penniless couple find a way to leave a party after they catch a burglar in their room in *Ways and Means. Still Life,* which became the film *Brief Encounter,* told of the bittersweet romance of a married man and a married woman.

The Theatre Guild's second failure of the season was William McNally's **Prelude to Exile** (11-30-36, Guild). Richard Wagner (Wilfred Lawson) is beset by a shrewish, jealous wife (Evelyn Varden), who also has no appreciation of his musical gifts. Wagner himself falls in love with Mathilde (Eva Le Gallienne), the wife of his benefactor (Leo G. Carroll). She inspires him to compose *Tristan and Isolde,* and almost succumbs to his plea to elope with him. But when she has second thoughts, she asks him, "Did the artist in you really need me, Richard? No! What he needed was his sense of frustration." Wagner is forced to go away—alone. After he has left, Mathilde tells Cosima Liszt von Bülow (Miriam Battista) that while her own life will hereafter be empty she will always have the opera's music to uplift her.

That Wycherley's Restoration comedy *The Country Wife,* which opened at Henry Miller's on December 1, could justify an eleven-week stay on twentieth-century Broadway was attributable almost solely to the acting skills of Ruth Gordon as Mrs. Pinchwife, who is determined to let herself be seduced by a charming philanderer. She brought to the role not merely her cacklely tones and her sly look or what Atkinson called her "artful naïveté," but "her awkward and beflustered gestures, her elaborate confidences turned straight into the faces of the audience, her falling voice, her alarms and studied raptures." If her supporting cast left something to be desired, a stage curtain set the proper mood, depicting a scene of seventeenth-century London, including one building clearly marked "School for Cuckolds."

The Holmeses of Baker Street (12-9-36, Masque) was an English play by Basil Mitchell, revised for American audiences by William Jourdan Rapp and Leonardo Bercovici. Holmes (Cyril Scott) is now an aging widower, raising bees in Scotland and visiting London only occasionally. On one visit he receives a package containing a magnificent queen bee. He would take it to Scotland, but his daughter, Shirley (Helen Chandler), to prevent his leaving London so soon, steals the cage with the help of a blowsy Mrs. Watson (Cecilia Loftus). Shirley does not seem to know that a notorious gang, the White X, have concealed the famous Medici pearl in the cage. She is kidnapped by gang members, but manages to escape and confound them. Anyway, she no longer has the pearl, which was cleverly hidden in one of Sherlock's pipes. For her efforts, Shirley is appointed the first woman detective at Scotland Yard. Critics found the play dim-witted, its problems aggravated by the fact that the gray-haired Scott, decades earlier a matinee idol, could not recall his lines.

Sam Harris, who had produced George S. Kaufman's first play of the season, also produced his second, this one written in collaboration with Moss Hart. They called their newest effort **You Can't Take It with You** (12-14-36, Booth). The Vanderhof clan is a wacky group of New Yorkers, presided over by curmudgeonly, seventy-five-year-old Martin Vanderhof (Henry Travers), who years ago took an elevator up to work, decided he did not like working, took the elevator back down, and has spent the intervening years attending commencements and collecting snakes. When a typewriter was delivered by mistake to the Vanderhof household, his daughter, Penelope Sycamore (Josephine Hull), appropriated it and has since been writing plays no one will produce. Her husband, Paul (Frank Wilcox), manufactures fireworks in the cellar. A Vanderhof granddaughter, Essie (Paula Trueman), practices ballet in the living room, while her husband, Ed (George Heller), plays the xylophone there and runs his printing press. Another granddaughter, Alice (Margot Stevenson), invites the parents of her rich fiancé, Tony Kirby (Jess Barker), to dinner. The Kirbys arrive one night early just as the home is raided by G-men who claim Ed has been printing seditious material and just as the basement fireworks explode. Everyone is hauled off to jail. After they are released Vanderhof attempts to explain his philosophy to the elder Kirby (William J. Kelly), pointing out that you can't take it with you and asking, "How many of us would be willing to settle when we're young for what we eventually get?" Vanderhof has also been hounded by the government for non-payment of income tax, but when the government learns that Vanderhof's wife once had used Vanderhof's name to bury a milkman who had made his home with them, it concludes Vanderhof is legally dead and not liable. Writing in the *New Yorker*, Robert Benchley allowed that he was quibbling when he complained that the comedy was not much of a play. Still, he called it "a very funny show. It is so funny that even when you are not laughing, you get a glow." A fistful of similar notices, followed in the spring by the Pulitzer Prize, pushed the hit into the season's longest run—837 performances.

A week was all Lillian Hellman's **Days to Come** (12-15-36, Vanderbilt) survived after almost unanimously negative reviews. For example, Anderson slammed it as "dreary, laborious and overwrought." The Rodmans' brush factory has been the principal source of employment in its small midwestern town, where everyone knows each other, for generations. But when labor troubles loom, a rather weak-willed Andrew Rodman (William Harrigan) is readily convinced by an associate, Henry Ellicott (Ned Wever), to call in strike-breakers, especially as the employees are heeding the tirades of Leo Whalen (Ben Smith), who "is in the business of hating." Rodman is unaware that Ellicott has had an affair with his wife, Julie (Florence Eldridge). Violence and bloodshed follow, and Whalen is jailed for a killing he did not commit. Julie, who has switched her affections to Whalen, helps gain his release. But more slaughter follows, leaving the town and the Rodmans permanently scarred. Andrew's neurotic sister, Cora (Frieda Altman), opens his eyes to everyone's true relationships and feelings. He tells them all they are free to go wherever they want or do whatever they like, but that what is left in the shattered homestead "is as much yours as it is mine."

Hellman's failure was all that separated one smash hit from a second, John Monks, Jr., and Fred F. Finklehoffe's **Brother Rat** (12-16-36, Biltmore). Unlike the season's earlier plays about life at a military academy, this was a light-hearted comedy. "Brother Rat" is a term of affection used among cadets at the Virginia Military Institute. At the moment few are held in more affection than the school's star pitcher, Bing Edwards (Eddie Albert). But Bing is worried. He is not certain that he can win the $200 award given the academy's best athlete, and he needs that cash since, against school rules, he is secretly married. Then he learns his wife is pregnant. He gives one buddy, Billy (Frank Albertson), $50 to put in his, Bing's, bank account, but Billy and another cadet, Dan (José Ferrer), bet the money on Bing's crucial game. Bing loses the game, and everything seems to fall apart for him. With commencement "practically here," his fellow cadets try to solace Bing. They suggest he name the forthcoming kid "Commencement." Bing holds up a telegram he has just received and responds, "Practically, hell! He *is here*." But then that means Bing has won $300 as the first father in the class. The *American*'s Gilbert Gabriel welcomed the comedy, which George Abbott directed, as "a double-quick-step march of jovial events by a company of immediately likable juveniles." It compiled 575 performances in New York.

The plot of Don Carle Gillette's **In the Bag** (12-17-36, Belmont) may have represented a bit of wishful thinking on the playwright's part. Bud Graham (Morgan Conway), a shoestring producer, agrees to put on a play written by the niece of a cemetery salesman, Jamaica Jones (Dudley Clements), if backing can be found. A bootblack (Don Anthony) and an Italian restaurant owner (Charles La Torre) provide the cash. The play, called variously *The Enchanted Lipstick* or *Lipstick Murder Mystery*, tells of a lipstick that makes men faint when kissed by a woman wearing it and is admittedly dreadful, but the critics love it. A cosmetic czar, fearful of repercussions in the industry, offers the producer and writer $103,000 to withdraw the hit. Among Gillette's lines was the question, "Where is a good place for a dead man who is alive to live?" The answer: "Philadelphia." The real critics handed Gillette's opus some of the season's most devastating notices, so it folded after half a week.

At the tiny Princess Theatre, now rechristened with a less romantic name, the FTP presented Lady Christine Longford's **Mr. Jiggins of Jigginstown** (12-17-36, Labor Stage). Mr. Jiggins (William Hallman) is a rich old man whose greedy relations are striving determinedly to have him remember them in his will. Instead, he leaves his money to build a schoolhouse.

Mr. Jiggins of Jigginstown may have called to mind Mrs. Wiggs of the Cabbage Patch when the playwright who had brought Mrs. Wiggs before the footlights in 1904 returned to the theatre after a long absence. Reviewers tried to be kind to Anne Crawford Flexner's **Aged 26** (12-21-36, Lyceum), appreciating its lofty intentions. But they still had to acknowledge its dullness. The latest in a rash of stage biographies, it departed from tradition by depicting Fanny Brawne not as a wanton, but as a decent young girl. John Keats (Robert Harris) encounters Byron (Charles Trexler) and Shelley (Anthony Kemble Cooper) at their publisher's office. Keats tells the pair his theory of poetry: "I think poetry should surprise by a fine excess—not by singularity. It should even strike the reader as an expression of his own thoughts, and appear almost as a remembrance." Keats meets and falls in love with Fanny (Linda Watkins), but his friends, Charles Armitage Brown (Kenneth MacKenna) and John Taylor (Matthew Boulton), dismayed at his failing health, persuade him to sail to Italy. He waves good-bye, unaware that he will never see England again but will die at twenty-six.

Charles Washburn, who collaborated with Clyde North on **All Editions** (12-22-36, Longacre), was a renowned press agent, representing, among others, George M. Cohan and George Abbott. So it was not too surprising that the central figure in the play was a former carnival barker metamorphosed into a press agent. The offices of Clarence "Fearlesso" Class (Walter N. Greaza) are the latest word in modernity. Into them come a motley assortment of figures looking to employ Class. These include a woman (Ruth Holden) who may or may not have been a former wife of his and who has now become a psalm-spouting evangelist seeking to blackmail Class into giving her free publicity. There are also a casket maker and a mortician who ask him to find a grotesquely ugly man willing to die and let them demonstrate how beautiful he can be made to

seem in his coffin. For them, Class scrounges up the Rhinoceros (John Ravold).

The first of three Maxwell Anderson plays to reach Broadway during the season was **The Wingless Victory** (12-23-36, Empire), which managed to run for 110 performances largely on the strength of Katharine Cornell's performance. The black sheep of his family, Nathaniel McQueston (Walter Abel) had sailed from Salem in 1773, promising not to return until he was wealthy. Twenty-seven years later he comes back a rich man but with a Christianized Malaysian wife, Oparre (Cornell), and their children. His puritanical family is willing to accept Nathaniel's wealth but not his non-white wife. Learning of some past misdeeds of his, they confront him with the choice of exposure or renouncing Oparre. He chooses to send the woman away. Since she fears that she will no longer be accepted back home, she boards a ship, gives her children poison, then drinks some herself. Concluding that Christ appeared too soon and that men are still not ready for him, she prays to one of her former gods, the "god of the lesser children of the earth,/ the black, the unclean, the vengeful." Nathaniel rushes in to tell her he has changed his mind, but it is too late. The first act was set in the McQuestons' spacious living room, with a wide, raised entrance hallway. But Cornell did not make her first entrance from the brightly lit hall. Instead, after the other characters had vacated the room, she appeared quietly from an unlit side door, in a sarong, with heavily braceleted arms and bare feet, and with dark body makeup. Critical opinion on the play was sharply divided, with Watts hailing its "eloquence and beauty" and Atkinson condemning it as "verbose" and "diffuse." But, with a few exceptions, Cornell was saluted, Gabriel calling her "most beautiful to see, most thrilling to hear, most memorable to meet in angry passion, in eloquent death. Confirm her is all we can as the foremost actress of our land." When business slackened, Cornell revived Shaw's *Candida* on March 10, giving fifty performances of it in repertory with Anderson's play.

More risible matters were presented when Max Gordon ushered in Clare Boothe's **The Women** (12-26-36, Ethel Barrymore). Bitchy Sylvia Fowler (Ilka Chase) persuades Mary Haines (Margalo Gillmore) to use her gossipy manicurist, Olga (Ruth Hammond), knowing full well that Olga will reveal the affair that Mary's husband, Stephen, is having. Mary's sensible mother (Jessie Busley) attempts to reason with her daughter, but, after Mary has an encounter with her husband's cheap inamorata (Betty Lawford), Mary insists on a divorce. She heads for Reno, falling in with a raffish crowd of would-be divorcées. Many of the women are catty, self-serving, and as unfaithful as the men they belittle. Mary is soon joined by Sylvia, whose husband

Act One: 1930–1944

has demanded she get a divorce after discovering her infidelity. From comments by her own young daughter (Charita Bauer), Mary eventually learns that Stephen's second marriage has been unsuccessful. She is prepared to take him back and also prepared to deal with her lady friends, announcing "I've had two years to sharpen my claws." The reservations expressed by some influential critics, notably Atkinson, who lashed out at its "stingingly detailed pictures of some of the most odious harpies ever collected in one play," hurt the box office at first. But highly favorable word of mouth soon had the all-women comedy selling out and kept it going for 657 performances.

Martin Flavin, who once had been considered among the great hopes of American playwriting, called it quits after the failure of his **Around the Corner** (12-28-36, 48th St.). Fred Perkins (Charles Coburn) is a hardware merchant who has gone bust in the Depression. His son (Milburn Stone) and his son-in-law (Boyd Crawford), both unemployed, attempt a holdup, but get cold feet during the crime and flee. Since they are well known in their small town, the sheriff (Cyrus W. Wendall), Fred's brother, calls to arrest them. But Fred reminds Amos that the youngsters are good boys, just hard up, and he is sure there are better times for everyone just around the corner. Amos lets the young men go.

Henri Bernstein's *L'Espoir* was offered to Americans in the H. M. Harwood translation that had pleased London under the title of **Promise** (12-30-36, Little). As so often happened, New Yorkers failed to share Londoners' tastes. The production is remembered only as marking the American debut of Cedric Hardwicke. He played Emile Delbar, whose second wife (Irene Browne) is a self-centered, querulous woman, ambitious for her own attractive daughter (Louise Platt), but neglectful of a homely stepdaughter (Jean Forbes-Robertson). When the young man (Frank Lawton) who has been engaged to the woman's daughter runs off instead with the stepdaughter, the woman goes to pieces. Her husband is far more philosophical.

The new year, 1937, began with the season's latest Shakespearean offering, *Othello,* on January 6 at the New Amsterdam. Walter Huston was starred, but critics lamented that his interpretation lacked the requisite fire and poetry. "He does not become enraged," one wrote, "he only becomes irritated." His voice was dismissed as "the raspy sound of a barker in a sideshow," while his makeup left him looking like "a burnt-cork Hoosier . . . a curly-headed imitation of the late Lew Dockstader." As Iago, Brian Aherne walked off with the best reviews for his bravura villainy. Robert Edmond Jones, who directed the Max Gordon production as well as designing it, was lauded for his scenery, including a spacious seafront in Cyprus, Desdemona's chamber as

seen through a balcony window, and a street scene in which black shadows loomed ominously against a yellow wall. The mounting ran only two and a half weeks, and when it closed the New Amsterdam, the last surviving legitimate theatre on 42nd Street, copied its neighbors by becoming a film house.

William A. Drake and Ludwig Lewisohn's translation of Franz Werfel's biblical spectacle **The Eternal Road** (1-7-37, Manhattan Opera House), which Max Reinhardt staged and Norman Bel Geddes designed, was said to have cost a staggering half million dollars to mount. For it, the mammoth auditorium was torn apart, with the proscenium arch removed, and the stage rebuilt on five levels to suggest a mountain road winding to heaven from the simple synagogue at its base. A Central European dictator is threatening his country's Jews with exile or extermination. While a raging mob shouts outside, a man (Harold Johnsrud) who has long denied his Jewish background and his young son (Sidney Lumet) flee into the synagogue for protection. The rabbi (Myron Taylor) comforts the boy by telling him the history of the Jews from Abraham (Thomas Chalmers) on and showing him how they have always overcome hatred. Kurt Weill composed the music, some of it prerecorded. That led to one critic's offering a complaint that would become pervasive decades later: "The amplification was too loud." The play attracted primarily Jewish audiences, but in New York they were numerous enough to allow the show to remain for 153 performances.

John Houseman and Orson Welles, having appropriated their early "Project 891" and made it the name of their branch of the FTP, brought out a highly praised mounting of Christopher Marlowe's *Doctor Faustus* at the Maxine Elliott on the 8th, with Welles—"robust . . . mobile and commanding"—in the leading role. Scenery was all but dispensed with, allowing the text and clever lighting to account for time and space. Puppets in a stage box were used for the Seven Deadly Sins. Real actors got close to the audience by sometimes performing on an apron set up over the orchestra pit, and made their entrances and exits using not merely the wings but trapdoors on stage and the auditorium itself. The result was a textbook classic turned into lively, imaginative modern theatre.

Maxwell Anderson's second show of the season was **High Tor** (1-9-37, Martin Beck). Like his first it was directed by Guthrie McClintic. Van Van Dorn (Burgess Meredith), fed up with civilization, is happy to flee to a hill he owns, overlooking the Hudson at Tappan Zee. After fighting with his sweetheart, Judith (Mab Maynard), he spends the night there in the company of an old Indian (Harry Irvine). The pair encounter bank robbers, land developers bent on buying the hill, and the ghosts of old sailors. Come morning, the ghosts disappear, the robbers are apprehended, and the developers make a satisfactory deal with Van, who is also reconciled with Judith. Although he may have sold out to the forces of progress, Van is assured by the Indian that in the long run it will not matter: "Nothing is made by men, but makes, in the end, good ruins." Watts praised what he deemed one of Anderson's "strangest and most arresting plays. A curious medley of fantasy, lyricism, symbolism, brooding philosophical meditation and slapstick farce." Mielziner's poetic settings, which included a swinging steam shovel not unlike Bel Geddes's earlier construction crane, were also lauded. Acting honors went to the pint-sized Meredith, with his curiously pixie-ish voice; Charles D. Brown, as a ghostly sea captain; and, in one of her rare American appearances, Peggy Ashcroft, as the captain's ghostly wife. Come spring the play won the New York Drama Critics Circle Award. It ran 171 performances.

Having sat on a hill overlooking the Hudson, first-nighters were transported two evenings later to an abandoned farm bordering on the Delaware. The farm, in Melvin Levy's **A House in the Country** (1-11-37, Vanderbilt), was owned by a gangster (Roy Gordon), who had used it as a hideaway during Prohibition. But his absentee ownership has not stopped Grandpa and Grandma Lotzgazel (Tom Powers and Fredrica Slemons) and their illegitimate granddaughter (Louise Campbell) from squatting there. When the gangster and his associates come to the farm, Grandpa figures out that they are up to no good, so he holds them with a shotgun until the game warden can arrest them. Powers, in a white wig and mustache, lacked the popularity and charisma to override thumbs-down notices.

More thumbs-down notices doomed Leopold L. Atlas's **But for the Grace of God** (1-12-37, Guild), which ran only until the Theatre Guild's subscription list was exhausted. With his father unemployed and his brother dying of tuberculosis, Josey Ademec (James McCallion) takes to crime to get money for his brother's medical expenses and, in an attempted holdup, kills the owner of the factory where his brother had worked. After Josey is arrested, he learns his efforts were in vain. His brother has died.

On several earlier occasions Samuel Shipman's plays had defied a sneering critical fraternity to achieve profitable runs. His latest effort, **Behind Red Lights** (1-13-37, Mansfield), written in conjunction with Beth Brown and based on her novel *For Men Only,* did it again, piling up a twenty-three-week run in the face of disdainful notices. It was given special pertinence by the ongoing hearings Thomas E. Dewey was conducting to expose New York City graft and corruption. The beautiful, blonde Norma King (Dorothy Hall) runs an exclusive Park Avenue brothel. Organized crime is trying to muscle in on her, while Sam Armstrong (Hardie Albright), a special state prosecutor, is attempting to enlist her in the battle against the gangsters. She refuses both offers until the hoods make trouble. At that point, realizing she has fallen in love with Armstrong, she agrees to help him. She is shot dead for her pains.

Frank Parker, one of the "golden voices" of radio, was lured to the stage as star of Robert Sloane and Louis Pelletier, Jr.'s **Howdy Stranger** (1-14-37, Longacre). He was cast as Elly Jordan, a Brooklynite walking and hitching his way west in hopes of a Hollywood career. Terrified of any sort of animal, he flees from a little prairie rabbit and seeks shelter at a Wyoming dude ranch, where his singing comes to the attention of Roy Chadwick (Louis Sorin), an agent, who brings him back to New York and lands him a job on radio as a singing cowboy, "Wyoming Steve Gibson." He assumes a western accent, carefully tailored for him by an expert on cowboy dialect, Joe Weinstein, and becomes so popular that his fan mail exceeds that for *Gang Busters*. Sam Thorne (Arthur L. Sachs), a jealous rival, aware of Elly's phobia, attempts to expose him, insisting that if he is the real thing he can participate in the Madison Square Garden rodeo. A hypnotist helps Elly overcome his fear long enough to break the record for bull-dogging and to win the hand of Jane Hardy (Dorothy Libaire), daughter of the ranch owners. Neither the comedy nor Parker was up to Broadway standards.

Certainly the writing and acting in the latest FTP venture were not up to snuff. Chet Jackson (Doe Doe Green), the protagonist of Conrad Seiler's **Sweet Land** (1-19-37, Lafayette), grateful to his white bosses for the opportunities accorded him, refuses to join a union. But when the whites resort to violence and call in the Klan to break up the black cotton workers' attempt at a strike, and after one of his pals is lynched, Chet changes sides.

Back downtown, George Brewer, Jr.'s **Tide Rising** (1-25-37, Lyceum) also placed small-town labor troubles front and center. Jim Cogswell (Grant Mitchell), his town's leading druggist, has to swallow his chagrin when his son, Dave (John D. Seynour), returns home with a wife, Ruth (Tamara), who is both a radical and a Jew. She stirs up the local millhands into striking. Violence erupts and Dave is killed. Jim is called in and forces both sides to compromise. Ruth heads off to see what trouble she can cause elsewhere.

And Now Good-Bye (2-2-37, Golden), Philip Howard's adaptation of James Hilton's novel, was also rejected. A married minister (Philip Merivale), sent to retrieve a runaway girl (Marguerite Churchill), falls in love with her and convinces her to elope with him. But she is killed in a train wreck. The clergyman, considered a hero because of his bravery at the accident scene, is welcomed home by a village ignorant of the facts. The Golden where the show opened was not the theatre that playgoers had known for a decade on 58th Street, but rather was a new name (and sixty years later a still ongoing name) for the former Masque in the heart of the Times Square theatre district.

Hardscrabble farmers were regularly depicted as peculiarly odd and immoral on the district's stages. Raymond Bond's **Thirsty Soil** (2-3-37, 48th St.) was no exception. The Warner family has abandoned Vermont to take up life on a bleak Nebraska farm. The father, Silas (Bond), is a deeply religious fanatic who refuses to take shelter during a tornado and is killed by the twister. The older son, Luke (Leon Ames), runs off to become a snake-oil salesman, returns to seduce his adopted sister, Milly (Ann Meril), and grudgingly marries her when she becomes pregnant. The younger son, Matt (George Makinson), falls in love with a girl above his station, Primrose Hurd (Greta Grandstedt), and loses her when her family moves away. Through all this, Ma Warner (Maude Allen) keeps her head and her hopes high.

New York had not seen a revival of Shakespeare's *Richard II* since Edwin Booth performed it in 1878. Now, on the 5th, an almost universally praised mounting confirmed Maurice Evans's newly won reputation and set him in the front ranks of American players. He played the bearded king as a foolish but engaging and ultimately pathetic figure. The *Mirror*'s Robert Coleman informed its readers that Evans "holds and dominates the stage . . . with rare eloquence, with a voice that is commanding and hypnotic, with diction that is a delight, and with plastic movement." Margaret Webster's direction was also well received, but the supporting cast and the stage pictures were deemed unexceptional. At the large St. James, the play held on for a highly respectable 133 performances.

If its eighty-nine performances were the fewest any of Maxwell Anderson's three novelties racked up during the season, the modest run of **The Masque of Kings** (2-8-37, Shubert) was by far the longest its producer, the Theatre Guild, enjoyed during its most horrendous year. The play attempted to solve the mystery of Mayerling, pitting a liberal young Crown Prince Rudolph (Henry Hull) against his reactionary father, the Emperor Franz Joseph (Dudley Digges). Rudolph, in part encouraged by his open-minded mother (Pauline Frederick), seizes power, but soon relinquishes it when he realizes he must kill his father if he is to retain his hold. He also discovers that his beloved mistress, Baroness Mary Vetsera (Margo), had been planted in his path by his wily father. He confronts her. She confesses the truth, "And now you see me as I see myself,/ a baggage, the

sort that might have sold you flowers/ or cleaned your rooms." But she insists that she has come to love him genuinely and will remain faithful. She kills herself, and when he finds her body, Rudolph commits suicide, too. The emperor is left to face a dismal future.

Royal battles were supplanted by middle-class strivings in Sara Sandberg's **Be So Kindly** (2-8-37, Little). With success in the garment industry, the Kadanskys of the Bronx have changed their name to Kadan and crossed the river to West End Avenue. Mrs. Kadan (Angela Jacobs) is determined to make good marriages for her kids. The marriage of selfish Clarisse (Jeanne Greene) strikes some rocks when her husband (Albert Hayes) has financial problems, but the more undemanding Della (Eva Langbord) latches on to a struggling writer (Franklin Gray) who comes into big money when Hollywood buys his book. The Kadans' son, Bert (John Call), weds the daughter (Edith Tachna) of his father's business rival, Lefkowitz, a man who has caused the elder Kadan (Francis Pierlot) to lose thousands of dollars by his price cutting.

Although it was a wintry February, Brooks Atkinson welcomed Mark Reed's **Yes, My Darling Daughter** (2-9-37, Playhouse) as "a light, summery comedy." Such praise helped the show run not only through the forthcoming summer, but into the following winter as well. Ann Whitman Murray (Lucile Watson) is aghast when she learns that her daughter, Ellen (Peggy Conklin), will spend a weekend with her handsome fiancé, Douglas Hall (Boyd Crawford). Ellen is shocked by her mother's reaction, since she knows her mother once had been among Greenwich Village's most notorious bohemians, and an advocate of freethinking and free love. Ellen's father (Charles Bryant) and her mother's admirer (Nicholas Joy) from the old Greenwich Village days have their own reasons for protesting Ellen's decision. Surprisingly, when Ellen and Doug return on Monday, it is Doug who becomes furious on learning everyone knows about the tryst. He insists that Ellen marry him immediately. Ellen looks to her mother for comfort, but mother's answer is unequivocal: "I think, when a man makes such a fuss over being seduced . . . a nice girl ought to marry him." Ellen agrees.

A father upset with his daughter's running off for a weekend liaison was also the theme of **Fulton of Oak Falls** (2-10-37, Morosco), which George M. Cohan based on *Yesterday's Lilacs*, a story by Parker Fennelly, and which briefly reactivated the once famous producing team of Cohan and Harris. Cohan was also starred. Ed Fulton comes for a sentimental weekend to the Bassett Lake Hotel, where he long ago had fallen in love with a girl whom he never saw again. To his chagrin, he discovers that his daughter, Betty (Francesca Lenni), is there alone with her sweetheart (Robert Light) instead of at a large, properly chaperoned gathering to which she told him she was going. Betty has spotted her father innocently flirting with a blonde vamp (Rita Johnson) and is ready to put the wrong construction on the affair when her father orders her home. Her sweetheart's proposal of marriage brings about a happy ending. While Richard Lockridge of the *Sun* noted that Cohan was, "as always, friendly and disarming and unaffectedly expert," he rued that "his play is, as his plays have so frequently been in recent years, disturbingly antiquated." Many critics could rarely resist itemizing Cohan's stage tricks, which this time included "his quizzical gleams out of the corners of his eyes, his absent-minded stroking of the forehead, his gurgling giggles and his jaunty exits under a good Broadway hat with a nobby topcoat flung over his arm." Increasingly, his tricks were not enough to induce a run. The comedy lasted a mere thirty-seven performances.

Two plays that ran half a week or less followed in short order. Jo Eisinger and Stephen Van Gluck's **A Point of Honor** (2-11-37, Fulton) professed to show how Peggy Shippen (Lillian Emerson), a diehard Philadelphia Tory, who actually loves Major Andre (Lloyd Gough), instead marries Benedict Arnold (Wilfred Lawson) to bring him over to the British side. Arnold's spiteful sister (Florence Reed) exposes the intrigue, but by then Peggy has come to love her husband and will aid him in any way she can.

As he had earlier in the season, the Yiddish comedian Joseph Buloff gathered some highly laudatory notices in a play the critics clobbered. This time it was Dan Goldberg's **Call Me Ziggy** (2-12-37, Longacre). Backstage at the Court Theatre in Chicago, Sidney Castle has just spent his last penny to keep his comedy, *Three In a Bed,* from closing before he can get a Hollywood offer for the property. One comes in the nick of time, and so does a bed company hoping to use the play for publicity purposes.

During the 1927–28 season Walter Hampden had scored a major success with a revival of Ibsen's *An Enemy of the People,* which ran for 127 performances. Ten years later enthusiasm for Hampden had waned noticeably, although no one questioned his high-mindedness. Moreover, Ibsen's plays were of an age at which they were generally belittled—"a somewhat outmoded vehicle," "somewhat wrinkled and gray-headed." So Hampden's latest revival of the work received merely polite notices when it came into the Hudson for two weeks beginning on the 15th, prior to a proposed tour.

The season's fourth examination of contemporary union agitation was John Howard Lawson's **Marching Song** (2-17-37, Bayes). Curiously it was housed at a rooftop theatre directly above where a similar if less left-wing play, *Tide Rising,* had been moved. In it, workers go on strike to force a company to take back a man (Grover Burgess) who has lost his home and been fired for his union activities. All the action occurred in Howard Bay's remarkable recreation of a rusting, abandoned factory, where a group of unemployed people have found shelter. The play was a quick flop, and marked the last new play by the radical Lawson (who ran off to a lucrative Hollywood job) and the last mounting by the similarly radical Theatre Union.

Without a knowing cast to bring out its virtues, Dion Boucicault's once ragingly popular *London Assurance* was given short shrift by both critics and playgoers when it was brought into the Vanderbilt on the 18th. The only "name" among the players was Ethel Barrymore's daughter, Ethel Barrymore Colt, who played Grace Harkaway.

For the second time in a little over a week, a picture of contemporary American-Jewish life was presented to Broadway. In this instance, Broadway liked what it saw. Arthur Kober's **Having Wonderful Time** (2-20-36, Lyceum) was set in a Jewish summer camp in the Berkshires, patronized by New Yorkers speaking a dialect and argot all their own. Thus one camper confesses that she is "a heavy water-drinkeh. Ten glasses is by me a notting." But the comedy's central figures are Teddy Stern (Katherine Locke), a Bronx stenographer who has come to Camp Kare-Free after falling out with an older man whom she had been dating, and Chick Kessler (Jules [later, John] Garfield), a proud but short-fused unemployed lawyer working as a waiter to meet expenses. Chick's eagerness and occasional rudeness at first put off Teddy, but after she is courted by an unscrupulous Lothario, Pinkie Aaronson (Sheldon Leonard), she comes to appreciate Chick's sincerity. When they agree to marry they realize that they are entitled to benefit from a policy covering newlyweds who first met at the camp—"Two weeks free vacation with positively no charge!" Critics peppered their reviews with complaints, lamenting the thinness of the plot, the unevenness of its effects on the audience, and the general unreadiness of the mounting, which had eschewed tryouts in favor of a few by-invitation-only previews. Douglas Gilbert concluded his *World-Telegram* review, "It is shameful to have to dismiss this fine effort as just an amusing comedy." But the play quickly caught on and ran for eleven months. In 1952, a musical version, *Wish You Were Here,* opened (with only some previews rather than a tryout), was generally panned, but also caught on and ran for a year and a half.

Two mountings by the Federal Theatre Project next claimed playgoers' attention. Arthur Arent's **Power** (2-23-37, Ritz), a new edition of the *Living Newspaper* series, escorted Mr. Average Consumer (Norman Lloyd) through a collection of dramatic sketches, film clippings, and protest songs tracing the history of commercial electricity from the days of Faraday and Edison, showing how business interests such as the "Insull Empire" exploited the public need for electrical power, and pleading for more government-sponsored TVAs. The play proved one of the FTP's most popular, running fifteen weeks at its small house and enjoying some brief revivals later.

With Barrie and Leona Stavis's **The Sun and I** (2-26-37, Adelphi), the FTP next turned from electrical power to political power to comdemn even benign dictatorship in the guise of the biblical story of Joseph. Pharaoh (Frederick Tozere) has allowed the alien Joseph (David Enton) to govern Egypt with an authoritarian hand. The carefully planned economy he foists on the nation brings prosperity and order, but considerable grumbling from a populace that sees itself as enslaved. Ousted by the Pharaoh, Joseph ponders what might have happened had he mingled more with the masses and listened to their ideas.

The latest London hit to find small favor with Americans was Barre Lyndon's **The Amazing Dr. Clitterhouse** (3-2-37, Hudson). Like Joseph Buloff before him, Cedric Hardwicke once again garnered good notices in a play that met with scant favor (though not as scant as Buloff's vehicles). Clitterhouse is a prominent London doctor who determines to explore the criminal mind at the moment it is committing a crime. He joins a gang of robbers, gets the information he seeks, but then discovers himself blackmailed by the robbers' fence (Clarence Derwent). He is forced to poison the man. With the police coming, he decides to pretend temporary insanity.

Mary Coyle Chase's **Now You've Done It** (3-5-37, Henry Miller's) had originally been presented months earlier by the FTP in Denver as *Me Third*. That title came from the fact that Harlan Hazlett (Walter Greaza), a candidate for Congress, is running under the motto "God first, the People second, Me third." Some sanctimonious politicians nearly scuttle his efforts until his mother (Evelyn Varden) hires Grace Dosher (Margaret Perry) to be the family maid. Grace, on parole from a Home for Incorrigibles, once had worked in the town's leading brothel, so when she recognizes the troublemakers as old customers, Hazlett's difficulties vanish. The play was the first of three Brock Pemberton would present during the month and, though it was a failure, was the only one of the three to run beyond two weeks. A few years down the road Pemberton, Chase, and their director, Antoinette Perry, would have a much better offering for playgoers.

A politician less lucky than Hazlett was the central figure in Bruno Frank's *Sturm im Wasserglas*, which James Bridie adapted for London as *Storm in a Teacup* and for New York as **Storm over Patsy** (3-8-37, Guild). A reporter (Roger Livesey), sent to write a puff interview with a Scotsman (Ian Maclean) standing for Parliament, is so annoyed by the man's refusal to help an Irish woman (Sara Allgood) keep her mixed-breed mutt—the Patsy of the title—after she fails to pay a license fee that he writes a savaging article instead. The whole matter goes to trial, and ends with the Scotsman being hooted and losing his wife (Claudia Morgan) to the reporter. For many, Leo G. Carroll stole the show as the puss-faced judge. The production closed out the Theatre Guild's hitless year.

Though Broadway had ventured a revival of *London Assurance*, the commercial theatre usually turned away from century-old plays, so it fell to the busy and venturesome FTP to make an evening out of three long-neglected curtain raisers from Boucicault's day: John Howard Payne's *Love in Humble Life*, Colin C. Hazlewood's *The Clock on the Stairs*, and Maddison Morton's *A Regular Fix*. The bill ran for a month at the 63rd Street Theatre, starting on March 9. (Up in Harlem, at the Lafayette on the 5th, the FTP had brought out an all-black revival of George Kelly's *The Show-Off*.)

Charles Coburn was the main attraction in Raymond Van Sickle's feeble **Sun Kissed** (3-10-37, Little). He was seen as the proprietor of Newberry Hall, a Los Angeles boardinghouse packed with eccentrics. But his real problem is his daughter (Francesca Bruning), who has run away from her psychologist husband (Russell Hardie). He comes after her, only to have the boarders create obstacles to a reunion. But hubby and wife finally are reunited.

The season then took a nosedive. March's remaining entries and April's first were all duds, only one managing to survive for even three weeks. In Randolph Carter's **Arms for Venus** (3-11-37, Golden), a Roman widow (Hortense Alden), preparing for suicide, fails to lock the door when she shuts herself up in her husband's tomb. The Emperor Nero (Walter Klavun) and an attractive soldier (Alan Davis) both enter and soon are wooing the woman. In time she capitulates to the soldier's blandishments.

In Joseph O. Kesselring's **Cross-Town** (3-17-37, 48th St.), Bumps Malone (Joseph Downing), the semiliterate son of a prizefighter, becomes a literary lion by plagiarizing long-forgotten magazine stories and rewriting them in the vernacular. When he is eventually exposed, he returns to the loyal wife he had deserted.

Even the freethinking FTP often echoed Broadway, when, as in *Thirsty Soil*, its mounting of Virgil Geddes's **Native Ground** (3-23-37, Venice) peopled a bleak Nebraska farm with a tainted family. A man appears at the Bentley farm, hoping to marry the Bentley daughter.

The man had once been Mrs. Bentley's lover, and she is forced to confess that he, and not her husband, is the girl's father. This does not stop the man and the girl from running off together. However, the girl later takes on a lover and has a child by him.

Sing Sing's celebrated warden, Lewis E. Lawes, collaborated with Jonathan Finn on **Chalked Out** (3-25-37, Morosco). The dying confession of a man (John Raby) shot in a prison break exonerates a death row inmate (Frank Lovejoy), who had been convicted of a murder, although he had merely owned the gun used in the killing, and fingers the real killer (Charles Jordan), the dying man's cellmate. The play was Brock Pemberton's second March offering.

North Bigbee and Walter Holbrook's **Farewell Summer** (3-29-37, Fulton) finds Keith Stuart (Lois Wilson) looking vainly for love. She adores her professor (Walter Gilbert), but he is a married man. Another likable suitor (James Todd) proves to be a philanderer. Preparing to leave her southwestern school for New York City, she gazes at a harvest moon and wonders if she is doomed to spinsterhood.

Walter Charles Roberts's **Red Harvest** (3-30-37, National), Pemberton's third presentation of the month, purported to be based on the diary of a nurse during the war. Episodic in nature, it recounted the struggles of nurses to move ever closer to the fighting. One nurse finds she is tending her dying brother. Another falls in love with a wounded private, but must watch his infection spread hopelessly. The chief nurse (Leona Powers) brings a high-hat surgeon (Frederic Tozere) to heel.

A second Bruno Frank play, this one translated by England's Hubert Griffith and Benn W. Levy as **Young Madame Conti** (3-31-37, Music Box), focused on an Austrian prostitute (Constance Cummings). Nella Conti falls in love with one (Patrick Barr) of her clients, overhears him say he hopes to live off her earnings, then shoots him. She is arrested and brought to trial, where the horrors of her past life are all rehearsed. Finally she is sentenced to be hanged. All this proves to be merely her fantasies as she sits in her luxurious apartment, awaiting her client. When he arrives, she shoots him.

Willie Chance was almost a stage-character name out of a bygone theatre, but it also was the name assigned the inveterate gambler in **Bet Your Life** (4-5-37, Golden). When a horse named Slow Poke wins his race, Willie's sweepstakes ticket is worth $150,000. He and his family live it up until the money is gone. Then a nag named Swaybag wins a race, so Willie (Lew Hearn) is rich again. The comedy's authors were another Willie, Willie Howard, the revue comedian, and Fritz Blocki, a onetime Chicago drama critic.

A then drama columnist and future critic, Ward More-house, was the author of **Miss Quis** (4-7-37, Henry Miller's). Liz Quis (Peggy Wood), a forty-two-year-old spinster who has worked for most of the nabobs in Fancy Gap, is left $700,000 by one of them, on the condition she try to clean up the town's corruption. She assembles all the elite and tells them, "I'm afraid under your guidance—the town will become just another blur on a map." She offers to buy them out, and, when they demur, she reveals she has the goods on them. Unfortunately the town's amiable gambler, Buster Niles (James Rennie), who has long admired Miss Quis, punches one of her opponents, who is killed when he falls. After the others perjure themselves at his trial, Miss Quis offers to meet their exorbitant terms if they will confess their misbehavior and leave town. They refuse. Buster is found guilty and told to move elsewhere. He sneaks back to propose to Miss Quis, but she rejects him, saying she must remain to fight Fancy Gap's battles. For all her charms, Wood, who was listed in the published text as co-author, could not keep the comedy on the boards above one month.

Bernard C. Shoenfeld's thinly veiled retelling of the John Barrymore–Elaine Barry affair was called **Hitch Your Wagon** (4-8-37, 48th St.). A would-be actress, Camille Schwartz (Dennie Moore), and her equally stagestruck mother (Dora Weissman) rescue the famous actor Rex Duncan (George Curzon) from a sanitarium where he is being dried out after his latest binge. They offer him love and chicken soup, but when he realizes that Camille is hopelessly untalented, he signs himself back into the sanitarium. She resumes her romance with a football player (Kenneth Roberts).

Victor Wolfson's **Excursion** (4-9-37, Vanderbilt) was a sleeper that might have run longer than 116 performances had it not arrived so late in the season. Richard Watts, Jr., hailed it as "a sort of exultant paean to the essential gallantry of the battered human spirit." For thirty years Cap'n Obediah Rich (Whitford Kane) has piloted the S.S. *Happiness* on its excursions between New Bedford and Coney Island. He has loved the task, even if his careful study of his passengers has left him unhappy: "Every Sunday morning, they come rushing down to this old boat—just as eager! An every Sunday night they come back—just as sad!" Since this is to be the ship's last voyage, Obediah's brother, Jonathan (J. Hammond Dailey), himself an old salt, suggests that instead of returning to New Bedford they head for an Eden-like island in the Indies. Obediah acquiesces. The passengers, a varied lot, are taken by surprise. The news allows several of them to sort out problems in their lives. But the Coast Guard intercepts the ship off the Virginia coast and forces it back. Still, the story has made Obediah a national hero, and the old tub is promised a new lease on life. Breakaway settings that slid back and forth allowed the action to alternate between the captain's cabin and a passenger deck. A 1951 musical version, *A Month of Sundays,* folded during its tryout.

The FTP's Jewish Theatre Unit presented Anne Bromberger's translation of Friedrich Wolf's **Professor Mamlock** (4-13-37, 63rd St.), in which a conservative German-Jewish surgeon is driven to suicide by the Nazis. Critics felt the playwright failed to bring out the drama innate in his theme.

Jean Ferguson Black's **Penny Wise** (4-19-37, Morosco) told how Penny Chase (Linda Watkins), advised by the former mistresses of her husband (Kenneth MacKenna) to do something about his unceasing philandering, invites his latest (Nancy Sheridan) to her home and tells her she has no objection to her sailing for Europe with him. That takes the wind out of her husband's sails.

A pathetically inept effort to recount the story of Duse and d'Annunzio, LeRoy Bailey's **Curtain Call** (4-22-37, Golden), renamed its central figures Isola Cassella (Ara Gerald) and Antonio Sebastiano (Guido Nadzo). Most of the play unfolded in Rome and Paris between 1894 and 1900, but a final scene—"an attempt . . . to capture some of the magic that is Helen Hayes' in her 'Victoria Regina' fadeout"—had the aged actress dying alone in an American hotel room twenty-five years later.

Bringing out plays all over the theatrical map, the FTP relit a famous Greenwich Village theatre for James Bridie's English drama **Tobias and the Angel** (4-28-37, Provincetown Playhouse). There was no admission charge for those who reserved seats to watch how the Archangel Raphael (Kirk Lucas) helped the timid son (Edwin Michaels) of the blind old Tobit (Harry Brooks) find courage and love.

The discovery of the crucified body of a hated army sergeant provokes the incidents in Ralph Spencer Zink's **Without Warning** (5-1-37, National). Army investigators at first would pin the killing on a civilian employee (Philip Ober), but soon come to understand that an officer (Don Dillaway) murdered the sergeant for refusing to share his smuggling profits. The killer himself is shot dead.

A small spate of revivals started with *Abie's Irish Rose* (5-23-22) at the Little on the 12th. It lingered only six weeks—by far the longest stand granted any of the spring resurrections. Brieux's examination of the problem of venereal disease, *Damaged Goods* (3-14-13), adapted by Henry Herbert from a translation by John Pollock, came into the 48th Street Theatre on the 17th and survived a single week.

The revivals were interrupted by the arrival of the season's last smash hit, yet another farce in a year that had not produced one major, long-running drama. George Abbott's mounting of John Murray and Allen Boretz's **Room Service** (5-19-37, Cort) was set in a modest New York hotel room. A shoestring producer, Gordon Miller (Sam Levene), has been camping out there and running up a $1200 bill for himself and his actors, thanks to his pliant brother-in-law, Joseph Gribble (Cliff Dunstan), whom he has sold a 10 percent interest in the show and who happens to be the hotel's manager. But now a supervising director is downstairs checking the books, so Gribble demands Miller pay up. Of course, he can't. He and his buddies are donning layers of clothing, intending to decamp, when Miller's not very bright playwright, Leo Davis (Eddie Albert), arrives from Oswego, having burnt all his bridges. Unable to flee, Miller decides on a ruse. First he makes it seem that Davis has the measles, and when that does not work, he announces that Davis has committed suicide. He begs for time, insisting he must attend to the funeral. In desperation the hotel helps finance the play. When the play becomes a hit, Miller tells the relieved supervising director (Donald McBride), "This may be the first hotel to win the Pulitzer Prize." Welcomed by Atkinson as "a very funny escapade in the helter-skelter vein of slapdash American fooling," the farce ran for 500 performances.

Even kids were not exempt from the FTP's highly slanted proselytizing, so Atkinson branded Oscar Saul and Lou Lantz's **The Revolt of the Beavers** (5-20-37, Adelphi) "a revolutionary bed-time story . . . a primer lesson in the class struggle." Two proletarian youngsters are carried by the North Wind to Beaverland, where they learn how a capitalistic beaver exploits his workers until the employees heed the cry "Beavers of the world, unite!"

Money Mad (5-24-37, 49th St.) may have seemed like the title of a novelty, but it proved to be merely Fritz Blocki's reworking of *Bet Your Life.* Willie Chance had become Lou Chance and was now portrayed by the Yiddish comedian Ludwig Satz. But only for a single performance.

A pair of producers brought out a pair of old murder mysteries, raising the curtain at the Majestic on the 31st for *The Bat* (8-23-20) and, two weeks later on June 14 at the same house, for *The Cat and the Canary* (2-7-22).

The season's final novelty was an FTP offering, which appeared between the two whodunits, George MacEntee's **The Case of Philip Lawrence** (6-7-37, Lafayette). The titular hero, having refused to take work as a railroad station redcap, accepts employment as a Harlem nightclub entertainer. His racketeer boss kills another hoodlum and frames Philip for the crime. But he is acquitted in court when his girlfriend testifies that she saw the killing and fingers the racketeer. The nightclub scenes made several critics long for the old days when black shows trafficked largely in lively strutting.

1937–1938

Production figures continued to drop. The *Times,* ignoring Federal Theatre Project offerings, counted seventy-four new plays; *Variety,* apparently taking into account some of them, tallied eighty-two. Thirty of these plays ran a week or less. Waving aside the implications of the ongoing numerical decline and the percentage of very short stays, most commentators were not unhappy. The new season seemed to them better balanced than the previous one. If there were considerably fewer of the deliciously madcap comedies the 1936–37 season had enjoyed, there were noticeably more good, substantial dramas. Several outstanding instances of fresh staging ideas also whetted interest.

The season got off to its slowest start in memory. Apart from two FTP presentations, not a single novelty raised its curtain in late June, July or August. For three months the seven holdover comedies that spanned the summer (considering the long-running *Tobacco Road* as a comedy) had the field to themselves.

Although only one of the FTP's two August offerings was unveiled in Harlem, both were by black writers. Hughes Allison's **The Trial of Dr. Beck** (8-9-37, Maxine Elliott's) told of a black doctor (Kenneth Renwick) accused of murdering his dark-skinned wife so that he might marry a light-skinned black. The case against him is based largely on his own writings, which suggest that if blacks and whites intermarry, within a few generations all Americans would be reasonably light-skinned. His dead wife's would-be lover is finally fingered as the real killer.

Dorothy Hallparn's **Horse Play** (8-28-37, Lafayette) seemed directed toward children. A black farmer (Doe Doe Green), threatened with foreclosure on his farm, takes his horse (played by men in costume) to Harlem. Animals from the zoo leave their cages and prevail on a circus master to stage a circus that includes the horse. The farmer earns the $200 needed to save his farm.

Not until late September did a commercial novelty brave Broadway. Gerald Savory's **George and Margaret** (9-22-37, Morosco) was a London success. An English family, awaiting the arrival of week-end guests (the George and Margaret of the title), sort out their own problems, including their son's desire to marry their serving girl. Only after the problems are resolved

are the guests announced (but never actually appear onstage). Cut-rate tickets allowed the comedy to last for eleven weeks, a far cry from its West End run.

In Valentine Davies's **Blow Ye Winds** (9-23-37, 46th St.) Hayden Chase (Henry Fonda), a rather dour young man who wants only to fish and sail, and Christine Lawrence (Doris Dalton), an ambitious scientific researcher who has rented his boat, fall in love, marry, then fall out of love when he refuses to give up his casual, roving life. In the end, they decide to try a reconciliation. Underplaying made the essentially adramatic piece seem monotonous. But the setting for the sailboat, which filled the stage at the beginning and close of the play, won applause.

The Lady Has a Heart (9-25-37, Longacre) was Edward Roberts's translation of an unspecified Hungarian play by László Bus-Fekete. The family of Count Mariassy (Lumsden Hare), the Conservative prime minister, has been served for four generations by Jean (Vincent Price) and his forefathers. Complications arise after Jean is elected to Parliament on a Socialist ticket and after he and the count's married daughter (Elissa Landi) fall in love. They leave for another country. Making her last Broadway appearance except for one musical was Hilda Spong, who had been a leading lady half a century before and who now was seen as the prime minister's wife. Cut-rate tickets once again helped a foreign play to an eleven-week run.

One week was all Kent Wiley's **On Location** (9-27-37, Ritz) could muster, even at a reduced $2.75 top. A Hollywood director (Leslie Denison) decides to make a movie about a rough-and-tumble gal (Katherine Hart) who runs an unproductive gold mine. When he discovers that most of her workers are WPA derelicts, he backs off. But love finally triumphs in the play's single setting of a rustic cabin in the Rockies. Wiley was a pen name for Samuel Ruskin Golding.

The season's first modest success was Gilbert Miller's production of another English play aided by cut-rate tickets, Terence Rattigan's **French Without Tears** (9-28-37, Henry Miller's). A group of young Englishmen studying French in preparation for the diplomatic service realize that their fellow student Diana Lake (Penelope Dudley Ward) is a flirt and a tease, so they noisily drop her. She is unconcerned, since Lord Heybrook is on the way. But then Lord Heybrook (Edward Ryan) turns out to be eleven years old.

The season's first modest hit was followed by its first sizable one, Maxwell Anderson's **The Star-Wagon** (9-29-37, Empire). Stephen Minch (Burgess Meredith) shrugs off complaints by his wife, Martha (Lillian Gish), that he is a poor breadwinner, still earning a mere $27.50 after all these years. Never mind that his boss, Duffy (Kent Smith), is ready to fire him for inventing a tire that will not wear out. Stephen has a better invention. He calls it his Star-Wagon, a device "that runs along on a thread of time" and can transport people back to better days. He employs the machine to return to his youth with Martha and relive the chance to wed a rich girl, Hallie Arlington (Jane Buchanan). The visit convinces Martha and him that they made the right decision. Look at how crotchety Hallie's husband has grown. Hallie's husband is Duffy. The show's six-month run was something of a surprise, considering the mixed notices it received. Richard Watts, Jr., of the *Herald Tribune* seemed to speak for both sides when he commented, "What the author . . . has done is to write a charming and touching little dramatic fantasy and then destroy three-quarters of its effectiveness by making it top-heavy with a pompous pseudo-intellectuality."

The black writer and composer Donald Heywood had time and again been subjected to scathing notices but had persisted in trying his luck on Broadway. He tried for one last time with **How Come, Lawd?** (9-30-37, 49th St.), which was so savagely slated that it was withdrawn after its second performance. Big Boy (Rex Ingram), a not very bright Alabama cotton picker, retains his faith in God even after his fellow unionists are mowed down and his girl (Hilda Rogers) is stabbed to death defending him. Black revival singing failed to add much color to the affair.

The Abbey Theatre Players, who had lost some of their best actors and who brought over little new, had a disappointing eleven-week stand. Their two novelties were Teresa Deevy's **Katie Roche** (10-2-37, Ambassador), in which an illegitimate, adopted child grows up to believe she is descended from elite parents and must be brought to realize that she is not, and Hugh Hunt's theatricalization of a Frank O'Connor story, **In a Train** (11-20-37), done in conjunction with *The Playboy of the Western World* and telling of jurors, witnesses, and even the acquitted defendant riding on a train back from Dublin after a murder trial. Other revivals were *The Far-Off Hills, The New Gossoon, Juno and the Paycock,* and *Drama at Inish* (done in America earlier as *Is Life Worth Living?*).

Ben Hecht set aside his biting humor when he supplied the Theatre Guild with **To Quito and Back** (10-6-37, Guild), the first of its season's offerings. The show was a flop, launching a second disastrous season for the Guild, albeit this season's plight was softened by one major success. To escape personal problems at home, Alexander Sterns (Leslie Banks), an American novelist, flees with Lola Hobbs (Sylvia Sidney) to Ecuador, where he enlists in a revolution led by the Communist Zamiano (Joseph Buloff). Later, guilt feelings, especially concerning his desertion of his wife, prompt

Sterns to go on a suicide mission. The play was dismissed by the *Times*'s Brooks Atkinson as "a sham battle of words and fine phrases." Several of his colleagues wondered why an American writer was played by an Englishman.

Rachel Crothers concluded her playwriting career with a smash hit, **Susan and God** (10-7-37, Plymouth). Prior to Broadway, the play had been plagued by hard luck, especially the death of Osgood Perkins, its leading man, during its Washington tryout. But with his understudy, Paul McGrath, given a golden opportunity of which he took full advantage, and the luminous Gertrude Lawrence in the lead, all turned out splendidly. Susan, heretofore vain and selfish, has returned from England converted to the idea that being open with God and your friends will solve all your problems. One problem she has resolved to do away with is her alcoholic husband, Barrie. Her friends are uncertain whether Susan is tired of Barrie because he drinks or Barrie drinks because Susan is tired of him. But Barrie approaches Susan, insisting he is on the wagon and will stay on the wagon if she spends the summer with him and their "girl scout gone wrong" daughter (Nancy Kelly). If he fails, he will not stand in the way of a divorce. He does slip off once, after Susan accuses him of having an affair with another woman. But Susan has learned tolerance and agrees to go on with the marriage. Richard Lockridge of the *Evening Sun* observed, "It doesn't need proving that Miss Crothers, theme or no theme, can write dialogue that humor glints on, and handle her situations and characters with a suave dexterity enchanting to watch." The play ran for nine months.

By contrast, Allan Scott's **In Clover** (10-13-37, Vanderbilt) disappeared after less than half a week. A city couple (Claudia Morgan and Myron McCormick) buy a house in the Connecticut countryside. They overpay for it, their well runs dry, demanding guests descend on them, and all other manner of difficulties nearly wreck their marriage before they decide to return to the sanity of city life.

The FTP used the same two theatres it had employed for novelties in August to offer revivals in October. At Maxine Elliott's on the 13th the group resurrected John Howard Lawson's expressionistic, jazz-decorated look at a coal-mine strike, *Processional* (1-12-25). Eugene O'Neill's four one-acters, generally performed together as *S.S. Glencairn,* were presented with an all-black cast at the Lafayette on the 29th. Young Canada Lee was Yank.

Stephen Powys's West End drama **Wise Tomorrow** (10-15-37, Biltmore) found absolutely no support on Broadway. Powys's heroine, a faded actress (Josephine Victor), remains a force in the theatre by her persistent influence on a protégée (Gloria Dickson). Even after the actress's death, the stipulations in her will continue her hold on the girl. Some critics detected a "malodorous" suggestion of lesbianism in the relationship.

Like *Wise Tomorrow,* John Lawrence's **Wall Street Scene** (10-18-37, Comedy) lasted for only three performances. But the play, telling of two unscrupulous, crooked speculators who worm their way into a respectable brokerage firm, was only listed for three playings. The producer and actors apparently hoped some major Broadway money would allow them to continue, but thumbs-down reviews destroyed their hopes.

The usually knowing George Abbott struck out with his production of Mrs. Bernie Angus's **Angel Island** (10-20-37, National). A handpicked group of unattractive guests are invited to an island by Leo Grainger (Carroll Ashburn). Most have gone bust in the Crash and are pleased to learn there may be buried treasure on the island. They also soon learn that the motorboat which could take them back to the mainland has broken down and the telephone wires have been cut. One by one the guests are murdered. Because he has a prison record, the most obvious suspect is the butler (Eric Wollencott), but the deranged killer finally is shown to be none other than Grainger.

In the face of mostly negative notices and despite its large cast and numerous scene changes **Many Mansions** (10-27-37, Biltmore), by Jules Eckert Goodman and his son, Eckert Goodman, survived for twenty weeks. In a dream, Peter Brent (Alexander Kirkland) receives a call to the ministry. He enters the church over the objections of his family and his sweetheart (Flora Campbell). His idealism, such as his attempts to attract poorer and younger parishioners and his defense of a fallen woman, quickly pits him against more pragmatic or cynical church officials. He refuses to compromise and is unfrocked. At one time or another in the play, the modern church was blamed for the rise of communism, fascism, and "all the rooted evils in the world." Monotonous organ music filled the auditorium during scene changes.

The first of three Shakespearean productions to arrive in short order closed out October, when *As You Like It* came into the Ritz on the 30th. The mounting had initially been done in summer stock by a group calling itself the Surry Players, and had drawn the attention of Dwight Deere Wiman, who moved it to New York. Although many of the players went on to successful careers, the consensus was that they were not yet ready for so difficult a challenge. Katherine Emery and Anne Revere, who had played the accused women in *The Children's Hour,* were Rosalind and Celia. Shepperd Strudwick was Orlando. They quitted the Forest of Arden after a mere two weeks.

When the curtain rose on S. N. Behrman's adaptation of Jean Giraudoux's **Amphitryon 38** (11-1-37, Shu-

bert), Jupiter and Mercury were seen lounging naked on a cloud and peering down at the beautiful women on the earth below. Of course, the gods' bodies were papier-mâché, but the smiling, chattering faces protruding from holes in the curtain belonged to Alfred Lunt and Richard Whorf. Jupiter has fallen in love with Alkmena (Lynn Fontanne), the wife of a general (Barry Thompson), so he comes down to earth and assumes her mortal husband's guise to woo her. When he leaves her pregnant with a child whom he has gotten her husband to agree to name Hercules, he blesses Alkmena with the gift of forgetfulness. Lockridge described Fontanne as "lovely in her robes . . . creating with inflections and little gestures an Alkmena full of wiles and tenderness, wit and devotion, and a touching humanity." The *Journal-American*'s John Anderson said Lunt's performance displayed "all the zest and energy and imagination of his best work." A nineteen-week run meant that the comedy was the Theatre Guild's lone big success during the season. The 1950 Cole Porter musical, *Out of This World,* followed the comedy closely, even to opening with Jupiter on a cloud, but claimed not to be based on the show.

There was little elegance but plenty of vitality in the playing of Clifford Odets's **Golden Boy** (11-4-37, Belasco). Mr. Bonaparte (Morris Carnovsky) is determined that his son, Joe (Luther Adler), should be a violinist, but Joe insists that the fastest way to escape from tenement life is with his fists, as a professional fighter. He enjoys some early victories in the ring, and when he breaks his hand and understands that he no longer can even think of a musical career, he rejoices, "Hallelujah. It's the beginning of the world." But that world turns sour after his girl, Laura (Frances Fuller), seems to desert him and after he kills a man in a bout. When Laura returns to console Joe, they drive off, but are killed in a crash. Praise for the play itself was somewhat muted, but Burns Mantle of the *Daily News,* among its admirers, felt it revealed "the best of the Odets genius for recreating a believable realism in both story and characters." The drama ran for seven months. It has enjoyed subsequent revivals and was made into a musical for Sammy Davis, Jr., in 1964.

Elswyth Thane's **Young Mr. Disraeli** (11-10-37, Fulton) added one more name to the list of English plays not made welcome in New York. The playwright recounted the disappointment of Disraeli (Derrick de Marney) at the reception of his first novel, his taking up politics, his switching from radicalism to conservatism, and his marriage to the widow (Sophie Stewart) of his best friend. Many first-stringers attended a dress rehearsal in order to be at a major Shakespearean revival opening the same night.

That Shakespearean entry led to one of the most

famous put-downs in American theatrical history, when John Mason Brown began his *Post* review, "Tallulah Bankhead barged down the Nile last night as Cleopatra—and sank." He went on to observe, "As the serpent of the Nile she proves no more dangerous than a garter snake . . . she seems nearer to a midway than to Alexandria." But his displeasure with the revival of *Antony and Cleopatra,* which came into the Mansfield on Wednesday the 10th and closed there on Saturday the 13th, was not confined to its star. Indeed his first paragraphs assailed the work of one Professor William Strunk, Jr., who not only bowdlerized much of the text but rearranged it capriciously—among other matters, opening the play in Rome rather than in Alexandria and reassigning Enobarbus's famous description of the queen and her barge to a lowly messenger. Aggravating matters was the unalluring, mechanical Antony of Conway Tearle.

Matters were quite different the next evening, prompting Mason to exclaim, "I come to praise 'Caesar,' not to bury it." He went on to hail this intermissionless *Julius Caesar,* the first effort by Orson Welles and John Houseman's newly established Mercury Theatre (once the hard-luck Comedy Theatre on 41st Street) as "the most exciting, the most imaginative, the most topical, the most awesome, and the most absorbing" mounting of the season. His mention of topicality came because the play was no longer set in ancient Rome but in modern Fascist Italy with the cast in neutrally colored uniforms or drab street clothes, frequently worn gangster-style with upturned collars and low-slung fedoras. The brick wall and piping at the rear of the stage were disclosed. In front of them some steps and some rearward-slanting platforms, suggesting "an abyss beyond," provided all the scenery. Dramatic lighting—"the miracle of enveloping shadows, knife-like rays, and superbly changing lights"—more often accounted for place or time or mood. Besides directing the play, Welles was its somber, lush-voiced Brutus. George Coulouris was an eloquent, forceful Marc Antony; Martin Gabel, anything but lean, a shrewd, purposeful Cassius; and Joseph Holland, a strutting, Mussolini-like Caesar. With so many critics echoing Mason's encomiums, the revival played to good business for 157 performances, eventually in repertory with other Mercury productions.

Aurania Rouverol's **Places, Please!** (11-12-37, Golden) was the latest in the season's half dozen three-performance flops. An actress (Lillian Emerson) from a famous old acting family gives up her career to marry a Boston Brahmin (Matthew Smith). When she finds that his family refuses to accept her, she leaves him, returns to the stage, and marries her stage manager (Don Dillaway). The play was the last to reach Broadway by

Rouverol, whose 1928 hit *Skidding* had inspired the then ongoing Andy Hardy series at MGM.

Dore Schary, who would someday head that Hollywood studio, was the young author of **Too Many Heroes** (11-15-37, Hudson), which survived for a fortnight. Jeb Williams (James Bell), a peaceable mill-worker, is ineluctably pressed into joining a lynch mob out to kill the confessed kidnappers and murderers of the mill superintendent's daughter. After it turns out that Jeb was the man who struck the blow that actually killed one of the kidnappers, Jeb's conscience plagues him. His attempts to help the dead man's widow (Shirley Booth) and to hand himself over for punishment turn the whole town against him and even cost him his wife (Elspeth Eric). Another lynch mob kills him after his wife accuses him of having an affair with the widow.

The Theatre Guild's second flop of the season was **Madame Bovary** (11-16-37, Broadway). Gaston Baty's adaptation of Gustave Flaubert's famous novel had been translated by Benn W. Levy. It employed a Greek-like chorus of six female "Companions" to help retell the story of the fun-loving Emma Bovary (Constance Cummings), her unhappy marriage to a dull, backwater doctor (Harold Vermilyea), her descent into adultery, and her eventual suicide.

One small, unexpected hit—though *Variety* estimated it closed in the red—was **Father Malachy's Miracle** (11-17-37, St. James), which Brian Doherty theatricalized from Bruce Marshall's novel. It featured Al Shean, the Jewish half of the old vaudeville duo of Gallagher and Shean, as a traditionalist Benedictine monk sent to assist at an Edinburgh church. The archly modern Anglican minister (Frank Greene) of a neighboring church insists that miracles are a totally bygone phenomenon and wagers with Father Malachy accordingly. To win his bet, the good father prays to God to transport the nearby, noisy Garden of Eden bar to a distant island. A patron leaving the bar hurries back in frightened and soaked. The pub-keeper rushes to the window and exclaims, "Christ Almighty! Sea Gulls." But the press of curiosity seekers, a lawsuit against the priest by the pub owner, and other problems finally prompt Father Malachy, on Christmas Eve, to pray to have the bar restored to its original location. The comedy chalked up 125 performances.

Three very short-run flops came next. The first to arrive was Stanley Young's pretentious blank-verse drama **Robin Landing** (11-18-37, 46th St.). The drama was set in a Kentucky trading post in 1770. Grant Eaton (Ian Keith) has lived there for years after leaving his wife and has even married an Indian, Sippi (Kathryn Grill). His first wife, Linda (Nan Sutherland), believing Grant dead, has married his unprincipled brother, Kane (Louis Calhern). By chance, they come across Grant in their travels, and the meeting leads to tragedy. Grant's half-breed son (Richard Paul Spater) is killed, Sippi leaves him to return to her tribe, and he is blinded in an attack by his brother. The village idiot (Fred Stewart) witnesses the attack and kills Kane. Linda opts to remain and support Grant, reassuring him, "There are still flowers for us not ridden under —/ There are still dreams."

Some of the season's most damning notices—"Plays like this make the theatre hang its head"—went to James Knox Millen's **The Bough Breaks** (11-19-37, Little). Although it had an inexpensive cast of only three, it survived for just three performances. Not until a boy's possessive mother (Eleanor Brent) drives him (Leon Janney) to suicide by her opposition to his marrying a girl (Cyrilla Dorne) he loves does she discover the girl is pregnant.

Henry Myers's **Work Is for Horses** (11-20-37, Windsor) struck most critics as no better. Cornelius Prentiss (Robert Keith) is content to let his wife (Connie Gilchrist) and daughter (Patricia Carroll) support him. Nor is he above trying to blackmail his daughter's boss (John Westley) after a boyfriend (Jack Warren) makes her pregnant. The blackmail fails, the daughter leaves home, and Cornelius is fearful that he might actually have to look for work. A bequest from an aunt relieves his worries.

Even Ethel Barrymore, coming out of a ballyhooed retirement, could not lure playgoers into Sidney Howard's **The Ghost of Yankee Doodle** (11-22-37, Guild), so the Theatre Guild suffered another flop. The action of the play occurs "eighteen months after the next world war" has begun. (England, France, and Russia are opposed to Germany, Japan, and Italy.) Sara Garrison, whose husband was killed in the last war, is an ardent pacifist and supports the American government's attempt to remain neutral. But the Garrison family business is threatened with bankruptcy if it cannot violate the neutrality act and sell armament to Japan. James Madison Clevenger (Dudley Digges), owner of a large newspaper chain and Sara's longtime suitor, hopes to win her over by having his papers advocate a war that would bring prosperity to the Garrisons' business. The plan backfires, with Sara sending him away. Of Barrymore, Atkinson wrote, not uncritically, "It is nice to have her back—unintelligible and shining as ever. She presides over the most attractive role with the patrician tossing of the head, the flashing eyes and the quiet grace of the Barrymore style." Even when the Guild's luck in selecting plays ran dry, it still offered fine physical productions and superb casts. In this instance, besides Barrymore and Digges, the cast included Frank Conroy, George Nash, Eliot Cabot, and Russell Hardie.

John Steinbeck's adaptation of his own novel **Of Mice and Men** (11-23-37, Music Box) won plaudits as "one of the most poignant and compelling dramas on any New York stage" from Sidney B. Whipple of the *World-Telegram,* and just before it concluded its six-month stand the New York Drama Critics Circle gave it the group's annual award for best play. According to Burns Mantle, the play "startled its first-night audience into upright sitting positions and such emotional quivers as no other Broadway audience since Jeanne Eagels cussed out a psalm-singing clergyman in 'Rain.' " Considering its somber theme, some playgoers might have been surprised to discover that it was produced by Sam Harris and directed by the master of comedy, George S. Kaufman. Lennie (Broderick Crawford) is a loving but infantile giant who has often killed pet mice accidentally with his crushing embrace. His loyal buddy and fellow migrant worker, George (Wallace Ford), has warned him to be careful, since one day it might not be an animal that he kills. Taking work at a ranch, they are told that the boss's sluttish daughter-in-law (Claire Luce) has been seen "givin' a couple of mule skinners the eye." One look at her prompts George to warn Lennie, "I seen 'em poison before, but I ain't seen no piece of jail bait worse than her. Don't you even smell near her!" But when the girl finds Lennie weeping over a puppy he has inadvertently killed and tries to soothe him, he grabs her, she screams, and in his fright he breaks her neck. George seeks out Lennie's hiding place and shoots him before the others can get to him.

Like Barrymore, another grand lady of the stage, Ina Claire, was having an off season. Indeed, apart from one last appearance in the 1950s, she would never again find an important Broadway hit. Her troubles began with Thomas Job's dramatization of Anthony Trollope's **Barchester Towers** (11-30-37, Martin Beck). Although Lockridge delighted at how she "deliciously italicizes the comedy with gestures and tosses of the head and unexpected inflections," a majority of his colleagues rued that she was "not properly cast" and "was not at her estimable best." As Madame Neroni, an expatriate returned home to her native England, she meddles in the affairs of the local church and even enjoys some cynical flirtations before returning to Italy and her Italian husband.

For the second time in little more than a month, George Abbott produced and directed a play by Mrs. Bernie Angus, and watched it quickly head for Cain's warehouse. Critics dismissed **Brown Sugar** (12-2-37, Biltmore) as an inept endeavor to create "a high-yellow 'Broadway.' " A black truckdriver (Juan Hernandez) falls in love with a "saffron-skinned" Harlem nightclub entertainer (Christola Williams) who is wanted by the police for drugging and killing a white playboy at the club. He attempts, with his wife's grudging consent, to hide the girl in his apartment. However, before long he is forced to grab a freighter for South America, the girl is arrested, and the wife (Beulah E. Edmonds) is left shaking her head. The play ran four performances.

The two plays that opened the next evening ran three and two performances respectively. **Merely Murder** (12-3-37, Playhouse), A. E. Thomas's stage version of a Georgette Heyer novel, attempted unavailingly to spoof murder mysteries. Scotland Yard suspects a flippant brother (Rex O'Malley) and sister (Claudia Morgan) of killing first one stepbrother and then another to ensure themselves an inheritance. But the killer turns out to be a golden-haired gold digger (Muriel Hutchinson) who hoped to marry the brother after he came into his inheritance. There were less criminal deaths in Charles George's **Love in My Fashion** (12-3-37, Ritz). A newly widowed Pamela Pennington (Luella Gear) has just buried husband number one—a philandering member of the First Families of Virginia, whom she forced to marry her at a shotgun wedding. She casts for and wins the hand of the mortician (G. Albert Smith) who buried her spouse, then, after he is killed in a train wreck, takes aim at the bachelor minister (Sherling Oliver) who presided at number two's service.

For some time now Ruth Draper, Cornelia Otis Skinner, and others had been offering Broadway one-woman shows. These entertainments usually consisted of a miscellany of sketches, on one or two occasions tied together by an overriding theme. Although Skinner was the only performer in **Edna His Wife** (12-7-37, Little), which she took from Margaret Ayer Barnes's novel, more than one critic looked at her vehicle as a "full-length drama." It offered eleven vignettes telling of the sad life of Edna Losser, a plain, fundamentally uninteresting woman who in 1900 rejects the proposal of a railroad brakeman and marries a man whose ambition and eye for a pretty woman by 1937 leave his loyal wife lonely and disappointed. Skinner played not only Edna, but Edna's friends, neighbors, and associates.

Critics suggested that the best thing about Norman Bel Geddes's presentation of Irwin Shaw's **Siege** (12-8-37, Longacre) was Bel Geddes's scenery. For a play about the Spanish Civil war he designed a high-rising fortress tower on a mountain peak. The set was on a turntable and pivoted to disclose tunnels dug out underground. In this Loyalist redoubt the aggressive former bullfighter Guiterra (Sheldon Leonard) seduces Teresa (Rose Hobart), wife of the would-be pacifist Diaz (William Edmunds). To flaunt his macho image, Guiterra volunteers to make a sortie for food for his besieged colleagues. The wounds he receives require that his leg be amputated. In his agony, he urges his fellows to sue for peace. Diaz, also changing his stripes,

puts Guiterra out of his misery, then leads what is surely a suicidal assault.

A cast of good players, including Lulu McConnell, Sylvia Field, and Ben Lackland, could do little to enliven Harry J. Essex and Sid Schwartz's **Something for Nothing** (12-9-37, Windsor). The Perkins family, avid contest players, think they can surely win the $100,000 prize offered by a chewing gum company for the best captions to a set of cartoons. After all, they have discovered that the contest's creator is their boarder, Mr. Scott (Lackland). Crooks, also looking to win the prize, complicate affairs. The Perkinses do win, but are disqualified when officials learn their daughter, Una (Field), is being courted by Scott.

An English play, Aimee and Philip Stuart's **Love of Women** (12-13-37, Golden), was also a quick flop. Vere (Valerie Taylor) and Brigit (Heather Angel) are writers who have lived and worked together for several years. This has led to speculation that they might be lesbians, causing Brigit's family particular concern. They are relieved when a young doctor (Hugh Sinclair) proposes marriage and is accepted. But Vere is desolate.

One performance was the lot of Murray Brown's **Fickle Women** (12-15-37, Nora Bayes). Like *Wise Tomorrow* before it, it was staged in hopes of attracting money to allow for a regular run, but once again savage notices buried the hopes. A prostitute takes pity on a woman forced into the trade by her white-slaver husband, cares for the woman's child, helps rehabilitate the woman, and shoots the husband.

Every season brings forth one or two plays that critics suggest might have been a hit in more knowing hands. Dorothy Day Wendell's **Tell Me Pretty Maiden** (12-16-37, Mansfield) was one such play. The author had earned her bread for many years by conducting and writing up interviews of celebrities for Chicago papers. A big new star, Margo Dare (Doris Nolan), is giving her history to the press. She tells them about romping in her jasmine-scented southern garden as a child and later attending a convent school. But as she recites these charming fictions, the audience is shown her real history, with her mother (May Buckley) hanging the wash outside their tenement and her brother (Charles Powers) scrambling over a fence to elude the police, and with her serving time in a reformatory. There is a modicum of truth in her saga of meeting her backer, but she does not reveal that the meeting occurred in a low-class nightspot while the man (Alan Bunce) was drunk. As the interview ends she is handed the latest newspaper, revealing that her brother was killed attempting to break out of prison.

The procession of flops was relieved by the arrival of Jed Harris's mounting of *A Doll's House* at the

Morosco on the 27th. Thornton Wilder had made the new translation and Ruth Gordon was starred. As had happened with several recent Ibsen revivals, some critics dismissed the play as "old hat," "a great deal of excitement about a dead issue," and "a little embarrassing now." Almost every critic also had some quibble about Gordon's interpretation, with most, perhaps, unhappy with her last-act transition from child-wife to independent woman. Overall, however, they admired her work. Many similarly praised Dennis King's complacent, patronizing husband, Sam Jaffe's shrewd, guileful Krogstad, and Paul Lukas's sympathetic Dr. Rank. Reservations did not deter theatregoers, so the play chalked up a remarkable 144-performance run.

The parade of failures resumed with Richard Carlson's **Western Waters** (12-28-37, Hudson), which, like *Robin Landing*, was set in eighteenth-century backwaters, this time on an Ohio River flatboat. A Massachusetts man, Josiah Cutler (Thomas Chalmers), and his family hope to become pioneers in the Ohio Valley. They have aboard a supposed parson, Rev. Barnabas Harpe (S. Thomas Gomez), unaware he is a French land agent planning to deprive the Yankees of their claim. A swaggering young man named Kaintuck (Van Heflin) joins the party and soon seduces Cutler's sex-hungry older daughter, Penelope (Joan Wheeler). But he wins the family's acceptance and gratitude when he agrees to marry the girl and then exposes Harpe.

Sheldon Noble's **One Thing After Another** (12-28-37, Fulton) was a comedy that misfired badly. A group of gangsters, needing $100,000, decide to kidnap a rich man's son and send three punks to carry out the kidnapping at a nightclub. By mistake they blackjack the mob's finger man and take him to a barn. The barn happens to be the very place where an heiress, Eloise Woodward (Ann Mason), has sent her friends on a treasure hunt. Thereafter it requires the rest of the evening to unravel complications.

Kurt Unkelbach's **Straw Hat** (12-30-37, Nora Bayes) was even less adept, ending the year on a distinctly sour note. The Eagle Beach Players is a New Hampshire summer stock group, about to put on its latest opus, *The Livid Sin*. The group is excited, since it has been assured that the author (Melbourne Ford), like George S. Kaufman, ends all his plays with a final curtain. News also has swept the group that a Hollywood talent scout (Gordon Peters) is in the audience. Louise (Sylvia Leigh) is prepared to do anything, absolutely anything, for a screen test. But she is rejected by the agent who thinks he spots more talent in her bashful, former farmboy beau, Ossie (Frederick A. Bell). He informs Ossie that you don't have to have acting ability to act in films. But Ossie proves so hammy that the agent

leaves the place empty-handed. One compensation: the play ran only an hour and forty minutes—including two intermissions.

Although they delighted in almost all of it, most critics were glad that a revival of Thomas Dekker's 338-year-old *The Shoemaker's Holiday,* which ushered in 1938 at the Mercury Theatre on January 1, also ran a mere ninety minutes—without intermission. Orson Welles and John Houseman had cut out much that would seem extraneous or incomprehensible to modern audiences, and Welles had staged the comedy in a fast-paced, bawdy style. John Mason Brown welcomed the "lusty, joyous creation. It bursts with the vitality of the age it mirrors." A stylized London street scene of tall, thin houses of unpainted wood served as a basic setting, while several curtains opened and closed now and then to produce smaller acting spaces. In Dekker's story, Rowland Lacy (Joseph Cotten) sends a substitute off to the wars so that he can remain in London in disguise and take a job as a shoemaker's apprentice in order to woo Rose Otley (Alice Front), whose father (John Hoystradt) opposes the match. Lacy takes work with Simon Eyre (Whitford Kane) and shares in the festivities at evening's end, when Eyre becomes Lord Mayor of London. Lacy's bested rival, Master Hammon (Vincent Price), marries another girl (Ruth Ford) on the rebound, only to have her first husband (Elliott Reid), presumed dead in battle, return home to reclaim her. In repertory with *Julius Caesar,* the comedy tallied sixty-nine performances.

J. B. Priestley's West End drama **Time and the Conways** (1-3-38, Ritz) ran about half as long. Mrs. Conway (Dame Sybil Thorndike) and her four daughters and two sons are celebrating the birthday of one daughter, Kay (Jessica Tandy). In a dream Kay envisions the dismal futures awaiting her and her siblings. She, for example, will not become a great novelist but merely write a sob-sister column for a newspaper and have an unhappy affair with a married man. So when her mother foretells bright futures for the whole family, Kay can say nothing.

Since all the actors in Vincent Duffy and Irene Alexander's **The Greatest Show on Earth** (1-5-38, Playhouse) represented animals, they were bedecked in fascinatingly stylized costumes that were basically ordinary street clothes deftly modified to suggest the animals they were portraying. Their makeup accentuated the transition. Critics also found humor and grace in the settings of the various animal cages, although they failed to specify what humor or what grace. The lone problem was the heavy-handed play itself. At the Norton Brothers' Circus, Slimy (Edgar Stehli), a writhing, hissing snake, goads the lions—Leo (Anthony Ross),

Laddie (Frank Lovejoy), Princess (Dorothy Patten), and Kitty (Margaret Perry)—to kill their keeper and escape. After the breakout ends in tragedy, Slimy moves on to see what trouble he can promote among the bears.

Horace Jackson's **Yr. Obedient Husband** (1-10-38, Broadhurst) told of the drinking, the wild spending, and the occasional skirt-chasing of Richard Steele (Fredric March)—he of the famous team of eighteenth-century scribblers Addison and Steele—and of how his behavior regularly exasperated his loving, loyal wife, Prue (Florence Eldridge). Possibly in revenge for having to slog through *The Spectator* in college, playgoers shunned the offering.

In Matt and Sam Taylor's **Stop-Over** (1-11-38, Lyceum), Bartley Langthorne (Sidney Blackmer), a fading actor, comes seeking peace and quiet at his retreat just off the Albany Post Road. He does not find it. First of all, pranksters have put up a sign saying "Tourists Accommodated," so unwanted visitors soon impose on him. Then Matt Scanlon (Arthur Byron), a gunman, appears. It turns out that he has come to console his wife (Alice Ann Baker), Langthorne's housekeeper, since their son is on trial for murder. But after Scanlon escapes and the others are persuaded to find lodgings elsewhere, Langthorne realizes the excitement has invigorated him.

Tortilla Flat (1-12-38, Henry Miller's) was the second Steinbeck novel to reach the stage during the season. But this time the novel had not apparently been conceived with the stage in mind, nor had Steinbeck himself adapted it. Jack Kirkland, of *Tobacco Road* fame, had assumed the task. The results were far from satisfactory, so the play folded after five performances. Danny (Edward Woods), by nature a hobo, is not pleased to learn that he has inherited property, even if the property is merely a couple of shacks. One of the local street women, Sweet Ramirez (Erin O'Brien-Moore), urges him to keep them and moves into one with him. Life soon becomes so complicated and pressing that Danny is relieved when one of the shacks burns. He decides to burn the other.

A fire in a tenement provided the opening and closing scenes of the fifth edition of the FTP's *Living Newspaper,* Arthur Arent's **One-Third of a Nation** (1-17-38, Adelphi). Its title came from Roosevelt's often-quoted remark in his second inaugural address to the effect that "one-third of a nation is ill-housed, ill-clad, and ill-nourished." The play, taking an average citizen (Clarence R. Chase) on a tour, professed to offer a history of residential real estate in America, but especially in New York, beginning with colonial land grants to Trinity Church, and moving on to the subsequent indifference of the church as well as such huge landowners as the Astors and the Wendells to the cheap housing built

on their land, the breeding of crime and disease in the slums, and the recent battle in Congress over the Wagner-Steagall Act, concluding with a plea for government-subsidized housing. Howard Bay's four-story, antiquated tenement building dominated the stage, with the forestage used for some other scenes. Motion pictures were employed to depict various real slums. Whether or not they agreed with its politics, most critics applauded the play's searing power. It became one of the FTP's major successes, running for 237 performances in New York alone (at an 83¢ top). Local problems were incorporated when it was mounted in other cities.

George Abbott was not having a good season. His third successive flop was John Baragwanath and Kenneth Simpson's **All That Glitters** (1-19-38, Biltmore). After the snooty Mrs. E. Mortimer Townsend (Helen Gardner) snubs a lady friend of the waggish Morgan "Muggy" Williams (Allyn Joslyn), Williams decides to get even. He picks up a Latin American streetwalker, Elena (Arlene Francis), and passes her off to Mrs. Townsend as a Spanish countess. The old lady falls for it, but so does Williams's close friend George Ten Eyck (Judson Laire), who elopes with Elena. Williams straightens out matters and gets an apology from Mrs. Townsend, on condition he does not tell the press how she was duped.

There was even less enthusiasm for Paul Hervey Fox and Benn W. Levy's **If I Were You** (1-24-38, Mansfield), which, according to its programs, had been "suggested by an idea" in a Thorne Smith novel, *Turnabout*. Overhearing her employer, Arthur Blunt (Bernard Lee), claim he is on the verge of finding a way to alter the sex of humans, Nora (Betty Field), an Irish maid, employs an old Irish curse to effect the change at once. Mrs. Blunt (Constance Cummings) becomes deep-voiced and wears pants, while Blunt speaks in trebly tones and dons laces. This provides all manner of awkward situations until Nora changes the couple back again.

An FTP group that had been performing older plays in Roslyn, New York, brought its repertory into Maxine Elliott's Theatre for a brief stand beginning January 25. The troupe offered Eugene O'Neill's *Diff'rent* (2-4-21), telling of the degeneration of an embittered spinster; George Bernard Shaw's *Pygmalion*; Clyde Fitch's *Captain Jinks of the Horse Marines* (2-4-01), spotlighting an American-born opera singer who returns from Europe to find romance with an officer who has bet friends that he can woo and win her; Shakespeare's *Coriolanus*; and one new anti-war play by the German refugee Ernst Toller, **No More Peace,** which was offered on January 28 in a translation by Edward Crankshaw and which had a few songs with W. H. Auden lyrics. On the heights of Mount Olympus, Napoleon (Douglas Campbell) contests the argument of St. Francis (Jay Velie) that the world truly wants peace. Napoleon manages to send a telegram to the little principality of Dunkelstein, announcing war has been declared. The populace immediately elects a dictator (Frank Daly), a small barber with a Charlie Chaplin mustache and whose name is Cain. Only when the barber is shown to have foreign blood does the war fever abate.

An English and an Irish play followed, and both were hits. Ian Hay's **Bachelor Born** (1-25-38, Morosco) centered on Charles Duncan (Frederick Leister), a housemaster at a small school. He entertains the three daughters of an old flame and their aunt (Phoebe Foster), all the while he is battling the Rev. Edmund Ovington (Philip Tonge), the school's troublesome headmaster, who is trying to oust him. The girls enlist the support of the students to help dispose of the headmaster and put Duncan in his place. The comedy ran a full year.

Another priest and another schoolmaster faced off in Paul Vincent Carroll's **Shadow and Substance** (1-26-38, Golden). Both the haughty, cold Canon Skerritt (Cedric Hardwicke) and the passionate, anti-clerical Dermot O'Flingsley (Lloyd Gough), who detest one another, are loved by the canon's serving girl, Brigid (Julie Haydon). A book by O'Flingsley provokes a riot in his village, during which Brigid is killed. Her death leads to an understanding and reconciliation between the two men. The play, first done at Dublin's Abbey Theatre, had been written off as a failure during its pre-Broadway tryout, but some reworking and glowing performances by the principals and supporting players such as Sara Allgood (as a country gossip) earned it a 274-performance run.

Two weeks earlier, Jack Kirkland, who had won success and fortune adapting an Erskine Caldwell novel, had failed with an adaptation of a John Steinbeck book. Now another Erskine Caldwell novel reached the stage, this time dramatized by Alfred Hayes and Leon Alexander. **Journeyman** (1-29-38, Fulton) was sourly received and departed after a five-week struggle. A hard-drinking, hard-gambling charlatan, Semon Dye (Will Geer), passes himself off as an itinerant preacher. Coming to the Horeys' down-and-out Georgia farm, he holds a revival meeting ("excitingly done with the congregation giving a good picture of what happens at a Holy Rollers' meeting"), wins money and a car from the farmer (Raymond Van Sickle), seduces the farmer's wife (Eugenia Rawls), then heads off for parts unknown after threatened with exposure by the farmer's more worldly ex-wife (Ruth Abbott).

The plot of Francis Edwards Faragoh's **Sunup to Sundown** (2-1-38, Hudson) was the sort generally embraced by the FTP. But the new protest drama was a commercial production, although hardly a successful one, closing after its first week. What that play protested was the use of child labor. Its action moved between two large tobacco barns. There Andy (Eugene Gericke), a youngster of about seventeen, runs away after learning he will not be allowed to marry Marta (Florence McGee), the fifteen-year-old Mexican girl he has made pregnant. The other youngsters attempt to have Andy's kid brother (Jack Jordan) take his place, but Mr. Brockwell (Carl Benton Reid), the farm owner, learns of the situation, sends Marta and her family away, and orders the other children back to work.

Two of the season's most memorable plays arrived on two successive evenings, albeit both, plagued by horrendously troubled tryouts, had almost closed on the road. The first had to fire its aging star, Richard Bennett, who could no longer remember lines, lost a second important player to illness, and offered Broadway first-nighters a new lead who had been allowed only a single previous performance in his role. At the other play, which received many unfavorable tryout notices, the producer-director had vicious battles with the author, the cast (one of whom he allegedly drove to suicide), and the unions. The first of the pair to arrive was **On Borrowed Time** (2-3-38, Longacre), Paul Osborn's dramatization of a Lawrence Edward Watkin novel. Gramps (Dudley Digges), a salty-tongued curmudgeon, is fearful that after his death, his wife, the cantankerous, sharp-spoken Granny (Dorothy Stickney), will place their young, orphaned grandson, Pud (Peter Holden), in the care of the boy's greedy, moralizing Aunt Demetria (Jean Adair). But Granny dies first, and when the Angel of Death, in the guise of Mr. Brink (Frank Conroy), seems to want Gramps to follow her, the old man chases him up an apple tree and fences him in. Gramps's careless description of the incident convinces Demetria and Dr. Evans (Clyde Franklin) that Gramps has become senile, prompting the doctor to certify that Demetria will hereafter be Pud's guardian. In despair, Pud runs away and climbs up the apple tree, from which he slips and falls. Gramps, seeing the lifeless Pud, releases Mr. Brink and joins them as they head out the garden gate. Mr. Brink tells Pud that they will all be together for eternity, and Pud asks how long eternity is. When Gramps informs him it is a "right smart piece of time," Pud replies that at least they will be together. Gramps assures Pud he is "damn right," at which a voice from heaven, sounding just like Granny's, demands to know why Gramps has to use such language in front of the boy. Hailed by Robert Benchley in the *New Yorker* as a "heart-warming, delightful play," the comedy-fantasy ran nearly ten months. It helped establish the reputation of its young director, Joshua Logan.

Act One: 1930–1944

. . .

Joshua [Lockwood] **Logan** (1908–88) was born in Texarkana, Tex. He studied at Princeton and with Stanislavsky in Moscow. In 1928 he was one of the founders of the University Players, with whom he remained for five years. His first solo directorial assigment on Broadway was in 1935 with *To See Ourselves*.

. . .

Audiences entering the theatre to see producer-director Jed Harris's mounting of Thornton Wilder's **Our Town** (2-4-38, Henry Miller's) were confronted with a bare, dimly lit stage. There was no curtain and no scenery, except for a few spartan chairs and tables. When the audience has assembled and the houselights are lowered, the Stage Manager (Frank Craven), wearing a battered fedora and fumbling with his pipe, saunters onstage, notices the playgoers, and tells them that they are in Grover's Corners, New Hampshire and that it is May 7, 1901. He gives the town's history and points out all the places of interest. He even lets Professor Willard (Arthur Allen) and Editor Webb (Thomas W. Ross) comment on the town's scientific and social backgrounds. Much of Act I, called "Daily Life," focuses on the ordinary pursuits of the town. The Webb family and that of Dr. Gibbs (Jay Fassett) soon claim primary attention, so Act II, "Love and Marriage," describes the courtship and wedding of Emily Webb (Martha Scott) and George Gibbs (John Craven). In Act III, "Death," the families attend the funeral of Emily, who has died in childbirth. (The austere scene, with the black-garbed cast all holding up black umbrellas, soon became the play's most famous moment.) Emily is offered a chance to relive any one special day in her life. She selects her twelfth birthday. But the return is painful, for she realizes that the living cannot appreciate how precious life's small moments really are. Moving back to the cemetery, she finds George crying at her grave. She muses to her mother-in-law (Evelyn Varden), who is buried alongside her, "They don't understand very much, do they?" "No, dear, not very much," Mrs. Gibbs responds. With that, the Stage Manager, who has signaled intermissions by inviting playgoers to go out for a smoke, sends the audience home. Most critics enjoyed the low-keyed acting, especially that of Craven, "the best pipe and pants-pocket actor in the business." And most fell in line with Robert Coleman of the *Daily Mirror*, who welcomed, "a great play, worthy of an honored place in any anthology of American drama," and who continued, "It captures the mind and spirit of this country as few plays of our time have." Like *On Borrowed Time*, the play ran for ten months. It received the season's Pulitzer Prize and made Wilder a name to be reckoned with in the theatre.

. . .

Thornton [Niven] **Wilder** (1897–1975) was born in Madison, Wisc., and educated at Yale and Princeton. His first full-length play, *The Trumpet Shall Sound* (1926), was a failure. But he won acclaim for his novels *The Cabala* (1926) and, more especially, *The Bridge of San Luis Rey* (1927). He then tried his hand at one-acters, several of which, including *The Long Christmas Dinner* (1931), became favorites with amateur groups.

. . .

A short-lived group, taking a name that had been used before and would be employed again, the Experimental Theatre, presented New Yorkers a chance to see Edwin Bjorkman's translation of August Strindberg's **The Bridal Crown** (2-5-38, Vanderbilt), in which a peasant girl (Aurora Bonney) hands over her baby to an old crone, with orders to kill and bury it, so that she may appear at her wedding as a virgin. The play gave only a single performance. Atkinson used the occasion of his review to take note of other offbeat mountings of the season. Although the celebrated Village playhouses of the twenties no longer attracted as much attention as they once had and the term "Off Broadway" had not yet gained wide currency, nonetheless all of Manhattan had small auditoriums doing interesting if short-lived work, and Burns Mantle in his *Best Plays* for the season, under the heading "Off Broadway," devoted five densely packed pages to recording the productions. Even *Variety* began to review some of the mountings in its "Plays on Broadway" section. The productions included, at various venues, a *Macbeth* with John Cromwell and Margaret Wycherly, *The Trojan Women* with Mildred Dunnock among the players, and a wide assortment of old and new plays.

The first of two Robert Ardrey plays—both failures—to premiere in February was **How to Get Tough About It** (2-8-38, Martin Beck). Matt Grogan (Kent Smith), a drifter and sometime union thug, seduces and deserts Kitty (Katherine Locke). She is taken in by the sympathetic Dan Grimshaw (Myron McCormick), who has turned an old scow into a houseboat. Later, when Matt attempts to reenter her life, Kitty at first succumbs to his blandishments, but then rejoins Dan and helps chase Matt out of town.

A not dissimilar story was told in Martin Berkeley's **Roosty** (2-14-38, Lyceum). The police foil a holdup, killing most of the robbers. One man, Stuff Nelson (William Harrigan), flees, but his young son, Roosty (James McCallion), is caught. A compassionate judge (William Fay) sends the boy to be looked after by Ed Shuster (Russell Hardie), an enlightened farmer about to wed a pretty schoolmarm (Katherine Emery). Ed and Roosty hit it off, but Stuff suddenly shows up, pretending his car has run out of gas and asking to stay the night. At first, Roosty leans toward leaving with his father. But in the end he decides to remain with Ed. McCallion received the sort of enthusiastic notices that promise stardom, but his Broadway career proved short and undistinguished.

Ina Claire and her largely British supporting cast enabled Frederick Lonsdale's pleasant but thin London high comedy **Once Is Enough** (2-15-38, Henry Miller's) to inch beyond the 100-performance mark. The incomparable comedienne played an English duchess whose husband (Hugh Williams) has fallen madly in love with a beautiful, blue-eyed married woman (Viola Keats). Although she refuses to divorce the duke, the duchess otherwise tells him he is free to run off if he cares to. By evening's end, the duchess has allowed her husband to see that blue-eyes is a gold digger, so the couple is reconciled.

Since the FTP's 1936 production of T. S. Eliot's *Murder in the Cathedral* had been taken off while still drawing good houses, Gilbert Miller risked reviving the play—at the Ritz on the 16th—with an English cast headed by Robert Speaight, who reportedly had played Becket more than 600 times in England. Miller lost his gamble, closing the drama after two and a half weeks.

Robert Ardrey's second play of the month was **Casey Jones** (2-19-38, Fulton). The curtain rose to show "a swaying, rattling locomotive pounding the rails." Casey (Charles Bickford) is fifty, and his eyesight is failing. Sometimes he goes through stop signals; at other times he stops when he imagines he sees such a signal, though none is there. He is finally relegated to a job in a dingy, backwater station. But it proves too unexciting for him, so he manages to flag down his old locomotive and climbs aboard. A subplot recounted the romance of Casey's daughter, Portsmouth (Peggy Conklin) and his fireman, Jed (Van Heflin). Allowances were made for Bickford, suffering from a bad case of laryngitis on opening night. Among Mordecai Gorelik's other highly praised settings was the exterior of a roundhouse. But critics felt that like all Ardrey's work, his latest, for all his sharp character studies, was "diffuse" or "spineless," and the direction of young Elia Kazan not much help. The Group Theatre mounting survived for three weeks.

Variety summed up the critical consensus about S. N. Behrman's **Wine of Choice** (2-21-38, Guild) when it observed, "In brilliance of dialog it measures up to his best writings, without providing the mirth that some others were accompanied with." As a result, it became the latest failure in the Theatre Guild's unfortunate season. The divorced Wilda Doran (Claudia Morgan) exclaims, "Think of it—after all these years to be suddenly so crowded with alternatives." The choices

she is speaking of are the two men courting her, the rich "Napoleon of indecision," Larry Sears (Donald Cook) and the new senator, Ryder Gerrard (Leslie Banks). But both men take a back seat with the arrival of Dow Christophsen (Theodore Newton), a young left-wing writer seeking a publisher for his muckraking novel about a sharecroppers' strike that failed. She falls in love with him, and although he is willing to go to bed with her, he deserts her. Left alone, she laments her fate to a charming Lithuanian refugee, Binkie Niebuhr (Alexander Woollcott). A lifelong bachelor with a penchant for matchmaking for other people, he assures her he is heir "to a tradition of patience and tenacity" and will no doubt find someone for her. Critics agreed that Woollcott, "a wee bit like a captive balloon," was the center of attention whenever he was onstage, but their comments on his playing were more kind than favorable.

Al Woods was as personally popular as Woollcott, but that did not save him from devastating notices and quick disaster when he produced a play that the FTP had tried out in California, Conrad Seiler and Max Marcin's **Censored** (2-26-38, 46th St.). The comedy was the first of seven successive openings, apart from two sponsored by the FTP, to run no more than a week and a half. Thanks to gangster backing, Art Richmond (Frank Lovejoy) is finally able to produce his blunt-spoken play about war and sex behind the lines (at a French bawdy house). The police, goaded by a frustrated old spinster, Miss Clutterbuck (Carolyne Norton), raid the show and haul Art and his actors into court. They are found guilty of salaciousness but a judge (Perce Benton) suspends the sentence if Miss Clutterbuck is allowed to rewrite and restage the show. She eliminates all the naughtiness and remounts a scene in the trenches with grass-carpeting and dainty flowerpots in the front line. The actors call a strike.

Katherine Dayton's **Save Me the Waltz** (2-28-38, Martin Beck) might have made the basis for a comic operetta but was hopeless as a straight comedy. To ensure a badly needed loan, the dictator (John Emery) of Jadlovia attempts to arrange a marriage between the Jadlovian Princess Claudine (Jane Wyatt) and Prince George (Leslie Barrie) of Holstein-Gastnau. Calling on the royal family, whom he had deposed, he falls in love with the princess himself. Her good influences prompt him to abandon his dictatorship and restore the monarchy. Leo G. Carroll and Mady Christians, as the droll, modest king and his charming if mischievously opportunistic queen, won the best notices.

Ernest Hammond (William Lynn), the hero of Edward Caulfield's **There's Always a Breeze** (3-2-38, Windsor), is a twittery bank clerk who never fails to wear his rubbers or carry his umbrella because "you never can tell when it'll rain." He stumbles upon his boss (Curtis Cooksey) and the boss's mistress (Sara Floyd) in a deadly argument. Attempting to grab the mistress's gun, Ernest apparently shoots and kills his boss. Although it takes some time before anyone will believe the milquetoast, his story eventually makes Ernest a celebrity. He receives fan mail from all across the nation, except, of course, Maine and Vermont. Fame starts to go to his head until it is discovered the fatal shot had been fired by someone else. Among the many applauded supporting players were the aging Cecilia Loftus as a boozy mother-in-law hoping to cash in on her son-in-law's notoriety by writing her memoirs, onetime silent-screen favorite Blanche Sweet as Ernest's baffled spouse, and young Hume Cronyn as an uproariously funny shyster lawyer.

The same evening, the FTP brought in the first of two March offerings that countered Broadway's doldrums. William Du Bois's **Haiti** (3-2-38, Lafayette) told how Napoleon's troops were sent to the island to put down a seemingly successful rebellion led by Toussaint L'Ouverture (Louis Sharp). The black insurgents are driven into the hills, where they wait until boredom and debauchery debilitate the whites, then, led by Henri Christophe (Rex Ingram), they drive out the French. With both the play and Ingram receiving highly laudatory notices, the drama ran in Harlem for twenty-one weeks at a 55¢ top.

Theatricalizations of the lives of English writers had failed recently in *Aged 26* and *Yr. Obedient Husband*; one failed again with Ernest Pascal and Edwin Blum's **I Am My Youth** (3-7-38, Playhouse). This time the central figure was William Godwin (Charles Waldron), the novelist and Socialist. Shelley (Frank Lawton) urges him to write a book countering what the poet sees as Malthus's pessimistic and reactionary theories. Shelley also deserts his wife to run off with Godwin's daughter, Mary (Sylvia Weld). Godwin's stepdaughter (Jean Bellows) is discovered to be having an affair with Byron. Fanny (Linda Watkins), who had always believed herself Godwin's child, commits suicide after learning that she is illegitimate. Godwin goes on with his writings.

Broadway had even less interest in Russian royalty when Jessica Lee and Joseph Lee Walsh's **Empress of Destiny** (3-9-38, St. James) attempted to show how Catherine (Elissa Landi), an obscure German, finding her new husband, Prince Peter (Glenn Hunter), hopelessly impotent and childish, arranged for his removal and turned herself into Catherine the Great. Covering forty-four years, the play was gorgeously costumed and set, but its physical attractions could not override its dullness.

For more than a decade, Lula Vollmer had been trying to recapture the applause she had received for *Sun-Up* (5-25-23) and *The Shame Woman* (10-16-23). She made one final, unavailing endeavor with **The Hill Between** (3-11-38, Little). Brent Robbins (Philip Ober), a mountain boy who left his home and became a successful city doctor, is married to a mean, selfish wife (Dorothy Patten). He takes her back to his mountains, where her worst nature comes out. She soon tries to seduce one (Philip Faversham) of his boyhood friends, who attempts suicide in shame. Brent would remain in the mountains, but his old love, Julie (Sara Haden), the selfsacrificing girl who long before had insisted he was meant for a better world, once again sends him on to the city.

The FTP's second March success was E. P. Conkle's **Prologue to Glory** (3-17-38, Maxine Elliott's). Although critics recognized that Conkle's drama was far more sentimentalized than John Drinkwater's earlier *Abraham Lincoln*, they found it equally compelling. The play examined a much earlier part of Lincoln's life than Drinkwater's drama had. Not wanting it said "I set all my life on a stump like him," young Abe (Stephen Courtleigh) leaves his father's farm to accept a job as a store clerk in New Salem, Illinois. He wins the respect of the townsfolk when he bests the town's boastful wrestling champ (Roderick Maybee) in a match. And he falls in love with Ann Mayes Rutledge (Ann Rutledge, said to be the original's great-grandniece), who helps with his book learning and manners. Before long he is running for office, promising to fight to have the Sangamon River diverted to allow for more river traffic. After Ann dies unexpectedly in an epidemic, Abe resolves to move on and to study law in Springfield. He asks friends to "Tell Pa and Ma I won't be back t'stump that land unless—Springfield don't agree with me!" Like *Haiti* up in Harlem, *Prologue to Glory* ran twenty-one weeks, albeit at a $1 top.

Even more so than Lula Vollmer, Clare Kummer had once been hailed as a bright hope of American playwriting, the mistress of high comedy. But her muse, too, had flown, although she continued to bring out occasional new pieces. **Spring Thaw** (3-21-38, Martin Beck), like several of her prior works, was written with her son-in-law, the tiny, dry-humored Roland Young, in mind. She did not serve him well this time. Young's Willie Granger, like Ina Claire's duchess, is saddled with a promiscuous spouse (Lillian Emerson), who complains to him, "You simply haven't an ounce of joie de vivre." And, like the duchess, Willie is surprisingly complaisant. Mrs. Grainger's latest is Georges Lebard (Guido Nadzo), a self-pitying pianist, given to theatrically preposterous suicide attempts. The pair decide to elope, but miss their boat. So they head off to Willie's cabin in the Adirondacks, where Willie has gone to be alone. Since only the bedroom is heated, all three crawl in bed together. But then Georges, who has a cold, also has second thoughts and decides to find romance with one of Willie's two sisters, both of whom have also invaded the cabin.

Joseph A. Fields and Jerome Chodorov, who would go on to better things, came a cropper with their satire on Hollywood, **Schoolhouse on the Lot** (3-22-38, Ritz). Peter Driscoll (Onslow Stevens), a banker sent to negotiate a $2 million loan at Mercury Pictures, learns that the studio's spoiled-brat, seven-year-old star, Dolly Shepard (Betty Philson), has screamed so loud because her teacher gave her bad grades that the teacher, Carol Birch (Mary Mason), is to be fired. Peter gives Dolly a much deserved spanking. The studio would sue him, but a compromise is reached, and Peter and Carol fall in love.

Ethel Barrymore's second vehicle of the season was **Whiteoaks** (3-23-38, Hudson), which Mazo de la Roche adapted from her own novel *Whiteoaks of Jalna*. It was a curious affair with Barrymore, "looking bewilderingly like her brother Lionel," made up to play a 101-year-old woman, "wearing a lace cap as if it were a matriarchal crown and brandishing her walking stick in sceptered majesty." Moreover, she appeared only in the first two of the play's three acts. The story was simple. The family of querulous, whiny Gran Whiteoaks maneuver to be named in her will, but, after she dies, they learn that she has left her money to Finch (Stephen Haggard), a seemingly unstable grandchild who wants to study music. Barrymore's tour de force kept the play in New York until July, and she took it out for a cross-country tour the following season.

Hardie Albright's **All the Living** (3-24-38, Fulton) was taken from Victor R. Small's *I Knew 3000 Lunatics*. Offering a variety of pictures, some amusing, some sad, of life in a mental institution, it used one story to tie all its divergent scenes together. Gilbert Kromer (Sanford Meisner) is convinced he has discovered a cure for one type of insanity, but the authorities will not allow him to test his Sulphur X on humans. A new staff member, John Merritt (Leif Erickson), takes the risk and succeeds in making a pathologically mute young boy (Alfred Ryder) talk. Merritt is discharged, but, in gratitude, Kromer backs away from his own courtship of a nurse (Elizabeth Young) whom he knows Merritt loves.

Having closed *Amphitryon 38* while it was still drawing profitable houses, the Lunts joined with the Theatre Guild to mount Stark Young's translation of Chekhov's *The Sea Gull* at the Shubert on the 28th. The Lunts hoped to use this tale of a self-centered actress and her coterie who bring despair to the artistic youngsters around them as part of a repertory with which they would tour the country in the following season. Perhaps surprisingly, although no effort was spared on the pro-

duction, the Lunts received some disappointing notices. No one questioned their brilliant technique, but some did lament that their interpretations—Lunt's Trigorin and Fontanne's Madame Trepleff—did not seem "to have been approached from within." More to many critics' liking were Richard Whorf's Constantine, Sydney Greenstreet's Dr. Sorin, and Uta Hagen's Nina.

Up on a rooftop theatre, Clemente Giglio offered New Yorkers **Pasquale Never Knew** (3-30-38, Nora Bayes), a play he supposedly wrote in Italian, then had translated and performed by actors who normally played in Italian for the Italian-American community. Giglio himself took the leading role of an immigrant father who is thrown for a loss when his lofty dreams for his young children all come to nought. New Yorkers chose not to accept the offering. The play lasted three performances.

Just short of two weeks later, the same playhouse was home to the lone performance of **Reunion** (4-11-38, Nora Bayes). The drama was written, produced, and backed by Harvard graduates, with coproducer Norman H. White, Jr., writing it under the pen name Ambrose Elwell, Jr. A young Harvard graduate (Andrew J. Fox, Jr.), despondent over the loss of his wife, sails for Germany and takes work with the Nazis, developing a poison gas. He remains unhappy, even though a co-worker (Dodee Wick), a pretty Michigan graduate, is clearly fond of him. Not until he returns home for his tenth reunion and meets a classmate's widow does he begin to get hold of himself.

George Abbott broke his short string of failures when he brought in what *Variety* hailed as "the funniest play of the season" and John Mason Brown called "a veritable Utopia of farce." Clifford Goldsmith's **What a Life** (4-13-38, Biltmore) is set in the office of Central High's principal. Henry Aldrich (Ezra Stone), a mischievous, fun-loving student who shows no promise of following his father to Princeton, has been summoned there. Instead of studying his *Hamlet,* he has been drawing a picture of a bespectacled whale, labeled Moby Bradley, which has fallen into the hands of the principal—Mr. Bradley (Vaughan Glaser). His mother (Lea Penman) also has been summoned to school, but she is willing to forget the matter and even to give Henry money to attend his junior prom if he does well in his history exam. That presents a problem. He tells the principal's secretary (Ruth Matteson) that his history book disappeared about three weeks ago. Asked why he failed to report it at the time, he replies, "I didn't need it then." He does well on the exam until it is discovered he cheated. To make matters worse, he is accused of stealing and hocking the school orchestra's instruments. But the police prove that Henry's rival (James Cormer) for a date with pert little Barbara Pearson (Betty Field) is the real thief. Henry finally does manage to get to the prom, even if he has to borrow their carfare from Barbara. The comedy piled up 538 performances, the season's biggest hit, and Burns Mantle predicted Broadway would hear more of Goldsmith. It never did, since his subsequent livelihood came from the long-running radio program suggested by the play.

Spring revivals began in earnest with two short-lived mountings. Estelle Winwood abandoned her tour of *Tonight at 8:30* to play Mistress Page in a hyper-active *The Merry Wives of Windsor,* which appeared at the Empire on the 14th. Many critics felt she and Effie Shannon as Dame Quickly were the mounting's sole redeeming features. An even more botched and undistinguished resurrection was that of *The Wild Duck* at the 49th Street on the 16th.

By contrast, Somerset Maugham's 1921 hit, *The Circle,* was given a skillful, glittering revival at the Playhouse on the 18th. Grace George was now the wife who had run off with her lover (Dennis Hoey) and years later returns to visit her since grown-up son (Bramwell Fletcher) just as his wife (Tallulah Bankhead) elects to run off with her own lover (John Emery). The consensus was that the play had not aged and possibly had even improved with time. Some critics held reservations about George's casting (she was deemed too good-natured) but Bankhead (in a role first played on Broadway by Winwood) was seen as recovering from her Cleopatra fiasco and giving what several reviewers thought was her best American performance to date. The comedy ran its prescheduled nine weeks.

Trojan Incident (4-21-38, St. James), Philip H. Davis's reworking of Homer and Euripides' tale of the plight of Troy's women following the fall of their city, mixed drama and dance. Davis's flowery dialogue and the rather savage dances of Helen Tamiris, who played Cassandra, failed to blend, so this FTP offering closed shop after twenty-six performances.

One of the lions outside the New York Public Library and several of the library's imposing rooms were settings for Robert Steiner and Harry Horner's **Escape This Night** (4-22-38, 44th St.). A refugee writer (Arnold Korff) and his wife (Ellen Hall) are hunted down by terrorists in the employ of a fascist dictator. The wife is shot and killed, but the husband is rescued at the last moment.

The Mercury Theatre's last production for the season was a revival of Shaw's treatise on the seeming inevitability of war, *Heartbreak House,* which it brought out at its playhouse on the 29th. Critics divided sharply on how well the play stood up, but for the most part approved of the playing. Orson Welles, in makeup "so thick that he almost seems to be wearing a mask," was hailed as the octogenarian Captain Shotover. (Some

commentators felt the makeup was meant to suggest Shaw himself.) A few thought that Vincent Price's Hector Hushabye was occasionally hammy, that George Coulouris's Boss Mangan was too much of a caricature, and that Geraldine Fitzgerald's Ellie was beautiful but mechanical. Mady Christians's affectionate Hesione Hushabye was universally applauded. The comedy gave six weeks' worth of performances as part of the troupe's repertory.

Last season the Theatre Guild had fallen one play short in the number of attractions it had promised its subscribers. To make up belatedly for the shortfall, it staged John Boruff and Walter Hart's dramatization of Dalton Trumbo's novel **Washington Jitters** (5-2-38, Guild). Half the subscribers saw the play during three weeks of previews (an unheard-of length for previews at the time), the remaining half during the three weeks that the play kept going after thumbs-down notices. A meek sign painter, Henry Hogg (Fred Stewart), delivering a sign marked "Co-ordinator" to one of the tri-lettered New Deal bureaucracies, is mistaken by a radio newsman (Anthony Ross) for the real co-ordinator and asked for his opinions. Suddenly embrazened, he offers his ideas of how to run the government. The newsman broadcasts his comments, and both the Administration and the opposition assume Henry is the head of the office. To please both sides, he promises the one to speak for a new bill and the other side to speak against it. When the error comes to light, it is decided that Henry cannot be fired, since he was never hired. Henry takes to the airwaves and denounces both parties. His speech is so effective that Republican and Democratic politicos alike approach him about running for president in 1940.

May's remaining two novelties were also failures. In Maxwell Selser's **Eye on the Sparrow** (5-3-38, Vanderbilt), a flighty widow (Catharine Doucet) returns from Europe to learn her children (Katherine Deane and Montgomery Clift) have sold virtually all the family possessions to pay off their late father's debts. They move to Greenwich Village, where the daughter flirts for a time with the idea of marrying for money and the son with radical politics, taking a job with the *Daily Worker.* The youngsters soon realize their foolishness. Meanwhile, mama discovers she still owns an almost priceless rug, agrees to help a German author with his book, and receives a proposal from a judge who long ago had been her suitor.

Writer Dan Goldberg, the up-and-coming producer Mike Todd, and the Yiddish comedian Joseph Buloff, who last season had worked together on *Call Me Ziggy,* tried and failed again with **The Man from Cairo** (5-4-38, Broadhurst), which Goldberg took from Yvan Noé's *Christian.* Once a month, Leon, an otherwise quiet, impecunious Budapest clerk, dons a dress suit, calls himself Istvan, and goes out on the town without his wife's knowledge. At the swank Café Rudolph he wins the affection of a beautiful demimondaine, Leni (Helen Chandler). But when Leni traces him to his apartment and learns that he is married, Leon is left to make matters up with his wife (Viola Roache). Some critics were unsure whether Buloff's marked Yiddish mannerisms were appropriate for the role, but they did applaud Frederick Fox's two settings, "both getting salvos of approval from the first-nighters."

At the tag end of the season, the FTP accorded playgoers a chance to see for the first time a relatively new Shaw play, his 1933 opus, **On the Rocks** (6-15-38, Daly's). It told of an English prime minister who decides the only way to save England is to introduce a totalitarian regime, but who quickly is forced out of office after implementing his schemes. Philip Bourneuf, unquestionably made up to resemble Shaw, won plaudits in the lead. Critics were less unanimous about whether Shaw's political debate really also made good theatre. Although some playgoers walked out in protest to the playwright's disparaging remarks about democracy, the comedy, in two separate engagements, tallied sixty-six performances.

1938–1939

The seemingly ineluctable decline of the American theatre continued into the new season. The *Times,* acknowledging that the statistics made "rather gloomy" reading, counted a mere sixty-five new plays; *Variety* tallied sixty-eight. (Neither apparently included the Federal Theatre Project offerings in their figures.) To the reasons for the drop, which had long included the Depression, radio, and films, one new culprit—albeit a temporary one—was added. The New York World's Fair opened on April 20. Initially, producers had hoped that visitors to the exposition would spend their evenings in the theatre. But attendance by out-of-towners at the fair at first was disappointing, and New Yorkers themselves elected to spend their money in Flushing rather than on Broadway. The result was that on two successive spring Saturdays, eleven shows closed—six one week, five the next.

The once busy summer months were, like last season, idle. Indeed, a three-month stretch elapsed between last season's final production and the new year's opener. That play was something of an oddity, a British drama, done in London as *Death on the Table,* whose central

figure was an American gangster. Several critics observed that Guy Beauchamp and Michael Pertwee, the authors of **Come Across** (9-14-38, Playhouse), put some noticeably dated American slang in the mouth of their Chicago hood, Mark Ryder (Arthur Vinton). Having been shot by rival mobsters, he goes to London to have the bullet removed secretly from his chest. To ensure no problems from the surgeon, he kidnaps the man's young son. But just as the surgery is ending, the lights go out. When they come on again, Ryder has been stabbed to death. Scotland Yard is able to pin the killing on one of Ryder's associates, who had hoped for a bigger share of the $500,000 Ryder has stashed away.

Better things might have been expected when the beloved old musical comedy comedian Fred Stone returned to the stage to play the title role in a revival of *Lightnin'* (8-26-18) at the Golden on the 15th. The amusing yarn about a chronic boozer and teller of tall tales had, for a time, been Broadway's long-run champ. John Golden, who had mounted the original, also produced the revival. Critics were kind to the grandfatherly Stone, whose "shaggy, tottery, warm-hearted" style still delighted his loyalists, but they felt the play showed its age. The mounting lingered for just seven weeks.

Several important critics also admired E. P. Ginty's **Missouri Legend** (9-19-38, Empire), on which Max Gordon and Guthrie McClintic lavished a careful staging. Thomas Howard (Dean Jagger) is a leading churchgoer in his small Missouri town. Away from the town he is better known as Jesse James. But even when fleeing a failed robbery he finds time to stop to give Widow Weeks (Mildred Natwick) the money she needs to prevent her home from being repossessed. Of course, he then lies in wait for the collector and repossesses his own cash. After he is tracked down and shot dead by one (Dan Duryea) of the Ford gang, Billy Gashade (José Ferrer) sings at his funeral of "the dirty little coward that shot Thomas Howard and laid poor Jesse in his grave." For all its perceived virtues, the drama could not find an audience.

Although few could perceive any virtues in **Dame Nature** (9-26-38, Booth), which Patricia Collinge drew from André Birabeau's French original, it ran precisely as long—six weeks. Two lonely youngsters meet when sixteen-year-old André Brisac (Montgomery Clift), whose unhappily married parents (Jessie Royce Landis and Onslow Stevens) pay him little attention, buys his school supplies at a store left to fifteen-year-old Leonie Perrot (Lois Hall) by her late aunt. Before long Leonie is pregnant. The news startles André's parents and brings about their reconciliation. They even agree to buy him his first pair of long pants.

The much liked May Vokes, once again in the role of a comic maid, could do nothing for Le Roy Bailey's

Thanks for Tomorrow (9-27-38, Nora Bayes). Her part was purely decorative, since the main story focused on a gambler (Robert Williams) and his blind sister (Eleanor Wells), and on a playboy (Ralph Holmes) and the playboy's sister (Mary Drayton). The gambler has lent the playboy $10,000 and stands to lose it after the playboy shoots a racketeer (Frederick Manatt). But the problems are straightened out, the blind girl regains her sight, and the men marry each other's sisters.

Although most playgoers assumed that Clare Boothe's **Kiss the Boys Goodbye** (9-28-38, Henry Miller's) spoofed the search for someone to play Scarlett O'Hara in *Gone with the Wind,* she muddied the waters in the preface to the play's published edition by insisting it was an attack on "Southernism," which she claimed "may possibly have been the inspiration or forerunner of Fascism." On a train taking Lloyd Lloyd (Millard Mitchell), a director, and his discovery, the southern belle Cindy Lou Bethany (Helen Claire), to Connecticut, a conductor (Wyman Holmes) suggests the girl who plays Velvet O'Toole will have to be "half Hepburn, half Bette Davis, half Myrna Loy." At the Connecticut home of Horace Rand (Philip Ober), an editor, she is slated to meet the film's producer, Herbert Z. Harner (Sheldon Leonard), known not all that affectionately to his colleagues as "God Almighty." Cindy Lou lays on her southern drawl, her southern upbringing, and her southern family connections, enticing all the men who are weekend guests at the home. Harner is ready to reject her, until one of the men antagonizes her and she butts him in the stomach like a nanny goat, just like her ol' southern mammy taught her to. Her passionate outburst prompts Harner to sign her. But when he attempts to seal the arrangement by seducing her, he is shot for his pains. The contract is torn up, and she heads off with a handsome polo player (Hugh Marlowe). Although most of his fellow aisle-sitters shared the view of the *Journal-American*'s John Anderson that "Miss Boothe has not come anywhere near the carbolic hilarity of 'The Women,' " most reviews nonetheless were money notices, winning the comedy 286 performances.

Perhaps the most interesting thing about Irving Gaumont and Jack Sobell's **30 Days Hath September** (9-30-38, Hudson) was its opening date. Edward (Gene Gericke), unwilling to wait for his mother's death, signs away his inheritance rights to a broker in return for an immediate payment. The rights finally wind up in the hands of a gangster (Willie Claire), leading Edward's mother (Leyla Taylor) to jump whenever a car backfires. It remains for Grandma Henny (Alison Skipworth) to calm her daughter, outwit the thugs, and allow Edward to marry.

The FTP launched its season with Theodore Pratt's **The Big Blow** (10-1-38, Maxine Elliott's). For the sake of his ailing mother (Dorothy Raymond), Wade Barnett (Kendall Clark) sells his Nebraska farm and moves to Florida cracker country. He turns successfully to scientific farming. His hard work and his sympathy for Clay (Doe Doe Green), an unjustly hunted Negro, earn him the enmity of his cracker neighbors. When a hurricane levels all the surrounding houses but not the one he has so sturdily built, Wade is granted a new respect. He finally marries Celie (Amelia Romano), the young orphan girl whom the leading cracker (Edwin Cooper) had accused Clay of attempting to rape. Welcomed as a well-written, finely staged melodrama, the play ran for 157 performances.

On the 3rd, Helen Hayes brought *Victoria Regina* into the Martin Beck, following a record-breaking cross-country tour. The play remained there for eleven weeks.

In Chester Erskins's **The Good** (10-5-38, Windsor) Harriet Eldred (Frances Starr), like her minister father, is a hard-hearted, unyielding moralist. Her cold sternness drives her sixteen-year-old son (Jarvis Rice) into the arms of a thirty-year-old choir master (Eric Kalkhurst), and her husband (Robert Keith) into bed with their maid (Florence Sundstrom). After she also sees to it that a young Jewish student (Douglas Parkhirst) is expelled for a $17 theft from school funds and the boy commits suicide, her husband tells her how much he has come to hate her. The beautiful Starr, once a Belasco favorite, was lost in a thankless role. But she only had to play it for a little more than a week.

That was all Joe Bates Smith's **The Devil Takes a Bride** (10-7-38, Cort) lasted, too. And it, too, centered on a vicious woman. Margaret Quimby (Jeannette Chinley) hates her cruel, possibly incestuous father (Louis Hector), so arranges with her lover (Anthony Ross) to kill him. By mistake her uncle (J. Arthur Young) is murdered, but she contrives to have her father convicted for the crime. Deserted by her lover, she is left to face the future alone.

The curtain rose on Moss Hart and George S. Kaufman's **The Fabulous Invalid** (10-8-38, Broadhurst) to disclose the glittering facade of a theatre. The year is 1900, and the Alexandria Theatre is about to open on 42nd Street. But the opening is marred by the death of one of the show's stars, Paula Kingsley (Doris Dalton), and the suicide of her husband and co-star, Laurence Brooks (Stephen Courtleigh). For the next thirty-eight years their ghosts, along with that of an old stage doorman (Jack Norworth), haunt the playhouse. They watch the productions and listen as, even in good times, the occupants bewail how critics, automobiles, films, radio, and unions are killing the theatre. With the coming of the Depression the theatre is turned over to grind movies, then to burlesque, and then is shuttered. But in front of its deteriorating facade a young man

(Lewis Howard), heading a new producing organization, vows to rejuvenate it and tells his associates, "They'll tell you that the theatre is dying. I don't believe it." He assures them anything that can bring them together and hold them together like their love of the theatre means the theatre cannot die. A cast of more than seventy performed numerous roles, enacting snatches from famous dramas and comedies of the past and even bits of musical numbers, with players impersonating George M. Cohan and a blackfaced Eddie Cantor. Posters of the old shows were also flashed on a screen from time to time. Some reviewers suggested that the Alexandria was meant to be the New Amsterdam, and the new group, something like the Mercury Theatre. The *Times*'s Brooks Atkinson spoke for many when he wrote that the play "is a handsome show that has grown out of an attractive impulse to serve the theatre. But it has taken the authors into a branch of writing they have not mastered yet." With its huge operating budget, the show was forced to close after sixty-five performances.

The main attraction at Leslie and Sewell Stokes's **Oscar Wilde** (10-10-38, Fulton) was the tour de force of pudgy Robert Morley in the title role. The play, which opened with Wilde and Lord Alfred Douglas (John Buckmaster) touring together in Algeria, was highlighted by the devastating trial after the writer sues Lord Alfred's father for accusing him of "masquerading as a sodomite," and ended with the ruined Wilde sitting dejectedly in a Paris café. To the surprise of Broadway's smart money, the London hit ran into the spring.

Another tour de force and another surprise success opened at the St. James two nights later, on the 12th, when Maurice Evans presented New Yorkers with their first uncut *Hamlet*. Performances began at 6:45, took a half-hour snack break at 8:15, then resumed until 11:15. Playgoers fearful of being bored were reassured by reviews such as John Mason Brown's in the *Post,* which advised them, "Only those who attend Maurice Evans' production of 'Hamlet' in its entirety will ever know how brief, and yet how exciting and unforgettable, almost every minute can seem." Brown further suggested that Evans's lack of physical presence was quickly overlooked and that his Dane was done in "colors unorthodox in their gaiety. . . . His sadness is in his heart rather than on his face." Despite her marked German accent, Mady Christians's Gertrude was "a triumph of acting," while Katherine Locke offered a poignant, clearly spoken, and intelligently conceived Ophelia. Margaret Webster's fresh direction was also praised, but critics were less taken with the scenery and costumes. At one of Broadway's largest theatres, the drama racked up ninety-six performances.

There was little enthusiasm for another English work, J. B. Priestley's **I Have Been Here Before** (10-13-38,

Guild). At a country inn, a visionary German scientist (Ernest Deutsch) warns a husband (Wilfrid Lawson) and wife (Lydia Sherwood) that the wife will soon run off with a young schoolmaster (Eric Portman), who is also staying there. The husband would kill himself until the scientist assures him that by not doing so he will be a wiser man in his next reincarnation.

Kenyon Nicholson suffered a quick failure with his **Dance Night** (10-14-38, Belasco), a play filled with youngsters and set in a New Jersey dance hall called Gantz's Grove Dansant and the woods around it. Hobie Morgan (Bert Conway), paroled from a reformatory where he had been sent for wounding Roy Titus (Lyle Bettger) after Roy had killed his dog, learns that his sweetheart, Jewel Hendricks (Mary Rolfe), is now engaged to Roy. The boys meet, and Roy attempts to bait Hobie, hoping he will misbehave and thus violate his parole. But even after Roy slugs him, Hobie shows such restraint that Jewel breaks her engagement and goes off with him.

For the second time in as many seasons, Abe Lincoln was the central figure in a major success. This time the play was Robert Sherwood's **Abe Lincoln in Illinois** (10-15-38, Plymouth). The drama was the first to be mounted by a new organization, the Playwrights' Company, which Sherwood, Maxwell Anderson, S. N. Behrman, Sidney Howard, and Elmer Rice had founded after being disillusioned with other producers, especially the Theatre Guild. At the log schoolhouse of Mentor Graham (Frank Andrews), Abe Lincoln (Raymond Massey) is saddened to learn that growing sectionalism prevented many from applauding Webster's plea for "Liberty and Union." A short time later, after his fiancée, Ann Rutledge (Adele Longmire), dies, he weds Mary Todd (Muriel Kirkland), whose fiercely possessive, shrewish nature hints at her eventual madness. He runs for senator from Illinois against the pro-slavery Stephen Douglas (Albert Philips), and soon finds himself a presidential candidate. His victory at the polls provides little elation, since Mary's behaviour and the country's divisive sectionalism have both grown worse. Boarding a train to leave for Washington, he tells those who have come to see him off of an ancient Eastern potentate who ordered his wise men to sum up all that was "true and appropriate" in a single sentence. That sentence was "And this too shall pass." He can only hope that such fatalism is not the real answer. Richard Watts, Jr. of the *Herald Tribune* called the drama "one of the most stirring of American plays. A beautiful and moving portrait of the greatest and most beloved of our national heroes," and he wrote of the lank, craggy Massey's work that "no performance in the modern theatre [was] more beautiful and understanding," adding, "In its sensitivity, its eloquence, its humor, its sympathy, its suggestion of the greatness and the essential sadness of the man, it is so true and magnificent." In the spring, the Pulitzer Prize was added to the play's laurels, helping it to run for more than a year. A 1993 revival failed.

In the four or five weeks that followed, not one of the novelties to raise its curtain lasted more than two weeks. Dorothy Bennett and Hannah Link's **A Woman's a Fool—(To Be Clever)** (10-18-38, National) was set on the terrace of a pink coral bungalow overlooking the sea in Bermuda. Jeff Foster (Ian Keith), a former matinee idol, and his wife, Christine (Vera Allen), have retired there to write plays. A beautiful girl appears, claiming to be Nina Suffieva (Haila Stoddard), an unemployed Russian actress. She hopes Jeff will write a part for her in his newest opus and maybe even come out of retirement to play opposite her. Christine soon recognizes that the girl is a fake and a tramp but, long aware of her husband's roving eye and heart, gives Nina enough leeway to encompass her own doom. Her plan succeeds. Just as things seem to be returning to normal, another beautiful young lady (Margie Ann Kaufman) appears and gushes over Jeff. All Christine can do is exclaim, "Oh, merciful heavens!"

Louis S. Bardoly, who wrote **Case History** (10-21-38, Lyceum), was a Cleveland surgeon, apparently trying to reconcile the dispute between regular physicians and faith healers. Dr. Jim Baker (Ned Wever) knows that Emily Pardee's daughter (Babs Savage) was not cured of polio by a Christian Science practitioner (Grace Fox), but is reluctant to argue with his friend. Unfortunately, Emily (Ruth Abbott) is so convinced of the efficacy of Christian Science that she refuses to allow her stepdaughter (Evelyn Mills) to be treated by physicians for a ruptured appendix until it is too late. When the despondent Emily takes to drink, Baker suggests that this is the time to turn to Christian Science, to allow it to minister to her soul, not her body.

Marcelle Maurette's **Madame Capet** (10-25-38, Cort) was translated into English by George Middleton at the behest of Eva Le Gallienne, who had seen it in Paris. The play dealt with the last fifteen years of Marie Antoinette's life, depicting her not as a frivolous, selfish woman, but as a loving mother and a sympathizer with the lot of the poor, caught unjustly in a revolution provoked by the greed and nastiness of her courtiers. She goes to the guillotine with her head high. Although the theatrical nobility of the part fitted the star's peculiar gifts, neither her acting nor gorgeous settings and costumes could override Middleton's leaden reworking.

Recent events in Germany were mirrored in Oliver H. P. Garrett's **Waltz in Goose Step** (11-1-38, Hudson). In an airplane as he is returning from an aborted coup attempt, the ranting, raving August, The Leader (Leo Chalzel), learns that the pilot (Joseph Straub) may

attempt to kill himself and everyone aboard by crashing the plane. With the help of his associate, Count Gottfried von Laidi [read Putzi Hanfstaengel] (Henry Oscar), the crash is averted. But then August realizes that von Laidi and the pilot, who has Jewish blood, are homosexual lovers. Von Laidi is forced to commit suicide.

Two days after he had scared much of America with his infamous *War of the Worlds* broadcast, Orson Welles spearheaded the Mercury Theatre's revival at its playhouse on the 2nd of Georg Büchner's *Danton's Death*, in a fresh translation by Geoffrey Dunlop. As he had with his other offerings, Welles drastically cut the play and offered it as another intermissionless ninety-minute entertainment. And once again, bare steps and platforms, imaginatively lighted, were substituted for traditional scenery. In the background skull-like masks filled the stage and suggested menacing mobs. Martin Gabel was cast as the revolutionary idealist who eventually falls victim to the cynical Robespierre (Vladimir Sokoloff). At the end of the play, curtains parted to show a guillotine, whose blade droped down accompanied by ominous drum rolls. Welles himself assumed the role of the booming-voiced prosecutor. Many critics felt that the drama was miscast and that the staging was becoming hackneyed. The off-putting notices, coupled with internal problems, brought an end to the year-old group, not long before considered the most exciting force in New York theatricals.

Hugh O'Connell, somewhat heftier after a spell in Hollywood, took the lead in Raymond Knight's **Run Sheep Run** (11-3-38, Windsor). He portrayed Wilkes Potter, a popular New York columnist, who regularly writes about the good old days he remembers in his small hometown, Parksburg, Illinois. But a trip back for a twenty-fifth high school reunion quickly disillusions him. Returning to New York, he discovers he has been followed by the daughter (Virginia Campbell) of his high school sweetheart (Regina Wallace). She would like to become his mistress, but he is content to wed the mistress (Ruth Weston) he already has.

Nor could William Bowers extract much fun from his look at college fraternity life in **Where Do We Go from Here?** (11-15-38, Vanderbilt). Members of the Alpha Tau fraternity at a small mid-western college are dismayed to learn that an alumnus will foreclose on the mortgage to their decrepit old house if they do not fork over $10,000. It takes a young Jewish student (Theodore Leavitt) from another fraternity to alert them to the fact that the alumnus is a swindler and help them out of their predicament.

The officers in Nathanael West and Joseph Schrank's **Good Hunting** (11-21-38, Hudson) could be perceived as even more puerile than the collegians. At his headquarters in an old French church, Brigadier General Hargreaves (Aubrey Mather) grows annoyed when the noise of his guns prevents his getting a sound sleep. He also forbids any discussion of the war at meals. His primpy wife (Estelle Winwood) unwittingly forwards a discarded order to advance. The troops move too far ahead, allowing the Germans to swing behind them. This leads to a meeting between the British and German generals who realize they are old friends and sit down for a friendly chat as the slaughter continues.

Leonard Ide's **Ringside Seat** (11-22-38, Guild) also tried vainly to be a clever satire—this time on Americans' fascination with sensational murder trials. (Philip Dunning was bruited as an uncredited co-author.) Orrin Sturgis (Grant Mitchell) thinks nothing of packing his wife (Lucia Seger) and daughter (Mary Rolfe) into the family car and driving to wherever the latest headline court case is being heard. That's why he turns up at a hotel in a small New York town. The defendant in the case is actually innocent and is being railroaded by gangsters and crooked politicians. Sturgis accidentally uncovers evidence to clear the man. By the trial's end Sturgis's daughter has fallen in love with a spunky reporter (Roy Roberts). The play marked Grant Mitchell's final Broadway appearance.

A lone modest hit, the Group Theatre's production of Clifford Odets's **Rocket to the Moon** (11-24-38, Belasco), relieved the procession of flops. Ben Stark (Morris Carnovsky), a dentist, is badgered by his pushy, shrewish wife (Ruth Nelson), who wants him to earn more money and celebrity by becoming a specialist. To relieve his unhappiness, Ben looks to his thoughtful secretary, Cleo Singer (Eleanor Lynn). Ben's rich father-in-law, the pince-nezed Mr. Prince (Luther Adler) [made up, some said, to resemble the noted financier, Bernard Baruch] also lusts after the girl. Cleo turns both down, especially after the older man tells her that Ben is "as mixed up as the twentieth century." With some reluctance, Ben accepts that he will have to stay with his wife, ruing, "What I don't know would fill a book." *Variety,* summing up the majority opinion, found the drama "less diverting than most predecessors by the same playwright" and "too long." The drama ran for seventeen weeks, grossing, according to the tradesheet, an estimated $110,000.

The sad parade of short-lived duds resumed with **Gloriana** (11-25-38, Little), which an uncredited adaptor took from Ferdinand Bruckner's *Elizabeth von England.* Elizabeth (Blanche Yurka) sends Essex (Boyd Crawford) to his death in the Tower after he is impolitic enough to manifest his shock on seeing her without her red wig and age-concealing makeup. Despite her subsequent success in her war with Spain, the queen resigns herself to a loveless future.

Leda Veerkind (Jeanne Dante) returns from school in Norman Macowan's **Glorious Morning** (11-26-38, Mansfield) to announce that she has had a vision in which God commanded her to make known that He and not the dictator of her homeland, Zagnira, is the supreme ruler. Her family, except for her devoted grandfather (Lee Baker), all tell her she must be quiet. She disobeys, and a religious fervor threatens to sweep the tiny nation. She, her family, and her friends are all led out to the public square to be shot. The drama, dismissed as "a preachment," was produced by Oscar Hammerstein, who made it known that he was dropping the "II" that had followed his name.

Miking and amplification would not become a bane of modern theatricals for several decades, but Victor Victor's **Soliloquy** (11-28-38, Empire) found a novel use for loudspeakers. Having won $100 in a bet and falling in love with a fellow employee (Helen Craig), Jimmy Mimms (John Beal), a bookkeeper saddled with a slovenly, pregnant wife (Ellen E. Lowe), slashes his wife's throat with a bread knife and makes it appear a suicide. A suspicious district attorney (Clarence Derwent) keeps his eye on Jimmy until he seems to give himself away. Brought to trial, he is convicted and sentenced to death. Throughout the evening a prerecorded sound track broadcast Jimmy's private thoughts as opposed to his public utterances.

The French playwright Jacques Deval is said to have written **Lorelei** (11-29-38, Longacre) in English. Whether that was the reason for its inadequacies is moot. Eric Rumpau (Philip Merivale), a Nobel-winning scientist from Leipsic, has left Germany to protest the Nazi regime and taken up residence in the French mountains, from where he propagandizes against the fascists. At the government's behest, his former student, Karen Von Singall (Doris Nolan), comes to lure him home, but instead falls in love with him. However, since her lover is being held hostage against her failing to return home, she does go back to Germany. Rumpau follows her, even though it means certain death. But he hopes his own sacrifice will speed the coming of the "Fourth Reich."

Although the two American novelties that opened next were both failures, neither had an embarrassingly short stand. Elmer Rice's "diffuse," "muddled," and "clumsy" **American Landscape** (12-3-38, Cort) survived for forty-three performances. At seventy-five, Captain Frank Dale (Charles Waldron) has decided to sell both his family's business and the family estate. He is ready to sell the estate to a German-American bund. His grandchildren beg him not to, and even the ghosts of his ancestors come to argue with him. These include Moll Flanders (Isobel Elsom), who tells him she is "by many removes" his grandmother, and Harriet Beecher

Stowe (Lillian Foster), who calls him a cousin. The ghosts also include a Revolutionary War captain (Charles Dingle) and Frank's own son, Anthony (George Macready), who was blinded and killed in the recent war. Tony pleads, "We fought for peace and there is no peace. Hatred walks the world and there is madness in high places. For God's sake, don't succumb to it!" Before he can definitely decide, Frank dies of a heart attack. His heirs agree not to sell.

Philip Barry's **Here Come the Clowns** (12-7-38, Booth) ran twice as long, although many critics admitted to being baffled about what the play really meant. "It hasn't the lucidity and the dramatic vigor necessary for success," Robert Coleman suggested in the *Daily Mirror*. The back room at Ma Speedy's Café des Artistes is reserved for performers and employees from Concannon's Globe Theatre, an old vaudeville house which it adjoins. On this night the customers include a ventriloquist and his wife, a dwarf, a song-and-dance team, and an illusionist. The illusionist (Leo Chalzel) insists he is not a magician since magicians deal in deception, while he is interested only in truth. "But truth is so often an illusion I must, you see, in truth call myself an illusionist." He goads the performers into doing their acts on the café's tiny stage and thus brings them face to face with reality. For example, the ventriloquist (Frank Gaby) is made to admit his wife (Hortense Alden) is an incorrigible lesbian, and so he will leave her. Dan Clancy (Eddie Dowling), an unhappily married stagehand, is looking for God, and seems to find Him only after he is accidentally shot. Knowing the wound is fatal, he philosophizes by asking who is not going to die. "Those who live and die like you" is one man's response.

An English importation, M. J. Farrell and John Perry's **Spring Meeting** (12-8-38, Morosco), was a near miss, falling just two performances shy of the charmed 100-performance mark. It told of an Irish country gentleman (A. E. Matthews) willing to spend a fortune on his horses and stables but not on his family. His daughters marry to be away from him, and the widowed mother (Gladys Cooper) of one of his new sons-in-law resolves to reform him.

At Harlem's Lafayette Theatre on the 16th, the FTP brought out an all-black revival of Shaw's *Androcles and the Lion,* with a program note comparing the persecution of the blacks to the persecution of Christians in ancient Rome. Negro spirituals were substituted for traditional Christian hymns. The offering ran for thirteen weeks. (One week later, at the Ritz, the FTP unveiled a version of **Pinocchio** for children of all ages, which many felt straddled the line between straight play and musical extravaganza.)

The uncut *Hamlet* aside, the season's most memorable revival may well have been Sutton Vane's tale of ship passengers who come to realize that they are dead and sailing for Eternity, *Outward Bound*. The presentation opened on the 22nd at the Playhouse with Helen Chandler and Alexander Kirkland as newlyweds, Bramwell Fletcher as the boozing Mr. Prior, Florence Reed as the snooty Mrs. Cliven Banks, Vincent Price as the Rev. William Duke, Louis Hector as a pompous businessman, and Thomas Chalmers as the Rev. Frank Thompson, whose task is to examine the passengers. All but the last two had made their first-act appearances when a bedraggled figure in a pork-pie hat, black alpaca cape, and tippet of fur and carrying a large knitting bag made a supposedly quiet entrance backing in from a side door. This was the indomitable charlady, Mrs. Midgit. According to report, when the audience recognized her, it broke out in a tumultuous "ten-minute ovation." For Mrs. Midgit was played by the much adored Laurette Taylor, returning to the stage after a seven-year bout with alcoholism. The next morning Anderson spoke of "the most breathtaking passages of acting I have ever seen. Seeing her begin it with a tremulous ballet of her hands, I tried to watch sharply enough to sleuth out the magic of such spellbinding, and then gave up, too misty-eyed, I'm afraid, to detect anything that can be explained." Brooks Atkinson devoted his entire Sunday follow-up to her, hailing her as "one of the theatre's great ladies" and begging her to watch her health and not take another extended vacation. Aided by such notices, the production ran for more than seven months.

The flops resumed with Louis E. Shecter and Norman Clark's **Window Shopping** (12-23-38, Longacre). While his father (George Sidney) is in the hospital, Jack Garfield (Philip Huston) decides to perk up business at Garfield's Department Store by having a pretty refugee (Gerta Rozan) dress for bed at night and for work in the morning in one of the store's windows. Business booms, and Jack marries the model. The plump Sidney had for years specialized in comic Jewish types, while Rozan was, in fact, a refugee. But they were given no chance to shine.

A group of Communists use an upstate New York farmhouse as offices from which to publish their magazine in Doris Frankel's **Don't Throw Glass Houses** (12-27-38, Vanderbilt). One rainy day some rich folk pop in after their limousine breaks down outside. The Commies have visions of riches, especially when a silly little debutante seems to be falling in love with one of them. But after a time each group goes its separate way. The play received some of the season's briefest, most dismissive notices, but still ran for two weeks—or twice as long as the evening's other two entries.

In William Du Bois's **Michael Drops In** (12-27-38,

Golden) Michael Dwyer (Onslow Stevens), a publisher, has regularly used a trellis from his penthouse to the apartment below to visit his attractive neighbor. But one day, not knowing she has temporarily sublet her flat to Judy Morton (Arlene Francis), a young writer from Idaho, he is surprised at whom he finds there. Audiences could guess the rest.

The evening's third and shortest-lived opening was Stanley Young's **Bright Rebel** (12-27-38, Lyceum), the latest in the recent rash of stage biographies of famous English writers—in this instance, Lord Byron (John Cromwell). Moving from 1809 to 1824, it told of his unloving mother (Jeanne Caselle), his vanity about his good looks and chagrin at his misshapen foot, his growing liberalism, his unhappy marriage to Annabelle Milbanke (Francesca Bruning), and his last days in Greece.

Critics split sharply on **The Merchant of Yonkers** (12-28-38, Guild), which Thornton Wilder took from Johann Nestroy's *Einen Jux will er sich machen,* in turn derived from John Oxenford's *A Day Well Spent.* Some reviewers saw it as "unrelentingly gay" and "the merriest kind of entertainment," while others slated it as imparting "a feeling of drugged boredom" or, at best, "a disappointment." Nor did they see eye to eye about Jane Cowl, who several felt could not handle its raucous-comedy demands. She was seen as the widowed Mrs. Levi, a matchmaker, who casts her sights on a Yonkers businessman (Percy Waram) all the while she is supposedly arranging for him to wed a milliner (June Walker). The plot grows complicated when the businessman's two clerks (Tom Ewell and John Call) close up shop and head out for a spree. The farce was withdrawn after five weeks. Nearly two decades later a revised, retitled version would be a smash hit.

A chorus singing "The Star-Spangled Banner" and a Man (Dean Jagger) and his Wife (Katherine Emery) plowing a field in the 1830s provided the opening tableau of Arnold Sundgaard and Marc Connelly's **Everywhere I Roam** (12-29-38, National). Over the next hundred years the Man and his Wife did not grow older, and more choral interludes and folk dances underscored and enlivened the salient moments of their lives. Johnny Appleseed (Norman Lloyd) teaches them how to farm successfully; the reaper and the railroad come to make life easier and make them richer. Then a pair of tricky profiteers, Jim and Jay (Paul Huber and Arthur Barnett), lure them into stock manipulations. They begin to live in luxury until the market crashes. At the end, again to the singing of "The Star Spangled Banner," they resume their simple farming. Most critics thought the first of the play's three acts was brilliant and exciting, but thereafter everything fell apart. They also had high praise for Robert Edmond Jones's scenery but, aside

from noting it offered sparse, stylized sets against a sky-blue background, offered no description.

Despite critics scoring it as "strangely unconvincing," and "a pretty routine sort of Negro melodrama," Dorothy and DuBose Heyward's somber **Mamba's Daughters** (1-3-39, Empire) remained before the footlights for twenty weeks. Of course, even naysayers confessed the evening was "given dignity and excitement by the beautiful performance of Ethel Waters," heretofore thought of as a revue singer. For killing a sailor who tried to cheat her, Hagar is given a suspended jail sentence and told not to come to Charleston again. She takes work on a plantation and sends her earnings back to her mother, Mamba (Georgette Harvey), to support the older woman and her own illegitimate baby. Years pass. To help an injured gambler (Willie Bryant) get medical attention, she violates her parole by taking him to a Charleston hospital. She is spotted and arrested. On leaving jail, she learns that the gambler has attacked her daughter (Fredi Washington). She has always known her daughter was someone special and does not want her hurt: "I ain't ever t'ink yo' like me an' Mamba. No, yo' is different, Lissa. But when a t'ing is done an' nothing can make um undone, yo' gots to go on jus' to go on livin'." She kills the gambler and then herself. Her friends sing a hymn assuring themselves that she is left in the hands "ob de kin' Sab-yor." Whether Waters and the other blacks kept to the rather heavily written dialect is uncertain, but the performance seems to have surmounted most difficulties.

Some critics were even harsher on George Abbott's production of Robert Buckner and Walter Hart's **The Primrose Path** (1-4-39, Biltmore), taken from Victoria Lincoln's novel *February Hill.* Many balked at what they perceived as an incredibly dirty show, a foulmouthed, "damnyankee variation" of *Tobacco Road.* It opens with 12-year-old Eva Wallace (Marilyn Erskine) telling a cat, "Lay still, you son-of-a-bitch." Except for the prissy, cold Maggie (Florida Friebus), the Wallace women, who live in a shanty in a small town near Buffalo, have been little better than prostitutes and thieves, albeit likable ones. There is Grandma (Helen Westley), her daughter Emma (Betty Garde), and Emma's other daughter, Clare (Betty Field). Emma has someway latched on to and married a toping Harvard graduate (Philip Wood), but he kills himself. However, all turns out well when little Eva looks to follow in the family's footsteps. While the comedy-drama's run fell far short of *Tobacco Road*'s, it nonetheless hung on for twenty-one weeks.

The Group Theatre's production of Irwin Shaw's **The Gentle People** (1-5-39, Belasco) ran almost as long in the face of mixed reviews. John Mason Brown found it "a very indifferent play, nothing more or less than a silly, creaking melodrama which sounds for all the world as if it were something Dion Boucicault had tossed off," but Burns Mantle in the *Daily News* hailed it as "taut and revealing." All Jonah Goodman (Sam Jaffe), an amiable Jew, and Philip Anagnos (Roman Bohnen), a Greek cook, want to do is go fishing in their skiff, which is docked at a Brooklyn pier. But a dapper, suave gangster, Harold Goff (Franchot Tone), demands $5 a week protection money. They give it to him. But then he learns they have saved up enough cash to buy a small motorboat. He beats Jonah into handing it over. Jonah also discovers that Harold plans to run off to Cuba with his daughter, Stella (Sylvia Sidney). At a Russian steam bath the men decide to kill him. Taking him out in their boat they do just that, recovering not only their money but several hundred dollars more. Because Harold had a gun, the police consider the matter justifiable homicide. The men give the extra money to charity, and Stella must be content with her old boyfriend, Eli Lieber (Elia Kazan). Many felt the play's high point was the scene in the steam bath, where the fat Lammanawitz (Lee J. Cobb), an anarchist whose dry-goods store has just gone bankrupt, bemoans his lot: "Sweat. The bankrupt's comfort. I sweat and the profit system comes out of my pores." Cobb delivered his lines with a marked Yiddish inflection, and several reviewers, who wished he had been given more to do, thought his clowning the best dialect bit in many years.

Paul Vincent Carroll's Irish drama **The White Steed** (1-10-39, Cort), while falling considerably short of the success his *Shadow and Substance* enjoyed last season, had a passable four-month run. When a well-loved, benevolent old canon (Barry Fitzgerald) suffers a crippling stroke, his place is taken by an intolerant religious fanatic (George Coulouris). A determined villager (Jessica Tandy) leads the opposition that prods the ill man to rise and teach his successor a lesson. Fitzgerald would make only a few more Broadway appearances before heading to a celebrated career in Hollywood; Tandy's "impressive intensity" furthered her path to stage fame, although there were even now some complaints about her high-pitched voice.

Dodie Smith's **Dear Octopus** (1-11-39, Broadhurst) failed to repeat its West End success on Broadway. A couple (Reginald Mason and Lucile Watson), on their golden anniversary, are content to learn that their son (Jack Hawkins) will marry his mother's companion (Lillian Gish), and that their daughter (Rose Hobart) has thrown over her French lover and returned to stay at home.

Just as Ibsen's plays were suffering through a period of disrespect, so, apparently, were those of his contemporary Oscar Wilde. "Distinctly too dated" and "too trifling" were some of the charges leveled at *The Importance of Being Ernest* when it was revived at the Vanderbilt on the 12th. Helping to gloss over the critical harrumphing were song-and-dance man Clifton Webb as Jack and big-eyed Estelle Winwood as Lady Bracknell. They led the laughter for five and a half weeks.

There was even less welcome for a French piece, when Sacha Guitry's *Le Nouveau Testament* opened on 45th Street in Edward Stirling's translation as **Where There's a Will** (1-17-39, Golden). Accidentally coming across her husband's will, a wife (Jessie Royce Landis) discovers that her best friend (Margaret Irving) is her husband's mistress and that her own lover (Donald Baker) is the woman's son. When matters come to a head, the husband (Stirling) stalks off with his secretary (Frances Reid), who he confesses is his illegitimate daughter.

The Rockefellers and others reportedly put up a then staggering $250,000 for Sam Harris and Max Gordon's lavish mounting in Rockefeller Center of George S. Kaufman and Moss Hart's **The American Way** (1-21-39, Center), which reputedly enlisted as many as 250 performers for its crowd scenes. The play opened with one on Ellis Island showing a ship docking and discharging its immigrants. Among the subsequent settings was a whole small-town square, whose stores changed with the changing times that moved from 1896 to the present. Torchlight processions rejoicing in election results, marching bands, villagers awaiting 4th of July fireworks, all filled the scene at one time or another. The story of this patriotic cavalcade begins with Martin Gunther (Fredric March), who had come over earlier to establish himself, meeting his wife (Florence Eldridge) and young children and seeing them through immigration. In Mapleton, Ohio, Martin has become a cabinetmaker, respected for his craftsmanship and integrity. McKinley's reelection gives way, among other things, to the July 4th outing in 1908, to the pleasures youngsters enjoy at a tennis club in 1914, and to the war clouds of 1917. When young Karl (David Wayne) enlists, Mrs. Gunther is upset that he might kill the children of her old German friends. But Martin insists Karl is right to go: "This country opened its arms to us, reared our children. Everything we have and everything that we are, we owe to America." Karl is killed in the war. Time continues to move on. Young war veterans parade home, Hoover is reelected, banks fail, and Roosevelt attempts to reassure the nation. (Critics reported that some first-nighters hissed a recording of a Roosevelt speech.) By 1938, Karl's son, Karl Jr. (Witner Bissell), cannot find work and decides to join other young German-Americans in a fascist bund. Martin enters as his grandson is taking the oath, tries to stop it, and is beaten to death. The whole town turns out for his funeral (a scene, according to *Variety,* dropped after opening night, but retained in a published version). For the second time in the season, Kaufman and Hart had largely jettisoned their biting humor and for this occasion created what the *Sun*'s Richard Lockridge hailed as "movingly patriotic . . . a gigantic spectacle, ordered and directed with extraordinary theatrical skill." Their efforts were rewarded with 244 performances (in two engagements separated by an extended summer layoff). Although nuances could scarcely be projected in the 4000-seat house, the critic nonetheless also welcomed the "rare simplicity" March and Eldridge brought to their roles. More than any of their earlier assignments, these made them important names on Broadway.

· · ·

Fredric March [né Frederick McIntyre Bickel] (1897–1975) was born in Racine and educated at the University of Wisconsin. He made his stage debut under his real name as the Prompter in *Deburau* in 1920. After adopting his new stage name, he appeared as leading man in a series of failed dramas, then became a Hollywood star before returning to Broadway last season in *Yr. Obedient Husband.* The handsome but stern-looking actor always retained a faint trace of the ham in his acting.

· · ·

Florence Eldridge [née Florence McKechnie] (1901–88) was born in Brooklyn and made her debut in 1918 as a chorus girl in musicals. In the 1920s she won major attention in such plays as *The Cat and the Canary* and *Six Characters in Search of an Author.* She married March in 1927. Her characterizations generally conveyed a motherly warmth.

· · ·

After setting aside his Hamlet, Maurice Evans turned to Falstaff and met further acclaim and success with his revival of *Henry IV, Part I* at the St. James on the 30th. Coleman found the production "a joyous and rewarding evening," and Evans's Falstaff "rich and flavorsome. It catches all the facets of the ingratiating knight's kaleidoscopic character." Welsey Addy was applauded for his Hotspur and Mady Christians for her Lady Percy. The rarely produced classic, under Margaret Webster's deft direction, stayed around for seventy-four playings.

Jeremiah (2-3-39, Guild), which Eden and Cedar Paul translated from Stefan Zweig's two-decade-old original and which John Gassner and Worthington Miner then adapted for American audiences, failed to raise the Theatre Guild out of its ongoing slump. The Israelites, crying out for war against their enemies, will not listen to the dire prophecies of Jeremiah (Kent Smith), who is attacked and imprisoned for questioning the policies of King Zedekiah (Arthur Byron), and who can take no satisfaction when he is proved right.

But a somewhat off-color comedy-drama, Jack Kirkland and Leyla Georgie's **I Must Love Someone** (2-7-39, Longacre), chalked up a six-month run in the face of generally negative notices. All the famous girls of the *Florodora* sextette are seeking love and having trouble finding it. Ann Gibson (Dorothy Libaire) kills the man (James Rennie) who has given her a venereal disease and is shielded from the police by her fellow chorines. Birdie Carr (Martha Sleeper) thinks she has found the man of her dreams in an automobile driver, Bob Goesling (Scott Colton), only to learn better. He simply wants her as another trophy. *Florodora*'s sextette scene and its song, "Tell Me, Pretty Maiden," were recreated, but not, according to the critics, very skillfully. One of the meteoric stars of the original musical's heyday—Ethel Jackson, America's first Merry Widow—had so small a role that critics passed over her in silence.

Mrs. O'Brien (Margaret Mullen) is not the central figure of Harry Madden's **Mrs. O'Brien Entertains** (2-8-39, Lyceum). That figure is her father, Tim Callahan (James Lane), who, to his snobbish daughter's annoyance, welcomes all manner of immigrants and helps mate them regardless of their national background. Among them, in George Abbott's racily staged picture of 1848 New York, is Patrick O'Toole (Harry Shannon). He ignores a beating by bigoted Know-Nothings and starts a quick rise in Tammany politics.

One of the season's most memorable plays was Lillian Hellman's **The Little Foxes** (2-15-39, National), which gripped New York playgoers for a solid year. The rapacious, hate-filled Hubbards dominate their small southern town at the turn of the century. Oscar (Carl Benton Reid) had married Birdie Bagtry (Patricia Collinge) for her family's money, but now the Hubbards need more money again. Oscar and his older brother, Ben (Charles Dingle), reluctantly offer their crafty sister, Regina (Tallulah Bankhead), one-third interest in a new cotton mill they are planning in return for a $75,000 loan. Regina's husband, Horace Giddens (Frank Conroy), refuses to lend the money, so Oscar prods his weakling son, Leo (Dan Duryea), into stealing Horace's bonds. The ensuing argument between Horace and Regina causes Horace to have a heart attack, but Regina ignores his plea for his medicine and lets him die. She then proceeds to blackmail her brothers and when they try to bargain, she refuses to hear them. "I'll take my seventy-five percent and we'll forget the story forever." She would then leave for Chicago and the good life, taking her daughter, Alexandra (Florence Williams), with her. But Alexandra, not the sugar water her mother had thought her, tells Regina that she is going her own way. All Regina can do is ask quietly if Alexandra would like to sleep in her room that evening. Alexandra, in turn, asks Regina if she is afraid of something. Although Atkinson felt that the play, unlike Hellman's *The Children's Hour,* was more melodrama than tragedy, others found it superior. Watts called it "a grim, bitter and merciless study, a drama more honest, more pointed and more brilliant." There was little disagreement over Bankhead; Watts, using several of the same adjectives he had employed about the play, went on to say she gave "the finest performance of her local career, a portrayal that is honest, merciless and completely understanding." Although she had been a promising actress and a celebrity for a decade and a half, her performance as Regina elevated Bankhead into high theatrical echelons.

. . .

Tallulah Bankhead (1903–68) was born in Huntsville into a prominent Alabama family—her uncle was a U.S. senator. She used her influence to land a walkon part in *Squab Farm* (1918). Films and ever larger Broadway assignments followed until she left for London in 1922 and remained there for eleven years. Mostly short-lived failures marked her return to America before she enjoyed a modest success in *Reflected Glory* (1936). A beautiful woman with a deep, almost baritone voice, she evinced a self-deprecating humor and too often eschewed the restraint that would have given her performances dignity and credibility.

. . .

The next three plays to open all ran a week or less. Bella and Sam Spewack could not elicit much fun from their needlessly complicated **Miss Swan Expects** (2-20-39, Cort). Josie Swan (Peggy Conklin) is a rattled-brained book reader at the House of Bretherton. Her husband, Bert (John Beal), is writing a biography of a famous businessman, but stands to have all his work go for nought when the man (Harry Antrim) balks at allowing it to be published. Josie tries various ploys, such as foisting a blonde siren (Ann Andrews) on him, before he comes around and also injects new money into the failing publishing house. At various points in the story Josie attempts to pay a cabdriver (William Bendix) by giving him copies of a banned, pornographic book in lieu of a fare and also has to deal with a Russian's fraudulent autobiography.

With a mere $600 budget for his lodge's entertainment, Harry Quill (Hume Cronyn) decides to invite some down-and-out veterans of the bygone two-a-day to comprise the show. He even agrees to let them stay at his house while they are rehearsing. His star is Gus Delancy (Joe Cook), once a Palace headliner, but now on his uppers. The vaudevillians all but eat Harry out of house and home before Harry is informed that the lodge has canceled the show night. Cook, a famed musical-comedy clown who had not been on Broadway

for five years, brought his preposterous inventions, his juggling, and his tall tales with him, but they could not save the day for Max Liebman and Allen Boretz's **Off to Buffalo** (2-21-39, Ethel Barrymore).

Several weeks after watching a play with 250 performers onstage, theatregoers could sit through a drama with a cast of just two (a great rarity at the time). **Close Quarters** (3-6-39, Golden) was taken by Gilbert Lennox from W. O. Somin's *Attentat* and had been a London hit. When circumstantial evidence might make it seem that a political radical (Leo Chalzel) has murdered his country's fascist dictator, he and his wife (Elena Miramova) commit suicide. They are no sooner dead than a radio broadcast reveals the killing has been pinned on someone else.

The Group Theatre revived Odets's *Awake and Sing!* at the Windsor on the 7th, using many of the same actors still employed in *Rocket to the Moon* and playing it in repertory forty-five times.

The season's second biblical drama, Lenore Coffee and William Joyce Cowen's **Family Portrait** (3-8-39, Morosco), fared better than its first. Critics held some reservations about the play itself, with Watts noting, "Despite a lack of the soaring eloquence that its theme demanded and the presence of a certain monotony, 'Family Portrait' is a drama of interest." Of far more interest to Watts and his colleagues was the performance of its star, Judith Anderson—"it would be impossible to imagine the role of the Mother much more beautifully played . . . a portrait of genuine spiritual beauty and fine dramatic authority." The Mother was, of course, Mary. Her other sons are furious that their brother and fellow carpenter has left them to go off preaching some silly doctrine. Mary herself does not understand his preachings but is sympathetic. His increasing notoriety upsets his siblings, who wish him dead, but they are sure it will all someday pass. Years after Jesus' execution, Mary confesses to one of her sons that she hopes he will name his first boy Jesus—"I'd like him not to be forgotten." The drama attained 111 performances.

Some very quick-closing fiascoes followed, the first two dealing with modern dictators or demagogues. Joe Marcy [Nathan Sherman] and Jacob A. Weiser's **First American Dictator** (3-14-39, Nora Bayes) recapitulated highlights in the life of Huey Long (Conrad Noles), albeit it changed the site of his assassination to the Capitol in Washington.

With names slightly altered, Richard Rohman's **Tell My Story** (3-15-39, Mercury) retold the saga of Mussolini, here called merely the Duke (Robert H. Harris), and his arranging for the killing of his idealistic, socialist opponent, Matteoti, here renamed Mateo (Gordon Nelson).

Mary McCarthy's **Please, Mrs. Garibaldi** (3-16-39,

Belmont) focused on Rosa Garibaldi (Dorothy Emery), pregnant by her boyfriend (William Rice). She is relieved when her parents (Ruth Amos and Giuseppe Sterni) seem to be understanding, but shocked that they think she ought to marry. Mama confesses she, too, had to marry Papa, and everything turned out just fine. So Rosa decides she will marry her lover. The play lasted just four performances, but McCarthy found fame with her other writings.

Like *Tell My Story,* John Stradley's **Stop Press** (3-19-39, Vanderbilt) lasted just a single performance. It was mounted by one of those idealistic theatrical groups that regularly spring up and quickly fall back. This one was called the Acting Company. The drama managed to draw several major critics even though it was only booked for a single playing, but hopes were high that backers would jump aboard so the drama might keep going (probably at something more than the $1.65 top asked for opening night). They and it didn't. The play depicted a typical 1930s conflict with a conservative newspaper owner (Houseley Stevens) taking the steel mills' side in a strike and his leftish son (Ralph Bell) favoring the union. The publisher dies of a stroke after his editor (Tony Kraber) prints pro-union articles and his reporters walk out to found their own paper (suggesting they didn't trust the son?).

The season's most enduring comedy has proved to be Philip Barry's **The Philadelphia Story** (3-28-39, Shubert), which delighted contemporary audiences for a full year. On the eve of her second marriage—this time to the self-made George Kitteredge (Frank Fenton)—Tracy Lord (Katharine Hepburn) finds herself doubly beset. First of all, her family, hoping to squelch a story about the philanderings of her father, who now lives in New York, has agreed to allow *Destiny* to send a writer, "Mike" Connor (Van Heflin), and a photographer, Elizabeth Imbrie (Shirley Booth), to cover the wedding. The leftish Mike insists that only in America can one find such young, rich, and rapacious women. Liz admits that even the idea of a Tracy Lord scares her, but when she asks, seemingly rhetorically, "Would I change places with her, for all her wealth and beauty?" she answers herself, "Boy! Just ask me!" Tracy's other problem is the unexpected reappearance of her ex, C. K. Dexter Haven (Joseph Cotten), who says her own god-like view of herself was the real cause of their breakup. She is disconcerted when George and Mike make similar statements. Having too much to drink at a prenuptial party, Tracy goes swimming in her pool, with Mike but without clothes. On learning of this, George demands an explanation and apology, or he will not go through with the wedding. Tracy gives him only a partial explanation, then sends him on his way. She requests the assembled wedding guests to wait

a few extra moments, since she has to change grooms. It will be Dexter at the altar with her once more. Atkinson saluted the work as "a gay and sagacious comedy" and suggested it gave Hepburn "an ideal part," which she played with "grace, jauntiness and warmth." Although her subsequent Broadway appearances were relatively few, she remained a potent draw whenever she did appear.

. . .

Katharine [Houghton] **Hepburn** (b. 1907) was born in Hartford, Conn, and educated at Bryn Mawr. She made her professional debut with a Baltimore stock company in 1928 and made her New York debut that same year, using the name Katherine Burns, in *Night Hostess.* She first gained theatrical acceptance in *The Warrior's Husband* (1932), but, apart from two brief failures, one of which did not even reach Broadway, spent the next six years as a screen star. Lithe, with a horsey beauty and a haughty accent, she was perceived to have succeeded as much by dint of glamor and dedication as by any exceptional acting abilities.

. . .

Even with much of its London cast still intact, Charles Morgan's **The Flashing Stream** (4-10-39, Biltmore) fared poorly in New York. On an isolated island, British researchers are trying to develop an aerial torpedo to shoot down planes. Most are unaware that the refusal of Commander Ferrers (Godfrey Tearle) to own up to his own mistaken calculation has cost the life of his friend and is impeding progress. But the dead friend's sister (Margaret Rawlings), herself a noted researcher, joins the party, detects the problem, convinces Ferrer to face up to it, and marries him. One reason given for the show's quick American failure was Tearle's startling resemblance to President Roosevelt, which allegedly distracted playgoers from the plot.

Charlotte Armstrong's **The Happiest Days** (4-11-39, Vanderbilt) was put down as "an honorable failure," an earnestly written and superbly acted drama, not quite well enough contrived and too unpleasant for success. It was based on a real incident that occurred in Jackson Heights a year earlier. After a seventeen-year-old girl (Uta Hagen) tells her seventeen-year-old sweetheart (John Craven) that she is pregnant, they discover that no justice of the peace will marry them. They cannot bring themselves to face their parents, so they agree that the boy will kill the girl, but he will survive to let the world know of their brief happiness. He is arrested, but acquitted by a compassionate jury.

Apparently learning from the success of the early Mercury Theatre productions, the Group Theatre offered William Saroyan's **My Heart's in the Highlands** (4-13-39, Guild) as an intermissionless eighty minute entertainment. Critics good-humoredly confessed to bafflement. Coleman tagged the play "the neatest surrealist crossword puzzle of the season," while Brown, less metaphorical, noted, "The air it admits may be cloudy, but it is moving and fresh, and pleasant to inhale." In Fresno in 1914, Ben Alexander (Philip Loeb), who considers himself "one of the greatest unknown poets living," holes up in a shack with his young son, Johnny (Sidney Lumet), and his mother (Hester Sondergaard), who speaks only Armenian. When Jasper MacGregor (Art Smith), a very old man playing a golden bugle, appears, telling everyone his and his family's hearts are all in the Scottish highlands regardless of where they themselves may be, the penniless Ben sends Johnny to beg bread and cheese from the grocer (William Hansen). Friends and neighbors come to listen to Jasper before guards arrive to return him to an old folks' home. Jasper dies, and Ben and Johnny find their shack sold out from under them. Heading onto the open road, Johnny muses to his father, "Something's wrong somewhere." The play was slated for only five performances, but an encouraging response prompted the Theatre Guild to enter the picture and offer seats to its subscribers at $1.75 top. As a result, the play ran for forty-four performances, and Saroyan, already known as a short-story writer, embarked on his meteoric theatrical career.

· · ·

William Saroyan (1908–81) was born in Fresno, where his Armenian parents were fruit farmers. He had little formal schooling and worked in odd jobs such as selling newspapers, delivering telegrams, and helping with vineyard harvests before calling attention to himself in 1934 with his short story *The Daring Young Man on the Flying Trapeze.*

· · ·

The season's last hit was one of its best, S. N. Behrman's **No Time for Comedy** (4-17-39, Ethel Barrymore). Linda Paige (Katharine Cornell) is a brilliant comedienne who has made all her important successes in fluff written for her by her toping husband, Gaylord Esterbrook (Laurence Olivier). So she is naturally concerned when Philo Smith (John Williams) appears and advises her that her husband has fallen under the influence of Smith's wife, Amanda (Margalo Gillmore), who has "a passion for developing latent powers" and whom he characterizes as "a Lorelei with an intellectual patter." Amanda, it seems, has convinced Gay that this day and age is no time for comedy and that he should try his hand at drama. Meeting Amanda, Linda warns her, "Sleep with him if you must, but don't spoil his style." Gay and Amanda decide to leave their spouses. Linda finds Gay packing and slyly suggests that the situation would make a good play. Gay agrees, although

he cannot think of how to end the play. When Amanda phones, impatiently demanding to know what is taking him so long, Gay realizes he has the perfect curtain. He hangs up on her. Watts wrote of Behrman, "His prose style is so graceful, his wit so sprightly, his mind so tolerant and his viewpoint so modest that he becomes the most winning of the drama's counselors." Calling her "the stage's most fascinating lady," he assessed Cornell as "enchanting throughout." He also lauded the rest of the cast, including the "admirable" Olivier, whom he saw as representing the finest in English acting skills. The comedy cost $21,000 to bring in, paid off almost at once, and ran for just short of six months.

The rest of the season was downhill.

Half a week was all **The Mother** (4-25-39, Lyceum) could muster. Written by Karel Capek just before his death and before the Nazi invasion of Czechoslovakia, and translated by Paul Selver and Miles Malleson, it told of a woman (Nazimova) who has lost her husband and four of her five sons in wars or war-related accidents. She is opposed to her last son (Montgomery Clift) going off to battle, but when the ghosts of her other men plead with her, she hands the boy a gun and bids him farewell. Her performances were the last Broadway appearances of Nazimova, an actress many felt never fully developed her remarkable talents.

Wuthering Heights (4-27-39, Longacre) was taken by Randolph Carter from Emily Brontë's great novel. Dealing only with the tragic love story of the mature Heathcliff (Don Terry) and Catherine (Edith Barrett), it was so ineptly written and so incompetently acted that critics shook their heads in disbelief.

But then Edward R. Sammis and Ernest V. Heyn's more original **Day in the Sun** (5-16-39, Biltmore) was no better. It featured Taylor Holmes, another player many critics felt never realized his full potential, but whom others saw as a very limited comedian at best. He was cast as Charlie Sumner, who spends all his spare time entering slogan contests. He is hailed as "the Truth Man of the Century" after he is able to testify in court that he saw a defendant working in the library at a nearby seat at the time the man supposedly committed a murder. Showered with attention and money, he earns the ire of his less lucky relations, who attempt to impugn his honesty. But he is vindicated.

The latest anti-Nazi play to bite the dust quickly was Burnet Hershey's **Brown Danube** (5-17-39, Lyceum). Critics were becoming a bit apologetic about having to pan one anti-Nazi play after another, but insisted there was nothing inherently undramatic in the subject and that a good one would probably be forthcoming. A family of liberal Catholic aristocrats are stopped from fleeing Austria after the Anschluss, largely because a former servant, now a Nazi commandant (Dean Jagger), covets one (Jessie Royce Landis) of their daughters. He would hold her brother hostage to ensure he has his way, but the Prince (Ernest Lawford) alludes to Jewish blood in the Nazi's background, forcing him to let the family go.

As it turned out, George Sklar's **Life and Death of an American** (5-19-39, Maxine Elliott's) marked the death of an American experiment, the Federal Theatre Project, which Congress put an end to a few days after the play's opening. The play was another of the cavalcades so popular recently. Jerry Dorgan (J. Arthur Kennedy) is born in 1900, becomes a good football player and an average student, but has to abandon his dream of becoming a scientist when his father (John Pote) dies. He takes work in an automobile plant and starts to rise until the Crash comes. Forced to accept a lesser job at less pay, he joins the union and is killed by police during a strike.

There were not many mourners for the FTP, except among dedicated leftists who stood to lose their jobs and their platforms. Investigators had dwelt not so much on the organization's patently radical leanings as on its corruption, incompetence, and waste. Yet the group was not without its finer moments. It had offered the first professional American mounting of *Murder in the Cathedral,* and it had undeniably spawned the Mercury Theatre. But not a single of its original native works, not even the highly praised *Prologue to Glory,* apparently lost in the miasma of its ragingly slanted propaganda pieces, found a permanent place on American stages. And apart from the members of the Mercury Theatre, precious few of its writers, directors, or performers moved on to better things on Broadway. (J. Arthur Kennedy, dropping his initial, did become an important player in many of Arthur Miller's essentially leftist dramas a decade or so later.)

"A new low for the season" and "The Lowest Depths," were some of the characterizations of the season's last play. **Clean Beds** (5-25-39, Golden) was said to have been written by one George S. George, who was given out to be one Youacca G. Satovsky, whom one reviewer "strongly suspected of being a couple of other fellows." Broadway scuttlebutt insisted Mae West had a hand in the writing. Murray (Nat Burns) runs a flophouse across the street from a brothel run by his wife (Fifi Louise Hall). A young man (Alfred Alderdie) comes to take lodgings at the seedy hostelry following a fight with his wife. Murray and his crooked buddies attempt to drug the man and then lure his wife (Helen Beverly) into white slavery. But another lodger (Joseph Holland), a besotted, tubercular old actor, foils the scheme.

1939–1940

Once again the count of new plays fell—*Variety* tallying sixty-two; the *Times* sixty. Since Congress had written finis to the Federal Theatre Project late last spring, only a handful of off-Broadway offerings might have been brought in to swell the totals. But Off Broadway was still not taken seriously, so its productions did not count. And once again, in a pattern that would become general for most ensuing seasons, no new plays opened in the summer. This year the ongoing World's Fair undoubtedly convinced many producers to hold off their openings. But just as the fair was preparing to close its first of two seasons, another diversion gripped potential playgoers. In early September, Germany invaded Poland, prompting England and France to come to Poland's aid by declaring war on the Nazis. World War II was under way. But at the same time, American industry had begun gearing up for the war President Roosevelt hoped to keep at bay, and this sudden increase in jobs signaled the first real signs of prosperity since the Crash. As a result, to Broadway's delight, business began to pick up perceptibly.

Some musicals aside, not until September 18 were critics and first-nighters summoned back to their posts, and that was to sit in judgment on the first of several revivals Leonard Sillman's New York Drama Festival promised. In the run of things, Sillman brought in only two mountings to the Empire. The first was *Journey's End,* R. C. Sheriff's much lauded English drama about officers in front-line trenches in 1918. Colin Keith-Johnston repeated his original role, with Reginald Mason, Glenn Hunter, and other respected players in support. Unfortunately, with Europe exploding once again, the timing could not have been worse. Two weeks later, on October 2, *They Knew What They Wanted* (11-24-24) was put on display. Featuring June Walker, Douglass Montgomery, and Giuseppe Sterni, this tale of a young waitress torn between a handsome stud and an old, loving vintner received divided notices and departed after three weeks.

In between the two revivals, one farce bucked critical put-downs to embark on a nearly seven-month run—much of it after it moved to a larger playhouse and dropped its top price from $3.30 to $1.10. Richard Maibaum and Harry Clork's **See My Lawyer** (9-27-39, Biltmore) was deemed by the *Journal-American*'s John Anderson to be "more athletic than amusing," and he wished "it were only funnier." For lack of work, the law offices of Lee, Russo and O'Rourke are a strange, unprofitably quiet place, where bread rolls are kept in the petty cash box and mustard in an inkwell. Things liven up after an eccentric, much divorced millionaire, Robert Carlin [read Tommy Manville] (Eddie Nugent), having first employed a freight elevator to bring it to the twenty-second floor, drives his car into the offices, hoping to settle up after knocking down the brother of the firm's receptionist. Instead, he plunks down $25,000 to retain Lee (Milton Berle), Russo (Gary Merrill) and O'Rourke (Millard Mitchell). All manner of mayhem ensues before the attorneys are relieved to learn that Carlin will take his business elsewhere. Although Berle was praised for showing unexpected restraint, the best notices went to tiny, startled-faced Teddy Hart, who played an ambulance chaser renting a rent-free desk in the firm's offices.

By now critics, taking the slow-moving elevator up to the Nora Bayes, had despaired of finding a noteworthy attraction on its stage, so they were not disappointed by the hopeless **Speak of the Devil** (10-6-39, Nora Bayes), which a seeming committee consisting of Dr. Van V. Alderman, Henry Cody, and Justus Schifferes derived from Goethe's *Faust*. Done on a black-curtained stage with only the simplest furniture and lighting, but with a choir chanting from offstage throughout much of the evening, it quickly disappeared.

Critics were, in fact, disappointed by Samson Raphaelson's **Skylark** (10-11-39, Morosco), but agreed that Gertrude Lawrence and her supporting cast turned it into fetching escapism. Thus John Mason Brown, writing in the *Post*, thought the play sounded like "a very inferior imitation of Philip Barry," but lauded Lawrence's ingratiating, disciplined performance as "a joy to watch." Lenya Kenyon is fed up with her husband's absorption in his work. Tony Kenyon (Donald Cook) has not taken a vacation in six years, and just before a party to celebrate their tenth wedding anniversary he informs Lenya she is to give up her beloved cook to the wife (Vivian Vance) of an important client, Mr. Valentine (Robert Burton). Lenya complains to a friend that marriages are only "anniversaries, starches and fats." To be even she runs off for a night-long ride with a lawyer (Glenn Anders) she knows to be Mrs. Valentine's lover. The outraged woman tells Tony, "I can assure you, after consulting my feminine intuition, that they're not picking daisies," and following some name-calling between the two ladies, Mrs. Valentine sees to it that Tony loses his job. Tony pretends to be happy, at last able to devote all his time to his wife. But his wife knows better. Heretofore childless, she decides to adopt a baby, unaware at first that Tony has planned the whole thing. Tony gets a fine new job, and Lenya has something to keep her occupied. Thanks to its star, the comedy ran out the season.

A group of young players who last season had brought their *As You Like It* from summer stock to Broadway now retraced their steps with Anton Chekhov's *The Three Sisters*. It opened at the Longacre on the 14th with a cast that included Katherine Emery, Anne Revere, Shepperd Strudwick, and Hume Cronyn. Cronyn won the highest praise as the ineffectual Andrei, but playgoers had only nine chances to see him.

George S. Kaufman and Moss Hart, reverting to the unrestrained comedy that had marked their earlier hits, scored big with **The Man Who Came to Dinner** (10-16-39, Music Box), a send-up of their friend, the writer, actor, and radio commentator, Alexander Woollcott. For the occasion he was rechristened Sheridan Whiteside (Monty Woolley), who is confined to a wheelchair and forced to convalesce at the home of the Stanleys, where he had slipped on the ice while leaving a dinner party. Cantankerous at best, the celebrated author is very unhappy about his plight and determined to see that the Stanleys (George Lessey and Virginia Hammond) are no less unhappy. Their simple, courteous inquiry about his health brings the reply, "I may vomit." Not only does he alienate the Stanley children from their parents, he even turns his nurse, Miss Preen (Mary Wickes), so misanthropic that she takes a job at a munitions factory in hopes of destroying the human race. To scotch a burgeoning romance between his secretary (Edith Atwater) and a local newspaperman (Theodore Newton), he invites a glamorous actress (Carol Goodner) to lure away the reporter. When she fails in her assignment he ships her off locked in a mummy case. He goes so far as to blackmail Mrs. Stanley by threatening to reveal her sister was once acquitted of a headline ax murder. Everyone is delighted when he recovers and can leave. But once again he slips on the ice. He is carried back into the home bellowing his promises of another six weeks of despotism. If Whiteside was indisputably Woollcott, the actress, called Lorraine Sheldon, was seen as Gertrude Lawrence, while two other characters, the suave Beverly Carlton (John Hoysradt) and the madcap Banjo (David Burns), were deemed to be spoofs of Noel Coward and Harpo Marx. With his elegantly pointed beard and sour hauteur, Woolley created a definitive Whiteside. He helped no end to make the comedy what the *Times*'s Atkinson referred to as "a roaring evening of literate hilarity" and to see to it that it ran 739 performances.

Toward the end of her long career, the late Mrs. Fiske had starred in *Ladies of the Jury* (10-21-29), a minor vehicle about a determined woman who by one method or another converts her eleven opposing jury members to her way of thinking. Now another great lady of the American theatre, Helen Hayes, at the height of her long career, came in with a similar play. (A third not unlike drama, *Good Men and True* [10-25-35], had featured a man as the decisive juror, but had failed.) Hayes's husband, Charles MacArthur, and his buddy Ben Hecht took **Ladies and Gentlemen** (10-17-39, Martin Beck) from an unspecified Hungarian play by Lászlo Bus-Fekete. A famous writer is on trial for allegedly pushing his wife over a cliff to her death so that he might be free to marry his paramour. For various reasons, some quite untoward, eleven of the jurors are determined to find the man guilty. Thus one juror (George Watts), a mortician, noting the defendant has no heirs, hopes to be allowed to bury the body if the man is sent to the chair. But Terry Scott, a famous movie producer's twenty-eight-year-old secretary, who sees her time on the jury as a vacation away from her overbearing boss, uses her logic, her feminine wiles, her knowledge of stage tricks, and all other means to have the man acquitted. She stages a fainting act to prove that one of the panel would not, as he claimed, instinctively have prevented her from falling, and she shows a snooty grande dame (Evelyn Varden), who heads a group hoping to censor Hollywood films—after, of course, first seeing the uncensored versions—that the lady will miss her opportunity to greet Mrs. Roosevelt if she does not allow the jury to reach a quick decision. Terry also has a brief, unfeigned flirtation with a married juror (Philip Merivale), but they go their separate ways after the acquittal. Only Hayes's presence allowed the comedy to run for thirteen weeks.

Elizabeth Reynolds Hapgood's translation of George Shdanoff's **The Possessed** (10-24-39, Lyceum), itself based on Dostoyevsky's novel, survived for merely a fortnight, telling of how a cynical, brutal revolutionist, Verkhovenski (Woodrow Chambliss), manipulates or murders his weaker or more idealistic opponents.

William Saroyan's **The Time of Your Life** (10-25-39, Booth) was viewed by Richard Lockridge of the *Sun* as "fantasy and gags and nitwit stories, bound together very lightly with melodrama; it is two-thirds delight, a third mere fumbling." The patrons at Nick's Pacific Street Saloon, Restaurant and Entertainment Place, which sits along San Francisco's seedy Embarcadero, include Murphy (Len Doyle), who also calls himself Kit Carson and spins tall tales about his life as an Indian fighter; Willie (Will Lee), a pinball addict who finally strikes a jackpot; Joe (Gene Kelly), a dancer longing to become a famous comedian; Dudley (Curt Conway), who tells his beloved on the phone that he will kill himself if she doesn't love him, then discovers he has dialed the wrong number and rejects the homely answerer (Nene Vibber) when she rushes to the saloon to comfort him; Wesley (Reginald Beane), a black who faints from hunger but plays a mean jazz piano after he is fed; and a harmonica-playing Arab (Houseley Ste-

vens), whose response to almost everything is "No foundation. All the way down the line." But most of the attention centers on the open-hearted, open-handed Joe (Eddie Dowling), who fosters a romance between his dull-minded sidekick, Tom (Edward Andrews), and Kitty Duval (Julie Haydon), a prostitute. Joe's philosophy is "In the time of your life, live, so that in that good time there shall be no ugliness or death for yourself or for any life your life touches." The melodrama Lockridge alluded to came when Nick (Charles De Sheim) is badgered by a vicious detective, Blick (Grover Burgess), who is finally shot by Kit Carson. The comedy ran just short of six months and, shortly after it closed, became the first play to win both the Pulitzer Prize and the New York Drama Critics Circle Award.

The same night as the Saroyan play premiered, a long-dark Village house relit briefly for Paul F. Treichler's **Cure for Matrimony** (10-25-39, Provincetown Playhouse). Mounted by a group of young, out-of-work actors based in Ohio, it was set on an island off the Maine coast and told of experiments conducted by a psychiatrist to see if men are monogamous or not. He puts up his wife and her friends as guinea pigs for his male subjects.

November began on a down note with Victor Wolfson's **Pastoral** (11-1-39, Henry Miller's). Ingebord (Ruth Weston), a refugee and mother of some grown children, and Genko (John Banner), a Bulgarian gunboat captain, have shocked their neighbors by living in sin on their Catskills chicken farm. Apart from the small change the chickens bring in, they make do—with a pair of colored servants—on the child-support money Ingebord's ex has been sending. Ingebord's daughter (Virginia Campbell) finds romance with a local farmer (Charles Lang), although Ingebord at first thinks she herself is being courted. When Ingebord's long-absent husband (Wilton Graff) suddenly turns up and reveals he has obtained a divorce, Ingebord and Genko decide to wed.

Some "extraordinary" scenery by Robert Edmond Jones was wasted on Vicki Baum and Benjamin Glazer's **Summer Night** (11-2-39, St. James), which reviewers waved off as a honky-tonk rehash of *Grand Hotel*. Jones framed the story in the gaudily lit entrance arch to an amusement park. Among his principal settings were a gloomy dance hall, where a marathon has been under way for thirty-four days, a pier, and the gambling room of a ship. Marion Bingham (Violet Heming), wife of a bankrupt banker (Louis Calhern), has come to the dance hall to check up on her lover, Melvyn Lockhart (Wesley Addy). Lockhart is a movie star who hopes to snatch some publicity by playing up to Ginger (Susan Fox), a contestant with a partner, Pat (Boyd Crawford), near collapse. Both Pat and Mr. Bingham have thoughts of suicide. But Jake (Lionel Stander), an ex-con who also has his eye on Ginger, shoots Lockhart, and this brings them all to their senses. Marion agrees to return to her husband and to pawn her jewels to save him; Pat, who has won some money on the gambling ship, and Ginger decide they now have enough to marry.

By the simple expedient of tickling an audience's ribs instead of preaching to it, Clare Boothe's **Margin for Error** (11-3-39, Plymouth) broke the jinx on anti-Nazi plays. Critical hemming and hawing was typified by Burns Mantle of the *Daily News,* who found the comedy "as full of holes as a sieve," but also "taut and tricky enough to be entertaining." Karl Baumer (Otto Preminger) is the Nazi consul in New York. He is also a blackmailer, a thief, and a double-crosser, who has the utmost contempt for America and its liberal democracy. His contempt turns to outrage and a fervent wish to break relations when a Jewish policeman, Officer Finkelstein (Sam Levene), is assigned to guard him. Finkelstein clearly does not do a proper job, since Baumer is murdered in a room filled with seeming supporters all listening to the broadcast of a Hitler speech. To increase Finkelstein's discomfort it is disclosed that he might have had several opportunities to prevent the killing, Baumer having been poisoned, and stabbed, and shot. Finkelstein finally pins the shooting and stabbing on two people with good reasons for killing the Nazi, and since Baumer was already dead from having mistakenly swilled from a glass he poisoned in hopes of murdering an associate and then blaming it on the Jews, Finkelstein exculpates the others. Finkelstein has just cleared up the whole matter when his captain, Mulrooney (Edward McNamara), appears. Mulrooney has never liked Baumer. Informed of the poisoning, stabbing, and shooting, he can only ask, "Did it kill him?" Although McNamara had a mere three sentences, his last line brought down the house as well as the curtain. But comic honors went to Levene, with his thickly New-York-Jewish-accented clowning. It was his last Broadway role for many years. The comedy ran out the season.

Wilson Starbuck's **Sea Dogs** (11-6-39, Maxine Elliott's) contained some of the foulest language heard till then in a Broadway drama, but all the profanity helped not an iota. Hard-drinking, abusive Captain Wickford (Joseph Macaulay) pays little heed to a fire in his ship's hold and refuses to treat the festering hand of a young crewman (James McCallion), a fugitive from a reform school who he knows can expose his dope smuggling. The chief mate (Russell Hardie), in love with the boy's sister, knocks out the captain and, with advice radioed from a distant surgeon, operates on the boy. In port, the boy is rushed to a hospital, where he dies, but not

before he and his mates have told authorities enough to have the captain arrested.

Theatrical columns of the time carried several paragraphs debating whether *Tobacco Road* would surpass the long-run record of *Abie's Irish Rose* on the 18th or whether it already had done so, since some sources questioned the number of performances the 1920s comedy had actually played. Naturally, no one could foresee that the next opening would in time make the matter somewhat moot. Howard Lindsay and Russel Crouse's **Life with Father** (11-8-39, Empire) had been culled from Clarence Day's short stories. The comedy was set in a comfortable New York brownstone in the 1880s. Clarence Day (Lindsay) has no doubt that he is the master of his family, which consists of his four red-headed sons and his wife, Vinnie (Dorothy Stickney). He is forever criticizing Vinnie's housekeeping, and his blustering tantrums have cost the Days maid after maid. During a visit by the Rev. Dr. Lloyd (Richard Sterling), father lets slip that he has never been baptized. This shocks mother, even though father insists he cannot be kept out of heaven on a mere technicality. Vinnie decides the oversight must be repaired, but Clarence steadfastly refuses until, in a weak moment when he is led to believe Vinnie is dying, he consents. To his dismay, Vinnie holds him to his promise. Heading in his Sunday best off to church, he bellows, "I'm going to be baptized, damn it!" Atkinson could not know how near he came to the truth when he noted, "Sooner or later every one will have to see 'Life With Father' . . . a perfect comedy . . . a darlin' play." Opening just after war had broken out again in Europe, its affectionate portrait of nineteenth-century home life evoked a past of simple values. In late June *Variety* reported it was the season's only hit to play at absolute capacity every performance since its opening. Before it closed, it had been done in New York alone 3224 times. The play's success confirmed the skills of Lindsay and Crouse, whose partnership had heretofore been confined to musicals.

. . .

Howard Lindsay [né Herman Nelke] (1889–1968) was born in Waterford, N.Y., and studied at Harvard. He began his career in the early years of the new century as an actor, but by the twenties occasionally directed plays as well. In 1933 he wrote the hit comedy, *She Loves Me Not,* then a year later first joined with Crouse to write the book for the musical *Anything Goes. Red, Hot and Blue!* (1936) and *Hooray for What!* (1937) followed before the pair turned to their new comedy.

. . .

Russel Crouse (1893–1966), a native of Findlay, Ohio, began his working days as a journalist, then tried his hand at acting and as a press agent for the Theatre Guild. In the early thirties he collaborated on the books for two failed musicals, prior to meeting Lindsay.

. . .

Once again, this time with the Group Theatre's production of his **Thunder Rock** (11-14-39, Mansfield), Robert Ardrey found himself characterized as a thoughtful, interesting writer who just could not quite make the grade theatrically. A disillusioned newspaperman, Charleston (Luther Adler), throws up his job and takes employment as a lighthouse keeper on an isolated island in Lake Michigan. The ghosts of the crew and passengers from a ship wrecked off the island eighty years before appear to him and convince him that for all its shortcomings American democracy is the world's best chance to struggle through to a better way of life. He opts to quit the island and return to an imperfect world.

A more personal struggle was the focus of Sidney Kingsley's **The World We Make** (11-20-39, Guild), which the playwright drew from Millen Brand's novel *The Outward Room.* Her quarreling, self-involved parents, whom she blames for giving her young brother a car in which he met with a fatal accident, have committed Virginia McKay (Margo) to a mental institution, where the head doctor (Rudolf Foster), tells her she has never developed emotionally beyond her brother's death. She flees the institution and, assuming the name Harriet Hope, takes a job in a laundry. When the arduous work would seem to be too much for her, a sympathetic employee, John Kohler (Herbert Rudley), brings her to his shabby rooms. They quickly fall in love. She becomes a model housekeeper for him, and they remain together even after she reveals her past. She tells him she will try to go on since "I want a place that's safe . . . where nothing can get at me." But when John's own younger brother, Jim (Joseph Pevney), is rushed to the hospital and dies, John goes to pieces. In helping him to come to grips with the problem, Harriet recognizes that she has triumphed over her own troubles. The play received sharply divided notices and lingered for only ten weeks.

Three much quicker failures followed. Some of the season's curtest reviews were handed Caroline North and Earl Blackwell's **Aries in Rising** (11-21-39, Golden). Martha Wood Baugh (Blanche Sweet) has brought her sugary daughter, Mattie Kate Baugh (Mary Mason), to New York, hoping talent scouts will spot her. On the advice of Madame Bernardi (Constance Collier), an eccentric astrologer who once had been a vaudevillian, Mattie assumes her mother's maiden name. After a hometown reporter (John Craven) plants a story suggesting she is the mistress of a senator, Mattie is given a screen test. But it turns out that mamma is the sort of actress Hollywood has been seeking.

There were more theatre folk in Gladys Hurlbut's **Ring Two** (11-22-39, Henry Miller's). Following her divorce, Mary Carr (June Walker) abandons her performing career and renovates an old Connecticut farmhouse. But she does not find the peace and quiet she seeks. Instead, she is descended upon by Durward Nesbitt (Tom Powers), her former leading man—who had been named as corespondent in her divorce—his new mistress (Betty Field), Mary's brash former agent (Edith Van Cleve), her onetime black servants and their family, and her daughter, Peggy (Gene Tierney), who is determined to reunite her parents. Sure enough, when Mary's ex (Paul McGrath) turns up and promptly gets lost in a snowstorm, Mary realizes how right Peggy has been.

In Justin Sturm's **I Know What I Like** (11-24-39, Hudson) Karl Hedstrom (John Beal), a struggling painter, wins rich Sandra Page (Helen Claire) away from a banker who has been courting her, even though Karl has painted a fake El Greco which an unscrupulous dealer (Gage Clark) has sold to Sandra as the real thing. Of course, Karl had not known the dealer's intentions.

The same critics who found many things to admire about Maxwell Anderson's **Key Largo** (11-27-39, Ethel Barrymore) also found much to complain about— "muddy and inconclusive," "bogged down by talk," "a tendency to induce indifference." But Paul Muni, returning from Hollywood after a seven-year absence, was garlanded on all sides for "the simple, masculine force and the lucidity that distinguish his acting." King McCloud recognizes that his side has lost the Spanish Civil War, so urges his men to join him in leaving. Led by Victor d'Alcala (José Ferrer), they refuse, and die in battle. Back in the States, King is riddled with guilt. Having visited the families of most of the dead men, he arrives at the lowly Florida hotel run by d'Alcala's blind father (Harold Johnsrud) and sister Alegre (Uta Hagen). He describes his visits to the dead men's families and his telling them the sad stories of how their boys died, adding, "and how I was alive—/ and I can see now it was natural/ they'd give me little thanks." The d'Alcalas are being menaced by gangsters. King would wave away the problem until, concluding his own life is now worthless, he kills one of the gangsters and is himself killed. His death spares two Indians whom a corrupt sheriff was attempting to frame for killings the gangster had committed. The play ran for 105 performances.

At least onstage, Ethel Barrymore was growing younger. In her last vehicle she had played a 101-year-old woman. In Noel Langley's somber drama **Farm of**

Three Echoes (11-28-39, Cort), set in South Africa, her Ouma Gerart was only ninety-seven. Ouma had killed her abusive husband, and now her daughter-in-law, Lisha (Ann Dere), murders her own abusive husband (McKay Morris), Ouma's son. Ouma's grandson (Dean Jagger), fearing history will repeat itself, refuses to marry until Ouma prods him into it. Brown praised Barrymore's "burning intensity, coupled with her lovely voice, her eloquent posture, and her manifest delight in the child's play she is trying to make adult," but his and other critics' plaudits could not lure in audiences.

Paul Osborn's **Morning's at Seven** (11-30-39, Longacre) ran forty-four performances—four performances less than Barrymore's vehicle. Although Mantle hailed it as "pleasant whimsey about pleasant people," his colleagues were less receptive, seeing it as falling "in the doldrums more frequently than it should" and even as "insupportably dreary." The backyards of the Swansons and the Boltons adjoin one another, a great convenience since Cora Swanson (Jean Adair) and Ida Bolton (Kate McComb) are sisters. A third sister, the unmarried Aaronetta (Dorothy Gish), lives with the Swansons and long has been in love with Theodore Swanson (Thomas Chalmers), with whom she once had a brief tryst. Her brother-in-law, Carl Bolton (Russell Collins), is subject to all manner of strange "spells." A fourth sister, Esther (Effie Shannon), lives nearby, but has to visit the others secretly since her husband (Herbert Yost) considers his in-laws "morons" and threatens to force Essie to live alone on her second floor if she sees them. The family differences and secrets boil over after the Boltons' forty-year-old son Homer (John Alexander), announces he will marry Myrtle Brown (Enid Markey), whom he has been seeing for many years and who has become pregnant. This allows Arry to leave the Swansons and move across the backyard to live with the Boltons, now that they have a spare room. Despite the play's failure, it was remembered with affection by many. A 1980 revival was cordially received and ran for more than a year.

December brought in several offerings which in later years might have been considered off-Broadway presentations, although two of these appeared in what had once been first-class playhouses. Arthur James Pegler and Charles Washburn's **She Gave Him All She Had** (12-1-39, Uncle Sam's Music Hall) was said to be a rehash of their *Little Lost Sister,* a drama alleged to have toured backwaters in 1913. Its venue was a cabaret-theatre in a converted restaurant. A starry-eyed heroine named Fanny Welcome comes to Chicago to earn a living but is lured by a dastardly, mustache-twirling villain into white slavery before she is rescued by a dedicated suffragette and finds safety in the embrace of the handsome hero. Variety acts entertained at intermission.

December really began on the 4th at the 44th Street Theatre when Maurice Evans returned in his full-length *Hamlet* after an extended tour. It added five more weeks to its record. With one exception, the rest of the month was a free fall.

Frederick Lonsdale found rough going with his **Foreigners** (12-5-39, Belasco). This West End importation told of a Jew (Richard Ainley) shunned by his fellow shipboard passengers. When the vessel is wrecked and the survivors take refuge on an island, the Jew's skills and industry make him dictator. Eventually the others leave on a rescue ship, but the Jew remains behind with a beautiful girl (Martha Scott) who had stowed away on the doomed vessel.

The heroine (Franciska Gaal) of Dorothy Cumming's **The Woman Brown** (12-8-39, Biltmore) goes resignedly to her death for a crime she did not commit. Mary Brown has come to hate her drunken but dangerously ill husband and love his foreman (Colin Keith-Johnston). A nurse (Helen Trenholme), who also covets the foreman, poisons a sleeping potion she has given Mary, but Mary inadvertently gives it to her husband. After she is sentenced, the foreman promises to raise her young son.

Harold Igo's **Steel** (12-19-39, Provincetown Playhouse) had been making the rounds of outlying theatres for nearly a decade. Critics mocked it as watered-down Eugene O'Neill. Hunky (Donald DeFore), a Polish immigrant steelworker, becomes convinced that steel is the modern god. He replaces the cross he has worn around his neck with a piece of steel. Fired for his union activities and his extremism, he kills a man during a strike. A giant crane picks him up and hurls him into a blast furnace.

The season's only play to fold ignominiously after a single performance was Lawrence Joseph Dugan's **Once upon a Time** (12-20-39, Labor Stage). Dugan had just left Yale, and his play spotlighted three young men climbing a mountain in search of their own disparate ideas of truth and the good life. A fourth young man attempts to have them kill each other and to seize all power, but the boys best him by following the advice of Mr. Moon to laugh away would-be dictators.

Lesley Storm's **Billy Draws a Horse** (12-21-39, Playhouse), which London had seen as *Tony Draws a Horse,* was viewed by critics as not much better. A woman (Hayley Bell) goes on a drinking binge after her physician husband (Arthur Margetson) punishes their son for drawing a sexually realistic horse on his office wall. But Grandma (Grace George) sets everything right after another of the boy's drawings wins an award. Billy never appears in the play.

Syd Porcelain's **Alternate Current** (12-22-39,

Daly's) survived for two performances. Set up as a play within a play, it described how a young woman tries to choose among three suitors, one (Porcelain) of whom is the playwright writing about it all. Critics who sat through the evening—and at least one acknowledged leaving after the first act—reported that some of the lines provoked responses from the audience, such as a character asking, "What's the matter?" and a first-nighter shouting back, "Plenty."

J. B. Priestley's London hit **When We Are Married** (12-25-39, Lyceum) provided some compensation. On their silver wedding anniversaries in 1909, three couples discover that the parson who married them was not authorized to do so. But just before eleven o'clock they learn that they are, indeed, wed in the eyes of the law. Played almost as farce by a cast that included Alison Skipworth, J. C. Nugent, Tom Powers, Estelle Winwood, Philip Tonge, Ann Andrews and Leona Powers, the entertainment delighted playgoers for twenty weeks.

Two weeks was all that Paul Vincent Carroll's Irish drama **Kindred** (12-26-39, Maxine Elliott's) stayed around. A mad poet (Wallace Ford), knowing his derangement is hereditary, refuses to wed his beloved Mary Griffin (Aline MacMahon), impregnates a serving girl, then commits suicide. Years later Mary, who has married the village grocer (Barry Fitzgerald) and had a son by him, meets a wandering fiddler (Arthur Shields) who preaches reform and who turns out to be the poet's bastard. She is torn between her devotion to her own family and some inexplicable attraction the fiddler has for her.

The old year's last entry, Gustav Eckstein's **Christmas Eve** (12-27-39, Henry Miller's), was gone by the time the new year came in. Julia McGlory (Katherine Locke), the daughter of a blustering, besotted Irish father (James Rennie) and a Polish mother, Hanka (Beth Merrill), is at once fascinated and repelled by the thought of sex, so she is reluctant to wed Peter Tor (Kent Smith), a plainspoken ironworker. But watching her mother give birth to the newest McGlory convinces her that marriage and sex are fine. Many critics were taken aback by the childbirth scene, however stylized. They were also puzzled by Jo Mielziner's setting of the McGlorys' modest apartment, which was designed to move sideways now and then to give a slightly different perspective to the action.

The new year's first entry quickly became the season's third smash hit comedy, James Thurber and Elliott Nugent's **The Male Animal** (1-9-40, Cort). Tommy Turner (Nugent) is a mild-mannered, thoughtful English professor at a large midwestern university. His ivory-tower world, however, is suddenly disrupted by two problems. For one, Joe Ferguson (Leon Ames), a former star football player at the school and an old flame of Turner's wife, Ellen (Ruth Matteson), comes back after a long absence for the big game of the season. Second, word has leaked out that Turner is to read to his class a letter the anarchist Vanzetti sent to Vanzetti's daughter before his execution. Since several faculty members have recently been dismissed for their red leanings, this could cause fireworks. An irate trustee (Matt Briggs) warns Tommy not to put ideas into students' heads. Coming to Tommy's defense, the dean (Ivan Simpson) assures the trustee, "I have been putting ideas into young people's heads for forty-two years with no visible results." Tommy's edginess about Joe leads to the two having a knock-down fistfight. However, Joe soon returns to his wife, and the letter proves harmless. Saluted by Richard Watts, Jr., in the *Herald Tribune* as "a singularly happy combination of Thurber's comic brilliance and Nugent's gift for human and likable characterization," the comedy ran for seven months.

A revival of Sean O'Casey's *Juno and the Paycock* at the Mansfield on the 16th featured Sara Allgood, Barry Fitzgerald and Arthur Shields in its principal roles. The consensus was that more nearly perfect players for the parts could not be found, so the drama did good business for thirteen weeks.

By contrast, nothing seemed right with **The Man Who Killed Lincoln** (1-17-40, Longacre), which Elmer Harris and Philip Van Doren Stern took from the latter's book. The drama recapitulated John Wilkes Booth's desire to revenge the Confederacy's defeat, his shooting of Lincoln, and his own subsequent killing. The writing was inept, the playing of Richard Waring as Booth and the supporting cast bombastic, and the staging, especially of the assassination scene, clumsy. Only the performance of Whitford Kane as Samuel Cox, who chides the fleeing Booth for his disservice to both the nation as a whole and the South in particular, received approval.

Closing after ninety-six performances, Elmer Rice's **Two on an Island** (1-22-40, Broadhurst) went down in the records as a near miss. Among those who delighted in it was the *World-Telegram*'s Sidney Whipple, who called it "a pleasant and unpretentious comedy of metropolitan life, ingeniously constructed and happily without an overburden of ponderous sociology." John Thompson (John Craven), a would-be playwright from Ohio, and Mary Ward (Betty Field), a New Hampshire girl hoping to become an actress, both arrive in New York and grab cabs—skeletonized cabs that were parts of Jo Mielziner's simplified, stylized settings. As the pair struggle to find themselves, their paths cross although they remain unaware of each other. Thus they are seated not far apart on the top deck of a sightseeing bus, and later John, who has taken a temporary job at an eatery counter, serves Mary coffee. They finally meet atop the

Statue of Liberty. Mary learns that the despairing John is ready to throw in the towel, and John realizes that Mary is in danger of falling for the snares of a lascivious producer (Luther Adler). They decide to help each other. Back at Penn Station two more youngsters arrive in New York and hail cabs. Rice filled his large cast with a variety of characters including a philandering artist, a union organizer, a tough sailor, and an old Jewish woman shunted aside by her newly rich daughter.

Two nights later a not dissimilar story unfolded in Arthur Wilmurt's **Young Couple Wanted** (1-24-40, Maxine Elliott's). Because her job as a schoolteacher prohibits her marrying, Catherine Daly (Arlene Francis) and her beau, Jed Jones (Hugh Marlowe), who ekes out a living selling toiletries door to door, room together without benefit of clergy until her parents learn of the situation and force the youngsters to wed. This costs Catherine her job. She and Jed try peddling jams that have been put up back home on the Jones farm, but big-city union troublemakers threaten to shut them down. So the youngsters abandon New York and head for the farm.

Most George Bernard Shaw plays were essentially debates. None more so than **Geneva** (1-30-40, Henry Miller's), touted as the playwright's fiftieth opus. The world's leading fascist dictators—Battler [read Hitler] (Maurice Colbourne), Bombardone [Mussolini] (Ernest Borrow), and General Flanco (John Turnbull)—are summoned to the League of Nations to defend their actions. Battler, who sports a small mustache and whose hair falls over his forehead, appears in a suit of medieval armor, with a swastika armband. Bombardone comes in a toga. Among those arguing the other side are a British minister (Lawrence Hanray), a Russian commissar (Earle Grey), a Jew (Beckett Bould), and a young woman (Jessica Tandy) who advocates living by Christ's teachings. Nothing is resolved, so the debate was silenced after two weeks.

In Catherine Turney and Jerry Horwin's **My Dear Children** (1-31-40, Belasco) Allan Manville, a much married matinee idol now living in Switzerland and having an affair with a countess (Tala Birell), is suddenly visited by his three daughters, Portia Trent (Patricia Waters), Miranda Burton (Lois Hall), and Cordelia Clark (Doris Dudley), none of whom he has seen before and each of whom has a different mother. All three girls are having problems with their marriages or their love lives and have called on him for help. Portia goes home after daddy cannot resolve her affair with Cordelia's ex. Miranda settles for one of daddy's friends. Cordelia requires a good spanking, but in the end agrees to act opposite her father in a new play. Just as Mrs. Midget's backing-in entrance last season had

provoked a storm of applause, so Manville's first appearance, doffing an overcoat to reveal evening trousers and a shirt, elicited a minutes-long ovation. For Manville was played by John Barrymore, returning to the New York stage after seventeen years. Some reviewers reported that he looked "weary" and "ravaged," but noted that the magnificent voice and the passionate eyes still shone through. There was general agreement that the play was a barely serviceable vehicle, but that Barrymore's light-hearted cavorting made it highly diverting. Critic after critic dwelled on his comic ad libs, ignoring the fact that weeks before *Variety* had reported the lines were actually in the script. Thus, pouring himself a drink, he turned to the audience and said he wished the stuff was real, and later advised patrons that one remark was "the lousiest line in the play." He also romped in a knee-baring Tyrolian costume and in a chef's apron and hat. But a hush fell on the theatre when he found occasion to insert Hamlet's "To be or not to be" speech. The play, which had run for thirty-three weeks in Chicago, was still doing good business when Barrymore grew tired of it, forcing it to close after 105 performances. They marked his last hours on a New York stage.

The Lunts, far more loyal and dependable, returned their *Taming of the Shrew* to the footlights at the Alvin on February 5 after a successful cross-country tour. They stayed for only one week.

One week was also all Broadway would allow Ayn Rand's adaptation of her own novel *We the Living,* renamed for the stage **The Unconquered** (2-13-40, Biltmore). The sullen Leo Kovalensky (John Emery), whose father has been killed by the authorities, and life-embracing Kira Argounova (Helen Craig) are Russian aristocrats struggling to survive in the Soviet Union in 1924. To permit the ailing Leo to have a Crimean rest cure, Kira gives herself to an OGPU agent, Andrei Taganov (Dean Jagger). Learning on his return of what she has done, Leo abandons her. Andrei, who is disgusted by the venality of his higher-ups, even though he himself has indulged in illegal speculation, kills himself. Kira, grabing her ermine coat, flees the country.

A number of critics compared Clifford Odets's **Night Music** (2-22-40, Broadhurst) to *Two on an Island.* A few also saw traces of Saroyan's newly voguish, undisciplined style in the work. Like the Rice play it used a large cast and multiple scenes to tell a story of a New York romance. Steve Takis (Elia Kazan), a young Greek-American boy with a chip on his shoulder and a flair for speechifying, has been sent to New York by his Hollywood employers to bring back some trained monkeys. When the monkeys steal a young actress's jewels, he is arrested. But a sympathetic, cancer-riddled detective (Morris Carnovsky) not only exculpates him, he helps Steve and the young actress (Jane Wyatt) become a pair. Steve decides to remain in New York. The play's action moved from a police station to a theatre, a hotel, the World's Fair, a restaurant, and an airport. Although critics had high praise for the actors, especially for Kazan's vibrant playing, they mostly agreed with Lockridge in dismissing the play as "minor Odets." It closed after two and a half weeks.

Dorothy Thompson, who had won fame for her books and newspaper columns assailing totalitarianism, and Fritz Kortner, a refugee playwright, combined their efforts for the short-lived **Another Sun** (2-23-40, National). George Brandt (Hans Jaray), a famous German Hamlet who has fled Germany to protest the arrest of his Jewish friends, and his live-and-let-live wife, Maria (Celeste Holm), now reside in New York. But Brandt finds it impossible to master English. Maria readily accepts a Nazi offer to return home, but Brandt elects to remain, even though the only work he can obtain is a $40-a-week job on radio—making animal noises.

Just as short-lived was John van Druten's **Leave Her to Heaven** (2-27-40, Longacre), which brought Ruth Chatterton back to New York after a fifteen-year hiatus. Although van Druten had moved to America, he set his play in England. Madge Monckton is married to a dour, much older man (Reynolds Denniston) and has taken on her chauffeur, Robert Ewen (Edmond O'Brien), as her lover. He proves so jealous that he bludgeons the husband to death. Upset and inebriated, Madge tells the police that she is the killer. But Robert also confesses. He is eventually sentenced to die, leading Madge to kill herself. Chatterton had a field day running the emotional gamut, but the play was too weak to sustain her.

Andrew Rosenthal's **The Burning Deck** (3-1-40, Maxine Elliott's) had originally been scheduled to open on Monday the 4th. Instead it advanced its first night and by the time Monday rolled around it was gone. On the veranda of a hotel on a Mediterranean island Rex Wolfson (Onslow Stevens), now a popular London playwright, runs into the wife (Vera Allen) and then infant son he had abandoned twenty years before in Davenport, Iowa. The boy, Rody (George Lloyd), has grown into a young man who wants to be a writer but is pressured by his mother to become a businessman. By the play's end, Rex has convinced his former wife to allow their son to remain on the island, try his hand at writing, and help a dying pianist (Mary Howes) with whom the youngster has been smitten.

Many aisle-sitters saw Allan Wood's **The Weak Link** (3-4-40, Golden) as an unimaginative blending of *Three Men on a Horse* and *Whistling in the Dark,* with Hume Cronyn as its sole saving grace. Peter Mason is a chess genius whose other hobby is spotting the weak points

in failed bank robberies. He offers his services to the Bankers' Protective Association, unaware the organization is a front for bank robbers. The thugs hold him and his girl (Peggy French) hostage and demand he design a flawless bank robbery. After his attempt to knock out his captors with sleeping pills misfires, he decides to give the gang a plan. However, he alerts the police by pasting a note on the back of the coat of one of the gangsters who is sent on an errand. He also tricks the hood left to guard him and his girl into running out on the fire escape, forgetting to remind the man that there is no fire escape.

By the time Ernest Hemingway's only play, **The Fifth Column** (3-6-40, Alvin), reached Broadway it had needed to be so heavily revised that Benjamin Glazer was listed as adaptor. Although many critics viewed it as disappointing, others agreed with Mantle's assessment—"a moving and exciting story of strong men in adventurous situations." Philip Rawlings (Franchot Tone), an American newspaperman, and Max (Lee J. Cobb), a German refugee, have been working to the point of exhaustion in Madrid to aid the Loyalists during the Civil War. In the middle of a bombardment, Philip, who is slightly in his cups, hears a woman scream in the next room and, when he goes to calm her, learns she is Dorothy Bridges (Katherine Locke), an American searching for her brother who is missing in the fighting. He seduces her, feels guilty about it, and would follow her to Paris until Max convinces him he must remain to continue the fight. The leading players all were praised, as was Lenore Ulric, once a Belasco star but now reduced to portraying a Moorish trollop—a latter-day Kiki—with whom Philip has spent time. The play, produced by the Theatre Guild, ran eleven weeks.

So scathing were the reviews for Ellis St. Joseph's **A Passenger to Bali** (3-14-40, Ethel Barrymore) that it had to be withdrawn after just four performances, although Walter Huston was its star and was showered with praise in a role that allowed him to range from a smiling, unctuous hypocrite to a bellowing madman. After the so-called Rev. Mr. Walkes sneaks aboard a freighter at Shanghai, its captain (Colin Keith-Johnston) discovers he is a man without a country whom authorities everywhere refuse to allow to disembark. Eventually he gets the Kanaka crew drunk on Holland gin and incites them to mutiny. But a typhoon arises—a typhoon that causes the ship to rock and lurch, and snaps a mast in two—and the captain orders the ship abandoned, but shoots Walkes rather than allow him into a lifeboat.

Jerome Mayer's **Goodbye in the Night** (3-18-40, Biltmore) begins on a foggy evening as Ollie (James Bell) escapes from a mental institution where he is being held as a homicidal maniac. He returns to his family farm, murders his brother, whom he blames for his problems, then later murders his brother-in-law and his former sweetheart. A woman, her daughter, and the girl's fiancé come to the farm looking for a night's lodging. They are forced to help bury one of the bodies, and Ollie, with the police closing in, tries unsuccessfully to pin the murders on them.

Much ballyhoo had been accorded Ellen Schwanneke, a leading German actress who reportedly had refused Hitler's personal request to remain in Germany and now was making her Broadway debut. Her vehicle was **A Case of Youth** (3-23-40, National), adapted by Wesley Towner from Ludwig Hirschfeld and Eugene Wolf's unspecified German original. She played Midge Mayflower, a young lady who discovers her musically inclined father's thoughtless appropriation of $10,000 from the bank where he works could send him to prison. She sells off the family furniture and, by one means or another, bamboozles his creditors into forgiving the remaining debt. A huge Great Dane, who spent much of the evening staring dolefully at the audience, almost stole the show. A few reviewers compared Schwanneke favorably with Elisabeth Bergner, but this quick-closing dud was her only New York appearance.

The terse, dismissive notices second-stringers handed **Separate Rooms** (3-23-40, Maxine Elliott's) suggested it too would fold shortly. Instead, by resorting to cut-rate tickets and a sexually exploitive ad campaign, this comedy, written by Joseph Carole and Alan Dinehart "in collaboration" with Alex Gottlieb and Edmund Joseph, proved the season's sleeper, sticking around for 613 performances. Jim Stackhouse (Dinehart) is a hardboiled gossip columnist. His playwright brother, Don (Lyle Talbot), on the other hand, is a softie married to a money-grubbing actress (Glenda Farrell). Don is husband in name only, since the lone male Pam will allow in her bed is her $400 pedigreed Chihuahua. To rectify matters, Jim threatens to expose Pam's rather sordid past. She comes around and in time even announces she is expecting a baby. Meanwhile, Jim has wooed and won his girl Friday, Linda (Mozelle Britton).

Ferenc Molnár, now a refugee, was in the audience for the revival of his *Liliom,* which was brought out at the 44th Street Theatre on the 25th. Most critics felt that the play had withstood the test of time, but, haunted by memories of Eva Le Gallienne and Joseph Schildkraut, were hardly unanimous about the new leads, Ingrid Bergman and Burgess Meredith. Those who admired them saluted Bergman's beauty and sensitivity and Meredith's vitality and intelligence. But the naysayers missed "the burning, smothered passion which smoldered" between the originals. Less generally welcomed was Elia Kazan's unsubtle Sparrow. The revival lingered for seven weeks.

Embellished by the splendid acting of Flora Robson, Isobel Elsom, and Estelle Winwood, Reginald Denham and Edward Percy's West End thriller **Ladies in Retirement** (3-26-40, Henry Miller's) captivated audiences for nineteen weeks. The kindhearted Leonora Fiske (Elsom), who has given up the stage and settled in the country, agrees to the request of her housekeeper, Ellen Creed (Robson), to invite Ellen's two batty sisters for a visit. The ladies, the battier of whom is Louisa (Winwood), quickly wear out their welcome but refuse to leave. When Leonora orders them to go, Ellen strangles her and hides her body in an unused bake oven. Ellen's sinister nephew (Patrick O'Moore) appears and, catching on, attempts to blackmail his aunt. But she retorts that the first murder is always the hardest. Still, she disappears, apparently hoping the police will blame her sisters.

Margery Sharp was an English novelist who adapted her novel *The Nutmeg Tree* for the stage as **Lady in Waiting** (3-27-40, Martin Beck) and allowed New Yorkers to enjoy it before Londoners did. Audiences first see Julia Packett (Gladys George) in her bath (with her back to playgoers) in a bathroom filled with antiques she hides there from her creditors. Julia is a beautiful, blonde if slightly vulgar actress, who has lived alone ever since handing her baby daughter over to her rich mother-in-law after her husband was killed in World War I. Now her presence is required in France to give approval to her daughter's marriage. On the Channel boat she has a flirtation with a handsome acrobat, Fred Genocchio (Leonard Penn) of the Flying Genocchios, and also meets a polished Englishman, Sir William Warring (Alan Napier). Arriving at her mother-in-law's home, she calls her daughter "my little Sue," only to have the priggish girl (Carol Curtis-Brown) reply, "I'm usually called Susan." She discovers that Sir William is also to be a houseguest, and, before long, Fred shows up to pursue his courtship. But Fred proves to be a worse prig than her daughter, and her daughter's fiancé (Stephen Ker Appleby) turns out to be a scoundrel. She sends them both on their way, then accepts Sir William's proposal. The play was almost a hit, running eleven weeks, and had no better luck when London saw it as *The Nutmeg Tree* the following year.

The Hanleys in Frank Gould's **The Scene of the Crime** (3-28-40, Fulton) are happy middle-class New York apartment dwellers until their son, David (Chester Stratton), takes to crime and is caught, convicted, and executed. Their grief is nothing compared to their feelings when David's ghost appears to comfort them but only succeeds in prompting his parents to gas themselves.

On April 1, Maurice Evans revived his celebrated *Richard II* at the St. James for a month, using many of the same players he had in his cast three years earlier.

Ethel Barrymore abandoned false wrinkles and wigs to play a woman her own age in Vincent Sheean's **An International Incident** (4-2-40, Ethel Barrymore). However, "her patrician profile, her lovely head, her far-set eye, her tenderly smiling mouth, the grace of her gestures, the poise of her movements, or the fog-bound lilt of her famous throaty voice" could not overcome a weak, aimless script. She was seen as the widowed Mrs. Charles Rochester, an American-born lady who has attained worldwide fame writing novels in England. On an American speaking tour she meets her second cousin once removed, Hank Rogers (Kent Smith), a newspaperman. Falling in love with her and fearing she is here merely to propagandize, he takes her to a Detroit strike scene in hopes of showing her blue-collar problems. At the picket line (never shown), she comes under police attack. The incident broadens her perspective but does not prevent her accepting a proposal from an aristocratic Englishman (Cecil Humphries). To suggest the similarities of New York, Chicago and Detroit, the club ladies of the three cities were played in each act by the same three ladies (Josephine Hull, Lea Penman, Eda Heinemann), while Stewart Chaney's three hotel suites simply rearranged the same walls and furnishings. Two weeks and the play was gone.

Less than a fortnight after they achieved success with *Ladies in Retirement*, Reginald Denham and Edward Percy went astray with **Suspect** (4-9-40, Playhouse). For many years the tight-lipped Mrs. Smith (Pauline Lord) has lived in seclusion in Cornwall with her son (Barton Hepburn). But her isolation ends when her son becomes engaged and his fiancée (Jane Lauren) arrives for a visit with her father (Wallis Clark) and godfather (Frederic Worlock). The latter, Sir Hugo Const, is a newspaper magnate who once had been a court reporter, and he recognizes Mrs. Smith as Margaret Wishart, who years earlier had been brought to trial for murdering her father and stepmother with an ax but had been let go in a Scottish court after a verdict of "not proven." Sir Hugo terrifies Mrs. Smith with his obvious attempt to get at the truth of her long-buried history, but she is finally able to convince him of her innocence. When the guests leave, Mrs. Smith takes out her old ax and begins chopping at some wood. Lord's "scattered, stifled, inarticulate" playing was "mesmeric" but, like Barrymore's, not enough to save an indifferent drama.

For their **Medicine Show** (4-12-40, New Yorker), Oscar Saul and H. R. Hays employed the "Living Newspaper" technique developed by the defunct Federal Theatre Project. The Statistician (Martin Gabel) uses not only statistics—such as 250,000 needless deaths each year and 1600 American counties without hospital facilities—but also slides, newsreel clippings, skits, and even a parody of *Alice in Wonderland* to assail the American Medical Association and campaign for socialized medicine.

Cute little Molly Picon, a leading light in Yiddish theatre, was described by one critic as "a darling" when she made her Broadway debut in Sylvia Regan's **Morning Star** (4-16-40, Longacre). She played the widowed Becky Felderman, who raises her children in a simple Lower East Side apartment. In 1910 she loses one daughter (Cecilia Evans) in the Triangle Shirt Waist factory fire; in World War I her only son (Ross Elliott) is killed. By 1931 she is saddled with her two surviving daughters; one (Jeanne Greene) is married to a wastrel songwriter (David Morris), and the other (Ruth Yorke) is an embittered harpy. But Becky keeps her chin up and finally agrees to marry her longtime boarder, Aaron Greenspan (Joseph Buloff). Like the more established Broadway names she followed, Picon could not help a helpless vehicle.

But then neither could a rising male luminary basking in his new Hollywood celebrity. John Garfield was starred in Albert Bein's **Heavenly Express** (4-18-40, National). Beneath a railroad trestle, three bearded hoboes huddle around a fire as the snow falls and reminisce about the Overland Kid, who died years ago jumping from a train while pursued by railroad men. Listening at a distance is one of the Kid's old buddies, Melancholy Bo (Curt Conway). Suddenly the Kid (Garfield) appears. He is now ticket-taker for the Heavenly Express, a train with a diamond as a headlight, platinum wheels, and the speed of a meteor. He has come to take Bo to Hobo Heaven and then will go to the home of Bo's mother, Betsy Graham (Aline MacMahon), and give her her ticket, too. At Betsy's—a boardinghouse for railroaders—he jumps from chair to table, sings songs while accompanying himself on his ukelele, and generally cavorts with the residents, especially Ed Peeto (Harry Carey), one of the few trainmen who showed kindness to hoboes. Finally he and Betsy depart. Several critics likened Garfield's athletic antics to Peter Pan's but, while commending his effort, felt the best work of the evening was Carey's. Carey, who had written and performed in the long-gone cheap touring shows, had not appeared on Broadway since 1909, instead making a career as a character actor in films.

The season's last dramatic hit was considered by many its best. "No one can complain about the theatre's being an escapist institution when it conducts a class in current events at once as touching, intelligent and compassionate" as Robert Sherwood's **There Shall Be No Night** (4-29-40, Alvin), Brown wrote. In Helsinki, neither the Nobel Prize–winning scientist Dr. Kaarlo Valkonen (Alfred Lunt), nor his American-born wife, Miranda (Lynn Fontanne), believes that the Russians will invade Finland. Their young son, Erik (Montgomery Clift), disagrees and is preparing to fight. He proves right when war soon breaks out. Miranda rejects her husband's plea for her to sail for safety in America. Erik is soon killed, and, learning the news, Kaarlo rips off his Red Cross armband and grabs a gun. A reluctant warrior, he nonetheless hopes that the war will not destroy civilization but rather will be "the long deferred death rattle of the primordial beast." He, too, is killed. Back in Helsinki, Miranda and Kaarlo's Uncle Waldemar (Sydney Greenstreet) prepare to burn their home if necessary in a scorched-earth gesture, but meanwhile she listens and muses as Waldemar plays an old Finnish melody on the piano. Watts observed, "Mr. Lunt has never been more moving nor more deeply impressive . . . , nor has Miss Fontanne ever appeared more earnestly and beautifully than as the loyal American wife. Here are characters of stature and intellectual capacity and honest emotion, and Mr. Lunt and Miss Fontanne indicate all of these qualities with splendid clarity." For the first time in memory, the Lunts sacrificed their traditional summer vacation in Wisconsin (or at least a good part of it) to play into the autumn. They then took the production on tour. After Finland's fall, Sherwood changed the setting to portray the German invasion of Greece. In the spring of 1941, the drama was given a Pulitzer Prize, having opened too late for consideration for the 1940 award. That meant that two plays from the same season had won the prize in two different years.

The current season's Pulitzer Prize winner, William Saroyan, did not fare so well with his second offering, **Love's Old Sweet Song** (5-2-40, Plymouth). A mischievous Greek-American messenger boy (Peter Fernandez) hands a forty-four-year-old, lovelorn spinster, Ann Hamilton (Jessie Royce Landis), a telegram suggesting that somebody named Barnaby Gaul will soon be coming to court her. So when an itinerant pitchman, old Doc Goodheart (Walter Huston), stops at her house, she assumes he is the man. Goodheart quickly comprehends the situation and strings along. But matters are complicated by a band of Okies—Pa and Ma Yearling (Arthur Hunnicutt and Doro Merande) and their fourteen children—who park themselves on Ann's lawn, steal her things, and eventually burn down her house. Still, old Doc is hanging around and love has blossomed. Among the play's absurdities was a *Time* salesman (Alan Hewitt) who pushes a subscription on the jobless, penniless Pa Yearling by reciting the long list of the magazine's editors and who walks away with a subscription signed with only two X's. And when old Doc lights some candles as part of his pitch for his snake oil, the Yearling kids burst out in "Happy Birthday."

Terence Rattigan and Hector Bolitho came a cropper with **Grey Farm** (5-3-40, Hudson), which served as the Broadway debut of Oscar Homolka, another German refugee. He played a farmer who has transferred the love he bore to his late wife to their only son (John Cromwell), although subconsciously he feels the boy was responsible for his mother's death at childbirth and he now harbors scarcely recognized homicidal urges. His son's announcement that he has become engaged snaps the father's mind. The old man strangles their servant girl (Maria Temple), then shoots himself.

Two one-week failures followed. The title of John Walter Kelly's **Out from Under** (5-4-40, Biltmore) was also the title of a sizzling novel written under a pseudonym by Joe Parker (John Alexander), a chubby, bored small-town Indiana editor. His wife (Ruth Weston), who does not know that he wrote the book but, like all her neighbors, has read it, is so taken by its suggestiveness that she contemplates having a fling with a New York banker (Philip Ober). At the same time, Joe's publisher sends a blonde beauty (Vivian Vance) to vamp him into doing a promotional tour. But the Parkers' booze-loving black maid (Viola Dean) gets Joe and his wife tipsy and cuddly, so everything comes out just fine.

The Strangler Fig (5-6-40, Lyceum) was adapted by Edith Meiser from John Stephen Strange's novel. A woman (Madeleine Clive) whose husband had been murdered some years before on an island off Florida invites all the people who were there at the time to come for another visit. One by one they are done away with until another woman (Meiser), who had loved and lost the dead man and who had provided the evening's comic relief, is exposed as the killer. At one point a character blurted out, "Good God, what a mess!" and at least two reviewers jumped on the line to express their sentiments about the play.

Having won fame in *Rebecca* and *Gone with the Wind,* Laurence Olivier and Vivien Leigh (not yet his wife) came to Broadway to offer their *Romeo and Juliet* at the huge 51st Street Theatre on the 9th. They were aghast at the notices received the next morning. "Much scenery: no play," Atkinson began his review. The scenery by Robert Edmond Jones was indeed beautiful but was set on a revolve that pushed much of the action upstage, unnecessarily far away from the audience. And in fact there was also too much play, for all the bits of business that Olivier as director added turned Shakespeare's "two hours traffic on the stage" into a more than three-hour production. Leigh was deemed beautiful but still too callow and inexperienced for her part, and Olivier's open-shirted, calisthenic Romeo chided as "mannered and affected." Edmond O'Brien was Mercutio; Cornel Wilde, Tybalt; Alexander Knox, Friar Laurence; and Dame May Whitty, the Nurse. With playgoers allegedly demanding refunds, the tragedy was taken off after thirty-six performances.

But then George M. Cohan met with even less luck, having to close his **The Return of the Vagabond** (5-13-40, National) at the end of its first week. The play was a sequel to *The Tavern* (9-27-20). Accompanied by the same lightning, thunder, and rain that had marked his entrances and exits twenty years earlier, the Vagabond (Cohan) returns to the same old tavern, meets the same old Tavern Keeper (E. J. Blunkall), the same old Governor (McKay Morris), his same not-so-old daughter (Celeste Holm), and her scared-of-lightning hubby (John Morny). He also traps a trio who have robbed a bank of $250,000, accepts a $10,000 reward for his actions, then hands the money over to the Tavern Keeper's Son (Fred Herrick), because he is a theatre buff. Cohan had fun at every turn. One of the robbers had disguised himself as a woman, so Cohan told his audience, "All my life I've had a desire to take a shot at a female impersonator." And he won an encouraging hand from the audience when, responding to one character's query as to why he was not abed, he remarked, "I'll never retire!" But the hokum simply did not add up to a good evening's entertainment. And, sadly, Cohan was unable to keep his promise not to retire, so these became his last Broadway appearances.

Fireworks on the James (5-14-40, Provincetown Playhouse) turned out to be John Cournos and Elizabeth McCormick's redaction of Chekhov's early *Platonov,* a story of an unstable, philandering teacher eventually driven to suicide. It was now reset in contemporary Virginia. Largely ignored, and panned by those who did review it, its two-week engagement apparently was cut short after a single week.

One week was also all that Percy Robinson's **At the Stroke of Eight** (5-20-40, Belasco) survived. First done more than a decade earlier in London as *To What Red Hell,* it told of a young man (Richard Waring) who suffers from memory lapses, but is able to confess to killing a prostitute and shoot himself in time to spare the son (Frank Maxwell) of a widow (Sara Allgood), a boy convicted of the murder on circumstantial evidence and slated to be executed.

Russian Bank (5-24-40, St. James), which programs said was written by Theodore Komisarjevsky and Stuart Mims, after an idea by Boris Said, told a tale not unlike *The Unconquered* had a few months before. To spare her aristocratic lover (Tonio Selwart), a prima donna (Josephine Houston) agrees to sleep with a doorman who has been newly appointed a Communist commissar (James Rennie). Years later, after they all have fled to America, the three meet at the Long Island estate of a Mrs. Cameron (Effie Shannon), where the prima donna is relieved to discover that the aristocrat no longer cares

that she has fallen for the ex-doorman. One scene was set in an apartment converted into a speakeasy-cabaret and allowed for some song-and-dance numbers. The play ran a week and a half, or half a week longer than the season's closer.

But then the Players' revival of Congreve's *Love for Love* at the Hudson on June 3 was only slated for a week. Barry Jones was Valentine; Bobby Clark, Ben; Leo G. Carroll, Scandal; Edgar Stehli, Tattle; and Cornelia Otis Skinner, Angelica. Supporting performers included Thomas Chalmers, Dudley Digges, Romney Brent, Peggy Wood, Violet Heming, and Dorothy Gish. A few dissenting voices aside—such as Atkinson, who branded the great comedy "moldy stuff"—reviewers endorsed both the play and the players.

1940–1941

For the eleventh successive year the number of new plays fell. *Variety* listed forty-nine; the *Times,* forty-eight. Mantle gave no figure but spoke with patent sadness of "a new low statistically," apparently unaware that a similar count had been given for 1901–02. Of course, that older tally did not include the numerous cheap touring shows packing in playgoers at neighborhood and backwater theatres, nor the many designed-for-touring dramas lighting up some of several thousand road houses. But cheap touring shows, killed by early silent films, had disappeared three decades earlier, while the road was a pathetic skeleton of its once robust self.

A revival of the five-year-old thriller *Kind Lady,* with Grace George again in the lead, launched the new season at the Playhouse on September 3. Applauded once more, it added another 105 performances to its record.

The theatrical year's first novelty was an importation from London, A. J. Cronin's **Jupiter Laughs** (9-9-40, Biltmore). A brilliant if abrasive scientist (Alexander Knox) is on the verge of important discoveries concerning mental illness. But when he drops his mistress (Nancy Sheridan), the wife of the head of his research facility, to court an attractive new assistant (Jessica Tandy), the rejected woman sets fire to his laboratory. The assistant dies trying to save the doctor's papers. He leaves dejectedly for foreign parts.

Elmer Harris's **Johnny Belinda** (9-18-40, Belasco) exemplified an increasingly rare phenomenon, a play which defies an all but universal drubbbing to become a hit. Richard Watts, Jr., of the *Herald Tribune* spoke for a majority of his colleagues when he dismissed the work as "antique melodrama," noting, "It contains all the clichés of its shopworn school of dramatic writing." In a small village on Prince Edward Island, a grim miller, Black McDonald (Louis Hector), sneers at his deaf-mute daughter, Belinda (Helen Craig), calling her a dummy. The lonely drudge is seduced by the village bully, Locky McCormick (Willard Parker), who then deserts her. But a young doctor, Jack Davidson (Horace McNally), comes on the scene, sets about teaching Belinda sign language, and learns her history. After her father is struck dead by lightning, the villagers persuade Locky to claim the baby. Belinda shoots him. Brought to trial, her pathetic story leads to her acquittal. She rushes into the doctor's arms, then cuddles the baby and speaks her first word—the baby's name, Johnny. The play ran out the season.

Critics let down Maxwell Anderson's blank-verse **Journey to Jerusalem** (10-5-40, National) more gently. The *Post*'s John Mason Brown observed, "His speech, no longer over-colored, is now merely without color. . . . His images have little beauty to them. His dialogue leaves the mind unfired." The public would not buy the play. Miriam (Arlene Francis) and Joseph (Horace Braham) have brought their twelve-year-old son, Jeshua (Sidney Lumet), to Jerusalem for Passover. A notorious thief, Ishmael (Arnold Moss), recognizes that the boy will grow up to be the Messiah. He warns that Herod, still fearful because of an old prophecy, has ordered all twelve-year-old Jewish boys slain, and Ishmael dies protecting him. Even Miriam, after a dream, realizes who her son is. For the time, however, Jeshua is content to dispute with the wise men in the temple. Jo Mielziner's austere but solid settings of Joseph's home, the roof of Herod's palace, a desert place, and the temple were made especially beautiful by his poetic lighting. Among the players, Moss received the best notices.

In England, where it closed before reaching London, St. John Ervine's **Boyd's Daughter** (10-11-40, Booth) had been known as *Boyd's Shop*. Her shopkeeper-father (Whitford Kane) would like his daughter (Helen Trenholme) to marry the village's new minister (Hiram Sherman), but she elects to wed a rival shopkeeper (William Post, Jr.). Kane and Sherman were able to salvage critical plaudits for their humane, humorous portrayals from the wreckage.

The season's second revival was the five-year-old *Blind Alley,* brought out at the Windsor on the 15th. Good notices saw to it that it lingered for eight weeks.

But an even better, more unexpected revival followed at the Cort on the 17th, when José Ferrer headed the cast of Brandon Thomas's forty-seven-year-old *Charley's Aunt.* This tale of an Oxfordian who, to help out a college friend, poses as an aunt from Brazil—"where

the nuts come from"—seemed as uproarious as ever and packed in theatregoers for seven months. Brown wrote of Ferrer, "He never loses sight of the all-important fact the guffaws are the reason and excuse for the monkeyshines he is up to. . . . Every embarrassment a college boy dressed up as a Victorian aunt would undergo—or cause—he has found a side-splitting way of expressing." Similar notices propelled Ferrer into the limelight.

· · ·

José [Vicente] **Ferrer** (1912–92) was born in Puerto Rico, but educated in New York and at Princeton. He made his professional debut in 1934, performing in melodramas on a showboat, and began acting on Broadway in the following year. He called attention to himself in *Brother Rat* (1936), *Missouri Legend* (1938), and *Mamba's Daughters* and *Key Largo* (1939). He was a dark-complected, heavy-featured, rich-voiced actor.

· · ·

The next night produced another hit, but one that was generally considered a major disappointment. Almost every critic compared George S. Kaufman and Moss Hart's **George Washington Slept Here** (10-18-40, Lyceum) unfavorably to the writers' earlier comedies. "You could," the *Sun*'s Richard Lockridge ended his notice, "considering everything, hope for a better play. Something, say, like 'The Man Who Came to Dinner.'" Still, even while making such comparisons, reviewers admitted that they had enjoyed themselves. So did the public for seven months. When Newton Fuller (Ernest Truex) tells his wife, Annabelle (Jean Dixon), that he has purchased the horribly dilapidating, abandoned farmhouse they are standing in and in which George Washington reputedly slept, she can only remark, "Martha wasn't a very good housekeeper." Since Fuller has relinquished the lease on their city apartment, they are forced to move in a month later. But then everything is ready—"except bedrooms, bathrooms, dining room, kitchen, floors, walls, ceilings—." There are other problems. All the wells they drill come up dry. Their daughter, Madge (Peggy French), has fallen for a married man, an actor in the local summer stock company. They have taken in Annabelle's bratty nephew (Bobby Readick) while his parents, getting a divorce, battle over his custody—each demanding the other take him. They are also visited by rich Uncle Stanley (Dudley Digges), an excruciating bore who becomes all the more painful when he confesses he is actually broke. Worse, a cantankerous banker-neighbor (David Orrick) threatens to foreclose on their mortgage, and the Fullers discover Washington never slept in the house—it was Benedict Arnold. But Uncle Stanley has been pretending to great wealth for so long that he has no trouble bamboozling the banker, so all ends happily.

Up in Harlem, Theodore Ward's **Big White Fog** (10-22-40, Lincoln) took an embittered view of black life in America. The play was set in Chicago and moved from 1922 to 1932. Victor Mason (Canada Lee) is an educated black man who has become a disciple of Marcus Garvey and invested his life savings with him. Garvey's downfall leaves him bankrupt. His family falls apart, and he is killed fighting eviction from his home.

Lawrence Langner and his wife, Armina Marshall, set their retelling of the legend of **Suzanna and the Elders** (10-29-40, Morosco) in an early nineteenth-century utopian religious community. John Adam Kent (Morris Carnovsky), the leader of Harmony Heights, selects the group's bashful bookkeeper, Brother Tupper (Howard Freeman), as the mate for Sister Suzanna (Haila Stoddard). But an outsider, Charles Owen (Paul Ballantyne), who has seen and fallen in love with Suzanna, joins the order so that he can woo her. His courtship ruptures the group, most of whom opt to return to the regular world, but he at least walks away with his darling.

Lawrence Riley's look at summer stock, **Return Engagement** (11-1-40, Golden), was a one-week flop. Two famous players, Elizabeth Emerson (Mady Christians) and Geoffrey Armstrong (Bert Lytell), had once been married but had fought so much that an acerbic associate, Ruth (Audrey Christie), was "surprised Tex Rickard never signed them up. Not that they needed anybody to promote *their* fights." Long since divorced, they now are guest stars at a Connecticut summer playhouse backed by rich Mrs. Faulkner (Leona Powers). When Geoffrey makes a play for Mrs. Faulkner, Elizabeth, who has come to realize that she still loves him, resorts to all manner of ploys—such as stealing his false teeth—to thwart and rewin him. A subplot had Mrs. Faulkner trying to force the company to give her stepdaughter (Caryl Smith) a major role. After all, Mrs. Faulkner observes, the girl has had only four lines all season—prompting Ruth to retort, "She remembered practically every one of 'em, didn't you, dear?" A young playwright (Thomas Coley) pretends to elope with the girl so that a genuinely talented ingenue (Augusta Dabney) whom he loves can have her part.

The next three novelties all centered on Hollywood, and all three bombed. In Lynn Starling and Howard J. Green's **Beverly Hills** (11-7-40, Fulton) Leonard Strickland (Clinton Sundberg) writes scenarios for Hollywood child stars, but his wife, Lois (Helen Claire) hopes to get him work on the new epic *Land of Cotton*. She approaches her friend, May Flowers (Violet Heming), once a silent-screen star and now married to the epic's producer, to help. May is man-crazy and goes after Leonard. Scandal erupts, but peace is restored after Leonard signs to write a film for Zanuck.

F. Hugh Herbert and Hans Kraly's **Quiet Please** (11-8-40, Guild) had an unusual opening and closing, which made some critics and playgoers uncomfortable. The entire theatre was supposed to be a movie set on which a play-within-a-film was being made, and the real audience, lectured at times by the bumptious director (Fred Niblo), was asked to pretend to be the extras constituting an imaginary audience. Cameramen and others scooted up and down the aisles. In between, the play told of the film's leading lady (Jane Wyatt), who is married to a philandering actor (Donald Woods). To teach him a lesson she sees to it he finds her apparently having an affair with a handsome filling station attendant (Gordon Jones). His roaming is cured. More than one critic rued that so talented and beautiful an actress as Wyatt could not find better roles.

The third Hollywood comedy, Florence Ryerson and Colin Clements's **Glamour Preferred** (11-15-40, Booth), was "a little duller, a little cheaper, a little more vulgar than its predecessors." Kerry Eldridge (Glen Langan), a dashing leading man on a personal appearance tour, encounters his old flame, Bonita (Betty Lawford), now unhappily married to a titled Englishman. Bonita decides to steal Kerry away from his wife, Lynn (Flora Campbell), who had given up her own important career when she married. Lynn sends for Bonita's husband (Robert Craven). It turns out he, too, is unhappily wed, but he agrees to assist Lynn in retrieving her beloved Kerry.

Some aura of its former celebrity clung to one Greenwich Village theatre, which could still attract critics to its offerings. So many of New York's aisle-sitters scurried down to sit in judgment on A. A. Milne's **Sarah Simple** (11-16-40, Provincetown Playhouse). They thought little of this tale of a wife (Joy Harrington), separated from her husband for eight years, who wins him back after she agrees to become the disguised corespondent in his attempt to divorce her.

Maurice Evans, Helen Hayes, and director Margaret Webster combined their talents to present playgoers with a robust, delightful *Twelfth Night* at the St. James on the 19th. A few critics insisted the comedy itself had a dismaying amount of languors, but Evans's Malvolio, an Elizabethan majordomo metamorphosed into "a 20th century cockney butler . . . more often than not in comic difficulties with his pronunciation," and Hayes's sprightly if unpoetic Viola were ample compensation. June Walker's bouncing, appealing Maria added to the fun. Wesley Addy was Orsino; Mark Smith, Toby; and Wallace Acton, Aguecheek.

Orville (Ezra Stone), the hero of Eugene Conrad and Zac and Ruby Gabel's **Horse Fever** (11-23-40, Mansfield), is an inventive young man. One of his brainstorms is to spike hamburgers with vodka to improve sales. For trying to sell them, his uncle winds up in jail. But Orville's real passion is animal psychiatry. At the track, the family's horse, Trilby, has refused to break from the gate. So Orville hides it in a piano crate, smuggles it into a hotel bathroom, and sets about treating it. He destroys the animal's mental block, but it still fails to win. The evening's best notices went to the beautiful black mare who played Trilby with great restraint and dignity.

Ethel Barrymore found the success she had been seeking for so long in Emlyn Williams's English drama **The Corn Is Green** (11-26-40, National). Miss Moffat is first seen in the small Welsh village of Glansarno, walking alongside her bike and dressed in a straw hat, a shirtwaist and tie, and long skirt, looking for all the world like a middle-aged Gibson girl. She is a spinster schoolmarm who encounters and deals with a variety of professional and local problems, but who finds her reward in her ability to rescue a young boy (Richard Waring) from a probably wasted life in the mines and set him on the path to great achievement as a writer. According to Watts, Barrymore, "with all that radiance of hers, all of her sly, twinkling humor," presented "a characterization of greatness and true nobility." In New York and on the road, the drama kept its star busy for two seasons.

A rash of failures ensued, none running more than three weeks. With the help of Philip Lewis, Eleanor Carroll Chilton adapted her novel *Follow the Furies* and called the dramatization **Fledgling** (11-27-40, Hudson). Once a devout Catholic, Grace Linton (Norma Chalmers) abandoned her faith when she married the atheistic Hugh (Ralph Morgan), a novelist who promised they would shine "light in dark places." He proved a scoundrel and hypocrite. In time, Grace comes down with a hopelessly wasting illness. To put her out of her misery, the Lintons' daughter, Barbara (Sylvia Weld), using a fountain pen, puts a deadly dose of nicotine in her mother's medicine. When her father callously points out that he is now free to marry his mistress, Barbara kills herself.

Elizabeth Barrett Browning aside, the lives of English literary figures seemingly had been of little interest to playgoers. That was the case once again with H. H. and Marguerite Harper's **Romantic Mr. Dickens** (12-2-40, Playhouse). In early manhood Dickens (Robert Keith) is prevented from marrying his beloved Dora Spenlow (Gertrude Flynn) by her snobbish father (Marshall Bradford). Years later, married to a nagging woman (Zolya Talma), he seeks out Dora but finds her not only married but grown fat and frumpy. He turns his attentions to a young actress (Diana Barrymore) until his wife threatens him with scandal.

The next play also examined a spouse's looking for extramarital affection, but with the sexes reversed. In 1936 Ferenc Molnár's one-acter *A cukrászné* (The Pastry-Baker's Wife) had been done in Budapest. Now a refugee in America, the playwright enlarged the script and had Emil Lengyel translate it and Gilbert Miller polish it. The result was **Delicate Story** (12-4-40, Henry Miller's). Mary Cristof (Edna Best), wife of a Swiss delicatessen proprietor (Jay Fasset), falls in love with a young soldier (John Craven) about to go to war and heads off for a ride in the countryside with him. Their car is involved in an accident, and news of it seems likely to create some unpleasantness. Then Mary discovers the boy is engaged to be wed. Best, "a sweet and lovable human who can wrinkle her nose," could not save so tenuous a piece.

Energetic, redheaded Lee Tracy had even less luck with Milton Lazarus's **Every Man for Himself** (12-9-40, Guild). Wally Britt, a screenwriter, wakes up after a four-day binge to find himself in a dress suit that is not his and a girl (Margaret Tallichet) in his bed wearing pajamas that are his. Before long his house is invaded by a flock of people, including a producer (John Gaullaudet) who wants Wally to retell him the plot he outlined and which Wally cannot recall, and who turns out to be the girl's fiancé, and a gangster (Wally Maher), who loves the girl. However, matters end happily enough when the girl discloses that she and Wally were married during the binge.

A woman courted by three men was also a central figure in Irwin Shaw's **Retreat to Pleasure** (12-17-40, Belasco). Norah Galligan (Edith Atwater), a lower-echelon executive with the WPA in Ohio, runs off rather than fire 10,000 employees. Back home she finds herself wooed by a handsome bohemian (Leif Erickson), a suave playboy (John Emery), and a tired businessman (Hume Cronyn). She runs away again, this time to Florida, where the men pursue her. Still in a tizzy, she rejects all three. Most critics singled out Cronyn's wistful manufacturer as the evening's top acting.

Edward Chodorov and H. S. Kraft's **Cue for Passion** (12-19-40, Royale) could not decide whether it wanted to be drama, whodunit, or farce. A nasty but famous novelist, John Elliott (George Coulouris), who was about to try his hand at acting, is found shot to death shortly after threatening his wife (Gale Sondergaard), a prominent magazine editor, with divorce. She insists the death was a suicide and convinces their associates to back her story. Police are sceptical and point a finger at a young lady (Claire Niesen) who was the last person known to see Elliott alive. But she produces a letter written by Elliott which reveals that he did commit suicide after all. Some Broadway smart money hinted that the leading characters were patterned after Sinclair Lewis and Dorothy Thompson. Sly, tiny Oscar Karlweis, a refugee, walked away with the best notices as the timid Belgian playwright whose play Elliott was to appear in.

Paul Vincent Carroll's fast-collapsing career hit bottom with his **The Old Foolishness** (12-20-40, Windsor). Several critics saw it as an allegory about the choices confronting Ireland. Maeve McHugh (Sally O'Neil) finds herself deserted by her farmer-lover (Sean Dillon), so asks his brothers—a businessman (Roy Roberts) and a poet (Vincent Donehue)—to explain his actions. In the end, Maeve runs off to sort matters out for herself.

The string of failures was cut short by the arrival of John van Druten's **Old Acquaintance** (12-23-40, Morosco), which ran for twenty-two weeks. Katherine Markham (Jane Cowl) is a novelist whose books are praised but sell few copies. She has long led a bohemian existence in Greenwich Village, with numerous lovers. Many of the books written by her acerbic friend, Mildred Watson Drake (Peggy Wood), have been best-sellers. Their friendship is seriously strained after Mildred's debutante daughter, Deidre (Adele Longmire), steals away Katherine's latest paramour (Kent Smith). But the women are sufficiently mature and intelligent to reconcile their differences. Cowl, "whose mellow voice is so tuneful and persuasive," brought her consummate skills and stage tricks to her part, while Wood surprised some observers by the artistry with which she suggested a vain, selfish, and unhappy woman. The play was set in New York—at Katherine's inexpensive apartment and Mildred's more lavish Park Avenue one—a small fact which could be seen as confirming that van Druten had settled in America permanently.

· · ·

John van Druten (1901–57) was born in London. He originally planned a career in law, which he practiced and taught for a time. Several of his early London hits found success in America—notably *Young Woodley* (1925), *There's Always Juliet* (1932), and *The Distaff Side* (1934).

· · ·

A far bigger hit came in several nights later. **My Sister Eileen** (12-26-40, Biltmore) was taken from Ruth McKenney's *New Yorker* stories by Joseph Fields and Jerome Chodorov. Calling it a "hilarious play," Sidney B. Whipple urged his *World-Telegram* readers to "do yourself a big favor" by seeing it. They did, so the comedy ran for more than two years, tallying 864 performances. (It later provided the inspiration for the 1953 musical *Wonderful Town*.) With some reluctance two Ohio sisters, Ruth (Shirley Booth) and Eileen Sherwood (Jo Ann Sayers), take a month's lease on a decrepit Greenwich Village basement apartment, described as "Alcatraz without a view of the bay." The acid-tongued Ruth hopes to sell her stories; the sweet

and pretty Eileen will try to become an actress. They are no sooner settled in than a loud explosion rocks the room and they learn a new subway is being blasted through directly below them. When a terrified Eileen asks Ruth what they are going to do, Ruth can only reply, "We're going to do thirty days!" Their apartment soon is invaded by "The Wreck" (Gordon Jones), an ex-football player fleeing his mistress's mother. Another fellow, Robert Baker (William Post, Jr.), likes Ruth's writings, but cannot persuade his boss at the *Manhatter* magazine to print them. Though she can find no work, Eileen is swamped with suitors. To get Ruth away, so that he can be alone with Eileen, Chick Clark (Bruce MacFarlane), a newspaper reporter, has Ruth cover his assignment to welcome a Brazilian navy ship. The sailors follow Ruth home, a fight breaks out, and Eileen is arrested for punching a policeman. The melee lands Eileen on the front page. She looks to get an acting job, while Ruth, who has fallen in love with Robert, takes work on Chick's paper. Booth was garlanded with praise. "No other actress on our stage," one critic commented, "can excel her when it comes to the precise firing of a Kaufman line." (George S. Kaufman had directed the comedy.) The role provided Booth with a major leg up.

· · ·

Shirley Booth [née Thelma Booth Ford] (1898–1992) was born in New York. She made her debut with the Poli Stock Company in Hartford in 1919. Six years later she was first seen on Broadway in *Hell's Bells*. A variety of roles followed before she scored a major success as a gangster's moll in *Three Men on a Horse* (1935). Although she grew somewhat stocky with the years, she never lost her singular baby-voice.

· · ·

Kenyon Nicholson and Charles Robinson's **The Flying Gerardos** (12-29-40, Playhouse) found little favor. Donna (Lois Hall), the youngest of a family of circus acrobats, comes under the spell of William Wentworth (Richard Mackay), a bookish graduate student. She causes consternation in the family by taking to reading and contemplating abandoning the troupe. A hot-tempered, croaky-voiced Mama Gerardo (Florence Reed) finagles Wentworth into giving up his studies and joining the act as a clown. Reed, sporting a red wig, employed her large bag of somewhat superannuated emotive tricks to color the evening.

Although most critics liked Elmer Rice's **Flight to the West** (12-30-40, Guild), they were far from seeing it, as the *Times*'s Brooks Atkinson did, as the equal of the playwright's *Street Scene*. Still, for all its rather unpleasant, debate-filled story, it lingered for 136 performances. The passengers aboard a Pan American Clipper, flying from Lisbon to New York, are a mixed lot, including Americans, war-scarred refugees, and Nazis. One American woman, Hope (Betty Field), a Gentile married to the Jewish Charles Nathan (Hugh Marlowe), is certain she has met Count Vronoff (Boris Marshalov) before and that he had a different name. He now claims he is heading for a professorship in California. Hope tells her suspicions to Louise Frayne (Constance McKay), a newspaperwoman, and, employing hints Hope offers, Louise cables back to Europe and learns that Vronoff is a probable spy. With the telegrams she has received she convinces the pilots to land the plane in Bermuda, where Vronoff is arrested. Once back in flight, a Belgian refugee (Lydia St. Clair), whose young son was killed and whose daughter crippled by Nazi bombings, and whose American husband was blinded in the attack, grabs a gun she has seen Vronoff hide under a seat and attempts to shoot Dr. Hermann Walther (Paul Henried), the only avowed Nazi aboard. But Nathan, attempting to stop her, is shot instead. When Walther is asked how he feels about having his life saved by a Jew, he boasts he himself would have thought twice before lunging for a gun, since his mind has not been "warped by the corrosive philosophy of liberalism and the insidious poisons of Jewish mysticism." Nathan, fortunately, gives every sign of recovering. Jo Mielziner's realistic recreation of the inside of a Clipper won huge applause.

The Lady Who Came to Stay (1-2-41, Maxine Elliott's) didn't, departing after just four performances. Kenneth White based his play on R. E. Spencer's novel. Three dark-minded spinster sisters, Emma (Mady Christians), Milly (Mildred Natwick), and Phoebe (Evelyn Varden), make life miserable for their widowed sister-in-law, Katherine (Beth Merrill), who lives with them. She dies, and so does Phoebe. Both ladies soon return as ghosts (bathed in green spotlights), and Katherine's spirit even plays an offstage piano. The surviving women would torture Katherine's children, but Milly dies—returning as a spotlighted ghost—and Emma's mind snaps, prompting her to set fire to their sunless, Victorian New York mansion. Critics were amazed that Guthrie McClintic would produce and direct such dross.

Two almost as short-lived flops came next. Not even a $2.75 top ticket could save Norman Rosten's **First Stop to Heaven** (1-5-41, Windsor). Eva Golden (Alison Skipworth) is determined to maintain her shabby Sixth Avenue boardinghouse, although her shiftless husband (Taylor Holmes) begs her to buy a chicken farm and authorities want to condemn the place to permit subway construction. (The same subway as in *My Sister Eileen?*) Her oddball tenants include a philosophizing razor-blade salesman, a small-time Italian gangster, and a daffy old lady who walks about planting tracts in people's pock-

ets. But the local building inspector (James Bell) finally prevails in emptying the place.

Mignon G. Eberhart, collaborating with Robert Wallsten, adapted her novel *Fair Warning* for the stage as **Eight O'Clock Tuesday** (1-6-41, Henry Miller's). His young wife (Celeste Holm) and his sister (Pauline Lord) find the body of the hateful Ivan Godden (McKay Morris) stabbed to death in his elegant library. Suspicion falls not only on the women but on Godden's neighbors, all of whom have good reasons for killing him. Detective Wait (Bramwell Fletcher) reenacts each suspect's version of what might have transpired (in flashbacks that keep restoring the corpse to life) until he pins the killing on an amiable doctor (Cecil Humphreys), whom Godden had prevented from marrying his sister. The once admired, wide-eyed Lord, with her "usual nebulous mannerisms, half-sentences, odd pauses and jerky nervousness," was never again to know her old acclaim, albeit she did later head the national tour of *The Glass Menagerie*.

The season's longest-running hit was Joseph Kesselring's **Arsenic and Old Lace** (1-10-41, Fulton). Broadway legend has it that Howard Lindsay and Russel Crouse, who produced the play, had a major hand in turning what Kesselring conceived as a serious thriller into a great comedy. Abbey Brewster (Josephine Hull) and her sister, Martha (Jean Adair), are two sweet old ladies. Never mind that their pastime is murdering lonely old men, whom they invite to their house and ply with elderberry wine laced with arsenic. Burying their victims would be a problem if their brother, Teddy (John Alexander), were not crazy, too. A heavy-set man with big teeth, a large mustache, and a pince-nez, Teddy thinks he is another, more famous Teddy. So he never walks up a flight of stairs. Instead, he bolts up San Juan Hill crying, "Charge!" Luckily, he is also digging a new lock for the Panama Canal in the cellar, and the graves he makes, for yellow fever victims, are merely additional excavations. Their nephew Jonathan (Boris Karloff) complicates matters when he appears with his strange cohort, Dr. Einstein (Edgar Stehli), since Jonathan is also a murderer and has left the body of his latest victim outside, in the rumbleseat of his car. He is resolved to dispose of the body in his aunts' home. Another nephew, Mortimer (Allyn Joslyn), is flabbergasted on learning of their activities. When Mortimer attempts to have the entire family committed to a mental institution, his aunts inform him that he cannot. He has been adopted and is not really one of them. He departs, relieved to learn that he is a bastard. Left alone with the man from the mental home, the ladies offer him a glass of their elderberry wine. (At a time of relatively healthy theatrical economics, one curtain call had a line of actors impersonating all the victims take a bow.) Lockridge told his readers, "You wouldn't believe homicidal mania could be such great fun." A flock of reviews like his propelled the comedy on to 1444 performances, while her notices established Josephine Hull as an enduring favorite.

• • •

Josephine Hull [née Mary Josephine Sherwood] (1886–1957) was born in Newtonville, Mass., and educated at Radcliffe. She studied for the stage with the popular nineteenth-century actress Kate Reingolds, then took work with stock companies, including Boston's Castle Square Theatre Company, and in a few Broadway failures. She retired when she married Shelley Hull and returned to the stage only after his death. In the 1920s she began to attract attention in such plays as *Fata Morgana* (1924), *Craig's Wife* (1925), and *Daisy Mayme* (1926). However, major acclaim did not come her way until *You Can't Take It with You* (1936). A tiny, heavy-set woman, she was best as dithering but lovable old ladies.

• • •

Lockridge must have recalled his own remarks two nights later, after a second murder-mystery-comedy, Owen Davis's **Mr. and Mrs. North** (1-12-41, Belasco), opened, since the play was drawn from *The Norths Meet Murder*, a novel which the critic and his wife, Frances, had written. Jerry North (Albert Hackett), a publisher, and his seemingly frazzle-brained wife, Pam (Peggy Conklin), return home from separate out-of-town trips to discover a body in their apartment. Before long a second body, that of their mailman, is found. When an inspector (Stanley Jessop) leaves no doubt about his suspicions—both bodies having been found in their apartment, no witnesses, and the Norths themselves reporting the dead men—Pam retorts, "We had to tell someone about it; we didn't want them." Several of the Norths' friends have motives for the killings. But when Pam discovers that one (Lewis Martin) of these friends, at the time of the first murder allegedly shelling lobsters to make a special recipe Pam had given him, had used canned lobster meat instead, his alibi is blown and the killings are solved. Critics liked the show, but suggested it might have fared better had it opened before *Arsenic and Old Lace*. Still, it ran a respectable twenty and a half weeks.

Lynn Riggs, a few years earlier considered one of the theatre's most promising writers, pleased virtually no one with **The Cream in the Well** (1-20-41, Booth). In 1906, in Indian Territory soon to become Oklahoma, the neurotic, incestuous Julie Sawters (Martha Sleeper) breaks up the engagement of her brother, Clabe (Leif Erickson), to Opal (Perry Wilson) and drives him to join the navy. She then badgers Opal into killing herself and turns the young man (Myron McCormick) who has married the girl into a drunkard. When Clabe returns home and confronts his sister, she commits suicide by jumping into a lake on their farm.

Barry Fitzgerald, making his final Broadway appearance, was the sole redeeming feature of Louis D'Alton's Irish drama **Tanyard Street** (2-4-41, Little). Although her husband (Lloyd Gough) returns home from fighting for Franco badly crippled, Hessy (Margo) is prepared to love and nurse him. But after he walks again and attributes his recovery to a miracle by the Virgin, he decides to become a priest, and the Church forces Hessy to swear to a future life of celibacy in order to admit the man. Fitzgerald portrayed the family's argumentative, lazy uncle.

If Philip Barry had not written **Liberty Jones** (2-5-41, Shubert) critics might have had a field day ridiculing it. Indeed some of their reviews bordered on the snide. But because of Barry's reputation most aisle-sitters were more tactful. Liberty Jones (Nancy Coleman)—she's a niece of Uncle Sam (William Lynn)—is ailing, and doctors of medicine, letters, divinity, and law seem unable to cure her. Worse, the three Shirts [Hitler, Mussolini, and Stalin?] want to dominate her. But all-American Tom Smith (John Beal) takes over, drives away the incompetents and malefactors, and brings about a cure. Even with the Theatre Guild's subscription list to support it, the play could not survive a full three weeks.

Jacques Deval's **Boudoir** (2-7-41, Golden) ran half as long. Deval, a Frenchman who had been working for several years in America, wrote the play in English, but critics were at a loss as to whether he meant it to be a melodrama or a spoof of one. Several cited it as the season's nadir. In the 1880s, in a magnificent Madison Avenue brownstone where she has been set up by rich Edgar Massuber (Taylor Holmes), the beautiful, scheming, and faithless Cora Ambershell (Helen Twelvetrees) takes on slick, mustachioed Enrico Palfieri (Henry Brandon), a man supposedly from Cairo, as a lover. Cora's butler, Gaylord (Staats Cotsworth), who once had been her husband until she deserted him for better things when he ran into trouble, recognizes Palfieri as a notorious strangler, given to leaving a cufflink beside the body of each woman he kills. Still smarting from Cora's past treatment of him, Gaylord says nothing about his discovery to her. The play ends with Palfieri removing a cufflink, then putting his hands around Cora's neck, ostensibly to help remove a necklace.

The critics who had attacked *Boudoir* as the season's low point reconsidered after sitting through Fred Herendeen's **Popsy** (2-10-41, Playhouse). All of Al Shean's old comic tricks could not enliven this tale of a mathematics professor, about to embark on a long-dreamed-of retirement trip to Hawaii after thirty-two years of teaching, who is abruptly descended upon by his three daughters. Two of the girls have walked out on their husbands; the third has split with her boyfriend. Not until the end of the last act are matters happily resolved and the professor able to sail.

Even critics who held reservations about Francis Swann's **Out of the Frying Pan** (2-11-41, Windsor) allowed that it had lots of bubbling moments and that first-nighters clearly enjoyed themselves. Six hopeful actors—three girls and three boys—all share an apartment they have leased directly above that of the famous producer Mr. Kenny (Reynolds Evans). They have even found an unused radiator pipe that lets them peer into his apartment. Dottie (Barbara Bel Geddes), the youngest and most naive of the group, is also the richest, and it is her money that largely maintains them. Their leader would seem to be Norman (Alfred Drake), a dedicated Stanislavskian. Into the midst of their customary bohemian mayhem pops Dottie's school chum, squeaky-voiced, nitwitty Muriel (Florence MacMichael). When, appalled at what she sees, she tells one of the girls, "Just because you're actors, you don't have to be crazy," she is informed, "It helps." Mr. Kenny has refused to see any of the youngsters at his office, but when, as an amateur chef, he comes to borrow some flour, the kids press him to watch their interpretation of his latest hit, *Mostly Murder*, a play Norman has characterized as "a burlesque of a satirical murder mystery." Their scream-filled performance, with Muriel given a Mickey Finn to make her a convincing corpse, brings on their landlady (Mabel Paige), the cops, and, by chance, Dottie's overly protective father (Henry Antrim). But it also convinces Kenny to cast them for the play's road company. This leads to Norman and Dottie's confessing their love for one another. The comedy ran thirteen weeks.

Rose Franken's **Claudia** (2-12-41, Booth), her first play since *Another Language* nine years before, was a far bigger hit, compiling 453 performances. In *PM* Louis Kronenberger assessed the play as "a quietly human story, sometimes sunlit, sometimes clouded over; a story which thrusts a touch of emotional reality into the abiding make-believe of the theater." David Naughton (Donald Cook), a prominent architect living on a colonial farm he has lovingly restored, would be more happily married if his wife, Claudia (Dorothy McGuire), were to grow up. Her mother-fixation and her doubts about her own sexual appeal have created problems. Matters come to a head after Claudia impulsively sells the farm to an opera singer (Olga Baclanova) and, dolled up in her sister-in-law's low-cut pajamas

and the opera singer's earrings, and bathed in fancy perfume, she has a brief flirtation with a young British author (John Williams). David is exasperated. Then Claudia learns that her mother (Frances Starr) is dying, and this news miraculously matures her. Indeed, her mother specifically calls it a miracle, adding, "It's just as if she were the mother and I were the child." Claudia returns the opera singer's check and settles down to become a proper wife. McGuire was hailed for playing "the title role lightly, suggesting at once the skimming quality of Claudia's mind and the steadfastness of her emotions." Oldtimer Starr brought to her part "her unfailing rightness of understanding and intonation and gesture." Cook was handed more perfunctory compliments.

S. N. Behrman, far more prolific than Franken, was not as fortunate with **The Talley Method** (2-24-41, Henry Miller's). Complaining that the playwright waxed much too serious after the first act and a half, Atkinson concluded, "As a master of comedy, it is his business to knock a little sense into the world by wit, humor and gleaming sapience." The widowed Dr. Axton Talley (Philip Merivale), a rigid, unfeeling surgeon, proposes marriage to his middle-aged patient Enid Fuller (Ina Claire), a liberal poet. She discovers that his young daughter (Claire Niesen) is a revolution-spouting soapboxer and that his son (Dean Harens), having flunked out of medical school, is courting a fan dancer. Relating easily to the children, she is able to set both of them on more profitable paths. But she soon comes to understand that the differences between her and Talley are irreconcilable. "Must we be separated, then, by points of view?" he asks. Her reply is "It is always point of view that separates people." Some critics felt that Claire, the stage's most adept high comedienne, was at sea in the play's less comic moments. Merivale was generally praised, as was Hiram Sherman in the ancillary role of an intellectual wastrel. But the numerous critical reservations confined the play to a seven-week run.

Critic after critic opened his (or her) review of Beatrice Alliot and Howard Newman's **Brooklyn Biarritz** (2-27-41, Royale) by describing Frederick Fox's setting, which recreated a slice of the Coney Island Beach, using real sand and littering it with crumpled papers, banana peels, and other oddments. To a man (and one woman), they were in no way as happy about the play. Snippets—much in the fashion of *Grand Hotel*—of the lives of a number of New Yorkers were presented. These folk included a proud, warm Jewish mother, her son who is studying for medical school, a hot-dog-stand owner, an Irish cop, and a fat, homely girl who goes from beach to beach and pretends to faint or to be drowning in order to get a lifeguard's attention. A melodramatic story framed the vignettes. A man (James

Todd), learning that his wife (Dorothy Libaire) has killed herself after being deserted by her lover (Bertram Thorn), strangles the man and dumps his body in the ocean. He then walks away, after tossing a wallet containing his own savings to a young man (Owen Lamont) who has been praying for enough money to permit him to marry his sweetheart (Ann Loring). Four performances sufficed.

One of the season's most memorable revivals was Shaw's *The Doctor's Dilemma,* which dealt with a physician confronted by the choice of saving a brilliant, scoundrelly artist or a talentless but good man. Guthrie McClintic staged it at the Shubert on March 11 for his wife, Katharine Cornell, with Raymond Massey (as Sir Colenso Ridgeon) and Bramwell Fletcher (as Louis Dubedat) in support. Reviewers split on their evaluation of the play itself and of the performers, but, despite a quibble here and a complaint there, they mostly gave the entertainment their thumbs up. Cornell as Jennifer Dubedat played "with the radiance which is hers alone. She proves that the size of a part has nothing to do with the fascination it can possess." Clarence Derwent, Whitford Kane, Cecil Humphries, and Colin Keith-Johnston brought lesser roles to life.

The howls (offstage) of a wild dog, heard even before the curtain rose, were supposed to add to the eeriness of Max Catto's English thriller **They Walk Alone** (3-12-41, Golden). Emmy Baudine (Elsa Lanchester), a seemingly mild-mannered Yorkshire girl, takes work as a maid on a farmstead. But it quickly becomes obvious that Emmy's real interests lie elsewhere. At midnight she can often be heard playing feverish fugues (offstage) on the local organ, and when that cannot occupy her, she is murdering (offstage) every local boy whom she has teased into making a pass at her. Of course, she is finally brought to justice. "There is quite a bit of pungent ham in little Mrs. Laughton," one critic observed, while another said her overwrought performance ran "the gamut from Baby Snooks to Ophelia and from Mrs. Rochester to King Lear. Janus could not make more faces than Miss Lanchester manages to make simultaneously."

An attempt to spoof William Saroyan (and, some said, Clare Boothe) went badly amiss in Lucille S. Prumbs's **Five Alarm Waltz** (3-13-41, Playhouse). In their elegant, modernistic Sutton Place digs, the successful playwright Brooke March (Louise Platt), "a female Noel Coward," and her unsuccessful novelist-husband, Adam Borguris (Elia Kazan), an untidy Bulgarian exhibitionist who romps around in nothing but a pair of blue shorts, constantly quarrel. When he calls her a superficial fraud, she challenges him to write a successful play. He puts together an amorphous tale about characters he has met—a moralizing prostitute, a sculp-

tor who plays "Chop Sticks" on the piano, and similar eccentrics. Jerry Manning (Robert Shayne), who long has hoped Brooke would divorce Adam and marry him, agrees to mount the play just to embarrass Adam. But the play is a big hit. So the couple go back to quarreling, this time about a refugee Chinese toddler Adam has brought home.

The reviews that Arthur L. Jarret and Marcel Klauber's **My Fair Ladies** (3-23-41, Hudson) received were no better than Prumbs's had been, but the comedy struggled on for a month before giving up. Two American chorus girls (Celeste Holm and Betty Furness), having been stranded by the war in London and having connived with a susceptible young man in the Foreign Office, have flown home carrying fake passports identifying them as Lady Keith-Odlyn and Lady Palfrey-Stuart. They are welcomed into the swank Mt. Kisco home of the Gages (Mary Sargent and Vincent Donehue), a pair of desperate social climbers whom they met aboard the Clipper. Doors to posh cocktail parties and other marvelous affairs all open to them until they are exposed by a boozy playboy who had backed some of the shows they had danced in. By that time, however, they have landed very eligible mates.

While most critics regretted that **Native Son** (3-24-41, St. James), which Paul Green and Richard Wright had dramatized from Wright's novel, lacked the full punch of the book, they still agreed that it was powerful theatre. Bigger Thomas (Canada Lee) is a lazy, uneducated, bullying black man, who hates whites. When he complains about having to wait to get into the bathroom in the morning, his sister (Helen Martin) berates him for letting his family live the way they do on relief. He barks back, "Relief didn't say more'n forty people have to use the same toilet every morning. . . . It's the way the white folks built these old buildings." He fantasizes about bombing Chicago and murdering people. And he uses a bread knife to kill rats, naming the dead ones after well-known white men. One he calls "Ol' Man Dalton," which proves ironic, since a social worker arrives to tell him she has, despite Bigger's criminal record, found him employment as Dalton's chauffeur. By accident, he kills the man's daughter (Anne Burr). In a panic, he burns the body and flees, but he is captured, tried, and sentenced to death. While he is awaiting execution, his fears are put to rest when he comes to believe that he has played at least a small part in destroying the security of the white world. At the final curtain he is staring blankly out at the audience, a spotlight on his face, from behind the bars of his grim prison cell. Orson Welles directed with "sledge-hammer impact and nerve-wracking excitement" and, as was his wont, played out all ten scenes without intermission. The settings, framed by drab brick walls, were spartan, and scene changes were accompanied by loud sound effects to heighten the tension. These deafeners included a wailing police siren, frantic boogie-woogie music, loud chimes, and the bellow of a fiery furnace. The play ran until July.

The season's shortest run—two performances—was the lot of **Gabrielle** (3-25-41, Maxine Elliott's), which Leonardo Bercovici took from Thomas Mann's short story "Tristan." At a Swiss sanitarium the consumptive Gabrielle (Eleanor Lynn) comes under the spell of the manipulative Detlev Spinell (John Cromwell), who persuades her to disobey doctors' orders to rest. The exertion kills her. Detlev believes he has done her a service, since she will never again have to face her demanding, insensitive husband (Harold Vermilyea).

As the season approached its end, a segment of New York theatre which was already being called "Off Broadway" in some circles sprang to life and received considerable newspaper attention. In December the Studio Theatre at the New School of Social Research had presented a largely assailed mounting of *King Lear* with Sam Jaffe in the title role. Now, on the 26th, it brought out a much praised presentation of **The Circle of Chalk.** This was a thirteenth-century Chinese drama, offered in an English translation of a German version. It featured petite Dolly Haas, one of many refugees finding employment in New York, as a Chinese maiden sold into bondage to the very man who has destroyed her family, but whom she learns to love and forgive. Similarly, the next night a group of Irish-American actors took over the Cherry Lane Theatre and brought out Padraic Colum's 1902 drama, *Broken Soil,* under a new title, **The Fiddler's House.** This story of an old itinerant fiddler, who convinces one of his daughters to accompany him as he resumes his wanderings, allowed the admired, resonant-voiced Augustin Duncan briefly to come out of the retirement his blindness had forced on him.

"The theatre found its voice last night . . . and gave us a play that shrivels anything else produced on Broadway this season," Kronenberger began his review of Lillian Hellman's **Watch on the Rhine** (4-1-41, Martin Beck). He continued, "It is a play about human beings and their ideological ghosts; a play dedicated to the deeds that they are called upon to perform, not the words they are moved to utter. It is a play whose final crisis, though peculiar to one man's life, is yet central to our own." Other critics, while complaining that Hellman's plot contrivances showed through, still attested to the play's power. Fanny Farrelly (Lucile Watson), a widowed matron in suburban Washington, will soon find her mansion rather crowded since she not only is housing the Roumanian Count de Brancovis (George Coulouris) and his wife, Marthe (Helen Tren-

holme), but is awaiting the arrival of her daughter, Sarah (Mady Christians), and Sarah's German husband, Kurt Müller (Paul Lukas), neither of whom she has seen for twenty years, and the three grandchildren she has never met. De Brancovis, who readily cavorts with Nazi diplomats, is aware that the American-born Marthe has long been out of love with him and has fallen for Fanny's apron-strung son, David (John Lodge). But his real interest at the moment is Kurt, whom, after rifling through his luggage, he identifies as a sought-after anti-Nazi refugee. He attempts to blackmail Kurt into handing over monies Kurt has collected to continue his anti-fascist efforts. Since Kurt knows he must use the money in hopes of freeing several associates recently captured by the Nazis, he kills the count. He changes his own plans and sets out to reenter Germany to try to effect the rescue. To his son (Eric Roberts) he observes that he must do such dangerous work so that the boy's generation will not know similar horrors: "All over the world, in every place and every town, there are men who are going to make sure it will not have to be." When the others, including Marthe, who will probably wed David, show their concern in their expressions, he reassures them that the men who wish to live have the best chance of doing so. The play ran 11 months.

Critics had no kind words for Abby Merchant's **Your Loving Son** (4-4-41, Little). A teenager (Frankie Thomas) comes home from summer camp to find his mother (Jessie Royce Landis) flirting with a young artist (Eddie Nugent) and his father (Jay Fassett) making a play for their upstairs neighbor (Ruth Lee). With the help of the neighbor's daughter (Charita Bauer), he sets matters aright.

A group calling itself the Experimental Theatre—a name that had been used several times before and would be employed again—briefly presented a pair of new plays and one revival at first-class houses. The revival, Margaret Webster's modern-dress *The Trojan Women,* opened at the Cort at a matinee on the 8th. Euripides' Greeks wore Nazi uniforms. Dame May Whitty was Hecuba; Webster herself, Andromache; while Walter Slezak and Tamara Geva were made to provide comic relief as Menelaus and Helen.

Laura and S. J. Perelman had small luck with their **The Night Before Christmas** (4-10-41, Morosco). Two hoods, the resourceful Otis (Forrest Orr) and the smiling but vacuous Ruby (George Matthews), buy a failing Sixth Avenue luggage store so that they can dig a tunnel into the bank next door. Their scheme is complicated by the untimely appearance of customers such as the famous actor Victor Immature (Dean Norton) and his police bodyguard, by a nearby jeweler (Louis Sorin) strolling in for a friendly chat, and by the decision of their girl, Denny Costello (Phillis Brooks), to go straight and marry the corner pharmacist. When they finally do blast their way through, they find they have emerged not in the bank but in the potato salad vat of a delicatessen. Typical of the Perelmans' lines was one of the gangster's remarking, "Wall Street lost a valuable man the day I entered reform school."

The Experimental Theatre's first novelty was George Harr's **Steps Leading Up** (4-18-41, Cort), a look at how crooked union officers attempt to thwart and take over an honest union.

By spring of 1941, positions had hardened on William Saroyan. Many leading critics, including Watts, Brown, and Atkinson, still remained loyalists. Nonetheless, unable to find a producer or angels, the playwright dug into his own pocket to stage what proved to be his last hit, albeit a modest one, **The Beautiful People** (4-21-41, Lyceum). Jonah Webster (Curtis Cooksey), a self-proclaimed minister, is given to preaching to unresponsive passersby on San Francisco street corners. He supports himself by forging the name of a former occupant of his house on annuity checks meant for that man. His daughter, Agnes (Betsy Blair), is called "St. Agnes of the Mice" because she believes that the mice who swarm over their house spell out her name with field flowers on her birthday. Her loving brother Owen (Eugene Loring), who writes books of just one word, even climbs a nearby church steeple to rescue a mouse for her. Another brother, Harold (Don Freeman), has gone to New York to play his cornet, although the family is certain they can hear his playing 3000 miles away. Samuel Leve's skeletonized setting depicted the run-down house with its small main room, its porch, and its yard. The play ran for 120 performances.

The Experimental Theatre concluded its season with George H. Corey's **Not in Our Stars** (4-25-41, Biltmore). It focused on Pibby Hoolihan (Harold Vermilyea), who hasn't worked since he lost his job as a trolley conductor when buses came in. His son is on parole and his daughter engaged to a man with no prospects. But the son-in-law-to-be finally lands a job as a policeman, and rich Cousin Willie forks up some long-promised charity, so life won't be too bad for Pibby, at least for a while.

Another off-Broadway entourage, the American Actors Company, allowed New Yorkers their first taste of Horton Foote with the youthful actor-playwright's **Texas Town,** put on at a nameless uptown West Side auditorium on the 29th. All the action occurs in a rather dingy drugstore. Ray Case (Foote) is mother-dominated and discontent with backwater life. He knows his neighbors think he is a malingerer. His only reason for remaining in his hometown is Carrie (Loraine Stuart), so, when she tells him she will marry his rival, he works up enough nerve to set out. Later Carrie has

second thoughts, but before she can reach Ray she learns he has been killed in an auto accident.

Even with John Barrymore's highly publicized daughter Diana in its cast, **The Happy Days** (5-13-41, Henry Miller's), which Zoë Akins adapted from Claude-André Puget's play, could not hold on for more than three weeks. A trio of young girls and a pair of boys whom two of the girls consider beaux have been left alone on one of the Thousand Islands while their families attend a funeral. To make the boys jealous the girls tell of meeting a fascinasting aviator in Quebec. Immediately thereafter, a pleasant and attractive aviator crash-lands on the island, and the girls all fall for him. Life returns to normal when he fixes his plane and flies away.

Not all off-Broadway offerings won critical respect. Critics blasted a vanity production, **When Differences Disappear** (6-2-41, Provincetown Playhouse), written, directed, and produced by Leonard A. Black, who also assumed the leading role—a character named Lenny who owns and operates a shabby luncheonette called Lenny's Hole in the Wall. There diners and employees debate on every conceivable subject, especially whether the United States should enter the war. After the Germans sink an American ship, the differences of opinion disappear.

For Broadway the season ended on a dire note, with Thomas A. Johnstone's **Snookie** (6-3-41, Golden)—"an ultimate low in adult entertainment," "The theater cannot sustain many such blows," "can be swept back under the carpet, safe, I imagine, even from desperate moths," "the stunned silence out front was so deep one could hear a joke drop." Cartoonists at the *New York Press* are a waggish lot, spending much of their day staring with binoculars at women in a hotel across the street, organizing an impromptu masquerade, or forming a jazz band to accompany a bespangled dancer named Stupid Stella (Betty Jane Smith) who arrives on a scooter. Their jobs are in jeopardy since their crusty managing editor (William Harrigan) has threatened to cut out all comics should he inherit the paper. To make certain the paper's childless heiress-apparent has a baby, the men send a job seeker (Laurence Weber) to help her—even if the baby has to be conceived in a test tube. By play's end, the baby is reported on the way. The play was allegedly produced by Olsen and Johnson, whose names did not appear on the program. Critics surmised they now knew why the clowns had turned their roles in *Hellzapoppin* over to summer replacements and hurriedly left town.

But the theatrical year's last word went to Off Broadway. Philip Yordan's **Any Day Now** (6-9-41, Studio) recounted the lives of a struggling Polish family in Chicago. The father has a barber shop on the ground floor. One son works for a crooked judge. The other son, Rudy (John Randolph), the play's central figure, is determined to succeed by hook or crook, but his crookedness backfires and nearly bankrupts the family. Fortunately his sister, a constant wisecracker, is able to save the day. Pert Kelton won kudos as a racketeer's wife in love with Rudy. A few years down the road, Yordan would take another play about a Polish family, rewrite it to depict black homelife, and come up with his only hit.

1941–1942

In the new season the count of novelties, which had been declining steadily for so many years, took a hopeful upward leap. *Variety* counted fifty-eight; the *Times*, fifty-seven. Of course, that was a far cry from the three-digit figures common in the twenties. The rising figure aside, the news was not good. Considerably fewer shows ran 100 performances or more—still a rule-of-the-thumb indication of success. Worse, there was no gainsaying that quality plummeted. No outstanding serious drama emerged, the season's hits consisting almost entirely of frothy comedies and thrillers. For the first—but not the last—time, no play was considered worthy of a Pulitzer Prize or a New York Drama Critics Circle Award. With America's mid-season entry into World War II—after the Japanese bombed Pearl Harbor on December 7—an argument could have been made to justify all the patently escapist offerings. Nonetheless, given the advance preparation required, playgoers might have rightly expected more demanding entries to come in throughout the winter. But great new dramas remained nowhere in sight.

The season began two nights after Labor Day with Carl Allensworth's **Village Green** (9-3-41, Henry Miller's), a comedy rushed in from a successful summer stock tryout. Homey, homely Frank Craven was starred as Judge Peabody, a Democrat who has made nine unavailing runs for office in his staunchly Republican New Hampshire town. In the midst of his latest campaign, a young artist (John Craven), who loves the judge's daughter (Laura Pierpont), paints a mural in the local post office and creates a hubbub by including a nude representation of the girl. The village is outraged. Although the judge is as shocked as anyone, he defends the artist's right to free speech. *Life* gets hold of the story and makes it a national issue. One by one the villagers fall behind the judge, so he wins the election.

Frederick Hazlitt Brennan's **The Wookey** (9-10-41, Plymouth) was set in wartime London, but its author

was said to be an American. As Mrs. Wookey (Nora Howard) says of her husband (Edmund Gwenn), "Got 'is own barge an' 'is own tug, too! If Downin' Street would listen ter Mr. Wookey they'd sive themselves all this muckin' about." But since Downing Street has refused to listen to him, he wants no part of the government or the war. Then his sister-in-law's fiancé is trapped at Dunkirk, so he takes his barge to join the rescue fleet. He is furious when his tug is seized by an oil company for non-payment for the fuel he used. But after Mrs. Wookey is killed in the blitz, he grabs a gun and heads off to do further battle. Producer Edgar Selwyn claimed that much of the show's $15,000 cost went to the British government for recordings of London sirens and the bombings. These deafening but telling effects, plus Jo Mielziner's collapsible (during the bombing) scenery, won huge applause. The play did good business until Pearl Harbor, after which grosses fell precipitously and forced its closing.

Michael Kallesser and Richard Norcross's **Brother Cain** (9-12-41, Golden) focused on a Polish-American miner (Frederic de Wilde) whose brothers and adoring mother have made sacrifices to send him to college. As a young lawyer he sues the mining company for compensation for his father's death. The company retaliates by firing his brothers and evicting his mother. When the family blames him, he walks out in disgust. As several reviewers noted, the play made the mistake of opening in a theatre next door to one where another, better mining drama, *The Corn Is Green*, was playing.

The first of a rash of comedy-mysteries to appear was Frank Gabrielson and Irvin Pincus's **The More the Merrier** (9-15-41, Cort). After his boss, Harvey Royal (Louis Hector), a famous newspaper publisher, heads off to run for governor without leaving him proper funds, Dan Finch (Frank Albertson), an assistant press agent, agrees to lodge some stranded travelers for the night for a fee in Royal's Colorado mansion. The guests include two hoping-to-retire-and-join-the-army gangsters (Teddy Hart and Millard Mitchell) and a corpse (Jack Riano) they have with them as well as an eccentric spinster (Doro Merande), a brash know-it-all ghostwriter (Keenan Wynn), and some more typical tourists. The corpse is put on roller skates to help move him and winds up in one bed after another. When Royal returns home and dumps the body from his own bed and over his balcony window, he is suspected of murder by his rival for the governorship, a famed prosecutor (Will Geer).

There was more of the same in Parker W. Fennelly's **Cuckoos on the Hearth** (9-16-41, Morosco). In a prologue a Maine character steps into a spotlight to announce he [she, in the printed text] will tell how Zadoc Grimes came to write *Horror at Harmony*

Hearth. The scene changes to the Carltons' Maine home as Donald Carlton (Carleton Young) is about to defy a winter storm and head for Washington to discuss his new secret gas with the government. Before he leaves, a sheriff (Percy Kilbride) comes to warn them that a homicidal maniac is on the loose. Mrs. Carlton (Margaret Callahan) and her retarded relation, Lulu Pung (Janet Fox), are left alone until Grimes (Howard Freeman), a cantankerous writer of mysteries who had been scheduled to stay with them during the summer, turns up several months late. Then three strange men appear, announcing that they are stranded and asking for shelter. They claim to be two traveling medicine-show men (George Mathews and Frederic Tozere) and a hitchhiking minister (Howard St. John), and they have with them, in a box, a fourteen-hundred-year-old Indian in a state of suspended animation. They almost convince Mrs. Carlton that she is not Mrs. Carlton but a woman who has left her real husband in a leper colony. Then a man (Henry Levin) [a mannish woman in the text] pops out of the box and announces he is the head of the insane asylum and the men are escapees. Only he turns out to be the homicidal maniac. The third act goes over the same period of time, in this case with the three men proving to be German spies prepared to steal Carlton's formula and with the sheriff popping out of the box and proving to be the escaped lunatic. Which story is the truth and which is Grimes's version? Despite thumbs-down notices, Brock Pemberton kept the show on the boards for sixteen weeks.

Gladys George was starred in Edwin B. Self's **The Distant City** (9-22-41, Longacre). She was seen as Mom Quigley, an atheistic former prostitute, whose life revolves around her son, Pete (Ben Smith), a garbage collector. Pete is willing to marry the girl (Gertrude Flynn) he loves even though she is pregnant by another man (Lester Penn). But that man kills her and frames Pete, who is sent to the electric chair. Forgetting her atheism, Mom prays to God that she be allowed to join her son in Heaven. Two performances and the play went to its own reward.

Ronald Jeans's **Ghost for Sale** (9-29-41, Daly's), which London had seen several years earlier, lasted four performances more, its stay perhaps prolonged by a $1.65 top. A man manages to make it seem that a mansion is haunted in order to force his brother to sell it to him, then, having succeeded, is scared away by other ghosts.

Matters improved to the extent that Arthur Sheekman and Margaret Shane's **Mr. Big** (9-30-41, Lyceum) ran for seven playings. This latest in the season's comedy-mysteries marked George S. Kaufman's inauspicious debut as producer. Critics looked back ruefully to the good old days of *The Spider* (3-22-27), which had

employed many of the same stage tricks first and more effectively. The play begins with actors in a play-within-a-play taking their bows and one of them dropping dead, murdered. (This led John Mason Brown, now with the *World-Telegram,* to observe "how wise" the authors were "to make their bid for applause at the play's start rather than at its finish.") The police order everyone to remain in the theatre. And the District Attorney (Hume Cronyn), who is running for governor and happens to be at the show, takes charge. He is heckled from the audience by a sarcastic lawyer (Florenz Ames) and at one point is lifted into the flies (prompting several critics to see as much *Hellzapoppin* in the play as *The Spider.*) Nor is he swift enough to prevent a second killing, but, after soliciting the audience's votes in his race, he does solve the crime.

The Theatre Guild found few takers when it revived Eugene O'Neill's *Ah, Wilderness!* at the Guild on October 2 with Harry Carey in the role George M. Cohan had originated, and with William Prince as Richard. Albeit Carey was applauded, it was generally felt he was not as warm and believable as Cohan had been. Even with a reduced $2.20 top, the play failed to run out the month.

In London Vernon Sylvaine's **All Men Are Alike** (10-6-41, Hudson) had been known as *Women Aren't Angels,* but the title may have been changed because the great musical comedy clown Bobby Clark was now starred in what had been a secondary role in the West End. Sylvaine's story had a philandering British marmalade tycoon (Reginald Denny) and his American partner, Wilmer Popday (Clark), head for a weekend in Surrey with some pretty women. They are barged in on by a gun-toting, jealous husband, spies, a Scotland Yard detective, a brattish young evacuee from the blitz and others. Clark, with his painted-on glasses, his stubby cigar, and his identifiable, loping stride, cavorted in kilts, in long underwear, and wearing a rug, but had to pack up his things and leave at the end of one month.

Anne of England (10-7-41, St. James) was Mary Cass Canfield and Ethel Borden's American redaction of another London show, Norman Ginsbury's *Viceroy Sarah.* A dull piece set amid the eighteenth-century splendors of the court of Queen Anne (Barbara Everest), it told how Sarah, the Duchess of Marlborough (Flora Robson) introduced her cousin, Abigail (Jessica Tandy), to the court and soon found herself supplanted by the wily girl. Abigail then persuades the queen to appease the country's French adversaries. Despite some fine acting, the play was withdrawn after one week.

So was the revival of another English play, a "golden oldie," Shakespeare's *As You Like It,* which first raised its curtain at the Mansfield on the 20th. Lemuel Ayers designed a Forest of Arden that resembled "a large, circular mound, something like an igloo with fallen arches. Slender trees are stuck in it and the unit is mounted on a turntable." Critics were most taken by Philip Bourneuf's "mettlesome and delightful" Jaques, with the *Times*'s Atkinson calling it "the best this column has ever seen," and Brown agreeing, almost in echo, that it was "by all odds the finest Jaques I have ever seen." Reviewers also had kind words for Alfred Drake's Orlando, but were not as pleased with Helen Craig's Rosalind.

Even though Sinclair Lewis set aside his writing for the moment to direct Jack Levin's **Good Neighbor** (10-21-41, Windsor), the play was the season's only entry to go down the drain after just one performance. When Dave Barron (Sam Byrd) comes back to his small southern town from time at sea and asks his mother, Hannah (Anna Appel), for the thousand dollars he had sent to her to save for him, he discovers the warmhearted Jewish woman has spent it all helping neighbors of every race and background. Worse, she is hiding a slightly retarded German-American boy (Arthur Anderson), falsely accused of being a Nazi and a murderer, from the Ku Klux Klan (called the Cavaliers in the play). But after a drunken black girl blurts out the truth, the hooded vigilantes kill Hannah.

One of the season's major disappointments was **Candle in the Wind** (10-22-41, Shubert), a drama by Maxwell Anderson, produced by the Theatre Guild and the Playwrights' Company, and staged by Alfred Lunt with Helen Hayes as star. *PM*'s Louis Kronenberger began his notice, "If there is anybody who still clings to the idea that Maxwell Anderson is one of the great men of our theater, I wish he would visit the Shubert and see *Candle in the Wind*. For in it Mr. Anderson has more than ever before given himself away, producing as ponderous and hollow a piece of high romantic rubbish as you would have found in a well-stocked Victorian library." Kronenberger was joined by several of his colleagues in assailing Lunt's painfully leisurely direction. Only Hayes's "powerfully pitched performance" supplied the requisite tension, although Tonio Selwart as the lone Nazi with human sympathies and Lotte Lenya as a refugee were also applauded. The plot was simple. Madeline Guest, a famous American actress in love with a French journalist-turned-soldier (Louis Borell) who has been captured, determines to rescue him. She employs cajolery and bribes to effect the rescue, but then finds that she herself is being held captive. Told by the Nazi commandant (John Wengraf) that America will be next after all Europe is enslaved, she replies that America is waiting—"there have been many wars between men and beasts. And the beasts have always lost, and the men have won." The drama recorded ninety-five performances.

Although George S. Kaufman and Edna Ferber's **The Land Is Bright** (10-28-41, Music Box) received somewhat better notices, it lingered for only seventy-nine performances. Those more or less in its corner included the *Journal-American*'s John Anderson, who reported, "It is a sort of grease paint massage of the new national ego—slick, flashy, superficial and trite, and yet in spite of all its obvious flaws, it is genuinely engrossing." Having amassed a $200,000,000 fortune, sometimes by unsavory means, Lacey Kincaid (Ralph Theadore) builds a magnificent mansion on Fifth Avenue and pays a seedy European count (Arnold Moss) $6,000,000 to marry his daughter (Martha Sleeper). But Lacey gets little chance to enjoy his new home, since he is killed by a man he wronged. Thirty years later, in the 1920s, a neurotic, thrill-crazy debutante granddaughter (Diana Barrymore) associates openly with bootleggers and other gangsters, so the second-act curtain concludes with another killing. By 1940 a new generation has developed a social conscience. It welcomes its cousin, the young count (Moss), who is fleeing the Germans, and it is proud that Lacey Kincaid II (John Draper) has enlisted in the army. Jo Mielziner, who designed the single setting (with changed furnishings in each act) for this play, along with the numerous set changes for the Anderson drama may have been startled to find himself receiving some disparaging notices on both accounts.

Norman Krasna's **The Man with Blond Hair** (11-4-41, Belasco), based loosely on an actual incident, told a story not unlike that in *Good Neighbor,* and ran one week instead of one performance. After two Germans escape from a Canadian prison camp, they are arrested in New York, where a policeman and some cohorts arrange for them to break free so that the cop and his buddies can recapture and beat them. One man escapes. The other, a handsome blond Aryan (Rex Williams), is hidden by a Jewish girl (Eleanor Lynn) in her mother's apartment. The girl fears that her boyfriend, one of the men planning the beating, will get into trouble for it. The German comes to admire American ways, rejects an opportunity to flee, and surrenders, hoping to be allowed to become an American after the war. (In the actual incident, the American Bund had helped the escapees return to Germany.)

The season's most enduring comedy was an importation, Noel Coward's **Blithe Spirit** (11-5-41, Morosco), in which the ghost of a man's first wife comes back to haunt his second marriage and arranges for his second wife to die in a car crash. When the ghost of wife number two joins the first wife to haunt him, he flees overseas. All the principals won rave reviews: Clifton Webb as the husband, Leonora Corbett as the first wife and Peggy Wood as the second, and Mildred Natwick as the eccentric medium who brings about all the trouble. The play ran a year and a half.

A. N. Langley, a South African who had become a Hollywood writer, was the author of the next short-lived flop, **The Walrus and the Carpenter** (11-8-41, Cort). Although he obligingly talked of a good many things in his play, his main attention was given to Essie Stuyvesant (Pauline Lord), a flibbertigibbet widow whose daughters are all having marital or fiancé problems and who is threatened with eviction for non-payment of rent. But a loyal, loving doctor (Nicholas Joy) brings about a happy ending when he proposes marriage to her. Once again Lord's singularly identifiable "breathless, absent-minded delivery" baffled some critics.

Despite critical complaints that it was desperately slow in getting started, Grace George found a season-long success in Isabel Leighton and Bertram Bloch's **Spring Again** (11-10-41, Henry Miller's). Nell Carter, exasperated with her husband, Halstead (C. Aubrey Smith), for his incessant hero worship of his father, the Civil War general Eliphalet Carter, helps write a debunking radio serial about the man. This threatens her otherwise happy marriage, especially when an aggressive film producer, William Auchinschloss (Joseph Buloff), pesters her for the screen rights. The wily gal allows Halstead to turn down the offer. George had fun throwing off lines such as "When someone asked me what I thought of Bergdorf-Goodman I said he's very good on the clarinet," and Smith also won his share of laughs. But Buloff, in his single brief, late appearance, stole the show, bemoaning that sociable if costly doctors have socialized medicine and responding to Halstead's seeming approval of Ronald Coleman to play his father, provided Coleman is a commanding actor, by informing him, "If we give an actor commanding words, he commands. To say nothing of the fact that if a man can command the salary Mr. Coleman commands he can command anything else."

Maurice Evans continued his series of Shakespearean revivals with *Macbeth*, which he unveiled at the National on the 11th. Although some critics, such as Brown, found Evans's thane a bit too intellectual, they nonetheless praised it. But their highest laurels were awarded to Judith Anderson's Lady Macbeth. Brown told his readers, "She projects it with a sulphurous villainy and an imagination unequaled by any of the Lady Macbeths of our time. She brings out the pathos too," and he added that her sleepwalking scene "is a masterpiece of invention and suspense; the kind of triumph only a truly remarkable actress could score." Margaret Webster directed the mounting, which went on to 131 performances.

The applause was muted for Guy Bolton and Somerset Maugham's emasculated theatricalization of Maugham's novel **Theatre** (11-12-41, Hudson). Since they continue to perform together, their public is unaware that Julia Lambert (Cornelia Otis Skinner) and her husband, Michael Gosselyn (Arthur Margetson), are divorced. At her age, Julia begins to be concerned about her fading looks, so indulges in a brief affair to reassure herself. But by the final curtain, she and her ex have decided to remarry. Thanks in good measure to the elegant Skinner's following, the play held the boards eight and a half weeks.

Two quick flops came next. **Little Dark Horse** (11-16-41, Golden) was Theresa Helburn's adaptation of a French play by André Birabeau. The family of a dying man (Grant Mills) learn that he has a son at military school. When the boy (R. V. Whitaker) is summoned home, they discover he is black (his father having served for a time in Africa). The boy is foisted off on a bullied bachelor uncle (Walter Slezak). Cecilia Loftus, making her final Broadway appearance, took the role of a tyrannical grandmother.

The central figure in Charl Armstrong's **Ring Around Elizabeth** (11-17-41, Playhouse) was the much harried Elizabeth Cherry (Jane Cowl), pressed on all sides by her insensitively demanding family and finally unable to cope with the problems. She tells a young adventurer (Barry Sullivan), "Life's a net you weave yourself to hold the things you care about together." It takes a bout of amnesia for her to see her family in perspective and put matters in order. Even the admired Cowl was attacked for overacting in her futile attempt to save the frenetic comedy.

The season's longest-run comedy—710 performances—was Jerome Chodorov and Joseph Fields's **Junior Miss** (11-18-41, Lyceum). Like such recent hits as *Life with Father, My Sister Eileen,* and the musical *Pal Joey,* it was derived from short stories that had originally appeared in the *New Yorker,* in this instance those by Sally Benson. "Youth in its most beguiling aspects brings joy and gayety to the new play . . . 'Junior Miss' has a warming glow about it," Richard Watts, Jr., rejoiced in the *Herald Tribune.* Thirteen-year-old Judy Graves (Patricia Peardon) is nothing if not imaginative. She begins an autobiographical essay she must write for school by describing her birth, "It was a wild stormy night and our family doctor fought his way through terrible rain to reach the bedside of my mother who hovered between life and death." No matter that Judy was actually born comfortably and easily at a swank hospital overlooking Central Park. She has also convinced herself that her father (Philip Ober) is having an affair with his boss's daughter, Ellen (Francesca Bruning), and that her Uncle Willis (Alexander Kirkland) is a reformed ex-convict. To right matters, Judy and her friend, Fuffy (Lenore Lonergan), conspire to mate Willis and Ellen. This infuriates Ellen's father, J. B. Curtis (Matt Briggs), who fires Mr. Graves. Things return to normal when Curtis mistakenly believes Graves has lured away one of Curtis's biggest accounts. Actually the Haskell Cummings (Billy Redfield) who is calling at the Graveses' apartment is the son of the man Curtis mistakes him for, and he is calling to pick up his date—Judy.

Some critics saw Alexander Greendale's **Walk into My Parlor** (11-19-41, Forrest) as a *Tobacco Road* about Italian-Americans in Chicago, others as hand-me-down Odets. Ilio Sarelli (Silvio Minciotti) is a struggling fruit peddler. His daughter (Helen Waren), an ardent unionist, is unhappily married to a man who refuses to join a union. His one son (Duane McKinney) works with him. Another son, Gino (Nicholas Conte), is a goldfish-eating counterfeiter who at one point holds a hot coal in his fist as self-punishment for seducing a sister-in-law and who lures his mother (Rosina Galli) into helping him pass his funny money. When the police close in, Gino flees. The rest of the family goes on along its dreary way. A $2.75 top was no help.

Matters were as bad or worse with Charles Rann Kennedy's turgid sermon, **The Seventh Trumpet** (11-21-41, Mansfield). Six stunned people sit before the newly bombed-out ruins of an ancient British chapel. They include a bobby (Peter Cushing) crippled while attempting to disarm a bomb at St. Paul's, Lady Madeleine (Carmen Mathews), who has taken it upon herself to nurse him, and her grandfather (Ian Maclaren), a wealthy industrialist who has become a monk. Lady Madeleine has also taken it upon herself to dub the bobby and tells him, "I verily believe that you are the only perfect knight of my life, Sir Percival." The group expostulates on the need for faith as Armageddon approaches. Soon they are joined by the German pilot (Alan Handley) who crash-landed after bombing the chapel. Their condemnation drives the aviator to kill himself just before another bombing attack destroys the others.

Sophie Treadwell's **Hope for a Harvest** (11-26-41, Guild) was almost as preachy but was redeemed in small measure by the performances of Fredric March and Florence Eldridge. After many years abroad, Carlotta Thatcher has been forced by the war to return to her California home. She finds her relations and friends, all old California stock, have gone to seed and look with bitterness on the "Wops and Japs" who have established prosperous farms by dint of their own industriousness. None is more bitter than Elliott Martin, a distant cousin whom Carlotta long has loved. He has had to sell off most of his once huge property and now

runs a small filling station. He complains to Carlotta of the shacks that have sprung up nearby, "All so shabby—and dirty—and dreary. Don't you remember how it used to be?—Now it's just a slum!" But Carlotta's purposefulness and determination reenergize Elliott, and they agree to put the old Thatcher property back in prime working order. Together they will have "a home and a harvest." March imbued Elliott with "a sullen strength," while Eldridge played "with admirable directness, simplicity and feeling."

A group of youngsters under the tutelage of Michael Chekhov and calling themselves the Chekhov Players Theatre had been touring college campuses and now brought in one of their mountings to the Little on December 2. Perhaps surprisingly, they did not offer Chekhov, but rather Shakespeare. And they offered one of his comedies that Broadway had seen a year before in far more experienced hands. A few of the players in their *Twelfth Night* went on to future fame—notably Beatrice Straight (Viola), Hurd Hatfield (Sir Andrew Aguecheek), and a young man listed in the program as Youl Bryner (Fabian). But even at a $2.20 top, New Yorkers wouldn't buy.

The season's most enduring thriller, like the season's most enduring comedy, was an importation. Called *Gaslight* in London and in a subsequent film version, Patrick Hamilton's **Angel Street** (12-5-41, Golden) scored 1295 performances, making it for many decades Broadway's longest-running foreign drama. (It remains today the second longest on record.) It told of a smooth, vicious husband (Vincent Price) who attempts to convince his wife (Judith Evelyn) that she, like her late mother before her, is losing her mind. But a sly inspector (Leo G. Carroll) latches on to the scheme and helps the wife thwart it. There were only three principals (plus two serving girls) in the cast of the single-setter, and there were no corpses, gunshots, or grisly hands appearing through walls. Instead the tension built steadily but quietly, reaching one celebrated peak when the inspector takes his leave but almost forgets his hat, resting tellingly on a desk. The unctuous Price, the dark, intense Evelyn, and the softly droll Carroll were all in top form.

Two days later, the Japanese bombed Pearl Harbor and, hours before the next play arrived, America declared war.

That first wartime entry was William Jay and Guy Bolton's **Golden Wings** (12-8-41, Cort). Set in an RAF service club and telling of several pilots, it might have seemed like a war tale. It was not. Instead, it told of a deadly love triangle. Two pilots, Rex and Tom (Lloyd Gough and Gordon Oliver), love the same woman (Signe Hasso), herself a pilot ferrying planes to the war zone. Rex is overheard threatening Tom not to come within his gunsights. So when the men go on a mission and Tom's plane is shot down under suspicious circumstances, Rex is headed for trouble.

(Another play scheduled to open during the same week was Lowell Barrington's **The Admiral Had a Wife.** But since it was a comedy detailing how a navy lieutenant [Alfred Drake], stationed at Pearl Harbor, contrives by means fair or foul to win a promotion, it was prudently called off.)

No further plays came in for two weeks, until John Bright and Asa Bordages's **Brooklyn, U.S.A.** (12-21-41, Forrest) opened. Suggested by District Attorney (later Mayor) William O'Dwyer's convicting the leaders of the notorious Murder, Inc., it watched as a variety of thugs went about their murderous ways. They include the inhuman but cynically named Smiley (Eddie Nugent), Dasher (Tom Pedi), who wishes his killings did not have to take him away from his Dodger games, and Philadelphia (Henry Lascoe), who can always find a humorous side to his thuggery. They pump one man full of bullets while he is sipping a Coke at a candy store and stab to death another man while he is covered with towels at a barber shop, then kill the squeamish barber. When news comes of the district attorney's indictments, the lady (Adelaide Klein) who runs the candy store where much of the action takes place decides life will be more peaceful running a brothel in California.

Some of the season's tersest and most damning notices went to Bernadine Angus's **Pie in the Sky** (12-22-41, Playhouse), in which a nearly bankrupt couple (Oscar Shaw and Luella Gear) attempt to marry off their son (Herbert Evers) to a blonde oil heiress. But the gentleman prefers brunettes. Since Shaw, Gear, and several of the other players had long been associated with musical comedies, a few critics suggested that should have been the route the story took. But none of them urged the matter strenuously.

The war came back to the stage with Fritz Rotter and Allen Vincent's **Letters to Lucerne** (12-23-41, Cort). At a Swiss school for rich young ladies, the war causes reassessments. Olga (Sonya Stokowski), a girl from Warsaw, has loved the brother of her German classmate, Erna (Grete Mosheim). The boy is a pilot in the Luftwaffe. When Olga's parents are killed in the bombing of Warsaw, she and the other girls turn against Erna. The mistress (Katharine Alexander) of the school pleads for understanding: "I'm not asking you to be tolerant of an enemy country—I'm asking you to be considerate of a human being!" Then a letter arrives for Erna, advising her that her brother crashed his own plane rather than bomb Warsaw. The girls reconsider their judgments.

Since most of the girls were played by youngsters with famous fathers or husbands, the first night was exceedingly posh, but after reviews came out branding the drama "dull" and "anemic," ticket sales dried up.

Even Clifford Odets could not make good in this disappointing season. Complaining that "the dynamite may have diminished in its power" in the writer's recent offerings, Brown went on to lament that it "has never been so dampened" as it now was. **Clash by Night** (12-27-41, Belasco) is set in the grubby Staten Island home of the slow-witted Jerry Wilenski (Lee J. Cobb) and his frustrated, secretly rebellious wife, Mae (Tallulah Bankhead). Jerry naively asks Mae to provide a room in their house for Earl Pfeiffer (Joseph Schildkraut), a handsome movie projectionist he has befriended. Before long, Mae and Earl are lovers. It takes Jerry some time to realize what has happened, but, when he does, he strangles Earl. Critics divided on whether or not Bankhead was miscast. They gave Schildkraut better notices. But virtually all agreed that Cobb was the show's main strength, with the *Sun*'s Richard Lockridge reporting, "Cobb brings to the character of the husband unusual comprehension and makes fully alive a pitiable, affecting human person."

Although most Americans were only beginning to be touched by the war, the year's last entry looked forward to the struggle to ensure the coming peace. Howard Koch and John Huston's **In Time to Come** (12-28-41, Mansfield) did so by recreating Woodrow Wilson's last battles. After a prologue showing Wilson (Richard Gaines) asking for a Declaration of War against Germany in 1917, the play demonstrated how his own personal quirks and stubborn idealism were no match for the self-serving interests of the international bigwigs who watered down his high-principled notions of a peace treaty and of his equally self-serving, isolationist political opponents at home who scuttled his drive to join the League of Nations. Even after being crippled by a stroke he insists, "Peace can be secured only by the unity of nations against aggression. This unity must be achieved." Bitter and exhausted, he has refused to see Colonel House (Russell Collins), the practical adviser who often spoke out courageously against the president's all too inflexible idealism. So after Wilson has left the room, his secretary, Joseph Tumulty (William Harrigan), quietly reads aloud a letter from House, suggesting future generations will more fully understand Wilson's greatness. Some critics had difficulty watching actors bring back to life public figures still fresh in many minds. Burns Mantle of the *Daily News* spoke for a number of his colleagues when he allowed that while "occasionally slow paced and wordy," the play itself was also "an always interesting and frequently stirring bit of dramatic history." Despite many similar notices the play could not find an audience.

The season failed to improve with the coming of the new year. Martha Hedman, now grown rather buxom, abandoned a decades-long retirement to perform the leading role of the insatiably dominating Norwegian-American mother in Arnold Sundgaard's **The First Crocus** (1-2-42, Longacre). In a small Minnesota town, Inga Jorisland bullies her weak husband (Herbert Nelson) and provokes her independently minded daughter (Barbara Engelhart) to leave home. Her pressure on her younger son (Eugene Schiel) to win a school prize for spotting the year's first crocus, a prize both his older brother and his sister have won in the past, prompts him to cheat, which causes a scandal when he is caught. So does her own unauthorized borrowing from school funds. Her husband has to sell his overcoat to pay back the money.

From Norwegian-Americans in Minnesota the theatre moved on to the Pennsylvania Dutch in Lancaster County, Pennsylvania, in Patterson Greene's **Papa Is All** (1-6-42, Guild). Papa (Carl Benton Reid) is a whip-cracking tyrant who refuses to allow Mama (Jessie Royce Landis) any modern amenities, calls his son, Jake (Emmet Rogers), stupid, and threatens to kill the surveyor who would court his daughter, Emma (Celeste Holm). So Jake takes him riding one day, conks his old man on the head, leaves their truck in the path of an oncoming train, and returns home to report that Papa is "all" [dead]. Mama immediately puts in plumbing and a telephone, only to have Papa return, alive and angry. But before he can do any damage he is arrested by a state trooper (Royal Beal). It seems he was hurled to safety, then got a gun and shot, but did not kill, the surveyor. So, one way or another, the family is rid of Papa, at least for the time being. The dialogue was in the Pennsylvania Dutch dialect. Thus Mama says, "Ach. I had wrong. I thought it was the telephone ringing, and it was Jake only. A doorbell he's made with the battery from the barn out." The *Post*'s Wilella Waldorf found the play "so fragile that it sometimes seems in danger of blowing itself away," but conceded that "it does supply a respectable number of laughs." Even so, it ran only until just after the Theatre Guild's subscriptions were exhausted.

Charles MacArthur became the latest well-known writer to come a cropper in the season when he offered **Johnny on a Spot** (1-8-42, Plymouth). His play was based on one by Parke Levy and Alan Lipscott, which itself had been drawn from a short story by George A. Hendon, Jr., and David Peltz. Governor Upjohn is running for senator of his southern state. He has promised his frantic, freewheeling campaign manager, Nicky Allen (Keenan Wynn), that he will give up his drinking and whoring during the campaign. When he fails to show up for a radio broadcast from his office on election eve, the desperate but resourceful Nicky decides to broadcast a recording the governor had made, hoping no one catches on. A friendly Doc Blossom (Will Geer) comes in while the recording is being played, and Nicky tells him to be quiet since the governor is speaking. Doc retorts, "Yeah, he's making one hell of a speech, considering he's dead." It turns out that the governor dropped dead while visiting a whorehouse. Nicky and his associates elect to keep the fact secret. They attempt to retrieve the body, lose it, find it again thanks to Doc's pet buzzards, and bring it to the office hidden in an iron lung. The opposition becomes suspicious, forcing Nicky to finally agree to a compromise that satisfies no one. But at least he can head off with the governor's pretty secretary (Edith Atwater). Critics dismissed the comedy as more frantic than funny. A 1994 revival by London's Royal National Theatre also failed.

A revival of Richard Brinsley Sheridan's *The Rivals* at the Shubert on the 14th had an all-star cast, with Mary Boland as Mrs. Malaprop, Walter Hampden as Sir Anthony, Haila Stoddard as Lydia, onetime musical comedy favorite Helen Ford as Lucy, and Philip Bourneuf as Sir Lucius O'Trigger. Critics split on their appraisals of the performances. Unanimously, they hailed Bobby Clark's Bob Acres as the runaway star of the evening. Clark employed quill pens as darts, used a pistol as a musical instrument, scampered over and under tables, and turned the eighteenth-century comedy into a madcap farce. Thanks in good measure to the Theatre Guild's subscribers, the production ran for fifty-four performances.

With draft-age men being called to the colors, Broadway was leaning more and more on younger players. This policy had worked well in *Junior Miss* and the musical *Best Foot Forward*. It failed with Louis Hoffman and Don Hartman's **All in Favor** (1-20-42, Henry Miller's). A teenaged-boys' club finds itself in financial difficulties—short the $30 rent for their basement club room. So they agree to take in girls. One of the girls (Frances Heflin) finds she has no money to get back home and is forced to spend the night at the club, in all innocence, with Wack Wack McDougal (Raymond Roe). Wack Wack's obnoxious kid brother, Peewee (Tommy Lewis), learns of the incident and threatens to blackmail everyone, especially when he also learns that the boys have pawned a $200 ring to raise further money. But then Peewee goes on a radio quiz show and wins big. By retrieving the ring and promising to remain silent, he buys his way into the club.

The easily spoofable William Saroyan was spoofed again in Samson Raphaelson's **Jason** (1-21-42, Hudson). Jason Otis (Alexander Knox) is the smug, priggish drama critic for the *Evening World*. His own world is shaken when a messenger boy, Mike Ambler (Nicholas Conte), a would-be playwright, comes to his apartment and lectures Otis on the critic's unnatural distancing of himself from the mass of humanity outside. Mike is nothing if not egocentric, apostrophizing, "Oh, Lord, You did a wonderful job when You made me and I want to thank You." He even urges the Lord to follow his own example and have mercy on those who will not understand him. For a time, Jason accepts Mike's challenge. Among those he meets is the comically soured-on-life Humphrey Crocker (E. G. Marshall), a former Met stagehand and sometime seaman. But then Jason discovers that his wife, Lisa (Helen Walker), has fallen for Mike. Furious, he dictates a scathing notice of Mike's play, *Hooray for the Madam*, calling him a plagiarizing half-wit. But when he realizes that Lisa still loves him, he writes a more balanced review. The real reviewers enjoyed the send-up of Saroyan, but took not-quite-mock umbrage at the depiction of the critic, one who, several were amused to note, dictated his reviews to a secretary in the leisurely comfort of his luxurious home. This time the public ignored the critics and allowed *Jason* a modest sixteen-week run.

The public also liked H. S. Kraft's **Cafe Crown** (1-23-42, Cort), which had some fun at the expense of another branch of New York theatre—the Yiddish stage. For Cafe Crown many read the celebrated Second Avenue eatery Cafe Royal, and for David Cole, the late Jacob Adler. Hymie (Sam Jaffe), the inexplicably well off waiter at the Cafe Crown has been an angel for many Yiddish productions, but he balks when the lordly Cole (Morris Carnovsky) saunters in, wearing a fur-lined coat and brandishing a silver-tipped cane, and tells Hymie that he is going to make another of his farewell appearances and would like Hymie's support for his modern version of *King Lear*. It will even include a part for Mrs. Cole, that of Mrs. Lear, so that she will not have to play with a Brooklyn rival, Mandelbaum. But having lost money when he backed a Shakespeare play about "Richard One-Two-Three," Hymie is loath to fork up cash for a Shakespearean piece about "an old Jew on Riverside Drive." To his own surprise, Cole obtains the money from a long-lost son (Whitner Bissell). He also backs down in his opposition to a Hollywood job for his son-in-law (Sam Wanamaker). Among the minor characters were a playwright (Eduard Franz) who is rewriting *Rain* with a Catskills setting and a reformed rabbi in place of the Protestant minister, and a critic (Daniel Ocky) who always composes his notice before he sees a production. The comedy ran for 141 performances. A highly praised off-Broadway revival in 1988 failed after it was moved uptown.

A dismayingly lengthy string of flops ensued. Like his former collaborator, Charles MacArthur, Ben Hecht had to face an ignominious defeat, in this case with **Lily of the Valley** (1-26-42, Windsor). The peg-legged Rev. Swen Houseman (Siegfried Rumann), a former Norwegian seaman whose church has burned down, is given permission to use a room in the morgue for his service. It takes him a while to realize that his new congregation consists of ghosts. They include an angry longshoreman (Myron McCormick), a scrubwoman (Minnie Dupree) who threw herself out of a window, a girl (Katharine Bard) who died on the eve of her first dance, and an old prostitute (Alison Skipworth). The minister goads one (David Hoffman) of the dead to reveal the whereabouts of a $40,000 cache. He retrieves it, but is killed by an insane morgue attendant (Will Lee). As the attendant is led away a heavenly concertina is heard playing a hymn and a light from above illumes the murdered man's body. Rejected by the critics with such adjectives as "half-baked" and "morbid," the fantasy left after one week.

The only nice things critics could say for **Solitaire** (1-27-42, Plymouth), which John van Druten extracted from Edwin Corle's novel, they reserved for Alfred Hitchcock's pudgy, shrill-voiced daughter, Pat. She delighted reviewers with her playing of twelve-year-old Virginia Stewart, who is neglected by her wealthy parents (Ben Smith and Sally Bates), so strikes up a friendship with Ben (Victor Kilian), a hobo who has made a home in the gulch below the Stewarts' Pasadena property after being kicked off a streetcar for carrying a pet rat in a cage. The friendship blossoms until some fascistic tramps attempt to make trouble and until news of a little girl's murder by a tramp reaches the community. Then the police arrest all the drifters and destroy their shacks. But Virginia prevails upon her father to bail out Ben and help him on his way.

A revival of *Hedda Gabler* at the Longacre on the 29th offered a new translation by Ethel Borden and Mary Cass Canfield and featured the slim, dark Greek actress Katina Paxinou. She received respectful but not enthusiastic notices. Her supporting cast included Margaret Wycherly (Juliana), Ralph Forbes (George), Cecil Humphreys (Judge Brack), and Henry Daniell (Eilert Lovborg). A week and a half, and they were gone.

The next celebrated writer to meet with disaster was Marc Connelly, whose **The Flowers of Virtue** (2-5-42, Royale) wilted after just four performances. In Mexico, General Orijas (Vladimir Sokoloff), backed by Nazi money, plans a fascist takeover of the country. But when he cripples a power plant, Grover Bemis (Frank Craven), a retired American engineer, quickly repairs it and is looked upon as a miracle-maker by the peasants, who send the general packing.

211

Lesley Storm's **Heart of a City** (2-12-42, Henry Miller's) spotlighted several of the girls who performed at London's famous Windmill Theatre, a house just off Shaftesbury Avenue that offered "non-stop" girlie revues and later boasted that it never missed a performance during the blitz. Carefree Judy (Gertrude Musgrove) loves the embittered, hard-drinking lyricist, Tommy (Romney Brent), but he loves the leading lady, Rosalind (Beverly Roberts), who suddenly has eyes only for an RAF pilot (Richard Ainley). About the time that Rosalind and her beau run off to be married, Judy and Tommy are killed in an air raid.

More than one critic could not resist having fun with the title of Leo Rifkin, Frank Tarloff, and David Shaw's **They Should Have Stood in Bed** (2-13-42, Mansfield), which featured former lightweight boxing champ Tony Canzoneri in the cast. Wheeler-dealer Al Hartman (Grant Richards) joins up with Barney Snedeker (Jack Gilford), a clientless lawyer, Sam Simkins (Sanford Meisner), who sells stolen clothing, and Harry Driscoll (Russell Morrison), a would-be private detective, to back a restaurant with the fighter Killer Kane as front man. To scrounge up money they decide to promote a bout between Kane and their not very bright chef, Henry Angel (Edwin Philips). Matters get complicated when both the boxer and the chef begin to pursue the boxing commissioner's wife (Peggy Meskell), when gangsters enter the picture after the entrepreneurs bet their bundle on the fight, and when neither contestant seems anxious to be socked.

In James Edward Grant's preposterous **Plan M** (2-20-42, Belasco), after Nazi spies kill General Sir Hugh Winston (Len Doyle), the British chief of staff, and substitute a look-alike, the royal family and the prime minister are kidnapped and the Germans replace the British plan to repel invasion with one of their own. The operation would have led to England's downfall had not the substitute made a pass at his secretary (Ann Burr), unaware she was the general's daughter.

Herbert Ehrmann's **Under This Roof** (2-22-42, Windsor) examined three decades in the life of a Massachusetts woman, Cornelia (Barbara O'Neil). In 1846 she rejects a proposal from Gibeon Warren (Peter Hobbs), a radical abolitionist, and instead weds his conservative brother, Ezra (Russell Hardie). Her young son (John Draper) is killed in the Civil War, and, in the prosperity that follows the war, Ezra becomes involved in shady railroad stock deals and is forced to flee. Later, ruined in a stock market crash, he returns home repentent. Cornelia, who by then has interested herself in the welfare of poor immigrants, takes him back out of a sense of charity.

One modest success interrupted the chain of failures. Hagar Wilde and Dale Eunson's **Guest in the House**

(2-24-42, Plymouth) was based on a story by Katherine Albert. Douglas (Leon Ames) and Ann Proctor (Louise Campbell) take in Ann's young niece, Evelyn Heath (Mary Anderson), who is said to be suffering from a dangerous heart ailment. Initially, Evelyn is as sweet as can be, but her vicious nature soon manifests itself. Her lies—such as stating that Douglas is having an affair with his secretary—and her serving as an unhealthy example for the Proctors' impressionable young daughter (Joan Spencer) drive Douglas to drink and Ann to the verge of a nervous breakdown. When they attempt to send her away, she rips her clothing and says she will claim Douglas attacked her. Fortunately, the Proctors' cagey Aunt Martha (Katherine Emmet) is around. Knowing of Evelyn's hysterical fear of birds, she shows the girl an empty bird cage and says the bird has escaped. As Evelyn starts to rush off to the safety of her room, Martha asks what makes her think the bird is not up there: "Birds fly, you know. They can go anywhere." The frantic Evelyn would run outside, but Martha reminds her there are thousands of birds in the open. Evelyn screams and her heart gives out; she drops dead.

A revival of James M. Barrie's *A Kiss for Cinderella* at the Music Box on March 10 was not made welcome. Screen favorite Luise Rainer was starred as the waif who dreams romantically about her local bobby (Ralph Forbes). But Rainer, with her thick accent and European tragic airs, was seen as all wrong for the role that Maude Adams had created.

Rowland Brown, best known for his screenplays for gangster films, was the author of **Johnny 2 X 4** (3-17-42, Longacre), a play which had no real story to tell but rather looked at the raffish times of a Greenwich Village speakeasy from its founding in 1926 to its closing at the end of Prohibition. Johnny (Jack Arthur) earned his nickname from the small portable piano he used to carry around. At his club are served up slices of the lives of his friends, his performers, and the inevitable gangsters, one of whom is shot there. The nightclub setting allowed the performers, who included a quartet known as the Yacht Club Boys, to sing their songs, high-kick their Charlestons, and play their trumpet and piano solos.

Gottfried Ephraim Lessing's 160-odd-year-old **Nathan the Wise** (4-3-42, Belasco), in a translation by Ferdinand Bruckner, received its first major Broadway hearing after an off-Broadway mounting was so well thought of that it was rushed uptown. A Christian knight (Alfred Ryder) who loves a supposed Jewess (Olive Deering) is outraged to discover she is merely the adopted daughter of Nathan (Herbert Berghof) and may not be Jewish at all. The Church would sentence Nathan to death, but since the action occurs in Muslim-occupied

Jerusalem, Saladin (Bram Nossen) summons the figures to his court, where he is impressed by Nathan's wisdom and tolerance. It soon develops that the knight and the girl are brother and sister, Saladin's own nephew and niece. (In this version, these last points were omitted, so the lovers could marry.)

Having met success with his adaptation of his own novel *Of Mice and Men,* John Steinbeck tried again by theatricalizing his latest best-seller, **The Moon Is Down** (4-7-42, Martin Beck), a book which like his earlier one, many had seen as a play awaiting transference to the stage. In doing so Steinbeck joined the ranks of outstanding writers to go awry during this dismal season. When invaders occupy a small mining town, the mayor's wife (Leona Powers) wonders if keeping "proper decencies" alive will not be the best policy. The thoughtful Colonel Lanser (Otto Kruger) assures her and her husband (Ralph Morgan) that the invasion is primarily a business matter and no unpleasantness will arise if the citizens remain peaceable. But the villagers refuse to remain quiet, and more and more occupiers are shot. When the colonel finally orders that the mayor himself be held hostage, the mayor, in lines echoing those in *Candle in the Wind,* tells the officer, "It is always that herd men win battles, but free men win wars. You will find it so, sir." He is led off. Although neither Germany nor Norway was specifically mentioned, it was generally understood that the story depicted the Nazi occupation of Norway. Some critics were taken aback by Steinbeck, who, in an effort to see good and evil on both sides, made his invaders, as Lockridge noted, "more sinned against than sinning," but all concurred that the dramatization was "disappointing." It survived for seventy-one performances.

Gussie Rogers (Beth Merrill) had hoped to inherit the restored New England colonial home which gave its name to Norma Mitchell and John Harris's **Autumn Hill** (4-13-42, Booth). After all, she had been a faithful companion for twenty years to the lady who owned it. But the old harpie left no will, so her nephew, Tony (Jack Effrat), inherits it. He lets Gussie stay on, and she falls in love with him. Although pretending to be an author, Tony actually is a counterfeiter and has his own abrasive girl (Elizabeth Sutherland). When a local clergyman gets wise to Tony's real work, Tony murders him. The police and the FBI close in. Tony pleads with Gussie to help him escape the electric chair, so Gussie shoots and kills him as the authorities pound on the door.

Paul Muni and Emlyn Williams also met with failure when Muni was starred in Williams's **Yesterday's Magic** (4-14-42, Guild). His alcoholism has reduced Maddoc Thomas, once a great Shakespearean actor, to work as Selfridge's Santa Claus. His devoted daughter, Cattrin (Jessica Tandy) wangles him a small part in a

musical, and his success there leads the great producer C. B. Cochran to give him a chance to play Lear. On the eve of his opening, Maddoc learns that Cattrin and her beau (Alfred Drake) plan to leave for America. He gets drunk and dies. A few critics wondered why playwrights depicting actors staging a comeback always seemed to have them play Lear (as in *Cafe Crown*), but no critic remembered that a very similar story, even to the play's being *King Lear,* had been used in *Success* (1-28-18).

Matters went badly downhill with Jo Eisinger and Judson O'Donnell's **What Big Ears** (4-20-42, Windsor). Gabby Martin (Taylor Holmes) and Joey Smithers (Edwin Philips) had been successful with a medicine show in which Joey dolled up as a woman to help sales. Now broke and in Hollywood, Joey is grabbed to play Whistler's Mother in a film. But Gabby, an inveterate gambler, signs Joey's name to some IOUs, then runs off to New York. The gangsters follow Joey to New York, where he has gone for his film's opening. In no time, people are running in and out of doors at a New York hotel room and hiding in closets before everything ends happily.

At the Shubert on the 27th, Katharine Cornell revived *Candida* for a third time, ostensibly for only four performances to benefit the Army Emergency Fund and the Navy Relief Society. Her cast included Mildred Natwick as Miss Garnett, Raymond Massey as Morell, Dudley Digges as Mr. Burgess, and Burgess Meredith as Marchbanks. So ecstatic were the reviews that the restoration was held over for three additional weeks.

Brooklyn Dodger fans were asked to believe that their beloved Bums had lost nine games in a row when the curtain rose on William Roos's **The Life of Reilly** (4-29-42, Broadhurst). One salient reason for these losses has been that their great southpaw, Rocket Reilly (Peter Hobbs), refuses to pitch after Mme. Waleska, a fortune teller whom he swears by and who never appears in the play, has warned him he will lose. Now she tells him he will kill someone before his next game, and, sure enough, he seems to shoot a small-time gambler (Loring Smith). Patrolman Cooper (Howard Smith) is such a Dodger rooter that he is even willing to take the blame for the killing himself rather than let Reilly miss a crucial game against the Giants. However, in the end it develops that the gambler was not really killed. No fewer than three newspaper critics quoted the same joke, in which the pitcher tells the policeman to arrest him and let him face the electric chair since he will at least be dying for something he believes in. When the cop asks him what that is, he replies, "Capital punishment." With gags like that, it was small wonder baseball fans and regular playgoers stayed away in droves.

Act One: 1930–1944

Fulton Oursler and his wife, Grace Perkins, were the authors of the latest thriller, **The Walking Gentleman** (5-7-42, Belasco). Although Doris Forrest (Arlene Francis), an actress, has divorced her actor-husband, Basil Forrest (Victor Francen), and has fallen in love with Dr. Blake (Richard Gaines), the psychiatrist she is seeing, she is irresistibly drawn back to her ex. He is currently working on a mounting of *Dr. Jekyll and Mr. Hyde*. After his leading lady is murdered, he asks Doris to take her place, and she agrees. But Dr. Blake has discovered several other strangled women in the actor's past and returns in time to rescue Doris from being his latest victim. Forrest quickly lights a poisoned cigarette he has pulled from his pocket and kills himself. Some critics questioned why Francen, a French refugee with a heavy accent, was cast in the role of an American actor.

Paul Vincent Carroll, whose once high-flying stock had completely collapsed, suffered another debacle with **The Strings, My Lord, Are False** (5-19-42, Royale). An open-minded Canon Courtenay (Walter Hampden) tends a motley variety of locals after the Germans bomb Clyde. Besides assisting such figures as a Communist (Art Smith) who believes God is a capitalistic invention, a Jewish refugee (Will Lee) who lost an arm at Dunkirk, and a self-sacrificing prostitute (Margot Grahame), he patches up affairs between a town councillor (Colin Keith-Johnston) and his fiancée (Ruth Gordon), a young lady who finds herself pregnant by another man.

Just as the season was coming to its sad end, one last smash hit suddenly appeared—Thomas Job's **Uncle Harry** (5-20-42, Broadhurst). At a backwater Canadian tavern in the early years of the century, a man (Joseph Schildkraut) sidles up to a traveler (Guy Sampsel) and insists on talking about murder, "because murder is a beautiful art if you look at it properly. Yes, that's the pathetic part of it." It is pathetic, he adds, because he has committed the perfect crime and has gone unpunished despite his numerous confessions. He is Harry Quincey, familiarly referred to as Uncle Harry, and he used to live with his two spinster sisters, the somewhat dreary Hester (Adelaide Klein) and the taunting, controlling Lettie (Eva Le Gallienne). A visit from Lucy (Leona Roberts), the girl he loved but whom his sisters stood in the way of his marrying and who is now about to marry someone else, is an unpleasant experience for him. After she leaves, he sends Lettie to the chemist to buy some poison to put their aging dog out of its agony. But later that evening, meeting the chemist at the tavern, Harry denies having sent Lettie and professes ignorance of the poison she bought. He also arranges for the Quinceys' servants to overhear a bitter fight between the sisters. So when Hester is found poisoned, Lettie is arrested, tried, and sentenced to death. Harry calls in Lucy and tells her that with one sister dead and the other about to be executed, he is free to marry her. But Lucy, who has seen through him, walks out. Overwhelmed with guilt and loneliness, Harry confesses to the prison governor (Colville Dunn), but is not believed. He demands his sister be called in. She will tell the truth. To Harry's horror, Lettie, who has resigned herself to dying, refuses to help, thus dooming Harry to a life of self-torture. "An admirably sinister murder play, slightly diabolical in its ingenuity and warranted to make the timid look hereafter with uneasy suspicion on all quiet little men" was Lockridge's happy assessment. A few critics had reservations about Schildkraut, but a majority suggested that he and Le Gallienne caught that tense, luminous interplay that they had brought to *Liliom* twenty years before. The play ran a solid year.

Unanimously disparaging reviews saw to it there was no run for a revival of William Gillette's *All the Comforts of Home* (9-8-90), which came into the Longacre on the 25th. Dorothy Sands, Celeste Holm and Nicholas Joy were among the actors recounting how a nephew, left in charge of his uncle's home while the uncle goes on vacation, rents out rooms to all manner of people. Watts found the play "pretty tedious fooling in our perhaps too sophisticated days."

A largely dismal season ended dismally indeed with Louis Vittes's **Comes the Revelation** (5-26-42, Jolson), a play set in upstate New York in 1827. To capitalize on a religious revival, Joe Flanders (Wendell Corey), a petty thief once arrested for stealing nightshirts from his neighbors' clotheslines, uses a book he has purchased for a dime to claim God has revealed to him that American Indians are the Lost Tribe of Israel. He announces God's further word has been given him on tablets of gold. His wife (Lesley Woods) is not hoodwinked and would expose him. But at the play's end he is leading his unquestioning followers on to Ohio. A not very subtle attack on the origins of the Mormon church, the play could not find an audience even at a $1.65 top for weekdays (and $2.20 on Saturday night). In fact, by opening on a Tuesday and closing the next night, it never even gave a Saturday performance.

1942–1943

Wartime brought problems and prosperity to Broadway. To save fuel, a dim-out was ordered. Marquees were left largely unlit, but while this lessened a certain sense of excitement and glamor, it did not hurt business. In fact, more plays ran beyond the benchmark 100-performance line, and even failures generally lasted a bit longer. Moreover, quality improved, although dramas were largely war dramas or patriotic pieces (including one brilliantly imaginative work) and comedies patent froth. Between the call of Hollywood and of Uncle Sam, much of the theatre's burgeoning male talent was drained away. Broadway looked increasingly to youngsters and oldsters, and with so many playwrights preoccupied with war work, increasingly to revivals. As a result the number of new plays resumed its plunge, falling to somewhere between forty-three and forty-seven novelties, depending on whose figure you accepted. But Americans' having more pocket money prompted producers to test higher prices. As the season progressed the standard $3.30 began to give way to $3.85.

As had been the case more often than not, the new season got off to a lame—albeit, for the first time in several years, early—start. Basil Beyea's **The Cat Screams** (6-17-42, Martin Beck), taken from a novel by Todd Downing, was set in a boardinghouse in a Mexican village, where an assortment of American travelers are abruptly quarantined by an epidemic. They include an old man (Harry Reid), his much younger wife (Doris Nolan), a writer who once was the wife's lover (Lloyd Gough), and a spinster (Mildred Dunnock) given to playing a piano and spouting poetry. One by one they appear to commit suicide, and just before each death the pension's cat screams. But at the close the deaths are apparently linked to the landlady (Lea Penman) and her drug trafficking. At that point a character blurts out, "I'm glad it's over. It's been a strain." Critics pounced on the lines to convey their own sentiments.

Andrew Rosenthal's **Broken Journey** (6-23-42, Henry Miller's) begins as two NBC war correspondents, Dan Hardeen (Warner Anderson) and Christina Landers (Edith Atwater), who long have been lovers, return to Dan's Ohio hometown after covering battles in Ethiopia, Spain, and Western Europe. Once back, Dan elects to marry his former sweetheart (Zita Johann), whose snobbish family had broken up their romance. At that moment, news of Pearl Harbor arrives, so Christina rushes back to work. But days later Dan hears Christina make a broadcast from Manila on Christmas Eve. He, too, hurries back to his job.

Continuing to have difficulties finding a producer, William Saroyan produced and directed a double bill of his shorter plays. **Across the Board on Tomorrow Morning** (8-17-42, Belasco) was set in Callaghan's, a bar on 52nd Street, and opened with a harpist (Lois Bannerman) entertaining the few patrons from her perch on a balcony. Those patrons comprise another of Saroyan's assortment of oddball habitués. They and a few employees include a philosophizing waiter (Canada Lee), who always bets on a horse named Tomorrow

Morning; two Filipino kitchen boys; a girl who rushes in to have a baby; and Maxwell Bodenheim, the celebrated Greenwich Village eccentric whom Saroyan allowed to play himself and recite his own poem, "Jazz Music." Near the end, proclaiming that "the glue that held the illusion together has run out," the characters agree that they all may well be dead and may have been dead for 1942 years. In **Talking to You,** Blackstone Boulevard (Lee), a black prizefighter who is reluctant to hurt good people, fights a midget (Andrew Ratousheff) dressed as Hitler, then finds himself deserted by everyone except a deaf white boy (Jules Leni).

Just as they had lit on the same telling lines in the season's opener, critics latched on to a line from Alec Coppel's West End drama **I Killed the Count** (9-3-42, Cort) to express their sentiments. That line was "This is getting ridiculous." A man is murdered, and Divisional Inspector Davidson (Louis Hector) is confronted by four suspects, each confessing to the killing and each, in a flashback recreating the crime, knowing undisclosed circumstantial evidence that appears to confirm the admission. Davidson is at a loss which person to arrest. Clarence Derwent won applause for his comic relief as a badgered witness anxious to leave and head off to clinch a business deal, but detained to reenact his part in each retelling.

A revival of *Tobacco Road* came into the Forrest on the 5th and lingered for a month.

Although virtually every critic compared it unfavorably with *Junior Miss*—"I am afraid it is a Junior Miss which belongs in the misses department," the *World-Telegram*'s John Mason Brown grouched—Josephine Bentham and Herschel Williams's **Janie** (9-10-42, Henry Miller's) was the season's first smash hit. Before it ran its course it chalked up 642 performances. Janie Colburn (Gwen Anderson) is a high schooler more or less fond of Scooper Nolan (Frank Amy) until her mother's widowed friend, Mrs. Lawrence (Linda Watkins), arrives for a visit with her Yalie son, Private Dick Lawrence (Herbert Evers), who is stationed at a nearby army base. Mr. Colburn (Maurice Manson) publishes the local newspaper and has written editorials opposing any mingling of the soldiers with the town's youngsters. But when Janie learns she and her girlfriends are to have the house to themselves one evening, she asks Dick to invite some of his friends to join them. What seems like his whole regiment turns up, and with the colored butler innocently agreeing to serve the boys hard liquor, mayhem ensues. Mr. Colburn is aghast until he learns that Janie has buttered the very man (Howard St. John) who can help Colburn get priorities for new printing presses. Of course, when Dick has to return to the war, Janie must return to Scooper. For many the play was stolen by skinny, deadpan Clare

Foley as Janie's younger sister, Elsbeth, who always demands no less than a nickel to leave the room when Janie is with a beau and who smugly informs anyone who will listen, "Once I grew four inches in a week."

Emlyn Williams's **The Morning Star** (9-14-42, Morosco) was an ongoing London hit that New York would not accept. It is bad enough that Mrs. Parrilow (Gladys Cooper) has had her home heavily damaged in the blitz, but her elder son, Cliff (Gregory Peck), a brilliant doctor and medical researcher, has gone to pieces, abandoning his work and his wife (Jill Esmond), taking up with a patent hussy (Wendy Barrie), and thinking about heading for Hollywood after a book he has written becomes a best-seller. But when his younger brother is reported killed in action, he gets hold of himself. Cooper won glowing notices, but the then unknown Peck received sharply divided ones ("left me cold," "promises to go far").

Another researcher (José Ferrer), the inventor of a machine to spread concealing smoke across a battlefield, might well have been driven batty by his wife (Uta Hagen) in S. M. Herzig's **Vickie** (9-22-42, Plymouth). Vickie Roberts, in the blue uniform of the AWCS (American Woman's Camp Service, an imaginary group patterned after numerous real ones), thinks nothing of taking over her husband's space for the convenience of her organization or of using his blueprints to wrap sandwiches for the boys. And when he is visited by an important dollar-a-year man come to examine the invention for the government, Vicki concludes the visitor is a spy and puts on a Mata Hari act to make him confess, while her hidden colleagues stand ready to rush into the room and capture him. Critics reported that Margaret Metzenauer, formerly with the Met, all but walked off with the play as an aria-yodeling cook.

Saroyan did convince Eddie Dowling to include one of his plays in the young season's second double bill, and many critics thought it much the best thing, however atypical, he had done. **Hello, Out There** (9-29-42, Belasco) is set in a small-town Texas jail where Photo Finish (Dowling), a gambler, is being held for a rape he is falsely accused of committing. In his loneliness he shouts, "Hello, out there" and is answered by the young girl (Julie Haydon) who cooks for the prisoners. They would become friends, but Photo Finish is lynched by the local vigilantes. The curtain raiser was a revival of G. K. Chesterton's twenty-five-year-old *Magic,* with Haydon as a girl who believes in fairies and Dowling as the conjurer who argues for the need for faith.

The cost of maintaining its huge cast and multi-scened production was probably as much a reason why Howard Lindsay and Russel Crouse's **Strip for Action** (9-30-42, National) jacked up its top ticket to $3.85 as

was the war-born prosperity. Its story was simple. Nutsy (Keenan Wynn) had been a burlesque comic before being drafted, so he decides to mount a good, old-fashioned burlesque show for his fellow recruits. That means heading to the War Department to get it to overrule a ban by some prudish officers. The show—stripteases and raunchy clowns—is a big hit with the soldiers. It was with burlesque-starved critics, too, who delighted that the authors were able to circumvent Mayor La Guardia's opposition to the genre (he had shut down all the town's burlesque shows). Of course, a few blocks north Mike Todd had done as much with the even more successful *Star and Garter,* with Bobby Clark and Gypsy Rose Lee heading the cast. But the bumps and grinds and, especially, Wynn and Joey Faye, running through such old burlesque routines as "Which Way Is Flugel Street?," were equally welcomed. Yet for some reason, the public was not all that interested, so the show closed after fourteen weeks.

Critics and public alike embraced Maxwell Anderson's war play, **The Eve of St. Mark** (10-7-42, Cort). Ignoring the reservations he had expressed about Anderson last season, *PM*'s Louis Kronenberger wrote, "Despite its faults, *The Eve of St. Mark* is the first play about the war that has any emotional impact and real humanity." It had been written for and presented by outlying regional theatre groups and called for only minimal furnishings and hints of settings presented against a curtained backdrop. The scheme was followed on Broadway. When Quizz West (William Prince) comes home on leave he brings with him his girl, Janet Feller (Mary Rolfe), a neighbor whom he had never paid much attention to until he met her in New York. She is made to feel welcome by the elder Wests (Matt Crowley and Aline MacMahon). Back at camp, Quizz remains faithful to her, even though his buddies take him to a local honky-tonk, and she remains loyal to him. When the war breaks out he is sent to the Philippines. Although he writes faithfully, he comes to her even more vividly in her dreams (the dream sequences were in blank verse, the rest of the play in prose). Then word comes that he has been killed in action. His mother tells Janet, "He was mine for a little while, but you'll always have him, even if he doesn't come back." Quizz's younger brothers (Carl Gose and Clifford Carpenter) announce that they have enlisted. Their father urges them to make better new worlds. Although the play ran for nine months, it never retained the allegiance or affection that the great War World I plays, Anderson's collaborative *What Price Glory?* or the English *Journey's End,* won, nor enjoyed the occasional revivals the British play still receives.

The revival of *Three Men on a Horse* that came into

the Forrest on the 9th, with William Lynn and Teddy Hart repeating their original roles, stayed around for less than four weeks.

A second revival, John Drinkwater's thirteen-year-old *Bird in Hand,* in which an innkeeper opposes the marriage of his daughter into the squirarchy, opened at the Morosco on the 19th but lasted only a single week.

John van Druten and Lloyd Morris's **The Damask Cheek** (10-22-42, Playhouse) garnered approving though not enthusiastic notices. Falling in line with a majority of his colleagues, the *Sun*'s Richard Lockridge concluded, "You could hardly, indeed, ask for more charm. You could hardly, on the whole, have less substance." In 1909, Rhoda Meldrum (Flora Robson), a thirtyish English spinster, has come to New York to spend time with her American relations and, with luck, find a husband. She has long loved her distant cousin, Jimmy Randall (Myron McCormick), but has never told her love. Jimmy is engaged to a flashy actress, Calla Longstreth (Celeste Holm). One night, having sipped too much champagne, Rhoda runs off for a spin in Central Park with a close friend (Zachary Scott) of Jimmy's. Her aunt (Margaret Douglass) is outraged and would send her away. In the discussions that follow Jimmy blurts out that he does not love Calla yet has "been spending the last three months trying not to say it to myself." That provokes Rhoda to ask Calla if she loves Jimmy. Calla admits that she is marrying for money, so Rhoda offers her $25,000 to give up Jimmy. Calla accepts, although some thoughtless words on her part lead to a hair-pulling struggle ("one of the best hair-pulling scenes I have ever witnessed," one critic rejoiced). Rhoda herself is about to leave when Jimmy proposes. Enough playgoers thought the comedy might be their cup of tea to keep it on the boards for twelve weeks.

The month's third revival was *Native Son.* With Canada Lee again playing Bigger, it began an eleven-week stand at the Majestic on the 23rd.

October's last novelty was Eric Hatch's **Little Darling** (10-27-42, Biltmore). Hatch, a successful screenwriter, found no luck on Broadway. Kenneth Brown (Leon Ames) is also a successful writer—of stories for women's magazines and of a hit play, *Old Letch,* which takes place entirely in a bedroom and which has been described as "the season's wickedest wow." But Brown is really a stuck-in-the-mud homebody. Then his spoiled-brat daughter (Barbara Bel Geddes), who looks on him as hopelessly stuffy, brings home her seventeen-year-old roommate (Phyllis Avery) and provokes him to taking the girl out for some wild times. But he soon comes to his senses and settles for marrying his loyal secretary (Karen Morley). Her charm and "uncommonly

pleasing voice" allowed Bel Geddes to walk off with the evening's acting honors. Runner up was Peter Goo Chong as a stereotypical Chinese servant, scurrying about giggling and saying, "Hello, bossy" or "Hello, missy," and singing a duet of "Belly Me on the Lone Plailie" with Brown.

In one of his last reviews before leaving to spend the war as a *Times* correspondent in China and Russia, Brooks Atkinson rued that there was little Katharine Hepburn could do for "a trifling play that is generally uneventful." That play was Philip Barry's **Without Love** (11-10-42, St. James). Patrick Jamieson (Elliott Nugent), the son of a career diplomat, has come to Washington in hopes of nudging Ireland out of its pro-Axis neutrality and into the Allies' corner. "When are you Irish going to quit acting so damned British?" he explodes. But his most immediate problem is finding housing. He has met Jamie Coe Rowan, a seemingly humorless, puritanical New England widow, who lives in the home of her late senator-father. She offers Patrick a room, but to squelch gossip they agree to marry. Of course, it will be a marriage in name only. And, of course, by eleven o'clock it is much more than that. Audiences had to be content ogling the "dazzling succession of frocks and peignoirs" Valentina designed for Hepburn. But the stars helped the play keep going for fifteen weeks.

The Barry play was produced by the Theatre Guild, and three nights later the Guild offered its subscribers a second play—and suffered one of its shortest-lived flops. Ketti Frings based **Mr. Sycamore** (11-13-42, Guild) on a story by Robert Ayre. Smeed's mailman, John Gwilt (Stuart Erwin), is so fed up with the dreariness of his daily route that he listens attentively to the town's librarian-poetess (Enid Markey) when she suggests he become a tree. Although his wife (Lillian Gish) at first opposes the idea, she finally acquiesces, so he digs a shallow hole, takes off his shoes and socks, steps into the hole, and refills it. Mrs. Gwilt brings a chair so that he can sit down until he takes root. She also brings him food and makes him a mustard plaster when he begins to sneeze. His fellow townsfolk mock him. Once or twice he is about to reconsider, but he eventually does take root. By play's end he has become a full-grown tree. Mrs. Gwilt sits underneath his shade, knitting and chatting with him.

Down in the Village, Edward Peyton Harris's **Homecoming** (11-16-42, Provincetown Playhouse) retold the biblical story of Noah in terms of Nate Eborn and his family, who are living in Greenville, North Carolina, just after the current war. Blind Augustin Duncan once again came out briefly from his enforced retirement to take the lead role.

A much more brilliant fantasy—or allegory—followed. It, too, touched on the Noah legend. The *Herald Tribune*'s new man, Howard Barnes, proclaimed, "Theater-going became a rare and electrifying experience" with the arrival of Thornton Wilder's "daffy and illuminating" **The Skin of Our Teeth** (11-18-42, Plymouth). Other assessments ranged from "provocative, and sometimes richly amusing" to the suggestion that it was "merely a stunt show" by one of the two of Broadway's eight major newspaper critics who saw it as nothing more than intellectualized Olsen and Johnson. After some brass band flourishes and some odd newsreels, including one showing a ring found by cleaning women and inscribed "To Eva from Adam Genesis 2-18," the curtain rises on the Excelsior, New Jersey, home of Mr. and Mrs. Antrobus (Fredric March and Florence Eldridge), where they live with their malevolent son, Henry (Montgomery Clift), and their giddy daughter, Gladys (Frances Heflin). They have a mammoth and a dinosaur for pets. Mr. Antrobus has invented the wheel and the alphabet, while his wife has discovered sewing and cooking. Despite the advance of the Ice Age and incessant human rapacity, the family survives. Not even their aggressive maid, Sabina (Tallulah Bankhead), can seduce Mr. Antrobus from his decent ways. Millennia pass. At an Atlantic City convention of the Ancient and Honorable Order of Mammals, Mr. Antrobus is elected president. A Cassandraic fortune teller (Florence Reed), who can foresee everything but finds the past a muddle, predicts disaster. Henry continues his murderous attacks, and Sabina is elected a beauty queen. Then a deluge threatens to engulf the world. Mr. Antrobus builds an ark and manages to get pairs of animals aboard. When the waters recede he sets out to build a better world. At this point Sabina starts her first scene again and, turning to the audience to whom she has directed numerous asides, tells them "This is where you came in. We have to go on for ages and ages. You go home. The end of the play isn't written yet." Awarded the Pulitzer Prize, the play ran just short of a year and has enjoyed many revivals.

Gladys Hurlbut's **Yankee Point** (11-23-42, Longacre) met with a cold shoulder. The Adamses live on the eastern seaboard. Mr. Adams (John Cromwell) is a former pacifist who is now a strong supporter of the war effort, much to the chagrin of his still-pacifist elder daughter (K. T. Stevens). His younger daughter (Dorothy Gilchrist) is engaged to a boy training with the air force. Mrs. Adams (Edna Best) is an air raid warden who captures a German spy hiding on the beach. When a few German bombers reach America, the family huddles under tables as the bombs fall nearby. Critics found the whole play dreary, but were especially annoyed at the idea that German planes might reach America.

The next of the season's many revivals was *Counsellor-at-Law,* which opened at the Royale on the 24th with Paul Muni again as star. Heartily received, it ran out the season.

S. N. Behrman's **The Pirate** (11-25-42, Martin Beck), adapted from Ludwig Fulda's *Der Seeräuber,* ran five months, thanks in large part to the acting and allure of the Lunts. Preceded by a tatterdemalion Negro band and drawn in a carriage by his fellow players, Serafin arrives at a West Indies town, steps out of the carriage, does a little dance, than heads for a visit to the mayor, Pedro Vargas (Alan Reed), whose permission he requires to perform. When permission is refused, Serafin lets the mayor know that he has recognized him as the long-sought pirate Estramudo. The mayor's wife, Manuela, is reading a romanticized biography of the pirate and dreams of being loved by him. But in no time Serafin woos and weakens Manuela. He tells her he must learn if she is a maiden—"For me it is as vital as a heartbeat to know"—and he points out her husband's failings and opens her eyes to his real history. The romance is tempestuous, with Serafin at one point walking a tightrope to enter Manuela's boudoir. Finally the actor hypnotizes Manuela into publicly revealing the truth about her husband, who is carted off to jail. Although critics enjoyed the Lunts, who were clearly having a lark, they were less pleased with the play. Lockridge observed, "It is the Lunts who are giving the party. . . . It's sort of a pity that Mr. Behrman couldn't come." Lemuel Ayers's gaudy, jauntily painted settings and Miles White's equally colorful costumes abetted the stars.

The Great Big Doorstep (11-26-42, Morosco) was Frances Goodrich and Albert Hackett's dramatization of E. P. O'Donnell's novel. Many critics dismissed it as a Cajun *Tobacco Road.* Commodore Crochet (Louis Calhern) lost his job as a riverboat captain when he fell asleep at the wheel and a load of mules was drowned. He was, he admits, even a failure on WPA. He tells his wife (Dorothy Gish), "The best plan I got is a big, big plan to let what gunna happen happen." One thing that has happened is that a magnificent white doorstep has drifted down the river and been claimed by them. But it looks funny in front of their shack. So they and their kids dream of buying the nice house next door, which is about to be sold off for $60 in back taxes. One scheme after another goes awry, including a loan from the commodore's brother (Clay Clement), when the check bounces. But Mother Crochet manages to scrounge up the money at the last minute thanks to some beautiful lily plants growing nearby.

Many critics felt that Daniel Lewis James's **Winter**

Soldiers (11-29-42, Studio) should have been brought uptown after its premiere at the New School for Social Research, but the high cost of its exceptionally large cast and multiple scenes militated against the transfer, so the play merely ran out its limited run at its initial venue. While some realistic German generals argue against attacking Russia, Hitler and his sycophants insist on launching the attack. Everywhere the troops turn, they are beset by saboteurs and bad weather. A hulking Croat masseur strangles an unsuspecting colonel; the Poles delay a train. Finally conceding defeat, the German marshal orders their tanks burned and the men to retreat. As he does, a voice from Radio Moscow announces, "Victory will be ours!"

As with *The Morning Star,* Norman Armstrong's **Lifeline** (11-30-42, Belasco) was a war drama that had succeeded on the West End but that Broadway would not accept. An all-male cast told the story of the tramp steamer *Clydesdale,* transporting fuel from Canada to England. The ship, which has left its convoy because of engine problems, sinks a submarine attempting to attack it, but is later set afire when dive bombers strafe it. The crew abandons ship. One lifeboat founders, but the men in the other return to the ship to put out the fire.

Sharply divided notices greeted a revival of the 1922 drama that gave the world the word "robot," *R. U. R.,* when it was brought out at the Ethel Barrymore on December 3. Since the producers had no money to spare, they closed the play after just four performances.

As far as New York was concerned the jinx besetting plays about baseball continued with **The Sun Field** (12-9-42, Biltmore), Milton Lazarus's theatricalization of Heywood Broun's novel. Judith Winthrop (Claudia Morgan), a Vassar-educated magazine writer, is totally and unexpectedly smitten after watching Tiny Tyler (Joel Ashley), the Yankees' home-run swatter, whom she compares to Thor casting thunderbolts. They are married, and Tiny gives up his drinking and loose living. He also stops hitting, costing the team a pennant by striking out at a crucial moment. (The game was heard over a radio, with famed sportscaster Bill Stern calling the plays.) Judith decides to leave him rather than let him destroy his career. But when she hears he has taken up with a notorious floozie, she returns. The play struck out after half a week.

Critics dismissed John Patrick's **The Willow and I** (12-10-42, Windsor) as mediocre melodrama coated with psychoanalytical balderdash. At the turn of the century, two sisters, the sweet Mara (Martha Scott) and the selfish Bessie (Barbara O'Neil), both love Robin Todd (Gregory Peck). When Mara announces that she and Robin will wed, Bessie attempts suicide. Mara grabs Bessie's gun, which goes off. Neither girl is hit, but Mara goes out of her mind. Bessie marries Robin,

but she is sufficiently remorseful to care for her deranged sister. Thirty years later Mara seems to regain her senses, but she mistakes her nephew (Peck) for his father, who had died some years before. The nephew, an artist, agrees to paint her picture.

The two sisters gave way to Chekhov's *The Three Sisters,* which Katharine Cornell and Guthrie McClintic presented at the Ethel Barrymore on the 21st. This rueful saga of the sisters' unfulfillable longing to visit Moscow featured an all-star cast, but the players meshed so beautifully that none was perceived as indulging in a star turn. Nonetheless, a number of aisle-sitters singled out Ruth Gordon's predatory sister-in-law. The sisters were played by Cornell as Masha, Judith Anderson as Olga, and Gertrude Musgrove as Irina. Alexander Knox was Baron Tuzenbach; McKay Morris, Captain Solyony; Dennis King, Vershinin; and Tom Powers, Kuligin. Howard Barnes, echoing the sentiments he expressed in his review of *The Skin of Our Teeth,* welcomed the mounting as another "rare experience in playgoing." The public patronized it for 123 performances at a high $3.85 top.

For the third time in the season a successful London war drama found no favor in New York. Terence Rattigan's **Flare Path** (12-23-42, Henry Miller's) confronted its actress-heroine (Nancy Kelly) with a choice of two men. One is an RAF pilot (Alec Guinness), whom she married on impulse during the blitz and who is now upset by the apparent loss of a close friend on a bombing mission. The other is her former lover (Arthur Margetson), an actor who fears his career is beginning to fade. She elects to remain with her husband. In his American debut, Guinness won good but not outstanding notices.

An American war drama, Allan R. Kenward's **Proof Through the Night** (12-25-42, Morosco), fared no better. Its all-women cast told of the last days of some nurses at Bataan. They comprise a typical theatrical assortment: a martinet, a former burlesque queen, a sappy southerner, a repressed lesbian, a girl whose neuroses lead to a nervous breakdown, and a fifth columnist. When the Japs arrive, the spy runs out to welcome them and is shot down in a storm of Jap bullets. Most reviewers merely mentioned in passing the girl who played the lesbian—Carol Channing.

Irving Brecher and Manuel Seff's **Sweet Charity** (12-28-42, Mansfield) hardly touched on the war and was staged by George Abbott, but its single hilarious scene could not carry it beyond its first week. The ladies of the Friendly Hand Club in a small Connecticut town are holding a dance to raise money for their pet project, a nursery for children of mothers doing war work. They have hired King Cole's renowned band, but the $2500 down he demands is attached just before they are about to pay it to him by the lawyer for a tot who slipped and broke his little leg at the nursery. This so upsets the gals that they filch cigarettes from a package a trumpet player has left on a table. The gals do not realize the cigarettes are actually reefers. High on marijuana, they try to go swimming in a water cooler, mistake a sprinkling can for a teapot and the president of the Chamber of Commerce's fedora for a teacup, and indulge in some wild jitterbugging, before the expected happy ending.

The war was brought home again to playgoers when the Theatre Guild offered **The Russian People** (12-29-42, Guild), which Clifford Odets adapted from Konstantin Simonov's play. Before the opening, critics were inundated with sheafs of material from the Russian embassy, detailing the twenty-seven-year-old Simonov's life, extolling the play as the greatest of Russian dramas, and otherwise thoughtlessly raising expectations. The result was a major letdown and a mere five-week run. The play showed in nine loosely related episodes what happens when the Germans occupy a Russian village. A spineless villager is appointed mayor by the occupiers, is despised by his wife, and finally shot by the Germans when he proves incapable. A shifty young man offers his services to the Germans but is shot by his uncle, a czarist officer. A doctor and a girl who loves a Russian officer both sacrifice their own lives.

There was a Russian sharpshooter in the next play to arrive on Broadway, but she was there to provide laughs. Most aisle-sitters expressed serious reservations about Joseph Fields's **The Doughgirls** (12-30-42, Lyceum), but *Variety,* which regularly took a hard-nosed look at a play's commercial possibilities, reported that the comedy "has everything in its favor for popular appeal, as an escapist, amusing farce-comedy, not the least of it being the neatly tempoed George S. Kaufman staging and three beauts as femme leads." The first of those beauts to be seen was Edna (Virginia Field), who learns that her old friend Vivian (Arleen Whelan) is about to become the new occupant of the Washington hotel suite from which she is being evicted. She gets Vivian to allow her to stay on. In short order they are joined by a third old buddy, Nan (Doris Nolan). All three gals have signed the register as married women, though none is married to the man she claims is her husband. Before long, Natalia (Arlene Francis), a Russian sniper, is imposed on them. She is a rugged young lady who has shot 397 Nazis and now takes short hikes—to Baltimore and back—for exercise. Complications spring up quickly. One of the lovers' wives appears, a marriage is delayed when divorce papers prove to be a report from a chemical laboratory, and a group of marines crowd in. Then an FBI man shows up and tells the women that eight agents have been checking

on "The Three Groomless Brides." It's been so hard on the agents that "two of them have enlisted as parachute jumpers and another one's having a nervous breakdown." At least Nan will not be groomless for long, since President Roosevelt has invited her to the White House to see her sweetheart get a medal. Natalia rushes out and grabs an Eastern Orthodox priest who marries Nan and her beau so that Nan will really be a married woman when she meets the president. The comedy kept Broadway laughing for 671 performances.

As Broadway entered the new year, business was good with *The Doughgirls, The Eve of St. Mark, The Pirate, The Skin of Our Teeth, The Three Sisters,* and *Without Love* all near or at capacity and grossing between $16,000 and $23,800. Longer runs were still prospering with takes between $6000 and $10,000.

The **Nine Girls** (1-13-43, Longacre) in Wilfred H. Pettitt's thriller were younger than the Washington ladies. In fact, they were sorority sisters spending time at a clubhouse in the Sierra Nevadas. One (Adele Longmire) of the girls, "from the wrong side of the tracks," has killed another to keep her from the boy she loves. A letter from the dead girl to a second sorority sister (Barbara Bel Geddes) forces the killer to kill again, stuffing the body in a closet. But a third sister (K. T. Stevens) instinctively suspects the murderer, who then tries to sabotage the girl's car. Failing this and tricked into a confession, the killer drinks poison. As with the season's earlier thrillers, some reviewers jumped on a single line in the play, "This would be funny if it weren't so horrible." They also suggested the entertainment, which started just before nine, had a noticeably long intermission, and finished at 10:30, short-changed audiences. But since the popular Al Woods returned to Broadway after a long absence to produce the play, critics let it down gently. Still, it survived only half a week.

The *Post*'s Wilella Waldorf began her review of **Dark Eyes** (1-14-43, Belasco), "Elena Miramova and Eugenie Leontovich, a couple of Russian actresses, have written a comedy . . . about a couple of Russian actresses trying to find a backer for their play about a couple of Russian actresses." No fewer than three of her colleagues employed similar openings. Actually the play concerned three Russian women, the worldly Natasha (Leontovich), the dreamy, pious Tonia (Miranova), and the assertive Olga (Ludmilla Toretzka), who cannot understand that they have committed a crime by handing the landlord who has evicted them for non-payment a check made out on a bank where they have no account. They are taken under the wing of Natasha's former lover, Prince Nicolai (Geza Korvin), who deposits them at the Long Island home of John Field (Jay Fasset), a dollar-a-year man. When he offers to underwrite the play, Tonia is pressed by the others to offer herself to him. She is startled by his refusal, but Olga explains, "The man has only exercised his God-given American right not to go to bed with a woman if he doesn't want to." In time, Field proposes marriage to Tonia. The comedy enjoyed a seven-month run.

Sidney Kingsley's **The Patriots** (1-29-43, National) ran only until mid-June, but then many playgoers probably read notices like that of Kronenberger, which observed that the work "is a rhetorical play whose issues are portrayed far more vividly than its men." On a ship returning from France, Thomas Jefferson (Raymond Edward Johnson) assures his daughter (Madge Evans) that he will not accept Washington's offer to become secretary of state. But the president (Cecil Humphreys), a fellow farmer and a homey man who loves to sneak out to fish, persuades him to assume the post. The major battle in the cabinet is with Alexander Hamilton (House Jameson), who has contempt for democracy and wants to emphasize a free market, even if that allows some shady speculators to become wealthy. Hoping to bring Jefferson on his side, he supports moving the capital to the Potomac. But Jefferson remains adamantly in favor of what Hamilton ironically decries as "wild illusions. Bill of rights! Freedom! Liberty! License! Anarchy!" The fight becomes bitter, although Jefferson attempts to keep it on a high level. He has placed his faith in the people and is confident of their ultimate victory. When Congress is fighting over who shall succeed John Adams, Hamilton is in a position to deny the vote to Jefferson. But sensing his own time is finished and admitting Jefferson's high-mindedness, he tells Jefferson he will throw his support to him.

The latest short-lived war play, Thomas Duggan and James Hogan's **The Barber Had Two Sons** (2-1-43, Playhouse), was set in occupied Norway. The barber is "Ma" Mathieson (Blanche Yurka), and her sons are Christian (Richard Powers), a patriotic sea captain who works with the underground, and Johann (Walter Brooke), a self-serving artist in love with a girl (Tutta Rolf) who is not unsympathetic to the Nazis. When the underground requires a German uniform, Ma allows a man whose wife has been raped by a German officer to slash the officer's throat when he comes for a shave. (Audiences laughed and applauded gleefully in expectation of what was about to happen.) But Ma learns that Johann and his girl are planning to betray the village and run off. Ma sees to it that Johann is taken as a hostage and shot to avenge underground killings. She herself shoots the girl.

The *Sun*'s Ward Morehouse, one of a number of new critics replacing men who had gone into the services or on to other wartime chores during the season, noted that with the arrival of **Counterattack** (2-3-43, Wind-

sor), Janet and Philip Stevenson's adaptation of Ilya Vershinin and Mikhail Ruderman's Russian original, "Forty-eighth Street has become theatretown's front line." *The Barber Had Two Sons* was next door; *The Eve of St. Mark,* across the street. After two Russian soldiers (Morris Carnovsky and Sam Wanamaker) capture seven German soldiers and a German nurse, they find they are all trapped by a cave-in in a cellar on the Eastern Front. A battle of wits and endurance ensues. Fortunately for the Russians, the Germans fall out among themselves. But fatigue is almost too much for the captors after three sleepless days and nights, and they are disheartened to hear German being spoken by men digging them out. However, the rescuers prove to be Russians.

Another new critic, the *World-Telegram*'s Burton Rascoe, opened his review of Stanley Young's **Ask My Friend Sandy** (2-4-43, Biltmore), "Roland Young is the only living person who can mumble in such a way as to make each word clear and distinct. He is as cute as a baby giant panda. He has manner, distinction, urbanity." What Young lacked, as he so often had lacked in his career, was a good vehicle. Harold Jackson is a book editor totally bored with life. So when Mrs. Jackson (Mary Sargent), helping in the war effort, brings home a brash private named Sandy (Norman Lloyd) for dinner, and when the soldier tells Jackson that in the postwar world money will be meaningless and that he might as well rid himself of his cash now, Jackson has no argument. After getting drunk on a mixture of scotch and rye and donning the blue uniform he had worn serving with the French in World War I, he takes Sandy, the missus, and all his servants for a night out in Harlem, then gives away his money. With that Mrs. Jackson walks out. Jackson would support himself as a taxi driver, but soon loses his job. He is selling off what is left of his furniture when his old associates tell him a book he wrote, *How to Be Happy on Less,* has become a best-seller. He's rich again.

Patricia Coleman's **The Moon Vine** (2-11-43, Morosco) was set in 1905 Louisiana and centered around a southern belle, Mariah Meade (Haila Stoddard), whose parents have forced on her an engagement with a missionary now off in Australia. An old neighbor, Danny Hatfield (Arthur Franz), returns home from what was supposedly a selling trip. In fact, he has become an actor and has returned home after his backwater troupe folded abruptly. Mariah gets a friend to write a letter claiming her fiancé has died in an Australian plague. Her grief is so dramatic that Danny is converted and would become a missionary himself. Learning the truth, he convinces Mariah to run off with him and employ her acting skills in another touring company.

Billie Burke had been missing from the Broadway

scene for a dozen years, so critics and playgoers were ready to welcome her back. Regrettably, like Roland Young, she chose an impossible vehicle. Walter Livingstone Faust, the author of **This Rock** (2-18-43, Longacre), was an oil company executive and a neophyte at playwriting. His inexperience showed. The British government imposes some of the children it has evacuated from London slums on the Stanleys (Nicholas Joy and Burke) at their large Tyneside estate. At first the fluttery Mrs. Stanley is aghast, but she soon comes to love the children. A subplot recounted the rocky romance of a bitterly leftish RAF pilot (Zachary Scott), the older brother of one of the slum children, and the Stanleys' daughter (Jane Sterling). Although Burke could still "pile up her words and purse her mouth and crinkle up her eyes," she could not save a dismal play.

Matters were different at the next opening, Florence Ryerson and Colin Clements's **Harriet** (3-3-43, Henry Miller's), with Helen Hayes as star. Lewis Nichols, Atkinson's replacement at the *Times,* commented, "It is good to have Miss Hayes back, in a play that by itself might not rank as a masterpiece, but which allows her to give a portrait that is." Harriet Beecher Stowe is first seen shortly after her marriage to a widower, Calvin Stowe (Rhys Stevens), being helped, perhaps more than she would care for, by her pompous, overbearing Beecher relations to settle into her Cincinnati cottage. Later she and her family move to Brunswick, Maine, where Calvin has been given a professorship. Ignoring all the distracting hubbub of family life, she writes *Uncle Tom's Cabin* after being moved by the plight of a runaway slave. Still, she is shocked when Lincoln is elected: "We have foist upon us a huckster from the backwoods." But during the war that Lincoln suggests her "little book" helped provoke, she meets the president and becomes an admirer: "One hour with our President has lifted my spirits," she tells a crowd as "The Battle Hymn of the Republic" is heard growing louder and louder. Thanks to Hayes, the drama ran eleven months.

For a fourth time this season, a hit London war drama failed in New York. Mary Hayley Bell's **Men in Shadow** (3-10-43, Morosco), revised for American audiences by Joseph Fields, unfolded in the loft of a deserted French mill. There a group of British and American airmen, who have been shot down, hide from the Nazis. They are led by a highly nervous American (Roy Hargrave), who kills several Nazis when they appear—one by shooting him, one by strangulation, and one by throwing him down the stairs—and who invariably gets sick afterwards. Learning that the Germans are going to occupy the mill, the men escape—taking along in a homebuilt stretcher one of their own who is unable to move.

The season's longest-running hit—957 performances—was George Abbott's staging of F. Hugh Herbert's **Kiss and Tell** (3-17-43, Biltmore). By the following season three road companies were taking the comedy across the country. Because the Archers (Robert Keith and Jessie Royce Landis) and the Pringles (Robert Lynn and Lulu Mae Hubbard) have not been on speaking terms ever since the Pringles allowed the Archers' sixteen-year-old daughter, Corliss (Joan Caulfield), to sell kisses at a fair alongside the Pringles' nearly eighteen-year-old daughter, Mildred (Judith Parrish), Mildred swears Corliss to secrecy when she elopes with Corliss's brother, Lenny (Richard Widmark), a lieutenant in the Air Force. Mildred is quickly pregnant, but it is only Corliss whom Mrs. Pringle sees leave the obstetrician. Mrs. Pringle gloatingly confronts Mrs. Archer with the news. Since she is sworn to secrecy, Corliss lets her parents think that the news is true and that their dim-witted neighbor, Dexter Franklin (Robert White), whose reaction to most news is "Holy Cow," is the father. When Mr. Archer confronts Dexter, Dexter, believing he is asking about Dexter's socking Corliss, assures him that it won't happen again, that Corliss was as much at fault as he, and that it was all in fun. Matters are properly resolved when Lenny writes home that he is getting a medal and confesses to the marriage.

Charles Schnee's **Apology** (3-22-43, Mansfield) starts when the Lecturer (Elissa Landi) comes onto a stage bare of anything but drapes and a lectern. After showing such pictures as how the earth might look from the moon and a view of the Brazilian jungles—to suggest what an infinitesimal thing man is—she embarks on a discussion of human frailty as exemplified by Albert Warner (Theodore Newton). Some bits of furnishings and hints of settings slide on- and offstage, and some stereopticon films are flashed on a screen to follow Albert as he rejects the girl he really loves, marries for money, betrays his friends, and abandons all scruples. Only late in life does he repent and attempt to make a better world for his daughter (Peggy Allardice). Most of the time the stage was dark with only spotlights playing on speaking figures. The drama lasted one week.

A revival of *Richard III* at the Forrest on the 24th, with George Coulouris in the title part, received thumbs-down notices and departed after eleven performances.

Sour notices also greeted **The Family** (3-30-43, Windsor), which Victor Wolfson took from parts of Nina Federova's best-seller. The family in question is a group of White Russians living in exile in Tientsin, China, in 1937 and presided over by a matriarchal grandmother (Lucile Watson). The boarders taken in to help make ends meet include an old professor and his wife, a fortune teller, a Chinese secret agent, and some noisy Japanese. But the central figure is Mrs. Parrish (Carol Goodner), an Englishwoman drinking to excess after the death of her son. She and Peter (Nicholas Conte), the older son of the exiles, dislike each other initially but soon fall in love. When the Japanese invade China, the household is broken up. Peter runs back to Russia but implies he will seek out Mrs. Parrish after the war, while she and the younger brother (Alec Englander) head for safety in England.

April's lone dramatic hit was James Gow and Arnaud d'Usseau's **Tomorrow the World** (4-14-43, Ethel Barrymore). The widowed Michael Frame (Ralph Bellamy), a university professor, has arranged to bring his nephew from Germany to America to live with him and his sister (Dorothy Sands). The boy is the son of another of his sisters, now dead, and her husband, a liberal killed by the Nazis. But Emil Bruckner (Skippy Homeier) has been brainwashed in the Hitler Youth. He proudly wears his Nazi uniform, insists his father committed suicide, and finds the fact that his uncle is seeing Leona Richards (Shirley Booth) "regrettable," since she is Jewish. He slashes the portrait of his father, tries to set each family member against the others, and nearly kills his cousin (Joyce Van Patten) when she comes across him attempting to steal his uncle's keys. Frame would send the boy away, but the compassionate Leona sees hope for him and convinces Frame to let him remain. The play recorded an even 500 performances and returned Bellamy, long a film name, to the stage.

. . .

Ralph Bellamy (1904–91) was born in Chicago and made his acting debut in 1922 on the Chautauqua Circuit in *Shepherd of the Hills*. After a long stint in stock, he first appeared on Broadway in *Town Boy* (1929). He quickly moved to Hollywood, where his smooth, slightly hard good looks frequently resulted in his being cast as the man who loses the girl at the end of the story.

. . .

A mere five performances sufficed for Irving Elman's **The First Million** (4-28-43, Ritz), which was brought out by Broadway's youngest producer. Reviewers gave Jimmy Elliott's age variously as eighteen or nineteen. They all gave his mounting the razz. Maw Boone (Dorrit Kelton) has promised her mentally defective sons that they and she will leave their Ozarks cabin and lead lives of luxury once their bank robberies have netted them $1,000,000. At the moment they have $980,000 hidden away in a butter churn. Then they learn that a nearby banker (Harlan Briggs) is sitting on $20,000 the government has given him to pay out to farmers who agree not to farm. The robbery goes awry, and they are

forced to kidnap the banker. (The banker, who has been embezzling government funds, proves to be as big a crook as the robbers.) But everything goes for naught when the family's one decent brother (Henry Bernard) burns all the money. As the curtain falls Maw is starting to plan for her second million.

Irwin Shaw's **Sons and Soldiers** (5-4-43, Morosco) could not make the grade either. Rebecca Tadlock (Geraldine Fitzgerald) is told that if she attempts to have a child, she will die. At that point she has a vision in which the children she hopes to have come to her and show her what will happen in their lives. Most important is her older son (Gregory Peck), who causes her to despair while he is growing up, but who later goes off to war feeling that even if he is killed, life has been worth living. Rebecca decides to ignore the doctors. All the action took place in Norman Bel Geddes's setting for the Tadlock home, with small flats dropping from the flies to signify other settings. The play was directed by Max Reinhardt, who co-produced it with Bel Geddes and Richard Myers.

Reviews weren't all that encouraging for Phoebe and Henry Ephron's **Three's a Family** (5-5-43, Longacre)—"some distance from being hilarious," "a third act preceded by a vacuum"—but the comedy defied critics and went on to play 497 performances. The tiny three-room apartment (only the living room is shown) of the Whitakers (Robert Burton and Ruth Weston) is cramped enough, what with Mrs. Whitaker's spinster sister, Irma (Ethel Owen), living there since Whitaker lost all her $1200 savings in the Crash. Then their daughter, Kitty (Katharine Bard), who has quarreled with her husband, moves in with her baby. She is followed in short order by her brother, Archie (Edwin Philips), and his overdue wife, Hazel (Dorothy Gilchrist). When Hazel goes into labor, Dr. Bartell (William Wadsworth) is summoned. They have to summon him, because he is the only neighborhood doctor not drafted and he has come out of retirement although he is deaf and almost totally blind. He bumps into and stumbles over the furniture and seems at times to be dozing. But Mr. Whitaker says there is no need to worry, since Bartell has delivered so many babies that he can now deliver them in his sleep. "Just the same," Irma retorts, "I think it would be a good idea to wake him up." The baby is duly delivered. What praise critics did allow they reserved for Wadsworth, who had been acting for fifty years—"single-handed he raises whatever parts of 'Three's a Family' get far off the ground."

The season ended with a miscast revival of *The Milky Way* at the Windsor on the 9th. Even at a $1.65 top, the comedy could not override the dismissive reviews.

1943–1944

Warborn prosperity was evident on Broadway. Attendance was up, and more shows were produced. The number of novelties jumped to the upper fifties. Quality was another matter. As far as introducing meritorious new dramas and comedies, the season was virtually a washout.

Because of additional money floating around, business during the summer perked, prompting several producers to risk hot-weather entries. The season's opener was Edward Chodorov's **Those Endearing Young Charms** (6-16-43, Booth). His friend Jerry (Dean Harens) introduces Lieutenant Hank Trosper (Zachary Scott) to Helen Brandt (Virginia Gilmore). Hank is a handsome, spoiled-rotten, reptilian navigator on a Flying Fortress. Helen is a pretty girl who sells lingerie in a New York City department store. When Hank sees that Helen has fallen madly in love with him at first sight, he prepares to take advantage of her before his two-day leave is up. But in two days and three acts he himself falls madly in love with Helen, so agrees to marry her. Critics saw the transition from louse to lover as preposterously abrupt. With former screen favorite Blanche Sweet, as Helen's mother, being the only other figure in this low-budget, four-character play, Max Gordon was able to keep the piece running for eight weeks in the face of negative notices.

The same stock group that had brought out a cheap-priced *The Milky Way* at the end of last season tried again with *Boy Meets Girl* at the Windsor on the 22nd. Two weeks and both the play and the troupe were gone.

Sheldon Davis's **Try and Get It** (8-2-43, Cort) lasted half as long. As he departs on an extended business trip, Thomas Barton (Albert Bergh) asks his mistress, Vivienne Gordon (Iris Hall), to entertain an old buddy of his. Vivienne, preferring a fling with some football players, hires sweet, innocent Sarah Smith (Margaret Early), a girl from a nearby bakery shop, to act in her stead. However, the old buddy sends his handsome, spoiled-rotten soldier-son (Donald Murphy) in his place. The boy sets out to seduce Sarah but, like Chodorov's Hank-the-navigator, has an eleven-o'clock change of heart. The production was Al Woods's last in a career that spanned half a century.

Although London had already embraced Martin Vale's **The Two Mrs. Carrolls** (8-3-43, Booth), New York's critics professed to have serious reservations about the play. Even the great Viennese favorite Elisabeth Bergner was criticized for over-emoting and under-projecting. Playgoers sided with their West End counter-

parts and gave the thriller a 585-performance run. Vale, a pen name for Marguerite Vale Veiller, widow of Bayard Veiller, told a simple story. In her home in prewar southern France, Sally Carroll is suddenly plagued by a mysterious illness. Sally is not aware of another problem, namely that her artist-husband, Geoffrey (Victor Jory), has fallen in love with their beautiful neighbor, Cecily Harden (Irene Worth). But when Geoffrey's first wife, Harriet (Vera Allen), meets with Sally, Harriet connects the two matters by pointing out that Geoffrey tried to kill her with a slow poison when he became enamored of Sally. Sally alerts a friend, Guy Pennington (Stiano Braggiotti), who locks up Geoffrey and phones the police. Geoffrey takes a fatal dose of his own poison.

The ten-year-old *Run, Little Chillun*, brought out at the Hudson on the 11th, was the season's second short-lived revival. It was the only non-musical entry between *The Two Mrs. Carrolls* and another British thriller, J. Lee Thompson's **Murder Without Crime** (8-18-43, Cort). This one failed to repeat its London success. When his mistress, Grena (Frances Tannehill), believes he is about to ditch her, she takes a knife and attempts to kill Stephen (Bretaigne Windust). In the struggle, Stephen grabs the knife, stabs her, then hides her body. But his psychopathic landlord, Matthew (Henry Daniell), suspects what has happened and sadistically attempts to drive Stephen to suicide. Stephen tries to kill Matthew and fails, then decides to have Matthew watch as he—Stephen—kills himself. But Matthew misunderstands, switches drinks, and dies from the poison Stephen had intended to swallow. With his dying breath he discloses that Grena did not die and she rushes in as Stephen looks on in horror.

Two archaic motifs failed to mix in **The Snark Was a Boojum** (9-1-43, 48th St.), which Owen Davis adapted from Richard Shattuck's novel. The will of an eccentric old man leaves his fortune to whichever niece or nephew's wife is the first to have a baby in his decaying mansion. Among the nieces is one who carries her husband's ashes in a briefcase. The nephews include a boozer, a pansy decorator, and a greeting-card writer (the show's producer had also produced *Three Men on a Horse*). News of an escaped homicidal maniac complicates matters, before a codicil is found which allows for a happy ending.

Thanks to some forcing, a revival of *Tobacco Road*, at the Ritz beginning on the 4th, ran for two months.

Early on in Elmer Rice's **A New Life** (9-15-43, Royale), the entire stage was masked by a black curtain, except for one small, square opening disclosing the blonde head of Edith Cleghorne (Betty Field). She is tired and in pain, for she is about to give birth. Edith had been a nightclub singer who, after a whirlwind courtship, had married Capt. Robert Cleghorne (George Lambert), an aviator now serving in the South Pacific and the son of a rich steel tycoon (Walter N. Greaza) and his overbearing wife (Merle Maddern). Robert's parents appear at the hospital and demand they be allowed to raise the infant. When Robert, on leave, shows up he at first sides with his parents. But after Edith says she will divorce him rather than put up with her impossible mother-in-law, he takes her side. Dismissed by Howard Barnes in the *Herald Tribune* as "too rarely dramatically moving or intellectually stimulating," the play hung on for nine weeks.

Albert and Mary Bein's **Land of Fame** (9-21-43, Belasco) looked at the conflict between the vicious Nazi occupiers of Greece and the local guerrillas, the latter forced to become as brutal as the invaders. Both use trickery, and it is an ancient Greek ruse which helps liberate a guerrilla leader (Norman Rose) when he is taken prisoner.

All for All (9-29-43, Bijou) proved to be merely Aaron Hoffman's *Give and Take* (1-18-23) rehashed by a committee posing as Norman Bruce. Jack Pearl, Lyle Bettger, and Harry Green headed the cast of comedians recounting this saga of a liberal son who persuades his conservative father to adopt modern business practices. It ran eleven weeks, defying yet another barrage of bad reviews.

Although Frederick Lonsdale's **Another Love Story** (10-12-43, Fulton) ran 104 somewhat forced performances, it lost money until it profited from the sale of picture rights. Curiously, this comedy by one of England's favorite playwrights was offered to America more than a year before Britain saw it. It dealt with several love triangles brought to light during a country weekend. Since Margaret Lindsay was co-starred, she was seen as a spunky gal who wins back her former fiancé (Philip Ober) by wrecking his plan to wed someone else. But for most critics and playgoers, the second co-star, Roland Young, in what proved to be his final Broadway appearance, provided what little spark the evening offered. He played a banker, quietly but desperately attempting to avoid marrying his boss's daughter (Fay Baker) and to continue his affair with his secretary (Jayne Cotter). He made audiences laugh with his insistently lugubrious wish that he were dead.

There were huzzas aplenty for the Theatre Guild's presentation at the Shubert on the 19th of *Othello*, which Margaret Webster staged with Paul Robeson, José Ferrer, and Uta Hagen in the leads. Robeson was praised for "a portrayal of great resonance, vitality and fluency," and Ferrer for his "extraordinary malevolence and conviction" and, perhaps contradictorily, for his "light touch," while Hagan was lauded for a death scene that was the play's most moving moment. Webster

herself made Emilia a fiery character. With generally ecstatic notices, the play ran nine months. Interestingly, *Variety*'s was a dissenting notice, slamming Robeson for often "expostulating rather ponderously in a monotone." The recording of the play suggests the tradesheet's was one of the few notices to assess his acting dispassionately.

Almost no one was dispassionate about Gypsy Rose Lee's **The Naked Genius** (10-21-43, Plymouth), which was directed by George S. Kaufman and whose advertisements assured playgoers that it was "guaranteed not to win the Pulitzer Prize." The play opens in the one-room apartment—complete with cook, butler, monkey, and rooster—of the famous stripteaser Honey Bee Carroll (Joan Blondell). It is just above a saloon, and many of the characters make their entrances and exits by way of the fire escape. Honey has allowed her name to be placed on a ghostwritten book which has become a bestseller but which she has never bothered to read. She has also agreed to wed her publisher's son. She pays for the wedding at her country estate, Naked Acres, by charging a $5 admission (part of which goes to charity but most of which her vulgarian mother [Phyllis Povah] pockets). At least the price includes a floor show (including Georgia Sothern in one routine). Like Tracy Lord, she also changes grooms at the last minute, settling for her old chum, a burlesque agent (Millard Mitchell). Among the supporting characters were battle-ax Bertha Belmore as a maker of rhinestone-encrusted G-strings, Doro Merande as a slatternly, acid-tongued ladies' room attendant, and Rex O'Malley as a "queenly hat designer" named Fred-Eric. (One John Frederics was a celebrated hat designer at the time.) But all the ingredients could not come together, so the comedy threw in the towel—or the G-string—after one month.

One week was all Aleen Leslie's **Slightly Married** (10-25-43, Cort) could survive. During that brief time it watched as Audrey Quin (Leona Maricle) pretended to be the mother of the baby her seventeen-year-old daughter (Patty Pope) has had by a nineteen-year-old soldier (Jimmie Smith). Seems that the youngsters thought getting a marriage license meant that they were legally married. The kids' proper marriage ends the confusions.

Some of the season's most damning reviews—"New Drama Low," "new depths of dismal entertainment," "new extreme of vacuity"—failed to keep playgoers, attracted by discounted tickets, away from Alice Gerstenberg's **Victory Belles** (10-26-43, Mansfield). The piece ran eleven weeks. Mrs. Stewart (Mabel Taliaferro), alarmed at reading that after the war there will be only four and a half men for every seven women, organizes parties of soldiers with her eligible daughter (Ellen Merrill) as hostess. The plan fails; no soldier jumps at the bait. So Mrs. Stewart's much divorced friend Flo (Barbara Bennett) organizes the local girls into a group called the Victory Belles. Complicating the plot was a butler (Addison Randall) who suddenly claims to be an FBI man and who arrests as a spy an army colonel (Raymond Van Sickle) he has knocked out.

Even Eddie Dowling could do nothing for Roy Walling's **Manhattan Nocturne** (10-26-43, Forrest). Peter Wade, a writer whose career and marriage are both on the skids, agrees to accommodate his wife's demand for a divorce by arranging for her to catch him with a corespondent in a seedy hotel. The girl (Terry Holmes) he selects turns out to be a prostitute suffering from amnesia. After examining their pasts the two believe they can salvage their lives by working together.

For the second time in the season a stock company was formed, hoping to produce cheap-priced revivals. In this instance the top price was to be $2.20 and the venue the long-dark New Amsterdam Theatre Roof. But after one week of *The Petrified Forest,* commencing on November 1, and a week of *Goodbye Again,* starting on the 9th, this troupe also bit the dust.

"Interesting but confusing" and "interesting, but it's muddled" were some of the critical comments about Rose Franken's **Outrageous Fortune** (11-3-43, 48th St.). Bert and Madeleine Harris (Frederic Tozere and Margalo Gillmore) have a satisfactory if cold marriage. Among the visitors at their home is Crystal Grainger (Elsie Ferguson). She assails Bert's unthinking pride in his Jewishness, "If you must be proud, be proud of what you are, not what you were born." She also shames Bert for his fury at his homosexual brother (Brent Sargent), who has driven his fiancée (Adele Longmire) to attempt suicide. Having given the family the benefit of her wisdom, she walks offstage and dies. Acting honors went to beautiful, throaty-voiced Ferguson and to gnomish Maria Ouspenskaya, who played an aged Jewish mother with a craving for pickled herring that embarrasses her more Americanized sons. The play ran ten weeks.

Lucille Prumbs's "downright moronic" **I'll Take the High Road** (11-9-43, Ritz) eked out a lone week. Judy Budd (Jeanne Cagney), a telephone operator at the Manson Aircraft Corp., overhears a conversation which proves that her boss is in cahoots with the enemy. So after she is elected "Miss Average Girl," she uses the speech she is asked to make to expose him. Her bravery wins her the hand of a corporal who has been a dashing Hollywood leading man (Michael Strong), but who grew up as the son of a Polish butcher in Manhattan.

Examining his offspring at the beginning of **The Innocent Voyage** (11-15-43, Belasco), Paul Osborn's theatricalization of Richard Hughes's novel *A High Wind in Jamaica,* Mr. Thornton (Guy Spaull) remarks, "We want the children to forget all about it. When they were returned to us in Jamaica, they were wild and unmanageable." He is referring to his youngsters, who, in 1860, were removed by pirates from a ship they were sailing on and lived with the pirates until they were rescued. In the meanwhile their lives were spared when the first mate (Herbert Berghof) talked the captain (Oscar Homolka) out of killing them. Unfortunately the play ignored the implications of Mr. Thornton's remarks, skipping over the inherent cruelty of the children that the book brought out, although one scene showed one of the little girls stabbing a bound seaman to death. Some critics lauded the physical production, but *Variety* said the play used much of the same scenery to depict several different ships and at times employed only a draped bare stage. The play ran as long as the Theatre Guild subscription list held out.

Short, scathing notices clobbered Alfred L. Golden's **Lady Behave!** (11-16-43, Cort), which nonetheless persisted in struggling along for three weeks. It dealt with a man (Jack Sheehan) whose ex (Pert Kelton) promises to return to him if he can successfully pretend to be a psychoanalyst whose apartment they have rented temporarily. Typical of the jokes was one character's remarking, "She's got in the neigborhood of a million bucks," and another character retorting, "A nice neighborhood."

By contrast, critics did joyous handsprings over Moss Hart's **Winged Victory** (11-20-43, 44th St.), saluting it as "masterly," "spine-tingling," and "a great and profoundly moving war play." Three boys—Allan (Cpl. Mark Daniels), Frankie (Pvt. Dick Hogan), and Pinky (Pvt. Don Taylor)—from Mapleton, Ohio, enlist in the air force, where they soon make friends with, among others, Irving (Pvt. Edmond O'Brien), a boy from Brooklyn, and Bobby (Pvt. Barry Nelson). Their lots vary. Pinky flunks his pilot's course, so has to settle for gunnery school. Frankie is killed in a training flight. Bobby's wedding is interrupted by a call to duty. Later the unlucky Pinky is seriously injured, but looks to survive. Still, they are game. One of the boys startles his buddies by promising them that when he leaves the army he'll still set his alarm for an early wake-up. Then he adds, when the alarm goes off he'll smash the clock and go back to bed for the rest of the day. Another soldier dresses up as Carmen Miranda for an impromptu show. At the end, Allan learns he has just become a father, so he sits down to write the boy a letter. Irving assures him that since most babies can't read, "You got time." But, in lines recalling the ending of several other recent war plays, Allan replies, "I'd like my kid to know how it was here tonight. . . . The world'll be better for our kids, Irv—huh?" The company comprised more than 300 men, a larger than usual pit band, and about thirty civilian women. Sgt. Harry Horner's settings moved from small-town Ohio, to various air force base locations, to a shabby hotel where the men's wives stand forlornly at a window watching a fly-by, and a South Pacific island. Some songs and incidental music were by Sgt. David Rose. The play ran for six months, then toured widely, earning millions of dollars for the Army Emergency Relief Fund.

But Broadway had fast tired of William Saroyan, so his latest play, **Get Away Old Man** (11-24-43, Cort), based loosely on his own experiences in Hollywood, was withdrawn after a week and a half. Patrick Hammer (Edward Begley), deciding that Harry Bird (Richard Widmark) is the world's greatest writer, hires him to do a picture inspired by "Ave Maria." Although Bird accepts, he fritters away his time with a philosophizing drunk (Glenn Anders), a pretty but naive extra (Beatrice Pearson), and other typical Saroyan characters.

Katharine Cornell had better luck with Dodie Smith's **Lovers and Friends** (11-29-43, Plymouth), which ran to twenty-one weeks of good business at the recently established (but not yet universal) $3.85 top. In 1918 in London's Regent Park, Stella, an actress, comes to tell Rodney Boswell (Raymond Massey), an officer on leave, that she has had to substitute for the friend he expected to meet. They fall in love and marry, but by 1930 Rodney has found a new passion, Martha Jones (Ann Burr), secretary to Edmund Alexander (Henry Daniell), a writer who is one of his legal clients. Stella reluctantly accepts the situation, returns to the stage, and takes up with Edmund. When he discovers that Martha is a pathological liar, Rodney would return to Stella. But Stella is not yet ready to take him back, although they have never been divorced. Twelve years later they meet again in Regent's Park and come to an amicable reunion. For all her fine support, the play was Cornell's, who "by her sheer artistry, makes Stella a memorable figure, attractive, intelligent and gracious." But critics saw the play itself as a comedown after the classics the star had been offering.

Critics could not fathom why Jed Harris produced **The World's Full of Girls** (12-6-43, Royale), which Nunnally Johnson derived from Thomas Bell's novel *Till I Come Back to You*. They could not even see how the play's title said much about the play. Before going off to serve in the marines, Miley (Berry Kroeger) visits the family with whom he boarded for several years in Brooklyn. Among the people he meets there is Sergeant Snyder (Harry Bellaver), who shows him where a buck-toothed Jap bit off two of his fingers. Later Miley agrees to spend a final night in his own Greenwich Village apartment with his old girl, Sally (Virginia Gilmore).

For the second time in less than two weeks a man

stood up by a date and settling for her friend provided the story for a Broadway hit. But this was what the *Times*'s Lewis Nichols called "the most delightful comedy of the season" and its longest-running hit (1557 performances), John van Druten's **The Voice of the Turtle** (12-8-43, Morosco). Like *Lovers and Friends* it asked for and got a $3.85 top. The three-character play was set in a three-room (plus bath) walk-up—with all three rooms (but not the bath) shown at once in Stewart Chaney's applauded setting. Olive Lashbrooke (Audrey Christie), an actress with a male friend in every city, stops by briefly at the apartment of a young, struggling actress-friend, Sally Middleton (Margaret Sullavan), to wait for a date she has asked to meet her there. But just before the date arrives, a richer, more promising man calls to ask Olive out. She agrees, letting it fall to Sally to entertain the soldier on leave whom Olive has just stood up, Bill Page (Elliott Nugent). Since Bill is well-to-do, he invites Sally to an expensive restaurant. She, in turn, allows him to spend the night at her place—in her brother's pajamas but in separate rooms. The next morning, Bill suggests that things are looking up and that "the voice of the turtle is heard in our land." When he explains to Sally that the quotation is biblical and that "turtles" means "turtle doves," she admits, "I could never understand the Bible. I don't see why they give it to children to read." Olive is rather annoyed to discover what has happened, but has to resign herself to the inevitable. That inevitability has Sally, who thanks to Bill has gotten over being dropped by a married producer, and Bill falling in love, and Bill's spending the remainder of his weekend leave in the flat. A revival at the 1995 Shaw Festival demonstrated that the comedy had lost none of its appeal.

Another soldier and another young lady found romance in Rose Simon Kohn's far less attractive **Pillar to Post** (12-10-43, Morosco). Working at a USO near an army base, Jean Howard (Perry Wilson) notices Lt. Don Mallory (Carl Gose) being nice to an old woman, so she hopes he will be nice to her, too. She asks him if he will help her get a room at a nearby motor court by pretending to be her husband, since the place will not accept single girls. He agrees. Complications set in when his colonel and the colonel's wife take the next cabin, and he is forced to introduce Jean as his bride. By the end of Act III she really will be.

The New York City Center of Music and Drama, a former Shriners' temple on 55th Street, taken over by Mayor La Guardia, began, on the 13th, what proved to be a years-long series of popular-priced revivals. The top ticket was just $1.65 at first. Plays chosen for the initial season were *Susan and God*, *The Patriots*, and *Our Town*.

The New York City Center of Music and Drama, a

For the single week that it survived, Pauline Jamerson

Act One: 1930–1944

and Reginald Lawrence's **Feathers in a Gale** (12-21-43, Music Box) attempted to extricate some fun from the long-abolished practice of vendue—the auctioning off of indigent local widows. Annabelle Hallock (Peggy Conklin) and two of her friends seem slated for the auction block. A kindly if rigid minister (Harry Ellerbe) loves Annabelle, but her heart is set on rough-hewn Capt. Barnabas (Norman MacKay). It takes the selfless minister to make matters right by pointing out the illegality of the vendue being held.

Listen, Professor! (12-22-43, Forrest) was Peggy Phillips's translation of a Russian comedy by Alexander Afinegenov in which a scholar (Dudley Digges), mired in his study of the seventh century, is forced into the modern world when his son's widow (Viola Frayne), on remarrying, foists the old man's granddaughter (Susan Robinson) on him.

Rose Franken, who heretofore had spaced her plays in a leisurely manner, now offered two in one season. Her second play of the current theatrical semester was **Doctors Disagree** (12-28-43, Bijou), which she took from her novelette *When Doctors Disagree,* developed in turn from her magazine serial *Women in White.* Dr. William Lathrop (Philip Ober) is willing to marry Dr. Margaret Ferris (Barbara O'Neil) if she will give up her practice and become a full-time homebody. She says no, but does allow "I would let you love me." Lathrop rejects her offer, responding, "I love you too much to love you." But after Dr. Ferris defies the warnings of her colleagues and successfully performs a dangerous brain operation on a young boy, Lathrop consents to allow her to continue her practice even after they wed.

Howard Rigsby and Dorothy Heyward's **South Pacific** (12-29-43, Cort) found Captain Dunlap (Wendell K. Phillips), a white man, and Sam Johnson (Canada Lee), a black seaman, drifting up to a Jap-held island after their merchant ship was torpedoed. The natives (all played by blacks) hide the captain but openly welcome Sam. "For once you are the wrong color," Sam tells his former superior. Even the Japs, who find out about Sam, are nice to him. He forms a liaison with a girl named Ruth (Wini Johnson) and strikes up a friendship with a native doctor (Louis Sharp). When American forces attempt a sortie on the island, the captain and the doctor join in trying to help them. Sam, saying he owes America and democracy nothing, refuses. The sortie fails, the captain and the doctor are hanged by the Japs, and the natives, including Ruth, turn against the increasingly swaggering Sam. He is shunned. So when, in a drenching rain, the Americans begin another assault, Sam shouts, "Capt. Dunlap, I'm coming!" and grabs a gun to do battle with the Japs. (No Japanese appeared in the play, but one's voice was heard over a loudspeaker.)

The new year's first entry, Ruth Gordon's **Over 21** (1-3-44, Music Box), was also its first hit. John Chapman of the *Daily News* welcomed it as "a delicious comedy of charm and several kinds of laughter—all good." As star, the bantam Gordon, with her sly smile, her slightly cackley voice, and her bag of comic acting tricks, glossed over any weak spots in her own script. Paula Wharton, a celebrated author, takes a cabin at a Florida motor lodge so that she can be near her husband, the almost fortyish newspaper editor, Max Wharton (Harvey Stephens), while he struggles through Officers' Candidate School. He could have a real struggle indeed since "the army has proved that over twenty-one you don't absorb any more." Of course, Paula has her own problems. The fridge makes ghastly noises, no light switch is in the same room as the light it governs, and the only way to open the window is to stamp on the floor. Furthermore, Max's old boss, the dapper publisher Robert Drexel Gow (Loring Smith), who always has a carnation in his buttonhole, is determined to get Max out of the service and back to the newspaper. However, when he comes on a second visit, Gow is in uniform, having offered the services his own service. He tells Paula, "Yesterday they accepted, so I turned in my carnation." He is chagrined to learn that Max, who graduated 271st in a class of 353, is determined to stay in the air force. But he does agree to Paula's odd compromise—she will edit his paper until Max returns. The comedy ran into the summer.

Another popular comedienne, homely, spindling Zasu Pitts, making her Broadway debut, lingered just as long, although her vehicle, George Batson's **Ramshackle Inn** (1-5-44, Royale), received a merciless critical drubbing. With her $3000 savings, Belinda Pryde, a spinster librarian, buys a rundown, seemingly deserted inn near Glouster, Massachusetts. She does not know it is used by gangsters to water down and store stolen whiskey. Before long, doors (there were ten of them in the set) open and shut mysteriously, screams are heard, the FBI enters the picture, and several characters are murdered. Finding one more body, Belinda asks, "Doesn't it get monotonous?" (a lead-with-one's-chin remark that critics again pounced on). Of course, in the end, Belinda bests the crooks and earns herself a $5000 reward for doing so.

On the other hand, Maxwell Anderson found his **Storm Operation** (1-11-44, Belasco) unrewarded by critics and public alike. The *Journal-American*'s Robert Garland dismissed it as "confused, diffused, remarkably uneven." In a landing barge alongside a transport ship that towers above it, Sgt. Peter Moldau (Myron McCormick), a former steelworker privately bitter at having to fight, exhorts his men to do their best in the North African invasion now in progress. He and those men

228

land safely enough and move on to Maknassy and then Mazzouna. In these desert redoubts, Peter meets and falls in love with Lt. Thomasina "Tommy" Grey (Gertrude Musgrove), a nurse who is also courted by a snobbish British officer, Capt. Sutton (Bramwell Fletcher). Sutton is further irked that because of a technicality he must take orders from the sergeant. After admitting that his carelessness cost the lives of some of his best soldiers, Peter asks Tommy to marry him. He says as a soldier, "You're just taking orders and eating rations and killing—and you're nothing—nothing!— unless you get a line on that blessed place back there where there are homes and children and peace." She accepts, and Sutton, impressed by Peter's candor and humanity, performs an impromptu wedding ceremony as German planes strafe the tent. The play ends as it began, with Peter in a landing barge giving a pep talk to soldiers before hitting the beaches—this time of Sicily. Critics praised the principals as well as Cy Howard, normally a writer on the Jack Benny show, for his performance as a double-talking Signal Corps man, whom the Arabs seem to understand better than the Yanks. Arab chants now and then provided a singular, mood-creating background.

Suds in Your Eyes (1-12-44, Cort), Jack Kirkland's dramatization of Mary Laswell's novel, made it two flops in a row. Beer-swilling Mrs. Feeley (Jane Darwell) invites a pair of friends to share the shack she has maintained at the junkyard she has run since her husband's death, decades ago. One is Miss Tinkham (Brenda Forbes), a twittery, lorgnetted old maid; the other is Mrs. Rasmussen (Kasia Orgazewski), a stout foreign mama in flight from a bullying daughter. They booze happily together, unite a pair of shy lovers, and, with the help of a stacked deck Miss Tinkham carries about, ward off the tax collector.

A third successive failure was Patrick Hamilton's English drama **The Duke in Darkness** (1-24-44, Playhouse), which used sixteenth-century French civil unrest as a background. The Duke of Laterraine (Philip Merivale) and his servant, Gribaud (Edgar Stehli), have been imprisoned by the Duke of Lamorre (Louis Hector), a member of the rival faction. To escape after several years, Laterraine feigns blindness. Lamorre holds a hot poker before his eyes, but Laterraine does not wince or even blink. While he thus is allowed to go free, the confinement has cost Gribaud his reason.

The short spell of flops was broken by a revival at the National on the 25th of *The Cherry Orchard*. Margaret Webster staged Irina Skariatina's fresh translation, and once again reunited Eva Le Gallienne and Joseph Schildkraut for the leads. There were quibbles here and there, with, for example, *PM*'s Louis Kronenberger opining Le Gallienne "shows deftness and intelligence, but somehow lacks temperament." Nonetheless, most concurred with Ward Morehouse of the *Sun,* who applauded "a rare contribution to the local theatrical season." The mounting ran twelve weeks.

Like several recent entries, Mary Orr and Reginald Denham's **Wallflower** (1-26-44, Cort) chalked up a nice stand—192 performances—in the face of critical headshaking. When the flirtatious, blonde Joy Linnet (Sunnie O'Dea) spurns Warren James (Joel Marston), "a wolf masquerading as a Princeton tiger," Warren asks her less pretty, brunette stepsister, Jackie (Mary Rolfe), out for a date. Jackie, used to being overlooked, is thrilled and accepts. So imagine the consternation of her father, Judge Andrew Linnet (Walter N. Greaza), who has been campaigning against increasing signs of juvenile deliquency and irresponsibility in Ironville, when he learns that Jackie and Warren have been seized in a police raid on a notorious roadhouse. The comedy ends happily when the youngsters show they had been married secretly just before the raid. Some critics were amused that the playwrights allowed their kids to use such even then antiquated slang as "jeeper-creepers" and "the berries."

Critics were not enthralled with the next novelty either, but respected its honesty and integrity, so, with some forcing, Edward Chodorov's second play of the season, **Decision** (2-2-44, Belasco), stayed around for twenty weeks. In the aftermath of race riots which he believes were promoted by his state's right-wing senator and the newspaper publisher who is under the politician's thumb, School Superintendent Riggs (Raymond Greenleaf) organizes a group of liberals to fight for truth and tolerance. When the publisher (Matt Crowley) meets with Riggs to discourage him, he is greeted with intemperate rudeness. Riggs tells him, "If I had the money and the inclination I believe I could establish a newspaper here and pay you well to print opinions directly opposed to those you hold now." As a result of his intransigence, Riggs is falsely accused of rape, jailed in protective custody, and lynched. His son, Tommy (Larry Hugo), who has returned wounded from the war, vows to keep up his father's battle, supported by an attractive teacher (Jean Casto) he will wed.

A long series of duds followed. In Ernest Pascal's **Peepshow** (2-3-44, Fulton), Jonathan Mallet (John Emery) would quietly cheat on his fiancée, Jessica Broome (Joan Tetzel), with a beautiful married woman, Leonie Cobb (Tamara Geva). He refuses to listen to His Conscience (David Wayne), whose clothes and mannerisms always parallel those of Jonathan. Jessica realizes what is happening after Jonathan and Leonie, coming home from a night on the town, are injured in an automobile accident. She visits him at the hospital, and with the help of His Conscience, who is nestled in bed alongside him, she persuades Jonathan to be good. Back home, when Jessica arrives to have dinner with him, they head for the bedroom, ungratefully slamming the door in the face of His Conscience.

The season's second superintendent of schools, Albert D. Bliven (Frank Wilcox), was a major character in E. B. Morris's **Take It as It Comes** (2-10-44, 48th St.). He and his clan have been selected by *Home and Fireside* as a model American family and not only get a spread in the magazine but appear on radio with the magazine's oleaginous editor, Dr. Witherspoon (Harold Moulton). Then a former neighbor, Anthony Pascuale (Tito Vuolo), leaves a package for safekeeping with the Blivens' Boy Scout son (Jackie Ayers). After Pascuale is machine-gunned to death by some of his fellow gangsters, the Blivens decide to open the package. They find $100,000 inside. This leads to all sorts of unsavory, anything but model, disagreements among the Blivens until Tommy does what every model American boy should do. He turns the package over to the police.

Although many critics regularly ignored what had begun to be called Off Broadway, several of them did pass judgment on the Rev. Thomas McGlynn's **Caukey** (2-17-44, Blackfriars'). Turning fact topsy turvy, it told of a rich, idealistic Negro (Clarence Q. Foster), who tries to better the lot of the poor, ignorant whites—or "caukies" (from Caucasian)—who inhabit the tenements he owns. His fellow Negroes insist his efforts will be futile, since nothing can be done to elevate these people.

Paul K. Paley's **Right Next to Broadway** (2-21-44, Bijou), the latest candidate for the season's worst play, was at least set right next to Broadway—in the garment district. There Paris-trained, wildly ambitious Lee Winston (Jeanette C. Chinley) takes over the company that her father, "Poppa" Weinstein (Leon Schachter), had built and announces she will offer "superfrocks" to sell at $16.75. But suppliers, out-of-town buyers, unionized workers, the OPA [Office of Price Administration], and others all throw monkey wrenches into her works. She settles for romance.

As Alonzo Price's **Mrs. Kimball Presents** (2-29-44, 48th St.) begins, players are celebrating a successful opening night with a small party in the dressing room of the young leading man, Dick Hastings (Michael Ames). A bailiff (Jesse White) who barges in, looking for another performer, Harold Burton (Arthur Margetson), is quickly shown the door. But the party soon moves to Dick's penthouse, which he calls Bachelor's Hall. His fellow performers are unaware that he is living far beyond his means by passing bad checks. His show's rich and socially prominent producer, Connie Kimball (Vicki Cummings), has her eye on Dick, so he plays up to her even though he really loves a girl named

Cynthia (Elizabeth Inglise). When the bailiff reappears, Harold pretends to be a butler. But it turns out that the bailiff is merely seeking to hand Harold a seven-year, $500-a-week contract with Paramount Pictures. And Dick, whose new hit allows him to pay back the bad checks, wins Cynthia after an understanding Connie learns the truth.

H. S. Kraft and Sam Jaffe had struck a small lode with *Cafe Crown* but came up empty-handed with **Thank You, Svoboda** (3-1-44, Mansfield), which Kraft adapted from John Pen's novel *You Can't Do That to Svoboda*. Svoboda is his Czech village's rather feeble-minded handyman, who lives off oddments his neighbors give him for cleaning their chimneys and performing similar tasks. When the German soldiers who occupy the village need to divert attention from their thievery, they claim Svoboda was attempting to blow up a bridge. He is sent to a concentration camp but is released after a time. Furious at the injustice done him, he returns home and destroys the bridge. Although all the characters were either Czech or German, Jaffe, alone in the cast, affected an accent.

John Boruff's **Bright Boy** (3-2-44, Playhouse) took place in a boys' prep school, where Allen Carpenter (Donald Buka) has been dumped by his unloving parents. After he is thrown in a lake by his mischievous classmates, he quietly vows revenge. He refuses to tattle on his dunkers, so wins their respect. He even lends them money to make up for the money which, unbeknownst to them, he has stolen from their rooms to force them to come to him. In gratitude, they make him class president. But the persistent kindness and faith his roommate (Charles Bowlby) has shown him eventually makes him repent his wickedness.

"I'm disappointed," "far from a perfect play," "not a great play," critics complained of S. N. Behrman's adaptation of Franz Werfel's **Jacobowsky and the Colonel** (3-14-44, Martin Beck). Still, most allowed that for all its faults it remained entertaining, so the comedy ran a full year. A haughty, not very bright Polish Colonel Stjerbinsky (Louis Calhern) is ordered to leave Paris, about to fall to the Nazis, and deliver important papers to the Allies, who will have a boat waiting for him on the coast of France. But he can think of no way of fleeing until a tiny, infinitely resourceful Jewish refugee, Jacobowsky (Oscar Karlweis), offers to let him drive a car he has just purchased. Seeing the officer is reluctant to ride with a Jew, Jacobowsky points out, "Instead of being in the enviable position of persecuting other people, you are persecuted yourself." Along with the colonel's orderly (J. Edward Bromberg), they flee Paris, but rather than hurry to the coast they first head into the German lines so that the colonel can pick up his beloved Marianne (Annabella). Thanks to the quick-thinking Jacobowsky they hoodwink the Germans and also obtain hard-to-find gasoline. But the Jew's cleverness, especially when the colonel realizes how impressed Marianne is by it, annoys the officer. "Less and less I like dis Jacobowsky," he wails. Yet when the time comes to take the boat for England, he insists that the Jew be given passage with him. Marianne, who is in less danger than the men, is left behind. Even those who held serious reservations about the comedy relished the charm, warmth, and "uncommonly delightful" performance of the pint-sized Karlweis, himself a refugee.

Another dramatization of a well-known novel launched a trio of failures. Eric Mawby Green and Edward Allen Feilbert based **The House in Paris** (3-20-44, Fulton) on Elizabeth Bowen's novel. It featured another refugee, the Russian-French Ludmilla Pitoeff, as Madame Fisher, who in 1900 had driven the young artist whom she loved to suicide. Eleven years later she agrees to raise the son he had by a much younger woman whom he never was able to propose to.

For both its stars and its playwright, Zoë Akins's **Mrs. January and Mr. X** (3-31-44, Belasco) represented their final Broadway bows. A wealthy but fluttery-minded widow, Mrs. January (Billie Burke), believing that communism is the coming way, rents half of a small two-family house in New England for $40 a month and decides to live there modestly with her fourteen trunks, her jewel case, her French maid, her cook, her butler, and her three children—each by a different marriage. Before long she has befriended her dour, taciturn landlord, Martin Luther Cooper (Frank Craven), who has been reluctant to rent to her, insisting that with $8000 a year he does not need more income. She replies, "Nonsense! Everybody needs money nowadays. Even the poor." She is sure she knows his name from somewhere, but cannot place it. They didn't meet on the Riviera, did they? No, it turns out that Cooper not long ago had been President of the United States. Three acts later Mrs. January has so brought the hidebound conservative to accept more liberal—albeit certainly not communistic—dogma, that it looks like his party may run him again. It also looks like Mrs. January will be heading for a fourth marriage. The crinkled, easy-going Craven and the still lovely, still flighty, redheaded Burke did their best, but it was not enough to save the comedy.

Horton Foote's **Only the Heart** (4-4-44, Bijou) had garnered some appreciative notices when it was presented off Broadway in late 1942, but failed to please on its belated move uptown. Set in the 1920s, it spotlighted a dominating mother (June Walker) whose obsession with controlling her family finally alienates her husband (Maurice Wells) and daughter (Eleanor Anton). Left alone in the world, she consoles herself with the knowledge that oil has been found on property she owns.

There wasn't even that much plot to **Chicken Every Sunday** (4-5-44, Henry Miller's), which Julius J. and Philip G. Epstein took from Rosemary Taylor's novel, and which many critics perceived as a hand-me-down *You Can't Take It with You*. At the moment, and that is 1916, Jim Blachman is the owner of Tucson's laundry, president of its horse-drawn streetcar line, and vice-president of a bank, but given his past fecklessness, Emily Blachman (Mary Philips) takes in boarders. They include a woman who monopolizes the bathroom, a widow who makes her son write poetry although he hates poetry, a New York beauty fleeing the Australian she has married and divorced several times, and a gentleman who persists in sneaking up the back stairs to the room of a lady, even after he has married her. A Blachman daughter is courted by a New Englander, provoking her very southern mother to warn, "There are no aristocrats north of Baltimore." Once again, wartime prosperity allowed a comedy to overcome indifferent notices. It ran more than nine months.

It went without saying who Dale Eunson meant to spoof in his **Public Relations** (4-6-44, Mansfield). In the days of the silents, Anita Sawyer (Ann Andrews) and Wallace Maxwell (Philip Merivale) had been the "Great Sweethearts" and "America's Most Happily Married Pair." And they lived in a magnificent Hollywood mansion they called the White House. After their divorce Anita retained ownership, remarried, and sat there clipping coupons, while Wallace roamed the world. Now he suddenly appears with a new wife (Yolanda Ugarte) and settles in for a visit. So does Anita and Wallace's recently married son (Michael Ames), who is a young film star, and Bubbles (Lynette Brown), a girl who is attempting to blackmail the boy. On top of these comes Wallace's long-forgotten daughter (Frances Henderson), hoping to give birth to her baby in the celebrated mansion. Between long phone calls to Hedda Hopper and Louella Parsons, all the problems are worked out. Betty Blythe, a famous silent-screen vamp, spent much of one act sprawled alluringly on a couch.

Late in the first act of George Seaton's—**But Not Goodbye** (4-11-44, 48th St.), which occurs in 1910, Sam Griggs (Harry Carey), a New England shipbuilder, hurries upstairs, dies of a heart attack, and comes back downstairs as a ghost. He is worried because he is afraid his partner will not tell his survivors of the $5000 profit they have made on a deal they have just pulled off. His long-dead father (J. Pat O'Malley) comes to him and urges him to move on to where he belongs. "I know how it is," he remarks. "You want to hang around for the funeral. Well, let me tell you, it's not what it's cracked up to be." None of the survivors sees the ghosts, but the pair conspire, aided apparently by a Higher Up, to trick the partner into revealing the truth and then dispose of him with a bolt of lightning.

Drama was rarely as popular as comedy. Although Lillian Hellman's **The Searching Wind** (4-12-44, Fulton) received many of the season's best notices, such as Kronenberger's hailing it as "a really rewarding serious play," it ran precisely as long as the far less admired *Chicken Every Sunday*—318 performances. In 1922 Alexander Hazen (Dennis King), a young American diplomat, complacently accepts Mussolini's take-over of Rome and begins a clandestine affair with Cassie Bowen (Barbara O'Neil), the best friend of his wife, Emily (Cornelia Otis Skinner). While the affair progresses through the twenties and thirties, Hazen continues to make excuses for the world's appeasements. But matters come to a head in 1944 when Cassie, who has not seen Emily for many years, comes to dinner at the same time that the Hazens' son, Sam (Montgomery Clift), who has returned from the war with a bad leg injury, announces that the leg will have to be amputated. Cassie confesses that she has hated Emily and wanted to take Alexander away from her; Emily reveals she knew of the affair; and Sam reads them all a letter from a dead buddy, berating the appeasers. Then he asks how you say you love your country, and his mother responds, "We're frightened of saying things like that now because we might sound like the fakers who do say them." Dudley Digges also won applause as Emily's father, a liberal publisher who has come to realize he, too, was not forceful enough. Like all of Hellman's plays to date, the drama was mounted by Herman Shumlin.

Hellman's earlier play *The Little Foxes* was called to mind by **Pretty Little Parlor** (4-17-44, National), which was written by one of the more promising juveniles of a few years back, Claiborne Foster. Whether she intended it for her own use or no, she did not in the end perform in it. Like the Hellman play it was set in a small town at the turn of the century, and its central figure might have been a twin sister to Regina. The ruthlessly ambitious Clothilde (Stella Adler) drives her husband (Sidney Blackmer) to drink, costs him his job with the railroad, and is unconcerned when he and her daughter (Marilyn Erskine), whom she has forced into an unwanted marriage, are drowned. She also steals an inheritance meant for her stepdaughter (Joan Tetzel), who leaves in disgust. But she may have met her match when she attempts to cozy up to the president (Ed Begley) of the railroad, a man as ruthless as she.

Somerset Maugham's eleven-year-old **Sheppey** (4-18-44, Playhouse) stirred no interest in New York.

Maugham's central figure, a London barber (Edmund Gwenn), elects to live strictly by Jesus' teachings after winning the Irish sweepstakes. His family attempt to have him committed, but he is spared that humiliation by the arrival of Death, in the person of a beautiful woman (Katherine Anderson).

The second ghost to caper on a Broadway stage during April was seen in Margaret Curtis's **A Highland Fling** (4-28-44, Plymouth), the season's third work written by an actress. Bekilted Charlie MacKenzie (Ralph Forbes), an eighteenth-century philanderer, has been assured by his wife (Frances Reid), now an angel, that he might still, two centuries late, gain a place in heaven if he returns to earth and redeems one seemingly incorrigible sinner. Back on earth, MacKenzie is visible only to children and "dafties." He falls in love with one village daftie, the looney Lady of Shalott (Curtis), known to villagers as Silly Shally. Superficially, MacKenzie appears to reform the crotchety, bibulous Rabbie MacGregor (Karl Swenson), and so gets to heaven. But finding it not to his liking, he returns to earth once more, only to discover Silly Shally has forgotten him. A subplot deals with an attempt to steal the Stone of Scone from Westminster Abbey.

The season's final success was Elsa Shelley's **Pick-Up Girl** (5-3-44, 48th St.) It looked at the problem of wartime juvenile delinquency and was set in a court devoted specially to the problem. The courtroom does not completely resemble a traditional courtroom. There is no jury box, the judge (William Harrigan) is not elevated haughtily above everyone else, and he wears no robes. The case at the moment concerns fifteen-year-old Elizabeth Collins (Pamela Rivers), who was caught entertaining a fortyish man (Arthur Mayberry) in her bedroom. Her mother works nights as a cook, and her father, after years of unemployment, has taken a job in California and plans to move his family there. Elizabeth's actions had been reported to the police by a neighbor, Mrs. Marti (Lily Valenty), worried that her violinist son, Peter (Marvin Forde), was coming under the girl's spell. Elizabeth, in turn, had clearly come under the influence of a louche eighteen-year-old, Ruth (Toni Favor). In session, each witness tries to blame the others for the situation. Only Peter would help Elizabeth, telling the judge that she behaved as she did "for the same reason that a hungry person will steal food. Betty was hungry for *fun*." During a recess, Betty and Peter plan to run away, but after she learns that she is infected with venereal disease, she agrees to submit to treatment. Noting it was "shocking, sometimes harrowing, and it minces no words," the *Post*'s Wilella Waldorf recommended the play solely for theatregoers with strong stomachs. It ran six months.

Another play that looked at juvenile delinquents,

Frederick Stephani and Murray Burnett's **Hickory Stick** (5-8-44, Mansfield), was so overwritten and so overheatedly performed that it alienated critics. The Truxton Vocational High School is where problem youngsters are shunted by the system. James Kirkland (Steve Cochran), a vet who had been wounded at Guadalcanal, comes there to teach, hoping kindness and persuasion will bring his students around. But an experienced colleague (Lawrence Fletcher) warns him such quixotic softness is dangerous. Nonetheless, it appears to work on Tony Pessolano (Vito Christi), probably because Tony's beloved elder brother had been in Kirkland's platoon. The teacher and the pupil become friends. But then another, vicious pupil, Steve Ames (Richard Basehart), a potentially brilliant youngster warped by fascistic leanings, menaces Kirkland. In a blind rage, Tony kills the boy. Kirkland is left uncertain how he can now help Tony.

Gerard M. Murray's **Career Angel** (5-23-44, National) had done well in an earlier mounting off Broadway, but was not strong enough for a more unyielding commercial run. When Brother Seraphim (Whitford Kane), an actor-turned-monk, bewails that the orphanage he runs has fallen on hard times financially, his gray-haired, gray-garbed Guardian Angel (Glenn Anders) appears and discloses where some valuable Civil War letters have been cached away. He also alerts Seraphim to the fact that Nazi spies are hiding ammunition in the building.

An odd double bill got nowhere. The bill opened with Noel Houston's one-acter **According to Law** (6-1-44, Mansfield), which, like *Career Angel,* had first been done off Broadway. Although his lawyer (Don Appell) is clearly able to show that Charlie Teague (Wardell Saunders), a Negro, has been framed for the rape he is accused of committing, a jury nonetheless finds him guilty and sentences him to death. The play was short and to the point, so won approval. The longer, second piece, Patti Spears's **A Strange Play,** described how a playwright (Ralph Clanton) discovers that the wife (Alicia Parnahay) of his friend (Richard Gordon) is cheating on the friend. He writes three versions of the story and its possible outcomes, and has the real figures enact them. That meant audiences had to sit through three repetitions of much the same dialogue.

J. C. Nugent was author, director, and star of **That Old Devil** (6-5-44, Playhouse). His wife (Luella Gear) and the townswomen have come to think of Jim Blair as a dull character. That is, they do until a pretty young English girl (Agnes Doyle) is foisted on the Blairs and shortly afterwards is found to be pregnant. Suddenly Jim is the center of some long-coveted attention. Matters return to normal after it is discovered that the father is a young local radical (Michael Ames), who has thrown eggs at superpatriots and who has been 4F until the army decides his color-blindness can be useful to them in the camouflage corps.

A large rathskeller-cum-theatre, which had been known by several different names and served a number of different functions, was rechristened the New York Music Hall and briefly served as home to a spoof of oldtime melodrama, Ralph Matson's **Broken Hearts of Broadway,** which opened on the 12th. Set in the 1890s, it told of a sweet, innocent heroine's rescue from a mustachioed Wall Street shark by a dashing, all-American hero. Musical olios enlivened intermissions.

In Frederick Jackson's **Slightly Scandalous** (6-13-44, National), taken from an earlier play by Roland Bottomley, Frances Stuart (Janet Beecher) has purchased a portrait of a distinguished-looking man at a London antique shop for four pounds ten and let her three children believe that it is a likeness of their late father. Actually each child has had a different sire—a stiff-necked English banker, a Polish pianist, and a French soldier. Now that the children have reached marriageable age, Frances feels they ought to be legitimatized. So she summons her three lovers—all of whom happen to be at hand—and asks her children to pick which one she should wed. The kids can't agree and are perfectly content to point to the painting.

Unmarried parents gave way to much married parents in F. Hugh Herbert's **For Keeps** (6-14-44, Henry Miller's). While her mother is on a Havana honeymoon with a new husband, fifteen-year-old Nancy Vanda (Patricia Kirkland) comes to spend time with her father (Frank Conroy), a commercial photographer who has just wed his fourth wife (Julie Warren), a twenty-six-year-old blonde beauty. Nancy falls instantly in love with daddy's handsome if 4F male model, Jimmy McCarey (Donald Murphy). So what if she has led him to think she is nineteen. Doesn't she smoke and drink cocktails and know several "words"? When Jimmy finds out the truth, he bolts. But the new Mrs. Vanda not only talks him into waiting until Nancy comes of age, she also convinces Mr. Vanda that he and she would be better for Nancy than Nancy's selfish, gallivanting mother.

The idea that honeymooners could safely fly off to Havana was a clear sign that the war was drawing to a close. Although the war lasted for another year, in the coming season Broadway would get hold of itself again. True, from here on, it would be increasingly dominated by the musical stage. Nonetheless, in the season ahead two dramatists emerged who would loom large over the American theatre for years to come.

ACT TWO
1944–1959

A SILVER AGE?

1944–1945

The new season was a very good one, a very prosperous one, and a very important one. More than sixty new dramas and comedies—a figure never again approached—tried their luck on Broadway. They provided what Burns Mantle termed "the most satisfying list of plays produced the last decade." Their quality, coupled with wartime prosperity, saw to it that playgoers agreed. New Yorkers and visitors packed playhouses, creating intermittent theatre shortages. And when producers realized that theatregoers were not balking at a doubling of the theatre ticket tax to 20 percent, they quickly began hiking basic ticket prices. Before long, straight plays were asking and getting a $4.20 top and even $4.80. As a result of all this, by season's end no fewer than twenty-four productions (out of ninety-odd plays, musicals, and revivals) had paid back their investors.

The season's importance lay in the fact that it introduced Broadway playgoers to the two most salient dramatists of the era. One, Arthur Miller, suffered a quick failure and had to wait for future recognition. The other, Tennessee Williams, enjoyed a smash hit, although some attributed his play's success to the luminous performance of its star.

The relatively busy summer got off to a dismal start with A. B. Shiffrin's attempt to find farcical possibilities in juvenile delinquency, **Love on Leave** (6-20-44, Hudson). Fifteen-year-old Lucy Wilson (Rosemary Rice), daughter of a man (Millard Mitchell) who writes authoritatively on child psychology and disciplining children, dons her elder sister's clothes and makeup, sneaks out her bedroom window in Astoria, and goes to Times Square, where she picks up a young sailor, Nick Hardy (John Conway). Nick, who loves his mother, his own kid sister, and chocolate sodas, sees through Lucy, so takes her home. But she claims she has been "seduced." The family, Nick's buddy, Lucy's louche girlfriend, and the police are all in a dither before the harmless truth comes out. "What's going on here anyway?" father Wilson inquires with some anguish. One critic observed, "We had wanted to ask the same question all evening."

The season's first long-run success (426 performances) was Agatha Christie's **Ten Little Indians** (6-27-44, Broadhurst), which she took from her mystery novel known variously as *The Nursery Rhyme Murders* or *And Then There Were None*, and which already had been seen in London as *Ten Little Niggers*. An ill-assorted group of people has accepted invitations to spend a weekend on the island retreat of a Mr. Owen, although none of them can say for sure that they know him. After they all arrive and are cut off from the mainland, a voice announces that each one of them has been guilty of somebody's death and that now they must pay for their crimes. Among the guests are a spinster (Estelle Winwood), a religious hypocrite who drove a servant girl to suicide; a surgeon (Harry Worth) who killed a patient by operating while he was drunk; a general (Nicholas Joy) who sent his wife's lover on a fatal mission; and a judge (Halliwell Hobbes) who sentenced an innocent man to die. The statues of ten Indians sit on a mantel over which is hung the old nursery rhyme. As, one by one, the guests—and servants—are murdered (poisoned, garroted, shot, pushed off a cliff, etc.), a statue is smashed. In time only two statues and the two youngest guests (Claudia Morgan and Michael Whalen) are left, so one of them must be the killer. But they discover the doctor had feigned his own death and is the actual murderer. He gets his comeuppance.

In recent seasons Chicago had welcomed several singularly salacious comedies. New York would see all three, this year or next. First to arrive was Frank Gill, Jr., and George Carleton Brown's **School for Brides** (8-1-44, Royale), which had reputedly delighted the West Coast as well as the Windy City. Jeff Conners (Warren Ashe), whose school for models is in financial trouble, decides to turn it into a school for brides. He wangles the six-times-married-and-divorced Frederick M. Hasty (Roscoe Karns) into propping up the place with $100,000, in return for which Hasty can make the next valedictorian his seventh wife. The tone of the evening was set by the girls in skimpy costumes, jokes about "Hasty marriages," and exclamations of "What a student body!" In the end, Hasty settles for the dean of students (Bernardine Hayes), famous for her onion sandwiches. The critics all got their knives out, but the public ignored the reviews and allowed the comedy to run into the following summer.

Critics were no happier with the next entry, but it, too, was a hit. If it did not run as long—only six months—it was because Mae West's **Catherine Was Great** (8-2-44, Shubert) had so huge a nut—prompted by its star, its large cast (sixty plus), and its many and lavish settings and costumes. Mike Todd's production was almost a musical extravaganza, without songs (albeit with some period dancing). The play began in a USO Recreation Room, where soldiers pondered what life in Russia must be like now and what it must have been like in Catherine's time. A revolving stage quickly turned back the centuries and revealed scenes in the high-ceilinged, gilded palace. As Catherine, the buxom, blonde West went through the motions of dealing with international problems, such as her difficulties with the Turks. But she was mostly preoccupied with bedding down any attractive man who crossed her path, such as Prince Potemkin, Gregory Orloff, or Ivan the Pretender. She generally got her man, although at her curtain call she apologized to her audience, "Catherine had 300 lovers. I did the best I could in a couple of hours." Her best, as Lewis Nichols noted in the *Times,* included "that smirk, that husky voice and what would be called a sinuous wriggle if she had not raised it to an art form." After New York, the play went on tour for the rest of the season.

A set of cursory, scathing reviews—the first of several such sets over the next weeks—slammed the stage door on Milton Herbert Gropper and Joseph Shalleck's **Good Morning, Corporal** (8-8-44, Playhouse). Dottie Carson (Charita Bauer), carried away by her desire to do something for the war effort, marries not one, but three men in uniform—a marine, a soldier, and a sailor. All are in their cups at the time of the weddings and immediately after are shipped out. But when the three return at the same time, problems crop up. "I'm Dottie," Dottie alerts one of them. "You certainly are," he responds.

Martin Bidwell's **Lower North** (8-25-44, Belasco) was perceived as a mite better. It studied youngsters attending a Quartermasters' School at a California naval training station. They include a lanky cowhand (Arthur Hunnicut), pining for his horse, Daisy; a trainee who can't get enough sleep; and one who sneers at the marines as "sea-going bell-hops." But the principal figure is Jim (Kim Spalding), who goes "over the hill" when he learns his wife is pregnant. Fortunately, his loyal buddies cover for him, and when he returns, his chief petty officer (Rusty Lane), a toughie-with-a-heart, pretends nothing happened.

Philip Yordan had found no takers for his play about Polish lowlife, so consented to allow some black players to perform it in Harlem. Its June premiere elicited a few laudatory notices and some excited word of mouth, prompting John Wildberg to move it to Broadway after director Harry Wagstaff Gribble had revised it by injecting humorous patches and giving it a happy ending. The result was the first native drama of the season to win general critical acclaim, **Anna Lucasta** (8-30-44,

Mansfield). The pious Joe (George Randol), unaware of his deepest yearnings for her, has ordered his daughter Anna out of his home and his life after catching her in bed with a man. But now Joe's old Alabama buddy has sent his young son, Rudolf, to Joe and asked Joe to find him a good wife. Since the family is on its uppers and Rudolf is coming to Pennsylvania with $800 in his pocket, Joe's sons-in-law force Joe to head for New York, seek out Anna, and bring her back as a bride for Rudolf. He discovers her (Hilda Simms) at Noah's Bar in Brooklyn, flirting with two sailors, and convinces her to come home. When Rudolf (Earle Hyman) arrives, he falls in love with Anna at once and she with him. She hides his money so the family cannot get their hands on it. Though she warns him he will marry her at his own risk, he does. But the appearance of one (Canada Lee) of the sailors and Joe's threats to expose Anna's past enrage her. She shouts, "If you so much as open your mouth to Rudolf, I swear to God I'll kill you." But Joe's revelation that he has already written the boy's father sends Anna hurrying back to Brooklyn. Rudolf comes searching for her there. On learning that her father has died, Anna agrees to go back with Rudolf. Even critics who held reservations about the play, including that few concessions were made to the change in racial background, lauded a sterling cast, which included Rosetta LeNoire and Frederick O'Neal. The drama compiled 957 performances.

The next three entries all garnered short, damning notices. None survived for more than three weeks. Lee Loeb and Arthur Strawn's **Sleep No More** (8-31-44, Cort) spotlighted a shady promoter, H. Clifford Gates (Robert Armstrong), who specializes in oddball inventions. Having failed miserably with a hair-growing machine that scalped its victim before exploding, he latches on to a pill, concocted by an Indiana yokel named William Jennings Brown (George Offerman, Jr.), designed to obviate the need for sleep. Just as Gates is about to close a $3,000,000 deal, Brown falls asleep during a demonstration ("joining," one critic noted, "large sections of the audience"). The men have to settle for a mere twenty-five grand when they learn the pill is at least good for worming dogs.

Catherine Chandler (Catharine Doucet), the villainess in Irving Kaye Davis's **Last Stop** (9-5-44, Barrymore), had, years before, helped murder the owner of an old ladies' home in order to gain control of it. Now the dead man's daughter (Minnie Dupree), a resident in the home, organizes the tenants to prevent Chandler from selling the fine old building and moving them to a firetrap. Besides not liking the play, reviewers complained that the old gals were sometimes inaudible.

In Leo Birinski's **The Day Will Come** (9-7-44,

National), when the Nazis overrun a Russian village they find the only resident left is an old Jew, Avrum Dovid (Harry Green), too busy with his prayers to flee. The officers, startled by his personal recollections of "that little fellow with the potbelly; what was his name? Oh, yes, Napoleon!" decide he must be the legendary Wandering Jew. Hoping to prevail on Hitler to end the war, they arrange for the two to meet. Hitler (Brandon Peters) claims his main objection to the Jews is that they founded Christianity; the Jew thanks Hitler for reuniting the Jews. But after Hitler orders the Jew shot, he himself goes ravingly mad.

Some of the season's most brutal notices were saved for Conrad Westervelt's **Down to Miami** (9-11-44, Ambassador). Two critics suggested it marked "a new low"; a third called it "one of the deadlier comedies of the new theatrical season"; a fourth found it unquestionably "the worst play of the season"; while a fifth branded it "a hallucination . . . the worst in years." According to the *Journal-American*'s Robert Garland, when a porter lumbered down into the smoking lounge to announce the second act, one playgoer piped up, "You couldn't make it the last act, could you?" The play was an *Abie's Irish Rose* with the sexes reversed. The Applegates have come to Miami's Rooney Square Hotel hoping to find a nice Christian wife for their banker son, Rufus (Charles Lang), currently a marine; their hometown neighbors, the department-store-owning Mandels, have come there looking for a nice Jewish boy for their daughter, Gloria (Elaine Ellis). They set their sights on another marine, Harry Katz (John Gould), whose father also owns a department store. Although the Mandels are major depositors in the Applegate bank, the Applegates snub them socially and are horrified when Rufus and Gloria fall in love. With the help of a fine Irish policeman (Brian O'Mara), who raises his tenor voice only to sing "Mother Machree," everything turns out just dandy. Harry even finds a love of his own.

The critics were unanimous in praising the first act of Terence Rattigan's London hit **While the Sun Shines** (9-19-44, Lyceum). Many even liked the second act. But they all felt the last act was a letdown. Rattigan depicted an amiable but not very bright English earl (Stanley Bell), a seaman in the Royal Navy, who brings home to his digs at the Albany a sozzled Yank officer (Lewis Howard) in hopes of foisting his tartish mistress (Cathleen Cordell) on him while he marries his heiress-fiancée (Anne Burr). The Yank confuses the bride-to-be with the mistress. A Free French officer (Alexander Ivo) also tries to court her. But, of course, she marries the earl. Wry, ultra-British Melville Cooper, at one point down on his knees in a crapshoot, stole the show as the bride's irresponsible father.

Harry Segall's **The Odds on Mrs. Oakley** (10-2-44, Cort) lacked even the saving grace of Rattigan's polished wit. When Susan and Oliver Oakley (Joy Hodges and John Archer) decide on a divorce they agree that each shall have charge of their beloved racehorse, Fanny, for three months at a time. In short order, Susan's gambler uncle (Morton L. Stevens) realizes that the horse wins whenever Susan is in charge and always loses during Oliver's term. So he and his buddies conspire to keep the couple from rewedding. Their plan fails, but not before Susan has almost compromised herself in an effort to have Fanny lose (so that she and Oliver can avoid outside interference). A radio broadcast describes the race, which Fanny wins after the initial winner is disqualified. The loser's gentlemanly owner refuses to go through with the bet on which Susan had risked her virtue in order to have the other horse entered.

Sharply divided notices (a "distinguished achievement"; "an awkward and jumbled piece of playwriting") could not attract playgoers to Herbert Kulby's **Men to the Sea** (10-3-44, National). While their men serve together on a destroyer, a group of navy wives share an apartment near the Brooklyn Navy Yard. Christabel (Toni Gilman), wife of the poetry- and Bible-spouting Duckworth (Randolph Echols), captain of a gun crew, has the hardest time, especially after she has had his baby and hears that he has been killed. She loses her mind for a time, walking in a nearby park and mistaking other sailors for her husband. Several of her apartment mates are more openly and cynically promiscuous, or are driven to infidelity by their loneliness. Only their black roommate (Mildred Smith) remains determinedly faithful. But while a section of the stage shows the girls enjoying a Christmas Eve party, the other half shows their men being killed in a dive-bombing attack on the ship.

The *Post*'s Wilella Waldorf, New York's only first-string female theatre critic, hailed Rose Franken's **Soldier's Wife** (10-4-44, Golden) as "simple, unpretentious, intelligent and full of a warm understanding." Most of her male colleagues were not so enthusiastic, though several allowed it would attract matinee ladies. It attracted enough of them and other playgoers to run until mid-May. John Rogers (Myron McCormick) has been furloughed home from the South Pacific to recuperate from some stomach wounds. He brings home the letters his wife, Katherine (Martha Scott), wrote him and tells her a dying buddy, whose father is a publisher, had read them and urged his father to publish them. Katherine has acknowledged that, for a soldier, "the coming back is almost as hard as the going away." But the money and celebrity her letters bring don't make life easier for John or her. She is strenuously courted by a worldly interviewer (Glenn Anders), while John is pursued by the interviewer's svelte editor (Lili Darvas). Both John and Katherine recognize the strain on the marriage, so agree to head for the country and a simpler life.

Everett T. George (Le Roi Operti), a celebrated publisher, comes to the rather seedy funeral home run by John MacGregor (Whitford Kane) and gives him $10,000, telling him, his not-as-naive-as-she-looks wife (Ruth McDevitt), and his equally unprosperous competitor, Manny Siegelmann (Al Shean), that he is about to be murdered and wants them to take care of his body—but not embalm it—after he is killed. He then collapses and dies. So much for the first act of Jane Hinton's **Meet a Body** (10-16-44, Forrest). The main suspects, George's former associates, turn up and are also murdered. There are the customary doors that open and shut seemingly unassisted and the screams in the dark, and once, late in the play, a policeman chases a deranged, mute dancer over the footlights, through the audience, and back onstage before shooting him. The killer turns out to be George, who, like the doctor in *Ten Little Indians,* was not really dead.

There was also an air of mystery about **The Visitor** (10-17-44, Henry Miller's), which Kenneth White took from the novel by Carl Randau and Leane Zugsmith. A seventeen-year-old, his arm in a sling, appears at the Cunningham home, claiming to be Bud Owen (Richard Hylton), who supposedly was drowned three years before but whose body was never located. Although he arouses the suspicions of his mother (Frances Carson) and his stepfather (Walter N. Greaza) by his curious lapses of memory, such as not recalling the name of his beloved dog, he finally proves to be the true Bud, and exposes Mr. Cunningham as the man who tried to kill him and plans to kill his mother for their money.

Several of the season's major American successes were derived from books. The latest to open was John van Druten's theatricalization of Kathryn Forbes's largely autobiographical *Mama's Bank Account* as **I Remember Mama** (10-19-44, Music Box). Two small revolving stages flanked a much larger revolve, and when the curtain rose audiences saw Katrin (Joan Tetzel) sitting at a desk on one of the side turntables, reading from the memoirs she has been writing. As she recalls growing up in turn-of-the-century San Francisco a cross-section of her home on Telegraph Hill can be seen, with glimpses of the street outside and the hills beyond. Mama (Mady Christians) is forever stashing away pennies in her home "bank account" to prepare for a rainy day, even though cantankerous Uncle Chris (Oscar Homolka) promises to leave his money to the family. Mama is the first to defend Aunt Trina (Adrienne Gessner) when the other aunts object to Trina's marrying. Mama also disguises herself as a hospital scrubwoman to visit a daughter after the girl's operation. When Uncle Chris dies the family discovers he has given all his money away to help crippled children. Worse, Mama confesses that there is no bank account. She had lied because "it is not good for little ones to be afraid." Katrin continues with her writing about the whole family, but insists, as she did at the start, "First and foremost, I remember Mama." Rodgers and Hammerstein's initial stab at producing was seen by the *Daily News*'s John Chapman as bringing to the theatre "the excitement of imagination and skill, of good writing, of good acting, of human warmth and human comedy." It chalked up 714 performances, and subsequently toured with Charlotte Greenwood as Mama.

"I'm precocious. It's my chief charm," boasts the titular heroine (Pat Hitchcock) of Whitfield Cook's **Violet** (10-24-44, Belasco). "It escapes me," retorts her much married father's latest intended (Helen Claire). In order to help smooth daddy's path to the altar, Violet summons his exes and all her siblings and stepsiblings to the Vermont farmhouse her laundryman (and would-be artist) father (Harvey Stephens) is carefully restoring. She creates some havoc but does eventually achieve her goal. Although the play survived only three weeks, the $100,000 MGM paid for film rights before the opening landed it squarely in the black.

Director-producer George Abbott enjoyed a much longer run (158 performances) with a farce by two film writers, Louis Solomon and Harold Buchman's **Snafu** (10-25-44, Hudson). The title stemmed from a wartime acronym which came from an expression that in more polite terms ran "Situation normal—all fouled up." Ronald Stevens (Billy Redfield) returns from the war very angry. It seems his commanding officer informed him, "Your mama wants you." For Richard was very much underage when he enlisted and still is. His parents (Russell Hardie and Elspeth Eric) are taken aback by the souvenirs he brings them—a bloodied Jap flag and a Jap officer's suicide sword. When his father attempts to tell him about the birds and the bees, Richard winds up telling the dropped-jawed old man things he never knew. He even describes the pictures the army shows recruits of what loose sex can lead to. "They scare the hell out of you," he admits. For a time Richard stands accused of attempting to seduce a young journalism student (Patricia Kirkland) with a wild imagination. But all ends happily after his former sweetheart (Bethel Leslie) embraces him and he prepares to head off again, this time with his parents' consent.

The smooth performances and popularity of two screen favorites, Miriam Hopkins and Victor Jory, allowed Samson Raphaelson's **The Perfect Marriage** (10-26-44, Barrymore) to run for eleven and a half weeks in the face of some softly dismissive notices. After ten years of seemingly happy marriage Dale and Jenny Williams recognize that they have become little more than "beautiful strangers." They both think about having flings and even about divorce before opting to struggle to make their marriage a deeper, enduring affair.

Just as superior new talent was about to burst on the American theatrical scene, a number of major oldtimers took their final bows. The last new play to reach Broadway by the once prolific Owen Davis was **No Way Out** (10-30-44, Cort), and it offered more than a hint of the cheap-priced touring melodramas on which he had cut his teeth so many decades earlier. Dr. Hilliard (Robert Keith) has married his mistress, after allowing her husband to die from lack of proper medical attention. But he squanders his newfound wealth in poor stock investments and is threatened by his broker with exposure. Knowing that his rich stepdaughter (Nancy Marquand) is dying of a rare malady, Addison's disease, Hilliard refuses to prescribe the one treatment that can save her. But the girl's chemist fiancé (Jerome P. Thor) has a sister (Irene Hervey) who is a physician and understands the situation. At first alarmed that her professional code of ethics prohibits her from inculpating Hilliard, she finds a last-minute way to get around it and bring Hilliard to justice.

Without acknowledging it, final bows were in order for the much beloved Ethel Barrymore, whose frequent lack of luck in picking suitable vehicles was manifest again in her last Broadway outing. **Embezzled Heaven** (10-31-44, National) was Lászlo Bush-Fekete and Mary Helen Fay's adaptation of Franz Werfel's novel. For thirty years Teta has been cook to the Countess Argan (Bettina Cerf). All that time she has carefully sent her hard-earned money to a nephew so that he can study for the priesthood and help her reach Heaven. But when she retires and returns to her native village she learns her nephew (Eduard Franz) is a scoundrel who has frittered away her money and joined a carnival. The shattered old woman makes a pilgrimage to the Vatican. She attracts the attention of the pope (Albert Basserman), who is passing by, and confesses to him, "I am not worthy of God's Grace, Holy Father. I have only one act of virtue. I tried to make a priest out of Mojmir." She then itemizes her "innumerable" sins, which seem pathetically petty, such as accepting bribes from the countess's grocer and lying about her own age. The pope has no sooner consoled her and gone than she dies. But one of his retinue tells onlookers that people like Teta, who are humble enough to seek the back door to Heaven, find that door to be Heaven's main gate. A prologue, set in 1912, allowed Barrymore to appear as a relatively young woman; the rest of the play showed

her a quarter of a century or more on. In *PM*, Louis Kronenberger wrote of Barrymore's performance, "There is more of the great lady than of the servant in her Teta; but the role is so passive that we can be glad she gives it that much character. She, who abounds in personality, should not in any case be asked to lend herself to picturesqueness. She cannot make the role real, even though she painstakingly subdues herself to it, but she makes it interesting because she is interesting." Nonetheless, her aging loyalists could support her for only fifty-two performances.

Far more acceptable to Broadway was the clowning of another oldtimer—also in his unrecognized farewell. The old vaudevillian Frank Fay returned after a long absence to play Elwood P. Dowd, the amiable boozer given to palling around with an invisible, six-foot-tall rabbit in Mary Chase's **Harvey** (11-1-44, 48th St.). Of course, Harvey was the rabbit. Matters come to a head when his flibbertigibbet sister, Veta Louise Simmons (Josephine Hull), and her haughty, homely spinster daughter, Myrtle Mae (Jane Van Duser), arrange for Elwood to meet Mrs. Chauvenet (Frederica Going), the local social arbiter. The dowager leaves hurriedly after Elwood insists on introducing her to Harvey, and a frustrated, furious Myrtle Mae demands Elwood be sent to the "booby hatch." There, at Chumley's Rest, Myrtle Mae is mistaken for the prospective patient. The confusion is soon cleared up, and Elwood is about to be admitted when the taxi driver (Robert Gist) who has brought them all to the mental home describes how nice the patients are when he brings them there, and how they act when they are "cured": "They crab, crab, crab. They yell at me to watch the lights, watch the brakes, watch the intersection. They scream at me to hurry." Veta decides she prefers to keep Elwood as harmless and lovable as he has been. So they all head home again—even Harvey. Fay was "quiet, wistful and detached, a master of timing and the sidewise glance"; Hull was her dithery, adorable self. The rest of the cast was as close to perfection as Broadway could come. The *Sun*'s Ward Morehouse greeted the play as "a quaint, capricious and enormously amusing comedy." Time has scoffed at those critics who suggested that without Fay the play would be nothing and has even justified the play's surprise selection for the season's Pulitzer Prize. It ran 1775 performances in New York alone.

Although it was considerably shorter than Barrymore's, Pauline Lord's career had enjoyed distinguished ups and suffered numerous downs. Her playing was more idiosyncratic—with her breathy, jerky speech mannerisms and nervous, sometimes inelegant gestures. Now she, too, was about to write finis to her Broadway record with Charlcie and Oliver Garrett's very short-lived **Sleep, My Pretty One** (11-2-44, Playhouse). Alice Sturdevant has been confined to her Gramercy Park home ever since her stroke on learning that her husband had gone down with the *Titanic*. But she is not alone there, since she has used all her Machiavellian tricks to keep her son (Harry Ellerbe) with her. His first fiancée fled on the eve of their wedding; the second fell mysteriously to her death from a fourth-floor window. When the forty-year-old Donald brings home a third prospective bride, Alice again tries to destroy the relationship. The girl (Julie Stevens) quickly sees through her and makes Donald face up to the truth. Alice drinks the poison she meant for the girl.

Devon Wainwright's friends can tell the state of her romantic life by the names of the new perfumes she markets—Autumn Glory. Crescendo, Morning Laughter. The heroine of **In Bed We Cry** (11-14-44, Belasco), which Ilka Chase adapted as a vehicle for herself from her own best-selling novel, lives in a world of high fashion and posh offices and apartments (albeit no bed appears onstage). After her husband (Frances DeSales) leaves the ambitious woman and is killed in the war, she takes up with a suave foreigner (Frederic Tozere) but eventually settles for a man (Paul McGrath) who has loved her long but quietly. Six weeks and the play was gone.

That was twice as long as Laurence Stallings's **The Streets Are Guarded** (11-20-44, Henry Miller's) lasted. Critics, baffled by the uncomfortable blend of mysticism and tough realism, deemed the work a far cry from Stallings's earlier *What Price Glory?* Recovering from his wounds at a naval hospital, a pharmacist (Morton L. Stevens) relives his experiences on a small Pacific island surrounded by Jap-held territory. He is stranded there with several other sailors, some fliers, and a Dutch nurse when a marine (Phil Brown) comes ashore. Something is odd about the man, including the strange wounds on his hands. But he engineers a raid on the nearest Jap base, bringing back much-needed medicine and a radio that allows the Americans to call in marine rescuers. Then he disappears.

George S. Kaufman (who also served as director) and John P. Marquand dramatized Marquand's affectionately satiric best-seller **The Late George Apley** (11-21-44, Lyceum) and delighted New York playgoers for just short of a year. Apley (Leo G. Carroll) is a Harvard-educated, very proper Bostonian Brahmin, who is content to believe that all that is good and worthwhile in life stems either from his city or his school. When he learns that his son, John (David McKay), is courting a girl from Worcester, he dejectedly informs his wife (Janet Beecher), "The girl—is a foreigner, Catherine!" Even worse, his daughter, Eleanor (Joan Chandler), is cavorting with a man who is a liberal, a bohemian, and

a Yalie. The best Eleanor can do is get her father to read Freud. This time Apley tells his wife, "It seems to be Dr. Freud's idea that sex very largely governs the lives of people—in other parts of the country." Eleanor has the gumption to marry her man, but John allows himself to be rushed off to Europe. Twelve years later, after Apley has died, John is seen to have turned into a rigid, tradition-bound Brahmin. Howard Barnes of the *Herald Tribune* saluted the play as "a brilliant comedy of manners," while Nichols applauded Carroll's "wonderful" performance, observing, "The part of Apley easily could have become caricature, but Mr. Carroll will have none of that. He plays the role honestly and softly."

Arthur Miller's playwriting debut, **The Man Who Had All the Luck** (11-23-44, Forrest), was a four-performance dud. Burton Rascoe told his *World-Telegram* readers, "This is not a play to knock you out of your seat, roll you in the aisles, cause you to dance in the street or throw your hat in the air. It is a much finer drama than that. It is an unique event," but his colleagues were less enthusiastic, dismissing the play as "incredibly turbid in its writing and stuttering in its execution," "neither compelling enough as theatre, nor significant enough, by a long shot, as drama," and "three addled acts." David Beeves (Karl Swenson) is a lucky man. When he despairs of fixing his car, a helpful mechanic comes along; when the father of a girl he is pursuing sets out to shoot him, the man is run over; when he buys a failing gas station, the state announces a major highway will go by it; and when he tries to raise minks, he succeeds despite everyone's warnings. Yet his kid brother, Amos (Dudley Sadler), laboriously trained by his sailor father (Jack Sheehan) to be a major-league pitcher, fails because of the old man's misjudgments. Why then is David so lucky? Playgoers had to provide their own answers.

Hand in Glove (12-4-44, Playhouse) was Charles K. Freeman and Gerald Savory's adaptation of Savory's novel *Hughie Roddis*. The curtain rises to allow audiences to watch as young Ramskill (George Lloyd) strangles a girl he has picked up on the docks, then savagely slices her. The murderous cockney has come to Yorkshire to find war work and taken a room with a woman known as Auntie B (Isobel Elsom). Auntie has an idiot nephew, Hughie (Skelton Knaggs), who collects sharp metal objects. So as he goes about his killings, Ramskill has little trouble casting suspicion on the boy. But he meets his match with the arrival from London of a Scotland Yard man (Aubrey Mather).

A Bell for Adano (12-6-44, Cort), taken from John Hersey's novel by Paul Osborn and praised by Barnes as "a triumphant drama," pleased audiences for nine full months. Being an Italian-American, Major Victor

Joppolo (Fredric March), head of the Allied Military Government in Adano, is sympathetic to needs of the Sicilian city. His haughty, far-off commanding officer is not and orders that carts not be allowed to impede traffic. Joppolo ignores the order. As punishment, he is advised he will be transferred. But before he goes he gives the villagers their fondest wish, a new bell to replace the one the Fascists had melted down for the war effort. Moments before he leaves, the new bell is tried out. "It shakes the whole damned building," Joppolo proudly tells his sergeant. Barnes also saluted March, who, he suggested, "gives the finest performance of his career . . . he concentrates on sincerity and intensity."

Neither the acting nor the writing redeemed Mary Orr and Reginald Denham's **Dark Hammock** (12-11-44, Forrest). "Dark Hammock" is the name of the Florida ranch where, in 1910, the young and beautiful former showgirl Coral Platt (Orr) is attempting to slowly murder her much older husband (Charles McClelland), hoping then to spend his $50,000 estate on her importuning lover back in New York. By grinding matchheads into his nightly eggnog she has reduced Platt to a wheelchair-bound cripple. On the very evening she plans to finish the job, Dr. Florence McDavid (Elissa Landi) and her comic-relief assistant, Amelia Coop (Mary Wickes), who have been sent to do research in the area by President Taft, seek shelter from a storm. McDavid quickly becomes suspicious of Coral and, at evening's end, tricks her into swallowing the lethal dose she meant for her husband.

The next evening the City Center revived Marian de Forest's stage version of Louisa May Alcott's classic *Little Women* (10-14-12). Throughout the season the city-owned house offered, at bargain prices, operas, revivals of old musicals, and return engagements of such recent offerings as *Harriet, The Cherry Orchard,* and *Othello.* One final revival came in at the start of spring.

What by December Morehouse was calling "the hit-contagion in the New York theater" added another happy instance with Norman Krasna's **Dear Ruth** (12-13-44, Henry Miller's). Being almost sweet sixteen and anxious to do her bit for the war effort, Miriam Wilkins (Leonore Lonergan) has taken to writing letters to a lonely soldier overseas. In fact, she has written him sixty letters. Only she has signed her older sister's name and enclosed her sister's picture. Home on leave, Lt. William Seawright (John Dall) comes seeking Ruth Wilkins (Virginia Gilmore) on the very day that Ruth has agreed to marry the stuffy Albert Kummer (Bartlett Robinson). Bill has a short two-day pass, but two days are all it takes for Ruth to fall in love with him and ditch Albert. Ruth's father (Howard Smith), a judge,

marries the couple, who hurry off to the briefest of honeymoons. They are no sooner gone than the doorbell rings. A young sailor—Harold Kobbermeyer (Peter Dunn)—comes looking for the Ruth Wilkins who has been writing him. Wondering how many correspondents Miriam has had, her dismayed parents can only shake their heads and moan, "Nooo!" Moss Hart's astute direction glossed over any weak spots. The pudgy young Lonergan, with her cracked voice and deadpan delivery, also helped the comedy ride merrily along for 683 performances.

"Grade B 'I Remember Mama'—if that" was one aisle-sitter's dismissal of **Sophie** (12-25-44, Playhouse), which George Ross and Rose C. Feld took from Feld's *New Yorker* stories, *Sophie Halenczik, American.* In her simple home along R.F.D. 4 near Ridgetown Connecticut, Sophie (Katina Paxinou), a Czech immigrant who has become a U.S. citizen, must arrange to wed her soldier son (Donald Buka) to the girl he has made pregnant, must overcome the patent bigotries of the proud Wasp (John McGovern) who stands to be the father-in-law of her daughter (Ann Shepherd), and must deal with her own sponging brother, "Uncle Anton" (Louis Sorin), and sister-in-law (Donna Keath). She manages to do it all.

Fear of having the old Wales Padlock Law imposed on them had decided the Shuberts against booking a new play about lesbianism. So Dorothy and Howard Baker's adaptation of Dorothy's novel, **Trio** (12-29-44, Belasco), had been forced to suspend its tryout and wait several weeks before finding a playhouse. When it finally opened, critics could not see what all the fuss had been about, assessing the drama as being "quietly effective but not at all sensational," "honest and serious," and "honest, straightfoward and [treating] its subject with dignity and restraint." For some years Pauline Maury (Lydia St. Clair), a neurotic, selfish professor of French literature at a western university, has kept her young protégée, Janet Logan (Lois Wheeler), unnaturally close to her by allowing the girl to share her apartment and credit for her writings. Ray Mackenzie (Richard Widmark), a graduate student hoping to become a filmmaker, falls in love with Janet. He is shocked when he realizes her situation and at first would break with her. But then he determines to open her eyes and win her. When he does and she agrees to marry him, Pauline abandons her fierce struggle to retain the girl and commits suicide. Despite the laudatory notices, city officials found the drama obscene and, by threatening to invoke the old law, forced the play to close after eight weeks.

Lindsay and Crouse, who, like Rodgers and Hammerstein, were as successful as producers as they were as writers, brought in 1945's first hit, John Patrick's **The**

Hasty Heart (1-3-45, Hudson). Five beds at an improvised hospital—a hut with a thatched roof—on the Burma front are occupied by an American (John Lund), an Australian (John Campbell), a New Zealander (Victor Chapin), an Englishman (Douglas Chandler), and a native (Earle Jones). The men are all companionable. Soon a sixth wounded soldier is brought in, an embittered young Scottish soldier, Lachlen (Richard Basehart), who has learned to hate anything he cannot have and who rejects the friendly camaraderie of his neighbors. They and the nurse, Margaret (Anne Burr), all know the soldier is dying. With time, they break down his reserve, until he discovers the truth about his condition. Then, believing they were kind to him out of pity, he again spurns them. But when he would leave, he comes to recognize the basic decency of the men and the genuine affection that Margaret has developed for him. Crying out that he does not want to die alone, he tells the nurse, "I've nae the time to squander on ma' pride. . . . If I moost beg ye tae take me back—then I beg ye." The others celebrate his decision. Most critics agreed with their colleague Garland, who characterized the work as "a tense, tough, tender play." It ran for 207 performances.

By contrast, Clare Kummer's **Many Happy Returns** (1-5-45, Playhouse) ran for only three, despite the presence of Hollywood's Mary Astor and Neil Hamilton at the head of the cast. Kummer, claiming unauthorized changes had hopelessly disfigured the comedy, unavailingly attempted to prevent its opening. Its very sour reviews the next day marked a sad Broadway farewell for a writer who once had been perceived as one of the American theatre's brightest hopes. Kummer's essentially simple story told how Cynthia Laceby calls Henry Burton's attention to herself by making a play for his married son. Henry goes to her apartment to offer her $10,000 to break off the affair, but is himself beguiled. However, since Henry also still has a loving wife, Cynthia's ploy fails.

Good Night, Ladies (1-17-45, Royale), Cyrus Wood's updated revamping of Avery Hopwood and Charlton Andrews's *Ladies' Night [in a Turkish Bath]* (8-9-20), had established a Chicago long-run record of 100 weeks. But this time around New York wouldn't buy the tale of a painfully shy man (James Ellison), taken out for a wild night on the town, who finds himself at a Turkish bath on the wrong evening. The farce left after ten weeks.

Nor would New Yorkers accept a stage version by Daphne Du Maurier of her famous novel (and equally famous film) **Rebecca** (1-18-45, Barrymore). The production starred Bramwell Fletcher and Diana Barrymore as the newlywed de Winters and Florence Reed as Mrs. Danvers, the servant who is sure that de Winter killed

his first wife. Although it had flourished handsomely on an extended pre-Broadway tour, it remained in New York for less than three weeks.

The parade of aging Hollywood celebrities hoping to resuscitate their careers with a stage success continued when Gloria Swanson, in her New York debut, and Conrad Nagel came to town in Harold J. Kennedy's **A Goose for the Gander** (1-23-45, Playhouse). Returning home unexpectedly, Katherine finds her husband, David, having breakfast with a beautiful, curvaceous blonde with the playful name of Suzy (Maxine Stuart). Katherine proclaims that what is sauce for the gander is sauce for the goose, so she invites three old flames— a Tarzan-like athlete (David Tyrell), a Noel Cowardy wit (Kennedy), and a dull but generous banker (John Clubley)—to her home. A disconcerting mixture of farce, comedy, and melodrama ensues before Katherine and David kiss and make up. Devastating reviews closed the play after a fortnight.

Shakespeare's rarely revived *The Tempest* was brought into the Alvin on the 25th. Margaret Webster's production was sometimes controversial, sometimes uneven, but all in all highly successful. Among the complaints were that too much emphasis was placed on the low comedy of Trinculo (George Voskovec) and Stephano (Jan Werich), that Vera Zorina's Ariel was too cold and ponderous, and that Canada Lee's Caliban was too snarlingly crude. But Arnold Moss's dignified, poetic Prospero held the evening together. Following a superbly recreated storm at sea, the action unfolded on a revolving stage that deftly moved the players from one part of the rocky, cave-strewn island to another. Webster transposed Prospero's famous "Our revels now are ended" speech to the final moments. As he told how we are all melted into air, the lights slowly dimmed and the surrounding actors disappeared, until the red-robed magician was silhouetted alone on the stage, then vanished with his closing words. For all the critics' qualifications, the comedy achieved a superb run of 100 playings.

Another of the season's returning soldiers was the central figure in László Bush-Fekete, Sidney Sheldon, and Mary Helen Fay's **Alice in Arms** (1-31-45, National). However, as the title suggested, the soldier was a woman—WAC Lieutenant Alice Madison (Peggy Conklin), sent back to her Linwood, Pennsylvania, home after contracting malaria. She is all set to marry her longtime sweetheart, Walter (Roger Clark), a ball-bearing executive. Before she can, Sergeant Steve Grant (Kirk Douglas), with whom she has enjoyed a fling overseas, and Colonel Benson (G. Albert Smith), a former commanding officer, both show up to court her. Since Steve was the best-looking and most personable of her three suitors, experienced playgoers knew early on that she would finally go to the altar with him. But thumbs-down reviews kept her from doing it for more than five performances.

Although Vincent Lawrence had never been hailed as effusively as Clare Kummer, several of his earliest comedies had been seen as offering great promise. The promise was never realized, so his last play, **The Overtons** (2-6-45, Booth), like some of his prior ones, was at best a modest success—running five and a half months. Because so much liquor was supposedly consumed during the action, two critics independently suggested the play was "poured" onto the stage, while Garland branded it "the drinkingest play I've ever seen." Some critics were also reminded of *The Perfect Marriage* (but, curiously, not of *A Goose for the Gander*). After eight years of happy wedded life, Cora "Nifty" Overton (Arlene Francis) spots a luscious blonde (Glenda Farrell) disrobing in the boathouse of her playboy husband (Jack Whiting)—known variously as Jack or "Friday." Drawing the wrong conclusion, she decides to have a fling of her own and maybe even break up the marriage. This delights some of the Overtons' cynical neighbors, who have long believed the pair's public happiness hid private problems. Naturally, all ends lovingly—in the couple's bedroom.

William McCleery's **Hope for the Best** (2-7-45, Fulton) was an even more modest hit, with 117 performances to its credit. Since McCleery was an editor at *PM*, its critic, Kronenberger, undoubtedly had to tread carefully. He concluded that the work was "a play of ideas and talk . . . and the talk must do duty for action." Michael Jordan (Franchot Tone) is a highly successful syndicated columnist, with an 11,000,000 readership. But he writes of small-town and old-stock lives rather than discussing the political situation he would prefer to survey. His fiancée, Margaret Harwood (Joan Wetmore), is a conservative political writer who is content to have Michael keep his more liberal views to himself. Then he meets a young, attractive war plant worker, Lucille Daly (Jane Wyatt), and she draws out a confession that once, when he "felt very pregnant with understanding," he wrote, but never published, some columns "to show how politics affects the average man's life in ways he doesn't understand." Lucille encourages him until he not only opts to change his style, but to change sweethearts as well.

Although it received its share of polite rejections (and these from several of the most important critics), Ruth Goodman and Augustus Goetz's **One-Man Show** (2-8-45, Barrymore) gathered in enough rave notices— "theatre as it should be," "profoundly entertaining," "an absorbing, intelligent and adult psychological drama," and "the most admirable sort of adult entertaining"— that the dismal one-month run of Jed Harris's mounting remains somewhat inexplicable. The play took up the old silver-cord motif, but with a difference—it was a father holding on tenaciously to his daughter. The father is Lucian Gardner (Frank Conroy), owner of a leading New York art gallery. By allowing Racine Gardner (Constance Cummings) to share every aspect of his work with him, he has, like the French professor of *Trio,* created an unnaturally close relationship—albeit in this case without apparent incestuous or other sexual connotations. He has carefully seen to it that burgeoning romances with one (Hugh Franklin) of the gallery's artists and with an older ladies' man (James Rennie) are quashed. But after a young diplomat (John Archer) from the State Department finally opens her eyes, Racine consents to marry him and go with him to Costa Rica.

A quartet of very short-lived flops followed. The first, Leslie Reade's English drama **The Stranger** (2-12-45, Playhouse), dealt with Jack the Ripper. Rumor has it that the killer is a young foreigner who wears a leather apron and carries a black bag. So when David Mendelsohn (Eduard Franz), a shoemaker who perfectly fits the description, first enters the meeting room of the International Workmen's Educational Club, suspicion falls on him. Critics complained that Reade laid incriminating evidence on too thickly, especially since at the very close of the play he implicated a gentleman (Morton L. Stevens) "who had hitherto taken no part in the conversation."

Signature (2-14-45, Forrest), which Elizabeth McFadden took from Melville Davisson Post's short story "Naboth's Vineyard," survived for only two performances. The play was set in 1856 Virginia and used the sounds of katydids and the sight of fireflies in the evening air to help create a hill-town setting. Rather than see her sweetheart, William Taylor (Bob Stevenson), condemned unjustly for murder, Alice Steuart (Anne Jackson) confesses to the crime, although she, too, is innocent. But John Cartwright (Donald Murphy), the shrewd young lawyer for the defense, soon realizes that Simon Kilrail (Frederic Tozere), a judge assigned to try the case, is the real killer—having murdered his rich cousin to inherit his lands. Cartwright slowly uncovers evidence to convict the jurist.

The distinguished Walter Hampden came badly a cropper when he starred in Edward Caulfield's lightweight **And Be My Love** (2-21-45, National). He played a bachelor actor, tired of acting, who meets a widowed scientist (Lotus Robb), also tired of her work. The two agree to run off for a time to the woman's Connecticut farm. But the sudden appearance of her daughter (Ruth Homond) and prudish spinster sister (Esther Dale) force the couple to pretend they are married. By the final curtain pretence has become reality. One big laugh came when Hampden, as the celebrated John Hogarth, insists on using a phony name, Henry Smith, which will mean nothing to their neighbors, only to discover to his mortification that the backwater neighbors have no idea who John Hogarth is.

Such was the temporary theatre shortage in this brilliant and prosperous season that the next play to come in used the same stage *And Be My Love* had hastily abandoned. But Sheridan Gibney's **Calico Wedding** (3-7-45, National) made an even hastier retreat. During the war, Captain George Gaylord (William Post), stationed at a radio listening post in Alaska, recalls incidents that took place seven years earlier, on his second wedding anniversary. His wife (Grete Mosheim), furious at his neglect of her because of his business interests and angrier still at his helping home a young girl who drank too much at a party, decides on a fling with a celebrated Antarctic explorer (Louis Jean Heydt). The comedy left the outcome up in the air.

Although Curt Goetz and Dorian Otvos's **It's a Gift** (3-12-45, Playhouse) was also a flop, it eked out a six-week run. Professor Herrmann (Goetz) and his wife (Valerie Van Martens) learn that his sister, whom he long ago had disowned for having a child out of wedlock, has died in Montevideo and left $750,000 to them and their twelve children on the condition that the eldest female in the family have an illegitimate child. The Herrmanns, their minister (Whitford Kane), and their eldest daughter, Atlanta (Julie Harris), hurry to Uruguay, where they first conclude that the sister had run bordellos but soon learn that she had become a famous singer and supported homes for orphaned or wayward girls. The professor, torn between his lofty morality and his greed, finally asks Atlanta to have a child with someone, but she is spared the humiliation when Mrs. Herrmann reveals that the ferryboat captain who married her and the professor had no legal right to do so. Thus she has had a dozen kids out of wedlock. That satisfies the will. Their minister then rights the old wrong.

The last original play of his that Philip Barry would see performed in his lifetime (he would also see an adaptation staged) was **Foolish Notion** (3-13-45, Martin Beck). Barry's name, the lure of Tallulah Bankhead, and the Theatre Guild's subscription list conspired to give the comedy a whopping $200,000 advance, but after reviews appeared and disappointed word of mouth was bruited about, ticket sales dropped off, so the production closed following 104 performances. Among the reviewers, Barnes deemed it "brittle, adolescent and pretentious"; Rascoe announced, "I was bored stiff by it." Having recognized that his actress wife, Sophie (Bankhead), had fallen in love with her longtime leading man, Gordon Roark (Donald Cook), Jim Hapgood (Henry Hull), albeit an American, enlisted in the British

army, was reported missing, and, after five years, was declared legally dead. But just as Sophie and Gordon prepare to tie the knot, a phone call advises them that Jim is about to return. They, Jim and Sophie's young adopted daughter (Joan Shepherd), and Sophie's father (Aubrey Mather) all fantasize on what the returning Hapgood will be like. Gordon sees him returning as the same old charming sot he always was; the daughter pictures him as a lovable father endangered on all sides; his father-in-law sees him as a heroic soldier in kilts; while all Sophie can think of is an urn filled with ashes. But when he returns, Jim makes no waves, for he has found a new love of his own. Sophie gratefully remarks, "You came because you knew I'd never be free of you until—you *have* freed me, Jim. How have you done it?" Jim confesses he had to free himself first. Sophie and Gordon now can wed.

A much bigger hit (320 performances), Howard Richardson and William Berney's **Dark of the Moon** (3-14-45, 46th St.), also had to override many negative or heavily qualified notices. Thus Morehouse reported, "It is a folk play of color, atmosphere and imagination, but with hardly enough substance for a full evening in the theatre." John (Richard Hart), the son of a witch and a buzzard, has looked down as he flies above the Smoky Mountains on his eagle, seen the beautiful blue-eyed, copper-haired Barbara Allen (Carol Stone), and fallen in love. So he begs the Conjur Man (Ross Mathew) to make him human. "No more ridin' with my eagle, . . . No more diggin' in the graveyard, no more yellin' in the night and a-screaming with the long high cry that splashes 'gainst the stars!" But the Conjur Man, unable to understand why the witch-boy would abjure 300 years of such delights before being turned into a mountain fog, demurs. John then begs the same favor of the Conjur Woman (Georgia Simmons). She consents, stipulating that if Barbara behaves unfaithfully before the first year is out, he will revert to a witch-boy. John and Barbara are married, but when their child proves to be a witch it is burned by the midwives. Her neighbors hold a revival meeting to save Barbara's soul, and there, on the last day of the year, she succumbs to the blandishments of Marvin Hudgens (John Gifford). As the scream of an eagle is heard, the witches hurry to the moon-bathed mountaintop to reclaim John. Fine acting and staging were enhanced by George Jenkins's evocative settings of a rustic cabin, a general store, a mountain-town square, and, best of all, a desolate, moonlit mountain peak, with its gnarled and twisted tree.

Donald Kirkley, drama critic for the Baltimore *Sun*, and Howard Burman, *Variety*'s Baltimore man, collaborated to no avail on **Happily Ever After** (3-15-45, Biltmore). A onetime medicine-show huckster, Homer Whatcoat (Gene Lockhart), has set himself up comfortably in Elkton, Maryland, refuge of so many elopers, and married 9999 couples. Most of these marriages have been performed with the help of his buddy, Charlie Porter (Parker Fennelly), whom he pays two bits a throw to act as witness. Just as he is about to perform his 10,000th ceremony, Whatcoat is exposed as a fraud. That would mean that 9999 couples from across the country are not legally wed. But, it turns out, before he entered the medicine-show racket he had been legitimately ordained. All's well. One much praised scene had Whatcoat attempting to marry a pair of exhausted marathon dancers, who would spring to life and go into their routine whenever a jitterbug record was played but collapsed instantly when the music was stopped.

The long-absent George Kelly returned to find small favor with his "slow and labored," "slight [but] interesting" **The Deep Mrs. Sykes** (3-19-45, Booth). "There are egotist women," Mr. Sykes (Neil Hamilton) proclaims. "And they say they're really much deadlier than the male because their egotism usually passes for mere feminine jealousy." Mrs. Sykes (Catherine Willard) believes unquestioningly in her intuition. So when a boozy neighbor (Jean Dixon) reports seeing white lilacs delivered to the newlywed singer across the street, Mrs. Sykes's intuition tells her that her husband sent them, and not even her own married son's confession that he ordered them can change her mind. The play carried on for nine weeks.

Kiss Them for Me (3-20-45, Belasco), which Luther Davis drew from Frederic Wakeman's novel *Shore Leave,* fared a bit better, lingering on for fourteen weeks. Crewson (Richard Widmark) and his naval air force pals, Mississip (Dennis King, Jr.) and Mac (Richard Davis), find themselves on leave from their carrier and take a swanky suite at a San Francisco hotel. (The hotel was called the St. Mark, combining parts of the names of two top hotels there, the St. Francis and the Mark Hopkins.) The men advise the management they want nothing but a jukebox, booze, and broads. They even give an obliging bellhop a card claiming they have hard-to-get nylon stockings in hopes of luring women up. But their best-laid plans go agley. A rich, stuffy shipbuilder (Robert Allen) presses them to speak to his workers, "paper navy" bureaucrats shower them with forms, and they are called in for physicals, after which two of them are told they can no longer serve. So the three sneak back to their carrier as it is about to sail. For most critics, the evening's high point was the bit assigned to a tartish nylons hunter named Alice. Rascoe delighted to note that in the role young Judy Holliday "achieves a great personal triumph (in fact, steals the show) with an impersonation which could easily have been made vulgar and farcical, but is, instead, touching and endearing."

Two revivals competed for attention the next Monday, the 26th. At the Barrymore, Katharine Cornell, who had been playing it for the troops abroad, brought back *The Barretts of Wimpole Street.* Brian Aherne was once again Robert Browning, and the same mutt she had always used was Flush. The revival lingered for eleven weeks. At the huge City Center *You Can't Take It with You* gave two weeks of performances at a $2.40 top with the beloved old musical comedy clown Fred Stone starred as Vanderhof and his dancing daughter Dorothy featured as Essie.

The season's final whodunit was Max Afford and Alexander Kirkland's **Lady in Danger** (3-29-45, Broadhurst). The play was set in Australia, where a Jap sympathizer and his chauffeur are both murdered by having a cat whose paw has been dipped in curare scratch them. The chauffeur's body falls out when a closet door is opened, so Monica Sefton (Helen Claire) is suspected. After all, she writes mysteries in which the killers use poison, and she was born in Japan. She is turned over to Dr. Gresham (Kirkland) for examination and, since he is the real killer, he tries to poison and hang her before he is nabbed in the nick of time.

The season's last success at one and the same time gave an admired old performer some final moments of glory and also introduced a major new playwright. Tennessee Williams's **The Glass Menagerie** (3-31-45, Playhouse) begins as a merchant sailor leans against the ironwork of a fire-escape landing, lights a cigarette, and quietly addresses the audience. He confesses that he has tricks in his pocket and up his sleeve, but assures everyone he is no magician. Instead of offering the illusion of truth, he will give them truth in the guise of illusion. For one, he will transport them back to the thirties, "when the huge middle-class of America was matriculating in a school for the blind," and his tale will be underscored with music, since "in memory everything seems to happen to music." His name is Tom Wingfield (Eddie Dowling), and he recalls times in the shabby tenement behind him, when he still resided there with his mother Amanda (Laurette Taylor), who lived in dreams of a probably imaginary past, and his crippled sister, Laura (Julie Haydon), who seemed to care only for her phonograph records and her collection of glass animals. His mother's nagging has long since driven their father to run away, although his smiling picture looks down upon them. With father gone, Amanda, between attempting to sell phone subscriptions for magazines and saluting those who do subscribe as Christian martyrs, now nags Tom about his smoking and his wasting money by going to the movies. She presses him as well to find a gentleman caller for his shy sister. So Tom invites Jim O'Connor (Anthony Ross), his co-worker at a warehouse, home to dinner.

Jim had gone to high school with Laura, who has had a secret crush on him ever since. The evening is a disaster. Jim persuades Laura to dance with him, only to break her favorite glass unicorn as they move about. Worse, Jim reveals he is engaged. After Jim leaves, Amanda scolds Tom, who rushes off to join the merchant marine. From his perch on the fire escape, he now admits he has little to show for his life but his memories, tells Laura to blow out her candles, and then bids the audience good-bye. "A performance that no lover of the theatre will dare to miss," "a joy to watch and hear," "an acting triumph" were some of the paeans garlanding Taylor, along with the more unintentionally ironic (since she died shortly after the play closed) "You can't describe a sunset" and "deathless." Kronenberger went into some detail: "She nags, she flutters, she flatters, she coaxes, she pouts, she fails to understand, and she understands all too well—all this revealed, most of the time, in vague little movements and half-mumbled words, small changes of pace, faint shifts of energy and masterfulness, quiet droopings of spirit." The rest of the cast was also praised, while the play itself was acknowledged "an event of the first importance" and "a masterpiece of make-believe." Almost immediately afterwards it won the New York Drama Critics Circle Award, then ran for 561 performances. Williams's career was brilliantly launched.

· · ·

Tennessee Williams [né Thomas Lanier Williams] (1911–83) was born in Columbus, Miss. His father was a violent, aggressive traveling salesman; his mother, the high-minded, puritanical daughter of a clergyman; his elder sister, a young woman often institutionalized in mental homes. He attended several universities before graduating from the State University of Iowa. Some of his earliest plays were produced at collegiate and regional playhouses. His first work to receive a major mounting was *Battle of Angels* (1940), which folded out of town.

· · ·

The rest of the season went downhill. Elliott Nugent's **A Place of Our Own** (4-2-45, Royale) rehashed the old liberal-vs.-conservative saga. The hidebound Charles Reddy (Robert Keith), hoping to keep his daughter (Jeanne Cagney) close to him, presents his newsman son-in-law David Monroe (John Archer), with a small-town newspaper as a wedding gift. But Reddy's attempts to determine the paper's editorial slant drive David, a Wilsonian idealist, to quit and almost wreck the marriage. A reconciliation follows when Reddy backs down.

In B. Harrison Orkow's **Star Spangled Family** (4-10-45, Biltmore), Sally Jones (Frances Reid), the widow of a war hero, provokes the ire of her former mother-in-law (Jean Adair) by remarrying. The old lady attempts to poison the mind of her eight-year-old grandson (Donald Devlin) against his mother and stepfather. But the stepfather (Edward Nugent) is a doctor. He recognizes that the older Mrs. Jones has slipped over the edge mentally. He gives her a tranquilizer, arranges for her to be committed, then carries his sleeping stepson up to bed.

Edward Chodorov's **Common Ground** (4-25-45, Fulton) was set in the music room of a war-damaged Italian castle. A USO show troupe is brought there after it is captured by the Nazis. The Jewish comedian (Philip Loeb) in the group is shipped off to a concentration camp, but the others are given their choice between propagandizing for the Nazis or being shot. They debate what to do until the rantings of a turncoat newspaperman (Paul McGrath) so disgust them that they all opt for the firing squad.

Half a week was all Broadway would grant Les White and Bud Pearson's **Too Hot for Maneuvers** (5-2-45, Broadhurst). Colonel Steve Hadley (Richard Arlen), newly discharged from the air force, takes over his family's dilapidating military academy just as a scandal breaks loose. Several important upperclassmen have been seen coming from Countess Rosini's "message parlor." The countess (Ellen Andrews) was famous for the "pigeon dance" she had performed at the World's Fair. Hadley personally goes to investigate and, after the requisite double entendres and misunderstandings, discovers the boys were merely trying to keep their weights down so that they could play on the basketball team.

A splendid performance by Montgomery Clift could not save Elsa Shelley's **Foxhole in the Parlor** (5-23-45, Booth). Dennis Patterson, a promising pianist whose career was interrupted when he was drafted, has been given a medical discharge from the army. He had gone to pieces after seeing his buddy blown to bits beside him. His former Greenwich Village neighbors, Tom and Ann Austen (Russell Hardie and Flora Campbell), would help rehabilitate him but first must fight off his callous sister (Grace Coppin), who would take him home and commit him to an institution. Dennis hears the voices of the dead crying for world peace. His recovery starts only when Tom's uncle (Raymond Greenleaf), a former U.S. senator and now a delegate to the U.N. meeting in San Francisco, agrees to read to the whole assembly there the messages Dennis has transcribed.

The season closed on a very sour note with Mary Orr and Reginald Denham's **Round Trip** (5-29-45, Biltmore). The play was set partially in Ironville, Ohio, the same imaginary town where the action of the couple's *Wallflower* had taken place. A conniving New

York actor, Clive Delafield (Edward Nugent), has been directing an amateur production in the town and trying to get the group's duenna, Sarah Albright (June Walker), to underwrite his new play. When she follows him back to New York, her irate husband, Edgar (Sidney Blackmer), rushes after her. He gets her back by first stealing Clive's girlfriend (Phyllis Brooks) and taking her to Ironville to make her his secretary. The pairings are properly restored at the end, with some help from the Albrights' precocious daughter (Patricia Kirkland).

1945–1946

Even though business remained generally strong at the box office and more and more plays were asking a $4.80 top, the number of new dramas and comedies dropped precipitously—by roughly 20 percent. *Variety* counted forty-eight novelties; the *Times,* forty-six. Broadway's ongoing decline had resumed after a wartime respite. Quality also sagged noticeably. Moreover, playgoers had many things to distract them, from the pressures of readjustment to peace to the upheavals caused by a postwar outbreak of labor unrest (including a New York newspaper strike, which very briefly did affect business adversely).

After World War I, Tin Pan Alley had poured out a rash of songs in which the loss of a beloved woman was generally acknowledged to have been a sublimated dirge for a son or husband killed in the war ("Oh, What a Pal Was Mary," "Old Pal, Why Don't You Answer Me?," "My Buddy"). The first postwar season following the Second World War began with a clutch of plays dealing with revenants—returning from the dead or the missing, albeit not necessarily lost in the war.

In Jacques Deval's **Oh, Brother!** (6-19-45, Royale), which starred Hugh Herbert—the jowly Hollywood comedian famous for his "woo-woo!"—the revenant was a fraud. Charles Craddock is a crook and a chess player, who needs $1000 to enter a chess tournament. While burglarizing a Daytona Beach house with two other thieves, Allen Kilmer (Don Gibson) and Sue Atkins (Susana Garnett), he discovers that the bathing beauty Marion Cosgrove (Arleen Whalen) can retain the Cosgrove fortune only if her long-lost brother, who years earlier had run off to Venezuela, cannot be found. Craddock has Kilmer pose as the missing heir. Neither Herbert's clowning nor Whalen's parading in an assortment of eye-popping bathing suits could compensate for the dreary complications that ensued.

Critics split sharply on Ralph Nelson's **The Wind Is Ninety** (6-21-45, Booth), but with a bit of forcing it spanned the hot weather for fourteen weeks. Don Ritchie (Wendell Corey) is killed when his fighter plane is shot down. But his spirit hurries back home to comfort his parents (Bert Lytell and Blanche Yurka) and wife (Frances Reid) before they receive official notice of his death. He is accompanied by the helpful ghost of the Unknown Soldier (Kirk Douglas). At first his family is unable to see or hear Don, and he listens while they reminisce about the little boy with the black eye and the lover who fell off a bench when his marriage proposal was accepted. But eventually, through telepathy, he lets them know that he will always be with them, a "living memory" who will return to soothe their woes whenever, in air force terms, the wind is ninety—that is, out of the east. Douglas's personable dead private walked off with the best notices for its warmth and sincerity.

The season began in earnest during the second week of September, even if, by week's end, John Chapman of the *Daily News* wailed, "The week beginning Monday, Sept. 10, 1945, should go into theatrical history books as one of the most disastrous of all time. Three plays have opened and have caused untold suffering." There were more revenants in Leslie Floyd Egbert and Gertrude Ogden Tubby's confusing **A Boy Who Lived Twice** (9-11-45, Biltmore), the first of the ignominious trio. After young Philip Hastings (John Heath) is killed in a fall from a horse, his mystical sister, Jeane (Anne Sargent), somehow manages to bring him back to life. But he returns with the soul of another man, Lt. John Ralston, who died in a plane crash in Illinois at the same moment that Philip was killed. It is reported that Ralston, who has also been revived, now believes he is Philip. After more complications it is shown that the men were actually twins, separated after birth by their father in a dispute with his wife.

No one brought Eugene Vale's **Devils Galore** (9-12-45, Royale) back to life following its dismal five-performance run. It, too, dealt with a return from the dead. After the philandering publisher Cecil Brock (George Baxter) is killed by a table lamp smashed into his skull by an irate young author, Effie Thurtson (Tony Eden), whom he tried to seduce, he is resurrected by the Devil's assistant (Ernest Cossart) on condition that he carry through the seduction. But plans go awry after the assistant, who concludes New Yorkers are more wicked than anyone in Hell, falls in love with Effie and helps her. He is denied a chance to return to Hell but receives word that St. Peter will assist him in getting into Heaven. The comedy's would-be humor was exemplified by the expletive, "Oh, the Heaven with you!"

Vera Mathews's **Make Yourself at Home** (9-13-45,

Barrymore) ran a mere four performances. The play had no revenant, unless a fading movie queen, hoping to revive her faltering career with a Broadway play, could be considered one. Mona Gilbert (Bernardine Hayes) and her fawning entourage barge into her swank Manhattan apartment and prepare to settle down, ignoring the fact that she has sublet it to a Wall Streeter and his mistress. Her play, *Seduction,* is slated by the critics, but becomes a hit after her brother punches the celebrated critic George Jean Norris at 21.

Matters improved a bit, but not all that much, with the arrival of Edmund Goulding's **The Ryan Girl** (9-24-45, Plymouth). Miley Gaylon (Edmund Lowe), a gangster wanted on murder charges, returns from hiding in Venezuela on learning that Lt. George Clark (John Compton), the son he had abandoned many years before, has won the Congressional Medal of Honor. He reasons that surely no one will prosecute the father of a hero. But when he attempts to expose the boy's past, George's mother, Venetia Ryan (June Havoc), a former *Follies* beauty who had also abandoned him, decides to protect her son's good name. She shoots and kills Miley, then she and her maid set everything up to make it seem a suicide.

The season's second fourteen-week run was chalked up by **You Touched Me!** (9-25-45, Booth), which Tennessee Williams had written with his lover, Donald Windham. The play, set in rural England, was suggested by D. H. Lawrence's story of the same name. Cornelius Rockley (Edmund Gwenn) is a besotted sea captain who had been forced to retire after allowing his ship to sink in the Caribbean. He is given to telling tall, off-color tales, such as the time he was seduced while shipwrecked by a beautiful, lustful porpoise. Cornelius lives with his mentally sadistic, "congenitally virginal" sister (Catherine Williard) and his young daughter, Matilda (Marianne Stewart), who is being molded in her aunt's merciless image. But he sees a way to alter matters for the better when his adopted son, Hadrian (Montgomery Clift), returns from service in the Royal Air Force. Hadrian awakes Matilda to the saner, happier world outside, and this promises some rosier years for Cornelius, too. Guthrie McClintic's direction and Motley's three-deckered set were praised, but reviewers differed on the play's merits, with the *World-Telegram*'s Burton Rascoe calling it "a work of art, edification and entertainment," while the *Times*'s Lewis Nichols saw it as "verbose and filled with lofty and long speeches."

The season's first smash hit was Arnaud d'Usseau and James Gow's **Deep Are the Roots** (9-26-45, Fulton). The play introduced another topic that would pop up several more times during the theatrical year: the place of blacks in white America. Brett Charles (Gordon Heath) grew up in the home of southern Senator Langdon (Charles Waldron), where his mother was a servant and where he was allowed to play with the senator's daughters, the elder Alice (Carol Goodner) and the younger Genevra (Barbara Bel Geddes). Now Brett has returned a decorated hero, but Langdon is outraged to hear that he may be given a scholarship to earn a doctorate. "Making a doctor of philosophy out of a nigger!" is preposterous to him. After all, Brett has been killing and bayoneting white men, and the senator is certain that such behavior has warped Brett's black soul. Indeed, Brett is not prepared to return to the humble ways forced on him in the past. He refuses to observe the verbal courtesies demanded of blacks at the post office and even enters the town library through the front door. So Langdon bribes a complacent black servant (Helen Martin) into backing his story that Brett has stolen a watch he gave to his prospective son-in-law (Lloyd Gough). Alice is dumbstruck at the charge and at first refuses to support the senator's demand for Brett's arrest. But after she learns that Genevra is in love with Brett, her deep-seated antipathy to blacks allows her to join in the charge. Brett is arrested and beaten. When he is put on a train and told not to come back, he jumps off the train and returns to the senator's home. There Genevra suggests they marry. Brett rejects the proposal but tells her, "We're both on the same side." Separately he and Genevra head out to make their own ways in the world. Critics had numerous complaints, such as the cheaply melodramatic touch of the false accusation, and the painting of all blacks as good but of most whites as tarnished with bigotry. Still, they conceded, as did Ward Morehouse in the *Sun*, that the evening provided "vibrant theatre." The drama ran for more thirteen months. It made a star of Barbara Bel Geddes.

. . .

Barbara Bel Geddes (b. 1922) was the daughter of Norman Bel Geddes and was born in New York. The blonde, somewhat horsey beauty made her debut as a walk-on in summer stock in 1940. She first appeared on Broadway the next year in *Out of the Frying Pan,* then toured for the USO as the overimaginative Judy in *Junior Miss.* Subsequent Broadway assignments were in *Little Darling, Nine Girls,* and *Mrs. January and Mr. X.*

. . .

Dan Totheroh, one of a handful of playwrights hailed early on as showing splendid promise but who never fulfilled playgoers' hopes, made one final Broadway stab with his **Live Life Again** (9-29-45, Belasco). Critics dismissed it as a jumbled, inept retelling of the Hamlet story. They also cited ponderous, unpoetic lines such as "I saw your light and blundered to it like a moth," or "My love is all I have to give—a thing quite poor." The play gave up after two performances. Mark Orme (Donald Buka) returns home from school to Bison Run, Nebraska, at the turn of the century, just in time to miss his mother's funeral. Believing his father (Thomas Chalmers) killed his mother in order to remarry, he vows on her grave to be revenged. But when he shoots his father, the dying man assures him of his love and brings about a futile reconciliation.

Superb acting almost made a hit of **Therese** (10-9-45, Biltmore), which Thomas Job adapted from Émile Zola's *Thérèse Raquin*. It ran for twelve weeks. Once again, in 1875 Paris, Therese (Eva Le Gallienne) and her lover (Victor Jory) murder her dreary, hat-trimming husband (Berry Kroeger) and settle into a guilt-ridden marriage. But the dead man's mother (Dame May Whitty), after suffering a stroke on discovering the truth, contrives to bring the pair down. All the principals were lauded, but the eighty-year-old Whitty was most highly praised, particularly for her acting in the final scene "where, helpless in an armchair, but with eyes blazing forth her hate, she dominates the situation so that the audience is breathless, aching with anticipation and excitement."

"The young season's flop crop continues to be as abundant as ragweed," *Variety* began its notice of Irwin Shaw's **The Assassin** (10-17-45, National). Curiously, although Shaw was an American, the play had already been seen in London. Even there, however, the time for its opportunistic story had passed, since Shaw was fictionalizing incidents surrounding the assassination of the traitorous French Admiral Darlan three years earlier. In Shaw's version Darlan was rechristened Admiral Marcel Vesprey (Roger de Koven). His duplicitous associate General Mousset (Clay Clement) has little difficulty persuading an ardent royalist, Robert de Mauny (Frank Sundstrom), to kill the admiral, especially after assuring him that he has arranged for de Mauny's subsequent escape. But following the assassination, Mousset reneges and de Mauny is shot.

Having voluntarily taken the rap for his bootlegger partner, Noll Turner (Luther Adler), Frankie Madison (Paul Kelly) has spent fourteen years in prison. At the beginning of Theodore Reeve's **Beggars Are Coming to Town** (10-27-45, Coronet) he has just been released and has come seeking Turner at the Avignon, the exclusive supper club that Turner runs. He assumes Turner will give him a 50 percent cut in the place. He also starts bossing people around, telling a newspaperman to scram and trying to pick up a prominent socialite. When Turner refuses to give Madison a share, Madison threatens mayhem. But Turner calmly shows him that

the club is an impersonal corporation and that he is merely its guiding light. A disgruntled Madison leaves, taking with him Florrie Dushaye (Dorothy Comingore), the club's leggy cigarette girl.

Although critics were clearly rooting for Mary Chase, they reluctantly had to turn thumbs down on her **The Next Half Hour** (10-29-45, Empire). The play left after a single week. Back during Holy Week in 1913, Margaret Brennan (Fay Bainter), a superstitious Irish immigrant, having turned up an ace of spades and accidentally come across some crepe used at her husband's funeral, is certain that someone's death is near after she hears a banshee cry. She fears that her older son, Pat (Jack Ruth), may be in mortal danger, since he is playing around with a married woman. She sends her younger son, Barney (Conrad Janis), to warn Pat, but Barney is killed when the woman's husband mistakes him for his brother. Margaret recognizes that you cannot tamper with fate and that "the next half hour always belongs to God."

Robert Turney's **The Secret Room** (11-7-45, Royale) was condemned by reviewers as farfetched and turgid. Leda Ferroni (Eleonora Mendelssohn), an Italian pianist who had been sent to Dachau by the Nazis, had the child she gave birth to there taken away from her, and then suffered a mental breakdown, gets Dr. Jackson (Ivan Simpson) to find her a place as a governess. So that the doctor cannot reveal her past, she smothers him with a pillow. At the home of the Beverlys she attempts to alienate the children from their mother (Frances Dee), and when the mother orders her to go away, she tries to strangle her. She is finally sent to an insane asylum. The secret room of the title was a room that the owners of the house supposedly knew nothing about and from which the children, who had stumbled upon it, watched Leda kill Jackson.

A fine performance by Judith Evelyn could not lift the season or Viña Delmar's **The Rich Full Life** (11-9-45, Golden) out of the doldrums. Lou Fenwick worries that her frail daughter, Cynthia (Virginia Weidler), who suffers from pernicious anemia, will be forced to lead a life even duller and more restricted than her own, so she is thrilled when Ricky Latham (Jonathan Braman), star of the high school swimming team, asks Cynthia to the senior prom. Against the warnings of Mr. Fenwick (Frederic Tozere) and her mother-in-law (Jessie Busley), she allows Cynthia to go to the dance in the pouring rain. Cynthia becomes deathly ill, but Lou calls Ricky to the girl's bedside, and together they bring on her recovery.

The Rugged Path (11-10-45, Plymouth) marked the return of two figures to Broadway. Playwright Robert Sherwood was back after spending five years working with Roosevelt in the White House; Spencer Tracy, after fifteen years in Hollywood. Tracy fared better than Sherwood. Howard Barnes spoke for many of the aisle-sitters when he told his *Herald Tribune* readers that Sherwood had created "a series of animated editorials rather than a challenging and absorbing play." On the other hand, Tracy was hailed as "splendid, exciting and admirable," "fine," and "solid." Having spent time in England, where he watched the English finally get up real spirit only after the Germans began bombing them, Morey Vinion returns to his job as editor of a newspaper in a middle-sized American city. He has become a convinced liberal and activist. But the paper is run by his weakling brother-in-law (Clinton Sundberg), who is largely influenced by its conservative, pacifist business manager (Lawrence Fletcher). Vinion, urged on by his liberal young Jewish protégé (Rex Williams), publishes an editorial advocating lend-lease to Russia. Since he cannot fire Vinion, the brother-in-law discharges the youngster. As a result Vinion decides to quit and join the navy. He tells his displeased wife (Martha Sleeper), "History has brought us all to a Great Divide, and every one of us has to make his own decision—whether to stay put, or to turn back, or to push over the ridge into the unknown." After America enters the war, the destroyer he serves on is sunk (a sinking effectively simulated "with loud speakers and gradually diminished lights"). Washed up on a small Philippine island, he is killed fighting off the Japs at Banana Beach. At the White House, he is posthumously awarded a medal, which his wife promptly hands over to those who fought with him on the island. Largely because of Tracy, the play ran for ten weeks.

On the 12th the City Center brought back last season's revival of *The Tempest* for three weeks at reduced prices. The same house also brought back the preceding year's *Little Women* for two weeks starting December 23.

Revenants returned in Harry Kleiner's **Skydrift** (11-13-45, Belasco). Just as they are about to jump, seven paratroopers are killed when their plane is hit and explodes. Overruling their sergeant (Alfred Ryder), who says they are better off remaining quietly dead, the men opt to visit their survivors. Two Italian-Americans (Zachary A. Charles and Carl Specht) discover their mother (Lili Valenti) cannot accept their deaths; one man (Arthur Keegan) finds his bride (Olive Deering) of one week hopelessly embittered; another (Eli Wallach) accuses his wife of infidelity; a corporal (Elliot Sullivan) talks of baseball to his son. Even the sergeant finally returns—to confront the girl who jilted him.

The season perked up conspicuously with the arrival of Howard Lindsay and Russel Crouse's **State of the Union** (11-14-45, Hudson), which garnered unanimous rave notices ("an adult, witty play about politics," "wins by a landslide," "a literate and amusing comedy"). It soon went on to win the Pulitzer Prize and chalk up 765 performances. The Republicans, out of power for a dozen years, are desperate to regain the White House. At the prodding of the influential James Conover (Minor Watson), they select an idealistic, millionaire airplane manufacturer, Grant Matthews (Ralph Bellamy). Of course, they are aware that his marriage to his wife, Mary (Ruth Hussey), is on the rocks and that he has become the lover of a powerful newspaper publisher, Kay Thorndike (Kay Johnson). Conover assures Mary that by occupying the White House with Grant she can remove Kay from the picture. There will be no ugliness of any sort. After all, there is only one basic difference between Democrats and Republicans: "They're in—and we're out!" At an important cocktail party, Mary has too much to drink. She points out that by pushing for the many foreign blocs in the country, the Republicans are cynically divisive. She suggests that they are willing to disunite the United Nations, and she asks how long it will be before the Republicans demand we forgive Germany in order to win the German-American vote. Matthews's idealism makes him appreciate Mary's comments, so he declines to run. He may even head an independent third party. (Many critics and playgoers saw more than a touch of the late Wendell Willkie in Matthews.)

Although some critics praised Harry Brown's **A Sound of Hunting** (11-20-45, Lyceum), others disliked it, and the public, no doubt tired of war stories, sided with the naysayers, so the drama closed after three weeks. Just as they are to be relieved, the eight members of the "lucky squad of iron men" led by Sgt. Mooney (Burton Lancaster), holding a position in a ruined house in Cassino, realize that one of their number has not returned for his share of the fruitcake sent the boys by the sister of Pfc. Muller (Kenneth Brauer) and must be trapped between the lines. He is Small, a distressingly inept "little guy with glasses," but the men, having come to believe that their unity has brought them their luck, determine to rescue him. Forgetting his incessant preoccupation with the girls of his dreams back around Bleecker Street, Pvt. Collucci (Sam Levene) heads out to the rescue. But he returns to report that Small is dead.

Some of the season's briefest and most scathing reviews went to Stanley Richards's **Marriage Is for Single People** (11-21-45, Cort), in which Lottie Disenhower (Gertrude Beach), a naive girl from the vineyards near Fresno, having fallen for the romantic line handed her by a rapscallion playwright-turned-naval-officer, comes to visit his family at their New York penthouse and winds up with the officer's nice kid brother.

"This fiendish season's withering touch has not even

spared the most engaging and adroit playwright of recent years," Louis Kronenberger began his *PM* review of John van Druten's **The Mermaids Singing** (11-28-45, Empire). After meeting pretty, young Dee Matthews (Beatrice Pearson) and her navy-man fiancé, Thad Greelis (Walter Starkey), at an out-of-town tryout of his latest comedy about infidelity, the playwright Clement Waterlow (Walter Abel) invites them to his suite for drinks. Thad is called away, allowing Dee to confess to Clement that she has fallen in love with him. He tells her he is married and has two daughters. But he admits to himself that he would enjoy a brief fling. For a time it appears he might succumb. But he finally acknowledges that the mermaids are not singing their songs of love for him, so he and Dee go their separate ways.

Strange Fruit (11-29-45, Royale) was Lillian and Esther Smith's dramatization of Lillian's best-seller. Critics agreed that the work became diffuse and lost much of its power in its transfer to the stage. Numerous noisy and prolonged scene changes also hurt the large-cast (more than thirty) production. In Maxwell, Georgia, Tracy Deen (Melchor Ferrer), the weakling son of the town's doctor, has an affair with a black girl, Nonnie Anderson (Jane White), but when she becomes pregnant he deserts her and embraces religion. To avoid further difficulties, he pays his father's somewhat retarded houseboy (Earl Jones) to marry the girl. Her outraged brother shoots and kills Tracy. Backwater Georgia justice demands a black be killed to atone for a white's murder, so, since the brother has fled, the local vigilantes lynch the houseboy.

Joseph Fields and Jerome Chodorov found few takers for **The French Touch** (12-8-45, Cort), their comedy that unfolded in a long-shuttered Parisian playhouse during the Nazi occupation. The once famous Roublard (Brian Aherne) and his last leading lady, his third wife, Giselle (Jacqueline Dalya), are so down and out that they sleep in a stage box. Then Roublard's first wife, Jacqueline (Arlene Francis), now the mistress of a Nazi officer (John Wengraf), shows up to offer to back the pair if Roublard will mount a piece of Nazi propaganda. He agrees, although he secretly resolves to change the ending of the play at the last minute to defy the Germans. His second wife, Odette (Madeleine Le Beau), also enters the picture to warn him his fellow players will boycott any pro-German work. Roublard is forced to reveal his plan. When the Nazi officer finds out about it, Roublard shoots him before going through with his suicidal performance.

It clearly needed more than deadpan, soft-spoken Charles Butterworth, with his trademarked unfinished sentences, to save John Cecil Holm's **Brighten the Corner** (12-12-45, Lyceum). Jeffrey Q. Talbot, a rich, eccentric inventor who has earned 1800 credits at the Massachusetts Institute of Technology by becoming a lifelong student there, pops in on his nephew (George Petrie) and his nephew's new wife (Phyllis Avery) to give them a $10,000 wedding gift and to promise them an additional $25,000 on the arrival of their first baby. But he manages to arrive just after the wife has stormed out in a huff and as a neighbor's wife (Lenore Lonergan) is using the nephew's shower because hers is on the blink. The nephew quickly introduces the neighbor's wife as his own, so when his own spouse comes contritely back an evening's worth of complications crop up. Butterworth even found occasion to repeat his famous "after-dinner speech," which he had performed decades before in the revue *Americana*.

For much of the war Maurice Evans had been touring the fronts offering his cut-down *Hamlet* to the troops. This "GI Version" eliminated such famous bits as the graveyard scene with its gravediggers and its "Alas, poor Yorick" speech, and was performed in nineteenth-century costumes. Although Kronenberger complained that Evans was "too purely elocutionary," most of his colleagues continued to sing the star's praises and also found kind adjectives for Thomas Gomez's Claudius, Lili Darvas's Gertrude, Thomas Chalmers's Polonius, and Frances Reid's Ophelia. The revival, the first of several soon to open, did seventeen weeks of excellent business at the out-of-the-way Columbus Circle Theatre starting on the 13th before heading for the road.

Elmer Rice abandoned his avant-garde, politically slanted playwriting to present Broadway with a totally commercial comedy and enjoyed one of his biggest hits. The *Journal-American*'s Robert Garland embraced **Dream Girl** (12-14-45, Coronet) as "the best in good, mean fun." The comedy followed a single long day in the life of Georgina Allerton (Betty Field). Georgina, who writes unpublishable novels and runs a small, unprofitable bookstore, awakes to confront the probability of more dreadful hours. To escape them she daydreams. The moment she turns on her radio as she dresses and hears the voice of a broadcasting psychiatrist, she imagines she is on the air with him, pouring out her problems. Her daydreams run to the likes of her becoming a streetwalker, of her having an affair with her brother-in-law (Kevin O'Shea), and of her enjoying a fling in Mexico with a lecherous book-jobber (Edmond Ryan). Her life changes only when she meets Clark Redfield (Wendell Corey), a young man who reviews books he hasn't read and hopes to be a sportswriter. He warns her about the nefarious consequences of all her daydreaming. By two in the morning they have gotten a justice of the peace to marry them. Sitting on a double bed in a Connecticut motel she quotes Kipling, "If you can dream and not make dreams your master," and she assures Clark that her life has turned into "some wonderful dream." Field, who was Mrs. Rice, spent almost the entire play onstage and maneuvered deftly around Jo Mielziner's numerous partial settings, which rolled in and out all evening long. The comedy ran for ten months.

Two plays opened the night after Christmas. First-stringers attended the novelty, S. N. Behrman's **Dunnigan's Daughter** (12-26-45, Golden). They were pleased with neither the play nor the performances. On the other hand, they were not extremely displeased. Most agreed with Wilella Waldorf, the retiring critic for the *Post,* who welcomed "the beguiling Behrman touches" but also found "nothing new nor particularly exciting." A ruthless entrepreneur, Clay Rainer (Dennis King), and his third wife, Ferne (June Havoc), the daughter of an Irish political boss who had facilitated Rainer's rise, are living in their home in Mexico while Rainer bribes officials to push peasants off their land so that he can go ahead with a huge project. She is wooed by a predatory Mexican artist with marked Communist leanings, Miguel Riachi (Luther Adler), who is painting a mural for Rainer. Then her old high school flame, Jim Baird (Richard Widmark), comes back into her life. He is now a State Department official fighting Rainer's land grab. He shows Ferne what her loveless husband is doing and also proves that Rainer was the cause of her father's suicide. When she opts to leave with Baird, Riachi bids her good-bye and tells her she has what few people get in life. "I know, Miguel," she replies, "the second chance."

It fell to second-stringers to review one of the season's major hits, a revival at the Barrymore of Shaw's *Pygmalion.* Since older actresses still regularly were cast as Eliza, no one balked at Gertrude Lawrence's assuming the part, especially since she brought her myriad charms and comic skills to the role. Raymond Massey's Higgins and Melville Cooper's dustman were also applauded. The comedy ran until June.

Critics divided sharply on Arthur Laurents's **Home of the Brave** (12-27-45, Belasco). Chapman called it the best drama yet about World War II; Rascoe was certain it would win the Pulitzer Prize. Others saw it as honest and intelligent, but inept and tedious. Pvt. Coen (Joseph Pevney), known to his friends as Coney, is brought to a field hospital suffering from paralysis of the legs, although he has no wounds. A psychiatrist (Eduard Franz) brings out the fact that the Jewish boy has long been obsessed with anti-Semitism and that he was momentarily glad when his best buddy was killed by the Japs. His buddy (Henry Bernard), in a fit of anger, had been about to call Coney a "lousy yellow Jew" but at the last moment had said "jerk." Coney's guilt at wishing his buddy dead had led to his paralysis. The doctor manages to cure the boy and send him

out in the world better able to confront it. Although Hollywood had long outclassed the theatre in its battle scenes, many critics said that the battle-scene flashbacks were the most gripping part of the drama. The play lingered in hopes of finding an audience, but finally closed after sixty-nine performances.

Vincent McConnor's **A Joy Forever** (1-7-46, Biltmore) proved to be a sixteen-performance dud. Embittered by the scandal that broke many years before when he painted his mistress (Dorothy Sands) in the nude, Benjamin Vinnicum (Guy Kibbee) has lived as a virtual recluse with her in a restored barn overlooking Fort Tryon. Then, suddenly, the critics remember him and his paintings become worth a fortune. He is offered a million dollars for them. Rather than return to the rat race, he gives the pictures away and resumes his quiet life.

The Theatre Guild's revival of Shakespeare's rarely done *The Winter's Tale,* brought into the Cort on the 15th, was coolly received by the press and ran only as long as the Guild's subscription list held out. The cast included Henry Daniell as Leontes, Jessie Royce Landis as Hermione, Florence Reed (who grabbed the best notices) as Paulina, Romney Brent as Autolycus, and Whitford Kane as the Old Shepherd.

Nor were there many cheers for Emmet Lavery's **The Magnificent Yankee** (1-22-46, Royale)—at least not for the play itself. But the universally lauded performances of Louis Calhern ("a characterization of insight, skill and believability") and Dorothy Gish ("a delight and a darling") kept the chronicle on the boards for the rest of the season. What the play chronicled were the highlights of the later career of Oliver Wendell Holmes, beginning with his and his wife's move to Washington in 1902 when he is appointed to the Supreme Court. It continued on to show his dealings with the young Harvard students appointed to assist him, his differences with Teddy Roosevelt (who never appears) and Henry Adams (Fleming Ward), his preparing for his fiftieth class reunion, visits from Owen Wister (Sherling Oliver) and Justice Brandeis (Edgar Barrier), the party held for his eightieth birthday, and, finally, the visit moments after his inauguration of Franklin Roosevelt. Told that President Roosevelt is downstairs, he asks querulously what Teddy Roosevelt could want of him now. But he soon realizes his error. The ninety-two-year-old Holmes turns his back to the audience so that he can face the door through which Roosevelt will come and draws himself up to prepare a soldier's salute for his guest.

There weren't many cheers, either, for Terence Rattigan's **O Mistress Mine** (1-23-46, Empire), but no one cared much since the production's real importance was that it brought the Lunts back to New York after they had spent most of the war years entertaining Londoners.

Part of their time there they had offered the same play as *Love in Idleness*. Unable for political reasons to obtain a divorce, Sir John Fletcher has simply been living with his mistress, Olivia Brown. Olivia's eighteen-year-old son, Michael (Dick Van Patten), had been evacuated to Canada at the start of hostilities. Now his return throws a monkey wrench into the couple's lives. He is not only an ardent left-winger but a prig as well, infuriated by what his mother is doing. Only after Michael finds a love of his own and she likes expensive high life, such as going to the Savoy, can he begin to understand his elders' relationship. By that time there is reason to hope the pair can be married. Barnes noted, "Miss Fontanne can keep a scene fascinating by merely making idle telephone calls to her friends or pounding a typewriter after her stage son has convinced her to mend her ways. Lunt can take mere wisps of a script and come up with a hilarious impersonation." No one could foresee that for the next dozen years the Lunts would appear in nothing but trite vehicles, only at the very end of their careers again finding a solid drama.

The season's second pair of same-night openings, like its first, brought in one hit and one flop. The hit was the season's long-run champ (1642 performances), Garson Kanin's **Born Yesterday** (2-4-46, Lyceum). Although critics applauded the comedy—"one of the more amusing occasions of the season," "a marvelous combination of wit and indignation"—they were quick to point out imperfections, and several insisted the play was not as good as *State of the Union*. Moreover, most seemed to agree with Barnes, who reported, "Douglas deserves most of the acting honors." Time has looked back more affectionately on the leading lady, whose playing, one critic did allow, was hilarious enough to call in the riot squad. Harry Brock (Paul Douglas), a crass, nouveau-riche junkman who always lives "at the top of his voice," is constantly embarrassed by the gaffes of his flat-toned and slightly raspy-lunged "dumb-blonde" mistress, Billie Dawn (Judy Holliday). He hires Paul Verrall (Gary Merrill), a young and handsome liberal writer, to tutor her. In short order Billie comes to see Harry as "not couth." She refuses to co-sign some important papers, prompting him to slap her. A hurt and angry Billie signs the papers, packs her bags, and, heading for the door, requests one last favor from Harry. When he surlily demands to know what the favor might be, she softly asks, "Drop dead?" But Harry soon misses her and wonders if he couldn't find somebody to make Billie dumb again. She returns for the rest of her things and stuns Harry by advising him that she has turned over to Paul incriminating papers capable of landing Harry in prison. Since he long ago had put most of his property in her name, she offers a compromise. The papers will not be made public, and she will sign

back his property to him—but only a bit each year, for as long as he behaves.

The evening's flop was **January Thaw** (2-4-46, Golden), William Roos's theatricalization of Bellamy Partridge's novel. Two liberal, very up-to-date New Yorkers, the highly social Marge Gage (Lulu Mae Hubbard) and her writer-husband, Herbert (Robert Keith), buy and modernize a rundown Connecticut farmhouse. They pay no attention to a clause in the deed of sale that states that the family who lived there years earlier still has the right to reside in the home as long as it chooses. After all, the Rockwoods moved away so many years before, they must be dead. But the Gages are no sooner settled in than the Rockwoods (Charles Middleton and Helen Carew) show up. They prove to be archly conservative Coolidge Republicans who prefer outhouses, chamber pots, and wood stoves. A clash of cultures ensues before an eleven-o'clock accommodation is reached. (In the original novel the Gages win out on a legal technicality.)

There were no city slickers in Kenyon Nicholson and Charles Robinson's **Apple of His Eye** (2-5-46, Biltmore), which critics felt was a sorry vehicle for Walter Huston, in what turned out to be his final Broadway appearances. But Huston's popularity and his own "flawless performance" propelled the comedy along for fourteen weeks. Sam Stover, a widowed Indiana farmer and Sunday school superintendent well into his fifties, hires attractive, twentyish Lily Tobin (Mary James) to keep house for him while his regular housekeeper is in the hospital. He soon is showing signs of being smitten by the girl. His nosy neighbor, Stella Springer (Doro Merande), and his selfish daughter-in-law (Mary Wickes) are shocked when he takes the girl out for a chop-suey dinner. At one point Stella calls him an old rooster, leading him to retort, "I may be an old rooster, Stella, but thank the Lord, I'm no old hen." However, when he tries to show off for Lily and hurts his back while wrestling a husky fireman at the local carnival, his family and neighbors demand he dismiss the girl. "Life is sure short and full of blisters," one sympathetic neighbor (Roy Fant) commiserates. Sam finally bows to all the pressure, but when Lily returns to Maple Lawn Farm to say farewell, he realizes how much he loves her and defiantly proposes marriage. Lily accepts.

During the war Jean Anouilh had offered Paris his version of Sophocles' tragedy about a girl who defies authority to bury her brother. Many Parisians saw it as a discreetly coded slap at their Nazi occupiers. Now Katharine Cornell brought this version of **Antigone** (2-18-46, Cort) to America in Lewis Galantiere's highly colloquial adaptation. The evening was performed in modern dress—the men in evening clothes and smoking cigarettes, the women in gowns—with only draperies and a few spare furnishings for scenery and without intermission. Critics found the hour-and-forty-minute entertainment "more interesting than satisfying," while Cornell, in an unheard-of situation, found herself outshone by the forceful Creon of Cedric Hardwicke. The play struggled along for sixty-four performances. Toward the end of its visit, Cornell, on April 3, began some performances of *Candida* in repertory with the tragedy. Hardwicke was Mr. Burgess; Marlon Brando, Marchbanks; Wesley Addy, Morell; and Mildred Natwick, Miss Garnett.

The season's third look at racial discrimination was Robert Ardrey's **Jeb** (2-21-46, Martin Beck). Jeb (Ossie Davis), a black man, returns from the war minus a leg but with a Silver Star and a Purple Heart. In a Negro bar in a northern city he is slipped a Mickey Finn and robbed. Returning to his Louisiana home, he seeks a job operating an adding machine. The open-minded owner of a mill, who has just fired a malingerer, agrees to hire him. But the malingerer spreads the rumor that Jeb is cavorting with a white girl. Jeb is run out of town. However, once back north again he decides he must return home and battle for his rights.

Then the season exploded in a bigger battle. Chapman called **Truckline Cafe** (2-27-46, Belasco) "the worst play I have seen since I have been in the reviewing business," and Nichols suggested the author wrote the play "with his left hand and, it is to be feared, in the dark of the moon." The other critics were equally severe. But since the author was Maxwell Anderson, he was not about to take such criticism lightly. He bought ads in the major papers calling the critics "so many incompetents and irresponsibles" and "a sort of Jukes family of journalism." The Jukes, it developed, were an upstate New York clan notorious for their history of poverty and crime. Anderson's play, set in a road stop between Los Angeles and San Francisco, told several stories at once. One dealt with an inebriated sailor (Karl Malden) who has too many girls on his hands. Another told of a veteran (Marlon Brando) who returns to seek out his unfaithful wife (Ann Shepherd), drags her to the cabin in which she had been unfaithful, and kills her. Anderson's principal story was similar, but with a happy ending. Anne (Virginia Gilmore), thinking her husband (Richard Waring) dead in the war, has an affair. When she learns her husband is alive, she has an abortion and takes a job as a waitress at the road stop, believing her husband will never find her there. He does, but since he, too, has been unfaithful, the couple are reconciled. For all the brouhaha, the play was withdrawn after thirteen performances.

Marie Baumer's **Little Brown Jug** (3-6-46, Martin Beck) died after five performances without any fuss. Broadway and filmdom's perennial Yankee, Percy Kilbride, was featured. When her perpetually besotted son-in-law (Ronald Alexander) refuses to grant her daughter (Marjorie Lord) a divorce, Irene Haskell (Katharine Alexander) slaps him. He loses his balance, falls through the window of a Maine cabin, and is killed. Ira (Kilbride), a slightly batty local handyman, witnesses the accident and threatens to claim the death was murder unless the women take him into their home. "You hit him, didn't you, and he died? You said you wanted to kill him, didn't you? That's what I would have to tell the police." Back in their Connecticut home, he drives away their servant and alienates them from their neighbors until the dead man's brother (Arthur Margetson) exposes him.

The villain of Robert and Sally Wilder's **Flamingo Road** (3-19-46, Belasco), which the couple took from Robert's novel, was far more malevolent. Titus Semple (Francis J. "Happy" Felton) is an obese, corrupt Florida sheriff and political boss, who spends most of his time in a rocking chair on the porch of a local hotel. He takes an immediate dislike to Lane Ballou (Judith Parrish), a girl who is stranded in his town after a carnival she has worked for as a cooch dancer folds and who has taken up with one of his henchmen. He has her fired from any job she gets, has her falsely arrested for prostitution, and sends her to prison. Later he attempts to frame a man (Philip Bourneuf) who would protect her. When she finally is driven to shoot him as he rocks smugly on the porch, an understanding local publisher (Will Geer) testifies that Semple's dying words were that he was shot by unknown men in a passing car. The play's only redeeming feature seems to have been its imaginative settings—the hotel porch, a prison yard, and some interiors—by Watson Barratt.

In early January 1922, the Theatre Guild had presented a mounting of Leonid Andreyev's *He Who Gets Slapped,* which told of a man who takes refuge from an unhappy marriage by becoming a clown in a circus and who kills himself and a young bareback rider with whom he has fallen in love when he learns her father is about to sell the girl to a dissolute rich man. The Guild revived the play at the Booth on the 20th in a new translation by Judith Guthrie and in a sumptuous staging by Tyrone Guthrie. Dennis King had the main role (rechristened "Funny" instead of simply "He"). Although several critics admired the play, most found its apparent subtexts as baffling as ever. Playgoers would not come, so the production closed after six weeks.

The much admired refugee comedian Oscar Karlweis was unable to save A. B. Shiffrin's dreary and obvious

I Like It Here (3-22-46, Golden). He played Willie Kringle, who takes a job as handyman at the home of a henpecked professor (Bert Lytell). Willie not only gets the man to stand up to his harridan wife (Beverly Bayne), but sees to it the daughter (Mardi Bryant) of the family weds the young taxi driver (William Terry) she loves instead of the sleazy politician (Donald Randolph) her mother would foist on her.

Walter and Jean Kerr's dramatization of Franz Werfel's **The Song of Bernadette** (3-26-46, Belasco) told of how a poor miller's daughter (Elizabeth Ross) at Lourdes in 1858 is addressed by the Virgin Mary, is scoffed at by family and friends for her claims, but helps give rise to the shrine there and enters a nunnery. Since a film version had recently been a huge success, the play found no takers and closed after three playings.

Years earlier Gustav Blum had enjoyed some lengthy runs on rooftop theatres with his cheap-priced attractions. He returned to producing to offer **Walk Hard** (3-27-46, Chanin) at a small auditorium high up in a Manhattan skyscraper and at a $3 top. The play, like *Anna Lucasta*, had first been done—two years before—by the American Negro Theatre in Harlem. Abram Hill adapted it from Len Zinberg's novel *Walk Hard—Talk Aloud*. It recounted the battles Andy Whitman (Maxwell Granville), a black prizefighter, must win to overcome the prejudice and gangsterism all around him. Mickey Walker, former welterweight and middleweight champion, made his acting debut as a happy-go-lucky pug. Broadway was not interested.

To many liberals the reactionary, patently bigoted McCormick-Patterson clan must have seemed like sitting ducks. Certainly they did to Sam and Bella Spewack. But their attempt to spoof them in **Woman Bites Dog** (4-17-46, Belasco) proved dismayingly unfunny and disappeared after five performances. Commander Southworth [read Colonel Robert R. McCormick of the *Chicago Tribune*] (Taylor Holmes) heads a leading Chicago newspaper. His brother, Major Southworth [read Joseph Medill Patterson of New York's *Daily News*] (Royal Beal) has a Manhattan tabloid. Their cousin Lizzie Southworth [read Cissy Patterson of the *Washington Times*] (Anne Shoemaker) is duenna of a Washington paper. Hopkins (Kirk Douglas), a decorated air force hero who has returned home to edit his small-town Danville newspaper and who was angered by the family's right-wing slanting of the news all during the war, decides to humiliate the commander. He comes to the commander's office and tells him that little Danville has been seized by the Communists, who have confiscated his and all other businesses in town. The commander, who sees red whenever the word "Communist" is mentioned, sends an ace reporter, Betty Lord (Mercedes McCambridge), to get all the horrific facts. She quickly realizes the whole thing is a hoax, but since she has just as quickly fallen in love with Hopkins and shares his disdain for her boss, she writes a series of fictionalized articles designed to humiliate the commander when the truth comes out. Taylor Holmes as the blustering publisher gave what many considered the funniest performance of his career, but it marked the end of that career—a career plagued by such poor choices of vehicles that he never realized the bright future predicted for him many decades earlier.

The Belasco, which had housed so many quick flops during the season, among them *Home of the Brave*, that wags were calling it the Fiasco, now hosted the season's second look at anti-Semitism, Don Appell's **This, Too, Shall Pass** (4-30-46, Belasco). During the war, Mac Sorrell (Sam Wanamaker) had saved the life of his closest soldier friend, Buddy Alexander (Walter Starkey), and had enjoyed a long correspondence with Buddy's sister, Janet (Jan Sterling). Mac and Janet had even become engaged by mail. But when he finally meets Janet and her family, and tells them he is Jewish, Janet's mother (Kathryn Givney) becomes so furiously intolerant that Mac rushes to leave. Buddy hurries out to stop him but is accidentally run over and killed by Mac's car. Mr. Alexander (Ralph Morgan) blames his wife for the tragedy, while Mac and Janet decide to wed despite her mother's unrelenting hatred.

For many, the most exciting and satisfying event of the season was the six-week engagement of England's celebrated Old Vic company, which opened its stand at the large Century on May 6. Four programs were offered: the two parts of Shakespeare's *Henry IV*, Chekhov's *Uncle Vanya*, and a double bill of Sheridan's *The Critic* and Sophocles' *Oedipus*. Some critics complained of a certain dragginess in the Russian play, but the other presentations were greeted ecstatically. Both the impeccable ensemble playing (virtually unknown in America) and individual performances were glowingly praised, among the latter Ralph Richardson's definitve Falstaff and Laurence Olivier's harrowing Oedipus, with its final bloodcurdling scream.

Along with revenants, the season's most recurring theme was America's racial problem. It cropped up for a fifth time in Maxine Wood's **On Whitman Avenue** (5-8-46, Cort). While her parents are away on vacation from their two-family home in a midwestern suburb, Toni Tilden (Perry Wilson), a liberal college student, rents the empty half of the house to Jeff Hall (Canada Lee), a decorated black war hero, and his family. (Note how often playwrights loaded their cases by making the black a decorated hero instead of just a more ordinary man.) Many of the neighbors are outraged, and, when her family returns, her mother (Ernestine Barrier) and brother (Martin Miller) side with the protesters, while her father (Will Geer) defends her. In the end, Hall and his family are forced to move back to a crowded, rat-infested inner-city apartment.

As far as Broadway was concerned the season ended glumly with Ben Hecht and Charles MacArthur's appropriately titled **Swan Song** (5-15-46, Booth), taken from an earlier, failed play by Ramon Romero and Harriet Hinsdale. Leo Pollard (David Ellen), a would-be pianist, was committed to a mental institution after the sudden, mysterious death of his sister, a far more promising pianist. Now released, he calls on his sister's professor (Theodore Goetz) to help him resume his career. But when he discovers that the professor's current favorite student (Jacqueline Horner) is a brilliant prodigy, he attempts to poison her. This leads the professor to trick him into confessing he murdered his sister and also probably the gardener (Ivan Simpson) from whom he stole the poison.

Off Broadway continued to slowly flex its wings all season. Among its leading organizations were the American Negro Theatre and the Blackfriars' Guild. The Guild closed its season with a play that had been awarded a National Theatre Conference prize two years before, Robert Anderson's **Come Marching Home** (5-18-46, Blackfriars'). It could be perceived as a poor man's *State of the Union*. An idealistic young college professor, home from the war, is pressured into accepting a draft to run for state senator. His party hopes to overthrow the entrenched machine. But when he realizes that his own party is as corrupt and cynical as the opposition, the professor backs off and considers running as an independent. A few more years would pass before Anderson won Broadway's attention.

1946–1947

"This has been a year of revivals, but not one of revival, in the theatre," Burns Mantle wailed. He was right. While the count of new plays remained roughly steady— at between forty-two and forty-six, depending on which tally was employed—the number of revivals, including musicals, soared to between seventeen and twenty-six. Of course, any healthy theatre ought to enjoy a good number of revivals, a testimony to its sense of balance and history. But the discouraging side of this picture was the paucity of novelties critics and playgoers could unstintingly rejoice in.

The season began drearily enough with N. Richard Nash's **Second Best Bed** (6-3-46, Barrymore), starring the long-absent Ruth Chatterton, who also served as co-producer and co-director. As the title hinted, the play dealt with Shakespeare (Barry Thomson) and Anne Hathaway. Shakespeare returns briefly from his busy London schedule to visit the wife he has left behind in Stratford. He finds she is in the process of seeking a divorce and plans to marry a local bailiff named Poggs (Ralph Forbes). There are some heated arguments, including Anne's breaking a demijohn over the playwright's head, and much quoting from his plays, before Will manages to foist the town trollop, Nell (Elizabeth Eustis), on Poggs and reclaim Anne. Folksinger Richard Dyer-Bennett strolled through the proceedings singing period songs while accompanying himself on a modern guitar.

The same night saw Maurice Evans bring back his GI version of *Hamlet* for two weeks at popular prices at the City Center.

Some still living theatrical figures, thinly disguised, were the subject of Milton Lewis and Julian Funt's **The Dancer** (6-5-46, Biltmore). The figures in question were Nijinsky, his wife, and his impresario, Sergei Diaghilev. Sergei Krainine (Anton Dolin), once the world's greatest ballet artist, has long been too mentally ill to perform and has been kept secluded by the perverted Aubrey Stewart (Colin Keith-Johnston) in a Paris apartment. The police suspect Krainine of murdering a prostitute but cannot prove it. His wife (Helen Flint), long denied access to him by Stewart, forces her way into the apartment determined to discover the whereabouts of a box for which she holds the key and which she believes contains the family's fortune. His daughter (Bethel Leslie) comes, hoping to learn if her father's insanity is hereditary. Stewart goads Krainine into killing the wife, then he himself is murdered by the dancer as the police close in. Dolin, not the best of actors, was allowed to perform a few brief dances to some "eerie" Paul Bowles music.

Claire Parrish's **Maid in the Ozarks** (7-15-46, Belasco), sometimes known as *Blue Mountain,* had been touring the country for five years, blithely advertising itself as "the worst play in the world," and chalking up amazingly long runs in defiance of critical shellackings. It did not attract a typically elegant Broadway first-night audience. Instead, as George Jean Nathan reported, it drew a crowd whose men "did not wear collars or ties and that, on its female side, looked as if it been fished out of Sheepshead Bay at low tide." He assailed the play as "dramatic halitosis." Two sisters, waitresses from Little Rock, come to a small burg in the Ozarks, where one of the girls, Lydia Tolliver (Johnee Williams), a former bigamist, has hooked a handsome mountaineer, Temple Calhoun (Jon Dawson). But after an evening's worth of jokes that another critic branded "a feast of coprophilia," she runs off with an artist (John Calvert) who painted her in the nude. Her sister (Gloria Humphries) settles in with Temple. Despite unanimous pans, the comedy lingered for thirteen weeks.

Ben Hecht and Charles MacArthur's *The Front Page* (8-14-28) was revived at the Royale on September 4, with Lew Parker as Hildy Johnson and Arnold Moss as Walter Burns. Most critics retained their fondness for this roughhouse comedy of newspaper life, but felt the cast and the staging lacked the requisite oomph. Ten weeks and it was gone.

The American League for a Free Palestine was the producer of **A Flag Is Born** (9-5-46, Alvin), the blatantly propagandistic pageant for which Hecht claimed sole authorship. At a graveyard somewhere in eastern Europe, Tevya (Paul Muni), an old Jew, and his frail wife, Zelda (Celia Adler), stop to rest on their way to Palestine. The exhausted man envisions a comfortable service in a fine synagogue, then talks with the biblical Saul (George David Baxter) about the need to fight for a Jewish homeland and finally heeds the advice of Solomon (Gregory Morton) to appeal to the Court of Nations, which merely promises to take the matter under advisement. First the weary Zelda dies, then Tevya. But a much younger Jew, David (Marlon Brando), whom the couple befriended, after rejecting the idea of killing himself, takes up Tevya's scarf as a banner and heads on to battle. While critics rejected the play, they admired the spectacle and, more especially, the fine acting of Muni and Brando. The play ran fifteen weeks.

Agatha Christie had no luck with **Hidden Horizon** (9-19-46, Plymouth), which she took from her own novel and West End play *Murder on the Nile*. A newlywed English lady (Barbara Joyce) is murdered while honeymooning on a Nile steamer. Then her maid (Edith Kingdon), who may point a finger at the murderer, is killed. A clergyman (Halliwell Hobbes) takes it upon himself to solve the crimes. Who is the killer? The husband's jilted mistress (Diana Barrymore), a leftish aristocrat (David Manners), a strange German doctor (Peter Van Zerneck), the husband himself (Blair Davies), or several other possible suspects? "It's a very bad business," the vessel's steward (Charles Alexander) notes, and critic after critic seized on the line to sum up his feelings.

Several critics also pointed out that if Louise Morgan (Barbara Robbins) had simply told her three young daughters she had married Tack Cooper (Russell Hardie) while vacationing in Mexico, there would have been no need for Frederick Kohner and Albert Mannheimer to waste their time with **The Bees and the Flowers** (9-26-46, Cort). But since she didn't, the oldest (Rosemary Rice) of the girls makes a play for Tack when he comes as a supposed guest to their house. The younger girls (Sybil Stocking and Joyce Van Patten) still hope their father, a foreign correspondent who deserted his clan, will return. By the final curtain the youngsters have accepted their new daddy.

Was **Obsession** (10-1-46, Plymouth) a "new" play or a revival? In October 1928, New Yorkers had applauded *Jealousy*, Eugene Walter's translation of Louis Verneuil's two-character Paris success *Monsieur Lambertier*, with Fay Bainter and John Halliday. Now this story of a newlywed man who decides his wife's relationship with her guardian has not been all it should have been and who rushes off to murder him was rewritten and its characters renamed by Jane Hinton. But Basil Rathbone and Eugenie Leontovich seemed miscast, so the production was quickly withdrawn.

A hot jazz combo is playing away as the curtain rises on Orin Jannings's **Hear That Trumpet** (10-7-46, Playhouse). The group consists of several somewhat embittered white war veterans and their more happy-go-lucky black clarinetist (Sidney Bechet). Erica Marlowe (Audra Lindley) gets her rich lover, Alonzo Armonk (Frank Conroy), to underwrite the group, but when he realizes that she has married the trumpeter, Dinger Richardson (Bobby Sherwood), he sets about to destroy it. He uses racial prejudice and obliging gangsters to create problems. Erica has no choice but to poison his tea and then attempt suicide. The drugged Alonzo is killed in an auto accident, but Dinger saves Erica in the nick of time. The combo is once again blaring away happily as the curtain falls. The play was the much admired Arthur Hopkins's last production, although later in the season he would direct a revival of one of his old hits.

Edmond Rostand's 1897 French classic, *Cyrano de Bergerac,* once again was welcomed by American critics and playgoers when José Ferrer presented himself in the leading role at the Alvin on the 8th. A pleased Louis Kronenberger observed in *PM* that the star had given it "all the dash and strut it needs, and gone on to exploit its color and humor, and not overplay its all too tempting pathos." A fine supporting cast and the "warm romantic colors and sweeping vistas" of Lemuel Ayer's settings added to the evening, which played to strong houses for just short of six months.

After more than a decade of silence, Eugene O'Neill offered a new play, **The Iceman Cometh** (10-9-46, Martin Beck). Back in 1912, Harry Hope's rather seedy bar can depend on its down-and-out, besotted habitués, who sit about sipping their booze and dreaming their improbable dreams of a better life. These regulars include a Harvard-trained lawyer, Willie Oban (E. G.

Marshall), a Boer War general, Piet Wetjoen (Frank Twedell), an unfrocked army captain, James Cameron (Nicholas Joy), an old newspaperman (Russell Collins), a former anarchist, Larry Slade (Carl Benton Reid), and one newcomer, a frightened young drifter, Dan Parritt (Paul Crabtree). And, of course, there is Harry (Dudley Digges), a former Tammany ward heeler, and his amiable barman, Rocky Pioggi (Tom Pedi). Their inertia is shattered by a visit from a traveling hardware salesman, Theodore Hickman (James Barton), familiarly known as "Hickey." Hickey informs the barflies that he is out for a toot, since his wife is busy with the iceman. He would make the others rid themselves of "the damned guilt that makes you lie to yourselves you're something you're not, and the remorse that nags at you and makes you hide behind lousy pipe dreams about tomorrow." Hickey's talk prompts Slade into goading Parritt into committing suicide. But his talk goes for naught when he confesses that he has murdered his wife and that the "iceman" is Death. The police remove Hickey, and the men return to their whiskey and their illusions, without which they cannot survive. Based on O'Neill's 1917 short story "Tomorrow," the four-hour-long play, which paused so that the patrons could have dinner, was generally welcomed by the critics, although many of them felt it could have been cut without damage. Thus Howard Barnes wrote in the *Herald Tribune* that the work was "mystical and mystifying. . . . The stuff of a great and moving tragedy gleams through scene after scene of the drama, but it has not been properly refined." Some critics also faulted Barton's Hickey, but all lauded realistic yet poetic settings by Robert Edmond Jones, which showed the bar and back room from two different perspectives. The play ran for 136 performances.

For the second time in the season a balladeer (James Robertson) attempted to embellish a failed comedy. Edward E. Paramore, Jr.'s **Mr. Peebles and Mr. Hooker** (10-10-46, Music Box), taken from a novel by Charles G. Givens, was set in Tennessee in 1939. Mr. Peebles (Howard Smith), dressed in overalls, pays a visit to Brother Alf Leland (Paul Huber), whose grandson, Wally (Tom Coley), is also considering becoming a preacher. The rich Mrs. Craine (Randee Sanford), whose husband (Neil McFee Skinner) is busy dynamiting union meetings, attempts to seduce the boy. She is prodded on to this "pleasure sinning" by the red-garbed Mr. Hooker (Rhys Williams), who likes to sit in his shack, heated even in the summer by a fiery stove, and look at pinups with a magnifying glass. All hell breaks loose after the dynamiting and after Wally spurns Mrs. Craine. There are riots, and a young carpenter (Jeff Morrow), who preaches peace and love and who calls Peebles "father," is nearly lynched. Mrs. Craine shoots Wally. But Peebles dons a gold cape, miraculously

cures Wally's wound, and performs other wonders. He has Wally and the young man's sweetheart (Dorothy Gilchrist) flee the area together. Then he takes a Stillson wrench, opens the sluice gates of a nearby dam, and floods the region. The clumsy allegory found no takers.

On the other hand, a magnificently beautiful if slightly stiff revival of Oscar Wilde's *Lady Windermere's Fan* came into the Cort on the 14th and ran until late April. The sumptuous settings and costumes were by England's Cecil Beaton. The regal Cornelia Otis Skinner was Mrs. Erlynne, and the glamorous Penelope Ward was Lady Windermere. Their supporting cast included Henry Daniell and Estelle Winwood.

A second revival, John Webster's blood-and-thunder *The Duchess of Malfi*, in an adaptation by W. H. Auden, was brought into the Barrymore the next evening, but did not fare nearly as well. Most reviewers reserved their kind words for Elisabeth Bergner in the title role. They considered Canada Lee's attempt to play the treacherous Bosola in whiteface as freakish.

Dale Eunson and Katherine Albert's **Loco** (10-16-46, Biltmore) told of Waldo Brewster (Jay Fassett), a successful, long-married Wall Street broker, who decides to have a fling with a beautiful, redheaded Conover model, Loco Dempsey (Jean Parker). He takes her to his hunting lodge in Maine, where she promptly comes down with the measles. While he is nursing her back to health, she talks him into forgiving his pregnant daughter (Elaine Stritch), whom he disowned for running off with a ballroom dancer, and into returning to his faithful if fluttery wife (Beverly Bayne). She even assures him she has no intention of making trouble for him. She's just a nice girl.

There were more obstreperous women in the latest revival of *Lysistrata*, which came into the Belasco on the 17th, employing the same Gilbert Seldes translation used back in 1930 and an all-black cast. Neither the players nor the staging was much applauded. Some critics were amused that the evening ended with the classically dressed performers doing a celebratory jitterbug.

John Golden returned to a theme he had often embraced when he produced Hagar Wilde's **Made in Heaven!** (10-24-46, Henry Miller's), a nice American marriage gone awry then restored. After a spat with his wife (Carmen Mathews) of ten years, Zachary Meredith (Donald Cook) runs off to a bar and seeks romance with a pretty redhead (Ann Thomas). His wife stumbles on the tryst and in revenge takes up with a suave foreigner (Louis Borel). But by the final curtain the Merediths are once again snug in their own home. Wilde derived the play from her own short story.

A revival of J. M. Synge's *The Playboy of the Western World* at the Booth on the 26th featured Burgess

Meredith in the leading role. Most aisle-sitters enjoyed his acting, but with caveats which varied from critic to critic. For many, Mildred Natwick's man-mad Widow Quin walked away with acting honors. Largely unnoticed in small roles were such future stars as Julie Harris and Maureen Stapleton. The revival lingered for ten weeks.

Like several other Noel Coward plays, his **Present Laughter** (10-29-46, Plymouth) was given dismissive notices on its initial outing and went on to become something of a classic. For a second time in a row—and in what would prove his last Broadway appearance—the lithe, slightly epicene Clifton Webb assumed a role Coward had first played in the West End. His Gary Essendine is an exceedingly vain, exceedingly popular leading man, pursued by a flock of beautiful women. After an evening of Cowardish repartee, he takes off with his former wife (Doris Dalton).

In Anita Loos's **Happy Birthday** (10-31-46, Broadhurst), Addie Bemis, a timid little Newark librarian, comes to the gaudily neoned Jersey Mecca Cocktail Lounge to warn the bank-clerk-of-her-dreams (Louis Jean Heydt) that her boozy, belligerent father (Robert Burton) is on the warpath. Daddy is filled with strange notions, which she remarks "come in bottles." Prompted by two of the bar's harpies (Grace Valentine and Enid Markey), she takes her first drinks, including a Pink Lady, a cocktail she has always been assured was "a tart's drink." Before long she is tangoing and fandangoing, watching as objects such as her tiny handbag grow out of all proportion, and staring at bottles which seem to light up in fascinating, glowing colors. She even has a brief love scene under the table. In the end, she weans the bank clerk from a brazen Jezebel, Myrtle (Jacqueline Page). Critics waved away the play as a claptrap vehicle, but rejoiced that its star, Helen Hayes, was having such a good time. Richard Watts, Jr., now critic for the *Post,* reported, "It is a vaudeville act, a one-women show, an actress' field day . . . and again you see that Helen Hayes, even if she is taking a kind of on-stage vacation, remains one of the great actresses of the world." Solely because of its star, the comedy ran for 614 performances.

Classic-style repertory returned to New York with the opening on November 6 of the American Repertory Theatre at the out-of-the-way International Theatre on Columbus Circle. Its guiding lights were three of the theatre's most dedicated ladies—Cheryl Crawford, Eva Le Gallienne, and Margaret Webster. Besides Le Gallienne and Webster, its roster of performers included Walter Hampden, Ernest Truex, and Victor Jory, plus, in small roles, such future stars as Eli Wallach and Anne Jackson. The opening bill was Shakespeare's *Henry VIII,* followed on the 8th by James M. Barrie's *What Every Woman Knows,* and on the 12th by Ibsen's *John Gabriel Borkman.* At first all the critics leaned over backwards to be kind and helpful, although their reviews varied greatly. But after a while an unhappy consensus began to seep through, suggesting that the selections were wrong, the plays often miscast, and the acting, at best, competent but disappointing. On December 19, the troupe offered a double bill of Shaw's *Androcles and the Lion* and Sean O'Casey's *Pound on Demand*; on February 27, Sidney Howard and Paul de Kruiff's *Yellow Jack*; and on April 5, the play that had almost saved Le Gallienne's earlier ensemble, her version of *Alice in Wonderland.* This last mounting enjoyed some success and ran, after pure repertory was largely jettisoned, for 100 performances. But by then, the enterprise was hopelessly doomed. An attempt to revive it the next season survived only for a short spell.

Dennis Hoey's **The Haven** (11-13-46, Playhouse), taken from a novel by Anthony Gilbert, spotlighted Edmund Durward (Hoey), a man who marries rich women and murders them for their money. His next victim would be Agatha Forbes (Valerie Cossart), until her landlady (Viola Roche) becomes suspicious. Those suspicions cost the landlady her life, and she is stuffed into a trunk onstage. But with the police hot on his trail, Durward swallows the poison he had intended for his bride.

Three superior plays arrived in quick succession and enlivened a season in desperate need of excitement. Hordes of unruly, screaming movie fans made it difficult for critics and playgoers to head in to see the return of Ingrid Bergman to live theatre. Her play was Maxwell Anderson's **Joan of Lorraine** (11-18-46, Alvin). On a bare stage, a play about Joan of Arc is starting rehearsals, with Mary Grey in the leading role and toughminded, obsessed Jimmy Masters (Sam Wanamaker) as its director. Mary's idea of Joan is far more idealistic than Jimmy's hardened, pragmatic approach. He is forced to show Mary the compromises he and she must make merely to get the show onstage. Mary finally accepts his approach, understanding that even Joan "will compromise in little things, in things that don't matter, but when it comes to her Voices and what she believes she will not tell one lie—or live one lie!" The rehearsals, with some costumes and scenery finally added, proceed, and Mary finds the proper fervor with which to imbue the part. Critics passed over the play with perfunctory compliments and concentrated on Bergman, who clearly surprised and awed them. The *World-Telegram*'s William Hawkins said she performed "without tricks," and continued, "She builds the two parts she is playing in a paralleled rise, until both have become realized selves. It is done with conviction and inner intensity." The play ran six months at its large house.

Act Two: 1944–1959

The same critics were never surprised by Ina Claire, who long since had been acknowledged as America's duenna of high comedy. Her gifts turned George Kelly's often observant, frequently delightful, and virtually plotless **The Fatal Weakness** (11-19-46, Royale) into a beguiling evening. According to Ward Morehouse of the *Sun,* she played her part "so archly, so artfully, so effortlessly that I'm now wondering how we managed to go through five long years without her." The weakness of the impossibly romantic Mrs. Espenshade is her penchant for attending weddings, even if she does not know either the bride or groom. Her daughter, Penny (Jennifer Howard), does not share her romantic notions. Indeed, she looks on her own husband, who loves her every bit as much as the day he married her, as "a case of arrested development." But troubles arise when Mrs. Espenshade learns that her husband (Howard St. John) is having a passionate affair with a female osteopath. A divorce is agreed to. Penny is shocked to discover that her mother is willing to "let go gracefully," and she sees her husband with new eyes. At the same time, her mother is planning to head off to enjoy herself at her former husband's second wedding. Largely because of its star, the comedy ran for 119 performances.

Lillian Hellman's **Another Part of the Forest** (11-20-46, Fulton) looked at *The Little Foxes*'s Hubbard clan twenty or so years before the action of that earlier hit. The new work was set in 1880. Marcus Hubbard (Percy Waram), who runs his family with a tightfisted, iron hand, made his money during the Civil War by blockade running and extortion. His sons, Ben (Leo Genn) and Oscar (Scott McKay), and his daughter, Regina (Patricia Neal), are determined to break free of his tyrannical rule. Ben finds a way when his slightly weak-minded mother (Mildred Dunnock) shows him proof that his father led Union forces to a spot where they could massacre a troop of local Confederates. A gloating, cynical Ben assures Marcus that he will plead with their neighbors to spare the old man's life, and he adds, "Better than that. I'll come tomorrow morning and cut you down from the tree, and bury you with respect." Marcus is forced to buy Ben's silence by handing over to him all his wealth. Regina is shocked to find Ben sitting in his father's chair and eating at his father's special table. But when she realizes what has happened, she ignores her father's suggestion to sit next to him. Instead, she moves her chair over to Ben's and pours his coffee. Brooks Atkinson, having resumed his seat as critic for the *Times,* lamented that the play seemed "a deluxe edition of a dime novel," but granted it had "great theatrical intensity." Although in recent years the play has enjoyed a number of reconsiderations, its initial run was a disappointing 182 performances.

But then Jean Paul Sartre's much ballyhooed *Huis-clos,* brought to Broadway in Paul Bowles's translation as **No Exit** (11-26-46, Biltmore), eked out a mere thirty-one performances after it received thumbs-down notices. The long one-acter—an hour and a half—was set in what seemed like a dismal hotel room in Hell. There a lesbian (Annabella), a vain, sensual woman (Ruth Ford) who killed her illegitimate child, and a sadistic wartime collaborator (Claude Dauphin) find themselves doomed to a horrid eternity together, since the lesbian cannot have the other woman, that other woman cannot seduce the man, and he can find no happiness with his roommates. Hell, in short, is other people.

Henry R. Misrock's **A Family Affair** (11-27-46, Playhouse) describes what happens after a young playwright (Joel Marston) writes a play about his parents' unsatisfactory marriage. As a result, the father (John Williams) runs off with his secretary (Jewell Curtis), and the mother (Ann Mason) dallies with a psychoanalyst (Frank Lyon). Even the writer's neighbors see themselves in minor characters. But everyone finally consents to forgive and forget.

Audiences first meet Moss Hart's **Christopher Blake** (11-30-46, Music Box) at the White House, where the president (Irving Fisher, made up to resemble Truman) is giving him an award. But when the president suggests that Christopher's parents must be very proud, there is an awkward moment until Christopher (Richard Tyler) informs him his parents are busy getting a divorce. Christopher then shoots and kills himself. But it is all a dream, a fantasy of the unhappy young teenager whose parents are, in fact, separating. He subsequently fantasizes that he is a great actor whose emoting drives his mother (Martha Sleeper) to teary repentance, then that he is a South American explorer who comes across his parents working in a poorhouse and tells them they are not his real parents. When a judge finally insists that Christopher choose between his mother and father (Shepperd Strudwick), he chooses to live with the latter. Not unlike Hart's story for the musical *Lady in the Dark,* several revolving stages were required for the clumsy, noisy scene changes. The *Journal-American*'s Robert Garland called the play "a showy showpiece which might have been a play of plays." Despite similar dismissals the production ran for 114 performances.

Greeted by far more embracing notices, such as John Chapman's saluting it in the *Daily News* as "a little treasure of a play," Ruth Gordon's autobiographical **Years Ago** (12-3-46, Mansfield) ran out the season. Back in 1913, Ruth Jones (Patricia Kirkland) has decided to become an actress after watching Hazel Dawn in *The Pink Lady.* To the dismay of her crusty father, Clinton (Fredric March), she rejects his plan for her to train as a physical education teacher. She also spurns the suit of a pleasant Harvard man (Richard Simon).

Not even being turned down by the Castle Square acting company discourages her. Her sole support, and that is somewhat reluctant, comes from her mother (Florence Eldridge), who begs her to "consider being normal." But in the end, Ruth brings even her father around, so while he has just lost his $37.50-a-week job and cannot give her the $50 he promised her for going-away money, he gives her his most prized possession, a spyglass from his younger seafaring days, to sell. Ruth assures her parents that once she is successful, she will return, "and every time we feel like it, we'll throw away fifty dollars." The comedy was dominated by March's droopingly mustachioed curmudgeon, who fights against bringing a telephone into the house and fears that hot air wafting from the family cat sitting on the radiator (called a register in the play) will give him malaria. His performance won him the newly established Antoinette Perry (later Tony) Award.

There were no awards for **Land's End** (12-11-46, Playhouse), Thomas Job's adaptation of a Mary Ellen Chase novel. Set in Cornwall between the wars, it watched as Derek Tregonny (Walter Coy), engaged to Ellen Pascoe (Helen Craig), allows himself to be seduced by Ellen's best friend, Susan Pengilly (Shirley Booth), then throws himself off the nearby cliffs in shame. The girls resolve not to let the incident destroy their friendship.

Christmas night brought in three openings. Most first-stringers opted for a comedy which some seasons ago several producers had optioned and announced for imminent production. None of the productions materialized until several years after a highly successful movie was made from the play. The film was called *Here Comes Mr. Jordan*, but Harry Segall's play retained its original title, **Wonderful Journey** (12-25-46, Coronet). A boxer named Joe Pendleton (Donald Murphy) comes to heaven fifty years ahead of schedule, so, with the help of a heavenly assistant, Mr. Jordan (Sidney Blackmer), is required to return to earth. First he is given the body of a murdered millionaire, and when that proves unsatisfactory, he becomes K. O. Murdock, the world champion. Critical kudos were reserved largely for Philip Loeb, who played Joe's mystified manager. Otherwise, critics suggested seeing the film.

Second-stringers who sat in judgment on Jacqueline Susann and Beatrice Cole's **Lovely Me** (12-25-46, Adelphi) also found little to cheer. It centered around Natasha Smith (Luba Malina), a four-time-married, fading Russian-emigré film star who is about to be "convicted" from her posh apartment for non-payment and so is seeking both a job singing in a nightclub and a fifth husband. She latches on to the supposedly wealthy head (Reynold Evans) of a dog-lovers' club known as the Tail-Bumpers. But the appearances of several past

husbands complicate matters. So do the hurryings in and out of her suite by a motley assortment of oddballs, none odder than Stanislaus Stanislavsky (Mischa Auer), a flagpole-sitter-turned-magician, who is frightened by his own tricks.

Although reviewed mostly by second-stringers, the evening's lone success proved to be a revival at the Belasco of George Manker Watters and Arthur Hopkins's *Burlesque* (9-1-27). This story of a boozy burlesque clown who cannot stand success on Broadway and ultimately returns to the cheap grind with his disillusioned but loyal wife starred Bert Lahr and featured Jean Parker. Lahr's traditional "gnong-gnong" mugging and his surprising poignancy in the play's most sentimental moments were highlights of the evening, as was the miniature burlesque show "complete with hot music, a deadpan rag-doll chorus, a wax-moustached tenor, a stripeuse (considerably restricted, of course) and Lahr himself as a comedy cop doing a scene with a sparsely clad chorine." The revival far surpassed the run of the original, compiling 439 performances.

Edward Mabley and Leonard Mins's **Temper the Wind** (12-27-46, Playhouse) unfolded in occupied Germany. Lt. Colonel Richard Woodruff (Thomas Beck) is assigned to help Reitenberg get back on its feet. He befriends the town's chief manufacturer, Hugo Benckendorff (Reinhold Schunzel), since he went to school with the man's son, a boy shot by the Nazis for his democratic sympathies. An American monopolist, Theodore Bruce (Walter Greaza), is also in town and has no qualms about working with such obvious Nazis as Erich Jaeger (Tonio Selwart). To Woodruff's chagrin, neither has Benckendorff. When the colonel puts his foot down, there is a riot. But since he has the American army behind him, he wins.

London had not welcomed Martha Gellhorn and Virginia Cowles's **Love Goes to Press** (1-1-47, Biltmore), so reviewers wondered aloud why anyone bothered to import it. Jane Mason (Joyce Heron) and Annabelle Jones (Jane Middleton) are war correspondents, sent to Italy, where Jane wheedles her ex, also a correspondent, away from an ENSA singer, while Annabelle falls for a British officer. But then both girls head off to an assignment in Asia.

Another female correspondent, the glamorous Danielle Forbes (Claire Trevor), comes illegally into the Russian-occupied part of Germany to ferret out an American who had broadcast for the Nazis during the war and now is hiding under an alias. She no sooner settles down at her dilapidating hotel in László Bush-Fekete and Mary Helen Fay's **The Big Two** (1-8-47, Booth) than she encounters Captain Nicholai Mosgovoy (Philip Dorn), a Russian officer also seeking the man. Ideological differences immediately crop up, and he threatens Danielle with arrest and deportation. But before long the pair have fallen in love. Soon thereafter Danielle weeds out the traitor (Eduard Franz), but arranges a hopeful compromise with Nicholai.

Neither Otto Kruger nor Jessie Royce Landis could do much for Hugh White's **Little A** (1-15-47, Henry Miller's). Late in life, "Little A," who was always under the thumb of his long-dead father, "Big A," learns that his son (Robert Wiley) is not his own but is the child his wife, Lucinda, had with his father and that his father had tricked him into marrying Lucinda. When he further discovers that the boy has attempted to seduce a young, orphaned music student (Ottilie Kruger) whom he is helping through school, he contemplates suicide. He rejects poisoning himself, so he hands Lucinda a gun and asks her to shoot him. She accidentally kills the son.

Arthur Miller's **All My Sons** (1-29-47, Coronet) examined a family torn apart by the father's behavior during the war. Since many of the airplane cylinder heads Joe Keller (Ed Begley) sold the government were knowingly defective, a number of pilots lost their lives in plane crashes. However, Keller managed to shift the blame to his partner, even though his own son Larry was engaged to the partner's daughter. Larry had been reported missing in action. But another son, Chris (Arthur Kennedy), is aware of a letter Larry wrote before his disappearance, in which Larry states he is so ashamed of his father's actions that he will not return from his next mission. An angry Chris shows his father the letter. Joe comes to see that in Larry's eyes the dead boys were "all my sons." The old man kills himself. Although Barnes suggested that the play demonstrated "more indignation than craftsmanship"—and, indeed, it was somewhat pat and cliché-riddled—most aisle-sitters rejoiced in "a play of high voltage," "a drama of force and passion." And several predicted a bright future for Miller, with Kronenberger garlanding him as "first among our new generation of playwrights."

. . .

Arthur Miller (b. 1915) was born in New York, grew up in a middle-class Jewish home in Brooklyn, and studied at the University of Michigan, where he won the Avery Hopwood Award for playwriting. He next took employment with the Federal Theatre Project, and later worked on documentary films after being rejected for service in the war. He won some acclaim with *Focus*, a 1945 novel about anti-Semitism. His first produced play, *The Man Who Had All the Luck* (1944), was a quick failure. With this second play his ardent leftist leanings came to the fore, and in his subsequent work his political philosophizing would frequently get the better of his carefully considered dramaturgy. Nonetheless, he still retained a better theoretical sense of

classic tragedy than any of his contemporaries, a fine gift for characterization, and an ear for modern dialogue.

. . .

The play also spurred the career of its director, Elia Kazan.

. . .

Elia Kazan (b. 1909) was born in Istanbul but raised in America. He attended Williams College and did graduate work at Yale before joining the Group Theatre as an actor. His first major directorial assignment was *Casey Jones* (1938), but real success came with *The Skin of Our Teeth* (1942). He then directed *Harriet* (1943) and *Deep Are the Roots* (1945). His work often combined stylization and realism, thus bringing a poetic bonus to his forceful theatricality.

. . .

The reviews, followed in the spring by the New York Drama Critics Circle Award, kept the play on the boards for 328 performances.

The next two plays both looked at returning soldiers and their wives or sweethearts, but with very different results. In Virginia Faulkner and Dana Suesse's **It Takes Two** (2-3-47, Biltmore), Todd and Connie Frazier (Hugh Marlowe and Martha Scott) were wed during the war, after which he was sent away. Now that he has been mustered out, they are thrilled to find a small apartment in Murray Hill. But personality clashes soon lead them to consider a divorce, especially after Todd's old buddy (Anthony Ross), a voluptuous blonde (Vivian Vance), and a "Mad Hatter" neighbor (John Forsythe) disrupt their lives. Naturally, the Fraziers kiss and make up at the close. Critics felt the playwrights should have concentrated on the disrupters and not on the lovers.

The same critics thought Norman Krasna's **John Loves Mary** (2-4-47, Booth) was merely a slickly contrived farce, but admired Josh Logan's brilliant staging and the superb comic playing, so allowed it would be a smash hit. It was, chalking up 423 performances. When John Lawrence (William Prince) returns home from the war, his sweetheart, Mary McKinley (Nina Foch), and her senator-father (Loring Smith) insist on an immediate wedding. That presents John with a problem, since he is already married. Of course, he doesn't love his English wife, Lily (Pamela Gordon). He has married her because she is the fiancée of Fred (Tom Ewell), the wartime buddy who saved his life, and marrying Lily was the only way to bring her into the country. John plans a quick divorce so that Fred can marry her. Unfortunately for John, Fred by this time has married another girl, who is about to make him a father. Matters are further complicated by a determined general (Harry Bannister) and John's former lieutenant (Lyle Bettger), a nasty blowhard who has since become a major in the usher brigade at the Paramount Theatre. John's problems are solved when Lily reveals she had been married before, to a lieutenant whose mother wrote her that he had died. One guess who the lieutenant was. At the curtain Fred is escorting Lily to see the new Dorothy Lamour picture at the Paramount. Ewell walked away with acting honors.

There was probably a good play in the sad saga of the woman executed for complicity in Lincoln's assassination, but John Patrick's **The Story of Mary Surratt** (2-8-47, Henry Miller's) wasn't it. Because Mary (Dorothy Gish) ran a boardinghouse where the conspirators met, she is caught up helplessly in the cry for blood. A senator (Kent Smith) who long ago loved her comes to her defense, but her son, who fled overseas to save his own neck and who could exculpate her, refuses to return, so she is condemned to hang after a blatantly unfair trial. As she is about to be led from her cell, she tells her defender, "How vain of me to have expected so much from this one life." Gish's appealing performance could not save a hollow play.

As far as novelties were concerned, the rest of the season went unremittingly downhill. A group of professionals calling itself the Experimental Theatre took over the long-dark Princess and mounted a series of plays, each for five performances. Although some major Broadway talent—such as José Ferrer—was involved in the staging and performances, none of the offerings was deemed worthy of being moved uptown.

A spurt of interesting revivals followed. While a few reviewers saw George Kelly's *Craig's Wife* (10-12-25) as dated when it was brought out at the Playhouse on the 12th, most felt it was still a powerful drama and admired Judith Evelyn in the title role. But the piece was withdrawn after two months.

Aisle-sitters were less pleased when Donald Wolfit and his English company came into the Century for three weeks, beginning on the 18th. He seemed to Americans an example of a long since superannuated, fustian school of emoting, and his supporting players were deemed unexceptional. His bills offered *King Lear, As You Like It, The Merchant of Venice, Hamlet,* and Ben Jonson's *Volpone.*

But another English ensemble provided what many considered the season's most brilliant revival. Led by John Gielgud, they brought their impeccable sense of stylized high comedy to Oscar Wilde's *The Importance of Being Earnest* at the Royale on March 3. Pamela Brown was Gwendolen; Robert Flemyng, Algernon; and Margaret Rutherford, Lady Bracknell. Reviews prompted the limited stay to be extended, so the comedy ran for ten weeks, until the group had another delicious mounting to offer.

William McCleery's **Parlor Story** (3-4-47, Biltmore) got bogged down in too much silken talk. Charles Burnett (Walter Abel) quits his job as editor of Mel Granite's newspaper to accept a professorship of journalism, hoping it will be a step toward becoming the university's president. Granite (Royal Beal) is furious, so when a young man (Richard Noyes) who hopes to marry Burnett's daughter writes an editorial in the campus paper espousing liberal views of marriage, Granite uses the editorial to pressure the governor (Paul Huber)—the man who must appoint the new president—to pass over Burnett. He almost succeeds, but Burnett finally finds himself in the president's office and with a new son-in-law.

The next two arrivals both ran a mere twenty-nine performances, despite the allure of their stars. In **The Eagle Has Two Heads** (3-19-47, Plymouth), Ronald Duncan's translation of Jean Cocteau's original, Tallulah Bankhead played the queen of a mythical country which she has ruled ever since her husband was assassinated on their honeymoon. Stanislas (Helmut Dantine), a dashing poet and revolutionary, climbs through her window in order to kill her. Before he can, voices of the palace police alert the queen, who, moved by the young man's resemblance to her dead husband, hides him. They quickly seem to fall in love, but when the guilt-ridden intruder swallows poison, she berates him, and he, in a fury, shoots her. Bankhead had a field day, traipsing about in gorgeous costumes, delivering several long speeches (one of which, fourteen minutes long, fell just short of the record established by Hickey's monologue in *The Iceman Cometh*), and then hurtling down a grand staircase after being shot.

The popular screen favorite James Mason could do no more for Jacques Deval's **Bathsheba** (3-26-47, Barrymore). In fact, his high-pitched, nasal voice and languid acting only underscored the play's weaknesses. King David spots the beautiful Bathsheba (Pamela Kellino) and soon seduces her, even though she is the wife of Uriah (Phil Arthur), one of his best warriors. She becomes pregnant, but then Uriah tells David that he has not slept with her and will not until he is victorious in battle. So David sends him to the front line and certain death.

Postwar housing shortages were global, as Thelma Schnee's translation of Konstantin Simonov's **The Whole World Over** (3-27-47, Biltmore) showed. An eccentric army bridge designer, Feodor (Joseph Buloff), and his daughter, Olya (Uta Hagen), who is also an engineer and who has lost her betrothed in the war, are forced to share lodgings with a handsome but embittered and widowed colonel (Stephen Bekassy), a third engineer. In no time, the resourceful Feodor has played matchmaker for the youngsters. Buloff won laughs by resorting to his whole bag of Yiddish mannerisms and stage tricks. Critics found few kind adjectives for the comedy, but it nonetheless held on for 100 performances.

The housing shortage also served as background for Frank Gould's **Tenting Tonight** (4-2-27, Booth). When a former serviceman (Richard Clark) and his wife (June Dayton) offer some other ex-GIs space in their small college-town home, they get more than they bargain for. Among the settlers-in are Phil Alexander (Dean Harens), an indefatigable ladies' man who brings a slew of friends and problems with him, and Joe Willinski (Joshua Shelley), who is more interested in bookies than in books. But Joe solves everyone's difficulties when he prevails on a local gangster (Henry Lascoe), who planned to convert an empty building into a nightery, to turn it instead into a dormitory.

James Parish's London drama **Message for Margaret** (4-16-47, Plymouth) was quickly hooted off the boards. A dying man's last words were said to have expressed his love for Margaret. Was he speaking of his wife Margaret (Mady Christians) or his mistress Adeline (Miriam Hopkins), whom he called Margaret for fear of forgetting himself in his sleep? The answer would seem to be that the farewell was meant for the wife.

There was a sadder farewell of sorts nine nights later when Ferenc Molnár gave Broadway the last new play he would offer it in his lifetime, **Miracle in the Mountains** (4-25-47, Playhouse). Set in the "Dark Carpathian Mountains" "about 100 years ago," it focused on a young, illegitimate boy whose father (Frederic Tozere), the village's mayor, has refused to acknowledge him and who accidentally kills him. The mayor attempts to foist blame for the boy's death on his mother (Julie Haydon). But a mysterious, saint-like man (Victor Kilian) appears from a nearby monastery to defend the mother. He does so by taking everyone to the bush beneath which the mayor had buried the body and bringing the boy back to life. He and the boy head off together toward the monastery. The play's three performances made it the season's shortest-lived failure.

Harry Thurschwell and Alfred Golden's **A Young Man's Fancy** (4-29-47, Plymouth) was set in a Connecticut summer camp for youngsters. Spoiled, bookish Dickie Crandell (Ronnie Jacobie) is lodged with four unholy terrors who badger him every way they can, until, with a counselor's encouragement, he strikes back by causing their cots to collapse, placing frogs in their beds, and painting their faces while they sleep. In return, he helps the counselor (Lynne Carter) land the camp's nice co-owner (Bill Talman). Ignoring critical pans and lured by cut-rate tickets, the public patronized the comedy for ten months.

By contrast, H. J. Lengsfelder and Ervin Drake's **Heads or Tails** (5-2-47, Cort) threw in the towel after

one month. It had attempted to stir up advance interest by promising any ticket buyers that they would become stockholders in the production and share in its profits. Reviewers were almost unanimous in calling it the season's worst play and giving it the shortest shrift, with Garland undoubtedly setting an unbeatable record for brevity. His review read simply, "No!" A married diplomat (Les Tremayne) and a stockbroker (Jed Prouty) flip a coin to see who will win the woman they both love. The loser is to commit suicide. At the same time, the diplomat's mother-in-law insures his life, with a special clause voiding the standard caveat about suicide. The play ends without any suicide but with the diplomat's returning to his wife.

Ivan Goff and Ben Roberts's **Portrait in Black** (5-14-47, Booth) was the season's final novelty. Believing they have committed the perfect crime in disposing of her invalided husband, Tanis Talbot (Claire Luce) and her lover, Dr. Philip Graham (Donald Cook), are aghast when they receive a letter saying their crime will be made public. They confront a bevy of suspects and, deciding that the Talbots' lawyer (Sidney Blackmer), who is known to love Tanis, is the writer, they kill him, too. Then they receive a second letter. When the doctor realizes that Tanis is writing the letters, he prepares to kill her and himself. Not only did reviewers find the play dull, they branded as ridiculous Luce's "death mask" makeup and B-picture posturing.

One last revival allowed the season to end happily when Gielgud's company offered Congreve's *Love for Love* at the Royale on the 26th. Critics admitted that the old play was not nearly as accessible for ordinary playgoers as Wilde's comedy had been and that the performance as a whole was not quite so glorious, but most were still delighted. Gielgud was Valentine; Pamela Brown, Angelica; Malcolm Keen, Sir Sampson; Robert Flemyng, Ben; and Adrianne Allen, Mrs. Frail. However, the evening was all but stolen by the Tattle of Cyril Ritchard, giving Americans a marvelous taste of the fops he would continue to portray until his death.

1947–1948

Contemporary historians could not agree either about the statistics or the quality of the new season. The number of new plays was given variously as forty-three or forty-four, making for a very slight rise or else a slight drop compared to the previous season—depending on what figure the source had offered a year ago.

Similarly, the new season was seen as "superior in quality" or marking "no appreciable improvement" over last year. However, most commentators concurred that Off Broadway was starting to come into its own, although the term still lacked a certain definition.

The season began, as most seasons do, not very encouragingly. Mary Boland, "an excellent comedienne, but a bad judge of plays," came and went in a single week in Harry Young's **Open House** (6-3-47, Cort), Broadway's latest gander at the postwar housing crunch. Rattlebrained Mrs. Barrett, living in genteel poverty, decides to take in some boarders despite local zoning laws prohibiting renters. She accommodates two veterans and one of their girls, telling suspicious neighbors that they are relations. But one neighbor reports the matter to the police, who raid the home and even accuse Mrs. Barrett of running a bordello. All ends happily after the uncle (Curtis Cooksey) of one of the renters proposes to the landlady.

There was general agreement that **Laura** (6-26-47, Cort), Vera Caspary and George Sklar's stage version of Caspary's novel, was patently inferior to the popular screen version. Once again, the beautiful Laura (K. T. Stevens) is briefly suspected of killing her friend and passing off the body, whose face was blasted beyond recognition, as herself before a handsome detective (Hugh Marlowe) pins the killing on a suave, decadent writer (Otto Kruger).

A group hoping to establish a repertory schedule at the City Center brought out Dion Boucicault's version of *Rip Van Winkle* (9-3-1866) on July 15 in a somewhat revised treatment by Herbert Berghof. Philip Bourneuf played the title figure, a part that had given Joseph Jefferson a meal ticket for more than a third of a century. Indifferent notices allowed Bourneuf to play the role for a mere two weeks, despite an attractive $2.40 top, and wrote finis to the producing group's ambitions.

Several critics pointed to the absurdity of what programs for Charles Raddock and Charles Sherman's **The Magic Touch** (9-3-47, International) called a "modest little New York apartment" filling the stage with a picture of spaciousness and no small luxury. Jeff Turner (William Terry), a $28.50-a-week stockboy at a publishing house, and his wife, Cathy (Sara Anderson), invite Jeff's boss, J. L. Thompson (Howard Smith), for dinner in hopes of wangling a raise. Seeing how resourcefully the youngsters live, he refuses to give Jeff the raise but has Cathy write a how-to book describing her methods. The book at first is a failure, and nearly ruptures the Turners' wedded bliss. But they kiss and make up after the book is a success. "If this is your idea of a joke, it's a very poor one," a character exclaimed. At least

one critic quoted the line to exemplify his own feelings. Adding financial injury to intellectual insult, the producer brought the play in with a top ticket of $6, the highest tag for a non-musical since the roaring twenties.

Critics also pounced on lines from Joseph Fields and Ben Sher's **I Gotta Get Out** (9-25-47, Cort), in this case to give readers some idea of its hopeless humor. They recorded such gems as "Let's form a bookie-of-the-month club," "I wouldn't give such a fur coat if I was an Eskimo," and the following snatch of dialogue:

She: Lend me $50 on account.
He: On account of what?
She: On account of I'm broke.

The bookie-of-the-month joke hinted at the play's racing milieu. Over his head in debt, young Timmie (John H. Conway) helps some bookies, chased from their poolroom above a police station, to find temporary quarters in the home of his sweetheart's aunt (Edith Meiser). This eventually leads to a police raid on auntie's, but the good woman, who soon shows a greater gift for picking winners than do the gamblers, gets the six grand she needs to underwrite a camp for poor kids by somehow legally renting space to the bookies for $6000. One setting moved the play briefly to Belmont. David Burns collected most of the evening's better notices as the bookie's boss. But the comedy got out after just four performances.

Theodore Ward's **Our Lan'** (9-27-47, Royale), which had won considerable laudatory word of mouth when offered the preceding season down in Greenwich Village, seemed far less effective on a larger, uptown stage. Larded with spirituals, it told of a group of blacks who had been granted their own island off Georgia during the Civil War by General Sherman, who had successfully raised cotton on the land but found difficulty selling to white buyers, and who now are told by the Johnson administration to move on. As the curtain falls they are preparing for obviously doomed battle with the Union forces coming to evict them.

The Heiress (9-29-47, Biltmore), Ruth and Augustus Goetz's theatricalization of Henry James's *Washington Square*, ran a solid year even though New York's two most prestigious newspaper drama critics, Brooks Atkinson of the *Times* and Howard Barnes of the *Herald Tribune*, stood united against it and the rest of their colleagues, who hailed it as "superb," "absorbing," and "something to cheer about." Rejecting the knowledge that her unloving father, Dr. Austin Sloper (Basil Rathbone), strongly opposes her entertaining Morris Townsend (Peter Cookson), the shy, slightly homely Catherine Sloper (Wendy Hiller) is not averse to the dashing young man's courtship. But after Townsend, a fortune hunter, learns that Sloper will disinherit his daughter if she weds, he jilts her. Following her father's death, when she has become wealthy in her own right, he returns. For a time the vengeful Catherine strings him along, then abruptly spurns him. The play ends with Townsend pounding at her door for admittance to her home and calling her name, as she, lamp in hand, slowly, resolutely ascends a long staircase to her bedroom and probable spinsterhood. Even those critics who supported the play took divergent stances on the playing, although Rathbone's smooth, icy father and Hiller's slightly sugary Catherine were generally well received.

Reviewers recalled that Donald Ogden Stewart had been a most promising writer before deserting to Hollywood, and they concurred that if his **How I Wonder** (9-30-47, Hudson) was any indication, all those years in the California sun had left him befuddled. Professor Lemuel Stevenson (Raymond Massey), an astronomer searching for a possibly undiscovered planet, frets over his own planet's bent toward atomic self-destruction. He discusses his concerns with the personification (Everett Sloane) of his own mind and with a strange, lovely redhead named Lisa (Meg Mundy), who may be a visitor from another planet, one destroyed by an atomic holocaust. He also does battle for his Negro watchman's brother, who has been jailed on trumped-up charges but actually for his attempts at unionization. Donald Oenslager's rooftop setting, with its observatory and its star-spangled sky, earned a solid round of applause, as did Massey's quiet, thoughtful performance.

There was nothing befuddled about William Wister Haines's **Command Decision** (10-1-47), and although no one hailed it as a great play, most fell in line with *PM*'s Louis Kronenberger, who wrote, "It puts on a good show which is all the better for being a serious one." Many of his colleagues are disturbed by Brig. Gen. K. C. Dennis (Paul Kelly), whom one of them describes as "a man so drunk with power he thinks he can cover anything he does with other people's blood." With Dennis ordering his bombers to fly far beyond the range of fighter protection, even some of his officers have balked at what they deem are suicide missions. Futhermore, he has disobeyed orders about which targets to bomb, deciding for himself the targets he will give priority. Yet he will not ask his men to do anything he himself would not do. He has even flown a captured enemy plane to learn its potential. When he is finally transferred to the Pacific, he confesses to his successor that their predecessor was driven to suicide by the job, and that he, too, often contemplated it. Taut, crisp acting by Kelly and a strong, all-male supporting cast added an extra punch to the drama.

Robinson Jeffers's nearly twenty-year-old **Dear Judas** (10-5-47, Mansfield) was finally given a Broadway hearing, only to have aisle-sitters agree it should have been left on the printed page. The blank-verse drama was done in modern dress, with Bach music for an accompaniment. Its single setting, the garden at Gethsemane, was an austere picture of tumbled crags and "a barren, malevolent-looking fig tree whose roots are like dragon's claws and whose branches are like the twisted fingers of the dead." Judas (Roy Hargrave) betrays Jesus (Ferdi Hoffman) not out of greed or hatred but because he fears that Jesus is turning away from his original ideals—"How hard he has grown toward suffering lately, and careless of the poor." But Jesus' apparent understanding of Judas's actions and the betrayer's own guilt drive Judas to hang himself. Margaret Wycherly was Mary.

An English horror play, Mary Hayley Bell's **Duet for Two Hands** (10-7-47, Booth), received a chilly reception in New York. A mad surgeon (Francis L. Sullivan) has given Stephan Cass (Hugh Marlowe) new hands after the young poet lost his in a mountain-climbing accident. But at the surgeon's isolated home on the storm-swept Orkneys, the poet begins to act strangely and also to fall in love with the surgeon's daughter (Joyce Redman). The doctor reveals the new hands are the hands of a demented murderer, who once tried to court his daughter, but when the doctor moves to forcibly cut them off, the hands reach out to choke him and he dies of a heart attack.

Two major revivals followed. First done in America forty-two years before, *Man and Superman*, Shaw's examination of the battle of the sexes and the place in that battle of a "life force," was a surprise smash hit all over again when Maurice Evans brought his splendid mounting into the Alvin on the 8th. Evans's John Tanner was lauded for its "gusto and vitality," and his supporting cast was also praised. A real, glittering 1904 Franklin motorcar added to the spectacle and period color. The comedy delighted New York audiences for nine months.

Although Robinson Jeffers's adaptation of Euripides' *Medea* ran only six and a half months after premiering at the National on the 20th, that was a remarkable record for a classic Greek tragedy. Its success was attributable wholly to the bravura performance of Judith Anderson. The *Post*'s Richard Watts, Jr., wrote of her, "Visually magnificent, she can be hideous, beautiful, frightening and infinitely sorrowful," and he concluded, "Hers is a portrayal . . . in the heroic tradition." Many saw director John Gielgud's rather flaccid Jason as the weakest of the evening's major performances (and he quickly relinquished the role), but had laurels for the eloquence of Florence Reed's apprehensive nurse.

By 1947, Broadway's increasingly brutal economics had largely negated the old rule-of-the-thumb which suggested that a show probably recouped its investment by the time it reached its 100th performance and thus could be classified as a hit. In any case, J. B. Priestley's **An Inspector Calls** (10-21-47, Booth) fell short of the charmed figure by five performances. The visit of an inspector (Thomas Mitchell) brings to light that Arthur Birling (Melville Cooper) and his comfortable family have all been guilty, directly or indirectly, in the suicide of a lower-class girl. The family breathes a sigh of relief when it is discovered the inspector was apparently a hoax, but then a phone call advises them another inspector is on his way to visit them. Not until forty-seven years later would the play enjoy a long run on Broadway.

John van Druten's **The Druid Circle** (10-22-47, Morosco) lingered for only seventy performances and never enjoyed a major reconsideration. Although van Druten had long since become an American citizen, many felt his latest offering was especially British. Leo G. Carroll's subdued performance as a frustrated, fusty professor and oldtimer Ethel Griffes's acting as his querulous mother were for them its saving graces. Professor White, a sexually repressed, embittered teacher at a rotting provincial university, comes across a love letter one (Walter Starkey) of his students has written to a girl (Susan Douglas), and he maliciously embarrasses them by reading it aloud in their class. The girl almost commits suicide. White comes to see the meanness and pettiness of his behavior, but not in time to save his job.

A third English play (considering van Druten's as one) gave Broadway a new hit and has, at least in England, been regularly revived ever since. Based on a genuine incident just before World War I, Terence Rattigan's **The Winslow Boy** (10-29-47, Empire) told of a thirteen-year-old naval cadet (Michael Newell) who is accused of stealing and cashing a five-shilling money order. His father (Alan Webb) jeopardizes his own health and his family's savings to prove the boy's professed innocence. The play's great moment came at the end of the first of its two acts with a blistering examination of the youngster by the famous barrister (Frank Allenby) whom the father has called in. Just as everyone is exhausted and resigned to the probability that the haughty lawyer, now preparing to leave, will refuse the brief, he quietly assures them that the boy is "plainly innocent" and that he accepts. He sees that right is done.

Two plays opened on the first Monday in November. Only the Theatre Guild's subscription list allowed its offering to outrun the single week the other survived. An old doctor (Sam Jaffe) and a younger one (John Archer) in Jan de Hartog's **This Time Tomorrow** (11-3-47, Barrymore) are both puzzled how a tubercular girl (Ruth Ford), dead by all medical criteria, remains alive. They conclude that her wish to be loved keeps her going, and, indeed, after the young doctor kisses her, she truly dies. Set in prewar Amsterdam, the play compounded its confusions by giving the girl psychic powers that allowed her to predict the Nazi invasion and the manner in which both men will die.

Conrad S. Smith's **Trial Honeymoon** (11-3-47, Royale) was so bad that many critics padded their reviews with examples of its misfiring humor. A character wiping a smudge off of a garment remarks, "One of those swallows must have taken a detour on the way back from Capistrano." Another suggests, "Let's go into the dark room and see what develops." The plot? Two California youngsters (Ellen Fenwick and Jack Fletcher) learn that they have scheduled their wedding a day before they can legally be wed. So they agree to spend a chaste evening in a bungalow at a motor lodge. The evening teaches the bride-to-be that her priggish husband-elect is not the man for her. She scurries off with the best man (Joel Thomas).

Although the same critics were not especially happy about F. Hugh Herbert's slickly contrived **For Love or Money** (11-4-47, Henry Miller's), they conceded that it was a crowd-pleaser. What's more, it introduced a beautiful young comedienne they all foresaw as a future star. The girl in question was Gene Lockhart's daughter, June, but her future lay almost exclusively with films and television. As Janet Blake, a dentist's assistant, she knocks on a strange Long Island door when her car breaks down in a rainstorm. The door and the mansion that goes with it belong to Preston Mitchell (John Loder), an aging matinee idol, whose conversation is sprinkled with dialogue from plays he appeared in. Although he observes all proprieties, he quickly realizes Janet is falling in love with him. He tries to discourage her. After all, his mistress and leading lady, the sharp-tongued—and sharp-toothed—Nita Havemeyer (Vicki Cummings), would not like the situation. He even tries to promote a romance between Janet and Bill Tremaine (Mark O'Daniels), his neighbor and godson. But in the end Preston recognizes he will settle in with the girl, especially after he has attempted to explain away everything to Nita, who is on the phone, only to have Janet, sitting beside him on a sofa, grab the phone and exclaim, "Preston—if you must talk to that woman—at least don't hog the covers!" Crowds were pleased for eight months.

St. John Ervine's 1929 hit, *The First Mrs. Fraser,* in which a woman who allowed her roving husband to divorce her finds that he wants her back, was revived in more modern dress at the Shubert on the 5th, with Jane Cowl as star. The consensus was that the comedy showed its age and, perhaps more unexpectedly, that

Cowl's once reined-in mannerisms (something critics had not previously harped on)—her exaggerated gestures, her repetitions, her frequent laughing at her own lines—were a bit out of hand. Henry Daniell was Mr. Frazer. The play's thirty-eight performances marked Cowl's last appearances before her death in a street accident.

Dorothy Gardner's **Eastward in Eden** (11-18-47, Royale) looked at Emily Dickinson in the light of recently discovered papers revealing that a married Philadelphia minister, Dr. Charles Wadsworth, was the wished-for lover whom the poetess wrote about. Wadsworth (Onslow Stevens) is puzzled that so pleasant a young woman as Emily (Beatrice Straight) is not married. She explains just what she is seeking in a husband: "It isn't so much a person that I want as a state of *Being,* the ecstasy of being understood." That would be her Eden. The pair correspond, but then he moves his family west. They have only one more, pleasant meeting, many years later. The play, condemned as "dramatically uneventful," closed after two weeks.

Although most reviewers proffered varying reservations, they generally approved of Katharine Cornell's resurrection of Shakespeare's *Antony and Cleopatra,* which she brought into the Martin Beck on the 26th. In the *Daily Mirror* Robert Coleman observed that "her performance is always under control, cleverly shaded, soft when it should be, robust when fitting." There was a suggestion that she lacked "the cunning animality and passion" that should be a part of the figure. Ironically, Lenore Ulric, who exuded just those qualities, served as Cornell's Charmian. Godfrey Tearle, seen by many as a Roosevelt look-alike, was a vigorous Antony. The gorgeously costumed but rather simply set mounting chalked up 126 performances.

December began with a smash hit, Tennessee Williams's **A Streetcar Named Desire** (12-3-47, Barrymore). Blanche Du Bois (Jessica Tandy), a woman trapped in illusions of past grandeur, comes to visit her sister, Stella (Kim Hunter), and her coarse, brutish brother-in-law, Stanley Kowalski (Marlon Brando). She is dismayed at the rough manner in which they live. By way of consolation, she believes she may find some romance with Stanley's lonely, kindly friend, Mitch (Karl Malden). When Blanche learns that Stella is pregnant, she warns her that she will spend her years like a local streetcar, traveling the seediest, most narrow streets. Stanley is furious on hearing about her comments, and he tells Mitch that Blanche has never been quite right in the head since her husband committed suicide after she found him in bed with another man. He also discloses that since then she has become a nymphomaniac and lost her teaching post for attempting to seduce a student. Stanley rapes Blanche, but Stella

will not believe her story and arranges to have her sent to an insane asylum. Blanche tells the doctor who comes for her, "Whoever you are—I have always depended on the kindness of strangers."

"Out of poetic imagination and ordinary compassion, he has spun a poignant and luminous story," Atkinson reported of Williams and his play. There were also kudos for Jo Mielziner's glowing, skeletonized setting of the Kowalskis' slummy home and for Elia Kazan's taut, tense direction. Time has also added luster to the performances, albeit not all reviewers were enthralled at the time. While Kronenberger noted that "no one is likely to underrate Marlon Brando's brilliant performance of the brother-in-law, the more astonishing for being like nothing else he has ever played," many of his colleagues passed over it with perfunctory remarks. Critics saluted Tandy as "compelling" and "glorious," but complained that she was not believable in the early scenes and had "a none-too-pleasant voice and a leaning toward monotony." The play won the Pulitzer Prize and the New York Drama Critics Circle Award, and ran 855 performances. After he left the production, Brando was never again seen onstage, but the drama launched Tandy on the road to stardom.

• • •

Jessica Tandy (1909–94) was born in England and made her first Broadway appearance in *The Matriarch* (1930). Thereafter the slim, sharp-voiced actress performed in films and made occasional, largely unnoticed returns to the stage. She was married to Hume Cronyn, with whom she often co-starred in later years.

• • •

For its second season, the Experimental Theatre moved across the street to Maxine Elliott's, a small, jewel-like but long-dark playhouse. Although it once had been considered a major theatre, it was now, albeit just around the corner from the busy Empire, deemed off Broadway. The group's first offering was Charles Laughton's translation of Bertolt Brecht's **Galileo** (12-7-47, Maxine Elliott's), with Laughton in the title role. Most critics had yet to understand Brecht's style of dramaturgy, so even the knowledgeable Atkinson dismissed the work as "loose and episodic" and as "pretentious." Two weeks later, down in the Village, in the very sort of auditorium that would come to typify Off Broadway, Barrie Stavis's **Lamp at Midnight** (12-21-47, New Stages) covered much of the same ground in more traditional fashion and won general critical approval. It ran there for over a month, while the Brecht offering generated little interest. Later in the season the Experimental Theatre, in conjunction with established producers, presented **A Long Way from Home** (2-8-48, Maxine Elliott's), Randolph Goodman and Walter Carroll's all-black, modern-dress version of Gorky's

The Lower Depths, reset in a North Carolina slum, and Halstead Welles's **A Temporary Island** (3-14-48, Maxine Elliott's), in which a seminary's bachelor president, ordered to chase a traveling circus out of the school's town, falls in love with one of the performers and almost abandons his post. Its impressionistic scenery consisted largely of drapes and "atmospheric set pieces." Another of the group's presentations met with some success and will be discussed when it opens in January.

Emmet Lavery's **The Gentleman from Athens** (12-9-47, Mansfield) was a one-week dud, despite some unusual preopening publicity the show received after Ginger Rogers's mother noisily complained that it was anti-American, Communist propaganda. Critics saw it as a *Born Yesterday* with the sexes reversed and without the earlier play's humor. The crude wine grower Stephen Socrates Christopher (Anthony Quinn), from Athens, California, decides to take over the Kilpatrick mansion in Virginia as his home while he serves in Congress, and he persuades pretty, sophisticated Lee Kilpatrick (Edith Atwater) to remain as his secretary. He tells her he is called "Sock," not so much because of his middle name as because "I sock first and explain later." It soon turns out he has bought his way into Congress, largely to be revenged on his local congressman who refused to help him. Deciding a bill to establish a United States of the World would bring him national recognition, he attempts to strong-arm it through. But his behavior alienates his associates, who dredge up his ballot-box chicanery and expel him from Congress. He can get back by blackmailing some important fellow members, but Lee convinces him to return to California and regain his seat by more high-minded methods.

Crime and Punishment (12-22-47, National), Rodney Ackland's dramatization of Dostoyevsky's novel, was given a beautiful mounting and was more than capably acted by a cast that included John Gielgud as Raskolnikoff and Lillian Gish as Katerina Ivanna. Unable to snare a public, it folded after only five weeks.

A heavy-handed revival at the Morosco on the 27th of Marcel Pagnol's 1930 success about a sweet man taught the virtues of corruption, *Topaze,* had Oscar Karlweis in the lead and Tilly Losch and Clarence Derwent in support. A notice attached to Ward Morehouse's review in the *Sun* stated, " 'Topaze' closed after its first performance Saturday night—the shortest run of the season thus far." The squib did not suggest what might amount to a shorter run.

Two interesting mountings away from the mainstream launched the new year. The Experimental Theatre offered Jan de Hartog's **Skipper next to God** (1-4-48, Maxine Elliott's), which brought John Garfield back briefly from films. Joris Kuiper is captain of an old Dutch ship carrying 146 Jewish refugees from Nazi Germany to South America. Despite the fact that the refugees have visas, they are denied admittance. Kuiper next sails for America, but when the navy attempts to turn him back he scuttles his ship so that his passengers can be brought ashore. Good notices and Garfield's drawing power allowed the mounting to be moved uptown, where it remained for two months, until Garfield had to return to Hollywood.

At the City Center a group led by José Ferrer, Richard Whorf, and Uta Hagen presented a series of bills at $2.40, beginning on the 8th with *Volpone.* This was followed by a revival of *Angel Street* on the 22nd, four one-act comedies by Chekhov on February 5, Ben Jonson's *The Alchemist* on May 6, and O'Neill's *S.S. Glencairn* on May 20. Each bill was offered for fourteen performances. Reviews were mixed.

Mainstream Broadway's new year got off to a dismal start with DeWitt Bodeen's **Harvest of Years** (1-12-48, Hudson). It focused on a determined Swedish-American widow (Esther Dale) who keeps on going at her San Joaquin farm, although one daughter takes to the bottle after the daughter's fiancé jilts her for her sister, a son's fiancée jilts him for his nephew, and all manner of other soap-operaish difficulties beset the widow.

Michael Clayton Hutton's English drama **Power Without Glory** (1-13-48, Booth) struck many as a poorly written variation on *An Inspector Calls,* since it, too, examined the effects on a family of a girl's death. Only this time the family is lower-class, living above their humble Thames-side shop, and there is no question that the family's weakling son (Peter Murray) has seduced his brother's bride-to-be (Hillary Liddell) and murdered the young tramp (Joan Newell) who would expose the relationship. Even those who disdained the play were awed by the individual performances and ensemble acting, yet no one in the cast went on to make a major name.

Pompous, reactionary Senator Cromwell (Carl Benton Reid) is all but struck dumb when his son, Matthew (John Archer), brings a bride into the family's Nob Hill mansion in Florence Ryerson and Colin Clements's **Strange Bedfellows** (1-14-48, Morosco). For the lady in question, née Clarissa Blynn (Joan Tetzel), is one of California's most vociferous suffragettes in this year of grace 1896. Before long she has gotten all the women of the house to lock their bedroom doors to the men until ladies everywhere are granted equal treatment. Belatedly, Matthew realizes that if Clarissa has her way, "man will become a vermiform appendix. He will shrivel up and blow away, and no one will miss us." The men head out to seek the comfort afforded by the painted women of the Barbary Coast before good sense is restored. Overriding its unexcited reviews, the comedy ran nearly seven months.

Perhaps recalling the strange, one-sentence squib at the end of his review of *Topaze,* Morehouse seemed to provide an answer when he commented on the next arrival, "If there were any justice the Mansfield's new piece would have given up after its first act." As it turned out, Elisabeth Cobb and Herschel Williams's **The Men We Marry** (1-16-48, Mansfield), which critics assailed as "the season's gabbiest play" and "constructed like a filibuster," went down in the records as the season's shortest-run novelty—three performances. To prevent the marriage of her daughter (Anne Sargent) to a poor medical student (John Hudson), a popular novelist (Shirley Booth) enlists her lady friends in a campaign to switch the girl's affections to a more suitable suitor. Mama fails, but not before jeopardizing her friends' marriages in the process.

Only Atkinson admired Peter Viertel and Irwin Shaw's **The Survivors** (1-19-48, Playhouse). His colleagues' unanimous pans doomed the melodrama to a single week's run. Returning to their Missouri ranch after being Confederate prisoners, Steve (Richard Basehart) and Morgan Decker (Kevin McCarthy) vow to resume their family's deadly feud with the neighboring Camerons, especially since they blame Tom Cameron (Anthony Ross) for their being captured during the war. Morgan's war wounds prove fatal before they can take any action, and Steve himself, reasoned with by the town's respected, peace-loving attorney, Vincent Keyes (Louis Calhern), is all but dissuaded from carrying out his vow. But goaded by malcontents on both sides, including Steve's prattling grandfather (Hume Cronyn), Steve and Tom shoot it out and both are killed. Boris Aronson's settings of a wild west hotel saloon and the ranch's veranda won general praise.

Strindberg's *Dodsdancen,* redacted by Peter Goldbaum and Robin Short as **The Last Dance** (1-27-48, Belasco), was also confronted by virtually unanimous pans and also withdrew after one week. Reset on a lush, semi-tropical island, it recounted how the vicious, hate-filled Edgar (Oscar Homolka) has destroyed any marital pleasure his wife (Jessie Royce Landis) may have hoped for. He sets out, as well, to destroy the ambitions of the well-meaning friend (Philip Bourneuf) who introduced the couple. But the rebellion of his daughter (Anne Jackson) provokes a fatal heart attack before he can do more damage. While rejecting the play, critics hailed Homolka: "He is evasive, surly, complacent and slimy. Much of the time he spends grinding his body sluggishly around in a chair. He has the indefatigable hypocrisy that can be infuriating, and his collapses are entirely convincing."

Michael Sayers's **Kathleen** (2-3-48, Mansfield) was another one-week failure. When Dublin's Kathleen Fogarty (Andree Wallace), who lives with her widowed father (Jack Sheenan) and two uncles, a priest (Whitford Kane) and a doctor (Frank Merlin), announces she is pregnant, she causes consternation. She really isn't; she just wants some excitement. She is bored with the poor man's son (James McCallion) and the clownish rich man's son (Henry Jones) who are courting her. Then she finds excitement and love with a handsome young soldier-engineer (Whitfield Connor).

Nor did the true Irish players from the Dublin Gate Theatre create much of a furor when they came in for a month's engagement at the Mansfield on the 10th. They offered *John Bull's Other Island,* Shaw's look at Irish-English relations, followed on the 17th by Denis Johnston's **The Old Lady Says "No!,"** in which an actor portraying Robert Emmet is accidentally knocked unconscious and dreams he is Emmet taking a dyspeptic look at modern Ireland. On the 24th the troupe unveiled Michael MacLiammoir's **Where Stars Walk,** in which two figures out of ancient Irish lore come back to life briefly as modern-day servants, before turning into white swans and flying off.

The sad parade of largely unwelcomed novelties continued with Joseph L. Estry's **Doctor Social** (2-11-48, Booth). Dr. Isaac Gordon (Al Shean), the dedicated old teacher of Dr. Farrar (Dean Jagger), is shocked to learn that Farrar will license his new serum to a big manufacturer instead of donating it to a charitable foundation. Farrar decides to demonstrate the serum's efficacy on Lee Manning (Haila Stoddard), disfigured by an explosion in her chemical laboratory. In doing so, he comes to realize that the serum will not only restore her skin but can cure the incipient cancer he has discovered in her. Since he has fallen in love with Lee, he heeds her pleas and donates the serum to charity.

Unwilling to admit defeat, Eva Le Gallienne attempted to revive the American Repertory Theatre. On the 16th at the Cort she brought out *Ghosts,* and on the 24th, *Hedda Gabler.* The mountings were condemned as "plodding and unimpressive," so after three futile weeks Le Gallienne finally accepted the inevitable and closed the shows.

The season enjoyed its biggest hit with **Mister Roberts** (2-18-48, Alvin), which Joshua Logan and Thomas Heggen took from Heggen's best-seller. Watts saluted the comedy as a "warm, full-blooded, hilarious and moving entertainment . . . a blessing to us all." For several years, Lt. Douglas Roberts (Henry Fonda) has served as a buffer between the crusty, unfeeling Captain Morton (William Harrigan) of the navy cargo ship *AK 601* and its bored, unhappy crew. The captain appears more interested in his palm trees than in his men, who often resort to mischief to release their frustrations. Thus the slightly loco Ensign Pulver (David Wayne) attempts to blow up the captain's quarters but merely destroys the vessel's laundry by accident. Roberts finally arranges to be transferred to another ship, despite the captain's efforts to retain him. Soon afterwards he is reported killed. News of his death goads the crew to unite forcefully against the captain. Taking matters into his own hands, Pulver pounds on the captain's door and informs him, "I just threw your palm trees overboard. Now what's all this crap about no movie tonight?" Fonda's "quiet, unforced" performance and those of his supporting cast helped keep the play on the boards for 1157 performances. Like Garfield, Fonda was returning to Broadway after a long spell in films, but unlike Garfield, he spent much of his later years onstage.

. . .

Henry [Jaynes] **Fonda** (1905–82) was born in Grand Island, Neb., and raised in Omaha, where he first appeared onstage in 1925. After performing with various stock companies for several years, the slightly twangy-voiced, lanky actor made his New York debut as a walk-on in *The Game of Love and Death* (1929). He then joined the University Players until 1932, when he returned to Broadway. Major attention spotlit him in 1934 as Dan Harrow, the canal man determined to return to the land, in *The Farmer Takes a Wife*. But after less successful appearances he headed for Hollywood in 1937 and for a decade was one of its most popular leading men.

. . .

A revival of six of the one-act plays (three a night) from Noel Coward's 1936 hit, *Tonight at 8:30,* raised its curtain at the National on the 20th with one of its two original stars, Gertrude Lawrence, heading the bills. Reviewers felt that many of the plays had not aged well and that even the better ones could have used the unique Lawrence-Coward electricity. With Graham Payn in the Coward parts, the plays lingered for only three weeks.

Long before playgoers had first heard of *Tonight at 8:30,* way back in 1929 in fact, radio audiences had begun to listen to a series of comic programs about Jewish life, *The Goldbergs*. The series had recently been ended, so its author and leading lady, Gertrude Berg, offered Broadway a play version, **Me and Molly** (2-26-48, Belasco). The *World-Telegram*'s William Hawkins spoke for most of his associates when he noted, "Her play is simple and homely, with a few tears and a lot of laughs. It never tries to be smart or original, and is at its best when it is most familiar." The year is 1919, and the Goldbergs have just moved into their new apartment in the East Bronx. Feeling he has imposed on them long enough, Uncle David (Eli Mintz) refuses to move in with them. Young Sammy (Lester Carr) is preparing for his bar mitzvah; his sister, Rosie (Joan Lazer), is thrilled to learn that there is a piano teacher in the building, since Mrs. Goldberg intends to buy a piano. Most important, Jake Goldberg (Philip Loeb) is planning to go into business for himself—the garment business. Mama has even given him an idea, when she complains, "Why shouldn't someone like me be able to go into a store and come out without being altered." Papa will specialize in off or odd sizes. But Mrs. Goldberg almost scuttles the plan when she matchmakes between the piano teacher (Margaret Feury) and a young friend (David Opatoshu) who had considered becoming Jake's partner. Now that he will have to support a wife, he prefers the relative safety of being a pharmacist. But after the opportunistic Cousin Simon (Louis Sorin), sensing a good thing, says he will become a partner, Mrs. Goldberg convinces Jake to go it alone. For all the friendly reviews, the comedy succumbed to the summer heat after 156 performances.

J. B. Priestley found no welcome with **The Linden Tree** (3-2-48, Music Box), in which an old professor refuses to retire, insisting that only the very old and very young can lift England out of its postwar doldrums. The professor was played by Boris Karloff, Hollywood's man of horrors, who this time eschewed any grisly makeup and delighted the few playgoers who saw him with his "sympathetic," "extraordinarily winning" performance. But his good notices could not lure sufficient audiences to get past the first week.

Rose Franken's **The Hallams** (3-4-48, Booth) ran only half a week longer. It looked at the same family the playwright had dealt with fifteen years before in *Another Language*. Now the grandson, Jerry (Dean Norton), returns from a sanitarium where he has been recovering from tuberculosis and brings with him a new bride, Ken (Katharine Bard), who herself has recovered from the disease. Jerry admits that the doctor warned him the marriage would be too exhausting, but he insists to his father (Royal Beal), "He's only my doctor, not my jailor." The marriage is also opposed by Jerry's grandmother, Mrs. Hallam (Ethel Griffes), who still dominates her clan, and by Jerry's mother, Etta (Mildred Dunnock). So when his exertions do kill Jerry, Etta blames Ken. But another of Mrs. Hallam's sons, Victor (Alan Baxter), persuades Ken to remain part of the family, and the long-suffering Mr. Hallam (John McKee) tells his wife, "This time, you must open your heart to her."

After a lapse of forty-three years, Shaw's *You Never Can Tell,* which nonetheless told of an ardent feminist's three children who finally meet the father they have not known, was mounted in an opulent Broadway production by the Theatre Guild at the Martin Beck on the 16th. Besides its colorful scenery and period costumes, its principal attraction was Leo G. Carroll's playing of a slyly observant waiter at the seaside resort where the story unfolds. Theatregoers were not interested, so the play departed after the Guild's subscription list was exhausted.

Having first been offered a little more than a month earlier by New Stages at its home in the Village, Jean-Paul Sartre's controversial **The Respectful Prostitute** (3-16-48, Cort), in a translation by Eva Wolas, was hurried uptown on the strength of excited notices and continued there for another ten months. In an unspecified southern city, the play's prostitute (Meg Mundy) initially balks at claiming that an innocent black man (John Marriot) has raped her and even attempts to hide the man from vigilantes. But offers of a comfortable life and southern social pressures eventually weaken her resolve. For many the evening's main attraction was the beautiful, redheaded Mundy, but her career was to be extremely brief. Because the piece was not full-length, Thornton Wilder's seventeen-year-old **The Happy Journey to Trenton and Camden** was added as a curtain raiser. Long popular with amateur groups, it described a family's reactions as its members ride along in the family car.

Allan Scott's **Joy to the World** (3-18-48, Plymouth) received mixed notices, but hung on until hot weather threatened. Played at breakneck speed, the comedy told of a young Hollywood wonder boy (Alfred Drake) who is hauled on the carpet after delivering a radio address which he had not bothered to read first and which was filled with liberal notions that are unpalatable to his film studio's higher-ups. He is threatened with the loss of his job if he does not issue a retraction. (This was the era of the House Un-American Activities Committee hearings and the Hollywood blacklists.) But, having met and instantly fallen in love with the beautiful girl (Marsha Hunt) who actually wrote the speech, he refuses to apologize. His career is saved when a famous film pioneer (Morris Carnovsky) asks him to take over his studio. The play was set in the wonder boy's huge, luxurious, and gadget-filled office. Early on he receives a phone call from Orson Welles. After tiring of Welles's long-winded oration, he plunks the receiver in a desk drawer and shuts the drawer so that he can go about his other business, but takes the receiver out at intervals for the rest of the play to offer Welles a few encouraging words before dropping it back in the drawer. Welles is still apparently yakking away at the play's end. Drake garnered excellent notices in his first essay of a major non-musical role since becoming a star.

A revival of *Macbeth* at the National on the 31st closed March on a down note. Much had been expected from Michael Redgrave and Flora Robson, but both, especially Redgrave, proved disappointments. Indeed,

Robson's "strangely placid" Lady Macbeth was characterized as "merely a disappointment, not at all a disaster." But Redgrave was assailed for his ranting and immoderation—he "either shouts his lines or delivers them with a querulous indecision."

There was even stronger critical headshaking after the opening of a fifteen-year-old English drama, a play that had been announced almost every season for production but until now never was brought to Broadway. Keith Winter's **The Rats of Norway** (4-15-48, Booth), like several other works imported during the season from London, was set at a school filled with unhappy faculty. One boozy instructor (John Ireland) has an affair with the unloved wife (Jeanne Stuart) of the headmaster (Colin Keith-Johnston); a younger instructor (William Howell) falls in love with a timid, dull music teacher (Rett Kitson). There is even a hint of repressed lust between the two instructors.

Matters failed to improve with Louis Paul's **The Cup of Trembling** (4-20-48, Music Box), which the playwright took from his own novel *Breakdown,* and in which the alcoholism of a celebrated newspaper writer (Elisabeth Bergner) nearly costs her both her career and her family. Happily a good psychiatrist (Philip Tonge) and friends (Arlene Francis and Anthony Ross) from Alcoholics Anonymous save the day. The play was weak enough, but critics long ago had become tired of the tiny refugee's excessively busy stage mannerisms ("she turns the part into a study of perpetual motion" "Miss Bergner's acting might benefit by a few delightful outbursts of repose").

The season's last smash hit was a revival at the Booth on the 28th of P. G. Wodehouse's adaptation of Ferenc Molnár's *The Play's the Thing,* which delighted audiences every bit as much as it had in 1926. Louis Calhern was the playwright who must find a way of rectifying matters for his composer-godson (Richard Hylton) after the young man overhears his sweetheart (Faye Emerson) chatting all too intimately with her pompous, not so young lover (Arthur Margetson). The piece ran along merrily for seven months.

May began with the arrival of Israel's Habimah company, performing, naturally, in Hebrew. The troupe offered four plays, starting with *The Dybbuk,* a look at the exorcising of an evil spirit, on the 1st; **David's Crown,** which was translated from Pedro Calderon de la Barca's Spanish drama by I. Lamdau, and which depicted murder and incest among King David's heirs, on the 8th; *The Golem,* centering on a medieval rabbi's molding and bringing to life a figure to confront the Inquisition, on the 15th; and *Oedipus Rex* on the 22nd.

In April a group calling itself the Six O'Clock Theatre had presented a bill of one-acters at Maxine Elliott's. One of the three plays was so favorably received that

Eddie Dowling hurried it and two replacement one-acters up to Broadway under the umbrella title **Hope's the Thing** (5-11-48, Playhouse). The principal attraction was Richard Harrity's **Hope Is the Thing with Feathers,** in which some homeless men in Central Park attempt to snare a duck from the lake and cook it for dinner. Instead, all they wind up with is a monkey from the nearby zoo. Harrity's two other plays were **Gone Tomorrow,** in which a family of Tenth Avenue Irish wait impatiently for an uncle to die and allow them to have a wake, and **Home Life of a Buffalo,** in which two aged, mediocre vaudevillians (played by Dowling and his wife, Ray Dooley) refuse to accept that vaudeville is dead. The move uptown was unsuccessful, so the bill folded after a single week.

Ladislas Fodor's **The Vigil** (5-21-48, Royale) ran only the least bit longer. In a courtroom supposedly shuttered for the Easter holidays, some ghostly figures in modern dress saunter in and put on trial a gardener for removing Christ's body from his tomb so that it would seem he had come back to life. A host of biblical figures testify (the season's second group of biblical figures to appear in modern dress), after which the judge tells the audience that it is the jury and must reach its own verdict.

The season's last novelty was another one-week flop, rushed to Broadway after causing a stir in a small venue far uptown. In Arthur Goodman's **Seeds in the Wind** (5-25-48, Empire) a group of children who have escaped the Nazi massacre of Lidice have taken refuge in a cave and plot to seize the world from the adults who have made such a mess of it. A Czech freedom-fighter (Tonio Selwart) stumbles on the cave, inadvertently causes dissension in the group, and so is put on trial, ostensibly for being an adult, but actually because the man has enchanted the sweetheart (Abby Bonime) of the group's rather surly leader (Sidney Lumet).

1948–1949

The new season was brilliant, arguably the last great season in the old Broadway tradition. True, the number both of total productions and of novelties had long since plummeted from Broadway's heyday. But at least this season the slide was momentarily halted and the count of novelties remained the same as last year. But what shows Broadway offered! Musicals included *Love Life, Where's Charley?, As the Girls Go, Lend an Ear, Kiss Me, Kate!,* and *South Pacific,* along with such short-run but often commendable failures as *Small Wonder,*

Magdalena, and *My Romance.* The list of new straight plays was equally noteworthy, as the season's history will show.

On the debit side, there were far fewer revivals, perhaps because highly praised new plays had prior claim to New York's stages. Nor did Off Broadway, unlike the preceding year, contribute much for uptown audiences. Worst of all, while $4.80 remained the standard top ticket for straight plays, costs of mounting them soared in the postwar inflation. It was not uncommon for relatively simple productions to be budgeted at a heretofore almost unheard-of $100,000 and to run out the season without recouping costs. Thus, by Broadway standards, these popularly applauded, longish-running shows were flops. The grim phenomenon would spread ominously in coming seasons.

On June 3, José Ferrer and the City Center concluded the series of revivals they had been presenting all through last season with their resurrection of the Capek brothers' *The Insect Comedy,* in the same Owen Davis version that Broadway had seen in 1922 as *The World We Live In.* Once again human life was reflected in the lives of various insect species. Like the company's other offerings it was given fourteen performances.

The season proper, following the pattern of most earlier seasons, got off to a drab start. None of the first five productions ran even a full two weeks. Bessie Breuer's **Sundown Beach** (9-7-48, Belasco) was a product of the year-old Actors' Studio, which several Broadway producers and directors had established as a training ground for young players. The young players fared far better than the playwright. At the Sundown Café, which is close by an air force hospital for mentally shattered fliers in Florida, a group of veterans and their women strive to put their futures in order. George (Edward Binns), whose war-bred neuroses seem incurable, kills himself after his unsympathetic wife (Cloris Leachman) walks out on him. It falls to Nancy (Phyllis Thaxter) to revitalize the discouraged Captain Arthur Bond (Warren Stevens). Ida Mae (Julie Harris), who has presented her husband (Stephen Hill) with a baby that is not his, wins him back with a promise of a dinner of collard greens, side meat, and black-eyed peas.

Marc Connelly's **A Story for Strangers** (9-21-48, Royale) was set in a small Michigan town in 1934. As a barber (Joseph Sweeney) and his manicurist (Joann Dolan) tell a traveling paint salesman (Edward Nannery) about the amazing reformation in their town, time and place move back on Ralph Alswang's turntables to a porch several months before. The local wimp, Norman (James Dobson), buys a spavined horse for $1.80 to help him deliver milk, but when the horse becomes dangerously ill, Norman, remembering a lecture about Roman deities, prays to the goddess of the stables to save it. A flash of lightning not only cures the horse (who is never seen onstage) but gives it the power of speech. In the end, the horse dies. However, by that time the whole town has been so impressed that everyone has mended his or her ways—the bookie becoming the honorable barber, and the town's former strumpet his manicurist. And Norman wins his beloved Bessie (Joan Gray), whose mother (Grace Valentine) had heretofore done everything in her power to prevent their marriage.

Although the season was still in its toddling clothes, critics were virtually unanimous that Albert Wineman Barker's **Grandma's Diary** (9-22-48, Henry Miller's) would grab the prize as its nadir. In fact, the header for Ward Morehouse's review in the *Sun* read simply "The Worst Ever." As was so often the case in such disasters, critics relished quoting particular gems, in this instance, such bon mots as "No woman forgets a husband very easily—unless he's living with her all the time" or "Every time I look at you I could hiccup." The play spotlighted a writer for a daytime soap opera who finds inspiration for its daily crises in her grandmother's diary and who must choose between her husband, returning from service in Japan with a lady friend in tow, and the tenor she has been having an affair with.

Gertrude Tonkonogy based her **Town House** (9-23-48, National) on John Cheever's *New Yorker* stories. Three young couples agree to share a once elegant New York brownstone. The snooty Tremaines (James Monks and June Duprez) hope to sell bonds to the rich publisher next door; the faddish, eggheaded Murrays (Hiram Sherman and Mary Wickes) hope the man will save their daughter's wildly progressive school from bankruptcy; and the Hylers (Reed Brown, Jr., and Peggy French) hope he will help them start a magazine. Only the Hylers appear to get their wish. Donald Oenslager's two-story setting revealed the house's living room, with its hall and formal staircase at the rear, and two small bedrooms on the second floor. One critic called it "a neck-cracker for anyone sitting in the first few rows."

Two noted wits, Norman Krasna and Groucho Marx, came badly a cropper with their **Time for Elizabeth** (9-27-48, Fulton). Elizabeth was not a lady, but Elizabeth, New Jersey, where old man McPherson (Leonard Mudie) has long dreamed of retiring. McPherson's plans for his golden years so seduce Ed Davis (Otto Kruger), the vice-president and general manager of the Snowdrift Washing Machine Company, where they both work, that, after twenty-eight years of devoted service, Ed packs it all in and heads with his family for Florida. He soon finds retirement deadeningly dull, and he is happy to accept his old boss's offer of a raise in pay to return to work.

Robert Morley and Noel Langley's London hit **Ed-ward, My Son** (9-30-48, Martin Beck) was a hit all over again in New York, chalking up 260 performances at the large house. It spanned thirty years from 1919 to 1948, and told of a man (Morley) who promises at the birth of his son that he will stop at nothing to make the world the boy's oyster. He commits arson, he lies, he steals, he blackmails, and he even drives his wife (Peggy Ashcroft) to drink to fulfill his pledge. The boy turns out to be a scoundrel, but dies as a fighter pilot during the war. The man's daughter-in-law (Dorothy Beattie) determines he will not spoil his grandson, whom she will keep from him. Edward never appears onstage. Although the pudgy Morley, with his how-now-brown-cow manner of speaking, dominated the play, Ashcroft and Leueen MacGrath, as the man's secretary-mistress, also won kudos.

Tallulah Bankhead and that "dark purple growl she uses for a voice" had a field day romping with Donald Cook through Noel Coward's *Private Lives*. They wrestled and hurled pillows at one another and turned Coward's reasonably sedate comedy into a brawling circus. The revival, which had been touring for much of the preceding season, settled (if that's not the wrong word) into the Plymouth for a seven-month run beginning October 4, even though a surprising number of critics, who loved the performance, lamented that the play was becoming hopelessly dated. Time was to prove them wrong.

Many critics would also have to reconsider their original judgments of Tennessee Williams's **Summer and Smoke** (10-6-48, Music Box). The *Times*'s Brooks Atkinson was virtually alone in finding it "tremulous with beauty," although he, like many of his colleagues, rued that Williams was writing little but "variations on the same theme." Other assessments ranged from the *Post*'s Richard Watts's polite "not one of his most successful works" to the *Daily News*'s John Chapman's harsh "mawkish, murky, maudlin and monotonous." In 1916, Alma Winemiller (Margaret Phillips), the prim daughter of Glorious Hill, Mississippi's minister, is at one and the same time repelled and fascinated by her handsome, amoral neighbor, Dr. John Buchanan, Jr. (Tod Andrews). She takes it on herself to teach him higher moral principles, while he attempts to get her to accept the realities of life and sex. Both are all too successful. By the time Alma has liberalized her views and assures John that the girl who had said "no" to him "doesn't exist any more, she died last summer—suffocated in the smoke from something on fire inside her," he has turned stuffily proper and become engaged. She allows a traveling salesman to pick her up. Even critics who assailed the play admired Jo Mielziner's magnificent setting, which showed a skeletonized view of Alma's Victorian home on the left, a skeletonized view of John's office and equally Victorian home on the right, and, in between, the town square, presided over by the statue of a kneeling angel. The generally negative notices and stiff competition confined the play's run to thirteen weeks.

Ruth Gordon, who had won some success two seasons before with an autobiographical look at an aspiring actress just before World War I, moved further back in time, to the turn of the century, to examine the difficult career of a totally imaginary player in **The Leading Lady** (10-18-48, National). For the sake of atmosphere, as if Oenslager's view of a plush Victorian town house and Mainbocher's gorgeous costumes were not enough, she restored to life such period figures as Clyde Fitch and young Maude Adams. Gerald Marriott (Ian Keith), a competent actor but nasty, egotistical man, married Gay (Gordon), a onetime chambermaid at Chicago's Palmer House, and made her his leading lady. Critics and audiences alike have generally come to agree that she far outshines him as a player. A savage review of his latest performance brings on a fatal heart attack. Left alone, Gay becomes despondent, and her career falters until a smitten young playwright (Wesley Addy) gives her new hope.

Broadway's romance with bygone days continued in **Life with Mother** (10-20-48, Empire), Howard Lindsay and Russel Crouse's sequel to *Life with Father.* The time is the 1880s, and Clarence Day (Lindsay) is confronted by myriad problems, including an alcoholic servant (Michael Smith), and a visiting cousin (Ruth Hammond) and her husband (Robert Emhardt) who are angry that a stock they bought on Clarence's recommendation has dropped in value. But the engagement of Clarence junior (John Drew Devereaux) creates a more vexing matter after the young man asks his mother (Dorothy Stickney) if he can borrow her engagement ring to give to the girl. She confesses that for all the rings father has bought her, he never gave her an engagement ring and "to this day, when people talk about engagement rings, I catch myself hiding my hand." Since tomorrow is their wedding anniversary she will ask him then to make good the oversight. But before she can do that she is visited by the widowed Bessie Logan (Gladys Hurlbut)—née Fuller. It develops that father was once engaged to Bessie Fuller and gave her a lovely engagement ring, which she still wears. The rest of the evening concerns mother's efforts, fruitful just before the final curtain, to appropriate the ring for herself. While many critics said the new work fell a trifle short of its predecessor, they nonetheless embraced it warmly: "a triumphant evening . . . a comedy of undiminished delight"; " . . . a new hit. A welcome hit. A terrific hit"; "Yes, the good old Days are here again. And welcome!" For all their praise,

the comedy ran only until June. Some commentators suggested that it simply met the fate of most sequels; others proffered that potential ticket buyers confused it with *Life with Father,* which they already had seen; still others said would-be patrons were discouraged by the numerous theatre parties that had bought out the comedy's earliest performances in advance; and some said Broadway simply could no longer sustain at one time so many good plays as the season produced. Whatever the reason, the mounting closed with a $40,000 loss on its $100,000 investment. A depressing hint of things to come.

Nearly a quarter of a century before, London had seen Richard Hughes's *A Comedy of Good and Evil.* Now New York saw it as **Minnie and Mr. Williams** (10-27-48, Morosco), with tiny, plump Josephine Hull elevated to stardom for the first time. Its setting was a turn-of-the-century Welsh village. The Devil sends an attractive young emissary named Gladys (Elizabeth Ross) to seduce the local parson (Eddie Dowling) and his wife, Minnie. Gladys presents the good woman with a pair of black stockings and a pair of bright red shoes, with the result that when Minnie sits down at the organ to play "Onward, Christian Soldiers" all her fingers will produce is "Frankie and Johnny." Even a local angel (Clarence Derwent), disguised as a fisherman, despairs of saving the minister. But when the man dies, Gladys, touched by the deep goodness of him and his wife, sees to it he gets into heaven.

Dorothy Heyward's **Set My People Free** (11-3-48, Hudson) moved further back in time than any other play so far in this rearward-looking season—to 1822 Charleston. For twelve years Denmark Vesey (Juano Hernandez), a former African prince who had been sold into slavery but had been able to purchase his freedom, has plotted to liberate all the slaves. He believes that the kindest, most humane slaveowners represent the biggest threat to his uprising. He would attack them first. In a way, his fears prove justified after George (Canada Lee), head slave on the plantation of the considerate Captain Wilson (Blaine Cordner), feels obligated to expose the plan. Based on real events, the play was dismissed as well-meaning but drab.

With Lili Darvas playing one of its leads, many critics saw the central figures in Edna Ferber and George S. Kaufman's **Bravo!** (11-11-48, Lyceum) as thinly veiled depictions of her and her husband, Ferenc Molnár. Zoltan Lazko (Oscar Homolka), a refugee Hungarian playwright, and his actress-wife, Rosa Rucker (Darvas), share a brownstone with several other refugees, including a former prince now working at the automat, an archduchess-turned-dressmaker, and a once important judge who today peddles candy. Lasko has taken to feeding the squirrels in the park, telling Rosa that the birds are the only public he still retains. The couple find themselves in trouble after they are willing to smudge the truth so that a former protégée (Christiane Grautoff), who has been in a mental hospital, can get past immigration. A chance meeting with Bernard Baruch (never shown) and his call to Washington bring about a happy ending. Unfortunately, the play held "very little of theatrical excitement or interest."

There was far less excitement or interest in Julie Berns's **For Heaven's Sake, Mother** (11-16-48, Belasco). When an aging actress (Nancy Carroll) finds that she is to become a grandmother and a mother at the same time, she attempts to foist her own baby on her daughter. Mrs. Rubin (Molly Picon) enters the picture, at first adding to the complications, but finally straightening out everything. Picon sang, danced, did a somersault, and employed some of her famous Yiddish mama routines from Second Avenue in a vain attempt to enliven the comedy.

Madeleine Carroll made her only Broadway appearance after becoming a Hollywood star when she returned to play the lead in Fay Kanin's **Goodbye, My Fancy** (11-17-48, Morosco). She took the part of Agatha Reed, a celebrated war correspondent who has become an equally celebrated, liberal congresswoman and who is now returning to her alma mater, Good Hope College for Women, to accept an honorary degree. Seeing her old room, which the college has carefully restored for her, drives her to tears. Her more hardboiled secretary, Grace Woods (Shirley Booth), refuses to succumb to such sentimentality. She prefers to ignore the past: "I was born in Newark, New Jersey. Every time I go through on a train, I pull down the shade." But the past returns for Agatha with a vengeance. The college's president is James Merrill (Conrad Nagel). He and she had been sweethearts in their college days, and she had been expelled for covering up for him. He has become a widower and a stuffy arch-conservative. Although he falls in love with Agatha again, and she with him, she is repelled by his politics, so threatens to disclose the truth about their past when he balks at the showing of a realistic war film which might promote pacificism. She heads off with a charming *Life* photographer (Sam Wanamaker), with whom she once had had a fling. Welcomed by Chapman as "a pungent, intelligent comedy being given just the right performance," the play ran for more than a year.

The next evening brought in another hit, Moss Hart's **Light Up the Sky** (11-18-48, Royale), although, like *Life with Mother,* its six-and-a-half month run was far shorter than its money notices suggested it would enjoy. Once again, Chapman spoke for most of his colleagues when he labeled the entertainment "a noisy and rollicking comedy." On the eve of a new play's Boston opening, its central figures assemble at the Ritz-Carlton suite of its leading lady, Irene Livingston (Virginia Field). They include the coarse-mouthed producer, Sidney Black (Sam Levene), his brassy wife, Frances (Audrey Christie), the swishy, lugubrious director, Carleton Fitzgerald (Glenn Anders), and the novice playwright, Peter Sloan (Barry Nelson). They gush sweetness and love to each other until they return from the first performance, which they believe to be a flop. Then a daggers-drawn name-calling session ensues. But when the reviews are all highly encouraging, the sweetness and camaraderie return. Each of the figures was superbly limned. Thus, when the stagily emotive Fitzgerald makes his first entrance, contemplating the opening just hours away, he announces, "I could cry." He makes the same statement at the play's end after learning that Black has booked six additional weeks of tryouts to save the show. In between, he blushingly covers his crotch when he hurriedly enters the suite in his pajamas and bathrobe and finds several women there, and he provokes the star's old pirate of a mother (Phyllis Povah) into a profane first-act curtain line as he describes the "withered crone, this hapless bag of bones . . . an unknown and unforgettable bit of human wreckage" whom he spied watching the dress rehearsal from the balcony, unaware it was she in disguise. Critics and playgoers also had fun identifying the famous stage figures the characters assuredly represented, with Black being Billy Rose; Frances, his wife Eleanor Holm; the vain, effusive Irene, Gertrude Lawrence; and Fitzgerald, Guthrie McClintic.

"One has to bide one's time at the Fulton, but there is a genuine satisfaction in doing so," Howard Barnes informed his *Herald Tribune* readers after the opening of N. Richard Nash's **The Young and Fair** (11-22-48, Fulton). Other reviewers said much the same thing, but the public chose not to find out for itself, so the play, in two slightly separated stands, totaled only forty-eight performances. At the Brook Valley Academy, a girl's junior college near Boston, a vicious student, Drucilla Eldridge (Doe Avedon), goads a weak-willed kleptomaniac, Nancy Gear (Julie Harris), into stealing money and jewels, but for a time pins the blame on a Jewish girl (Lois Wheeler) who refuses to be subservient to her. Since her father is a rich trustee at the school, Drucilla feels she can get away with whatever she contrives. And the headmistress, Sara Cantry (Frances Starr), fearful of losing her job, is too timid to right matters. But Frances Morritt (Mercedes McCambridge), an alumna who is returning to teach at the school, finds her sister, Patty (Patricia Kirkland), another student, is also being fingered as a suspect. Frances uncovers the true story, gives the headmistress a piece of her mind, and leaves, taking her sister with her. The entire cast was praised, but Harris won the most applause for her hysterical confession scene.

November's third hit was Robert McEnroe's **The Silver Whistle** (11-24-48, Biltmore). The denizens of a home for the aged run with genteel tightfistedness by the church next door are a sorry, unhappy lot. Caustic old Mrs. Hanmer (Doro Merande) tells the superintendent (Eleanor Wilson) that the dump spends just enough money on the residents to keep them alive, so it can boast of the church's charity. Then into their midst bounces a shabbily garbed man who identifies himself as Oliver Erwenter (José Ferrer), who has a birth certificate stating he is seventy-seven years old, and who carries with him a caged rooster. He tells them he has done everything and traveled everywhere. Among his achievements he became an associate professor at a university at thirty-four. But then he read Omar Khayyam, who advocated a carefree, joyous life, and a student asked him what would happen if he tried to live by Omar's precepts. "Throwing the book into the wastebasket, I turned to the blackboard and wrote: 'By God, I'll find out!' " He jumped through a window and off he went. Erwenter quickly brings gaiety and new purpose to the lives of the old folk. But then he is exposed. His real name is Wilfred Tashbinder, and he is not yet fifty. He found the birth certificate in a trashbin. The oldsters are shattered, but Erwenter rejuvenates them a second time by assuring them he now knows that a ripe old age can be fun. Then he heads off to new adventures. Ferrer's "brilliant bravado impersonation" glossed over the show's weak spots and helped it run for 216 performances.

Critics and first-nighters, as they had at the opening of *Joan of Lorraine*, had to force their way through a thick horde of screeching film fans when Charles Boyer made his Broadway debut in **Red Gloves** (12-4-48, Mansfield), which Daniel Taradash took from Jean-Paul Sartre's *Les Mains sales*. Critics came away highly impressed with Boyer's artistry. In the *Post*, Richard Watts, Jr., commended him as "a superb actor, powerful, intelligent, imaginative and resourceful, without a trace of film nonsense or pretentiousness about him." However, John Lardner of the short-lived *Star* did complain that he sometimes "talks a little too much as though he had a hot pomme de terre in his mouth," a complaint that would grow more frequent with his subsequent stage appearances. Hugo (John Dall), a wealthy young man who has joined the ranks of the Communists in some unidentified Middle European country, is ordered to kill Hoederer, the party leader. He takes work as the man's secretary, but when he confronts Hoederer with a gun, the leader coolly faces him down, takes the gun from him, and places it quietly on his desk. However, Hugo later stumbles on Hoederer

kissing Hugo's wife (Joan Tetzel) and, in a fury, slays him. The dying Hoederer exonerates him, calling the death not a political killing but a crime of passion. For all their admiration of the star, most critics found the drama faulty. Despite an advance sale listed variously between $130,000 and $300,000, ticket purchases soon slumped, and the play was withdrawn after 113 performances.

Negative tryout notices put a crimp in the advance sales for Maxwell Anderson's **Anne of the Thousand Days** (12-8-48, Shubert), although the first Broadway appearance of Rex Harrison since he had soared to fame in films provided something of a cushion. But Anderson used the tryouts to turn the play around. Joining a majority of his colleagues, William Hawkins wrote in the *World-Telegram,* "This is a great love story, and Anderson tells it with lustiness and grand excitement." "Harrison," he went on, "is both coarse and compellingly romantic as Henry. His voice is guttural and his gait a royal swagger." Harrison's English co-star, Joyce Redman, was seen as giving a performance of "rare beauty." Tiring of both his queen and his mistress, Henry VIII lusts after his mistress's younger sister, Anne Boleyn. He determines to divorce Queen Catherine and marry Anne, even if it means defying the Church of Rome. Initially, his most vociferous opposition stems from Anne herself, since she would marry Percy, Earl of Northumberland (Robert Duke). Henry forces Percy to marry another woman, and when Percy dies shortly after the marriage, Anne blames Henry. Nevertheless she recognizes that she is falling in love with him. They wed, but their life together starts to fall apart after Anne gives birth to a girl. Deciding another queen is more likely to present him with a male heir, he gives Anne the choice of exile or death. So that her daughter Elizabeth may one day ascend the English throne, Anne opts for death. After she is gone, Henry muses, "It would have been easier to forget you living than to forget you dead." The drama ran for nine months.

Edwardian England provided the setting for **Make Way for Lucia** (12-22-48, Cort), John van Druten's theatricalization of E. F. Benson's novels. In the small town of Tilling in 1912, Mrs. Emmeline Lucas, whose pretensions to Italianate ways make her call herself Lucia (Isabel Jeans), rents the home of Miss Mapp (Catherine Willard) for the summer. The prying, domineering Mapp is the town's social arbiter, but the coy, disarming Lucia, aided by her outrageously foppish friend, Georgie Pillson (Cyril Ritchard), sets out to seize hegemony and does. The play's humor proved too specialized for most Americans.

Variety used its review of Jean Kerr's **Jenny Kissed Me** (12-23-48, Hudson) to comment on the theatre's changing economic picture. Its notice began, "A few years ago there would have been a place on Broadway for an innocuous little comedy like 'Jenny Kissed Me.' In the bygone days of reasonable production costs, such a play would have been operated for about $4,000–$5,000 a week and would have pleased enough people to have had a moderately profitable run." Since those days were gone, the new comedy folded after less than three weeks. In that time it looked at crusty old Father Moynihan (Leo G. Carroll), whose loyal housekeeper (Frances Bavier) convinces him to take in her orphaned, eighteen-year-old niece, Jenny (Pamela Rivers). Hoping to get her off his hands and into the arms of a willing neighbor (Brennan Moore), the priest buys some fashion magazines and attempts to glamorize the girl. But on her own she lands Michael Saunders (Alan Baxter), a thirty-four-year-old school inspector.

For the umpteenth time, Ernest Truex found himself in a comedy unworthy of his talents. "As one of the theatre's ablest portrayers of the meek and mild he can rise above the banality of his lines with the lifting of an eyebrow, a diffident shake of the head. He can shrivel his frame in fear, clutch at pillars and hide behind flower vases so that you forget the tasteless situation into which he has been thrown." His Japhet Meadowbrook in Ronald Telfer and Pauline Jamerson's **Oh, Mr. Meadowbrook!** (12-26-48, Golden) is a still virginal, middle-aged English taxidermist who agrees to follow the advice of his doctor and find sex on a visit to America. At the Connecticut home of a playwright (Harry Ellerbe), Meadowbrook goes after the man's neglected wife (Grace McTarnahan) and a sharp-tongued woman of the world (Vicki Cummings), but scores only with his host's Scottish maid (Sylvia Field).

That same evening several first-string critics deserted Broadway to assess an offering in the Village. **The Victors** (12-26-48, New Stages) was Thornton Wilder's translation of the voguish Jean-Paul Sartre's drama. It recounted the efforts of some captured Resistance fighters to deceive their Vichy captors, only to discover that they have a traitor in their midst. Those critics who did write up the play were increasingly annoyed at Sartre's depersonalized, puppet-like figures.

The next evening another French play sharply divided the critics, one of whom rejoiced that it would be the season's most talked about success while another dismissed it as tremendously disappointing. But after a dangerously slow start, Maurice Valency's adaptation of Jean Giraudoux's **The Madwoman of Chaillot** (12-27-48, Belasco) caught on and ran for 368 performances. In modern-day Paris, the demented Countess Aurelia (Martita Hunt) still believes she is living at the turn of the century and dresses accordingly—and flamboyantly. So do her three cronies, the madwomen of Passy (Estelle Winwood), St. Sulpice (Nydia West-

man), and La Concorde (Doris Rich). Advised by a philosophic ragpicker (John Carradine) that the President (Clarence Derwent) and his associates are searching for oil under Paris and are prepared to destroy the city to obtain it, she invites the men to her apartment and suggests that the oil lies down in the well beneath her cellar. She has, in fact, learned that the well is actually a bottomless pit from which there is no escape, so once the men are in it, she slams the lid on them. Hunt, an English actress, Winwood, and Derwent walked off with many of the acting laurels.

A third French play was Sacha Guitry's **Don't Listen, Ladies** (12-28-48, Booth), in Stephen Powys's translation. Critics not only waved away the comedy, but felt its English star, Jack Buchanan, was far more comfortable in musicals. When Daniel Bachelet's wife (Moira Lister) claims she spent the evening stuck atop a ferris wheel, he suspects her fidelity; she suspects his after finding a love note in his coat pocket. Daniel's first wife (Adele Dixon), wanting him back, tries unsuccessfully to make trouble. Commentators, who may have thought the ferris wheel a novel motif, were probably too young to recall its use in two 1903 comedies, *The Earl of Pawtucket* and *Who Is Brown?*. The comedy lingered for only two weeks.

Three even shorter-lived failures followed. For no apparent reason, Garson Kanin set his **The Smile of the World** (1-12-49, Lyceum) in 1923, shortly after Harding's death. Years earlier, Supreme Court Justice Boulting (Otto Kruger) had been an ardent liberal, but he has long since turned into a stuffy reactionary, furious at the ongoing liberalism of Justices Holmes and Brandeis. His new law clerk is Sam Fenn (Warren Stevens), an attractive young man who is very much of Boulting's old liberal stripe. An affair soon blossoms between Fenn and Mrs. Boulting (Ruth Gordon). She sees in him all she once admired in her husband. Boulting becomes aware of the affair and offers no objection, but he is shocked into reconsidering his whole position after learning that Fenn and Mrs. Boulting may go off together.

Edward Percy's long-run London hit **The Shop at Sly Corner** (1-18-49, Booth) found no favor among New Yorkers. Decius Heiss (Boris Karloff), a onetime inmate of Devil's Island, now runs a London antique shop as a front for his fencing activities. He strangles a young employee (Jay Robinson) who tries to blackmail him. After an initial police investigation appears to exonerate Decius, a more purposeful-looking inspector (Reginald Mason) comes into the shop. The frightened Decius kills himself with a poisoned dart, only to find out that the policeman merely came to consider purchasing a suit of armor.

Like *Summer and Smoke*, Joseph Hayes's **Leaf and**

Bough (1-21-49, Cort) had first been presented at Margo Jones's Dallas playhouse—one of the earliest important American theatres erected in arena style. The connection was underscored by Carl Kent's skeletonized settings, which showed the kitchen of the Warren farmhouse on one side of the stage and Campbell's living room on the other. The self-consciously respectable Warrens are aghast to hear that their daughter, Nan (Coleen Gray), is in love with Marc Campbell (Richard Hart), son of a besotted, lowlife family. Her father (Anthony Ross) drives Nan from home, but then Mark attacks her after his malicious brother, Glenn (Charlton Heston), impugns her fidelity. Mark quickly becomes contrite and begs, "Let me make a life for you, Nan—with my hands, with my heart, with all my love." The youngsters are reconciled. Critics felt Rouben Mamoulian's over-heated direction brought additional problems to a some-times thoughtfully written but largely faulty play.

Many of the same critics gave high marks to Bernard Reines's **Forward the Heart** (1-28-49) for its sincerity, but for little else. David Gibbs (William Prince), a blinded veteran, returns after several years of hospital-ization to his family's fashionable Boston home, where his mother's maid, Julie (Mildred Joanne Smith), teaches him typing and other useful skills. Before long he is in love with her, which outrages his supposedly progressive mother, since Julie is a Negro. Even David hesitates. But after careful consideration he decides to defy convention and propose to the girl. Telling him society is not yet ready for mixed marriages, she runs off. He packs his bags, resolved to seek her out.

A pair of revivals followed. The first, at the Coronet on February 5, brought back Mae West in her old romp *Diamond Lil* (4-9-28). Chapman saluted the star as "the most gifted female impersonator since Julian Eltinge" and reported that she and her play had him and the audience "laughing fit to—if you'll pardon the expres-sion—bust." This hokey saga of a resourceful madam looked to be a smash hit again, but three weeks after the opening West broke her ankle, and the show had to shut down until June. Reopening as the hot weather approached, it never quite regained its initial box-office vigor. Nonetheless it frolicked along for 181 perfor-mances.

On the 8th at the Booth, Broadway saw a "stream-lined" version of Shakespeare's *Richard III,* which first had been mounted by the quickly defunct Boston Reper-tory and which starred Richard Whorf, who also de-signed the settings and costumes. His settings consisted of double arches, lots of gray drapes, and a handful of set pieces. One unusual trick was to turn a red spotlight on Richard whenever he committed or thought about bloodshed. The staging was especially fast-paced. But a majority of favorable reviews—"a great and vibrant

show," "an invigorating production"—could not lure in the public.

Reviews were anything but kind to Jean Pierre Au-mont's *L'Empereur de Chine* when the Theatre Guild offered it to Broadway in Philip Barry's adapation as **My Name Is Aquilon** (2-9-49, Lyceum). Several aisle-sitters were reminded of *The Silver Whistle,* since the central figure was a suave, glib young man (Aumont) given to inventing all manner of fictitious stories about himself. He wheedles himself into the good graces of a rich black marketeer (Lawrence Fletcher) and tries to seduce every woman in sight. But he finally wins the abiding love of the black marketeer's daughter (Lilli Palmer), even after he is exposed as a fraud.

Willy Loman (Lee J. Cobb), the protagonist of Arthur Miller's **Death of a Salesman** (2-10-49, Morosco), is also something of a fraud as he speaks of better days gone by and how he was once so highly appreciated by his employers. His life has been devoted to his work, his wife, Linda (Mildred Dunnock), and his sons, Happy (Cameron Mitchell) and Biff (Arthur Kennedy). He cannot admit to himself that his sons will never amount to much, nor that Biff has never gotten over his disgust at finding his father in a hotel room with a prostitute. After the sixty-three-year-old Willy loses his job, he spurns the suggestion of rich old Uncle Ben (Thomas Chalmers) that he try a new life in Alaska. Instead, he commits suicide by crashing his car in hopes that his $20,000 insurance will pay off the mortgage and give his boys a better chance. At Willy's funeral, a neighbor characterizes him as "a man way out there in the blue, riding on a smile and a shoeshine. And when they start not smiling back—that's an earthquake." But the long-suffering Linda can only cry that they are at last "free and clear."

The morning-after notices were unanimous raves. Given a few extra days' time to think, John Mason Brown concluded that the "play is the most poignant statement of man as he must face himself to have come out of our theatre," only to add, "Mr. Miller's play is a tragedy modern and personal, not classic and heroic. Its central figure is a little man sentenced to discover his smallness rather than a big man undone by his greatness." He further remarked, "Mr. Cobb's Willy Loman is irresistibly touching and wonderfully unspar-ing. He is a great shaggy bison of a man seen at that moment of defeat when he is deserted by the herd and can no longer run with it. Mr. Cobb makes clear the pathetic extent to which the herd has been Willy's life. He also communicates the fatigue of Willy's mind and body and that boyish hope and buoyancy which his heart still retains." The rest of the cast, fluently directed by Elia Kazan, was highly praised, as was Jo Miel-ziner's skeletonized reconstruction of both floors of the

Lomans' shabby home, in and around which all the action occurred, and Mielziner's poetic lighting. The play, awarded both the Pulitzer Prize and the New York Drama Critics Circle Award, compiled 742 performances.

A revival of Sidney Howard's *They Knew What They Wanted* (11-24-24) at the Music Box on the 16th received a handful of highly enthusiastic reviews, but they were outnumbered by ones expressing far less satisfaction. Many saw the play as thin or dated. Paul Muni was starred as the old Italian vinegrower who courts trouble when he attempts to woo a young waitress by sending her a photograph of his handsome foreman and claiming it is a picture of himself. Atkinson spoke for a majority with his complaint that Muni's overfussy acting was "academic. The meticulous details are on the surface." Fred Stone's youngest daughter, Carol, was Amy, and Edward Andrews was Joe.

Unanimous pans—"a cumbersome and muddled drama," "exasperatingly disappointing," "the season's biggest disappointment"—meant that the reported $200,000 advance sale Clifford Odets's **The Big Knife** (2-24-49, National) had comfortably in its till would not be able to save it. Years earlier Odets had gained Broadway's sneers by deserting it for Hollywood's gold and now he garnered further contempt by biting the hand that he had chosen to have feed him. Prodded by his wife (Nancy Kelly), Charlie Castle (John Garfield), a disgruntled film star, would throw over Hollywood. But his studio's ruthless boss, Marcus Hoff (J. Edward Bromberg), reminds him that the studio has covered up for the fact that a drunken Charlie killed a little girl while out driving with a floozie. The floozie, Dixie Evans (Joan McCracken), was given a long-term contract, but has since hit the bottle and is proposing to squeal. Charlie balks at Hoff's plan to murder the girl and at an alternate scheme to divorce his wife and marry Dixie, since a wife cannot testify against her husband. If he fails to go along, the studio will hold him to his fourteen-year contract but give him no self-respectable work. His acting days are over. Recognizing that he is trapped, Charlie tells his wife, "I pledge you a better future. It begins tonight," and he runs upstairs and kills himself. The play ran for 108 performances.

Reviews for Robert Pyzel's **Anybody Home** (2-25-49, Golden) were even harsher. A pompous Westchester lawyer (Donald Curtis) finds his wife (Phyllis Holden) is having an affair with a playboy (Roger Clark), who struts around in riding clothes. Only after the wife's sister (Katherine Anderson) appropriates the playboy can the couple resume their marriage. Adding to the play's absurdities was a view from the setting's window of Westchester's magnificent alpine mountain peaks.

Nor did most critics relish Samuel Spewack's **Two**

Blind Mice (3-2-49, Cort), which brought yet another fading film star, Melvyn Douglas, back to Broadway. Watts advised his readers that the play "certainly has its comic points . . . but its mockery is only intermittently satisfying." When Tommy Thurston, a newspaperman, visits his ex-wife's Aunt Lettie (Laura Pierpont) he makes the startling discovery that the Office of Seeds and Standards, where the old gal works, was abolished years ago but that since nobody bothered to send official notification Lettie and her equally gray-haired buddie, Chrystal (Mabel Paige), have been running it together ever since. They make ends meet by renting one room to a luscious blonde (Jane Hoffman) who gives rhumba lessons in it, and another room to a pants presser. They also collect fees from the parking lot. Members of the armed forces come to claim the space, but Thurston bamboozles them into believing they are to help the ladies in a supersecret project. He gives the ladies further credence by wangling them a French medal and an invitation to the White House. And when the economy-minded Senator Kruger (Frank Tweddell), who had led the campaign to close down the office, appears on the scene, Thurston informs him that the senator's not very bright nephew (Elliott Reid) has been acting as courier for the old ladies. The office is reinstated, and Thurston is reunited with his ex (Jan Sterling). For all the disparaging notices, the comedy ran twenty weeks.

James B. Allardice's "lively slapstick farce" **At War with the Army** (3-8-49, Booth) ran nineteen weeks. What little plot it seemed to have dealt with attempts in 1944 by First Sergeant Robert Johnson (Gary Merrill) to get himself transferred out of a boring Kentucky training camp and overseas to some action. But army red tape and a waitress (Maxine Stuart) at the local PX, who claims she is pregnant with his child, present three acts of hurdles. Among the other characters were a whistle-mad staff sergeant (Mike Kellen), a pathetically lost, seemingly mute private (Tad Mosel), and a captain (William Mendrick) whose wife (Sara Seegar) somehow learns about his orders before he does. However, many thought the play was stolen by a Coca-Cola machine, which refused to work most of the evening, then at the very end made a grand show of clattering and wildly regurgitating its bottles and nickels all over the orderly room.

The season's last hit was Sidney Kingsley's **Detective Story** (3-23-49, Hudson). The *Daily Mirror*'s Robert Coleman rejoiced that the melodrama "has heart, thrills, and humanity to recommend it. You won't find a dull moment." Detective McLeod (Ralph Bellamy) of the 21st Precinct in New York City is a fanatically committed policeman. His notions of law and justice are often as warped as those of the hoodlums he so despises. He seems to believe that all suspects are guilty until proven innocent. Worse, even when suspects are acquitted in court, he insists that "there is a higher court," and that he is it. But his world collapses after he learns that his wife (Meg Mundy) had an abortion by a shady doctor (Harry Worth) whom he just has manhandled. He purposely walks into a suspect's gun and is shot dead. Boris Aronson created a vivid picture of a detective squad room, endlessly crowded by police and suspects. Among the large, excellent supporting cast many picked out Lee Grant for her pretty little shoplifter. The play chalked up 581 performances.

Dalton Trumbo's **The Biggest Thief in Town** (3-30-49, Mansfield) survived for less than two weeks. Bert Hutchins (Thomas Mitchell), a funeral director in Shale City, Colorado, is on his uppers, so when he learns that John Troybalt, the town's preposterously rich old skinflint, has died, he and his boozy cohort, Dr. Stewart (Walter Abel), steal the body and prepare to give it an expensive burial. He even buys an $8000 coffin in which to bury the man and envisions a $12,000 profit on the ceremony. But in short order an arm pops out from beneath the sheet under which the corpse had been transported. Troybalt (William J. Kelly) is quite alive. And he gleefully confesses that he's been diddling his books, that he's completely broke, and that all his enterprises will go bust when the truth comes out. His estate would not have a penny to pay toward his interment. But then Troybalt really dies. A rival funeral director insists he has the right to bury the dead man, though he agrees to purchase the coffin from Hutchins—for $15,000. Hutchins assures him, "From now on it's your funeral."

Given the largely rave notices accorded Herman Wouk's **The Traitor** (4-4-49, 48th St.) and its superb cast—only Atkinson dissented—the adroit thriller should have been another hit. Instead it languished for a little more than eight weeks before surrendering. Lee Tracy—"dynamic, vital, shrewd, knowing and strangely graceful"—played Captain Gallagher, who was removed from command of his ship after an accident and assigned to naval intelligence. He now must find out who is betraying atomic secrets to the Russians. Toward this end he visits a distinguished professor, Tobias Emanuel (Walter Hampden), who has balked at his university's demand to take a loyalty oath. Gallagher soon shows him that his young associate, Allen Carr (Wesley Addy), is the traitor, a misguided idealist who is not a Communist but is willing to help the enemy in hopes that an atomic stalemate will bring about world peace. Emanuel offers Carr two options: "Stand your ground as a traitor, Allen, because you believe in what you did—or work with Gallagher, because it's your duty as an American." Carr agrees to cooperate and lures the head Russian spy

(John Wengraf) to a rendezvous. Realizing what is happening, the spy kills Carr but is shot dead by government agents as he attempts to flee out a window. A chastened Emanuel signs the loyalty oath.

Mirroring the season's depressing start, the season's last six plays all ran a week or less. Virtually the only thing critics could praise in Mervyn Nelson's **The Ivy Green** (4-5-49, Lyceum) was Stewart Chaney's "stunning period setting, that of the drawing room at Tavistock House, with its grand winding stairway." For the play dealt with thirty-four years in the life of Charles Dickens (Daniel O'Herlihy), painting an ugly picture of his disloyalty to his first wife (Judith Evelyn), his capitulating to her selfish sister (Carmen Mathews), and his abandonment of Mrs. Dickens for a young actress (June Dayton).

In George Batson's **Magnolia Alley** (4-18-49, Mansfield) the widowed Laura Beaumont (Jessie Royce Landis), even during those rare times when she is sober, is not at all particular about the boarders she accepts at her rundown rooming house on a back street in a southern city. Thus her unpleasant daughter, Nita (Anne Jackson), deserts her husband, Andy (Jackie Cooper), a small-time prizefighter, runs off with a wrestler, returns when she is broke, steals $500 from the lodgings' prostitute (Bibi Osterwald), and heads off again. But Laura's religiously fanatic helper (Julie Harris) and Laura herself apparently do find love, the latter with a man (Fred Stewart) who was once an army chaplain.

Peggy Wood was grossly miscast as a harridan mother-in-law who wrongly believes her hard-studying, veteran son-in-law (Douglas Watson) is unfaithful to her daughter (Judy Parrish), and acts to break up the marriage. She gets her comeuppance at the end of Thomas Coley and William Roerick's **The Happiest Years** (4-25-49, Lyceum).

Matters were equally unfunny in Will Glickman and Joseph Stein's **Mrs. Gibbons' Boys** (5-4-49, Music Box). Just as timid Lester MacMichaels (Francis Crompton) is about to propose to gushing, nitwitty Mrs. Gibbons (Lois Bolton), the sons she dotes on show up. They are Rudy (Tom Lewis), who is on parole, the flashily dressed Rodla (Ray Walston), and Francis X. (Richard Carlyle). The last two have newly escaped from prison by hiding in a garbage truck, and they have brought with them Horse Wagner (Royal Dano), who likes throwing people through windows. They hold MacMichaels and Mrs. Gibbons hostage until mama talks them into giving themselves up.

Another doting mother (Fay Bainter) and another troubled son (Jay Robinson) were the central figures in Mignon and Robert McLaughlin's **Gayden** (5-10-49, Plymouth). After young Gayden Sibley has tormented his mother's houseguest (Carol Wheeler), getting her to cancel her wedding plans and then sneeringly spurning her, his uncle (Clay Clement) warns Mrs. Sibley that Gayden is insane, possibly murderously so. Gayden's loving mother is willing to agree, but not to do anything about it, even though the uncle suggests that someday she may be the boy's victim.

Mr. Adam (5-25-49, Royale), Jack Kirkland's dramatization of Pat Frank's novel, ended a superb season in dire fashion. Because he was deep in a lead mine when an atomic holocaust sterilized every other man in the world, Homer Adam (James Dobson) is alone capable of repopulating the globe. At first his bosomy, southern cutie of a wife (Elisabeth Fraser) is vehemently opposed to his doing so. But she withdraws her opposition after he demands that all dictators resign and all armies be abolished as preconditions.

1949–1950

Any notions that the new season could repeat the brilliance of the preceding one were brutally disabused early on. Continually inflating production costs so discouraged producers from gambling on an always risky Broadway reception that the number of new plays crashed by nearly 30 percent—a wrenching drop. Fewer than thirty new plays came before the footlights. Moreover, not even half of these were original American works. The others were either English pieces, adaptations from the French, or dramatizations of novels. (The total of new plays, revivals, and musicals was fifty-seven—far and away the lowest figure thus far in the century.) To add to the gloom, the drop in quantity was accompanied by a marked falling-off in quality, so with straight plays starting to ask for a $6 top, attendance also took a beating. Proportionately fewer shows repaid their investments.

Although off-Broadway groups presented a few interesting importations during the summer, Broadway brought out nothing at all, and when its season finally began—exceptionally late—in early October, it, too, leaned heavily on foreign works. The first to arrive, at the prestigious Empire on the 3rd, was a classic—albeit a surprising number of critics openly expressed bewilderment about its centuries of praise. This production of Shakespeare's *Twelfth Night* had originated at the Michigan Drama Festival and featured Arnold Moss as Malvolio, Carl Benton Reid as Sir Toby Belch, Francis Reid as Viola, and Nina Foch as Olivia. The verdict was competent but unexciting, and the run was confined to forty-six performances, even at a come-on

$3.60 top. Nonetheless, the revival marked the producing debut of a man who would become probably Broadway's most prolific producer in ensuing years, Roger Stevens. (His arrival was some compensation for the deaths during the season of such old stalwarts as William A. Brady, Arthur Hopkins, and Brock Pemberton.)

. . .

Roger [Lacey] **Stevens** (b. 1910) was born in Detroit and studied for a while at the University of Michigan. By the time he made his rather tardy entry onto the theatrical scene, he had amassed a private fortune in real estate.

. . .

During its long London run, W. Douglas Home's **Yes, M'Lord** (10-4-49, Booth) had been known as *The Chiltern Hundreds*. The West End title would have been meaningless to most Americans, but the new one was little help. Only the popularity of eighty-year-old A. E. Matthews nudged the comedy on for eleven weeks. He played an earl much impoverished thanks to the new Labour government. His daughter-in-law-elect (Elaine Stritch) demands her husband-to-be (Hugh Kelly) find a job. The young man decides to stand for Parliament—on the Labour ticket. But he is defeated by his Conservative opponent—the family's butler (George Curzon).

Maurice Evans, playing in contemporary dress for the first time since he became a major star, met with disappointment when he unveiled a Terence Rattigan double bill consisting of **The Browning Version** and **Harlequinade** (10-12-49, Coronet). His co-star was Edna Best. In the drama, a mediocre schoolteacher, whose mean-mouthed wife has been openly unfaithful and who is about to retire, finds a moment of touching happiness when a young student (Peter Scott-Smith) affectionately presents him with a copy of Browning's translation of *Agamemnon*. The comedy depicted the confusion into which a famous but aging acting couple are thrown in the midst of their touring revival of *Romeo and Juliet*, when the man's long-forgotten daughter by an earlier marriage suddenly appears, carrying her own baby. The bill ran less than nine weeks.

Monserrat (10-29-49, Fulton), Lillian Hellman's translation of Emmanuel Robles's French drama, fared no better. Learning that one of his officers, Monserrat (William Redfield), has helped Simon Bolivar elude capture, Monserrat's commanding officer, Izquierdo (Emlyn Williams), devises a fiendish revenge. He rounds up six innocent people and tells Monserrat they will die, one at a time, unless he reveals where Bolivar has fled. As they are shot, Monserrat's will weakens, but one of the hostages—a young peasant girl (Julie Harris)—eloquently reinforces his determination. While the play was dismissed as mechanical and uneven, Williams's cold, cynical Izquierdo was highly praised, as was Harris's fiery big moment. With her special charisma she called attention to herself merely standing quietly against a wall with the other hostages and watching the action.

The season's first hit was another importation. Marcel Achard's *Auprès de ma blonde* was presented to Broadway in S. N. Behrman's version as **I Know My Love** (11-2-49, Shubert). Even those critics who had reservations about the play minimized them. After all, the Theatre Guild production starred the Lunts, celebrating their twenty-fifth anniversary as an acting team. A delighted Richard Watts Jr., wrote in the *Post,* "Miss Fontanne and Mr. Lunt play every scene and manage each speech and gesture with such ease and brilliance that it is happiness just to watch them. . . . There is a warmth about them, a sense of effortless gayety, a rich and mellow humanity, which gives their playing a quality that causes the theatre to glow." The play itself opens with an anniversary in 1939, the golden wedding of the Chanlers. But all is not well, and before long Mr. Chanler, whose granddaughter (Betty Caulfield) wants to marry simply for love, has ordered his own weak daughter (Katharine Bard), the mother of the girl, and his snobbish, embittered son (Geoffrey Kerr) out of the house. Fifty years earlier Lucy Talbot had defied her own father (Noel Leslie) to wed Tom Chanler, then a penniless graduate student. Over the years, after taking charge of the Chanler family business, Tom had driven his artistic brother (Henry Barnard) to suicide and made no effort to stop Lucy's brother (Hugh Franklin) from drinking himself to death, but nothing impairs the love Lucy retains for Tom. The Lunts made their first entrance descending a staircase as a slightly doddering, gray-haired couple, but the next act began with them, fifty years earlier, just as they are engaged, and subsequent scenes took them through the years up to 1920. The play ran until the Lunts returned to Wisconsin at the beginning of June.

The first original American play of the season was Doris Frankel's **Love Me Long** (11-7-49, 48th St.). It wasn't much to boast of. Several reviewers saw it as a rehash of the plot of *Private Lives,* without an iota of Coward's style or wit. Through some error two pair of newlyweds, the Kennedys (Russell Hardie and Shirley Booth) and the Skinners (George Keane and Anne Jackson), have both rented the same apartment. It turns out Mr. Skinner and Mrs. Kennedy had once been husband and wife, and by the final curtain it looks as if they will be again.

A revival of Strindberg's *The Father,* in a translation by Robert L. Joseph, raised its curtain at the Cort on the 16th. Raymond Massey was the much put-upon captain; Mady Christians, his vicious wife who drives him to an early grave by suggesting he is not truly the father of her child; and Grace Kelly, that daughter. The critics split on this one, although a majority seemed to feel the mounting lacked the requisite fire and steel. Young Kelly was welcomed as a promising player.

A great, established player came somewhat a cropper in the season's second look at Spanish history. **That Lady** (11-22-49, Martin Beck) was Kate O'Brien's dramatization of her own novel *For One Sweet Grape.* Having lost an eye in a duel when she was merely fourteen, Princess Anna de Mendoza y de Gomez (Katharine Cornell) must wear a patch over one eye. But that does not prevent a romance between her and Antonio Perez (Torin Thatcher), the secretary of state. King Philip II (Henry Daniell), one of her former lovers, is jealous. He forces Perez to flee and walls the princess up in a windowless room in her own castle. As usual, Cornell herself was praised, with Atkinson reporting to his *Times* readers, "This is one of her finest pieces of work—beautifully and lovingly detailed, both modest and imperious, all grace and sincerity." Rolf Gérard's somber-hued costumes and settings, recreating the sixteenth-century Spanish court, also won plaudits for their elegance and, in the case of the settings, for their sense of spaciousness. But the play was trounced as woeful and tedious.

So was Alexander Knox's **The Closing Door** (12-1-49, Empire). Knox was a Canadian actor who had won celebrity playing the title role in an American film biography of Woodrow Wilson. He wrote the new show as a vehicle for himself and his wife, Doris Nolan. Vail Traherne is a dangerous mental case, but clever enough to elude his wife's attempts to institutionalize him until he nearly kills their young son (Jack Dimond) by bashing him over the head. Only then does he agree to enter a mental hospital.

Benn W. Levy's London hit **Clutterbuck** (12-3-49, Biltmore) ran out the season, telling of two couples (Arthur Margetson and Ruth Ford, and Tom Helmore and Ruth Matteson) on a luxurious cruise. The wives have mixed feelings when they spot a man (Charles Campbell)—the Clutterbuck of the title—with whom they both once had flings in Venice; the husbands are equally thrown off balance when they realize they both had affairs with the man's new, baby-talking wife (Claire Carleton). Clutterbuck himself remains silent throughout the evening.

There was no disguising that William Walden's **Metropole** (12-6-49, Lyceum) was a send-up of *The New Yorker* magazine and its famous founder and editor, Harold Ross. Only Ross was now called Frederick M. Hill (Lee Tracy), and Hill's magazine gave the show its name. But Hill's world nearly comes crashing down after a very rich tycoon decides to start a rival publication to be called *The Gothamite.* He not only steals many of Hill's best writers, but is on the brink of wedding Hill's former wife (Edith Atwater). Hill eventually triumphs, even reclaiming his ex. The comedy was hardly a triumph, tying with a later entry for the season's shortest run—two performances.

More superb Rolf Gérard settings and costumes—this time often in gaudy, gilded colors—and several splendid performances kept a revival of Shaw's *Caesar and Cleopatra* on the boards for eighteen weeks following its opening on the 21st at the National. Cedric Hardwick was an aloof yet witty Caesar; Lilli Palmer, a delightfully kittenish Cleopatra; Bertha Belmore, an unexpectedly restrained Ftatateeta; and, best of all for many, Arthur Treacher, an intensely English, belligerently respectable Britannus.

Because a majority of his colleagues agreed with Ward Morehouse's assessment in the *Sun* of Garson Kanin's **The Rat Race** (12-22-49, Barrymore) as "a comedy with atmosphere, showmanship—and no heart at all . . . a hollow and strident hodge-podge," the play lingered for only ten and a half weeks. Her husband ran out on her and she hasn't had much luck as a rhumba contestant or taxi dancer, so Helen Brown (Betty Field) is deeply pessimistic. By contrast, Gus Hammer (Barry Nelson), a wide-eyed saxophone wizard from the Midwest, has come to New York full of hope. The two have rooms in the same boardinghouse, and soon meet. At one point Helen questions Gus, asking him if he smokes or drinks. His response to both questions is no, but he quickly adds that the answer to her next question will be yes. Though Gus's beloved saxophone is stolen, he and Helen look to work out some accommodation together. Donald Oenslager's imaginative, multi-leveled setting showed part of the rooming house's interior, its exterior, and a glimpse of the street and of a garden across the way. From her window in the rooming house, the landlady (Doro Merande) joined with Mac (Joseph Sweeney), who sat in the garden, to act as a chorus, commenting on Gus and Helen's problems and those of the others who crossed their paths.

After an eight-year absence, Grace George returned to the stage as co-star of Rosemary Casey's **The Velvet Glove** (12-26-49, Booth). Although she has the support of the salty but invalided Monsignor Burke (Walter Hampden) and the feisty Sister Monica (Jean Dixon), Mother Hildebrand is at first at a loss how to make the bishop (John Williams) change his mind about expelling from the school system she oversees a fine young history teacher (James Noble) who has supposedly been preaching leftist doctrines. She wins the man's reinstatement after persuading some rich local ladies to withhold donations for the bishop's pet seminary project. John Chapman's verdict in the *Daily News*, finding

the comedy "nice, and pleasant, . . . but slight," was echoed by most of his colleagues, as was his praise of the cast. Buttressed by the notices, the comedy appealed to largely Catholic audiences for nineteen weeks.

Only Ralph Alswang's split-stage setting, showing a young boy's bedroom on one side, a family living room on the other, and a largely empty, all-purpose area in between and in front of the rooms, won general commendations in the morning-after notices for Sarett and Herbert Rudley's **How Long till Summer** (12-27-49, Playhouse). Josh Jeffers (Josh White, Jr.), a black youngster, has such lurid nightmares and so verges on the brink of hysteria after his white buddy's father has chased him away and threatened him that his own father (Josh White), a lawyer with ties to shady white businessmen, abandons the quest he had undertaken at the suggestion of his associates for a congressional seat and decides to expose the men and to face the consequences. "Misguided," "muddled," and "hopeless" were some of the adjectives that doomed the play to a week's run.

With Maurice Evans now in charge, the City Center placed four bills on its boards between year's end and early February. Each was slated for a two-week run. The first was Oliver Goldsmith's *She Stoops to Conquer* on the 28th with Celeste Holm as Kate and Brian Aherne as Young Marlow. It was replaced on January 11 by *The Corn Is Green,* with Eva Le Gallienne. The final offering, on February 8, was *The Heiress,* with Basil Rathbone in his original role and Margaret Phillips and Edna Best in support. The house's third offering, in late January, was such a marked success that it will be discussed in more detail in its proper sequence.

The new year got off to a splendid start with Carson McCullers's dramatization of her own novel **The Member of the Wedding** (1-5-50, Empire). Frankie Addams (Julie Harris) is a lonely, sensitive twelve-year-old girl. She lives in a small southern town with a widowed father (William Hansen), who ignores her, and Berenice Sadie Brown (Ethel Waters), the family's warm, understanding, four-times-married Negro cook. Berenice, along with Frankie's bespectacled six-year-old cousin, John Henry West (Brandon de Wilde), makes life bearable for the girl until her brother, Jarvis (James Holden), returns from the army and asks her to be a member of his wedding. An elated Frankie tells John Henry, "I know that the bride and my brother are the 'we' of me." But her joy is shattered when she discovers that she cannot accompany the newlyweds on their honeymoon, as she had expected to do. Although John Henry dies of meningitis and Berenice leaves to take on a fifth husband, early stirrings of adolescent romance promise better days. Whatever they thought of the play, and their evaluations ran from "rare and special" to "shaky," critics were elated by the three principal performances. Waters's Berenice, generally perceived as the high point in her variegated career, was "a masterpiece of comedy and pathos . . . Lines roll from her lips with such genuine emotion there can never be a false lilt to her speech. . . . [Her] laugh is a trumpet of pure joy." Eight-year-old de Wilde "won all the hearts in the audience last evening; for he is resourceful and self-contained." But for many the star of the evening was Harris: "She must be fractious, fantastic and ugly, heroic in her own mind, antagonistic and presumptive, utterly unreasonable, and with all of that, always touching. Miss Harris does it with extraordinary success, with lightning changes and inner consistency." The play won the New York Drama Critics Circle Award, ran 501 performances, and made Harris a name to be reckoned with.

. . .

Julie [née Julia Ann] **Harris** (b. 1925) was born in Grosse Point, Mich., and educated at the Yale School of Drama. The slightly elfin actress made her Broadway debut in *It's a Gift* (1945). She subsequently gained critical attention and approval in a series of short-lived flops.

. . .

While many reviewers applauded **The Enchanted** (1-18-50, Lyceum), which Maurice Valency took from Jean Giraudoux's *Intermezzo,* the public would not buy it, apparently feeling last year's not dissimilar grotesqueries of Chaillot's Madwoman and her cronies sufficed. Isabel (Leueen MacGrath), a French schoolmarm, falls in love with the Ghost (John Baragrey) of a man who committed murder, then killed himself. She comes to believe that he and his fellow ghosts have something to teach her and her pupils. News of this outrages the local townfolk, especially the Inspector (Malcolm Keen), and almost everyone is soon up in arms against her. But the handsome young Supervisor (Wesley Addy), who loves her, exorcises the Ghost. When the shock seemingly kills Isabel, a compassionate Doctor (Russell Collins) and the Supervisor's protestations of love revive her.

Neither critics nor playgoers bought Mel Dinelli's **The Man** (1-19-50, Fulton), although many admired Dorothy Gish's acting. Her widowed Mrs. Gillis rents rooms in her old, no longer fashionable Victorian mansion. Trouble starts after she hires a handyman, Howard Wilton (Don Hanmer), unaware he is a psychopath always on the move because he can never remember whether or not he killed someone at his last job or home. He menaces several locals, kills Mrs. Gillis's dog, locks her in her house, and finally murders her.

Even those critics who confessed to not being able to understand all of it conceded that T. S. Eliot's **The Cocktail Party** (1-21-50, Henry Miller's) was an important play. In "simple and elegant, rather than soaring and vivid" blank verse, the American expatriate told about a psychiatrist (Alec Guinness) who reconciles a husband (Robert Flemyng) and wife (Eileen Peel), and sends the man's mistress (Irene Worth) to a martyr's death as a missionary. He suggests that all anyone can do in life is make the best of a bad deal. Guinness won accolades metamorphosing from the gin-drinking singer of raucous ballads in the opening act's cocktail party to a correct, attentive Harley Street shrink in the second half. Cathleen Nesbitt also garnered laurels as a snooping matron. For all its difficulties, the play became one of the season's rages and ran a full year.

The next week ushered in one quick flop and three hits. The lone flop, William Berney and Howard Richardson's **Design for a Stained Glass Window** (1-23-50, Mansfield), was set in Elizabethan England. Having to choose between two partners in a butchery for a husband, Margaret (Martha Scott) selects John Clitherow (Charlton Heston). His associate, Robin Flemming (Ralph Clanton), reacts to her choice by leaving the enterprise, renouncing Catholicism, winning riches alongside Drake, and becoming the Earl of Hartford, one of the queen's favorites. So when Margaret is truthfully accused of hiding Catholic priests and encouraging popery, he leads the vendetta against her. She manages to send her son to safety in France, but she herself is condemned to death.

The first of the week's trio of hits was **The Happy Time** (1-24-50, Plymouth), which Samuel Taylor dramatized from Robert Fontaine's novel. The *Journal-American*'s Robert Garland celebrated it as "an entrancing new comedy of life, love and adolescence." Bibi (Johnny Stewart) is the teenaged son of a Scottish Maman (Leora Dana) and a French-Canadian Papa (Claude Dauphin). Maman worries that Bibi will be corrupted by Papa's pleasure-loving brothers, the dashing, lady-killing Uncle Desmonde (Richard Hart) and the toping Uncle Louis (Kurt Kasznar), who carries a wine-filled water cooler about with him. Perhaps Maman has some grounds for concern, for Bibi dotes on Desmonde's blonde fiancée, Mignonette (Eva Gabor), a former acrobat's assistant, and steals her nightgown. After Bibi sheepishly admits to the theft, the newly engaged Desmonde presents him with his no longer needed collection of women's fancy garters. But Papa takes them from him, admonishing him, "If you wish to be a man who collects garters, do not do it second-hand." Just then a girl (Marlene Cameron) whose braces and prim hairdo had made Bibi indifferent to her walks in—her braces gone and her hair beautifully styled. Bibi's voice breaks as he tries to speak about her. The comedy enjoyed a 614-performance run and subsequently was made into a popular musical.

The third in the City Center's series of revivals was Shaw's only play set in America, his drolly jaundiced look at Revolutionary times, *The Devil's Disciple*. Evans was Dick Dudgeon and Dennis King the show-stealing General Burgoyne. Following its opening on the 25th, most aisle-sitters concurred with Atkinson's salute to "the skill, gusto and warm humor of the acting in this uproarious escapade," so the play quickly sold out. The cry for an extension was answered when the play reopened at the Royale on February 25. There it ran out the season, but because of union demands, including totally new scenery and costumes, the mounting did not make money.

Another revival, at the cort on the 26th, also ran out the season and toured at length, but allegedly only made money because the star tore up her huge weekly paychecks. That star was Katharine Hepburn, and her vehicle was Shakespeare's *As You Like It*. Critics of the period were on an anti-Shakespearean-comedy kick, so words and comments such as "potboiler," "silly," "a rather sorry comedy," and "might have been written for May Day at a girls' boarding school" were sprinkled through their notices. Even Hepburn came in for some disparaging remarks, especially about "that Down East Granny's voice of hers," "her not-too-pleasant voice," or a voice "a little hard and shallow for Shakespeare's poetry." But the same critics who perceived her as unready for Shakespearean foolery conceded that she delighted her audience in a mounting so lavish it smacked of nineteenth-century staging. Of the star's supporting company, William Prince's Orlando, Cloris Leachman's Celia, and Whitford Kane's Corin received the most prominent attention.

Only their old favorite Lee Tracy and one sturdy supporting comedienne, Vicki Cummings, grabbed favorable notices from the critics in Walter Bullock and Daniel Archer's **Mr. Barry's Etchings** (1-31-50, 48th St.). Mr. Barry is a warmhearted man who repairs kids' toys for them, dabbles in his garden, and does expert engraving. Learning of a number of needy local charities, he engraves $50 bills and presents the organizations as many of them as they need. Initially no one seems to notice the small change Mr. Barry has made in his own counterfeits, giving the heretofore dour Grant a pleasant smile. But some professional counterfeiters, led by a notorious lady hood, "Fifty" Ferris, catch on and attempt to horn in. So do a group of T-men, headed by Tom Crosby (Scott McKay). Since both groups pretend they are from *Life*, Barry becomes a little suspicious. He holds the gangsters at the point of a toy gun. And Tom, having fallen in love with Barry's

daughter (Gaye Jordan), will try to obtain a presidential pardon for his future father-in-law.

Whatever it lost in its transfer from the printed page to the stage, **The Innocents** (2-1-50, Playhouse), William Archibald's theatricalization of Henry James's *The Turn of the Screw,* was compensated for by a brilliant mounting. The curtain rose on one of Jo Mielziner's most memorable settings—of an English country home in the 1880s: "Its simple enormity dwarfs the people, as a huge staircase swings up around a curved wall, a great window reveals gloomy trees, a huge Oriental chest and a mantel dominate the moss color brocaded walls and dim Chinese paintings brood from above." The mansion is occupied only by a secretive housekeeper (Isobel Elsom), two orphaned youngsters, Flora (Iris Mann) and Miles (David Cole), whose guardian wants nothing to do with them, and their new governess, Miss Giddens (Beatrice Straight). An indescribable terror pervades the home. She soons learn that the children are haunted by the ghosts of a former governess and the woman's lover, who had been a butler there. She manages to send Flora away, but when she tries to rid Miles of his obsession, the shock kills the boy. She can only rationalize that he is at least free. Peter Glenville's fluid direction "retained a suppressed atmosphere of ominous unrest and strain throughout the play." The drama ran out the season.

Leaving Arnold Manoff's **All You Need Is One Good Break** (2-9-50, Mansfield), comedian Milton Berle was overheard to remark that it should have been called *All You Need Is One Good Act*. The "disorderly and hysterical" nature of the play was underscored by set designer Samuel Leve's "rumbling his gadget scenery [showing frowsy street scenes and interiors] around at a great rate under [Peggy] Clark's swooping spots." Compounding the confusion, a substantial portion of the dialogue was in Yiddish. Marty Rothman (John Berry) is a flashy, ne'er-do-well shipping clerk so busy dreaming of striking it rich with a lucky bet that he cannot help his ailing mother (Anna Appel), his impoverished father (Reuben Wendorff), his dance-mad sister (Ellie Pine), or even himself. He winds up in jail, having a nervous breakdown.

The lone original American work (as opposed to adaptation) to score a success during the season was William Inge's **Come Back, Little Sheba** (2-15-50, Booth). Yet the play itself was not well received by most critics. The *Herald Tribune*'s Howard Barnes called it a "straggling play," while the *Daily Mirror*'s Robert Coleman suggested it was an "underwritten drama" containing "the synopsis for a good play, but the author hasn't filled in the scenario." However, critics were in virtual agreement about the excellence of its two stars' performances. Atkinson saw Shirley Booth as superb, explaining, "She has the shuffle, the maddening garrulity and the rasping voice of the slattern, but withal she imparts to the role the warmth, generosity and valor of a loyal and affectionate woman." Sidney Blackmer as her worn-down, patient husband, who does not explode until the play is almost finished, did "his best job in recent years." Doc is an alcoholic, temporarily on the wagon. He was forced to give up medical school to marry Lola. But they soon lost their child and Doc has had to be content as a chiropractor. Lola has become a sloven, forever dreaming of past days, and especially of their cute, white puppy, Sheba, who ran away long ago. She moons, "I'll soon be forty. Those years have vanished—vanished into thin air. Just disappeared—like Little Sheba." After they take in Marie (Joan Lorring), an attractive college girl, as a boarder, Doc starts resenting her beaux, unaware that he is jealous of them. He grows furious when she appears to ditch a trusting young man for a dumb athlete, so goes on a bender. Home from the hospital, he and Lola return to their humdrum ways. The play ran for 190 performances and launched Inge's Broadway career.

. . .

William [Motter] **Inge** (1913–73) was born in Independence, Kans., and educated at the University of Kansas. He served as a schoolteacher and as an actor before accepting the post of drama critic for the St. Louis *Star-Times* in 1943. He left the paper after Margo Jones presented his first play, *Farther Off from Heaven* (1947), at her celebrated Dallas theatre.

. . .

Arthur Laurents's **The Bird Cage** (2-22-50, Coronet) required a two-tiered setting (by Boris Aronson) to show the various sections of the nightclub which gave the play its title. A few aisle-sitters thought the setting was the best thing about the evening. They rejected the play as "chiefly sound and fury." Wally Williams (Melvyn Douglas) is the club's cruelly self-serving owner. He betrays and destroys a decent partner (Sanford Meisner), smashes the fingers of another partner (Laurence Hugo) who loves to play the piano, drives his socialite wife (Maureen Stapleton) to drink, and tries to force his son (Wright King) to have sex with a woman who spurned him. When he realizes he has alienated everyone who cared for him, he sets the nightclub on fire.

Luminous performances by Fredric March and his wife, Florence Eldridge—especially the latter—were not sufficient to save **Now I Lay Me Down to Sleep** (3-2-50, Broadhurst), Elaine Ryan's stage version of Ludwig Bemelmans's novel. When World War II breaks out, General Leonidas Erosa, who has been living at Biarritz, hires a broken-down Greek freighter, packs it with his wines, good food, and his other belongings,

and heads with his coterie back to his native Ecuador. First among his motley band is his prim, prudish English mistress, Miss Leonora Graves—a woman he met when he saved her from suicide and whose numerous subsequent attempts he has regularly foiled. Though she is a dutiful mistress, Erosa is hardly loyal. After he dies in an Ecuadorian earthquake, Miss Graves prepares to return to England. But a baby—Erosa's latest illegitimate offspring—is left on her doorstep, so she consents to remain and raise it. Bemelmans was known for his identifiably stylized drawings, and, while he did not design the settings, Wolfgang Roth's scenery recaptured his style.

Most critics never liked *Tobacco Road,* and they liked it even less when it was revived at the 48th Street Theatre on the 6th with an "All Negro Cast." One week and it was gone.

For the umpteenth time this season some beautiful acting illumined a lacklustre play. But since Helen Hayes, giving a "fragrant, lacy performance," led the cast that brought to life **The Wisteria Trees** (3-29-50, Martin Beck), the mounting was able to struggle on for twenty-one weeks. The drama was merely Joshua Logan's transfer of Chekhov's *The Cherry Orchard* to the turn-of-the-century American South. Madam Ranevskaya became Lucy Andree Ransdell; her brother Gaev, Gavin Andree (Walter Abel); and the upstart Lopahin, who argued futilely for the cherry orchard to be broken up into saleable lots, the self-made Yancy Loper (Kent Smith), who urges Lucy to consign her wisteria plantation to the same fate.

Even the acting in **Cry of the Peacock** (4-11-50, Mansfield), the season's second two-performance fiasco, was assailed by some critics. The play was Cecil Robson's adaptation of Jean Anouilh's *Ardèle ou la Marguerite.* The General (Raymond Lovell) and his demented wife (Lili Darvas) call a family conference to see what can be done to prevent his hunchbacked sister from wedding a hunchbacked teacher. Another sister (Marta Linden) arrives with both her husband (Oscar Karlweis) and her lover (Philip Tonge) in tow. The General's son (Peter Brandon) comes with the sister-in-law (Patricia Wheel) the young man wants to steal. Before the assemblage can take action, word is received that the hunchbacks have killed themselves. Cecil Beaton provided the players with an extravagantly elaborate baroque château and colorful 1912 outfits.

Elsa Shelley's **With a Silk Thread** (4-12-50, Lyceum) described how a nasty, jealous surgeon (Philip Huston) becomes nice and understanding after his actress-wife (Claire Luce) has an affair with an attractive young performer (Phil Arthur) who played Marchbanks to her Candida. Critics found the motivations baffling, but did like Watson Barratt's beach-house setting, with real sand around it and the sea heard thundering "like a fleet of angry bombers."

Happily, everything fell into place in the season's last hit, a revival at the Imperial on the 24th of James M. Barrie's *Peter Pan*. Jean Arthur, "looking and sounding pleasantly like Mary Martin," was a "boyish and engaging" Peter; Boris Karloff, employing "a grand manner that is pure story book," was a "captivating" Hook. Diminutive Joe E. Marks's Smee was also singled out for praise. Ralph Alswang and Motley were applauded, respectively, for their settings and costumes, while Leonard Bernstein's music was heard as "fascinatingly unworldly and tinkling." The beloved show added 321 more performances to its ongoing record.

The season's final novelties comprised a quickly folding double bill. Kenneth White's **Freight** (4-26-50, Fulton) was set in a freight car where nine frightened Negroes are fleeing from a lynching. A knife-wielding southern cracker (Glen Gordon) climbs aboard and begins to taunt the blacks. But they turn the tables after seizing the knife, belittling him with the ultimate humiliation that a white man isn't worth killing. The drama had received encouraging word of mouth when it had been done earlier in Harlem by the American Negro Theatre, but lost its punch in the relative vastness of even a small Broadway house. The other half of the bill gave New Yorkers their first chance to see a play by the Englishman who, even more noisily than T. S. Eliot, was attempting to bring back poetry to the modern stage. Christopher Fry's blank-verse comedy, **A Phoenix Too Frequent** reused a motif popular since classical times. In ancient Rome, a widow (Nina Foch), along with her loyal servant (Vicki Cummings), is sitting sacrificially in her recently deceased husband's tomb awaiting her own death, when a handsome centurion (Richard Derr) enters. The widow and the soldier are instantly taken with each other, so when they discover that the body the soldier was supposed to be guarding has disappeared, they put the woman's dead husband in its place and go off arm in arm.

The call to restore poetry to the stage would be relatively short-lived. Another innovation would have a longer life. Although the acidulous George Jean Nathan characterized the newly voguish arena staging or theatre-in-the-round as "an economical device for getting out of renting a high-priced regular theatre and palming off the economy as something very special in the way of art," the sort of theatre in which the stage is in the center and the audience surrounds it still flourishes. Broadway first saw it when just this sort of playhouse was shaped out of a ballroom in the Edison Hotel. The play selected to inaugurate the new Arena on May 31 was George Kelly's *The Show-Off*. Curiously, the lead

was given to Lee Tracy, who had played a supporting role in the original 1924 production, and who, at fifty-two, was considerably too old for the lead. Furthermore, critics who had constantly praised him felt this time he failed to impart the necessary hard-core nastiness to his Aubrey Piper. The comedy was withdrawn after three weeks.

1950–1951

Although the number of novelties spurted during the season—the count given variously as somewhere between forty-three and forty-six—there was little cause for optimism. The Pulitzer committee felt no new play was worthy of its award—only the fifth time in more than forty years that it had passed over a season's new dramas. And the dearth of quality was aggravated by a continuing economic crunch. The day when a play that ran 100 performances could reasonably expect to recoup its costs and be considered a commercial hit were gone forever. Thus *Billy Budd* and *The Autumn Garden*, both of which inched past the 100-performance mark, closed with losses of $105,000 and $70,000 respectively, while the relatively low-budget *Second Threshold* ran for 126 performances yet wound up $30,000 in the red.

The summer months were a bit busier than they had been of late, though they produced nothing exciting. The Arena, the new theatre-in-the-round at the Edison Hotel, brought out Shakespeare's *Julius Caesar* for its second offering on June 20th. While Marc Antony (Alfred Ryder) turned and turned to harangue the surrounding crowd, noisy responses rang out from actors rushing through the audience on all sides. The production, indifferently received, ran for a month with Basil Rathbone as Cassius, Joseph Holland as Brutus, and Horace Braham as Caesar. One curious aspect of the play's reviews was the critics' comments on the tragedy. Last season they had disparaged Shakespearean comedy; now some major ones were unhappy with his more serious work. Howard Barnes of the *Herald Tribune* belittled it as "a second-rate Shakespearean classic," while in the *Times* Brooks Atkinson advised his readers to "Skip the first half," which he suggested got bogged down in excessive exposition.

A group headed by Sam Wanamaker and Terese Hayden, and calling itself the Festival Theatre, began what was supposed to be a succession of four programs with **Parisienne** (7-24-50, Fulton), Ashley Dukes's transcription of Henri Becque's comedy. It told of a scheming young lady (Faye Emerson) who aids the political ambitions of her lover (Francis Lederer) by having a number of affairs. The group's second effort was a revival at the same house on August 7 of Ibsen's *The Lady from the Sea.* Luise Rainer, the once celebrated film star, played a woman almost seduced from her marriage by a sailor she loved long ago. Both mountings were greeted coolly and ran for two weeks apiece.

Garson Kanin threw his hat into the ring early on with **The Live Wire** (8-17-50, Playhouse). A group of vets, all would-be actors, share a quonset hut with a stunning view of the Manhattan skyline. They add to their number a pleasant-looking young man, Leo Mack (Scott McKay). Leo soon proves to be an unprincipled heel, lying, deceiving, and back-stabbing to land a big Hollywood contract with the help of a slick, high-powered agent (Murvyn Vye).

The Festival Theatre's third effort, at the Fulton on the 21st, was Lynn Riggs's **Borned in Texas,** which turned out to be a revival of his twenty-year-old *Road-side.* Its reception was so chilly that it was pulled after one week, and the company abandoned its plan for a fourth show.

James Bridie's London hit **Daphne Laureola** (9-18-50, Music Box) was perceived as a mediocre vehicle for its magnetic star, Dame Edith Evans. She won kudos as the fiftyish wife of a much older man (Cecil Parker). She consoles herself for her disappointing marriage with snifters of brandy, a fling with an ardent young Pole (John Van Dreelen), and, after her husband's death, by running off with his brawny chauffeur (Peter Williams). But Evans's good notices—"serenely triumphant," "grace and style"—could not lure in American play-goers.

The season's first hit came from a famous French playwright, long resident in California, who was attempting his initial effort in English. Louis Verneuil's **Affairs of State** (9-25-50, Royale) was purportedly written as a vehicle for its star, Celeste Holm. George Henderson (Shepperd Strudwick), appointed as a senator from Colorado to fill out the term of a man who died in office, now hopes to run for a full term. But his old friend, Philip Russell (Reginald Owen), a former secretary of state, warns him he cannot win since he is not married. True, marriage is like a besieged fortress, with those inside anxious to get out and those outside pining to get in. He suggests that his niece, Irene Elliott, currently serving as Henderson's temporary secretary, be presented, at least in public, as the senator's wife. Meanwhile, since Russell is aware that Henderson is having an affair with his young wife (Barbara O'Neil), he works behind the scenes to defeat him. But Irene, who protests that any superior woman "has a thousand charms I'll never have and she does a million things I've never done," is as wily as her uncle. So, while

falling in love with Henderson, she makes herself so charming and so indispensable that Henderson finally proposes marriage. He also wins an appointment as under secretary of state. Mrs. Russell, allowing it is much simpler to recover from a wounded love than a happy memory, embarks on a round-the-world trip with her husband. In the *Daily Mirror,* Robert Coleman welcomed the entry as "a slick, suave and amusing drawing-room comedy" and Holm's transformation from the bookish schoolmarm to the poised and attractive wife as "perfect." Propelled by such notices, the comedy ran for 610 performances.

Owen Crump's **Southern Exposure** (9-26-50, Biltmore) reportedly broke the four-year attendance record at Margo Jones's famed theatre in Dallas, but when she brought it to New York it met with swift rejection. Richard Watts, Jr., dismissed it in the *Post* as "a rather negative little antic." A young Vermont Yankee (Cameron Mitchell), whose satire on Natchez's racial situation has been banned there, comes to the southern city spoiling for a fight. Under the name John Salguod, he rents a room from a genteelly impoverished spinster, Penelope Mayweather (Betty Greene Little). She all but faints when she discovers who he is and warns him to keep hidden. Before long is he captivated by the old gal and by her rich, youthful, and attractive relation, Carol Randall (Pat Crowley). He proposes to Carol after weaning her away from her worthless fiancé and helps Penelope get a $5000 advance on her sensation-packed diary.

For the second time in the still new season, a great British actress won laurels in a far less than great play. The play was Lesley Storm's London hit **Black Chiffon** (9-27-50, 48th St.); the actress, Flora Robson. Robson was cast as a comfortably well-off woman of heretofore good character who seemingly inexplicably steals a black chiffon nightgown shortly before the wedding of her son (Richard Gale). A psychiatrist (Anthony Ireland) concludes that she has an unnatural attachment to the boy and hoped the scandal would wreck the wedding plans. Brought to her senses, she accepts a quiet prison term rather than make a destructive public issue of the matter. Solely on the strength of Robson's playing, the drama ran for fourteen weeks.

The year's second hit was Wolcott Gibbs's **Season in the Sun** (9-28-50, Cort). Since Gibbs was the *New Yorker*'s drama critic, his newspaper colleagues might have been accused of bending over backward to be kind to him, but since the public soon agreed with the virtually unanimous raves, such as John Chapman's hailing it as "a grand evening of laughter" in the *Daily News,* everyone was happy. Everyone also knew the sort of magazine its hero worked for, even if it was not mentioned by name. But George Crane (Richard

Whorf), a recovering alcoholic, is determined to quit the magazine and write a book denouncing New York City's corrupting influences. He and his wife, Emily (Nancy Kelly), have taken a bungalow on Fire Island. George's serenity is interrupted time and again. His eccentric landlady (Grace Valentine) announces she takes out the window screens whenever she has to rent to fairies, "so's they can *fly* in and out." A luscious blonde, Deedy (Joan Diener), appears with George's old drinking buddy, John Colgate (King Calder), a famous correspondent. And shortly after the Cranes are visited by their aggressively straitlaced summer neighbors, the Andersons (Eddie Mayehoff and Doreen Lang), Colgate brings over a notorious New York madam, Molly Burden (Paula Lawrence), who discloses that Mr. Anderson is one of her best customers. Horace Dodd [Arthur Dodd in many programs] (Anthony Ross), Crane's crusty editor, also shows up. What appears to be a brief fling between Deedy and George drives Emily away and George back to the bottle. The play ends with the Cranes reconciled, but with Deedy turning her blandishments onto Dodd, who seems determined to sit out a hurricane on the island. Knowing playgoers read real names into the fictitious ones: for example, Polly Adler for Molly Burden and Harold Ross for Horace or Arthur Dodd. The comedy ran for 367 performances.

Once again, for the third time this season, an English actress walked off with critical garlands although her play was slammed, only this time she had to share them with two male associates. In Aldous Huxley's **The Gioconda Smile** (10-7-50, Lyceum), Henry Hutton (Basil Rathbone), who had taken on a young, pretty second wife (Marian Russell), is condemned to be hanged for killing his rich, invalided first wife. But, in the nick of time, a perceptive, sly doctor (George Relph) gets Janet Spence (Valerie Taylor), who had hoped to wed Hutton herself, to confess to the poisoning. Taylor, Rathbone, and Relph were all hugely applauded, but the drama survived only five weeks.

Having met with marked success for their earlier propaganda dramas, James Gow and Arnaud d'Usseau tried and failed with **Legend of Sarah** (10-11-50, Fulton), a comedy meant to spoof family pride. Minerva Pinney (Marsha Hunt), after fighting with her lover (Tom Helmore), a biographer of the debunking school, returns to Pinneyfield and proposes to turn the town into another Williamsburg, in honor of Sarah Pinney, who delayed General Howe and thus saved Washington's army during the Revolution. But on seeing the manner in which the greedy town banker (Philip Coolidge) hopes to take advantage of her scheme, and how ready her associates are to dispossess an old man (Joseph Sweeney) from his family's ancestral home, Minerva has second thoughts. When her feisty mother

(Ethel Griffes) discloses that Sarah was merely a promiscuous tramp and Howe merely another bed partner, Minerva scuttles her plans and is reunited with her lover.

John Steinbeck met with instant failure after critics tore apart his **Burning Bright** (10-18-50, Broadhurst). Its story was simple. At fifty Joe Saul (Kent Smith) despairs of Mordeen (Barbara Bel Geddes), his young wife, ever presenting him with a child. She realizes that he is sterile, so she sleeps with his new associate, Victor (Martin Brooks), and becomes pregnant. When Joe Saul discovers the truth he is devastated. But then, concluding "there is a shining," accepts that the world must be repopulated one way or another. Critics assailed the writing, which was in "a pretentiously archaic language that is not realistic and yet never manages to scale the heights of true blank verse." Moreover, although the character names remained the same, the settings and the figures' occupations changed capriciously in each of the three acts. Act I was set at a circus where the three performed; Act II on a farm where they worked; and Act III took them onto a ship at sea.

"Unevenly limp" was William Hawkins's assessment in the *World-Telegram and Sun* of the revival of Shaw's antiwar comedy *Arms and the Man* at the Arena on the 19th. Not only did he and his colleagues find fault with the performances, but many slammed the play itself as "an oppressive bit of foolery," "not much fun, having neither bite nor vigor," or "a museum piece." Yet, with no little forcing, this mounting, which offered Francis Lederer as Bluntschli, Lee Grant as Raina, and Sam Wanamaker as Sergius, ran for 110 performancres. (A few days later, Shaw's *Mrs. Warren's Profession* was revived off Broadway at the Bleecker Street Playhouse on the 25th with Estelle Winwood as Mrs. Warren and John Loder as Sir George. Only Winwood walked away with good notices.)

John Patrick's **The Curious Savage** (10-24-50, Martin Beck) was set in "The Cloisters," a comfortable, homey institution for wealthy, harmless mental patients. These include a statistician (Robert Emhardt) who can only play a few notes on the violin but believes himself a virtuoso, a fine pianist (Hugh Reilly) who will not perform because he believes his face was scarred in the war, and a woman (Gladys Henson) with a long list of pet hatreds who refuses to answer questions. Into this group, three grasping grandchildren bring Mrs. Savage (Lillian Gish). They are concerned not because she dyes her hair bright blue or because she insists on carrying about a teddy bear, but because she is giving away her $10,000,000 inheritance to make people happy. Before long she is popular with the inmates and the staff, so the head nurse (Flora Campbell) fakes a burning of Mrs. Savage's irreplaceable, negotiable bonds, thus ridding her of the grandchildren. When Mrs. Savage says she would like to remain, the doctor (Sydney Smith) warns her that the peace she finds there is like the reflection of the moon on a dark lake—destroyed by any slight disturbance on the surface. Responding that she wants what everyone wants—to want nothing—Mrs. Savage agrees to return to the real world and try to make people happy there. Critics were delighted with Gish and most of her supporting players, but found the comedy only intermittently entertaining.

The English were not having a happy season on Broadway. For the week and a half that it survived, Frederick Lonsdale's **The Day After Tomorrow** (10-26-50, Booth) described the attempts of a self-assured American millionairess (Beatrice Pearson) to help a down-and-out family of English lords and ladies, and to marry one (Ralph Michael) of them. She is brought to earth by their insistence that she take them as they are—without her money. (By chance, the heiress, like Mrs. Savage, was said to be worth $10,000,000.) Melville Cooper earned some of the best notices as a quizzical lord.

The titular heroine (Jessica Tandy) of Samson Raphaelson's **Hilda Crane** (11-1-50, Coronet) returns to live with her mother (Beulah Bondi) in her small hometown of Winona, Illinois, after a series of marital and professional failures in Chicago and New York. She is wooed by Henry Ottwell (John Alexander), a stodgy businessman who has loved her for many years, and by Charles Jensen (Frank Sundstrom), a professor who wants her only as a mistress. At her mother's behest, she chooses Ottwell, although she does not love him. Ottwell's mother (Evelyn Varden) attempts to dissuade Hilda by offering her any one of several substantial rewards and says, if necessary, she will expose Hilda's louche past. But Hilda angrily retorts, "I've never done anything in my life that I didn't believe in at the time," and vows she will stop at nothing to wed the woman's son. The argument drives Mrs. Ottwell to an early grave. Two years later, an unhappily married Hilda decides to go out for a night on the town with Jensen. Ottwell learns of this, only to beg Hilda not to look down on him if he forgives her. Despairing of her future, Hilda swallows a handful of sleeping pills. The evening received generally excellent notices. Raphaelson's effort was hailed as "an interesting play," "his finest play," and "powerful drama." Of Tandy, Hawkins wrote, "In her playing a remarkable lyrical quality of hope mingles with growing hopelessness. She has a warmth here that is entirely unlike her portrayal of the remote neurotic of 'Streetcar.'" Yet, possibly because the two major morning papers were not in its corner, the play struggled along for seventy performances.

Christopher Fry's blank-verse London hit **The Lady's Not for Burning** (11-8-50, Royale) ran more than twice as long, propelled in part by the brief rage for Fry's consciously artificial style and in part by the lush performing of a fine cast headed by John Gielgud and Pamela Brown. Thomas Mendip, a usually misanthropic soldier, who, because he is tired of life, has confessed to a murder he did not commit, comes to the aid of Jennet Jourdemayne, a beautiful lady falsely accused of witchcraft. A compassionate justice (Peter Bull) spares them both and allows the pair to go off arm in arm.

Two of the season's most memorable hits followed in short order. Reviews for Clifford Odets's **The Country Girl** (11-10-50, Lyceum) were mixed, ranging from "a tense and absorbing play" through "runs down a small hill, but does so in a bravura manner" to "almost embarrassing . . . we couldn't bring ourselves to believe in it." Yet even the naysayers generally conceded that the three principals gave electrifying performances. An ambitious young director, Bernie Dodd (Steven Hill), overrides the objections of his author and producer and hires Frank Elgin (Paul Kelly) to star in a new play. Elgin is considered a has-been, having destroyed his career by his drinking. He blames his problem on his wife, Georgie (Uta Hagen), who he insists became a suicidal alcoholic after the death of their daughter. When Frank prods Georgie into seeking a raise and long-term contract for him from Dodd, the director concludes she is also a meddler and orders her to stay away. But Elgin turns up on opening night too drunk to act, and Dodd learns from Georgie who is the real would-be suicide. Elgin sobers up in time to make a hit at the New York premiere. Although Georgie has grown to admire and even love Dodd, she promises Frank she will stick by him so long as he does not make her unhappy. She warns him, "You, Frank, have to be strong enough to bear that uncertainty." The play ran for seven months.

John van Druten's **Bell, Book and Candle** (11-14-50, Barrymore) opened four nights later and closed on the same evening as the Odets play. Atkinson assured his readers he meant no pun when he called the comedy "completely enchanting." Gillian Holroyd (Lilli Palmer), a lovely, kittenish witch, employs her black arts to get whatever she wants. And right now she wants Shep Henderson (Rex Harrison), the dashing publisher in the next apartment. He promptly knocks on her door, falls in love with her, and shortly afterward proposes. To further please him, Gillian conjures up an author he has been trying to nab. But the happy arrangement looks to be spoiled by Gillian's brother (Scott McKay) and aunt (Jean Adair), both of whom are also witches. Although the brother has retired he promises, "I'll make a farewell appearance, to stop this!" And they spill the beans to Shep. So that she may keep him, Gillian herself gives up witchery, a sacrifice she insists ought to prove to Shep that she is only human. Harrison and Palmer, husband and wife at the time, were applauded on all sides as "beguiling," with Harrison proving "a farceur of extraordinary talent, giving the victim exactly the bewildered touch the script demanded" and Palmer "warmly winning."

A flock of flops came in next. Audiences arriving at Paul Crabtree's intermissionless **A Story for a Sunday Evening** (11-17-50, Playhouse) saw no curtain, and a bare stage in front of them. When the houselights dim, David (Crabtree) explains he has rented the theatre for a single Sunday run-through of a play he is writing. It is a triangle play with David as the husband, Evelyn (Cloris Leachman) as his wife, and Beatrice (Nan Martin) as the other woman. All during the run-through the characters interrupt the action to complain that the dialogue or incidents are not true to life and to suggest changes. Leachman copped the few good notices the evening received.

Matters were no better at Victor Wolfson's **Pride's Crossing** (11-20-50, Biltmore). The wealthy, aristocratic Bayard Goodale died, leaving a half interest in his house to his servant-mistress, a lusty Polish girl named Zilla (Tamara Geva), by whom he had a young son (Donny Harris). Zilla has remained to take care of the widowed Mrs. Goodale (Mildred Dunnock), but after Zilla learns that the Goodale grandson (Robin Michael) has a weak heart she goads her own son into playing roughly with the boy, in hopes the exertion will kill him. Then Mrs. Goodale's son (John Baragrey) brings a schoolteacher (Katharine Bard) into the picture. She divines Zilla's scheme, so convinces the youngster's father to remove him. She leaves with them. Zilla is left to look after her own youngster and Mrs. Goodale, who may have some sort of neurotic attachment to the servant girl.

William Dinner and William Morum's **Edwina Black** (11-21-50, Booth) was the latest London hit to find no favor in New York. Its story was not unlike that of an earlier importation which also failed, *The Gioconda Smile*. After Edwina's death it is discovered that she was poisoned. A Scotland Yard detective (Michael Shepley) learns that Mr. Black (Robert Harris) and Edwina's companion, Elizabeth Graham (Signe Hasso), had purchased an Italian villa together. Did they kill Edwina? Or did the Blacks' unsmiling servant, Ellen (Marjorie Rhodes), who was devoted to the dead woman, but who knew how unhappy she was? Or could it be that Edwina found a way of committing suicide? If she did, she could have enjoyed a belated revenge, since the detective's questions turn the lovers against each other.

The consensus was that John Vanbrugh's 254-year-old *The Relapse; or, Virtue in Danger,* which romped into the Morosco on the 22nd, showed its age. This saga of a sex-mad lady (Madge Elliott) luring away the husband (John Emery) of her cousin (Ruth Matteson) amid the similar antics of a flagrantly loose society was made entertaining primarily by the brilliant playing of Cyril Ritchard as Lord Foppington. He cavorted in a huge periwig, "which features a blond pompadour of altitude only slightly superior to Ethel Merman's" and moved "in a switching, jittery strut that shows off his feathers and curls and laces to ostentatious advantage." Chapman added, "His voice has an incredible range of meaningful inflections and his gift for hilarious pantomime is worthy of a Mack Sennett comedian." Yet such artistry in such a play remained caviar for the general, so the mounting closed after thirty performances.

Although it was a hit in its Paris home, in London, and in numerous other European theatrical capitals, **Ring Round the Moon** (11-23-50, Martin Beck), a "charade" which Christopher Fry translated from Jean Anouilh's *L'Invitation au château,* failed to delight New York audiences. The cynical Frederic (Denholm Elliott) decides to derail the plans of his shy twin brother Hugo (also Elliott), to wed a brash heiress (Neva Patterson) by introducing him to a ballet dancer (Stella Andrew). Despite the inevitable unforeseen complications, the plan works—and the heiress latches on to Frederic. Among the supporting cast Oscar Karlweis took honors as a rich man whose every attempt to lose his money only makes him richer. Gorgeous 1912 costumes, an elegant tango, sparkling incidental music by Francis Poulenc, and gaudy, sketchy Raoul Dufy curtains enhanced the period charm.

"When Josephine Hull and Ernest Truex fail to keep a comedy from foundering, it is a sure bet that there is something exceedingly awry in the writing," Barnes began his notice of Samuel Spewack's **The Golden State** (11-25-50, Fulton). His fellow critics agreed it was a mighty dull affair. Mrs. Morenas, a wacky but lovable little old lady, has for years been in court pressing her claim to all of Beverly Hills and Hollywood, which she insists rightfully has come down to her from a very distant Spanish relation. The costs don't bother her since, as she remarks, "of course, my credit is good. I owe everybody in town." Meanwhile, she runs a boardinghouse. One of her boarders is an unsuccessful prospector, Tim White, who freezes like a bird dog whenever he approaches a lode. One day he freezes out in Mrs. Morenas's back yard. Sure enough, there is gold in the ground. He and his landlady are certain they are rich. But the gold turns out to be flecks he himself had carelessly dropped, and in the end matters are back where they began.

Although the American National Theatre and Academy had been chartered by Congress in 1935, it was not until a postwar reorganization that it began to make a mark. In 1950 it rescued the Guild Theatre from radio broadcasting, renamed it, and embarked on an ambitious production program. Its initial attraction was Robinson Jeffers's retelling of the Greek legends of Agamemnon and his family in **The Tower Beyond Tragedy** (11-26-50, ANTA). The play had been written a quarter of a century earlier and had been produced nine years before at an open-air theatre in California with Judith Anderson as star. Anderson recreated her Clytemnestra for Broadway. The play began with the voice of the playwright Aeschylus (Robert Harrison) coming over a loudspeaker to provide some background. From there followed the traditional account of Clytemnestra's murder of her husband (Frederic Tozere), and of its avenging by their children (Philip Huston and Marion Seldes), with the body of Clytemnestra tumbling down the blood-soaked stairs. The play was looked upon as "less than completely satisfying," but Anderson's emoting, in her thundering Medea manner, with its "moments of lightning-like magic," was deemed "superb." The play ran for a month.

ANTA's second offering also featured a dysfunctional family, this time some lower-class Irish-Americans from Chicago. Phillip Pruneau's **The Cellar and the Well** (12-10-50, ANTA) had caused a stir when first offered by the Erie Playhouse, and now was presented at matinees (nine of them) while Jeffers's opus continued in the evenings. Before she breaks her own neck falling down the cellar stairs, loathsome, harridan Grandmother Mayo (Eda Heinemann) goads her boorish, boozy son (Eric Mattson) into mistreating his wife (Dorothy Sands), which drives the woman into the arms of their shy boarder (Henderson Forsythe) and nearly precipitates tragedy.

Four revivals closed out the year. ANTA's third presentation, at its playhouse on the 24th, was Ben Hecht and Charles MacArthur's 1932 hit, *Twentieth Century,* with José Ferrer and silent screen star Gloria Swanson in the leads. No one was surprised that Ferrer "never misses a trick," but Swanson's hellcat, "darting swiftly around the set, tossing off the vernacular with snarling vitality and giving the vanity all its deliberate humor without burlesquing it," was an unexpected bonus in this "jubilant revival." Its reception was so enthusiastic that the comedy was hurriedly moved to another theatre, where it rolled on merrily for seven months.

For several reasons, *King Lear*'s fate was less happy, following its premiere at the National on the 25th. Still on their anti-Shakespeare kick, a number of critics belittled the tragedy as "not an actable play," "a trap for the stars who venture to tackle the title role," and "Shakespeare's most macabre and muddled drama." Many also felt that Louis Calhern lacked the required

fire for the king, and they disagreed on the merits of Martin Gabel's Kent, Arnold Moss's Gloucester, Wesley Addy's Edgar, and Nina Foch's Cordelia. For all that, the play managed to eke out a six-week stand.

Perhaps because Shaw had died less than two months before at the age of ninety-four, critics dropped their recent carpings and were kind to him when his *Captain Brassbound's Conversion* was brought out at the City Center on the 27th. Nonetheless, by far the most laudatory notices were accorded to Edna Best for her Lady Cicely, whose innocence and sweetness on her travels defeat brigands, British law and the American navy.

Ibsen's *An Enemy of the People* raised its curtain at the Broadhurst on the 28th, in a new version by Arthur Miller. Critics felt that Miller's inclusion of words and expressions such as "lousy" and "burned up," and his underscoring of the soapbox anger in Ibsen's already angry drama, were little help to Fredric March, who played Stockmann, the unwelcomed crusader against pollution. March's wife, Florence Eldridge, played Mrs. Stockmann, while Morris Carnovsky was the town mayor—Stockmann's brother and chief foe.

Since Philip Barry had died in late 1949, Robert Sherwood took it upon himself to complete **Second Threshold** (1-2-51, Morosco). Despondent because his daughter, Miranda (Margaret Phillips), and son, Jock (Frederick Bradlee), have drifted away from him, Josiah Bolton (Clive Brook) contemplates suicide. But a thoughtful young doctor (Hugh Reilly), who understands Bolton's problem, talks Miranda out of sailing off to an English marriage. She helps revitalize her father and agrees to marry the doctor, who had been her childhood playmate. Although the relatively short drama was greeted with such salutations as "fine and memorable" and "thoughtful and moving," the public failed to respond heartily, granting the play only a sixteen-week run.

But Federico García Lorca's **The House of Bernarda Alba** (1-7-51, ANTA) was clearly not at all Broadway's cup of tea. It told of a domineering mother (Katina Paxinou) who lords it over her brood of unhappy daughters. When she shoots the man (never seen in this all female cast) who plans to elope with the youngest daughter (Kim Stanley), she causes the girl to commit suicide.

A revival at the City Center on the 10th of Kaufman and Ferber's tale of the-show-must-go-on, *The Royal Family* (12-28-27), garnered some unsought publicity when John Emery, who was playing the John Barrymore-like Anthony Cavendish, tripped on opening night and tore his ankle ligaments. He finished the performance after his foot was taped up, but John Baragrey assumed the part for the rest of the two-week run.

Darkness at Noon (1-13-51, Alvin) was Sidney

Kingsley's theatricalization of Arthur Koestler's best-seller. After Rubashov (Claude Rains) is brought into prison he has time to review his life. He was a dedicated Communist who believed that any means were justified if in the end they promoted his social program. As a result, he unconcernedly sent many people, even friends and lovers, to their deaths. And he rose to be a commissar. But now time has passed him by, and a new, more ruthless coterie, exemplified by the brutish OGPU interrogator, Gletkin (Walter J. Palance, later Jack Palance), is in charge. With them the means have become an end in themselves. Hounded into submission, Rubashov begs forgiveness from the "hundred and eighty million fellow prisoners" whom he sent to exile or death. When Gletkin asks him if he has a last wish, he responds, "To die." The play won the New York Drama Critics Circle Award, but its unrelieved starkness prevented its running beyond the end of spring.

Two performances sufficed for Joseph Kesselring's **Four Twelves Are 48** (1-17-51, 48th St.). In each of three generations of the Bawke family, who are Osage Indians, a daughter has given birth at the age of twelve to an illegitimate girl. Now the current twelve-year-old (Pat Crowley), having been kissed by a young boy, announces she is pregnant. Of course, she is not. Among the fine players caught in this mess were Anne Revere as the family matriarch and Ernest Truex, "in tobacco makeup and black braids," as Uncle Snake Tooth, who has made a fortune in oil and owns a Rolls-Royce with a built-in bathroom.

Producer Eddie Dowling took on the role of Hilary, the sharp-tongued but good-hearted shop owner, in A. B. Shiffrin's **Angel in the Pawnshop** (1-18-51, Booth). Lizzie (Joan McCracken), fleeing a marriage to a murderous gangster, comes seeking escape by donning some sixteenth-century costumes from Hilary's stock and dreaming of better, long-bygone times. Hilary and a young writer, Timothy Spangle (Herbert Evers), attempt to bring her back into the present. But they succeed only after a shootout between the gangster (Clark Williams) and Hilary leaves the gangster dead and Hilary dying. McCracken, a popular, petite Broadway dancer, was allowed several light choreographic turns as she fantasized about the past. The play itself was sluggish and succumbed after eleven weeks.

At the City Center on the 24th, Maurice Evans brought back the *Richard II* with which he had first impressed Broadway in 1937. For its limited two-week return, it impressed once again.

Critics were not nearly as impressed with the second Ibsen of the season, the rarely staged *Peer Gynt*, which was offered for a month at the ANTA, beginning on the 28th. John Garfield was starred. Conceding the play was difficult to stage at best, many felt neither Lee

Strasberg's direction nor Garfield's playing imparted thrust and poetry to the mounting. Supporting players included Mildred Dunnock as Aase, Karl Malden as the Buttonmolder, and January's second Broadway dancer, Sono Osato, as Anitra.

A revival on February 1 at the Golden of *The Green Bay Tree,* with its implications of homosexuality carefully muted, offered Joseph Schildkraut as the sybarite and Denholm Elliott as the young man he would bring under his sway. Despite generally favorable notices, playgoers failed to line up at the box office, so the show closed after two and a half weeks.

Although they rued that he continued to be preoccupied with neurotic women, most critics rejoiced that Tennessee Williams was at least telling his latest saga with comic relish. Atkinson concluded, "Mr. Williams can compose in the halcyon style as well as the somber one. Now we can be sure that he is a permanent source of enjoyment in the theatre." The heroine of **The Rose Tattoo** (2-3-51, Martin Beck) was Serafina della Rosa (Maureen Stapleton), who lives on the Gulf Coast between New Orleans and Mobile in a community largely of Sicilian-Americans and who keeps the ashes of her beloved husband, a truck driver, in her parlor. But her idealized memories of him are totally false. Some neighbors have told her that her husband, who had a rose tattoo on his breast, "had put on my head the nanny-goat's horns." She is shattered. Then another truck driver, Alvaro Mangiacavallo (Eli Wallach), comes into her life. He, too, has a rose tattoo on his chest. Confirming the truth about her husband, he soon restores her warmth and ebullience with his own goodness and even gets her to throw away the urn. Happy again, she encourages the romance of her daughter (Phyllis Love) and a young sailor (Don Murray). Enlivened by the dynamic performances of Stapleton and Wallach, the comedy ran nine months.

• • •

[Lois] **Maureen Stapleton** (b. 1925) was born in Troy, N.Y. and studied with Herbert Berghof before making her Broadway debut in a 1946 revival of *The Playboy of the Western World*. She was described as having "big show-girl eyes, a small mouth, . . . a radiance, and a voice that combines harridan and chamber music with layers of 'cello and violin."

• • •

Eli Wallach (b. 1915) was a Brooklyn native who never lost his Brooklyn accent or mannerisms. He made his Broadway debut in 1945 and subsequently performed with the American Repertory Theatre.

• • •

Ti-Coq (2-9-51, Broadhurst), a Canadian play, had been popular there and in some parts of the United States before heading to New York. Its author and star was Gratien Gélinas, who had become a star on Canadian radio as Fridolin and who was now writing and performing under that name. He played the titular hero, a young Canadian soldier who is abashed because he was both illegitimate and an orphan. He falls in love with Marie-Ange (Huguette Oligny), and she promises to wait until he returns from the war, so he heads off dreaming of the large family of instant relations his marriage will bring him. But on his return he finds that Marie-Ange has wed another man. A benevolent padré (Jacques Auger) consoles him the best he can. For all its success elsewhere, New Yorkers were uninterested.

Enough playgoers were interested in **Billy Budd** (2-10-51, Biltmore), Louis O. Coxe and Robert Chapman's stage adaptation of Herman Melville's novel, to keep it going for thirteen weeks. The diabolical John Claggart (Torin Thatcher), master-at-arms on the H.M.S. *Indomitable,* attempts to cause trouble for Billy Budd (Charles Nolte), a young, very innocent sailor. He inadvertently destroys himself as well as Billy. For when he falsely accuses Billy of stirring up treason, Billy strikes him and accidentally kills him. A court-martial would acquit the youngster, as, in his heart, would Capt. Vere (Dennis King), but the captain nonetheless insists that the law demands a seaman who killed a superior hang. A comprehending Billy forgives the captain and as he climbs the ratlines to his death cries out, "God bless Captain Vere!"

As soon as the curtain rises on Elmer Rice's **Not for Children** (2-13-51, Coronet) a tuxedoed Elijah Silverhammer (Keene Crockett) steps before the footlights to deliver a long introduction in the course of which he notes that the audience may be about to sit through the only performance of Elmer Rice's new play. "In fact," he adds, "to put it in Mr. Rice's own words: 'After to-night, we may be playing exclusively to invisible audiences.' " The words almost came true, for in the wake of what must have been the most savaging notices of Rice's career—"he has written a satire without revealing any trace of satirical sense," "a bore," "a formless charade," "confused and adolescent"—this play, written in 1934 but never produced till now, closed after seven performances. An anti-theatre professor (Elliot Nugent) and a pro-theatre lecturer (Betty Field) stand before rostrums, one on each side of the proscenium, and comment on a play (or is it plays?) supposedly being rehearsed onstage. As in *A Story for a Sunday Evening,* the actors who are playing the characters in the play and the characters themselves argue with each other—and, now, with lecturers as well.

There were twenty-nine performers and twenty-six scenes in **The Small Hours** (2-15-51, National), the first collaboration of George S. Kaufman and his new, young wife, Leueen MacGrath. Donald Oenslager's

settings moved the action from a publisher's opulent home to a rival's posh dining room, a private railroad car, a glimpse of Florida, and elsewhere. (One result of all the scenery and costumes, and the upkeep of a large cast, was that when the show closed after twenty performances it was $120,000 in the red.) Shy, self-deprecating Laura Mitchell (Dorothy Stickney) is convinced she cannot help or even keep up intellectually or emotionally with her family. Her publisher-husband (Paul McGrath) is flirting with a man-crazy author (Polly Rowles); her latently homosexual son (Michael Wager) is jailed for smoking marijuana; and her brash daughter (Joyce Lear) seems to be rushing into an unfortunate marriage. But after someone points out to Polly, "You are no different from anybody else—everybody is lonely," she gains self-confidence and starts to straighten out her family. The *Herald Tribune*'s Otis L. Guernsey, Jr., rated the entertainment "scattered and indecisive."

Earlier in the season a batch of London hits had transferred to Broadway, only to quickly flop. Another such failure was added to the list with Charlotte Hastings's **The High Ground** (2-20-51, 48th St.). One of its leading players was Leueen MacGrath, the co-author of its immediate predecessor. She played Sarat Cairn, a gifted painter who is being taken to prison following her conviction for murdering her worthless brother. But a flash flood forces her and her escorts to seek shelter at a convent. There, a nun, Sister Mary Bonaventure (Margaret Webster), taking time to review the case, exculpates Sarat and shows that an attractive local physician (Tom Helmore) is the actual killer.

Two plays that followed were among the season's most quickly shuttering duds, surviving four and two performances respectively. Walter Macken, a physically towering actor from Dublin's Abbey Theatre, was brought over to play one of the leads in Michael Malloy's Irish folk play **The King of Friday's Men** (2-21-51, Playhouse). In late eighteenth-century Ireland, Una Brehony (Maggie McNamara) is happily betrothed to timid Owen Fennigan (Mac McLeod), so when Caesar French (Frederic Tozere), the lord of the manor, demands that she be brought to him as a tally woman—a mistress—she knows that Owen would be unable to defend her. Her devoted uncle (Ian Martin) enlists Bartley Dowd (Macken), a bruiser with a penchant for swinging his shillelagh, to do Owen's work for him. He kills French, but falls in love with Una at the same time. Still, the grateful Una remains loyal to Owen.

The season's harshest notices went to Joseph Schulman, William H. Lieberson, and Martin R. Lieberson's **Springtime Folly** (2-26-51, Golden). Some cloak-and-suiters form the Lullaby Dress Company to make and market a maternity outfit called "Springtime Folly," a design for "swell women." But they mistakenly cut it from a pattern that does not allow its wearer to swell. All the garments come back to them, and they have to think up another use for them. They apparently do.

Mary Rose, James M. Barrie's tale of a young woman who returns unaged after years in a mysterious otherworld, was revived at the ANTA on March 4 with the beautiful Bethel Leslie in the title role. Leo G. Carroll and Patricia Collinge were among her supporting players. Many of the reviews were raves, and several critics admitted to liking the play better than when they first saw it in late 1920. Nonetheless, it lingered for only seventeen performances.

By contrast, notices for Lillian Hellman's Chekhovian **The Autumn Garden** (3-7-51, Coronet) ranged from Hawkins's "engrossing" to Atkinson's "boneless and torpid." It ran for 101 performances. The play was set in a tarnished summer boardinghouse on the Gulf Coast. Among the people there are a crusty grandmother (Ethel Griffes), her daughter-in-law (Margaret Barker) and her effete grandson (James Lipton), a daydreaming general (Colin Keith-Johnston) and his silly wife (Florence Eldridge), and a lonely, philosophic banker (Kent Smith). Into their midst comes a failed, third-rate painter (Fredric March) who riles the calm waters with his aggressive meddling. He is the catalyst for all manner of soul-searching, but how much good any of it does is moot. The landlady's immigrant helper (John Lorring) tells the banker that none of the guests try their best. But, allowing they are all lonely, he warns her, "You should be careful because maybe lonely people are the only people who can't afford to cry." The landlady (Carol Goodner) herself has long loved the artist, but he has been unresponsive and continues to be so. When she looks for comfort to the banker, who, in turn, has long loved her, he apologizes. He only fooled himself and her, he says, when he thought he loved her.

A four-character comedy, F. Hugh Herbert's **The Moon Is Blue** (3-8-51, Henry Miller's) chalked up the season's longest run—924 performances. Donald Gresham (Barry Nelson), an up-and-coming architect, and pretty Patty O'Neill (Barbara Bel Geddes) meet on the observation tower of the Empire State Building. Before long she has agreed to come to his apartment and cook dinner for him. She makes certain that he understands she is a virgin and intends to remain one. But her questions about his sex life, which bring out the fact that he has just broken off with a girl who always starts crying into her fifth daiquiri, prompt Don to accuse Patty of being preoccupied with sex. "But don't you think it's better for a girl to be preoccupied with sex than occupied?" she asks. The rakish, tart father (Donald Cook) of the girl Don has broken with

appears, initially to confront Don. However, he is soon so taken with Patty that he starts to make a play for her. Patty's policeman-father (Ralph Dunn), having learned where she is, shows up just long enough to slug Don. But after the expected contretemps, Don and Patty meet again on the observation tower the next afternoon and agree that a real romance like theirs happens once in a blue moon. Although critics found the comedy very slight, they were still, in that theatrically healthier day and age, willing to concede it was the sort of carefree fun playgoers needed and wanted. Bel Geddes was applauded for her projection of "eager, inquisitive youth," and Nelson for doing so charmingly with the "difficult part of a nice young man, a thankless job in any play." For many, the nasal-voiced Cook, revealing himself as "a master farceur," stole the show.

One of the few things critics agreed on in reviewing the revival of *Romeo and Juliet* that opened at the Broadhurst on the 10th was Oliver Messel's magnificent settings of "a beautiful, hot Mediterranean town, in units that changed with wide contrast" from crenellated exteriors to draped interiors. They disagreed sharply on the merits of film star Olivia de Haviland's Juliet—"thin and mechanical," "a softly spoken, carefully studied interpretation"—with a solid majority not in her favor. Her Romeo, Douglas Watson, and her other support also generally disappointed the aisle-sitters. Taken off after forty-nine performances, the production was the biggest money loser among the season's non-musicals, with a then staggering $330,000 going down the drain.

But initial costs were such that even a low-budget revival of Benn Levy's 1931 comedy, *Springtime for Henry,* lost money ($30,000) after a fifty-three-performance run that began at the Golden on the 14th. The star was the rather epicene Edward Everett Horton, a popular film comedian who had been touring with the comedy off and on, especially in summer playhouses, for eighteen years.

A third revival, this time of *The Green Pastures* at the huge Broadway on the 15th, was also a costly flop, dropping $200,000 in its forty-four-performance stand. And yet the revival reaped unanimously favorable notices, with Chapman, for example, hailing it as "the great American folk play." At worst, critics agreed that no one could replace the original Richard Harrison as De Lawd, but still gave William Marshall high marks for his interpretation.

Naturally there were no expectations that Molière's *L'Ecole des femmes* would linger long after it raised its curtain at the ANTA on the 18th, for the whole mounting had been imported from Paris with Louis Jouvet as star and was done in French. Christian Bérard's playful settings and costumes were an added touch. Even critics who confessed to knowing little or no French suggested it would be a treat for knowledgeable playgoers. It was, for three weeks.

ANTA was also responsible for the next revival, Clifford Odets's 1940 failure, *Night Music,* which opened on April 8 at its playhouse. Critics hadn't liked it in 1940, and they didn't like it again. So the play left after a single week.

Atkinson began his morning-after review of Scott Michel's **Angels Kiss Me** (4-17-51, National) by placing it in the same bottom drawer as *Four Twelves Are 48* and *Springtime Folly,* although he could not know at the time that it would join the pair in the ignominious distinction of having the season's shortest runs—two performances each. A young man (Alan Manson) who has fought his way from the slums to a high position in the newspaper-distributing business decides all he now needs is a socialite wife. So he marries an attractive tobacco heiress (Maryanna Gare), unaware of her family's history of suicide. He must later stop his pregnant wife from jumping into a lake and cure her bent, a task for which he receives no help from the girl's vicious, warped aunt (Madeline Clive).

Davis Snow's **The Long Days** (4-20-51, Empire) eked out three performances. A beautiful luminary of yesteryear, the now gray-haired but still lovely Frances Starr, played a domineering New England mother, who has driven her husband and three sons to drink and has had a rebellious daughter-in-law committed to an insane asylum. One son is in jail; another returns briefly for a visit to the family's old farm. But that stay is marred when his mother goes mad after accidentally killing the lone son (Jeffrey Lynn) who had loyally remained with her.

No doubt Margaret Webster asked for trouble when she had some players in her free-wheeling revival of *The Taming of the Shrew* at the City Center on the 25th sing snatches of songs from *Kiss Me, Kate!* This led at least two critics to claim Cole Porter's musical was superior to Shakespeare's comedy. Since most of the critics were left cold by Claire Luce's Kate, Ralph Clanton's Petruchio, or the other players' interpretations, that meant plenty of empty seats during the two-week stand.

Her late neighbor and landlady has bequeathed Nancy Willard (Sarah Churchill), the heroine of John Cecil Holm's **Gramercy Ghost** (4-26-51, Morosco), the ghost (Richard Waring) of Nathaniel Coombs. He's a nice ghost, a Revolutionary soldier who was shot by Redcoats on the site of Nancy's Gramercy Park apartment before he could deliver General Washington's message, and the general, annoyed that Nathaniel had stopped on his way to flirt with a wench, has seen to it

that he cannot enter heaven. Nancy's problem is that no one else can see or hear Nathaniel. In fact, her stuffy fiancé, Parker Burnett (Robert Smith), is ready to have her sent to a booby hatch. Fortunately, a personable reporter, Charley Stewart (Robert Sterling), who has come to interview Nancy about her late landlady, is sympathetic. After some other ghosts sneak Nathaniel into heaven so that he can present his case, and after it turns out that Burnett is a distant descendant of the man to whom Nathaniel was supposed to deliver his message, the ghost vanishes. That allows Nancy and Charley to go off together. Neither Winston Churchill's daughter nor the comedy set critics celebrating, but it survived for an even 100 performances.

On the other hand, Edmund Wilson's arcane **The Little Blue Light** (4-29-51, ANTA) lasted a mere two weeks after critics axed it with such assessments as "flubdub," "a disorderly dramatic grab-bag," and "If 'The Little Blue Light' is a joke, it is no laughing matter!" Sometime in "the not-remote future," when communism is deemed a far-right menace and when power groups are fighting each other in a bid for total world control, the last crusading editor, Frank (Melvyn Douglas), struggles to expose the danger. He does not even know that his host, Gandersheim (Burgess Meredith), and his own wife, Judith (Arlene Francis), are in league with the leader of one of the power groups. In the end, all three are destroyed when Frank inadvertently turns on the flashlight whose little blue spot annihilates everything around. Only the Gardener (Martin Gabel) remains, and he discloses to the audience that he is Ahasuerus, the Wandering Jew. He laments that "even in this black night of blasphemy I cannot yet die or rest."

The season's last novelty, Donald Bevan and Edmund Trzcinski's **Stalag 17** (5-8-51, 48th St.), was also its last hit. A closeness naturally develops among the American soldiers held in a German prison camp. They include the rather oddball, cynical Stosh (Robert Strauss), who must walk around in his only clothing, his long underwear. However, one soldier, Sefton (John Ericson), remains aloof and critical. So when the Germans foil an escape attempt the others conclude he is the spy they know the Germans have planted in their midst. They give him a vicious beating. But he is not the spy, and shortly afterward he stumbles on the truth. Therefore, when the men arrange for another escape attempt, by one prisoner (Mark Roberts) they have heard may be tortured by the Nazis, Sefton fingers the spy, Price (Laurence Hugo), who in a panic gives himself away. While the would-be escaper starts to leave, the others chase Price out the door as a diversion. Although he yells "Schiess nicht" to the guards, he is gunned down.

Most reviewers proffered varying objections, but nevertheless recognized audiences would enjoy the comedy-melodrama. It ran for more than a year (472 performances) and led to a popular television series, *Hogan's Heroes*.

Three revivals closed out the season. *Dream Girl* came into the City Center on the 9th, with Judy Holliday in the lead. Disappointing expectations, her performance was seen as too broad and burlesqued to be acceptable, even making allowances for the mammoth auditorium.

Getting Married, Shaw's not very lively debate on the pros and cons of wedded life, ended ANTA's first busy year when it opened at its playhouse on May 13. Peggy Wood, Bramwell Fletcher, Arthur Treacher, Guy Spaull, and John Buckmaster headed the cast.

At the City Center on the 23rd, *Idiot's Delight* was offered with the irresistible Lee Tracy and the witty and sparkling Ruth Chatterton in the roles created by the Lunts. But several aisle-sitters bewailed that the comedy was starting to show its age.

1951–1952

Quantitatively the number of novelties held steady in the new season. But although the *Daily News*'s John Chapman, writing as editor of the *Best Plays* series, thought the theatrical year had been "not too bad," he acknowledged that his colleagues generally put a less kind value on it. The public apparently agreed with the dissenters. Only one play ran for more than a year, and only four others ran even six months, with one of these, *Gigi*, still ending up in the loss column despite 219 performances.

Seasons rarely got off to flying starts, and this season was no exception. Echoing one of last year's features, it began with a London hit that found no welcome on Broadway. Aimee Stuart's **Lace on Her Petticoat** (9-4-51, Booth) was set in 1890 Scotland and examined the problem of class distinctions. Rich, neglected Alexandra Carmichael (Perlita Neilson) befriends Elspeth McNairn (Patsy Bruder), the daughter of one of her titled parents' poor cottagers. But after Elspeth's widowed mother (Neva Patterson) sacrifices to buy her daughter a petticoat so that she may attend Alexandra's birthday party, Alexandra is ordered to rescind her invitation. Accepting a proposal from a local man (Jeff Morrow) who wants to make a better life in the New World, Mrs. McNairn, Elspeth, and he prepare to sail for Canada.

A revival of *Diamond Lil*, with Mae West naturally heading the cast, lit up the huge Broadway on the 14th and stayed for eight and a half weeks.

Kenyon Nicholson said farewell to the New York stage with **Out West of Eighth** (9-20-51, Barrymore), which lingered a mere four performances. Virginia Beamer (Barbara Baxley), a manicurist at Manhattan's lowly Rialto Plaza Hotel, has been in love with Eddie Todd (Richard Carlyle), a former pug and bellhop who now is a dude rancher in the Poconos. But when a rodeo comes into Madison Square Garden and many of the cowpokes stay at her hostelry, she falls head over heels for jut-jawed Lash Castro (Robert Keith, Jr.), a real bronco-buster who likes his steaks bloody. There is a Marx–Brothers–like chase through a hotel corridor and a horse is stashed away in a closet before Eddie wins back Virginia.

Kate Scott (Nancy Kelly), the heroine of A. B. Shiffrin's **Twilight Walk** (9-24-51, Fulton), is a mystery writer who believes that psychopathic killers need sympathetic attention rather than strong-arm treatment, so she sets out to uncover and redeem a young man (Charles Proctor) whose resentment of his overbearing mother has driven him to strangle women in Central Park. The two meet by a bridge in the park, but luckily for the writer a caustic plainclothesman (Walter Matthau) has been keeping a watchful eye open and comes to her rescue.

The season's first longish run—199 performances—went to Howard Lindsay and Russel Crouse's **Remains to Be Seen** (10-3-51, Morosco), which critics deemed everything from "a rousing hit" to "a sophomoric escapade." A notorious crusader against pornography, whose apartment is cluttered with naughty literature and art, is found dead there. A doctor (Warner Anderson) ascribes the death to an accidental overdose of insulin. But when an undertaker comes to collect the body, the corpse has a knife stuck into it. Jody Revere (Janis Paige), a niece who sings with a band and who hates her uncle, walks into the ensuing mayhem, having been summoned beforehand by the dead man's attorney, Benjamin Goodman (Lindsay). Jody answered the summons only because she thought the attorney was the famous bandleader. She quickly finds herself falling in love with Waldo Walton (Jackie Cooper), the apartment building's young, patently unworldly janitor, who does, however, play a mean drum. She also finds herself menaced by a woman (Madeleine Morka) who appears in the darkened apartment after entering from a secret passage hidden behind some bookcases. In the end, it turns out that the Japanese butler (Harry Shaw Lowe) stabbed his already dead employer in order to bring the police into the picture, since he was aware that the doctor was the real killer. The doctor confesses to lusting after the dead man's mistress, whom the dead man kept in an adjoining building. Goodman has fallen in love with Jody and proposes. But she tells him he will be better off marrying a virgin—just like she is about to do. And she heads out with a delighted if not fully comprehending Waldo.

Just as the critics split on the Lindsay-Crouse opus, so they split on the Theatre Guild's revival of Shaw's *Saint Joan,* which came into the Cort on the 4th. Uta Hagen had the title role. William Hawkins of the *World-Telegram and Sun* proclaimed, "Miss Hagen has that rare gift of creating spiritual energy in the theater, then controlling it at will. She has the authority to compel an audience into silent attention." Conversely, the *Daily Mirror's* Robert Coleman suggested "her portrayal of the hapless Maid of Orleans failed to glow, and a tricky little squeak in her voice proved distracting." Most critics passed over her supporting cast with perfunctory salutes, while the settings and costumes were waved aside as "attractive but not dramatically impressive." The revival ran for four months.

Melvyn Douglas and Signe Hasso, both with screen celebrity to cash in on, were probably the reason that Edward Mabley's "very feeble striving after the comic spirit," **Glad Tidings** (10-11-51, Lyceum), held on for 100 performances. Steve Whitney is a former foreign correspondent who has become the editor of a magazine owned by the woman he is about to marry, Ethel Nash (Haila Stoddard). Without warning, one of his old flames, Maud Abbott, a famous, flamboyant film star, reenters his life, bringing with her the nineteen-year-old daughter, Claire (Patricia Benoit), who she tells him is half his. When Ethel foolishly turns nasty about the matter, Steve packs the other women into his car and heads for Cape Cod.

One off-beat attraction that nonetheless drew all the major critics was Christopher Fry's **A Sleep of Prisoners,** which was brought out on the 16th at the uptown St. James's Church. The blank-verse drama told of four British soldiers being held by the enemy in an abandoned church. After one of the men attempts to strangle another, the four fall asleep and dream of the incident, one in terms of Cain and Abel, another in terms of King David and Absalom, a third envisioning the story of Abraham and Isaac, and the last relating the incident to the Fiery Furnace. The play was given thirty-one times.

Last season a rich young actor named Jay Robinson had underwritten the costs of *The Green Bay Tree's* revival with the understanding that he would play one of the two leads, but he was asked to withdraw during rehearsals and did so. Now he appeared in **Buy Me Blue Ribbons** (10-16-51, Empire), a play written at his behest by Sumner Locke Elliott and recounting the matter. Only Jay Robinson became Jordan Sable, a onetime child film star, whom his agent (Gavin Gordon) described as "a Lucky Luciano in knee-pants." Sable

hopes to make a comeback by starring himself in a poetic drama. But he is so inept he is forced to leave, and the play becomes a hit without him. At the final curtain, he is attempting to get publicity for himself by announcing he will start again from the bottom and has accepted a walk-on in a Shakespearean revival.

Like Douglas and Hasso, Ann Sothern and Robert Cummings were Hollywood names, but they were only able to keep László Bush-Fekete and Mary Helen Fay's **Faithfully Yours** (10-18-51, Coronet) before the footlights for eight and a half weeks after its critical drubbing. The play was based on Jean Bernard-Luc's *Le Complexe Philemon,* leading Chapman to wish everyone involved "better Luc next time." Dr. Peter Wilson (Philip Bourneuf), a $50-an-hour psychiatrist who longs to get her to his Poconos hideaway, convinces the highly susceptible Vivian Harding that if her husband still loves her as much as he says he does after ten years of marriage he must be in desperate need of analysis. This leads hubby to conclude that the little woman needs some sessions on a couch. The wife is finally brought to her senses and the shrink sent packing.

One critic attributed so many film names rushing to Broadway to Hollywood's panic over inroads being made by the newly popular television. The next in the parade of glamor figures to try her chances again on the boards was Ginger Rogers. Her vehicle was Louis Verneuil's **Love and Let Love** (10-19-51, Plymouth), which critics perceived as a rueful comedown from his not-all-that-great hit of last season, *Affairs of State.* Dismayed that her prosaic, drab sister, Ruth (Rogers), was able to steal a dashing artist from her, the beautiful actress Valerie King (also Rogers) asks Charles Warren (Paul McGrath), a diplomat whom she has long considered a confidant, to marry her. Although he is fond of Valerie, he gently leads her into the arms of Fred Stevens (Tom Helmore), a doctor who has long loved her.

On October 22 a single reading was given at Carnegie Hall of Shaw's **Don Juan in Hell,** which was actually the third act of *Man and Superman,* but which had never been done in New York before, either as part of the play or as a separate entity. Seated on stools and dressed in modern evening clothes, Charles Laughton was The Devil; Charles Boyer, Don Juan; Cedric Hardwicke, the Statue; and Agnes Moorehead, Donna Anna. The entertainment was seen as a brilliant debate, and a brilliant debate is always good theatre. Such were the ecstatic morning-after notices that plans for numerous appearances elsewhere were canceled and the company brought into the barn-like Century Theatre on November 29 for a brief run. It subsequently returned to the smaller Plymouth in April. In all, 105 readings were given in New York during the season.

The season's longest run—632 performances—went to Jan de Hartog's **The Fourposter** (10-24-51, Barrymore). Among the aisle-sitters, only the *Journal-American*'s Robert Garland remarked on its resemblance to *The First Fifty Years* (3-13-22), the earliest two-character comedy surveying the history of a marriage. In 1890, Michael (Hume Cronyn) carries his new bride, Agnes (Jessica Tandy) across the threshold of their bedroom and places her in its fourposter bed. He tries to kiss her, but she points out the door is still open. She orders him to turn around while she undresses, and later she is shocked to learn that he wears a nightcap. She also puts a pillow saying "God Is Love" on the bed. With time the setting changes. First, a cradle appears in the bedroom; later the washstand disappears, since an indoor bathroom has been installed. The marriage, too, changes. Michael seems jealous of the attention the first baby receives. As the children grow up, he and Agnes quarrel over how to raise them. Then he nearly loses his head over another woman. A few years on, Agnes thinks briefly of leaving. By 1925, with both children married and gone, they give up the house. But not before Agnes has left her "God Is Love" pillow for the newlyweds slated to follow them—and Michael, perhaps more thoughtfully, has left them a bottle of champagne on his side of the bed. The new critic for the *Herald Tribune,* Walter Kerr, thought the play "a shade too plain and a shade too familiar for a thoroughly winning evening in the theatre." But he wrote of Tandy, "The actress brings as much fire to some first-act roughhouse as she does delicacy to the play's closing moments. As if her loveliness were not enough, she is a performer of spirit and rare tartness." About Cronyn, he wrote, "There is a quality of unction in Mr. Cronyn's acting style which puts him at his best in his vainer and more pompous moments . . . he is always an intelligent actor." The play's tremendous success, possibly more than any other two-character piece, opened the sluice gates to such attractions as an answer to the theatre's growing economic squeeze. (It was subsequently made into the 1966 musical *I Do! I Do!*.) The comedy also allowed Cronyn to take his place alongside his wife and thus let them become the "latter-day, lesser Lunts."

. . .

Hume Cronyn (b. 1911) was born in London, Ontario. He performed in Canada and in stock in Washington, took courses at the American Academy of Dramatic Arts and elsewhere, then joined the Barter Theatre as performer and director. A small man with a long face and prominent mouth and teeth, he made his Broadway debut in *Hipper's Holiday* (1934), subsequently appearing in, among others, *Boy Meets Girl* (1936), *Room Service* (1937), *High Tor* (1937), and *The Three Sisters*

(1939). Before acting opposite his wife in this latest play, he had directed her in *Hilda Crane* (1950).

. . .

Arthur Carter's melodrama **The Number** (10-30-51, Biltmore) told of Sylvia (Martha Scott), a pleasant but not especially intelligent woman, who is currently separated from her dull husband, and takes a job as a clerk with a big-time gambler (Murvyn Vye). She is conned by a smooth-talking bettor (Dane Clark) into helping him cheat her boss. After the bettor is rubbed out, she is left to put her life back together again.

Only the two major morning newspapers, the *Herald Tribune* and the *Times,* disliked Maxwell Anderson's **Barefoot in Athens** (10-31-51, Martin Beck), with the latter's Brooks Atkinson reporting that it was not merely barefoot, "but heavy-footed and slow." Yet that may have been enough to prompt the public to reject the drama, which folded after less than a month. Socrates (Barry Jones) "likes to go up and down the streets questioning and doubting." He even deliberates long over whether he should shave in the morning. But with Athens having been seized by the Spartans, his fellow citizens are in a mean mood. He is brought to trial for attempting to corrupt the city's youth with his philosophy and condemned to death. Pausanias (George Matthews), the King of Sparta, takes a liking to the old man and offers him shelter in the Spartan court. But he retorts that he "must wrangle and make inquiries" in his usual way, or else he prefers to drink the hemlock. After praying with his acid-tongued but loving wife, Xantippe (Lotte Lenya), he does just that.

Several critics suggested that the best thing about Joel Wyman's **Dinosaur Wharf** (11-8-51, National) was Samuel Leve's two-level setting of an abandoned East River dock and the barge moored alongside it. Paula (Lois Wheeler) lives on the barge with her father (Harrison Dowd), a retired captain, and is in love with Will (Leo Penn), a longshoreman fighting corrupt union rule. He advocates fighting violence with violence, while Paula espouses peaceful means. But when Charlie (James Gregory), the vicious union boss, shoots at Will and kills Paula's father by mistake, she stabs him in the back. He runs from the barge up onto the dock before dropping dead. Reviewers condemned the overacting, the underdirecting, and pretentious lines such as Paula's "My feet are wet; my shame can't dry them."

Broadway's indifference to London successes was seen again when Roger MacDougall and Otis Bigelow's **To Dorothy, a Son** (11-19-51, Golden) came and went in one week's time. Unaware that his Mexican divorce from an eccentric American girl he married in Samoa is not valid, Evelyn Ridgeway (Ronald Howard), a composer of film music, has married Dorothy (Stella

Andrew). She is about to give birth when his ex (Hildy Parks) shows up. It seems her uncle has left Evelyn a million dollars if his wife has a son within a year of the old man's death; otherwise the ex inherits everything. At first it looks as if Dorothy has given birth a few hours too late, but then the time difference between England and America is taken into account. Evelyn is a millionaire.

Carl Leo's all-American **Never Say Never** (11-20-51, Booth) fared no better. Coralie Jones (Anne Jackson), a would-be poet and freethinker, has been living with Alex Wesley (Hugh Reilly), a profesional ghostwriter, in a cramped apartment on lower Fifth Avenue. At her insistence they have been living there without benefit of clergy. So she has Alex move out temporarily and hides all signs of his occupancy when Lester B. Sprawls (Don Briggs), her hometown beau from back in Idaho Falls, pops in for a visit. But Lester proves so dull and inadvertently makes so many problems that once he is gone, Coralie is happy to marry Alex.

Aisle-sitters found much to fault in **Gigi** (11-24-51, Fulton), Anita Loos's adaptation of Colette's novel, but still recommended it highly. Thus Kerr concluded, "Colette's saucy tale is hard to beat down, and the show as a whole emerges as a gay little trinket." What made this saga of a young Parisian beauty who finds real romance despite her aunt's efforts to turn her into a bejeweled courtesan were the delightful settings and costumes and some capital performances. First among these were the "sensitive and endearing" work of a then largely unknown Audrey Hepburn in the title role, and the elegance and beauty of Cathleen Nesbitt, who played the aunt. As mentioned earlier, the comedy ran for more than six months without recouping its investment.

Another adaptation, which opened four nights later and closed on the same late May night as the Loos-Colette play, was the second adaptation in a row to win the New York Drama Critics Circle Award. John van Druten took his **I Am a Camera** (11-28-51, Empire) from some short stories by Christopher Isherwood. Isherwood (William Prince), then a struggling young writer, sits in his room at Fraulein Schneider's, recording his impressions of a Berlin raked by ominous Nazi rioting. He attempts to be objective, noting, "I am a camera, with its shutter open, quite passive." Some of this carefully nurtured passivity is disturbed when he is introduced to Sally Bowles (Julie Harris), a charming, mercurial English girl who sings at a local nightclub. Neither her demand that Isherwood never question her about her past nor her becoming pregnant by another man seriously affects the friendship they develop. Only the growing turmoil outside sunders them. He elects to depart, but Sally, as apolitical as she is amoral, chooses

to remain. The play was welcomed as "an amusing and moving evening," but the principal kudos went to Harris's "fascinating full-length portrait"—"in every scene of pretense, in every gay, bird-like gesture, there is always the shadow of the heartbreaking figure Sally Bowles really is."

Nina (12-5-51, Royale) was Samuel Taylor's adaptation of a French farce by André Roussin. The hypochondriacal Adolphe (Alan Webb) comes to the apartment of Gerard (David Niven), the lover of his wife, Nina (Gloria Swanson), prepared to shoot him. But he develops such a nasty cold there that Gerard persuades him to remain until he feels better. Much to Nina's chagrin, the men are soon fast friends. Adolphe decides the best course is to poison Nina and Gerard decides to leave the country. On his way to the airport he is struck by a truck, so Nina and Adolphe agree to nurse him back to health. Webb garnered virtually all of the better notices as "a Milquetoast engrossed in delicious idiocies," while Niven received the short end of the critical stick. Swanson, who had loudly protested during the play's tryout that she wanted to be released from a patent dud, was seen as miscast.

Many critics felt that Katharine Cornell had miscast herself when she revived Somerset Maugham's *The Constant Wife* at the National on the 8th. "The qualities that make her admirable keep her from being really at home in the crisp and brittle world of sin that Mr. Maugham inhabits with so much style," Atkinson observed. Hawkins felt Ethel Barrymore had been "infinitely more wicked" in the original 1926 New York mounting, while Chapman dismissed the star as "pallid." Yet this comedy about a loyal wife who finally resolves to give a philandering husband a taste of his own medicine found enough of an audience to run for 138 performances. Brian Aherne, Grace George (in her farewell appearances), and John Emery were the main supporting players.

Elmer Rice, whose best days were permanently behind him, suffered a one-week flop with **The Grand Tour** (12-10-51, Martin Beck). Richard Watts, Jr., of the *Post* regretted that the play "never quite manages to achieve more than a mild glow of wistful romance." Having inherited some money from her father, Nell Valentine (Beatrice Straight), a New England schoolmarm past her prime, embarks on an extended European trip. She falls in love with Raymond Brinton (Richard Derr), a handsome banker she meets aboard ship. They decide to do the Continent together. But Nell eventually discovers that besides being a divorced father of two children, Raymond has embezzled $60,000. She convinces him not only to return to his family, but to accept her legacy and use it to make restitution and avoid jail.

The play ends with a subdued Nell showing slides of her recent holiday to her pupils.

Ghosts failed to provide the hoped-for amusement in John Patrick's **Lo and Behold** (12-12-51, Booth). A Nobel-laureated writer (Leo G. Carroll) makes a will leaving a third of his estate to a young doctor, a third to preserve his home as a future haunt for himself, and a third to Harvard to ensure his wishes are carried out. Then he eats himself to death. When he returns home as a ghost he finds three other ghosts in the house: the caustic Minnetonka Smallflower (Doro Merande), who had been pushed off a Lover's Leap; the noisily liberal southerner Honey Wainwright (Cloris Leachman), who had shielded her lover from a rival and defied the rival to shoot; and Kenneth Moore (Roy Irving), a musician. Together the four watch as the doctor (Jeffrey Lynn) and the dead writer's pretty cook (Lee Grant) fall in love.

The next of the season's numerous successful adaptations was **Point of No Return** (12-13-51, Alvin), which Paul Osborn took from John P. Marquand's best seller. Although Charles Gray (Henry Fonda) assures his wife, Nancy (Leora Dana), that he is not, figuratively speaking, running for office, she says he's polishing apples whether he knows it or not. For Charles is a candidate for promotion to the vice-presidency of the Stuyvesant Bank, with the slick, conniving Roger Blakesley (Bartlett Robinson) as his principal rival. A business matter sends Charles back to his boyhood home in Massachusetts, where he recalls his past. He had courted and seemingly won Jessica Lovell (Patricia Smith), but her aristocratic father (Colin Keith-Johnston) had scotched the affair. His own father had quoted Jonathan Swift to him: "Ambition often puts men upon doing the meanest offices: so climbing is performed in the same posture with *creeping*." These memories allow Charles to recover his old sense of integrity, but he is still surprised to learn that he has received the promotion and that Roger was at no time really a serious prospect. He vows never to creep or to polish apples again. A careful theatricalization, a stylish, multi-scened mounting and a fine cast headed by Fonda all ensured success. Hawkins commented, "Fonda is so right as the banker it is almost too easy to take him for granted. He has the calm, the concern and warmth and puzzlement of all young men who abandon romantic ideas to bolster up reliable traditions." The production ran for 364 performances.

The most glittering opening-night audiences of the season were on hand when the Oliviers (Laurence Olivier and Vivien Leigh) came into the magnificent Ziegfeld Theatre on the 19th to offer their interpretation of Shaw's *Caesar and Cleopatra*, then the next evening began alternating it with Shakespeare's *Antony and Cleopatra*. The productions were sumptuous, with the rather cut Shakespeare speeded up further by using a revolving stage. Of the stars, Leigh clearly won the palm, moving deftly from the whimsical, childish, and virginal youngster to the "great figure of tragedy." Olivier was chided for occasional inaudibility, while critics carped that his serious approach to Caesar was "at the expense of some of the wit and raillery." Nor did his Antony, which was better received, have the proper "feeling of broken greatness." Still, the seventeen-week engagement played to packed houses.

Legend of Lovers (12-26-51, Plymouth) was Kitty Black's adaptation of Jean Anouilh's *Eurydice*. Having met in a bus station, an itinerant accordionist (Richard Burton) and a young, provincial actress (Dorothy McGuire) enjoy a brief fling before the girl is killed in a bus accident. Back at the station, a mysterious traveler (Noel Williams) promises to restore her to the musician if he will not look at her until daybreak. He does look, and she disappears, so he commits suicide in order to be with her in death. Burton, who had made his Broadway debut only last season, was hailed as a most promising actor even though reviewers said his performance was hampered by misdirection and a gloomy, monotonous text.

The same evening, the City Center unveiled its revival of Ibsen's *The Wild Duck* with Maurice Evans as Hjalmar, Kent Smith as Gregers, Mildred Dunnock as Gina, and Hollywood's Diana Lynn as Hedvig. Slammed by the critics, it did disappointing business during it's two-week stand. It was followed on January 9 by a more welcomed *Anna Christie* (11-2-21). Although critics suggested that the play was not one of O'Neill's best and that Celeste Holm lacked the emotional weight for the lead, the production was moved briefly after its initial two-week stand to a small Broadway house, but failed to flourish there.

When Amanda Phipps (Leueen MacGrath) is asked by a judge (Reynolds Evans) who is marrying her if she "takes this man" Martin Vellabrook (Glen Langan) to be her wedded husband, she asks him to repeat the question, then after a moment's hesitation decides maybe she won't. So begins MacGrath and George S. Kaufman's **Fancy Meeting You Again** (1-14-52, Royale). For it develops that in various guises over bygone millennia Amanda has been marrying the same man, but really wanting another (Walter Matthau). It had happened when she was a cavewoman and he a caveman; she a noble Egyptian and he the playboy of the Nile; and she a Roman matron while he was a philosophy-spouting shepherd. Now that she is a famous sculptor, she prefers him as the celebrated archaeologist and art critic Sinclair Heybore. Warned that this is her final reincarnation and that she must nab him now or never, she resorts to her memories of her time as an Egyptian to help Sinclair find a missing temple, and thus wins him. Waspish Margaret Hamilton and lovable, slightly doddering Ruth McDevitt (called by one writer "the poor woman's Josephine Hull") aided the festivities. Nonetheless, critics bewailed that there "isn't enough fun to fill the evening." The play went into the record books as a one-week dud.

The season's Pulitzer Prize, but with it a run of only 161 performances, went to Joseph Kramm's **The Shrike** (1-15-52, Cort). Jim Downs (José Ferrer) is wheeled into a hospital ward after a failed suicide attempt. He has been despondent because he cannot obtain a job as a theatrical director. Taking advantage of her legal status, his vicious, estranged wife, Ann (Judith Evelyn), determines to keep him there until he comes back to her. She quietly turns the hospital staff against him and agrees to his release only after he promises to abandon a warm, loving girl with whom he has been having an affair. Exhausted into submission, he accepts Ann's terms. On the phone he requests she come pick him up. He concludes the conversation by total surrender: "Thank you, dear. You won't be long—will you?"

The second O'Neill play to be revived during the season was *Desire Under the Elms* (11-11-24), which was brought out at the ANTA on the 16th. Most critics hailed the play, but held reservations about the performances of Karl Malden as the patriarchal Ephraim, Douglas Watson as his son Eben, and Carol Stone as Abbie Putnam, who has married the old man but has a child by the son. The drama lingered for six weeks.

The venerable saw that it is difficult enough to revive a hit, but virtually futile to revive a flop was exemplified again by the City Center's mounting on the 23rd of Clemence Dane's 1934 failure, *Come of Age,* with Judith Anderson in her original role. As before, Anderson was admired and the play was not.

Another London hit to suffer Broadway's quick rejection was Enid Bagnold's **Gertie** (1-30-52, Plymouth). The youngest daughter (Glynis Johns) of an improvident English scholar is sufficiently ambitious and shrewd to use the visits to her home of an American film writer (Polly Rowles) and a New York producer (Albert Dekker) to obtain a hearing for a play by her shy, older sister (Patricia Wheel).

S. N. Behrman's **Jane** (2-1-52, Coronet), which he took from Somerset Maugham's story and which London and the Continent had already seen, split New York's critics. Their evaluations ran from an "hilarious hit" to "after an agreeably funny first act, woefully thin on invention." But they generally allowed that the performances were first-rate. For all that, the comedy could not get beyond its 100th performance. Athough Willie and Millicent Tower [read Maugham and his estranged wife, Syrie] (Basil Rathbone and Irene Browne) have long been separated, they are still friends who see each other whenever Willie is in England. But Millicent is annoyed that her dowdy, blunt-spoken, widowed sister-in-law, Jane Fowler (Edna Best), has invited herself for a visit. Millicent complains to Willie, "She looks twenty years older than I do and she's perfectly capable of telling anyone she meets that we were at school together." When she arrives, Jane shocks her hostess by announcing her engagement to a young architect (Philip Friend). The marriage is short-lived. So Jane goes after Lord Frobisher (Howard St. John), a newspaper magnate whom Millicent wants for herself, and badgers him into marrying her.

Although one-man shows were nothing new, they were now about to burst on an economically strapped Broadway. First to arrive was Emlyn Williams as **Charles Dickens** (2-4-52, Golden), with the star made up as the famous author and reading excerpts from his works, much as Dickens himself had done when he toured American lecture circuits in 1867. Most reviewers said it made for an interesting enough evening, but the *Journal American*'s often crabby John McClain was outraged at the $4.80 top and concluded his notice, "Is this THEATRE? I wonder." It satisfied atypical audiences for six weeks.

Lines such as "I'll believe it when I hear it in black and white" and "Rome wasn't burnt in a day" were among the reasons several critics gave for calling Lillian Day and Alfred Golden's **Collector's Item** (2-8-52, Booth) the season's worst play. A family of international art dealers persuade a young restorer (James Gregory) to refurbish an antique French sedan chair for a nasty Washington hostess. Detesting the purchaser, the young man builds a potty into the seat, then elopes with the sweetheart (Gaye Jordan) of one of the dealers. Three performances sufficed.

Rex Harrison and Lilli Palmer could not make a hit out of Christopher Fry's blank-verse English drama **Venus Observed** (2-13-52, Century), in which an aging duke, a widower with a love of astronomy, decides to marry one of his three former loves. But before he can, the daughter of his somewhat dishonest estate manager subtly woos and wins him.

In Mary Chase's **Mrs. McThing** (2-20-52, ANTA) the snooty Mrs. Howard V. Larue II (Helen Hayes) cannot figure out why her young son, the wildly pampered and heretofore difficult Howay (Brandon de Wilde), has suddenly become so obsequiously well behaved. Then she learns that because she turned away Mimi (Lydia Reed), a poor, shabbily dressed little girl who longed to play with Howay, Mimi's mother, a witch named Mrs. McThing, has replaced the real Howay with "a stick." The real Howay now works as a dishwasher at the Shantytown Pool Hall Lunchroom, and gangsters, led by the mother-pecked Poison Eddie

Shellenbach (Jules Munshin), who run the joint soon invite him to become a member of their mob. For further snobbishness, Mrs. Larue herself is made into a scrubwoman at the lunchroom and another "stick" substituted for her at home. Later the gangsters plan to rob the Larue estate. But after Howay convinces his mother to be nice to Mimi, matters turn out just fine. Although the witch is forced to give up Mimi, the newly liberalized Mrs. Larue assures the youngster that she will live with them like a daughter. Chapman typified the majority ayesayers when he embraced the comedy as "another big load of cheer" and thanked Hayes for "the most resourceful, the most endearing performance imaginable." Albeit the play had initially been announced for a customary ANTA run of two weeks, everyone knew it would be extended in the face of so many laudatory notices. By the time it closed, it had run for 350 playings.

That was 346 more performances than Lexford Richards's **Dear Barbarians** (2-21-52, Royale) achieved. An explosively temperamental, totally selfish young musician (Donald Murphy) has refused to marry the girl (Cloris Leachman) with whom he has been living, arguing that the unhappy marriage of his parents (Nicholas Joy and Violet Heming) should serve as a warning. Only after the girl shows him he is a chip off the old block, and after he realizes that his parents, for all their bickering, love each other, does he consent to wed.

Sylvia Rayman's **Women of Twilight** (3-3-52, Plymouth) was the latest London drama to bomb in New York, running just one week. It told of a home for unwed mothers run by a vicious woman (Mary Merrall), who often underfeeds her charges and forcibly gives the babies up for adoption until she is exposed by one of her victims. First nighters had to wade through a noisy picket line set up to protest the producers' importing the original London scenery instead of building it anew in America.

Cornelia Otis Skinner's **Paris '90** (3-4-52, Booth) was a one-woman show essentially in the Ruth Draper tradition, but whereas Draper had performed on a bare stage, Skinner employed elegant costumes and scenery, and music by Kay Swift, to ornament her largely unconnected skits about turn-of-the-century Paris. She impersonated, among others, grande dames, a streetwalker (her least effective effort), a touring Boston schoolmarm, and even Yvette Guilbert.

A generally praised revival of Clifford Odets's *Golden Boy,* brought into the ANTA on the 12th, featured John Garfield—in his last appearance before his early death—as the violinist-turned-prizefighter and Lee J. Cobb as his father. It ran for seven weeks.

Even critics who did not care for George Tabori's **Flight into Egypt** (3-18-52, Music Box) let it down gently, seeing it as an honest, intelligent attempt to look at an ongoing problem. The Engels—father (Paul Lukas), mother (Gusti Huber), and young son (Voytek Dolinski)—have traveled all across Europe for six years and finally taken lodgings in a seedy Cairo hotel while awaiting visas to America. "With all this agony you could build a cathedral," one character remarks. But when Mr. Engel, crippled in the war, is denied a visa, he decides he has had agony enough and kills himself so that his wife and son can find a home in the New World. Along with the principal actors, Jo Mielziner's setting of the hotel—the long, receding arches of the lobby, part of the bar, and a section of the Engels' cramped, shabby room—won universal praise. But the plight of the displaced interested only sufficient playgoers to remain before the footlights for six weeks.

There was even less interest in Sigmund Miller's **One Bright Day** (3-19-52, Royale). The manufacturer (Howard Lindsay) of a painkiller is caught in a dilemma when some of the pills prove toxic. Should he warn the public or hope that a second death will not occur before all the pills are quietly called back? To further his anguish, he realizes his daughter's fiancé (Walter Matthau) has been tampering with the pills' formula and hopes to replace his prospective father-in-law as company chief. Many of the best notices went to Glenn Anders as the company's waspish playboy director.

A week and a half was all Broadway would grant Harvey Haislip's **The Long Watch** (3-20-52, Lyceum). Because Lt. Lennox (Sonia Sorel) is such a rigid martinet, Susie Blake (Christine White) must go AWOL to spend a night with her husband. As a result she falls asleep on her watch in the communications room of a naval rescue unit and fails to pick up a distress call. The rescue craft sent out later is piloted by her husband. It runs short of fuel and crashes, so Susie's husband is killed. She, in turn, commits suicide. Lennox is left to reconsider her unyielding policies. Strangely, none of the performers mentioned was featured. That honor fell to Walter Abel, who was cast as the women's salty, reluctant overseer.

Truman Capote served as the adaptor for his own novel **The Grass Harp** (3-27-52, Martin Beck), which most reviewers felt had been better off left between the original hardcovers, and which survived for a little more than one month. Unhappy with the treatment she receives at home at the hands of her materialistic, power-hungry sister, Verna (Ruth Nelson), Dolly Talbo (Mildred Natwick) takes refuge in a tree house, accompanied by a young cousin (Johnny Stewart), a maid (Georgia Burke), and, eventually, a thoughtful, philosophical judge (Russell Collins). She remains there until Verna falls on hard times and a reconciliation of sorts is brought about.

George Westman (Sidney Blackmer), the central figure in Irving Elman's **The Brass Ring** (4-10-52, Lyceum), is a highly successful executive who continually asks himself whether he would have been happier had he not thrown over his bohemian life in Paris years ago with a giddy young artist named Corliss. He urges his daughter (Bethel Leslie) to have a Parisian fling before wedding a rich man's son; and after his own son (Douglas Watson) gets into trouble with his secretary he is helpful and not displeased. But then he meets Corliss again. Only she is now Mrs. Potter (Helen Dumas), a flighty matron. So he concludes everything happens for the best. In flashbacks Watson and Leslie played the young George and Corliss.

The more influential newspaper critics thought little of Horton Foote's **The Chase** (4-15-52, Playhouse), with Atkinson regretting it "does not make much impression." Sheriff Hawes (John Hodiak) dislikes using his gun; he prefers to bring in criminals peaceably. Even Bubber Reeves (Murray Hamilton). Bubber is an escaped killer whom Hawes had helped send to jail before and who has vowed to kill Hawes. Hawes tracks Bubber to an isolated cabin where Bubber's wife (Kim Stanley) has been living with another man. When persuasion fails to move Bubber, Hawes is forced to shoot him. Despite José Ferrer's fine staging, the play languished for a month before shuttering.

So did a revival of Shaw's *Candida*, which came into the National on the 22nd. It represented Olivia de Haviland's second attempt to make a mark for herself on the stage, and like her earlier one it failed. Bramwell Fletcher was her Mr. Burgess, with the rest of the cast less well known.

At the start of William Marchant's **To Be Continued** (4-23-52, Booth), Claude Franklin (Neil Hamilton) and his mistress, Dolly (Dorothy Stickney), are celebrating twenty-five years of unwedded bliss. Then Dolly, who has come to resent his going home to his wife every weekend and who is goaded by a friend (Luella Gear) newly abandoned by her own longtime lover, gets the notion that Claude ought to divorce his wife and wed her instead. The wife (Jean Dixon) shows up to confront Dolly, and, by the time they have had it out, matters are left where they were at the start.

All previous candidates for the season's worst play were set aside with the arrival of Charles Horner and Henry Miles's single-performance fiasco, **Hook 'n' Ladder** (4-29-52, Royale). A trio of fire-engine salesmen (well, actually one of them is a saleswoman) attempt to bribe a hick town into buying a broken-down fire engine only to discover that honesty is the best policy. Kerr noted that throughout the evening Vicki Cummings kept muttering, "We're all in this mess together," leading him to observe that her remark "left

a reviewer with practically nothing more to say." But then he went on to add his now classic remark, "It's plays like 'Hook 'n' Ladder' that give failures a bad name."

Three revivals followed, and only the first was a hit. That was James Thurber and Elliott Nugent's 1940 success, *The Male Animal*, which romped into the City Center on the 30th for a two-week stay, with Nugent recreating his original role and with Martha Scott and Robert Preston as his co-stars. The brisk, athletic Preston all but stole the show, especially with his hilarious recounting of his famous "Statue of Liberty" football play. Hawkins proclaimed, "This show is becoming a minor classic." With his fellow aisle-sitters unanimously echoing his sentiments, the comedy was hurried into the Music Box. It stayed around for 317 performances, thereby comfortably outrunning the original.

The Music Box became available because a revival of *Much Ado About Nothing*, which opened on May 1, folded after four performances. Claire Luce and Antony Eustrel repeated the Beatrice and Benedick they had done at Stratford-on-Avon several seasons earlier but were not well liked. The best notices went to the Dogberry of Melville Cooper, who once again found himself the saving grace of an otherwise graceless evening.

At the City Center on the 14th, the Thurber-Nugent comedy was replaced by the Deval-Sherwood hit of 1936, *Tovarich*. This time the critics were in anything but agreement over the revival's merits. With such fine players as Herbert Berghof, Uta Hagen, Paula Lawrence, and Romney Brent in the cast it played out its slated two-week stand, then closed.

The season's third one-person show was **Conscience** (5-15-52, Booth), which Claude Vincent and A. M. Klein took from Pedro Bloch's Portuguese original. The lone person in the cast was Maurice Schwartz, a refugee from the largely moribund Yiddish theatre. He appeared as a failed writer who returns home from his mistress's to find his wife and his children are gone, then belabors his shrewish spouse and his miserable in-laws for the rest of the evening. With almost fiendish exuberance Schwartz figuratively chewed the scenery and literally tore to shreds some books and papers in the writer's library.

The theatrical year ended with two plays arriving on the same night. Emery Rubio and Miriam Balf's **Sunday Breakfast** (5-28-52, Coronet) was the sole novelty. George Decker (Anthony Ross) is an ineffectual Connecticut jeweler living over his shop with his harridan wife (Margaret Feury), his drifting, jobless grown son (Douglas Watson), his sluttish grown daughter (Cloris Leachman), and his often abused and neglected six-year-old daughter (Jada Rowland). The youngster runs away from home, but is brought back by a kindly state trooper (Jim Nolan), who suggests the family sit down to Sunday breakfast and try to work out their problems. The attempt fails, but George does promise the youngster to take her to Maine—someday.

The City Center finished its season with Edna Best and the long absent Helen Gahagan in Katharine Dayton and George S. Kaufman's 1935 hit, *First Lady.* Even those critics who enjoyed it suggested it was becoming a bit frayed around the edges and noted that the authors, who had added up-to-date references to Betty Grable and Dick Tracy, must have thought so, too.

By the time this last pair closed, two weeks later, Broadway was in the dumps. Only seven non-musical plays were running, none was near capacity, and several had posted closing notices. The heftiest grosses were reported by *Point of No Return,* but it was taking in only about $25,000 out of a possible $37,000. Point of small returns might have described the situation.

On the other hand, small beginnings could lead to larger, more important things. Off Broadway had never died, but certainly had dwindled to a pale reflection of its vigorous self in the 1920s. Now the first major stirrings of a renaissance could be perceived—if only in retrospect. During the season, a group calling itself the Loft Players had traveled down from Woodstock, New York, and established itself at a tiny venue called the Circle in the Square. Their first offering, a revival of *Dark of the Moon,* made no waves. But in March they presented a reconsideration of Tennessee Williams's *Summer and Smoke,* staged by an unknown director, José Quintero, and featuring an unknown actress, Geraldine Page, as Alma. Once the belated notices began to appear (Atkinson didn't get around to it until late April), the group, Quintero, and Page could no longer be called unknown.

1952–1953

Much of the commentary at season's end was evasive or at least equivocating. Reactions to the just terminated theatrical year ran from "so-so" to "it has not been a particularly auspicious one" to the assessment by the *Best Plays*'s new, brahmin editor, Louis Kronenberger, that no small part of the season's interest rested with the controversies several plays provoked rather than with the plays themselves. But then there were far fewer new plays to think about. The number of novelties was listed variously between twenty-nine and thirty-four. By way of compensation, business was somewhat better,

and therefore the runs, at least of several hits, were longer than in the prior year.

The season opened with Hugh Hastings's **Seagulls over Sorrento** (9-11-52, Golden), a long-running London success that survived in New York for only a week and a half. The play dealt with the lives of some British able seamen who volunteer to perform hazardous experiments on an isolated island in the Scapa Flow. One is killed and another meets his wife's lover before their time is up and they prepare to return to the mainland.

Nor was Broadway all that delighted with Stanley Young's theatricalization of Dickens's *Pickwick Papers* as **Mr. Pickwick** (9-17-52, Plymouth), which retained many of the novel's most celebrated incidents but often seemed to be caricaturing caricatures. At least Estelle Winwood got a big hand as Mrs. Leo Hunter, reciting "Ode to an Expiring Frog." George Howe was Pickwick, and Clive Revill was Sam Weller.

The British tinge to the early season continued with a revival of Somerset Maugham's 1928 failure, *The Sacred Flame,* at the President on October 6. The story of a mother who kills her hopelessly invalided son rather than have him learn his own brother has seduced his wife failed again, although Frances Starr won kudos as the mother.

Italy was the setting for several plays (and one short-lived musical) which came in next. Edmund Beloin and Henry Garson's **In Any Language** (10-7-52, Cort) spotlighted Hannah King (Uta Hagen), a faded Hollywood star who comes to Italy hoping to revive her career by appearing in some arty new-realism flicks. She bombs. But at least she wins back the love of an American flier (Walter Matthau) whom she had wed during the war. Critics were delighted to discover Hagen's gift for comedy, and a number of them admitted that the audience had a grand time, but most still did not like the comedy, and neither, apparently, did the public at large.

Alfred Drake and Edward Eager were the translators of Ugo Betti's **The Gambler** (10-13-52, Lyceum), in which Drake, far better known as a leading man in musicals, also assumed the main role. He played David Petri, who stands accused of murdering his wife, if only by wishing her dead, and who comes to realize that he actually loved the woman he believed he hated. Critics gave the play short shrift but lauded Drake's "moving sincerity, admirable technical resource and amazing semblance of conviction."

At the Pensione Fioria in Venice, the locale for Arthur Laurents's **The Time of the Cuckoo** (10-15-52, Empire), young Eddie Yaeger (Donald Murphy) nearly loses his wife (Geraldine Brooks) after she learns that he has enjoyed a fling with the proprietress (Lydia St.

Clair). But theirs are not the only disillusionments. A lonely American spinster, Leona Samish (Shirley Booth), has come to Venice to see the sights and, not incidentally, to look for romance. She believes she has found it with a suave, handsome Italian, Renato de Rossi (Dino Di Luca), but he turns out to be not only a married man with children, but a sponger, who leaves Leona to shell out for the supposed gift of jewelry he gave her. The proprietress berates her, telling her that her disappointment really comes because she thinks "so much of money and so little of yourself." A sadder, wiser Leona heads out to see some more sights, commenting forlornly, "In Italy, everything molta bella." Critics were none too happy with the play, seeing it as an uncomfortable mixture of high comedy and tearjerker drama, but saluted Booth for investing the evening with "the sweetness and glow and simplicity of her acting." The play was the first hit of the season, running for 263 performances. Whether, as claimed, it was the theatre's 279th attraction, it was the last show to play the venerable Empire on Broadway. Shortly after the play closed, the house was demolished. In 1965 the show became a Richard Rodgers musical, *Do I Hear a Waltz?*

The high school boys in Mary Chase's **Bernardine** (10-16-52, Playhouse) meet regularly in the back room of the Shamrock, a 3.2 beer parlor in an unidentified western city. They dream of being loved by a slightly older, beautiful, somewhat beat-up-looking figment of their imaginations whom they have named Bernardine Crud: "When she walks down the streets, her eyes flash a message—live on, boy, dream on—I'm waiting for you." One of the boys, Buford "Wormy" Weldy (Johnny Stewart), thinks he has come across her in Enid Lacey (Beverley Lawrence), who owns a '53 Cadillac convertible and invites him to her apartment. But given his opportunity, Wormy becomes gauche and embarrassed, especially after discovering that Enid is a friend of his parents. Not to worry, for Wormy may well have found Bernardine Crud in the person of Jean Cantrick (Camilla DeWitt), who calls him to come to her rescue after a date has stranded her. Brooks Atkinson wrote in the *Times:* " 'Bernardine' is deficient in everything that does not matter much [such as its drab scenery]. But Mrs. Chase is wonderful with things that are important. She knows her characters thoroughly and forgives them for being human. She has the kind of humor that does not consist in telling jokes but in having a sweet and hospitable sense of proportion." The comedy ran twenty weeks, but failed to recoup its costs.

On the other hand, Shaw's very late (1935) **The Millionairess** (10-17-52, Shubert) ran only ten and a half weeks, but wound up happily in the black. Of course, thanks to its star, Katharine Hepburn, it packed the large musical comedy house for much of that time

and did so at a $6 top. Having made a botch of her marriage to a macho athlete, the oh-so-wealthy heroine latches on to a rather epicene man-about-town (Cyril Ritchard), whom she throws down a flight of stairs after he makes a careless, disparaging remark about her daddy, and she finally settles for a soft-spoken, idealistic Egyptian doctor (Robert Helpmann). Not every critic rejoiced at Hepburn's ceaselessly dynamic, whirlwind performance, and, indeed, Ritchard came off best for his "wonderfully droll" antics as the bumbling Englishman "wavering pleasantly between the coy and the resentful."

Two more English shows followed. The second longest run of the season—552 performances—went to Frederick Knott's **Dial 'M' for Murder** (10-29-52, Plymouth). Having wed Margot (Gusti Huber) for her money, Tony Wendice (Maurice Evans) decides to kill her for it. He blackmails a criminal (Anthony Dawson) into murdering the woman, but instead Margot reaches for a pair of scissors and stabs her would-be killer to death. The resourceful Tony then manages to get his wife convicted of murder, but an even more resourceful detective (John Williams) and Margot's lover (Richard Derr) are not so sure that she is guilty. The detective sees to it that Tony's carelessness about a key trips him up. Evans could clip appreciative day-after notices. Thus William Hawkins in the *World-Telegram and Sun* reported, "Evans dominates the performance. . . . He is thoroughly unpleasant, yet retains a superficial charm that reasonably takes in his associates. Whenever the ice gets thin for him it is quite remarkable how he is able to show his apprehension to the audience without tipping off the people of the story." Cleverly contrived and tautly staged, the play gave Broadway the thriller it had been seeking.

But the day when a two-handkerchief tearjerker could find a sufficient audience, especially at matinees, was gone, so while Terence Rattigan's **The Deep Blue Sea** (11-5-52, Morosco) compiled 132 performances, it wound up in the red. Hester Collyer (Margaret Sullavan) unsuccessfully attempts suicide when she realizes that her lover, a selfish test pilot (James Hanley) for whom she threw over a dull but loving husband (Alan Webb), is an ineffectual man who may well leave her. Her still loyal husband is found and proves willing to help her recover. But after sending the pilot off to a dangerous job in South America, yet remaining unable to return to her husband, she attempts suicide a second time. In this instance, a neighbor (Herbert Berghof), a strange doctor who has been disallowed from practicing, saves her and gives her the courage to go on living. The play was seen as the effective ladies' matinee claptrap that it was, although many critics felt no need for such plays on contemporary Broadway. Of the beautiful, blonde

Sullavan, who was returning to the stage after a lapse of some years, Walter Kerr wrote in the *Herald Tribune* that "the actress, delicately fetching as before, does a dozen small things which illuminate the minor moods of the piece. The awkward shyness with which she withdraws her instinctively preferred hand from her former husband, her strained attempt to be gay when she is actually drained of all emotion, . . ." but Kerr continued on to complain that regrettably "the depths of Hester's despair are never fully sounded."

The Climate of Eden (11-6-52, Martin Beck) was Moss Hart's dramatization of Edgar Mittelholzer's novel *Shadows Move Among Them*. A majority of critics found it too complex and only intermittently moving. The action takes place around the home and church of the Reverend Gerald Harmston (John Cromwell), a most unorthodox, freethinking minister, living with his family in the jungles of British Guiana. That family includes two daughters, the younger, impressionable Olivia (Penelope Munday), and the more mature Mabel (Rosemary Harris). Into their midst comes a patently disturbed young man, Gregory Hawke (Lee Montague), who may have murdered his wife and who does at one point menace the daughters. This does not prevent Olivia from becoming enamored of him, and she is furious when she learns he and Mabel have fallen in love. She even announces that Mabel has been killed by a bushmaster, a small snake with a most deadly neurotoxic venom. The minister has gotten Gregory to see that his wife committed suicide and to understand that he must stop blaming himself. Once Olivia's false alarm is disposed of, Gregory and Mabel can start to plan for a better life ahead. The minister is left to console Olivia by assuring her that Gregory will "never be without part of us and part of this place" and that it is time to cast away her girlhood. The play was the first in which Harris called New Yorkers' attentions to her great acting skills.

A pair of foreign ensembles furthered the international air that Broadway had displayed for so much of the season. Jean-Louis Barrault and Madelaine Renaud brought in their Paris troupe on the 12th at the Ziegfeld. They opened with a double bill of Marivaux's **Les Fausses Confidences,** in which a young man wins the hand of a lovely lady despite the machinations of her highborn family and friends, and Jacques Prevert's pantomime **Baptiste**, in which a Pierrot-like figure woos a beautiful statue. Subsequent attractions included **Le Procès,** a French theatricalization of Kafka; a double bill of Molière plays, **Amphitryon** and **Les Fourberies de Scapin**; Feydeau's classic farce **Occupe-toi d'Amélie;** Anouilh's **La Répétition;** and *Hamlet* (in French). Most critics admitted that they were scarcely

fluent in French, but allowed that the troupe was an exemplar of brilliant concerted acting.

At a second musical comedy house, the Mark Hellinger, the National Theatre of Greece, led by Katina Paxinou and Alexis Minotis, arrived on the 19th to offer two Sophocles tragedies, *Electra* and *Oedipus,* done in modern Greek. Like the Frenchmen, the troupe was well-received.

The season's biggest hit was George Axelrod's **The Seven Year Itch** (11-20-52, Fulton), which John Chapman welcomed in the *Daily News* as "a grand and goofy comedy and it will relieve the dolors of even a Stevenson voter." With a bagful of such notices and good word of mouth spreading quickly, the play soon settled in for a run of 1141 performances. Richard Sherman (Tom Ewell) finds himself on edge while summer bacheloring. He is a wildly imaginative paperpack publisher, whose wild imagination has him, in short order, fantasizing about a little marital infidelity. Just then a flowerpot that belongs to the beautiful tenant upstairs falls from her balcony and nearly conks him. That leads to his meeting the girl (Vanessa Brown), and the meeting leads to more Walter Mittyish dreams. In one, his wife (Neva Patterson), on learning of his philandering, takes time out from making a cherry pie to shoot him. With his dying breath he pleads for a cigarette, only to have the little woman remind him, "You know what Dr. Murphy told you about smoking!" His fantasies and the voice of his conscience (coming out from a loudspeaker) keep him on the straight and narrow. Ewell was applauded every bit as much as the play: "Tom Ewell brings an almost inexhaustible supply of unlikely leers, majestic attitudes and frantic palpitations. Whether he is waltzing around the room in his new-found freedom, or dreaming such enchanting dreams over what is going to happen when the doorbell rings that he doesn't hear the doorbell when it does ring, Mr. Ewell is extraordinarily funny."

Melvyn Douglas was funny enough in Ronald Alexander's **Time Out for Ginger** (11-26-52, Lyceum) to help the show stay alive for 248 performances. Most critics were not excited by the play itself, although many did grant there was an audience for such entertainments. Atkinson, in one of the more encouraging reviews, concluded that although the comedy "is a little unsteady on its pins, it is fresh, warm-hearted and funny." Since Howard Carol, a banker, has spoken publicly in favor of more freedom of expression and behavior for high school students, his three high-school-aged daughters decide to hold him to his words. Two rebel against having to take gym. The third, the youngest, tomboyish Ginger (Nancy Malone), takes the opposite tack and wins a place on the football team. She also wins national notoriety, which for a brief time threatens Carol's job. After Ginger scores a winning touchdown, her proud father inadvertently calls her "son" and confesses, "When I heard the coach say, 'Send Carol in,' I almost ran out onto the field myself." This helps Ginger decide that being a girl is more fun. Mrs. Carol (Polly Rowles) suggests that it may be not too late for Howard and her to try to have a boy.

John van Druten had no luck with **I've Got Sixpence** (12-2-52, Barrymore), his look at two girls who are roommates and their quests for romance and happiness. The more worldly girl, Doreen (Vicki Cummings), settles for the security of a devoted Catholic, Robert Gallagher (Bert Thorn). The free-spirited Inez (Viveca Lindfors) is almost driven to suicide by her relationship with Peter Tyndall (Edmund O'Brien), a writer and ex-Communist soured on everything. He is the sort who announces, "I've got a feeling here inside of me, like a bird beating its wings." The couples are aided, and occasionally confused, by the writer's virtually blind aunt (Patricia Collinge) and a self-important guru (Paul Lipson) who speaks pompously of the "all effulgent." Richard Watts, Jr., writing in the *Post*, dismissed the piece as "simply not credible."

Many critics felt the same way about N. Richard Nash's clumsily symbolic **See the Jaguar** (12-3-52, Cort). Most of his fellow townsfolk are in debt to Brad (Cameron Prud'homme), who owns the local store. Brad is not a nice man, gloating as he displays caged animals around him. When batty Mrs. Wilkins (Margaret Barker), who has kept her inarticulate son (James Dean) locked in her ice house, dies, he has the boy seized and caged. Brad hopes to locate the $900 Mrs. Wilkins is supposed to have hidden somewhere. Some of the money would go to pay off her debt to him. But Brad's independent daughter, Janna (Constance Ford), and her sweetheart, Dave (Arthur Kennedy), a high-principled schoolteacher, set out to free the boy. Dave is shot and killed in the process. Half a week and the play disappeared.

Robert Finch's **Whistler's Grandmother** (12-11-52, President) grabbed no better notices but survived three weeks at its tiny house, possibly on the strength of Josephine Hull's lure. To get out of the rain, a little old lady pops into Eddie's saloon and props herself up a bit awkwardly on a bar stool. When Eddie (Lonny Chapman) asks her what she'll have, she responds, "What's nourishing?" Before long this little old gal realizes that she may be the answer to Eddie's prayers. She has overheard Eddie and his fiancée, Joy (Peggy Nelson), a hoofer, quarrel and split up because Joy longs for a more comfortable, homey place than Eddie has. The old gal—her name is Kate—agrees to redo the rooms above the bar in cozy Victorian fashion and to pose there as Eddie's grandmother. The barflies can move in as friends of the family. By the time the hoax is exposed, Joy is willing to concede "it's realer than if it was not really real."

John D. Hess's **The Grey-Eyed People** (12-17-52, Martin Beck) was another of the season's half-week duds. Chapman noted that Ibsen, and Thurber and Nugent, had handled the same basic plot more skillfully. John Hart (Walter Matthau) loses his job as a TV advertising executive for coming to the defense of his old college buddy (Tony Bickley), a man long disillusioned by the communism he once embraced but refusing to disclose the names of his former associates. Although the play was billed as a comedy, Hart did not get back his job.

"Still taut and pertinent" was Atkinson's evaluation of a revival of Lillian Hellman's 1934 melodrama, *The Children's Hour*, at the Coronet on the 18th with Kim Hunter and Patricia Neal in the leading roles. Yet while most of his colleagues shared Atkinson's high opinion of the play and the acting, and while the drama ran out the season, it wound up in the red—a further instance of Broadway's increasingly chilling economic picture.

The new year began with the third five-performance flop in little more than a month, Mary Orr and Reginald Denham's **Be Your Age** (1-14-53, 48th St.). Gwendolyn Holly (Hildy Parks), a young college girl, shocks her father (Loring Smith) by informing him she has broken her engagement to the boy next door (Dean Harens) and instead plans to marry Eliot Spurgeon (Conrad Nagel), a psychologist who had been her father's schoolmate. Before Gwendolyn comes to her senses, her father thinks about a fling with his young secretary (Martha Randall)—although he admits it may cost him "a lot of puffing"—and the boy next door mulls over an engineering job in Brazil.

Peter Ustinov's **The Love of Four Colonels** (1-15-53, Shubert) is set in occupied Germany and begins with colonels (Larry Gates, Robert Coote, George Voskovec, and Stefan Schnabel) from the four occupying powers trying to figure out why they cannot penetrate a mysterious castle nearby. A strange man (Rex Harrison) appears, offering to gain them entrance and help them. The officers do not recognize him as the devil's emissary. Nor are they aware that the attractive woman (Leueen MacGrath) who pops up almost simultaneously is an angel. Each of the officers is given an opportunity to wake and win the sleeping beauty (Lilli Palmer) who lies in the castle, and each contemplates wooing her in a manner typical of his country. The Frenchman sees her as an eighteenth-century lass of the boulevards, the Russian as something out of Chekhov, the Englishman as a noble, virginal Elizabethan, and the American as a tough, slangy moll. None wins her, albeit all are told they can try again in another hundred years. The uneven but largely diverting London hit ran for 141 performances.

Zasu Pitts, as the shrieking servant made famous in the original production by May Vokes, was the principal attraction in a revival of *The Bat* (8-23-20) at the National on the 20th. Critics divided on whether the mystery-thriller about an old lady (Lucile Watson) who rents a summer place that had once belonged to a possibly murdered banker could still give playgoers the creeps or whether it had become dated. Playgoers elected not to find out for themselves, so the production was withdrawn after three weeks.

In Viña Delmar's **Mid-Summer** (1-21-53, Vanderbilt), Val (Mark Stevens), his wife, Lily (Geraldine Page), and their precocious daughter, Carlo (Jenny Hecht) are living from hand to mouth in a seedy 14th Street hotel room. The year is 1907. Lily, a half-illiterate ex-waitress, longs for the comfort and security of a little white house on Staten Island, luxuries she has never enjoyed, but Val has quit teaching to try his hand in the highly uncertain fields of songwriting and vaudeville. Lily has trouble understanding Val's willingness to take risks. He tells her it is for his own self-respect. And when he asks her if she understands the meaning of the word, she replies, "It's what made my mother die over somebody else's wash tubs because she wouldn't take charity." However, in the end, for all her own uncertainties, Lily goes along with Val's wishes. Robert Coleman told his readers in the *Daily Mirror* that the play was "no literary masterpiece. It rambles a little, and some of the dialogue is less than eloquent," but for Coleman and his fellow aisle-sitters the evening was made worthwhile by its leading lady: "Miss Page reminds us a little of Pauline Lord. She has the same high-pitched, wispy voice, hands that flutter effectively in moments of frustration, a choppy, puzzled manner in delivering lines." Banner after banner proclaimed Page a new star, but she could not carry the drama beyond 109 performances nor on to commercial success.

• • •

Geraldine Page (1924–87) was born in Kirksville, Mo. She studied at the Goodman Theatre School in Chicago and with Uta Hagen before coming to playgoers' attention in a 1952 revival of *Summer and Smoke* at the Circle in the Square. In her early years she often subscribed to the nervous, inelegant mannerisms of the method school.

• • •

Since parallels between the Salem witch hunts of 1692 and the McCarthyite ones of the 1950s were so obvious, Arthur Miller had a readymade theme for

The Crucible (1-22-53, Martin Beck). Abigail Adams (Madeleine Sherwood) is the promiscuous niece of the Reverend Samuel Parris (Fred Stewart). She is employed by John and Elizabeth Proctor (Arthur Kennedy and Beatrice Straight) until Mrs. Proctor fires her. In revenge, she accuses Elizabeth of being a witch. Her charges are given ample credence in the highly emotionalized atmosphere of the time. Proctor comes to his wife's defence, but in the process admits to adultery with Abigail. He refuses to sign a confession, even though it means death: "I speak my own sins. I cannot judge another . . . I have no tongue for it." Most critics hailed the work, but the two most influential critics of the morning dailies, Atkinson and Kerr, expressed reservations. Both compared it unfavorably to Miller's earlier *Death of a Salesman*, with Kerr branding it "a step backward into mechanical parable" and Atkinson ruing that the new work was "not of that stature and it lacks that universality." But, always the gentleman, he ended his notice, "On a lower level . . . it is a powerful play and a genuine contribution to the theatre." The tragedy ran six months, but closed on the wrong side of its ledgers.

A work of far less merit but with one unforgettable performance ran for 645 playings. The comedy was Sylvia Regan's **The Fifth Season** (1-23-53, Cort); the performance that of pint-sized, sad-faced Menasha Skulnik, who had been a comic star of the Yiddish theatre in its last heyday. He was seen as Max Pincus, better known as Pinkie, who is one half of the failing garment firm of Goodwin-Pincus. Pinkie is the practical one. Thus, much as he admires a model, he shrugs, "I think I'll fire her altogether. Who needs a model? Somebody is buying our garments?" The other half of the firm is Johnny Goodwin (Richard Whorf), a supersalesman but a goodtime Charlie and playboy. Even in the struggle to save the firm, he finds occasion to court a beautiful woman (Phyllis Hill), so Pinkie must pretend she is his own inamorata to dissuade Mrs. Goodwin (Augusta Roeland) from leaving Johnny. There was no concealing that the play was hackwork. But Skulnik's cornucopia of shrugs, whines, grimaces, and other gestures made it hilarious. Thus he described a minor friend not as a friend—with his hands palms out and raised above his head—but as a friend—with his hands cupped in front of his belt.

William Stucky's **Touchstone** (2-3-53, Music Box) dealt with the still sensitive subject of a young Negro boy (Josh White, Jr.) who causes a stir in his small southern community by claiming a vision has told him that a once polluted swimming hole has been miraculously cleansed and now has healing powers. Scientific tests prove that the waters have, in fact, become pure. When a rich, white liberal (Ian Keith), who has helped the boy's father (Ossie Davis) through medical school, attempts to stop his dying granddaughter (Patty McCormack) from testing the waters, the boy tries to bring her there on his own. He is foiled and the girl dies. But racial harmony is strengthed by the incident.

On the 4th, the New York City Center began its winter season, now under the direction of Albert Marre, with Shakespeare's rarely done *Love's Labour's Lost.* Reset in Edwardian times, the revival featured Joseph Schildkraut as Don Adriano, Kevin McCarthy as Berowne, and Philip Bourneuf as Holofernes. Although all but two critics were delighted with the offering, the two displeased critics were Atkinson and Kerr. So there was no cry to extend the run beyond the initially scheduled two weeks.

George Tabori's **The Emperor's Clothes** (2-9-53, Barrymore) told of an intellectual (Lee J. Cobb), living in the Hungarian police state of the 1930s, who has been dismissed from a university for his liberal pronouncements. His very young son (Brandon de Wilde), who has become disillusioned by his father's refusal to fight the authorities, attempts to enlist other children in a mock subversive group. Using this as an excuse, the police arrest the father and torture him. But he regains his child's respect by not breaking under the torture. The principals, including Maureen Stapleton as the intellectual's wife, were praised, but the drama was seen as squandering its opportunities.

A fine revival of Paul Osborn's 1938 hit, *On Borrowed Time,* which came into the Playhouse on the 10th, was turned into something special by the performance of a beloved old comedian famous for his singular amalgam of wistfulness and toughness, seventy-seven-year-old Victor Moore, as Gramps. Moore, Kerr reported, "will have no truck with second-rate sentimentality, that fey archness, which might easily invade the role. He indulges the boy with magnificent sobriety, explaining that birds don't carry watch-fobs in a tone that hasn't a trace of fatherly patronage in it." Leo G. Carroll was Mr. Brink, and Beulah Bondi, Granny. Yet for all the critical hat-throwing, the comedy ran only ten weeks.

The brief vogue for readings, begun with last season's *Don Juan in Hell,* continued with Stephen Vincent Benet's **John Brown's Body** (2-14-53, New Century). Accompanied this time by a chorus and a pair of dancers, the principals, each reading a number of parts, were Judith Anderson, Raymond Massey (whose recitations naturally included anything to do with Lincoln), and Tyrone Power. The reading chalked up sixty-five performances, closing primarily because of the players' Hollywood commitments.

The hit of the City Center's winter season was Shaw's infrequently revived *Misalliance.* Enlivened by Cyril Ritchard's zesty, high-styled staging, the comedy, first done on Broadway in 1917, was brought out again on the 18th with a cast that included Barry Jones, Roddy McDowell, and Dorothy Sands. It was hailed by Richard Watts, Jr., in the *Post* as "a theatrical treat," and was hurriedly moved to the Ethel Barrymore for a regular run—which continued on merrily until the end of June. Merrily for playgoers, at least, but not for the producers. Without the lure of a Hepburn and the higher top ticket she commanded at a much larger house (this mounting asked a mere $3 top and yet had to resort to twofers) and because unions demanded sets and costumes be recreated for the move to a mainstream playhouse, the comedy wound up as a money-loser.

Both the Pulitzer Prize and the New York Drama Critics Circle Award for the season went to William Inge's **Picnic** (2-19-53, Music Box). Kronenberger, discussing the drama in his *Best Plays* introduction, noted, "Mr. Inge's naturalistic round dance of frustrated, unfulfilled, life-hungry women catches something of the mischance and misbegottenness of life itself," but he slammed what he—and some of his colleagues—deemed Josh Logan's overheated, unsubtle direction. On a sultry Labor Day morning in a small Kansas town, Hal Carter (Ralph Meeker), a cocky, muscle-bound young vagrant, strays into the Owenses' backyard and disrupts the lives of the family. He goads Rosemary (Eileen Heckart), the spinster sister of Mrs. Owens (Peggy Conklin), into forcing her reluctant gentleman friend (Arthur O'Connell) to marry her, and he breaks the heart of the tomboy younger daughter, Millie (Kim Stanley), by cajoling the older daughter, Madge (Janice Rule), into abandoning her rich boyfriend (Paul Newman) and running away with him. Madge asks her mother what one can do with the love one feels: "Where is there you can take it?" A defeated Mrs. Owens acknowledges, "I never found out." So Madge agrees to follow Hal, even though she may have to support herself to do so. The drama closed only after 477 performances.

A revival of *The Merchant of Venice* raised its curtain at the City Center on March 5 to conclude that playhouse's winter season. Luther Adler, following in the footsteps of his famous father, was Shylock, but neither he nor the rest of the mounting elicited any wild handclapping.

My 3 Angels (3-11-53, Morosco), which Sam and Bella Spewack took from Albert Husson's *La Cuisine des anges,* was one of several shows this season to run long yet go down as a commercial failure. Although it played for ten months (344 performances), it could not recoup its costs. In 1910, three convicts (Walter Slezak, Jerome Cowan, and Darren McGavin) from Devil's Island are assigned to help around the Ducotels' home and store in French Guiana. Joseph (Slezak), the convicts' spokesman, is appalled by the conditions of Mr. Ducotel's books. He tells the dismayed fellow (Will Kuluva) that while he—Ducotel—is an honest man, his books make him look like a crook. And he proposes to change all that so Ducotel's books will be crooked but Ducotel himself will seem like an honest man. After all, everybody is a bit crooked; only the convicts have had the misfortune to be caught. The men not only merely doctor the books, but do away with the Ducotels' adversaries, leaving the family better off than they had been before the convicts came on the scene.

Delightful fantasy gave way to muddled symbolism and allegory with the arrival of the season's most controversial drama, Tennessee Williams's **Camino Real** (3-19-53, National). Although all the action took place on a tropical-looking plaza, with the Siete Mares Hotel on one side and some Skid Row-like buildings opposite, Gutman (Frank Silvera), the hotelkeeper, who served as narrator, insisted each of the eighteen scenes represented a separate "block." Among the characters to appear and to mingle with an assortment of beggars and rogues are Casanova (Joseph Anthony), Camille (Jo Van Fleet), and Lord Byron (Hurd Hatfield), but the main figures are Kilroy (Eli Wallach), a Gypsy (Jennie Goldstein) and her daughter, Esmeralda (Barbara Baxley). Every now and then streetcleaners pass by, collecting dead bodies. The Gypsy insists that "the Camino Real is a funny paper read backwards!" and that her sluttish daughter becomes a virgin again with each new moon. Kilroy is a Golden Gloves champ, who has hocked his gloves to pay for his trip but at least retains a heart that is genuine solid gold. He is a patsy, but what can he do about it? Hawkins welcomed the play as "a brilliant and riotous adventure," but Chapman, speaking for an irritatedly vociferous majority, branded it a "wotsit" and whined, "It induced in this observer an acute state of misery." Theatregoers agreed with the naysayers, so the play closed after sixty performances.

Broadway gave Andrew Rosenthal's **Horses in Midstream** (4-2-53, Royale) only four hearings. Having met Marie Louise (Lili Darvas), a beautiful French novelist, in a Paris pharmacy and fallen instantly in love with her, Charles Pine (Cedric Hardwicke), a successful New England businessman, made her his mistress and deserted his family. The pair have lived together on Elba for thirty-one years. But when a granddaughter (Diana Lynn) he has never before seen suddenly appears and tells him she is engaged to a man she does not love, so would like to run off the way he did, Pine feels it incumbent upon himself to dissuade her.

A botched revival of the 1937 hit *Room Service* drew

mixed reactions after it opened at the Playhouse on the 6th. It remained around for two weeks, with a still unknown Jack Lemmon cast as the baffled young playwright.

Even beautiful and beautifully gowned Constance Bennett was no reason for wasting time on George Batson's **A Date with April** (4-15-53, Royale). Bennett was seen as a composer of modern music who has been having an on-again, off-again affair with a world-traveling novelist (Edmon Ryan). For a time the novelist believes that the composer is having a fling with a handsome movie star (Herbert Evers) who has asked her to write a score for his next film, while she thinks the writer is pursuing a nightclub dancer. Matters are resolved satisfactorily shortly before eleven o'clock.

On the 20th at the tiny Bijou, Emlyn Williams returned in his Dickens makeup. But rather than always repeating last season's variegated bill, he spent many of his appearances reading excerpts solely from *Bleak House*. Old bill or new, he read for three weeks.

Steve Allen, a popular TV comic, was the main attraction at John G. Fuller's **The Pink Elephant** (4-22-53, Playhouse). The play was set in three adjoining Kansas City hotel rooms. Jerry Elliot is a former newspaperman turned speechwriter for a stuffy politician. He hopes his writings will earn him enough to buy a small boat and a retreat in the Bahamas. Then he meets a pretty girl (Patricia Barry) who has learned of a scheme in which some mossback Republicans hope to discourage Eisenhower from naming a Democrat to an important post ("It's like Westbrook Pegler waltzing with Eleanor Roosevelt!"). They have decided to smear the candidate. Together Jerry and the girl burst their bubble and find romance.

The season's closing play, Richard Condon's **Men of Distinction** (4-30-53, 48th St.), was another dud and also reflected current events—in this case the sensational Mickey Jelke case, in which a rich young man rented high-priced prostitutes to well-heeled clients. Peter Hogarth (Robert Preston), a ruthless publicist; Carleton Pelter (Chandler Cowles), a rich young man who manages a string of call girls; and the foxy August Volpone (Martin Ritt), a notorious racketeer, are all on the list of the blustering, cigar-chomping D.A., Daniel Gaffney (David Burns), for indictment. But the men see to it that the vain Gaffney gets his own big TV spot, and they all then conspire to set up a meek tax expert, Marvin Flynch (Ralph Bunker), as their fall guy. Some idea of the play's humor was one character picking up a copy of *Popular Mechanics* and asking another, "Have you ever known a really popular mechanic?" Among the lesser players, Orson Bean walked away with honors as a go-getting television producer, "complete with crewcut, hypnotic grin, and magnificently swiveling jaw."

1953–1954

It was another good-bad year on Broadway. The *Times* at season's end skipped its chance to comment on the year's quality. Instead it noted only that once again the number of new plays jumped to forty. (*Variety* counted forty-two novelties.) Both observed that, thanks to a pickup in business, a slightly larger proportion of productions (fourteen in all) ran beyond the 100-performance mark, although only eleven of them repaid their investments. As to quality, Kronenberger remarked in the *Best Plays,* "Not in many years had Broadway known a season boasting such a large number of pretty good plays." Of course, with his haughtier-than-thou attitude, the adverbial "pretty" governed his thinking, so he was happy to balance every play's virtues against its not always apparent-to-others faults. But even Kronenberger had to concede that for the first time since the twenties Off Broadway came back into its own as an exciting venue for serious, mainstream writing.

After a career that spanned thirty years without a single critical success, Myron C. Fagan said farewell to Broadway with **A Red Rainbow** (9-14-53, Royale). It was produced by his son Bruce, possibly because no established producer would touch it. A celebrated columnist (Robert Middleton) is murdered and in a series of flashbacks is shown to have been a sometime fascist, a Communist, and a blackmailer, leaving the detective (Howard Smith) who solves the mystery to allow the killer to walk away with a pat on the back. Fagan filled his story with all manner of right wing charges, such as that Harry Hopkins knowingly sold the Russians atomic secrets. This led the *Post*'s Richard Watts, Jr., to paraphrase Samuel Johnson and call patriotism "the last refuge of the bad playwright."

End As a Man (9-15-53, de Lys) was Calder Willingham's adaptation of his own novel. Reviews such as that of Brooks Atkinson in the *Times,* which called the drama "uneven though remarkably interesting . . . sharp and alive," prompted the play's transfer after a month to an uptown house. The two runs gave it a record of 139 performances, not enough to recoup costs. Jocko de Paris (Ben Gazzara), a cadet at a military academy, can smile and smile and still be a villain, since his father is a major trustee of the school. Jocko lords it over and often torments his fellow cadets, even

throwing one of them down a flight of stairs. He would employ the more pliable in a scheme to wreck the academy, but when he is exposed he is kicked out despite his father's position. The evening was capped by Gazzara's superb performance, combining "a lazy insinuating control with a hint of restlessness which is just this side of hysteria."

In London the Lord Chamberlain banned the playing at regular West End theatres of F. Tennyson Jesse and H. M. Harwood's version of Jesse's novel **A Pin to See the Peepshow** (9-17-53, Playhouse). New York's critics killed it on this side of the Atlantic after a single performance. The play was based on an actual early-1920s murder in which the young lover of a very slightly older woman stabbed to death her much older husband. Because of letters she had written him, seemingly goading him on, she was hanged as well as he. In the play the lover (Roger Moore) bludgeons the husband (Bill Griffis) to death, and the wife (Joan Miller), for all her protestations of innocence, is again condemned along with her lover.

For the most part, the largely white theatregoing public still remained indifferent to black plays, so while Louis Peterson's **Take a Giant Step** (9-24-53, Lyceum) won endorsement from a majority of the critics, it survived for only nine and a half weeks. Robert Coleman of the *Daily Mirror* was among the applauders, observing, "It has a vitality, a raciness, and an emotional impact that we found irresistible." Confronted by the ire of his strict, middle-class parents (Frederick O'Neal and Estelle Evans) after he is expelled from school for smoking a cigar in the men's room, Spencer Scott (Louis Gossett) goes to a bar to get drunk, allows a prostitute (Pauline Myers) to take him back to her room, but has to admit to her that he is too scared to do anything. He pays her the $2.39 he has and rushes away. Later he begins to find himself with a pretty housemaid (Dorothy Carter), whom his mother hires after his beloved, no-nonsense grandmother (Estelle Hemsley) dies. When Mrs. Scott gets wind of the matter, she fires the girl. But Spencer is also disturbed by his rejection by his white playmates. He tells his mother, "Let's just both try to forget it happened and go on to something else."

The Strong Are Lonely (9-29-53, Broadhurst) was Eva Le Gallienne's adaptation of a play by Fritz Hochwalder that reportedly had been a Continental success. In colonial Paraguay the Jesuits have established a self-productive community for the natives which might someday be reasonably autonomous. But the neighboring landowners bring pressure on the authorities and the Church to quash the movement. Victor Francen played the idealistic Jesuit leader; Dennis King, the spokesman for Spanish authority; and Philip Bourneuf, the emissary from Rome. Critics admired the play's high mindedness, but too many also found it tedious. One week and it was gone.

The season's longest-running drama was Robert Anderson's **Tea and Sympathy** (9-30-53, Barrymore). At the New England boys' school he attends, Tom Lee (John Kerr) is thought of as an "off horse," a boy whose shyness sets him apart from his classmates and even leads to whispers of homosexuality. His own father (John McGovern) is no help. Neither is the sanctimonious, aggressively masculine headmaster, Bill Reynolds (Leif Erickson). Tom's problems come to a head after he is cast as a girl in a school play. The lone person who understands Tom and is willing to provide more than the expected tea and sympathy is Reynolds's wife, Laura (Deborah Kerr). She assails her husband for persecuting the boy in order to mask his self-doubts about his own masculinity. Then she discreetly offers herself to Tom, telling him, "Years from now—when you talk about this—and you will!—be kind." In the *Daily News,* John Chapman summed up the sentiments of most of his colleagues when he wrote, " 'Tea and Sympathy' has been beautifully written . . . and last evening it was most beautifully acted." The play ran for 712 performances.

Conversely, New Yorkers had no time for a play which had long delighted Paris and London, **The Little Hut** (10-7-53, Coronet), Nancy Mitford's Anglicization of André Roussin's French original. Shipwrecked on a desert island in their best evening clothes, the husband (Roland Culver) and the lover (Colin Gordon) of the sole lady survivor (Anne Vernon) agree to share a little hut they have built, with each man living there with the woman on alternate weeks. When a brawny stranger appears, the wife mistakes him for an island prince, though he is merely the sunken ship's cook in disguise. Before a ménage à quatre can develop, a rescuing ship appears.

Rosemary Casey's **Late Love** (10-13-53, National) was a near miss, departing after ninety-five performances. Graham Colby (Neil Hamilton) is a widower, an author, and a stuffed shirt. No smoking is allowed in his elegant country drawing room, guests must be punctual, radio and television are banned, and nothing stronger than sherry can be served. He insists, for public consumption, that he does all this to please his demanding mother (Lucile Watson). But Constance Warburton (Arlene Francis), an artist sent by his publisher to paint his portrait, unearths the truth. She helps his daughter (Elizabeth Montgomery) elope with his secretary (Cliff Robertson), and takes mama for a fling in New York.

The season's biggest hit was John Patrick's theatrical-ization of Vern Sneider's novel **The Teahouse of the August Moon** (10-15-53, Martin Beck). Walter Kerr greeted it in the *Herald Tribune* as "a brightly colored comic-strip with a bland, broad grin on its face and a healthy share of mockery in its heart." In time it went on to win both the Pulitzer Prize and the New York Drama Critics Circle Award, and to run happily for 1027 performances. The wily little Sakini (David Wayne) comes before a bamboo curtain to explain that he and his fellow Okinawans have never had to leave home to obtain culture—it has been brought to them over the centuries by succeeding waves of conquerers. The Americans are merely the latest. The Yanks' do-it-by-the-book leader, Colonel Wainwright Purdy III (Paul Ford), is not pleased to learn that a new officer, Captain Frisby (John Forsythe), has been foisted on him, because the young man has bungled every other assignment handed to him. Purdy tells Frisby, "My job is to teach these natives the meaning of Democracy and they're going to learn Democracy if I have to shoot every one of them." [Compare this line with a similar, wittier one in *Of Thee I Sing:* "The people of this country demand John P. Wintergreen for president, and they're going to get him whether they like it or not."] He assigns Frisby the tasks of building a school in Tobiki and otherwise helping the natives there. No market develops for cricket cages the natives manufacture, but then Frisby discovers they can make a wicked brandy from sweet potatoes. The village starts to prosper. What's more, the villagers have decided democratically to build a teahouse instead of a school. News of this leaves Purdy almost apoplectic. He arrests Frisby and orders the teahouse demolished. The demolition is no sooner complete than Purdy is advised that the teahouse is being hailed in Washington as a prime example of "American 'get-up-and-go.' " Fortunately, Sakini and his friends have only dismantled the building and hidden the materials, so the edifice is hastily reassembled to await arriving congressmen and newspaper photographers. The play was gorgeously and ingeniously mounted, with the teahouse reassembled quickly as the audience watched. Top-notch performances, especially by Wayne and the hilariously deadpan, pompous Ford, added to the amusement. In 1970 the play was musicalized unsuccessfully as *Lovely Ladies, Kind Gentlemen.*

There was some demolition of sorts in Nathaniel Benchley's **The Frogs of Spring** (10-20-53, Broadhurst), but it failed to prove funny enough to sustain the comedy. Charles Belden (Hiram Sherman) and James Allen (Anthony Ross) take down the fence that separates the small yards behind their brownstones, leaving them with a one-tenth-of-an-acre playground for their families. They build a tree house for the kids that the kids don't want and bring in a portable swimming pool that promptly threatens a flood. These and other mishaps—neighbors are born mishaps—drive the men to drink, causing Belden to be arrested for drunkenness and to lose his job. But all ends reasonably happily, though the families contemplate restoring the fence.

Dorothy Parker and Arnaud d'Usseau combined their disparate talents for **The Ladies of the Corridor** (10-21-53, Longacre), a play with several crackerjack scenes that allowed for a number of memorable performances. The ladies are mostly middle-aged, many are widows, and they all live alone in an apartment-hotel catering to their ilk. Mrs. Gordon (June Walker) and Mrs. Lauterbach (Vera Allen) have accepted their situations and use gossip, borrowed books, and trips to the movies to pass the time. The savage Mrs. Nichols (Frances Starr) keeps her grown son (Shepperd Strudwick) at her beck and call by blackmailing him. Mildred Tynan (Betty Field), a dipsomaniac who has a sleazy affair with one of the bellhops, does a running dive out of a window to her death. Most interesting of all is Lulu Ames (Edna Best), who almost snares a younger man (Walter Matthau) for herself until her nattering and nagging drive him away. There were intermittent flashes of the famed Parker humor (asked if a friend has lost weight, one of the gals replies she must have, since she's been dead for some years), but the drama never truly built or caught hold for any length of time.

Janet Green's London hit **Gently Does It** (10-28-53, Royale) found few takers in New York. A man (Anthony Oliver) murders his elderly wife (Phyllis Povah) only to discover that she has not had time to change her will in his favor. He tries the same gambit on a second, more earthy wife (Brenda Bruce), an ex-barmaid who gives him lots more trouble. But he is finally undone by a third woman (Joyce Heron), who has supposedly won the Irish Sweepstakes and is actually the sister of his first victim.

The reception was not truly all that much better for F. Hugh Herbert's **A Girl Can Tell** (10-29-53, Royale). The play begins with Jennifer (Janet Blair) showing her daughter her scrapbook. In flashbacks she recalls all the various suitors she had—a college senior, a CPA, a young surgeon, a moth ball manufacturer, an advertising man, and so on. At the play's end the audience learns which boy Jennifer chose.

Ouida Rathbone adapted bits and pieces from several Conan Doyle stories so that her husband, Basil, could have a new vehicle in **Sherlock Holmes** (10-30-53, New Century). He had already appeared as Holmes in sixteen films and for many years in a radio series. This time the adventures revolved about an attempt to steal the Bruce-Partington submarine plans. An opera favorite, Jarmila Novotna, was Irene Adler, while Thomas Gomez was Moriarty. Stewart Chaney's highly praised settings included 221B Baker Street, a foggy square, and a chalet overlooking the Reichenbach Falls. For the play, when Holmes and Moriarty battle it out to the death, only Moriarty tumbles to his doom. But the dramatization displeased those who count the most, so it left after three playings.

Although everyone sang paeans to Lillian Gish for her performance—"a triumph of skill and spirit," "fine and sensitive"—in Horton Foote's **The Trip to Bountiful** (11-3-53, Henry Miller's), most agreed with Watts that the play was "neither dramatically stirring nor fully realized." The play closed after five weeks. Upset at her unpleasant life in Houston with her weakish son (Gene Lyons) and his vulgar, selfish wife (Jo Van Fleet), Carrie Watts decides to run back home to her roots in a small town called Bountiful. She tells an attractive young woman (Eva Marie Saint) whom she meets at the bus station that her hands long to "feel the need of dirt." When she arrives at the bus stop nearest to Bountiful, a sheriff (Frank Overton) wants to arrest her on orders from her son and daughter-in-law, who are on the way to get her. But she talks him into letting her have a look at the old homestead, now deserted and falling into ruins. Seeing it, she tells him, "When you've lived longer than your house or your family, maybe you've lived too long." The son and daughter-in-law appear. The son has made his wife promise that she will be more considerate of his mother in the future, but just how happily they will live together from here on is moot.

Thanks to clever manipulation by producer-director Joshua Logan, Norman Krasna's **Kind Sir** (11-4-53, Alvin) wound up in the hit column. The potent lure of its stars, Mary Martin and Charles Boyer, had packed tryout houses and had allowed the play to come to Broadway with a purported $600,000 advance. Capacity at the large musical comedy house at a $6 top was more than $39,000 weekly. Then the New York reviews appeared. Kerr called Martin "incontestably dazzling," he labeled Mainbocher's costumes for her "breath-taking stuff," and he also noted, "Above the two stars towers Jo Meilziner's setting [of a posh apartment], daring the actors to outshine it." Then he concluded glumly that for all of this "Krasna has provided a kiddie-car" as a vehicle. (Kerr felt Boyer's appearance "was a downright tragic waste.") The plot could not have been simpler. Jane Kimball, a luminous stage star, falls in love with Philip Clair, a very rich, foreign-born financier and diplomat. She would like to marry him, but he is only interested in an affair. "Life follows art," Jane notes. "There isn't a situation in life that hasn't its formula in the theatre. Including the one we're in now." In the theatre, Jane has her way by the end of the last act. By the start of the new year, grosses had plunged to about $30,000 per week, so a closing notice was posted before losses could pile up, and the comedy left after 166 performances.

But Howard Teichmann and George S. Kaufman's **The Solid Gold Cadillac** (11-5-53, Belasco) stayed and stayed, lingering until it had given 526 performances. Mrs. Laura Partridge (Josephine Hull) is a sometime actress who hates doing Shakespeare because you never get to sit down unless you are a king. She also owns some shares of the mammoth General Products Corporation. At a stockholders' meeting she meekly raises her hand and inquires if she may ask a few questions. Those few questions are enough to prompt a badly shaken board of trustees to give her the nominal post of head of shareholder relations. She takes her job very seriously, answering all queries and sometimes writing or phoning shareholders just to say a friendly hello. The company has not been getting much government business since its former president, Edward L. McKeever (Loring Smith), left for a Washington cabinet post (at which time he was forced to make a multimillion-dollar profit by selling his shares in order to accept the new job). [McKeever was seen as a parallel of General Motors's Charles E. Wilson, who made a profit selling his stock so that he could accept a post in Eisenhower's cabinet.] Laura heads off to meet McKeever. Before long Laura and he are linked in what the papers would have readers believe is a scandalous romance, but was actually an innocent rendezvous. The scandal gives the trustees, who have been milking the company in McKeever's absence, their chance to fire Laura. She sits down to clean out her desk, but then at the annual meeting she discovers the shareholders have turned their proxy votes over to her. "Aren't they the darlingest people?" she asks the trustees. Then, pointing an accusatory finger at them, she informs them, "Gentlemen, you're fired!"

One of the play's best moments came with a drop curtain disclosed after the scandal breaks. It depicted the front pages of all the New York papers of the time. The tabloids splashed full-page photos of Laura and McKeever emerging from a hotel. All but one of the regular papers gave the incident bold headlines. That holdout paper's front page was devoted entirely to other local, national, and international developments, with the scandal clearly not news that's fit to print. At the same time, sly, nasal Fred Allen, who served by way of recordings as a commentator on the comedy, promised the audience that if there was not a happy ending, the producer, Max Gordon, would refund their money— only to add, "And a fat chance there is of that!" Admittedly the comedy had its ups and downs, but Hull's performance was an unqualified joy. Cleaning

out her desk after her firing, she has found one bright red rubber shoe in a drawer and is hunting for the mate: "Humming a nice fireside tune, she keeps delving into one drawer after another, coming up with a coffee pot, a piggie bank and other incongruous articles—looking puzzled, astonished and worried by turns. . . . Mrs. Hull is terrific." Sadly, it was her last role before her death.

Among the season's more interesting offerings down in the Village was Victor Wolfson's adaptation of his own novel *The Lonely Steeple* as **American Gothic** (11-10-53, Circle in the Square). It told of a saddened woman (Clarice Blackburn) who never stops loving the husband (Jason Robards, Jr.) who married her at his father's insistence, then ran out on her.

The plot of Samuel Taylor's **Sabrina Fair** (11-11-53, National) wasn't much more complicated than *Kind Sir*'s had been, but it had so much more wit and high-comedy style that it ran twice as long—318 performances. Sabrina Fairchild (Margaret Sullavan), the bright, up-and coming daughter of the Larrabees' chauffeur (Russell Collins), returns home from a diplomatic stint in Paris and promptly finds she has three suitors, a wealthy French sportsman (Robert Duke), the Larrabees' younger, lazy son, David (Scott McKay), and their more achieving elder son, Linus junior (Joseph Cotten). Since Cotten was Miss Sullavan's co-star, audiences could guess which one she wanted. What they might not have foreseen is that after telling him, "I should always have a husband or a small animal about," she, not he, pops the question. But by then she has learned that her father, having carefully been buying stock in the Larrabees' company ever since the bottom of the Depression, is a millionaire himself. The comedy was capitally acted by a cast that also included the sharp-tongued Luella Gear, the radiantly beautiful Cathleen Nesbitt, and the wry John Cromwell.

That same evening, José Ferrer again assumed the reins at the City Center and began his programs with a revival of his brilliant *Cyrano de Bergerac*. Douglas Watson was his Christian, and Arlene Dahl his Roxane. The Rostand was followed on the 25th by *The Shrike*, on December 9 by *Richard III*, and on the 22nd by *Charley's Aunt*.

The latest British hit to displease New Yorkers was Roger MacDougall's **Escapade** (11-18-53, 48th St.). It told of an ineffectual pacifist (Brian Aherne) who must watch his more resourceful children become militant pacifists, even to accidentally shooting a teacher and purposely stealing an airplane in order to drop leaflets on a U.N. meeting.

The next evening a group of Spanish-speaking actors began a three-week stand at the Broadhurst. They offered a repertory of seven plays, among them such

Spanish classics as *Don Juan Tenorio, El alcalde de Zalamea,* and *La vida es sueño.*

In 1939, George M. Cohan had tried out a Sidney Howard comedy, deemed it unsuited for New York, so closed it on the road. Now T. Edward Hambleton and Norris Houghton, having taken over the dark Yiddish Art Theatre at Second Avenue and 12th Street and rechristened it, launched their exciting new venture by giving the play another hearing. **Madam, Will You Walk** (12-1-53, Phoenix) told of Mary Doyle (Jessica Tandy), the reclusive, guilt-ridden daughter of a corrupt Tammany politician who died while serving time in Sing Sing. Her gloomy world is suddenly lit up by a visit from Dr. Brightlee (Hume Cronyn), whose somber black suit is lined with bright red and whose shadow mysteriously reveals horns and a cloven foot. Of course, he is the devil in disguise. But he is a good devil, only wanting to bring some excitement and improvement to the world. He escorts Mary on a tour of Manhattan's after-dark spots, including Central Park and a night court. Although Brightlee falls in love with her, she quickly finds that she prefers a hackie (Robert Emmett) who hopes to becomes a hoofer. The Phoenix was a full-sized house with a full-sized stage, but all the plays at the theatre were to be brought out for limited runs and at a $3.60 top. Hailed as "just about right" for the circumstances, and "sparked" with "understanding performances," the play's six-week stay inaugurated the new enterprise handsomely.

Another Mary, Mary Prescott (Katharine Cornell), was the heroine of the next new play to arrive, Howard Lindsay and Russel Crouse's **The Prescott Proposals** (12-16-53, Broadhurst). Mary is the American delegate to the United Nations, and she has proposed that the bickering nations concentrate for a time on "areas of agreement" and set their squabbling aside. But on the eve of her speech, a Czech delegate (Bartlett Robinson), who years earlier had been her lover, pays her a visit and drops dead in her apartment. This angers the Russian delegate (Ben Astar), who believes she may have been encouraging the Czech to defect. He threatens to make her whole history with the dead man public. Fortunately, he has a last-minute change of heart, especially after Mary quietly reminds him of some things in his own past. With that matter out of the way, Mary is free to continue her romance with Elliott Clark (Lorne Greene), the famous television commentator. Like Sabrina Fairchild before her, she pops the crucial question, telling the startled Clark, "You see, I've become famous for proposals." While critics dismissed the play as "markedly lightweight," they delighted in Cornell's elegant, seemingly effortless acting. She was able to keep the vehicle alive for 125 performances—not enough to pay back its costs.

Conversely, Edward Chodorov's **Oh, Men! Oh, Women!** (12-17-53, Henry Miller's) proved highly profitable during its 382-performance run. Despite a title that several critics felt was singularly off-putting, it provided, according to William Hawkins of The *World-Telegram and Sun,* "some of the season's loudest laughs." Shortly before Alan Coles (Franchot Tone), a popular society psychoanalyst, is to wed Myra Hagerman (Betsy von Furstenberg), he discovers from a particularly distraught, pugnacious patient (Larry Blyden) that Myra has been leading a very active and not highly selective sex life. The patient tells him that a man "would have to be blind, deaf and dumb—or so stuck on her physically that he could swallow baloney all the time!" Coles further learns, from the emotionally overwrought wife (Anne Jackson) of a famous film star (Gig Young) who is angry with the effect Coles's therapy is having on his wife, that the actor intends to seduce Myra before the wedding, just to see if Coles "can take it as well as dish it out." Coles realizes he must analyze his own reactions to all this news. He does, in time for a happy ending aboard a ship carrying him and Myra to their honeymoon.

Two duds followed, starting with Lenard Kanter's **Dead Pigeon** (12-23-53, Vanderbilt). Having been railroaded into prison by her gangster lover, Sherry Parker (Joan Lorring) promises to squeal on the hoods if the D.A. shortens her sentence. She is taken to a hotel room where she is guarded by two cops. Both are corrupt and willing to kill her for a fee, but after one, Detective Ernest Brady (Lloyd Bridges), falls in love with her, he prevents his buddy (James Gregory) from carrying out the killing.

Some of the season's harshest and shortest notices went to Jean Lowenthal's **Sing till Tomorrow** (12-28-53, Royale). An unsuccessful Philadelphia pharmacist, more interested in fishing than in minding the store, learns not only that his second wife has been unfaithful to him with his own son and that the young man has written a play satirizing his father, but that the pharmacy is no longer saleable.

Jane Bowles's **In the Summer House** (12-29-53, Playhouse) was also a flop, folding after fifty-five performances, but many critics praised its honesty and intelligence, although they granted it made for a talky and not always gripping evening. On the California coast, the embittered Mrs. Eastman-Cuevas (Judith Anderson) despises her daughter, Molly (Elizabeth Ross), who spends most of her time mooning in a vine-covered summer house. She is also contemptuous of the tippling, life-denying Mrs. Constable (Mildred Dunnock). Mrs. Eastman-Cuevas marries a rich Mexican (Don Mayo) but, detesting his large and noisy family, walks out on the marriage. Her daughter has also married, but by threatening to disclose that the girl had pushed Mrs. Constable's daughter (Muriel Berkson) over a cliff and thus murdered her, she forces Molly to live with her again. For want of anywhere better to go, Mrs. Constable comes along, too. Jane's husband, Paul, composed the incidental music.

Unlike Mrs. Eastman-Cuevas, Mr. Horace Pennypacker, Jr. (Burgess Meredith), president of the Pennypacker Prime Pork Products Co., is an amiable man and a good family man. In fact, in Liam O'Brien's **The Remarkable Mr. Pennypacker** (12-30-53, Coronet), he is such a good family man that he keeps one family in Wilmington, Delaware, and a second a short train ride away in Philadelphia. Since the year is 1890 and since one (Phyllis Love) of Mr. Pennypacker's Wilmington daughters is newly engaged to the son (Michael Wager) of a fluttery minister (Glenn Anders), news of Mr. Pennypacker's arrangement causes some consternation. But the highly liberal Mr. P. cannot understand the fuss. After all, he dresses in plus fours, and he is a member of the Darwin League, a single-taxer, a feminist, and chairman of a committee to bring no less a fellow liberal than George Bernard Shaw to America. He quotes Saint Thomas à Kempis—"Those who travel, seldom come home holy"—to his Wilmington clan, and adds, "My children have been educated to the responsibility that when one of them wants to get married, he or she makes the decision, picks the partner, and that's that." In a vote, his seven Wilmington children decide he is wrong but ask him to stay with them anyway. As the play ends he is preparing to find out what his Philadelphia brood think of the matter. The "uproarious" comedy managed to run for seven months without recouping its costs.

The new year began with **Mademoiselle Colombe** (1-6-54, Longacre), Louis Kronenberger's gifted translation of Jean Anouilh's *Colombe*. Since Julien (Eli Wallach) has been called up for military service, he entrusts his sweet little wife, Colombe (Julie Harris), to his mother, Mme. Alexandra (Edna Best), then a popular turn-of-the-century Parisian actress. By the time Julien returns, Colombe has adapted all the irresponsible ways of the Paris art world, including sleeping around. Nor is she shy about revealing her new world to Julien. An epilogue reverts to the first days of Julien and Colombe's marriage, when they were promising each other eternal loyalty and happiness. The play had its languors, so its scintillating acting, including Sam Jaffe as Mme. Alexandra's harassed secretary, and its gorgeous Boris Aronson settings of the less elegant parts of an elegant Parisian theatre, could not draw patrons. It closed after a seven-and-a-half-week struggle.

Fay and Michael Kanin's more New Yorkish **His and Hers** (1-7-54, 48th St.) ran two weeks longer,

thanks probably to its stars. A couple of divorced playwrights (Robert Preston and Celeste Holm) learn they have both come up with the same idea for a play and go to court over who has the right to the story. A judge (Donald McKee) orders them to collaborate on the effort, and, as no one was surprised to see, by curtain time the pair has reconciled.

After his **Bullfight** (1-12-54, de Lys) was offered down in the Village, critics hailed Leslie Stevens as a playwright of great promise. Although he soon afterwards sold out to more commercial interests, the play was, indeed, a fine maiden effort. Domingo del Cristobal Salamanca (Hurd Hatfield), the son of a famous bullfighter, is an evil genius. He prods his sweet, unprepared brother Esteban (Mario Alcalde), into the ring and to his death. Then he coldly sets out to see what additional mischief he can stir up.

A Pin to See the Peepshow and Diana Morgan's **The Starcross Story** (1-13-54, Royale) earned the dubious distinction of being the only plays of the season to shutter after their first night. Lady Starcross (Eva Le Gallienne) is determined to perpetuate the memory and legend of her husband, who died on a polar expedition, by assisting with a new film biography of the man. Anne Meredith (Mary Astor), his mistress, has different ideas, and shows that the dead explorer was a selfserving scoundrel. But Lady Starcross prevails.

For its second offering, on the 19th, the Phoenix Theatre brought out Shakespeare's rarely done *Coriolanus* with film favorite Robert Ryan in the lead and Mildred Natwick as his mother. Although many felt that Ryan was too unpoetically oriented for his assignment, they mostly agreed that John Houseman's lively staging glossed over the star's inadequacies, and they were grateful to see a full mounting of the tragedy. It ran for the preordained six weeks.

One of the season's major hits—it ran a solid year—was Herman Wouk's adaptation of part of his bestselling novel *The Caine Mutiny* as **The Caine Mutiny Court-Martial** (1-20-54, Plymouth). Kerr noted that the drama "is a theatrical adventure which builds to a second-act climax of such hair-raising intensity that you are sure nothing, and no one, can ever top it. Someone then proceeds to top it." Lt. Stephen Maryk (John Hodiak) is on trial for seizing command of the U.S.S. *Caine* during a typhoon. Maryk contends that he did so because the commander, Captain Queeg (Lloyd Nolan), had panicked. His lawyer, Lt. Barney Greenwald (Henry Fonda), who is a stickler for naval discipline, nonetheless takes the lone realistic course open to him, and turns the defense into an attack on Queeg. He soon has Queeg contradicting himself and playing nervously with two metal balls. The court acquits Maryk but suggests that Greenwald reprimand himself for his irresponsible approach, which the judge advocate had branded "shyster tactics." But an admiring Maryk tells Greenwald that the lawyer "murdered Queeg," and Greenwald bitterly agrees. At a celebration afterwards, Greenwald makes a brief appearance. He tells Maryk he thinks the lieutenant is guilty, but he places the real blame for the problems on Lt. Keefer (Robert Gist), who had goaded Maryk into action. Throwing his drink in Keefer's face, he stalks out.

A mother who stalks in was the most memorable character in Don Appell's **Lullaby** (2-3-54, Lyceum), especially since she was played hilariously by a "rampageous" Mary Boland in her last Broadway appearances. Much to their own amazement, Johnny (Jack Warden) and Eadie (Kay Medford) find themselves in a second-rate Scranton, Pennsylvania, hotel room—on their honeymoon. Eadie is a nightclub cigarette girl who never expected to find love; Johnny is a mother-dominated thirty-eight-year-old truck driver who never truly believed he could cut the apron strings. As they lean back on the bed, Eadie jokingly suggests, "I could be arrested for kidnappin'!" Their idyll is shattered with the arrival the next morning of Johnny's mother, who announces she was right to assume that something terrible had happened and insists on calling Eadie "Bubbles." She sticks with them when they move into an apartment, warning that Eadie's encouraging Johnny to purchase his own truck can lead to ruin and urging them to sleep separately after Eadie comes down with a cold. The newlyweds finally flee to Long Island, telling mother she can enjoy visiting hours, from two to five—once a month. The small cast was saluted, but critics could not get too excited about what was at best "a cheerful little comedy." It went to its reward after forty-five performances.

Its ninety-six performances made Ruth and Augustus Goetz's adaptation of André Gide's **The Immoralist** (2-8-54, Royale) another of the season's near misses. Immediately after his father's funeral, Michel (Louis Jourdan) is prodded by Marceline (Geraldine Page) to marry her. They leave France and settle in a North African village. There his real sexual leanings come to the fore. He is menaced by a slimy young Arab blackmailer (James Dean), but a more understanding, older Arab homosexual, a professor (David Stewart), advises him to face the facts of his bent nature. He confesses to Marceline and sends her back to France but, on learning that she is carrying his child, returns home to be with her. Once again critics applauded the players, but had divided feelings on the play. The prudish Chapman announced that he was "embarrassed" by this "clinical drama about a sex deviate." The more compassionate Atkinson hailed the evening as "austere, crushing and genuine."

Down in the Village, there were kudos for Alfred Hayes's theatricalization of his own novel **The Girl on the Via Flaminia** (2-9-54, Circle in the Square), which was subsequently brought uptown but failed to gain an audience there. In newly liberated Rome, a young American corporal (Leo Penn) finds love with a poor Italian girl (Betty Miller), possibly driven into his arms by her need for shelter and affection. After she is branded as a prostitute, he questions her so sharply that she runs off. He heads after her, fearing she may be ready to commit suicide.

As a play, T. S. Eliot's **The Confidential Clerk** (2-11-54, Morosco) proved a major disappointment, with Atkinson dismissing it as "ordinary" and Watts opining that it would not increase the playwright's stature. Sir Claude Mulhammer (Claude Rains) believes his private secretary, Colby Simpkins (Douglas Watson), is actually his illegitimate son. He also knows that Lucasta (Joan Greenwood) is his illegitimate daughter. His wife, Lady Elizabeth (Ina Claire), similarly is aware that she had a son out of wedlock but doesn't recall what became of him. Although Lucasta loves Colby, fears about consanguinity drive her into the arms of a belligerent young man named B. Kaghan ((Richard Newton). Matters end satisfactorily enough after B. is shown to be Lady Elizabeth's misplaced son. What made the comedy a 117-performance success in New York was the fine cast, headed by Claire, America's duenna of high comedy, in her final Broadway appearances. Kerr noted that the star, "still looking like a dazzling line-drawing from the most fashionable magazine of the '20s, is delectable beyond belief as she scrunches up in a chair, glazes her eyes, and accepts as her son a breezy youngster she detests."

Elmer Rice continued to come a cropper with all his latter-day plays such as **The Winner** (2-17-54, Playhouse). For the second time in the season a widow (Jane Buchanan) and the dead husband's mistress (Joan Tetzel) battle it out. Only this time the widow is the vindictive one, the dispute is over the man's estate (left to the mistress) and not over his reputation, and the mistress wins. Afterwards she discards a suitor (Whitfield Connor) who had been panting after her newfound riches and accepts a proposal from the widow's handsome lawyer (Tom Helmore). "Mighty loquacious" was Hawkins's unhappy verdict.

The titular heroine of **Ondine** (2-18-54, 46th St.), which the faithful Maurice Valency translated from Jean Giraudoux's original, is a water nymph (Audrey Hepburn) who falls in love with a human, a dashing medieval knight (Mel Ferrer), but when he dies in her arms after wedding a more ordinary girl, she is summoned back to the domain of the Water King. Alfred Lunt staged the play with consummate elegance. Its beautiful costumes were by Richard Whorf, and its equally imaginative settings—with sea urchins rising out of a crystal fountain, with barred windows inexplicably flying open, and with birds and dogs and armor appearing out of nowhere—were by Peter Larkin. Yet somehow, all of this could not call up the requisite theatrical magic. It was, as one critic lamented, a jewel box to look at but a trial to sit through. Nonetheless it drew packed houses for much of its 157-performance run, one week grossing $42,292, which *Variety* called "a new record for a straight play," and went into the books as a hit.

On the other hand, Charles Morgan's London drama **The Burning Glass** (3-4-54, Longacre) lasted less than a month. An English scientist (Scott Forbes) discovers a way to harness the sun's energy for a limitless source of power. His wife (Maria Riva) and his associate (Walter Matthau) help reconstruct his experiment after he is kidnapped by enemy agents. Since he refuses to divulge his secrets, he is released. He also refuses to give his own government his plans, unless it needs them to overcome some dire developments. Rather than run a risk of being kidnapped himself, the associate commits suicide.

On March 10, down at the Theatre de Lys, a mounting of *The Threepenny Opera* opened. It ran for only ninety-five performances, but cries for its return, especially from Atkinson, were so persistent that it was brought back in September of 1955 and ran for 2611 performances. More than anything else, this production along with the works being offered at the Circle in the Square and at the Phoenix signaled the vigorous resurrection of Off Broadway.

Jean Kerr and Eleanor Brooke's **King of Hearts** (4-1-54, Lyceum) opened to generally favorable notices, delighted audiences for 278 performances, yet reportedly closed in the red. Larry Larkin (Donald Cook) is a fervently egomaniacal cartoonist, famous for his strip about Snips, a philosophic, sweet little boy, and Snips's dog, Runtie. Whenever Larry says the smallest thing that might be considered clever or original, he commands his loving secretary, Dunreath (Cloris Leachman), to make a note of it. Thus, after a lady once told him that he had not a split personality, but a shattered one, he replied that in that case he would have a group photo taken of himself. Since he is about to embark on a European holiday with Dunreath, he hires a ghost cartoonist, Francis X. Dignan (Jackie Cooper), a man so modest that he admits that "where other men falter I fall flat on my face" and that he recently managed a non-profit organization that hadn't set out to be non-profit. Larry complicates his own life by adopting a small boy (Rex Thompson), naming Dunreath as guardian so that he cannot be sued if anything goes wrong.

Naturally, by curtain time, Dunreath and Dignan are a pair.

Although Jerome Chodorov and Joseph Fields's **Anniversary Waltz** (4-7-54, Broadhurst) was not nearly so witty or fresh, it was so slickly and knowingly written that it rolled along gaily for 615 performances. Watts condemned the comedy as "machine-made," while Atkinson termed the authors "mechanics." Clearly, theatregoers couldn't have cared less. On his fifteenth wedding anniversary, a slightly boozy Bud Walters (Macdonald Carey) lets slip to his kids that he and their mother (Kitty Carlisle) had enjoyed pre-marital sex. Matters are made worse when their little daughter, Debbie (Mary Lee Dearring), blurts out the news on national television. Bud promptly smashes the set with his foot. But fifteen years of marital bliss are too much to allow a sixteen-year-old indiscretion to destroy it, so all ends happily.

The season's final novelty, Julian Funt's **The Magic and the Loss** (4-9-54, Booth), ran less than four weeks. It focused on an aggressive, unhappy businesswoman (Uta Hagen), who cannot keep a husband (Robert Preston), a lover (Lee Bowman), or even her teenaged son (Charles Taylor), who elects to live with his father.

Several critics, while admiring the individual performances in the Phoenix Theatre's revival of *The Sea Gull*, which opened on the 11th, remarked that the players' inability to catch fire as an ensemble underscored the need for permanent repertory companies in America. The stellar cast included Judith Evelyn as Madame Arkadina, Montgomery Clift as her son, Sam Jaffe as her brother, Kevin McCarthy as Trigorin, Maureen Stapleton as Masha, and June Walker and Will Geer as her parents. The play did near-capacity business for much of its five-week run.

Indeed, late-season business was good on Broadway, although illness or other contractual obligations were removing such stars as Josephine Hull, Henry Fonda, Margaret Sullavan, Joseph Cotten, and Deborah Kerr. *The Caine Mutiny Court-Martial, Ondine, The Solid Gold Cadillac, Tea and Sympathy,* and *Teahouse of the August Moon* were among the attractions above, at, or close to capacity. One small assist may have come from the U.S. government, which finally halved the wartime ticket tax, so that, for example, a $4.80 ticket was reduced to $4.40.

1954–1955

Although the slump in the number of novelties offered to Broadway resumed—most sources this season agreeing on a count of thirty-four—the news was not entirely gloomy. Despite the drop, no fewer than fifteen comedies and dramas traipsed beyond the once charmed 100-performance mark. That the charm had long since lost its potency was attested to by the fact that only nine of these wound up as commercial successes—repaying their original investments. More happily, the season was constantly and, in one way, surprisingly interesting. The surprise was the marked return to "good old-fashioned theatre, toward rousing second acts, toward stately, plump Recognition Scenes." Added to this was the ongoing "great resurgence" of Off Broadway.

Indeed, Off Broadway was alive and kicking even during the summer months when many uptown playhouses remained dark. Thus Paul Green, the Pulitzer Prize author who had been spending much of his recent years creating summer historical pageants, was represented by three one-acters tied together as **Salvation on a String** (7-6-54, de Lys). His look at courtship on a southern farm, **The No 'Count Boy,** had been floating around since the mid-twenties. **Supper for the Dead** was seen as a confused look at the violence voodoo can lead to, while **Chair Endowed** was a grim examination of domestic misery. The bill failed.

But enough New Yorkers were interested in Robinson Jeffers's retelling of Euripides' *Hippolytus* as **The Cretan Women** (7-7-54, Provincetown Playhouse) to keep it before the footlights for three months. As he had been doing for twenty-five hundred years, young Hippolytus (William Andrews) once more resisted the temptations thrown in his path by his lascivious stepmother (Jacqueline Brookes) and paid for his virtue with his life—slain onstage this time—when his father (Charles Aidman) believed Phaedra's false charges. Only in Jeffers's version the virtuous Hippolytus was not all that virtuous, since he resisted his stepmother because he preferred to sleep with men.

And Broadway's first novelty was not all that novel. Late in the 1943–44 season Frederick Jackson's *Slightly Scandalous* had come and gone hurriedly. Normally that would have been the end of the matter. But a French playwright, Marc-Gilbert Sauvajon, somehow turned the Broadway flop into a Paris hit, then Alan Melville adapted the newer version for London. Now it returned to Broadway as **Dear Charles** (9-15-54, Morosco) and provided the latest opportunity for theatregoers to watch Tallulah Bankhead play Tallulah Bankhead. The former lovers she had to choose from in order belatedly to legitimatize her children were Robert Coote, Werner Klemperer, and Hugh Reilly. Of course, for most audiences the whole show was the croaky-voiced star, "batting those big eyes with the long lashes, undulating around the furniture, grinning, roaring, putting saucy inflections into innocuous lines."

She was show enough to keep the comedy spinning merrily for twenty weeks, not sufficiently long to let it recoup its cost.

The Metropolitan Opera House was the surprise venue for a Victorianly lavish revival of *A Midsummer Night's Dream,* which concert impresario Sol Hurok brought in on the 21st. An Old Vic production, it featured two players celebrated primarily as dancers, Robert Helpmann and Moira Shearer, as Oberon and Titania. Both were extolled for their remarkably clear, well-projected diction. Stanley Holloway's comic Bottom was also praised. While running a mere twenty-nine performances (not at all bad considering the size of the house), the production nonetheless made money.

Walter Macken's **Home Is the Hero** (9-22-54, Booth), an Irish play with its Irish playwright in the lead, found no welcome, so departed after a month. Five years in prison have not mellowed Paddo O'Reilly, who still attempts to noisily lord it over his tippling wife (Glenda Farrell), his brazen daughter (Peggy Ann Garner), and his crippled son (Donald Harron). But time has given Paddo's family the wherewithal to stand up to him. Thwarted, he heads out alone for parts unknown.

The father (Ed Begley) in Robert Anderson's **All Summer Long** (9-23-54, Coronet), taken from Donald Wetzel's novel *A Wreath and a Curse,* is also crude, choleric, and not very effectual. The mother (June Walker) is an incorrigible sentimentalist. But their older son, Don (John Kerr), albeit embittered that an automobile accident has left him too crippled to continue as a basketball player, lovingly acts as a surrogate parent to his eleven-year-old brother, Willie (Clay Hall). The two boys work together to keep rising flood waters from destroying their home. The waters burst through, but their joint efforts have strengthened their fraternal ties. Jo Mielziner's setting of a tree-draped riverbank, overhung with spindly branches and silvery leaves, and with a skeletonized house to one side, won high praise. The play itself was called "intelligent" and "careful," but never exciting. It lingered for sixty performances.

One of Off Broadway's most highly praised offerings during the season was a revival at the Cherry Lane on the 30th of *The Way of the World.* Gerry Fleming and Louis Edmonds were Millamant and Mirabell, but the most memorable performances were those of Fritz Weaver and Nancy Wickwire as Fainall and Marwood. (Weaver distinguished himself again late in the season when the Phoenix mounted a few special matinees of John Webster's *The White Devil.*) The Restoration comedy ran for 122 performances.

Uptown, Harry Kurnitz's "smooth and pleasant comedy" **Reclining Figure** (10-7-54, Lyceum) ran just two performances less, but still closed in the red. Sam Ellis's boss, the famous dealer in old masters Jonas Astorg, never calls a painting a painting, but rather "the final distillation of genius, or a monument to man's attainment of the unattainable." Determined to break away and start a gallery devoted solely to struggling young painters, Sam (Mike Wallace) unearths a heretofore unknown Renoir and flies from Paris to California to sell it to Lucas Edgerton (Percy Waram), the multimillionaire inventor and manufacturer of Tingle, a leading soft drink that one character decribes as a mixture of lemon juice and Alka Seltzer. After all, Edgerton already owns forty-seven Renoirs and would undoubtedly enjoy having another to stash away in his vaults far from the eyes of a public incapable of appreciating it. What poor Sam—doubly poor since he has given a bad check to buy the oil—doesn't know is that the painting is a fake and that Astorg (Martin Gabel) has purposely allowed him to "discover" the masterpiece so that he can keep his hold on Edgerton by exposing the fraud. By the time the truth emerges, Edgerton's daughter (Georgiann Johnson) has fallen in love with Sam. She sees to it that all ends happily for everyone.

There was hardly any happy ending in Norman A. Brooks's **Fragile Fox** (10-12-54, Belasco). During the Battle of the Bulge, the craven Captain Erskine Cooney (Andrew Duggan) is given to cowering under his cot, swilling booze, and sending his men to certain death on wasteful missions. Several times, Lieutenant Costa (Dane Clark) has to be talked out of killing him by the more deliberate Lieutenant Woodruff (Don Taylor), but after Costa himself is sent to his death by Cooney, Woodruff does shoot and kill him. This does not sit well with Colonel Bartlett (James Gregory), who knows the whole story but also knows that Cooney's father holds the key to Bartlett's rise in state politics. He forces Woodruff to claim that Cooney died a hero. "You've got to like war plays—if you do, this is a good one," John McClain of the *Journal-American* suggested. Not enough playgoers agreed to give the drama a run.

But then the public wouldn't buy Max Shulman and Robert Paul Smith's "ingratiating and amiable" **The Tender Trap** (10-13-54, Longacre). It ran for 102 performances, and ended up in the hit column solely because of the sale of its movie rights. A resignedly married Joe McCall (Robert Preston), a research chemist for a pharmaceutical house, hopes his new cold cure will allow him to break away on his own (shades of *Reclining Nude*). His wife's demands for wall-to-wall carpeting and braces for the kids' teeth won't prove so onerous if he can be his own boss. While tests are being conducted in New York, he stays there with Charlie Reader (Ronny Graham), a childhood buddy who has remained a business associate. Joe is flabbergasted to hear all the calls Charlie gets from girls and to see all

the girls pop up to Charlie's apartment bearing gifts. Joe asks him what special something he has. Charlie retorts, "It ain't what I got, it's what I ain't got—a wife." Before long Joe is flirting with one (Kim Hunter) of Charlie's girls, a gal who has fiddled with Toscanini, but only in the back row. Meanwhile, Charlie cavalierly plays the field. By the time Joe learns that his discovery is a bust (further shades of *Reclining Nude*) and that he must go back to wall-to-wall carpets and kids' braces, Charlie has fallen into the tender trap set for him by a pert lab assistant (Janey Riley).

Robert Ardrey's **Sing Me No Lullaby** (10-14-54, Phoenix) got the Village playhouse's second season off to a sour start. In the witch-hunting climate of the early fifties, Mike Hertzog (Jack Warden) has been hounded out of his scientific work by the FBI because he was a committed leftist in the thirties. His fine war record is conveniently ignored. Finding himself stymied, he decides to move to Russia, although he knows he will be no better off there. His decision prompts his old buddy (Richard Kiley) to reenter the political arena. The buddy does so despite the strenuous opposition of his own reactionary mother (Jessie Royce Landis). The play left after thirty performances.

So did Horton Foote's **The Traveling Lady** (10-27-54, Playhouse), which Richard Watts, Jr., rejected in the *Post* as "real and honest, but not very moving." Georgette Thomas (Kim Stanley) comes with her young daughter (Brooke Seawell) to a small Texas town to await the release from prison of her husband (Lonny Chapman), a third-rate bandleader with a propensity for lawlessness. But she soon discovers that he has been released on parole without telling her and that he is in more hot water and liable to return to prison. So she finds romance with an attractive widower (Jack Lord) and heads off with him. What redeemed the evening for some was Stanley's playing. Espousing the then voguish method school of acting, she "twists her fidgety fingers, moistens her lips in desperation and stumbles over all the things she would like to say."

Stanley was followed by an even more famous advocate of the method school, Geraldine Page, who was starred in N. Richard Nash's **The Rainmaker** (10-28-54, Cort). Although her thin voice and jittery mannerisms underlined her allegiance, she delighted critics with an unexpected flair for comedy. The play itself was seen as romantic hokum, with the *Herald Tribune*'s Walter Kerr harking back to the heyday of Otis Skinner and Holbrook Blinn for its like. In the era of crystal sets and Essex automobiles, the Currys have two problems. One is the prolonged drought devasting their western ranch. The other is Lizzie Curry, who, to the dismay of her father and brothers, seems destined for spinsterhood. Then along comes Bill Starbuck (Darren

McGavin), who promises to bring on the rain for a $100 advance. The menfolk are willing to gamble, but Lizzie balks. "Lizzie girl," Starbuck tells her, "once in your life you gotta take a chance on a con man!" In short order he has shown Lizzie how to let down her hair, think of herself as beautiful, and enjoy love. But then File (Richard Coogan), the sheriff's assistant who has long loved Lizzie in silence, comes to arrest Starbuck as a traveling bunco artist. Starbuck meekly hands back the $100 advance, but File, understanding the change he has wrought in Lizzie, lets him leave. File and Lizzie acknowledge their love. Just then it begins to thunder and lightning. Starbuck rushes back in to reclaim his money, then heads off again. Although the play ran only 125 performances, it was classed among the commercial successes.

By contrast, Noel Coward's **Quadrille** (11-3-54, Coronet) ran 150 performances, but closed in the red. Its story was not at all complicated. In the Europe of the 1870s, an American businessman (Alfred Lunt) and an English marchioness (Lynn Fontanne), whose wife (Edna Best) and husband (Brian Aherne) have eloped together, set out to bring the lovers back, but in due time conclude they prefer each other. Critics were increasingly unhappy with the Lunts' vehicles, of which this was seen as an often dreary example. The Lunts themselves were another matter. The *Daily Mirror's* Robert Coleman spoke for his colleagues, as well as himself, when he wrote, "Miss Fontanne is quite gorgeous and irresistible. . . . It is a joy, indeed, to study her changes of mood and heart." He continued, "Lunt is superb, too, as the bluff, uncouth, well-meaning American empire builder. He has a magnificent episode in which he describes his boyhood, his dreams and their realization. In the theatre we have encountered nothing more touching since that memorable scene in Zoe Akins' 'Declasse,' where Claude King, another fine actor, recounted his rise from newsboy to Wall Street tycoon." Best's sniveling, flouncing Boston renegade added immeasurably to the fun. So did Cecil Beaton's period costumes and settings.

Off Broadway was spreading uptown as well as down. On the 10th, in the Jan Hus Auditorium, a converted chapel on 74th Street, a group calling itself the Shakespearewrights came up with a joyously lively recounting of *Twelfth Night*. Thomas Barbour made a memorable Malvolio, but the whole cast fell easily into the merry spirit of the play. On February 22, the company brought out *The Merchant of Venice*. The group would enjoy several years of deserved popularity.

There was precious little gaiety in Graham Greene's **The Living Room** (11-17-54, Henry Miller's). Torn between her passionate love for a married man (Michael Goodliffe) and the demands of the Catholic Church,

Rose Pemberton (Barbara Bel Geddes) takes the only escape she believes available to her. She commits suicide. Twenty-two performances sufficed.

A mere twenty sufficed for a revival on the 18th at the Holiday of *Abie's Irish Rose*, which years before had compiled 2327 performances to establish a 1920s long-run record. Most critics in those bygone days hadn't found the comedy funny, nor did their successors—at least not intentionally funny. But, perhaps surprisingly, several remarked on its compensatory virtues of "heart and humanity." In the same 1920s the Holiday had been known as the Gaiety. Situated smack on Broadway in the center of Times Square, it was rescued briefly and fitfully over the season from long service as a film house.

The quest of two Jewish sisters for husbands was the subject of Theodore Reeves's **Wedding Breakfast** (11-20-54, 48th St.). The more lovable sister (Virginia Vincent) and her complacent beau (Harvey Lembeck) are saving so that they can have a proper nest egg before they wed. After the more aggressively intellectual sister (Lee Grant) is thrown over by an ambitious young doctor, her sister's beau arranges for her to meet his cousin (Anthony Franciosa), who works at his father's hardware store. The snobbishly cultured girl's attempt to remake the boy in her own image nearly scuttles the romance. But by evening's end, both couples are ready for the altar. The comedy was larded with Newyorkese such as "You don't know yet, but tomorrow night I'm thinking strapless." Hailed by William Hawkins in the *World-Telegram and Sun* as "hilarious and poignant," it ambled along for 113 performances without repaying investors.

Although Constance Ford was supposed to be the star of Justin Sturm's **One Eye Closed** (11-24-54, Bijou), she took ill shortly before opening night, so producer Haila Stoddard went on in her place for all three Broadway playings. She was seen as a woman married to a worthless Yale graduate and writer (Tom Helmore). He is so impecunious that he and his wife are forced to live in a stable owned by the horse that munched oats on one side of the stage for much of the evening. Hubby has at least won a 1903 Winton—a sidewinder with a rear entrance—in which he rides off to a costume party dressed as a convict. An old buddy (John Baragrey), a dashing Harvard grad who has escaped from prison, comes to the stable in real convict clothes. For a time, the wife feels herself drawn to the rascal, but eventually opts to remain with her husband.

There were hosannas aplenty for **The Bad Seed** (12-8-54, 46th St.), which Maxwell Anderson adapted from William March's novel. Welcomed by Kerr as "a genuine fourteen-carat, fifteen-below chiller," it went on to grip audiences for 332 performances. When Mrs.

Penmark (Nancy Kelly) discovers a medal which had belonged to a drowned little boy and which her nine-year-old daughter, Rhoda (Patty McCormack), had coveted, she begins to wonder about the seemingly sweet, innocent child. In time she comes to realize that the girl has burned to death a janitor (Henry Jones) who could have pointed a finger at her and that years earlier she had shoved an old lady down a fire escape to obtain a crystal ball from her. Since Mrs. Penmark has also learned that her own mother was a criminally insane murderess, she gives Rhoda an overdose of sleeping pills, then shoots herself. Mrs. Penmark dies, but Rhoda is saved and promises baskets of kisses to her unsuspecting rescuers.

Two more hits followed in quick succession. Sidney Kingsley's **Lunatics and Lovers** (12-13-54, Broadhurst) was set in a suite in a cheap West 48th Street hotel. Pudgy, beady-eyed Dan Cupid (Buddy Hackett) traffics in watered-down perfumes, French postcards, and other seedy deals—and keeps out of jail through political connections such as Judge Sullivan (Dennis King). The judge's mistress (Vicki Cummings) would desert him for a rich, philandering dentist (Arthur O'Connell), so Dan persuades the judge to have a fling with the dentist's wife (Mary Anderson). The dentist and his wife soon tire of the sordid goings-on; the judge retrieves his lady friend; and Dan settles down with a heart-of-gold (Sheila Bond). The play divided the critics, with Brooks Atkinson taking a middle road in the *Times,* where he observed, "There is some funny stuff in 'Lunatics and Lovers.' Unfortunately, there is some labored stuff, too." But the public kept the box office busy for 336 performances.

There was an even larger public for Agatha Christie's **Witness for the Prosecution** (12-16-54, Henry Miller's), which held playgoers on the edge of their seats for nineteen months. An amiable young married man (Gene Lyons) is accused of murdering a middle-aged woman for her money. At his trial, he, his famed barrister (Francis Sullivan), and everyone else are stunned when the testimony of his foreign-born wife (Patricia Jessel) goes far to implicate him. Then a somewhat bedraggled cockney woman appears in the barrister's chambers and offers him letters showing the wife wanted a conviction so that she could run off with a lover. Put back on the stand, the wife breaks down, and the man is acquitted. Afterwards, the wife confesses that she was the cockney, disguised so that no one would recognize her. She had feared favorable testimony by a foreigner would not have moved an English jury. The startled barrister can only wonder at the lengths a wife will go to help an innocent husband, but she startles him further by assuring him her husband is guilty.

However, when she discovers he is also unfaithful, that proves too much. There in the courtroom, she grabs a convenient knife and kills him.

Neither of the two flops that followed, separated by a revival, ran a full week. **Portrait of a Lady** (12-21-54, ANTA) was William Archibald's theatricalization of Henry James's novel in which a naive American lady (Jennifer Jones) comes to England and foolishly marries an unscrupulous American expatriate (Robert Flemyng) instead of the colorless English lord she ought to have wed.

At the City Center on the 22nd, Helen Hayes returned in what she often stated was her favorite play, James M. Barrie's *What Every Woman Knows,* thus giving theatregoers a chance to see her highly praised Maggie Wylie for two more weeks.

During the Philadelphia tryout of A. B. Shiffrin's **Black-Eyed Susan** (12-23-54, Playhouse), in lieu of a legitimate second-act curtain, Vincent Price turned to the audience and smirkingly remarked, "I have a line here, but I'm not allowed to say it in Philadelphia." When the comedy reached New York the line was altered to read "even in New York" rather than simply "Philadelphia." The change attested to Shiffrin's lack of wit and originality. This "new high in low taste" told of a girl (Dana Wynter) who comes to a waggish, philandering neurologist to ask for help in conceiving a child. He helps her in the most obvious way he can, and when he is informed of his success, he stares out over the footlights for a moment and then comments, "I guess this is what is known as a pregnant pause." His behavior prompts his loyal, loving assistant (Kay Medford) to flirt with the girl's husband (Charles Boaz).

The critics split wildly over what proved to be Clifford Odets's last Broadway play, **The Flowering Peach** (12-28-54, Belasco). Atkinson called it Odets's finest; Kerr dismissed it as "repetitive and apparently rudderless." But everyone loved tiny, growly- or whiny-voiced Menasha Skulnik, who played the biblical Noah in a buttoned blue undershirt and crescent-shaped chin whiskers, and made him "a delightful old mule." Noah is amazed and baffled by God's choosing him to build and populate an ark. "You sure you don't mean some other man?" he asks. But Noah is dutiful and brings his whole squabbling clan aboard as well as pairs of every animal, even a gitka, an animal so small that only God could have considered making it or worrying about it. When the waters subside, Noah thanks God for sparing him, although his beloved wife, Esther (Berta Gersten), died during the ordeal. But, hoping that man has learned humility, he asks God for a sign that God will not destroy the world again. God grants Noah a beautiful rainbow. [An arc for an ark?] The play ran 135 performances, but, rather than a final multi-tinted rainbow of its own, it closed in a puddle of red ink. It subsequently became the 1970 Richard Rodgers musical *Two by Two*.

Anastasia (12-29-54, Lyceum), Guy Bolton's redaction of Marcelle Maurette's French drama, ran twice as long as Odets's play and was a hit primarily because of its "transcendent" recognition scene. "Pure romantic theatre," Hawkins rejoiced, "as we all too rarely see nowadays." In Berlin in 1926, an unscrupulous Russian prince (Joseph Anthony) and his cronies have taken under their wing a frail, possibly demented girl (Viveca Lindfors) who was saved from committing suicide after jumping into a river and who claims she is the lone Romanoff child to have escaped the slaughter of the czar and his family at Yekaterinburg. Hoping to get their hands on the czarist wealth still banked in Sweden, the men coach the girl on all the details they can think of about Anastasia. Then they have her confront the Dowager Empress (Eugenie Leontovich). At first, the old woman is sceptical. Slowly, she grows less and less certain of what to believe. Finally, with the girl on her knees and tugging at the Empress's skirts, the Empress finds herself laughing, crying, and scolding all at once. But, is she right to be convinced? Whatever the critics thought of the rest of the play, they singled out and extolled this scene. Kerr, otherwise one of the naysayers, recalled, "The players have fought through the sequence with utter integrity, given it weight and dignity and disturbing belief. For the time, we are genuinely touched." In 1965 the play was turned into the unsuccessful musical *Anya*.

The new year, 1955, was launched by two revivals. *The Fourposter* came into the City Center on January 5, with Tandy and Cronyn again in their old parts. Down at the Phoenix on the 11th, Shaw's *The Doctor's Dilemma* was brought back with a cast that included Roddy McDowall as Dubedat, Geraldine Fitzgerald as his wife, and Shepperd Strudwick as Ridgeon.

Back uptown the year's first novelty, Sam and Bella Spewack's **Festival** (1-18-55, Longacre), was a short-lived flop. Max Granada (Paul Henried) is a famous musical impresario who hates music and musicians. At the moment, his pet peeve is Sasha Rostov (George Voskovec), a famous pianist who is refusing to perform at a Mexican music festival. Into Max's palatial California sunroom pops Sally Ann Peters (Betty Field), a young, determined piano teacher with a supposed child prodigy (Abbott Lee Ruskin) in tow. To get him a hearing—and possibly a place in the Mexican program—she claims that Rostov is the boy's father. That leads to all manner of complications before the happy ending in which Max sets aside his dislike of musicians long enough to propose to Sally Ann.

The City Center's winter program continued with an "all-star" revival of *The Time of Your Life* on the 19th. The cast included Franchot Tone, Myron McCormack, Lonny Chapman, Harold Lang, Biff McGuire, John Carradine, Gloria Vanderbilt, and Paula Laurence. Both the play and the playing were welcomed by the critics, but there was no call to extend the engagement beyond its initially slated two weeks.

Several critics suggested that Ronald Alexander's **The Grand Prize** (1-26-55, Plymouth) might have been a more attractive comedy had its leading man been more pleasantly limned and less indifferently played. A television script writer (Nancy Wickwire), surveying the small apartment of Lu Cotton, secretary to the president of a New York perfume house, observes, "I never knew there were so many poor, dreary little girls, living around the city in such bad taste." Nevertheless, by answering a few inane questions and performing some basic chores, Lu (June Lockhart) wins the top prize on a TV show called "Boss for a Day." That means her somewhat randy, not unhandsome boss, Bob Meredith (John Newland), must be at her beck and call for twenty-four hours. His hope that those twenty-four can be consecutive hours does not sit well with Lu. Still, by the next morning she has changed her mind and thrown over the baffled advertising man she was engaged to. Tow-headed, quivery-cheeked, startled-eyed Tom Poston was cast as the rejected suitor and stole the show. He had not only a capital drunk scene, but a hefty share of the best lines. Thus he tells Bob that in advertising two things are necessary. First, you've got to have no opinions, but you must be definite about them. Second, you must stay permanently frightened. Later, when he cannot find Lu, he calls the morgue and asks, "Who's new?" But Poston alone could not save the show.

Off Broadway, the season's longest run went to what Atkinson saluted as "a perfect off-Broadway piece," **Thieves' Carnival** (2-1-55, Cherry Lane). The comedy was Lucienne Hill's translation of Jean Anouilh's *Le Bal des voleurs*. At a French spa an English lady and her two nieces are pursued for their money and jewels by a trio of thieves and a gold-digging father and son. With the lady's amused connivance, the thieves win.

The City Center's winter season concluded on the 2nd with a revival of *The Wisteria Trees*, in which Helen Hayes once again appeared as Lucy Ransdell.

John Cecil Holm's **The Southwest Corner** (2-3-55, Holiday), taken from Mildred Walker's novel, begins when Marcia Elder (Eva Le Gallienne), an eighty-three-year-old Vermont widow, decides to take in a companion to help defray her rising expenses. Regrettably she picks Bea Cannon (Enid Markey), a seemingly sweet, slightly flighty, and garrulous woman, who soon is exposed as viciously greedy and manipulative. She would auction off her host's beloved possessions and send her to an old-folks' home, but a heart attack brought on by the excitement of the auction kills her. Marcia and her loyal handyman (Parker Fennelly) can face a safe if somewhat bleak future together. Despite Markey's brilliant performance, too much talk and insufficient theatrical electricity doomed the adaptation.

But there was all the theatrical electricity any playgoer could want in **The Desperate Hours** (2-10-55, Barrymore), which Joseph Hayes dramatized from his own novel. A "slam-bang melodrama with a glowering figure behind every door and a nervous finger on every trigger," "a whirlwind melodrama, with no time for breath or wonder," "rousing theatre, good old-fashioned theatre," and "shatters the nerves" were some of the morning-after assessments. To hide out while awaiting delivery of some money, three escaped convicts take over the Hilliards' Indianapolis home. Their ringleader, Glenn Griffin (Paul Newman), wants the money not only to complete their escape but to pay a hired gunman to kill an Indianapolis policeman (James Gregory) he detests. At various times, Glenn, his brother, Hank (George Grizzard), or the third escaper, Robish (George Mathews), pistolwhip Mr. Hilliard (Karl Malden), kill a trashman (Wyrley Birch) who has become suspicious, and prevent the Hilliards' young son (Malcolm Brodrick) from escaping out of his upstairs bedroom. But Hank loses his life attempting to flee alone, and Robish is later shot by the police. Finally Hilliard tricks Glenn into taking an unloaded gun, while he confronts him with a loaded one. Adding to the excitement were Howard Bay's settings, which showed a cross-section of the two-story home and also brought on police venues at times. Although the thriller ran for more than six months, *Variety* listed it among the season's commercial failures.

Critics mentioned other books and plays which told the same basic story as Jacques Deval and Lorenzo Semple, Jr.'s **Tonight in Samarkand** (2-16-55, Morosco), but none seemed to recall the once ragingly popular *Eyes of Youth* (8-22-17). Like the heroine of that play, Nericia (Jan Ferrand), a tiger tamer with a circus touring French bywaters, asks the show's fortune teller, Sourab Kayam (Louis Jourdan), to read her future and tell her whom she should wed. She herself would marry a juggler, but Sourab warns that he would be faithless, and both, in any case, would die in the sinking of the *Holandia*. Then she might marry a rich man, but he, too, is fated to drown with his wife on the same ship. To escape such destinies, Nericia consents to

marry Sourab, who has secretly loved her. But her happiness is destroyed after she finds herself in Le Havre and learns that she and Sourab are booked to sail on the ship.

Metaphysics of a different sort reared its head in Paul Vincent Carroll's **The Wayward Saint** (2-17-55, Cort). A canon (Liam Redmond) who can talk to animals and can make plums grow on cherry trees is exiled to a remote country parish after his bishop (William Harrigan) becomes disturbed by his unworldly attributes. There the canon is tempted by a baron (Paul Lukas) who is actually the devil's emissary. He nearly succumbs to the temptations, but his prayers save him.

Only the lures of Katharine Cornell and film favorite Tyrone Power kept Christopher Fry's blank-verse **The Dark Is Light Enough** (2-23-55, ANTA) on the boards for nine weeks. During the 1848 uprising in Hungary against Austria, Countess Rosmarin shelters her worthless son-in-law at her own peril and receives no gratitude. But when she dies he realizes he must face his enemies alone. Most reviewers were not impressed with Power, to whom Cornell had given roles before he became a screen star. But Cornell was saluted as lovely to look at and a quiet joy to hear: "The measure of her grace and skill may be taken by the fact that her final scenes—in which, dying, she enunciates the humane little thoughts which are meant to make a tattered universe tolerable—are her best."

Back in October, in a small, cramped venue in which the audience sat on two sides of the stage, a young man named David Ross had offered a highly lauded revival of *The Dybbuk,* which ran for 103 performances. On February 25 at the same 4th Street Theatre, he brought out an equally commended mounting of *The Three Sisters.* The title roles were played by relatively unknown actresses, but several better-known men were also cast, notably Philip Loeb as Tchebutykin and Morris Carnovsky as Andrey. This mounting chalked up 102 playings and allowed Ross to begin to carve a niche for himself, first as a fine producer of Chekhov and later as an advocate of Ibsen.

Divided notices greeted the Phoenix Theatre's revival on March 1 of *The Master Builder.* Oscar Homolka was its Solness; Joan Tetzel, its Hilda.

March's only two uptown entries were both major hits. Atkinson thought William Inge's **Bus Stop** (3-2-55, Music Box) was better than *Picnic*, while Kerr hailed it as the season's best play. Passengers from a bus stranded by a blizzard have gathered at a combination bus stop and restaurant, operated by a hard-nosed woman named Grace (Elaine Stritch) in a small Kansas town. One of the riders is a strumpety nightclub "chantoosie," Cherie (Kim Stanley). Another is a loudmouthed, sexually eager cowboy, Bo Decker (Albert Salmi), who is bent on pestering Cherie until he get what he wants from her. Initially, Cherie attempts to avoid Bo, but the long stopover forces her to deal with him. By the time the bus is ready to move on, Cherie has brought out Bo's underlying gentleness and humility. When he informs her that he is virgin enough for two, she replies, "Thass the sweetest, tenderest thing that was ever said to me." They board the bus together, with their fellow travelers applauding their newfound romance. The play ran for 478 performances, without collecting any of the season's major prizes.

The two most prestigious awards of the era, the Pulitzer Prize and the New York Drama Critics Circle Award, went to Tennessee Williams's **Cat on a Hot Tin Roof** (3-24-55, Morosco), which Watts termed "a play of tremendous dramatic impact" and which subsequently moved on to compile 694 performances. The Pollitts have assembled at their Mississippi Delta plantation to celebrate the birthday of the family patriarch, Big Daddy (Burl Ives). But the gathering only serves to exacerbate family tensions. Margaret (Barbara Bel Geddes), a woman of strong passions and determination, who is frustrated by the lack of affection accorded her by her detatched, alcoholic husband, Brick (Ben Gazzara), reveals to him that she had an affair with his closest friend, Skipper, even though she knew Skipper was a homosexual. The affair drove Skipper to drink and suicide. Big Daddy also assails Brick, suggesting his drinking stems from his refusal to help Skipper because he shared the dead boy's homosexual tendencies. Infuriated, Brick reveals that Big Daddy is dying of cancer. Maggie knows that there is no will, and, fearing that Big Daddy may now disinherit Brick and her, she lies that she is pregnant. Throwing away Brick's liquor, she says, "We can make that lie come true. And then I'll bring you liquor, and we'll get drunk together, here, tonight, in this place that death has come into!" Mildred Dunnock headed the supporting cast as Big Mama.

Having called attention to himself with an adventuresome off-Broadway entry, Leslie Stevens moved into the mainstream with a piece of disappointing hackwork, **Champagne Complex** (4-12-55, Cort). After a worried fiancé (John Dall) calls in a psychiatrist (Donald Cook) because his girl (Polly Bergen) insists on stripping every time she drinks champagne, the girl ditches the boy and agrees to wed the doctor. The three-character comedy stayed around for only three weeks.

The season's last hit was Jerome Lawrence and Robert E. Lee's **Inherit the Wind** (4-21-55, National), which the *News*'s John Chapman lauded as "one of the most exciting dramas of the last decade." Despite fictitious names assigned various characters, it was openly based on the famous 1925 Scopes "monkey" trial in Tennessee, and made no secret that its Drummond, Brady, and Hornbeck actually were Clarence Darrow, William Jennings Bryan, and H. L. Mencken. With a modest schoolteacher, Bertram Cates (Karl Light), brought to trial for violating his state's law against teaching evolution, the flamboyant orator and politician Matthew Harrison Brady (Ed Begley) comes to the trial scene to help the prosecution and smilingly addresses his enthusiastic supporters in Hillsboro's town square. When he and the crowd leave the square empty with only the newspaperman Hornbeck (Tony Randall) lounging there, a lone figure trudges up from the railroad station: "weary, puffing, mopping his neck, walking as though there were holes in his shoes and the pavement were hot." Hornbeck recognizes the great defense lawyer Henry Drummond (Paul Muni), but not a word is spoken as the curtain falls. The trial quickly becomes a circus, in which Drummond devastates Brady. But after the trial ends, with Cates found guilty and assessed a token fine, the exhausted, humiliated Brady dies. Drummond surprises Hornbeck by coming to the defense of the dead man and the Bible: "You never pushed a noun against a verb except to blow up something," he says, insisting that every man has the right to be wrong and that Brady's mistake was that "he was looking for God too high up and far away." Superbly acted, the play proved the season's longest-running drama, closing with 806 performances to its credit.

Virtually every critic compared Roald Dahl's **The Honeys** (4-28-55, Longacre) to *Arsenic and Old Lace*— and none of the comparisons was favorable. Two darling little ladies (Dorothy Stickney and Jessica Tandy) are married to irascible, nasty twins (both played by Hume Cronyn). Noticing how happy a friend has been ever since her husband fell or was pushed from a window, the pair decide to kill the brothers. Rotten oysters and a malfunctioning elevator fail to do the trick, but a bludgeoning with a frozen leg of lamb and some tiger whiskers in orange juice do the jobs nicely, thank you.

Although it had run for months at a small Los Angeles playhouse, Baruch Lumet and Henry Sherman's **Once upon a Tailor** (5-23-55, Cort) lasted only a single week in New York as the season's finale. Set in Austrian backwaters in the 1880s, it described how a poor tailor (Oscar Karlweis), needing money to save his elder daughter from having her husband leave her for want of a dowry, attempts to drum up some cash by serving as a matchmaker, albeit the violinist he would pair with a rich man's daughter is the very boy his own daughter loves.

1955–1956

"Qualitatively and quantitatively," the *Times* commented at season's end, "it has been one of the most successful in a decade." In his *Best Plays* Louis Kronenberger rated it "the most rewarding in years." Dissenters could point to a paucity of good musicals, albeit the two best were *My Fair Lady* and *The Most Happy Fella*. And among straight plays, however good, a discouraging number came from overseas or were adaptations of novels or even television shows. Why the *Times* was so happy about the quantity of shows is more puzzling, since its figure of thirty-nine new plays (*Variety* counted thirty-five) was nowhere near a few recent highs. And its seemingly lofty total of eighty-eight productions stemmed from its considering each offering of some major foreign repertory groups individually.

However, business was good. No fewer than sixteen shows ran more than 100 performances, though only eleven of these repaid their investors. Ticket prices inched up in two ways. Since the federal government had halved its wartime tax from 20 to 10 percent, New York City rushed in with a 5 percent surcharge. Thus a $4.00 ticket, which had cost $4.80 with the older tax, then $4.40, jumped up to $4.60. Producers, crying that the new tax would kill business, promptly hiked prices on their own. The best seats for straight plays went up to $5.75 and, in one instance, $6.90.

Revivals launched the season. A star-packed mounting of *The Skin of Our Teeth* returned from delighting the Continent to offer New Yorkers a three-week chance to see it. It opened at the ANTA on August 17 with Mary Martin as Sabina, Helen Hayes as Mrs. Antrobus, George Abbott—having allowed Alan Schneider to direct—as Mr. Antrobus, and Florence Reed as the Fortune Teller.

The City Center brought out a pair of Shakespearean dramas. On September 7 it unveiled its highly praised *Othello,* with William Marshall as the Moor and Jerome Kilty as Iago. Critics were less happy with *Henry IV, Part I,* which premiered on the 21st with Kilty as Falstaff.

Between the two Shakespeare openings a sensational debut took place. Marcel Marceau, a French mime, came into the Phoenix on the 20th and single-handedly sparked a vogue for mime in America. A small, reedy man with the most supple and imaginative body movements, his character of BIP performed in a battered high hat surmounted by a flower.

In London several of the greatest English players had helped make N. C. Hunter's Chekhovian **A Day by the Sea** (9-26-55, ANTA) a memorable experience. In New York some of our finest players—two of whom were English-born naturalized Americans—could not satisfy critics or theatregoers. A self-involved career diplomat (Hume Cronyn), who years earlier spurned a chance to wed a lovely woman (Jessica Tandy) lest she hamper his rise, now belatedly and futilely courts the widow. His mother (Aline MacMahon) and a boozy doctor (Dennis King) devoted to the mother watch and philosophize on the affair.

Although Arthur Miller's double bill of **A View from the Bridge** and **A Memory of Two Mondays** (9-29-55, Coronet) ran for 148 performances, it was not a commercial hit. The latter play was a curtain raiser that looked at turnings in the lives of some warehouse employees during the Depression. One leaves to try college; another, albeit poetically inclined, grows bitter about life; others find solace in after-hours drinking and lechery. The major critics agreed that the evening's main drama, written to some extent in blank verse, was a tragedy manqué. In the *Herald Tribune* Walter Kerr bewailed it missed "that last note of exultation" that might have made it a major work, while in the *Times* Brooks Atkinson rued, "Mr. Miller's blunt, spare characterizations . . . are not big enough for big tragedy." Eddie Carbone (Van Heflin), a Brooklyn longshoreman, has agreed to take in for a time Marco (Jack Warden) and Rodolpho (Richard Davalos), two of his wife's nephews, who are illegal immigrants, and get them work on the piers. Marco tells the family that he had to come here so that he could support his wife and children back home: "If I stay there they will never grow up./ They eat the sunshine." But it is the blond and strikingly handsome Rodolpho who unwittingly causes problems when he falls in love with Eddie's orphaned niece, Catherine (Gloria Marlowe). She loves him, too, but Eddie himself secretly loves the girl—probably more than he realizes. He tries to convince her that the boy wants to marry her so he can become an American citizen and, when that fails to dissuade her, tries to suggest that Rodolpho is homosexual. Stymied, Eddie informs immigration authorities about the men. Before the brothers can be deported, however, Marco kills Eddie. To underline a sense of Greek tragedy, Miller employed a lawyer (J. Carroll Naish) as a sort of one-man chorus, and Boris Aronson designed a set showing the Carbone apartment and the area around it that included stylized hints of Greek stairways and columns.

Another sad, undeserving failure was **The Young and Beautiful** (10-1-55, Longacre), which Sally Benson derived from some F. Scott Fitzgerald short stories. In 1915 Chicago, Josephine Perry (Lois Smith) is a rich, spoiled "tearing speed," a dangerously blasé teenager who loses interest in a boy the moment she gets him to kiss her. She laments, "I wish there were some place else—and something besides boys—and somebody else besides me." She would woo an older, wiser young man (Douglas Watson), who works for her father, but he is on to her and sends her on her way. Finally a fine, handsome member (James Olson) of the Lafayette Escadrille falls in love with her. Although he would be ideal, she loses him when she tells him his kisses don't excite her. She is left to go out with pretentious Travis de Coppet (Peter Brandon), who affects a cape and a walking stick. Given "a perfect production" with an elegant setting of a scrollwork-and-velveteen drawing room, lovely costumes, and a fine, Maxixe-dancing cast, the play still could not find an audience.

But there was enough of an audience to give **Tiger at the Gates** (10-3-55, Plymouth) a six-and-a-half-month run. The play was Christopher Fry's reworking of Jean Giraudoux's elegantly pessimistic *La Guerre de Troie n'aura pas lieu*. One great warrior, the noble Hector (Michael Redgrave), has little problem convincing another, Ulysses (Walter Fitzgerald), to take Helen (Diane Cilento) home and thereby avoid a war between Troy and Athens. But, for their own selfish reasons, Trojan politicians, businessmen, and the swayable populace all clamor for battle and blood. So there is irony in the original French title.

There was all matter of symbolism in Ugo Betti's *Delitto all'isola delle capre*, which Henry Reed translated simply as **Island of Goats** (10-4-55, Fulton), but New York's critics were thrown for a loss to figure out what the symbolism symbolized. A good-looking young stranger (Laurence Harvey) appears on an island and promptly seduces a woman (Uta Hagen), her daughter (Tani Seitz), and her sister-in-law (Ruth Ford). But after he falls down a well, the trio taunt him and leave him to drown. The play was memorable mainly for its massive, towering Jo Mielziner setting of a crumbling mill, with striking vertical lines and a faint shaft of light coming from a gap in the ceiling.

"By shunning any trace of theatricality or emotional excess, the playwrights have made the only-too-true story deeply moving in its unadorned veracity," the *Post*'s Richard Watts, Jr., wrote of Frances Goodrich and Albert Hackett's **The Diary of Anne Frank** (10-5-55, Cort). The drama, which eventually won both the Pulitzer Prize and the New York Drama Critics Circle Award and which ran for 717 performances, was based on the actual, best-selling diary of a young Dutch Jew who died at the hands of the Nazis. A short time after the war, Otto Frank (Joseph Schildkraut) returns with his former stenographer, Miep Gies (Gloria Jones), to the gabled attic where Mr. Kraler (Clinton Sundberg) had hidden Frank, his family, and other Jews from the Gestapo. There Frank discovers the diary kept by his thirteen-year-old daughter, Anne (Susan Strasberg). It recalls the hours they spent crowded into the small space, often in tense silence lest they give away their whereabouts. Frank remembers both happy moments, such as a Chanukah celebration, and bitter ones, such as catching a fellow Jew stealing their food. The announcement of Allied landings brings hope of a quick rescue, but shortly before the liberation, the hiding place is betrayed. Anne and the others are sent to the gas chambers. Only Frank escapes. He reads the last lines of the diary: "In spite of everything," Anne writes, "I still believe people are really good at heart." "She puts me to shame," a bitter Frank confesses. The cast was hailed as "unfalteringly admirable."

In Edmund Morris's **The Wooden Dish** (10-6-55, Booth), white-haired, mustached old Pop Dennison (Louis Calhern) is so doddering that he sometimes sets fire to his bed. He eats from a wooden dish since he is given to accidentally breaking china. Living in their Texas home with his weak-willed son (Gordon Tanner) and his unhappy daughter-in-law (Polly Rowles), he is a source of constant worry. Indeed, he causes the woman so much grief that she considers running off with a boarder (John Randolph). But before they can put the old man in a home, he volunteers to move into one. Calhern, in his last Broadway appearance before his fatal heart attack, played "with fine vim and freshness," but couldn't save an unlikable play. Perhaps surprisingly, not a single newspaper critic called to mind a much better, earlier play with a similar story, Kaufman and Ferber's *Minick* (9-24-24).

But several critics did recall *The Yellow Jacket* (11-4-12) in their notices of Aldyth Morris's **The Carefree Tree** (10-11-55, Phoenix), for Morris was attempting to employ Chinese theatrical conventions to tell a saga of ancient China. That meant no scenery, stylized props, and, of course, a helpful property man (Jerry Stiller). Thankfully, it also allowed for some gorgeous costumes—the mounting's saving grace. A northern Dowager Empress (Blanche Yurka) balks at the Princess (Janice Rule) marrying a southern warrior (Farley Granger), whose family has long been feuding with hers. But love triumphs.

The Faust legend was transferred to modern Hollywood in George Axelrod's **Will Success Spoil Rock Hunter?** (10-13-55, Belasco), which defied critical headshakings to run gaily on for thirteen months. Thus William Hawkins, of the *World-Telegram and Sun*, complained it was "a jerky piece, up and down like a scenic railway and too spasmodic to ever get rolling." George MacCauley (Orson Bean) is a twenty-seven-year-old nebbish and virgin, sent by his fan magazine to interview the nation's sex symbol, Rita Marlowe

(Jayne Mansfield). At her St. Regis suite he meets Irving LaSalle (Martin Gabel), ostensibly an agent but actually the devil in modern dress. Irving grants George any wish he wants—at 10 percent of his soul for each wish granted. Before long George is partnered with the luscious Rita in and out of bed. He runs her studio and even wins an Oscar. But when the brawny football star whom Rita had walked out on threatens to make mincemeat of George, the boy realizes he is running out of wishes and will soon belong to the devil. However, George had used up one of his wishes to compensate Mike Freeman (Walter Matthau) for stealing Rita from him and wangling the right to do the screenplay for Mike's lone Broadway work, a Pulitzer Prize-winning drama. He has gotten the devil to come up with another great manuscript for Mike, including all the revisions Mike will have to make during the tryouts. Mike, who has described himself as "a playwrote. That's a playwright who hasn't written anything lately," is so grateful that he agrees to become Irving's "client" in George's stead. George can be a nebbish again.

Edith Sommer's **A Roomful of Roses** (10-17-55, Playhouse) told of a mother (Patricia Neal) who had given up her daughter (Betty Lou Keim) to her husband when she divorced him and remarried. Now the unloving father has sent the girl back to her mother because he, in turn, wants to remarry. It takes two acts for the mother to overcome the girl's hostility.

Down in the Village at the 4th Street Theatre on the 18th, David Ross continued his Chekhov series by presenting Stark Young's version of *The Cherry Orchard*. Nancy Wickwire's Varya, and George Ebeling's Lopahin won many of the best notices.

The season's comedy champ was **No Time for Sergeants** (10-20-55, Alvin), which Ira Levin took from Mac Hyman's novel. "You'll find nothing funnier the length of Broadway," Robert Coleman told his *Daily Mirror* readers. Enough playgoers agreed to keep the comedy around for 796 performances. Will Stockdale (Andy Griffith), an innocent, trusting Georgia hillbilly, is drafted into the Air Force. Cantankerous Sergeant King (Myron McCormick) takes an instant dislike to him and sets out to make his life miserable. He orders him to clean the company's latrine, telling him that the latrine is "kind of the captain's hobby; when it sparkles, the captain sparkles too." So Will makes the latrine shine, but also blurts out King's remarks to the captain (Ed Peck), who threatens to strip King of his rank and leave him a PLO—permanent latrine orderly. Deciding he must get Will out of his squad, King gives him answers to a classification test, only to have Will mate the answers to the wrong questions. Later Will is presumed lost when his plane inadvertently flies into an atomic test. But when Will blithely shows up at a ceremony awarding him a posthumous medal, he is given a medal to keep his mouth shut.

By contrast to his enthusiasm for the Levin-Hyman comedy, Coleman dismissed William Marchant's **The Desk Set** (10-24-55, Broadhurst) as "a featherweight comedy." Nonetheless, he acknowledged that "you couldn't hear many of the punch lines for the howls." Most of those howls were evoked by Shirley Booth, whose warmth and exceptional comedic talents kept audiences delighted and the show running profitably for nine months. She brought down the house "reciting a perfectly deadpan piece of office chatter in the rhythms of 'Hiawatha'" and found all sorts of hilarious intonations for the single word "puce." Bunny Watson is the mainstay of the reference department at the International Broadcasting Company—"the network with a heart." There's scarcely a fact she and her loyal girls don't have at their fingertips. But then the president's know-it-all nephew (Byron Sanders) convinces him to replace the staff with an Emmerac, an Electro-Magnetic Memory and Research Arithmetical Calculator. It will save 6240 man-hours in Bunny's department alone. After all, the nephew smugly tells Bunny, people are outmoded. Bunny politely responds, "I wouldn't be a bit surprised if they stop making them." But the new machine gives out reviews of a film called *King Solomon's Mines* when asked for information on the Watusis and confuses Corfu with curfew. So the jobs are saved, and Bunny even wins a proposal of marriage from a corporate vice-president (Frank Milan).

The next evening the famed Comédie Française began a brief stand at the Broadway offering five plays in three bills: **Le Bourgeois Gentilhomme**; **Arlequin poli par l'amour** and **Le Barbier de Seville**; and **Le Jeu de l'amour et du hasard** and **Un Caprice.**

Enid Bagnold's English comedy **The Chalk Garden** (10-26-55, Barrymore) was October's sixth and final hit. A concerned grandmother (Gladys Cooper) hires a woman (Siobhan McKenna), who subsequently seems to have been a convicted murderess, to look after her granddaughter (Betsy von Furstenberg), a neglected young lady given to wild prevarication. The woman, whose conviction may have been unjust, helps salvage the granddaughter and the grandmother's difficult garden, both of which need a special kind of attention. Fritz Weaver was commended as a daffy, grumpy servant.

Some of the season's harshest notices went to Leonard Lee's **Deadfall** (10-27-55, Holiday). A woman (Joanne Dru), angry that a man (John Ireland) she knows murdered her husband has been acquitted, plots revenge. Donning a red wig and assuming a new personage, she manufactures an array of clever evidence, then makes it seem that the man has killed the redhead. As her real self, she even takes the stand against him. Her ploy works.

The next evening a group called the Shakespearean Theatre Workshop, headed by someone named Joe Papp, brought out *As You Like It* at a church on 6th Street near the East River. On December 15 the group added *Romeo and Juliet* to its schedule.

Shots were heard before the curtain rose on **The Heavenly Twins** (11-4-55, Booth), an uncredited adaptation of Albert Husson's *Les Pavés du ciel*. When the curtain went up there was svelte Faye Emerson in a white satin gown, a gun in her hand and her husband (Jean Pierre Aumont) on the floor. But he soon bounces back up, since he had put blanks in the cartridge. After she shoots him again, this time with bullets that work, he turns into a grandfather clock. Next, she shoots his charming illegitimate son (also Aumont), who has refused to have an affair with her. Then she awakes—it was all a nightmare.

A growing, more true-to-life nightmare—drug addiction—was the theme of Michael V. Gazzo's **A Hatful of Rain** (11-9-55, Lyceum). Johnny Pope (Ben Gazzara), wounded in the war, was treated with drugs and became an addict. He kicked the habit but now has relapsed. He often walks the streets at night seeking a fix, and has been brutalized by his pushers when he cannot pay. Neither his pregnant wife (Shelley Winters) nor his self-preoccupied father (Frank Silvera) is aware of the problem. His wife is even thinking of leaving him. Only his brother, Polo (Anthony Franciosa), knows and has exhausted his savings providing Johnny the money he needs for his drugs. As matters deteriorate Johnny promises to quit "tomorrow," but Polo retorts, "It's been tomorrow for months, Johnny; the calendar never moves." Not until matters come near to hitting bottom and his wife and father discover the truth does Johnny allow his wife to call the police to come to take him for detoxification, even if that means time in jail. Propelled by an "unbearably powerful" performance by Gazzara, the drama ran nearly a full year.

Down at the Phoenix, the playhouse inaugurated a "New Directors' Series" with another critical look at life in a military academy, Arthur Steuer's **The Terrible Swift Sword** (11-15-55, Phoenix). The first new director was Fred Sadoff. Steuer's play pitted a cynical plebe (Conrad Janis) against an inhumane sergeant (Arch Johnson), who nearly kills the boy by holding his head in a bucket of water. But the series soon came to naught.

Critics trudged down to the Village again the next evening for Jacquetta Hawkes and J. B. Priestley's **Dragon's Mouth** (11-16-55, Cherry Lane), in which four quarantined yacht passengers use the time to probe their inner feelings.

There were far more public shrivings in **The Lark** (10-17-55, Longacre), Lillian Hellman's redaction of Jean Anouilh's drama. An impatient Warwick (Christopher Plummer) wants to rush the trial of Joan (Julie Harris) so that she can be burned at the stake, but an older, more compassionate Cauchon (Boris Karloff) insists she be heard out. For her part, Joan insists that St. Michael, "in a beautiful clean robe that must have been ironed by somebody very careful," appeared to her and ordered her to shake France and lead it to freedom. He directed her to Baudricourt (Theodore Bikel) who, in turn, was to lead her to the Dauphin (Paul Roebling). Of course, in time the trial goes against Joan, who makes her peace with Warwick before she is led to the fire. Critics praised Hellman's tough, no-nonsense translation and the supporting cast. There was also special praise for Jo Mielziner's imaginative designs; basically "steps on different levels against a cyclorama. With a few props, a slide projector, and skillful lighting, he evokes a whole section of France." But it was Harris's girlish, impassioned maiden that grabbed the lion's share of garlands: "none have brought to the role such fragile and beguiling sincerity," "a triumphant performance," "I've never seen a finer portrayal of Joan." The play ran seven months.

In the Village, Edward Justus Mayer's **The Last Love of Don Juan** (11-23-55, Rooftop) told how the don is shattered to discover a famous lady is just as happy to go to bed with a smelly pastry chef as with him.

Uptown, the hits continued to pile in. Carolyn Green's "wild and enjoyable" **Janus** (11-24-55, Plymouth) brought playgoers back to its own version of modern-day Greenwich Village, where every summer Jessica (Margaret Sullavan) and Denny (Claude Dauphin) have walk-ups one above the other, joined by a convenient dumbwaiter. They are married, but not to each other. Jessica is wed to a West Coast shipping magnate and Denny to a termagant in Massachusetts, but each summer the pair collaborate on writing sexy historical novels and are "faithfully unfaithful" to their spouses. They are abetted by a useful literary agent (Mary Finney), a woman with the "courage of her commissions." Whenever Jessica needs Denny she pounds the ceiling with a broomstick and he shoots down the dumbwaiter. Their lives become complicated when Jessica's husband (Robert Preston) suddenly appears and when a man (Robert Emhardt) from the IRS accuses Denny of filing false income tax returns by not taking enough deductions. By play's end, nothing has really changed, although everyone is a bit more worldly wise.

Once more back down to the real Village, where the Circle in the Square did itself proud on December 1 with an admired revival of the 1927 importation *The Cradle Song*.

Several nights later, big-time audiences were transported back to the Yonkers and Manhattan of the 1880s. They had been there before and met the same characters when Thornton Wilder had initially, and unsuccessfully, offered his work to Broadway as *The Merchant of Yonkers.* Now revised and retitled **The Matchmaker** (12-5-55, Royale), it provided Broadway with one of the gayest romps in years, thanks in good measure to Tyrone Guthrie's madcap staging. Dolly Levi (Ruth Gordon), a self-confessed "woman who arranges things," has promised the rich, pompous Yonkers merchant Horace Vandergelder (Loring Smith) to prevent his niece (Prunella Scales) from eloping with a poor artist, Ambrose Kemper (Alexander Davion). She has also promised Horace to find him a young wife. Don't you believe it for a minute! Even though she is pushing a pair of supposed candidates (Eileen Herlie and Esme Church), she is really pushing only a third—Dolly Levi herself. All the figures—the lovers, the candidates, Vandergelder's furtively gallivanting clerks (Arthur Hill and Robert Morse), along with her and Vandergelder—meet down by the Battery at the Harmonia Gardens Restaurant. There she reveals herself, telling the dismayed merchant, "you go your way (*Points finger.*) and I'll go mine (*Points finger in same direction.*)" In no time at all everyone is paired according to Dolly's plans. With the delightfully raucous and vulgar Gordon in the forefront, the farce, which John Chapman of the *Daily News* hailed as "the funniest thing on Broadway," ran 486 performances and was subsequently made into the enormously successful 1963 musical *Hello, Dolly!* Years later the same Nestroy play also became the source of Tom Stoppard's London hit *On the Razzle.*

. . .

Tyrone Guthrie (1900–71), the great British director, long associated with the Old Vic, first came to America in 1936 to direct *Call It a Day,* then returned ten years later to stage a revival of *He Who Gets Slapped.* Henceforth he shuttled regularly between the West End and Broadway. He was largely responsible for the creation in 1953 of the Shakespeare Festival Theatre in Stratford, Ontario, and a decade thereafter of the Guthrie Theatre and Guthrie Theatre Foundation in Minneapolis.

. . .

The play was one of the earliest hits of producer David Merrick.

. . .

David Merrick [né Margulois] (b. 1911) was born in St. Louis and trained as a lawyer, before taking work with Herman Shumlin. His first successful venture was the musical *Fanny* in 1954. Within a few seasons he became far and away the most active producer on Broadway, remarkable for the variety of works he presented and for the outrageous methods he often employed to publicize them.

. . .

On the 11th at the Phoenix, Tyrone Guthrie was also the stager of a highly lauded revival of *Six Characters in Search of an Author,* which he and Michael Wager had retranslated. A fine cast, including Wager, Whitfield Connor, Katharine Squire, Natalie Schafer, and Kurt Kasznar, aided the production in staying alive for sixty-five performances, the longest for any of the season's attractions at the playhouse.

Two Irish plays closed out the year. Both were failures, although the quiet, unballyhooed one ran the longer. Frank Carney's **The Righteous Are Bold** (12-22-55, Holiday) told of a priest (Denis O'Dea) who exorcises a possessed girl (Irene Hayes) at the expense of his own life. It lingered for sixty-eight performances.

The second Irish drama, Sean O'Casey's **Red Roses for Me** (12-28-55, Booth), had a highly vociferous coterie of boosters who tried desperately if unavailingly to keep it running beyond twenty-nine playings. In 1913 Dublin, a young Protestant artist (Kevin McCarthy) loves a greedily ambitious Catholic girl (Joyce Sullivan). When a transportation strike erupts, she urges him to earn money as a strike-breaker. Instead, he joins the workers and is killed for his pains. Down with the play went Howard Bay's richly constructed and dramatically crowded settings of a modest Dublin home, a street and bridge, and a church grounds.

The titular hero (Alfred Lunt) and heroine (Lynn Fontanne) of Howard Lindsay and Russel Crouse's **The Great Sebastians** (1-4-56, ANTA) were a second-rate mind-reading act caught in Prague at the time of the Communist takeover. Since the pair had eaten lunch with Jan Masaryk hours before his death, the authorities attempt to hold them until they sign statements claiming the politician had spoken to them of suicide. They refuse, and resort to some of their stage tricks to elude their captors and flee to freedom. As was regularly the case in recent years with the Lunts' vehicles, neither the story nor the writing was exceptional. All that mattered were the stars. The play began with Lunt, in evening clothes, strolling through the aisles, borrowing possessions from playgoers, and calling out to a be-gowned, blonde-wigged, and blindfolded Fontanne onstage to identify the objects. One critic wrote of Lunt in subsequent scenes, "Keep an eye on him as he mesmerizes a buffalo-type general with the secret of turning lead into gold, treats a suspect telephone as though it were a red-hot stove, and brags genially about breaking the house record at the Palladium the week Danny Kaye happened to be playing there. It's necromancy, all right." The same reviewer wrote of Fontanne, "Trapped behind barred doors for a nervous evening, she tucks a napkin into her Mainbocher gown, deftly spears away a hefty slice of her husband's dinner, and coolly mocks a bully with a haughty 'We're ever so frightened' in superb disdain." At a new $6.90 top for a straight play, the drama set house records, pulling in more than $40,000 a week.

Three remarkable revivals followed on Broadway, although one actually wasn't a revival.

With himself as director and star, Orson Welles brought a roaring, frantically propelled *King Lear* into the City Center on the 12th for a two-and-a-half-week stand. Not even his having to perform in a wheelchair, since he had broken an ankle in rehearsal, daunted him. Viveca Lindfors was his Cordelia. Typical of his lush hamming was his big early scene with his daughters: "Here, Mr. Welles, letting his lip curl slyly behind a story-book beard, has his faithful retainers unroll an enormous map, a map large enough to walk on. Mr. Welles does walk on it, as he apportions the land to those scoundrels, Regan and Goneril. More than that. As he begs Cordelia for a loving word, the map is stretched taut and tempting across his breast, only beard and eyes glowering above it. Then, when Cordelia has stuck to her guns, he charges right through it, splitting Britain open like a paper-hoop in a three-ring circus." (Uptown, the next evening, the Shakespearewrights revived *A Midsummer Night's Dream* at the Jan Hus Auditorium and were greeted by a divided press.)

More hilarious still than Welles was the tiny, sour-faced musical comedy comedienne Nancy Walker in Noel Coward's 1927 fluff, *Fallen Angels,* which came into the Playhouse on the 17th. Coward's story told of two unhappily married ladies who fall to quarreling and get drunk while awaiting the appearance of a French lover they had both enjoyed years before. (The other lady was played by Margaret Phillips.) "Thanks to Nancy Walker's terribly funny performance," Kronenberger wrote, "*Fallen Angels* was worth reviving as it had never been worth producing when new." Walker became entangled in a telephone cord which finally catapulted her through a door—and whatever she hit on the other side catapulted her right back. She fought with a gold lamé stole as she tried to replenish an empty cocktail glass, then stirred the cocktail with her lavalliere. And she was staggered by the weight of her arm's-length cigarette holder. Every attitude she struck, struck back. But her humor was not merely visual. She managed to pack a complete history of a failed marriage into the deceptively simple "I'm fond of Fred, too." The production ran seven months without repaying its investors.

No one expected Canada's Stratford Festival Theatre's production of Christopher Marlowe's **Tamburlaine the Great** to show a profit, and it didn't. Although some careless reviewers referred to Tyrone Guthrie's lushly baroque mounting as a revival when it came into the Winter Garden on the 19th, it wasn't. Strictly speaking, the three-and-a-half-centuries-old drama was being given its first professional New York playing, with Anthony Quayle as a magnificently voiced and fiercely virile hero. Of course, the play could only appeal to a limited audience, so had to be satsified with a twenty-performance stand.

Despite some glowing notices—"an engrossing melodrama that moves into the realm of ideas," "a taut and strikingly topical melodrama with disturbingly thoughtful overtones," "a bombshell"—Henry Denker and Ralph Berkey's **Time Limit!** (1-24-56, Booth) was listed as a commercial failure when it shuttered after 127 performances. A major (Richard Kiley) with a heretofore unblemished history turned into a Communist mouthpiece after fourteen months in a North Korean prison camp. At his trial, a curious judge advocate (Arthur Kennedy) determines to find out if there was any hidden reason for the man's becoming a turncoat. At first the major is uncooperative, demanding the trial be allowed to take its course. But the judge advocate eventually learns that the fear of eighteen of his fellow prisoners being put to death prompted the major's behavior. Ralph Alswang's skillful use of backlighting allowed the military courtroom to quickly become a barbed-wired prison camp during revealing flashbacks.

Several critics pounced on the same bad joke to exemplify problems Sam Levene faced when he played the lead in Allen Boretz and Ruby Sully's **The Hot Corner** (1-25-56, Golden). Levene was seen as Fred Stanley, a onetime big-league baseball manager, whose foul mouth and hot temper have confined him to the bush leagues for a decade. Now he has a chance to return and manage Detroit if his team wins in its league. Everything depends on his star pitcher, Lefty McShane (Don Murray), in the crucial game. But after the local peanut vendors set up a picket line and Lefty refuses to cross it, all hell breaks loose. Since this was a comedy, a happy ending followed. The bad joke? One character insists, "I'm a general manager," so another character retorts, "Well, go manage some generals." Five performances and the play was gone.

Back down in the Village, David Ross continued his admirable Chekhov series at the 4th Street Theatre on the 31st with *Uncle Vanya.* George Voskovec had the title role, while Franchot Tone was the doctor. Clarence Derwent and Signe Hasso were among the supporting players.

Theodore Apstein's **The Innkeepers** (2-2-56, Golden), which replaced Levene's vehicle at the same house, ran one performance less than its predecessor—four. Ever since David McGregor (Darren McGavin)

Act Two: 1944–1959

lost his State Department job because his wife, Amy (Geraldine Page), had been a member of the Communist party for a few months when she was seventeen, the couple has drifted aimlessly and now manages a shabby inn in Mexico, where David also dabbles in archaeology. But when a pregnant Amy demands that she and David move back to the States, David, increasingly despondent and disheartened, refuses. So Amy goes back without him.

Most reviewers saw that, basically, **Middle of the Night** (2-8-56, ANTA), which Paddy Chayefsky expanded from one of his television plays, was a drab mediocrity—one critic branded it "soapera"—made capital theatre by Edward G. Robinson's quiet yet authoritative performance. Chayefsky, reverting to an expressionistic fad dating back to Robinson's earlier days on the stage, listed the characters in the program as The Manufacturer, The Girl, and so on. But in the actual play, they were given names. Betty Preiss (Gena Rowlands) has come to her mother's apartment to escape an unhappy marriage and has called the office where she works to tell them she inadvertently took with her some important papers. Her boss, Jerry Kingsley, a widower who finds himself increasingly lonely and fatigued, arrives to pick them up. Betty pours out her whole sad story to him, and he impulsively asks her to dinner, then calls himself a jerk for doing so. But a romance soon springs up between the couple, even though she is only twenty-four and he is fifty-three. Betty's mother (June Walker) and Jerry's daughter (Anne Jackson) both oppose the liaison. Only Jerry's son-in-law (Martin Balsam) is sympathetic. For a time Betty tries a reconciliation with her husband, only to have it fall apart. But after she tells Jerry, "What I have with you is fulfillment," Jerry proposes and she accepts. The play ran 477 performances and was the last commercially successful comedy or drama of the season.

For the second time in the season, a vengeful relative of a dead man plots to kill a murderer who looks otherwise to get off scot-free. This time the plotting took place in Emlyn Williams's **Someone Waiting** (2-14-56, Golden), but once again critics wouldn't buy it. Convinced that his son was hanged for a crime the boy did not commit, the dead boy's father (Leo G. Carroll) takes a job as a tutor at the home of his son's best friend (Robert Hardy), who he is convinced is the real killer. It turns out that the friend's father (Howard St. John) is the actual murderer, and the only way the dead boy's father can implicate the man is to allow himself to be murdered. He does so.

The next night the City Center revived *A Streetcar Named Desire* and unleashed a storm of controversy by casting Tallulah Bankhead as Blanche. Played before a "notably epicene" first-night audience, it left critics at loggerheads about the star's interpretation: "she . . . kidded the pants off it" "Miss Bankhead can't quite manage to be the troubled and tremulous nymph whom the author created" "one of the most extraordinarily shattering performances of our time." Playgoers had only two weeks to judge for themselves.

The Ponder Heart (2-16-56, Music Box), Joseph Fields and Jerome Chodorov's "recklessly charming" theatricalization of a whimsical Eudora Welty story, ran eighteen weeks, yet couldn't close in the black. Lovable, eccentric Uncle Daniel Ponder (David Wayne) takes on a child bride, Bonnie Dee (Sarah Marshall), and to delight her fills his home with all manner of modern electrical appliances, even though he has no electricity. However, after Bonnie Dee's weak heart fails her during a terrible storm, a politically ambitious district attorney (Will Geer) accuses Uncle Daniel of murdering the girl. At his trial, Uncle Daniel provides the prosecutor with some unexpected help, such as publicly hailing his opening remarks as "one of the most movin' and beautiful pleas I ever heard to a jury." But when he insists that Bonnie Dee died of Love on realizing she was in his arms, his fellow townsmen are quick to acquit him.

Down at the Phoenix on the 21st, the house raised its curtain on a double bill of Strindberg: *Miss Julie* and *The Stronger*. The bills starred Viveca Lindfors. In the former she played a rich bourgeoise who makes sexual passes at a servant (James Daly) and is given her comeuppance by him. In the latter she played a man's mistress who is lectured to and ultimately humiliated by his wife (Ruth Ford).

Back uptown there was nothing to rejoice about at **Debut** (2-22-56, Holiday), Mary Drayton's stage version of Isabel Dunn's novel *Maria and the Captain*. Maria (Inger Stevens) is a South Carolina tomboy until she meets Wyn Spaulding (Tom Helmore), a Boston writer come down to do research on southern aristocrats. She even decides to glue on a beard before making her debut, but Wyn employs his razor to help make her presentable. Before long she has thrown over her southern beau, Dabney Beauchamp Featherstone III (Charles McDaniel), for Wyn, who turns out to be Winthrop Spaulding IV.

Some lovely Cecil Beaton costumes and settings for an eighteenth-century French château were the most attractive features of Hugh Mills's **Little Glass Clock** (3-26-56, Golden). His rivals order the newlywed Comte de Montfort (Douglas Watson) to arms in hopes of making free with his bride (Eva Gabor), but she gets him to send a substitute, disguise himself as a priest, and baffle her other suitors, who include Louis XV (George Curzon).

Broadway found few takers for Norman Rosten's

adaptation of Joyce Cary's novel **Mister Johnson** (3-29-56, Martin Beck), in which the misfirings of all the attempts of an amiable young African (Earle Hyman) to be like the whites around him lead to his accidentally killing a man while he is drunk. He cannot understand why he should be hanged for the crime.

Come April 3, the Phoenix Theatre ended its season on an up note with a fine revival of Turgenev's *A Month in the Country,* in Emlyn Williams's translation. This story of an older woman falling in love with her child's young tutor featured Uta Hagen and Al Hedison in the roles.

One critic suggested Bill Hoffman's **Affair of Honor** (4-6-56, Barrymore) was an attempt "to combine Bernard Shaw with sex." Whatever it was, it didn't work. After the colonists blow up a Vermont bridge during the Revolution, Major "Mad Dog" Rogers (Dennis King) orders several hostages taken. They will be shot—unless a pretty tavern barmaid (Betsy Palmer), whose brother is one of the hostages, spends the night with the officer. She agrees, but by the next morning she has given him cause to regret his insistence. Among the pseudo-Shavian epigrams were such lines as "He's a right to be a lecher; he's a gentleman" and "Have the good sense to show a little stupidity."

The season's most talked-about and controversial play—no small part of the controversy hinged on its meaning—was Samuel Beckett's **Waiting for Godot** (4-19-56, Golden). Coleman's description of the plot ran, "Gogo [Bert Lahr] and Didi [E. G. Marshall], a pair of Weary Willies, wait hungrily by a roadside for a mysterious Godot to appear. He never does. . . . They encounter a sinister bully [Kurt Kasznar] who drives an overburdened, moronic servant [Alvin Epstein] about with a whip." After admitting bafflement as to what all this signified, Coleman reported that he "kept thinking of those wonderful two-a-dayers, Moss and Frye. At the good old Palace and other such temples of entertainment, they anticipated 'Waiting for Godot' via their inimitable skit, 'How High Is Up?' They took only 15 brief minutes in their quest for sense in nonsense. Beckett takes over two hours." Not all day-after criticism fell in line with Coleman. "Theatregoers . . . cannot ignore it" and "continuously fascinating" were other assessments. Although he is said to have later confessed to not understanding much of what he was speaking, Lahr, one of the theatre's great musical comedy clowns, gave an exceptionally touching, seemingly knowing performance. But Broadway didn't want Beckett's play, so it was withdrawn after fifty-nine performances. In time, its seminal importance in disposing of so many stage conventions was recognized.

But then neither did Broadway want such light-hearted, obvious malarkey as the revival of the 1932 hit *Goodbye Again,* which came into the Helen Hayes on the 24th. It lasted only a single week, despite the presence in its cast of such skilled farceurs as Donald Cook as the famous writer, Hiram Sherman as the imposed-upon husband, Polly Rowles as the eager-to-be-faithless wife, and Tom Poston as the unctuously overbearing attorney.

A new comedy, Alex Gottlieb's **Wake Up, Darling** (5-2-56, Barrymore), fared no better. After his wife (Barbara Britton) wins a role in a new musical comedy about the Civil War, Don Emerson (Barry Nelson), a highly paid perfume-ad writer, discovers he has problems. It seems that the show's creator (Russell Nype), a crew-cut, bespectacled Yalie who calls himself the "poor man's Cole Porter," is a virgin intent on losing his virginity with Emerson's wife. Matters are set to rights by evening's end. Among the supporting players, Kay Medford walked away with honors as a perennially inebriated secretary. Having just sworn, "May the ceiling fall on me if I take another drink," she looks up—and bits of ceiling fall on her.

Off Broadway continued to excel primarily at revivals, and none was more important during the season than the mounting on May 8 at the Circle in the Square of Eugene O'Neill's 1946 opus, *The Iceman Cometh.* Almost single-handedly the production helped resurrect the playwright's fading reputation and propelled director José Quintero and leading man Jason Robards, Jr., to the forefront of their professions.

. . .

José [Benjamin] **Quintero** (b. 1924). A native of Panama, he studied at the University of Southern California. Subsequently, he directed summer stock before calling attention to himself with his sensitive stagings at the Circle in the Square, including the earlier *Summer and Smoke* that brought Geraldine Page to fame.

. . .

Jason Robards, Jr. (b. 1922). Son of a popular film star, the dark, somewhat weather-beaten-looking actor was born in Chicago. He studied at the American Academy of Dramatic Arts and with Uta Hagen prior to making his first professional appearances in the late 1940s.

. . .

Atkinson called Quintero "a remarkably gifted artist" and, lauding Robards's interpretation as better than the original, observed, "Jason Robards, Jr. plays Hickey, the catalyst in the narrative, like an evangelist. His unction, condescension and piety introduce an element of moral affectation that clarifies the perspective of the drama as a whole." In the wake of many similar notices, the play ran 565 performances.

The season ended in disappointment. The curtain rose on Leslie Stevens's **The Lovers** (5-10-56, Martin Beck) to reveal what Kerr labeled and described as "a breath-taking visual image: a peasant with a scythe stands poised on a jagged series of rocks before a vast curved universe that seems to stretch to world's end." What followed was a drama that sharply divided the critics, who considered it everything from "an impressive work of art" to "stuffy and ineffectual." A monk (Hurt Hatfield) is asked to bury some corpses whom his church would deny interment. He is given their history. After a local lord (Darren McGavin) has exercised his *droit du seigneur,* he and the young girl (Joanne Woodward) fall in love. "I felt the pupils of my eyes open," she tells the man. Nonetheless, dismayed by her duplicity toward her new husband (Mario Alcalde), she runs out to the fields and throws herself upon the scythe. Her husband and the lord then battle to their deaths. Hearing the story, the monk decides defiantly to bury the three bodies. An exceptionally costly work to mount and operate, it was closed after just four playings and before playgoers could truly decide what they thought of it.

1956–1957

It was, at best, an uneven season that led to disparate evaluations. In the *Best Plays* Louis Kronenberger slapped it down as "depressingly bad." *Variety* deemed it merely "n.s.g." (read, not so good). The *Times,* in its year-end review, passed up the chance to pass judgment. If there were areas of agreement they were on the growing strength of Off Broadway and the ongoing revival of Eugene O'Neill—a resurrection which gave the season its finest "new" play. At the box office a slow inflation continued. More plays asked and received a $6.90 top, while a $4.60 top became virtually extinct. The combination of a rise in prices and a drop in quality allowed only thirteen novelties and two revivals to run beyond 100 performances, and only seven of these made a profit.

With theatre-folk celebrating the centennial of Shaw's birth, a number of Shavian treats regaled New York. The Phoenix was first off the mark with its mounting of *Saint Joan* on September 11. Siobhan McKenna was Joan. Many critics hailed her as the most vigorous, and believable of all Joans they had ever seen, but a determined minority branded her Joan as little more than a petulant Irish scrubwoman. In three slightly separated engagements, the revival chalked up seventy-seven performances.

The fading, short-lived vogue for readings gave a dying gasp with Sean O'Casey's thinly veiled look at

his own youth in **Pictures in the Hallway** (9-16-56, Playhouse). Aline MacMahon was among the principals.

Uptown at the Jan Hus Auditorium a revival of *Take a Giant Step* opened on the 25th to excellent notices and virtually ran out the season.

John Boruff's **The Loud Red Patrick** (10-3-56, Ambassador) managed to last for ninety-three performances in the face of sharply divided notices. In 1912 Cleveland, Patrick Flannigan (Arthur Kennedy) is a forty-five-year-old widower with four daughters. He professes to be an advanced thinker, going so far as to observe, "We stand at the threshold of a new era of progress when the female will become something more than a mere breeder of the species." He is even liberal enough to hold family councils where everybody has the same number of votes as his or her age. That means he has only to bribe his youngest daughter to have enough votes to carry any motion. But his freethinking is sorely tested when his oldest daughter (Peggy Maurer) wants to marry the scion of the Gas Works, an outfit that Patrick detests. His refusal to consent leads the girl to declare "war," and by evening's end Patrick has surrendered "on all fronts." David Wayne grabbed most of the laughs as Mr. Finnegan, a sponger who balks at working, ostensibly so that he won't have any income to pay as alimony to his ex, and who lives in an alcove in the Flannigan home.

Some stabs at pseudo-poetic prose and odd purple lighting effects couldn't save Norman Vane's **Harbor Lights** (10-4-56, Playhouse). By spouting fraudulent yarns about his own maritime adventures, a divorced man (Robert Alda), who is merely a hand on a tugboat, takes advantage of his court-allowed visits to his young son (Peter Votrian) to try to turn the boy against his stepfather (Paul Langton). Film star Linda Darnell played the boy's mother. The drama ran four performances.

A small idea of how daringly far-reaching Off Broadway could be was offered the same night down on 27th Street at the Davenport Theatre, where a revival of Mary Austin's even more pseudo-poetic look at the hopeless love of an Indian medicine woman, *The Arrow Maker* (2-27-11), was ventured. But the drama had failed forty-five years before, and it failed again now.

Two performances was all that Broadway permitted Scott Michel's **Sixth Finger in a Five Finger Glove** (10-8-56, Longacre). But then the comedy itself was as off-putting as its title. Matt Holly (Jimmie Komack) runs a small-town "swap shop." His naivete helps him outwit those who would trick him, and it turns out he owns the whole burg.

Matters looked up for playgoers with the arrival of William Douglas Home's London hit **The Reluctant**

Debutante (10-10-56, Henry Miller's). A real-life mother and daughter, Adrianne Allen and Anna Massey, played mother and daughter in the comedy. Mrs. Broadbent wants Jane to wed a shakoed guardsman, while the rebellious girl wants to marry a seeming cad. Of course, before long the guardsman is shown to have clay feet, while the supposed cad is actually a high-minded duke. Many of the evening's best laughs came from the sly, throwaway humor of Wilfrid Hyde White's husband and father. Unfortunately, although the comedy ran for 134 performances, its investors were unable to recoup their money.

Too Late the Phalarope (10-11-56, Belasco), taken by Robert Yale Libott from Alan Paton's novel, dealt with an inarticulate, white South African policeman (Barry Sullivan), whose philandering with a black girl (Ellen Holly) not merely violates the law, but infuriates his aged Afrikaner father (Finlay Currie) and plays havoc with his marriage to his cold wife (Laurinda Barrett).

One of Off Broadway's biggest successes during the season was Walt Anderson's **Me, Candido!** (10-15-56, Greenwich Mews). It looked at an aspect of New York City life heretofore largely neglected uptown—the influx of Puerto Ricans. Candido (Jose Perez) is an orphan and a street waif, taken in by a warmhearted couple, the Gomezes. Then bureaucrats enter the picture. The Welfare Department demands Candido be enrolled in school, but the school says he cannot enter until the Gomezes legally adopt him. Next, the Welfare Department claims that the Gomezes' income is too small to allow them to adopt the boy. But all ends happily—happily enough to permit the comedy to run for twenty weeks.

"Crazy-mixed-up" was an expression of the day, and several aisle-sitters thought Paul Nathan's **Double in Hearts** (11-16-58, Golden) exemplified the term. It told how "a crazy-mixed-up television script editor [Billy Redfield], his sensible but growing-impatient estranged wife [Neva Patterson], a stunning and spectacularly neurotic model [Julia Meade] who falls for him, and the compulsive lecher [Laurence Hugo] in whose bachelor apartment he's doing his trauma-dodging and drinking" finally decide which man will pair with which girl.

The season's second Shaw revival was one of his lesser plays, *The Apple Cart,* in which a future English king threatens to abdicate and run for Parliament to teach his ministers democracy. A Theatre Guild offering, it opened at the Plymouth on the 18th. King Magnus was played with great verve and charm by Maurice Evans, but while the revival ran 124 performances, it closed in the red.

London's famed Old Vic came into the Winter Garden on the 23rd for a three-month stand, bringing with it four Shakespeare plays—*Richard II, Romeo and Juliet, Macbeth,* and *Troilus and Cressida.* Paul Rogers, John Neville, Jeremy Brett, Rosemary Harris, and Claire Bloom were among the principals of a troupe deemed still very fine but no longer at its early postwar peak.

London also gave New York Terence Rattigan's **Separate Tables** (10-25-56, Music Box). Two one-act plays were both set in the same slightly frayed seaside hotel. In the first, a frigid, shallow woman (Margaret Leighton) attempts to win back her former spouse (Eric Portman), a drunken, has-been politician who spent time in prison for attempting to murder her. In the second, a spinster (Leighton) approaching middle age persists, over objections by her mother (Phyllis Neilson Terry), in pursuing a "Major" (Portman), even after he is exposed as a misfit non-combatant who has molested women in dark film houses. Whatever the weaknesses in the plays, superb acting by a cast composed mainly of members of the original West End production made for compelling theatre so the bill ran for 332 performances.

F. Hugh Herbert suffered a three-performance dud when he turned Eduardo de Filippo's *Filumena Marturano* into **The Best House in Naples** (10-26-56, Lyceum). Filomena (Katy Jurado), a prostitute, having bamboozled Domenico Soriano (Rino Negri) into making her his mistress, now wheedles him into wedding her. Only then does she tell him about her three sons—one of whom is his. Neither his threats nor his cajolings can make the woman reveal which boy is which.

An all-star revival of Shaw's *Major Barbara* at the Martin Beck on the 30th delighted most critics and ran for 232 performances. (Despite which, like *The Apple Cart,* it closed in the red.) Frog-voiced Glynis Johns made an engaging heroine; director Charles Laughton, waddling "softly about [and] mildly dispensing the author's paradoxical darts," was a memorable Undershaft; Burgess Meredith was Adolphus Cusins; Eli Wallach, the cockney Bill Walker; and Cornelia Otis Skinner, an elegant Lady Britomart.

A single performance dominated the next entry. The entry was **Auntie Mame** (10-31-56, Broadhurst), which Jerome Lawrence and Robert E. Lee derived from Patrick Dennis's best-seller. The performance was that of a film favorite, tall, willowy Rosalind Russell. She played an unconventional, widowed aunt who takes over her orphaned nephew (Jan Handzik as a boy; Robert Higgins as a young man) and gives him an unconventional upbringing while traipsing around the world and allowing herself to be courted. The action ran from 1929 to 1946. "The title part is so long," one critic commented, "so strenuous and requires such range and personality that it's hard to imagine anyone less dynamic and versatile playing it. With Miss Russell, it looks easy. In fact she achieves the magic of making it seem not work at all, but just spontaneous fun." The comedy ran for 639 performances and in 1966 became the hit musical *Mame*.

Terence Rattigan's second offering of the season, **The Sleeping Prince** (11-1-56, Coronet), didn't fare as well as his first, although its superb cast was headed by Michael Redgrave, Barbara Bel Geddes, and Cathleen Nesbitt. It described the brief, fascinating fling the Prince Regent of Carpathia had, while in London for the 1911 coronation, with an American chorus girl. Nesbitt was seen as the eccentric but worldly wise Grand Duchess. In 1963 it was musicalized unsuccessfully by Noel Coward as *The Girl Who Came to Supper*.

Playgoers were wafted from 1911 London to Moscow in the 1860s with Rodney Ackland's translation of Alexander Ostrovsky's **Diary of a Scoundrel** (11-4-56, Phoenix), in which a cynical opportunist (Roddy McDowall) keeps a diary ridiculing the pretensions of the bourgeoisie he works with and, when the diary falls into their hands, finds it has made him a hero.

By general agreement the season's high point was Eugene O'Neill's **Long Day's Journey into Night** (11-7-56, Helen Hayes). The play had been written by the author years before his death and proscribed from public performance until at least a quarter of a century after his funeral, but his greedy, self-serving widow released it prematurely to a thankful world. The *Herald Tribune*'s Walter Kerr hailed it as "a stunning experience," while his colleague, the *Post*'s Richard Watts, Jr., deemed it "magnificent and shattering." Among the minority naysayers was Robert Coleman, who dismissed the drama in the *Mirror* as "over-long Chekhov." Actually, little happens in this glimpse of a single day in the lives of the Tyrone family in 1912. James Tyrone (Fredric March) is a famous actor and tightwad who squandered his talents on the safety of a popular potboiler and his money on bad land investments. His wife, Mary (Florence Eldridge), has taken to drugs, but has recently returned home from a cure. His older son, James junior (Jason Robards, Jr.), is boozy wencher and wastrel. His younger son, Edmund (Bradford Dillman), wants to be a writer. (The family, of course, paralleled O'Neill's own.) But amidst the family's daily accusations and shrivings, Mary quietly takes to drugs again, while Edmund learns that he is consumptive. In searching for why they are the way they are, the Tyrones blame the past for much of their behavior, but when James demands that Mary forget the past, she retorts, "How can I? The past is the present, isn't it? It's the future, too. We all try to lie out of that but life won't let us." And the drama concludes with her recalling her first meeting with James and how she fell instantly in love with him. The cast was superb, especially Robards and March,

the latter's own touch of hamminess exactly right for the elder Tyrone. The nearly four-hour-long play won all the season's major awards and ran for 390 performances.

A revival of *The Teahouse of the August Moon* was mounted for a limited engagement at the City Center, starting on the 8th. A girl, Rosita Diaz, was cast as Sakini. It was followed on the 21st by *The Glass Menagerie*, with Helen Hayes as Amanda. On December 5 *Mr. Roberts* was restored to the stage with Charlton Heston in the lead and Orson Bean as Ensign Pulver.

Child of Fortune (11-13-56, Royale), Guy Bolton's dramatization of Henry James's *Wings of the Dove*, was a twenty-three-performance failure. Pippa Scott played the innocent American heiress who is victimized by some snooty English aristocrats but wreaks vengeance on them from her deathbed.

Robert Alan Aurthur's **A Very Special Baby** (11-14-56, Playhouse) was even less well received, collapsing after a mere five performances. Unlike his brothers, who are flourishing professionals, Joey Casale (Jack Warden) is a thirtyish failure, who lives with his domineering father (Luther Adler) and his older, spinster sister (Sylvia Sidney), a woman also under her father's thumb. His father has kept Joey home by pampering him, insisting he is a very special baby—the youngest in his family, whose mother died giving him birth. But his father's real feelings rush to the surface after Joey begs for some money in order to leave home and to start a small business with his wartime buddy (Jack Klugman). The old man refuses, shouting, "It's your fault I'm alone. . . . You son-of-a-bitch, you killed my wife." Joey heads out on his own. The play was originally slated to star Ezio Pinza, but he was forced to withdraw when struck down by his last illness. With him went the play's heretofore large advance sale.

N. Richard Nash's **The Girls of Summer** (11-19-56, Longacre) centered around a sexually repressed older sister (Shelley Winters) and her more normal younger sibling (Lenka Peterson). The older woman is pursued by a man (Arthur Storch) who is probably a latent homosexual. All hell breaks loose after the younger girl brings home a cocky, Jaguar-driving stranger (Pat Hingle), a construction foreman, who unleashes the older sister's sexual furies. The voguish term "crazy-mixed-up" again emerged in notices to describe both the play and its characters. But audiences were not interested, regardless of some fine acting, particularly by Winters.

Cordelia Drexel Biddle and Kyle Crichton's *My Philadelphia Father*, a best-selling anecdotal history of Mrs. Biddle's socialite father, Anthony Drexel Biddle, was theatricalized by Crichton as **The Happiest Millionaire** (11-20-56, Lyceum). Some of the anecdotes, such as

Biddle's passion for boxing and alligators, were transposed to the stage, while the play itself was tied together by the romance of Cordelia (Diana van der Vlis) and tobacco heir Angier Duke (George Grizzard). The play ran for seven months, primarily on the lure of Hollywood's Walter Pidgeon in the title role. Called "disarming" and "just about ideal" for the part, he was "headstrong, noisy and boastful [but] also a gentleman, and fleetingly humble when something penetrates that athletic exterior of his." Yet despite its run, the play went into the record books as a flop.

Down on East 6th Street, at the now rechristened Shakespeare Workshop, the newly organized or rechristened New York Shakespeare Festival Theatre, with Joe Papp at its head, brought out one of the bard's most rarely offered works, **Titus Andronicus,** on December 2. "A bloody bore" was Brooks Atkinson's curt rejection in the *Times.* He also noted that it was the first professional mounting of the tragedy in New York, and suggested he would not be unhappy if it were the last.

A space ship, filled with glowing and flashing lights, buzzers, all manner of futuristic gadgets, and jet propulsion sound effects, was the setting for Arch Oboler's **Night of the Auk** (12-3-56, Playhouse). The ship's crew (including Claude Rains and Christopher Plummer) are returning from the first manned mission to the moon when they learn that an atomic war has destroyed the earth and so they themselves are doomed. Plagued by "elliptical, bombastic" dialogue, the sci-fi fantasy ran only a single week.

Eric Bentley's translation of Bertolt Brecht's *Der gute Mensch von Sezuan* as **The Good Woman of Setzuan** (12-18-56, Phoenix) garnered divided notices. It told of the troubles besetting a prostitute (Uta Hagen) after she is given money by gods grateful that she alone would offer them shelter when they came to Setzuan seeking to find one good person. She is forced to disguise herself as her hard-hearted male cousin and become an exploitive employer. The play ran three weeks.

Audrey and William Roos's more commercially slanted **Speaking of Murder** (12-19-56, Royale) ran only half again as long. It was set in a dark-paneled, two-story library of a rich man's house. That man, Charles Ashton (Lorne Greene), lost his first wife when she fell to her death from a balcony. Now he is remarried, to a beautiful film star, Connie Barnes (Neva Patterson). What Charles does not know is that his first wife was murdered by her old friend Annabelle Logan (Brenda de Banzie), who has served to raise Charles's children since the killing and who secretly craves to wed Charles. His second marriage has infuriated her. She tells a toping old acquaintance, Mrs. Walworth (Estelle Winwood), who is blackmailing Annabelle with

a letter which could prove her guilt, "When someone takes what belongs to you . . . you do what is necessary to get it back." In this case that means shoving Connie into a soundproof vault, slyly suggesting that Charles's son (Bill Quinn), who resents his stepmother, did it, and stating that at the time she was visiting Mrs. Walworth. But when it is learned that a drunken Mrs. Walworth was accidentally struck and killed by a car several hours before the vault incident, it becomes obvious what Annabelle has been up to. She dashes off.

The title role of Julie Berns and Irving Elman's **Uncle Willie** (12-20-56, Golden) was taken by pint-sized, lugubrious-miened Menasha Skulnik. In the turn-of-the-century Bronx, Uncle Willie contrives to send passage money to a niece (Arline Sax) in Russia so that she can come to America. Never mind that he has never heard of her before. A niece is a niece. He arranges a marriage for her and wangles a mortgage so that she can have a home of her own a few blocks away—"in the country." He also tries to soothe the hurt feelings of an Irish family who take half of the two-family dwelling. When things go wrong, he is branded a meddler, but all winds up satisfactorily. Typical of Willie's yarns was one about sharing a farm with a farmhand. They exchanged places in alternate years since neither could afford to pay the other. "We made a living that way," he recalls. The comedy ran eighteen weeks, not long enough to allow it to pay back investors.

However belatedly, New Yorkers got to see Sean O'Casey's **Purple Dust** (12-28-56, Cherry Lane) even if it meant trudging down to the Village to watch it. Two smug Englishmen (Harry Bannister and Paul Shyre) make fools of themselves trying to become Irish country gentlemen. After a flood wrecks their carefully restored mansion and their mistresses desert them, they decide they would be better off back in truly civilized England. The comedy ran out the season.

Beautiful Faye Emerson brought the old year to a close when she appeared in Howard Richardson and William Berney's **Protective Custody** (12-28-56, Ambassador). The drama had drawn mixed notices and no attendance out of town and so had folded on the road. But the star persuaded some friends to bankroll a New York opening. They underwrote her for only three performances. Dolly Barns is a celebrated syndicated columnist who is kidnapped by the Russians. They hope to brainwash her into writing articles more favorable to them. Her tormentors are a subtle, chilling English renegade (Fritz Weaver) and a more physically brutal ex-Nazi (Thayer David). They snip off her hair and dress her in sackcloth and for a time seem to break her will. But she eventually escapes to tell her tale. Peter Larkin's scenes of a grim former convent were set on two revolving stages, one within the other and turning in opposite directions, which allowed for some dramatic effects.

Robert Sherwood had opened his career with a play about a woman who gives herself to an enemy general in order to deter his invasion. His last play, **Small War on Murray Hill** (1-3-57, Barrymore), was produced posthumously and told a similar story. Only this time, instead of ancient Rome, the setting was Revolutionary New York. General Howe (Leo Genn) tells his associates that the colonists are "a dangerous lot, with inherited criminal instincts and an undeniable gift for homicide. And—worse—they are fuzzy-minded idealists." But the truth is, the suave officer has a soft spot for the rebels. So when Mary Murray (Jan Sterling), who resides in Manhattan on the Heights of Inklenberg and whose husband (Joseph Holland) is an ardent loyalist, offers the general some alcoholic refreshment and a comfortable bed, the general is not averse to dallying, although he realizes that this will allow Putnam and Washington to unite and cost the British dearly. He suggests that the Heights be renamed Murray Hill. An unusual show curtain, displayed before the comedy began and between scene changes, showed a map of the area, with colored arrows indicating ever changing troop movements. Called "small but appealing," "a bit disappointing," and "tired," the comedy was withdrawn after only a week and a half.

A revival of the Jonson-Zweig-Langner *Volpone*, first done in America in 1928, was one of Off Broadway's major delights during the season after it opened at the Rooftop Theatre on the 7th, with Howard da Silva in the title role and Alfred Ryder as Mosca. It ran for 130 performances.

Back uptown, a young playwright, who for years had been considered among the theatre's most promising writers, came sadly a cropper. According to Coleman, Arthur Laurents "mistook pretentiousness for depth, obfuscation for the poetic" in **A Clearing in the Woods** (1-10-57, Belasco). Coming to Oliver Smith's "necromantic forest," Virginia (Kim Stanley), who is running away from her own unhappiness, encounters herself as a child (Barbara Myers), as a young girl (Anne Pearson), and as a younger woman (Joan Lorring). She also meets her father (Onslow Stevens) and the other important men in her life. She is finally made to see that she has demanded an unrealistic perfection from everyone: "Most of us aren't capable of being stars, only of refusing *not* to be. . . . It's not very sweet to accept that you're just another groundling." Most critics found Stanley's nervous, method-school acting "plastic in its flow of images, emotionally alive and searching."

Brilliant comic clowning by Ralph Richardson and Mildred Natwick immeasurably enhanced Lucienne Hill's translation of Jean Anouilh's **Waltz of the Torea-**dors (1-17-57, Coronet). An aging, lecherous general, saddled with a nagging wife who pretends to all manner of illnesses and two daughters whom he describes as "misbegotten frumps," finds his latest would-be conquest (Meriel Forbes) stolen from him by his own secretary (John Stewart), a young man who turns out to be his own illegitimate son.

An all-black *Waiting for Godot*, with a cast including Earle Hyman, Geoffrey Holder, and Rex Ingram, opened at the Barrymore on the 21st and shuttered on the 26th.

The Phoenix brought in Shakespeare's *Measure for Measure* on the 22nd, using the sets, costumes, and many of the players seen the previous summer at Stratford, Connecticut's American Shakespeare Festival Theatre. Among the players were Morris Carnovsky, Nina Foch, Arnold Moss, Hiram Sherman, and Richard Waring. Rouben Ter-Arutunian's costumes were perceived variously as "late-eighteenth or even early nineteenth century," "Franz-Josefian," or "semi-modern"; his settings were basically curtains described as looking like huge Venetian blinds. On February 20th, using much of the same scenery and many of the same players, with Pernell Roberts brought in to play Petruchio, the house presented *The Taming of the Shrew*.

The Hidden River (1-23-57, Playhouse) was Ruth and Augustus Goetz's dramatization of Storm Jameson's novel. Several Resistance fighters had been betrayed and tortured to death during the war. Many suspected Uncle Daniel Monnerie (Dennis King) because he had played cards with and entertained a Nazi general who had been a prewar friend. As a result, Daniel has spent time in prison. Now newly released, the weary old man is shunned by most of his family. But his older nephew, Jean (Robert Preston), discovers the culprit was his own kid brother, Francis (Peter Brandon), who did it to save the Monnerie lands. So Jean orders everyone to confine Francis to the property and shoot him if he attempts to leave. Some splendid acting could not override a critical turndown. The play survived for two months.

Another off-Broadway hit was New York's first professional glimpse of Shaw's late comedy **In Good King Charles's Golden Days** (1-24-57, Downtown). The comedy had the sometimes disguised king debating with such contemporaries as Newton, Fox, Kneller, and, of course, Nell Gwynn. Before it closed it had given 182 performances.

Despite its somewhat off-putting theme, Graham Greene's **The Potting Shed** (1-29-57, Bijou) ran out the season. A spiritually dead James Callifer (Robert Flemyng) is given a new zest for living after it is discovered he has submerged the fact that he had committed suicide as a child and was brought back to life by a priest (Frank Conroy), an uncle who had offered up his own faith to ensure the boy's resurrection. A stellar cast included Sybil Thorndike, Lewis Casson, and Leueen MacGrath.

For the second time in the season an attempt to bring a Henry James novel to the stage failed. Not even "a bold and booming" Tallulah Bankhead could infuse it with sufficient vitality to keep it before the footlights beyond a week and a half. In this case the novel was *The Europeans,* and Randolph Carter's stage version was called **Eugenia** (1-30-57, Ambassador). A baroness and her dilettante brother (Scott Merrill) come to America, seeking security. Although the brother makes a good marriage, the baroness finds nothing of value and sets off to have fun in Venice, but only after putting some stuffy Boston Brahmins in their place.

At the Winter Garden, starting on the same night, a great French acting couple, Jean-Louis Barrault and Madeleine Renaud, and their entourage managed to offer eight attractions (two in double bills) in less than three weeks. Besides their own version of the Jonson-Zweig *Volpone,* they presented **Cristophe Colomb,** *Le Misanthrope,* **Les Nuits de la colère,** combined with **Feu la Mère de Madame, Intermezzo,** and **Le Chien du jardinier** along with **Les Adieux,** this last an assemblage of bits and pieces from other productions not brought over.

Gore Vidal's "droll" **Visit to a Small Planet** (2-7-57, Booth), an extended version of his earlier TV play, begins with Roger Spelding (Philip Coolidge) and his friend, General Tom Powers (Eddie Mayehoff), conversing in the Spelding living room in Manassas, Virginia. Spelding is a famed TV commentator about to make a broadcast proving that UFOs are hoaxes. That would relieve the asinine Powers, since he has just been kicked upstairs at the Pentagon and placed in charge of detecting UFOs. Their chat is interrupted when a UFO lands on the Spelding lawn. Into the Spelding living room dashes a man brandishing a sword and dressed in a Civil War uniform. He is Kreton (Cyril Ritchard), and he is dismayed to learn that he is nearly a hundred years too late for the Battle of Bull Run. He is, he admits, a man from another dimension, a suburb of time. The Earth is his hobby. Human mores amuse him: "You revel in public slaughter: you pay to watch two men hit one another repeatedly, yet you make love secretly, guiltily and with remorse . . . too delicious!" For excitement, he uses his extra-terrestrial powers to try to start another world war. But Spelding's daughter (Sarah Marshall), whom Kreton has taught unworldly powers of concentration, employs them to summon his superiors to take him back to his own planet. He promises next time to return in 1861, only he hopes on that occasion the South will win the war. Mayehoff stole many scenes as a semi-idiotic bore with "nasal

whines, blurts and whinnies," but Ritchard dominated the evening with his "rich and rollicking" performance. The comedy ran just short of one year.

The Tunnel of Love (2-13-57, Royale), Joseph Fields and Peter DeVries's theatricalization of DeVries's novel, ran exactly one year, and did so in the face of some critical warnings that playgoers could find the subject offensive. A suburban couple, Augie and Isolde Poole (Tom Ewell and Nancy Olson), are seemingly unable to have a child of their own, so decide to adopt one. Unfortunately, the girl (Sylvia Dansel) from the adoption agency comes to visit them immediately after Isolde has stormed out in a huff. Augie tells the girl that for the moment his wife has left him to his own devices, and he asks her, "Will you be one of my devices?" She will. In short order she is pregnant, just as Mrs. Poole discovers that she, too, is to have a baby. The expected blow-up follows, but everything is put to rights and Mrs. Poole insists she and Augie give up the suburbs for a saner life in Manhattan.

In a healthier theatrical economy, the 100-performance run of Ronald Alexander's **Holiday for Lovers** (2-14-57, Longacre) would very likely have meant that the show had earned a profit. Not anymore, so the comedy was one of the season's flops. But then most critics agreed with the *World-Telegram and Sun*'s Tom Donnelly, who found it "as stimulating as a whole-wheat lollipop." Bob and Mary Dean (Don Ameche and Carmen Mathews) are packing for their first trip to Europe. When Bob asks Mary if she is excited, she answers, "Everytime I think of it I gasp, like I used to when I first met you." They are taking their younger daughter, Betsy (Sandra Church), with them and plan to visit their older daughter (Ann Flood), who is studying music in France. There they learn that the girl has given up her lessons to wed her instructor's son (Rene Paul). And Betsy soon falls in love with a young American expatriate painter (Thomas Carlin). Even Mary finds herself romantically inclined. Just before leaving for home, she closes the drapes in their suite, places a Do Not Disturb sign on the door, and asks Bob to carry her over the threshold like he once did.

Arnold Schulman's **A Hole in the Head** (2-28-57, Plymouth), a stage version of Schulman's TV play *The Heart Is a Forgotten Hotel,* ran only half again as long as Alexander's comedy, but did wind up in the black. It received divided notices, and critics could not even decide on its genre. Thus Atkinson saluted it as "a tender and humorous drama," while Watts waved it away as "a scattered and rather ramshackle comedy." Sidney (Paul Douglas), an improvident widower, is attempting to hold on to both his failing, rundown Miami Beach hotel and his young son, Ally (Tommy White). His well-heeled brother, Max (David Burns), from whom Sidney hopes to borrow $5000, and his sister-in-law, Sophie (Kay Medford), try to marry off Sidney to a young widow (Lee Grant). When this fails they attempt to take Ally back to New York with them, believing he will receive a better upbringing there. But the boy elects to remain with his father.

Revivals continued to be Off Broadway's forte. On March 5, Pirandello's *Right You Are [If You Think You Are]* was given at the Carl Fisher Hall, with Erik Rhodes in the lead and a young Vincent Gardenia in the cast. **Three Plays by John Millington Synge** (3-6-57, Theatre East) was the name given to a triple bill consisting of *In the Shadow of the Glen*, *The Tinker's Wedding*, and *Riders to the Sea*. Welcomed by the critics, the bill ran out the season, though none of its players went on to future renown.

Good as Gold (3-7-57, Belasco) was John Patrick's dramatization of Alfred Toombs's novel. It was also a four-performance dud. A young scientist with the sticky moniker Benjamin Franklin (Roddy McDowall) discovers that when dirt is mixed with gold it can grow a cabbage big enough to overshadow a Chevrolet or a carrot as large as a guided missile. All sorts of complications ensue after he appeals to Congress to allow him to use the gold in Fort Knox to save the world from hunger. Long-faced Paul Ford played one of his typical pompous blusterers—this time a congressman—while Zero Mostel was seen as a Washington-wise hobo who uses the local jail for his hotel.

Matters were hardly any better at John McLiam's **The Sin of Pat Muldoon** (3-13-57, Cort), which ran a mere five performances. Pat Muldoon (James Barton) renounced his religion following the death of his young son. Afterwards, he blew most of his savings on entertaining a Mexican floozie and then had a heart attack. Now on his deathbed in his California home, he is berated by his shrewish wife (Katherine Squire) and harridan older daughter (Elaine Stritch). But before he dies—unrepentant—he sees to it his younger daughter (Patricia Bosworth) can tie the knot with an amiable Mexican boy (Gerald Sarracini).

Resorting again to Rouben Ter-Arutunian's Venetian-blind curtains and to costumes which critics again termed everything from "pseudo-Edwardian" to "vaguely modern," the Phoenix brought out John Webster's gory *The Duchess of Malfi* on the 19th. Jacqueline Brookes had the title role; Hurd Hatfield and Joseph Wiseman were her vicious brothers; and Pernell Roberts, the treacherous Bosola. More than one critic warned the squeamish to remain home, but said stronger-stomached playgoers might have a ripsnorting time. The play held on for three weeks.

The *Daily News*'s John Chapman spoke for a majority of naysayers when he suggested that Tennessee Williams's **Orpheus Descending** (3-21-57, Martin Beck) "lacks discipline." In 1940 the drama had been called *Battle of Angels* and had been the first Williams work to be given a professional production, but it had folded on the road. The new version was said to represent a substantial rewriting. Val Xavier (Cliff Robertson), a handsome stud wearing a snakeskin jacket and toting a guitar, finds himself stranded in a small southern town after his car goes bad. He takes work at a dry-goods store owned by the dying Jabe Torrance (Crahan Denton) and his Italian wife, "Lady" (Maureen Stapleton). The passionate woman reveals to Val that Jabe had bought her in "a fire sale," after he and his fellow Klansmen had burned down her father's winery and her father had died fighting the blaze. The town's young nymphomaniac (Lois Smith) unsuccessfully attempts to seduce Val. But he takes pity on the unhappy "Lady" and offers her solace instead. Her husband manages to crawl down the stairs and shoot and kill her. Val is lynched and thrown to the dogs who have been heard howling all through the play. Stapleton's "superb performance of the widest variety . . . so skillfully done that there is no evidence of the gear-shifting such a performance demands of a player" and Boris Aronson's "poetic" skeletonized setting of the store and its environs were hugely applauded, but could not inch the drama beyond sixty-eight performances.

Stanley Mann and Roger MacDougall's **Hide and Seek** (4-2-57, Barrymore) was another of the season's one-week duds. It described the problems that crop up after it is believed that a youngster (Peter Lazer) has stolen a radioactive egg from a laboratory where his father (Barry Morse) is working for the British government on a project to create mutations before birth. The incident provokes the father into quitting his job.

Sadly, in 1957 classic French farce was out of vogue in America. As a result, **Hotel Paradiso** (4-11-57, Henry Miller's), Peter Glenville's redaction of Georges Feydeau and Maurice Desvallières's *L'Hôtel du Libre Échange*, struggled for three months, despite a superb cast and staging, before throwing in the towel. To escape his battle-axe wife (Vera Pearce), a henpecked husband (Bert Lahr) takes his neighbor's neglected spouse (Angela Lansbury) to a seedy hotel for a tryst. All manner of people interrupt the couple, including the neglectful husband (John Emery), who is there to exorcise some reputed ghosts. Lahr, of course, was the center of the fun: "Mr. Lahr hurls women to the floor in animal passion, tosses off a bit of a tango, hides delicately and inadequately behind a palm-frond—and each majestic or cowardly attitude is a joy to behold."

A bravura performance by hefty, beady-eyed Walter Slezak may have been the only good reason for seeing Norman Ginsbury's **The First Gentleman** (4-25-57,

Belasco). It depicted scenes from the life of England's Prince Regent—who later became George IV—and his futile attempt to wed his daughter (Inga Swenson) to the not overly bright William of Orange (John Milligan). She prefers Leopold of Saxe-Coburg (Peter Donat) and wins the day. But it costs her her life when she dies after giving birth to a stillborn child (thus setting the path for Victoria to ascend the throne). Slezak stormed about in a top hat and scarlet hunting coat and had fun riding a child's tiny rocking horse.

People had precious little fun in Eugene O'Neill's **A Moon for the Misbegotten** (5-2-57, Bijou). The play was reputed to be the last O'Neill wrote and, like Williams's earlier entry, had been tried out some years before but closed on the road. The action takes place in 1923, eleven years after the occurrences in *Long Day's Journey into Night*. A homely but warm Josie (Wendy Hiller) and her waspish-mouthed Irish father, Phil Hogan (Cyril Cusack), are tenants on the hardscrabble farm owned by the Tyrones. The Tyrones' elder son, James (Franchot Tone), has promised he would not sell the place out from under them. Hogan, knowing James's drunken ways, is not so certain that he will keep his word, so he tries to get Josie to seduce the man. After James stands her up for a date at the ramshackle farmhouse, she seems willing to go along. But then he appears contritely and unburdens himself about the haunting agony of having to escort his mother's body back on a train. He falls asleep in her lap. When he wakes in the morning, both recognize that they cannot go on together. She sends him on his way, and once he is out of sight she remarks compassionately, "May you have your wish and die in your sleep soon, Jim, darling," adding, "May you rest forever in forgiveness and peace." Although Watts suggested that the drama offered "further proof that Eugene O'Neill was one of the titans of the theatre," most of his colleagues disagreed. Atkinson called the play "tired," while Kerr thought "O'Neill seems to have lost all sense of theatre." The drama was withdrawn after sixty-eight performances.

As was usually the case, the season ended with a thud. In this instance it came from Tony Webster's **The Greatest Man Alive!** (5-8-57, Barrymore). Jauntily humming "The Camptown Races," Amos Benedict (Dennis King), a seventy-two-year-old failure, takes a rope from his bureau drawer and sets about to hang himself. He steps off his chair to write a proper suicide note, then moments later climbs down again to correct his spelling. Finally he steps back up on the chair, places his derby hat at a rakish angle, and prepares to die. Naturally, since this is the opening of the comedy, he doesn't. He is interrupted by a young girl (Kathleen Maguire) doing door-to-door research for a food manu-

facturer. In short order the police and the clergy arrive to add their bit to the confusion. In the end, Amos is left contemplating an even showier way of leaving this world—with Fourth of July sparklers, a military band playing on the phonograph, and his neighborhood buddy (Russell Collins) blowing taps on a bugle.

1957–1958

Quantitatively, there was no change between the new season and the last. Depending on whose count you accepted, somewhere between thirty-seven and thirty-nine new plays were offered. However, this year only thirteen slipped past the 100-performance mark, and only eight of these were commercially successful. Yet despite the drop in longer runs, most commentators were excited about the season. The *Times* called it "one of the legitimate theatre's most noteworthy seasons in years," while Louis Kronenberger in the *Best Plays* series praised it as "outstandingly good." Still, he immediately went on to modify his rapture, insisting that two rather than three cheers were sufficient. A look at his selection shows one reason why. Only three of his ten plays were original American works. The remainder were either adaptations or importations. And certainly for many who sat through the season, in retrospect performances often remain more memorable than the plays themselves.

Joe Papp, moving his Shakespearean troupe out to Central Park, presented three offerings, beginning on June 27: *Romeo and Juliet, Two Gentlemen of Verona,* and *Macbeth*. In the last, Colleen Dewhurst made an admirable Lady Macbeth.

On Broadway the season got off to a late start. Thomas W. Phipps's **Four Winds** (9-25-57, Cort) was a short-lived dud. Davina Mars (Ann Todd) is a very spoiled rich girl. She has her own four-engine plane, a yacht, and homes everywhere you can think of. She also has had three husbands who married her for her money. Now she is on the verge of wedding a fourth gold digger (Peter Cookson). An amiable, altruistic young writer (Robert Hardy) takes a liking to her and attempts to set her straight by suggesting she spend some time alone on a Wyoming ranch, far from all her parasites. But she quickly accepts that her ways are too ingrained. Whatever must be, she cannot change.

A couple of entries attempted to resuscitate the moribund vogue for readings. Neither succeeded. First to try was Paul Shyre's adaptation of Sean O'Casey's autobiographical **I Knock at the Door** (9-29-57, Belasco), which looked at the playwright's Dublin boyhood. Aline MacMahon and Staats Cotsworth headed the company of six.

The season's first hit gave Broadway a taste of the dramas being created by Britain's highly ballyhooed coterie of "angry young men." Their premier spokesman at the time was John Osborne, and his work was the appropriately titled **Look Back in Anger** (10-1-57, Lyceum). Jimmy Porter (Kenneth Haigh) is a slovenly, articulately embittered owner of a small candy shop, whose pregnant wife (Mary Ure) must be the audience for most of his tirades. When she has had enough, she leaves him. For a time, an attractive redheaded actress (Vivienne Drummond) takes her place. But Jimmy and his wife have an uneasy reconciliation after she loses her baby. Their Welsh friend, Cliff Lewis (Alan Bates), helps them to get together before he, too, heads off. All of the principals received good notices—Haigh for his impassioned performance, Bates for his quieter one. Only Bates would have much of an American career subsequently.

Miss Lonelyhearts (10-3-57, Music Box) was Howard Teichmann's theatricalization of Nathanael West's novel. A neophyte (Fritz Weaver) from the *Chronicle*'s city room is appointed to write a column of advice for the lovelorn. Although he expresses little real interest in the position, he soon finds he is "afflicted with idealism—the 20th century bubonic plague" and takes a personal interest in those who write to him. He starts preaching that love is the answer to all problems. This prompts him to drop his own girl and begin an affair with one of his correspondents. For his pains, he is shot to death by the woman's furious husband. Weaver's "gentle, understanding" performance won kudos, as did Pat O'Brien's as a blaspheming editor with a long-buried heart of gold. Equally lauded was Jo Mielziner's "ingenious setting . . . a collection of towering, off-angle, semi-cylinders, on which lantern slides project locales in the blink of an eye." But for all its virtues, the production lasted a mere week and a half.

The season's second reading, **A Boy Growing Up** (10-7-57, Longacre), could be seen as either a one-man or a two-man show. For its creator, Emlyn Williams, sat alone onstage in a simple blue suit, reading and acting out bits from the autobiographical stories of the early life of another artist, Dylan Thomas. Although critics praised the reading, the public stayed away. Two weeks and it was gone. But Thomas would be represented again on Broadway a week later.

Down at the Phoenix, a revival of a nineteenth-century favorite, *Mary Stuart*, opened on the 8th to critical plaudits with Irene Worth in the title role and Eva Le Gallienne as Queen Elizabeth. For the occasion Friedrich Schiller's drama was given a new translation by Jean Stock Goldstone and John Reich. It ran for seven weeks.

Molly Kazan's **The Egghead** (10-9-57, Barrymore) ran for less than three. After a blindly idealistic professor (Karl Malden) is questioned by the FBI about a former student, the angered teacher invites the man (Lloyd Richards), a Negro, to speak. The man insists he is not a Communist and tells the professor, "You should spend one day in my skin." But the Negro proves treacherous, for he is still a dedicated Red. The professor's wife (Phyllis Love) exposes him. A contrite professor is forced to apologize, and vows to fight lunatic fringes on both ends of the political spectrum. (Since Kazan's husband, Elia, had recently denounced some of his former Communist buddies, a few critics hinted that there were autobiographical touches in the drama.) Critics divided on whether the play could stand on its own.

Communism and democracy provided the background for the season's next hit, Peter Ustinov's London comedy **Romanoff and Juliet** (10-10-57, Plymouth). When the son (Gerald Sarracini) of the Russian ambassador (Henry Lascoe) to the smallest country in Europe falls in love with the daughter (Elizabeth Allen) of the American ambassador (Fred Clark) there, Cold War animosities rear their ugly heads. The boy is asked to believe that any girl so interested in clothing might be undesirable, while the girl is heard to complain that the boy's refusal to go to a nightclub is suspicious. However, the country's patient, worldly-wise, pince-nezed head of state (Ustinov) sees to it the couple are united at the altar of the Holy Unorthodox Church.

Dylan Thomas's writings were brought to life on Broadway for the second time this season when his radio drama, **Under Milk Wood** (10-15-57, Henry Miller's), was given a full-blown presentation. The diffuse drama, with more than sixty characters (actors took as many as four roles during the evening) was described by one reviewer as "a midnight-to-midnight prowl of a seedy Welsh fishing village," filled with lecherous, loutish, and larcenous inhabitants. The play was dismissed as too uneven and too macabre, so was withdrawn after five weeks.

Herman Wouk's **Nature's Way** (10-16-57, Coronet) did only a mite better, surviving for seven and a half weeks. The *Daily News*'s John Chapman spoke for many when he complained that the play was "never quite sure if it should be a comedy or a farce." Billy Turk (Orson Bean), a young composer with one Broadway smash to his credit, lives with his wife, Maggie (Betsy von Furstenberg), in an apartment which he characterizes as a cross between "early newlywed and late nouveau riche." Actually, he has been wed only four months, although Maggie is six months pregnant.

Maggie subscribes to a doctor (Robert Emhardt) who insists births be done without medication or any other unnatural inducements. When Billy discovers that he owes the government $50,000 in back taxes for which he hasn't the money, he agrees to head off to Venice with his lavenderish librettist (Scott McKay) to work on his new show away from his mother-in-law (Audrey Christie) and other distractions. Rumors that he is cavorting there with a princess bode ill, but he returns to New York to audition for backers, and at the party Maggie goes into labor. Since the doctor is nowhere in sight, a swishy, but knowing, waiter (Joe Silver) delivers the infant—a boy. Beatrice Arthur stole many of the best laughs as a pushy, opportunistic interior decorator, whose brick wall—built to hide a real brick wall—comes crashing down at the party.

Most aisle-sitters gave William Saroyan's **The Cave Dwellers** (10-19-57, Bijou) rave reviews, with Brooks Atkinson calling it in the *Times* "one of the most enchanting stories he has ever told." But the public would not buy it, so it closed after ninety-seven performances. Some homeless people have taken refuge in an abandoned theatre that is slated to be demolished to make way for a housing project. They include The King (Barry Jones), a former clown, The Queen (Eugenie Leontovich), once an actress, and The Duke (Wayne Morris), an ex-boxing champ. They tell themselves they are "of the theatre," but stretch the point to give shelter to an attractive Girl (Susan Harrison), since she long ago had recited the Pledge of Allegiance in public. The Queen informs The Girl that love is the secret to success in the theatre, and The King agrees, stating how much better the world would be if there were more love in it. But he also accepts a more baffling reality: "This is the world, this is us, this is all there is, and we do not understand." Into their midst comes an animal trainer (Gerald Hiken) with his pregnant wife (Vergel Cook) and his trained bear (Ronald Weyand). When the baby is born, The Duke runs off to steal milk for it, and is chased back to his refuge by the milkman's mute assistant (John Alderman). Then The Wrecking Crew Boss (Clifton James) comes to tell them they must leave but, taking pity on them, gives them a long weekend to find new shelter. The Girl, though she had first professed love for The Duke, leaves with the mute. Then the others depart, too, with the hopeful King in their wake.

Monique (10-22-57, Golden) was taken by Dorothy and Michael Blankfort from the same French novel by Pierre Boileau and Thomas Narcejac that had provided the source for the celebrated French film *Diabolique*. It had little of the film's punch. A gun salesman (Denholm Elliott), married to a loveless spouse (Maureen Hurley), is shown a seemingly foolproof method of killing his wife by a sinister doctor (Patricia Jessel). But the wife

appears to return from the dead, driving the man to suicide. Was it a scheme of the two women to be rid of the man?

Far uptown, the Shakespearewrights brought out a vigorous *Julius Caesar* on the 23rd and were rewarded with a run of 114 performances.

One of the most famous of all 1920s murder cases—the Loeb-Leopold affair, in which two wealthy, well-educated young men killed a cousin of one of them for the sheer fun of it—had been made into a popular novel by Meyer Levin and now was dramatized under the same title, **Compulsion** (10-24-57, Ambassador). But whether Levin himself or Robert Thom was responsible for the stage version was open to some dispute. It took nearly fifty actors three and a half hours to reenact the events. Drops and insets against the background of a large ramp allowed for multiple scene changes. Only now the boys were called Judd Steiner (Dean Stockwell) and Artie Strauss (Roddy McDowall), and the famed lawyer who got them off with life sentences, Clarence Darrow, became Jonathan Wilk (Michael Constantine). Largely favorable notices helped the drama play on for 140 performances. Nonetheless, it went down in the records as a commercial failure.

There were few favorable notices for Carson McCullers's **The Square Root of Wonderful** (10-30-57, National). Molly Lovejoy (Anne Baxter) has been twice married to and twice divorced from Philip Lovejoy (William Smithers). He is a selfish, emotionally disturbed writer whose single success came from writing up his mother's memories. Mother (Jean Dixon) herself is no prize package, with even Philip acknowledging that she's "a babbling old horror." Now Molly has met a kindly architect (Philip Abbott), and although her ex demands she and he try a third marriage, she opts for a probably better life with her newfound love.

In the growing economic squeeze in which the theatre was caught, Sam Locke's **Fair Game** (11-2-57, Longacre) ran for more than six months (217 performances) yet closed in the red. True, the critics didn't care for it, except as a vehicle for Sam Levene. Yet many felt Levene made it worthwhile. Thus Frank Aston wrote in the *World-Telegram and Sun*, "Shrugging, rolling his eyes, gesticulating with palms up, roaring or pleading with his tin-lined voice, fighting phones, daring double pneumonia on his double terraces, back-slapping competitors who he hopes will drop dead . . . Mr. Levene makes it all seem at least 10 times funnier than it is." In fact, from the title and the story, Levene's character was probably not meant to be the star part. Susan Hamarlee (Ellen McRae), a young, beautiful divorcée, comes to New York to attend school. Harry Bohlan (Robert Webber), the brother of the woman from whom she is subletting her apartment, takes an immediate liking to her, helps her get a job as a model so that she can support herself, but warns her that if she lets on she is divorced she will be considered fair game. Certainly Harry's boss at Winkler's Frocks, Lou Winkler (Levene), thinks she is. But then he has trouble telling the good girls from the bad—except that the good ones talk dirtier. He tells Susan, "You're NOT selling your body. You're renting your figure." Despite the inducements Lou and others offer, Susan settles for the likable Harry.

Off Broadway continued on its venturesome way, sometimes with success, sometimes not so happily. At the Phyllis Anderson on the 5th, an attempt to reevaluate an earlier triumph, David Belasco's *The Girl of the Golden West,* met with sharp disdain. But two nights later **Clerambard** (11-7-57, Rooftop) was joyously welcomed. Norman Denny and Alvin Sapinsley adapted it from Marcel Aymé's French original. It recounted the frustrating attempts of an irascible, hectoring man (Claude Dauphin), following a visit from the spirit of St. Francis, to lead a Christ-like life. The comedy ran for 194 performances.

Uptown, Broadway did not do quite as well, in one sense, with another translation from the French. **Time Remembered** (11-12-57, Morosco) was Patricia Moyes's anglicization of Jean Anouilh's *Léocadia,* and while it ran for seven months (248 performances), like *Fair Game* it failed to pay back its investors. However, this time most critics were squarely in its corner. Seeing her princely nephew (Richard Burton) moping over the death of a beloved ballerina who was accidentally strangled by her own scarf, a countess (Helen Hayes) recreates on the grounds of her château all the spots at which her nephew had cavorted with the dancer and hires a look-alike milliner (Susan Strasberg) to take the dead girl's place. The youngsters fall in love. Hayes's "portrayal of the sweet and mildly dotty aunt" was "a gem of beguiling humor, gentle and gallant, but still salty and gaily scornful when necessary." Burton's early glowerings and stammerings gave way to a long last-act soliloquy, delivered with "precision and power." Beautiful settings and costumes caught the play's romantic mood to a tee.

Only Noel Coward's personal attraction kept his **Nude with Violin** (11-14-57, Belasco) on the boards for eleven weeks. Playing the part of a butler to a deceased painter, he was made up to look vaguely Oriental. One running gag had the multi-lingualed servant carrying on brief phone conversations in French, German, Spanish, Russian, Chinese, and Yiddish. For all his knowing acting skills, Coward was caught up in a play with little plot and less real wit. It seems the painter was a wag who foisted on a gullible public paintings not his. One of his "masterpieces" was, indeed, painted by the butler's twelve-year-old son. To fill out the booking, Coward also gave a handful of performances of his *Present Laughter.*

Proffering various reasons, critics held strong reservations about Morton Wishengrad's unyielding drama **The Rope Dancers** (11-20-57, Cort), but they all admired the performances. Since the play's principals included Siobhan McKenna, TV's Art Carney, and filmdom's Joan Blondell, audiences supported it for just short of six months (189 performances)—once again not enough to allow the production to close in the black. Margaret Hyland (McKenna) is a resolute, deeply religious woman, who has separated from her glib-tongued, feckless husband, James, and who has just moved into a shabby tenement with her unfortunate daughter, Lizzie (Beverly Lunsford). The girl was born with six fingers on one hand and has since developed St. Vitus's Dance. Margaret, who has blamed the girl's problems on the fact that James was drunk and just returned from a whorehouse when the child was conceived, is a stern mother, insisting, "To work is to pray." When the girl has a fit, a warmhearted new neighbor (Blondell) calls in a local Jewish doctor (Theodore Bikel). He attempts an operation to remove the extra finger, but under such primitive conditions, Lizzie dies. Complaining that strong women like herself have no chance against the James Hylands of the world and finally admitting to her own lustful desires, Margaret is reunited with her husband.

At the Heckscher Theatre on the 26th Joe Papp brought out a *Richard III* with an unknown George C. Scott playing the usurper as a sardonic knave. Scott would come into his own later in the season. In January the troupe brought out *As You Like It.*

On the 27th, when Broadway essayed an English classic, William Wycherley's *The Country Wife,* it did so at so large a theatre—the Adelphi, normally given over to musicals—that several critics, forgetting the large houses in which it initially played, bewailed a loss of intimacy and subtle comic effect. Still, Julie Harris's naively unprincipled Mrs. Pinchwife, Laurence Harvey's dry, virile Horner, and Pamela Brown's glittering Lady Fidget all won hearty applause. But the public came for only five and a half weeks.

Look Homeward, Angel (11-28-57, Barrymore), which Ketti Frings derived from Thomas Wolfe's novel, was hailed by Richard Watts, Jr., in the *Post* as "a rich, beautiful, moving and full-bodied play." Most of his colleagues agreed, so at season's end it was awarded not only the Pulitzer Prize but the New York Drama Critics Circle award as well. It is 1916 in Altamont, North Carolina, where the greedy, manipulative Eliza Gant (Jo Van Fleet) lords it over her family and the guests at her boardinghouse, a rambling frame building with an electric sign above the door that proclaims

"Dixieland." Her much-imposed-upon younger son, Eugene (Anthony Perkins), is a moonstruck, sensitive boy; her sculptor-husband (Hugh Griffith) is a blustering, toping man; while her older son, Ben (Arthur Hill), is dying of consumption. Eugene wants to go to college, but his mother lyingly insists she hasn't the money to send him. However, when Ben dies he leaves Eugene his small bankroll. At the same time, Eugene learns that his calf-love romance with a pretty boarder (Frances Hyland) can come to naught. Telling his mother that he is grateful for all she has done, he itemizes his gratitude, thanking her "for every hour of loneliness I've had here, for every dirty cell you gave me to sleep in, for ten million hours of indifference, and for these two minutes of cheap advice." As she watches helplessly, he stalks out.

Down at the Phoenix, Karel Capek's story of a woman who has learned the way to eternal life, *The Makropoulos Secret,* was presented in Tyrone Guthrie's new version on December 3. Eileen Herlie played the lead. Greeted with disappointing notices, the drama lingered for just one month.

"Wonderfully evocative: warm, troubled and deeply moving" was Walter Kerr's assessment in the *Herald Tribune* of William Inge's **The Dark at the Top of the Stairs** (12-5-57, Music Box). Since most of his fellow critics and their public agreed, the play ran for 468 performances. The Floods are a lower-middle-class family, residing in a small Oklahoma town in the 1920s. Rubin Flood (Pat Hingle) is a harness salesman, in an era when automobiles are destroying the market for harnesses. His wife, Cora (Teresa Wright), is the daughter of a schoolteacher and has married below her station. Because Rubin is away so much she considers herself little better than a widow. Their children are Reenie (Judith Robinson), a teenager, and Sonny (Charles Saari), a ten-year-old who is afraid of the dark. The family's humdrum existence is shaken by three events: Cora's sister, Lottie (Eileen Heckart), comes for dinner and confesses she is frigid; Reenie's date at a dance, a young Jewish boy (Timmy Everett), leaps to his death from a fourteenth-story window after being humiliated by an anti-Semite; and Rubin comes home to announce he has lost his job since his employer is going out of business. The incidents bring about some understanding and compassion, and with them the small hope of a happier life.

Down in the Village, a "blunt, sobering" adaptation of **The Brothers Karamazov** (12-8-57, Gate) garnered kudos for its fidelity and fine acting, so ran for 165 performances.

Aldous Huxley, working in conjunction with Beth Wendel and Alec Coppel, dramatized his own novel **The Genius and the Goddess** (12-10-57, Henry Miller's). A preoccupied, older Nobel Prize winner (Alan Webb) invites an attractive young colleague (Michael Tolan) to stay with him and his much younger, beautiful wife (Nancy Kelly). When the wife's mother dies and the scientist becomes dangerously ill, the distraught wife is driven into the younger man's arms. But after the scientist recovers, his contrite colleague insists on leaving and accepting a post in a distant country. Some fine acting could not rescue a tedious play.

Sol Stein's **A Shadow of My Enemy** (12-11-57, ANTA) was the second flop in a row to run less than a week. It was also the season's second play to be a thinly veiled recounting of a famous trial. In this case it was the trial of Alger Hiss, who had been accused by Whittaker Chambers of hiding his Communist past. For the play, Hiss was called Horace Smith (Gene Raymond), while Chambers became Augustus Randall (Ed Begley). The most interesting aspect of the production was Donald Oenslager's set designs, which one critic described as "a waffle iron stage—a circular affair which does not turn but moves up and down like the top of a waffle cooker" and another saw as "a vast double disc out of which an entire courtroom can be lowered into view."

Critics were embarrassed for Shirley Booth when she appeared in one of the year's worst plays, Michael Plant and Dennis Webb's **Miss Isobel** (12-26-57, Royale). Yet for all the savage pans the play received, Booth was able to keep it going for nearly seven weeks. She played the part of a gray-haired, seventy-year-old lady who lives in a rundown mansion in San Francisco and takes in boarders. But something snaps when she finds her shrewish spinster daughter (Nancy Marchand) rifling her room. In several steps she becomes younger and younger, turning back in her own mind into the bride from Australia that she had been half a century before and finally into a baby-talking little girl. Before she is institutionalized she gives away the money her daughter had been seeking to a boarder's young son (Peter Lazer). The romance of the boy's widowed mother (Kathleen Maguire) and a blinded Korean war veteran (Robert Duke) provided a subplot.

Two double bills, both off Broadway, began the new year. **Garden District** (1-7-58, York) consisted of two Tennessee Williams one-acters, **Something Unspoken** and **Suddenly Last Summer.** The former was the lesser of the pair and told of two southern ladies living together but unable to face reality. The latter dealt with a once beautiful, now aging woman (Hortense Alden) who tries to force her niece (Anne Meacham) to have a lobotomy to make her disclaim the horrible story of the death of the woman's son. But truth serum reveals the story is true. The boy was a homosexual who used beautiful women to lure handsome men. When his mother became too old to attract men, he traveled with his cousin. But on one exotic island, his lusts got out of hand and he was killed and cannibalized by some native youths. The program ran out the season.

Downtown many playgoers received their first exposure to Eugene Ionesco with a double bill of **The Chairs** and **The Lesson** (1-9-58, Phoenix). In *The Chairs* a couple (Joan Plowright and Eli Wallach), both in their nineties, keep bringing additional chairs onstage so that a multitude of imaginary guests can listen to an important lecture. But after they themselves sneak off, the speaker (Kelton Garwood) arrives and speaks gibberish. In the other play a professor (Max Adrian) stabs to death an unresponsive student (Plowright) just as he has those who came before her. He is whetting his knife for his next pupil as she (Plowright) appears.

The new year's first big hit on Broadway was William Gibson's **Two for the Seesaw** (1-16-58, Booth). It was still a relative rarity for the time, a two-character play, but most critics concurred with the *Post*'s Robert Coleman, who saw it not as a money-saving stunt but as "a whale of a hit, a bittersweet joy ride." Since his wife has started divorce proceedings back in Omaha, Jerry Ryan (Henry Fonda) has come to New York to try his fortunes as a lawyer there. But he finds himself lonely and adrift in the big city, so he telephones a young girl for a date. She proves to be a warmhearted but aggressively bohemian Jewish girl from the Bronx, Gittel Mosca (Anne Bancroft). A somewhat awkward romance ensues. At one point she complains, "You know what you got too much of? A lack of self-confidence." Although they clearly like each other, in the end their disparate backgrounds and disparate interests send them on their separate ways. Fonda was hailed for his expected understated performance, which in this instance was seen as a perfect foil for the lively, lovely Bancroft: "With tousled black hair, a slouching walk and a mouth that matches her hands in expressiveness, she is the most engaging gamin to light up a stage in many a semester." The play enjoyed 750 performances.

Off Broadway, Maxim Gorky's **The Courageous One** (1-20-57, Greenwich Mews), in an adaptation by Miriam Goldina, won critical applause and ran nearly 100 performances. It told how a family, led by a younger, adopted son, rebels against the domination of a tryannical father.

On the 21st France's brilliant Marcel Marceau came into the City Center for a month-long stand with a new bill of pantomimes.

The other side of the world, Australia, also contributed to the season. Ray Lawler's **Summer of the 17th Doll** (1-22-58) had been a huge hit in its homeland and in London, but New York wanted none of it. Two sugarcane workers, having finished their seven-month

stint up north, return to a Melbourne suburb for their five-month annual layoff. This will be the seventeenth year they have done so, and, as always, one of the men, Roo (Kenneth Warren), brings his lady friend a Kewpie doll. But Roo then learns that next year he will be replaced in the fields by a younger man. His buddy, Barney (Lawler), finds that his own lady friend has run off and married. The men confront the inevitability of a different life as they grow older.

Samuel Beckett's **Endgame** (1-28-58, Cherry Lane) delighted enough lovers of unconventional theatre to run for 104 performances in the Village. In his dingy, gloomy room a blind man (Lester Rawlins), wearing a hard hat and raggy clothes, spews out bitter harangues to his long-suffering slave (Alvin Epstein) and his two white-faced parents (P. J. Kelly and Nydia Westman), both of whom are confined in ashcans.

The lives of seven career girls sharing a large, cheap apartment was the subject of Mel Tolkin and Lucille Kallen's **Maybe Tuesday** (1-29-58, Playhouse). The girls ran the customary gamut. One, who never appears, is always either on the phone or in her bubble bath. Another (Myra Carter) thrives on salacious readings. A third (Brett Somers) is a cynic. A fourth (Zohra Lambert) is accident-prone. But the principal girl is Katy (Patricia Smith), who is pregnant but doesn't seem to realize it. Happily, her nice young man (Richard Derr) eventually leads her to the altar. Stealing the show was frumpy Alice Ghostley as a married woman who descends on the girls to coax them into marriages, but has the opposite effect when she tells them of hastily defrosted meals, sore backs from housework, and being late for the theatre, though "you can always find someone to tell you what happened in the first act." New Yorkers had only five chances to miss this one's first act.

Even the *Journal-American*'s frequently cranky John McClain had to concede that Dore Schary's **Sunrise at Campobello** (1-30-58, Cort) was "an enormously moving and gratifying experience." He predicted it would last for many terms. Actually, it ran for over a year, compiling 558 performances. In August of 1921 Franklin Delano Roosevelt (Ralph Bellamy) complains of back pains following a swim at the family's summer retreat on Campobello Island. In short order he is totally paralyzed. But he is a fighter and after a few days can move his torso and arms. Only his legs remain useless. Fearing fire, he teaches himself to crawl to an exit. He is removed to his home in New York City, where his wife, Eleanor (Mary Fickett), and his loyal adviser, Louis Howe (Henry Jones), understand his desire to continue in politics and are ready to assist him. After all, as he tells Eleanor, "invalidism—even temporary—is very lonely." His domineering mother (Anne Seymour), who hates politics and politicians, wants him to retire. But the others win out. His chance comes when Al Smith (Alan Bunce) asks him to put Smith's name in nomination during the 1924 Democratic convention. At the convention he carefully gauges the distance between his seat and the podium, then struggles to his feet and to the podium, and smiles and waves at the cheering crowd. Despite what seemed like some pompous speeches, Bellamy would not be "lured into a rhetorical trap." Citing such small touches as Bellamy's rocketing "his wheelchair away from his stamp collection to pick up something he has dropped," Kerr concluded, "The performance, in the sensitivity of its balance between hero-worship and simple honesty, is superb."

The Infernal Machine (2-3-58, Phoenix) was Alfred Bermel's adaptation of Jean Cocteau's French original. It was Cocteau's modern retelling of the Oedipus legend. The New York production featured a film in which Claude Dauphin offered background and other comments. Oedipus (John Kerr) is revealed as a determined, callous go-getter who tricks the Sphinx (Joan McCracken) into giving up her secret, then deserts her and runs headlong into the embrace of a youth-hungry Jocasta (June Havoc). But when the truth comes out he is forced to blind himself in penance. American actors were deemed not up to the artificial high style Cocteau required, so the drama was withdrawn after five weeks.

Many critics suggested the best thing about **Winesburg, Ohio** (2-5-58, National), taken by Christopher Sergel from Sherwood Anderson's book, was Oliver Smith's "whopper of a set," a stark, constructivist masterpiece which "filled the stage with a huge three-story representation of the hotel interior, with a summer house at one side and a glimpse of the town at the other." The story reminded several reviewers of *Look Homeward, Angel,* with the attitude of the mother reversed. She (Dorothy McGuire), too, runs a small-town hostelry, but she is willing to make large personal sacrifices so that her young son (Ben Piazza) can head off to Chicago and try his hand at writing. What seemed moving between the covers did not seem at all gripping onstage. The play ran a week and a half.

Ira Levin's **Interlock** (2-6-58, ANTA) had to be content with a half-week's run after some of the season's harshest reviews. Although Mrs. Price (Celeste Holm) is confined to a wheelchair, her malice is unrestrained. When her immigrant housekeeper (Rosemary Harris) introduces her handsome fiancé (Maximilian Schell), a baker's assistant who longs to be a classical pianist, into Mrs. Price's Gramercy Park mansion, Mrs. Price takes advantage of a lovers' spat to separate the couple and keep the young man for herself.

Critics didn't think much more highly of the next play, John Osborne's second of the season, **The Enter-**

tainer (2-12-58, Royale), "a grubby, rambling" affair picturing the ineluctable decline of a seedy, immoral, third-rate music-hall performer. But they granted that it made for a memorable evening in the theatre thanks to a gaudy performance by Laurence Olivier: "He sings in the nasal tones that are usual in the lower ranks of the profession; he tells blue jokes in a cheap accent. . . . His shoulders swivel with a kind of spurious bravado. Wearing his hat at a flashy angle, swinging his stick smartly, Mr. Olivier is the very model of the worn-out, untalented music-hall performer." Joan Plowright and Brenda de Banzie were cast as the man's hapless daughter and wife. The play enjoyed a profitable limited engagement of twelve weeks.

Max Wilk's **Cloud 7** (2-14-58, Golden) lingered around for only a week and a half. In that time it recounted two days in the life of a young executive who has decided on an exceedingly early retirement. Preferring to build furniture in his basement, Newton Reece (Ralph Meeker) throws up his position superintending the dehydration and packaging of cookie mixes at United Foods. A sheaf of bills quickly forces him to return to work at a better salary. But when he remains dissatisfied, his wife (Martha Scott) agrees to struggle along with him at home for better or worse. Beady-eyed John McGiver walked off with the best laughs and notices as Reece's boss, a man who sees everything as a wicked plot concocted by his huge rival, General Foods.

The last new Maxwell Anderson show to be given a Broadway hearing (albeit one more new play would be mounted off Broadway next season) was a joint theatricalization with Brendan Gill of Gill's novel **The Day the Money Stopped** (2-20-58, Belasco). A playboy son (Richard Basehart), all but cut out of his father's will, confronts his self-consciously respectable lawyer-brother (Kevin McCarthy), "a cold shower and daily chapel man" during his years at Yale, and his more humane sister (Mildred Natwick) with some possibly unsavory incidents in their father's past—such as driving their mother to suicide and siring a child out of wedlock. The confrontation results in something of an understanding. The play survived a mere four performances.

Arthur Bartley (Burt Brinckerhoff), the young hero of James Leo Herlihy and William Noble's **Blue Denim** (2-27-58), has trouble relating to his rigid father (Chester Morris), a retired army officer, and his somewhat light-headed mother (June Walker), so is quick to find solace in the arms of pretty Janet Willard (Carol Lynley). But he becomes frightened when he learns that she is pregnant. His hustling friend, Ernie Lacey (Warren Berlinger), forges Arthur's father's signature to a check that allows Janet to have an abortion. After the truth emerges, it produces some brief fireworks but, more important, lets Arthur and his parents learn how to accept each other more openly and confidently. The play deftly caught the teenage lingo of the day. When Ernie first wants to get rid of Janet, whom he sees as interfering with his and Arthur's card game, he barks, "Look, Snow White—eat a poison apple, will you?" (One critic heard that last part as "will yuh," an interesting observation since much of the dialogue, was, in fact written to convey the teenagers' slovenly pronunciations.) Reviewers also applauded Peter Larkin's ingenious set, which managed to squeeze comfortably onstage the Bartleys' living room, basement, and backyard. But the aisle-sitters disagreed on the merits of the work itself, seeing it as "a mere piece of theatricality—and a somewhat distasteful one" or "a warm and fulfilling evening." The comedy ran twenty-one weeks, yet closed still in the red.

Off Broadway continued to be willing to explore bygone American theatre, even long-neglected failures. It met with remarkable success when it took a chance on Edwin Justus Mayer's *Children of Darkness* (1-7-30), which had failed to please playgoers initially despite laudatory reviews. The Circle in the Square brought it out for reconsideration on the 28th. This look at how a mercenary jailkeeper provides special considerations to certain prisoners for a properly high fee gave major pushes to the careers of Colleen Dewhurst as the jailer's lascivious daughter and George C. Scott as the icily wry titled prisoner. The revival scored 301 performances.

When Ann Williams (Mary Healy) catches her husband, David (Peter Lind Hayes), a chemistry professor at Columbia, kissing one of his students, she rushes to book a plane for Reno. In desperation, David calls in his buddy, Michael Haney (Ray Walston), a TV writer, and begs him to find a way to make Ann change her mind. That's the situation at the start of Norman Krasna's **Who Was That Lady I Saw You With?** (3-3-58, Martin Beck). Michael's brainstorm is to have the two of them claim they are secret special agents for the FBI and that the girl was a foreign spy. Before long real FBI agents are sucked into the plot, as are real foreign spies. The latter, who have learned of David's false claim, kidnap him and take him to a cellar at the Empire State Building. Made to believe he is in a submarine, he pulls levers and turns knobs, hoping to scuttle the vessel. He nearly destroys the building before the genuine agents rush in to his and its rescue. Ann is forgiving, especially as David has bought her a necklace of cultured pearls—"As against uncultured pearls, which say 'ain't.' " Coleman spoke for most of his fellow reviewers when he called the comedy "just the entertainment tonic the doctor ordered for Spring." With the baby-faced Healy and his gorgeous wife, Mary, who were popular radio and TV comics, the production ran

six months—only to close without fully reimbursing its investors.

At the Martinique Theatre, just off Herald Square, a revival of Arthur Miller's *The Crucible* won excited notices and ran for 571 performances.

The Phoenix followed with a revival of *Two Gentlemen of Verona*, which raised its curtain on the 18th. This rather stately mounting from the Canadian Stratford Festival received mixed notices but held on for a month.

So did Arnold Moss's two-and-a-half-hour condensation of Shaw's nine-hour-long play cycle, *Back to Methuselah*, in which Shaw argued the virtues of longevity. The Theatre Guild, which had presented the whole shebang back in the twenties, produced the shortened revival at the Ambassador on the 26th. Moss himself, Tyrone Power, Faye Emerson, dancer Valerie Bettis, Richard Easton, and Arthur Treacher had the principal roles.

The Phoenix closed its season, at least as far as plays done in English were concerned, with Donald Harron's translation of Heinrich von Kleist's *The Broken Jug* on April 1. Harron reset this story of a judge who is trying a man for breaking a woman's favorite jug, but who turns out to be the culprit himself, in 1812 Canada. Like its Shakespearean companion, it was a mounting initially offered at Canada's Stratford Festival. Subsequently, the house presented several bills of Molière plays as performed by Le Théâtre du Nouveau Monde.

Broadway took the title of John G. Fullers's **Love Me Little** (4-15-58, Helen Hayes) to heart, so the comedy lasted only one week. A young girl (Susan Kohner), whose father (Donald Cook) writes sexy novels, decides to learn about sex for herself. She almost succumbs to some wolfish boys, but in the end, along with her father, concludes it is better to be the pursuer than the pursued.

To celebrate Israel's tenth anniversary, Katharine Cornell produced Christopher Fry's **The firstborn** (4-30-58, Coronet), which looked at the struggles Moses (Anthony Quayle) endured before deciding to lead his people to a promised land. Cornell, who assumed the part of Pharaoh's sister, was praised for her charm and regal aspect, but won relatively scant attention. Quayle's Moses grabbed acting honors. In the face of divided notices for the play itself, the production ran five weeks.

An elaborate retelling of *Jane Eyre*, which came into the Belasco on May 1, fared only a bit better, eking out a six-and-a-half-week stand. It was offered and allegedly written by a wealthy dabbler in the arts, Huntington Hartford. Its Victorian story was given an expensive Victorian-style mounting that included a spectacular fire scene. Eric Portman made a fine Rochester, and Blanche Yurka an excellent Mrs. Fairfax, but Jan Brooks was deemed a lackluster Jane.

For once, a season did not end on a down note. The theatrical year's last entry allowed the Lunts to make their farewell appearance in the first play of incontestable merit that they had offered in a distressingly long while. The play was Maurice Valency's translation of Friedrich Duerrenmatt's **The Visit** (5-5-58, Lunt-Fontanne), and it was presented at the old Globe theatre, a large musical comedy house redecorated and renamed for the occasion. A musical comedy top of $8.05 was asked and gotten, so that although the drama ran only 189 performances, it ended up as a commercial success. But then money and what it can do were the evening's theme. In Duerrenmatt's story an old lady, now very rich, returns to her Swiss hometown, where she offers the sleepy village and its inhabitants a stupendous fortune of a billion marks on one condition—that they kill the man who years ago betrayed her after making her pregnant. He is the man everyone expects to be the town's next mayor, but the villagers' greed allows them to hound him to his death. Although Lunt received considerable pre-opening publicity—such as describing his debate with himself as to how many pebbles he should remove from his shoe in one scene (he decided on three)—Fontanne received the more detailed, glowing notices. Kerr wrote: "The regal, tight-lipped smile is familiar. What is new is almost unspoken, an inexplicable hatred that seems to eat itself alive and thrive on nourishment as Miss Fontanne listens glassily to every plea that might save Mr. Lunt, as she languidly exhales snowdrifts of cigar-smoke while listening to a foolish rhapsody, as she fixes her eyes on a raised rifle and coolly, imperiously talks it and its owner down. The malice is alive, implacable even when it is invisible, a source of enormous, chillingly felt, strength. This is as much mesmerism as acting." (As part of their subsequent farewell tour, the Lunts returned in the play for a two-week stand at the City Center in March of 1960.)

1958–1959

Variety and the *Times* agreed that thirty-seven new plays were offered on Broadway during the season—essentially the same figure as the two prior years. But the daily noted the startling fact that, for the first time, a rising Off Broadway surpassed the uptown total. As to quality, there were some differences of opinion, with the lofty Louis Kronenberger, as editor of *Best Plays,* lamenting the paucity of "the dramatic high voltage of something new, fresh, vibrant." Still, as it almost always did, Broadway offered lots to please all but the most hypercritical. Clearly, the public thought so. Even though producers began cautiously testing a $7.50 top, no fewer than ten Broadway plays ran for more than six months, albeit two of these, reflecting the theatre's swelling economic strains, closed in the red.

The high summer months brought in nothing but a return of *Auntie Mame,* this time with Sylvia Sydney in the lead. She lingered at the City Center for three weeks starting on August 11.

The raging popularity of television quiz shows and the scandals beginning to erupt about them gave fodder to Broadway playwrights no less than twice during the season. Although most critics found Phoebe Ephron's **Howie** (9-17-58, 46th St.) pleasant, they regretted it wasn't pleasant enough. So it lasted a mere five performances. A couple of critics saw hints of George Kelly's *The Show-Off* in it. To his beleaguered in-laws (Leon Ames and Peggy Conklin), Howie Dickerson (Albert Salmi) is an unemployed, unemployable know-it-all—the sort of man only a wife (Patricia Bosworth) could love. "Are we too old to run away from home?" the in-laws ask each other. But when he becomes a contestant on *Dollars for Scholars,* Howie's heretofore infuriating knowledge lands him in the big time until he himself points out a wrong answer that was overlooked and spurns a $15,000 prize. A friendly FBI agent (Conrad Fowkes) brings about a happy ending.

Off Broadway's first hit of the season was James Forsyth's **Heloise** (9-24-58, Gate). It told the well-known tragedy of Heloise (Mitzi Hoag) and Abelard (Eugene Miles). Young Abelard has become one of the most famous teachers in medieval Paris, but then he falls in love with his beautiful pupil, the niece of the fussy, mincing Canon Fulbert (Sol Serlin). Learning that she has had a baby, the angered canon orders the mother and child exiled and has Abelard castrated. Heloise retreats into a nunnery. Hailed as a compassionate, well-written recounting of the tale, the drama ran for seven months.

Back on Broadway, a second five-performance dud, N. Richard Nash's **Handful of Fire** (10-1-58, Martin Beck), also had some good points, the critics agreed. When Manuel (James Daly), the corrupt gambling-house owner in a small Mexican town, discovers that Maria (Joan Copeland), an innocent girl whom he would make his mistress over the protestations of the bordello queen (Kay Medford) who loves him, is herself falling in love with a filthy little peon, Pepe (Roddy McDowall), who photographs tourists on his burro in front of the gambling house, he orders the burro shot, the camera wrecked, and Pepe roughed up. A sympathetic Maria washes Pepe's bloody face in the horse trough. She assures him the horses will never mind. Pepe decides to become a tough, outgangstering Manuel. His attempts are not very successful, but he and Maria reach an understanding. The cast and the play's better moments won applause, as did Jo Mielziner's single, impressionistic setting, "suggesting a stageful of steps."

The next night brought in what for many was the season's most noteworthy success, Eugene O'Neill's **A Touch of the Poet** (10-2-58, Helen Hayes). Brooks Atkinson began his review in the *Times,* "Given Eugene O'Neill and a cast of superb actors, the effect on the stage is electric." In the late 1820s, Cornelius Melody (Eric Portman) keeps an inn near Boston. He is a tyrannical, often drunk Irishman, living off memories of his past importance. As a young soldier he had fought alongside Wellington at Waterloo and apparently had risen to the rank of major. He dominates his submissive, loving wife, Nora (Helen Hayes), and his more forthright, aggressive daughter, Sara (Kim Stanley). Melody considers his Yankee neighbors beneath contempt, so after Sara is spurned by the son of a rich New Englander, he sets out to avenge the slight. Instead, he is beaten and humiliated. Returning home, he severs his last link with the past by shooting his beloved old mare. "The Major's passin' to his eternal rest has set me free to jine the Democrats," he tells his wife and daughter, "and I'll vote for Andy Jackson, the friend av the commen men like me, God bless him." There were numerous complaints about Portman's careless enunciation, but otherwise he and the rest of the cast received glowing notices. Hayes's "shrunken, shabby biddy" was particularly admired, as was Betty Field's depiction of a haughty American aristocrat. The drama chalked up 284 playings.

According to some notices, Chekhov's **Ivanov** (10-7-58, Renata) had never before been given a professional performance in New York. An off-Broadway production changed that. But this saga of a charming scoundrel (Paul Stevens), whose misbehavior finally leads to his suicide, so entertained the critics that the public subsequently supported the play for 183 performances.

Prolonged drunk acts are tricky business, but Tom Poston's brilliant handling of one helped Abram S. Ginnes and Ira Wallach's **Drink to Me Only** (10-8-58, 54th St.) struggle along for seventy-seven performances. He played Miles Pringle, whose law firm has him drink two quarts of whiskey in twelve hours to prove that their playboy client (Paul Hartman) still had a few of his wits about him after he himself did so and then shot his latest wife in her rear. Miles's handling of his liquor wins him the law case and a partnership in the firm.

One of the season's biggest hits was David Merrick's sumptuous mounting of **The World of Suzie Wong** (10-14-58, Broadhurst), which Paul Osborn took from Richard Mason's novel. Against Jo Mielziner's "daz-

zling blue-red landscape . . . knife-edged Oriental panels drip from the heavens, side panels slip silkily away to reveal drenched umbrellas battering their way through a rainstorm, a kaleidoscope of enormous painted butterflies, baskets of geese, scarlet rickshaws and bobbing lanterns is eternally ready to spin its gaudy way across the Broadhurst stage." In Hong Kong, Richard Lomax (William Shatner), a young artist, is not discouraged when he discovers that Susie Wong (France Nuyen), a pretty girl he has come to like, is a prostitute. Although Susie is willing enough to talk about her trade and continue to ply it, Richard prefers to paint her and reform her. He is unmoved when Kay Fletcher (Sarah Marshall) would lure him away to a more respectable life. Critics lambasted the banal dialogue ("Why are you telling me all this?") and the simplistic story, but allowed the public would enjoy it. The public did, for 508 performances.

Jean Vilar's Théâtre National Populaire, which included the screen idol Gerard Philipe in its roster, came into the Broadway on the same evening for a three-week engagement, offering five French classics: *Lorenzaccio, Le Triomphe de l'amour, Marie Tudor, Don Juan,* and *Le Cid.* Notices were laudatory and attendance gratifying.

Suzie Wong attracted a much larger public than did Howard Teichmann's **The Girls in 509** (10-15-58, Belasco), which lingered for only 117 performances after being gently knocked by the critics. Noting that "our family has looked down on his for generations," Aunt Hetty (Peggy Wood) and her spinsterish niece, Mimsy (Imogene Coca), had fled to the seclusion of an elegant hotel suite after learning of Roosevelt's first election. A quarter of a century later the hotel has become seedy and is about to be demolished. The girls are its last tenants. They are disillusioned when they learn that the Republicans are now as liberal as the Democrats. Adding to their woes, Aunt Hetty has long believed that she is broke. But when some stocks she has plastered on their walls turn out to be worth a fortune, the ladies decide to face the world again.

The acting was the redeeming feature in T. S. Eliot's **The Family Reunion** (10-20-58, Phoenix) A young man, who is haunted by the notion that he may have brought about his wife's death, comes home to a family reunion only to realize that his mother is as haunted and disturbed by her past as he is about his. Fritz Weaver was praised for his delineation of the young man, but oldtimers Florence Reed and Lillian Gish won still more striking encomiums as the ruthless matriarch and an aunt.

The public disagreed with a majority of critics who felt Harry Kurnitz's **Once More, with Feeling** (10-21-

58, National) "fails to meet its potential," so it did good enough business to run out the season. At the urgings of his harassed manager (Walter Matthau), Dolly Fabian (Arlene Francis) agrees to be reunited with Victor Fabian (Joseph Cotten), a temperamental conductor whose outlandish tantrums have relegated him to small-time orchestras. The reunion is rocky at first, but as experienced playgoers could have guessed from the start, everything ends harmoniously. For many, Matthau won comic honors, constantly ruing that he had rejected the chance to manage Leonard Bernstein and forever bringing down on his own head such curses as "May I manage a Wagnerian opera company and may I have to feed them at my own expense."

Read today, Samuel Taylor and Cornelia Otis Skinner's **The Pleasure of His Company** (10-22-58, Longacre) seems hardly much funnier than Kurnitz's play, until one recalls the virtually perfect playing of its original cast. On the eve of his daughter Jessica's wedding, Biddeford "Pogo" Poole (Cyril Ritchard) returns after a fifteen-year absence, during which he has had three wives ("I'm not very retentive, am I?") and won fame as a globe-trotting playboy. In the interval, Jessica (Dolores Hart) has been raised by her mother Katherine (Skinner), her stepfather, Jim Dougherty (Walter Abel), and her crusty grandfather (Charles Ruggles). Her betrothed (George Peppard) has persuaded her to move their honeymoon from Paris to Hawaii, so he can attend a cattle auction there, and has run off from a party in order to doctor an ailing prize bull. What with Pogo's manifest charms and gifts of persuasion, it doesn't take much for him to convince Jessica to delay the wedding for a year and join him on his international hops. The comedy kept playgoers laughing for 474 performances.

Television quiz shows came to the fore again in Norman Barasch and Carroll Moore's **Make a Million** (10-23-58, Playhouse). Sid Gray, the very unhappy producer of a popular quiz show, learns it may be canceled since his prize contestant, a southern hillbilly (Anne Wedgeworth) with a flawless memory for most facts, is becoming visibly pregnant but is unmarried. The only fact she can recall about the soldier with whom she spent a night in a hotel room is that his first name was John. With help from a Pentagon general (Don Wilson), the soldier (Conrad Jenis) is located. Sid tries to have him stage a fake suicide, but that goes comically awry, so the brash, cocky John finally consents to wed the girl. In one of the evening's biggest laughs he spots a rare begonia which Sid has been lovingly nurturing for eight years and snaps it off for a boutonniere. But most of the laughs came from the comedy's star, Sam Levene, who "meets each new

thrust with a desperate shrug, a skyward roll of his eyes, an unbelieving scowl, and the most eloquent and hopeless hands in show business." The play ran for more than nine months without recovering its costs.

Maxwell Anderson ended his career on a down note—off Broadway. His **The Golden Six** (10-25-58, York) looked at the attempts of Augustus Caesar's six grandsons to ascend the throne after his death. The mad Caligula (Roger Evan Boxill) wins the race, watched from a distance by the more humane, horrified Claudius (Alvin Epstein). "Not up to the level of Mr. Anderson's most memorable dramas" was the critical verdict.

Slapped with some of the season's worst notices, **Patate** (10-28-58, Henry Miller's) made no attempt at a run. Irwin Shaw's translation of Marcel Achard's Paris hit closed after one week. Tom Ewell was seen as an eccentric, unsuccessful inventor who is always borrowing funds from a childhood buddy (Lee Bowman), now grown rich and contemptuous of his onetime playmate. Then the inventor discovers that the man would seduce his daughter. He confronts him with the letters he has found, but the boulevardier's patently insincere threat to kill himself melts the inventor's resolve.

Like several other of the season's hit comedies, Leslie Stevens's **The Marriage-Go-Round** (10-29-58, Plymouth) does not read as delightfully as memory recalls it. Again, its stars no doubt glossed over its failings. In this case the stars were two screen favorites, Charles Boyer and Claudette Colbert, assisted by luscious, curvaceous Julie Newmar. The play starts with Paul Delville, a professor of cultural anthropology, and his wife, the dean of women, each at a podium on one or another side of the stage, lecturing on modern sexual mores. Both use the same example, the time a beautiful Swedish girl came into the Delville home and asked Paul to father her child. The wife's jealousy and concern prompt her to take up with another professor (Edmon Ryan). But for all the circling of the turntable at center stage, little happens. The wife does not run off with the other man, and, when the wife sneeringly asks the Swede if her husband flunked his test, the husband barks, "I did not flunk! I did not even take the exam!" The comedy ran just over a year.

Two other fine players, Hume Cronyn and Jessica Tandy, could do little for **The Man in the Dog Suit** (10-30-58, Coronet), which Albert Beich and William H. Wright theatricalized from an Edwin Corle novel. Oliver Walling is a milquetoast who has married into a family of go-getters. Then, when he and his wife are slated to attend a costume ball as Columbine and Harlequin, he is mistakenly sent a fierce dog outfit. The disguise emboldens him, so he thereafter insists on wearing the costume around the house and even to work at the bank, where it gives him enough nerve to turn down a loan request from his overextended brother-in-law. Finally, he persuades his wife to follow him to Oregon and to lead a quiet life in a woodland retreat. For many, Carmen Mathews performed the remarkable feat of nearly stealing the show from Cronyn with a brilliant scene as his tipsy sister-in-law.

John Osborne and Anthony Creighton's **Epitaph for George Dillon** (11-4-58, Golden) was another short-lived flop. George (Robert Stephens) is a scoundrel quick to take advantage of kindly people. He is also a mediocre playwright, not above compromising his writings to achieve some middling success in the hinterlands. Soon enough he is brought around to reciting his own epitaph, a confession of his true worthlessness. An attempt to revive the play after its first closing led to a second unsuccessful stand.

There was no second chance for Speed Lankin's **Comes a Day** (11-6-58, Ambassador) which starred Judith Anderson as an aggressive mother determined to marry her daughter (Diana van der Vlis) to a rich man and not to the attractive, modest boy (Brandon de Wilde) the girl loves. But the rich man proves to be a demented sadist, which allows the girl to run off with her sweetheart and relegates the mother to an unhappy life with her failure of a husband (Arthur O'Connell). For once, Anderson found the show stolen from her—by George C. Scott's playing of the psychopath. He made his first entrance sucking a lime and later beheaded the pet bird of the girl's brother. When the stresses became too much for him, he pulled out a knife, confessed to killing his own pet dog, and lay writhing helplessly on the floor.

The first of the season's two modern retellings of the Hamlet story appeared off Broadway. Bernard Kops's **The Hamlet of Stepney Green** (11-13-58, Cricket) was set in London's heavily Jewish East End. Hamlet became David Levy (Dino Narizanno), and his father, Sam (Michael Gorrin), a herring merchant. But this time the ghost of the murdered man is not vindictive. Rather he helps David and Chava (Blanche Marvin) wed and reconciles the young man to his mother and new stepfather. Despite comments by some baffled reviewers the play ran twenty-one weeks, continuing long after its uptown counterpart had folded.

Divided notices greeted the Actors' Studio's revival of Sean O'Casey's look at Dublin during the 1920 uprising, *The Shadow of a Gunman*, at the Bijou on the 20th. The cast included William Smithers and Susan Strasberg.

A second off-Broadway drama to garner mixed notices yet still compile a respectable run (125 performances) was Barrie Stavis's rather thirtyish bit of agit-prop, **The Man Who Never Died** (11-21-59, Jan Hus), which harked back to the teens to look at the biased trial and possibly unjust execution of the famed Wobblie leader Joe Hill (Mark Gordon). At one point in the proceedings cast members ran up and down the aisles carrying empty, battered beer buckets and begging playgoers for nickels and dimes to help underwrite Hill's defense.

Harking back even further, Milton Geiger's **Edwin Booth** (11-24-58, 46th St.) attempted to chronicle the life of America's most famous nineteenth-century tragedian, with one of the nation's leading contemporary players, José Ferrer, in the title role. The famous *Tribune* critic William Winter (Lorne Greene) served as narrator, starting with a very young Booth (Stephen Franken) carefully tending his unruly, drunken actor-father (Ian Keith), stopping to watch Booth's triumphs, his response to the horror of Lincoln's assassination by his brother (Richard Waring), and moving finally to his last days. Settings were more suggestive than complete, and many felt the performances, even Ferrer's, much the same—never capturing anywhere near the full man.

The second modern-day Hamlet to appear in short order was Tony Burgess (John Kerr). In Elmer Rice's **Cue for Passion** (11-25-58, Henry Miller's), he returns from a stint in the Orient to learn that his father was killed in a puzzling automobile accident and that his mother (Diana Wynyard) has hastily married a longtime friend. As in Kops's retelling, most things turn out for the better. Tony's bullet merely grazes old Doc Gessler [read Polonius] (Russell Gaige), and Lucy [read Ophelia] (Joanna Brown) does not go mad and die. Tony's mother advises him to take a trip until he can calm his nerves, and he consents to do so. Some critics, such as Richard Watts, Jr., of the *Post*, saw the drama as "a striking play"; others, among them the *Daily Mirror*'s Robert Coleman, dismissed it as "a high-falutin', windy reworking of the Shakespeare masterpiece." Theatregoers sided with the latter, so the play lasted only five weeks.

One of Off Broadway's hits during the season was the production of Brendan Behan's **The Quare Fellow** (11-27-58, Circle in the Square), a loosely plotted, somewhat polemical look at how prisoners and guards react to a forthcoming execution. Done on a bare stage, with a rear wall bearing the warning "Silence," it nonetheless made for a powerful evening in the theatre, so ran for sixteen weeks.

Matters did not turn out any better for Daphne Bau (Janice Rule) than they had for Tony Burgess. The pregnant, well-to-do heroine of Michael V. Gazzo's **The Night Circus** (12-2-58, Golden) flees to the seedy Jolly Roger Bar to escape marriage with the stuffy young executive who is the father of her baby. She takes up with a tough merchant seaman (Ben Gazzara) and has an impassioned fling with him, only to be deserted by him when he realizes that in the long run they are incompatible. Since her father (Shepperd Strudwick) suffers a fatal heart attack on discovering what she has done, Daphne finds herself alone in the world. Both Gazzara and Rule received the sort of notices that in healthier times might have granted the drama a run, but the play itself was slammed and folded after a single week.

Another brilliant performance helped a somewhat more attractive play run for twenty-five weeks, not long enough, in its case, to pay back investors. **The Disenchanted** (12-3-58, Coronet) was Budd Schulberg and Harvey Breit's dramatization of Schulberg's best-seller and was suggested by the life of F. Scott Fitzgerald. Only now he was called Manley Halliday (Jason Robards, Jr.). His once glittering career behind him, Halliday has reluctantly accepted a large fee to write the screenplay for *Love on Ice* in conjunction with a Halliday-worshipping tyro, Shep Stearns (George Grizzard). Yet inspiration will not come. Taking again to the bottle, Halliday relives his halcyon days and sometimes knife-edged moments with his strange wife, Jere (Rosemary Harris). The boozing proves too much and he dies, but not before leaving a note for his young partner warning, "A second chance—that was our delusion. A first chance—that's all we have." Robards was lauded for his "flawless" portrayal of "a sensitive man who is slowly falling to pieces."

Back in 1926, a revival of John Ford's Caroline tragedy *'Tis Pity She's a Whore* was hooted off the stage as "England's dirtiest play." But when it was brought back at the Orpheum on the 5th—still advertised somewhat prudishly as *'Tis Pity She's a . . .* — this saga of incest between a brother and sister was generally received with more understanding and compiled 204 performances at its off-Broadway berth.

Like *The Disenchanted*, S. N. Behrman's diffuse **The Cold Wind and the Warm** (12-8-58, Morosco) received mostly glowing notices, had a passable run of fifteen weeks, and went down in the record books as a commercial failure. Behrman derived the play from his thinly disguised chronicle of his own youth, *The Worcester Account*. The Jewish community in Worcester is very Jewish indeed, with its Jewish love of culture, its Jewish outlook on life, and its Jewish speech mannerisms. There's Ida (Maureen Stapleton), the matchmaker, always ready to assure clients, "You'll get!" There's the not very prosperous Dr. Nightingale (Vincent Gardenia), whose first love is his oboe. And there's the youthful Tobey (Timmy Everett), a would-be musician and composer, taken under the wing of the philosophic and kindly Willie (Eli Wallach), who is, as

Tobey recalls, "always preoccupied with mystery—the mystery of life—the mystery of death," and whom Tobey considers the most life-enhancing person he has ever met. But Willie's philosophy and life-giving have their limits. When he is spurned by the trampish widow (Carol Grace) he adores, he rejects an offer of marriage from the sweet, compassionate Leah (Suzanne Pleshette) and commits suicide.

On the 9th London's famed Old Vic began a five-week stand at the Broadway, offering three Shakespeare plays: *Twelfth Night, Hamlet,* and *Henry V.* Among the players were Barbara Jefford, Judi Dench, Joss Ackland, and Laurence Harvey.

For the second time in the season Fritz Weaver won garlands for a performance in a play the public found difficult. This time it was for his playing of the degenerate priest who knows he should renounce his post but finds himself trapped, in Denis Cannan and Pierre Bost's adaptation of Graham Greene's **The Power and the Glory** (12-10-58, Phoenix).

The season's Pulitzer Prize went to Archibald MacLeish's blank-verse drama **J.B.** (12-11-58, ANTA). Inspired by the Book of Job and set in Boris Aronson's somber, billowing circus tent, it spotlighted J.B. (Pat Hingle), a wealthy businessman who seemingly lacks nothing in life. Strolling through the great traveling circus that is the world, he comes to the attention of Mr. Zuss (Raymond Massey), a downtrodden balloon seller, and Nickles (Christopher Plummer), a sardonic popcorn vendor. After Nickles assumes the Satanmask and Zuss the Godmask, the pair confront J.B. His blessings are taken from him one by one—his money lost, his children killed, his body diseased, his wife deserting him. But when he refuses to condemn God, his wounds are healed. He concludes, "We *are*—and that is all our answer./ We are, and what we are can suffer . . . / But . . . what suffers, loves." Critics were not blind to the drama's limitations, but Walter Kerr, writing in the *Herald Tribune,* observed, "If they keep the evening at some remove from wholly touching drama, they do nothing to rob it of its fascination as sheer theatre." The play ran for 364 performances.

Although Alec Coppel's **The Gazebo** (12-12-58, Lyceum), taken from his and Mary Coppel's short story, delighted many aisle-sitters and ran 218 performances, it closed in the red. Elliott Nash (Walter Slezak) is a mystery writer, who admits his profession allows him to enjoy some "delicious fantasies," including killing off his friends and enemies in print. But when he believes his wife (Jayne Meadows) is being blackmailed, he invites the blackmailer to his home, shoots him, and buries the body beneath the foundations of a gazebo under construction. However, since his house has been sold and the new owners do not want the gazebo, his crime looks to be exposed. In fact, the corpse is dug up. But it develops that Elliott's shot missed and the man died of a heart attack, so Elliott gets off scot-free.

John Gielgud brought in his one-man show **Ages of Man** (12-28-58, 46th St.) for a five-week engagement. It consisted of readings from Shakespeare related to youth, manhood, and old age.

The old year ended with the arrival of Eleanor and Leo Bayer's **Third Best Sport** (12-30-58, Ambassador), which had been touring successfully for many months and held on tenaciously in New York for ten weeks in the face of some of the year's most thumbs-down notices. No doubt the appeal of its star, Celeste Holm, and the Theatre Guild's still reasonably healthy subscription list helped it hang around. According to the Bayers, conventions are America's third favorite sport—after sex and baseball. Following her marriage to a rising executive (Andrew Duggan), Helen Sayre is informed that her life must center around assisting her husband to climb in the company and to abet the company itself in all its projects. But after being made to don a nurse's uniform and minister to drunks at a convention, and following some harsh words with other company wives, she convinces her husband to devote only forty hours a week to his work and spend the rest of the time as a family man, at home, where she will stay.

Two ongoing, off-Broadway Shakespearean groups added some zest to very early 1959. At their new digs at the Players' Theatre on January 2, the Shakespeare-wrights offered a noisy, jet-propelled *King Lear*. Perhaps more satisfyingly, at the Heckscher on the 13th, Joseph Papp presented *Antony and Cleopatra* with George C. Scott as a "noble" if "tongue clicking and facial twitching" warrior and Colleen Dewhurst as a "voluptuous, fiery, viperish and regal" queen.

The same evening the soon-to-be-controversial Living Theatre presented three Wiliam Carlos Williams one-acters under the covering title **Many Loves.** Judith Malina was starred in all three plays, first as a slut attempting to get rid of one lover and take on another, then as a prowling lesbian, and finally as an unloving young mother. The bill caught on and ran out the season.

Rashomon (1-27-59, Music Box), the celebrated Japanese film, was whipped into theatrical form by Fay and Michael Kanin. Once again the story told of a Samurai who is murdered after, apparently, his wife has been attacked by a brigand. At a court, four disparate versions of the incident are given: one by the brigand (Rod Steiger), one by the wife (Claire Bloom), one by the ghost of the murdered man (Noel Williams), and the other by a frightened woodcutter (Akim Tamiroff), who happened to be passing by. Beautifully

mounted by Oliver Messel—"a crumbling mass of wall, a jungle gaining depth because of a turntable, a rain storm, a sun burst"—the drama remained for eighteen weeks, but closed at a loss.

The large-cast, multi-scened **Tall Story** (1-29-59, Belasco), which Howard Lindsay and Russel Crouse took from Howard Nemerov's novel *The Homecoming Game,* ran only for 108 performances, but reportedly wound up in the black. Many critics agreed it suffered from some sluggish exposition but had lively and funny second and third acts. Ray Blent (Robert Elston), whom one faculty member has described as a "juvenile deliquescent," is the superstar of Custer College's basketball team. The refusal of his beloved June (Nina Wilcox) to marry him until he can support her properly drives him to accept money to throw the big game. So that he cannot play, he purposely flunks two major exams. But then he blurts out the truth and attempts to return the cash. His avuncular physics professor (Marc Connelly) and his absurdly high-minded ethics professor (Hans Conried) are both pressured into giving him token re-exams while the game is in progress. Naturally he passes and all ends happily. Lindsay and Crouse had fun twitting both sides of college life. Thus the coach (Mason Adams) dreams of a college where there is no faculty, since teachers spend too much time on education. He is not surprised that students are mixed up. Conversely, the lofty ethics prof complains, "I've been at the Faculty Club, an organization composed entirely of gentlemen who have lost their faculties."

Since William Faulkner had dramatized his own novel **Requiem for a Nun** (1-30-59, Golden)—according to some in conjunction with leading lady Ruth Ford—it received respectful, if sharply divided, notices. Thus Frank Aston of the *World-Telegram and Sun* concluded, "It proves how harsh, raw and stunning the mature theatre can be," while in the *Daily News* John Chapman insisted that the play "is so serious about itself that it may impress many people. But not me." A wild southern belle (Ford) had dabbled in prostitution before making a satisfactory marriage. Her devoted colored maid (Bertice Reading) had also once been a prostitute. The maid kills one of the belle's young children and hopes the killing will help her bring to light the two women's sordid pasts and let them atone for their sins. Although the belle does reveal her own history in pleading with the governor (House Jameson) to spare the maid, her pleas are in vain. The maid resigns herself to her fate, while the belle recognizes that, unable to believe in forgiveness, she and everyone about her are doomed. Once again, the Theatre Guild's subscription list allowed the play to survive for five weeks, but most playgoers preferred their Faulkner between hardcovers, if they preferred him at all.

Aided by the fine acting of mostly unknown performers, a revival of Arthur Miller's version of Ibsen's *An Enemy of the People* came to Off Broadway at the Actors Theatre and settled in for a season-long run.

Some equally fine acting uptown could not propel Norman Corwin's **The Rivalry** (2-7-59, Bijou) beyond ten weeks. With Nancy Kelly, as Mrs. Douglas, serving as narrator, the evening recreated the famed Lincoln-Douglas debates. Martin Gabel made a finicky yet compassionate Douglas; Richard Boone, a warm, wise, cliché-free Lincoln. But playgoers apparently had had their surfeit of debates, however theatrical the best might be.

Nor were they interested in the Lizzie Borden story, particularly after most critics gave Reginald Lawrence's **The Legend of Lizzie** (2-9-59, 54th St.) forty whacks. Anne Meacham was seen as a highly neurotic, frustrated Lizzie, who is almost surely guilty but is acquitted on the testimony of friendly neighbors. A startling, multi-leveled setting by one Ballou depicted the Bordens' cluttered home, the streets of Fall River, and the courthouse. Two performances and the drama was gone.

On the other hand, thanks to capital performances by its two stars, Leonard Spigelgass's "splendidly cornfed comedy" **A Majority of One** (2-16-59, Shubert) ran for 556 performances. Mrs. Jacoby (Gertrude Berg) is an aging Brooklyn widow, who has never forgiven the Japanese for the death of her son in the war. But when her diplomat son-in-law (Michael Tolan) is assigned to Japan, she agrees to accompany him and her daughter (Ina Balin) to his post. On shipboard, she is rude to a polite Japanese gentleman, Koichi Asano (Cedric Hardwicke), who would be kind to her. Learning of the reason for her resentment, he finds a way to let her know that his own sailor son and his own daughter, a nurse at Hiroshima, did not survive the war either. A friendship blooms—Asano even entertains Mrs. Jacoby at an elaborate Oriental dinner in his home—until it appears to stand in the way of her son-in-law's diplomatic mission. She returns home, but Asano, being an important businessman, manages to wangle a U.N. post in New York, where he promises to continue his courtship. Berg won applause for her customary playing of a warmhearted, New York-accented Jewish matron, while Hardwicke surprised many with his convincing portrayal of an Oriental.

Down at the Phoenix on the 24th a revival of George Farquhar's *The Beaux' Stratagem,* in which two gay blades stoop to conquer, featured June Havoc as Mrs. Sullen and won mixed notices.

There was little interest in Kieran Tunney and John Synge's Irish drama **God and Kate Murphy** (2-26-59, 54th St.)—known in its homeland as *A Priest in the Family.* (Synge was the nephew of the more famous playwright.) Kate (Fay Compton) had promised God to make her next-born son a priest if God helped her find the money to buy a pub. She kept the promise with disastrous results, for her older son (Mike Kellin), who had wanted to become a priest, was forced to abandon his calling and sank into alcoholism, while her younger boy (Larry Hagman) was made to enter the Church against his will. Both men denounce her.

Nor was New York delighted with **Look After Lulu** (3-3-59, Henry Miller's), which Noel Coward took from Georges Feydeau's *Occupe-toi d'Amélie.* It recounted the adventures of an engaging cocotte (Tammy Grimes) while her lover is away on military maneuvers. Besides the pencil-thin, squeaky-voiced Grimes, the cast included Roddy McDowall as the lover's friend, assigned to look after the girl, Kurt Kasznar as a pompous, libidinous prince, and Polly Rowles as a middle-aged duchess on the prowl for young cavaliers. To make assurance of success doubly sure, Cyril Ritchard directed and Cecil Beaton designed the gaudy period settings and costumes. But nothing is ever sure in the theatre, so the farce closed after five weeks.

Two smash hits followed. The first was Tennessee Williams's **Sweet Bird of Youth** (3-10-59, Martin Beck). Under the name of Princess Pazmezoglu [sometimes listed as Kosmonoplis], the alcoholic, drug-addicted, fading screen star Alexandra Del Lago (Geraldine Page) comes to a small Gulf Coast town with her handsome gigolo, Chance Wayne (Paul Newman). Wayne had grown up in the town but had fled after giving the political boss's daughter a venereal disease. A vengeful Boss Finley (Sidney Blackmer) has never forgotten. When Alexandra discovers that her success in her latest film suggests she is about to make a major comeback, she deserts Chance, telling him, "You've gone past something you couldn't afford to go past; your time, your youth, you've passed it. It's all you had, and you've had it." Accepting the validity of the pronouncement, Chance abandons the idea of running after her, and resigns himself to waiting for the Boss's men to come to castrate him. Page, who heretofore had played largely mousey, soft-spoken women, startled some with her stentorian, commanding interpretation. Elia Kazan directed, and Jo Mielziner designed the scenery, which included a giant upstage screen that showed pictures of Boss Finley rousing his cronies. Kerr noted that "Mr. Williams' newest play is a succession of fuses, deliberately—and for the most part magnificently—lighted." Greeted with so many similar notices, the drama ran for 375 performances.

Aided by equally welcoming notices—"a lovely play," "most illuminating," "a moving and impressive drama"—and at season's end by the New York Drama Critics Circle Award, Lorraine Hansberry's **A Raisin**

in the Sun (3-11-59, Barrymore) ran even longer—530 performances. Lena Younger (Claudia McNeil) hopes to use the $10,000 she will receive from her late husband's life insurance policy to move her large, three-generation family out of the black ghetto. But her son, Walter (Sidney Poitier), appropriates much of the money and invests it in a liquor store, hoping to make a quick killing. Before long, however, his partner absconds with the funds, leaving the family shattered. A white man (John Fiedler) approaches Walter, representing the white neighbors they would have had, and offers to pay Walter to drop his plans to move. A bitter Walter tells his family, "There ain't nothing but taking in the world and he who takes most is smartest." But Lena and the rest of her brood insist he show some pride. He finally agrees to reject the offer. The family will move and hope for the best. In 1973 the play was musicalized as *Raisin*.

The season's only single-performance dud was Sigmund Miller's **Masquerade** (3-16-59, Golden). Thanks to her rearing by a highly warped mother (Glenda Farrell), Amy Grenville (Cloris Leachman) can bring no real passion or love to her marriage to her doctor-husband (Mark Richman). She would commit suicide after a frustrated attempt to have an affair with her husband's brother (Gene Lyons), but her still loving husband sets out to teach her how to live a more normal, happier life.

Pearl S. Buck's **A Desert Incident** (3-24-59, Golden) received even more severe notices than Miller's play had. Indeed, several critics insisted it marked the season's nadir. But probably because of Buck's name, the drama eked out almost a full week's run. It dealt with scientists working on a super-secret project labeled "Pilgrim." In their desert enclave, where sexual desires seem to override scientific curiosity, the Polish wife (Sylvia Daneel) of an American scientist (Shepperd Strudwick), who is determined the research will be devoted to war-like applications, falls in love with the man's colleague, a British pacifist (Paul Roebling), who opposes exploring military uses. In the end, the American is apparently brought around to the Englishman's way of thinking.

Off Broadway, Hal Holbrook found a decades-long meal ticket when he painted wrinkles on his face, donned a white wig and mustache, and read from America's favorite humorist in **Mark Twain Tonight!** (4-6-59, 41st St.).

Postwar Japanese-American relations had been treated lightly and successfully some weeks back. Now a look at a wartime meeting of two enemy soldiers found few takers. Shimon Wincelberg's **Kataki** (4-9-59, Ambassador) had only two characters—the two soldiers. A young American, Alvin (Ben Piazza), parachutes to safety, landing on a desolate islet in the Pacific. He finds a lone Japanese soldier, Kimura (Sessue Hayakawa), already there. At first their natural hostilities manifest themselves, but the men quickly recognize there is no point in trying to kill one another. Alvin even employs his limited supply of sulfa drugs to heal Kimura's horrible leg wound. In short order they become friends, and one of the few words that Kimura learns is "frendu." But when American forces land on the island, Alvin rushes off, shouting to them that he is a friend, and leaving Kimura behind to commit hari-kari. Although Hayakawa had almost no lines, while Piazza had to conduct a running monologue, most critics felt Hayakawa came away with acting honors.

The season ended with **Triple Play** (4-15-59, Playhouse), a bill of actually four one-acters, starring Hume Cronyn and Jessica Tandy. Many critics saw Tennessee Williams's **Portrait of a Madonna** as an early study for *Streetcar*. An aging spinster goes gaga after fantasizing that a former suitor has returned to rape her. Chekhov's *Some Comments on the Harmful Effects of Tobacco* found a henpecked man professing to deliver a lecture against smoking but actually rattling on about the tyranny of his wife. Sean O'Casey's *A Pound on Demand* depicted the attempts of a pair of soused bucks (Biff McGuire played the second man) to withdraw money from their postal savings. In this one Tandy portrayed a prissy lady endeavoring quietly to write a letter while the men make their disturbance. O'Casey's **Bedtime Story** described how a prudish, straitlaced bachelor falls into the clutches of a roguish trollop. The evening proved no exception to the rule that Broadway playgoers have little time for bills of one-acters.

ACT THREE
1959–1969

DECLINE

1959–1960

Long before the season's first play arrived, the new theatrical year got off on the wrong foot. On June 2, Actors' Equity called the first general strike since 1919. Although the walkout ended on the 12th, it set a troubling tone for the rest of the year. At the season's other end, statisticians could not agree on numbers. *Variety* saw the count of new plays rise by one to thirty-eight; the *Times* said it dropped to thirty-four. And there was little celebration of quality. In fact, in sharp contrast with last season, only four plays surpassed the 200-performance mark, while only five others slipped beyond the 100-performance figure. Time and again, critics suggested the acting was far better than the play. When prizes were announced, the Pulitzer committee bestowed its award on a musical (*Fiorello!*), only the third occasion it saw fit to do that.

Off Broadway remained reasonably active all summer, and produced one of its more memorable dramas early on. Jack Gelber's **The Connection** (7-15-59, Living Theatre) was done as a play (or, more accurately, movie shooting) within a play. Leach (Warren Finnerty) and his fellow drug addicts are holed up in his "pad" waiting for Cowboy (Carl Lee) to bring them a fresh supply of narcotics. Cowboy arrives with innocent Sister Salvation (Barbara Winchester) who has helped him elude the police in the naive hope that she can reform the men. She can't. Much like actors in last season's *The Man Who Never Died,* cast members walked through the aisles panhandling, and, foreshadowing many plays of the 1960s, they shouted all manner of obscenities. Actors were also shown receiving their fix while seated on a toilet. A jazz combo provided atmospheric music. Hailed by Kenneth Tynan in the *New Yorker* as "the most exciting new play that off-Broadway has produced since the war," the drama compiled 711 performances.

During the fifties Shakespeare was common fare at summer festivals and elsewhere. About the time most festivals were shuttering for the year, Broadway was offered one especially memorable mounting. Done with almost nineteenth-century opulence, the revival of *Much Ado About Nothing* at the Lunt-Fontanne on September 17 starred John Gielgud and Margaret Leighton. By a notable coincidence, several major critics employed the identical description of their performances—"quicksilver." Among supporting players George Rose received a big hand for his droll Dogberry.

Off Broadway also presented a worthy reconsideration. On the 21st at the 4th Street, David Ross restored Chekhov's *The Three Sisters,* which ran out the season.

Given the many laudatory notices it received from the most influential critics—"lively, interesting, colorful showmanship," "extraordinarily interesting"—Jerome Lawrence and Robert E. Lee's **The Gang's All Here** (10-1-59, Ambassador) should have been a hit. It wasn't, running for a modest 132 playings and closing at a loss. Just as they had in 1927 with *Revelry,* playgoers rejected this thinly veiled recounting of the Harding scandals. At a deadlocked convention, the conniving politician Walter Rafferty (E. G. Marshall) assures his fellow manipulators that he will reveal his dark horse candidate when enough palms are sweating. That dark horse, an Ohio senator who rose from being a small-town publisher, is Griffith P. Hastings (Melvyn Douglas), and he is unaware of what the backroom men have planned. Hastings is the sort of man whose speeches you see rather than hear, since you watch the handsome man orate but rarely listen to his banal words. Sure enough, he is nominated and elected, and proves putty in his cronies' hands—often signing for them documents he has not read. He is happy to run off in the evenings from his hectoring wife, "the Duchess" (Jean Dixon), and play cards and entertain floozies at a house on L Street. Almost before he knows it, his administration is engulfed in scandal. Stunned by the measure of it and his inability, for all his good will, to put an end to it, he steals deadly pills from his doctor's bag, and takes them with his soup. He begs his wife, "Don't spoil my chance to be on a two-cent stamp!"

Off Broadway and Broadway again vied for attention with revivals. At the Gramercy Arts Playhouse on the 5th, Tennessee Williams's *Orpheus Descending* received such favorable notices that it ran out the season.

At the Coronet on the 6th, *The Great God Brown* (1-23-26), Eugene O'Neill's look at men's split personalities, baffled critics as much as it had more than three decades earlier. With Fritz Weaver and Robert Lansing in the leads, it also baffled many playgoers for a month.

Some of the year's most disparaging notices and one of its shortest runs (three performances) fell to **Moonbirds** (10-9-59, Cort), John Pauker's adaptation of Marcel Aymé's Paris hit. The wispy son-in-law (Wally Cox) of the headmaster (Michael Hordern) of a school for dim-witted children finds he can turn obnoxious people into birds, and later, when the moon changes phases, into snails. In the end, all the folk are restored to their human conditions. Hordern walked away with the comic honors.

There was even more glowing praise for the principals in **Chéri** (10-12-59, Morosco), derived by Anita Loos from Colette's stories of a cocotte's son. Instead of marrying for money, as his mother brought him up to do, Frederick "Chéri" Peloux (Horst Buchholz) falls in love with Lea de Lonval (Kim Stanley), a cocotte his mother's age. The romance lasts from 1911 to 1929, by which time Lea is grown old and fat. At this point, Frederick visits the apartment of a drug dealer (Lili Darvas) and there shoots himself. Despite the brilliant, moving acting, many considered the play a waste of talent. It folded after seven weeks.

Lorenzo Semple, Jr.'s **Golden Fleecing** (10-15-59, Henry Miller's) survived for ten and a half weeks, thanks in good measure to another hilarious performance by Tom Poston. Poston was Lt. Ferguson Howard, an officer on a top-secret electronics ship, U.S.S. *Elmira*. On leave in Venice, with a compliant ensign (Robert Carraway) and technical whiz kid (Robert Elston), he and his buddies decide to break the bank at a casino by flashing the winning numbers to the ship and having the ship's advanced computers tell them which numbers to bet on next. Their cantankerous admiral (Richard Kendrick) provided complications; the admiral's lovely daughter (Suzanne Pleshette) and another beautiful girl (Constance Ford) provided more complications and romance. The not quite licit winnings are turned over to charity.

A brilliant revival of Shaw's *Heartbreak House* at the Billy Rose on the 18th garnered extolling notices but lasted for only fourteen weeks and went down in the ledgers as a flop. Maurice Evans was Captain Shotover; Sam Levene, Boss Mangan; Dennis Price, Hector Hushabye; Alan Webb, Mazzini Dunn; Pamela Brown, Lady Utterword; and Diana Wynyard, Mrs. Hushabye.

Although a few critics quibbled about the quality of the play, most agreed with the *Post*'s Richard Watts, Jr., that William Gibson's **The Miracle Worker** (10-19-59, Playhouse) was "a deeply impressive drama" made into electrifying theatre by its performers. Having graduated from Boston's Perkins Institute for the Blind after her own sight had been restored, the orphaned Annie Sullivan (Anne Bancroft) arrives at the Tuscumbia, Alabama, home of short-tempered Captain Keller (Torin Thatcher) and his soft wife (Patricia Neal) to become teacher-companion for their young daughter, Helen (Patty Duke). Helen, who is deaf, dumb, and blind, is a wildly undisciplined, unkempt, but iron-willed child. It requires all of Annie's persistence, and

sometimes a touch of savagery, to begin to bring the girl around. At one point an attempt to get Helen to use a spoon properly leads to a tussle that nearly wrecks the dining room. Not until Helen is later drenched and manages to spell out the word "water" can Annie feel she has reached her. A friendship slowly develops which will release Helen from her lonely, dark world. Bancroft was "forthright, explicit, funny and enormously endearing" in a role which often required her to be uncompromisingly steely and tough. Duke's sightless "she-devil" also won sympathy. The drama ran for 719 performances.

More fine performances could not turn Joe Masteroff's **The Warm Peninsula** (10-20-59, Helen Hayes) into a hit. Having come to Miami Beach in search of some excitement, homely Ruth Arnold (Julie Harris) observes herself in a mirror and asks plaintively, "Wouldn't you think that just once some one might have said to himself, 'What the hell, whistle at her!'" Ruth has taken an apartment with glamorous Joanne de Lynn (June Havoc), a kept woman who once had been Alice Faye's stand-in and is bored with her lover. Ruth does have a brief moment with a handsome gigolo (Farley Granger), who subsequently spurns her, while Joanne has an affair with a garage attendant (Larry Hagman), who is married and fleeing the fact that he inadvertently allowed his little daughter to drown. Eventually, Ruth heads back to Milwaukee to marry her co-worker at a hardware store. Joanne is quite capable of looking after herself.

In London Robert Bolt's **Flowering Cherry** (10-21-59, Lyceum) had been a prize-winning, long-run success. In New York it was withdrawn after half a week, following reviews which suggested it was a second-rate British *Death of a Salesman*. Jim Cherry (Eric Portman) is a boastful liar who has failed in the insurance business and dreams of running his own orchards. He is not above stealing money from his wife (Wendy Hiller) and accusing his son (Andrew Ray) of the theft. He suffers a fatal heart attack when his wife walks out on him. Hiller and Portman received rave reviews, although complaints again emerged about Portman's diction.

In 1956 Paul Shyre had presented a six-player reading based on John Dos Passos's *U.S.A.* off Broadway. Set at the turn of the century, it followed the rise of a small town hustler to the moneyed world of big time public relations. The reading was revived on the 28th at the off-Broadway Martinique and this time ran out the season.

No such good fortune awaited Dore Schary's preachment **The Highest Tree** (11-4-59, Longacre), which even the Theatre Guild could not keep on the boards for a full three weeks. It told of a blue-blooded atomic scientist (Kenneth MacKenna) who learns that he is dying of leukemia and has only six months to live. He decides to campaign against atomic testings.

Early in Paddy Chayefsky's **The Tenth Man** (11-5-59, Booth) the sexton (David Vardi) of a shabby, skylit orthodox synagogue in a converted store hurries out into the streets to round up a tenth man so that his paltry handful of worshippers can have a minyan to allow them to proceed with their service. He enlists Arthur Brooks (Donald Harron), a young passerby who is a disillusioned lawyer, whose marriage is on the rocks, and who has just come off a long bender. He admits he had "taken up with one mistress after another for no other reason than I wanted to feel guilty towards my wife." The worshippers are troubled when one of the congregation, Foreman (Jacob Ben-Ami), brings with him his disturbed granddaughter, Evelyn (Risa Schwartz), a schizophrenic whose parents would return her to an asylum. Foreman is convinced that the girl is possessed of a dybbuk, a vengeful spirit from the dead. In this instance the dead person is a girl whom Foreman violated decades ago. The rest of the small congregation urge Foreman to take her to a celebrated rabbi but, when that rabbi cannot be found, agree to attempt the exorcism on their own. As the ceremony progresses, a piercing scream shakes the synagogue. It develops that, unexpectedly, the rite has cleansed Arthur of his demons. He decides to take Evelyn under his wing in hopes of curing her, especially since the pair have had a long discussion in the rabbi's office during which Evelyn recounted her sad history and bared her soul. The drama was lightened by Jewish humor. Recalling Walter Matthau's curses in last season's *Once More, with Feeling,* one worshipper exclaims, "My daughter-in-law, may she grow rich and buy a hotel with a thousand rooms and be found dead in every one of them." In the *Herald Tribune,* Walter Kerr saluted the drama as "a work of the creative imagination . . . [an] uncompromising haymaker." It ran for 623 performances.

Tonight We Improvise (11-6-59, Living Theatre), Claude Fredericks's translation of Luigi Pirandello's drama, gave the off-Broadway ensemble a second hit for its season's repertory. Ostensibly dealing with the lives of a volatile Sicilian family, it actually was merely another of the playwright's attempts to discern what is fiction and what is reality, with the director and his players sometimes stopping proceedings to argue among themselves or with their audience. It chalked up 176 performances.

For a second time running, Broadway looked at a glimpse of Jewish life. In this case, **Only in America** (11-19-59, Cort) was Lawrence and Lee's adaptation of Harry Golden's best-selling autobiography. Coming from New York to Charlotte, North Carolina, the very

Jewish, cigar-puffing Golden (Nehemiah Persoff) sets out to publish *The Carolina Israelite* and shocks many, in the process, by hiring a Negro secretary. His views are often controversial and against the southern grain. Yet for an outspoken man, he is strangely reticent when a dedicated, cultured segregationist (Shepperd Strudwick) asks him to become a member of the local school board, or when he has to defy a bigoted state senator (Harry Holcombe). It soon develops that he has a dark secret. Golden had spent time in prison for illegally manipulating some money. He quickly realizes that his neighbors could not care less. Once again Jewish humor was sprinkled through the entertainment. Told a lion is loose, Golden inquires, "Is that good for Jews or bad for Jews?" But this time everything did not add up happily, so the production closed after less than a month.

There was even less enthusiasm and a shorter run in store when the Phoenix Theatre revived *Lysistrata* on the 24th, giving it a rambunctious, slapstick treatment that one critic dismissed as a low point for the house. Dudley Fitts made the adaptation.

But the heretofore praised William Inge also came a cropper with his skimpy, dull **A Loss of Roses** (11-28-59, Eugene O'Neill). Like all Inge's plays it was set in a Midwest town. Kenny Baird (Warren Beatty) would seem to have a crush on his widowed mother (Betty Field). Her feelings about him are more ambivalent. When a woman (Carol Haney) who long ago had helped his mother nurse him and now gets $100 a week for appearing in cheap porno films pays a visit, Kenny beds her for a night but is savage to her in the morning. She unsuccessfully attempts suicide, and he decides to leave home in hopes of finding himself.

Some not dissimilar themes were seen in an importation from London, Peter Shaffer's **Five Finger Exercise** (12-2-59, Music Box). However, this time sharp writing and fine ensemble playing led to a ten-month run. A philistine British furniture manufacturer (Ronald Culver) and his artistically pretentious wife (Jessica Tandy) have settled into an edgy marriage. The father worries that their nineteen-year-old son (Brian Bedford) is overeducated. They also have a younger daughter (Juliet Mills). A German (Michael Bryant), fleeing from the home of his still ardently Nazi parents, is hired to tutor the girl. Before long it becomes obvious that mother, daughter, and possibly even son have fallen in love with the man. Asked to leave, he attempts suicide.

Two more unhappy people were the focal point of Robert Anderson's **Silent Night, Lonely Night** (12-3-59, Morosco). John (Henry Fonda) and Katherine (Barbara Bel Geddes) meet on Christmas Eve at a quiet New England inn. She is there because her son has been ill at the school he attends nearby. He is about to be released, and she hopes to put him on a plane so that he can spend the holidays overseas with his philandering businessman-father. Although John at first tells Katherine his wife is dead, he finally admits that he has come to visit her at a mental institution down the road. She went insane after their daughter died, a death for which John blames himself. He says he is not asking for pity, but is deeply moved when she in turn says she is. In short order the couple spend the night together before heading their separate ways. As token remembrances he gives her a penny and she gives him a handkerchief. For all the fine playing, most aisle-sitters concurred with John McClain's assessment in the *Journal-American* that the drama "lacks dramatic impact." Still, the lure of its stars kept it in front of the footlights for 124 performances.

Several critics saw Lonnie Coleman's **Jolly's Progress** (12-5-59, Longacre), which the playwright adapted from his own novel *Adams' Way,* as an updated *Pygmalion,* interwoven with America's growing preoccupation about racial matters. After his ex-wife's latest husband violates Jolly (Eartha Kitt), a disheveled, almost illiterate black gamin, David Adams (Wendell Corey) decides to educate her in his home. His old schoolmarm (Anne Revere) is called in to help. Together they chase away the Ku Klux Klan and polish Jolly enough to send her off for further schooling in Philadelphia. This "well-meaning mediocrity" survived for only nine performances.

Many critics were not much kinder to Jean Anouilh's *L'Hurluberlu,* which New Yorkers saw in Lucienne Hill's translation as **The Fighting Cock** (12-8-59, ANTA). But the lure of Rex Harrison as the crusty, De Gaulle-like old soldier defiantly battling progress kept the play alive for eleven weeks. Roddy McDowall as the pragmatic son of a war profiteer and Arthur Treacher as a blundering man of the world won applause for their support.

An even bigger attraction from Hollywood, sultry Lauren Bacall, kept George Axelrod's **Goodbye, Charlie** (12-16-59, Lyceum) alive and kicking for 109 performances. After George Tracy (Sydney Chaplin) has given a rather equivocal eulogy for his late pal Charlie, the meager handful of guests at the service leave. George's eulogy had to be equivocal, since Charlie was something of a self-serving louse who had been shot by another friend when Charlie was caught in bed with the friend's wife on the friend's yacht. Wearing only the friend's raincoat, Charlie had vainly tried to flee out of a porthole. As George is about to leave, a beautiful girl, dressed only in a raincoat, appears. She insists she is Charlie and spiels off abundant facts to prove it. It turns out that God has punished Charlie by forcing him to return to earth as a woman and learn what it is like to deal with men such as he was. Complications arise when George falls madly in love with the new Charlie. Finally the repentant revenant begs forgiveness. George will find a more comfortable romance with a Charlie-girl look-alike. Several critics lambasted the show as a one-joke affair, and a dirty joke at that. But they almost all loved Bacall. In the *Times* Brooks Atkinson suggested the star's "good, slam-bang performance" was "a cross between a female impersonator and Tallulah Bankhead." He later threw in Lon Chaney and Mae West for good measure. Chaplin also won fine notices, as did Sarah Marshall, playing the vinegary wife who was the cause of Charlie's downfall.

As a fill-in for the prematurely closed *Lysistrata,* the Phoenix hauled out a revival of *Pictures in the Hallway* on the 26th, with Mildred Dunnock heading the cast of readers.

A powerful, superbly played courtroom drama, Saul Levitt's **The Andersonville Trial** (12-29-59, Henry Miller's), ran until June, but closed without recouping all its costs. The play dealt with the patently biased trial of Henry Wirz, the Swiss immigrant held liable for the horrors and 14,000 deaths at the Andersonville, Georgia, prisoner-of-war camp during the Civil War. Wirz's lawyer (Albert Dekker) vainly pleads for a postponement, insisting that the mood of the country just four months after Lincoln's assassination precludes a fair hearing—"it swells the charge of murder against the defendant to gigantic size." The presiding judge, General Lew Wallace (Russell Hardie), refuses to accept the argument. Although he time and again leans over to be impartial, he shares the nation's anger. The defense counsel regularly pokes holes in the stories of witnesses brought forth by the youthful, ambitious, and acrimonious judge advocate, Lt. Col. Chipman (George C. Scott), who persistently disregards the defense's principal plea, that Wirz (Herbert Berghof) was merely following orders and that any army man should understand and respect that. Instead, Chipman harps on the fundamental inhumanity of Wirz's actions. Patently foredoomed, Wirz is sentenced to death by the court.

The titular figure of Arthur Kober and George Oppenheimer's **A Mighty Man Is He** (1-6-60, Cort) is never seen, albeit his voice is heard barking orders over an intercom system in his luxurious New York apartment. He is a Broadway producer with an incessantly roving eye. When he is injured in an automobile accident and a lady's traveling case is discovered in the car, his wife (Nancy Kelly) assumes it belongs to his regular mistress (Polly Rowles). Learning that it is, rather, the property of a blonde chippy (Diana van der Vlis) from the chorus of his latest show , she joins with his older mistress to send the girl packing. In the process, the mistress sees the light and leaves the husband to his wife. The drama was the first of three early 1960 novelties on Broadway to run half a week or less.

Fritz Weaver, moving from role to role without ever finding the great part in the great production to ensure his stardom, played the title figure in the Phoenix Theatre's presentation of Ibsen's *Peer Gynt*. The mounting, in a translation by Norman Ginsbury, opened on the 12th. During the drama's three-and-a-half-hour running time, critics decided the play was really not all it was touted to be. It was, they concluded, second-rate, pretentious Ibsen. But the mounting and the playing were received respectfully and continued on for a month.

Like *A Mighty Man Is He,* Katherine Morrill's **A Distant Bell** (1-13-60, Eugene O'Neill) survived a mere five performances. In the mid-1930s, a widowed mother (Martha Scott) returns to her small-town New England home after spending time in a mental institution. She confronts her three daughters, who have little love for her. She also confronts a family tragedy, since two of the girls love the same newspaperman (Andrew Prine). One (Evans Evans) of these locks the other (Phyllis Love) in a closet, which unhinges the girl's mind. She is committed to the same asylum her mother had been in, flees, and dies of exposure. The mother then leaves home, possibly to return to the asylum herself.

Off Broadway, a bill of two one-acters confirmed the theatrical skills and eccentricities of a foreign writer and introduced a promising native dramatist. All that happens in Samuel Beckett's **Krapp's Last Tape** (1-14-60, Provincetown Playhouse) is that its lone character (Donald Davis), a crotchety old man, listens to a tape recording made in happier, more youthful days. In Edward Albee's **Zoo Story,** Jerry (George Maharis), a shabbily dressed, aggressively hostile beatnik, accosts Peter (William Daniels), a mild-mannered publisher who is sitting, reading on a park bench, and begins to unburden himself of his feelings and history. He tells of a boardinghouse dog, unmoved by kindness but reached for an impersonal modus vivendi by an act of cruelty. It becomes clear that Jerry wishes to die. He tries to monopolize the bench and to force Peter into a fight. Finally, calling Peter "a pathetic little vegetable," he goads him into picking up his knife. Peter holds it at arm's length, defensively. So Jerry rushes at it and impales himself on it, thus achieving the death he so desired. The double bill ran for 532 performances.

Uptown, the parade of flops continued with a two-performance fiasco, **Cut of the Axe** (2-1-60, Ambassador), which Sheppard Kerman took from Delmar Jackson's novel. When a young woman of questionable virtue is apparently murdered, a corrupt politician (Thomas Mitchell) tries to get the authorities to railroad or have lynched two innocent vagrants since he himself

was with the girl at the time of her death. To his chagrin his henchmen turn against him, the dead woman being one man's daughter-in-law. At the close, everyone goes free, after it is shown that the girl accidentally killed herself when she fell on a kitchen knife.

The Deadly Game (2-2-60, Longacre) was James Yaffe's theatricalization of Friedrich Duerrenmatt's novel *Die Panne*. In an isolated, snowbound Swiss chalet, three retired court officials (Ludwig Donath, Claude Dauphin, and Max Adrian) agree that even the most seemingly innocent person can be a murderer at heart. When a traveling American salesman, Howard Trapp (Pat Hingle), whose car has plowed into a snowbank, appears at their door, they invite him to join them in a mock trial. He will be the defendant. Before the evening is finished they have convinced him that, half knowingly, he brought on his boss's fatal heart attack. Trapp rushes out and drives himself over a precipice. Days later, his wife (Frances Helm) shows up to explore what happened, so the men invite her to play the same parlor game.

Thumbs-down notices assailed Sidney Sheldon's **Roman Candle** (2-3-60, Cort). Mark Baxter (Robert Sterling) is a scientist about to leave for Alaska to watch trials of a missile he has worked on. At his Washington apartment he goes to mix himself a martini, only to discover he is out of vermouth. At that very moment his beautiful neighbor, Elizabeth Brown (Inger Stevens), appears with a full bottle. Her ESP told her of the problem. It also informs her who will win at the races that day, that the first missile trial will be a bust (Eisenhower can putt that far), that a second will succeed, and that Mark will not marry the girl he is engaged to but will marry her instead. She also knows that before that happens she will be mistaken for a Russian spy. And, boy, is she right! In the times-never-change department, several critics singled out the same joke: "There's no expense too unnecessary for the army."

Alone on the stage in a simple white-fringed black dress in **A Lovely Light** (2-8-60, Hudson), Dorothy Stickney employed the poetry and letters of Edna St. Vincent Millay to recreate the woman's life from a young, hope-filled girl in Maine through her early struggles and disappointments, her happy marriage, and her less happy widowhood. The engagement was limited to two weeks as part of an extended tour, which played college campuses as well as legitimate theatres.

Two off-Broadway hits opened three nights later. Both went to ancient times and familiar figures for their stories. Jack C. Richardson's **The Prodigal** (2-11-60, Downtown) told how Orestes was loath to get involved in his parents' difficulties but how circumstances forced him to avenge his unloved, antiquated father's death, because he himself was "not great enough to create something better." **Between Two Thieves** (2-11-60, York) was Warner LeRoy's adaptation of Diego Fabbri's *Processo a Gesú*. Done in contemporary dress, it looked at Jesus' trial and its aftermaths in term of modern mores.

For the second time in as many seasons, a mad Roman emperor strutted his horrific moments on a New York stage. In Justin O'Brien's translation of Albert Camus's **Caligula** (2-16-60, 54th St.), Kenneth Haigh portrayed the boy king who wanted to be the first ruler to purposely dehumanize himself so that he might use unlimited power in an unlimited way. Will Steven Armstrong's constructivist setting had a series of free-hanging stairways arranged about the bottom fragment of a huge, ornate column. At the play's end, Caligula jumps from these stairs onto the swords of his aroused enemies.

The nation's growing racial problems were brought to light again in **The Long Dream** (2-17-60, Ambassador), derived by Ketti Frings from Richard Wright's novel. Tyree Tucker (Lawrence Winters), a black undertaker, has made himself a small fortune in his Mississippi town by toadying to whites and allowing the Chief of Police (R. G. Armstrong) to share in his profits from the dance hall and bordello he also owns. But after the bordello burns down with forty-two people trapped inside, the future looks bleak for Tucker. His son, "Fishbelly" (Al Freeman), who has long had contempt for his father's practices, is killed defending him. The boy's death prompts the father to vow to reform and never again grovel.

New York City's black life was on view in **The Cool World** (2-22-60, Eugene O'Neill), Warren Miller and Robert Rossen's stage version of Miller's novel, which a number of critics suggested was a lame *West Side Story* without music. Since the former leader of the Crocodiles has become a hopeless drug addict, Duke Custis (Billy Dee Williams) moves to take over. He wins the affection of the group's in-house prostitute (Alease Whittington), who charges $1.50 a throw and gives a third of that to the Crocodiles' war chest. But Duke is convinced he needs a gun to be in command, so he agrees to sell narcotics to earn the $32.50 needed. Yet once he gets the gun and heads the rumble against the rival Wolves, he finds the teachings of his mother (Lynn Hamilton) and grandmother (Eulabelle Moore), with whom he lives, preclude him from pulling the trigger. Nonetheless, in the wake of the battle, the police come to take him away. Although some critics singled out lines such as the grandmother's "When a husband gets lost in Harlem, he stays lost," others complained that it was "tedious to have every speech begin with 'Man!'" Playgoers didn't care either way,

so the play closed after two performances—three fewer than *The Long Dream*.

For two weeks beginning on the 23rd, the New York City Center played host to the Piccolo Teatro di Milano's production of Carlo Goldoni's *The Servant of Two Masters*. Aisle-sitters concurred that it was not necessary to understand Italian to enjoy the buffoonery. But an appreciation of English added nothing to Benn Levy's pretentious, blank-verse London drama **The Tumbler** (2-24-60, Helen Hayes), which looked at a female, modern-day Hamlet. Returning from her wanderings around the world, Lennie (Rosemary Harris) takes refuge from a storm in a barn, where she is seduced by Kell (Charlton Heston). He turns out to be her stepfather, whom her mother (Martha Scott) married hastily after her father's mysterious death. Within a day, Lennie has driven Kell to hang himself.

The new year's first solid success was Lillian Hellman's **Toys in the Attic** (2-25-60, Hudson). John Chapman of the *Daily News* welcomed it as "a smackingly vigorous drama." Carrie (Maureen Stapleton) and Anne Berniers (Anne Revere) are a pair of old maids living in genteel poverty. They have few pleasures except their ne'er-do-well brother, Julian (Jason Robards, Jr.). When he brings home a child bride (Rochelle Oliver) and seems on the verge of making an illicit fortune, the sisters become frightened of losing him. The battles between the sisters and the wife drive the sisters apart. Anne points out Carrie's not so well hidden feelings about Julian, "You lusted and it showed." Julian's scheme to get rich starts to fall to pieces. And after a vengeful Carrie goads Julian's wife into disclosing some philandering by Julian, the aggrieved husband has Julian brutally beaten and slashed. No one gives much credence to Julian's pledge to start over again. Robards gained the highest praise for his Julian, "so sweetly and insensitively determined to make everybody share his good fortune." The play won the New York Drama Critics Circle Award and ran for 556 performances.

Critics didn't think much of Josh Logan's slammed-home mounting of Daniel Taradash's **There Was a Little Girl** (2-29-60, Cort), but applauded Henry Fonda's daughter, Jane, in her debut. She was seen as Toni Newton, who has a falling-out with her latest beau (Dean Jones) and runs off, only to be seized and raped. To her horror she finds that the police, her family, and her friends all imply that she asked for it. She seeks out the rapist (Sean Garrison) and must be content with his assurance that she put up quite a struggle.

On March 1, the Phoenix brought out *Henry IV, Part I*. Donald Madden's Hotspur, Eric Berry's Falstaff, and Fritz Weaver's king were generally admired, but Edwin Sherin was deemed a weak-voiced, listless washout as

Prince Hal. A basic setting had twin flights of stairs leading to a gallows-like platform. William Steven Armstrong, who designed *Caligula*'s stepped setting, created this one, too.

What one critic called "the year's most impressive cast" was conspicuously wasted on **The Good Soup** (3-2-60, Plymouth), Garson Kanin's redaction of Félicien Marceau's huge Paris hit. Unfortunately something got lost in the sea-crossing, so the comedy lingered for less than three weeks. Marie Paul (Ruth Gordon), an aging cocotte, sitting in a casino, recounts her life to a bored croupier (Jules Munshin). She tells of getting a rich married man to buy her a bistro, marrying a handsome waiter and, after he is killed, learning she is pregnant. She traps a rich mama's boy into wedding her, but years later is surprised by her husband in the arms of their daughter's new spouse. Set loose with a modest income, she is on the prowl for another rich man. Assuming one or more roles were Diane Cilento (as the young Marie Paul), Mildred Natwick, Sam Levene, and Ernest Truex.

Jean Genet's **The Balcony** (3-3-60, Circle in the Square), in Bernard Frechtman's translation, was set, during a revolution, in a brothel where men come not only to satisfy their sexual needs but to play out their social fantasies. The men and the girls don huge, often grotesque costumes to bring to life these daydreams. Acting honors went to Nancy Marchand as the icy madam and Salome Jens as a girl pretending to be a pony. The play ran 672 performances and, along with the Beckett and Albee double bill, spotlighted the new theatre of structured meaninglessness that would characterize much of the advanced writing of the decade.

On the 8th, the Lunts, as part of their farewell tour, began a two-week stand at the City Center in *The Visit*.

Patricia Jourday's **Semi-Detached** (3-10-60, Martin Beck) was a Canadian drama about two families who occupy the two parts of a semi-detached home. One, Catholic, is life-loving and rising in the world. The other, Protestant, is bigoted and, having lost their drugstore, on the way down. The families' two young sons do not share their prejudices. The boys build a boat together but take to arguing, and one is drowned in the tussle. The Protestant daughter further fuels the fire by falling in love with a married Catholic man. The problems finally reconcile the families.

Just as the Lunts were writing finis to their great careers, Katharine Cornell came in to close out hers. Her vehicle was Jerome Kilty's adaptation of the famed, verbally tempestuous correspondence of George Bernard Shaw and Mrs. Patrick Campbell as **Dear Liar** (3-17-60, Billy Rose). Cornell, "unruffled in red velvet . . . ingratiating in demure black (with white stole) or in

Cecil Beaton olive," made a regal, albeit not all that fiery, actress. (She was suffering from laryngitis on opening night.) Brian Aherne was Shaw. Besides reading from the letters, they performed snatches from *Pygmalion* and *The Apple Cart*. Their New York stand of fifty-two performances concluded a sixty-six-city tour.

Beverly Cross's English drama **One More River** (3-18-60, Ambassador) found no audience in America. When the captain of a tramp steamer dies, the sadistic first mate (Alfred Ryder) takes over, but after he blinds a young cabin boy (David Winters) by throwing boiling water at him, the crew rebels. They would kill him, but for the reasoned protests of the bo's'n (Lloyd Nolan). He persuades the men to lock up the mate and turn him over to authorities at the next port. The need for that is precluded when the mate dies in a fall.

The season's last hit was its most entertaining comedy, Gore Vidal's **The Best Man** (3-31-60, Morosco). Kerr praised it as "a knockout." William Russell (Melvyn Douglas), a gentlemanly liberal of the old school, and Joseph Cantwell (Frank Lovejoy), a calculating, unscrupulous senator, are leading candidates for the presidential nomination of their party. To boost his own chances, Cantwell leaks to the press a damaging psychiatric analysis once made of Russell. A feisty ex-president, Arthur Hockstader (Lee Tracy), tells Cantwell, "It's not that I mind your being a bastard. . . . It's your being such a *stupid* bastard, I object to." Hockstader switches to the Russell camp, where he urges they make public Cantwell's secret history of homosexuality. Russell demurs, withdrawing from the race in favor of a third candidate. Many contemporaries read Adlai Stevenson, Joe McCarthy, and Harry Truman into the characters of Russell, Cantwell, and Hockstader. The comedy ran 520 performances.

The season's third two-performance bomb was George Panetta's **Viva Madison Avenue!** (4-6-60, Longacre). Joe Caputo (Buddy Hackett), a wacky maverick director of TV commercials, is given a chance to direct a full-length story, with orders that he save his hero at the end for additional adventures. Instead, he lets the hero die. Barhounds drown their sorrow at the man's death in so many extra orders of the sponsor's beer, and critics so praise the program, that Caputo himself becomes a hero. The childish, pouting Hackett was a popular nightclub and television comic.

There were echoes of *A Mighty Man Is He* in **A Second String** (4-13-60, Eugene O'Neill), which Lucienne Hill dramatized from a Colette novel. Only in this instance a disillusioned wife (Shirley Booth) decides it would be politic to share her philandering playwright-husband (Jean Pierre Aumont) with his mistress-secretary (Nina Foch). They shared for less than a month.

On the 18th, the Phoenix followed its *Henry IV, Part I* with *Part II*. Using the same set and the same principal actors, the new mounting received much the same notices as the earlier one.

The season's last play was a French drama come by way of England: Jean Giraudoux's *Pour Lucrèce,* which Christopher Fry anglicized as **Duel of Angels** (4-19-60, Helen Hayes). Infuriated at the cold, sanctimonious behavior of an aggressively upright lady (Vivien Leigh), a more louche lady (Mary Ure) drugs her, leaves her in a compromising position in a brothel, and allows her to believe she was raped. The supposed rapist is killed, and the good woman commits suicide.

1960–1961

It wasn't the best of seasons. "Depressing" and "bleak" were words that cropped up in assessments at the season's end. The number of new plays continued to slide, and whether one accepted *Variety*'s figure of thirty-three or the *Times*'s twenty-nine, it represented the lowest total in living memory. Morever, so much of what was good in the season came from overseas.

Apart from the first American appearance of Japan's *Grand Kabuki,* which began a three-week stand at the City Center on June 2 and delighted critics with its exotically stylized presentations, the hot-weather months were unproductive. The City Center itself helped rekindle matters when it brought back the French pantomimist Marcel Marceau on September 6. He, too, was given a three-week engagement.

The World of Carl Sandburg (9-14-60, Henry Miller's) was a staged reading devised by Norman Corwin from the poet's writings and had Bette Davis, Leif Erickson, and Clark Allen to recite the lines.

The *Times*'s new critic, Howard Taubman, spoke for many when he branded Brendan Behan's Irish play **The Hostage** (9-20-60, Cort) "a grabbag of wonderful and dreadful prizes." Set in a brothel where some Irish militants are holding a British soldier in retaliation for the arrest of an Irish terrorist, it gave glimpses of the raffish life of lower-class Dublin in such characters as a toothless old crone, a one-legged revolutionary, two flaming homosexuals, and a redheaded tart. The play ran for 127 performances—not long enough to pay back its costs.

John Vari and Rodney Ackland's London comedy hit **Farewell, Farewell, Eugene** (9-27-60, Helen Hayes)

was even more clearly not to Broadway's tastes. In 1915 Manhattan, two old maids (Margaret Rutherford and Mildred Dunnock), who have been scraping together enough to visit their brother, Eugene, in South Africa, find their serenity disturbed when a younger cousin (Leueen MacGrath) announces that she hopes to wed a man who is socially and intellectually her inferior. The boxy, dowdy, rubber-faced Rutherford won the best notices, although one or two critics rued that her muggings were excessive. The comedy survived for a single week.

But the West End also gave Broadway the season's first hit, Shelagh Delaney's **A Taste of Honey** (10-4-60, Lyceum). Delaney was a youngster, a sometime theatre usher, who had written the play at nineteen just to prove she could do so. Deserted by the Negro sailor (Billy Dee Williams) who rendered her pregnant, and largely neglected by her sluttish mother (Angela Lansbury), Josephine (Joan Plowright) finds consolation and affection in her relationship with an amiable homosexual, Geoffrey (Andrew Ray). Illuminated by the glowing performances of Lansbury and Plowright, the play ran for 376 performances.

France provided the next hit, Lucienne Hill's translation of Jean Anouilh's **Becket; or, The Honor of God** (10-5-60, St. James). The play recounted the well-known history of Henry II's (Anthony Quinn) raising his roistering friend Becket (Laurence Olivier) to archbishop despite the man's warning that as a churchman he would place the interests of God and the Church first, and of Becket's ultimate martyrdom for his stance. Quinn's loutish king won high praise, but Olivier's Becket was even more garlanded: "The courtier is limned with elegance and spirit; the man of God has dedicated simplicity and sad, consoling wisdom." David Merrick's production—Merrick had also sponsored the Delaney play—ran for six months. When it returned briefly in the spring, Olivier was seen as the king and Arthur Kennedy as Becket.

Although **The Wall** (10-11-60, Billy Rose), Millard Lampell's dramatization of John Hersey's best-seller, ran almost as long—twenty-one weeks—it went down in the records as a commercial failure. Like Behan's play, it used a thin story line—in this case the tale of a lone-ish resistance fighter (George C. Scott) and the devotion of a determined woman (Yvonne Mitchell) to him, even though she knows him to be married—to frame slices of life in the Warsaw ghetto as Nazi cruelties provoke the doomed uprising. Most lauded among the players was Joseph Buloff, as a pathetic little peddler who bravely pretends to be his rabbi so that the rabbi might be spared.

One of the few off-Broadway plays to run more than 100 performances during the season was Paul Shyre's dramatized reading of Sean O'Casey's third autobiographical novel, **Drums Under the Windows** (10-14-60, Cherry Lane). Called Sean Casside here, the future playwright receives his first exposure to Shakespeare and Shaw, and bitterly contemplates his impoverished sister's funeral.

Not even screen favorite Jack Lemmon could earn a run for **Face of a Hero** (10-20-60, Eugene O'Neill), Robert L. Joseph's theatricalization of Pierre Boulle's novel. In his small, corrupt southern town, young Harold Rutland, Jr. (George Grizzard), has always considered himself above the law, a position which has earned him the venomous enmity of the town's police captain (Albert Dekker). So when a trollop with whom the boy was known to cavort turns up drowned, the captain has little difficulty persuading a rising prosecutor, David Poole (Lemmon), to throw the book at him. Poole does and succeeds. What Poole keeps silent about is that he himself had watched the pregnant girl commit suicide and had done nothing to stop her. But at least the town is now rid of two undesirables.

Tiny, doleful-faced, and gravel-voiced Menasha Skulnick had only little better luck with his vehicle, Florence Lowe and Caroline Francke's **The 49th Cousin** (10-27-60, Ambassador). The former Yiddish stage star's personal popularity kept the play on the boards for three months. Isaac Lowe is a widowed, retired spectacle manufacturer, living in Syracuse at the turn of the century with his three unmarried daughters (Martha Scott, Evans Evans, and Marian Winters). They are unmarried because of Isaac's German-Jewish mentality: no man, but especially a Russian Jew, or, worse, a Goy, is good enough for his children. Unfortunately a Russian Jew (Gerald Hiken) and a young Christian (Paul Tripp) are the very men two of the girls love. In the show's most hilarious scene, the daughters trick him into donning formal clothes to greet members of his synagogue who are coming to call on him. He believes the visitors will ask him to become the church's president. Instead, they ask him to find another synagogue, since they have grown annoyed at his behavior. The shock helps liberalize Isaac's outlook.

Arthur Laurents's **Invitation to a March** (10-29-60, Music Box) was yet another play that had the sort of run—113 performances—which in healthier times would have suggested at least a modest profit, but which now meant it closed in the red. Reviewers looked on the comedy as a retelling of the Sleeping Beauty story in very modish dress and with characters stopping to address asides to the audience. Camilla Jablonski (Celeste Holm) owns a pair of beach houses on the South Shore of Long Island. She lives in one of them with her illegitimate son, Aaron (James MacArthur), and rents out the other to summer people. This summer she has rented the place to a widow (Madeleine Sherwood) with a daughter, Norma (Jane Fonda), who seems unhappily engaged to the stuffy son (Tom Hatcher) of the rich Tucker Grogans (Eileen Heckart and Richard Derr). When the Grogans come to visit it turns out that Mr. Grogan is Aaron's father. A match of wits develops between Camilla and Mrs. Grogan, while an impassioned kiss from Aaron awakes Norma from her indifference and shows her where her future lies. Critic after critic proclaimed that Heckart stole the show, dressed in gaudy pants, sporting a piccolo-sized cigarette holder, and dropping barbed remarks everywhere ("Tucker, a conversation is not a monologue, you know").

The Phoenix began its season on November 1 with a well-received mounting of Oliver Goldsmith's *She Stoops to Conquer*.

For the second year in a row, Englishman Benn W. Levy came a cropper when one of his London plays, **The Rape of the Belt** (11-5-60, Martin Beck), was transported to New York. As Hera (Peggy Wood) and Zeus (John Emery) watch from pedestals on either side of the proscenium, Heracles (Philip Bosco) and his buddy Theseus (Joseph Bova) descend upon the Amazons to seize the royal jeweled belt. Antiope (Constance Cummings) and Hippolyte (Joyce Redman), who rule jointly, seem loathe to fight, until an infuriated Hera goads them on. Nonetheless, the victory goes to the men.

New Yorkers also had relatively little time for Agatha Christie's **The Mousetrap** (11-5-60, Maidman) when it was offered off Broadway, even though it was already in a record-breaking eighth year in London and would continue to run on there for decades. (It is still running at this writing in 1996.) The mystery stranded a number of people in a snowbound guest house. Each is a suspect in a killing in London earlier in the day. In the end, as in the bygone American hit *The Bat,* the supposed detective turns out to be the killer. Although the mystery ran six months, that was a far cry from what many had expected.

David Ross, who had won laurels primarily for his fine Chekhov revivals, brought out a remounting of Ibsen's *Hedda Gabler* at the 4th Street on the 9th with Anne Meacham in the leading role. More laurels followed, as did a season-long run.

Tennessee Williams tried his hand at comedy in **Period of Adjustment** (11-10-60, Helen Hayes), grabbed notices such as Robert Coleman's in the *Mirror,* which called it "packed with laughs . . . tender and touching," and eked out a modest hit with a 132-performance run. Ralph Bates (James Daly) is sitting alone in his home on Christmas Eve because his wife has taken their child and run back to her parents. His beer-drinking and TV-watching are interrupted by the noisy arrival of his old pal George Haverstick (Robert Webber) and George's bride, Isabel (Barbara Baxley). Isabel is very upset, since George has gotten the shakes on his first honeymoon night and hasn't been able to do anything. Ralph volunteers that his own wife had initially suffered from "psychological frigidity." He says a period of adjustment is necessary before most marriages settle down to work. Still, George suggests he and Ralph head out to a better life in the West. Ralph's angry in-laws (Nancy R. Pollock and Lester Mack) arrive with a policeman (Charles McDaniel) in tow to reclaim some of their daughter's belongings. And Dorothea Bates (Rosemary Murphy) appears in their wake. The arguments and discussions become heated, but after a while both couples are reconciled.

Lawrence Roman's **Under the Yum-Yum Tree** (11-16-60, Henry Miller's) received more divided notices than had Williams's comedy, ran longer (173 performances), but wound up in the loss column. Robin Austin (Sandra Church) sublets the comfortable Frisco "sin-bin"—with its wonderful view of the Bay Bridge—that her Aunt Irene (Nan Martin) is leaving to accept a teaching post in Sacramento. Robin hopes to persuade her lawyer-suitor, Dave Manning (Dean Jones), to move in with her for a pre-marital but platonic relationship. At first reluctant, he consents when he realizes that her landlord and neighbor, Hogan (Gig Young), is a dashing lecher. But one evening after Robin and Dave have downed a few, Dave fears he can no longer restrain himself and runs out. Returning the next morning, he is led by circumstances to believe that Robin may have spent the night with Hogan. It develops that Irene did. Robin and Dave agree to head for Reno—to get married there. Hogan announces that he, like Irene, is moving to Sacramento.

More mixed reviews greeted **Advise and Consent** (11-17-60, Cort), which Loring Mandel dramatized from Allen Drury's best-seller. But its 212-performance run allowed it to wind up in the black. The President (Judson Laire), something of a wheeler-dealer, nominates William Huntington (Staats Cotsworth), to be secretary of state. But an idealistic young Senator Anderson (Richard Kiley) leads the opposition, upset that Huntington has refused to admit to some Communist leanings in his youth. The demagogic Senator Van Ackerman (Kevin McCarthy) discloses in turn that during the war Anderson had had a homosexual relationship with a sailor. Saying, "Sometimes the clutter gets too much," Anderson kills himself. When the vote in the Senate is tied, the Vice President (Tom Shirley) casts the deciding vote—against Huntington.

Another dramatized novel won both the Pulitzer Prize and New York Drama Critics Circle Award, although

it, too, garnered sharply divided notices. **All the Way Home** (11-30-60, Belasco) was Tad Mosel's stage version of James Agee's *A Death in the Family*. Comments on it ranged from the *Daily News*'s John Chapman's "it lacks strength and unity" to the *Post*'s Richard Watts, Jr.'s "a somber and beautiful play." Back in 1915, Jay Follet (Arthur Hill) is a country boy, more or less indifferent to religion, who has made a happy marriage with his city-bred, devoutly Catholic wife, Mary (Colleen Dewhurst). They are drawn all the closer by the warmth of their extended family. Of course, they have problems. Jay had been a heavy drinker, although he now is on the wagon. And, despite Jay's objections, Mary has been reluctant to explain to their young son, Rufus (John Megna), what it means that she is pregnant again. So when Jay is killed in a car crash, apparently while driving under the influence, Mary must deal with her own grief and her son's. She concludes resignedly, "People fall away from us, and in time, others grow away from us. This is simply what living is." And she decides to explain her condition to the boy. Among the supporting players, special praise was accorded Lillian Gish as a sweet, almost deaf grandmother and Aline MacMahon as a compassionate aunt.

There were very few favorable notices for James Costigan's **Little Moon of Alban** (12-1-60, Longacre), but numerous bouquets for its star, Julie Harris. She was seen as Brigid Mary Mangan, a young Irish lass whose sweetheart (Robert Redford) is ambushed and killed during the uprisings of the early 1920s. On his death she joins a religious order and is assigned to ministering to wounded British soldiers. She finds herself nursing the very lieutenant (John Justin) who led the ambush. He is sarcastic, atheistic, and, at first, near death. Doctors tell Brigid her prayers must have pulled him through. Although he falls in love with her, she opts to remain with her order.

Good notices for another fine performer, David Wayne, could do little for Norman Barasch and Carroll Moore's **Send Me No Flowers** (12-5-60, Brooks Atkinson). George Kimball is a hopeless hypochondriac, who misinterprets an overheard remark by his family doctor (Frank Merlin) and assumes he is dying. In one of his wild flash-aheads he sees his beloved wife (Nancy Olson) peddling pencils on a freezing night in front of Carnegie Hall and losing a nickel on each six she sells. He nobly prepares to leave his widow as well off as possible, observing, "I'm in lousy shape now, but I'll be all right when I'm gone." When his fears prove groundless, he is slapped with another worry, since his wife wonders if his strange behavior isn't his way of covering up an affair. Heywood Hale Broun was applauded as a cheerful grave salesman.

A sourly received revival of Sean O'Casey's *The Plough and the Stars* began a month-long stand at the Phoenix on the 6th.

Canada was the source and setting for Robertson Davies's short-lived **Love and Libel; or, The Ogre of the Provincial World** (12-7-60, Martin Beck). The playwright adapted the work from his own novel *Leaven of Malice.* When the Bridgetowers and the Vambraces, who have been acting like the Capulets and the Montagues for thirty years, read a newspaper squib about a young love-match between the families, they suspect the boozy, cold-plagued church organist (Dennis King) of planting the story. He denies it, but the story does lead to a wedding and the families' reconciliation. Not only did the players help move about the screens that served as basic settings, but, as in *Invitation to a March,* they regularly stopped to address the audience. Among the supporting cast, Gene Saks corralled laughs as a "human relations engineer" attempting to explain the Oedipus complex to a professor of the classics.

Perhaps not suprisingly, the hero of Ira Levin's **Critic's Choice** (12-14-60, Barrymore) was a celebrated if imaginary New York drama critic. But Parker Ballantine (Henry Fonda) has a problem, since his wife (Georgann Johnson) has decided to write a play. He waves away the plot—something about life with her eccentric old uncle—warning, "In Boston tryouts alone it's already folded twelve times." And he gets so angry when the play progresses and is accepted for Broadway that he starts to write a snide book about it. The Ballantines nearly are split asunder after he insists, against her express wishes, on reviewing the play, which he pans savagely. But all is forgiven after he apologizes for not having helped her while she was struggling and she realizes that she was wrong to attempt to push him out of his position as a professional critic. Light fluff, beautifully staged, it ran nearly six months only to close at a loss.

The new year was launched with Derek Prouse's translation of Eugene Ionesco's **Rhinoceros** (1-9-61, Longacre), which told of a town where virtually all the people come to believe that they are rhinoceroses and act accordingly. Only one man (Eli Wallach), meek but reasonable, refuses to be convinced, even after his sweetheart (Anne Jackson) joins the herd. The evening's most commanding performance was that of hefty Zero Mostel as the most conspicuous convert, snarling, grunting, bellowing, and charging across the stage. Indeed, his performance was so remarkable that Walter Kerr, in the *Herald Tribune,* opened his review by reversing matters and insisting that "an extremely talented rhinoceros played Zero Mostel." Yet for all the kudos

and in the face of a 240-performance run, the play was recorded as one of the season's commercial failures.

Uptown above the main theatre district, Edward Albee's **The American Dream** (1-24-61, York) was premiered as part of a double bill that also included a musical. Although Mommy (Jane Hoffman), a domineering middle-class wife, and Daddy (John C. Becher), a wealthy, henpecked husband, have apparently long since killed their adopted son, who did not turn out to be to their liking, they plan to adopt another. This one (Ben Piazza) proves to be the twin of the dead boy. At least the young man can develop an understanding relationship with Grandma (Sudie Bond), who is complacently awaiting her own death. The play ran for 372 performances.

The Phoenix Theatre received some of the best notices it had garnered in a long while when, on the 27th, it bravely reached back and revived a long-neglected American melodrama, Dion Boucicault's *The Octoroon* (12-6-1859). It followed to her ultimate suicide, so as not to become the property of a slave-owning villain, the sad history of a regal octoroon loved by the upright hero. The revival was given forty-five performances, only three fewer than the run of the original production more than a century earlier.

Brooks Atkinson's wife, Oriana, had written a witty best-seller covering Atkinson's years as foreign correspondent in wartime Moscow and called it *Over at Uncle Joe's.* Using the book as a starting point, Howard M. Teichmann freely adapted it, changed the leading characters' names to Jake (Myles Eason, made up to look like the bespectacled, pipe-smoking Atkinson) and Julia Ryan (Claudette Colbert), invented some incidents, and christened his play **Julia, Jake and Uncle Joe** (1-28-61, Booth). The pivotal incident related how Jake is arrested and imprisoned for spying after he is caught bird-watching and how Julia pretends to have valuable atomic secrets in order to hoodwink Stalin (Boris Mashalov) into releasing him. Slammed by Atkinson's old colleagues, the comedy was withdrawn after a single performance.

One of Off Broadway's more interesting novelties was Michael Shurtleff's **Call Me by My Rightful Name** (1-31-61, One Sheridan Square). It dealt with the love of a white boy (Robert Duvall) and a black boy (Alvin Ailey), both friends, for the same white girl (Joan Hackett). Although the black boy feels that he and all blacks are grossly misunderstood ("I can't belong to your magic circle. . . . The rest of the world doesn't believe in magic. Not even you.") and the white boy seemingly gets the white girl, the girl does bring about some reasonably good feelings among the three of them.

The drama, suggested by S. P. Foutz's novel *The Whipping Boy,* ran for 127 performances.

Mary Chase was heard from one last time with **Midgie Purvis** (2-1-61, Martin Beck). Critics didn't think much of the rambling comedy, but several thought that its star, Tallulah Bankhead, had a glorious field day in the title part. She made her first entrance parading down a curving staircase in a tiara and gorgeous furs, only to be told by her son (William Redfield) that her getup and behavior are ridiculous for an eighty-year-old woman and will mar his chances with his potential in-laws. Hurt, Midgie dresses in rags and runs off to become governess to some young children. Bankhead, sliding down and clambering back up a firehouse pole, sliding rear end first down a bannister, and riding high in a swing, has a whopping time with the more understanding tots before her son agrees to accept her as she is.

Some of the season's worst notices went to **How to Make a Man** (2-2-61, Brooks Atkinson), a comedy derived by William Welch from a Clifford Simak short story. In the almost utopian world of 1991 liquor can be downed in capsule form, people have four-day weekends, and closed-circuit home TV can disseminate odors. When the Knights (Barbara Britton and Tommy Noonan) send away for a mechanical pet dog, they are shipped a robot by mistake. The robot, Albert (Peter Marshall), proves uniquely intelligent and a boon to the family, but the manufacturer sues to get it back. In court the Wrights are defended by two more robots. They lose, so at Albert's suggestion, before returning him Mrs. Wright removes the tube that serves as his superior brain. He will now be a very ordinary robot, with merely a name and serial number.

At the City Center on the 7th, Hamburg's Deutsches Schauspielhaus brought in an austere mounting of the first part of Goethe's *Faust.* It played for its slated two weeks.

Rabindranath Tagore's **The King of the Dark Chamber** (2-9-61, Jan Hus) was an allegory about an Indian queen's search for her reclusive husband. Despite its exotic nature, it ran out the season.

Sam Spewack suffered a humiliating single-performance failure with his **Once There Was a Russian** (2-18-61, Music Box). Catherine the Great (Françoise Rosay) foists the very Yankee John Paul Jones (Albert Salmi) on the conniving, currently out-of-favor Prince Potemkin (Walter Matthau). But most of Potemkin's ploys to cut down Jones—drinking him under the table, saddling him with a discarded mistress, forcing him to show his mettle at sea—go awry. When Jones finally leaves, Potemkin can only sigh what a much better world it would be without foreigners. Critic after critic reported that the biggest laugh came from the

same line—although none reported it in precisely the same words. According to one reviewer it went, "You need aid. I am an American and you're going to get aid whether you want it or not."

The Comédie Française came into the City Center on the 21st for a three-week stand with a five-plays-in-four-bills program. The troupe opened with a Molière double bill, *L'Impromptu de Versailles* and *Les Fourberies de Scapin,* then moved on to *Tartuffe,* Racine's *Britannicus,* and Georges Feydeau's *Le Dindon.*

Come Blow Your Horn (2-22-61, Brooks Atkinson) introduced a new name to Broadway, Neil Simon. Suddenly appearing at the apartment of his brother, Alan (Hal March), Buddy Baker (Warren Berlinger), who has just turned twenty-one, announces he has run away from home. He has balked at his domineering Jewish parents' denying him his fun and freedom. He wants to live the way Alan does. Both young men still work for their father in his artificial fruit business, so the old man (Lou Jacobi) is not long in showing up. He is, in his own sarcastic way, understanding: "You work very hard two days a week and you need a five-day weekend. That's normal." When Alan tells of being on the ski slopes and trying—unsuccessfully—to phone a client from there, Baker's admiration knows no bounds. He tells Alan he ought to be in the Olympics. The verbal sparring goes back and forth. But in the end Baker keeps his sons in the business with him, accepts Alan's choice for a bride, and allows Buddy to live away from home. Like many critics, Kerr reported "a blockbuster response on the part of the customers, whether the jokes were satisfying, so-so or seedy," and he concluded plaintively, "We can only yearn for the years of Anne Nichols' maturity." With even those reviewers who disliked the comedy acknowledging that first-nighters loved it, the play ran for 677 performances and launched Simon on his career.

· · ·

[Marvin] **Neil Simon** (b. 1927) was born in the Bronx and educated at New York University. He began his career as a radio- and television-script writer, and subsequently turned to the stage by writing skits for summer camp revues. His sketches were also seen in *Catch a Star* (1955) and *New Faces of 1956.*

· · ·

To replace the failed musical that had accompanied *The American Dream,* the producers brought out another Albee play which Europe had already welcomed, **The Death of Bessie Smith** (3-1-61, York). Bessie Smith, the famed black singer, never appears in the work. Instead, her death, coming because whites in a southern hospital in 1937 refuse her proper treatment for injuries sustained in an automobile accident, is seen through the eyes of a nurse in charge of admissions. Initially the woman represents the arrogant, bigoted stand of the era's southland, but as the hour-long play progresses she comes to be shaken by doubts about its fundamental decency. At the play's end she is crooning, crying, and laughing all at once.

Unlike Parker Ballantine earlier in the season, Walter Kerr did not write the review of his wife's play for his newspaper. But the gal who did and all Kerr's other colleagues handed Jean Kerr's **Mary, Mary** (3-8-61, Helen Hayes) the kind of hats-in-the-air notices that virtually ensured a long run. In the *World-Telegram and Sun,* Frank Aston observed of the author and her play, "With vixenish, vinegarish vigor she has written an ironclad hit." The public agreed, keeping the comedy on the boards for 1572 performances. Bob McKellaway (Barry Nelson) shows his fiancée, Tiffany Richards (Betsy von Furstenberg), reviews of his latest book, and tells her his ex-wife used to ask why his books were so good that "a hundred thousand people wouldn't read them." An incessant fusillade of similarly barbed remarks had led him to leave her. Now he has to meet with her again, to straighten out some tax problems. When Mary (Barbara Bel Geddes) appears, she is as caustic as ever. At the same time, an old friend named Dirk Winsten (Michael Rennie) arrives. He is a fading film star who is deserting Hollywood—"the sinking ship leaving the rats." Dirk's romantic advances to Mary let Mary and Bob recognize that they still love each other. Mary even manages to swallow her latest barb in mid-sentence.

The Devil's Advocate (3-9-61, Billy Rose) was Dore Schary's transcription of Morris L. West's best-seller. A dying English monsignor (Leo Genn) is sent to Calabria to see if the late Giacomo Nerone is deserving of sainthood. In flashbacks, it turns out that Nerone was actually a deserter (Edward Mulhare) from the British army during the war, and as much sinner as saint. On his own deathbed, the monsignor equivocates in his conclusions. Some critics felt Genn played his part too brazenly. But unanimous raves greeted Sam Levene for his portrayal of the sceptical but good-hearted Jewish doctor who had been relegated to the village by the Fascists. The drama lingered for a little more than three months.

The Importance of Being Oscar (3-14-61, Lyceum) was a one-man show allowing the Irish actor Michael Mac Liammoir to give a sort of biography of the man by reading from Wilde's private and published writings.

Although Hugh Wheeler's **Big Fish, Little Fish** (3-15-61, ANTA) ran only 101 performances and went down as a commercial failure, it was one of the year's most critically acclaimed plays. In the *Journal-American,* John McClain hailed it as "funny, yet strangely profound. It is first-class theatre." Having long

since been dismissed from his college post because of a sex scandal, William Baker (Jason Robards, Jr.) has settled into a job in a minor publishing house. His limited social life centers on a coterie of quarreling, parasitic nonentities—"barnacles" is the honest assessment by one of them. Learning that Baker is in line for a better position overseas, they fight tooth and nail against the move. When the position falls through, Baker nonetheless decides to pick up and leave. But he offers his hangers-on a farewell party, asking them, "What the hell's the point of life, if you're not fond of your friends?" A performance directed with silken elegance by John Gielgud included Hume Cronyn as Baker's old-maidish admirer and Martin Gabel as a pushy but failed small-time publisher.

The Phoenix ended its year with an applauded revival of *Hamlet,* offering young Donald Madden in the lead. It ran, beginning on the 16th, for one more performance than did Wheeler's play.

Even reasonably long runs could not ensure that a play would close with a profit. That was the sad fate of Henry Denker's **A Far Country** (4-4-61, Music Box), which Taubman reported "enriches a season that badly needs enriching," and which ran for 271 performances. Preparing to leave Nazi-occupied Vienna in 1937, Sigmund Freud (Steven Hill) recalls an 1893 case that helped establish his reputation. Elizabeth von Ritter (Kim Stanley) is so crippled that she can only walk with the aid of crutches. In a last desperate attempt at a cure, since all other doctors have failed, she is brought to Freud. When his attempts at hypnotism achieve nothing, he allows the girl to talk on and on, hoping something will give him a clue. His methods are scoffed at by his anti-Semitic colleagues. But after Elizabeth is made to understand that she longed for her sister's death in order to marry her brother-in-law, her newfound knowledge permits her to walk again.

Allegory, expressionism, fantasy, and reality were thrown about in kaleidoscopic fashion all through Jean Genet's "brilliantly sardonic" **The Blacks** (5-4-61, St. Marks), in a Bernard Frechtman translation and featuring an all-black cast. Several high-and-mighty figures in white masks (suggesting the ruling white world) look down from their perch on a group of minueting blacks, who announce they have killed a white woman. The whites put them on trial, but the blacks' stories are inconsistent, and they finally admit no one has been killed—yet. But they also announce their claim represented a diversion while blacks prepare to slaughter whites and take over the world. With the white-masked figures murdered, the blacks express their hope for a better future. The 1960s were about to explode in revolutionary rhetoric and violence, so the play appealed to a large segment of a certain public. By the time it closed it had run for 1408 performances, then an off-Broadway record for a non-musical.

By contrast, a Broadway look at black-white relations lasted for only a single week. Jack Kirkland adapted **Mandingo** (5-22-61, Lyceum) from Kyle Onstott's novel. The setting is the Maxwells' Alabama plantation in 1832. Warren Maxwell (Franchot Tone), who breeds slaves for a living, thinks nothing of using a little black boy for a footstool. Trouble arises after his son (Dennis Hopper) marries the oversexed, incestuous Blanche (Brooke Heyward). She comes to believe that neither her husband nor her brother can satisfy her, so she takes up with one of Maxwell's more favored slaves, Mede, the Mandingo (Rockne Tarkington). Learning of the situation, Maxwell sets out to kill the black. When his son tries to protect the slave, Maxwell shoots and kills both of them.

The season ended with the quick failure of Jerome Lawrence and Robert E. Lee's **A Call on Kurpin** (5-25-61, Broadhurst), taken from the novel by Maurice Edelman. Jonathan Smith, a writer of articles on science, comes to Russia as a tourist, but also hopes to meet with V. V. Kurpin (George Voskovec), the Russian leading research on building a nuclear-driven spacecraft. The men had worked together at an American university before Russian authorities, by threatening his aged mother, had forced Kurpin to return to the USSR. The CIA enlists Smith's help in getting Kurpin out of the country. For many, Eugenie Leontovich walked off with the entertainment as the old mother, still dressing in pre-WWI clothing, talking as if the czar were still on the throne and as if Wilson were still president.

1961–1962

Although the number of novelties rose somewhat during the season—up one to thirty-four according to *Variety*, up seven to thirty-six by the *Times*'s count—there was little cause for rejoicing. Overall quality again was disappointing at best. And once more, many of the most interesting new works came from overseas. Indeed, during this theatrical year, several newsworthy American works were mounted by cautious Broadway producers only after they had first been acclaimed in Europe. But playgoers did have one small compensation. For the third season in a row, ticket prices did not increase. As a rule, $6.90 remained the weekday top while the weekend top stayed at $7.50.

Off Broadway continued busy all summer long, even if the only entry to chalk up a sizable run (169 perfor-

mances) before late September was Arnold Weinstein's **Red Eye of Love** (6-12-61, Living Theatre), which looked back from a distant millennium on the more or less contemporary dilemma of a young lady (in a fifty-story, all-meat department store, where there is even a department selling spoiled meat) who loves both a successful butcher and an ineffectual dreamer.

Uptown the lights came on first at the City Center on September 19 to offer theatregoers the Greek Tragedy Theatre (Piraikon Theatron) in three classics: *Electra*, *The Choephori*, and *The Eumenides*. The group remained for two weeks.

Off Broadway followed swiftly with two successful revivals. On the 21st at the 4th Street Theatre, David Ross brought out Ibsen's *Ghosts*; on the 25th Shaw's *Misalliance* was brought back at the Sheridan Square.

Broadway proper began to relight with Ossie Davis's **Purlie Victorious** (9-28-61, Cort). Robert Coleman of the *Mirror* referred to this hilarious send-up of black and white stereotypes as "burlesque without strippers." Purlie Victorious Judson (Davis) returns to Cotchipee County determined to wrest back control of the barn-cum-chapel in which his ancestors used to preach and which he will convert into a pulpit from which to raise the cry for black power. To this end he has brought with him Lutiebelle Gussie Mae Jenkins (Ruby Dee) to pose as a dead cousin who should have inherited the property which the unregenerate Confederate and boss of the land, Ol' Cap'n Cotchipee (Sorrell Booke), has seized. When Lutiebelle questions Purlie's intentions, he responds with outrage, "You're a disgrace to the Negro profession!" Of course, Cotchipee, despite his southern-colonel getup and his bullwhip, is not hopelessly reactionary. He is perfectly willing to allow "negras" to go to school—so long as all they take is "a coupla courses in advanced cotton picking." Purlie's trickery nearly backfires, but with the help of Cotchipee's liberal young son (Alan Alda), he gets title to the church. Among the more memorable subsidiary characters was Gitlow Judson (Godfrey M. Cambridge), Cotchipee's personal Uncle Tom, always willing to assent to the old man's most preposterous statements or fall on his knees to sing "Ol' Black Joe." The comedy ran more than seven months (261 performances), yet, in Broadway's increasingly difficult economic crunch, failed to pay back investors. It was subsequently made into the 1970 musical *Purlie*.

Like *Purlie Victorious*, Harold Pinter's London hit **The Caretaker** (10-4-61, Lyceum) had the sort of run (twenty-one weeks) that in an economically healthier theatre would have ensured a profit, but now it, too, closed in the red. Although it was somewhat new to them, Pinter's elliptical style did not throw most critics. They gave the show rave notices. It told of two young, down-and-out brothers (Robert Shaw and Alan Bates) who befriend a shabby tramp (Donald Pleasence) and offer him shelter. But his behavior is so unsociable and demanding that they finally send him on his way.

Lieutenant Stanley Poole (Darren McGavin), who represents one-third of the title of James and William Goldman's **Blood, Sweat and Stanley Poole** (10-5-61, Morosco), is desperate to retain his rank, but won't if he fails the army's new high school and college equivalency tests. To this end, he's stealing his supply room blind, and bribing his venal captain (John McMartin) to doctor the test records. The captain, in turn, is selling the loot and using the money to buy a Jaguar. But then Poole is assigned a highly educated misfit, Pvt. Oglethorpe (Peter Fonda), who catches on to the scheme and offers to tutor Poole so he won't have to steal any more. When the horrified captain realizes what has happened, he alters Poole's answers and flunks him. Poole and his buddies wreck the Jaguar, which sends the captain to the very mental ward Oglethorpe had come from. The comedy ran eleven weeks.

John Patrick's **Everybody Loves Opal** (10-11-61, Longacre) ran less than three, but for many years remained a favorite in amateur theatres. Opal Kronkie (Eileen Heckart) is a bag lady who lives alone in a dilapidating house on the edge of a dump. The house is cluttered with junk, such as a chipped copy of the Venus de Milo and a cheap portrait of Opal's grandmother, framed in a tire. Three crooks (Brenda Vaccaro, Donald Harron, and Stubby Kaye), who manufacture and sell ersatz perfume and who are on the run from the police, wheedle their way into staying with Opal. Of course, they have contempt for a congenital optimist who "greets each day with such determined good will the sun never sets—it flees." Pretending to take her in as a partner, they insure her for $10,000 and try to kill her. They rig a Rube Goldberg invention to allow the ceiling to fall on her, try to run her over, and finally try to poison her. Each attempt misfires. By then the crooks have come to respect her, and she, having caught on to their plans, tells them they were unneccesary since she had more than enough cash hidden away in the house.

Karl Wittlinger's two-character **Do You Know the Milky Way?** (10-16-61, Billy Rose) had been well received in numerous foreign theatrical centers, but New York wanted nothing of it. It spotlighted a veteran (Hal Holbrook) who, learning that he is officially listed as dead, has taken on another soldier's identity, only to discover the other man is a wanted criminal. At a mental institution he writes an autobiographical drama in which he plays himself, while the resident doctor (George Voskovec) assumes all the other roles.

A Shot in the Dark (10-18-61, Booth) was Harry Kurnitz's adaptation of Marcel Achard's Paris hit *L'Idiote*. It was also the first Broadway play of the season to close—after just short of a year—with a profit. A maid (Julie Harris) has been found, passed out, nude, and with a gun in her hand, close by the body of her chauffeur-lover. A young magistrate (William Shatner), on his first case and prodded by his superiors to wrap it up quickly, starts to believe her protestations of innocence. But after he learns that she had recently become the mistress of her rich and famous banker-employer, he wonders whether she or the banker committed the murder, so he calls in the man (Walter Matthau). The banker proves ludicrously pompous. When he blurts out that he never loved the girl, she, hurt, says she now understands why he so often sneaked into his wife's room when he was supposedly at his club. This leads to the revelation that the wife (Louise Troy) has a lover, and that the wife, a descendant of Attila the Hun, did the shooting, thinking it was her husband in the bed. Harris as the blunt, raffish, but somewhat vulnerable girl and Matthau (who took over the part on short notice after Donald Cook died during the tryout) as the stuffed shirt gave deliciously comic performances.

Steven Gethers's short-lived and unlamented **A Cook for Mr. General** (10-19-61, Playhouse) was set on a South Pacific island during the war. The ulcer-beset general (Roland Winters) is in charge of a group of misfits, including the Greek-born Tomas Agganis (Bill Travers), who cooks up succulent feasts of lamb guts, goat bladders, and canned sparrows. They are having a glorious time until a higher-ranking general (John McGiver) makes a surprise inspection. He finds his subordinate doing a wild Greek dance, while the cook, who slugs anyone who touches him, slugs his aide (James Karen). This leads to a court-martial, during which the cook reveals his own sad history and all is forgiven.

An even shorter-lived failure was Hugh Wheeler's **Look: We've Come Through** (10-25-61, Hudson). A mousey, homely little culture bug, Belle Dort (Collin Wilcox), would love to have an affair with the husband (Clinton Kimbrough) from whom her pretty actress-roommate (Zohra Lampert) is separated. It doesn't work out. The actress and her husband are reconciled and head for Hollywood. So Belle must seek solace with Bobby Kraweig (Ralph Williams), a hairdresser whose not deeply buried homosexual leanings have found no outlet with a handsome young sailor (Burt Reynolds).

Frederick Knott's **Write Me a Murder** (10-26-61, Belasco) was a good enough thriller to run profitably for six months. The play is set in the magnificently paneled, high-ceilinged library of Rodingham Manor. It is a room filled with a collection of guns and swords and other even more menacing old weapons. Clive Rodingham (Denholm Elliott), on his uppers, has sold the estate on which his family has lived for 500 years to an insensitive, grasping upstart, Charles Sturrock (Torin Thatcher). Sturrock arrives with his wife, Julie (Kim Hunter), at the same time that Clive's younger brother, David (James Donald), appears. Both Julie and David are writers, and together they write a short story about an apparently detection-proof murder, which makes it seem that an intruder is the killer. The pair quickly fall in love and decide to carry through the scheme to rid themselves of Charles. But before they can, Charles is killed in a car accident. A year later, after a failed American marriage, Clive returns to England and discovers that David and Julie have wed and that they have adopted Charles's plans to develop the property. He attempts to blackmail David, so David follows through with the original murder scheme—but with Clive as the victim. Then Julie, who has been down to London, returns with a surprise. She has submitted their story to a paper, where it won the prize and has been published this very morning. Two Scotland Yard men, she tells him, were reading it on the train. The men now come to the house.

The season's lone one-performance dud was Waldemar Hansen's **The Garden of Sweets** (10-31-61, ANTA). Its title came from the candy store and ice cream parlor run in a city on the Great Lakes by Ana "Manna" Zachariadis (Katina Paxinou), who years before sent her husband packing and has raised her three sons with an iron hand. One has run off to become a sponge fisherman, one a florist and gambler, and one a drunkard. Realizing she is unloved, she dies of a heart attack, but the children gathered for her funeral can hear her spirit intoning, "My name is Ana. Where is Ana now?" Down the drain with the play went Boris Aronson's highly lauded setting: "a veritable cave with descending stalactites of tinted crystal and ascending stalagmites of piled-up lozenge jars meeting each other in the central air like so many decayed teeth."

Graham Greene's London hit **The Complaisant Lover** (11-1-61, Barrymore) ran a hundred performances more than Hansen's play, but still failed to return much of its investment. In it, a pleasant but weak dentist (Michael Redgrave), a complaisant husband, attempts to persuade the bookseller (Richard Johnson) who has been his wife's (Googie Withers) lover to continue the relationship and not rock the boat. But the bookseller is not prepared to be a complaisant lover.

Paddy Chayefsky's **Gideon** (11-9-61, Plymouth) ran more than twice as long (236 performances) after being welcomed by Howard Taubman in the *Times* as "a graceful conceit tinged with innocent wonder and wise laughter," yet also went down in the books as a commer-

cial failure. The Angel (Fredric March) of God exhorts Gideon (Douglas Campbell), a young farmer, to lead his people against the Midianites. At first Gideon is sceptical, but when the Angel performs miracles and gives him the winning battle plan, Gideon accepts that the Angel is in fact Jehovah. However, Gideon later balks at slaying the elders of Succoth. His head has been swelled by praise, and he has come to attribute his success not to God but to "historico-economic, socio-psychological forces." The Angel is left to rue that Man, for all his professed belief in God, believes first in himself.

For many, the season's most satisfying play was Robert Bolt's London success **A Man for All Seasons** (11-22-61, ANTA), a work of solid craftsmanship made luminous by Paul Scofield's quiet, commanding performance in the title part. Thomas More is a thoughtful man with no desire for a showy martyrdom, but he accepts his fate with dignity rather than acquiesce to allowing Henry VIII (Keith Baxter) to divorce Catharine of Aragon or to signing an oath of supremacy which would establish the king instead of the pope as head of the English Church. The drama was accorded a year-and-a-half run.

A revival of Sean O'Casey's *Red Roses for Me* opened at the Greenwich Mews Theatre on the 27th, received embracing reviews, and continued on for 176 performances.

Spurning the suggestion of her fiancé that they have pre-marital sex, Eileen Taylor (Pat Stanley), the heroine of Norman Krasna's **Sunday in New York** (11-29-61, Cort), comes to the Manhattan apartment of her pilot-brother, Adam (Conrad Janis), to seek reassurance that she did the right thing. She firmly believes that she is "the only twenty-two-year-old virgin alive." Her brother assures her that she behaved properly and that he himself does not sleep with women. On a bus, her clothes become snared with those of a nice young newspaperman, Mike Mitchell (Robert Redford), and a romance quickly blossoms until he starts telling the sort of joke which she takes as a prelude to a pass. But they meet again and get caught in the rain. After Eileen discovers a red nightgown and black brassiere in her brother's closet, she decides to loosen up. But just then the fiancé (Ron Nicholas) shows up and finds Mike in little more than a bathrobe. Mike pretends to be Adam until Adam complicates matters by also appearing. (Adam tells Eileen that the "loophole" in his vow was the word "sleep.") In short order, the fiancé heads out, leaving Eileen and Mike to plan their futures. Although the play employed the basic setting of Adam's apartment, by clever lighting and some maneuvering, its furnishings were made to serve also as a New York bus, a film house, two different restaurants, and a Ferrari. Once again in this depressing season, the play had a reasonably lengthy run (just short of six months) yet closed with a loss.

Daughter of Silence (11-30-61, Music Box), Morris L. West's dramatization of his own novel, appeared almost concurrently with the book, but held little interest for playgoers. The story unfolded in contemporary Italy. A young attorney, Carlo (Rip Torn), against the advice of his father-in-law (Emlyn Williams), a self-made, very powerful lawyer who is now the leading figure in his village, agrees to take on the case of a teenager (Janet Margolin) who has killed the man who raped and helped murder her mother during the war. The defendant and the unhappily married Carlo begin to fall in love. But the girl is found guilty and, though she is given a light sentence, goes mad, leaving Carlo to make an accommodation with his cold, selfish wife (Joanne Linville).

On December 12 at One Sheridan Square, a generally acclaimed revival of *The Hostage* began what developed into a 565-performance run.

Most critics had serious reservations about or cared little for Phoebe and Henry Ephron's **Take Her, She's Mine** (12-21-61, Biltmore). Referring to its lack of dramatically exciting incidents, Walter Kerr began his review in the *Herald Tribune,* "The problem with the new comedy at the Biltmore is that it hasn't got a problem." But the public made up its own mind about this formulaic comedy, and kept it before the footlights for 404 performances. Art Carney's droll mugging and George Abbott's fast-paced direction helped the multiscened piece no end. Frank Michaelson (Carney) seems shocked and bewildered that his bright, wholesome daughter, Mollie (Elizabeth Ashley), has gone off to college. Even his understanding wife (Phyllis Thaxter), his disheveled younger daughter (June Harding), and rhumba lessons can provide only small comfort or distraction. He is further baffled when he learns about Mollie's truculently self-assured Harvard beau (Richard Jordan). But Frank is no exception to the sad truth that fathers must reconcile themselves to losing their darling daughters.

Mother and son rather than father and daughter were the central theme of **First Love** (12-25-61, Morosco), which Samuel Taylor derived from Romain Gary's largely autobiographical novel *Promise at Dawn.* Looking back on his youth, Romain (Hugh O'Brian) meets with himself as a boy (Claude Gersene) and as a young man (Rex Thompson), but most of all he recalls his relationship with his Russian-born, Polish-raised francophilic mother (Lili Darvas), an indomitable woman determined her son will be a great hero, a great writer, a great diplomat, and a great lover. He achieves many of her ambitions, but only after she herself is dead.

Several critics were awed that O'Brian, best known as a TV cowboy, could give so sensitive a performance. But he and his celebrity could not draw in enough playgoers for a run.

There was more history in Terence Rattigan's West End hit **Ross** (12-26-61, Eugene O'Neill), which was a thinly veiled recounting of the last years of Lawrence of Arabia. Under the name of Ross (John Mills), the famed soldier who had helped lead the Arabs in their wars for independence has enlisted in the RAF. But he is clearly a troubled recruit. In flashbacks his adventures in the Middle East are relived, most distressingly his capture by the Turks and the shrewd Turkish governor (Geoffrey Keen) who recognizes that the quickest way to break his will is to defile him homosexually, thus exposing his deepest fears about himself. Like so many other plays of the period, it enjoyed a decent stand (twenty weeks), only to close in the red.

But Tennessee Williams's **The Night of the Iguana** (12-28-61, Royale) earned both critical praise and a profit, although it proved to be the last Williams opus to do either. "A beautiful play," "one of Tennessee Williams' saddest, darkest and most comtemplative plays," and "Williams . . . at the top of his form" were among the salutations, and even Kerr, who branded the work "unsatisfactory," confessed to being "very much moved." At a seedy resort on the west coast of Mexico in 1940, the Reverend T. Lawrence Shannon (Patrick O'Neal) is escorting a batch of tourists. Actually he has long since been defrocked for committing fornication and heresy in the same week. Also at the resort are Hannah Jelkes (Margaret Leighton), a woman who ekes out a living drawing charcoal sketches and watercolors, and her ninety-seven-year-old grandfather, Nonno (Alan Webb), "the oldest living and practicing poet on earth." For a brief time a romance would seem to blossom between Hannah and Shannon, and he does oblige her by releasing an iguana some natives have tethered beneath the porch. "Now another one of God's creatures is going down to swim in that liquid moonlight," he tells her. But in the end the old man dies and Hannah decides to move on. Shannon will stay around to help manage the place for the resort's feisty owner (Bette Davis), who struts about in tight dungarees and an open shirt, and he'll service her or the women guests as need be. By the time it closed, the drama had recorded 316 performances.

Despite some feeble disclaimers, there was no question that Leo Lieberman's **The Captains and the Kings** (1-2-62, Playhouse) clearly reflected the problems Admiral Hyman G. Rickover had come up against in his struggles to have the American navy introduce nuclear-propelled submarines. Like Rickover, Captain Kohner (Dana Andrews) must sweep aside not merely the dangerous conservatism of top navy brass such as Admiral Bradley (Conrad Nagel), but the anti-Semitism of his fellow officers and of a corrupt senator (Charles Ruggles) who would scuttle Kohner's plans by revealing unsavory information about the captain's son. At first, the nuclear trials, with Bradley's more progressive son (Peter Graves) in command, seem a disaster. But everything works out as Kohner hoped it would.

The season's third army play featured its third bright, misfit recruit. He appeared in Ernest Kinoy's dramatization of Mark Harris's novel **Something About a Soldier** (1-4-62, Ambassador). Saying that the boy is a "luxury" who has too much latent talent to be put at risk by an army for which he is clearly unsuited, the sympathetic Capt. Dodd (Kevin McCarthy) sees to it that Pvt. Jacob Epp (Sal Mineo), né Epstein, is hurried into a mental ward and then given his discharge. For his pains, Dodd himself is reposted overseas, where he is killed in the war.

Joseph Kramm's **Giants, Sons of Giants** (1-6-62, Alvin) was deemed even less acceptable. A French-born scientist (Claude Dauphin), whose cruel father had left him with a nasty inferiority complex, now lives in a modest-sized American city. His charms and skills have won the respect of his wife (Nancy Kelly), his neighbors, and his colleagues. Together they raise the $1,000,000 he needs to open a clinic he long has dreamed of. But his decades-old paranoia surfaces, proves brutally destructive, and drives him over the brink into madness.

Another in the parade of short-lived flops was **The Egg** (1-8-62, Cort), which Robert Schlitt adapted from Félicien Marceau's Paris hit. It focused on a young man (Dick Shawn) who has drifted aimlessly for years before marrying and settling down. Although he himself is not especially faithful, he is outraged to learn his wife (Paddy Edwards) has taken a lover (Frederick Rolf). He first blackmails the lover, then shoots his own wife, frames the man for the crime, and rejoices in his conviction.

Economic necessity had forced the Phoenix Theatre Company to abandon its superb, full-sized playhouse far down on Second Avenue, and to move to a tiny venue uptown. Its first attraction there had been an English play which, like so many West End works, failed to find favor in New York. Its second offering was an American play that was more encouragingly received, Frank D. Gilroy's **Who'll Save the Plowboy?** (1-9-62, Phoenix), Dying from a wound he received in the war fifteen years ago while rescuing a buddy, Larry Doyle (William Smithers) decides to visit the man and see if his own sacrifice was worth the effort. The man is Albert Cobb (Gerald O'Loughlin), whose openly expressed dreams of running a farm had earned him the nickname of "Plowboy." But Larry quickly learns that Albert has failed as a farmer and at everything else he has tried, and has made a mess of his marriage. Albert even goes so far as to hire a neighborhood kid to pose as the son he had told Larry he named after him. A sadder, wiser Larry goes home to die.

Yet another captivating performance by the debonaire Cyril Ritchard could not push **Romulus** (1-10-62, Music Box), Gore Vidal's reworking of Friedrich Duerrenmatt's comedy, beyond a two-month stand. This Romulus has purposely wangled his way to the throne by marrying the hereditary empress (Cathleen Nesbitt) so that he could have the pleasure of being the emperor to preside over a decadent Rome's ultimate, well-deserved downfall. He gaily prepares to surrender to the Gothic barbarians at the gates. But when he is visited by the Gothic leader, Ottaker (Howard Da Silva), he discovers that the man admires most of what Rome stands for. A disillusioned Romulus takes himself off to raise chickens in the quiet countryside.

A drama from and about Trinidad, Errol John's **Moon on a Rainbow Shawl** (1-15-62, East 11th St.), won good notices and a 105–performance run off Broadway. The drama looked at residents in a slum shortly after the war. A prostitute promises to give up her trade when she is given an engagement ring. A young girl is awarded a scholarship to a good high school, but her plans to attend are shattered after her father is arrested for stealing money with which to buy her uniform and books. An embittered trolley-bus driver (James Earl Jones) runs off to England, leaving behind a pregnant girl.

Back on Broadway, Santha Rama Rau's adaptation of E. M. Forster's famous novel **A Passage to India** (1-31-62, Ambassador) received generally favorable notices, but struggled along for 109 performances before throwing in the towel. Its story centered on a rising Indian doctor (Zia Mohyeddin), eager to accommodate his Anglo-Saxon associates. But his reputation and career are destroyed when a hysterical English girl (Anne Meacham) accuses him of attacking her. Although she recants her charges in court, he recognizes that Indians and Englishmen must live in separate worlds.

The Old Vic came into the City Center for a six-week stay beginning on February 6. Its *Macbeth,* with John Clements and Barbara Jefford in the leads, was not well liked. But its *Romeo and Juliet,* with John Stride and Joanna Dunham in the title roles and with Franco Zeffirelli's unconventional and lively staging, and its *Saint Joan,* with Jefford as the maid, were applauded by most critics.

The Aspern Papers (2-7-62, Playhouse) was Michael

Redgrave's theatricalization of Henry James's novel. It received divided assessments and lingered for ninety-three performances. An American publisher (Maurice Evans), hoping to uncover the lost papers of a dead poet, courts both the man's aged mistress (Françoise Rosay) and her spinster niece (Wendy Hiller). But his playing so cynically both ends against the middle costs him his objective.

Garson Kanin's **A Gift of Time** (2-22-62, Barrymore) was one more dramatized book. Its source was Lael Tucker Wertenbaker's autobiographical *Death of a Man*. Learning that he is dying of cancer, Charles Christian Wertenbaker (Henry Fonda) resolves to live until he is no longer self-sufficient or able to enjoy life, and then to kill himself. As the days go by, doses of morphine must be increased, and he suddenly can no longer type or strum his guitar. After a fall, he realizes his end is near. His loving, supportive wife, Lael (Olivia de Haviland), hands him a razor blade, hugs him, and whispers, "I love you—please die." Fonda's fine, under-stated performance was what playgoers expected of him, but de Haviland's strong, humane wife surprised many and gave her the applause she had heretofore vainly sought in the theatre. Even so, the stars could not keep so somber an evening on the boards beyond its ninety-second playing.

The Phoenix came up with its most talked-about production by offering an American play that had already grabbed kudos overseas, Arthur Kopit's **Oh Dad, Poor Dad, Mamma's Hung You in the Closet and I'm Feelin' So Sad** (2-26-62, Phoenix). This "pseudo-classical tragifarce" was a choice American example of the theatre of the absurd. When Madame Rosepettle (Jo Van Fleet) arrives at a Caribbean hotel she is accompanied by her customary entourage—her pet piranha, the stuffed corpse of her husband, and her stammering, neurotic son, Jonathan (Austin Pendleton). A wide-eyed, determined professional babysitter, Rosalie (Barbara Harris), joins them, and immediately decides that the baby she most wants to sit with is Jonathan. Unfortunately for her, her advances panic the boy and he smothers her to death. Returning to the disarrayed bedroom, Mamma looks around and asks, "What is the meaning of this?" The play chalked up 454 performances.

The cigar-puffing title figure (George C. Scott) of Ira Levin's **General Seeger** (2-28-62, Lyceum) had raised his boy to be a soldier, whether the boy liked it or not. Now he is about to attend the dedication of a building named for his late son, who reputedly had thrown himself on a grenade to save the lives of his fellow workers at a testing laboratory. But the general's resentful daughter-in-law (Dolores Sutton) steps up to reveal

that her husband had hated army life, hated his father, and, in fact, had killed himself. The boy's mother (Ann Harding), Seeger's long-neglected wife, reluctantly confirms the facts. However, the army will not listen to the truth and insists on proceeding with the dedication. His dreams gone up in smoke, Seeger refuses to attend the ceremony and resigns his commission. Two performances and the play was gone.

Robert L. Joseph's **Isle of Children** (3-16-62, Cort) ran only a bit longer—eleven performances. Richard Watts, Jr., in his *Post* review called the drama "a child's version of 'A Gift of Time,' but without its skill." His colleagues agreed, albeit most had the highest praise for its star, Patty Duke. She was seen as a precociously bright fourteen-year-old who knows she will soon die of an incurable heart malady. Her father (Noel William) and she are resigned to the fact, but her mother (Norma Crane) insists on dragging her from doctor to doctor in vain hope of a miracle cure. Just before she dies her parents consent to stage a playlet she has written. It concerns an Oriental monarch, anxious to be remembered after his death, but fearful he has done nothing to keep his memory alive.

If death dissuaded playgoers from lining up at the box office, so did an affirmation of life, Alice Cannon's **Great Day in the Morning** (3-28-62, Henry Miller's). Her work was set in St. Louis in 1928, in the garish if shabby kitchen of Phoebe Flaherty (Colleen Dewhurst). It is a kitchen hung with portraits of Al Smith and Charles Lindbergh, and where Phoebe makes her home brew. For eighteen years the hot-tempered, good-hearted woman has rejected her church and fought with friends, neighbors, and relations. But she finally consents to attend the confirmation of her young niece, Sis (Peggy Burke), and she heads off to the ceremony with a new hope for the future.

Broadway's last hit of the season was Herb Gardner's **A Thousand Clowns** (4-5-62, Eugene O'Neill). Young Nick (Barry Gordon), deserted by his uncaring mother, has been raised by his independent, iconoclastic, unemployed uncle, Murray Burns (Jason Robards, Jr.). Two social workers are sent to report on the situation. Murray's wisecracks and sneers infuriate the prissy Albert (William Daniels), who storms out vowing to have the boy removed from Murray's care. But the other worker, Sandra (Sandy Dennis), approves of remarks about Nick by Murray—"I want him to be sure he sees all the wild possibilities." And she quickly falls in love with him, spending the night in his apartment. She also goads him into seeking a job, since otherwise he is certain to lose the boy. At first, Murray snappishly turns down all offers. Then the popular television clown Leo "Chuckles" Herman (Gene Saks), for whom Murray used to work, comes and confesses that ratings have dropped since Murray stopped writing the show. To keep Nick, Murray agrees to go back with Leo. Hailed by John Chapman of the *Daily News* as "a standout comedy in any season," the play compiled 428 performances.

Down at the 4th Street Theatre on the 11th, David Ross's Ibsen series continued with *Rosmersholm*. Nancy Wickwire played Rebecca West in a mounting that remained for 119 performances.

Broadway's final novelty was a four-performance fiasco. In Henry Denker's **Venus at Large** (4-12-62, Morosco) the screen's most fabulous sex symbol, Olive Ogilvie [read Marilyn Monroe] (Joyce Jameson), comes to New York to try her luck on the stage. She is encouraged by Mick Mandelbaum [read Arthur Miller] (Jack Bittner), a playwright who has not fared well in Hollywood, and by Mr. Kronheim [read Lee Strasberg] (Boris Tumarin), the egomaniacal, theory-spouting head of a school for youthful performers. But in the end Olive recognizes her limitations and returns west. David Wayne won laughs as the Presbyterian agent who has become more Jewish than his Jewish associates— "Something new on the face of the earth, a wandering Presbyterian." And Ernest Truex was applauded as an impatient Hollywood mogul.

The mainstream season closed with a one-week visit, beginning May 14 at the Cort, of the Royal Dramatic Theatre of Sweden. The company offered two Strindberg dramas—*The Father* and *Miss Julie*—and one by O'Neill, *Long Day's Journey into Night*. The productions were well received, even though some of the performers, harking back to a bygone tradition, were in their sixties and seventies yet played characters as young as twenty-five.

Off Broadway provided the season's last success, a double bill. The curtain raiser was Joseph Carroll's **The Barroom Monks** (5-28-62, Martinique), which allowed audiences to sit in on sometimes baffling conversations by habitués of a contemporary Irish-American bar in Chicago. The main part of the evening was devoted to Frederic Ewen, Phoebe Brand, and John Randolph's adaptation of James Joyce's highly autobiographical **A Portrait of the Artist as a Young Man.** The scenes of his youth in a religious household, his difficult times at a Jesuit college, and his early struggles as a writer were again relived. The bill was performed 300 times.

1962–1963

Once more, it was not a very good season. In his second year as editor of the *Best Plays,* Henry Hewes lamented,

"The deterioration of the New York climate for theatrical production . . . became mercilessly apparent in a 1962–63 season generally regarded as the worst." Only two of Hewes's ten best were native dramas (although a third was an American play which failed off Broadway). Even the Pulitzer committee turned its back on the stage, though not without controversy.

Depending on whose tally was accepted, somewhere between thirty-four and thirty-six novelties premiered on Broadway. As with last season, the one piece of good news for playgoers was that ticket prices held steady.

Little excitement was generated either on or off Broadway until mid-September. The season's first hits were unveiled downtown. William Snyder's **The Days and Nights of Beebee Fenstermaker** (9-17-62, Sheridan Square) encompassed several years in the life of its heroine who, believing the "future's as bright as a button and nothin' can stand in my way," comes to New York to try her hand as a writer. She is neither especially sharp nor well organized. One romance with interesting possibilities comes to naught, so she eventually settles for the consoling presence of a boy (Robert Duvall) who never got beyond the eighth grade and whose own father has just fired him from his auto body shop. (By way of counterpoint, glimpses were offered of the squabbles among her mother and aunts back home.) For all its garrulousness (and some of Beebee's speeches were extended monologues), the play ran out the season.

Back in 1908, competing versions of Ferenc Molnár's *The Devil* had opened on the same evening. Now two versions of a Bertolt Brecht play raised their curtains one night apart off Broadway. The first to appear was **Man Is Man** (9-18-62, Living Theatre), Gerhard Neilhaus's translation of Brecht's somewhat diffuse and more politically strident 1954 revision of his 1926 original. **A Man's a Man** (9-19-62, Masque) was Eric Bentley's adaptation of the earlier version. In both versions the simple, harmless Galy Gay is brainwashed into believing he is the fearsome Jeriah Jip. By a second coincidence both versions ran for 175 performances.

On Broadway the season began with Ronald Millar's adaptation of C. P. Snow's novel **The Affair** (9-20-62, Henry Miller's). Although he hates both Donald Howard (Keith Baxter) and Howard's openly Communistic leanings, Julian Skeffington (Donald Moffat), a staunch conservative and devout Catholic, leads the cry for fairness to the man when Howard is accused of doctoring a photograph for his thesis on nuclear physics. After a hearing by Howard's peers, a seemingly happy outcome pleases everyone except Howard's implacable wife (Brenda Vaccaro). The play lingered for 116 performances without paying back its investors.

Garson Kanin's **Come On Strong** (10-4-62, Morosco) survived a mere thirty-six playings, despite the presence of two Hollywood names, Carroll Baker and Van Johnson, at the head of the cast. Since Herbert Lundquist, an unemployed actor with whom she has been having an affair, refuses to marry her, Virginia Karger ups and leaves him, and weds a middle-aged man who promptly drops dead on their wedding night. Herbert and Virginia meet again two years later. He is now trying to make arty documentary movies, and she is the mistress of a celebrated film producer. Nothing comes of the meeting. But two years on, after she has become a star and he is a photographer for *Life,* their paths again cross, and they resume their old romance.

Sharp divisions were exposed in the reviews of Edward Albee's **Who's Afraid of Virginia Woolf?** (10-13-62, Billy Rose). In the *Post,* Richard Watts, Jr., called it "the most shattering drama I have seen since O'Neill's 'Long Day's Journey Into Night.' " In the *Times,* Howard Taubman concluded that the "new work, flawed though it is, towers over the the common run of contemporary plays." The *Daily News*'s John Chapman growled, "It is three and a half hours long, four characters wide and cesspool deep." Martha (Uta Hagen) is an unfulfilled, foul-mouthed woman who is wed to George (Arthur Hill), a quiet college professor. She has long held it against him that he never lived up to his early promise or to the success of her father, who had been president of the college. Matters come to a head one night after the pair, neither quite sober, return from a party and Martha announces she has invited a young couple new to the school over for a nightcap. They turn out to be Nick (George Grizzard) and Honey (Melinda Dillon). Under the influence of more booze and under the guise of "fun and games," the evening erupts into a session of mordant sadomasochism. By the time the embarrassed and upset youngsters leave, George has been provoked to publicly demolish Martha's most cherished illusion—that the childless couple has a son. Helped by winning the New York Drama Critics Circle Award, the drama ran for 664 performances. (Several important Pulitzer judges had also voted for the play but were overruled. They resigned noisily.)

Another less than ideal marriage might have been seen as the background for **Seidman and Son** (10-15-62, Belasco), which Elick Moll theatricalized from his own novel. Morris Seidman (Sam Levene) has run a successful business in the garment industry and hopes his son (Stewart Moss) will take it over. But the boy yearns to be a poet and a do-gooder. He even loses an account by questioning a southern customer's attitude toward blacks. Morris's daughter (Alberta Grant) is flaky, and wears a medallion with St. Christopher on one side and a Star of David on the other. Morris's wife (Frances Chaney) is a hectoring health-food nut

who walks around the house in curlers. When she demands to know if Morris will be home for dinner, he responds exasperatedly, "If I live. If not, I'll call you." No wonder Morris spends some time at the apartment of his attractive, young, but unhappy designer (Nancy Wickwire), if only to show her a little understanding and tenderness. Mrs. Seidman, protesting her loyalty, has no choice but to accept his story of what happened. So he promises to take her to Italy—when next year's line is finished. And Seidman himself must accept his son's living according to his own ambitions. Greeted as a mediocre comedy made delightful by the surefire, very New Yorkish Levene, the play ran for twenty-seven weeks without showing a final profit.

Naturally there was no profit at all to show at Bernard Evslin's **Step on a Crack** (10-17-62, Barrymore), the first of the season's three single-performance flops. A wife (Pauline Flanagan) is upset when her roving-eyed husband (Gary Merrill), a small-town doctor, hires a beautiful receptionist (Maggie McNamara), so her neurotic son (Donald Madden) kidnaps the girl, ties her to a chair in a toolshed, and lights a pile of firecrackers at her feet. The girl is saved at the last minute, but the boy's mind snaps completely.

Sidney Kingsley came a cropper with **Night Life** (10-23-62, Brooks Atkinson), which the *Journal-American*'s John McClain characterized as "a sort of 'Grand Hotel' transported to an after-hours key club." Kingsley's characters included a youthful attorney (Jack Kelly), whose career is on the skids because of his drinking; the attorney's girl (Salome Jens), who has strong lesbian leanings; an ex-gangster turned union leader (Neville Brand), determined to win national power; the club's singer (Carol Lawrence), who has fallen for the labor boss; and a kind, aging businessman (Walter Abel) and his flighty wife (Carmen Mathews). Trouble explodes when the union hood attempts to knife the lawyer, but instead kills the businessman who intervenes. Both Lawrence, a singer better known in Broadway musicals, and Bobby Short, a boîte pianist, entertained with atmospheric songs.

Jack Sher's three-character **The Perfect Setup** (10-24-62, Cort) clearly wasn't, so folded after five performances. In that time it recounted the adventures of a high-priced public relations counsel (Gene Barry), who thinks he has contrived an ideal world with a wife (Jan Sterling) in Westchester and a department store buyer as a mistress (Angie Dickinson) in Manhattan. When push comes to shove and he is forced to choose, he chooses to remain with his wife.

Like *Seidman and Son,* **Tchin-Tchin** (10-25-62, Plymouth) had a good run (twenty-eight weeks), yet closed in the red. The play was Sidney Michaels's freehanded adaptation of François Billetdoux's Paris hit.

Not all critics admired the essentially two-character play, but they saluted the poignant yet wryly humorous performances of its stars, Margaret Leighton and Anthony Quinn. They were seen as a seemingly graceless wife and a rough-hewn construction contractor whose spouses have run off with each other. She persuades him to move in with her and help her consume the cases of whiskey she has bought. Their awkward idyll transports them to Rockefeller Center, a cheap hotel room, and a "dream-haunted" street beneath the Queensboro Bridge.

Another adaptation, **The Fun Couple** (10-26-62, Lyceum), which Neil Jansen and John Haase took from Haase's novel, told of younger love gone slightly awry. Gill Stanford (Bradford Dillman), a pill peddler, has married Tish (Jane Fonda), an ad illustrator, four hours after meeting her on a Mexican vacation. He quickly discovers to his dismay that Tish wants all life to be "one great big surprise party." By carrying some of her notions to their illogical (or is it logical?) extremes, he teaches her to face up to a mundane reality. The comedy, which received harsh notices, was withdrawn after five performances.

The season's third play to inch over the six-month mark yet still go down as a commercial failure was Joseph Hayes's **Calculated Risk** (10-31-62, Ambassador). Hayes took the work from an English play by George Ross and Campbell Singer. A vicious corporate raider (Gerald O'Loughlin) is attempting to take over an old New England company, Armstone Mills. Someone on the board is clearly feeding him crucial information. But Julian Armstone (Joseph Cotten), the latest member of his family to lead the firm, determines to unmask the informant. That means he must give up his beloved hunting and fishing, and get down to work—something he has heretofore been reluctant to do. Julian not only succeeds in finding out who the disloyal board member is, he also mends his shaky relationship with his neglected wife (Patricia Armstrong).

The Foo Hsing Theatre was a group of young Formosan drama students. In two slightly separated engagements, the first beginning on November 12 at the Longacre, they presented a pair of Chinese plays, their titles translated as **The Beautiful Bait** and **The White Snake.** Highly stylized characterizations were acted out in resplendent costumes and meager, suggestive scenery. In all, the youngsters gave twenty-four performances.

Off Broadway followed with two interesting revivals. On the 14th at the Theatre Four, David Ross reverted to Chekhov, offering *The Cherry Orchard* with Marion Winters as the mistress of the doomed estate, Bramwell Fletcher as her brother, and Richard Waring as Lopahin. At the Heckscher on the following evening, Joseph Papp brought out *Macbeth* with largely unknown players

in the major roles. The former mounting ran for sixty-one performances, the latter for 116.

Some memorable acting by suave, mustachioed Charles Boyer kept S. N. Behrman's silky if virtually plotless **Lord Pengo** (11-19-62, Royale) on the boards for 175 playings, but that wasn't enough to allow it to close with a profit. There was no hiding that Pengo was actually the famous art dealer Joseph Duveen. In fact, Behrman had based his play on his own *New Yorker* series "The Days of Duveen." Pengo has been selling masterpieces to American millionaires at huge sums, but insisting "no matter what you pay for the priceless, you are getting it cheap." And he rarely fails to make a sale. But then, as his loyal secretary (Agnes Moorehead) and his unhappy son and heir, Derek (Brian Bedford), agree, selling is almost a part of his religion, like prayers. Derek finally breaks away and leaves to paint the sort of modern works his father detests. However, they are reunited shortly before Pengo's near-at-hand death. What is more, by then Pengo has realized his longtime dream of seeing a national gallery of art established in Washington.

Back down in the Village a double bill by Harold Pinter began a six-month stand. The plays were **The Dumbwaiter** and **The Collection** (11-26-62, Cherry Lane). In the former a pair of not very bright crooks are waiting in the basement of an abandoned restaurant for information about their next job when the dumbwaiter begins to bark orders for fancy food. They attempt unsuccessfully to oblige. Afterwards, one of the crooks is attacked. In the second play a married couple and two homosexual men argue about an alleged adultery.

In Sumner Arthur Long's **Never Too Late** (11-27-62, Playhouse), Harry Lambert (Paul Ford) is a crusty codger, the sort who replies to his wife's asking if he likes her new hat, "Keep it, anyway." He and Edith Lambert (Maureen O'Sullivan) are a middle-aged couple who share their house with their twenty-four-year-old daughter, Kate (Fran Sharon), and Kate's husband, Charlie (Orson Bean), whom Harry has reluctantly given work at his lumber yard but whom he abominates. An always annoying world becomes suddenly almost impossible for Harry when he learns that Edith is pregnant. To add insult to injury he learns that for wood with which to build a new nursery, Edith has turned to a rival, cheaper firm. Harry takes to wearing dark glasses so, he claims, he won't see everyone laughing at him. But after a drunken toot with Charlie, a modus vivendi is reached. Critics saw the play as essentially a one-joke farce that was made uproarious by the frustrated defiance of Bean and, most of all, by Ford. One critic wrote of the long-faced, deadpan comedian, "He is the most mournful-looking man alive, with the sad,

sad eyes of a mistreated dog and a face which has been permanently frozen into lines of bereavement—and he has a perfectly terrible time in this jolly little play." This jolly little play ran for 1007 performances.

Orson Welles had adapted Herman Melville's **Moby Dick** (11-28-62, Barrymore) for the stage some while earlier and performed it briefly in London. Now with Rod Steiger in the lead, it was offered to New York, which wanted no part of it. Welles's treatment had a group of late nineteenth-century strolling players sit down to rehearse their version of the story of a sea captain who loses his life attempting to wreak vengeance on a whale which years before had severed his leg. This approach meant several of the players doubled in brass. Scenery consisted of a few platforms, ladders, and some furled canvas swinging from the flies.

Nor did Broadway care much for Herman Raucher's **Harold** (11-29-62, Cort). A grocer (Nathaniel Frey), an elevator operator (Don Adams), and a waiter (John Fiedler) combine forces to assist Harold (Anthony Perkins), the gauche, painfully girl-shy brother of their old buddy, in gaining some social graces and winning the swank debutante of his dreams. To tutor Harold, they hire a bevy of instructors, such as the proprietor of a Chinese restaurant (Stephen Cheng), who will teach the boy about European wines. And they enlist a homely but sweet young girl, Iris Munger (Rochelle Oliver), for a practice date. At the real ball with the real deb, Harold is a failure, but by then he has come to love Iris, so all ends happily.

Most critics came down hard on Seyril Schochen's pompous, pretentious look at the John Brown legend, **The Moon Besieged** (12-5-62, Lyceum). Her Brown (Charles Tyner) is a fiery rabble-rouser, who convinces his followers that all his actions are God-directed. But his youngest son, Oliver (Ted van Griethuysen), guilt-ridden by the murders his father had once ordered him to commit, and the boy's Quaker bride (Kathryn Hays) have strong pacifist leanings. They beg Brown to free the slaves but not to shoot at anyone. Brown seems to acquiesce. Was Brown deceiving his son, or was he betrayed at Harpers Ferry? Critics admitted to uncertainty about the ending, and the public had little chance to decide for itself, since the drama's first performance was also its last.

Off Broadway went far afield—to New Zealand—for James K. Baxter's **The Wide Open Cage** (12-10-62, Washington Square), which looked at how a middle-aged man takes on the role of father confessor to a motley assortment of folk. Perhaps surprisingly, the play found something of an audience, surviving for 110 performances.

Before the next work opened on Broadway, New York's newspapers closed shop because of a strike that would last several months. The major critics found other, sometimes specially set up, but basically less broadly accessible, outlets for their reviews, while a few took to the air to read their critiques. Still, the damage to business was incalculable, and aficionados of at least one play were to claim it was denied success because of the strike.

The relations of fathers and sons in business had been examined comically in several plays in recent seasons. Now Leslie Weiner's **In the Counting House** (12-15-62, Biltmore) essayed a more serious look—at least for the four performances it ran. Max Hartman (Howard Da Silva), a blustery but warmhearted man, has made his Miss Julie lingerie firm into one of the garment district's more prosperous affairs. His liberal, forty-year-old son, Woody (Sydney Chaplin), has worked with him for some time but now has grown unhappy, especially since his marriage is in trouble and he is falling in love with his attractive secretary (Barbara Murray). Woody's struggle to choose between the women and the struggle's effect on his work occupied much of the play.

Tiger, Tiger, Burning Bright (12-22-62, Booth) was Peter S. Feibleman's adaptation of his own novel *A Place Without Twilight*. That gloomy place, sandwiched in between a pair of cemeteries on the edge of a New Orleans swamp, is the home of a black woman, Mama Morris (Claudia McNeil). Two of her children live with her, a shy, repressed daughter (Ellen Holly) and a spastic son (Al Freeman, Jr.). A framed telegram on the wall states that another son was killed in Korea. That leaves her third, supportive son, Clarence (Alvin Ailey), who supposedly works for the telegraph company, as her mainstay. But her world comes tumbling down when she discovers that Clarence is actually a burglar and a male prostitute, and that he faked the telegram to spare her the knowledge that the "dead" boy is actually in prison for murder.

The comedy that legend has said was hardest hit by the lack of convenient reviews was S. J. Perelman's **The Beauty Part** (12-26-62, Music Box). True, its star, Bert Lahr, was showered with encomiums, and much of Perelman's eclectic, eccentric wit was savored. But the consensus was that it was not as consistently hilarious a tour de force for a great clown as Sid Caesar's musical vehicle, *Little Me,* which had opened slightly more than a month before. Lance Weatherwax (Larry Hagman), now that his father, Milo Leotard Allardyce DuPlessis Weatherwax (Lahr), has informed him that the Weatherwaxes' marriage "has blown a gasket," decides to make his way in the world on his own. But everywhere he roams, he discovers he is wanted only for the Weatherwax name and the Weatherwax millions. Among the people he encounters are

Hyacinth Beddoes Laffoon, the harridan publisher of pulp magazines ("not one of those cockamamie affairs that Henry Luce runs"); Harry Hubris, a movie mogul aiming to make a film about the friendship between John Singer Sargeant and Vincent Youmans; Nelson Smedley, the John Bircher ice cream tycoon, who sees Communist conspiracies on all sides and feels frigid although he is bundled up in a mansion kept at 118 degrees; and Herman J. Rinderbrust, a TV judge more interested in mugging for the cameras than in dispensing justice. (All these figures were played by Lahr). At the close Lance marries the sexy gold digger (Patricia Englund) whom his mother (Alice Ghostley) acknowledges to be a cheap little tramp, while Milo throws money out into the audience. The comedy struggled along for eighty-five performances before folding.

On January 1, 1963, the City Center brought back the great French mime Marcel Marceau for three weeks.

Maxwell Maltz, a plastic surgeon who also dabbled in writing, was the author of **Hidden Stranger** (1-8-63, Longacre), a preposterous and confusing play ("so dreadfully inept that it takes on a kind of repulsive fascination") derived from his short story "Dr. Pygmalion." A famous plastic surgeon (Torin Thatcher), with an alcoholic past and his wife's suicide on his conscience, is lured to an Italian villa by a contessa (Joan Miller) whose husband's face was mutilated in a fire. But the count (Sam Locante) refuses treatment, believing he is being punished by God. So the wife asks the plastic surgeon to scar her face. But when the count realizes that the doctor is falling in love with his wife, he consents to the surgery. His mission accomplished, the lonely doctor departs.

That same evening, the Circle in the Square revived O'Neill's *Desire Under the Elms* with George C. Scott as Ephraim, Colleen Dewhurst as Abbe, and Rip Torn as Eben. The drama played out the season.

Another Italian villa and its surroundings (in a beautifully suggestive, stylized setting by Jo Mielziner) were the scene of Tennessee Williams's **The Milk Train Doesn't Stop Here Anymore** (1-16-63, Morosco). Dying of cancer, the drug-addicted, six-time-widowed Flora Goforth (Hermione Baddeley) is dictating her memoirs into microphones and recording machines scattered about her mansion. If her recollections sometimes drive her to tears, she is not averse to a good cry. After all, she asks the machine, "Who *else* would cry for me?" Her work is interrupted by the arrival of a beautiful, pallid young poet named Chris Flanders (Paul Roebling), who soon reveals that he is known as the Angel of Death because rich old women always seem to die in his presence. Flora warns him not to expect charity from her—that milk train no longer stops at her villa. But he refuses her demand to have sex with her. She

sends him on his way, only to resign herself to the inevitable and call him back. Although it bore all his trademarks, the play was perceived as one of Williams's "lesser plays." Mildred Dunnock's wonderful portrayal of a rival grande dame helped the drama linger for sixty-nine performances.

From England came a magnificent revival of Sheridan's *The School for Scandal,* which opened at the Majestic on the 24th with John Gielgud as Joseph, Ralph Richardson as Peter Teazle, and Geraldine McEwan as Lady Teazle. Greeted by hat-tossing notices, the mounting chalked up sixty performances at the large house.

The season's last one-performance fiasco was Avraham Inlender's **On an Open Roof** (1-28-63, Cort). It dealt with the difficulties encountered in the marriage of an offensively defensive Puerto Rican lawyer and his New England wife as they struggled in their cold-water Manhattan "penthouse."

The King's English was heard again on Broadway in John Barton's **The Hollow Crown** (1-29-63, Henry Miller's), which culled various sources to briefly chronicle the lives and loves of Britain's monarchs from William the Conqueror through Victoria. Programmed as a "revue," it did contain some harpsichord interludes, but consisted primarily of recitations by eight formally dressed players—headed by Max Adrian and Dorothy Tutin—sitting in a drawing-room-like setting.

Critics viewed William Inge's **Natural Affection** (1-31-63, Booth) with considerable distaste. Watts dismissed it as "a slice-of-life drama that revels in degradation." When her fifteen-year-old son, Donnie (Gregory Rozakis), is released from reformatory, where he had been sent for theft and battery, his mother, Sue (Kim Stanley), is confronted with a dilemma. Sue is a successful career woman, a buyer for a Chicago department store, and she has shared her apartment and bed with a handsome ne'er-do-well, Bernie Slovenk (Harry Guardino). Now she must decide whether to continue the affair or devote her time to helping rehabilitate her son. In a strange fashion, the men choose for her. Bernie leaves after a fling with a nymphomaniacal neighbor (Monica May), while Donnie, sensing that his mother would have preferred Bernie to remain, wantonly stabs to death a girl in the apartment hallway.

Off Broadway David Ross pursued his generally admired Chekhov and Ibsen revivals with the mounting at Theatre Four on February 2 of *A Doll's House.*

But Off Broadway also happily explored new playwrights, so Murray Schisgal's double bill of two-character one-acters, **The Typists** and **The Tiger** (2-4-63, Orpheum), was one of the season's surprise delights. In the former Paul (Eli Wallach), a new employee, is being shown how to type mailing addresses by Sylvia

(Anne Jackson). They exchange small talk, sometimes arguing, sometimes joking, sometime analyzing themselves. Thus Paul confesses that deep down he has wanted to feel sorry for himself, while Sylvia retorts that most likely he really wants others to feel sorry for him. As they chat and type, the years fly by. They are still typing and chatting away twenty years later. In the second play, Ben has kidnapped Gloria and brought her to his dingy, messy basement. Ben is not a rapist but a sadly psychopathic philosopher (he has awarded himself a degree in "comprehensive ontology") and wants to share his laments about the uniformization of the world with someone. He proves curiously attractive to Gloria, and, when he releases her, they agree to meet again. Only next time, Gloria says, she will clean up his slovenly digs. The bill ran for six months.

Slammed by the critics, George Tabori's adaptation of Max Frisch's **Andorra** (2-9-63, Biltmore) hung around for only a week. A schoolteacher (Hugh Griffith) has passed off his illegitimate son (Horst Buchholz) as a Jew he saved during the war. But the man is forced to tell the boy the truth when the boy falls in love with his half-sister. In a fury, the boy announces he will always be a Jew. His stance costs him his life during an anti-Semitic interlude. Only too late do the villagers learn the truth.

With a little forcing, Peter Ustinov's **Photo Finish** (2-12-63, Brooks Atkinson) ran out the season. The hefty Ustinov played a wheelchaired, bearded, eighty-year-old writer who is penning his reminiscences. As he does so he confronts his raffish sixty-year-old self (Dennis King), a man worrying about how long he can maintain his sexual prowess, his more self-confident forty-year-old self (Donald Davis), and his hope-filled self (John Horton) at twenty. He also has an ironic confrontation with his long gone father (Paul Rogers) and foretells that not-so-old man's death. Then, too, there is his wife of all seasons (Eileen Herlie). Finally he meets himself as a newborn.

The titular figure (Alfred Drake) of Jack Richardson's **Lorenzo** (2-14-63, Plymouth) headed a group of strolling players trouping across the map of sunny Renaissance Italy. He feels he is above the petty squabbles all around him. But he soon finds himself caught between opposing sides after a duke (David Opatoshu) attempts to drain the local swamps and convert them to farmland. Before long, Lorenzo has watched his children, his wife, and his friends be murdered or carried off. He then is killed in a duel with the leader (Fritz Weaver) of the local mercenaries. Waved aside as a major disappointment, the play was withdrawn after half a week.

Kay Medford, she of the "whining, quavering voice and a permanently soured expression," was probably the only reason to sit through Frank Tarloff's **The Heroine** (2-19-63, Lyceum). Medford was seen as Sylvia Barr, whose husband (Joe Silver) has lost all confidence in himself and his sex drive as well. To reassure and reinvigorate him, she hires a call girl (Beverly Bentley) to pose as a beautiful, respectable innocent who professes to be overwhelmed by the man. The ploy works so well that to Sylvia's chagrin by evening's end her husband is seeking other beautiful, respectable innocents.

Off Broadway *The Importance of Being Earnest* was given a pleasant revival at the Madison Avenue on the 25th and ran out the season. One interesting bit of casting was the old screen and stage favorite Melville Cooper in the relatively minor role of Rev. Chasuble.

Leonard Spigelgass's **Dear Me, the Sky Is Falling** (3-2-63, Music Box) was based on a story by Gertrude Berg and James Yaffe, and starred the plump Berg in another one of her lovable Jewish mother roles. Libby Hirsch's self-preoccupied husband (Howard Da Silva) wants to sell his business and their suburban home, and move away to Florida. As if that isn't a problem enough, their daughter, Debbie (Jill Kraft), is ready to ditch her attractive, young attorney beau (Michael Baselson) and take up with a work-fleeing beatnik (Ron Leibman). Employing some advice from a sympathetic psychiatrist (William Daniels) and her own chicken-soup common sense, Libby sets matters aright. At one point she describes the menu she has been planning for her daughter's wedding as "simple but filling," and that, Walter Kerr said in his CBS review, perfectly described the comedy. The play compiled 146 performances without breaking even.

Along with the Jews, the Irish had for decades been a mainstay of the theatre, so it was not altogether unexpected for a comedy about Irish life to follow one about Jewish carryings-on. Only Will Greene's **The Riot Act** (3-7-63, Cort) wasn't to many playgoers' liking. Katie Delaney (Dorothy Stickney) is a devoted Irish mother of three sons. She tries to govern them with an iron hand at the same time she attempts to be understanding and modern. Thus she allows each boy occasionally to have the apartment to himself for a date—but with the understanding "blinds up, lights on." Never mind that her three sons are all policemen. She even takes under her wing a little Puerto Rican lad (Alexandro Lopez) who belongs to a switchblade gang and allows a beer-swilling neighbor (Ruth Donnelly) to move in with her.

Three superior revivals added sparkle to the season. The first, *Six Characters in Search of an Author,* was brought out at the Martinique on the 8th with a cast of unknowns and ran for 528 performances.

The other two remountings were on Broadway. The Actors' Studio, the voguish training grounds for selected young players, enlisted some of their best-known members for an all-star *Strange Interlude* (1-30-28) at the Hudson on the 11th. The cast included William Prince as Charles Marsden, Franchot Tone as Professor Leeds, Geraldine Page as Nina, Ben Gazzara as Edmund Darrell, Pat Hingle as Sam Evans, Betty Field as Sam's mother, and Jane Fonda as Madeline Arnold. Critics had mixed feelings about both the cast and the play, but theatregoers showed sufficient interest to keep the long drama on the boards for seventy-two performances.

Most critics agreed that *Too True to Be Good,* which Broadway had first seen in 1932, was very minor Shaw indeed. But with a superb cast consisting of Lillian Gish, Eileen Heckart, Glynis Johns, Robert Preston, Cyril Ritchard, David Wayne, Ray Middleton (from the musical theatre), and Cedric Hardwicke, the comedy, which raised its curtain at the 54th Street on the 12th, ran until the hot weather. However, it did so without showing a final profit.

On the other hand, **Enter Laughing** (3-13-63, Henry Miller's), Joseph Stein's theatricalization of Carl Reiner's novel, ran a full year and did make money. Howard Taubman of the *Times* branded it as "marvelously funny." It was the latest glimpse of New York Jewish life. David Kolowitz (Alan Arkin) is a nebbish, who works for the patient if exasperated Mr. Freeman (Irving Jacobson) at the shop where Freeman manufactures machines for hat makers. David's adoring parents (Sylvia Sidney and Marty Greene) want him to be a druggist, but David is stagestruck. He enrolls in a school run by a seedy, boozy old actor (Alan Mowbray), a school where students are expected to pay for their "scholarships." His attempts to act (he even naively reads the stage directions as if they were dialogue) are so bad that the old actor is driven to extra-long swigs from his bottle. But the man's sexy daughter (Vivian Blaine) develops a crush on David and helps him through an embarrassing opening night. Any sensible youngster would recognize not merely his limitations, but his utter lack of talent. Not David, who persists in telling his loyal girl (Barbara Dana), "I'm an actor." Arkin had fun wrestling with a tuxedo and playing with greasepaint, and, of course, hilariously misreading some of his lines.

But Broadway was not ready to reconsider its long neglect of *The Lady of the Camellias.* Dumas's classic was given a new adaptation by Giles Cooper and Terrence McNally, and starred Susan Strasberg and John Stride as the doomed lovers. The mounting opened at the Winter Garden on the 20th and was withdrawn after a week and a half.

Broadway was also becoming surfeited with plays about Jews, so Lillian Hellman closed her playwriting career on a disastrously sour note. "Dismal and dull"

was the assessment of the *World-Telegram and Sun*'s Norman Nadel on **My Mother, My Father and Me** (3-23-63, Plymouth). In several ways the effort was unusual for Hellman, for not only was it a comedy but it was derived from a book—Burt Blechman's *How Much?* Bernie Halpern (Anthony Holland) is a guitar-strumming beatnik. His father (Walter Matthau) is a shoe manufacturer constantly fretting about the possibilities of bankruptcy. His featherbrained mother (Ruth Gordon) is no help to the old man, since she is a compulsive shopper. His tough grandmother (Lili Darvas) is put out to pasture in an old-folks' home. Deciding that perhaps the Indians have been able to override the American rat race, Bernie heads west, where he is last seen selling native baubles in Albuquerque.

Like the central figure in *Lorenzo,* the mother (Anne Bancroft) in **Mother Courage and Her Children** (3-28-63, Martin Beck) is caught between opposing armies, and, since she is a camp-following peddler, has perhaps considered herself immune to the worst horrors of war. While she pushes from the rear, her sons pull her wagon from site to site and her mute daughter sits atop all the shabby goods. One by one, the children are taken from her. Her daughter dies after bravely climbing a rooftop and wildly beating a drum to warn sleeping villagers of an impending massacre. So the weary Mother Courage is left to trudge on alone. Bancroft played "with surface impassivity through which gleam heartiness and cunning, and, at the right rare moments, emotion." For all its virtues, Eric Bentley's version of the Bertolt Brecht drama could not lure playgoers beyond fifty-two performances.

But then Irwin Shaw's **Children from Their Games** (4-11-63, Morosco) lasted merely half a week. "In a sick age, we need sick men to guide us," growls Melvin Peabody (Martin Gabel). Gabel is a vitriolic misanthrope, who finds some reason to complain about everything. Thus he is furious that his ulcer means he cannot use the new wonder drug that might cure his gout. With nothing going right, he sends for his wartime buddy, Sidney Balzer (John McMartin), to help him commit suicide. Fortunately, Balzer is in no way a sick man, and by hypnotizing Peabody, Balzer causes him to have sufficiently pleasant dreams to implant a new, more optimistic outlook on life.

On the 14th at the Lyceum, John Gielgud brought back his *Ages of Man* for a week's stand, allowing his admirers to hear him again recite excerpts from Shakespeare's plays and sonnets dealing with youth, manhood, and old age.

England also offered us Charles Dyer's **Rattle of a Simple Man** (4-17-63, Booth). A millworker (Edward Woodward) from Manchester on holiday in London is picked up by a prostitute (Tammy Grimes) and taken back to her drab flat. But he proves to be a mother's boy, a forty-two-year-old virgin, so all of the girl's efforts to excite him apparently come to naught.

The last long run (239 performances) of the season off Broadway went to Kenneth H. Brown's **The Brig** (5-15-63, Living Theatre). It purported to show a day in the lives of marines confined to a cramped jail. They are beaten by sadistic guards, made to yell at the top of their lungs, and forced to do inhumanly exhausting exercises and to ask permission to cross any of the white lines scattered everywhere on the small floor. One prisoner cracks under the strain and is removed in a straitjacket.

The season on Broadway ended with a sex farce that Paris had relished, that had toured the States profitably for nearly ten years, but that New York soon rejected. **Pajama Tops** (5-31-63, Winter Garden) was Mawby Green and Ed Feilbert's reworking of Jean de Letraz's *Moumou*. When his wife, Yvonne (Leslie Vallen), learns that Georges Chauvinet (Richard Vath) is planning to go away for an evening with blonde, luscious Babette Latouche (June Wilkinson), she invites Babette to the Chauvinet home. There both Georges's swishy pal, Leonard Jolijoli (Cliff Hale), and Babette's husband (James Winslow) show up to create complications. One unforeseen result is that after spending some time alone with Babette, Leonard reappears speaking in a baritone voice and displaying distinctly mannish mannerisms.

1963–1964

Although tallies of how many novelties reached Broadway in the new season ranged widely from thirty-five to forty-two (a sharper discrepancy than usual), there was little disagreement that the theatrical year once again was largely lackluster. No fewer than six entries folded after their first performance. And at season's end neither the Critics Circle nor the Pulitzer committee saw fit to garland an American play. (Oddly enough, one of this season's late entries did win both prizes next year).

Off Broadway remained relatively busy all summer and produced one reasonably long-run hit during the warm weather, Lewis John Carlino's **Cages** (6-13-63, York), a double bill of one-acters. Both plays featured Jack Warden and Shelley Winters. In **Snowangel** John escorts Connie, a prostitute, back to her place at four in the morning but shocks her by asking her to dress and talk like the one girl he ever loved. At first Connie is outraged, but after she recalls her own unfulfilled love—an illegal immigrant who showed her a happy

time before he was caught and sent back to Mexico—the pair reach an accommodation. The husband in **Epiphany** is a bird specialist who attempts to break loose from his dominating wife, a woman who makes no bones about her suspicions of his homosexuality. He brandishes a razor-like metal beak and cackles, but then, unfortunately and literally, lays an egg. The victorious wife assures her humbled "henny-penny" that she will take care of him. The bill lingered for 176 performances.

On the same evening, Joe Papp began his summer series of Shakespearean plays in Central Park. Starting with *Antony and Cleopatra,* he moved on to *As You Like It* on July 11 and *The Winter's Tale* on August 8. Among the players, in major or minor roles, were Colleen Dewhurst, Michael Moriarty, Charles Durning, Salome Jens, and James Earl Jones.

On August 27, *Oh, Dad, Poor Dad . . . ,* which had been touring regular road houses since its off-Broadway run, came into the Morosco for a six-week stand with Hermione Gingold and Sam Waterston in the leads.

The season's first novelty on Broadway, Hugh and Margaret Williams's **The Irregular Verb to Love** (9-18-63, Barrymore), was a harbinger of the rush of West End plays to reach New York during the fall. About the same time that his wife, Hedda (Claudette Colbert), is released from prison, to which she had been sent for blowing up a fur store in protest against the killing of animals, Felix Rankin (Cyril Ritchard) must also confront his pregnant daughter (Kathryn Hayes) who insists on remaining unwed, and his beatnik-novelist son (Robert Drivas) who returns from Sardinia with a child-bride-to-be (Margot Bennett) who can speak only Greek. Since Felix himself has had a little fling while his wife was incarcerated, he must show tolerance all around. The play ran for 115 performances.

That was five performances more than a highly urbane but perhaps too esoteric French comedy ran. Pamela Hansford Johnson and Kitty Black were credited with translating Jean Anouilh's **The Rehearsal** (9-23-63, Royale). At an elegant château, some Frenchmen decide to mount a performance of Marivaux's old classic *The Double Inconstancy.* They enlist a serving girl (Jennifer Hilary) for one of the roles. But when the count (Keith Michell) shows signs of falling in love with the maid, the countess (Coral Browne) and his mistress (Adrienne Corri) conspire to have the count's alcoholic friend (Alan Badel) seduce the girl.

The first American novelty of the year was also its first single-performance failure. Robert Thom based his **Bicycle Ride to Nevada** (9-24-63, Cort) on Barnaby Conrad's novel *Dangerfield.* Its story was suggested by the painful last years of Sinclair Lewis. Winston Sawyer

(Franchot Tone) remained on the wagon for many months in order to write his latest book. But now, recognizing the work as a failure, he is boozing heavily again and seems near death. His long-neglected son (Richard Jordan) suddenly appears, chases away the young, loving girl (Lois Smith) who has been sustaining the writer, and vents all his spleen on his father. The confrontation proves too much for Sawyer.

The season's first commercial hit was John Osborne's **Luther** (9-25-63, St. James), with young Albert Finney giving "dignity and grandeur" to the title part. The play covered the years from Luther's induction into the Augustinian Order of Eremites in 1506, through his rebellion against Roman Catholic corruption, and ended in 1527, when, now an ex-monk and married, he whispers his hopes for the baby's future to his newborn son.

Another commercial hit, largely because it was so cheap to mount and maintain, was **Spoon River Anthology** (9-29-63, Booth), in which six players read poems culled by Charles Aidman from Edgar Lee Masters's famous book of verses about small-town life. Among the dead brought back to life were a father bitter that his daughter is hopelessly blind, and the girl herself, who leads a perfectly happy life for all her sightlessness. The readings were given 111 times.

The season's third British importation, Arnold Wesker's **Chips With Everything** (10-1-63, Plymouth), was well received and ran for nineteen weeks, yet wound up in the red. A group of conscripts arriving at an RAF training station are mostly middle- or lower-class, but one (Gary Bond) comes from a more elite background. He tries bravely to stoop to win the respect of the others, but in the end, prodded by some snobbish officers, realizes he must be himself. Alan Dobie won acting honors as a loud, tough drill corporal.

Broadway wanted nothing to do with David Turner's West End hit **Semi-Detached** (10-7-63, Music Box). It folded after a mere two weeks. The tellingly named insurance salesman Fred Midway (Leonard Rossiter) has raised himself and his family from his seedy beginnings to lower-middle-class respectability and a semi-detached home. Now he aims to rise to the upper middle class and a detached house. He will do so by what he insists is the only sure method, having no time for the truth or other scruples. Thus he encourages one daughter (Bridget Turner) to divorce a husband who has lost his inheritance and marry a richer man. He has similar plans for his other children.

With the cooler weather having arrived, Joe Papp moved his Shakespearean troupe indoors and offered *Twelfth Night* at the Heckscher on the same night.

Also off Broadway, Henry Reed's translation of Ugo Betti's **Corruption in the Palace of Justice** (10-8-63, Cherry Lane) won sufficient plaudits and patronage to

run for 103 performances. Erzi must conduct an inquiry in the name of the Lord High Chancellor to find which of six judges is guilty of corruption. While only one judge appears guilty of the specific charge, all are shown to be sorely tainted.

The next British entry was Peter Shaffer's double bill, **The Private Ear** and **The Public Eye** (10-9-63, Morosco). In the former a shy young man (Brian Bedford) mistakenly believes an attractive girl (Geraldine McEwan) shares his intellectual interest in fine music. He is left alone after she proves to be more interested in his brash friend (Barry Foster). In the second play a distraught husband (Moray Watson) hires a rather vulgar Greek-monickered detective (Foster) to find out with whom his wife (McEwan) is having an affair. It develops that she is not unfaithful, but simply addicted to horror movies. Despite fine writing and superb acting, the bill was withdrawn at a loss after twenty weeks.

Even more so than the first American play to make a brief appearance on the boards this season, the next two native works openly mirrored historical people. Henry Denker's **A Case of Libel** (10-10-63, Longacre) was taken from Louis Nizer's autobiographical *My Life in Court,* and, more specifically, from the chapter dealing with Quentin Reynolds's suit against columnist Westbrook Pegler. Besides claiming he is a secret Communist, Boyd Bendix (Larry Gates) has accused his former friend, the famous foreign correspondent Dennis Corcoran (John Randolph), of being an "immoral, yellow-bellied degenerate." Such wild charges are typical of the right-wing columnist. Corcoran persuades an exhausted Robert Sloane (Van Heflin) to forgo a vacation and take his case. Sloane is unable to convince the one man (Richard McMurray) who could prove that Bendix's charges have damaged Corcoran to be a witness, so he must establish that the accusations are intentionally malicious. He does this by showing that Bendix used lunatic-fringe publications as sources and that he carefully selected the most destructive words to embellish probably fictional incidents. He also gets Bendix to agree that some quotations could only have been written by a "Communist-leaning, party-lining lout" and then shows the quotations are from Bendix's own writings. After the jury awards Corcoran only one dollar in compensatory damages, but hundreds of thousands in punitive damages, Corcoran congratulates Sloane on bringing the matter to a happy conclusion. Sloane, not so content, warns that the battle will have to be fought time and again in the future. Although the drama was hailed by the *Journal-American*'s John McClain as a "salutary success," and ran for seven months, it was reputed to have closed without recouping all of its initial costs.

Robert Noah's **The Advocate** (10-14-63, ANTA) was

a one-week failure that reexamined the often-told story of the Sacco-Vanzetti case, in which a pair of Italian-born anarchists were tried, convicted, and put to death for a killing they most likely did not commit. Noah looked at the affair from the viewpoint of Warren Curtis (James Daly), a New England blue-blood who sacrifices a chance for quick promotion by taking on the case. Much of the script, including Vanzetti's final statement to the court, was said to have been taken verbatim from trial transcripts.

The French actress Marie Bell won praise when she came to the Brooks Atkinson on the 20th for a two-week stand, offering a pair of Racine tragedies, *Phèdre* and *Bérénice*.

The idea of spoofing labor unions and their self-serving leaders appealed to many critics, but these same men felt that Howard Teichmann's **A Rainy Day in Newark** (10-22-63, Belasco) failed to pull it off. Many of the reviewers suggested the leading figure was a light-hearted send-up of the Teamsters' notorious Jimmy Hoffa. John "Black Jack" T. Kodiak (Eddie Mayehoff), grounded in New Jersey because of bad weather, decides to help with negotiations at the Lamb Clock Factory, which his thugs have organized on the principle that "anything that runs on wheels belongs in my union." His demands—such as a twelve-hour work week—are so outrageous that the exasperated owner (Dody Goodman) simply hands over the business to him. As a capitalist, Kodiak changes sides completely, prompting his employees to walk out and lock in him and his lawyer (John McMartin). "Taft and Hartley," he cries, "wherever you are—Help!" Before long he has handed back the business to its former owner and headed off to less troublesome pastures. One week and the play was gone.

A much more fully realized comedy became the season's runaway hit. The *Daily News*'s John Chapman referred to Neil Simon's **Barefoot in the Park** (10-23-63, Biltmore) as a "hurricane of hilarity." Newlyweds Corie (Elizabeth Ashley) and Paul Bratter (Robert Redford), fresh from a happy honeymoon at the Plaza, move into a dilapidating walk-up where a broken window in the skylight allows the snow to fall through and where you turn off the radiator to get heat. It's truly quite a walk up to reach the walk-up—five flights or six, if you count the stoop outside. The couple's first visitors are Corie's mother, Mrs. Banks (Mildred Natwick), and their eccentric neighbor, the gourmet and lothario Victor Velasco (Kurt Kasznar). Corie unwittingly invites the pair to dinner on the same night, but, when the oven fails to work, Victor takes them to a wild Albanian restaurant on Staten Island. Everyone enjoys him- or herself except Paul, whom Corie accuses of being such a stuffed shirt that he would like to sleep with his tie on. Corie decides she wants a divorce. But when her mother shows up in Victor's bathrobe after having spent the night at his place, and after Paul, soused, reveals he has obligingly danced barefoot in the park, Corie realizes how much she loves Paul and his sane, quiet ways. A running gag throughout the show was the characters' various reactions to climbing six flights of stairs. Thus an old delivery man can do nothing but quiver and shakily point to where Corie must sign for a package. Rave notices and word of mouth kept the comedy on the boards for 1530 performances.

A majority of critics had almost as much high praise for **The Ballad of the Sad Café** (10-30-63, Martin Beck), Edward Albee's sensitive and sometimes poetic transcription of Carson McCullers's story. But playgoers, for the most part, were uninterested, so the play was removed from the boards after fifteen weeks. In a small southern town, the Amazonian Miss Amelia Evans (Colleen Dewhurst), who dresses in mannish shirts, dungarees and boots, has thrown her much smaller husband out of her bed and out of the combination store-café-and-home she owns. Her hunchbacked, dwarfed Cousin Lymon (Michael Dunn) appears. She takes him in and quickly displays a certain motherly affection for him. But after a time her husband, Marvin (Lou Antonio), returns from a spell in prison. Lymon instantly develops a crush on him. A knock-down-drag-out fight erupts between Miss Amelia and Marvin, which Miss Amelia seems on the verge of winning until Lymon interferes on Marvin's behalf. The two men head off together. When a customer comes into Miss Amelia's store, the humiliated proprietress would charge the woman $1.05 for a soda, explaining it's "five cents for the coke, and a dollar . . . for lookin' at the freak." Miss Amelia closes the store and lives reclusively from then on.

A somewhat unusual off-Broadway success was **In White America** (10-31-63, Sheridan Square), Martin B. Duberman's compilation of white and black statements on American race relations through the centuries, from the writing of an eighteenth-century ship's doctor on the slave trade and Thomas Jefferson's views on blacks through a report of the treatment of black troops in World War II and a young black girl's attempt to enter an all-white high school in 1957. The dramatic reading ran for 493 performances.

Off Broadway, a revival of *The Immoralist* at the Bouwerie Lane on November 7 found favor and ran for 210 performances.

Broadway continued to traffic in plays about thinly disguised historical figures. There was no question that the **Arturo Ui** (11-11-63, Lunt-Fontanne) of the drama which George Tabori took from Bertolt Brecht's original was a portrait of Adolf Hitler. Even Christopher Plummer's makeup in the title part underscored the fact. Ui is a small-time Brooklyn hood who comes to Chicago and employs all manner of devious or vicious means to take over the cauliflower trade. From there it is a small step to bigger and uglier things. Rouben Ter-Arutunian framed his stylized black and white settings and costumes in a proscenium festooned with bare light bulbs, giving an ironically cynical midway air to the brutal story. But neither critics nor theatregoers seemed too interested, forcing the play to leave after a single week.

Some more possibly veiled biography was seen in Terence Rattigan's **Man and Boy** (11-12-63, Brooks Atkinson). At least a number of critics saw parallels in it to the life and death of the infamous Swedish match king, Ivar Kreuger. In 1934, with his world collapsing around him, and with even his wife (Jane Downs) and closest friend and adviser (Geoffrey Keen) turning against him, the famous Roumanian financier Gregor Antonescu (Charles Boyer) arrives at the Greenwich Village basement apartment of his long-neglected son. He hopes for some sort of reconciliation, but realizes that the boy's good looks would appeal to a homosexual client whose support he desperately needs. The boy, who of course is shocked, tries to be supportive without prostituting himself. Recognizing the hopelessness of the situation, Antonescu kills himself. Some critics admired Boyer's suave, probing performance, but others complained his speech was growing increasingly thick and unintelligible. The drama lingered for seven weeks.

One Flew over the Cuckoo's Nest (11-13-63, Cort), which Dale Wasserman based on Ken Kesey's novel, stayed around for only ten weeks, but enjoyed a prosperous afterlife in regional theatres and in films. Its raffish, extroverted hero (Kirk Douglas), given a choice of prison or a spell in a mental institution for a crime he has committed, opts for the insane asylum, assuming it will be a short-termed lark. What he does not bargain for is the sadistic, tyrannical head nurse (Joan Tetzel), who is not beyond ordering a lobotomy for the man to force him into line.

Lewis John Carlino, having met with success off Broadway earlier in the season, had another small success there with **Telemachus Clay** (11-15-63, Writers Stage). For this "collage," a cast of eleven, sitting on stools on an otherwise bare stage, recounted the adventures of an illegitimate young man seeking both his natural father and fame as a film writer.

Three dismal comedies followed one another over a month's time on Broadway. The first two were so bad they were hurried away immediately after their first night; the third hung on for a week and a half. In between the arrival of the first two, the nation was thrown into shock by President Kennedy's assassination.

In Owen G. Arno's **Once for the Asking** (11-20-63,

Booth) a suburban housewife, Mrs. Goolsby (Dorothy Sands), discovers that she is a fairy who can fulfill anyone's wish for twenty-four hours. She helps a struggling advertising copywriter (Scott McKay) become an overnight success on Madison Avenue. She also tranforms his boss into the pigtailed little sister he wanted to be, turns a girl into a goldfish, and allows a frustrated hausfrau a fling in Hollywood. Typical of the dialogue was the copywriter's daughter's telling her father that a fairy had moved in next door, and his retorting, "Where did you learn that dirty language?"

Irving Cooper's **Have I Got a Girl for You!** (12-2-63, Music Box) was, as its title might have suggested, Broadway's latest look at New York Jewish life. Joe Garfield (Simon Oakland) lives in the Bronx with his mother (Nancy R. Pollock) and is a devoted athletic instructor at an East Side school. He loves another teacher (Karen Thorsell), a girl as dedicated as he is. But mama dreams of bigger things for him, both matrimonially and elsewhere in the world. He gets his way after making a case for his profession on television and after all his mother's friends call her to tell her what a hero her boy is.

When Buzzy Pringle (Dennis Cooney), a high school senior, announces he has eloped with his next-door neighbor, Rosemary Cotts (Alberta Grant), a junior, his parents (Larry Parks and Mary Fickett) in Anita Rowe Block's **Love and Kisses** (12-18-63, Music Box) are thrown off base. So are his older sister (Susan Browning) and her fiancé, Freddy Winters (Bert Convy). But all ends happily. Among the "jokes" in this comedy, which the *Times*'s Howard Taubman dismissed as "not advanced enough for a none-too-bright 12-year-old," were daddy's response to the news that the young bride can bake pizzas—"Datsa nice."

There was some noticeable improvement in Ronald Alexander's gag-filled **Nobody Loves an Albatross** (12-19-63, Lyceum), as well as another delightful portrayal of a likable scalawag by Robert Preston, who had few equals in the type. The three-times-married Nat Bentley admits privately that he is "one of the greatest liars who ever lived" and "a man of five-minute loyalties." In fact, he is a self-promoting television writer who regularly takes credit for the work of hope-filled, desperate youngsters he bamboozles into creating scripts for him. When his shenanigans are exposed and he is ordered to write an original television comedy about a young girl and her love for animals, he simply plagiarizes an old Shirley Temple film. Caught out again, he loses the sweet secretary (Carol Rossen) who might have married and helped him. But the curtain falls with his flimflamming another TV bigwig (Leon Janney) into giving him a high-paying position. Representative of the gags was his comeback to his precocious little daughter, who informs him his last wife was not all that attractive: "I never told you this, but now you're old enough to know. She was a female impersonator." For all Preston's domination of the evening, several scenes were stolen by mole-faced Phil Leeds as an eccentric inventor who has perfected a marvelous laugh machine, which he treats almost as a wife. The comedy ran out the season, but wound up in the loss column.

On Broadway, the year closed with a look back at a twenties and Depression phenomenon. June Havoc took her **Marathon '33** (12-22-63, ANTA) from her autobiographical *Early Havoc*. June (Julie Harris) has abandoned her unhappy career in a rapidly dying vaudeville world. Wearing a short skirt, white socks, and scuffed shoes and carrying all her possessions in a paper bag, she comes to a seedy dance hall where a sign warns "No Spitting or Cat Calls" and where a dance marathon is about to start. She accepts an offer of $5 to sing with the band (Conrad Janis and his Tail Gate 5), but is wheedled by the clownish Patsy (Lee Allen), a professional marathon chaser, into being his partner. Their struggle against their competitors is often degrading and nasty, with some rivals even trying to drug Patsy and others. Toward the end, June is dragging an all but unconscious Patsy around the dance floor. Even with that, they don't win. Harris's "valiant, touching and real" June was considered one of her finest achievements, as was her mimicry of Florence Reed's reciting the "I survived" speech from *The Shanghai Gesture*. But patrons would not come, so the play folded after six weeks.

Off Broadway did have one surprise success at year's end when the Circle in the Square brought out Edith Hamilton's version of Euripides' *The Trojan Women* on the 23rd. Mildred Dunnock was its highly lauded Hecuba. The tragedy played on for a remarkable 600 performances.

The new year, 1964, began strangely. On the 1st at the Brooks Atkinson, David Merrick ventured a revival of last season's failed *The Milk Train Doesn't Stop Here Anymore*. Tennessee Williams had revised his text, which now starred Tallulah Bankhead, and featured Tab Hunter and Ruth Ford. Critics saw no improvement, some suggesting the new version was worse than the original. When the production closed after four performances, so did Bankhead's stage career. Many felt that for all her glamor and notoriety, she had rarely realized her true potential.

Enid Bagnold's **The Chinese Prime Minister** (1-2-64, Royale) told of an aging, soon-to-retire actress (Margaret Leighton) who longs for the sort of highly respected last years supposedly accorded to old Chinese statesmen. But neither her sons nor her husband (John Williams), who reappears suddenly after a decades-long

absence, promise her real satisfaction on that score. Alan Webb won kudos as an ancient, doddering servant.

Dylan (1-18-64, Plymouth), Sidney Michaels's redaction of several biographies of the late Welsh poet Dylan Thomas, looked at his American tours, his irresponsibility, his drunkenness, his death, and the notion that, for all his patent flaws, he would be remembered long after most of his sober, more responsible contemporaries were forgotten. All the action took place on or around some spiraling ramps, with Alec Guinness making a touching, believable poet. Thanks in good measure to the star, the play ran nineteen weeks.

Down in temporary quarters on Washington Square the Repertory Theatre of Lincoln Center began what most playgoers hoped would be a long and bright future with its mounting of Arthur Miller's **After the Fall** (1-23-64, ANTA Washington Square). Most playgoers were unaware of the dismal history of similar, earlier projects; but they did know that the new play was another among the season's thinly veiled biographies—or in this instance, autobiography. More or less as in *Dylan,* the stage was given over to artistically grouped steps and ramps. Coming down and addressing the audience, Quentin (Jason Robards, Jr.), a successful lawyer in his forties, begins his reminiscences by telling it he had come to feel "I was merely in the service of my own success. It all lost any point." Clearly the women in his life have been pivotal. There was his troubled mother (Virginia Kaye), resentful that her husband had lost his money trying to save his business; his first wife, Louise (Mariclare Costello), who valued her independence above all; and his prospective third wife, Helga (Salome Jens), still scarred by her life in Nazi Germany. But most of all there was his second wife, Maggie [read Marilyn Monroe] (Barbara Loden), a beautiful but insecure cabaret singer who cannot understand the demands of truly affectionate love and who ultimately commits suicide. Critics divided in assessing the work, with Walter Kerr calling it "seriously incomplete" in the *Herald Tribune,* while the *World-Telegram and Sun*'s Normal Nadel hailed it as "a beautiful, remarkable play." By far the most popular of the the three pieces that would shortly be performed in repertory fashion, it compiled 208 performances.

At the City Center, a revival of *A Man for All Seasons* began a fortnight's stand on the 27th with a largely undistinguished cast.

On February 3 at the Little, the Habimah, Israel's national theatre, opened a two-month visit with its production of *The Dybbuk*. Subsequent mountings were Ben-Zio Tomer's look at young European refugees attempting to acclimate to life in Israel, **Children of the Shadows,** brought out on the 26th, and Hanoch Bartov's not dissimilar examination of all ages of immigrants endeavoring to adjust, **Each Had Six Wings,** which opened on March 11. Performances were given in Hebrew.

In Richard Dougherty's **Fair Game for Lovers** (2-10-64, Cort) Chester Witten (Leo Genn), a writer, believes that at eighteen his daughter, Prudence (Pegeen Lawrence), is too young and too inexperienced to wed a twenty-three-year-old graduate student, Benny (Alan Alda), so Prudence and Benny decide to live together, out of wedlock, in her room in her father's swank East Side home. Before long, daddy consents to their marrying. The generally panned comedy hung on for only a week.

Although it earned some better notices, with the *Post*'s Richard Watts, Jr., observing it "is neither moving nor particularly dramatic, but it discusses important historical and political matters arrestingly," Paddy Chayefsky's **The Passion of Joseph D.** (2-11-64, Barrymore) survived for two weeks. Looking at Russia from 1917 to Lenin's death in 1924, the drama followed the rejection by Stalin (Peter Falk) of God, his subsequent adoration of his wife (Elizabeth Hubbard), and his rejection of even her after he sets up Lenin (Luther Adler) as his idol. But at Lenin's death, he forgets his mentor's comment—"You have a good mind, don't restrict it to cunning"—and embarks on his ruthless quest for total power.

The fourth of the season's single-performance flops was John Sherry's **Abraham Cochrane** (2-17-64, Belasco). Hoping to make his wife (Nancy Wickwire) feel guilty and thus return to their marriage bed, Roger Balcon (Peter Adams) brings home a handsome wartime buddy, Abraham Cochrane (Bill Travers), and unobtrusively encourages the pair to have an affair. Before he goes on his own unconcerned way, Cochrane wreaks havoc with the marriage, seducing not only the wife but her dying mother (Ann Harding) as well.

The season's second big comedy hit (982 performances) was Muriel Resnik's **Any Wednesday** (2-18-64, Music Box). Most critics were only modestly impressed with the novice's playwriting, but felt the direction and the delicious clowning of the comedy's four players—particularly wispy, blonde Sandy Dennis—glossed over any imperfections. John Cleves (Don Porter) is a conceited, lecherous, hopelessly spoiled businessman who has set up his young, somewhat oddball mistress, Ellen Gordon (Dennis), in a posh "executive suite" which he claims as a tax deduction. For two years they have been spending every Wednesday together at the flat. An innocent secretary gives the keys of the suite to Cass Henderson (Gene Hackman), who is unhappy with the way Cleves is dealing with the Henderson firm that Cleves has bought into. She also gives keys to Cleves's wife (Rosemary Murphy), who comes in unexpectedly and at first mistakes Ellen for Cass's wife. The childishly pampered behavior of Cleves when the foursome try to play a harmless game is ridiculous enough. But then the cat is really out of the bag after Cass learns of the tax write-off and Mrs. Cleves of the true relationships. Appalled at Cleves's puerile, petulant reaction, his wife leaves him, agreeing only that if he wants to get together he can call her—"Any Wednesday." And there is the possibility of wedding bells for Ellen and Cass.

The Repertory Theatre of Lincoln Center brought out its second offering at the ANTA Washington Square on the 20th. The play was Eugene O'Neill's *Marco Millions* (1-9-28). Hal Holbrook was Marco; David Wayne, Kublai Khan; and Zohra Lampert, Kukachin. The drama was waved away on several sides as "among [O'Neill's] least successful works," but, more important, the acting of the ensemble was coming to be perceived as awkwardly uneven. Still, the mounting was kept on the bills for forty-nine playings.

On the 25th at the City Center, the Théâtre de France, under the direction of its star, Jean-Louis Barrault, began a three-week visit. Besides one musical, the troupe offered Beaumarchais's *Le Mariage de Figaro*, Racine's *Andromaque*, and a double bill of Barrault's **Salut à Molière** and Ionesco's **Le Piéton de l'air.**

Pickets were so numerous and voluble at the opening night of **The Deputy** (2-26-64, Brooks Atkinson) that police had to be called in and patrons were kept from going out on the sidewalk during intermission. Jerome Rothenberg translated the drama from Rolf Hochhuth's German original. Repelled by the Nazis' deportation and extermination of the Jews, a young priest (Jeremy Brett) makes a personal appeal to Pope Pius XII (Emlyn Williams) to speak out. But the pope, fearing for the Church's own interests, balks at any forceful denunciation. The saddened priest pins a Star of David on his garment and prepares to go along with the Jewish deportees. Although some critics felt the drama, however powerfully acted, was not worth all the brouhaha, it ran for 316 performances.

Athol Fugard, the author of **The Blood Knot** (3-1-64, Cricket), was a South African white. His play dealt with half-brothers, one light-skinned (J. D. Cannon), one quite black (James Earl Jones). They live lovingly in a shack in the wrong part of town, but the light-skinned one dreams of passing as a white man. A letter from a female pen pal brings to the surfaces latent differences and causes them to confront the struggles of their race. The highly praised drama ran for 240 performances.

Although several critics thought that S. N. Behrman's **But for Whom Charlie** (3-12-64, ANTA Washington Square) was the most fully and happily realized of the scripts offered by the Repertory Theatre of Lincoln Center to date, the public disagreed, so its forty-seven performances were the fewest won by any of the group's first-season mountings. Seymour Rosenthal (Jason Robards, Jr.), to compensate for the ways his late, crass movie-mogul father had made his millions, has set up a foundation to help struggling writers. Grateful for the courtesies Charles Taney (Ralph Meeker) had shown him while they were students together at Yale, he appoints the go-getting, opportunistic Charlie to head the group. But arguments, as much over women as over other matters, finally goad Seymour into asserting his own authority. David Wayne won many of the best notices as an old writer, with only one early success to his name, who has made milking foundations into an art.

A Murderer Among Us (3-25-64, Morosco), the season's latest one-performance fiasco, was George White's adaptation of Yves Jamiaque's Paris hit. Having been released after serving ten years for a killing it was subsequently proved he did not commit, elfin Jerome Lahutte (Pierre Olaf) tells his fellow townsmen that he feels he is entitled to commit one murder with impunity and that, accordingly, he will eliminate the most worthless of the town bigwigs. Since all the nabobs are well aware of their own failings, they attempt to get Jerome to assassinate the town's nasty banker (Severn Darden). Jerome demurs, so the others kill the banker and frame Jerome for the crime.

The three young would-be filmmakers (Gino Conforti, Lawrence Pressman, and Martin Sheen) in Jerry Devine's **Never Live over a Pretzel Factory** (3-28-64, Eugene O'Neill) actually live in a boiler room beneath a Chinese restaurant. When no inspectors are around, one boiler is revealed to be a closet, and packing cases open up into reasonably uncomfortable chairs. The boys need $5000 to film their short about two possible lovers who pass each other without recognizing the possibilities. Then into the cellar pops a boozy screen star (Dennis O'Keefe) fleeing the agent who would put him aboard a ship so that he can sail to make a Western in Morocco. He promises to dig up the cash. In short order, a Mt. Kisco madam with three of her girls, a four-piece combo, and a building inspector all cram in to create complications. But everything winds up happily. At one point the agent dashes in to exclaim that the star's ship has sailed. The star responds, "Was I on it?" He only had to ask the question for nine performances.

Like Off Broadway, Broadway itself looked at the problems of faraway South Africa, perhaps sensing that some of its difficulties were becoming our own. Alan Paton had already won huge success in America with his novels about his homeland. Now he joined with Krishna Shah to write **Sponono** (4-2-64, Cort). Sponono (Cocky Tihotlhalemaje) is a personable but dangerously amoral, even criminal young black. Having been convicted of stealing and of raping the girl who was to marry his best friend, he has been sent to a reformatory. The institution's dedicated white principal (Michael Goodliffe) tries to inculcate white ideals of behavior, but Sponono and his black buddies seem, for the most part, incapable of either understanding or observing them. The boys go so far as to hold a mock trial to condemn the principal for his lofty notions.

On the 5th Eva Le Gallienne's latest attempt at a permanent repertory, the National Repertory Theatre, which was touring the country, came into the Belasco with two offerings, *The Seagull* and *The Crucible*. Both received at best a polite approval from the critics, but little support from New York playgoers. Le Gallienne and a faded screen star, Farley Granger, were the best-known players.

But another revival caused a sensation. In John Gielgud's mounting of *Hamlet* at the huge Lunt-Fontanne Theatre on the 9th, all the characters were in modern street dress for what supposedly was a sceneryless rehearsal of the drama. The Dane was acted by one of filmdom's most sizzling stars, Richard Burton, supported by such players as Alfred Drake as Claudius, Hume Cronyn as Polonius, Eileen Herlie as Gertrude, William Redfield, Barnard Hughes, George Rose, and George Voskovec in lesser roles, and the recorded voice of Gielgud as the Ghost. Ophelia was played by Linda Marsh. Theatregoers were not discouraged by some reviewers who insisted that Burton was "without feeling" or that the play, and not the performers or direction, remained the thing. Nor were they put off by the upped top tickets of $8.80 for weekdays and $9.90 for weekends. Audiences helped the play establish a new Broadway long-run record for the tragedy—137 performances—and close with a decent profit.

Similarly, two more glamorous Hollywood names—Paul Newman and his wife, Joanne Woodward—were clearly the reason that James Costigan's **Baby Want a Kiss** (4-19-64, Little) ran for a profitable 145 performances. Critics discerned in this baffling three-character (plus one dog) play hints of the Theatre of the Absurd, Albee, Thurber, Pirandello, and a slew of other disparate influences. A celebrated film couple pay a visit to an old buddy (Costigan) and at his prodding live out revealing fantasies about themselves and their happy-unhappy marriage.

Another look at black-white relationships, James Baldwin's **Blues for Mister Charlie** (4-23-64, ANTA), ran a tad longer, 148 performances, without proving profitable. Taubman thought the sceneryless drama was "not a tidy play . . . but it throbs with fierce energy and passion." It opened on the same day that Baldwin's own novel version of the story was published. A white man (Rip Torn) dumps the body of a black he has killed and exclaims, "May every nigger like this nigger end like this nigger—face down in the weeds!" The white man is a redneck named Lyle Britten, and the boy he has killed is the northern-educated, rebellious son (Al Freeman, Jr.) of the local minister (Percy Rodriguez). Albeit it is a foregone conclusion that his neighbors will acquit Britten, both the whites and blacks perjure themselves in court to bolster their sides. Even Parnell (Pat Hingle), who is sympathetic to the plight of the blacks and is editor of the local paper, feels the tug of racial loyalty. A flashback after the acquittal shows that Britten shot the boy because the boy refused to say "sir" to him and demanded to be treated like an equal.

Inevitably, some wags suggested that **The Sunday Man** (5-13-64, Morosco), which Louis Bardoly took from Ferenc Dunai's Hungarian original *A Nadrag,* might have been titled *Any Other Sunday.* A married businessman (David Brooks) keeps a typist (Vivienne Martin) as mistress and visits her every other Sunday. On this particular visit he is shocked to learn that she is pregnant and angry to see that she has accidentally smeared butter on his pants. Complications, much as they had in *Any Wednesday,* consist of the unexpected arrival of the man's wife (Jen Nelson), of a young man (Stephen Strimpell) who loves the typist, and of a fat, older man (Dean Dittmann) who covets the businessman's position. The three men find themselves trying to exchange pants so that the businessman can have a pair of unbuttered trousers. The comedy was the season's sixth and final one-performance failure.

Mixed but largely favorable notices greeted England's Royal Shakespeare Company when it came into the mammoth New York State Theatre for two weeks beginning on the 18th. Its presentations consisted of *King Lear* (with Paul Scofield as the king, Irene Worth as Cordelia, and Alec McCowen as the Fool) and *The Comedy of Errors* (with McCowen and Ian Richardson as the two Antipholuses).

Three weeks was all that Broadway would grant **The White House** (5-19-64, Henry Miller's), A. E. Hotchner's vignettes of presidents and first ladies. Helen Hayes, Fritz Weaver, and James Daly headed the cast. Among the twelve characterizations Hayes offered were her Mary Todd Lincoln, on trial for her sanity, and Edith Wilson, attempting to influence her husband and hide the effects of his stroke. Weaver was seen, among other roles, as Andrew Jackson, ruing that he had not shot Clay nor hanged Calhoun, and Abe Lincoln, parrying Stephen Douglas's stances.

Lesley Storm's London hit **Roar Like a Dove** (5-21-

64, Booth) survived a mere two and a half weeks, telling in that time of the American wife (Betsy Palmer) who, having given her Scottish lord of a husband (Derek Godfrey) six daughters, refuses to try for a seventh child in hopes it will be a boy and heir. But with the help of her parents (Jessie Royce Landis and Charles Ruggles) the lord prevails on her to try once more. A bagpipe player announces the resulting good news at the final curtain.

Broadway and Off Broadway each had one final hit up their sleeves. Kerr ended his notice of Frank D. Gilroy's **The Subject Was Roses** (5-25-64, Royale), "Too bad, really, that the prize-giving season is just over. Small in outline as this occasion is, recognition is due in every direction." And, sure enough, at the end of the 1964–65 season, the play, which ultimately ran for 832 performances, won not only the Pulitzer Prize and the New York Drama Critics Circle Award, but also found inclusion in that season's *Best Plays.* Mustered out of the army, Timmy Cleary (Martin Sheen) returns to his parents' drab, lower-middle-class Bronx apartment. The Clearys are anything but happily married, although out-and-out explosions are infrequent. Like many wives in similar positions, Mrs. Cleary (Irene Dailey) looks down on a husband who she feels never lived up to his earlier promise, and Mr. Cleary (Jack Albertson) resents her family and her refusal to give him the sexual satisfaction he still requires. With Timmy back, they both fight each other to win his favor. But Timmy is not deceived. He remembers such battles from his childhood and how ill they had made him, and he says, "From the day I left this house I was never sick. Not once. Took me a long time to see the connection." So he informs his parents that he is leaving home and will live with a friend. Scarred by their own infighting, the Clearys have no choice but to agree.

Englishwoman Ann Jellicoe's "fresh, darting, smiling" **The Knack** (5-27-64, New) ran for 685 performances, aided immeasurably by Mike Nichols's droll staging and a fine cast of young players. Colin (Roddy Maude-Roxby) is so awkward with girls that there seems little chance he will ever win pert little Nancy (Alexandra Berlin) away from Tolen (George Segal), a dashing ladies' man with a knack for getting around women, until his artist friend, Tom (Brian Bedford), tries to lend a helping hand. Even then as he shouts a defiant "I'll show you" to Tolen, Colin fails to catch Nancy while chasing her around a small bed. Tolen grabs her, but after Colin warns him he'll kill him if he touches her, Tolen rushes out a window. Was he truly fearful of Colin, or had he spotted the luscious young lady who had just sauntered past the window?

1964–1965

By now the pattern of the sixties seemed to have been clearly established. In short, it was another largely discouraging season. Fewer than forty new plays opened on Broadway. The *Times* counted a mere thirty-one. True, there were no one-performance disasters this year, and eight plays closed with a hundred or more performances to their credit, yet when all was said and done only four new plays, all comedies, finished with a profit.

The hottest months saw only revivals. Beginning on June 16, Joe Papp's New York Shakespeare Festival offered *Hamlet, Othello,* and Sophocles' *Electra* at its open-air playhouse in Central Park and toured the boroughs with *A Midsummer Night's Dream.* Players included such stars as Julie Harris (Ophelia) and such rising figures as James Earl Jones (Othello). On October 12, the company's *Othello,* in reaction to the high praise it had earlier received, was moved indoors to the Martinique, where it ran out the season. The group's unusual Greek offering had no sooner closed than the Greek Tragedy Theatre (Piraikon Theatron) returned to these shores for two weeks, starting on August 31 at the City Center, to present *Medea* and its version of Sophocles' drama.

The season proper was launched with a belated New York presentation of Jean Anouilh's 1937 Paris success, **Traveller Without Luggage** (9-17-64, ANTA), in a translation by Lucienne Hill. Having spent eighteen years in a mental hospital after snapping during WWI, Gaston (Ben Gazzara) is released and sets out to find his past. He believes he has always been a good, peace-loving man, but the family who claims him for its own can show him only his history of violence and meanness. Rather than accept this, he lets himself believe he is the nephew of a sweet little boy (Jeffrey Neal) who insists he is the older man's "uncle." Even with a second world war intervening to create similar situations, New Yorkers would not accept the play.

But they were even less welcoming to Don Appell's lone-week, two-character dud, **A Girl Could Get Lucky** (9-20-64, Cort). Penny Moore (Betty Garrett) is a thirty-five-year-old secretary who reads the *Times* and high-quality paperbacks. Andy Willard (Pat Hingle) is a forty-one-year-old taxi driver who reads the *Daily News,* works out on barbells, and is a health food nut. Penny invites Andy to dinner in her $90-a-month apartment (kitchen, dining alcove, living room, and bedroom). Love blossoms, and marriage follows. So do

bickering and separation. But by the final curtain the pair are reunited.

Ira Wallach's **Absence of a Cello** (9-21-64, Ambassador) ran fifteen weeks only to close in the red. Andrew Pilgrim (Fred Clark), a distinguished scientist, has lost so much money on his own experiments that he feels he must take a job with a large corporation. But he has always lived informally, dispensing with ties and other constricting clothing, and happy to take time off to play his beloved cello. His wife (Ruth White) has written some scholarly books. But they are advised that they must hide their intellectuality and informality if he is to land the position. So the cello and the wife's books are stashed away, while a TV set and some *Reader's Digest*s are given conspicuous places, and out come the long-neglected ties. Then an uncomfortable Andrew rebels, insisting on being himself. He gets the job anyway.

Poor Sam Levene! For all his hilarious skills and great popularity, he was never to find a real post–*Guys and Dolls* hit, not even when he appeared in a comedy by no less than Saul Bellow. But, then, Bellow was primarily a novelist and was inexperienced as a playwright. His new work was called **The Last Analysis** (10-1-64, Belasco). Philip Bummidge, né Bumovich, was a famous comic known to his once adoring public as "Bummy." But his popularity plummeted, and he was forced to retire. Now, hoping to find what went wrong and resurrect his career, he pays for a closed-circuit television show which will be beamed from his luxurious loft to a convention of psychiatrists at the Waldorf. In it, he relives his life—backwards from the present to his birth—thus remeeting his relations, his friends and his enemies. The evening's highlight was his birth, with his colleagues as a sort of black-robed Greek chorus commenting on the struggles of baby Philip to come into the world and a very adult baby Philip mugging and responding accordingly.

Off Broadway fared a mite better on the same night with George Panetta's **Kiss Mama** (10-1-64, Actors' Playhouse), helped by the presence in the cast of a popular singer, Julius La Rosa. Since her Italian-Catholic son, George, married his Jewish bride (Rose Gregorio) in a civil service, Mama (Augusta Ciolli) yearns for a proper wedding in the parish church. She strives even harder after learning that the couple are expecting, since otherwise the baby might be born without a soul. The comedy chalked up 142 playings.

If Saul Bellow's inexperience had hurt his comedy, all of Samuel Taylor's heretofore successful efforts counted for naught when he brought out **Beekman Place** (10-7-64, Morosco). Unlike Bellow's Bummidge, the great violin virtuoso Christian Bach-Nielsen (Fernand Gravet) is happily retired. That is, he is happy until an old friend (Arlene Francis) of his wife (Leora Dana) shows up and reminds everyone of an affair she and the violinist had in wartime England. She brings with her the militant, ban-the-bomb daughter (Carol Booth) of that liaison. But the shock of disclosure and the excitement of supporting the daughter's protests revitalize Christian, so he decides to resume his career.

In Friedrich Duerrenmatt's **The Physicists** (10-13-64, Martin Beck), which New Yorkers heard in James Kirkup's translation, two great scientists, Herbert Beutler (Hume Cronyn) and Ernst Ernesti (George Voskovec), feign madness and claim to be Newton and Einstein, in order to gain admission to a mental institution where Johann Mobius (Robert Shaw) is housed. Mobius, another great scientist, insists he receives personal messages from Solomon. The others are convinced that he, too, is faking in order not to have to work on death-delivering projects. But when the men believe they have cleared up the mystery, they are told by the doctor (Jessica Tandy) in charge of the establishment that they are all genuinely insane (all three have strangled their nurses) and will remain there to do her bidding.

Lorraine Hansberry's **The Sign in Sidney Brustein's Window** (10-15-64, Longacre) ran for only 101 performances even though a group of Broadway figures from, alphabetically, James Baldwin through Shelley Winters took out a large advertisement lamenting the lack of patronage and urging playgoers to see the work. Brustein (Gabriel Dell) lives in a Greenwich Village apartment with his part Irish, part Greek, part Cherokee wife, Iris (Rita Moreno). He devotes himself to editing a neighborhood newspaper in which he attempts to get a supposedly idealistic politician (Frank Schofield) elected. This causes a breach between him and his wife. She also has a sister (Cynthia O'Neal) who is a prostitute and in love with a Negro ex-Communist (Ben Aliza), and another sister (Alice Ghostley) who has made a rich marriage. The one sister kills herself after the Negro leaves her; the politician proves treacherous as soon as he is in office; and Iris storms out. But Brustein is not willing to give up his fight for what he believes is right: "Everytime we say 'Live and let live'—death triumphs."

Although London had liked it, New York would not embrace Iris Murdoch and J. B. Priestley's **A Severed Head** (10-28-64, Royale). A wine merchant (Robin Bailey) moves smoothly between his mistress (Jessica Walters) and his wife (Heather Chasen), but before long the wife's psychoanalyst (Paul Eddington), the merchant's sculptor-brother (Robert Milli), and the psychoanalyst's half-sister (Sheila Burrell) all enter the picture, and the six people engage in a round dance of marital and extramarital affections.

At the ANTA Washington Square, the Repertory Theatre of Lincoln Center began its second season on the 29th with a mounting of Thomas Middleton and William Rowley's 342-year-old **The Changeling,** in what was billed as its first professional American playing. Having gotten the mercenary De Flores (Barry Primus) to murder the man she is supposed to marry but does not love, Beatrice (Barbara Loden) finds herself forcibly seduced by the killer. She therefore orders a virginal servant to take her place on the night she marries the man she does love. By evening's end, Beatrice and De Flores have joined the corpses littering the stage. Critics liked neither the blood-and-thunder melodrama nor its uneven, uninspired playing, so the piece was withdrawn after thirty-two performances.

Prize-winning novelist Edwin O'Connor's **I Was Dancing** (11-8-64, Lyceum) survived only half as long, although it was much more happily performed. And for the second time in a matter of weeks, a novelist-turned-playwright offered a comedy about a retiree. Its central figure was bow-tied, mustachioed Waltzing Dan Considine (Burgess Meredith), a seventy-year-old retired hoofer, who hopes to impose himself on the married son (Orson Bean) whom he has ignored for most of his life. He even fakes a heart attack when the son would send him to St. Vincent's Smiling Valley for Senior Citizens, especially since it means he would have to put up with his gabby, preachy sister (Pert Kelton), a resident there. But the son has a mind and determination of his own.

The season's first comedy hit was Murray Schisgal's three-character **Luv** (11-11-64, Booth). A scruffy, despondent Harry Berlin (Alan Arkin) has climbed the railing and is about to commit suicide by jumping off a bridge. Just then, his dapper, seemingly cockily successful old college buddy, Milt Manville (Eli Wallach), strolls by and nonchalantly gets Harry to change his mind, climb down, and crumple his suicide note. But it soon turns out that Milt, caught in an apparently hopeless marriage and longing to wed another girl, has come to the same bridge for the same purpose. In a moment of inspiration Milt decides to solve both their problems by foisting his wife, Ellen (Anne Jackson), on Harry. His plan works at first. Harry and Ellen wed, and so do Milt and his young lady friend. However, a few months later Milt's bride has left him and he wants Ellen back. His two attempts to murder Harry by pushing him off the bridge both end with Milt's falling in the river. Nonetheless, he and Ellen are eventually reconciled. Harry is left to climb a lamppost to escape a vicious dog. Welcomed in this disappointing season by the *Herald Tribune*'s Walter Kerr as "the answer to a theatregoer's prayer," the comedy ran for 901 performances.

There was little rejoicing when Edna St. Vincent Millay's twenty-seven-year-old **Conversation at Mid-**

night (11-12-64, Billy Rose) was given its first major New York airing. Still, this talky, blank-verse drama, in which seven men are seen and heard palavering during an imaginary evening, was let down gently by the critics. The men include a Negro (Al Freeman, Jr.), a priest (John Randolph), a writer (Sandy Kenyon), and a young ad man (Hal Englund) who is having trouble with his love life. But the three principal talkers, who nearly come to blows at one point, are a conservative capitalist (Larry Gates), a determined Communist (James Patterson), and a middle-of-the-road liberal (Eduard Franz). The latter suggests, "All soil is rock under the wafted seed of Reason;/ Whenever it falls, it falls on stony ground." The conversations were repeated for only half a week.

Some critics also regretted having to reject **Poor Bitos** (11-14-64, Cort), and it was withdrawn after seventeen playings. The entertainment was Lucienne Hill's translation of Jean Anouilh's Paris success. A group consisting largely of aristocrats, all dressed incongruously in modern formal evening wear and eighteenth-century wigs, have assembled for dinner, pretending to be figures from late eighteenth-century France. They take it upon themselves to bait another guest, the local prosecutor, Bitos (Donald Pleasence), who arrives dressed as Robespierre. He is a poor boy who has made good, but has never gotten over his hatred of those born to wealth and easy living. Although one (Diana Muldaur) of the guests is sympathetic enough to warn him of the others's plans, he leaves assuring her he will be avenged on all his betters.

The season's second comedy hit was Bill Manhoff's two-character **The Owl and the Pussycat** (11-18-64, ANTA). In the wee hours of the morning a young girl pounds on the door of Felix Sherman (Alan Alda), pleading that she needs help and for him to let her in. When he finally, grudgingly does, she quickly changes her tune, calling him a "rat fink pansy," "a slimy snail," and "a bedbug." Actually, he's none of these. Felix is merely a book-store clerk who hopes to be a successful writer. But, having spied on her with his binoculars, he has reported her to her landlord for plying her trade at all hours with the blinds up. Her trade? Well, although Doris (Diana Sands) insists she is a model, she resorts to prostitution to make ends meet. Now, her landlord having thrown her out and seized her money, she has only seventy-two cents to her name. She insists she will stay the night. That night lasts for a month, during which time the pair become close, have fallings-out, make up, then fight again. Finally, they go their separate ways, but not until he has made her get a respectable job, and she has helped him see he has merely the smallest talent as a writer. Much ballyhoo was accorded the fact that Sands was black and the casting color-

blind. There is no mention of race in the text. Richard Watts, Jr., the critic for the *Post,* called the play "a most winning little comedy," and even those who held reservations concurred that it was deliciously acted. The comedy ran merrily for 427 performances.

P. S. I Love You (11-19-64, Henry Miller's), which lingered a week and a half, was Lawrence Roman's anglicization of André Roussin's *L'Amour qui ne finit pas.* Set in France, it spotlighted the rather foolish wife (Geraldine Page) of an American diplomat (Lee Patterson). For a time the woman dreams of running off to Italy with a married Frenchman (Gilles Pelletier) who has been writing her mash notes, but then her husband makes her see the light.

Lovers of German drama—in German—had two weeks in which to enjoy the Schiller Theater of West Berlin when the ensemble came into the huge New York State Theater on the 24th to offer Schiller's *Don Carlos* and Carl Zuckmayer's send-up of the harsh orderliness and excessive red tape of the kaiser's days, **The Captain of Koepenick.**

Given the laudatory notices William Hanley's three-character **Slow Dance on the Killing Ground** (11-30-64, Plymouth) received—"big-league," "taut and passionate," "Christmas has come early to Broadway"— one might have expected it to be a hit. It wasn't, folding sadly after an eleven-week struggle. Just as Glas (George Rose) is closing up his small, tawdry combination magazine and confectionary shop in the shadow of the Brooklyn Bridge late one evening, a jivey but somewhat menacing young black (Clarence Williams III) enters. He is dressed in a close-fitting suit with a velvet collar, a small-brimmed, high-crowned hat, a short cape, and dark glasses. Fearing a holdup, Glas tells him there is nothing much to steal and he's not afraid of being robbed. But the boy, who gives his name as Randall, does not seem to be bent on thieving and even mentions he is supposed to have a 187 IQ. The pair soon enter into a conversation which starts to expose their histories. Glas, insisting he is not a Jew, tells of fleeing the Nazis. The boy also seems to be fleeing something. Before long Rosie (Carolan Daniels) enters. She has lost her way while seeking a back-alley abortionist. She, too, joins the revelatory conversation, which eventually brings out that Glas was a Communist who left his Jewish wife and son to their fate when he ran off, and that the black boy has murdered his mother. Glas accepts that he must live the remainder of his life with his guilt, Randall understands that he must head back out to almost certain death, and Rosie more clearly realizes the unpleasant choices confronting her.

In Dore Schary's **One by One** (12-1-64, Belasco) two paraplegics confined to wheelchairs fall in love. Kathy (Sharon Laughlin) was crippled after slipping from a tree when she was ten years old. Jason (Donald Madden) had a promising athletic career devastated by polio. Still, he can swim well enough to save Kathy, who has fallen from a pier, and his love for her gives hope of curing his crushing bitterness. But Kathy's spinster sister (Michaele Myers) is jealous, while Jason's father (Richard McMurray), kidding himself that Jason will someday make a full recovery, believes Jason should wait until then before choosing a bride. Fortunately, the lovers prevail. The play received thumbs-down notices and closed at the end of its first week.

Jean Kerr's **Poor Richard** (12-2-64, Helen Hayes) had a curious fate. It opened to very mixed reviews, with some critics seeing it as a joy; some as good, but not up to *Mary, Mary*; and a few panning it. (Judith Crist, who was substituting on the *Herald Tribune* for Mrs. Kerr's husband, Walter, was probably the harshest.) Thereafter, the show struggled along for a modest run of 118 performances, yet wound up as one of only four plays to close with a profit during the season. Its story was not all that complex. A reputedly bibulous young English poet, Richard Ford (Alan Bates), has come to America to help publicize his surprise best-seller, a book of poems written as a sort of memorial to his late wife. His publisher (Gene Hackman) sends his secretary, Catherine Shaw (Joanna Pettet), to help the writer, not knowing that Catherine has long had a crush on him and promptly announces to the startled author that he will marry her. She is soon disillusioned to realize that he apparently never really loved his late wife, but later, after she sees his reaction to a letter his dying wife had written to the publisher, comprehends his actual feelings. Mrs. Kerr offered two endings, one in which they conclude they must go their separate ways (the one performed) and one in which they seem to be heading for the altar. But she also offered the Wildean bon mots that her admirers had come to expect from her, lines such as "There is no despair like the despair of a man who has everything" or "No one has yet found a way to drink for a living." Decades later, when Texas governor Ann Richards wowed the Democratic Convention with her quip about Bush having been born with a silver foot in his mouth, no one apparently recalled the all but identical line in this play.

Not everyone agreed with the *Times*'s Howard Taubman that Arthur Miller's **Incident at Vichy** (12-3-64, ANTA Washington Square) "returns the theatre to greatness," but most, nonetheless, were pleased. One by one the people who have been rounded up in Vichy are either determined to be Jews and sent off to a concentration camp, or else are found to be Aryans and released. When only two are left in the waiting area,

the doctor (Joseph Wiseman), who is a Jew and had come out of hiding to seek medication for his wife, and the Austrian prince (David Wayne) confront each other. The prince insists he has never been an anti-Semite and is sympathetic to the plight of the Jews. But the doctor points out that even with the best of intentions everyone harbors hatreds and that the prince has been welcoming to known bigots. To the prince's stammered apologies, the doctor retorts, "It's not your guilt I want, its your responsibility—that might have helped." The mortified prince allows the doctor to escape by giving him his own pass.

Probably the sole cogent reason for seeing Susan Slade's **Ready When You Are, C.B.!** (12-7-64, Brooks Atkinson) was another winning performance by Julie Harris. An insecure and penny-pinching young actress, who found her $58-a-month West Side apartment by following up obituaries, sublets it to a famous, rising screen-idol-in-hiding (Lou Antonio) for $300 a week. She stays on to help him since, as he claims, he sleepwalks. They have a brief love affair, but when he returns to Hollywood, she recognizes the romance is over. Even so, she now has a happier outlook on life. Estelle Parsons won applause as the actor's gaudy mistress. The title came from a humorous story told in the play about the time Cecil B. De Mille staged a magnificent scene, only to discover afterwards that his cameraman had not filmed it.

Off Broadway, two early Harold Pinter plays, **The Room** and **A Slight Ache** (12-9-64, Writers Stage), began what proved to be a ten-month stand. In the former, a truckdriver's wife (Frances Sternhagen) feels menaced by visitors after her husband goes off to work, most particularly by a blind black man who may represent death. In the latter, a strange matchseller brings out the emptiness in the life of a cold writer (Henderson Forsythe) and his more compassionate wife (Sternhagen).

Playgoers again had to trek downtown to another double bill, this one by LeRoi Jones, consisting of **The Slave** and **The Toilet** (12-16-64, St. Marks). The first dealt with a revolutionary black (Al Freeman, Jr.) who blows up the home of his former wife, a white woman now married to a professor. The second told of a group of young black students beating up a white boy who has sent a love note to their leader. The plays, heavy in the foulest language, played 151 performances.

Uptown, Bill Naughton's London hit **Alfie!** (12-17-64, Morosco) failed to amuse New Yorkers. A young cockney lecher (Terence Stamp) delights in telling the audience about his cynical, love-'em-and-leave-'em way with his "birds."

Nor did playgoers embrace Eugene O'Neill's **Hughie** (12-22-64, Royale). The work was actually an hour-long, intermissionless one-acter in which one of its two characters does most of the talking. That character is "Erie" Smith (Jason Robards), an old, pretentious Broadway sport, who walks in during the small hours of a 1928 summer morning to the lobby of the seedy hotel where he resides and tells the bored night clerk (Jack Dodson) how he used to regale the former clerk, Hughie, with his tales of big bets and dates with dolls from the *Follies*. He admits the tales were tall, indeed, but insists that poor, luckless Hughie lapped it up. Hell, "if every guy along Broadway who kids himself was to drop dead there wouldn't be nobody left." The play survived for six and a half weeks.

Edward Albee's **Tiny Alice** (12-29-64, Billy Rose) hung on for twenty-one weeks, without repaying investors. The *Daily News*'s John Chapman criticized it as "wordy and unclear," while Kerr concluded, "In such a play it is easy for both author and audience to get lost." Miss Alice (Irene Worth), who is the world's richest woman, bequeaths $2 billion to the Catholic Church with the stipulation that the mysterious lay brother Julian (John Gielgud) be sent to her home to accept the money. Although he admits to having spent six years in a mental institution, he is seduced by Alice, then dies, crying out, "God, Alice . . . I accept thy will."

The new year was launched off Broadway with a revival of the popular old thriller *The Cat and the Canary* (2-7-22). It compiled 141 performances following its premiere at Stage 73 on January 4.

The next evening the City Center offered New Yorkers the Polish Mime Theatre. The troupe remained at the auditorium for two weeks.

Critics were beginning to observe that incoming new plays often had more producers than players. Such was certainly the case with Enid Rudd's two-character **Peterpat** (1-6-65, Longacre). In a sense, there were three characters, since a smiling lady named Louise Rush sat in an upper box playing merrily away at an organ before the curtain went up, during intermission, and while the silhouetted principals changed costumes between scenes. Peter (Dick Shawn), an unsuccessful writer of mysteries, and Pat (Joan Hackett), having lived together for three years, decide to marry shortly before their child is due. Problems arise after Peter's books are bought for TV serialization and he takes on a mistress. This leads Pat to opt for divorce. But Peter follows her to their summer home, where all is made right again.

Matters went further downhill with Ben Starr's **The Family Way** (1-13-65, Lyceum). A widowed young actress (Colin Wilcox) finds that her pre-teen son (Michael Kearney) has been passing out pictures of her and inviting men to stay with her. Seems the boy longs for a father and has been told by a friend (Christopher

Mann) that he would get one if a man got his mother in the family way. The woman finds her own new husband in her attractive agent (Jack Kelly).

The Repertory Theatre of Lincoln Center received some of its best notices to date when it mounted Richard Wilbur's translation of Molière's *Tartuffe* on the 14th. Michael O'Sullivan had the title role. By season's end the piece had been repeated more than seventy times.

An off-Broadway revival of *A View from the Bridge,* which opened at the Sheridan Square on the 28th with Robert Duvall and Jon Voight in the principal roles, received generally rave notices and remained for 780 performances.

Having run five years in Paris and currently in its third year in London, Marc Camoletti's **Boeing-Boeing** (2-2-65, Cort) seemed a logical contender for a Broadway run as well. But old-fashioned, slambang sex farce was out of vogue, so the entertainment survived in New York a mere three weeks in Beverly Cross's translation. For some time at his apartment overlooking Orly Airport, Bernard (Gerald Harper) has enjoyed the favors of three stewardesses—one American (Diana Millay), one French (Susan Carr), and one German (Joanna Morris). He can do this, since the girls' schedules never seem to overlap. Each has been led to think of herself as his one and only. But a sudden spell of bad weather and scheduling changes bring the girls together, with a frantic Bernard enlisting his buddy, Robert (Ian Carmichael), to help him out of his mess. Since Bernard's apartment sported seven doors, audiences knew pretty much what to expect.

When the Moscow Art Theatre began a month-long engagement at the City Center on the 4th, it brought with it Mikhail Bulgakov's dramatization of Gogol's look at corruption in nineteenth-century backwaters, **Dead Souls,** two Chekhovian revivals, *The Cherry Orchard* and *The Three Sisters,* and one modern work, Nikolai Pogodin's **Kremlin Chimes,** in which Lenin struggles to secure the revolution in 1920. Reviews were courteous, but a far cry from those the company had garnered in its initial American appearances more than forty years before.

Two other revolutionaries, Juan and Eva Peron, provided the inspiration for Jerome Lawrence and Robert E. Lee's failed **Diamond Orchid** (2-10-65, Henry Miller's). Having been ditched by the senator (Bruce Gordon) who had been keeping her, Paulita (Jennifer West) latches on to a rising young officer, Jorge Salvador Brazo (Mario Alcalde), and prods him on to greater things. Before her early death, she uses her influence with the army and the unions to help Brazo become dictator and to enrich her own coffers.

Bill Naughton's second West End comedy to reach Broadway in two months was **All in Good Time** (2-

18-65, Royale). Like the first, it was rejected by New Yorkers. Bookish young Arthur Fitton (Brian Murray) and his bride, Violet (Alexandra Berlin), seem unable to consummate their marriage after six weeks. Word of their predicament mortifies Arthur's blustering father (Donald Wolfit). The youngsters' parents offer varying suggestions on how to remedy the matter, but, as the title suggests, things right themselves in good time.

The characters in Jack Weinstock and Willie Gilbert's tricky **Catch Me if You Can** (3-9-65, Morosco) were given no names in the program to add to the air of mystery. At an A-frame in the Catskills, a Detroit advertising man (Dan Dailey) claims his wife has run off during their honeymoon. But a local detective (Tom Bosley) brings in a young woman (Bethel Leslie) who insists that she is the wife, and a parish priest (George Matthews) confirms her identity. Nonetheless, the man says it isn't so. The murder of a local delicatessen man (Eli Mintz) complicates the affair, before a solution is reached.

The season's longest-running comedy hit—964 performances—was Neil Simon's **The Odd Couple** (3-10-65, Plymouth). Taubman observed of Simon, "His skill—and it is not only great but constantly growing—lies in his gift for the deliciously surprising line and attitude. His instinct for incongruity is faultless. It nearly always operates on the basis of character." Praise was also accorded the sour-faced Walter Matthau as a "master of the slow burn," and the "delicate yet manly verve" of Art Carney. Sportswriter Oscar Madison's apartment is a pigsty. Dirty dishes, empty bottles, overflowing ashtrays, and yellowing newspapers clutter the place. Pants hang from bookshelves and ties from skewed Venetian blinds. This doesn't seem to upset Oscar (Matthau) or his cronies when they gather for their regular poker game. Then their meticulous fellow player, Felix Ungar (Carney), appears, announces he has split with his wife, and swallows what proves to be a batch of harmless pills. He moves in with Oscar, but his compulsive neatness quickly leads to arguments. At one point, as Felix tries desperately to clean up the place, Oscar purposely empties ashes on the floor. But after the men date some sisters (Monica Evans and Carole Shelley) who live in the building, Felix decides to move in with one of the girls. His stay, however, has not been without its effects. When the poker games resume, Oscar warns the players to be careful with their ashes. After all, this is his apartment, not a pigsty.

"The Tabernacle of Truth and Love," a small church occupying a seedy Harlem storefront, is the setting for much of James Baldwin's **The Amen Corner** (4-15-65, Barrymore). It was established by Sister Margaret (Bea Richards) following the death of her infant daughter. Since then, she has been attempting to get her recalcitrant young son (Art Evans) to walk in her pious path. Then her long-missing husband (Frank Silvera), a life-loving jazz musician, turns up to claim the boy's allegiance and seemingly shatters Sister Margaret's security. Her fellow sisters and brothers at the church turn against her, leaving her to realize that her faith is best served by ministering to her husband and child.

Terrence McNally's **And Things That Go Bump in the Night** (4-26-65, Royale) was savaged by the critics and lasted for only two weeks. The family of Ruby (Eileen Heckart), a demented old singer or actress, is lodged in a cellar bomb shelter protected by an electrified fence. The family consists of the all but speechless Fa (Clifton James), Grandfa (Ferdi Hoffman), who longs for the sanity and serenity of an insane asylum, daughter Lakme (Susan Anspach), and homosexual son Sigfrid (Robert Drivas), who lures an unsuspecting visitor (Marco St. John) to the lair. The visitor is electrocuted trying to escape. Ruby takes heart, shouting, "We will survive!"

In Evan Hunter's **A Race of Hairy Men!** (4-29-65, Henry Miller's) two college students (Martin Huston and Brandon de Wilde) plan to invite two girls to a cold-water flat they have borrowed in lower Manhattan, and seduce the girls there. But when the girls appear, although one of the youngsters seems anxious to be ravaged, they all realize that they are too naive and too good-natured for so cynical an enterprise. Four performances and the play was gone.

The season on Broadway ended with a revival of *The Glass Menagerie* at the Brooks Atkinson on May 4. Maureen Stapleton was Amanda; George Grizzard, her son; Piper Laurie, the daughter; and Pat Hingle, the Gentleman Caller. Critics felt the play held up beautifully, and, while no one could recapture the special magic of Laurette Taylor, the cast was excellent. Helped by money notices, the drama ran for 175 performances.

Off Broadway also had one late long run when Eric Bentley's translation of Bertolt Brecht's **The Exception and the Rule** (5-20-65, Greenwich Mews) was coupled with a Langston Hughes gospel song-play to create a double bill. Brecht's highly slanted tale described the travels of a suspicious, grasping merchant-capitalist and his trusting, generous coolie as the two traipse about in search of oil concessions. The bill compiled 141 performances.

1965–1966

The parade of disappointing seasons continued. Only somewhere between thirty-three and thirty-eight new plays opened, and the few truly memorable works all came from overseas. Neither the Pulitzer committee nor the Drama Critics Circle bestowed their awards on any native effort. In the former instance, it meant that no Pulitzer Prize had been awarded in three out of the last four seasons. If things were bad onstage, playgoers occasionally found some small relief at the box office, where a cut in the tax on theatre tickets reduced prices fractionally. Of course some producers tried to keep the difference for themselves, with the result that top tickets, heretofore basically uniform, now could be $7.00, $7.20, $7.25, or $7.50. In a few instances, such as *The Impossible Years,* patrons did not benefit, since the comedy's producers did away with a cheaper weekday top and asked $7.50 for all performances. That ticket buyers did not balk probably alerted producers to the possibilities of even higher prices in the near future. Adding to Broadway's problems was yet another newspaper strike, cutting off easily accessible notices for many weeks early in the theatrical year.

While Broadway estivated, Off Broadway flourished. American playgoers were given their first opportunity to see another new British playwright, John Arden, when the Theatre Company of Boston brought in **Live Like Pigs** (6-8-65, Actors' Playhouse). The Sawney family, little better than untamed Gypsies, are given shelter in a housing project in the north of England, but their loud, filthy ways disgust their more prissy, pretentious neighbors, the Jacksons. In time the Sawneys bring some of the Jacksons down to their lower standards, rather than the other way around. The play ran through the summer.

A double bill of revivals that opened the next evening at the Cherry Lane ran a month longer, not closing until the end of October. The bill consisted of *Krapp's Last Tape* and *The Zoo Story.*

The next night the New York Shakespeare Festival launched its summer season at the open-air Delacorte in Central Park. Three of Shakespeare's rarer plays were mounted, starting with *Love's Labour's Lost* and followed on July 7 by *Coriolanus* and on August 4 by *Troilus and Cressida.* For those not willing to trek to the park or preferring more common fare, the group's mobile units toured all summer long, presenting *Henry V, The Taming of the Shrew,* and *Romeo and Juliet.* No truly major names of the time were featured, although some, such as James Earl Jones and Michael Moriarty, subsequently made more or less notable careers.

Two one-acters by Arkady Leokum, **Friends** and **Enemies** (9-16-65, Theatre East), also enjoyed some modest acclaim, and a modest run of 139 performances. In the former an old scholar is put upon by a malevolent student; in the latter, a meek waiter proves to be a better investor than his obnoxious, supposedly market-wise patron.

By the time Broadway proper was ready to unveil its first new works, the newspapers had gone on strike again. Actually, the earliest attraction was not all that novel, since William Hanley's **Mrs. Dally** (9-22-65, Golden) was in reality two one-acters, the first of which, **Mrs. Dally Has a Lover,** had been done off Broadway three years before. Each play had only two characters. Mrs. Dally (Arlene Francis) is a forty-two-year-old, coarsely accented New Yorker not too happily married to a boorish cab driver. She loves the sort of great poetry and good music for which her husband has no time. Trying to arouse similar interests in a crude, inarticulate young man (Robert Forster), the son of a neighbor, she finds she must settle for a brief, unsatisfactory fling. **Today Is Independence Day,** which unfolds six months later in July, looks at the woman and her husband (Ralph Meeker) trying to itemize clearly their marriage's better and worse points and, by doing so, reaching an accommodation. The surprising thing about the evening was Francis's remarkable performance, with the normally velvet-voiced, suave actress purposely eschewing the studied poise and elegant accent with which she was identified. The low-budget affair, produced by Francis's husband, Martin Gabel, hung on for fifty-three performances.

The often crass, cackly-voiced Ruth Gordon was both star and author of **A Very Rich Woman** (9-30-65, Belasco), and her husband, Garson Kanin, served as producer and director. The play, which one wag called "Queen Lear," was taken from an unidentified French work by Philippe Hériat. Mrs. Lord is a seventy-five-year-old Boston widow given to spending so freely that her two greedy daughters (Joan Wetmore and Carrie Nye) and her equally greedy son-in-law (Peter Turgeon) have her kidnapped and placed in a mental institution. For a time she is confined to a barren, poorly lighted cell, with her pleas ignored. But she eventually wangles her way free and gives her brats their comeuppance. A remarkable roster of distinguished veteran supporting players included Ethel Griffies, Madge Kennedy, Ernest Truex, and Raymond Walburn, but they could not help a severely flawed entertainment achieve more than a three-and-a-half-week run.

Perhaps William Goodhart was fortunate that his **Generation** (10-6-65, Morosco) opened during the newspaper strike, since such critical barbs as "exasperating," "pretty thin," and "intermittently amusing" were not likely to encourage playgoers to line up at the box office. But with reviews not readily available, and with the popular and dependably understated Henry Fonda as star, playgoers did just that. The comedy ran out the season, chalking up 299 performances. When advertising man Jim Bolton arrives to visit his daughter, Doris (Holly Turner), a bride of one week, he discovers that she is nine months pregnant. Just as bad, his anti-establishment son-in-law, Walter (Richard Jordan), who wears beaded necklaces instead of ties and who has contempt for doctors, lawyers, and advertising men, plans to deliver the baby himself. Jim barks at the boy, "If you don't believe in anything, what the hell's the idea marrying my daughter and starting a family!?" And he warns he will force Walter into "the System." To that end, he secretly calls in an old buddy, an obstetrician (A. Larry Haines), and a colleague, a young lawyer (Don Fellows). It's lucky he summoned the doc, because the delivery proves difficult. But once the baby is born, Walter is determined to have another child as soon as possible and probably look after the birth himself then.

Al Morgan's **Minor Miracle** (10-7-65, Henry Miller's) was virtually stillborn, folding after half a week. Father Britt (Lee Tracy) is a parish priest with a small church in the Yorktown section of Manhattan. He spends much of his mornings figuring bets at the local races and giving his choices to his devoted housekeeper (Pert Kelton). Shortly after he scoffs at the claim of a young boy to have seen the Blessed Virgin in the church, a new lithograph of Christ's head appears to shed tears. The news spreads, crowds follow, and a famous TV bishop (Dennis King) tries to capitalize on the furor. But the wetness is shown to have come from a mistake in the printing inks. For the lively, redheaded Tracy, long a favorite of the critics, the show marked his farewell appearances.

Four players, one woman and three men, were all that were required for Donald Hall's **An Evening's Frost** (10-11-65, Theatre de Lys), which embellished its recounting of Robert Frost's life with readings from his poetry. The evening remained off Broadway for 132 performances.

Although the doomed English playwright Joe Orton would in time become something of an icon, his first Broadway exposure with **Entertaining Mr. Sloane** (10-12-65, Lyceum) was given singularly short shrift. For all the turmoil erupting in the decade, New York's critics could not yet fathom Orton's very black, louche humor. A pasty-faced young man (Dudley Sutton) rents a room in the home of a fortyish woman (Sheila Hancock), and immediately both she and her homosexual brother (Lee Montague) seduce the boy. Then their half-blind Dadda (George Turner) blurts out that the guest is a sought-after murderer, so the boy murders him. With that the sister and brother blackmail the boy into continuing to service them.

The season's second comedy hit, Bob Fisher and Arthur Marx's **The Impossible Years** (10-13-65, Play-

house), like its first, was deemed "not funny enough" by the critics. And, like the first, it dealt with the generation gap. The father in this case is Dr. Jack Kingsley (Alan King), a psychologist currently working on a book advising parents how to deal with their children. His own experiences with his two teenaged daughters are themselves unnerving, especially those with his almost-eighteen-year-old daughter, Linda (Jane Elliott). She is the sort of girl, he admits to his wife (Janet Ward), who could drive him back to his own analyst. He finally orders her to stop dating one especially oddball, randy youngster (Terrence Logan), only to have her take up with odder and randier specimens. To the Kingsleys' profound shock, a local doctor (Michael Vale) informs them that Linda is no longer a virgin. The shock for Mrs. Kingsley is so great that at her next bridge game she inadvertently bids "three no virgins." To make matters worse, they discover that Linda has been secretly wed. Happily, it turns out her husband is the nice, clean-cut ghost writer (Bert Convy) who has been helping the doctor with his book. King was a popular nightclub and TV comedian, and his celebrity no doubt was a factor in the comedy's running for 670 performances.

Once again, with Michael Dyne's **The Right Honorable Gentleman** (10-19-65, Billy Rose), a London hit became a New York failure, although in this instance the drama, based on a genuine Victorian scandal, did struggle on for 118 performances. Sir Charles Dilke (Charles D. Gray) is a rising politician with a good chance to become prime minister. But after it is revealed that he has had an affair not only with the wife (Sarah Badel) of a member (Henderson Forsythe) of Parliament, but with her mother (Coral Browne) and several other women as well, his career is destroyed.

For the critics, the opening on the 21st of the Vivian Beaumont Theatre at Lincoln Center far overshadowed the first offering which the Repertory Theatre of Lincoln Center offered there. While that was probably inevitable, the reception accorded the mounting was ominous, boding ill for the future of a group already assailed for its unevenness and whose roster offered none of the major names heretofore on it. The opening production was director Herbert Blau's translation of Georg Büchner's look at the French revolution, *Danton's Death*. John Chapman dismissed it in the *Daily News* as "madly noisy," and the *Post*'s Richard Watts, Jr., thought the theatre and Jo Mielziner's settings for the drama vastly superior to the "somewhat futile play" itself, while, in the *Herald Tribune*, Walter Kerr, rejecting the drama and, more especially, its staging, concluded, "All that is left to us is to hope."

One play that London and New York did agree on was Peter Shaffer's **The Royal Hunt of the Sun** (10-

26-65, ANTA), although its 261-performance run was not sufficient to let it recoup all of its investment. The drama told how the illiterate, irreligious Pizarro (Christopher Plummer), with only 160 men, conquered the Inca Empire so easily because the Inca ruler, Atahuallpa (David Carradine), mistook him for a sun god. Yet even Pizarro comes to realize after the Inca's murder that he has ruined a fascinating civilization, bequeathing it only "greed, hunger and the Cross." A stage filled with colorful period costumes and masks added to the sense of spectacle, as did such devices as waving huge red cloths to signify a bloodbath.

There was more history in Robert Nemiroff's **Postmark Zero** (11-1-65, Brooks Atkinson), which was derived from *Last Letters from Stalingrad,* a collection of letters written to be sent home by German soldiers in Russia but allegedly never delivered. They described the futile hopes and very real agonies of the men, such as a youngster watching as one by one he loses his fingers both to frostbite and enemy bullets. Newsreel films of the battle and large still photographs underscored the writings. But the gruesome subject was best left between the covers, so the play departed after a single week.

The next play did not fare as well. Eleanor Harris Howard and Helen McAvity's **Mating Dance** (11-3-65, Eugene O'Neill) was the first of three one-performance duds during the season, even though it starred the once popular screen favorite Van Johnson. He played a publisher who wants a divorce from his wife (Marion Winters), but since she is running for the Senate she demands he remain publicly faithful until after the election. However, because he has been seen around with an attractive young lady (Marian Hailey), his wife hires a "beard" (Richard Mulligan) to pose as the lady's beau and divert the scandal seekers. Who would pair with whom at the final curtain became obvious early on.

Jack Richardson's **Xmas in Las Vegas** (11-4-65, Barrymore) did a little better, lasting half a week. Every Christmas Bostonian Edward T. Wellspot (Tom Ewell) takes his eccentric family to Vegas so he can drop another bundle. His clan includes his wife (Shannon Bolin), who sees Episcopal angels hovering everywhere; his daughter (Judy Frank), a much married nymphomaniac; his son (Joe Ponazecki), who can't decide between committing suicide or living in Boston; and his dissolute brother (Heywood Hale Broun), always dreaming about bygone orgies and binges. This year Edward latches on to a widow (Mabel Albertson) whose luck has been phenomenal. But when she tries to help him, her lucky streak deserts her. He goes back home with empty pockets again.

Two attractions flourished off Broadway. William

Alfred's blank-verse **Hogan's Goat** (11-11-65, St. Clements Church) was lauded by the *Times*'s Howard Taubman for its "shapeliness, clarity and glowing power," and ran on for 607 performances. The year is 1890, and the ambitious, opportunistic Irish immigrant Matthew Stanton (Ralph Waite) is certain he will be nominated for mayor of Brooklyn. He is certain because the current incumbent, Mayor Quinn (Tom Ahearne), is wallowing in scandal for his blatant corruption. But Stanton himself has an Achilles' heel. For three years he has been living with Kathleen (Faye Dunaway) after a supposed civil ceremony, and the religious Kathleen is begging him for a proper church wedding. But that would offend other devout neighbors, who would perceive the relationship as "three years' fornication." Then Agnes Hogan, the woman with whom Stanton had been living before he took up with Kathleen, dies, and Quinn rifles her belongings to recover a certificate proving she was Stanton's legitimate wife. When this is revealed, Kathleen would storm out. In the tussle that follows she is either pushed or accidentally falls down the stairs and is killed. As Stanton, his hopes destroyed, prepares to give himself up to the police, a priest (Barnard Hughes) wails, "Cry for us all!" The priest's exclamation became the title of an unsuccessful musicalization in 1970.

By contrast, Douglas Turner Ward's double bill **Happy Ending** and **Day of Absence** (11-15-65, St. Marks) was light-hearted spoofing. In the first, two black maids lament that the rich white couple that has employed them is planning a divorce. This means they will no longer be able to steal the most expensive food to fill their freezer, or the finest clothes for their and their men's closets. But things turn out for the best when they receive a phone call notifying them that the divorce has been called off. In the second play, acted entirely by blacks in whiteface, a half-black southern town is thrown into turmoil after all its blacks abruptly disappear—even the ones who have been passing as white. White women can't figure out how to make breakfast, factories are forced to close, and the frustrated police are "denied their daily quota of Negro arrests." But one day later the blacks return as mysteriously as they disappeared, and everything falls into place again. The bill pleased theatregoers for 504 performances.

The Devils (11-16-65, Broadway) was John Whiting's theatricalization of Aldous Huxley's *The Devils of Loudon.* In 17th-century France, a debonair young priest (Jason Robards) is accused by a secretly lustful young prioress (Anne Bancroft) of being Satan's tool and having possessed her. In the hysteria that follows he is sent to a preordained judgment, since everyone who crosses his path has some self-serving or misguided reason to condemn him. Most critics felt that both the writing and, perhaps more unexpectedly, the acting were hollow. The play remained at its large berth for eight weeks.

The next evening the French pantomimist Marcel Marceau returned for yet another visit and regaled playgoers at the City Center for three weeks.

For several seasons, the Association of Producing Artists had been drawing attention to itself at venues off Broadway. Now, on the 23rd, it came into the Lyceum with a warm, scintillating revival of *You Can't Take It with You*. Although, among the cast, only Rosemary Harris (who played Alice) went on to lasting fame, the ensemble acting was a joy and helped the still admired comedy run for seven months.

John Osborne's London hit **Inadmissible Evidence** (11-30-65, Belasco) was also a hit in New York, closing with a profit after 166 performances. It looked on the intellectual, emotional, and spiritual disintegration of a self-made lawyer (Nicol Williamson). He finds himself alone after alienating his clients, his family, and his friends. The play was a tour de force for Williamson, requiring him to be onstage for virtually the whole evening, but he carried it off triumphantly. He was spelled by another player for the matinees.

Joan Drayton's **The Playroom** (12-5-65, Brooks Atkinson) was set in an old but posh New York apartment house known as the Montana, which many playgoers read as the famous Dakota. Judy (Karen Black), a teenager resentful of her stepmother, and four of her friends, who call themselves the "Filthy Five," connive to kidnap her ten-year-old stepsister (Christopher Norris) and hide her in a little-used turret of the building. The others eventually talk Judy into trying to kill the youngster, who, in her innocence, is delighted to be playing with her elders and has no clue to her own peril. Fortunately, she is rescued in time.

There were no timely rescues in John Webster's horrific Elizabethan horror tragedy *The Duchess of Malfi*, which was done in modern dress on the 6th at the Circle in the Square and continued on for 152 performances.

The season's second lone-performance dud was Charles Horine's **Me and Thee** (12-7-65, Golden). The Carters (Durward Kirby and Barbara Britton) send their difficult young son (Randy Kirby), who has been arrested for a college prank, to a psychiatrist (Charles Braswell), only to be told by the doctor that the boy is perfectly normal but that they are absurdly inhibited. So Mrs. Carter dons some colorful, sexy clothes, while Mr. Carter tries to take up with a young girl (Carolan Daniels) and get her drunk. He discovers that while she is amorous when sober, when drunk she is a model of decorum. She and the Carters' son head off to the library together.

The season's biggest hit followed. **Cactus Flower**

(12-8-65, Royale) was Abe Burrows's adaptation of Pierre Barillet and Jean Pierre Gredy's Paris success. Now that Julian (Barry Nelson), a dentist, has decided to marry his sweet, slightly suicidal mistress, Toni (Brenda Vaccaro), he has a problem. After all, he has lied to her that he is married. Since Toni insists on meeting the poor woman she is about to supplant, Julian must come up with a "wife." To this end he enlists his barbed-tongued, super-efficient nurse, Stephanie (Lauren Bacall). But Stephanie, who has quietly loved Julian for some time, is so efficient that she winds up walking down the aisle with him. Toni settles for a nice boy (Burt Brinckeroff) from the apartment next door. Although the beautiful Vaccaro gave a wonderful performance, the show was Bacall's. Norman Nadel wrote in the *World-Telegram and Sun,* "Not many actresses can be grim and endearing at the same time; Miss Bacall is both, and she tops off the combination with a straight-faced comic delivery which not only sets her role sparkling but which makes anyone else in the scene look good." David Merrick's production played 1234 performances, still an American record for a Continental comedy.

The Repertory Theatre of Lincoln Center was plagued by another batch of thumbs-down notices after it unveiled its revival of *The Country Wife* at the Vivian Beaumont on the 9th. The only performer to move on to better things from the mounting was Stacy Keach, who played Horner.

A second notable David Merrick production followed several weeks later. Most people referred to Geoffrey Skelton and Adrian Mitchell's adaptation of Peter Weiss's **The Persecution and Assassination of Marat as Performed by the Inmates of the Asylum of Charenton Under the Direction of the Marquis de Sade** (12-27-65, Martin Beck) simply as **Marat/Sade.** The title of the play, allegedly based on a true incident in which de Sade (Patrick Magee), then an inmate in 1808, staged this and similar works, gave much of the plot away. Ian Richardson impersonated Marat, and Glenda Jackson, the murderous Charlotte Corday. The evening was made memorable by Peter Brook's free-flowing, imaginative staging, set on a high, raked, almost bare stage, with characters often entering and exiting from trapdoors in the floor, while the man (Clifford Rose) in charge of the institution and his family watched smugly from a platform onstage left. Although the large-cast mounting ran for only 144 performances, Merrick's careful husbanding allowed it to close with a profit.

None of the next four Broadway plays ran a full week. The title of James Kirkwood's screwy comedy **UTBU** (1-4-66, Helen Hayes) stood for "Unhealthy To Be Unpleasant." The person who saw to that was William Uggims (Alan Webb), a blind man who wreaks havoc with his cane on flowerpots, lamps, and anything else in his path, and who is dedicated to ridding the world of nasty people. One of the people he does away with is an obnoxious stage mother (Constance Ford) who threatens to burn her little daughter's Raggedy Ann doll if the child muffs a line. But his main objective at the moment is the greased-haired, mustachioed, and pinstriped J. Francis Amber (Tony Randall), an actor-author determined to poison his demented ninety-four-year-old mother (Thelma Ritter) to get enough money to mount his new show. Uggims blasts the man to smithereens but then mistakes a window for a door, so falls to his own death. Comedienne Nancy Walker was hailed for her comically inventive staging and dour Margaret Hamilton for her sarcastic maid, but they weren't enough to save the flawed comedy.

Off Broadway, Alvin Aronson's **The Pocket Watch** (1-5-66, Actors Playhouse) bucked not only the Broadway doldrums uptown but a highly negative review by the *Times*'s new critic, Stanley Kauffmann, to go on to a 725-performance run. Set in 1953 in the suburban Boston home of a largely unsuccessful Jewish immigrant and his loving wife (who dies by the play's end), it told of their uncomfortable struggles with their two daughters, their son-in-law, and their grandson (who leaves just before the final curtain to make a better world for himself).

There apparently was not much nice to be said for Edward Albee's dramatization of James Purdy's novel **Malcolm** (1-11-66, Shubert), which Watts dismissed as "a simply awful play." Fifteen-year-old Malcolm (Matthew Cowles) sits in front of a hotel, waiting for a long-lost father, who may, in fact, be long dead. He is taken under the wing of an aging pederast (Henderson Forsythe) who tells him he must experience the real world and introduces him to various figures: a man (John Heffernan) claiming to be 192 years old and his retired-streetwalker of a wife (Estelle Parsons); a selfish, depraved rich couple (Ruth White and Wyman Pendleton); an arty young couple (Donald Hotton and Alice Drummond); and a sexually desperate singer (Jennifer West), who literally loves the boy to death.

Some of the season's worst notices went to Harry Tugend's **The Wayward Stork** (1-19-66, 46th St.), which starred film and TV favorite Robert Cummings, in extravagantly dyed red hair. A radiologist, who has been sterilized by his work, and his wife (Lois Nettleton) long for a baby and settle on artificial insemination by the sperm of another red-haired man (Bernie West). But the wife's widowed sister (Arlene Golonka) seems to have been inseminated by mistake. Then the mistake turns out to have been a mistake, as did the play itself.

Matters were even more confused and banally developed in Irene Kamp's **The Great Indoors** (2-1-66,

Eugene O'Neill). Arnolt Zend (Curt Jurgens) had managed in Nazi Germany to hide the fact that he was a Jew and to prosper there. His Christian wife, however, had been shipped off to her death for opposing the Nazis. Now living in the American South and, apparently, guilt-ridden about his former behavior, he defiantly adopts a Negro (Clarence Williams III) and also meets up with his German son (Hans Gudegast), who considers himself a Jew. Lost in this muddle was Geraldine Page as Zend's brothel-managing mistress.

The string of flops was broken by Frederick Knott's **Wait Until Dark** (2-2-66, Barrymore), which scared patrons for eleven months. Three men invade the Greenwich Village basement apartment of the Hendrixes looking for a doll, which the Hendrixes do not realize is stuffed with a fortune in heroin. Regrettably for the blind Mrs. Hendrix (Lee Remick), her husband is away. The men cajole and threaten and, for a time, fall out among themselves. One (Val Bisoglio) of the men eventually runs off; the second (Mitchell Ryan) is stabbed to death by the third, Harry Roat (Robert Duvall). He then menaces the woman, who flicks off the lights and thus gives herself a small advantage in the pitch-dark apartment. When Roat lights a match she threatens to throw gasoline on him, but he contrives to open a refrigerator door and by its light grab her knife. She eventually grabs another knife, unplugs the refrigerator, and kills Roat just as the police and her husband arrive.

The Repertory Theatre of Lincoln Center's next offering was Justin O'Brien's translation of Jean-Paul Sartre's **The Condemned of Altona** (2-3-66, Vivian Beaumont), in which a German munitions manufacturer (George Coulouris), who has built his enterprise into a postwar giant, wants to see that his heirs inherit the company, but understands that the war has left his oldest son a deranged recluse, living in an attic and believing that crabs will take over the world. Perhaps significantly, Coulouris, who was listed as a "guest" artist, received the best notices.

The Comédie Française made a return visit, moving in on the 8th for a three-week stand at the City Center, and bringing with it revivals of Molière's *L'Avare,* Pierre Corneille's *Le Cid,* and Georges Feydeau's *Un Fil à la patte,* as well as the American premiere of Henri de Montherlant's tale of a prince who enthrones his murdered bride as his queen when he is crowned, **La Reine Morte.**

Another French play, Jean Racine's *Phèdre,* was revived at the Greenwich Mews on the 10th with Beatrice Straight in the title role and Mildred Dunnock as Oenone, and ran an even 100 performances.

A revival of a far more recent foreign play, *The Deadly Game,* did a mite better, compiling 105 performances in a run at the Provincetown Playhouse beginning on the 13th.

David Merrick had his third hit in relatively short order when he mounted Brian Friel's Irish play **Philadelphia, Here I Come!** (2-16-66, Helen Hayes). A youngish man named Gareth O'Donnell (Patrick Bedford) is about to emigrate to America. With the help of his inner, private self (Donal Donnelly) he explores his reasons for leaving. In part, these include his desire to escape his dour, uncommunicative father (Eamon Kelley) and the girl he loved but lost to another man. He and his private self also ponder on whether or not he will be truly happy in America.

Thanks largely to the aging screen favorite Ray Milland, Jack Roffey's English courtroom thriller **Hostile Witness** (2-17-66, Music Box) enjoyed a twenty-week run, although it closed still in the red. Critics divided sharply on Milland's stage abilities, but his public didn't seem bothered by any shortcomings. A distinguished attorney is accused of murdering the jurist who he believes accidentally ran over and killed his daughter. When his own defense attorney (Michael Allison) resigns in protest to the man's constant interference, he assumes his own defense. At first his own witnesses seem to incriminate him, but he eventually turns the tables and points to the real murderer.

Tennessee Williams, sinking badly in the esteem of many reviewers—"[he] has completely broken with the world of reality," "this brilliant talent is sleeping"— came badly a cropper with his double bill of one-acters **Slapstick Tragedy** (2-22-66, Longacre). **The Gnadiges Fraulein** told how a frowsy keeper (Kate Reid) of a rundown boardinghouse on the Florida Keys and a visiting gossip columnist (Zoe Caldwell) chatter away while a guest (Margaret Leighton), a seedy, ancient vaudevillian who used to catch fish with her teeth in her act, has her eyes gouged out vying with some raucous cockaloony birds for fish at a nearby pier. **The Mutilated** recounted the battle between one New Orleans prostitute (Reid), newly released from prison, and a rival (Leighton) who has recently had her breasts removed. In both plays, the dangerously alluring stud, another Williams cliché, was played by James Olsen. In the former he was an Indian; in the latter, a sailor. The bill lasted for only one week.

One critic rechristened David Rayfiel's **Nathan Weinstein, Mystic, Connecticut** (2-25-66, Brooks Atkinson) "The Perils of Sam Levene." Another observed, "This is the second time in less than two years . . . that Mr. Levene has been miscast in a non-realistic role because the part was Jewish and funny." Having presented her father (Levene) with the huge Alpine horn he has longed for, Rachel Weinstein (Zohra Lampert) gets into a fight with him, conks him, and is committed to a mental institution. But the sympathetic Nathan has second thoughts, releases her, and takes her to visit a 101-year-old lady (Estelle Winwood), who used to run a dairy farm and now is a bootlegger. She advises reconciliation, even with his stodgy son (Robert Berand) who, Nathan complains, "wore a vest before he could walk." In the boy's case everyone remains far apart, but the daughter finds romance of sorts with the local police chief (Saeed Jaffrey), an exchange visitor from Korea. Levene could not keep the work on the boards beyond its third performance.

That was two performances more than were accorded the season's final lone-performance fiasco, Oliver Hailey's **First One Asleep, Whistle** (2-26-66, Belasco). Elaine (Salome Jens), a voluptuous woman who supports herself by doing TV commercials, is the unwed mother of a seven-year-old daughter (Marya Zimmet). Looking to provide herself with a man and her daughter with a stepfather, she takes up with a bookseller (Frank Converse), a "Don Juan from Doubleday," who claims his own child bride has left him. But after he is reunited with his spouse, Elaine is back on square one.

Like his friend Tennessee Williams, William Inge was never again to know a Broadway hit. His latest opus, **Where's Daddy?** (3-2-66, Billy Rose), folded after twenty-two performances. His hero, Tom (Beau Bridges), like Hailey's heroine, makes a living doing television commercials. He was an orphan, found in a bar when he was fifteen by an effeminate but kindhearted man (Hiram Sherman) and raised by him. Tom makes a young girl (Barbara Dana) pregnant and agrees to marry her so that the child will be legitimate, but also gets the girl to agree that they will put the child up for adoption and then get a divorce. The baby's arrival changes his thoughts.

Thanks in good measure to two capital performances by its stars, James Goldman's **The Lion in Winter** (3-3-66, Ambassador) ran ninety-two performances but, with so short a run, it went down in the record books as a commercial failure. A premature death having claimed his eldest son and heir apparent to the English throne, Henry II (Robert Preston) must decide which of his surviving sons will replace him. To help with the choice, he temporarily releases his long-imprisoned queen, Eleanor (Rosemary Harris), although he knows she prefers the older Richard (James Rado) to the younger John (Bruce Scott), toward whom Henry is leaning. The king, the queen, Richard, John, and the devious middle son, Geoffrey (Dennis Cooney), incessantly jockey for position, sometimes with murderous thoughts. As Eleanor says, "We all have knives. It is eleven eighty-three and we're barbarians." In disgust, for a time Henry contemplates marrying his mistress, Alais (Suzanne Grossman), and begetting another son with her. To that end he locks up the three princes and considers killing them. But Eleanor, before she must return to her confinement, finally persuades him to let history run its own course. Both Preston and Harris were splendid comedians, but Preston brought a surprisingly virile credibility to his dramatic moments, while Harris contributed her beauty and elegant readings.

Another superior comedian, basset-faced Paul Ford, could do little to save Jerome Chodorov's **3 Bags Full** (3-6-66, Henry Miller's), which the playwright adapted from a French comedy by Claude Magnier. An engaging if nasty young man (Joe Ponazecki) tells his employer, a sporting goods tycoon (Ford), that he has stolen half a million dollars from him and will return it only when the tycoon allows the young man to marry his daughter and to be given a permanent job. Half the loot, in jewels, is in one bag; half, in cash, in another, identical bag. What the young man does not know is that the girl (Leigh Taylor-Young) he loves is only pretending to be the tycoon's daughter. The real daughter, pregnant; a chambermaid, in apparently a similar state; two more young men; and a third identical bag—this one with the maid's lingerie—provide complications.

John Arden's second play of the season was done off Broadway. **Serjeant Musgrave's Dance** (3-8-66, Theatre de Lys) had been a sensation in London seven years before but was now first reaching Broadway. In the early 1800s three army privates, all deserters and led by the charismatic Musgrave, bring with them a dead soldier's skeleton when they come to a troubled Midlands town, ostensibly to recruit but actually to argue for peace. One of the four is killed in a squabble, and the others soon are carted off by authorities to the gallows. The drama ran for 137 performances.

Back uptown the season drifted to a close with three novelties (at least to Broadway), two revivals, and two visits by more foreign troupes. J. A. Ross's **Happily Never After** (3-10-66, Eugene O'Neill) launched the parade. Several critics pointed out that J. A. stood for Judith Ann and that her husband was the play's producer. She looked at an unhappy family summering on Long Island. The second wife (Barbara Barrie) of the paterfamilias (Gerald O'Loughlin) seems unable to have children. His daughter (Karen Black) by his former wife announces she is living in sin with a British physicist. His niece (Rochelle Oliver) is married to his Wall Street partner (Ken Kercheval), but the couple is contemplating divorce because the husband gargles noisily with a mouthwash the girl detests. After half a week, the clan took its troubles elsewhere.

At the City Center, the puppet theatre of Japan, Bunraku, came for two weeks on the 15th, offering several bills from a repertory of eighteenth- and early nineteenth-century plays.

At the Longacre Hal Holbrook brought back his *Mark Twain Tonight!* on the 23rd and stayed around for eleven weeks.

The Repertory Theatre of Lincoln Center closed its first season at what was to be its "permanent" house with Eric Bentley's translation of Bertolt Brecht's **The Caucasian Chalk Circle** (3-24-66, Vivian Beaumont). A prologue suggests that everything always works out for the best in the modern Soviet Union thanks to wise Communist government. Thus men willing to develop some land are given it rather than those who would exploit it. The rest of the play illustrated the need for allowing the best man—or, in this instance, the best woman—to win. The wife of a rich governor has abandoned her baby, so a kitchen maid quietly adopts it. When the real mother decides she wants the baby back, a judge orders the women each to grab one end of the child and pull at it. Whoever pulls the baby to herself will win it. But the maid, reluctant to hurt the infant, refuses. She is granted custody. Kauffmann noted that because the drama required "neither the high style of Wycherley nor the high-acting virtuosity of the Büchner or Sartre plays" the mounting was especially successful. Audiences seemed to agree, granting it ninety-three performances.

Gwen Davis's **The Best Laid Plans** (3-25-66, Brooks Atkinson) was taken off the boards after three playings. A conniving young lady (Marian Hailey) has fallen hard for the playwright (Edward Woodward) in the next apartment. She has learned he wants to study suicidal former junkies and to this end has visited a psychiatrist (Kenneth Mars) who has agreed to let him sit in on group therapy sessions. So our young lady contrives to become one of the group, even if she must make up a totally phony history to do so. For a while, her plans go agley, but she eventually wins her man.

Germans followed the Japanese into the City Center on April 5 for a two-week visit. The Bavarian State Theatre opened with a double bill of Goethe's story of the cuckolding of a thieving innkeeper, **Die Mitschuldigen,** coupled with Büchner's **Woyzeck,** which told how an unworldly young man is driven to murder his beloved wife after he discovers she has been unfaithful. The second bill was Gerhart Hauptmann's **Die Ratten,** a sort of Teutonic *Lower Depths*. A woman, living in a crowded hovel and desperate for a child, adopts one and pretends it is her natural baby. The truth comes out after the real mother is murdered, and this drives the woman to suicide.

The season ended with John Gielgud starring in his own adaptation of Chekhov's *Ivanov*. The hero shoots himself when his no-longer-loved wife dies following the revelation of his infidelty with a wealthy, younger woman. Reviews were disappointing, so the play, which opened at the Shubert on May 3, remained before the footlights for only six weeks.

1966–1967

Thanks to a creeping inflation in ticket prices, Broadway grossed more than $55,000,000 during the new season, a record up to its time—and one, of course, created in large part by Broadway's successful musicals. But that was virtually all the good news to report. By general agreement the season marked another dismal year for American playwriting. Of the ten top entries awarded a place in the annual *Best Plays,* only three were by American dramatists (and one of these came from Off Broadway). Three others were musicals—admittedly American—and the remaining four were British. At season's end the New York Drama Critics Circle passed over native entries and crowned a British play as the year's top offering. And the total number of new plays also plunged, to thirty or less.

Adding to Broadway's woes was the abrupt and all but simultaneous closure of three of New York's major newspapers—the *Journal-American,* the *World-Telegram and Sun,* and the *Herald Tribune*—which departed the scene between the end of last season and the opening of the new one. For a very brief spell the three survived in a single mongrel amalgamation called the *World Journal Tribune.*

The first modest run of the season—137 performances—went to an importation presented off Broadway, Arnold Wesker's **The Kitchen** (6-13-66, 81st St.). Abandoning the redneck toughs he had played so often, Rip Torn was featured as an excitable chef whose frustration at not being able to sleep with the married waitress he adores, coupled with some casual insults, drives him over the edge and into a violently destructive rampage.

Up in Central Park, at the Delacorte, the New York Shakespeare Festival began its summer stand on the 15th with *All's Well That Ends Well,* then moved on to *Measure for Measure* and *Richard III.* Its mobile theatre toured the five boroughs with *Macbeth.*

Broadway's first offering of the theatrical year was a commerical hit (that is, it paid off its initial investment) even though it opened to largely negative notices and ran only 132 performances. Norman Nadel, critic for the short-lived *World Journal Tribune,* spoke of the "cold, untouching malevolence" of Edward Albee's **A Delicate Balance** (9-22-66, Martin Beck), while Walter Kerr, now the *Times*'s new critic, saw "hollowness...of-

fered to us on an elegantly lacquered empty platter." Sitting after dinner in their plush library, Agnes (Jessica Tandy) confides to her husband Tobias (Hume Cronyn), that she sometimes frets about losing her mind. But Tobias is quick to assure her that he knows no saner woman. Then in short order their serenity is interrupted by the appearance of Agnes's younger sister, Claire (Rosemary Murphy), a bitter, malicious alcoholic; the panicky arrival of Harry (Henderson Forsythe), Tobias's best friend, and Harry's wife, Edna (Carmen Mathews), who confess they are terrified by something they cannot put their finger on; and by the return of Agnes's and Tobias's daughter, Julia (Marian Seldes), after the breakup of her fourth marriage. The visits force Agnes and Tobias to reevaluate all their relationships and to recognize that they must maintain a delicate balance between sanity and madness. Adding to the play's elusive nature and the sense that it was an intellectual exercise rather than a dramatic theatre piece was such stilted, and often convoluted, dialogue as Claire's "I apologize that my nature is such to bring out in you the full force of your brutality." Long after the drama closed, it was awarded the Pulitzer Prize.

Much had been expected of Tyrone Guthrie's revival of Kaufman and Ferber's 1932 hit, *Dinner at Eight,* which opened at the Alvin on the 27th. The star-packed cast included June Havoc, Walter Pidgeon, Ruth Ford, Arlene Francis, Robert Burr, Jeffrey Lynn, Darren McGavin, Phil Leeds and Blanche Yurka. But something went askew and words such as "fragmentary", "contrived" and "disappointment" larded the morning-after notices. The revival hung on for 127 performances, but closed in the red.

Another usually successful director, George Abbott, could not breathe the requisite life into Keith Waterhouse and Willis Hall's English comedy **Help Stamp Out Marriage!** (9-29-66, Booth). The play, which had been known in the West End as *Say Who You Are,* folded after two and a half weeks. In that brief time, it recounted how, every Friday, Sarah (Valerie French) drags her husband, David (Roddy Maude-Roxby), to the cinema in order to leave their flat free so that her friend, Valerie (Ann Bell), can pursue an assignation with Stuart (Francis Matthews), all the while pretending that this is her flat and that she is married to David, and thus cannot wed Stuart. Naturally the foursome eventually come together and an evening of complications follows.

On the same night, the City Center launched its season of revivals, starting with Odets's *The Country Girl.* Joseph Anthony was the alcoholic, suicidal actor; Jennifer Jones, his wife; and Rip Torn, the determined director. *The Rose Tattoo* followed on October 20, with Maureen Stapleton recreating her original role and Harry

Guardino in support. Judith Anderson closed the series, beginning on November 3, playing the title role in Maxwell Anderson's *Elizabeth the Queen.*

Peter Weiss's uncompromising look at the trial of the Auschwitz defendants was offered in Jon Swan and Ulu Grosbard's translation as **The Investigation** (10-4-66, Ambassador). The entire original text was excerpted verbatim from trial records. Houselights were kept on during the whole evening, and, during the performance, floodlights along the proscenium and directed out to the audience were turned on, suggesting playgoers and actors alike were equally involved. Onstage an austere setting ranged the defendants in two upper tiers, the accusers (including the only two women in the cast) on a lower tier, and the attorneys and judge in what should have been the raised orchestra pit. An evening reliving unrelenting horrors, it nonetheless lured patrons for 103 performances and managed to close in the black.

A West End success, Frank Marcus's **The Killing of Sister George** (10-5-66, Belasco), ran twice as long and also joined the season's parade of New York hits. Sister George is not a real person. Rather she is a character, a lovable nurse, on a BBC soap opera. But she is played by June Buckridge (Beryl Reid), a cigar-smoking, gin-swilling lesbian. At home, June lords it over her slavey, Childie (Eileen Atkins), a neurotic girl who clings to her doll and whom June punishes for missteps by making the girl eat leftover cigar butts and drink June's dirty bath water. But June is apparently also so difficult at work that the powers that be decide to kill off her character. In its stead, she is offered the role of a cow in a children's program. June loses her battle to keep Sister George alive and also loses Childie to a rival lesbian (Lally Bowers), a BBC executive. At the final curtain she is left alone, practicing bovine sounds.

Last season the young Irish playwright Brian Friel had scored a success with a play about an Irish youth heading for life in America. This season he came a cropper with a play about an elderly Irish woman returning to her homeland after fifty-two years in the States, **The Loves of Cass McGuire** (10-6-66, Helen Hayes). The play was given its world premiere in New York. Cass (Ruth Gordon) has lived raffishly abroad and now hopes to spend her last years with her brother and sister-in-law, to whom she has been faithfully sending $5 a month over the decades. But the brother wants no part of her and gives her back the money, which he has set aside, so that she can enter an old-age home. At the home she tells her history to the other patients and listens to their possibly spurious memories. Dennis King won applause as one of the patients, looking back lovingly on his wife who drowned during their honeymoon (or did she run away with another man?).

Gordon, given many asides to the audience, was chastized for playing Ruth Gordon, with her cackly voice, her erratic accenting of lines, and all her other old tricks.

The Repertory Theatre of Lincoln Center initiated its season on the 13th with a roustabout revival of Ben Jonson's look at swindlers and gulls, *The Alchemist.* Two more revivals followed. Federico García Lorca's *Yerma,* which New York had first seen off Broadway in 1952, was given in a new W. S. Merwin translation on December 8. It told of a woman who longs to have a child and is driven to strangling her husband when he refuses to cooperate. On April 13 Anthony Quayle was featured in Charles Laughton's adaptation of Bertolt Brecht's *Galileo.* (One new play was offered in February and will be dealt with at that time.) Critics divided in their reactions to the mountings, but the overall impression was a sense of nagging disappointment. By mid-January, Herbert Blau, one of the company's two directors, resigned, another signal that the troubled enterprise was probably doomed.

A West End hit, Henry Livings's **Eh?** (10-16-66, Circle in the Square), enjoyed a season-long run off Broadway in good measure because of the performance of young Dustin Hoffman, who had called attention to himself in earlier off-Broadway productions. Hoffman, whom one critic labeled a cross between "Ringo Starr and Buster Keaton" and whom he hailed as "one of the most agile and subtly controlled comedians around," played Valentine Brose, a strangely inner-directed young man who wangles a job in a push-button-controlled factory, honeymoons there with his exasperated bride (Alexandra Berlin), and finally pushes all the wrong buttons in rebellion against impersonal automation.

We Have Always Lived in the Castle (10-19-66, Barrymore) was Hugh Wheeler's dramatization of Shirley Jackson's novel. After being acquitted for the arsenic poisoning of her parents and other members of her family, Constance (Shirley Knight) has lived in shunned isolation in her Vermont home with two more survivors of the incident, her aging uncle (Alan Webb) and her fifteen-year-old sister, Merricat (Heather Menzies). A long-lost cousin, Charles (Phillip Clark), reappears to court Constance. But when he and a local black boy (William Sims) are poisoned it becomes evident that Merricat is the real killer. The play opened on one Saturday night and closed on the next.

Roger Milner's English comedy **How's the World Treating You?** (10-24-66, Music Box) fared a bit better, eking out a five-week run. Frank More (James Bolam) is a born loser. In the first act he loses his regiment and his pants; in the second he is forced to marry a girl he has made pregnant; in the third act, with his marriage a failure and hating his job as a washing-machine salesman, he finally succeeds—at committing suicide. Most of the performers in the cast played different roles in each act. Thus Patricia Routledge was a Blimpish colonel's man-eating wife, a woman who wears her dresses on backwards so that she will look attractive from the rear while dancing and who cannot see that her daughter is pregnant, and a lady named Rover who helps maintain a home for would-be suicides.

Saul Bellow's second attempt at playwriting met with no more success than his first. **Under the Weather** (10-27-66, Cort) was a bill of three two-character one-acters (a third player appeared briefly in one part). Shelley Winters and Harry Towb were the principals. In the first play Harry, a widower, is determined to avoid the clutches of Flora, a widow. He purposely lets the air out of some tires, then pleads a bad heart. So Flora pumps up the tires. But that doesn't prevent Harry from having to be carried away on a stretcher. In the second play a distinguished nuclear physicist visits an old flame and struggles for a second glimpse of an embarrassingly placed birthmark he had seen on the girl when they were youngsters. In the last of the trio, an aging prostitute hopes to lure her lone surviving customer, a man nearing eighty, into a more permanent relationship by baking him a soufflé. But the soufflé fails to rise, and the man stalks away.

Another set of three one-acters enjoyed a long success off Broadway, where Jan-Claude van Itallie's **America Hurrah** (11-6-66, Pocket) ran for 634 performances. The evening was subtitled "Three Views of the U.S.A.," but all three plays suggested that what some Americans looked on with affection and pride, others viewed with indifference and even hatred. In **Interview,** masked, grinning interviewers hurl cold, impersonal questions at some unemployed persons before all the characters are caught up in a fugue of street noises and small incidents. **TV** unfolded in the viewing room of a rating company where three employees talk casually about this and that (and one nearly chokes on a chicken bone), while on the TV actors with striped faces run through a daily diet of news, songs, soaps, and old films. In **Motel** a large female doll known as the Motel-Keeper speaks of the history and virtues of fine lodgings and also indulges in aimless patter about "catnip, club feet, canisters, bannisters," at the same time that a couple of oversized dolls, who have paid for a room, wantonly deface and destroy it.

The season's longest run for a full-length comedy—598 performances—went to Woody Allen's **Don't Drink the Water** (11-17-66 Morosco) even though many reviewers, acknowledging that it was "filled with funny lines" and "moved the audience to great laughter," lamented that the lack of real plot and character develop-

ment meant "the final result falls disturbingly short of satisfaction." The Hollanders—father (Lou Jacobi), mother (Kay Medford), and daughter Susan (Anita Gillette)—take refuge in the American embassy of an Iron Curtain country after being chased by secret police for supposedly snapping unauthorized pictures. While the ambassador is out of the country, the embassy is being run by his notoriously incompetent son, Axel (Anthony Roberts). The loud, cranky Mr. Hollander is a caterer from Newark, New Jersey, who boasts he was "the first to make bridegrooms out of potato salad," and he is anxious to return home because he cannot trust his partner's operating the business properly without him. At first, to no small extent because of Axel's blunderings, everything goes awry. But eventually Mr. and Mrs. Hollander make their escape disguised as a visiting sultan and his wife. Susan, having fallen in love with Axel despite his obvious shortcomings, can remain safely behind after a priest (Dick Libertini), who has been living as a refugee in the embassy for six years, marries the couple. The dour, blustering Jacobi and the sad-faced, scratchy-voiced Medford garnered most of the laughs.

The rising star of the APA (Association of Producing Artists Repertory Company) shone brightly during the season, although like all such ambitious enterprises on Broadway it was soon doomed to disappear. Along with such fine players as Clayton Corzatte, Keene Curtis, Will Geer, and Rosemary Harris, the troupe, under the guidance of Ellis Rabb, was joined by Helen Hayes when it inaugurated its new season on the 21st at the Lyceum with *The School for Scandal.* Corzatte was Charles; Rabb, Joseph; Sydney Walker, Sir Peter; Harris, Lady Teazle; and Hayes, Mrs. Candour. The next evening brought out the company brought out Pirandello's *Right You Are (If You Think You Are),* with Walker as Ponza, and Hayes as the old woman who may or may not be his mother-in-law. For the most part the company—for its choice of plays, its mounting of them, and its performances—received the sort of glowing notices that the Lincoln Center troupe could only dream about. In December they offered one "new play," then brought back works they had performed earlier off Broadway or elsewhere—*The Wild Duck* (January 11), *You Can't Take It with You* (February 10), and *War and Peace* (March 21).

Generally dreadful notices prompted Michael Stewart's **Those That Play the Clowns** (11-24-66, ANTA) to call it a run after four performances. A group of down-and-out, quarreling strolling players are lodged at a Danish inn, wondering where their next meal will come from since the public has tired of seeing them in *Violated at Vespers, Two Monks and a Minx,* or *The Duchess Debauched.* Their luck seemingly changes when a young prince invites them to perform at the castle, asking only that they add sixteen lines or so that he has written to the famous play of *The Murder of Gonzago*. He wants the play performed before his mother, the queen, and his uncle, the new king. When the king takes umbrage at the play the actors rush back to the inn, but soldiers come to arrest them, and they have to indulge in some real swordplay before they can escape. Alfred Drake and Joan Greenwood were starred—and wasted—as the leading strollers.

A British play, David Halliwell's **Hail Scrawdyke!** (11-28-66, Booth), lingered twice as long—one week. The play had been known in London as *Little Malcolm and His Struggle Against the Eunuchs*. A misfit, red-bearded art student, Malcolm Scrawdyke (Victor Henry), having been kicked out of the Huddersfield School of Art, plots with three other young malcontents to take over first Huddersfield, then England, and finally the world. They form the neo-Nazi Party of the Dynamic Erection, adopt a swastika-like emblem, act out in pantomime their savage fantasies, and finally beat up a young girl who has told them off. But Scrawdyke soon alienates his followers, one by one, and after the last is gone he attempts suicide. When this fails, he embarks on a damning self-appraisal.

Early on in David Westheimer's **My Sweet Charlie** (12-6-66, Longacre) Charles Roberts (Louis Gossett), an articulate young Northern black lawyer, fleeing after accidentally killing a redneck who attacked him during a civil rights demonstration, breaks in through the shuttered windows of what he believes to be a deserted summer cottage on the Gulf Coast. He immediately finds that he is not alone, for an all but illiterate girl, illegitimately pregnant, has also taken refuge there to hide from her poor-white-trash father. At first the girl is fearful and contemptuous of the black, who must "talk dumb" to her to slowly win over her confidence and sympathy. He admits, for example, that, like all blacks, he is specially partial to watermelons. Eventually the pair develop a genuine if platonic affection for one another. So when the girl needs help with a difficult birth, Charlie sacrifices his freedom and life to bring in aid. Jo Mielziner's cottage, set on pilings in the sand, won applause. And many critics agreed with Richard Watts, Jr., of the *Post* when he called the drama "remarkably poignant." But the public wouldn't come, forcing the play to close after just thirty-one playings.

Virtually no one cared for Abe Einhorn's **Agatha Sue, I Love You** (12-14-66, Henry Miller's), which folded after half a week. Two down-and-out gamblers, Jack (Corbett Monica) and Eddie (Ray Walston), living on one graham cracker and half a Coke a day in a fleabag hotel run by a harpyish proprietress (Betty Garde), decide to steal and pawn the guitar owned by

Agatha Sue (Lee Lawson), a young folksinger in the next room. She mistakes Jack's attentions for a proposal of marriage and offers to move in with them and to lend them her meager savings to bet on a sure thing, Flaming Arrow. As she kneels in prayer, Agatha Sue asks God to bless mother, father, Uncle Harry—and Flaming Arrow. Sure enough, the horse wins big. But Jack uses his winnings to buy a loud pinstripe suit and to latch on to a blonde floozie (Renee Taylor). A sadder but wiser Agatha Sue heads off to a singing engagement in Chicago.

The APA's lone "novelty" of the season was **We, Comrades Three** (12-20-66, Lyceum), Richard Baldridge's rearrangement of Walt Whitman's poetry to examine his life and his views on slavery and the Civil War. The three comrades represented Whitman himself at three different periods—as a disheveled, troubled youth (Marco St. John), as a more self-confident middle-aged man (Sydney Walker), and as a venerable oldster (Will Geer). Helen Hayes also appeared, as a character called simply Mother, dressed in a red and blue cloak spangled with white stars and with a crown on her head and a sword and mirror in her hands. The evening ended with the strains of "The Battle Hymn of the Republic" rising to a crescendo. The entertainment was the only one of the group's productions during the season to receive generally thumbs-down notices.

Critics felt pretty much about Neil Simon's three-character **The Star-Spangled Girl** (12-21-66, Plymouth) the way they had felt about Woody Allen's comedy—that it was loaded with hilarious one-liners but had merely a wisp of a plot to hold them together. Douglas Watt assessed it in the *Daily News* as "Simon's most contrived effort to date." Simon's two young men, Andy Hobart (Anthony Perkins) and Norman Cornell (Richard Benjamin), are living on their uppers in a rundown studio apartment overlooking San Francisco Bay. Together they publish a protest magazine, *Fallout,* with Norman writing all the articles under various pseudonyms and Andy handling the business end by using a variety of accents to fend off creditors who phone and by going for terrifying joy rides with their harridan landlady (never seen) on her motorcycle. Not only could their landlady be a first cousin to the gal in *Agatha Sue,* but their starvation diet is not much different from that of the other comedy's gamblers. Norman's most recent lunch has consisted of a sardine on a frozen waffle, which leaves just three ice cubes and a light bulb in the refrigerator for tomorrow's meals. But like the gamblers, the men have a pretty neighbor. She is blonde, pert Sophie Rauschmeyer (Connie Stephens), newly moved in and a superpatriot if there ever was one. She is shocked to think the boys could find anything to protest about in so wonderful a country. Norman falls instantly in love with her, but soon enough she has fallen for Andy. That causes a breach between Andy and Norman, who briefly consider abandoning the magazine. Happily, Sophie eventually throws over the marine she has been engaged to and allows that there is always room for protest in democracy. She goes so far as to assist the men in getting out the publication, showing her newfound enthusiasm by singing "The Battle Hymn of the Republic," in which she is joined by a seemingly heavenly chorus (an echo from the Lyceum?), as the men look on, dumbfounded. The boyish Perkins and the deadpan Benjamin won enthusiastic notices, but Stephens was assailed in some quarters for overzealous playing. Although the comedy was a hit, its 261-performance run was far shorter than those of Simon's earlier successes.

Perhaps curiously, a somewhat enigmatic English drama, Harold Pinter's **The Homecoming** (1-5-67, Music Box), ran a couple of months longer, not closing until it had been performed 321 times. Reviewers, many of whom voted to accord it the New York Drama Critics Circle Award later in the year, could recount the basic story, but were uncertain what lay under the surface or what the numerous Pinterish silences meant. Pinter's scene was a shabby house in a lower-class North London area. The house is home to coarse, nasty Max (Paul Rogers), a retired butcher, his servile brother (John Normington), a chauffeur, and Max's two sons, Lenny (Ian Holm), a pimp, and Joey (Terence Rigby), a would-be boxer. The men are visited by Max's third son, Teddy (Michael Craig), a philosophy professor in America, and Teddy's wife, Ruth (Vivien Merchant). Before long Ruth is propositioning the other men and even smooching with them in Teddy's presence. Teddy decides to return home alone, while Ruth will remain with his family, apparently dabbling in prostitution to contribute to their till.

Another English play, Pauline Macaulay's **The Astrakhan Coat** (1-12-67, Helen Hayes), found very few takers. Claud (Roddy McDowall), a naive waiter, answers an ad which has offered an astrakhan coat for sale. He is greeted by the epicene James (Brian Bedford) and James's twin cronies, the equally epicene Alain (Job Stewart) and Alain's mannishly garbed sister, Barbara (Carole Shelley). Claud does not realize that the three have robbed and murdered a diamond merchant, hidden the body, and are setting him up as the fall guy. Claude is taken in by the police, but to his surprise finds he enjoys all the attention he is receiving. Lacking sufficient evidence, the police release him and send him home to his bed-sitter. There he finds the three killers awaiting him and he asks to be allowed to join them. They are pleased to agree, never letting on that they

have committed another murder and are preparing to frame him for that one, too.

A pair of still shorter-lived Broadway flops followed, separated only by one moderately popular off-Broadway entry and another misadventure at the Lincoln Center Repertory. According to a program note quoted by several critics, sheepish, easily panicked Soupy Sales had been featured in 5,370 television shows. But his Broadway outing in Lee Minoff and Stanley Price's **Come Live with Me** (1-26-67, Billy Rose) kept him before New York footlights for only four performances. His Chuck Clark is a divorced writer, living in London and working there on a screenplay for a film about Hannibal. An obliging neighbor (Michael Allison) suggests he import an au pair girl to make his life more pleasant. Grabbing at the idea, he brings over pretty little Ingeborg (Hanne Bork) from Denmark. But his former wife (Nan Martin), his film producer (Sorrell Booke), a rival au pair girl (Yvonne Constant), and his neighbor all complicate the situation before Chuck decides to make his relationship with Ingeborg more permanent. Besides the almost inevitable drunk scene and hangover scene, the nervous, easily flustered Chuck manages to pour a box of Rice Krispies all over the room and deal with such lines as "I don't care if you get Skippy-Peanut-Butter to play Scipio Africanus."

The Deer Park (2-1-67, de Lys) was Norman Mailer's theatricalization of his best-selling novel. It found only a modest audience down in the Village, so closed after 128 performances. Mailer framed his bitter spoof of Hollywood in the boozy dream of an air force flier, Sergius O'Shaugnessy (Gene Lindsey). Among the butts of the author's darts was the geat movie mogul Teppis (Will Lee, made up to resemble Louis B. Mayer), who sits on a golden throne, complete with hidden toilet, stabbing his fingers at his subordinates as he rules his studio like an absolute despot. Stars, fading directors, and agents all had their moment in the uncomfortable spotlight.

Leo Lehman's **The East Wind** (2-9-67, Vivian Beaumont) was the second foreign play of the season to be given a world premiere in New York and the lone novelty of the Lincoln Center Repertory Theatre's program. Two Hungarian refugees from the same village, after wandering separately about the world, meet again in London and decide to open a delicatessen. But the past keeps haunting the men. (The play begins with Zauber [Michael Granger], who talks loudly and feels little, stopping the more introspective Konarski [George Voskovec] from hanging himself, then moves backward and forward in time.) Even a seemingly happy marriage to an Englishwoman (Estelle Parsons) who can make a wonderfully reassuring pot of tea cannot stop Konarski's growing unhappiness. He finally manages to kill himself, though his spirit returns to give some comfort to his associate and his widow.

Harry Cauley's **The Paisley Convertible** (2-11-67, Henry Miller's), which had already played on the waning summer circuits, lasted for just nine performances on Broadway. After six weeks of marriage, Amy and Charlie Rogers (Joyce Bulifant and Bill Bixby) both wonder if the other was virgin when they wed. After all, Amy, in art class, had made drawings of a handsome nude, who later gave her a spare room in his apartment, while Charlie, an intern, had actually been engaged. Both the figures (Jed Allan and Betsy von Furstenberg) out of their past reappear to add fuel to the situation, as does Amy's mother (Marsha Hunt). But husband and wife are finally able to satisfy each other on all counts. The convertible of the title was not a car, but a sofa-bed in the couple's one-room flat.

Another English attraction to find favor and profit on Broadway was Peter Shaffer's bill of one-acters **Black Comedy** and **White Lies** (2-12-67, Barrymore). In the latter, a curtain raiser written for the Broadway mounting, a fraudulent fortune teller (Geraldine Page) is bribed by a singing group's thuggish manager (Donald Madden) to suggest a discouraging future to the young singer (Michael Crawford) who has his eye on the manager's girl. But the victim turns out not to be all that gullible, and the fortune teller has her pride. For the role, Page donned a black wig and a false nose. In the main piece, Shaffer resorted to what he suggested was an old Chinese stage trick—having the stage fully lit when the characters are supposedly moving about in total darkness. Conversely, the stage then becomes dark when the scene is supposedly bright. Sitting in real darkness (and imagined bright lights), Brinsley Miller (Crawford), an opportunistic young sculptor, and his current fiancée, Carol Melkett (Lynn Redgrave), are awaiting Brinsley's first meeting with Carol's colonel-father. To make his situation look more prosperous, Brinsley has "borrowed" without permission some fancy furnishings from a swishy, vacationing neighbor. But a fuse blows out leaving the pair in total darkness (on a now brightly lit stage). In short order, papa (Peter Bull) appears, as do the irate neighbor (Madden), a former flame (Page), and an assortment of other characters. The fun came from watching the characters try to move around or find seats, slipping up and down the stairs, or angrily poking a finger at someone actually standing several feet to their rear. The bill chalked up 337 performances.

Norman Krasna, whose Broadway successes were all long behind him, had a three-week dud with **Love in E-Flat** (2-13-67, Brooks Atkinson). Howard (Hal Buckley), the stage's second intern within a week, is having an affair with Amy (Kathleen Nolan), the teacher who has the apartment below his. Suspicious of her fidelity, he has her flat bugged. Amy catches on, so purposely allows Howard to hear her tell her sister (Marcia Rudd) of a rich lover who will take her to El Morocco or away on his yacht and of a concern that she may, in fact, be pregnant. Naturally the lovers kiss and make up at the end, after Howard has landed a job as house physician at a large company. Among the evening's jokes were the sister's exasperated question, "How can I sit here and not say anything?" followed by Amy's reply, "Just don't move your lips and nothing will come out."

On the next evening, the Bristol Old Vic also began a three-week stand, pre-booked as such at the City Center, offering a trio of Shakespearean plays—the season's second *Measure for Measure, Hamlet,* and *Romeo and Juliet.* Although the company was greeted by little critical hat-tossing, its mountings were welcomed as competent and not uninteresting.

There was still less enthusiasm when the Swedish actress Ingrid Thulin assumed the lead in Arnold Sundgaard's **Of Love Remembered** (2-18-67, ANTA). The drama moved back and forth over thirty years' time to unveil the unhappy life of a Norwegian girl. Inga is seduced by a wealthy mill owner (George Gaynes), then cast off by him after he finds his son, Ansgar (Toralv Maurstad), unaware of the relationship, would marry her. The couple move to Minnesota. There their son (James Olson), when grown, falls in love with a girl (Janet Ward) who deserts him as he starts to go blind. A family friend (William Traylor) woos Inga and, after she spurns him, discloses her history to Ansgar. The distraught husband kills himself. The play threw in the towel after a week.

Before the next Broadway opening, no fewer than three of Off Broadway's entries held major interest. Barbara Garson's **MacBird** (2-22-67, Village Gate) used the skeleton of *Macbeth* to savagely spoof Lyndon Johnson and his relations with the Kennedys, going so far as to suggest that Johnson had a hand in John Kennedy's assassination. Thus, when Lady MacBird goes mad, she sprays aerosol deodorant all around to mask the stench of MacBird (Stacy Keach) and his foul deeds, and cries, "Out, damned odor, out." Kennedy was seen here as John Ken O'Dunc, while other contemporary figures became Earl of Warren and Wayne of Morse. Although some critics and playgoers were offended, enough supporters turned out to keep the show on the boards for 386 performances.

John Herbert's **Fortune and Men's Eyes** (2-23-67, Actors Playhouse) ran only four performances less. It depicted life in a Canadian prison, and how the lack of normal sexual outlets drives inmates into homosexuality, which some discover they can enjoy or at least accept. Indeed, the play's most striking character was Queenie, a swish not unwilling to dress up in drag for a prison Christmas show. But other prisoners find ways of refusing to admit what they have been driven to. As with most prison plays, there was also a sadistic guard.

John Wilson's English drama **Hamp** (3-9-67, Renata), taken from an episode in a J. L. Hodson novel, recounted the seemingly ineluctable journey of one basically decent English soldier from his frightened desertion of his post during the World War I battle of Passchendaele after several years of dutiful service to his death before a firing squad. The drama ran for 101 performances.

The first performance of Lee Thuna's **The Natural Look** (3-11-67, Longacre) was its last. Reedy Harris (Brenda Vaccaro), a working wife who heads the advertising end of a large cosmetic firm, discovers that the former girlfriend (Zohra Lampert) of her doctor-husband, Barney (Gene Hackman), is prepared to mother him in Reedy's absence. So Reedy takes to serving hubby breakfast in bed and whistling "Tiptoe Through the Tulips" as she merrily picks up after him. But she soon realizes that Barney does not want to be mothered or too assertively wifed, so Reedy goes back to her work. Eighty-six-year-old Ethel Griffes won applause as the dominating duenna (read Helena Rubinstein) of the cosmetic firm, as did Jerry Orbach as a treacherously self-serving young executive.

The season's longest run—756 performances—went to yet another of the year's many bills of one-acters, Robert Anderson's **You Know I Can't Hear You When the Water's Running** (3-13-67, Ambassador). This time the bill consisted of four playlets. Watts saluted them as "notably fine comic and dramatic episodes." In **The Shock of Recognition,** Jack Barnstable (George Grizzard) is a successful playwright, somewhat squeamish about using profanity, but determined to have a nude scene in his latest play. He claims the shock of seeing how ugly the nude male is will force a more sensible viewpoint on playgoers. (Nude scenes had become not uncommon, especially off Broadway. The original *Marat/Sade* had offered Broadway a brief glimpse of dorsal nudity, and the touring company of the play, which had begun an engagment at the Majestic in January, had even more. Next season the musical *Hair* would present a bit of frontal nudity.) But the fundamentally prudish Barnstable gets more than he bargains for when an overeager actor (Martin Balsam) is willing to strip totally during an interview. **The Footsteps of Doves** describes how Harriet (Eileen Heckart) forces her husband, George (Balsam), to take her

to a bedding store to buy twin beds to replace the double bed she insists they are too old to use anymore. At first George refuses to go along with the change, but after meeting a luscious young typist (Melinda Dillon) who is looking for a double bed, he agrees. He will move the old double bed to the young typist's apartment. **I'll Be Home for Christmas** has Chuck (Balsam) and Edith (Heckart) arguing over how to raise their children, only to realize that their own marriage has been empty and that the children will go their own ways regardless of which parent wins the argument. In **I'm Herbert,** Herbert (Grizzard) and Muriel (Heckart), a very elderly couple, both of whom have been married several times, try in vain to remember their early love affairs and to get the names of all their spouses straight.

"Play absent," "the barest outline of a play," and similar dismissals sealed the fate of Frank D. Gilroy's **That Summer—That Fall** (3-16-67, Helen Hayes), a retelling of the classic Phaedra story. Only this time the stepmother is Angelina Capuano (Irene Papas), the second wife of a Lower Manhattan restaurant owner (Richard Castellano), and the object of her fatal attraction is her husband's handsome, athletic, if illegitimate son Steve (Jon Voight). For a time she struggles desperately to avoid a liaison. After she kills herself in despair, Steve drives off to his own death in the family car.

The season's second one-performance fiasco was Lonnie Coleman's **A Warm Body** (4-15-67, Cort). Homer (Kevin McCarthy), a fortyish, much married anthropologist who specializes in the pygmies of the Congo, meets Kate (Lois Markle), a prim, thirtyish newspaper columnist, whose own sex life has been none too satisfactory. At her apartment he tells her that "a warm body is a stand-in for somebody real," but before long the possibility grows that their relationship can become the real thing.

The Newquists in Jules Feiffer's **Little Murders** (4-25-67, Broadhurst) are clearly typical New York apartment dwellers. They keep the air-conditioner on in February to drown out all the street noises, pay little attention to the heavy breathers who regularly pester them with phone calls, and usually duck whenever snipers start shooting. True, one son didn't duck and was killed while out walking at 97th and Amsterdam. Now Patsy (Barbara Cook), the Newquists' determined daughter, brings home the nerdish Alfred Chamberlain (Elliott Gould). He has some bruises on his face because he never bothers to resist when anyone chooses to beat him up. "I daydream all through it," he tells the Newquists. But, in her determination, Patsy plans to marry and change Alfred—to make him see that there are things worth reacting to. Indeed, immediately after the marriage, a sniper shoots Patsy dead, and six months later, after 345 similar unsolved murders, Alfred finally does react. He joins Patsy's father (Heywood Hale Broun) and her effeminate brother (David Steinberg) in shooting out the window at passersby. This makes Patsy's mother (Ruth White) happy to see everyone laughing again. Largely negative notices—"could use more deftness and body," "needlessly distasteful"—prompted the producer to close the show after one week, but a little over a year and a half later a long-running off-Broadway revival would bring about some reconsideration.

An ANTA-sponsored touring repertory company came into the ANTA on May 1 to showcase for New Yorkers mountings it had been presenting across the nation. New Yorkers were unimpressed. The plays offered were Molière's *Imaginary Invalid,* O'Neill's *A Touch of the Poet,* and three of the one-acters from Noel Coward's *Tonight at 8:30—Ways and Means, Still Life,* and *Fumed Oak.*

As was so often the case, the season ended on a distinctly down note. William F. Brown's **The Girl in the Freudian Slip** (5-18-67, Booth) spotlighted a psychiatrist (Alan Young) who has written a play called *Linda Stone Is Brutal.* He has based the play on one of his own patients. She (Susan Brown) gets wind of it and comes to his office-apartment in a sexy leopard-skin outfit to discuss the matter. When the doctor's wife (Marjorie Lord) walks in she conveniently misconstrues what she sees, leading to several scenes of complications before everything is resolved. Four playings and the comedy, like the season it closed, was history.

1967–1968

Theatrically speaking, there was both good news—some of it deceptively so—and bad news. The count of new plays took a sharp leap up, to between forty-one and forty-seven, depending on whose statistics were followed. For the fourth year running a new total record gross, a smidgen under $59,000,000, was set. Moreover, since there were no blockbuster musicals this season except the late-arriving *Hair,* a bigger share of the figure came from comedies and dramas. At the same time, though, inflation, which had been creeping along for several seasons, suddenly heated up. The $6.90 top disappeared, and prices of $7.50, $8.00, and $8.50 became commonplace. One play even asked and got $9.90 and $10.90. So the higher gross did not necessarily reflect more ticket sales. Also, once again, imports all but dominated the scene. Neither the New York

Drama Critics Circle nor the Pulitzer judges deemed any native effort worthy of their main awards. Nonetheless, a few superior American plays did emerge.

For many local theatregoers, the New York Shakespeare Festival got the season underway on June 7 at Central Park's Delacorte Theatre with a mounting of *The Comedy of Errors.* Two even more rarely done plays followed: *King John* on July 5 and *Titus Andronicus* on August 2. The troupe's mobile unit trekked about the boroughs with a contemporary non-Shakespearean favorite, Ben Jonson's *Volpone.* In the casts, playing larger or smaller roles, were such performers as Olympia Dukakis, Charles Durning, and Raul Julia. Later in the season, the company offered additional works at its newly converted permanent quarters in Lower Manhattan.

At the Sheridan Square Playhouse, a pleasant if unexceptional *Arms and the Man* began a 189-performance run with John Heffernan as Bluntschli.

On Broadway proper, only one attraction braved the summer heat, Peter Ustinov's **The Unknown Soldier and His Wife** (7-6-67, Vivian Beaumont). Skipping across the centuries—with stops in ancient Rome, the Crusades, the French and American Revolutions, and World War I—a baffled but dutiful young soldier (Christopher Walken) is killed and buried in a nameless grave. This satisfies the self-righteous ruler-general (Brian Bedford) and confirms the dire but mealymouthed pronouncements of the oracle-priest (Howard Da Silva) of the moment. Other age-spanning characters included the insatiable munitions inventor (Bob Dishy) who comes up with such supposedly war-deterring devices as the crossbow, the guillotine, and poison gas, and the soldier's pregnant wife (Melissa C. Murphy). Despite reservation-filled notices, the blackish comedy hung on for 148 performances, only to close in the red.

Ira Levin's **Dr. Cook's Garden** (9-25-67, Belasco) received such negative notices that it survived for only a single week. Dr. Cook (Burl Ives) is the beloved hometown physician in Greenfield Center, Vermont, a man proud of his lovely garden from which all weeds are quickly removed. Young Dr. Tennyson (Keir Dullea), who looks on Cook as a father figure and who has just completed his own internship, comes to pay the older man a visit. Browsing through Cook's files he notices that many of Cook's deceased patients have an "R" on their cards and have died somewhat puzzlingly. Tennyson soon realizes that Cook has been killing off the terminally ill, the disabled, the ugly, and the nasty, weeding out what he considered undesirable villagers much as he weeded his garden. When Tennyson confronts him with his discovery, Cook attempts to poison him with sodium cynanide. The young man tricks him into providing an antidote. Before he can do

Act Three: 1959–1969

any more mischief or be exposed, Cook dies of a heart attack.

Bill Naughton's **Keep It in the Family** (9-27-67, Plymouth) lasted only half a week. When it first had been done in London, it had been called *Spring and Port Wine* and had been set in contemporary Yorkshire. The American version was set in the Boston of twenty years ago. Frank Brady (Patrick Magee) is a savage martinet, ruling his wife (Maureen O'Sullivan) and children with an iron first. For example, he has the mackerel that his daughter balked at eating placed before her at every meal, refusing to serve her anything else until she eats it. In time the family rebels—a rebellion that at heart does not totally displease Brady.

Alfonso Paso was said to be a leading Spanish playwright, but his **Song of the Grasshopper** (9-28-67, ANTA), as translated by William Layton and Augustin Penon, failed to impress Broadway. Like Naughton's opus, it ran only half a week. Aristobulo (Alfred Drake) is an idler who likes nothing better than to lounge, with his hat partially covering his face, on the sofa in his crumbling home while his loyal daughter (Diana Davila) looks after his cats and his illegitimate children. His lazy life is abruptly disturbed when the wife (Jan Ferrand) from whom he has been separated for seventeen years reappears, bringing with her an attractive young man (Ben Piazza), who woos and wins away the daughter. Aristobulo and his wife are reconciled, and she agrees to give up her mansion and come live with him again.

Critics who had been puzzled last season by the meaning of Harold Pinter's *The Homecoming* were even more perplexed when his earlier play **The Birthday Party** (10-3-67, Booth) was offered belatedly to New York. Stanley (James Patterson) is a failed pianist who is afraid to confront the world. He lives in semi-squalor in a boardinghouse run by an ineffectual couple (Ruth White and Henderson Forsythe). Two sinister figures, a sycophantic Jew (Ed Flanders) and a dour, thuggish Irishman (Edward Winter), appear, ostensibly to hold a birthday party for Stanley. They browbeat him with a volley of cruel questions, a rough game of blind man's buff, and by breaking his glasses. Reduced to little more than a zombie, Stanley is taken away by the men. By now, Pinter's reputation and following were enough to allow the play to remain on the boards for 126 performances, but they were insufficient to permit the work to recover its costs.

Two very short-lived flops followed. The first ran for three performances; the second, for only one. Eric Nicol's Canadian play **A Minor Adjustment** (10-6-67, Brooks Atkinson) was the first of several scheduled to open shortly dealing with the generation gap. Cameron Clark (Austin Willis), a paper tycoon, feels his son,

Cam junior (Paul Collins), is too young to marry his high school sweetheart, so he arranges with his public relations man, Ron Webster (William Redfield), to fix up the boy with Ron's mini-skirted, high-booted artist-girlfriend, Gilian (Joan Darling). The two men will watch the seduction over closed-circuit television. Junior's reaction is only partially what his father had hoped. While he puts off any marriage plans, he heads off to work in a Chinese commune, a trip underwritten by a CIA front group.

In the one-shot fiasco, Mary Mercier's **Johnny No-Trump** (10-8-67, Cort), Harry Armstrong (Pat Hingle) believes his nephew, the would-be poet Johnny Edwards (Don Scardino), is a born loser, a young man with no trumps to play in life. Harry's opinion counts for something, since Johnny and his schoolteacher mother, Florence (Sada Thompson), have lived with him ever since Johnny's alcoholic father ran away to live a bohemian life as a painter. But Johnny cannot get along with his elders, except for one of his teachers—"I call her Georgia because she is a peach." He decides to pack and live somewhere on his own. Just then his father (James Broderick) turns up. The older men read some of Johnny's poems and decide they are quite good. When Mrs. Edwards is killed in an automobile accident, the three men settle in resignedly in the now all-male household.

Despite some laudatory notices, John Bowen's **After the Rain** (10-9-67, Golden), which Bowen had adapted from his own novel and which had already been mounted in London, could not find a market on Broadway. In the year 2169, 200 years after the great, world-destroying flood of 1969, a lecturer (Paul Sparer) tells his listeners about the aftermath while a group of prisoners acts out his tale. A few survivors take to a raft sponsored by a breakfast cereal called Glub, which claims that men can live on Glub alone. The group is dominated by one man (Alec McCowen), who at first seeks social supremacy but soon attempts to establish himself as a god. Although he is eventually assassinated, his writings survive and become canonized and the world becomes theocratic.

Off Broadway had a smash hit with Bruce Jay Friedman's **Scuba Duba** (10-10-67, New). The *Times*'s new critic, Clive Barnes, hailed it as "the most polished and certainly the most hilarious American comedy since Arthur Kopit's 'Oh, Dad, Poor Dad.' " His wife having run off with a black frogman, Harold Wonder (Jerry Orbach) is alone in the French château he has rented. Back home, Harold wrote copy for billboards—"the true urban folk-literature of the sixties." But now, all he has for company—and a security blanket—is the scythe he carries around with him. For comfort he phones his psychiatrist and his mother. (During these

418

conversations, life-sized cutouts of the figures drop from the flies.) By way of additional consolation he invites over his mauve-bikinied neighbor (Brenda Smiley). But her bluish stories and her descriptions of her life with her girlfriend and that girl's lover are not much help. He constantly yells threats and racial insults out the window to the frogman, who is apparently too far away to hear. When the wife (Jennifer Warren) returns briefly, she brings with her not one, but two black men (Cleavon Little and Rodney K. Douglas), which only further exacerbates the supposedly liberal Harold's befuddled prejudices. The wife and her men soon head away, leaving Harold once more to yell out the window his threats to date the neighbor and never speak to his wife again. The comedy played on for 962 performances.

By George (10-12-67, Lyceum) was a one-man show, with Max Adrian made up to look like George Bernard Shaw and reading from the letters, essays and criticism Shaw had written between the ages of thirty-eight and ninety-three. The show had already been done in London, but New York critics felt that the figure onstage was almost always Adrian and rarely Shaw. Two weeks and it was gone.

Reviewers were somewhat more taken with Stephen Levi's two-character drama **Daphne in Cottage D** (10-15-67, Longacre), seeing Levi as an extremely promising writer who had not written a fulfilling play. Two lonely people, Daphne (Sandy Dennis) and Joseph (William Daniels), meet at a New England summer resort. After a time they fence at lovemaking, but when Joseph tries to kiss Daphne, she rips his shirt and sends him away. He later returns, and the pair confess their dark secrets to one another. She is the widow of a movie star and has lost custody of her young son. "You may have noticed—I'm not a mother; I'm something much, much more—I'm a drunk," she tells him. He reveals that he has run away from his home after accidentally killing his own young son in an auto mishap. Even if they can't make love, Joseph can at least decorate her cottage for her boy's hoped-for visit. However, he is no sooner gone than she tears down the decorations and sits alone on the floor playing the xylophone she has bought for the youngster who will probably not come.

Last season, *Those That Play the Clowns* had told the Hamlet story tangentially from the viewpoint of the traveling players whom Hamlet had enlisted. The play had been a quick failure. Now the prince's story was seen from another viewpoint and gave Broadway its first real hit of the year. **Rosencrantz and Guildenstern Are Dead** (10-16-67, Alvin) was America's introduction to the young British playwright Tom Stoppard. The foggy-minded pair (Brian Murray and John Wood), who have really not known the prince very well and whose

names Hamlet (Noel Craig) gets mixed up, come to Elsinor and watch the goings-on there uncomprehendingly. They accept unthinkingly the command of the king (Roger Hamilton) to spy on the prince, and sail away with a sealed letter, never realizing that Hamlet has switched epistles and that they are carrying their own death warrants. The play chalked up 420 performances.

Another British play—another hit, this one running for 321 performances. Robert Danvers (Gig Young), the central figure in Terence Frisby's **There's a Girl in My Soup** (10-18-67, Music Box), is an egocentric, middle-aged food writer. He's also something of a ladies' man, whose most recent lady (Rita Gam) has just walked out on him. So at a party he picks up mod (in the lingo of the time), nineteen-year-old Marion (Barbara Ferris), who has newly split with a drummer her own age, and takes her back to his posh apartment. Her open amusement at his romantic ploys does little for his *amour propre,* but he does manage to take her off to France for a fling. Even so, she finally rejects his marriage proposal and reunites with her drummer boy.

The City Center offered New Yorkers a chance to see a pair of revivals at bargain prices, beginning on the 19th. The initial attraction was *Life with Father,* with Dorothy Stickney recreating her original role as Mother Day and Leon Ames as Father. *The Tenth Man* was brought back on November 8 and featured John Kerr in the title role. Each play ran three weeks.

Also on the 19th, the Jewish State Theatre of Poland began a two-month stand at the Billy Rose, offering a pair of bills. The first was Jacob Gordin's *Mirele Efros,* in which a doting, generous mother is plagued with greedy sons; the second was Brecht's *Mother Courage and Her Children.* The troupe's star, Ida Kaminska, was hailed for her understated yet illuminating playing.

Deadpan, put-upon Paul Ford was deemed the saving grace of Henry Denker's generation-gap comedy **What Did We Do Wrong?** (10-22-67, Helen Hayes). Having raised his son on Dr. Spock and *The Reader's Digest,* Walter Davis, Sr., a manufacturer of television aerials, is appalled when Walter junior (Russell Horton) comes home from college a tie-dyed-in-the-wool, guitar-strumming hippie, bearded and slovenly. Deciding to fight fire with fire, Walter senior dons a shaggy black wig and clothes which he has splattered with "instant dirt." He parades through town brandishing a placard demanding respect for parents and even threatens to set fire to himself on the steps of his wife's beloved Lincoln Center. Young Walter gets the point. Ford, "at the peak of his delightful and distinctive comic skills," could not keep the comedy going beyond six weeks.

Ostensibly Michael McClure's **The Beard** (10-24-67, Evergreen) was a two-character play in which the shades of Jean Harlow (Billie Dixon) and Billy the Kid (Richard Bright) explore the implications of sexual relationships. But playgoers who sauntered down to 11th Street were treated to a mixed-media mounting that also included filmed scenes and a three-man group singing and strumming raga-rock. The affair remained around for 100 performances.

At the Vivian Beaumont, the troubled Repertory Theatre of Lincoln Center briefly hit the jackpot with its revival of *The Little Foxes* on the 26th. Not only did most critics feel that Lillian Hellman's melodrama had withstood the test of time, but they had kudos for the superb cast, including Anne Bancroft as Regina, George C. Scott as Ben, E. G. Marshall as Oscar, Margaret Leighton as Birdie, and Austin Pendleton as Leo. Since the season had essentially been booked in advance, Mike Nichols's mounting was moved in time to a regular Broadway theatre. In all it ran for 100 performances. Subsequent revivals, with less prestigious casts and less critical acclaim, were *Saint Joan* on January 4, *Tiger at the Gates* on February 29, and *Cyrano de Bergerac* on April 25.

When he died, Eugene O'Neill had left a nine-hour-long rough draft for **More Stately Mansions** (10-31-67, Broadhurst). The drastically cut-down version which America saw (Sweden had seen an earlier abridgement) was the work of director José Quintero, who had been responsible for so much of O'Neill's rehabilitation. The new play had been planned as part of the lengthy cycle O'Neill had envisaged and was slated to come chronologically immediately after *A Touch of the Poet*. Con Melody is dead, and his daughter, Sara (Colleen Dewhurst), has married a prosperous local businessman, Simon Hartford (Arthur Hill). But Simon has deep emotional problems. To begin with he is torn between a high idealism and an inbred, aggressive greed. Worse, he has a love-hate relationship with his dominating if fantasy-prone mother (Ingrid Bergman). A battle is soon waged between the women for the affection and loyalty of the pathetically vacillating Simon. Critics agreed that, at least as seen onstage, the play was distinctly lesser O'Neill. On the other hand, most reviewers had high praise for Bergman and, more especially, Dewhurst, although they generally felt Hill was defeated by his difficult, uncertain part. For all the critical complaints, the mounting managed to run for 142 performances and, thanks to careful husbanding, show a profit.

Amram Ducovny and Leon Friedman's **The Trial of Lee Harvey Oswald** (11-5-67, ANTA) postulated what might have happened if Jack Ruby's shot had missed and Oswald had survived. Audiences entering the auditorium saw a spotlighted, emotionless Oswald (Peter Masterson) seated in Robin Wagner's otherwise empty, stylized courtroom. When the trial did commence, theatregoers also discovered they were addressed as if they were the jury. The first act gave the prosecution case as presented by a clearly bigoted southerner (Clifton James). The second act offered Oswald's wild, confused defense, in which he insisted that he was set up by the CIA and that a pair of Cubans were the real killers. The drama was a quick failure.

So was J. J. Coyle's **The Ninety-Day Mistress** (11-6-67, Biltmore). Having been raised by an embittered, feminist mother (Ruth Ford) after her father ran off to raise pineapples and sons in Hawaii, Leona Hastings (Dyan Cannon) has little time for men. In fact, she insists no affair can continue for more than ninety days—or nights—after which the romance has to cool. Then she meets a nice young man (Martin Milner) from the Midwest. She is about to discard her rigid notions and marry him, when she learns he is a detective hired by her father to spy on her mother. But after her father (Walter Abel) appears and shows her that her mother's version of the family breakup was untruthful and self-serving, she goes ahead with her marriage plans.

Critics looked on Peter Ustinov's second comedy of the season, **Halfway Up the Tree** (11-7-67, Brooks Atkinson), as an English *What Did We Do Wrong?*. General Sir Mallalieu Fitzbuttress (Anthony Quayle) returns from four years in Malaya to find that his unmarried daughter (Margaret Linn) is pregnant and that his son (Sam Waterston), who has been sent down from Oxford, is now a bearded, guitar-toting hippie in love with a friend of indeterminate sex ("Lesley"). His response, not unlike Walter Davis, Sr.'s, is to stage his own rebellion, which he does by taking to a tree outside his home. He grows his own beard and gets his own guitar. An accommodation is reached after the youngsters both agree to make normal marriages. The comedy struggled on for eight weeks before calling it a run.

Down in the Village, the Nigerian playwright Wole Soyinka, who at the time was imprisoned in his homeland, scored some small success with a double bill consisting of **The Trials of Brother Jero** and **The Strong Breed** (11-9-67, Greenwich Mews). In the former, the curtain raiser, a fraudulent prophet keeps his followers in line by predicting dire consequences if they do the things they want to do. The longer play told how a young schoolteacher, learning that he is to be the annual scapegoat and ritually sacrificed as his village's offering to its gods, attempts unavailingly to escape his fate. The bill remained at its berth for 115 playings.

Three weeks was all the first new Russian play to reach Broadway in many seasons could manage. **The Promise** (11-14-67, Henry Miller's) was Ariadne Nicolaeff's translation of Aleksei Arbuzov's original. In besieged Leningrad, Lika (Eileen Atkins), who wants

420

to be a medical specialist, takes refuge in a bomb-damaged apartment belonging to Marik (Ian McShane), a bridge engineer. So does Leonidik (Ian McKellen), a would-be poet. Both men fall in love with Lika before they head off to battle. After the war Marik returns a bemedalled hero; Leonidik, minus one arm. More out of pity than love, Lika marries Leonidik. But thirteen years later Leonidik is a failed writer and an alcoholic, and Lika is merely an ordinary practitioner. Marik suddenly reemerges and, though he, too, has not realized his promise—to become a great engineer—he persuades Leonidik to depart and leave Lika to him.

The Circle in the Square came up with a season-long success on November 21 when it offered playgoers Euripides' *Iphigenia in Aulis,* in a translation by Minos Volanakis and with Irene Papas as Clytemnestra.

Back in 1955 in *Will Success Spoil Rock Hunter?,* George Axelrod had a character who had written one successful play and referred to himself as a "playwrote." In Carl Reiner's **Something Different** (11-28-67, Cort), Bud Nemerov (Bob Dishy) had written a very successful play twelve years earlier and had not been able to come up with anything since then. He finally decides that what inspired him the first time was working in his mother's Bronx kitchen with his mother sitting around and nagging him. So he attempts to recreate his mother's kitchen in his suburban mansion, even to bringing in cockroaches and hiring a voluptuous blonde actress (Maureen Arthur) to impersonate his mother. Unfortunately the play he now writes is so bad that it could succeed only "with Marlon Brando and Sophia Loren to do it in the nude." But his wife (Linda Lavin), who has presented him with "twins"—one white, one black—and who has had a conspicuous affair with the exterminator (Gabriel Dell) who has been providing Bud with the bugs, suggests that life has been too healthy to provide him inspiration and that he must lead the "sick" existence he led while under his mother's thumb. When she agrees to make things as sick as possible for Bud, his inspiration returns. Although reviewers liked the basic idea, they felt Reiner was not fully able to carry it through. Nonetheless, the play held on for thirteen weeks.

Edward Albee's name helped his new play, **Everything in the Garden** (11-29-67, Plymouth), which he took from the recent English drama by Giles Cooper, to linger on for eight-four performances. With Richard (Barry Nelson) and Jenny (Barbara Bel Geddes) scraping by in their suburban home and with Richard refusing to allow Jenny to earn pocket money by taking a part-time job, it proves not very difficult for a suave Englishwoman, Mrs. Toothe (Beatrice Straight), to persuade Jenny to receive carefully selected men in her bed during the day while Richard is away at work.

Richard stumbles on the truth, then is further shocked to discover that several neighboring wives are also plying the trade. A local artist (Robert Moore) threatens to explode the whole sorry tale and is suffocated and buried for his pains. At the final curtain, Richard and Jenny are sitting forlornly on their sofa, aware they have wrecked their lives.

The APA began its season with George Hauger's translation of Michel de Ghelderode's **Pantagleize** (11-30-67, Lyceum). On May 1, Pantagleize (Ellis Raab), a shy writer for a fashion magazine, awakes to celebrate his fortieth birthday. Going for a walk, he innocently gives some revolutionaries the secret phrase that is to launch the revolution. Before he realizes what is happening, he is sucked into the melee, made the leader, and, when the uprising is crushed, led before a firing squad. Once again, most critics hailed the troupe as New York's best hope for enlightened, well-presented repertory. But the group had an even bigger delight in store for playgoers when it revived George Kelly's *The Show-Off* (2-5-24) on December 5. The "company moved into the realm of pure, joyous art," the *Daily News*'s John Chapman proclaimed. Helen Hayes, "looking dowdy and lumpy, with a gray topknot on her gray hair, and wearing severe spectacles," walked away with the most enthusiastic notices as the crusty Mrs. Fisher.

There were more raves for **Spofford** (12-14-67, ANTA), which Herman Shumlin theatricalized from Peter DeVries's novel *Reuben, Reuben*—"an evening of delightful humor and a great deal of sly wisdom," "a wise, sly, witty and ingratiating exposure of life in exurbia." And there were equally laudatory adjectives showered on the play's star, Melvyn Douglas. Yet, though the play survived for six months, it went down in the record books as a commercial failure. Spofford is an old, widowed chicken farmer who has watched in dismay as his small, friendly farming community has been taken over by rich folk escaping from the city. He is given to philosophical observations. Thus, when a socialite quotes Tennyson to him, he tells the audience, "Reading Tennyson is like drinking liqueur. You're likelier to get sick on it than drunk." And observing one particularly cold, snobbish newcomer, he concludes, "Women with flat backsides lack warm natures." After his granddaughter (Penelope Windust) is spurned by the new society, he decides to examine it more closely, so he takes odd jobs at their homes. Before long, he has learned enough to write a devastating tell-all book about the upstart exurbanites. They get wind of it, and, though he is the only Democrat in town, they make him First Selectman in return for not publishing his stories.

The season's second one-man show was Patrick Garland's **Brief Lives** (12-18-67, Golden), taken from the writings of a seventeenth-century London name-dropper, John Aubrey. Roy Dotrice, in a shaggy white wig and layers of filthy clothing, made room for himself on a cluttered stage, to portray the gossipy Aubrey at seventy-one, shortly before his death. Two weeks sufficed to satisfy New Yorkers.

Downtown at Joe Papp's New York Shakespeare Festival Public Theatre, a quite outré, ninety-minute, modern-dress version of *Hamlet* provoked critical ire when it opened on the 26th. Even some of the names were changed, with Hamlet's two former buddies becoming Rosencraft and Guilderstone. The production, which offered Martin Sheen in the title role, began with the king and queen in bed, a seemingly naked Hamlet handcuffed in a coffin at their feet, and the three bickering over a blanket. The mounting was withdrawn after seven weeks.

The new year, 1968, started with the APA's latest offering, Eugene Ionesco's **Exit the King** (1-9-68, Lyceum), another ninety-minute, intermissionless drama, covering the last hour and a half in the life of a monarch (Richard Easton). His old queen (Eva Le Gallienne) favors telling him the truth about his illness, but his young queen (Patricia Connelly) rejects the idea and tries to force him to go on living. Critics were more respectful of the mounting than they had been of the NYSF *Hamlet* but not much more pleased.

Another of the season's many English plays, Charles Dyer's two-character **Staircase** (1-10-68, Biltmore), was set in a slummy Brixton hairdresser's shop and centered on the two homosexuals who run it. The marcelled Charles (Eli Wallach) is waspish and peacocky; pudgy, bald Harry (Milo O'Shea) is soft and motherly. The men are constantly squabbling, with Charles sniping about Harry's mother, who lives with the men, and Harry retorting by questioning whether the daughter Charles claims he has was really his. For a time, after Charles is summoned to court to explain why he dressed as a woman in public, Harry seems to have the upper hand. Broadway didn't buy this one.

A second two-character play, Lawrence Holofcener's **Before You Go** (1-11-68, Henry Miller's), proved even less attractive. The heavy rain that is falling on the steps outside can be clearly seen in Stanley Fish's Greenwich Village basement apartment. So can the feet of a young woman caught in the rain. Stanley (Gene Troobnick) invites her (Marion Seldes) to come in and dry off. He, it turns out, is a buyer in his uncle's store by day and a sculptor by night; the girl is a would-be actress obsessed with psychoanalytical jargon. As everyone in the audience knew they would be, the pair were in bed together by evening's end.

Although Jay Allen was an American, her adaptation of Muriel Spark's **The Prime of Miss Jean Brodie** (1-

16-68, Helen Hayes) had first been a hit in London. Now brought to New York, it starred Zoe Caldwell as a well-meaning but pretentious Edinburgh schoolmarm in the 1930s. She tells her young ladies that they are all the *crème de la crème* and are destined for wonderful things. Her love affairs would appear to be either platonic or vicarious. Thus she foists one of her pupils on a married but philandering art teacher whom she herself dotes on. Unfortunately, her romantic notions of fascism and her glowing appraisals of Franco and Mussolini bring about her downfall after she inspires another of her girls to head off to fight in Spain, where the girl is killed. Caldwell was applauded for bringing out the character's humorous nuances, with Barnes adding that she "flounces onto the stage like a sparrow with illusions of grandeur . . . and her lilting Scots voice picks over her consonants with the languid deliberation of a dowager picking over a box of candy." Walter Kerr, in his Sunday column, garlanded the evening as "the most attractive and most satisfying of the season," thereby helping it to run for 378 performances.

A double bill of one-acters introduced theatregoers to Israel Horovitz, a young writer whom many critics saw as most promising. The evening's curtain raiser, **It's Called the Sugar Plum** (1-17-68, Astor Place), had a somewhat oddball Harvard student woo and win a young lady (Marsha Mason) whose skateboarding fiancé he has just fatally run over. In the main piece, **The Indian Wants the Bronx,** an East Indian, new to the city and possibly lost, is waiting for a bus at an isolated bus stop. Two teenaged toughs (one played by Al Pacino) appear and, at first, merely tease the foreigner. In short order, however, when no bus arrives, their teasing turns into vicious tormenting, then ends with their beating and slashing the man. By the time the bill closed it had run for 204 performances.

Reviewers split on judging Robert Anderson's **I Never Sang for My Father** (1-25-68, Longaere). Some disliked it, condemning it as "heavy" or "soap opera," while admirers praised its integrity and welcomed it as "fine theatre." Addressing the audience, much as Spofford had done earlier, forty-year-old Gene Garrison (Hal Holbrook) remarks, "Death ends a life, but it doesn't end a relationship." The relationship Gene is referring to is that he had with his selfish, self-centered father (Alan Webb). The older man—he is nearly eighty—wants his widowed son to remain close by, ostensibly because Gene's ailing, adoring mother (Lillian Gish) needs him, but actually because he wants to dominate and rely on him. This becomes even clearer after the mother dies and Gene proposes to move to California to wed again. It is a move Gene's sister (Teresa Wright) strongly supports. The father is outraged and turns against Gene, much as he had turned against his own drunken, unloving father and against his own daughter after she disobeyed him by marrying a Jew. Gene moves west, but eventually brings his failing father to live with him. Yet when the man dies there has been no genuine reconciliation. Gene can only repeat the comment he made at the start. The play struggled along for 124 performances before folding.

Keith Baxter all but stole Samuel Taylor's **Avanti!** (1-31-68, Booth) as a resourceful, amoral, bisexual Roman fixer, but couldn't earn the show a run. Alexander "Sandy" Claiborne (Robert Reed), a St. Louis businessman, comes to Rome to arrange to return his father's body to America. His father had been killed in a car crash. An Englishwoman had been killed in the same crash, and her daughter, Alison Ames (Jennifer Hillary), has come to Italy to claim her remains. Sandy and Alison soon realize that their parents, although married to others, had been lovers for many years, meeting once each year for a tryst in Italy. Italian red tape prolongs their stays. Sandy, who barks, "The world doesn't stop between one and four," can't get the Italians to see that. With the good offices of the American embassy, he finally is introduced to young Baldassare "Baldo" Pantaleone (Baxter), and Baldo eventually breaks through the bureaucratic tangle. However, by that time Sandy and Alison have become lovers, even though she knows he is married. When Sandy's comely, down-to-earth wife (Betsy von Furstenberg) arrives, Alison assumes the affair is ended. But Sandy pleads that they do what their parents did and meet once a year in Italy. Although she has her doubts they will really see each other again, Alison agrees.

Despite its unpleasant subject, Peter Nichols's London hit **A Day in the Death of Joe Egg** (2-1-68, Brooks Atkinson) hung on till mid-June, in some measure because of a striking performance by Albert Finney—although he left the cast in mid-April. Joe (Susan Alpern) is short for Josephine, a hopelessly retarded ten-year-old. Her parents, Bri (Finney) and Sheila (Zena Walker), have not institutionalized the girl and have attempted to deal with their problems as light-heartedly as possible. But Bri eventually cannot take it any longer. After failing in an apparent attempt to kill the child, Bri packs his things and heads off. Like several other leading characters during the season, Bri spent much of the evening addressing the audience. In a novel departure, a small onstage jazz band played incidental music.

Whatever reservations they held, most aisle-sitters approved of Arthur Miller's four-character, intermissionless **The Price** (2-7-68, Morosco). Typically, Chapman hailed it as "an absorbing play," so, with its low running budget, it continued on for a little more than a year, compiling 429 performances. Two brothers, estranged for sixteen years, meet again in the jampacked attic of the brownstone they once called home. The building is about to be demolished, and a used-furniture man (Harold Gary) has been called in to buy the old, dust-laden stuff. One brother, Victor (Pat Hingle), has been a policeman, taking on the job and sacrificing his chance for an education to look after his father, who had been destroyed in the Crash. The other brother, Walter (Arthur Kennedy), refused to help and went on to become a successful doctor. Victor suggests that Walter failed in his obligations, but Walter retorts that their father was not as down and out as Victor insisted he was and that Victor enjoyed his self-imposed martyrdom. Indeed, Victor has had a good marriage to his long-suffering, goading wife (Kate Reid) and raised a fine young son, while Walter's marriage has fallen apart and he has had a nervous breakdown. The brothers part again, without totally resolving their differences.

The season's smash hit was Neil Simon's **Plaza Suite** (2-14-68, Plymouth), a bill of three one-acters. "All three of the plays are richly funny," Richard Watts, Jr., wrote in the *Post,* "and they have a way of rising on an increasing scale of humor." With such notices to prod them, theatregoers flocked to the entertainment for 1097 performances. All three plays were set in Suite 719 at New York's famed Plaza Hotel. Karen (Maureen Stapleton) and Sam Nash (George C. Scott), the central figures in **Visitor from Mamaroneck,** have booked the same suite they had during their honeymoon twenty-four years before. But Karen discovers that Sam has taken on his secretary (Claudette Nevins) as a mistress, so when he departs for a rendezvous with the girl, she is left alone with a bottle of champagne and two glasses. In **Visitor from Hollywood,** the suite is occupied by blond, smirking Jesse Kiplinger (Scott), now a Hollywood celebrity, who has invited his New Jersey high school sweetheart to visit him. Muriel (Stapleton) has become a slightly dowdy suburban matron. But she has followed his career, and he has only to start pouring drinks and dropping names to lure her to bed with him. The evening's best playlet was **Visitor from Forest Hills.** With just minutes to go until her $8000 wedding, Mimsey Hubley (Nevins) locks herself in her bathroom and refuses to come out. Frantic attempts by her mother, Norma (Stapleton) and increasingly exasperated father Roy (Scott), are unavailing. Roy goes so far as to try breaking down the door and climbing out on a ledge to enter by the bathroom window. He merely succeeds in getting drenched in a downpour and shredding his rented cutaway. After all of Roy's hectic but futile efforts, the groom (Bob Balaban) turns up, quietly tells Mimsey, "Cool it," and gets her to head for the ceremony. Both

Act Three: 1959–1969

Stapleton and Scott were better known as dramatic players, so they surprised many audiences with their comic skills. Stapleton's were more subdued, but Scott gave free rein to "a maniacal gift for wild, uninhibited rough-house farce."

By contrast, some of the season's most savage put-downs—"depressing," "junk," "very sad and very sick"—and one of its shortest runs—seven performances—was the lot of Robert Alan Aurthur's **Carry Me Back to Morningside Heights** (2-27-68, Golden). Seymour Levin (David Steinberg), a young Jew guilt ridden by his country's treatment of blacks, insists Willie Nurse (Louis Gossett), a black law student, take him on as a slave. He is so insistent that Willie finally does. Seymour turns out to be a competent housekeeper and a decent cook of his family's soul food, such as steamed carp. Of course, when Seymour "borrows" a pen, the blacks observe that the whites walk away with anything not nailed down, and when he is caught spooning with a white girl in a neighboring apartment, they accept that whites are only animals. In time, Seymour is sold down the corridor to a black bus driver (Johnny Brown).

The latest of the season's many importations from London was William Francis's **Portrait of a Queen** (2-28-68, Henry Miller's), a loosely structured survey of Queen Victoria's reign, from her coronation to 1900, drawn from the letters, diaries, and writings of Victoria herself and her contemporaries. Dorothy Tutin's Victoria won the highest praise, while Dennis King's skillfully portrayed Disraeli was also approved.

Up at Lincoln Center's smallish secondary playhouse, a new drama managed to overcome indifferent notices to run for 127 performances. Audiences learned early on that the Young Man (David Birney) who was the hero of Ron Cowen's **Summertree** (3-3-68, Forum) was killed in Vietnam. Scenes moved back and forth across the years to offer glimpses of his life. He wants to be a pianist and is supported in his ambition by his highly possessive Mother (Priscilla Pointer). His salesman Father (Philip Sterling) scoffs at such notions, insisting he become a money-making businessman. His Girl (Blythe Danner) is compliant but uncommitted.

The Guide (3-6-68, Hudson) was Harvey Breit and Patricia Rinehart's very short-lived dramatization of R. K. Narayan's novel. A pair of escaped convicts, Raju (Zia Mohyeddin) and Bhabani (Titos Vandi), have taken shelter in a neglected Indian temple. Because of Raju's clever glibness, he is mistaken for a holy man. The local villagers beg him to bring rain to end their drought. At first, when nothing happens, angry villagers kill Bhabani. But the rains come in time to save Raju's neck and his reputation as a saint in villagers' eyes.

The parade of failures that would march on uninter-

ruptedly to season's end—at least on Broadway—continued with Gore Vidal's "predictable and rather desultory" **Weekend** (3-13-68, Broadhurst). Polls show that Senator Charles Magruder (John Forsythe), with 28 percent of the delegates in his favor, will have a reasonable lead at the forthcoming Republican convention over Nixon, Rockefeller, or Reagan. Naturally this delights everyone around him, including his cold wife (Rosemary Murphy) and his affectionate secretary-mistress (Kim Hunter). Then Magruder's obnoxious son (Marco St. John), a long-haired, turtlenecked academic who has been studying in England, returns home, bringing with him a fiancée—a black girl (Carol Cole). Consternation and shock reign. Magruder contemplates withdrawing from the race. But the news has leaked out and, to general surprise, the public has no objections. In fact, 61 percent will vote for Magruder. Mrs. Magruder asks what about the bigots. "They're in the suburbs," she's told, while the votes are in the cities.

Consternation and shock of a different sort reigned a few nights later when the late Joe Orton's London comedy **Loot** (3-18-68, Biltmore) premiered. It would take some more years for the controversial dramatist to be installed in the pantheon of major contemporary playwrights. For the time being critics were either left aghast or warned that their readers would be. The body of the late Mrs. McCready remains at her home, awaiting burial and attended by her grieving, devoutly Catholic husband (Liam Redmond). She has apparently been poisoned by her homicidal nurse (Carole Shelley). Her androgynous son and the undertaker's assistant (Kenneth Cranham and James Hunter), who have jointly just robbed a bank, show up, looking for a place to hide the money. So does a rather unconventional detective (George Rose). The boys place the money in the coffin after hiding the corpse in a closet. Farcical pandemonium ensues before all the characters except the father agree to divvy up the loot. The poor, innocent old man is hustled off to jail.

The APA concluded its season with Eva Le Gallienne's translation of *The Cherry Orchard*, which opened on the 19th. Uta Hagen was Madame Ranevskaya, and, in an unusual bit of casting, musical comedy comedienne Nancy Walker was Charlotta, the governess given to showing magic tricks.

At the City Center on the same night, the Vienna Burgtheater began a three-week stand, presenting four plays. **Professor Bernhardi** was Arthur Schnitzler's look at pre-WWI anti-Semitism in Austria, where a Jewish doctor is assailed for preventing a priest from administering last rites. Hermann Bahr's *Das Konzert,* offered to Broadway in 1910 by David Belasco, recounted how an aging, philandering musician is brought to his senses by his devoted wife. Schiller's *Maria*

Stuart had been a nineteenth-century favorite in America. Johann Nestroy's *Einen Jux will er sich machen* had been seen in New York as *The Merchant of Yonkers* and *The Matchmaker,* the latter the springboard for *Hello, Dolly!*

Paul Foster's **Tom Paine** (3-25-68, Stage 73) was a production of the celebrated La Mama troupe, which had been performed by them in London and Edinburgh before being given its New York premiere. The loosely structured drama covered the highlights in the life of the arrogant, alcoholic, yet brilliant Paine (Kevin O'Connor)—his arrival from England at the age of thirty-eight, his publication of *Common Sense,* his return to his homeland and the great success of of *Rights of Man,* his fleeing the island to avoid a charge of treason, his unavailing attempt to save Louis XVI in France (which nearly costs him his own life), and his final, unwelcomed return to American with his burial there in an unconsecrated grave. Enough embracing notices caught the public's attention to allow the work to compile 295 performances.

Tennessee Williams received few compliments for his three-character **The Seven Descents of Myrtle** (3-27-68, Barrymore). Even Jo Mielziner's skeletonized, cramped two-story dwelling failed to please reviewers. Lot Ravenstock (Brian Bedford), a mother-crushed, weak, and dying young man, brings his new bride, Myrtle (Estelle Parsons), home to his flood-ravaged Mississippi farm. On his release from a hospital, he had seen her, a failed carnival performer and singer, on television, when she had been crowned "Take-Life-Easy-Queen," and had wed her in a TV ceremony a day or so later. Now he hopes she can wheedle the rights to his land back from his hip-booted, stud half-brother, the part-Negro Chicken (Harry Guardino), to whom he had willed the property after his death. She fails again. As Lot, dressed in his mother's bed clothes and wearing a blond wig, dies in a parlor chair, Myrtle attempts to make eggs, bacon, and home-fries. But the onrushing waters force her and Chicken to seek the safety of the roof.

While Broadway was languishing, Off Broadway still had one more hit to unveil, Mart Crowley's **The Boys in the Band** (4-15-68, Theater Four). It elicited some interesting comparisons. Watts suggested it "makes the recent 'Staircase' seem a study in reticence," while Barnes observed, "It makes Albee's 'Who's Afraid of Virginia Woolf?' seem like a vicarage tea party." Michael (Kenneth Nelson) has invited five of his homosexual friends to a birthday party for a sixth, Harold (Leonard Frey). He tells Donald (Frederick Combs), the first to arrive, that the party will be "screaming queens singing 'Happy Birthday'. . . the same old tired fairies you've seen around since day one." But the

sought-after privacy of the affair is destroyed by the unwanted appearance of Michael's old college buddy, the straight, married Alan (Peter White). An outburst from Emory (Cliff Gorman), the most camp of the guests, prompts Alan to slug him. In the melee that follows, Michael, who has been on the wagon, downs too much booze, bringing out the meanest side of him. He suggests they all play a game in which each person must call the one he has most truly loved and confess that love. Alan, whom Michael had branded a repressed homosexual, is prodded into joining the game, but when he makes his call, and Michael grabs the phone to see who he is talking to, Michael discovers Alan has called his own wife. This breaks up the party and leaves Michael shattered. The play ran for an even 1000 performances.

George Panetta's **Mike Downstairs** (4-18-68, Hudson) began as a folksy New York comedy and ended in the realm of sci-fi-fantasy. Mike (Dane Clark), the unoffical mayor of Mulberry Street, is called Mike Downstairs because he spends all his time helping his neighbors around the street. For instance, he does everything in his power to help fat Joe (Leonardo Cimino) lose weight, so Joe's lady friend will love him. But the Authorities (John Tormey and Alan Peterson) appear and alert the neighborhood to the atomic menace, pushing people to build shelters and practice drills. Mike, who feels all this is nonsense, watches in horror as his friends become increasingly paranoid. Then, suddenly, a big explosion causes everyone to die slowly while loudspeakers blare out Jerome Kern's "The Night Was Made for Love."

Critics were even less taken with Lewis John Carlino's Pirandellish, two-character **The Exercise** (4-24-68, Golden). An Actor (Stephen Joyce) and an Actress (Anne Jackson) meet to rehearse a play. Since they once had been lovers, each gives a self-serving account of the romance as well as recalling other incidents in his or her life. Before long their real histories and the parts they are to play become confusingly intertwined. What is the truth and what fiction?

Rolf Hochhuth's **Soldiers** (5-1-68, Billy Rose), in a translation by Ronald D. MacDonald, was set in the ruins of a Coventry cathedral. To celebrate the 100th anniversary of the Geneva Convention, Dorland (Colin Fox), a former bomber pilot turned playwright, puts on an anti-war drama he has written. It accuses Churchill (John Colicos), under the baleful influence of Lord Cherwell (Joseph Shaw), of agreeing to bomb innocent civilians and to allow the prickly General Sikorski (Eric House) to be killed in order to appease the Russians. The play had been banned in London, and found only the most meager audiences in New York.

The season's second one-performance dud was Arthur

Alsberg and Robert Fisher's **Happiness Is Just a Little Thing Called a Rolls Royce** (5-11-68, Barrymore). Walter Bagley (Pat Harrington), a struggling young lawyer and a member of Alcoholics Anonymous, splurges on a Rolls to surprise his bride (Hildy Parks). Appalled at the extravagance, she walks out. Then Walter discovers a youthful waif (Alexandra Berlin) sleeping in the car and takes her home with him. Walter's boss (John McGiver), spotting the car, assumes that Walter is being sought by rival firms, so offers him a partnership and a minimum of $30,000. The waif leaves, and Walter effects a reconciliation with his wife now that he is on a more solid financial footing.

Frank D. Gilroy's three-character **The Only Game in Town** (5-20-68, Broadhurst) disappointed critics, who suggested that for all his promise he still wrote thin plays—"dangerously slender," "underneath it isn't very rich." Joe Grady (Barry Nelson), a piano player on the Vegas Strip and himself an inveterate gambler, begins an affair with Fran Walker (Tammy Grimes), a dancer at one of the clubs. He is soon in love with her, but she warns him that she is waiting for her wealthy lover to obtain a divorce. But when the man (Leo Genn) finally appears, Fran realizes that she now loves Joe, so she sends him on his way. Joe almost blows it by losing his $3,600 savings in a single night, but after he parlays $10 into $18,000 all is right again.

For all practical purposes the Gilroy drama closed out the season. However, on the 28th at Henry Miller's, the Teatro Stabile di Genova [Genoa] came in briefly to delight Italian-speaking playgoers with Carlo Goldoni's **The Venetian Twins (I Due Gemelli Veneziana),** in which two long-separated twins, one doltish, one sharp, cross paths and unleash myriad misunderstandings.

1968–1969

Last season's exciting leap in the number of new plays mounted on Broadway was not repeated in the current theatrical year. In fact, the figures plummeted to somewhere between twenty-eight and thirty-four, again depending on whose accounting was accepted, and never more would Broadway welcome anywhere near forty new plays in a single season. One immediate reason for this season's drop in figures was that only about a third the number of foreign plays that Broadway had seen last year came in during the new session. Yet these few apparently were responsible for a disproportionate percentage of the year's quality. Half of the ten works

selected for the latest edition of the *Best Plays* were of foreign origin. By way of compensation, all the season's major awards went to the same drama—an American one.

The New York Shakespeare Festival launched its summer outing at the open-air Delacorte in Central Park on June 11 with *Henry IV, Part I* and followed a week later with *Henry IV, Part II*. On one occasion the two works were presented together on the same evening, in a performance running from 7 p.m. to 3 a.m. In August the troupe brought out *Romeo and Juliet*. Players included Sam Waterston (Prince Hal), Stacy Keach (Falstaff), Charlotte Rae (Mistress Quickly and the Nurse), and Martin Sheen (Romeo).

Down in the Village on the 12th the Circle in the Square offered a revival of *A Moon for the Misbegotten* with Salome Jens as Josie and Mitchell Ryan as James. The well-received mounting played on until the beginning of December.

There were some scandalized outcries the next evening, not far away, with the opening of Rochelle Owens's look at bestiality, **Futz** (6-13-68, de Lys). Cyrus Futz is a young farmer enamored of his favorite pig, Amanda. His church has refused to allow him to marry the animal, but he, being a religious boy, is careful to read the Bible to her. However, his narrow-minded fellow villagers are uncomprehending, so a local tramp, spurned by Futz, has little difficulty persuading her brothers to murder him and his pig. Amanda never appears onstage. The "shouting abandon" of Tom O'Horgan's mounting pleased some and distressed others, but the production stimulated enough interest to survive for 233 performances.

At the Vivian Beaumont in Lincoln Center, the Compagnie du Théâtre de la Cité de Villeurbanne (from Lyons, France) popped in on the 25th for a brief stand to regale francophone playgoers with *The Three Musketeers, George Dandin,* and *Tartuffe*.

Brian Friel's **Lovers** (7-25-68, Vivian Beaumont) was a pair of one-acters. In **Winners,** a narrator (Art Carney) describes the seemingly idyllic outing of a pregnant girl (Fionnuala Flanagan) and her soon-to-be-husband (Eamon Morrisey), only to reveal that they accidentally drowned at day's end. They were winners because they never had to face the future's disappointments. The central figure of **Losers** is Andy (Carney), beset by a fanatically religious harridan (Grania O'Malley), the mother of his fiancée and eventual wife (Anna Manahan). She is constantly praying to God and St. Philomena. So when Andy learns that the Vatican has removed Philomena from its roster of accepted saints, he happily informs his mother-in-law in revenge for all her meddling. She is forced to find another saint, but neither she nor her daughter will reveal who that saint is. Andy is a loser because he must go on living, disdained by the women in his home.

No doubt some confusion was created when the next entry, another bill of one-acters, was called **Lovers and Other Strangers** (9-18-68, Brooks Atkinson). The playlets, by Renee Taylor and Joseph Bologna, were untitled. In the first, an inept young seducer (Ron Carey) must be shown the ropes by the supposedly innocent girl (Zohra Lampert) he was attempting to woo. The second play described the efforts of a long-married woman (Taylor) to sexually rearouse her husband (Gerald S. O'Loughlin). The next play watched as a bride-to-be (Mariclare Costello) calmly put to rest her beau's (Marvin Lichterman) panicky wish to call off the wedding. The fourth and final playlet told of parents (Richard Castellano and Helen Verbit) attempting to salvage the rocky marriage of their son (Bobby Alto) and daughter-in-law (Candy Azzara). Friel's bill ran till the end of November and went into the records as a hit; the Taylor-Bologna works ran nine weeks and were deemed a commercial failure.

Several critics remarked that the large police presence, keeping order among a sizable and noisy band of Cuban refugees protesting outside the theatre, provided more excitement than did Jack Gelber's blantantly pro-Castro **The Cuban Thing** (9-24-68, Henry Miller's). Its story, intermingled with newsreel films of Castro's revolution, recounted how a wealthy, initially pro-Batista family comes to believe in the society which Castro is setting up. Rip Torn was the head of the family, and Raul Julia, the servant who becomes Castro's spokesman and spy in the house, and eventually weds the family's daughter (Maria Tucci). The play's first night was its last.

Don C. Liljenquist's **Woman Is My Idea** (9-25-68, Belasco) was allegedly based on a true story about a real figure in Salt Lake City in the 1870s. John Rocky Park (John Heffernan), a Mormon, but a confirmed bachelor, gives shelter to a beautiful young lady (Lara Parker) whose home had been burned down and who is said to be dying. She begs the man to marry her so that she can say she is married when she goes to heaven. In a careless moment, he consents, then hurries off to foreign parts. However, on his return he is chagrined to discover his bride hale and hearty. Luckily for him, his chagrin lasted only five performances.

There was self-deception of a different sort in Robert Shaw's English drama **The Man in the Glass Booth** (9-26-68, Royale). Arthur Goldman (Donald Pleasence), a very rich German-born American Jew, who had once been a concentration-camp inmate, allows himself to be taken for a long-sought Nazi, kidnapped to Israel, and

put on trial. Although witnesses appear, willing to testify against him, and he himself makes numerous anti-Jewish comments, it soon develops he merely further wants to bring home to the world the Nazi horrors and is willing to make a sacrifice of his own life to that end. A perplexed judge dismisses him. Pleasence's bravura performance, Harold Pinter's staging, and the play itself received generally laudatory notices. Yet, while it ran out the season, it failed to make the list of commercial successes.

Theater 69, a producing unit headed by Richard Barr and Edward Albee, began a month-long series of productions with a double bill of Albee one-acters, **Box** and **Quotations from Chairman Mao Tse-Tung** (9-30-68, Billy Rose). Since there was no intermission between the two works, many felt that Albee obviously meant them to have some connection, although that connection was hardly clear. No character appears in the first play, but from a twenty-foot square box glowing in black light, the voice of a speaker (Ruth White) is heard delivering statements such as "When art begins to hurt, it's time to look around." In the second play, four figures appear on what may be the deck of an ocean liner. Chairman Mao (Wyman Pendleton) recites lines from his own scriptures; an Old Woman (Sudie Bond) declaims the poem "Over the Hill to the Poorhouse"; a Long Winded Lady (Nancy Kelly) runs on about her personal problems; while a Minister (George Bartenieff) hangs about saying nothing. Subsequent bills included the pairing of *The Death of Bessie Smith* with *The American Dream,* and Beckett's *Krapp's Last Tape* with Albee's *The Zoo Story.* The final attraction was Beckett's *Happy Days,* which had been seen before off Broadway and which opened on October 12. It featured a woman, slowly sinking into the ground, chatting away to a neighbor about her happy-unhappy world.

"A big, robust drama," "a whirlwind," and "the most unabashed dramatic outburst we have had since 'Long Day's Journey Into Night,' " were some of the laurels with which critics crowned Howard Sackler's **The Great White Hope** (10-3-68, Alvin). At season's end both the New York Drama Critics Circle and the Pulitzer committee agreed—giving it their awards. It was no secret that Jack Jefferson (James Earl Jones) represented the first black heavyweight champion, Jack Johnson. Like him, this Jack has gone to Australia to win the title. On the ship returning home he has met a white girl, Eleanor "Ellie" Bachman (Jane Alexander), and made her his mistress. In America the whites are outraged by the relationship and by his "smart-ass remarks," and they determine to find a great white hope to best him. But he keeps winning, so those who are out to get him take another tack. He is arrested and sentenced to prison for violating the Mann Act—transporting someone across state lines for immoral purposes. Before he can be jailed, he and Ellie flee the country. Overseas more bigots and his own arrogance keep him in trouble, and these difficulties cause him to lose his temper and turn on Ellie—"evvy time you pushes dat pinch up face in fronna me, Ah sees where it done got me." Despondent, she commits suicide. An emotionally defeated Jack consents to take a fall in his next bout in Havana, in return for the dropping of all charges back home. He keeps to the agreement, but not before brutally turning his opponent into little more than living pulp. Besides praising the play, the critics also had affirmative words for James Earl Jones. Clive Barnes wrote in the *Times,* "Mr. Jones pounded into the role, spitting and shouting. He rolled his eyes, he stamped on the ground, he beat his chest, he roared with pain and even when he chuckled it seemed like thunder. Here was Jack, larger than life. . . . If anyone deserves to become that occasional thing, a star overnight, then Mr. Jones deserves no less."

. . .

James Earl Jones (b. 1931) was born in Mississippi. He studied at the University of Michigan and with Lee Strasberg, then made his Broadway debut in *Sunrise at Campobello* (1958). He called attention to his skills when he took on such roles as Caliban, Macduff, and Othello at the New York Shakespeare Festival. His deep, rich bass voice and strong presence helped make his performances memorable.

. . .

With so many people in its corner, the drama ran for 556 performances.

Having returned several weeks earlier with holdovers from its previous season, the APA brought out the first of its new revivals, T. S. Eliot's *The Cocktail Party,* at the Lyceum on the 7th. This was followed by Molière's *The Misanthrope,* O'Casey's *Cock-A-Doodle Dandy,* and *Hamlet,* with the group's director, Ellis Rabb, in the title part. O'Casey's play, a very late one, was new to Broadway, although it had been done off Broadway in 1958. It told of a woman who magically becomes a rooster which is chased out of its community by superstitious fun-haters who perceive it as a devil. For several years, the APA had been associated with the old Phoenix Theatre group in its productions. Unfortunately, by season's end, financial problems, despite generally receptive notices, forced an end to the alliance and also an end to the still so promising repertory ensemble. Both groups would survive separately for a time, operating in more traditional fashion.

Hugh and Margaret Williams's London comedy **The Flip Side** (10-10-68, Booth) found no welcome in New York. A young publisher (David McCallum) and his wife (Monica Evans) are entertaining an author (Don Franks) and the writer's wife (Gwyda Donhowe) at their home. The freethinking author convinces everyone to swap spouses. For a time, the exchange seems to work. But after a few months, the couples recognize that their original pairings were best.

Off Broadway a bill of Harold Pinter's one-acters earned a happier reception. Both had initially been seen on British television. In **Tea Party** (10-15-68, Eastside) a highly successful, self-made manufacturer of bidets is brought down by his inability to deal with his cold new wife, his brother-in-law, his voluptuous if sphinxlike secretary, and others who cross his path. **The Basement** begins with a man chuckling over a book of erotic art. A friend and that friend's girl arrive, but soon seem more interested in making love together than in being sociable with their host. Before long the men are dueling with milk bottles and alignments switch back and forth.

Critics were not sure what to make of Joseph Heller's loose, enigmatic **We Bombed in New Haven** (10-16-68, Ambassador). The *Post*'s Richard Watts, Jr., called it "a play on an anti-war theme with overtones of Pirandello." A group of actors are rehearsing a drama about some airmen. They have been assigned to bomb Constantinople, even though a few protest that Constantinople no longer exists. It long has been Istanbul. Some are doomed to die, but insist on coming back to life. The men are told their next target is Minnesota. An often baffled Captain Starkey (Jason Robards) is in charge of matters, albeit overseen by The Major (William Roerick), who insists on following the script. Starkey is apparently having an affair with Ruth (Diana Sands), a Red Cross worker, who hands out coffee and doughnuts. Toward the end, Starkey's son (Gene Sandur) comes on the scene. This puzzles Starkey, who insists the boy was only born "just a little while ago." When Starkey is forced to order him on a mission that certainly means his death, the boy warningly compares himself and his father to Absalom and David. Then Starkey turns to the audience, reminds them this is merely a play, and sends them home. The work, by the author of the popular, ironic best-seller *Catch-22,* struggled on for ten and a half weeks.

Rockefeller and the Red Indians (10-24-68, Barrymore) was an English play by Ray Galton and Alan Simpson, derived from an unidentified French comedy by René de Obaldia. The evening began with the popular English comic Frankie Howerd coming before the audience and telling them they are about to see a performance by the East Grinstead Repertory Company of a play on the American Wild West written by some Englishmen who have never been to America and, in fact, have never been been outside of East Grinstead.

The play abounds in all the clichéd characters of film and TV Westerns: the toping doctor, the determined wife, the weak son, the dance-hall prostitute, the untried sheriff, and the comic redskin, spouting such typical Western speech as "Would you care to join us for tea and some cucumber sandwiches?" It ends with the hero, John E. (for Emery) Rockefeller (Howerd), who with his family has been waiting for an Indian attack, discovering oil on his land. Not to American tastes, the spoof was withdrawn after half a week.

The Repertory Theatre of Lincoln Center relit the Vivian Beaumont on November 7 with a *King Lear* that brought Lee J. Cobb back to the stage after a long absence. Both the production and Cobb's performance were deemed competent but uninspired. Even chillier notices greeted the company's second mounting, a novelty, William Gibson's **A Cry of Players** (11-14-68, Vivian Beaumont). Back in the 1580s in a muddy English village, a young man named Will (Frank Langella) bridles at the restraints his family's skinning and tanning business, the local authorities, and his purposeful wife, Anne (Anne Bancroft), impose on him. To savor some freedom, he poaches and wenches whenever he can. Then a band of strolling players comes to town to perform one of Christopher Marlowe's works. This inspires Will to want to be an actor and playwright, so he runs off to London to try his luck. Nowhere in the play was the name Shakespeare mentioned.

Reviews were distinctly mixed, and, if anything, a bit on the unfavorable side when Off Broadway's Circle in the Square presented a bill of one-acters on Broadway. Three young playwrights had a hand in **Morning, Noon and Night** (11-27-68, Henry Miller's). **Morning** was by Israel Horovitz. A black family, thanks to pills they swallowed the night before, wake up to find themselves white. A joy-filled mother (Charlotte Rae) insists they are home free—"Ain't nobody gonna believe we was anything 'cept what we look." Then a white neighbor (John Heffernan) appears and accuses their son (Robert Klein) of leaving his daughter pregnant. A fight ensues, and when the neighbor confesses he is also a black man who took the pill, the family kill him, shout that all whites should be killed, and, tossing black paint on themselves, celebrate their blackness. Critics complained of Horovitz's excessive profanity. Most preferred the next piece. Terrence McNally's **Noon** was set in a loft. A variety of sexual types come there, responding to an ad placed by someone named Dale that promises "culmination of your most sensuous desires." One is a homosexual (Heffernan), who tries to get a young man (Klein) to undress, but the boy is more interested in finding a woman. A nymphomaniac (Jane Marie Robbins) shows up, announcing that she is in a hurry because she is double parked. Then a couple (Rae and Sorrell Booke) arrive, dressed in leather and carrying whips. But all the visitors leave unfulfilled when Dale never comes. In Leonard Melfi's **Night,** a small cluster of mourners attend a nighttime burial, each convinced he or she was the dead person's best friend. Then a man (Klein) arrives to bury his dog. Reviewers threw up their hands after trying to decipher this one.

Popular as he was, Milton Berle could not keep Herb Gardner's "talky," "overloaded" **The Goodbye People** (12-3-68, Barrymore) on the boards beyond its first week. Hoping against hope, a very old Max Silverman decides to come out of retirement and reopen his weatherbeaten old fruit-drink stand, Max's Hawaiian Delicacies, on the boardwalk at Coney Island even though it is mid-winter. But he has trouble raising the money, since his old cronies are dead and their sons, with voices "born for telephones," will not help: " 'Goodbye,' will *they* do a job for you on 'Goodbye!' " Neither a strange young man (Bob Dishy) nor Max's daughter (Brenda Vaccaro) can help much, either.

On the other hand, Dustin Hoffman, fresh off his film triumph in *The Graduate,* helped Murray Schisgal's **Jimmy Shine** (12-5-68, Brooks Atkinson) run 153 performances and close in the black. Jimmy is a painter living in a rundown, untidy loft. His earlier life flashes before him. He has failed in everything—he even spells the word F-A-L-E-D. His best school friend (Charles Siebert), who talked him into becoming an artist and promised to share his digs with him, has instead gone on to be a money-chasing businessman and married the girl (Susan Sullivan) Jimmy loved. His visit to a whorehouse is disastrous, and he loses his job in a fish market because he won't kill fish. In the end he is left with the company of a cheap, promiscuous streetwalker (Rose Gregorio). Several songs and dances were inserted in the evening, prompting one reviewer to jokingly refer to it as a musical. But critics concurred on Hoffman's "richly enjoyable performance . . . most of the time gleamingly inarticulate, and yet still possessed of that wayward intelligence . . . an image, even a projection of much of contemporary youth."

Off Broadway also had something of a hit in Joseph Dolan Tuotti's **Big Time Buck White** (12-8-68, Village South). The piece had begun life in a theatre workshop in the Watts district of Los Angeles. It was a curious work, with an abrupt mid-stream change of tone. It took place in the meeting room of BAD—Beautiful Allelujah Days—a charity dedicated to helping poor blacks. However, most of the blacks are there simply to sponge off the organization. And they are stereotypically comic blacks of the old "Miller and Lyles and Two Black Crows" school, with lines such as "Who you callin' nigger, nigger?" and "Hey, man, don't you never call Sunset Boulevard a street!" But the organization's head, Big Time Buck White (Dick Williams), struts in, and after haranguing his listeners with a call to self-reliance and to fight for one's rights, he takes questions from the audience. Although several actors were planted in the audience, many of the questions were spontaneous and serious, and the actor portraying the speaker improvised legitimate answers. The play ran for 124 performances and was subsequently turned into an unsuccessful musical.

A prestigious regional group, the Minnesota Theater Company, under Tyrone Guthrie's direction, came in for a brief visit, beginning with John Lewin's compact adaptation of Aeschylus' entire *Oresteia* as **The House of Atreus** (12-17-68, Billy Rose). The drama was performed by an all-male cast, wearing masks and elevated shoes. Thus Douglas Campbell's Clytemnestra "looks seven feet tall and has a face that is a kind of gigantic cartoon of grinning evil." The troupe's second bill, brought out on the 22nd, was Brecht's *The Resistible Rise of Arturo Ui.*

Between these two openings one novelty came and went quickly. Douglas Taylor's **The Sudden and Accidental Re-Education of Horse Johnson** (12-18-68, Belasco) spotlighted a warehouse man (Jack Klugman) who gives up his job and determines to find himself by staying at home and reading the great masters of philosophy. He sees himself turning into another Gandhi. Horse has been inspired to do this by an unemployed apple picker (Mitchell Ryan) he met at a bar. But after the man tries to seduce the pretty sister (Jill Clayburgh) of Horse's wife (Kathleen Maguire), Mrs. Johnson has no problem convincing Horse to return to a more practical routine.

The old year's last gift to Broadway was the season's longest-running hit, **Forty Carats** (12-26-68, Morosco). Jay Allen adapted the comedy from the Paris hit of Pierre Barillet and Jean-Pierre Gredy, and it lingered on for 780 performances. Although Ann Stanley (Julie Harris) is grateful that a young passerby, Peter Latham (Marco St. John), lends her a sleeping bag after her car breaks down in Greece, she soon forgets the matter until Peter reappears at her New York apartment for a date with her seventeen-year-old daughter, Trina (Gretchen Corbett). However, Peter, who is twenty-two, and Ann, who is forty but tries to pass for thirty-six or thirty-eight when she thinks she can get away with it, soon find themselves in love. At the same time, forty-five-year-old Eddy Edwards (Franklin Cover), who has been Ann's suitor, looks with new eyes at Trina. All this upsets Ann's former husband (Murray Hamilton), but Ann's widowed mother (Glenda Farrell), while bemused, is more accepting when the oddly matched couples decide to head for the altar.

Off Broadway got the new year going with two interesting productions. Robert Nemiroff drew **To Be Young, Gifted and Black** (1-2-69, Cherry Lane) from the writings of the late Lorraine Hansberry. The play used a simple, white-ramped stage and photographic blow-ups as a setting for the dramatist's reminiscences of her life, beginning in a modest Chicago home, and excerpts from her plays. Cicely Tyson, Barbara Baxley, and John Beal were among the cast members.

Three nights later the Circle in the Square revived Jules Feiffer's failure of two seasons back, *Little Murders,* and met with a year-long success. Vincent Gardenia and Linda Lavin played the father and daughter.

Broadway had a more modest success with an English play, **Hadrian the Seventh** (1-8-69, Helen Hayes), which Peter Luke took from the fantasy-bathed semi-autobiographical writings of Frederick William Rolfe, alias Baron Corvo. For a long time Rolfe (Alec McCowen) has been rejected in his attempts to become a priest, but then he not only is ordained but is suddenly made the first English pope since the Middle Ages. He attempts to be a singularly humane pope, walking the streets to meet the people and selling the Vatican treasures to obtain money to feed the poor. However, it is all a dream, and the closing moments find Rolfe again in his lonely London room. McCowen, capturing "all the qualities that make the poor fellow both impossible and endearing," aided the entertainment in running for 166 performances.

Scenes of nude, homosexual lovemaking may have allowed Gus Weill's double bill of one-acters, **Geese** (1-12-69, Players), to keep going off Broadway for 336 performances. The young boys who have sex together in **Parents and Children** do so because one of the lads believes his parents are happy only when they are having sex. In the play which gave the evening its name, two somewhat older girls, a farmer's daughter and a college student, are provoked by the loveless lives of their heterosexual parents. "Love can come in varieties, you know," one of the girls exclaims, "but it's still love."

Some of the season's worst notices were handed to **Fire!** (1-28-69, Longacre), by a writer working under the nom de plume John Roc. In a cavern or a tomb—described variously by critics as Aztec, Egyptian, or Inca—a bearded, booted guru attempts to get all his listeners to "vote for fire," claiming a fiery holocaust will destroy and renew the world. One man (Rene Auberjonois) resists, but is finally brought forcibly into line. The play survived for five performances.

Almost equally dismissive reviews were accorded Jerome Weidman's **The Mother Lover** (2-1-69, Booth), which lasted for only one playing. Seymour (Larry Blyden) visits his mother (Eileen Heckart) in Queens every Sunday, not because he loves her, but because he hopes to persuade her to die so he can inherit her money. The lonely woman rents a room in her home to a girl (Valerie French) who has fled to America from a Christine Keeler-like scandal in London. Initially the girl is sympathetic to the older woman, but eventually she sides with the son and assists him in killing her.

Lonne Elder III's **Ceremonies in Dark Old Men** (2-4-69, St Marks) was one of several plays mounted for limited engagements during the season by the Negro Ensemble Company, but its reception was such, with some critics comparing Elder to a young O'Casey, that it was quickly revived at the Pocket Theatre on April 28 and ran for 320 performances. Russell B. Parker, a onetime dancer and now a lackadaisical Harlem barber, is supported mainly by his more ambitious daughter. He insists "looking for a job can be very low-grading . . . and it's worse after you get the job." The daughter proudly calls herself the only real working person in the house. One son is more or less withdrawn from society; the other is a small time shoplifter. But after the boys mix a batch of corn whiskey they call Black Lightning, a Harlem sharpy named Blue Haven, set on kicking the whites out of the area, horns in on their brewing and tries to go big time. For a while the affair flourishes, but the boys are soon gunned down.

Another off-Broadway mounting to find favor was one more of the season's numerous bills of one-acters, **Adaptation** and **Next** (2-10-69, Greenwich Mews). The former was by Elaine May, the latter by the busy Terrence McNally (who had several additional less long-running plays done off Broadway during the season). May's play compared life to a television game show, with the Contestant (Gabriel Dell) moved back and forth across the squares in reaction to his behavior in the various phases of his life, from his birth to his death. Thus he is temporarily assigned to the Isolation Square after he makes a remark which offends a black boy at his "sub-standard but equal" school. In the McNally play a fat, fortyish man (James Coco), who insists he is too old and in too poor physical condition for an army physical, is nonetheless perturbed when he fails it.

Whatever they thought of Woody Allen's playwriting gifts, other critics agreed with Barnes when he observed that Allen's performance turned **Play It Again, Sam** (2-12-69, Broadhurst) "into a cheerful virtuoso romp." The public concurred, too, keeping the play before the footlights for 453 performances. Allen Felix is a bespectacled nerd, whose wife, Nancy (Sheila Sullivan), has left him and who dines by sucking on frozen TV dinners (an echo of *The Star-Spangled Girl*). But the shade (Jerry Lacy) of Humphrey Bogart—in a trench-coat and a snap-brim gray hat, hands in his pockets and speaking with a slight lisp—appears to him, warns him, "Kid, somewhere in life you got turned around," and

starts to set him straight. At first, Allen still manages to either do or say the wrong thing, but in time Bogie's instructions pay off. Not only does he have a brief fling with the wife (Diane Keaton) of his best friend (Anthony Roberts), but when a new neighbor (Barbara Brownell) knocks on his door and asks to use his phone, he knows just what to do and say.

On the 24th, the National Theatre of the Deaf began a two-week stand at the Longacre. Bills, done in panto-mime and sign language for deaf playgoers but with readers speaking the material for others in the audience, consisted of short pieces by Chekhov (*On the Harm-fulness of Tobacco*), Sheridan (*The Critic*), Kabuki, and commedia dell'arte as well as several original compilations.

With a single exception, although the theatrical year still had three months to run, none of the novelties presented on Broadway proper from now till the end of the season ran longer than one week. Don Petersen's **Does a Tiger Wear a Necktie?** (2-25-69, Belasco) took place at a rehabilitation center for young drug addicts isolated on a river island off a large city. A dedicated, turtlenecked teacher (Hal Holbrook) tries to redeem the youngsters. One interesting inmate is a menacing but bright youth (Al Pacino), hopelessly torn by the tragic outcome of his search for his long-lost father. A black boy (Roger Robinson), who is released, promises to wait for the black prostitute (Lauren Jones) he met and fell in love with at the center, although her chances for rehabilitation seem dim.

Hollywood writer Julius J. Epstein fared no better with his comedy about a Hollywood writer, **But, Seriously . . .** (2-27-69, Henry Miller's). Walter London (Tom Poston) is a weak-willed man whose wife (Bethel Leslie) has long since lost her respect for him because of his wishy washy ways. An ambitious district attorney (Dick Van Patten) tries to get him to appear as a witness against a fading actor (Robert Mandan) confronted with a rape charge. A vengeful producer (Steven Graves), bitter that his wife (Sally Gracie) once had a fling with the actor, urges Walter to cooperate. But Walter absolutely refuses, and his tough stance restores his wife's respect and love for him. Even Poston's by now standard drunk scene was no help.

In a program note, Leonard Spigelgass confessed that **The Wrong Way Light Bulb** (3-4-69, Golden) was semi-autobiographical. Like Epstein and Walter London and Spigelgass himself, Harold Axman (James Patterson) is a scriptwriter. His distinctly liberal notions are put to the test when he inherits and moves into an aging Brooklyn apartment house, which still retains some of its older Jewish tenants but also houses newer black and Puerto Rican renters. Vandalism and racial and religious hatreds are rife. An elderly Jewish lady

(Nancy R. Pollock) has her wrists broken when she is mugged in the hallway. A Puerto Rican girl (Miriam Colon), to whom Harold is attracted, causes problems because she wanted the apartment he moved into. And a white-hating young black (Laurence Cook) burns down the adjoining Turkish bath, which Harold had also inherited. Harold himself, in disgust, thinks about burning down the apartment house to collect the insurance, but decides better. The title came from the special hallway bulbs which can only be screwed in counterclockwise and so cannot work in normal lamps, thereby discouraging their theft by tenants.

The **Zelda** (3-5-69, Barrymore) of Sylvia Regan's play of the same name was not a woman, but a catastrophic hurricane that Alexander Hartman (Ed Begley), a retired Long Island druggist, insists is coming to end life on earth as he and his family have known it. That family includes his wife (Lilia Skala), a left-wing son (Tom Keena), a nouveau-riche, materialistic son (Alfred Sandor), a cute grandson (Bobby Benson), and two daughters-in-law (Nita Talbot and Renee Roy). Despite the derision of his family and friends, he buys and outfits a boat. So when, sure enough, the storm does come, he and those he has taken aboard can ride out the flood. The jokes in the play, often Jewish in tone, were on the order of "He can't have paranoid symptoms. They were taken out when he was a boy."

Away from the Broadway mainstream, the Repertory Theatre of Lincoln Center found itself being praised for its mounting of **In the Matter of J. Robert Oppenheimer** (3-6-69, Vivian Beaumont). Curiously, though the work had an American theme, it was by a foreign playwright, Heinar Kipphardt, and was offered in a translation by Ruth Spiers. The drama reviewed the famous, or infamous, hearing by the Atomic Energy Commission on the scientist. The soft-spoken, thoughtful Oppenheimer (Joseph Wiseman) has been called "the Father of the Atomic Bomb," but after seeing its effects on Hiroshima has turned against it and against the notion of developing an even more horrendous H-bomb. Since he had briefly embraced Communism in the thirties and retains many notoriously left-wing friends, his detractors, in the chill of the McCarthy era, ask if he isn't still a secret Communist, hoping to let Russia gain the lead in future research. The hearing's decision is a rather unsatisfactory compromise: the judges deem Oppenheimer a loyal American but deny him further security clearance.

Back on Broadway, the season slogged on with its second and final one-performance flop, Lyle Kessler's **The Watering Place** (3-12-69, Music Box). A Vietnam War veteran (William Devane) pays a visit to the family of a dead soldier he claims to have been his buddy. The family consists of the Mother (Vivian Nathan), who

carries around her Bible but refuses to attend church; the Father (Ralph Waite), proud that at sixty-seven he is still a vigorous athlete; and a daughter-in-law, Janet (Shirley Knight), who has used a pillow to make herself seem still pregnant after her miscarriage. The soldier breaks the Father's pitching arm in a baseball game, then exposes Janet's fraud and makes her really pregnant. This drives the Mother batty. She grabs the discarded pillow and begins crooning to it. Having wreaked such havoc, the visitor quietly leaves.

Several aisle-sitters thought the setting—a Coca-Cola bottling plant piled high with Coke bottles—was the most interesting thing about Laird Koenig's three-character **The Dozens** (3-13-69, Booth). During a revolution in the African country of Chaka, a black American nightclub singer (Paula Kelly) and her manager-husband (or lover) (Al Freeman, Jr.) take refuge in the bottling plant. The deposed, twenty-four-year-old president (Morgan Freeman) of the country also seeks to hide there. He confesses to the singer that he has long been her admirer and tries to persuade her to remain with him. But she elects to stay with her fellow American. Some of the humor came from the president's predilection for placing nude statues of himself everywhere. There is even one in the plant. In the course of the evening the agent hangs the singer's wig on the statue—on its very public private parts.

Cop-Out (4-7-69, Cort) was a bill of two one-acters by John Guare, who had called attention to himself last season off Broadway with a play called *Muzeeka*. In **Home Fires,** a German-American policeman (MacIntyre Dixon) comes to bury his wife on the day after the World War I armistice. He has anglicized his name to Smith, but that doesn't lessen the resentment of the bigoted funeral director (George Bartenieff). The policeman's daughter (April Shawhan) has retained the German spelling, but her snooty brother (Charles Kimbrough) now spells his name Smythe. For all his airs, he is merely an agent for animal acts, while his equally nose-in-the-air girl (Carrie Nye) turns out to be the maid who draws Anna Held's celebrated milk baths. The title piece dealt with the relations between several policemen and the women in their lives. All the men were played by Ron Leibman; all the women by Linda Lavin. The police types were a serious cop who allows himself to be sterilized in the name of progress, and a cop who fantasizes that he is a big, two-gun crimebuster. Lavin's ladies included a slinky nightclub hostess, a legless police informer, a latter-day Marilyn Monroe, and a placard-waving protester.

Another young playwright who would move on to better things was Lanford Wilson. His **The Gingham Dog** (4-23-69, Golden) recounted the last days in the failing marriage of a white architect (George Grizzard) from Kentucky and a black New Yorker (Diana Sands). She resents his designing cheap housing developments for blacks and has come to hate all whites. A visit by her sharp-tongued sister-in-law (Karen Grassle) exacerbates matters. The husband's final attempt at a reconciliation fails when the wife insists she has a lover in the bedroom.

At the Lunt-Fontanne on May 1, just days after the APA repertory closed, a second *Hamlet* came to town. This starred the British actor Nicol Williamson as a bearded, lower-class-accented, angry Dane. Most critics didn't care for the interpretation.

The New York Shakespeare Festival had been presenting non-Shakespearean novelties all season long at its downtown headquarters. It scored a major hit with Charles Gordone's **No Place To Be Somebody** (5-4-69, Public), and for the second time during the season a black playwright was hailed as one of a new generation of promising dramatists. Johnny Williams (Nathan George) is an unprincipled, white-hating black bar owner resolved to make it big in the underworld. All he is waiting for is his beloved mentor, Sweets Crane, to get out of prison. But when Sweets (Walter Jones) comes out, though he still enjoys showing off his skill as a pickpocket, he has no heart for vying with bigtime hoods. So Johnny takes up with a white girl (Laurie Crews) whose father, a judge, has papers that could incriminate Johnny's Italian rivals. He gets her to steal the papers. In the showdown that follows even Sweets is drawn in. He stabs one of the mobsters before he himself is shot to death. Johnny then kills the two gangsters. In despair, Johnny provokes an effeminate black playwright, Gabe Gabriel (Ron O'Neal), into killing him. Alone and dressed as a woman, Gabriel tells the audience, "My black anguish will fall on deaf ears." The drama compiled 250 performances.

Reviewers were none too pleased with the Repertory Theatre of Lincoln Center's final offering of the season on the 8th-a leaden mounting of Molière's *The Miser* in translatin by writers listed almost anonymouly H. Baker and J. Miller.

On the other hand, a revival of Ben Hecht and Charles MacArthur's ribald look at newspapermen, *The Front Page* (8-14-28), at the Barrymore on the 10th, occasioned critical hat-tossing: "a classic American comedy," "hilarious," "a rollicking, tempestuous hit." Robert Ryan was Walter Burns and Bert Convy, Hildy Johnson. Response to the reviews was such that, after a prolonged summer hiatus, the initially limited engagement was open-ended, and the comedy, now with Helen Hayes as Mrs. Grant, ran on for a total of 222 performances.

The following evening was a sad one off Broadway, where Tennessee Williams's **In the Bar of a Tokyo Hotel** (5-11-69, Eastside Playhouse) was relegated after

no producer would mount it on Broadway. An "inferior little drama" typified next-day reactions. A painter (Donald Madden) is quickly going to seed in his struggle to recapture his early artistry. His sexually promiscuous wife (Anne Meacham), unable to cope, summons his agent (Lester Rawlins) from the States to take him back home. Once he is gone, she must confront her own aging and loneliness. The play struggled on for three weeks before giving up.

The next night saw the premiere of **De Sade Illustrated** (5-12-69, Bouwerie Lane), which Joseph Bush took from the Marquis de Sade's *Philosophy in the Boudoir*. The story told of the sexual education of a young girl by friends of various sexual persuasions. Slides, motion pictures, rock 'n' roll, and Mozart all aided the fully dressed players in unveiling the tale. The play gave 120 performances. (Oddly enough, a second play, using the same source and de Sade's original title, appeared a little more than a week later, but hurriedly departed.)

For the umpteenth time, the season on Broadway ended with a flop. This year it was Phoebe and Henry Ephron's **My Daughter, Your Son** (5-13-69, Booth). A California television writer (Robert Alda) and his actress-wife (Vivian Vance) have a daughter (Lee Lawson) who lives in New York with her beau (Gene Lindsey), a writer for *Newsweek*. The boy's father (Bill McCutcheon) is a dentist, and his mother (Dody Goodman) a flibbertigibbet. By means of transcontinental phone calls, the parents prod the youngsters into a wedding and happily proceed to arrange the event. The comedy stuck it out for six weeks.

In the following spring—the spring of 1970—the Pulitzer committee did a doubly unexpected thing. First, for only the second time, it gave its award to a show that had actually opened very late in the preceding season. More startling, for the first time ever it gave the award to an off-Broadway attraction, *No Place to Be Somebody*. Admittedly the play, between two long off-Broadway engagements, had been presented briefly at a Broadway playhouse. But that almost certainly did not figure in the committee's thinking. Regardless of the reasoning, the decision was a landmark—as good a sign as any of how the American theatre was changing. In a perspicacious summary in his 1968–69 *Best Plays*, months before the award was announced, Otis L. Guernsey, Jr., had called the theatrical year just ended "a season of transition," continuing, "In 1968–69, at last, you could see plainly that an old theater tradition was dying, and a new one was being born; but the process was still in its early stages."

The old days, when elegantly dressed playgoers entered an elegant auditorium and, on the rising of the curtain, saw elegantly garbed players in an elegant setting, were fast disappearing. Playgoers' elegant dress went first, with the tuxedos and evening gowns that had been standard, especially on weekends, giving way to more everyday businesslike attire during the Second World War. With time this changed, too, so, as the seasons progressed, more and more slovenly playgoers sat unconcernedly even in the orchestra.

"Well-made" plays and realistic three-walled settings still abounded, but increasingly so did loose-structured works and all but sceneryless mountings. The notion that the footlights (themselves quickly vanishing) represented an unseen fourth wall was discarded. With greater regularity actors spoke directly and for long stretches to the audience (not merely in the quick asides of yesteryear). Now and then the action erupted in all corners of the auditorium itself. (Again, stooges in a box or in the balcony were a time-honored device, but never before on this level.) Any number of new entries dealt in depth with subjects—homosexuality, bestiality, politically and socially explosive matters—that could only have been hinted at decades earlier. Nudity and prolific profanity were growing commonplace.

Inevitably, ticket prices had to reflect national inflation as a whole. But something more sinister and devastating soon began cropping up. For centuries there had been a one-to-four, and occasionally a one-to-six, ratio between the best orchestra seats and places in the upper balcony. That is, when an orchestra seat cost $6.00, a balcony seat went for $1.00 or $1.25 or, most likely, $1.50. But within a few years there would be precious little difference between the price of an orchestra seat and a balcony seat. True, some "half-price" seats were usually available, but they could not be obtained by walking up to a box office in a sheltered lobby. Instead, they were gotten by waiting in long lines at a special ticket booth exposed to the wind and the rain and the sleet. The higher prices and the often uncomfortable inconvenience discouraged many younger, less affluent or less hardy theatre lovers. Thus a heretofore loyal and important segment of playgoers was gradually being lost.

Many playgoers, unsure of their way around theatres, relied on critics for advice. With the coming of the Depression, critical stances had toughened, ostensibly to protect would-be ticket buyers from throwing away hard-earned cash on undeserving works. But by the sixties, when in fact, with the folding of so many dailies, there were fewer critics to rely on, a particularly nasty, brahmin breed of critics—not unlike the old George Jean Nathan—emerged. Their notices often suggested that they were more interested in seeing how smart-alecky and arrogantly vicious they could be, rather than in assisting readers to select the sort of play the readers might enjoy. Beyond question, some more hesitant would-be theatregoers were discouraged by these reviews and their business lost.

And if fewer playgoers meant fewer plays, and fewer plays meant fewer playgoers, they also meant fewer playhouses. This soon became especially true of road cities, where tryouts and post-Broadway tours once had kept so many fine old theatres lit, and so many local audiences happy. But as tryouts and post-Broadway tours disappeared, so did the theatres. For example, Philadelphia had had as many as ten playhouses during the twenties. In the forties, fifties, and sixties, five survived. Later on, only one served the city's needs. (Philadelphia was luckier than many other cities, for two more of its former legitimate theatres remain—one owned and used by a school and still booking an occasional attraction, the other becoming the city's major regional playhouse.) More and more, devoted theatregoers had to trek to New York to see plays.

True, regional theatres sprouted up everywhere. But they could provide only a partial answer. First of all, with rare exceptions, they were tiny compared with the old legitimate playhouses. Second, many haughtily eschewed the sort of popular entertainments so many theatregoers sought, instead offering conspicuously arty or provocative productions. And the "off-Broadway" style playhouses, both in New York and elsewhere, which generally were even more arty and provocative, tended to be shabby or at least uncomfortable venues, usually in out-of-the-way locations. Still, as even many playwrights who once felt more comfortable on Broadway sought refuge in these little outlets, regional theatres did become saviors to the American stage.

Of course, cities suffered another blight. Areas not far from the center of town and once home to middle-class Jews and Irish, both strong playgoers, after World War II deteriorated into inner-city slums, filled with inhabitants who had little interest in the theatre and so dangerous that suburbanites often feared driving through them on their way to the theatre. To paraphrase an old advertisement, getting there became half the problem. Indeed, theatre districts themselves, especially around Broadway, became hangouts for sordid and occasionally genuinely menacing figures.

So, in its own changed and, in some cases, decimated way, the theatre goes on. It probably will for the foreseeable future. But how many rich, memorable experiences it can provide remains moot.

INDEX

The index is divided into two major sections. The first covers the plays discussed in the book; the second, the people.

PLAYS   The Play index lists the plays treated in the book and has a subsection that lists sources (foreign plays, foreign and domestic novels, poems, or short stories) for many of the plays. A foreign play that was a source and was also presented on Broadway in its native tongue is listed in both sections. Most plays mentioned in passing, especially in mini-biographies, and musicals noted as being derived from plays discussed are not indexed.

PEOPLE   Playwrights and authors whose works served as sources are listed in the People index, as are producers, directors, designers, and the occasional composer or choreographer, but because listing all performers mentioned would have made the index excessively large, only those players mentioned six or more times are included. However, celebrated foreigners, performers best known in other fields (musicals, vaudeville, films), and a few deemed of special interest for other reasons have been included in spite of the six-or-more rule. Thus, exceptions have been made for some old-timers whose careers came to a halt during these years, for young actors and actresses just embarking on what became fine careers, and for a handful of players who had brief glory, but then died young or faded from the scene. Critics per se have not been indexed; they appear solely if they wrote or worked on plays dealt with in this volume. Players in off-Broadway mountings are cited only if they went on to subsequent celebrity, and indexed then in accordance with the criteria just mentioned. Page numbers in bold print indicate mini-biographies. The People index has a subsection that lists producing organizations. Only those places where the group is mentioned in our discussion of a play are cited. Readers can often surmise what other plays the group produced by noting the theatre where the play was mounted. Thus, almost all plays produced at the Guild Theatre were Theatre Guild offerings.

PLAYS

435

Index

Index

Index

Index

Index

Index

Index

Index

Index

Index

Index

Index

Index

SOURCES

Index

Index

PEOPLE

Index

Index

Index

Index

Index

Index

Index

Index

Index

Index

Index

Index

Index

Index

Index

Index

ORGANIZATIONS

Index

ABOUT THE AUTHOR

Gerald Bordman is the author of numerous books, including the following published by Oxford University Press: *American Theatre: A Chronicle of Comedy and Drama, 1914-1930* (1995), *American Theatre: A Chronicle of Comedy and Drama, 1869-1914* (1994), *American Musical Theatre: A Chronicle, Second Edition* (1992), *Jerome Kern: His Life and Music* (1980), *Days to be Happy, Years to be Sad: The Life and Music of Vincent Youmans* (1982), *American Musical Revue: From The Passing Show to Sugar Babies* (1985), *The Oxford Companion to American Theatre, Second Edition* (1992), *American Operetta: From H.M.S. Pinafore to Sweeney Todd* (1981), *American Musical Comedy: from Adonis to Dreamgirls* (1982), and *The Concise Oxford Companion to American Theatre* (1987).